Chevrolet
Lumina & Monte Carlo Automotive Repair Manual

by Jeff Kibler, Jay Storer and John H Haynes

Member of the Guild of Motoring Writers

Models covered:

All Chevrolet Lumina and Monte Carlo models 1995 through 1999

(8C3 - 24048)

ABCDE
FGHIJ
KLMNO
P

Haynes Publishing Group
Sparkford Nr Yeovil
Somerset BA22 7JJ England

Haynes North America, Inc
861 Lawrence Drive
Newbury Park
California 91320 USA

About this manual

Its purpose

The purpose of this manual is to help you get the best value from your vehicle. It can do so in several ways. It can help you decide what work must be done, even if you choose to have it done by a dealer service department or a repair shop; it provides information and procedures for routine maintenance and servicing; and it offers diagnostic and repair procedures to follow when trouble occurs.

We hope you use the manual to tackle the work yourself. For many simpler jobs, doing it yourself may be quicker than arranging an appointment to get the vehicle into a shop and making the trips to leave it and pick it up. More importantly, a lot of money can be saved by avoiding the expense the shop must pass on to you to cover its labor and overhead costs. An added benefit is the sense of satisfaction and accomplishment that you feel after doing the job yourself.

Using the manual

The manual is divided into Chapters. Each Chapter is divided into numbered Sections, which are headed in bold type between horizontal lines. Each Section consists of consecutively numbered paragraphs.

At the beginning of each numbered Section you will be referred to any illustrations which apply to the procedures in that Section. The reference numbers used in illustration captions pinpoint the pertinent Section and the Step within that Section. That is, illustration 3.2 means the illustration refers to Section 3 and Step (or paragraph) 2 within that Section.

Procedures, once described in the text, are not normally repeated. When it's necessary to refer to another Chapter, the reference will be given as Chapter and Section number. Cross references given without use of the word "Chapter" apply to Sections and/or paragraphs in the same Chapter. For example, "see Section 8" means in the same Chapter.

References to the left or right side of the vehicle assume you are sitting in the driver's seat, facing forward.

Even though we have prepared this manual with extreme care, neither the publisher nor the author can accept responsibility for any errors in, or omissions from, the information given.

NOTE

A **Note** provides information necessary to properly complete a procedure or information which will make the procedure easier to understand.

CAUTION

A **Caution** provides a special procedure or special steps which must be taken while completing the procedure where the Caution is found. Not heeding a Caution can result in damage to the assembly being worked on.

WARNING

A **Warning** provides a special procedure or special steps which must be taken while completing the procedure where the Warning is found. Not heeding a Warning can result in personal injury.

Acknowledgements

Wiring diagrams provided exclusively for Haynes North America, Inc. by Valley Forge Technical Communications.

© **Haynes North America, Inc. 1998, 1999**

With permission from J.H. Haynes & Co. Ltd.

A book in the Haynes Automotive Repair Manual Series

Printed in the U.S.A.

ISBN 1 56392 370 X

Library of Congress Catalog Card Number 00-100317

Contents

Haynes photographer, mechanic and author with 1997 Chevrolet Monte Carlo

Introduction to the Chevrolet Lumina and Monte Carlo

The models covered by this manual are available in two and four-door sedan body styles.

Engines used in these vehicles include the 3.1 liter, 3.4 liter DOHC and a 3.8 liter (3800) V6 engine. All models are equipped with Multi-port fuel injection (MPFI). 1996 and later models are equipped with the On Board Diagnostic Second Generation (OBDII) computerized engine management system that controls virtually every aspect of engine operation. OBDII is designed to keep the emis-

sions system operating at the federally specified level for the life of the vehicle. OBDII monitors emissions system components for signs of degradation and engine operation for any malfunction that could affect emissions, turning on the Service Engine Soon light if any faults are detected.

The transversely mounted engine transmits power to the front wheels through an electronically controlled four-speed automatic transaxle via independent driveaxles.

Suspension is independent in the front,

utilizing coil springs with struts and lower control arms to locate the knuckle assembly at each wheel. The rear suspension features strut/coil spring assemblies, trailing arms and lateral link rods.

The rack-and-pinion steering unit is mounted behind the engine with power-assist as standard equipment.

The brakes are disc at the front and disc or drums at the rear, with power assist standard. An Anti-lock Braking System (ABS) is standard on most models.

Vehicle identification numbers

Modifications are a continuing and unpublicized part of vehicle manufacturing. Since spare parts manuals and lists are compiled on a numerical basis, the individual vehicle numbers are essential to correctly identify the component required.

Vehicle Identification Number (VIN)

This very important identification number is stamped on a plate attached to the left side of the dashboard and is visible through the driver's side of the windshield (see illustration). The VIN also appears on the Vehicle Certificate of Title and Registration. It contains valuable information such as where and when the vehicle was manufactured, the model year and the body style.

VIN engine and model year codes

Two particularly important pieces of information found in the VIN are the engine code and the model year code. Counting from the left, the engine code letter designa-tion is the 8th digit and the model year code letter designation is the 10th digit.

On the models covered by this manual the engine codes are:

M	3.1L V6
X	3.4L V6
K	3.8L (3800) V6

On the models covered by this manual the model year codes are:

S	1995
T	1996
V	1997
W	1998

Engine identification numbers

The engine identification number(s) are found on a pad on the left side of engine block by the transmission bellhousing (see illustration).

Automatic transaxle identification number

The transaxle ID number on 3T40 models is stamped into the top of the casting by the shift lever (see illustration). The transaxle ID number on 4T60-E and 4T65-E models is stamped onto a plate which is riveted to the right rear corner of the transaxle housing.

Vehicle Emissions Control Information label

This label is found in the engine compartment. See Chapter 6 for more information on this label.

The Vehicle Identification Number (VIN) is visible through the driver's side of the windshield

V6 engine identification number locations

A   Engine ID number   B   VIN number

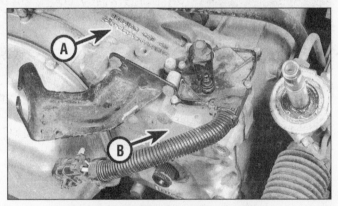

Transaxle identification number locations

A   VIN number   B   Transaxle ID number

Buying parts

Replacement parts are available from many sources, which generally fall into one of two categories - authorized dealer parts departments and independent retail auto parts stores. Our advice concerning these parts is as follows:

Retail auto parts stores: Good auto parts stores will stock frequently needed components which wear out relatively fast, such as clutch components, exhaust systems, brake parts, tune-up parts, etc. These stores often supply new or reconditioned parts on an exchange basis, which can save a considerable amount of money. Discount auto parts stores are often very good places to buy materials and parts needed for general vehicle maintenance such as oil, grease, filters, spark plugs, belts, touch-up paint, bulbs, etc. They also usually sell tools and general accessories, have convenient hours, charge lower prices and can often be found not far from home.

Authorized dealer parts department: This is the best source for parts which are unique to the vehicle and not generally available elsewhere (such as major engine parts, transmission parts, trim pieces, etc.).

Warranty information: If the vehicle is still covered under warranty, be sure that any replacement parts purchased - regardless of the source - do not invalidate the warranty!

To be sure of obtaining the correct parts, have engine and chassis numbers available and, if possible, take the old parts along for positive identification.

Maintenance techniques, tools and working facilities

Maintenance techniques

There are a number of techniques involved in maintenance and repair that will be referred to throughout this manual. Application of these techniques will enable the home mechanic to be more efficient, better organized and capable of performing the various tasks properly, which will ensure that the repair job is thorough and complete.

Fasteners

Fasteners are nuts, bolts, studs and screws used to hold two or more parts together. There are a few things to keep in mind when working with fasteners. Almost all of them use a locking device of some type, either a lockwasher, locknut, locking tab or thread adhesive. All threaded fasteners should be clean and straight, with undamaged threads and undamaged corners on the hex head where the wrench fits. Develop the habit of replacing all damaged nuts and bolts with new ones. Special locknuts with nylon or fiber inserts can only be used once. If they are removed, they lose their locking ability and must be replaced with new ones.

Rusted nuts and bolts should be treated with a penetrating fluid to ease removal and prevent breakage. Some mechanics use turpentine in a spout-type oil can, which works quite well. After applying the rust penetrant, let it work for a few minutes before trying to loosen the nut or bolt. Badly rusted fasteners may have to be chiseled or sawed off or removed with a special nut breaker, available at tool stores.

If a bolt or stud breaks off in an assembly, it can be drilled and removed with a special tool commonly available for this purpose. Most automotive machine shops can perform this task, as well as other repair procedures, such as the repair of threaded holes that have been stripped out.

Flat washers and lockwashers, when removed from an assembly, should always be replaced exactly as removed. Replace any damaged washers with new ones. Never use a lockwasher on any soft metal surface (such as aluminum), thin sheet metal or plastic.

Fastener sizes

For a number of reasons, automobile manufacturers are making wider and wider use of metric fasteners. Therefore, it is important to be able to tell the difference between standard (sometimes called U.S. or SAE) and metric hardware, since they cannot be interchanged.

All bolts, whether standard or metric, are sized according to diameter, thread pitch and length. For example, a standard 1/2 - 13 x 1 bolt is 1/2 inch in diameter, has 13 threads per inch and is 1 inch long. An M12 - 1.75 x 25 metric bolt is 12 mm in diameter, has a thread pitch of 1.75 mm (the distance between threads) and is 25 mm long. The two bolts are nearly identical, and easily confused, but they are not interchangeable.

In addition to the differences in diameter, thread pitch and length, metric and standard bolts can also be distinguished by examining the bolt heads. To begin with, the distance across the flats on a standard bolt head is measured in inches, while the same dimension on a metric bolt is sized in millimeters (the same is true for nuts). As a result, a standard wrench should not be used on a metric bolt and a metric wrench should not be used on a standard bolt. Also, most standard bolts have slashes radiating out from the center of the head to denote the grade or strength of the bolt, which is an indication of the amount of torque that can be applied to it. The greater the number of slashes, the greater the strength of the bolt. Grades 0 through 5 are commonly used on automobiles. Metric bolts have a property class (grade) number, rather than a slash, molded into their heads to indicate bolt strength. In this case, the higher the number, the stronger the bolt. Property class numbers 8.8, 9.8 and 10.9 are commonly used on automobiles.

Strength markings can also be used to distinguish standard hex nuts from metric hex nuts. Many standard hex nuts have dots stamped into one side, while metric nuts are marked with a number. The greater the number of dots, or the higher the number, the greater the strength of the nut.

Metric studs are also marked on their ends according to property class (grade). Larger studs are numbered (the same as metric bolts), while smaller studs carry a geometric code to denote grade.

It should be noted that many fasteners, especially Grades 0 through 2, have no dis-

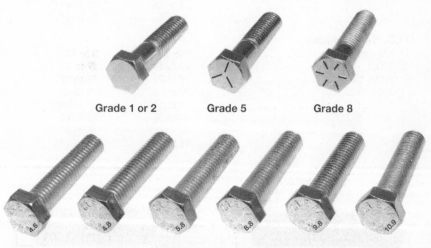

Grade 1 or 2   Grade 5   Grade 8

Bolt strength marking (standard/SAE/USS; bottom - metric)

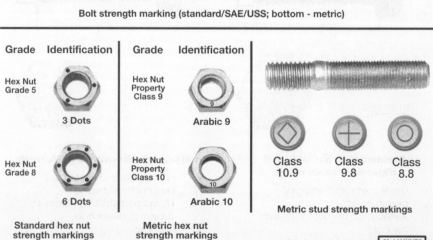

Grade	Identification	Grade	Identification
Hex Nut Grade 5	3 Dots	Hex Nut Property Class 9	Arabic 9
Hex Nut Grade 8	6 Dots	Hex Nut Property Class 10	Arabic 10

Standard hex nut strength markings

Metric hex nut strength markings

Class 10.9   Class 9.8   Class 8.8

Metric stud strength markings

tinguishing marks on them. When such is the case, the only way to determine whether it is standard or metric is to measure the thread pitch or compare it to a known fastener of the same size.

Standard fasteners are often referred to as SAE, as opposed to metric. However, it should be noted that SAE technically refers to a non-metric fine thread fastener only. Coarse thread non-metric fasteners are referred to as USS sizes.

Since fasteners of the same size (both standard and metric) may have different strength ratings, be sure to reinstall any bolts, studs or nuts removed from your vehicle in their original locations. Also, when replacing a fastener with a new one, make sure that the new one has a strength rating equal to or greater than the original.

Tightening sequences and procedures

Most threaded fasteners should be tightened to a specific torque value (torque is the twisting force applied to a threaded component such as a nut or bolt). Overtightening the fastener can weaken it and cause it to break, while undertightening can cause it to eventually come loose. Bolts, screws and studs, depending on the material they are made of and their thread diameters, have specific torque values, many of which are noted in the Specifications at the beginning of each Chapter. Be sure to follow the torque recommendations closely. For fasteners not assigned a specific torque, a general torque value chart is presented here as a guide. These torque values are for dry (unlubricated) fasteners threaded into steel or cast iron (not aluminum). As was previously mentioned, the size and grade of a fastener determine the amount of torque that can safely be applied to it. The figures listed here are approximate for Grade 2 and Grade 3 fasteners. Higher grades can tolerate higher torque values.

Fasteners laid out in a pattern, such as cylinder head bolts, oil pan bolts, differential cover bolts, etc., must be loosened or tightened in sequence to avoid warping the component. This sequence will normally be shown in the appropriate Chapter. If a specific pattern is not given, the following procedures can be used to prevent warping.

Initially, the bolts or nuts should be assembled finger-tight only. Next, they should be tightened one full turn each, in a criss-cross or diagonal pattern. After each one has been tightened one full turn, return to the first one and tighten them all one-half turn, following the same pattern. Finally, tighten each of them one-quarter turn at a time until each fastener has been tightened to the proper torque. To loosen and remove the fasteners, the procedure would be reversed.

Component disassembly

Component disassembly should be done with care and purpose to help ensure that the parts go back together properly. Always keep track of the sequence in which parts are removed. Make note of special characteristics or marks on parts that can be installed more than one way, such as a grooved thrust washer on a shaft. It is a good idea to lay the disassembled parts out on a clean surface in the order that they were removed. It may also be helpful to make sketches or take instant photos of components before removal.

When removing fasteners from a component, keep track of their locations. Sometimes threading a bolt back in a part, or putting the washers and nut back on a stud, can prevent mix-ups later. If nuts and bolts cannot be returned to their original locations, they should be kept in a compartmented box or a series of small boxes. A cupcake or muffin tin is ideal for this purpose, since each cavity can hold the bolts and nuts from a particular area (i.e. oil pan bolts, valve cover bolts, engine mount bolts, etc.). A pan of this type is especially helpful when working on assemblies with very small parts, such as the carburetor, alternator, valve train or interior dash and trim pieces. The cavities can be marked with paint or tape to identify the contents.

Whenever wiring looms, harnesses or connectors are separated, it is a good idea to identify the two halves with numbered pieces of masking tape so they can be easily reconnected.

Gasket sealing surfaces

Throughout any vehicle, gaskets are used to seal the mating surfaces between two parts and keep lubricants, fluids, vacuum or pressure contained in an assembly.

Metric thread sizes	Ft-lbs	Nm
M-6	6 to 9	9 to 12
M-8	14 to 21	19 to 28
M-10	28 to 40	38 to 54
M-12	50 to 71	68 to 96
M-14	80 to 140	109 to 154

Pipe thread sizes		
1/8	5 to 8	7 to 10
1/4	12 to 18	17 to 24
3/8	22 to 33	30 to 44
1/2	25 to 35	34 to 47

U.S. thread sizes		
1/4 - 20	6 to 9	9 to 12
5/16 - 18	12 to 18	17 to 24
5/16 - 24	14 to 20	19 to 27
3/8 - 16	22 to 32	30 to 43
3/8 - 24	27 to 38	37 to 51
7/16 - 14	40 to 55	55 to 74
7/16 - 20	40 to 60	55 to 81
1/2 - 13	55 to 80	75 to 108

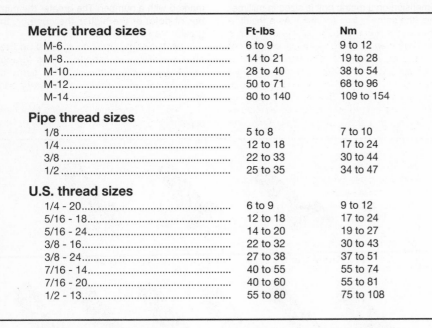

00-2 HAYNES

Standard (SAE and USS) bolt dimensions/grade marks

G　Grade marks (bolt strength)
L　Length (in inches)
T　Thread pitch (number of threads per inch)
D　Nominal diameter (in inches)

Metric bolt dimensions/grade marks

P　Property class (bolt strength)
L　Length (in millimeters)
T　Thread pitch (distance between threads in millimeters)
D　Diameter

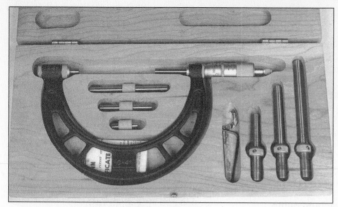

Micrometer set

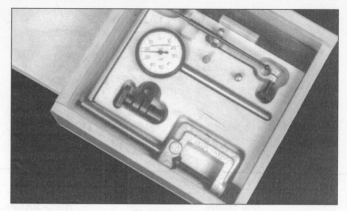

Dial indicator set

Many times these gaskets are coated with a liquid or paste-type gasket sealing compound before assembly. Age, heat and pressure can sometimes cause the two parts to stick together so tightly that they are very difficult to separate. Often, the assembly can be loosened by striking it with a soft-face hammer near the mating surfaces. A regular hammer can be used if a block of wood is placed between the hammer and the part. Do not hammer on cast parts or parts that could be easily damaged. With any particularly stubborn part, always recheck to make sure that every fastener has been removed.

Avoid using a screwdriver or bar to pry apart an assembly, as they can easily mar the gasket sealing surfaces of the parts, which must remain smooth. If prying is absolutely necessary, use an old broom handle, but keep in mind that extra clean up will be necessary if the wood splinters.

After the parts are separated, the old gasket must be carefully scraped off and the gasket surfaces cleaned. Stubborn gasket material can be soaked with rust penetrant or treated with a special chemical to soften it so it can be easily scraped off. A scraper can be fashioned from a piece of copper tubing by flattening and sharpening one end. Copper is recommended because it is usually softer than the surfaces to be scraped, which reduces the chance of gouging the part. Some gaskets can be removed with a wire brush, but regardless of the method used, the mating surfaces must be left clean and smooth. If for some reason the gasket surface is gouged, then a gasket sealer thick enough to fill scratches will have to be used during reassembly of the components. For most applications, a non-drying (or semi-drying) gasket sealer should be used.

Hose removal tips

Warning: *If the vehicle is equipped with air conditioning, do not disconnect any of the A/C hoses without first having the system depressurized by a dealer service department or a service station.*

Hose removal precautions closely parallel gasket removal precautions. Avoid scratching or gouging the surface that the hose mates against or the connection may

leak. This is especially true for radiator hoses. Because of various chemical reactions, the rubber in hoses can bond itself to the metal spigot that the hose fits over. To remove a hose, first loosen the hose clamps that secure it to the spigot. Then, with slip-joint pliers, grab the hose at the clamp and rotate it around the spigot. Work it back and forth until it is completely free, then pull it off. Silicone or other lubricants will ease removal if they can be applied between the hose and the outside of the spigot. Apply the same lubricant to the inside of the hose and the outside of the spigot to simplify installation.

As a last resort (and if the hose is to be replaced with a new one anyway), the rubber can be slit with a knife and the hose peeled from the spigot. If this must be done, be careful that the metal connection is not damaged.

If a hose clamp is broken or damaged, do not reuse it. Wire-type clamps usually weaken with age, so it is a good idea to replace them with screw-type clamps whenever a hose is removed.

Tools

A selection of good tools is a basic requirement for anyone who plans to maintain and repair his or her own vehicle. For the owner who has few tools, the initial investment might seem high, but when compared to the spiraling costs of professional auto maintenance and repair, it is a wise one.

To help the owner decide which tools are needed to perform the tasks detailed in this manual, the following tool lists are offered: *Maintenance and minor repair, Repair/overhaul* and *Special*.

The newcomer to practical mechanics should start off with the *maintenance and minor repair* tool kit, which is adequate for the simpler jobs performed on a vehicle. Then, as confidence and experience grow, the owner can tackle more difficult tasks, buying additional tools as they are needed. Eventually the basic kit will be expanded into the *repair and overhaul* tool set. Over a period of time, the experienced do-it-yourselfer will assemble a tool set complete enough for most repair and overhaul procedures and will add tools from the special category when it is

felt that the expense is justified by the frequency of use.

Maintenance and minor repair tool kit

The tools in this list should be considered the minimum required for performance of routine maintenance, servicing and minor repair work. We recommend the purchase of combination wrenches (box-end and open-end combined in one wrench). While more expensive than open end wrenches, they offer the advantages of both types of wrench.

> *Combination wrench set (1/4-inch to 1 inch or 6 mm to 19 mm)*
> *Adjustable wrench, 8 inch*
> *Spark plug wrench with rubber insert*
> *Spark plug gap adjusting tool*
> *Feeler gauge set*
> *Brake bleeder wrench*
> *Standard screwdriver (5/16-inch x 6 inch)*
> *Phillips screwdriver (No. 2 x 6 inch)*
> *Combination pliers - 6 inch*
> *Hacksaw and assortment of blades*
> *Tire pressure gauge*
> *Grease gun*
> *Oil can*
> *Fine emery cloth*
> *Wire brush*
> *Battery post and cable cleaning tool*
> *Oil filter wrench*
> *Funnel (medium size)*
> *Safety goggles*
> *Jackstands (2)*
> *Drain pan*

Note: *If basic tune-ups are going to be part of routine maintenance, it will be necessary to purchase a good quality stroboscopic timing light and combination tachometer/dwell meter. Although they are included in the list of special tools, it is mentioned here because they are absolutely necessary for tuning most vehicles properly.*

Repair and overhaul tool set

These tools are essential for anyone who plans to perform major repairs and are in addition to those in the maintenance and minor repair tool kit. Included is a comprehensive set of sockets which, though expensive, are invaluable because of their versatil-

Dial caliper

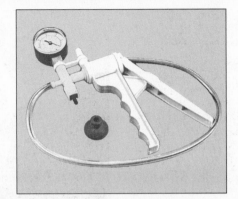

Hand-operated vacuum pump

Timing light

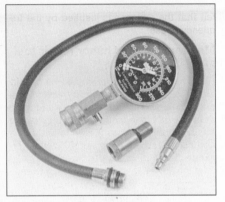

Compression gauge with spark plug
hole adapter

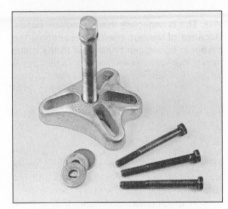

Damper/steering wheel puller

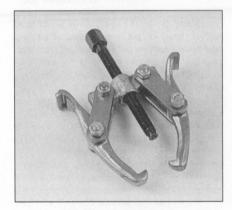

General purpose puller

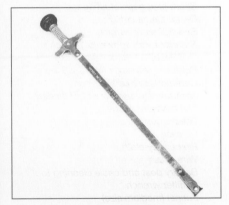

Hydraulic lifter removal tool

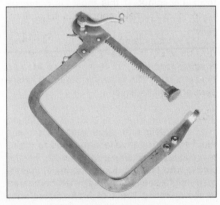

Valve spring compressor

Valve spring compressor

Ridge reamer

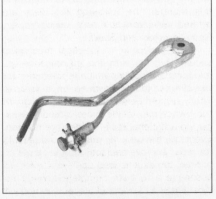

Piston ring groove cleaning tool

Ring removal/installation tool

Ring compressor

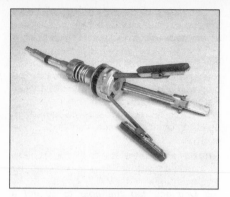

Cylinder hone

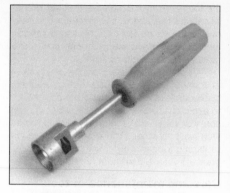

Brake hold-down spring tool

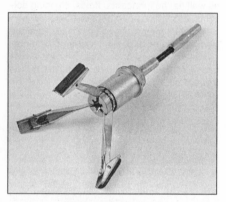

Brake cylinder hone

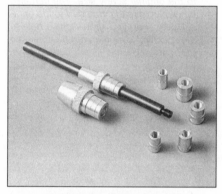

Clutch plate alignment tool

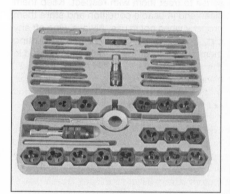

Tap and die set

ity, especially when various extensions and drives are available. We recommend the 1/2-inch drive over the 3/8-inch drive. Although the larger drive is bulky and more expensive, it has the capacity of accepting a very wide range of large sockets. Ideally, however, the mechanic should have a 3/8-inch drive set and a 1/2-inch drive set.

Socket set(s)
Reversible ratchet
Extension - 10 inch
Universal joint
Torque wrench (same size drive as sockets)
Ball peen hammer - 8 ounce
Soft-face hammer (plastic/rubber)
Standard screwdriver (1/4-inch x 6 inch)
Standard screwdriver (stubby - 5/16-inch)
Phillips screwdriver (No. 3 x 8 inch)
Phillips screwdriver (stubby - No. 2)
Pliers - vise grip
Pliers - lineman's
Pliers - needle nose
Pliers - snap-ring (internal and external)
Cold chisel - 1/2-inch
Scribe
Scraper (made from flattened copper tubing)
Centerpunch
Pin punches (1/16, 1/8, 3/16-inch)
Steel rule/straightedge - 12 inch
Allen wrench set (1/8 to 3/8-inch or 4 mm to 10 mm)
A selection of files
Wire brush (large)

Jackstands (second set)
Jack (scissor or hydraulic type)

Note: *Another tool which is often useful is an electric drill with a chuck capacity of 3/8-inch and a set of good quality drill bits.*

Special tools

The tools in this list include those which are not used regularly, are expensive to buy, or which need to be used in accordance with their manufacturer's instructions. Unless these tools will be used frequently, it is not very economical to purchase many of them. A consideration would be to split the cost and use between yourself and a friend or friends. In addition, most of these tools can be obtained from a tool rental shop on a temporary basis.

This list primarily contains only those tools and instruments widely available to the public, and not those special tools produced by the vehicle manufacturer for distribution to dealer service departments. Occasionally, references to the manufacturer's special tools are included in the text of this manual. Generally, an alternative method of doing the job without the special tool is offered. However, sometimes there is no alternative to their use. Where this is the case, and the tool cannot be purchased or borrowed, the work should be turned over to the dealer service department or an automotive repair shop.

Valve spring compressor
Piston ring groove cleaning tool
Piston ring compressor
Piston ring installation tool

Cylinder compression gauge
Cylinder ridge reamer
Cylinder surfacing hone
Cylinder bore gauge
Micrometers and/or dial calipers
Hydraulic lifter removal tool
Balljoint separator
Universal-type puller
Impact screwdriver
Dial indicator set
Stroboscopic timing light (inductive pick-up)
Hand operated vacuum/pressure pump
Tachometer/dwell meter
Universal electrical multimeter
Cable hoist
Brake spring removal and installation tools
Floor jack

Buying tools

For the do-it-yourselfer who is just starting to get involved in vehicle maintenance and repair, there are a number of options available when purchasing tools. If maintenance and minor repair is the extent of the work to be done, the purchase of individual tools is satisfactory. If, on the other hand, extensive work is planned, it would be a good idea to purchase a modest tool set from one of the large retail chain stores. A set can usually be bought at a substantial savings over the individual tool prices, and they often come with a tool box. As additional tools are needed, add-on sets, individual tools and a larger tool box can be purchased to expand the tool selection. Building a tool set gradually allows the cost of the tools to be spread over a longer period of time and gives the mechanic the freedom to choose only those tools that will actually be used.

Tool stores will often be the only source of some of the special tools that are needed, but regardless of where tools are bought, try to avoid cheap ones, especially when buying screwdrivers and sockets, because they won't last very long. The expense involved in replacing cheap tools will eventually be greater than the initial cost of quality tools.

Care and maintenance of tools

Good tools are expensive, so it makes sense to treat them with respect. Keep them clean and in usable condition and store them properly when not in use. Always wipe off any dirt, grease or metal chips before putting them away. Never leave tools lying around in the work area. Upon completion of a job, always check closely under the hood for tools that may have been left there so they won't get lost during a test drive.

Some tools, such as screwdrivers, pliers, wrenches and sockets, can be hung on a panel mounted on the garage or workshop wall, while others should be kept in a tool box or tray. Measuring instruments, gauges, meters, etc. must be carefully stored where they cannot be damaged by weather or impact from other tools.

When tools are used with care and stored properly, they will last a very long time. Even with the best of care, though, tools will wear out if used frequently. When a tool is damaged or worn out, replace it. Subsequent jobs will be safer and more enjoyable if you do.

How to repair damaged threads

Sometimes, the internal threads of a nut or bolt hole can become stripped, usually from overtightening. Stripping threads is an all-too-common occurrence, especially when working with aluminum parts, because aluminum is so soft that it easily strips out.

Usually, external or internal threads are only partially stripped. After they've been cleaned up with a tap or die, they'll still work. Sometimes, however, threads are badly damaged. When this happens, you've got three choices:

1) *Drill and tap the hole to the next suitable oversize and install a larger diameter bolt, screw or stud.*
2) *Drill and tap the hole to accept a threaded plug, then drill and tap the plug to the original screw size. You can also buy a plug already threaded to the original size. Then you simply drill a hole to the specified size, then run the threaded plug into the hole with a bolt and jam nut. Once the plug is fully seated, remove the jam nut and bolt.*
3) *The third method uses a patented thread repair kit like Heli-Coil or Slimsert. These easy-to-use kits are designed to repair damaged threads in straight-through holes and blind holes. Both are available as kits which can handle a variety of sizes and thread patterns. Drill the hole, then tap it with the special included tap. Install the Heli-Coil and the hole is back to its original diameter and thread pitch.*

Regardless of which method you use, be sure to proceed calmly and carefully. A little impatience or carelessness during one of these relatively simple procedures can ruin your whole day's work and cost you a bundle if you wreck an expensive part.

Working facilities

Not to be overlooked when discussing tools is the workshop. If anything more than routine maintenance is to be carried out, some sort of suitable work area is essential.

It is understood, and appreciated, that many home mechanics do not have a good workshop or garage available, and end up removing an engine or doing major repairs outside. It is recommended, however, that the overhaul or repair be completed under the cover of a roof.

A clean, flat workbench or table of comfortable working height is an absolute necessity. The workbench should be equipped with a vise that has a jaw opening of at least four inches.

As mentioned previously, some clean, dry storage space is also required for tools, as well as the lubricants, fluids, cleaning solvents, etc. which soon become necessary.

Sometimes waste oil and fluids, drained from the engine or cooling system during normal maintenance or repairs, present a disposal problem. To avoid pouring them on the ground or into a sewage system, pour the used fluids into large containers, seal them with caps and take them to an authorized disposal site or recycling center. Plastic jugs, such as old antifreeze containers, are ideal for this purpose.

Always keep a supply of old newspapers and clean rags available. Old towels are excellent for mopping up spills. Many mechanics use rolls of paper towels for most work because they are readily available and disposable. To help keep the area under the vehicle clean, a large cardboard box can be cut open and flattened to protect the garage or shop floor.

Whenever working over a painted surface, such as when leaning over a fender to service something under the hood, always cover it with an old blanket or bedspread to protect the finish. Vinyl covered pads, made especially for this purpose, are available at auto parts stores.

Anti-theft audio system

General information

1   Some of these models are equipped with THEFTLOCK audio systems, which include an anti-theft feature that will render the stereo inoperative if stolen. If the power source to the stereo is cut with the anti-theft feature activated, the stereo will be inoperative. Even if the power source is immediately re-connected, the stereo will not function.
2   If your vehicle is equipped with this anti-theft system, do not disconnect the battery, remove the stereo or disconnect related components unless you have either turned off the feature or have the individual ID (code) number for the stereo.

Disabling the anti-theft feature

3   Press the stereo's 1 and 4 buttons at the same time for five seconds with the ignition on and the radio power off. The display will show SEC, indicating the unit is in the secure mode (anti-theft feature enabled).
4   Press the MIN button. The display will show "000".
5   Press the MIN button to make the last two numbers appear.
6   Press HR to display the first one or two numbers of your code. The numbers will be displayed as entered.
7   Press AM/FM. If the display shows "_ _" you have successfully disabled the anti-theft feature. If SEC is displayed, the code you entered was incorrect and the anti-theft feature is still enabled.

Unlocking the stereo after a power loss

8   When power is restored to the stereo, the stereo won't turn on and LOC will appear on the display. Enter your ID code as follows; pause no more than 15 seconds between Steps.
9   Turn the ignition switch to ON, but leave the stereo off.
10   Press the MIN button. "000" should display.
11   Press the HR button to make the last two numbers appear, then release the button.
12   Press the HR button until the first one or two numbers appear.
13   Press AM/FM. SEC should appear, indicating the stereo is unlocked. If LOC appears, the numbers you entered were not correct and the stereo is still inoperative.

Jacking and towing

Jacking

Warning: *The jack supplied with the vehicle should only be used for raising the vehicle when changing a tire or placing jackstands under the frame. Never work under the vehicle or start the engine while the jack is being used as the only means of support.*

The vehicle must be on a level surface with the wheels blocked and the transmission in Park. Apply the parking brake if the front of the vehicle must be raised. Make sure no one is in the vehicle as it's being raised with the jack.

The head of the jack should fit squarely in the notch on the rocker flange at either the front or rear of the vehicle

Remove the jack, lug nut wrench and spare tire from the trunk compartment.

To replace the tire, use the tapered end of the lug wrench to pry loose the wheel cover. **Note:** *If the vehicle is equipped with aluminum wheels, it may be necessary to pry out the special lug nut covers. Also, aluminum wheels normally have anti-theft lug nuts (one per wheel) which require using a special "key" between the lug wrench and lug nut. The key is usually in the glove compartment.* Loosen the lug nuts one-half turn, but leave them in place until the tire is raised off the ground.

Position the jack under the side of the vehicle at the indicated jacking points. There's a front and rear jacking point on each side of the vehicle **(see illustration)**.

Turn the jack handle clockwise (the lug wrench also serves as the jack handle) until the tire clears the ground. Remove the lug nuts and pull the tire off. Clean the mating surfaces of the hub and wheel, then install the spare. Replace the lug nuts with the beveled edges facing in and tighten them snugly. Don't attempt to tighten them completely until the vehicle is lowered or it could slip off the jack.

Turn the jack handle counterclockwise to lower the vehicle. Remove the jack and tighten the lug nuts in a criss-cross pattern. If possible, tighten the nuts with a torque wrench (see Chapter 1 for the torque values). If you don't have access to a torque wrench,

have the nuts checked by a service station or repair shop as soon as possible. **Caution:** *The compact spare included with these vehicles is intended for temporary use only. Have the tire repaired and reinstall it on the vehicle at the earliest opportunity and don't exceed 50 mph with the spare tire on the car.*

Install the wheel cover, then stow the tire, jack and wrench and unblock the wheels.

Towing

We recommend these vehicles be towed from the front, with the front wheels off the ground. If it's absolutely necessary, these vehicles can be towed from the rear with the front wheels on the ground, provided that speeds don't exceed 35 mph and the distance is less than 50 miles; the transaxle can be damaged if these mileage/speed limitations are exceeded.

Equipment specifically designed for towing should be used. It must be attached to the main structural members of the vehicle, not the bumpers or brackets.

Safety is a major consideration when towing and all applicable state and local laws must be obeyed. A safety chain must be used at all times.

The parking brake must be released and the transaxle must be in Neutral. The steering must be unlocked (ignition switch in the Off position). Remember that power steering and power brakes won't work with the engine off.

Booster battery (jump) starting

Observe these precautions when using a booster battery to start a vehicle:

a) *Before connecting the booster battery, make sure the ignition switch is in the Off position.*

b) *Turn off the lights, heater and other electrical loads.*

c) *Your eyes should be shielded. Safety goggles are a good idea.*

d) *Make sure the booster battery is the same voltage as the dead one in the vehicle.*

e) *The two vehicles MUST NOT TOUCH each other!*

f) *Make sure the transaxle is in Neutral (manual) or Park (automatic).*

g) *If the booster battery is not a maintenance-free type, remove the vent caps and lay a cloth over the vent holes.*

Connect the red jumper cable to the positive (+) terminals of each battery. **Note:** *The vehicles covered in this manual are equipped with a remote positive terminal. This terminal is located in the left (driver's) side of the engine compartment, covered by a red plastic cap* **(see illustration)**.

Connect one end of the black jumper cable to the negative (-) terminal of the

booster battery. The other end of this cable should be connected to a good ground on the vehicle to be started, such as a bolt or bracket on the body.

Start the engine using the booster battery, then, with the engine running at idle speed, disconnect the jumper cables in the reverse order of connection.

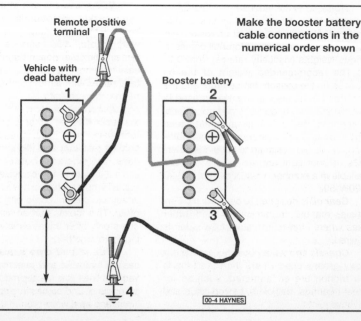

Make the booster battery cable connections in the numerical order shown

Remote positive terminal

Vehicle with dead battery

1

Booster battery

2

3

4

00-4 HAYNES

Automotive chemicals and lubricants

A number of automotive chemicals and lubricants are available for use during vehicle maintenance and repair. They include a wide variety of products ranging from cleaning solvents and degreasers to lubricants and protective sprays for rubber, plastic and vinyl.

Cleaners

Carburetor cleaner and choke cleaner is a strong solvent for gum, varnish and carbon. Most carburetor cleaners leave a dry-type lubricant film which will not harden or gum up. Because of this film it is not recommended for use on electrical components.

Brake system cleaner is used to remove grease and brake fluid from the brake system, where clean surfaces are absolutely necessary. It leaves no residue and often eliminates brake squeal caused by contaminants.

Electrical cleaner removes oxidation, corrosion and carbon deposits from electrical contacts, restoring full current flow. It can also be used to clean spark plugs, carburetor jets, voltage regulators and other parts where an oil-free surface is desired.

Demoisturants remove water and moisture from electrical components such as alternators, voltage regulators, electrical connectors and fuse blocks. They are non-conductive, non-corrosive and non-flammable.

Degreasers are heavy-duty solvents used to remove grease from the outside of the engine and from chassis components. They can be sprayed or brushed on and, depending on the type, are rinsed off either with water or solvent.

Lubricants

Motor oil is the lubricant formulated for use in engines. It normally contains a wide variety of additives to prevent corrosion and reduce foaming and wear. Motor oil comes in various weights (viscosity ratings) from 0 to 50. The recommended weight of the oil depends on the season, temperature and the demands on the engine. Light oil is used in cold climates and under light load conditions. Heavy oil is used in hot climates and where high loads are encountered. Multi-viscosity oils are designed to have characteristics of both light and heavy oils and are available in a number of weights from 5W-20 to 20W-50.

Gear oil is designed to be used in differentials, manual transmissions and other areas where high-temperature lubrication is required.

Chassis and wheel bearing grease is a heavy grease used where increased loads and friction are encountered, such as for wheel bearings, balljoints, tie-rod ends and universal joints.

High-temperature wheel bearing grease is designed to withstand the extreme temperatures encountered by wheel bearings in disc brake equipped vehicles. It usually contains molybdenum disulfide (moly), which is a dry-type lubricant.

White grease is a heavy grease for metal-to-metal applications where water is a problem. White grease stays soft under both low and high temperatures (usually from -100 to +190-degrees F), and will not wash off or dilute in the presence of water.

Assembly lube is a special extreme pressure lubricant, usually containing moly, used to lubricate high-load parts (such as main and rod bearings and cam lobes) for initial start-up of a new engine. The assembly lube lubricates the parts without being squeezed out or washed away until the engine oiling system begins to function.

Silicone lubricants are used to protect rubber, plastic, vinyl and nylon parts.

Graphite lubricants are used where oils cannot be used due to contamination problems, such as in locks. The dry graphite will lubricate metal parts while remaining uncontaminated by dirt, water, oil or acids. It is electrically conductive and will not foul electrical contacts in locks such as the ignition switch.

Moly penetrants loosen and lubricate frozen, rusted and corroded fasteners and prevent future rusting or freezing.

Heat-sink grease is a special electrically non-conductive grease that is used for mounting electronic ignition modules where it is essential that heat is transferred away from the module.

Sealants

RTV sealant is one of the most widely used gasket compounds. Made from silicone, RTV is air curing, it seals, bonds, waterproofs, fills surface irregularities, remains flexible, doesn't shrink, is relatively easy to remove, and is used as a supplementary sealer with almost all low and medium temperature gaskets.

Anaerobic sealant is much like RTV in that it can be used either to seal gaskets or to form gaskets by itself. It remains flexible, is solvent resistant and fills surface imperfections. The difference between an anaerobic sealant and an RTV-type sealant is in the curing. RTV cures when exposed to air, while an anaerobic sealant cures only in the absence of air. This means that an anaerobic sealant cures only after the assembly of parts, sealing them together.

Thread and pipe sealant is used for sealing hydraulic and pneumatic fittings and vacuum lines. It is usually made from a Teflon compound, and comes in a spray, a paint-on liquid and as a wrap-around tape.

Chemicals

Anti-seize compound prevents seizing, galling, cold welding, rust and corrosion in fasteners. High-temperature ant-seize, usually made with copper and graphite lubricants, is used for exhaust system and exhaust manifold bolts.

Anaerobic locking compounds are used to keep fasteners from vibrating or working loose and cure only after installation, in the absence of air. Medium strength locking compound is used for small nuts, bolts and screws that may be removed later. High-strength locking compound is for large nuts, bolts and studs which aren't removed on a regular basis.

Oil additives range from viscosity index improvers to chemical treatments that claim to reduce internal engine friction. It should be noted that most oil manufacturers caution against using additives with their oils.

Gas additives perform several functions, depending on their chemical makeup. They usually contain solvents that help dissolve gum and varnish that build up on carburetor, fuel injection and intake parts. They also serve to break down carbon deposits that form on the inside surfaces of the combustion chambers. Some additives contain upper cylinder lubricants for valves and piston rings, and others contain chemicals to remove condensation from the gas tank.

Miscellaneous

Brake fluid is specially formulated hydraulic fluid that can withstand the heat and pressure encountered in brake systems. Care must be taken so this fluid does not come in contact with painted surfaces or plastics. An opened container should always be resealed to prevent contamination by water or dirt.

Weatherstrip adhesive is used to bond weatherstripping around doors, windows and trunk lids. It is sometimes used to attach trim pieces.

Undercoating is a petroleum-based, tar-like substance that is designed to protect metal surfaces on the underside of the vehicle from corrosion. It also acts as a sound-deadening agent by insulating the bottom of the vehicle.

Waxes and polishes are used to help protect painted and plated surfaces from the weather. Different types of paint may require the use of different types of wax and polish. Some polishes utilize a chemical or abrasive cleaner to help remove the top layer of oxidized (dull) paint on older vehicles. In recent years many non-wax polishes that contain a wide variety of chemicals such as polymers and silicones have been introduced. These non-wax polishes are usually easier to apply and last longer than conventional waxes and polishes.

Conversion factors

Length (distance)

Inches (in)	X 25.4	= Millimetres (mm)	X 0.0394	= Inches (in)
Feet (ft)	X 0.305	= Metres (m)	X 3.281	= Feet (ft)
Miles	X 1.609	= Kilometres (km)	X 0.621	= Miles

Volume (capacity)

Cubic inches (cu in; in³)	X 16.387	= Cubic centimetres (cc; cm³)	X 0.061	= Cubic inches (cu in; in³)
Imperial pints (Imp pt)	X 0.568	= Litres (l)	X 1.76	= Imperial pints (Imp pt)
Imperial quarts (Imp qt)	X 1.137	= Litres (l)	X 0.88	= Imperial quarts (Imp qt)
Imperial quarts (Imp qt)	X 1.201	= US quarts (US qt)	X 0.833	= Imperial quarts (Imp qt)
US quarts (US qt)	X 0.946	= Litres (l)	X 1.057	= US quarts (US qt)
Imperial gallons (Imp gal)	X 4.546	= Litres (l)	X 0.22	= Imperial gallons (Imp gal)
Imperial gallons (Imp gal)	X 1.201	= US gallons (US gal)	X 0.833	= Imperial gallons (Imp gal)
US gallons (US gal)	X 3.785	= Litres (l)	X 0.264	= US gallons (US gal)

Mass (weight)

Ounces (oz)	X 28.35	= Grams (g)	X 0.035	= Ounces (oz)
Pounds (lb)	X 0.454	= Kilograms (kg)	X 2.205	= Pounds (lb)

Force

Ounces-force (ozf; oz)	X 0.278	= Newtons (N)	X 3.6	= Ounces-force (ozf; oz)
Pounds-force (lbf; lb)	X 4.448	= Newtons (N)	X 0.225	= Pounds-force (lbf; lb)
Newtons (N)	X 0.1	= Kilograms-force (kgf; kg)	X 9.81	= Newtons (N)

Pressure

Pounds-force per square inch (psi; lbf/in²; lb/in²)	X 0.070	= Kilograms-force per square centimetre (kgf/cm²; kg/cm²)	X 14.223	= Pounds-force per square inch (psi; lbf/in²; lb/in²)
Pounds-force per square inch (psi; lbf/in²; lb/in²)	X 0.068	= Atmospheres (atm)	X 14.696	= Pounds-force per square inch (psi; lbf/in²; lb/in²)
Pounds-force per square inch (psi; lbf/in²; lb/in²)	X 0.069	= Bars	X 14.5	= Pounds-force per square inch (psi; lbf/in²; lb/in²)
Pounds-force per square inch (psi; lbf/in²; lb/in²)	X 6.895	= Kilopascals (kPa)	X 0.145	= Pounds-force per square inch (psi; lbf/in²; lb/in²)
Kilopascals (kPa)	X 0.01	= Kilograms-force per square centimetre (kgf/cm²; kg/cm²)	X 98.1	= Kilopascals (kPa)

Torque (moment of force)

Pounds-force inches (lbf in; lb in)	X 1.152	= Kilograms-force centimetre (kgf cm; kg cm)	X 0.868	= Pounds-force inches (lbf in; lb in)
Pounds-force inches (lbf in; lb in)	X 0.113	= Newton metres (Nm)	X 8.85	= Pounds-force inches (lbf in; lb in)
Pounds-force inches (lbf in; lb in)	X 0.083	= Pounds-force feet (lbf ft; lb ft)	X 12	= Pounds-force inches (lbf in; lb in)
Pounds-force feet (lbf ft; lb ft)	X 0.138	= Kilograms-force metres (kgf m; kg m)	X 7.233	= Pounds-force feet (lbf ft; lb ft)
Pounds-force feet (lbf ft; lb ft)	X 1.356	= Newton metres (Nm)	X 0.738	= Pounds-force feet (lbf ft; lb ft)
Newton metres (Nm)	X 0.102	= Kilograms-force metres (kgf m; kg m)	X 9.804	= Newton metres (Nm)

Vacuum

Inches mercury (in. Hg)	X 3.377	= Kilopascals (kPa)	X 0.2961	= Inches mercury
Inches mercury (in. Hg)	X 25.4	= Millimeters mercury (mm Hg)	X 0.0394	= Inches mercury

Power

Horsepower (hp)	X 745.7	= Watts (W)	X 0.0013	= Horsepower (hp)

Velocity (speed)

Miles per hour (miles/hr; mph)	X 1.609	= Kilometres per hour (km/hr; kph)	X 0.621	= Miles per hour (miles/hr; mph)

Fuel consumption*

Miles per gallon, Imperial (mpg)	X 0.354	= Kilometres per litre (km/l)	X 2.825	= Miles per gallon, Imperial (mpg)
Miles per gallon, US (mpg)	X 0.425	= Kilometres per litre (km/l)	X 2.352	= Miles per gallon, US (mpg)

Temperature

Degrees Fahrenheit = ($°C \times 1.8$) + 32

Degrees Celsius (Degrees Centigrade; °C) = ($°F - 32$) x 0.56

*It is common practice to convert from miles per gallon (mpg) to litres/100 kilometres (l/100km), where mpg (Imperial) x l/100 km = 282 and mpg (US) x l/100 km = 235

Safety first!

Regardless of how enthusiastic you may be about getting on with the job at hand, take the time to ensure that your safety is not jeopardized. A moment's lack of attention can result in an accident, as can failure to observe certain simple safety precautions. The possibility of an accident will always exist, and the following points should not be considered a comprehensive list of all dangers. Rather, they are intended to make you aware of the risks and to encourage a safety conscious approach to all work you carry out on your vehicle.

Essential DOs and DON'Ts

DON'T rely on a jack when working under the vehicle. Always use approved jackstands to support the weight of the vehicle and place them under the recommended lift or support points.

DON'T attempt to loosen extremely tight fasteners (i.e. wheel lug nuts) while the vehicle is on a jack - it may fall.

DON'T start the engine without first making sure that the transmission is in Neutral (or Park where applicable) and the parking brake is set.

DON'T remove the radiator cap from a hot cooling system - let it cool or cover it with a cloth and release the pressure gradually.

DON'T attempt to drain the engine oil until you are sure it has cooled to the point that it will not burn you.

DON'T touch any part of the engine or exhaust system until it has cooled sufficiently to avoid burns.

DON'T siphon toxic liquids such as gasoline, antifreeze and brake fluid by mouth, or allow them to remain on your skin.

DON'T inhale brake lining dust - it is potentially hazardous (see *Asbestos* below).

DON'T allow spilled oil or grease to remain on the floor - wipe it up before someone slips on it.

DON'T use loose fitting wrenches or other tools which may slip and cause injury.

DON'T push on wrenches when loosening or tightening nuts or bolts. Always try to pull the wrench toward you. If the situation calls for pushing the wrench away, push with an open hand to avoid scraped knuckles if the wrench should slip.

DON'T attempt to lift a heavy component alone - get someone to help you.

DON'T rush or take unsafe shortcuts to finish a job.

DON'T allow children or animals in or around the vehicle while you are working on it.

DO wear eye protection when using power tools such as a drill, sander, bench grinder, etc. and when working under a vehicle.

DO keep loose clothing and long hair well out of the way of moving parts.

DO make sure that any hoist used has a safe working load rating adequate for the job.

DO get someone to check on you periodically when working alone on a vehicle.

DO carry out work in a logical sequence and make sure that everything is correctly assembled and tightened.

DO keep chemicals and fluids tightly capped and out of the reach of children and pets.

DO remember that your vehicle's safety affects that of yourself and others. If in doubt on any point, get professional advice.

Asbestos

Certain friction, insulating, sealing, and other products - such as brake linings, brake bands, clutch linings, torque converters, gaskets, etc. - may contain asbestos. Extreme care must be taken to avoid inhalation of dust from such products, since it is hazardous to health. If in doubt, assume that they do contain asbestos.

Fire

Remember at all times that gasoline is highly flammable. Never smoke or have any kind of open flame around when working on a vehicle. But the risk does not end there. A spark caused by an electrical short circuit, by two metal surfaces contacting each other, or even by static electricity built up in your body under certain conditions, can ignite gasoline vapors, which in a confined space are highly explosive. Do not, under any circumstances, use gasoline for cleaning parts. Use an approved safety solvent.

Always disconnect the battery ground (-) cable at the battery before working on any part of the fuel system or electrical system. Never risk spilling fuel on a hot engine or exhaust component. It is strongly recommended that a fire extinguisher suitable for use on fuel and electrical fires be kept handy in the garage or workshop at all times. Never try to extinguish a fuel or electrical fire with water.

Fumes

Certain fumes are highly toxic and can quickly cause unconsciousness and even death if inhaled to any extent. Gasoline vapor falls into this category, as do the vapors from some cleaning solvents. Any draining or pouring of such volatile fluids should be done in a well ventilated area.

When using cleaning fluids and solvents, read the instructions on the container carefully. Never use materials from unmarked containers.

Never run the engine in an enclosed space, such as a garage. Exhaust fumes contain carbon monoxide, which is extremely poisonous. If you need to run the engine, always do so in the open air, or at least have the rear of the vehicle outside the work area.

If you are fortunate enough to have the use of an inspection pit, never drain or pour gasoline and never run the engine while the vehicle is over the pit. The fumes, being heavier than air, will concentrate in the pit with possibly lethal results.

The battery

Never create a spark or allow a bare light bulb near a battery. They normally give off a certain amount of hydrogen gas, which is highly explosive.

Always disconnect the battery ground (-) cable at the battery before working on the fuel or electrical systems.

If possible, loosen the filler caps or cover when charging the battery from an external source (this does not apply to sealed or maintenance-free batteries). Do not charge at an excessive rate or the battery may burst.

Take care when adding water to a non maintenance-free battery and when carrying a battery. The electrolyte, even when diluted, is very corrosive and should not be allowed to contact clothing or skin.

Always wear eye protection when cleaning the battery to prevent the caustic deposits from entering your eyes.

Household current

When using an electric power tool, inspection light, etc., which operates on household current, always make sure that the tool is correctly connected to its plug and that, where necessary, it is properly grounded. Do not use such items in damp conditions and, again, do not create a spark or apply excessive heat in the vicinity of fuel or fuel vapor.

Secondary ignition system voltage

A severe electric shock can result from touching certain parts of the ignition system (such as the spark plug wires) when the engine is running or being cranked, particularly if components are damp or the insulation is defective. In the case of an electronic ignition system, the secondary system voltage is much higher and could prove fatal.

Troubleshooting

Contents

Engine and performance

1 Engine will not rotate when attempting to start

1   Battery terminal connections loose or corroded. Check the cable terminals at the battery; tighten cable clamp and/or clean off corrosion as necessary (see Chapter 1).

2   Battery discharged or faulty. If the cable ends are clean and tight on the battery posts, turn the key to the On position and switch on the headlights or windshield wipers. If they won't run, the battery is discharged.

3   Automatic transaxle not engaged in park (P) or Neutral (N).

4   Broken, loose or disconnected wires in the starting circuit. Inspect all wires and connectors at the battery, starter solenoid and ignition switch (on steering column).

5   Starter motor pinion jammed in driveplate ring gear. Remove starter (Chapter 5) and inspect pinion and driveplate (Chapter 2) at earliest convenience.

6   Starter solenoid faulty (Chapter 5).

7   Starter motor faulty (Chapter 5).

8   Ignition switch faulty (Chapter 12).

9   Engine seized. Try to turn the crankshaft with a large socket and breaker bar on the pulley bolt.

2 Engine rotates but will not start

1   Fuel tank empty.

2   Battery discharged (engine rotates slowly). Check the operation of electrical components as described in previous Section.

3   Battery terminal connections loose or corroded. See previous Section.

4   Fuel not reaching fuel injectors. Check for clogged fuel filter or lines and defective fuel pump. Also make sure the tank vent lines aren't clogged (Chapter 4).

5   Faulty ignition module. (Chapter 5).

6   Low cylinder compression. Check as described in Chapter 2.

7   Water in fuel. Drain tank and fill with new fuel.

8   Dirty or clogged fuel injectors.

9   Faulty idle control system (Chapter 4).

10   Faulty emissions or engine control systems (Chapter 6).

11   Wet or damaged ignition components (Chapters 1 and 5).

12   Worn, faulty or incorrectly gapped spark plugs (Chapter 1).

13   Broken, loose or disconnected wires in the ignition circuit.

14   Broken, loose or disconnected wires at the ignition coil(s) or faulty coil(s) (Chapter 5).

15   Timing chain or belt failure or wear affecting valve timing (Chapter 2).

3 Starter motor operates without turning engine

1   Starter pinion sticking. Remove the starter (Chapter 5) and inspect.

2   Starter pinion or driveplate teeth worn or broken. Remove the inspection cover on the left side of the engine and inspect.

4 Engine hard to start when cold

1   Battery discharged or low. Check as described in Chapter 1.

2   Fuel not reaching the fuel injectors. Check the fuel filter and lines (Chapters 1 and 4).

3   Defective spark plugs (Chapter 1).

4   Intake manifold vacuum leaks. Make sure all mounting bolts/nuts are tight and all vacuum hoses connected to the manifold are attached properly and in good condition.

5   Faulty idle control system (Chapter 4).

4   Faulty emissions or engine control systems (Chapter 6).

5 Engine hard to start when hot

1   Air filter dirty (Chapter 1).

2   Bad engine ground connection.

3   Fuel not reaching the injectors (Chapter 4).

4   Loose connection in the ignition system (Chapter 5).

5   Faulty idle control system (Chapter 4).

6   Faulty emissions or engine control systems (Chapter 6).

6 Starter motor noisy or engages roughly

1   Pinion or flywheel/driveplate teeth worn or broken. Remove the inspection cover and inspect.

2   Starter motor mounting bolts loose or missing.

7 Engine starts but stops immediately

1   Loose or damaged wiring in the ignition system.

2   Intake manifold vacuum leaks. Make sure all mounting bolts/nuts are tight and all vacuum hoses connected to the manifold are attached properly and in good condition.

5   Faulty idle control system (Chapter 4).

4   Faulty emissions or engine control systems (Chapter 6).

8 Engine 'lopes' while idling or idles erratically

1   Vacuum leaks. Check mounting bolts at the intake manifold or plenum for tightness. Make sure that all vacuum hoses are connected and in good condition. Use a stethoscope or a length of fuel hose held against your ear to listen for vacuum leaks while the engine is running. A hissing sound will be heard. A soapy water solution will also detect leaks. Check the intake manifold or plenum gasket surfaces.

2   Leaking EGR valve or plugged PCV valve (Chapter 6).

3   Air filter clogged (Chapter 1).

4   Leaking head gasket. Perform a cylinder compression check (Chapter 2).

5   Worn timing chain or belt (Chapter 2).

6   Camshaft lobes worn (Chapter 2).

7   Valves burned or otherwise leaking (Chapter 2).

8   Ignition system not operating properly (Chapters 1 and 5).

9   Dirty or clogged injectors (Chapter 4).

10   Faulty idle control system (Chapter 4).

11   Faulty emissions or engine control systems (Chapter 6).

9 Engine misses at idle speed

1   Spark plugs faulty or not gapped properly (Chapter 1).

2   Faulty spark plug wires (Chapter 1).

3   Wet or damaged ignition components (Chapter 1).

4   Short circuits in ignition, coil(s) or spark plug wires.

5   Faulty emissions or engine control systems (Chapter 6).

6   Clogged fuel filter and/or foreign matter in fuel. Replace the fuel filter (Chapter 1).

7   Vacuum leaks at intake manifold or plenum or hose connections. Check as described in Section 8.

8   Low or uneven cylinder compression. Check as described in Chapter 2.

9   Clogged or dirty fuel injectors (Chapter 4).

10   Leaky EGR valve (Chapter 6).

11   Faulty emissions or engine control systems (Chapter 6).

10 Excessively high idle speed

1   Sticking throttle linkage (Chapter 4).

2   Idle speed incorrect (Chapter 4).

3   Faulty idle control system (Chapter 4).

4   Faulty emissions or engine control systems (Chapter 6).

11 Battery will not hold a charge

1   Drivebelt defective or not adjusted properly (Chapter 1).

2   Battery cables loose or corroded (Chapter 1).
3   Alternator not charging properly (Chapter 5).
4   Loose, broken or faulty wires in the charging circuit (Chapter 5).
5   Short circuit causing a continuous drain on the battery (Chapter 12).
6   Battery defective internally.
7   Faulty regulator (Chapter 5).

12   Alternator light stays on

1   Fault in alternator or charging circuit (Chapter 5).
2   Drivebelt defective or not properly adjusted (Chapter 1).

13   Alternator light fails to come on when key is turned on

1   Faulty bulb (Chapter 12).
2   Defective alternator (Chapter 5).
3   Fault in the printed circuit, dash wiring or bulb holder (Chapter 12).

14   Engine misses throughout driving speed range

1   Fuel filter clogged and/or impurities in the fuel system. Check fuel filter (Chapter 1) or clean system (Chapter 4).
2   Faulty or incorrectly gapped spark plugs (Chapter 1).
3   Incorrect ignition timing (Chapter 5).
4   Disconnected ignition system wires or damaged ignition system components (Chapter 1).
5   Defective spark plug wires (Chapter 1).
6   Emissions or engine control system components faulty (Chapter 6).
7   Low or uneven cylinder compression pressures. Check as described in Chapter 2.
8   Weak or faulty ignition coil(s) (Chapter 5).
9   Weak or faulty ignition system (Chapter 5).
10   Vacuum leaks at intake manifold or plenum or vacuum hoses (see Section 8).
11   Dirty or clogged fuel injector (Chapter 4).

15   Hesitation or stumble during acceleration

1   Ignition timing incorrect (Chapter 5).
2   Ignition system not operating properly (Chapter 5).
3   Dirty or clogged fuel injectors (Chapter 4).
4   Low fuel pressure. Check for proper operation of the fuel pump and for restrictions in the fuel filter and lines (Chapter 4).
5   Emissions or engine control system components faulty (Chapter 6).

16   Engine stalls

1   Faulty idle air control valve (Chapter 4).
2   Fuel filter clogged and/or water and impurities in the fuel system (Chapter 1).
3   Damaged or wet ignition system wires or components.
4   Faulty idle control system (Chapter 4).
5   Emissions or engine control system components faulty (Chapter 6).
6   Faulty or incorrectly gapped spark plugs (Chapter 1). Also check the spark plug wires (Chapter 1).
7   Vacuum leak at the intake manifold or plenum or vacuum hoses. Check as described in Section 8.

17   Engine lacks power

1   Incorrect ignition timing (Chapter 5).
2   Check for faulty ignition wires, etc. (Chapter 1).
3   Faulty or incorrectly gapped spark plugs (Chapter 1).
4   Air filter dirty (Chapter 1).
5   Spark timing control system not operating properly (Chapter 5).
6   Faulty ignition coil(s) (Chapter 5).
7   Brakes binding (Chapters 1 and 9).
8   Automatic transaxle fluid level incorrect, causing slippage (Chapter 1).
9   Fuel filter clogged and/or impurities in the fuel system (Chapters 1 and 4).
10   EGR system not functioning properly (Chapter 6).
11   Use of sub-standard fuel. Fill tank with proper octane fuel.
12   Low or uneven cylinder compression pressures. Check as described in Chapter 2.
13   Air (vacuum) leak at intake manifold or plenum (check as described in Section 8).

18   Engine backfires

1   EGR system not functioning properly (Chapter 6).
2   Ignition timing incorrect (Chapter 5).
3   Vacuum leak (refer to Section 8).
4   Damaged valve springs or sticking valves (Chapter 2).
5   Intake air (vacuum) leak (see Section 8).

19   Engine surges while holding accelerator steady

1   Intake air (vacuum) leak (see Section 8).
2   Fuel pump not working properly.
3   Faulty idle air control system (Chapter 4).
4   Emissions or engine control system components faulty (Chapter 6).

20   Pinging or knocking engine sounds when engine is under load

1   Incorrect grade of fuel. Fill tank with fuel of the proper octane rating.
2   Ignition timing incorrect (Chapter 5) or problem in the ignition system (Chapter 5).
3   Carbon build-up in combustion chambers. Remove cylinder head(s) and clean combustion chambers (Chapter 2).
4   Incorrect spark plugs (Chapter 1).
5   Knock sensor system not functioning properly (Chapter 6).

21   Engine diesels (continues to run) after being turned off

1   Idle speed too high (Chapter 4).
2   Ignition timing incorrect (Chapter 5).
3   Incorrect spark plug heat range (Chapter 1).
4   Intake air (vacuum) leak (see Section 8).
5   Carbon build-up in combustion chambers. Remove the cylinder head and clean the combustion chambers (Chapter 2).
6   Valves sticking (Chapter 2).
7   Valve clearance incorrect (Chapter 1).
8   EGR system not operating properly (Chapter 6).
9   Leaking fuel injector(s) (Chapter 4).
10   Check for causes of overheating (Section 27).

22   Low oil pressure

1   Improper grade of oil.
2   Oil pump regulator valve not operating properly (Chapter 2).
3   Oil pump worn or damaged (Chapter 2).
4   Engine overheating (refer to Section 27).
5   Clogged oil filter (Chapter 1).
6   Clogged oil strainer (Chapter 2).
7   Oil pressure gauge not working properly (Chapter 2).

23   Excessive oil consumption

1   Loose oil drain plug.
2   Loose bolts or damaged oil pan gasket (Chapter 2).
3   Loose bolts or damaged front cover gasket (Chapter 2).
4   Front or rear crankshaft oil seal leaking (Chapter 2).
5   Loose bolts or damaged valve cover gasket (Chapter 2).
6   Loose oil filter (Chapter 1).
7   Loose or damaged oil pressure switch (Chapter 2).
8   Pistons and cylinders excessively worn (Chapter 2).
9   Piston rings not installed correctly on pistons (Chapter 2).

10 Worn or damaged piston rings (Chapter 2).
11 Intake and/or exhaust valve oil seals worn or damaged (Chapter 2).
12 Worn valve stems.
13 Worn or damaged valves/guides (Chapter 2).

24 Excessive fuel consumption

1 Dirty or clogged air filter element (Chapter 1).
2 Incorrect ignition timing (Chapter 5).
3 Incorrect idle speed (Chapter 4).
4 Low tire pressure or incorrect tire size (Chapter 10).
5 Fuel leakage. Check all connections, lines and components in the fuel system (Chapter 4).
6 Dirty or clogged fuel injectors (Chapter 4).
7 Problem in the fuel injection system (Chapter 4).

25 Fuel odor

1 Fuel leakage. Check all connections, lines and components in the fuel system (Chapter 4).
2 Fuel tank overfilled. Fill only to automatic shut-off.
3 Charcoal canister filter in Evaporative Emissions Control system clogged (Chapter 6).
4 Vapor leaks from Evaporative Emissions Control system lines (Chapter 6).

26 Miscellaneous engine noises

1 A strong dull noise that becomes more rapid as the engine accelerates indicates worn or damaged crankshaft bearings or an unevenly worn crankshaft. To pinpoint the trouble spot, remove the spark plug wire from one plug at a time and crank the engine over. If the noise stops, the cylinder with the removed plug wire indicates the problem area. Replace the bearing and/or service or replace the crankshaft (Chapter 2).
2 A similar (yet slightly higher pitched) noise to the crankshaft knocking described in the previous paragraph, that becomes more rapid as the engine accelerates, indicates worn or damaged connecting rod bearings (Chapter 2). The procedure for locating the problem cylinder is the same as described in Paragraph 1.
3 An overlapping metallic noise that increases in intensity as the engine speed increases, yet diminishes as the engine warms up indicates abnormal piston and cylinder wear (Chapter 2).To locate the problem cylinder, use the procedure described in Paragraph 1.
4 A rapid clicking noise that becomes

faster as the engine accelerates indicates a worn piston pin or piston pin hole. This sound will happen each time the piston hits the highest and lowest points in the stroke (Chapter 2). The procedure for locating the problem piston is described in Paragraph 1.
5 A metallic clicking noise coming from the water pump indicates worn or damaged water pump bearings or pump. Replace the water pump with a new one (Chapter 3).
6 A rapid tapping sound or clicking sound that becomes faster as the engine speed increases indicates "valve tapping" or stuck valve lifters. This can be identified by holding one end of a section of hose to your ear and placing the other end at different spots along the rocker arm cover. The point where the sound is loudest indicates the problem valve. Adjust the valve clearance (Chapter 1).
7 A steady metallic rattling or rapping sound coming from the area of the timing chain cover indicates a worn, damaged or out-of-adjustment timing chain. Service or replace the chain and related components (Chapter 2).

27 Overheating

1 Insufficient coolant in system (Chapter 1).
2 Water pump drivebelt defective or out of adjustment (Chapter 1).
3 Radiator core blocked or grille restricted (Chapter 3).
4 Thermostat faulty (Chapter 3).
5 Electric cooling fan blades broken or cracked (Chapter 3).
6 Radiator cap not maintaining proper pressure (Chapter 3).

28 Overcooling

Faulty thermostat (Chapter 3).

29 External coolant leakage

1 Deteriorated/damaged hoses or loose clamps (Chapters 1 and 3).
2 Water pump seal defective (Chapters 1 and 3).
3 Leakage from radiator core or header tank (Chapter 3).
4 Engine drain or water jacket core plugs leaking (Chapter 2).
5 Leak at engine oil cooler (Chapter 3).

30 Internal coolant leakage

1 Leaking cylinder head gasket (Chapter 2).
2 Cracked cylinder bore or cylinder head (Chapter 2).

31 Coolant loss

1 Too much coolant in system (Chapter 1).
2 Coolant boiling away because of overheating (Chapter 3).
3 Internal or external leakage (Chapter 3).
4 Faulty radiator cap (Chapter 3).

32 Poor coolant circulation

1 Inoperative water pump (Chapter 3).
2 Restriction in cooling system (Chapters 1 and 3).
3 Water pump drivebelt defective or out of adjustment (Chapter 1).
4 Thermostat sticking (Chapter 3).

Automatic transaxle

Note: *Due to the complexity of the automatic transaxle, it's difficult for the home mechanic to properly diagnose and service this component. For problems other than the following, the vehicle should be taken to a dealer service department or a transmission shop.*

33 Fluid leakage

1 Automatic transmission fluid is a deep red color. Fluid leaks should not be confused with engine oil, which can easily be blown by air flow to the transaxle.
2 To pinpoint a leak, first remove all built-up dirt and grime from the transaxle housing with degreasing agents and/or steam cleaning. Drive the vehicle at low speeds so air flow will not blow the leak far from its source. Raise the vehicle and determine where the leak is coming from. Common areas of leakage are:

a) *Pan (Chapters 1 and 7)*
b) *Filler pipe (Chapter 7)*
c) *Transaxle oil lines (Chapter 7)*
d) *Speedometer gear or sensor (Chapter 7)*
e) *Vacuum modulator (Chapter 7)*

34 Transaxle fluid brown or has a burned smell

Transaxle overheated. Change the fluid (Chapter 1).

35 General shift mechanism problems

1 Chapter 7 deals with checking and adjusting the shift linkage on automatic transaxles. Common problems which may be attributed to poorly adjusted linkage are:

a) *Engine starting in gears other than Park or Neutral.*
b) *Indicator on shifter pointing to a gear other than the one actually being used.*
c) *Vehicle moves when in Park.*

2 Refer to Chapter 7 for the shift linkage adjustment procedure.

36 Transaxle will not downshift with accelerator pedal pressed to the floor

Throttle Valve (TV) cable out of adjustment (Chapter 7).

37 Engine will start in gears other than Park or Neutral

Park/Neutral switch malfunctioning (Chapter 7).

38 Transaxle slips, shifts roughly, is noisy or has no drive in forward or reverse gears

There are many probable causes for the above problems, but the home mechanic should be concerned with only one possibility - fluid level. Before taking the vehicle to a repair shop, check the level and condition of the fluid as described in Chapter 1.

Correct the fluid level as necessary or change the fluid and filter if needed. If the problem persists, have a professional diagnose the probable cause.

Driveaxles

39 Clicking noise in turns

Worn or damaged outer CV joint. Check for cut or damaged boots (Chapter 1). Repair as necessary (Chapter 8).

40 Knock or clunk when accelerating after coasting

Worn or damaged CV joint. Check for cut or damaged boots (Chapter 1). Repair as necessary (Chapter 8).

41 Shudder or vibration during acceleration

1   Excessive inner CV joint angle. Check and correct as necessary (Chapter 8).
2   Worn or damaged CV joints. Repair or replace as necessary (Chapter 8).
3   Sticking inboard joint assembly. Correct or replace as necessary (Chapter 8).

Brakes

Note: *Before assuming that a brake problem exists, make sure . . .*
a) *The tires are in good condition and properly inflated (Chapter 1).*

b) *The front end alignment is correct (Chapter 10).*
c) *The vehicle isn't loaded with weight in an unequal manner.*

42 Vehicle pulls to one side during braking

1   Incorrect tire pressures (Chapter 1).
2   Front end out of line (have the front end aligned).
3   Unmatched tires on same axle.
4   Restricted brake lines or hoses (Chapter 9).
5   Malfunctioning brake assembly (Chapter 9).
6   Loose suspension parts (Chapter 10).
7   Loose brake calipers (Chapter 9).
8   Contaminated brake linings (Chapters 1 and 9).

43 Noise (high-pitched squeal when the brakes are applied)

Front disc brake pads worn out. The noise comes from the wear sensor rubbing against the disc. Replace pads with new ones immediately (Chapter 9).

44 Brake roughness or chatter (pedal pulsates)

Note: *Brake pedal pulsation during operation of the Anti-Lock Brake System (ABS) is normal.*
1   Excessive front brake disc lateral runout (Chapter 9).
2   Parallelism not within specifications (Chapter 9).
3   Uneven pad wear caused by caliper not sliding due to improper clearance or dirt (Chapter 9).
4   Defective brake disc (Chapter 9).

45 Excessive pedal effort required to stop vehicle

1   Malfunctioning power brake booster (Chapter 9).
2   Partial system failure (Chapter 9).
3   Excessively worn pads (Chapter 9).
4   One or more caliper pistons or wheel cylinders seized or sticking (Chapter 9).
5   Brake pads contaminated with oil or grease (Chapter 9).
6   New pads installed and not yet seated. It will take a while for the new material to seat.

46 Excessive brake pedal travel

1   Partial brake system failure (Chapter 9).

2   Insufficient fluid in master cylinder (Chapters 1 and 9).
3   Air trapped in system (Chapters 1 and 9).
4   Excessively worn rear shoes (Chapter 9).

47 Dragging brakes

1   Master cylinder pistons not returning correctly (Chapter 9).
2   Restricted brakes lines or hoses (Chapters 1 and 9).
3   Incorrect parking brake adjustment (Chapter 9).
4   Sticking pistons in calipers (Chapter 9).

48 Grabbing or uneven braking action

1   Malfunction of proportioner valves (Chapter 9).
2   Malfunction of power brake booster unit (Chapter 9).
3   Binding brake pedal mechanism (Chapter 9).
4   Sticking pistons in calipers (Chapter 9).

49 Brake pedal feels spongy when depressed

1   Air in hydraulic lines (Chapter 9).
2   Master cylinder mounting bolts loose (Chapter 9).
3   Master cylinder defective (Chapter 9).

50 Brake pedal travels to the floor with little resistance

Little or no fluid in the master cylinder reservoir caused by leaking caliper or wheel cylinder pistons, loose, damaged or disconnected brake lines (Chapter 9).

51 Parking brake does not hold

Check the parking brake (Chapter 9).

Suspension and steering systems

Note: *Before attempting to diagnose the suspension and steering systems, perform the following preliminary checks:*
a) *Check the tire pressures and look for uneven wear.*
b) *Check the steering universal joints or coupling from the column to the steering gear for loose fasteners and wear.*
c) *Check the front and rear suspension and the steering gear assembly for loose and damaged parts.*

d) Look for out-of-round or out-of-balance tires, bent rims and loose and/or rough wheel bearings.

52 Vehicle pulls to one side

1   Mismatched or uneven tires (Chapter 10).
2   Broken or sagging springs (Chapter 10).
3   Front wheel alignment incorrect (Chapter 10).
4   Front brakes dragging (Chapter 9).

53 Abnormal or excessive tire wear

1   Front wheel alignment incorrect (Chapter 10).
2   Sagging or broken springs (Chapter 10).
3   Tire out-of-balance (Chapter 10).
4   Worn shock absorber (Chapter 10).
5   Overloaded vehicle.
6   Tires not rotated regularly.

54 Wheel makes a "thumping" noise

1   Blister or bump on tire (Chapter 1).
2   Improper shock absorber action (Chapter 10).

55 Shimmy, shake or vibration

1   Tire or wheel out-of-balance or out-of-round (Chapter 10).
2   Loose or worn wheel bearings (Chapter 10).
3   Worn tie-rod ends (Chapter 10).
4   Worn balljoints (Chapter 10).
5   Excessive wheel runout (Chapter 10).
6   Blister or bump on tire (Chapter 1).

56 Hard steering

1   Lack of lubrication at balljoints, tie-rod ends and steering gear assembly (Chapter 10).
2   Front wheel alignment incorrect (Chapter 10).
3   Low tire pressure (Chapter 1).

57 Steering wheel does not return to center position correctly

1   Lack of lubrication at balljoints and tie-rod ends (Chapter 10).
2   Binding in steering column (Chapter 10).
3   Defective rack-and-pinion assembly (Chapter 10).

4   Front wheel alignment problem (Chapter 10).

58 Abnormal noise at the front end

1   Lack of lubrication at balljoints and tie-rod ends (Chapter 1).
2   Loose upper strut mount (Chapter 10).
3   Worn tie-rod ends (Chapter 10).
4   Loose stabilizer bar (Chapter 10).
5   Loose wheel lug nuts (Chapter 1).
6   Loose suspension bolts (Chapter 10).

59 Wander or poor steering stability

1   Mismatched or uneven tires (Chapter 10).
2   Lack of lubrication at balljoints or tie-rod ends (Chapters 1 and 10).
3   Worn shock absorbers (Chapter 10).
4   Loose stabilizer bar (Chapter 10).
5   Broken or sagging springs (Chapter 10).
6   Front wheel alignment incorrect (Chapter 10).
7   Worn steering gear clamp bushings (Chapter 10).

60 Erratic steering when braking

1   Wheel bearings worn (Chapters 8 and 10).
2   Broken or sagging springs (Chapter 10).
3   Leaking wheel cylinder or caliper (Chapter 9).
4   Warped brake discs (Chapter 9).
5   Worn steering gear clamp bushings (Chapter 10).

61 Excessive pitching and/or rolling around corners or during braking

1   Loose stabilizer bar (Chapter 10).
2   Worn shock absorbers or mounts (Chapter 10).
3   Broken or sagging springs (Chapter 10).
4   Overloaded vehicle.

62 Suspension bottoms

1   Overloaded vehicle.
2   Worn shock absorbers (Chapter 10).
3   Incorrect, broken or sagging springs (Chapter 10).

63 Cupped tires

1   Front wheel alignment incorrect (Chapter 10).
2   Worn shock absorbers (Chapter 10).
3   Wheel bearings worn (Chapters 8 and 10).
4   Excessive tire or wheel runout (Chapter 10).
5   Worn balljoints (Chapter 10).

64 Excessive tire wear on outside edge

1   Inflation pressures incorrect (Chapter 1).
2   Excessive speed in turns.
3   Front end alignment incorrect (excessive toe-in or positive camber). Have professionally aligned.
4   Suspension arm bent or twisted (Chapter 10).

65 Excessive tire wear on inside edge

1   Inflation pressures incorrect (Chapter 1).
2   Front end alignment incorrect (toe-out or excessive negative camber). Have professionally aligned.
3   Loose or damaged steering components (Chapter 10).

66 Tire tread worn in one place

1   Tires out-of-balance.
2   Damaged or buckled wheel. Inspect and replace if necessary.
3   Defective tire (Chapter 1).

67 Excessive play or looseness in steering system

1   Wheel bearings worn (Chapter 10).
2   Tie-rod end loose or worn (Chapter 10).
3   Steering gear loose (Chapter 10).

68 Rattling or clicking noise in rack and pinion

Steering gear clamps loose (Chapter 10).

Notes

Chapter 1
Tune-up and routine maintenance

Contents

Specifications

Recommended lubricants and fluids

Note: *Listed here are manufacturer recommendations at the time this manual was written. Manufacturers occasionally upgrade their fluid and lubricant specifications, so check with your local auto parts store for current recommendations.*

Engine oil	
Type	API grade SG, SG/CC or SG/CD multigrade and fuel-efficient oil
Viscosity	See accompanying chart
Automatic transmission fluid	Dexron III Automatic Transmission Fluid (ATF)
Engine coolant	50/50 mixture of water and the specified ethylene glycol-based (green color) antifreeze or "DEX-COOL", silicate-free (orange-color) coolant - DO NOT mix the two types (refer to Sections 4, 11 and 27)
Brake fluid	DOT 3 brake fluid
Power steering fluid	GM power steering fluid or equivalent
Chassis grease	SAE NLGI no. 2 chassis grease

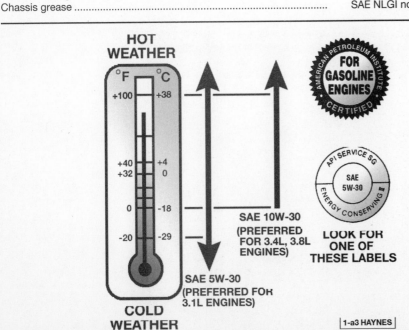

Engine oil viscosity chart - For best fuel economy and cold starting, select the lowest SAE viscosity grade for the expected temperature range

1-a3 HAYNES

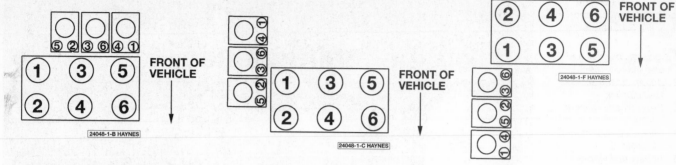

Cylinder location and coil terminal
identification diagram - 3.1L engine

Cylinder location and coil terminal
identification diagram - 3.4L engine

Cylinder location and coil terminal
identification diagram - 3.8L engine

Capacities*

Engine oil (with filter change)	
3.1L	4.5 to 5.0 qts
3.4L	5.5 to 6.0 qts
3.8L	4.5 to 5.0 qts
Fuel tank	
All (except 3.1L)	17.1 gallons
3.1L	16.1 gallons
Cooling system	
1995 through 1996	
3.1L (with 3T40 transmission)	12.7 qts
3.1L (with 4T60-E transmission)	12.5 qts
3.4L (with 4T60-E transmission)	12.7 qts
1997 on	
3.1L	11.6 qts
3.4L	12.3 qts
3.8L	11.6 qts
Automatic transmission (fluid and filter replacement)	7 qts

*All capacities approximate. Add as necessary to bring to appropriate level.

Ignition system

Spark plug type and gap	
1995	
3.1L	AC type R44LTSM or equivalent @ 0.060 inch
3.4L	AC type R42LTSM or equivalent @ 0.045 inch
1996 through 1997	
3.1L	AC type 41-940 or equivalent @ 0.060 inch
3.4L	AC type 41-919 or equivalent @ 0.045 inch
1998	
3.1L	AC type 41-940 or equivalent @ 0.060 inch
3.8L	AC type 41-921 or equivalent @ 0.060 inch
Firing order	
3.1L	1-2-3-4-5-6
3.4L	1-2-3-4-5-6
3.8L	1-6-5-4-3-2

General

Radiator cap pressure rating	15 psi
Brake pad lining wear limit	1/8 inch
Brake shoe lining wear limit	3/32 inch

Torque specifications

Ft-lbs (unless otherwise indicated)

Automatic transmission pan bolts	90 to 100 in-lbs
Engine oil drain plug	15 to 20
Spark plugs	
3.1L	132 in-lbs
3.4L	132 in-lbs
3.8L	15 to 20
Wheel lug nuts	100

Typical engine compartment components - 3.1L engine

1 Ignition coil pack and spark plug wires
2 Automatic transmission fluid dipstick
3 Brake master cylinder reservoir
4 Engine compartment fuse block No. 2
5 Battery (not visible)
6 Windshield washer fluid reservoir
7 Upper radiator hose
8 Air filter housing
9 PCV valve
10 Engine oil dipstick
11 Engine oil filler cap
12 Spark plugs (front side)
13 Lower radiator hose
14 Radiator cap
15 Engine compartment fuse block No. 1
16 Power steering fluid reservoir
17 Engine coolant reservoir
18 Drivebelt

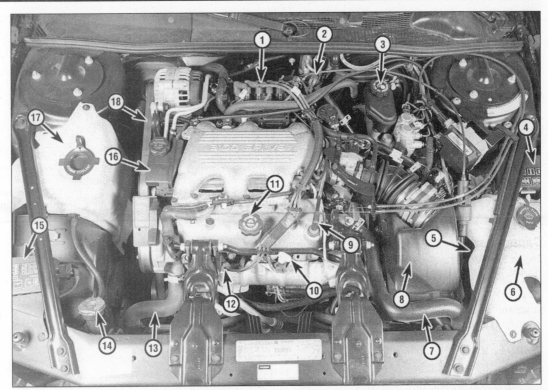

1

Typical engine compartment components - 3800 engine

1 Automatic transmission fluid dipstick
2 Brake master cylinder reservoir
3 Engine compartment fuse block No. 2
4 Battery (not visible)
5 Windshield washer fluid reservoir
6 Air filter housing
7 Upper radiator hose
8 Spark plugs (front side)
9 Engine oil filler cap
10 Engine oil dipstick
11 Lower radiator hose
12 Radiator cap
13 Engine compartment fuse block No. 1
14 Ignition coil pack and spark plug wires
15 PCV valve
16 Engine coolant reservoir
17 Drivebelt
18 Power steering fluid reservoir (not visible in photo; below alternator)

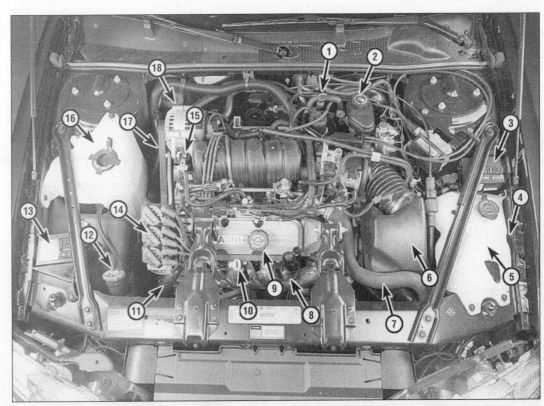

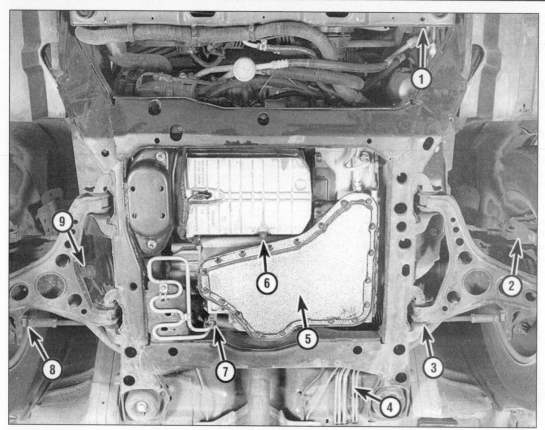

Typical front underside components

1 Radiator drain plug (not visible)
2 Front brake caliper
3 Lower control arm bushing
4 Fuel lines
5 Automatic transaxle fluid pan
6 Engine oil drain plug
7 Steering gear
8 Tie-rod end
9 Driveaxle

Typical rear underside components

1 Fuel filler pipe and hose assembly
2 Exhaust hanger
3 Muffler
4 Rear brake hose
5 Trailing arm bushing
6 Fuel tank
7 Lateral link rod
8 Shock/strut assembly
9 Stabilizer bar bushing

1 Chevrolet Lumina and Monte Carlo Maintenance schedule

The following maintenance intervals are based on the assumption that the vehicle owner will be doing the maintenance or service work, as opposed to having a dealer service department do the work. Although the time/mileage intervals are loosely based on factory recommendations, most have been shortened to ensure, for example, that such items as lubricants and fluids are checked/changed at intervals that promote maximum engine/driveline service life. Also, subject to the preference of the individual owner interested in keeping his or her vehicle in peak condition at all times, and with the vehicle's ultimate resale in mind, many of the maintenance procedures may be performed more often than recommended in the following schedule. We encourage such owner initiative.

When the vehicle is new it should be serviced initially by a factory authorized dealer service department to protect the factory warranty. In many cases the initial maintenance check is done at no cost to the owner (check with your dealer service department for more information).

Every 250 miles or weekly, whichever comes first

Check the engine oil level (Section 4)
Check the engine coolant level (Section 4)
Check the windshield washer fluid level (Section 4)
Check the brake fluid level (Section 4)
Check the tires and tire pressures (Section 5)

Every 3000 miles or 3 months, whichever comes first

All items listed above plus:
Check the power steering fluid level (Section 6)
Check the automatic transmission fluid level (Section 7)
Change the engine oil and filter (Section 8)
Lubricate the chassis (Section 9)

Every 6000 miles or 6 months, whichever comes first

All items listed above plus:
Check and service the battery (Section 10)
Check the cooling system (Section 11)
Inspect and replace, if necessary, all underhood hoses (Section 12)
Check the engine drivebelt (Section 13)
Inspect the suspension and steering components and the driveaxle boots (Section 14)
Check the brakes (Section 15)*
Rotate the tires (Section 16)
Inspect the exhaust system (Section 17)

Every 12,000 miles or 12 months, whichever comes first

Inspect the throttle linkage (Section 18)
Inspect and replace, if necessary, the windshield wiper blades (Section 19)
Inspect the seat belts (Section 20)
Replace the air filter (Section 21)

Every 30,000 miles or 24 months, whichever comes first

All items listed above plus:
Inspect and replace, if necessary, the PCV valve (Section 22)
Inspect and replace, if necessary the spark plug wires (Section 23)
Replace the spark plugs (conventional [non-platinum] spark plugs) (Section 24)
Replace the fuel filter (Section 25)
Inspect the fuel system (Section 26)
Service the cooling system (drain, flush and refill) (green-colored ethylene glycol anti-freeze only) (Section 27)

Every 60,000 miles or 48 months, whichever comes first

Change the automatic transaxle fluid and filter (Section 28)**
Inspect and replace, if necessary the timing belt (3.4L V6 engines) (Chapter 2B).
Note: *After 60,000 miles, the timing belt should be inspected every 15,000 miles.*

Every 100,000 miles or 5 years, whichever comes first

Replace the spark plugs (platinum-tipped spark plugs) (Section 24)
Service the cooling system (drain, flush and refill) (orange-colored "DEX-COOL" silicate-free coolant only) (Section 27)

If the vehicle frequently tows a trailer, is operated primarily in stop-and-go conditions or its brakes receive severe usage for any other reason, check the brakes every 3000 miles or three months.

**If operated under one or more of the following conditions, change the automatic transmission fluid every 30,000 miles:*

In heavy city traffic where the outside temperature regularly reaches 90-degrees F (32-degrees C) or higher
In hilly or mountainous terrain
Frequent trailer pulling

2   Introduction

This Chapter is designed to help the home mechanic maintain the Chevrolet Lumina and Monte Carlo models with the goals of maximum performance, economy, safety and reliability in mind.

Included is a master maintenance schedule (page 1-6), followed by procedures dealing specifically with each item on the schedule. Visual checks, adjustments, component replacement and other helpful items are included. Refer to the **accompanying illustrations** of the engine compartment and the underside of the vehicle for the locations of various components.

Servicing your vehicle in accordance with the mileage/time maintenance schedule and the step-by-step procedures will result in a planned maintenance program that should produce a long and reliable service life. Keep in mind that it's a comprehensive plan, so maintaining some items but not others at the specified intervals will not produce the same results.

As you service your vehicle, you'll discover that many of the procedures can - and should - be grouped together because of the nature of the particular procedure you're performing or because of the close proximity of two otherwise unrelated components to one another.

For example, if the vehicle is raised, you should inspect the exhaust, suspension, steering and fuel systems while you're under the vehicle. When you're rotating the tires, it makes good sense to check the brakes since the wheels are already removed. Finally, let's suppose you have to borrow or rent a torque wrench. Even if you only need it to tighten the spark plugs, you might as well check the torque of as many critical fasteners as time allows.

The first step in this maintenance program is to prepare yourself before the actual work begins. Read through all the procedures you're planning to do, then gather up all the parts and tools needed. If it looks like you might run into problems during a particular job, seek advice from a mechanic or an experienced do-it-yourselfer. **Caution:** *The stereo in your vehicle may be equipped with an anti-theft system. Refer to the information at the front of this manual before performing any procedure which requires disconnecting the battery cable.*

3   Tune-up general information

The term tune-up is used in this manual to represent a combination of individual operations rather than one specific procedure.

If, from the time the vehicle is new, the routine maintenance schedule is followed closely and frequent checks are made of fluid levels and high wear items, as suggested throughout this manual, the engine will be kept in relatively good running condition and the need for additional work will be minimized due to lack of regular maintenance. This is even more likely if a used vehicle, which has not received regular and frequent maintenance checks, is purchased. In such cases, an engine tune-up will be needed outside of the regular routine maintenance intervals.

The first step in any tune-up or diagnostic procedure to help correct a poor running engine is a cylinder compression check. A compression check (see Chapter 2, Part B) will help determine the condition of internal engine components and should be used as a guide for tune-up and repair procedures. If, for instance, a compression check indicates serious internal engine wear, a conventional tune-up won't improve the performance of the engine and would be a waste of time and money. Because of its importance, the compression check should be done by someone with the right equipment and the knowledge to use it properly.

The following procedures are those most often needed to bring a generally poor running engine back into a proper state of tune.

Minor tune-up

Check all engine related fluids (Section 4)
Clean, inspect and test the battery (Section 10)
Check the cooling system (Section 11)
Check all underhood hoses (Section 12)
Check and adjust the drivebelts (Section 13)
Check the air filter (Section 21)
Check the PCV valve (Section 22)
Inspect the spark plug wires (Section 23)
Replace the spark plugs (Section 24)

Major tune-up

All items listed under Minor tune-up plus . . .
Replace the air filter (Section 21)
Replace the spark plug wires (Section 23)
Replace the fuel filter (Section 25)
Check the fuel system (Section 26)

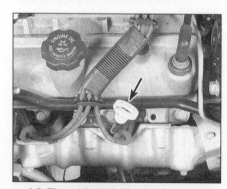

4.2 The engine oil dipstick (arrow) is located on the front side of the engine on all models

Check the ignition timing (Chapter 5)
Check the charging system (Chapter 5)
Check the EGR system (Chapter 6)

4   Fluid level checks (every 250 miles or weekly)

Note: *The following are fluid level checks to be done on a 250 mile or weekly basis. Additional fluid level checks can be found in specific maintenance procedures which follow. Regardless of intervals, be alert to fluid leaks under the vehicle which would indicate a problem to be corrected immediately.*

1   Fluids are an essential part of the lubrication, cooling, brake and windshield washer systems. Because the fluids gradually become depleted and/or contaminated during normal operation of the vehicle, they must be periodically replenished. See *Recommended lubricants and fluids* at the beginning of this Chapter before adding fluid to any of the following components. **Note:** *The vehicle must be on level ground when fluid levels are checked.*

Engine oil

Refer to illustrations 4.2, 4.4 and 4.6

2   The engine oil level is checked with a dipstick **(see illustration)**. The dipstick extends through a metal tube down into the oil pan.

3   The oil level should be checked before the vehicle has been driven, or about 15 minutes after the engine has been shut off. If the oil is checked immediately after driving the vehicle, some of the oil will remain in the upper part of the engine, resulting in an inaccurate reading on the dipstick.

4   Pull the dipstick from the tube and wipe all the oil from the end with a clean rag or paper towel. Insert the clean dipstick all the way back into the tube and pull it out again. Note the oil at the end of the dipstick. Add oil as necessary to keep the level above the ADD mark in the cross hatched area of the dipstick **(see illustration)**.

5   Do not overfill the engine by adding too much oil since this may result in oil fouled spark plugs, oil leaks or oil seal failures.

6   Oil is added to the engine after removing

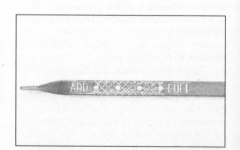

4.4 The oil level should be at or near the upper hole or in the cross-hatched area on the dipstick - if it's below the ADD line, add enough oil to bring the level into the upper hole or top of the cross-hatched area

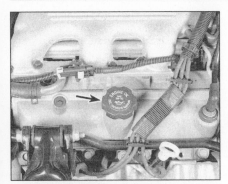

4.6 The engine oil filler cap (arrow) is clearly marked and threads into the tube on the valve cover - turn it counterclockwise to remove it

4.9 The coolant reservoir is located on the right (passenger's) side of the engine compartment - the coolant level can be checked by observing it through the translucent reservoir

4.14 Flip the windshield washer fluid cap (arrow) up to add fluid

a twist-off cap located on the valve cover **(see illustration)**. A funnel may help to reduce spills.

7   Checking the oil level is an important preventive maintenance step. A consistently low oil level indicates oil leakage through damaged seals, defective gaskets or past worn rings or valve guides. If the oil looks milky in color or has water droplets in it, the cylinder head gasket may be blown or the head or block may be cracked. The engine should be checked immediately. The condition of the oil should also be checked. Whenever you check the oil level, slide your thumb and index finger up the dipstick before wiping off the oil. If you see small dirt or metal particles clinging to the dipstick, the oil should be changed (see Section 8).

Engine coolant

Refer to illustration 4.9

Warning: *Do not allow antifreeze to come in contact with your skin or painted surfaces of the vehicle. Flush contaminated areas immediately with plenty of water. Do not store new coolant or leave old coolant lying around where it's accessible to children or pets - they're attracted by its sweet smell. Ingestion of even a small amount of coolant can be fatal! Wipe up garage floor and drip pan coolant spills immediately. Keep antifreeze containers covered and repair leaks in the cooling system immediately.*

Caution: *Never mix green-colored ethylene glycol anti-freeze and orange-colored "DEX-COOL" silicate-free coolant because doing so will destroy the efficiency of the "DEX-COOL" coolant which is designed to last for 100,000 miles or five years.*

8   All vehicles covered by this manual are equipped with a pressurized coolant recovery system. A plastic coolant reservoir located at the front of the engine compartment is connected by a hose to the radiator assembly. As the engine warms up and the coolant expands, it escapes through a valve in the radiator cap and travels through the hose into the reservoir. As the engine cools, the coolant is automatically drawn back into the cooling system to maintain the correct level.

9   The coolant level in the reservoir should be checked regularly. **Warning:** *Do not*

remove the radiator cap or the reservoir cap to check the coolant level when the engine is warm. The level of coolant in the reservoir varies with the temperature of the engine. When the engine is cold, the coolant level should be at or slightly above the COLD mark on the reservoir **(see illustration)**. Once the engine has warmed up, the level should be at or near the HOT mark. If it isn't, add coolant to the reservoir. To add coolant simply flip up the cap and add a 50/50 mixture of ethylene glycol based green-colored antifreeze or orange-colored "DEX-COOL" silicate-free coolant and water (see **Caution** above).

10   Drive the vehicle and recheck the coolant level. If only a small amount of coolant is required to bring the system up to the proper level, water can be used. However, repeated additions of water will dilute the antifreeze and water solution. In order to maintain the proper ratio of antifreeze and water, always top up the coolant level with the correct mixture. An empty plastic milk jug or bleach bottle makes an excellent container for mixing coolant. Do not use rust inhibitors or additives.

11   If the coolant level drops consistently, there may be a leak in the system. Inspect the radiator, hoses, filler cap, drain plugs and water pump (see Section 11). If no leaks are noted, have the radiator cap or coolant reservoir cap pressure tested by a service station.

12   If you have to remove the radiator cap, wait until the engine has cooled completely, then wrap a thick cloth around the cap and turn it to the first stop. If coolant or steam escapes, let the engine cool down longer, then remove the cap.

13   Check the condition of the coolant as well. It should be relatively clear. If it is brown or rust colored, the system should be drained, flushed and refilled. Even if the coolant appears to be normal, the corrosion inhibitors wear out, so it must be replaced at the specified intervals.

Windshield washer fluid

Refer to illustration 4.14

14   Fluid for the windshield washer system is located in a plastic reservoir on the left side

(driver's side) of the engine compartment **(see illustration)**. In milder climates, plain water can be used in the reservoir, but it should be kept no more than two-thirds full to allow for expansion if the water freezes. In colder climates, use windshield washer system antifreeze, available at any auto parts store, to lower the freezing point of the fluid. Mix the antifreeze with water in accordance with the manufacturer's directions on the container. **Caution:** *Do not use cooling system antifreeze - it will damage the vehicle's paint.*

15   To help prevent icing in cold weather, warm the windshield with the defroster before using the washer.

Battery electrolyte

16   All vehicles covered by this manual are equipped with a battery which is permanently sealed (except for vent holes) and has no filler caps. Water does not have to be added to these batteries at any time.

Brake fluid

Refer to illustration 4.18

17   The brake fluid level is checked by looking through the plastic reservoir mounted on the master cylinder. The master cylinder is mounted on the front of the power booster unit in the left (driver's side) rear corner of the engine compartment.

18   The fluid level should be at or near the base of the reservoir filler neck **(see illustration)**. If the fluid level is low, wipe the top

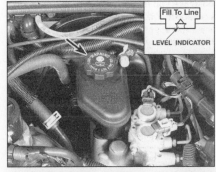

4.18 The fluid level inside the brake fluid reservoir can easily be checked by observing the level after unscrewing the cap - if necessary, add additional fluid until it reaches the top of the level indicator - DO NOT OVERFILL

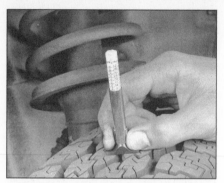

5.2 Use a tire tread depth gauge to monitor tire wear - they are available at auto parts stores and service stations and cost very little

UNDERINFLATION

CUPPING

OVERINFLATION

INCORRECT TOE-IN
OR EXTREME CAMBER

Cupping may be caused by:
- Underinflation and/or mechanical irregularities such as out-of-balance condition of wheel and/or tire, and bent or damaged wheel.
- Loose or worn steering tie-rod or steering idler arm.
- Loose, damaged or worn front suspension parts.

FEATHERING DUE
TO MISALIGNMENT

5.3 This chart will help you determine the condition of the tires, the probable cause(s) of abnormal wear and the corrective action necessary

of the reservoir and the lid with a clean rag to prevent contamination of the system as the lid is pried off.

19   When adding fluid, pour it carefully into the reservoir to avoid spilling it on surrounding painted surfaces. Be sure the specified fluid is used, since mixing different types of brake fluid can cause damage to the system. See *Recommended lubricants and fluids* at the front of this Chapter or your owner's manual. **Warning:** *Brake fluid can harm your eyes and damage painted surfaces, so use extreme caution when handling or pouring it. Do not use brake fluid that has been standing open or is more than one year old. Brake fluid absorbs moisture from the air. Excess moisture can cause a dangerous loss of braking effectiveness.*

20   At this time the fluid and master cylinder can be inspected for contamination. The system should be drained and refilled if deposits, dirt particles or water droplets are seen in the fluid.

21   After filling the reservoir to the proper level, make sure the lid completely snaps in place to prevent fluid leakage.

22   The brake fluid level in the master cylinder will drop slightly as the pads at each wheel wear down during normal operation. If the master cylinder requires repeated replenishing to keep it at the proper level, this is an indication of leakage in the brake system, which should be corrected immediately. Check all brake lines and connections (see Section 15 for more information).

23   If, when checking the master cylinder fluid level, you discover one or both reservoirs empty or nearly empty, the brake system should be bled (see Chapter 9).

5   Tire and tire pressure checks (every 250 miles or weekly)

Refer to illustrations 5.2, 5.3, 5.4a, 5.4b and 5.8

1   Periodic inspection of the tires may spare you the inconvenience of being stranded with a flat tire. It can also provide you with vital information regarding possible problems in the steering and suspension systems before major damage occurs.

2   The original tires on this vehicle are equipped with 1/2-inch wide bands that appear when tread depth reaches 1/16-inch, indicating the tires are worn out. Tread wear can be monitored with a simple, inexpensive device known as a tread depth indicator **(see illustration)**.

3   Note any abnormal tread wear **(see illustration)**. Tread pattern irregularities such as cupping, flat spots and more wear on one side than the other are indications of front end alignment and/or balance problems. If any of these conditions are noted, take the vehicle to a tire shop or service station to correct the problem.

4   Look closely for cuts, punctures and embedded nails or tacks. Sometimes a tire will hold air pressure for short time or leak down very slowly after a nail has embedded itself in the tread. If a slow leak persists, check the valve stem core to make sure it's tight **(see illustration)**. Examine the tread for

an object that may have embedded itself in the tire or for a "plug" that may have begun to leak (radial tire punctures are repaired with a plug that's installed in a puncture). If a puncture is suspected, it can be easily verified by spraying a solution of soapy water onto the suspected area **(see illustration)**. The soapy solution will bubble if there's a leak. Unless the puncture is unusually large, a tire shop or service station can usually repair the tire.

5   Carefully inspect the inner sidewall of each tire for evidence of brake fluid. If you see any, inspect the brakes immediately.

6   Correct air pressure adds miles to the lifespan of the tires, improves mileage and enhances overall ride quality. Tire pressure cannot be accurately estimated by looking at a tire, especially if it's a radial. A tire pressure gauge is essential. Keep an accurate gauge in the vehicle. The pressure gauges attached to the nozzles of air hoses at gas stations are often inaccurate.

5.4a If a tire loses air on a steady basis, check the valve core first to make sure it's snug (special inexpensive wrenches are commonly available at auto parts stores)

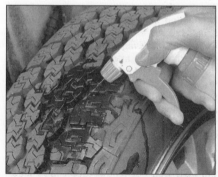

5.4b If the valve core is tight, raise the corner of the vehicle with the low tire and spray a soapy water solution onto the tread as the tire is turned slowly - leaks will cause small bubbles to appear

5.8 To extend the life of the tires, check the air pressure at least once a week with an accurate gauge (don't forget the spare)

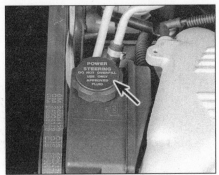

6.2 The power steering fluid reservoir (arrow) is located on the right (passenger's) side of the engine compartment - turn the cap counterclockwise for removal (3.1L and 3.4L location shown)

6.6 The marks on the dipstick indicate the safe fluid range

7   Always check tire pressure when the tires are cold. Cold, in this case, means the vehicle has not been driven over a mile in the three hours preceding a tire pressure check. A pressure rise of four to eight pounds is not uncommon once the tires are warm.

8   Unscrew the valve cap protruding from the wheel or hubcap and push the gauge firmly onto the valve stem **(see illustration)**. Note the reading on the gauge and compare the figure to the recommended tire pressure shown on the label attached to the inside of the glove compartment door. Be sure to reinstall the valve cap to keep dirt and moisture out of the valve stem mechanism. Check all four tires and, if necessary, add enough air to bring them up to the recommended pressure.

9   Don't forget to keep the spare tire inflated to the specified pressure (refer to your owner's manual or the tire sidewall).

6   Power steering fluid level check (every 3000 miles or 3 months)

Refer to illustrations 6.2 and 6.6

1   The power steering system relies on fluid which may, over a period of time, require replenishing.

2   The fluid reservoir for the power steering pump is mounted on the front of the engine by the engine drivebelt **(see illustration)**.

3   For the check, the front wheels should be pointed straight ahead and the engine should be off.

4   Use a clean rag to wipe off the reservoir cap and the area around the cap. This will help prevent any foreign matter from entering the reservoir during the check.

5   Twist off the cap and check the temperature of the fluid at the end of the dipstick with your finger.

6   Wipe off the fluid with a clean rag, reinsert it, then withdraw it and read the fluid level. The level should be at the HOT mark if the fluid was hot to the touch **(see illustration)**. It should be at the COLD mark if the fluid was cool to the touch.

7   If additional fluid is required, pour the specified type directly into the reservoir, using a funnel to prevent spills.

8   If the reservoir requires frequent fluid additions, all power steering hoses, hose connections, the power steering pump and the rack and pinion assembly should be carefully checked for leaks.

7   Automatic transaxle fluid level check (every 3000 miles or 3 months)

Refer to illustrations 7.3 and 7.6

1   The automatic transmission fluid level should be carefully maintained. Low fluid level can lead to slipping or loss of drive, while overfilling can cause foaming and loss of fluid.

2   With the parking brake set, start the engine, then move the shift lever through all the gear ranges, ending in Park. The fluid level must be checked with the vehicle level and the engine running at idle. **Note:** *Incorrect fluid level readings will result if the vehicle has just been driven at high speeds for an extended period, in hot weather in city traffic, or if it has been pulling a trailer. If any of these conditions apply, wait until the fluid has cooled (about 30 minutes).*

7.3 The automatic transmission fluid dipstick (arrow) is located at the rear of the engine compartment on all models

3   With the transmission at normal operating temperature, remove the dipstick from the filler tube. The dipstick is located at the rear of the engine compartment **(see illustration)**.

4   Carefully touch the fluid at the end of the dipstick to determine if the fluid is cool, warm or hot. Wipe the fluid from the dipstick with a clean rag and push it back into the filler tube until the cap seats.

5   Pull the dipstick out again and note the fluid level.

6   If the fluid felt cool, the level should be within the lower marks on the dipstick **(see illustration)**. If it felt warm or hot, the level should be within the cross-hatched upper areas on the dipstick. If additional fluid is required, pour it directly into the tube using a funnel. It takes about one pint to raise the level from the lower mark to the upper edge of the cross-hatched area with a hot transmission, so add the fluid a little at a time and keep checking the level until it's correct.

7   The condition of the fluid should also be checked along with the level. If the fluid at the end of the dipstick is a dark reddish-brown color, or if the fluid has a burned smell, the fluid should be changed. If you're in doubt about the condition of the fluid, purchase some new fluid and compare the two for color and smell.

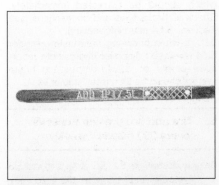

7.6 With the automatic transmission at normal operating temperature, the fluid level must be maintained within the cross-hatched area on the dipstick, between the upper and lower holes

1

8   Engine oil and filter change (every 3000 miles or 3 months)

Refer to illustrations 8.2, 8.7, 8.12 and 8.14

1   Frequent oil changes are the best preventive maintenance the home mechanic can give the engine, because aging oil becomes diluted and contaminated, which leads to premature engine wear.

2   Make sure you have all the necessary tools before you begin this procedure **(see illustration)**. You should also have plenty of rags or newspapers handy for mopping up any spills.

3   Access to the underside of the vehicle is greatly improved if the vehicle can be lifted on a hoist, driven onto ramps or supported by jackstands. **Warning:** *Do not work under a vehicle which is supported only by a hydraulic or scissors-type jack.*

4   If this is your first oil change, get under the vehicle and familiarize yourself with the locations of the oil drain plug and the oil filter. The engine and exhaust components will be warm during the actual work, so try to anticipate any potential problems before the engine and accessories are hot.

5   Park the vehicle on a level spot. Start the engine and allow it to reach its normal operating temperature. Warm oil and sludge will flow out more easily. Turn off the engine when it's warmed up. Remove the filler cap from the valve cover.

6   Raise the vehicle and support it securely on jackstands. **Warning:** *Never get beneath the vehicle when it is supported only by a jack. The jack provided with your vehicle is designed solely for raising the vehicle to remove and replace the wheels. Always use jackstands to support the vehicle when it becomes necessary to place your body underneath the vehicle.*

7   Being careful not to touch the hot exhaust components, place the drain pan under the drain plug in the bottom of the pan and remove the plug **(see illustration)**. You may want to wear gloves while unscrewing the plug the final few turns if the engine is hot.

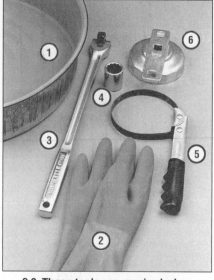

8.2 These tools are required when changing the engine oil and filter

1 **Drain pan** - *It should be fairly shallow in depth, but wide to prevent spills*
2 **Rubber gloves** - *When removing the drain plug and filter, you will get oil on your hands (the gloves will prevent burns)*
3 **Breaker bar** - *Sometimes the oil drain plug is tight, and a long breaker bar is needed to loosen it*
4 **Socket** - *To be used with the breaker bar or a ratchet (must be the correct size to fit the drain plug)*
5 **Filter wrench** - *This is a metal band-type wrench, which requires clearance around the filter to be effective*
6 **Filter wrench** - *This type fits on the bottom of the filter and can be turned with a ratchet or breaker bar (different-size wrenches are available for different types of filters)*

8   Allow the old oil to drain into the pan. It may be necessary to move the pan farther under the engine as the oil flow slows to a trickle. Inspect the old oil for the presence of metal shavings and chips.

9   After all the oil has drained, wipe off the drain plug with a clean rag. Even minute metal particles clinging to the plug would immediately contaminate the new oil.

10   Clean the area around the drain plug opening, reinstall the plug and tighten it to the specifications listed at the beginning of this Chapter.

11   Move the drain pan into position under the oil filter.

12   Loosen the oil filter **(see illustration)** by turning it counterclockwise with the filter wrench. **Note:** *Oil filters on 3.1L and 3.4L engines are located on the front side of the engine block, while the oil filter on 3.8L engines is located on the rear side of the engine block next the crankshaft pulley.* Use a quality filter wrench of the correct size and be careful not to collapse the canister as you apply pressure. Once the filter is loose, use your hands to unscrew it from the block. Just as the filter is detached from the block, immediately tilt the open end up to prevent the oil inside the filter from spilling out. **Warning:** *The exhaust system may still be hot, so be careful.*

13   With a clean rag, wipe off the mounting surface on the block. If a residue of old oil is allowed to remain, it will smoke when the block is heated up. Also make sure that none of the old gasket remains stuck to the mounting surface. It can be removed with a scraper if necessary.

14   Compare the old filter with the new one to make sure they are the same type. Smear some clean engine oil on the rubber gasket of the new filter and screw it into place **(see illustration)**. Because overtightening the filter will damage the gasket, do not use a filter wrench to tighten the filter. Tighten it by hand until the gasket contacts the seating surface. Then seat the filter by giving it an additional 3/4-turn.

15   Remove all tools, rags, etc. from under the vehicle, being careful not to spill the oil in the drain pan, then lower the vehicle.

16   Add new oil to the engine through the oil filler cap in the valve cover. Use a funnel, if necessary, to prevent oil from spilling onto the top of the engine. Pour three quarts of fresh oil into the engine. Wait a few minutes to allow the oil to drain into the pan, then check the level on the oil dipstick (see

8.7 The engine oil drain plug is located at the rear of the oil pan - it is usually very tight, so use a socket or box-end wrench to avoid rounding off the hex

8.12 The oil filter is usually on very tight as well and will require a special wrench for removal - DO NOT use the wrench to tighten the new filter!

8.14 Lubricate the oil filter gasket with clean engine oil before installing the filter on the engine

9.1 Materials required for chassis and body lubrication

1   **Engine oil** - *Light engine oil in a can like this can be used for door and hood hinges*
2   **Graphite spray** - *Used to lubricate lock cylinders*
3   **Grease** - *Grease, in a variety of types and weights, is available for use in a grease gun. Check the Specification for your requirements*
4   **Grease gun** - *A common grease gun, shown here with a detachable hose and nozzle, is needed for chassis lubrication. After use, clean it thoroughly!*

Section 4 if necessary). If the oil level is at or near the upper hole on the dipstick, install the filler cap hand tight, start the engine and allow the new oil to circulate.

17   Allow the engine to run for about a minute. While the engine is running, look under the vehicle and check for leaks at the oil pan drain plug and around the oil filter. If either is leaking, stop the engine and tighten the plug or filter.

18   Wait a few minutes to allow the oil to trickle down into the pan, then recheck the level on the dipstick and, if necessary, add enough oil to bring the level to the upper hole.

19   During the first few trips after an oil change, make it a point to check frequently for leaks and proper oil level.

20   The old oil drained from the engine cannot be re-used in its present state and

9.6 Lubricate the transaxle shift linkage (arrow) with clean engine oil

should be discarded. Check with your local refuse disposal company, disposal facility or environmental agency to see whether they will accept the oil for recycling. Don't pour used oil into drains or onto the ground. After the oil has cooled, it can be drained into a suitable container (capped plastic jugs, topped bottles, milk cartons, etc.) for transport to one of these disposal sites.

9   Chassis lubrication (every 3000 miles or 3 months)

Refer to illustrations 9.1 and 9.6

1   All suspension and steering joints are factory sealed and DO NOT require lubrication, however other various chassis components such as hood and door hinges, door locks, parking brake cable guides and transaxle shift linkage require regularly scheduled lubrication. Specific materials and equipment are needed to perform these tasks **(see illustration)**.

2   Open the hood and smear a little chassis grease on the hood latch mechanism. Have an assistant pull the hood release lever from inside the vehicle as you lubricate the cable at the latch.

3   Lubricate all the hinges (door, hood, etc.) with engine oil to keep them in proper working order.

4   The key lock cylinders can be lubricated with spray graphite or silicone lubricant, which is available at auto parts stores.

5   Lubricate the door weatherstripping with silicone spray. This will reduce chafing and retard wear.

6   For easier access under the vehicle, raise it with a jack and place jackstands under the frame. Make sure it's safely supported by the stands. Then clean and lubricate the transaxle shift linkage with engine oil **(see illustration)**.

7   Clean and lubricate the parking brake cable guides and levers. This can be done by using a grease gun. **Note:** *DO NOT lubricate the parking brake cables, as this will deteriorate the plastic coating used to prevent the cables from rusting.*

10   Battery check, maintenance and charging (every 6000 miles or 6 months)

Refer to illustrations 10.1, 10.4, 10.5a, 10.5b and 10.5c
Warning: *Hydrogen gas is produced by the battery, so keep open flames and lighted tobacco away from it at all times. Always wear eye protection when working around the battery. Rinse off spilled electrolyte immediately with large amounts of water. When removing the battery cables, always detach the negative cable first and hook it up last!*
Caution: *If the radio in your vehicle is equipped with an anti-theft system, make*

sure you have the correct activation code before disconnecting the battery.
1   Battery maintenance is an important procedure which will help ensure you aren't stranded because of a dead battery. Several tools are required for this procedure **(see illustration)**.
2   A sealed battery is standard equipment on all vehicles covered by this manual. Although this type of battery has many advantages over the older, capped cell type, and never requires the addition of water, it should still be routinely maintained according to the procedures which follow.

Check

3   The battery is located in the left front corner of the engine compartment beneath the windshield washer fluid reservoir. To access the battery, first remove the engine compartment support brace and the windshield washer fluid reservoir as

1

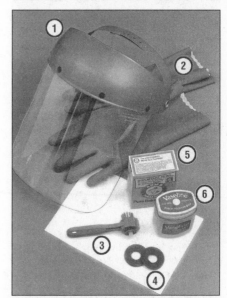

10.1 Tools and materials required for battery maintenance

1   **Face shield/safety goggles** - *When removing corrosion with a brush, the acidic particles can easily fly up into your eyes*
2   **Rubber gloves** - *Another safety item to consider when servicing the battery - remember that's acid inside the battery!*
3   **Battery terminal/cable cleaner** - *This wire brush cleaning tool will remove all traces of corrosion from the battery and cable*
4   **Treated felt washers** - *Placing one of these on each terminal, directly under the cable end, will help prevent corrosion (be sure to get the correct type for side-terminal batteries)*
5   **Baking soda** - *A solution of baking soda and water can be used to neutralize corrosion*
6   **Petroleum jelly** - *A layer of this on the battery terminal bolts will help prevent corrosion*

10.4   Check the tightness of the battery cable terminal bolts

10.5a   A tool like this one (available at auto parts stores) is used to clean the side terminal type battery contact area

10.5b   Use the brush to finish the cleaning job

10.5c   The result should be a clean, shiny terminal area

described in the battery removal procedure in Chapter 5.

4   Check the tightness of the battery cable terminals and connections to ensure good electrical connections and check the entire length of each cable for cracks and frayed conductors **(see illustration)**.

5   If corrosion (visible as white, fluffy deposits) is evident, remove the cables from the terminals, clean them with a battery brush and reinstall the cables **(see illustrations)**. Corrosion can be kept to a minimum by using special treated fiber washers available at auto parts stores or by applying a layer of petroleum jelly to the terminals and cables after they are assembled.

6   Make sure that the battery tray is in good condition and the hold-down clamp bolt is tight. If the battery is removed from the tray, make sure no parts remain in the bottom of the tray when the battery is reinstalled. When reinstalling the hold-down clamp bolt, do not overtighten it.

7   Information on removing and installing the battery can be found in Chapter 5. Information on jump starting can be found at the front of this manual. For more detailed battery checking procedures, refer to the *Haynes Automotive Electrical Manual*.

Cleaning

8   Corrosion on the hold-down components, battery case and surrounding areas can be removed with a solution of water and

baking soda. Thoroughly rinse all cleaned areas with plain water.

9   Any metal parts of the vehicle damaged by corrosion should be covered with a zinc-based primer, then painted.

Charging

Warning: *When batteries are being charged, hydrogen gas, which is very explosive and flammable, is produced. Do not smoke or allow open flames near a charging or a recently charged battery. Wear eye protection when near the battery during charging. Also, make sure the charger is unplugged before connecting or disconnecting the battery from the charger.*

10   Slow-rate charging is the best way to restore a battery that's discharged to the point where it will not start the engine. It's also a good way to maintain the battery charge in a vehicle that's only driven a few miles between starts. Maintaining the battery charge is particularly important in the winter when the battery must work harder to start the engine and electrical accessories that drain the battery are in greater use.

11   It's best to use a one or two-amp battery charger (sometimes called a "trickle" charger). They are the safest and put the least strain on the battery. They are also the least expensive. For a faster charge, you can use a higher amperage charger, but don't use one rated more than 1/10th the amp/hour rating of the battery. Rapid boost charges that claim to restore the power of the battery

in one to two hours are hardest on the battery and can damage batteries that aren't in good condition. This type of charging should only be used in emergency situations.

12   The average time necessary to charge a battery should be listed in the instructions that come with the charger. As a general rule, a trickle charger will charge a battery in 12 to 16 hours.

13   Remove all of the cell caps (if equipped) and cover the holes with a clean cloth to prevent spattering electrolyte. Disconnect the negative battery cable and hook the battery charger leads to the battery posts (positive to positive, negative to negative), then plug in the charger. Make sure it is set at 12-volts if it has a selector switch.

14   If you're using a charger with a rate higher than two amps, check the battery regularly during charging to make sure it doesn't overheat. If you're using a trickle charger, you can safely let the battery charge overnight after you've checked it regularly for the first couple of hours.

15   If the battery has removable cell caps, measure the specific gravity with a hydrometer every hour during the last few hours of the charging cycle. Hydrometers are available inexpensively from auto parts stores - follow the instructions that come with the hydrometer. Consider the battery charged when there's no change in the specific gravity reading for two hours and the electrolyte in the cells is gassing (bubbling) freely. The specific gravity reading from each cell should be very close to the others. If not, the battery probably has a bad cell(s).

16   Some batteries with sealed tops have built-in hydrometers on the top that indicate the state of charge by the color displayed in the hydrometer window. Normally, a bright-colored hydrometer indicates a full charge and a dark hydrometer indicates the battery still needs charging. Check the battery manufacturer's instructions to be sure you know what the colors mean.

17   If the battery has a sealed top and no built-in hydrometer, you can hook up a digital voltmeter across the battery terminals to check the charge. A fully charged battery should read 12.5-volts or higher.

---

11   Cooling system check (every 6000 miles or 6 months)

Refer to illustration 11.4

Caution: *Never mix green-colored ethylene glycol anti-freeze and orange-colored "DEX-COOL" silicate-free coolant because doing so will destroy the efficiency of the "DEX-COOL" coolant which is designed to last for 100,000 miles or five years.*

1   Many major engine failures can be attributed to a faulty cooling system. If the vehicle is equipped with an automatic transmission, the cooling system also cools the transmission fluid and plays an important role in prolonging transmission life.

2   The cooling system should be checked with the engine cold. Do this before the vehicle is driven for the day or after the engine has been shut off for at least three hours.

3   Remove the radiator cap by turning it to the left until it reaches a stop. If you hear any hissing sounds (indicating there is still pressure in the system), wait until it stops. Now press down on the cap with the palm of your hand and continue turning to the left until the cap can be removed. Thoroughly clean the cap, inside and out, with clean water. Also clean the filler neck on the radiator. All traces of corrosion should be removed. The coolant inside the radiator should be relatively transparent. If it is rust colored, the system should be drained and refilled (see Section 27). If the coolant level is not up to the top, add additional antifreeze/coolant mixture (see Section 4).

4   Carefully check the large upper and lower radiator hoses along with any smaller diameter heater hoses which run from the engine to the firewall. Inspect each hose along its entire length, replacing any hose which is cracked, swollen or shows signs of deterioration. Cracks may become more apparent if the hose is squeezed **(see illustration)**.

5   Make sure all hose connections are tight. A leak in the cooling system will usually show up as white or rust colored deposits on the areas adjoining the leak. If wire-type clamps are used at the ends of the hoses, it may be wise to replace them with more secure screw-type clamps.

Check for a chafed area that could fail prematurely.

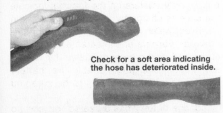

Check for a soft area indicating the hose has deteriorated inside.

Overtightening the clamp on a hardened hose will damage the hose and cause a leak.

Check each hose for swelling and oil-soaked ends. Cracks and breaks can be located by squeezing the hose.

11.4 Hoses, like drivebelts, have a habit of failing at the worst possible time - to prevent the inconvenience of a blown radiator or heater hose, inspect them carefully as shown here

6   Use compressed air or a soft brush to remove bugs, leaves, etc. from the front of the radiator or air conditioning condenser. Be careful not to damage the delicate cooling fins or cut yourself on them.

7   Every other inspection, or at the first indication of cooling system problems, have the cap and system pressure tested. If you don't have a pressure tester, most gas stations and repair shops will do this for a minimal charge.

12 Underhood hose check and replacement (every 6000 miles or 6 months)

General

1   **Warning:** *Replacement of air conditioning hoses must be left to a dealer service department or air conditioning shop that has the equipment to depressurize the system safely. Never remove air conditioning components or hoses until the system has been depressurized.*

2   High temperatures under the hood can cause the deterioration of the rubber and plastic hoses used for engine, accessory and emission systems operation. Periodic inspection should be made for cracks, loose clamps, material hardening and leaks. Information specific to the cooling system hoses can be found in Section 11.

3   Some, but not all, hoses are secured to the fittings with clamps. Where clamps are used, check to be sure they haven't lost their tension, allowing the hose to leak. If clamps aren't used, make sure the hose hasn't expanded and/or hardened where it slips over the fitting, allowing it to leak.

Vacuum hoses

4   It's quite common for vacuum hoses, especially those in the emissions system, to be color coded or identified by colored stripes molded into each hose. Various systems require hoses with different wall thicknesses, collapse resistance and temperature resistance. When replacing hoses, be sure the new ones are made of the same material.

5   Often the only effective way to check a hose is to remove it completely from the vehicle. If more than one hose is removed, be sure to label the hoses and fittings to ensure correct installation.

6   When checking vacuum hoses, be sure to include any plastic T-fittings in the check. Inspect the fittings for cracks and the hose where it fits over the fitting for distortion, which could cause leakage.

7   A small piece of vacuum hose (1/4-inch inside diameter) can be used as a stethoscope to detect vacuum leaks. Hold one end of the hose to your ear and probe around vacuum hoses and fittings, listening for the "hissing" sound characteristic of a vacuum leak. **Warning:** *When probing with the vacuum hose stethoscope, be careful not to allow your body or the hose to come into* *contact with moving engine components such as the drivebelt, cooling fan, etc.*

Fuel hose

Warning: *Gasoline is extremely flammable, so take extra precautions when you work on any part of the fuel system. Don't smoke or allow open flames or bare light bulbs near the work area, and don't work in a garage where a natural gas-type appliance (such as a water heater or clothes dryer) with a pilot light is present. Since gasoline is carcinogenic, wear latex gloves when there's a possibility of being exposed to fuel, and, if you spill any fuel on your skin, rinse it off immediately with soap and water. Mop up any spills immediately and do not store fuel-soaked rags where they could ignite. When you perform any kind of work on the fuel system, wear safety glasses and have a Class B type fire extinguisher on hand. The fuel system is under pressure, so if any lines must be disconnected, the pressure in the system must be relieved first* (see Chapter 4 for more information).

8   Check all rubber fuel lines for deterioration and chafing. Check especially for cracks in areas where the hose bends and just before fittings, such as where a hose attaches to the fuel filter and fuel injection unit.

9   High quality fuel line, specifically designed for high-pressure fuel injection applications, must be used for fuel line replacement. Never, under any circumstances, use regular fuel line, unreinforced vacuum line, clear plastic tubing or water hose for fuel lines.

10   Spring-type clamps are commonly used on fuel lines. These clamps often lose their tension over a period of time, and can be "sprung" during the removal process. As a result spring-type clamps should be replaced with screw-type clamps whenever a hose is replaced.

Metal lines

11   Sections of steel tubing often used for fuel line between the fuel pump and fuel injection unit. Check carefully for cracks, kinks and flat spots in the line.

12   If a section of metal fuel line must be replaced, only seamless steel tubing should be used, since copper and aluminum tubing do not have the strength necessary to withstand normal engine vibration.

13   Check the metal brake lines where they enter the master cylinder and brake proportioning unit (if used) for cracks in the lines and loose fittings. Any sign of brake fluid leakage calls for an immediate thorough inspection of the brake system.

13 Drivebelt and tensioner check and replacement (every 6000 miles or 6 months)

Drivebelt

Refer to illustrations 13.2, 13.5a and 13.5b

1   A single serpentine drivebelt is located at the front of the engine and plays an

1

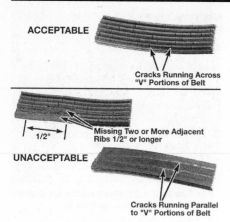

ACCEPTABLE

Cracks Running Across
"V" Portions of Belt

1/2"

Missing Two or More Adjacent
Ribs 1/2" or longer

UNACCEPTABLE

Cracks Running Parallel
to "V" Portions of Belt

**13.2 Small cracks in the underside of a
serpentine belt are acceptable -
lengthwise cracks, or missing pieces are
cause for replacement**

important role in the overall operation of the engine and its components. Due to its function and material make up, the belt is prone to wear and should be periodically inspected. The serpentine belt drives the alternator, power steering pump, water pump and air conditioning compressor.

2   With the engine off, open the hood and use your fingers (and a flashlight, if necessary), to move along the belt checking for cracks and separation of the belt plies. Also check for fraying and glazing, which gives the belt a shiny appearance **(see illustration)**. Both sides of the belt should be inspected, which means you will have to twist the belt to check the underside.

3   Check the ribs on the underside of the belt. They should all be the same depth, with none of the surface uneven.

4   The tension of the belt is maintained by the tensioner assembly and isn't adjustable. The belt should be checked at the mileage specified in the maintenance schedule at the front of this Chapter, if the belt shows noticeable damage or wear during these checks it should be replaced.

5   To replace the belt on 3.1L and 3.8L engines, rotate the tensioner counter-clockwise to release belt tension **(see illustration)**. To replace the belt on 3.4L engines, rotate the tensioner clockwise to release belt

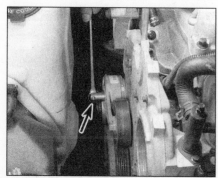

**13.9 Remove the retaining bolt (arrow)
located at the center of the tensioner
assembly**

**13.5a On 3.1L and 3.8L engines rotate the
drivebelt tensioner (arrow) counterclockwise to remove or install the belt**

tension. Note the routing of the belt before removing it. **Note:** *These models have a drivebelt routing decal on the engine to help during drivebelt installation* **(see illustration)**. *If the decal is missing, make a sketch.*

6   Remove the belt from the auxiliary components and slowly release the tensioner.

7   Route the new belt over the various pulleys, again rotating the tensioner to allow the belt to be installed, then release the belt tensioner.

Tensioner

8   Remove the engine drivebelt as described above in steps 5 and 6.

3.1L and 3.4L engines

Refer to illustration 13.9

9   On 3.1L and 3.4L engines, simply remove the tensioner retaining bolt **(see illustration)** and detach the tensioner assembly from the front of the engine. **Note:** *It may be necessary to detach and position the coolant recovery reservoir aside to allow access to the tensioner retaining bolt.* Installation is the reverse of the removal procedure.

3.8L engine

Warning: *If you're removing the tensioner from a 3.8L engine, wait until the engine has cooled completely before beginning the job.*

10   Drain the engine coolant (see Section 27).

11   Move a large container under the front

**14.3a Inspect the lower control arm
bushings and balljoint . . .**

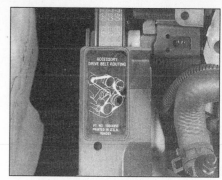

**13.5b A serpentine drivebelt routing
diagram is located on the engine
(3.1L V6 shown)**

of the engine to catch the coolant and remove the heater hose adapters with the heater hoses attached from the drivebelt tensioner assembly.

12   Detach the drivebelt tensioner retaining bolts and remove the tensioner assembly from the vehicle. Installation is the reverse of the removal procedure.

13   Refill the cooling system (see Section 27), start the engine and check for leaks.

14 Steering, suspension and driveaxle boot check (every 6000 miles or 6 months)

Refer to illustrations 14.3a, 14.3b, 14.3c, 14.3d and 14.6

1   Indications of a fault in these systems are excessive play in the steering wheel before the front wheels react, excessive sway around corners, body movement over rough roads or binding at some point as the steering wheel is turned.

2   Raise the front of the vehicle periodically and visually check the suspension and steering components for wear. Because of the work to be done, make sure the vehicle cannot fall from the stands.

3   From under the vehicle check for loose bolts, broken or disconnected parts and deteriorated rubber bushings on all suspension and steering components **(see illustrations)**. Check the power steering

**14.3b . . . the front and rear stabilizer bar
bushings . . .**

14.3c . . . and the tie rod ends for deteriorated bushings and torn grease seals

14.3d Check the steering gear boots for cracks and leaking steering fluid

14.6 Check the driveaxle boots for cracks and/or leaking grease

1

hoses and connections for leaks. Check the shock absorbers or leaking fluid or damage.

4   Have an assistant turn the steering wheel from side-to-side and check the steering components for free movement, chafing and binding. If the steering doesn't react with the movement of the steering wheel, try to determine where the slack is located.

5   The driveaxle boots are very important because they prevent dirt, water and foreign material from entering and damaging the constant velocity (CV) joints. Oil and grease can cause the boot material to deteriorate prematurely, so it's a good idea to wash the boots with soap and water.

6   Inspect the boots for tears and cracks as well as loose clamps **(see illustration)**. If there is any evidence of cracks or leaking lubricant, they must be replaced as described in Chapter 8.

15 Brake check (every 6000 miles or 6 months)

Note: *For detailed information of the brake system, refer to Chapter 9.*
Warning: *Brake system dust may contain asbestos, which is hazardous to your health. DO NOT blow it out with compressed air, inhale it or use gasoline or solvents to remove it. Use brake system cleaner only.*

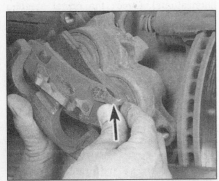

15.3 The disc brake pads are equipped with wear indicators that contact the disc and make a squealing sound when the pad has worn to its limit

1   In addition to the specified intervals, the brakes should be inspected every time the wheels are removed or whenever a defect is suspected. Raise the vehicle and place it securely on jackstands. Remove the wheels (see *Jacking and towing* at the front of the manual, if necessary).

Disc brakes

Refer to illustrations 15.3, 15.5 and 15.7

2   Disc brakes can be checked without removing any parts except the wheels. Extensive disc damage can occur if the pads are not replaced when needed.

3   The disc brake pads have built-in wear indicators **(see illustration)** which make a high-pitched squealing sound when the pads are worn. **Caution:** *Expensive damage to the disc can result if the pads are not replaced soon after the wear indicators start squealing.*

4   The disc brake calipers, which contain the brake pads, have an inner pad and outer pad in each caliper. All pads should be inspected.

5   Each caliper has a "window" to inspect the pads **(see illustration)**. If the pad material has worn to about 1/8-inch thick or less, the pads should be replaced.

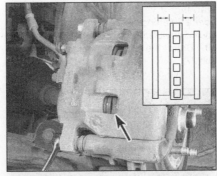

15.5 With the wheels removed, the brake pad lining can be inspected through the caliper window (arrow) and at each end of the caliper - If the pad is bonded to the metal backing plate, measure the pad thickness from the outer surface to the metal backing plate, as shown here; if the pad is riveted to the metal backing plate, measure from the pad outer surface to the rivet head

6   If you're unsure about the exact thickness of the remaining lining material, remove the pads for further inspection or replacement (see Chapter 9).

7   Before installing the wheels, check for leakage and/or damage at the brake hoses and connections **(see illustration)**. Replace the hose or fittings as necessary, (see Chapter 9).

8   Check the condition of the brake disc. Look for score marks, deep scratches and overheated areas (they will appear blue or discolored). If damage or wear is noted, the disc can be removed and resurfaced by an automotive machine shop or replaced with a new one. See Chapter 9 for more detailed inspection and repair procedures.

Drum brakes

Refer to illustrations 15.14 and 15.16

9   Raise the vehicle and support it securely on jackstands. Block the front tires to prevent the vehicle from rolling; however, don't apply the parking brake or it will lock the drums in place.

10   Remove the wheels, referring to *Jacking and towing* at the front of this manual if necessary.

11   Mark the hub so it can be reinstalled in the same position. Use a scribe, chalk, etc. on the drum, hub and backing plate.

12   Remove the brake drum (see Chapter 9 if necessary).

13   With the drum removed, carefully clean the brake assembly with brake system

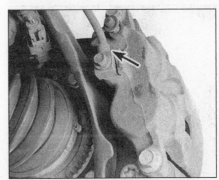

15.7 Check for any sign of brake fluid leakage at the line fittings (arrow) and the brake hoses

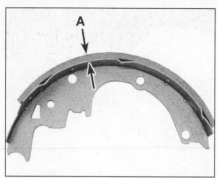

15.14 If the lining is bonded to the brake shoe, measure the lining thickness from the outer surface to the metal shoe, as shown here; if the lining is riveted to the shoe, measure from the lining outer surface to the rivet head

cleaner. **Warning:** *Don't blow the dust out with compressed air and don't inhale any of it (it may contain asbestos, which is harmful to your health).*

14   Note the thickness of the lining material on both front and rear brake shoes. If the material has worn away to within 3/32-inch of the recessed rivets or metal backing, the shoes should be replaced **(see illustration)**. The shoes should also be replaced if they're cracked, glazed (shiny areas), or covered with brake fluid.

15   Make sure all the brake assembly springs are connected and in good condition.

16   Check the brake components for signs of fluid leakage. With your finger or a small screwdriver, carefully pry back the rubber boots on the wheel cylinder located at the top of the brake shoes **(see illustration)**. Any leakage here is an indication that the wheel cylinders should be overhauled immediately (see Chapter 9). Also, check all hoses and connections for signs of leakage.

17   Wipe the inside of the drum with a clean rag and denatured alcohol or brake cleaner. Again, be careful not to breathe the dangerous asbestos dust.

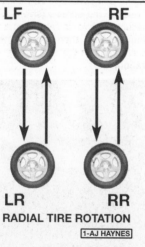

LF   **RF**

LR   **RR**

RADIAL TIRE ROTATION

1-AJ HAYNES

16.2   Tire rotation diagram

15.16   Check for fluid leakage at both ends of the wheel cylinder dust boots

18   Check the inside of the drum for cracks, score marks, deep scratches and "hard spots" which will appear as small discolored areas. If imperfections cannot be removed with fine emery cloth, the drum must be taken to an automotive machine shop for resurfacing.

19   Repeat the procedure for the remaining wheel. If the inspection reveals that all parts are in good condition, reinstall the brake drums, install the wheels and lower the vehicle to the ground.

Parking brake

20   The parking brake is operated by a foot pedal and locks the rear brake system. The easiest, and perhaps most obvious, method of periodically checking the operation of the parking brake assembly is to park the vehicle on a steep hill with the parking brake set and the transmission in Neutral (be sure to stay in the vehicle during this check!). If the parking brake cannot prevent the vehicle from rolling, it needs service (see Chapter 9).

16   Tire rotation (every 6000 miles or 6 months)

Refer to illustration 16.2

1   The tires should be rotated at the specified intervals and whenever uneven wear is noticed.

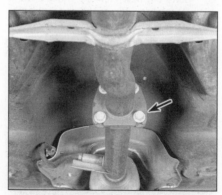

17.2a   Check the flange connections (arrow) for exhaust leaks - also check that the retaining nuts are securely tightened

2   Refer to the **accompanying illustration** for the preferred tire rotation pattern.

3   Refer to the information in *Jacking and towing* at the front of this manual for the proper procedures to follow when raising the vehicle and changing a tire. If the brakes are to be checked, don't apply the parking brake as stated. Make sure the tires are blocked to prevent the vehicle from rolling as it's raised.

4   Preferably, the entire vehicle should be raised at the same time. This can be done on a hoist or by jacking up each corner and then lowering the vehicle onto jackstands placed under the frame rails. Always use four jackstands and make sure the vehicle is safely supported.

5   After rotation, check and adjust the tire pressures as necessary and be sure to properly tighten the lug nuts.

17   Exhaust system check (every 6000 miles or 6 months)

Refer to illustrations 17.2a and 17.2b

1   With the engine cold (at least three hours after the vehicle has been driven), check the complete exhaust system from the engine to the end of the tailpipe. Ideally, the inspection should be done with the vehicle on a hoist to permit unrestricted access. If a hoist is not available, raise the vehicle and support it securely on jackstands.

2   Check the exhaust pipes and connections for evidence of leaks, severe corrosion and damage. Make sure that all brackets and hangers are in good condition and tight **(see illustrations)**.

3   At the same time, inspect the underside of the body for holes, corrosion, open seams, etc. which may allow exhaust gases to enter the interior. Seal all body openings with silicone or body putty.

4   Rattles and other noises can often be traced to the exhaust system, especially the mounts and hangers. Try to move the pipes, muffler and catalytic converter. If the components can come in contact with the body or suspension parts, secure the exhaust system with new mounts.

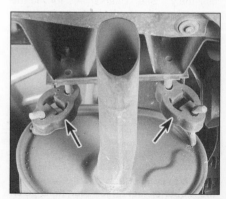

17.2b   Check the exhaust system hangers (arrows) for damage and cracks

18.2 Check the throttle linkage for binding

19.3 Gently pry off the trim cap and check the tightness of the wiper arm retaining nut

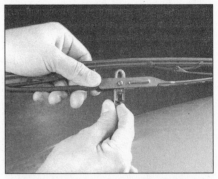

19.5 Press on the release tab, then push the blade assembly down and out of the hook in the arm

18 Throttle linkage check (every 12,000 miles or 12 months)

Refer to illustration 18.2

1   At the specified intervals the throttle linkage should be inspected for kinks, binding and misalignment.

2   Starting at the throttle body in the engine compartment, with the engine OFF, grasp the throttle lever and open it to the full throttle position **(see illustration)**. Quickly release your hand from the throttle lever and note the amount of time it takes the throttle lever to return to the idle position. If the lever returns quickly to the idle position the throttle linkage is in proper working order. If the lever returns slowly to the idle position, inspect the accelerator cable or cruise control cable for kinks or signs of binding. Also check the cable retaining brackets for missing retaining clips. **Note:** *Never lubricate the accelerator or cruise control cable as this will destroy the protective plastic coating on the outside of the cable.* If signs of kinks or binding exist in the cable assembly, replace the cable as described in Chapter 4.

3   If there's no evidence of binding in the cable assembly, remove the cables from the throttle lever and repeat the test described in Step 2. If the throttle lever returns slowly to the idle position with the cables detached, the problem lies in the throttle body assembly. See Chapter 4 for further inspection of the throttle body assembly.

19 Wiper blade inspection and replacement (every 12,000 miles or 12 months)

Refer to illustrations 19.3, 19.5 and 19.6

1   The windshield wiper and blade assemblies should be inspected periodically for damage, loose components and cracked or worn blade elements.

2   Road film can build up on the wiper blades and affect their efficiency, so they should be washed regularly with a mild detergent solution.

3   The action of the wiping mechanism can loosen the bolts, nuts and fasteners, so they should be checked and tightened, as necessary, at the same time the wiper blades are checked **(see illustration)**.

4   If the wiper blade elements (sometimes called inserts) are cracked, worn or warped, they should be replaced with new ones.

5   Lift the arm assembly away from the glass for clearance, press on the release lever, then slide the wiper blade assembly out of the hook in the end of the arm **(see illustration)**.

6   Use needle-nose pliers to compress the blade element, then slide the element out of the frame (claws) and discard it **(see illustration)**.

7   Compare the new element with the old for length, design, etc.

8   Slide the new element into the frame (claws), notched end last and secure the claw into the notches of the blade element.

9   Reinstall the blade assembly on the arm, wet the windshield and test for proper operation.

20 Seat belt check (every 12,000 miles or 12 months)

1   Check the seat belts, buckles, latch plates and guide loops for obvious damage and signs of wear.

2   See if the seat belt reminder light comes on when the key is turned to the Run or Start position. A chime should also sound.

3   The seat belts are designed to lock up during a sudden stop or impact, yet allow free movement during normal driving. Make sure the retractors return the belt against your chest while driving and rewind the belt fully when the buckle is unlatched.

4   If any of the above checks reveal problems with the seat belt system, replace parts as necessary.

21 Air filter replacement (every 12,000 miles or 12 months)

Refer to illustration 21.1a and 21.1b

1   The air filter is located inside the air cleaner housing at the left (driver's) side of the engine compartment. To remove the air filter, release the screws **(see illustration)** that secure the two halves of the air cleaner housing together, then separate the cover halves and remove the air filter element **(see illustration)**.

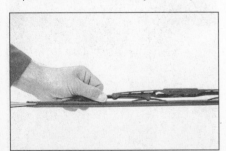

19.6 Use needle-nose pliers to compress the rubber element, then slide the element out - slide the new element in and lock the blade assembly fingers into the notches of the wiper element

21.1a Remove the screws and separate the cover from the air cleaner housing

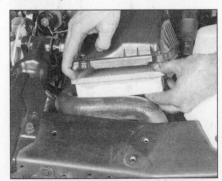

21.1b Lift the cover up and slide the element out of the housing

1

2   Inspect the outer surface of the filter element. If it is dirty, replace it. If it is only moderately dusty, it can be reused by blowing it clean from the back to the front surface with compressed air. Because it is a pleated paper type filter, it cannot be washed or oiled. If it cannot be cleaned satisfactorily with compressed air, discard and replace it. While the cover is off, be careful not to drop anything down into the housing. **Caution:** *Never drive the vehicle with the air cleaner removed. Excessive engine wear could result and backfiring could even cause a fire under the hood.*

3   Wipe out the inside of the air cleaner housing.

4   Place the new filter into the air cleaner housing, making sure it seats properly.

5   Installation of the housing is the reverse of removal.

22   Positive Crankcase Ventilation (PCV) valve check and replacement (every 30,000 miles or 24 months)

Check

3.1L and 3.4L engine

Refer to illustration 22.1

1   On 3.1L engines the PCV valve is located in the forward valve cover **(see illustration)**. On 3.4L engines the PCV valve is located in the intake manifold just behind the throttle body assembly.

2   With the engine idling at normal operating temperature, pull the valve (with hose attached) out of the rubber grommet in the intake plenum or valve cover.

3   Place your finger over the end of the valve. If there is no vacuum at the valve, check for a plugged hose, manifold port, or the valve itself. Replace any plugged or deteriorated hoses.

4   Turn off the engine and shake the PCV valve, listening for a rattle. If the valve doesn't rattle, replace it with a new one.

3.8L engine

Refer to illustration 22.5

5   On 3.8L engines the PCV valve is located in the intake manifold under the MAP

22.1 The PCV valve on 3.1L engines is located in the valve cover

sensor at the front (passenger side) of the engine **(see illustration)**.

6   To check the valve it must first be removed (see Step 12). Then shake the PCV valve, listening for a rattle. If the valve doesn't rattle, replace it with a new one.

Replacement

3.1L and 3.4L engine

7   To replace the valve, pull it out of the end of the hose, noting its installed position and direction.

8   When purchasing a replacement PCV valve, make sure it's for your particular vehicle, model year and engine size. Compare the old valve with the new one to make sure they are the same.

9   Push the valve into the end of the hose until it's seated.

10   Inspect the rubber grommet for damage and replace it with a new one if necessary.

11   Push the PCV valve and hose securely into position.

3.8L engine

Refer to illustration 22.13, 22.14 and 22.15

12   Detach the fuel injector cover (see Chapter 4).

13   Disconnect the electrical connector from the MAP sensor and unclip the MAP sensor from the PCV valve access cover **(see illustration)**.

14   Press downward on the PCV valve

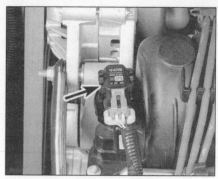

22.5 The PCV valve on 3.8L engines is located at the front of the intake manifold below the MAP sensor (arrow)

access cover and rotate it counterclockwise to remove it **(see illustration)**.

15   To replace the valve, pull the PCV valve and O-ring assembly from the intake manifold noting its installed position and direction **(see illustration)**.

16   When purchasing a replacement PCV valve, make sure it's for your particular vehicle, model year and engine size. Compare the old valve with the new one to make sure they are the same.

17   Installation of the valve is the reverse of removal.

23   Spark plug wire check and replacement (every 30,000 miles or 24 months)

Refer to illustrations 23.4 and 23.8

Note 1: *On 3.1L engines the engine must be rotated forward (towards the front of the car) to allow access to the right side (rear) spark plugs or plug wires. See Chapter 2A for the engine rotation procedure.*

Note 2: *On 3.4L engines the upper intake manifold must be removed first to allow access to the right side (rear) spark plugs or plug wires. See Chapter 2B for the intake manifold removal procedure.*

Note 3: *On 3.8L engines the fuel injector cover must be removed first to access the right side (rear) spark plugs or plug wires.*

22.13 Disconnect the electrical connector and unclip the MAP sensor from the PCV valve access cover

22.14 Press down on the PCV valve access cover, rotate it counterclockwise then pull up to remove it (be sure to check the O-ring and replace it if necessary)

22.15 Remove the PCV valve and the O-ring from the intake manifold

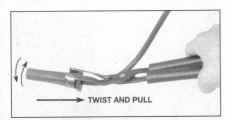

23.4 Using a spark plug boot puller tool like this one will make the job of removing the spark plug boots much easier

1   The spark plug wires should be checked and, if necessary, replaced at the same time new spark plugs are installed.

2   The easiest way to identify bad wires is to make a visual check while the engine is running. In a dark, well-ventilated garage, start the engine and look at each plug wire. Be careful not to come into contact with any moving engine parts. If there is a break in the wire, you will see arcing or a small spark at the damaged area. If arcing is noticed, make a note to obtain new wires.

3   The spark plug wires should be inspected one at a time, beginning with the spark plug for the number one cylinder, (see the specifications section at the beginning of this Chapter), to prevent confusion. Clearly label each plug wire with a piece of tape marked with the correct number. The plug wires must be reinstalled in the correct order to ensure proper engine operation.

4   Disconnect the plug wire from the first spark plug. A removal tool can be used, or

23.8 Remove each spark plug wire from the ignition coil packs - check for corrosion and a tight fit

you can grab the wire boot, twist it slightly and pull the wire free. Do not pull on the wire itself, only on the rubber boot **(see illustration)**.

5   Push the wire and boot back onto the end of the spark plug. It should fit snugly. If it doesn't, detach the wire and boot once more and use a pair of pliers to carefully crimp the metal connector inside the wire boot until it does.

6   Using a clean rag, wipe the entire length of the wire to remove built-up dirt and grease.

7   Once the wire is clean, check for burns, cracks and other damage. Do not bend the wire sharply or you might break the conductor.

8   Disconnect the wire from the coil pack. Pull only on the rubber boot. Check for corrosion and a tight fit **(see illustration)**. Reinstall the wire.

9   Inspect each of the remaining spark plug wires, making sure that each one is securely fastened on each end.

10   If new spark plug wires are required, purchase a set for your specific engine model. Pre-cut wire sets with the boots already installed are available. Remove and replace the wires one at a time to avoid mixups in the firing order. Should a mix up occur refer to the Specifications at the beginning this Chapter.

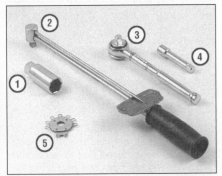

24.2 Tools required for changing spark plugs

1   *Spark plug socket* - This will have special padding inside to protect the spark plug's porcelain insulator

2   *Torque wrench* - Although not mandatory, using this tool is the best way to ensure the plugs are tightened properly

3   *Ratchet* - Standard hand tool to fit the spark plug socket

4   *Extension* - Depending on model and accessories, you may need special extensions and universal joints to reach one or more of the plugs

5   *Spark plug gap gauge* - This gauge for checking the gap comes in a variety of styles. Make sure the gap for your engine is included

24.5a Spark plug manufacturers recommend using a wire type gauge when checking the gap - if the wire does not slide between the electrodes with a slight drag, adjustment is required

24   Spark plug check and replacement (see maintenance schedule for service intervals)

Refer to illustrations 24.2, 24.5a, 24.5b, 24.8, 24.9 and 24.10

Note 1: *On 3.1L engines the engine must be rotated to allow access to the right side (rear) spark plugs or plug wires. See Chapter 2A, Section 4, for engine rotation procedure.*

Note 2: *On 3.4L engines the upper intake manifold must be removed first to allow access to the right side (rear) spark plugs or plug wires. See Chapter 2B for the intake manifold removal procedure.*

Note 3: *On 3.8L engines the fuel injector cover must be removed first to access the right side (rear) spark plugs or plug wires.*

1   All vehicles covered by this manual are equipped with transversely mounted V6 engines which locate the spark plugs on the side of the engine at the front and the rear of the engine compartment. The left side (front) spark plugs can be reached from the front of the vehicle while the right side (rear) spark plugs are located between the engine and the firewall. Removal of the right side (rear) spark plugs requires special removal procedures (as noted above) to be performed first to allow access to the right side (rear) spark plugs or plug wires.

2   In most cases, the tools necessary for spark plug replacement include a spark plug socket which fits onto a ratchet (spark plug sockets are padded inside to prevent damage to the porcelain insulators on the new plugs), various extensions and a gap gauge to check and adjust the gaps on the new plugs **(see illustration)**. A special plug wire removal tool is available for separating the wire boots from the spark plugs, and is a good idea on these models because the boots fit very tightly. A torque wrench should be used to tighten the new plugs. It is a good idea to allow the engine to cool before removing or installing the spark plugs.

3   The best approach when replacing the spark plugs is to purchase the new ones in advance, adjust them to the proper gap and replace the plugs one at a time. When buying the new spark plugs, be sure to obtain the correct plug type for your particular engine. The plug type can be found in the Specifications at the front of this Chapter and on the Emission Control Information label located under the hood. If these two sources list different plug types, consider the emission control label correct.

4   Allow the engine to cool completely before attempting to remove any of the plugs. While you are waiting for the engine to cool, check the new plugs for defects and adjust the gaps.

5   Check the gap by inserting the proper thickness gauge between the electrodes at the tip of the plug **(see illustration)**. The gap between the electrodes should be the same as the one specified on the Emissions Control Information label or as listed in this

1

24.5b To change the gap, bend the *side* electrode only, as indicated by the arrows, and be very careful not to crack or chip the porcelain insulator surrounding the center electrode

24.8 Use a special spark plug socket with a long extension to unscrew the spark plugs

24.9 Apply a thin coat of anti-seize compound to the spark plug threads

Chapter's Specifications. The wire should slide between the electrodes with a slight amount of drag. If the gap is incorrect, use the adjuster on the gauge body to bend the curved side electrode slightly until the proper gap is obtained **(see illustration)**. If the side electrode is not exactly over the center electrode, bend it with the adjuster until it is. Check for cracks in the porcelain insulator (if any are found, the plug should not be used).

6   With the engine cool, remove the spark plug wire as described in Section 23 from one spark plug. Pull only on the boot at the end of the wire - do not pull on the wire. A plug wire removal tool should be used if available.

7   If compressed air is available, use it to blow any dirt or foreign material away from the spark plug hole. A common bicycle pump will also work. The idea here is to eliminate the possibility of debris falling into the cylinder as the spark plug is removed.

8   The spark plugs on these models are, for the most part, difficult to reach so a spark plug socket incorporating a universal joint will be necessary. Place the spark plug socket over the plug and remove it from the engine by turning it in a counterclockwise direction **(see illustration)**.

9   Compare the spark plug with the chart shown on the inside back cover of this manual to get an indication of the general

running condition of the engine. Before installing the new plugs, it is a good idea to apply a thin coat of anti-seize compound to the threads **(see illustration)**.

10   Thread one of the new plugs into the hole until you can no longer turn it with your fingers, then tighten it with a torque wrench (if available) or the ratchet. It's a good idea to slip a short length of rubber hose over the end of the plug to use as a tool to thread it into place **(see illustration)**. The hose will grip the plug well enough to turn it, but will start to slip if the plug begins to cross-thread in the hole - this will prevent damaged threads and the accompanying repair costs.

11   Before pushing the spark plug wire onto the end of the plug, inspect it following the procedures outlined in Section 23

12   Attach the plug wire to the new spark plug, again using a twisting motion on the boot until it's seated on the spark plug.

13   Repeat the procedure for the remaining spark plugs, replacing them one at a time to prevent mixing up the spark plug wires.

25 Fuel filter replacement (every 30,000 miles or 24 months)

Refer to illustrations 25.3 and 25.5
Warning: *Gasoline is extremely flammable, so take extra precautions when you work on any part of the fuel system. Don't smoke or allow*

open flames or bare light bulbs near the work area, and don't work in a garage where a natural gas-type appliance (such as a water heater or clothes dryer) with a pilot light is present. Since gasoline is carcinogenic, wear latex gloves when there's a possibility of being exposed to fuel, and, if you spill any fuel on your skin, rinse it off immediately with soap and water. Mop up any spills immediately and do not store fuel-soaked rags where they could ignite. The fuel system is under constant pressure, so, if any fuel lines are to be disconnected, the fuel pressure in the system must be relieved first (see Chapter 4 for more information). When you perform any kind of work on the fuel system, wear safety glasses and have a Class B type fire extinguisher on hand.

1   Relieve the fuel system pressure (see Chapter 4).

2   Raise the vehicle and support it securely on jackstands.

3   The fuel filter is mounted to the floor pan just in front of the fuel tank **(see illustration)**.

4   Use compressed air or carburetor cleaner to clean any dirt surrounding the fuel inlet and outlet line fittings.

5   Once all the dirt has been removed, depress the white plastic quick-disconnect tabs and detach the inlet line from the fuel filter **(see illustration)**. **Note:** *Have spare rags or a small container to catch or wipe up extra gasoline which will spill from the filter assembly.*

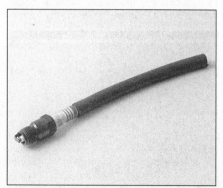

24.10 A length of snug-fitting rubber hose will save time and prevent damaged threads when installing the spark plugs

25.3 The fuel filter (arrow) is located underneath the vehicle in front of the gas tank

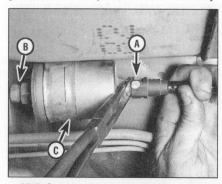

25.5 Squeeze the white plastic quick-disconnect tabs together and pull the inlet line (A) away from the filter, then detach the outlet line (B) from the fuel filter - unbolt the filter mounting bracket (C) to remove the fuel filter

26.4 Check the fuel filler lines (arrows) for cracks and deterioration and the hose clamps for tightness

27.4a Remove the radiator cap (arrow) by pushing downward and rotating it counterclockwise

27.4b Use a screwdriver to open the bleeder screw (arrow) on the thermostat housing, two or three turns

6   Use an open end wrench to steady the outlet side of the filter and a flare nut wrench to unscrew the fuel line nut, then separate the outlet line from the filter while noting the installed position of the O-ring. Using a flare nut wrench will help to avoid rounding the corners off of the fuel line nut.

7   Detach the fuel filter mounting bracket bolt and remove the fuel filter.

8   Installation is the reverse of removal. **Note:** *Be sure to install a new O-ring on the outlet line before reassembling.*

26   Fuel system check (every 30,000 miles or 24 months)

Refer to illustration 26.4

Warning: *Gasoline is extremely flammable, so take extra precautions when you work on any part of the fuel system. Don't smoke or allow open flames or bare light bulbs near the work area, and don't work in a garage where a natural gas-type appliance (such as a water heater or clothes dryer) with a pilot light is present. Since gasoline is carcinogenic, wear latex gloves when there's a possibility of being exposed to fuel, and, if you spill any fuel on your skin, rinse it off immediately with soap and water. Mop up any spills immediately and do not store fuel-soaked rags where they could ignite. The fuel system is under constant pressure, so, if any fuel lines are to be disconnected, the fuel pressure in the system must be relieved first (see Chapter 4 for more information). When you perform any kind of work on the fuel system, wear safety glasses and have a Class B type fire extinguisher on hand.*

1   The fuel system is most easily checked with the vehicle raised on a hoist so the components underneath the vehicle are readily visible and accessible.

2   If the smell of gasoline is noticed while driving or after the vehicle has been in the sun, the system should be thoroughly inspected immediately.

3   Remove the fuel filler cap and check for damage, corrosion and an unbroken sealing imprint on the gasket. Replace the cap with a new one if necessary.

4   With the vehicle raised, inspect the fuel tank and filler neck for cracks and other damage **(see illustration)**. The connection between the filler neck and tank is especially critical. Sometimes a filler neck will leak due to cracks, problems a home mechanic can't repair. **Warning:** *Do not, under any circumstances, try to repair a fuel tank yourself (except rubber components). A welding torch or any open flame can easily cause the fuel vapors to explode if the proper precautions are not taken.*

5   Carefully check all rubber hoses and metal lines leading away from the fuel tank. Check for loose connections, deteriorated hoses, crimped lines and other damage. Follow the lines to the front of the vehicle, carefully inspecting them all the way. Repair or replace damaged sections as necessary.

27   Cooling system servicing (draining, flushing and refilling) (see maintenance schedule for service intervals)

Refer to illustrations 27.4a, 27.4b and 27.6

Warning: *Make sure the engine is completely cool before performing this procedure.*

Caution: *Never mix green-colored ethylene glycol anti-freeze and orange-colored "DEX-COOL" silicate-free coolant because doing so will destroy the efficiency of the "DEX-COOL" coolant which is designed to last for 100,000 miles or five years.*

1   Periodically, the cooling system should be drained, flushed and refilled to replenish the antifreeze mixture and prevent formation of rust and corrosion, which can impair the performance of the cooling system and cause engine damage.

2   At the same time the cooling system is serviced, all hoses and the radiator cap should be inspected and replaced if defective (see Section 11).

3   Since antifreeze is a corrosive and poisonous solution, be careful not to spill any of the coolant mixture on the vehicle's paint or your skin. If this happens, rinse it off immediately with plenty of clean water. Consult local authorities about the dumping

of antifreeze before draining the cooling system. In many areas, reclamation centers have been set up to collect automobile oil and drained antifreeze/water mixtures, rather than allowing them to be added to the sewage system.

4   With the engine cold, remove the radiator cap, reservoir cap and the air bleed screws (if equipped) **(see illustrations)**.

5   Move a large container under the radiator to catch the coolant as it's drained.

6   Drain the radiator by opening the drain plug at the bottom of the radiator **(see illustration)**. If the drain plug is corroded and can't be turned easily, or if the radiator isn't equipped with a plug, disconnect the lower radiator hose to allow the coolant to drain. Be careful not to get antifreeze on your skin or in your eyes.

7   After the coolant stops flowing out of the radiator, remove the lower radiator hose and allow the remaining fluid in the upper half of the engine block to drain.

8   While the coolant is draining from the engine block, disconnect the hose from the coolant reservoir and remove the reservoir (see Chapter 3 if necessary). Flush the reservoir out with water until it's clean.

9   Remove the thermostat from the engine (see Chapter 3). Then reinstall the thermostat housing without the thermostat. This will allow the system to be back flushed.

10   Reinstall the lower radiator hose and tighten the radiator drain plug.

11   Disconnect the upper radiator hose, then place a garden hose in the upper

27.6 The drain plug (arrow) is located at the lower left corner of the radiator

radiator inlet and flush the system until the water runs clear at the upper radiator hose.

12   In severe cases of contamination or clogging of the radiator, remove the radiator (see Chapter 3) and have a radiator repair facility clean and repair it if necessary.

13   When the coolant is regularly drained and the system refilled with the correct antifreeze/water mixture, there should be no need to use chemical cleaners or descalers.

14   To refill the system, install the thermostat, reconnect any radiator hoses and install the reservoir and the overflow hose.

15   Be sure to use the proper coolant (see **Caution** above). The manufacturer recommends adding GM cooling system sealer part number 3634621 any time the coolant is changed. Slowly fill the radiator with the recommended mixture of antifreeze and water to the base of the filler neck. On models without a radiator cap, add coolant to the coolant reservoir. Wait two minutes and recheck the coolant level, adding if necessary. Close the bleed screws (if equipped) when the coolant issuing from them is free of bubbles. **Note:** *The low coolant light may illuminate after the draining and flushing procedure has been completed. Start the engine and let it run until it reaches normal operating temperature, then let it completely cool down. Repeat this procedure two more times until the light goes out.*

16   Keep a close watch on the coolant level and the cooling system hoses during the first few miles of driving. Tighten the hose clamps and/or add more coolant as necessary. The coolant level should be a little above the HOT mark on the reservoir with the engine at normal operating temperature.

28   Automatic transaxle fluid and filter change (every 50,000 miles)

Refer to illustrations 28.7, 28.10a, 28.10b and 28.12

1   At the specified time intervals, the transaxle fluid should be drained and replaced. Since the fluid will remain hot long after driving, perform this procedure only after everything has cooled down completely.

2   Before beginning work, purchase the specified transaxle fluid (see *Recommended lubricants and fluids* at the front of this Chapter) and a new filter.

3   Other tools necessary for this job include jackstands to support the vehicle in a raised position, a drain pan capable of holding several quarts, newspapers and clean rags.

4   Raise and support the vehicle on jackstands.

5   With a drain pan in place, remove the front and side transaxle pan mounting bolts.

6   Loosen the rear pan bolts one turn.

7   Carefully pry the transaxle pan loose with a screwdriver, allowing the fluid to drain **(see illustration)**.

8   Remove the remaining bolts, pan and gasket. Carefully clean the gasket surface of the transaxle to remove all traces of the old gasket and sealant.

9   Drain the fluid from the transaxle pan, clean the pan with solvent and dry it with compressed air. Be careful not to lose the magnet.

10   Remove the filter and pry out the seal **(see illustrations)**.

11   Push a new filter seal fully into its bore,

28.7 After removing the front and side pan bolts, loosen the rear bolts and allow the fluid to drain, then remove the bolts and lower the pan from the vehicle

then install the new filter.

12   Make sure the gasket surface on the transaxle pan is clean, then install the magnet and a new gasket **(see illustration)**. Put the pan in place against the transaxle and install the bolts. Working around the pan, tighten each bolt a little at a time until the final torque figure is reached.

13   Lower the vehicle and add the specified amount of automatic transmission fluid through the filler tube (see Section 7).

14   With the shift lever in Park and the parking brake set, run the engine at a fast idle, but don't race it.

15   Move the shift lever through each gear and back to Park. Check the fluid level.

16   Check under the vehicle for leaks during the first few trips.

28.10a Pull the filter straight down to remove it

28.10b Pry out the old seal

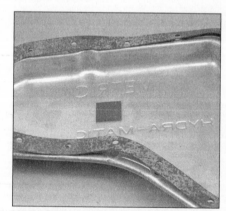

28.12 After cleaning the pan, place the magnet in position and install the gasket

Chapter 2 Part A
3.1L V6 engines

Contents

Specifications

General

Cylinder numbers (drivebelt end-to-transaxle end)	
Front bank (radiator side)	2-4-6
Rear bank	1-3-5
Firing order	1-2-3-4-5-6
Displacement	3.1 liters (189 cubic inches)

FRONT OF VEHICLE

Cylinder location and coil terminal identification diagram - 3.1L engine

24048-1-B HAYNES

Torque specifications

Ft-lbs (unless otherwise indicated)

Camshaft sprocket bolt	
1995	74
1996 and 1997	81
1998	103
Cylinder head bolts	
First step	
1995 through 1997	33
1998	37
Second step	Rotate an additional 90-degrees (1/4-turn)
Exhaust manifold-to-cylinder head bolts	12
Exhaust heat shield bolts	89 in-lbs
Exhaust crossover pipe nuts	18
Flywheel/driveplate-to-crankshaft bolts	
1995	59
1996 and 1997	61
1998	52
Intake manifold (lower)-to-cylinder head bolts/nuts	115 in-lbs
Oil pan bolts/nuts	
To block	18
Side bolts	37
Oil pump mounting bolt	30
Rocker arm bolts	
1995	18
1996 and later	
Step 1	168 in-lbs
Step 2	Rotate an additional 30-degrees
Timing chain cover bolts	
1995	
Small	18
Large	41
1996 and 1997	
Small	15
Large	35
1998	
Small	15
Medium	35
Large	41
Timing chain damper bolts	
1995	18
1996 and later	15
Valve cover-to-cylinder head bolts	89 in-lbs
Vibration damper bolt	76
Front engine mount-to-bracket nuts	35
Front mount bracket-to-oil pan bolts	43
Rear engine mount nuts to transaxle bracket	35
Rear engine mount-to-chassis nuts	35
Torque strut through-bolt nuts	35
Left strut mount to cylinder head bolts	52
Right strut mount to block	37

1   General information

This Part of Chapter 2 is devoted to in-vehicle repair procedures for the 3100 V6 engine. These engines utilize cast-iron blocks with six cylinders arranged in a "V" shape at a 60-degree angle between the two banks. The overhead valve aluminum cylinder heads are equipped with replaceable valve guides and seats. Hydraulic lifters actuate the valves through tubular pushrods.

The engines are easily identified by looking for the designations printed on the aluminum intake plenum, directly on the top.

All information concerning engine removal and installation and engine block and cylinder head overhaul can be found in Part D of this Chapter. The following repair procedures are based on the assumption that the engine is installed in the vehicle. If the engine has been removed from the vehicle and mounted on a stand, many of the steps outlined in this Part of Chapter 2 will not apply.

The Specifications included in this Part of Chapter 2 apply only to the procedures contained in this Part. Part D of Chapter 2 contains the Specifications necessary for cylinder head and engine block rebuilding. **Note:** *On models equipped with the Theftlock audio system, be sure the lockout feature is turned off before performing any procedure which requires disconnecting the battery.*

2   Repair operations possible with the engine in the vehicle

Many major repair operations can be accomplished without removing the engine from the vehicle.

Clean the engine compartment and the exterior of the engine with some type of degreaser before any work is done. It'll make the job easier and help keep dirt out of the internal areas of the engine.

Depending on the components involved,

it may be helpful to remove the hood to improve access to the engine as repairs are performed (refer to Chapter 11 if necessary). Cover the fenders to prevent damage to the paint. Special pads are available, but an old bedspread or blanket will also work.

If vacuum, exhaust, oil or coolant leaks develop, indicating a need for gasket or seal replacement, the repairs can generally be done with the engine in the vehicle. The intake and exhaust manifold gaskets, timing chain cover gasket, oil pan gasket, crankshaft oil seals and cylinder head gaskets are all accessible with the engine in place.

Exterior engine components, such as the intake and exhaust manifolds, the oil pan (and the oil pump), the water pump, the starter motor, the alternator and the fuel system components can be removed for repair with the engine in place.

Since the cylinder heads can be removed without pulling the engine, valve component servicing can also be accomplished with the engine in the vehicle. Replacement of the timing chain and sprockets is also possible with the engine in the vehicle, although camshaft removal can not be performed with the engine in the chassis (see Part D of this Chapter).

Several in-vehicle repair procedures that involve components on the rear (firewall) side of this engine require a preliminary step, called "rotating" the engine (see Section 4).

In extreme cases caused by a lack of necessary equipment, repair or replacement of piston rings, pistons, connecting rods and rod bearings is possible with the engine in the vehicle. However, this practice is not recommended because of the cleaning and preparation work that must be done to the components involved.

---

3 Top Dead Center (TDC) - locating

Refer to illustration 3.8

1   Top Dead Center (TDC) is the highest point in the cylinder each piston reaches as it travels up-and-down when the crankshaft turns. Each piston reaches TDC on the compression stroke and again on the exhaust stroke, but TDC generally refers to piston position on the compression stroke.

2   Positioning the piston(s) at TDC is an essential part of certain procedures such as timing chain/sprocket removal and camshaft removal.

3   Before beginning this procedure, be sure to place the transaxle in Park, apply the parking brake and block the rear wheels. Raise the front of the vehicle and support it securely on jackstands.

4   Remove the spark plugs (see Chapter 1).

5   When looking at the drivebelt end of the engine, normal crankshaft rotation is clockwise. In order to bring any piston to TDC, the crankshaft must be turned with a socket and ratchet attached to the bolt threaded into the center of the vibration damper on the crankshaft.

6   Have an assistant turn the crankshaft with a socket and ratchet as described above while you hold a finger over the number one spark plug hole. **Note:** *See the cylinder numbering diagram in the specifications for this Chapter.*

7   When the piston approaches TDC, air pressure will be felt at the spark plug hole. Instruct your assistant to turn the crankshaft slowly.

8   Insert a plastic pen into the spark plug hole **(see illustration)**. As the piston rises the pen will be pushed out. Note the point where the pen stops moving out - this is TDC.

9   After the number one piston has been positioned at TDC on the compression stroke, TDC for any of the remaining pistons can be located by repeating the procedure described above and following the firing order.

---

4 Valve covers - removal and installation

Removal

Front cover

Refer to illustration 4.10

1   Disconnect the negative battery cable from the battery. **Note:** *On models equipped with the Theftlock audio system, be sure the lockout feature is turned off before performing any procedure which requires disconnecting the battery.*

2   Remove the air cleaner assembly (see Chapter 4).

3   Remove the thermostat bypass pipe clip nut.

4   Remove the transaxle vacuum modulator pipe assembly.

5   Disconnect the right engine mount strut at the engine (see Section 17).

6   If necessary, remove the spark plug wires from the spark plugs (see Chapter 1). Be sure each wire is labeled before removal to ensure correct reinstallation.

7   Detach the spark plug wire harness clamps from the coolant tube.

8   Remove the PCV tube from the valve cover.

9   Drain the coolant (see Chapter 1), and disconnect the coolant bypass pipe. **Note:** *This is not necessary on 1998 models.*

10   Loosen the valve cover mounting bolts **(see illustration)**. **Note:** *Some models are equipped with special bolts. Remove them with a T-30 Torx driver.*

11   Detach the valve cover. **Note:** *If the cover sticks to the cylinder head, use a block of wood and a hammer to dislodge it. If the cover still won't come loose, pry on it carefully, but don't distort the sealing flange.*

Rear cover

Engine rotation

Refer to illustrations 4.14 and 4.15

12   **Note:** *For removal of the rear cover (and for some other engine procedures), the engine must be rotated forward.*

13   Remove the air cleaner duct and air cleaner (see Chapter 4).

14   Remove the bolts in the two engine torque strut mounts on the radiator side of the engine **(see illustration)**. Swing the struts away from the radiator.

15   Attach a ratcheting strap to the front side of the engine and ratchet the strap to tilt

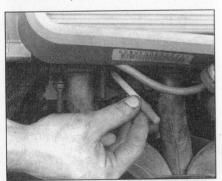

3.8 A plastic pen inserted in the number one spark plug hole can be used to determine the highest point reached by that piston

4.10 Loosen the valve cover mounting bolts (arrows indicate three) - the bolts will stay with the cover

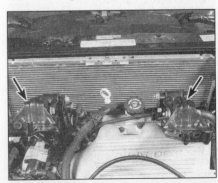

4.14 Remove the bolts in the torque strut mounts, then swing the mounts and struts (arrows) out of the way

4.15 While rotating the engine forward with a prybar, use a ratcheting strap to hold the engine, to better access components at the rear of the engine

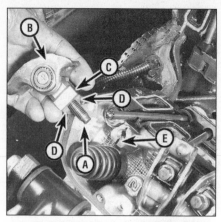

5.1 These engines use rocker arm bolts, stamped roller rocker arms, and rocker arm pedestals - they are kept as an assembly by a small sleeve between the bolt and the pedestal - note the projections on the pedestal; they fit into grooves in the head

A   Rocker arm bolt
B   Rocker arm
C   Rocker arm pedestal
D   Pedestal projections
E   Grooves in the head

5.2 A perforated cardboard box can be used to store the pushrods to ensure they are reinstalled in their original locations - note the label indicating the transaxle end of the engine

the engine toward the radiator side **(see illustration)**. **Note:** *Attach the front end of the strap under the front bumper and tighten the strap. Use a large prybar inserted through the bracket for the torque strut mount to rotate the engine forward while cinching up the ratcheting strap.*

Cover removal

16   Disconnect the negative battery cable from the battery.
17   Remove the air cleaner assembly (see Chapter 4).
18   Disconnect the EGR valve and move it aside (see Chapter 6).
19   Remove the ignition coil assembly (see Chapter 5) and its mount, which on 1998 models also includes the solenoids for the vacuum canister and purge control (see Chapter 6). Tag all disconnected wires and hoses.
20   Remove the serpentine drivebelt (see Chapter 1).
21   Remove the black plastic cover from the shock tower.
22   Remove the alternator and the alternator brackets (see Chapter 5).
23   Detach the breather hose from the PCV valve.
24   Remove the spark plug wires from the spark plugs (see Chapter 1). Be sure each wire is labeled before removal to ensure correct reinstallation.
25   Remove the bolts and detach the valve cover. **Note 1:** *Some models are equipped with special bolts. Remove them with a T-30 Torx driver.* **Note 2:** *If the cover sticks to the cylinder head, use a block of wood and a hammer to dislodge it. If the cover still won't come loose, pry on it carefully, but don't distort the sealing flange.*

Installation

26   The mating surfaces of each cylinder head and valve cover must be perfectly clean when the covers are installed. Use a gasket scraper to remove all traces of sealant or old gasket material, then clean the mating

surfaces with lacquer thinner or acetone (if there's sealant or oil on the mating surfaces when the cover is installed, oil leaks may develop). The valve covers are made of aluminum, so be extra careful not to nick or gouge the mating surfaces with the scraper.
27   Clean the mounting bolt threads with a die if necessary to remove any corrosion and restore damaged threads. Use a tap to clean the threaded holes in the heads.
28   Apply a dab of RTV sealant to the two joints where the intake manifold and cylinder head meet.
29   Place the valve cover and new gasket in position, then install the bolts. Tighten the bolts in several steps to the torque listed in this Chapter's Specifications.
30   Complete the installation by reversing the removal procedure. If the engine was rotated to access the rear cover, return the engine to normal position and reattach the through-bolts in the engine torque struts, and torque them to Specifications. Start the engine and check carefully for oil leaks at the valve cover-to-head joints.

---

5   Rocker arms and pushrods - removal, inspection and installation

Refer to illustrations 5.1 and 5.2

Removal

1   Beginning at the drivebelt end of one cylinder head, remove the rocker arm/pedestal assemblies **(see illustration)**. Store each set of rocker arm components separately in a

marked plastic bag to ensure they're reinstalled in their original locations. The 1996 and later rocker arms have the pedestal mount "captured" on the rocker arm bolt by a metal sleeve inside. The components can be separated if necessary by tapping the bolt out of the pedestal, but normally all components for a particular valve will stay as an assembly.
2   Remove the pushrods and store them separately to make sure they don't get mixed up during installation **(see illustration)**. **Note:** *Intake and exhaust pushrods are different lengths. Intake pushrods are 5.68 inches long, while exhausts are 6.0 inches long. They may also have color codes to easily tell them apart.*

Inspection

3   Inspect each rocker arm for wear, cracks and other damage, especially where the pushrods and valve stems make contact.
4   Check the pivot seat in each rocker arm and the pivot ball faces (1995 models). Look for galling, stress cracks and unusual wear patterns. If the rocker arms are worn or damaged, replace them with new ones and install new pivot balls as well. Make sure the rollers operate freely on 1996 and later rocker arms.
5   Make sure the hole at the pushrod end of each rocker arm is open.
6   Inspect the pushrods for cracks and excessive wear at the ends. Roll each pushrod across a piece of plate glass to see if it's bent (if it wobbles, it's bent).

Installation

7   Lubricate the lower end of each pushrod with clean engine oil or moly-base grease and install them in their original locations. Make sure each pushrod seats completely in the lifter socket.
8   Apply moly-base grease to the ends of the valve stems and the upper ends of the pushrods.
9   Apply moly-base grease to the pivot

6.4 This is what the typical air hose adapter that threads into the spark plug hole looks like - they're commonly available at auto parts stores

6.7 While the valve spring tool is compressing the spring, remove the keepers with a small magnet or pliers

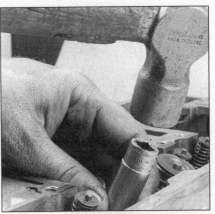

6.13 Tap the new seal in place on the guide with a socket

2A

balls/pedestals to prevent damage to the mating surfaces before engine oil pressure builds up. Install the rocker arm/pedestal assemblies and bolts and tighten them to the torque listed in this Chapter's Specifications. As the bolts are tightened, make sure the pushrods engage properly in the rocker arms. Also, make sure the projections on the bottom of the pedestals fit into the grooves on the head before tightening the bolts (see illustration 5.1).

10 Install the intake manifold and valve covers.

6 Valve springs, retainers and seals - replacement

Refer to illustrations 6.4, 6.7, 6.13 and 6.15
Note: *Broken valve springs and defective valve stem seals can be replaced without removing the cylinder head. Two special tools and a compressed air source are normally required to perform this operation, so read through this Section carefully and rent or buy the tools before beginning the job.*

1 Remove the valve cover (see Section 4).
2 Remove the spark plugs from the cylinders which have the defective components. If all of the valve stem seals are being replaced, all of the spark plugs should be removed.
3 Turn the crankshaft until the piston in the affected cylinder is at top dead center (see Section 3). If you're replacing all of the valve stem seals, begin with cylinder number one and work on the valves for one cylinder at a time. Move from cylinder-to-cylinder following the firing order sequence (see this Chapter's Specifications).
4 Thread an adapter into the spark plug hole (see illustration) and connect an air hose from a compressed air source to it. Most auto parts stores can supply the air hose adapter. **Note:** *Many cylinder compression gauges utilize a screw-in fitting*

that may work with your air hose quick-disconnect fitting.
5 Apply compressed air to the cylinder. **Warning:** *The piston may be forced down by compressed air, causing the crankshaft to turn suddenly. If the wrench used when positioning the number one piston at TDC is still attached to the bolt in the crankshaft nose, it could cause damage or injury when the crankshaft moves.* The valves should be held in place by the air pressure. If the valve faces or seats are in poor condition, leaks may prevent air pressure from retaining the valves - a "valve job" is necessary to correct this problem.
6 If you don't have access to compressed air, an alternative method can be used. Position the piston at a point approximately 45-degrees before TDC on the compression stroke, then feed a long piece of nylon rope through the spark plug hole until it fills the combustion chamber. Be sure to leave the end of the rope hanging out of the engine so it can be removed easily. Use a large breaker bar and socket to rotate the crankshaft in the normal direction of rotation (clockwise) until slight resistance is felt.
7 Stuff shop rags into the cylinder head holes above and below the valves to prevent parts and tools from falling into the engine, then use a valve spring compressor to compress the spring. Remove the keepers **(see illustration)** with small needle-nose pliers or a magnet.
8 Remove the spring retainer and valve spring, then remove the valve guide seal.
9 Wrap a rubber band or tape around the top of the valve stem so the valve won't fall into the combustion chamber, then release the air pressure.
10 Inspect the valve stem for damage. Rotate the valve in the guide and check the end for eccentric movement, which would indicate the valve stem is bent.
11 Move the valve up-and-down in the guide and make sure it doesn't bind. If the valve stem binds, either the valve is bent or the guide is damaged. In either

6.15 Keepers don't always stay in place, so apply a small dab of grease to each one as shown here before installation - the grease will hold the keepers in place on the valve stem

case, the head will have to be removed for repair.
12 Reapply air pressure to the cylinder to retain the valve in the closed position, then remove the tape or rubber band from the valve stem.
13 Lubricate the valve stem with engine oil and install a new valve guide seal. An appropriate-size socket can be used to install the new seal, just don't force it once it bottoms **(see illustration)**.
14 Install the spring in position over the valve. **Note:** *The large end of the spring goes toward the cylinder head.*
15 Install the valve spring retainer. Compress the valve spring and carefully install the keepers in the groove. Apply a small dab of grease to the inside of each keeper to hold it in place if necessary **(see illustration)**. Remove the pressure from the spring tool and make sure the keepers are seated.
16 Disconnect the air hose and remove the adapter from the spark plug hole. If a rope was used instead of air pressure, turn the crankshaft counterclockwise and pull the rope out of the cylinder.
17 Install the spark plug(s) and hook up the wire(s).
18 Install the valve cover(s).

7.4 Remove the intake plenum mounting bolts (arrows)

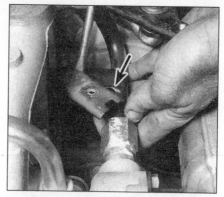

7.7 Remove the bolt and pull out the heater pipe (arrow) from the lower intake manifold - use a screwdriver under the bracket to twist the pipe until it comes out of the fitting

7.8 Disconnect the thermostat bypass hose (arrow) from the pipe

19   Start and run the engine, then check for oil leaks and unusual sounds coming from the valve cover area.

7   Intake manifold - removal and installation

Removal

Refer to illustrations 7.4, 7.7, 7.8, 7.9a and 7.9b

1   Disconnect the negative battery cable from the battery. **Note:** *On models equipped with the Theftlock audio system, be sure the lockout feature is turned off before performing any procedure which requires disconnecting the battery.*

2   Tag and disconnect the hoses/wires attached to the intake plenum and throttle body (see Chapter 4).

3   Refer to Chapter 6 and remove the EGR valve-to-plenum bolts.

4   Remove the intake plenum mounting bolts and remove the plenum with the throttle body attached **(see illustration)**. Relieve the fuel system pressure and remove the fuel rail and injectors (see Chapter 4).

5   Label and disconnect any remaining wires, fuel and vacuum lines from the lower intake manifold.

6   Remove the valve covers (see Section 4).

7   Remove the bolt and pull the heater pipe from the transaxle end of the lower intake manifold **(see illustration)**.

8   Disconnect the thermostat bypass hose from the bypass pipe **(see illustration)**.

9   Remove the manifold mounting bolts and nuts, then separate the manifold from the engine **(see illustrations)**. Don't pry between the manifold and heads, as damage to the soft aluminum gasket sealing surfaces may result. If you're installing a new manifold, transfer all fittings and sensors to the new manifold.

10   Loosen the rocker arm nuts/bolts, rotate the rocker arms out of the way and remove the pushrods that go through the manifold gaskets (see Section 5).

Installation

Refer to illustrations 7.13a and 7.13b

Note: *The mating surfaces of the cylinder heads, block and manifold must be perfectly clean when the manifold is installed. Gasket removal solvents are available at most auto parts stores and may be helpful when removing old gasket material that's stuck to the heads and manifold (since the manifold is*

made of aluminum, aggressive scraping can cause damage). Be sure to follow the directions printed on the container.

11   Lift the old gaskets off. Use a gasket scraper to remove all traces of sealant and old gasket material, then clean the mating surfaces with lacquer thinner or acetone. If there's old sealant or oil on the mating surfaces when the manifold is installed, oil or vacuum leaks may develop. Use a vacuum cleaner to remove any gasket material that falls into the intake ports or the lifter valley.

12   Use a tap of the correct size to chase the threads in the bolt holes, if necessary, then use compressed air (if available) to remove the debris from the holes. **Warning:** *Wear safety glasses or a face shield to protect your eyes when using compressed air!*

13   Apply a 3/16-inch (5 mm) bead of RTV sealant to the front and rear ridges of the engine block between the heads, then install the intake manifold gaskets against the heads **(see illustrations)**.

14   Install the pushrods and rocker arms (see Section 4).

15   Carefully lower the manifold into place and install the mounting bolts/nuts finger tight. First tighten the four vertical bolts (in the middle of the manifold) then the four angled bolts (at the ends). **Note:** *Coat the bolt threads with thread sealing compound.*

7.9a Intake manifold mounting bolt locations (arrows)

7.9b Pry the manifold loose at a casting boss (arrow) - don't pry between the gasket surfaces!

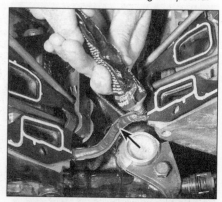

7.13a Apply a bead of sealant to the end ridges between the heads (arrow indicates ridge at transaxle end)

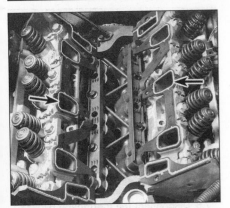

7.13b Install the intake gaskets (arrows) against each cylinder head

8.11 Remove the bolt (A) from the top of the right-side torque strut mount (B), then pull it forward off the locating pin (C)

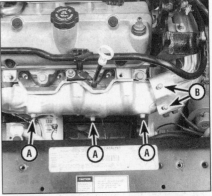

8.12 Remove the screws (A) and the exhaust heat shield, then remove the exhaust crossover heat shield (B indicates the two front bolts, others are at the rear manifold)

16   Tighten the mounting bolts until they're all at the torque listed in this Chapter's Specifications. **Caution:** *To prevent oil leaks, tighten the vertical bolts first to ensure that the lower manifold stays centered on the gaskets, then tighten the angled bolts.*

17   Install the remaining components in the reverse order of removal.

18   Change the oil and filter and refill the cooling system (see Chapter 1). Start the engine and check for leaks.

8   Exhaust manifolds - removal and installation

Removal

Front manifold

Refer to illustrations 8.11, 8.12, 8.13 and 8.14

1   Disconnect the negative battery cable from the battery. **Note:** *On models equipped with the Theftlock audio system, be sure the lockout feature is turned off before performing any procedure which requires disconnecting the battery.*

2   Remove the air cleaner assembly and duct (see Chapter 4).

3   Allow the engine to cool completely, then drain the coolant (see Chapter 1) and

disconnect the coolant bypass tube, if necessary.

4   Remove the upper and lower radiator hoses.

5   Remove the tie straps from the heater outlet pipe and ignition wire harness, and remove the heater outlet pipe.

6   Remove the automatic transaxle vacuum modulator pipe (below the crossover pipe).

7   Remove the coolant reservoir (see Chapter 3).

8   Remove the serpentine drivebelt (see Chapter 1).

9   Unbolt the air conditioning compressor and position it out of the way, leaving the hoses connected to it (see Chapter 3). **Warning:** *The air conditioning system is under high pressure. DO NOT loosen any fittings or remove any components unless the system has been discharged. Air conditioning refrigerant must be properly discharged into an EPA-approved container at a dealer service department or an automotive air conditioning facility. Always wear eye protection when disconnecting air conditioning system fittings.*

10   Remove the through-bolts from the engine torque struts and secure the engine in a "rotated" position (see Section 4).

11   Unbolt the right-side engine torque strut mount (there is a bolt at the top, the bottom is held by the compressor mounting bolts your removed in Step 9), and pull it forward from its locating pin **(see illustration)**.

12   Remove the manifold heat shield **(see illustration)**.

13   Remove the crossover pipe heat shield, then unbolt the crossover pipe where it joins the front manifold **(see illustration)**. You should first apply penetrating oil to the fastener threads - they're usually rusted. **Note:** *After removing the three nuts, pull the crossover pipe back (the flexible joint toward the rear will allow some movement) and remove the three studs. There are hex portions on the studs. If the studs are not removed from the manifold, it is difficult to pull the manifold from the cylinder head because the manifold is also mounted on studs.*

14   Remove the mounting bolts and detach the manifold from the cylinder head **(see illustration)**.

Rear manifold

Refer to illustrations 8.21, 8.22a and 8.22b

15   Perform Steps 1 through 8 as for the front manifold.

2A

8.13 Unbolt the crossover pipe where it joins the front manifold (arrows)

8.14 Remove the six nuts (arrows indicate the upper three) from the exhaust manifold studs

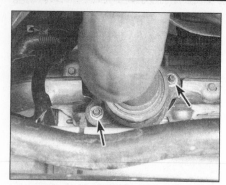

8.21 Remove the two nuts (arrows) holding the exhaust pipe to the rear manifold

8.22a Loosen these bolts (arrows) at the rear of the front suspension subframe

8.22b Remove these bolts (arrows) and lower the front suspension subframe with a hydraulic jack

16   Disconnect the oxygen sensor electrical connector (see Chapter 6). Remove the EGR tube from the rear manifold (see Chapter 6).

17   Remove the through-bolts from the engine torque struts and secure the engine in a "rotated" position (see Section 4).

18   Unbolt the crossover pipe where it joins the rear manifold. **Note:** *You may have to apply penetrating oil to the fastener threads - they're usually corroded.*

19   Remove the heat shield from the rear exhaust manifold.

20   Set the parking brake, block the rear wheels and raise the front of the vehicle, supporting it securely on jackstands.

21   Working under the vehicle, remove the exhaust pipe-to-manifold bolts **(see illustration)**. **Note:** *You may have to apply penetrating oil to the fastener threads - they're usually corroded.*

22   It will be necessary to lower the drive-train/front suspension frame assembly to remove the rear exhaust manifold. Place a floor jack under the frame front center crossmember. Loosen the rear frame bolts - DO NOT REMOVE THEM! Remove the front frame bolts and lower the front of the frame **(see illustrations)**.

23   Remove the bracket bolt on the automatic transaxle dipstick tube and move the tube aside.

24   Unbolt and remove the rear exhaust manifold.

Installation (front or rear)

Refer to illustration 8.26

25   Clean the mating surfaces to remove all traces of old gasket material, then inspect the manifold for distortion and cracks. Warpage can be checked with a precision straightedge held against the mating flange. If a feeler gauge thicker than 0.030-inch can be inserted between the straightedge and flange surface, take the manifold to an automotive machine shop for resurfacing.

26   Remove the exhaust manifold inner heat shield (the gasket material is part of the inner heat shield) and examine the gasket areas for signs of corrosion or leakage **(see illustration)**. If the shield/gasket seems reusable, reinstall it, lace the manifold in position and install the mounting bolts finger tight.

27   Starting in the middle and working out toward the ends, tighten the mounting bolts a little at a time until all of them are at the torque listed in this Chapter's Specifications.

28   Install the remaining components in the reverse order of removal. On rear manifold installations, raise the front suspension subframe with a hydraulic jack and retighten the bolts to this Chapter's Specifications.

29   Start the engine and check for exhaust leaks between the manifold and cylinder head and between the manifold and exhaust pipe.

---

9   Cylinder heads - removal and installation

Refer to illustrations 9.3, 9.13, 9.16a, 9.16b and 9.19

Caution: *Allow the engine to cool completely before loosening the cylinder head bolts.*
Note: *On engines with high mileage and during an overhaul, camshaft lobe height should be checked prior to cylinder head removal (see Part D of this Chapter for instructions).*

Removal

1   Disconnect the negative battery cable from the battery. **Note:** *On models equipped with the Theftlock audio system, be sure the lockout feature is turned off before performing any procedure which requires disconnecting the battery.*

2   Remove the air cleaner assembly (see

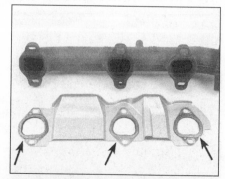

8.26 Examine the gasket areas (arrows) of both sides of the inner heat shield - if bad, the whole shield must be replaced

Chapter 4) and then remove the intake manifold as described in Section 7.

3   If you're removing the front cylinder head, remove the oil dipstick tube mounting bolt **(see illustration)**.

4   Disconnect all wires and vacuum hoses from the cylinder head(s). Be sure to label them to simplify reinstallation.

5   Disconnect the spark plug wires and remove the spark plugs (see Chapter 1). Be sure the plug wires are labeled to simplify reinstallation.

6   Detach the exhaust manifold from the cylinder head being removed (see Section 8).

7   Remove the valve cover(s) (see Section 4). On the front cylinder head, remove the engine torque strut brackets from the head.

8   Remove the rocker arms and pushrods (see Section 5).

9   Using the new head gasket, outline the cylinders and bolt pattern on a piece of cardboard. Be sure to indicate the front (drivebelt end) of the engine for reference. Punch holes at the bolt locations. Loosen each of the cylinder head mounting bolts 1/4-turn at a time until they can be removed by hand - work from bolt-to-bolt in a pattern that's the *reverse* of the tightening sequence **(see illustration 9.19)**. Store the bolts in the cardboard holder as they're removed - this will ensure they are reinstalled in their original locations, which is absolutely essential. Note which ones are studs and their location.

10   Lift the head(s) off the engine. If resistance is felt, don't pry between the head and

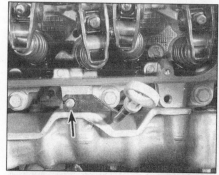

9.3 Remove the bolt (arrow) holding the oil dipstick tube to the front cylinder head

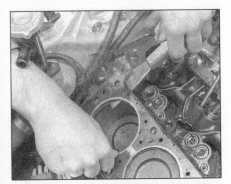

9.13 Remove the old gasket and carefully scrape off all old gasket material and sealant

9.16a Position the new gasket over the dowel pins (arrows) . . .

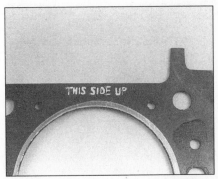

9.16b . . . with the correct side facing up

block as damage to the mating surfaces will result. Recheck for head bolts that may have been overlooked, then use a hammer and block of wood to tap up on the head and break the gasket seal. Be careful because there are locating dowels in the block which position each head. As a last resort, pry each head up at the rear corner only and be careful not to damage anything. After removal, place the head on blocks of wood to prevent damage to the gasket surfaces.

11 Refer to Chapter 2, Part D, for cylinder head disassembly, inspection and valve service procedures.

Installation

12 The mating surfaces of each cylinder head and block must be perfectly clean when the head is installed.

13 Use a gasket scraper to remove all traces of carbon and old gasket material **(see illustration)**, then clean the mating surfaces with lacquer thinner or acetone. If there's oil on the mating surfaces when the head is installed, the gasket may not seal correctly and leaks may develop. When working on the block, it's a good idea to cover the lifter valley with shop rags to keep debris out of the engine. Use a shop rag or vacuum cleaner to remove any debris that falls into the cylinders.

14 Check the block and head mating surfaces for nicks, deep scratches and other damage. If damage is slight, it can be removed with a file; if it's excessive, machining may be the only alternative.

15 Use a tap of the correct size to chase the threads in the head bolt holes. Dirt, corrosion, sealant and damaged threads will affect torque readings.

16 Position the new gasket over the dowel pins in the block. Some gaskets are marked TOP or THIS SIDE UP to ensure correct installation **(see illustrations)**.

17 Carefully position the head on the block without disturbing the gasket.

18 Clean the bolt threads and install the bolts in the correct locations - two different lengths are used. Here's where the cardboard holder comes in handy.

19 Tighten the bolts, using the recommended sequence **(see illustration)**, to the torque listed in this Chapter's Specifications. Then, using the same sequence, turn each bolt the amount of angle listed in this Chapter's Specifications.

20 The remaining installation steps are the reverse of removal.

21 Change the engine oil and filter (see Chapter 1).

10 Valve lifters - removal, inspection and installation

1 A noisy valve lifter can be isolated when the engine is idling. Hold a mechanic's stethoscope or a length of hose near the location of each valve while listening at the other end. Another method is to remove the valve cover and, with the engine idling, touch

each of the valve spring retainers, one at a time. If a valve lifter is defective, it'll be evident from the shock felt at the retainer each time the valve seats.

2 The most likely causes of noisy valve lifters are dirt trapped inside the lifter and lack of oil flow, viscosity or pressure. Before condemning the lifters, check the oil for fuel contamination, correct level, cleanliness and correct viscosity.

Removal

Refer to illustrations 10.5, 10.6a, 10.6b and 10.7

3 Remove the valve cover(s) and intake manifold as described in Sections 4 and 7.

4 Remove the rocker arms and pushrods (see Section 5).

5 Remove the bolts holding the roller lifter guide to the block, and remove the two roller lifter guides **(see illustration)**. Mark the guides as to which side they came from.

6 There are several ways to extract the lifters from the bores. A special tool designed to grip and remove lifters is manufactured by many tool companies and is widely available, but it may not be required in every case. On newer engines without a lot of varnish buildup, the lifters can often be removed with a small magnet or even with your fingers. A machinist's scribe with a bent end can be used to pull the lifters out by positioning the point under the retainer ring in the top of each lifter **(see illustrations)**. **Caution:** *Don't use pliers to remove the lifters unless you intend*

9.19 Cylinder head bolt TIGHTENING SEQUENCE (reverse the sequence when loosening the bolts)

10.5 Remove the bolts (A) and pull up the roller lifter guides (B)

10.6a A magnetic pick-up tool . . .

2A

10.6b ... or a scribe can be used to remove the lifters

10.7 Store the lifters in order to ensure installation in their original locations

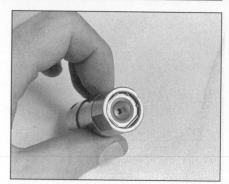

10.10a Check the pushrod seat in the top of each lifter for wear

to replace them with new ones (along with the camshaft). The pliers may damage the precision machined and hardened lifters, rendering them useless.

7   Before removing the lifters, arrange to store them in a clearly labeled box to ensure they're reinstalled in their original locations. Remove the lifters and store them where they won't get dirty **(see illustration)**.

Inspection, installation and adjustment

Refer to illustrations 10.10a and 10.10b

8   Parts for valve lifters are not available separately. The work required to remove them from the engine again if cleaning is unsuccessful outweighs any potential savings from repairing them.
9   Clean the lifters thoroughly with solvent and dry them thoroughly, without mixing them up.
10   Check each lifter wall and plunger seat for scuffing, score marks or uneven wear **(see illustration)**. Check the rollers carefully for wear or damage and make sure they turn freely without excessive play **(see illustration)**. If the lifters walls are worn (not very likely), inspect the lifter bores in the block. If the pushrod seats are worn, inspect the pushrods also.
11   When reinstalling used lifters, make sure they're replaced in their original bores. Soak new lifters in oil to remove trapped air. Coat all lifters with moly-base grease or engine

assembly lube prior to installation.
12   The remaining installation steps are the reverse of removal.
13   After reassembly, the lifters and rocker arms must be adjusted on 1995 models (later models are not adjustable). See Section 5 for adjustment procedure.
14   Run the engine and check for oil leaks.

---

11 Crankshaft front oil seal - removal and installation

Caution: *On some engines a rubber sleeve connects the inertia weight to the vibration damper hub. Take care when working on the vibration damper that you do not accidentally shift the inertia weight's position relative to the sleeve or damper, as this will upset the tuning of the vibration damper.*

Removal

Refer to illustrations 11.7, 11.8 and 11.9

1   Disconnect the negative battery cable from the battery. **Note:** *On models equipped with the Theftlock audio system, be sure the lockout feature is turned off before performing any procedure which requires disconnecting the battery.*
2   Loosen the lug nuts on the right front wheel.
3   Raise the vehicle and support it securely on jackstands.

4   Remove the right front wheel.
5   Remove the right front inner fender splash shield (see Chapter 11).
6   Remove the serpentine drivebelt (see Chapter 1).
7   On automatic transaxle equipped models, remove the driveplate cover and position a large screwdriver in the ring gear teeth to keep the crankshaft from turning while an assistant removes the vibration damper-to-crankshaft bolt **(see illustration)**. The bolt is normally very tight, so use a large breaker bar and a six-point socket.
8   Pull the damper off the crankshaft with a bolt-type puller **(see illustration)**. Leave the Woodruff key in place in the end of the crankshaft. **Caution:** Don't use a jaw-type puller that applies pressure to the outer ring of the damper, as this will damage it.
9   Note how the seal is installed - the new one must be installed to the same depth and facing the same way. Carefully pry the oil seal out of the cover with a seal puller or a large screwdriver **(see illustration)**. Be very careful not to distort the cover or scratch the crankshaft! Wrap electrician's tape around the tip of the screwdriver to avoid damage to the crankshaft.

Installation

Refer to illustrations 11.10 and 11.11

10   Apply clean engine oil or multi-purpose grease to the outer edge of the new seal, then install it in the cover with the lip (spring

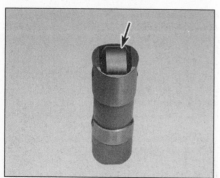

10.10b The roller on the roller lifters must turn freely - check for wear and excessive play as well

11.7 Remove the vibration damper-to-crankshaft bolt (arrow) - it's very tight, so use a six-point socket and a breaker bar

11.8 Use a puller that bolts to the vibration damper hub; jaw-type pullers will damage the vibration damper

11.9 Carefully pry the old seal out of the timing chain cover - don't damage the crankshaft in the process

11.10 Drive the new seal into place with a large socket and hammer

11.11 The damper keyway must be aligned with the Woodruff key (arrow) in the crankshaft nose

side) facing IN. Drive the seal into place **(see illustration)** with a large socket and a hammer (if a large socket isn't available, a piece of pipe will also work). Make sure the seal enters the bore squarely and stop when the front face is at the proper depth.

11 Installation is the reverse of removal. Be sure to apply multi-purpose grease to the seal contact surface of the damper hub (if it isn't lubricated, the seal lip could be damaged and oil leakage would result). Align the damper hub keyway with the Woodruff key **(see illustration)**.

12 Tighten the vibration damper-to-crankshaft bolt to the torque listed in this Chapter's Specifications.

13 Reinstall the remaining parts in the reverse order of removal.

12 Timing chain cover, chain and sprockets - removal and installation

Cover removal

Refer to illustrations 12.5, 12.13, 12.15a, 12.15b, 12.18a and 12.18b

1 Disconnect the negative battery cable from the battery. **Note:** *On models equipped with the Theftlock audio system, be sure the lockout feature is turned off before performing any procedure which requires disconnecting the battery.*

2 Loosen, but do not remove, the water pump pulley bolts, then remove the serpentine drivebelt (see Chapter 1).

3 Remove the water pump pulley (see Chapter 3).

4 Remove the vibration damper (see Section 11).

5 Unbolt the drivebelt tensioner **(see illustration)** and idler, if equipped.

6 Drain the coolant and engine oil (see Chapter 1).

7 Remove the alternator and loosen the mounting bracket (see Chapter 5).

8 Unbolt the power steering pump (if equipped) and tie it aside (see Chapter 10). Leave the hoses connected.

9 Unbolt the flywheel/driveplate cover below the transaxle.

10 Remove the starter (see Chapter 5).

11 Remove the engine strut and bracket from the front cylinder head. Refer to Chapter 3 and remove the engine cooling fan assembly, unbolt the air-conditioning compressor and set it aside without disconnecting the refrigerant lines, then remove the compressor mounting bracket.

12 Remove the front exhaust manifold (see Section 8).

13 Remove the hood (see Chapter 11). Support the engine from above with an engine support fixture **(see illustration)**.

14 Remove the oil pan (see Section 13). **Note 1:** *This procedure requires engine support from above and the lowering of the*

front suspension subframe with a hydraulic jack. Make sure you have these tools or rent them before beginning the procedure. **Note 2:** *The front cover can be removed with the oil pan in place, but the pan must be removed for a good installation to seal against the bottom of the front cover.*

15 Disconnect the coolant hoses from the bypass pipe and water pump, and remove the coolant bypass pipe from the front cover **(see illustrations)**.

16 Unbolt the spark plug wire shield at the water pump.

17 Disconnect the electrical connector at the crankshaft position sensor (see Chapter 6).

12.5 The drivebelt tensioner is secured to the timing chain cover by a bolt (arrow)

12.13 Support the engine with an engine support fixture and chains to the front and rear engine lifting eyes (arrows)

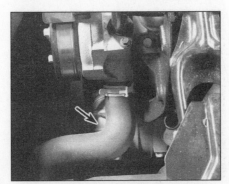

12.15a Disconnect the radiator hose (arrow) from the water pump housing

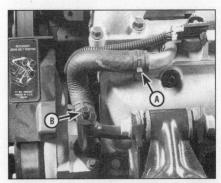

12.15b Disconnect the hose at the intake manifold pipe (A), then remove the bolt (B) at the bypass and pull the bypass from the front cover

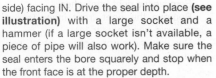

2A

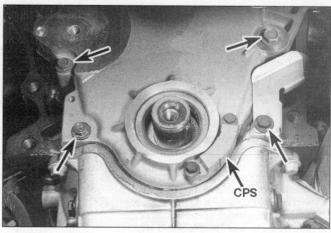

12.18a Timing chain cover bolt locations (arrows), upper . . .

12.18b . . . and lower (arrows) - the crankshaft position sensor (CPS) should be unbolted and laid aside

18   Remove the timing chain cover-to-engine block bolts **(see illustrations)**.
19   Separate the cover from the engine. If it's stuck, tap it with a soft-face hammer, but don't try to pry it off.

Timing chain and sprockets

Inspection

20   The timing chain should be replaced with a new one if the engine has high mileage, the chain has visible damage, or total freeplay midway between the sprockets

exceeds one-inch. Failure to replace a worn timing chain may result in erratic engine performance, loss of power and decreased fuel mileage. Loose chains can "jump" timing. In the worst case, chain "jumping" or breakage will result in severe engine damage.

Removal

Refer to illustrations 12.22 and 12.26

21   Remove the timing chain cover (see Steps 1 through 19).
22   Temporarily install the vibration damper bolt and turn the crankshaft with the bolt to

align the timing marks on the crankshaft and camshaft sprockets. When aligned at TDC for number 1 piston, the crankshaft sprocket timing mark should align with the mark on the bottom of the chain tensioner plate, and the small hole in the camshaft sprocket should be at the 6 o'clock position, aligned with the timing mark in the top of the chain tensioner plate **(see illustration)**.
23   Remove the camshaft sprocket bolt. Do not turn the camshaft in the process (if you do, realign the timing marks before the bolt is removed).
24   Use two large screwdrivers to carefully pry the camshaft sprocket off the camshaft dowel pin. Slip the timing chain and camshaft sprocket off the engine.
25   Timing chains and sprockets should be replaced in sets. If you intend to install a new timing chain, remove the crankshaft sprocket with a puller and install a new one. Be sure to align the key in the crankshaft with the keyway in the sprocket during installation.
26   Inspect the timing chain damper (guide) for cracks and wear and replace it if necessary. The damper is held to the engine block by two bolts **(see illustration)**. The damper should be reinstalled before installing the new timing chain and sprockets.
27   Clean the timing chain and sprockets with solvent and dry them with compressed

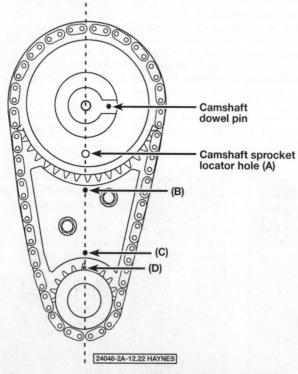

Camshaft
dowel pin

Camshaft sprocket
locator hole (A)

(B)

(C)

(D)

24048-2A-12.22 HAYNES

12.22 The timing marks on the sprockets should align as shown - a straight line should pass through the center of the camshaft, camshaft sprocket timing hole (A), the upper mark on the tensioner (B), the lower mark on the tensioner (C), the crankshaft sprocket timing mark (D) and the center of the crankshaft

12.26 The timing chain damper (guide) is retained by two bolts (arrows)

air (if available). **Warning:** *Wear eye protection when using compressed air.*

28 Inspect the components for wear and damage. Look for teeth that are deformed, chipped, pitted and cracked.

Installation

29 If the camshaft has turned at all since removal of the sprocket, turn the camshaft to position the dowel pin at 3 o'clock. Mesh the timing chain with the camshaft sprocket, then engage it with the crankshaft sprocket. The timing marks should be aligned as shown in **illustration 12.22.** **Note:** *If the crankshaft has been disturbed, turn it until the "O" stamped on the crankshaft sprocket is exactly at the top.*

30 Install the camshaft sprocket bolt (make sure the dowel hole in the sprocket is aligned with the dowel pin in the camshaft) and tighten to the torque listed in this Chapter's Specifications.

31 Lubricate the chain and sprocket with clean engine oil.

Cover installation

32 Use a gasket scraper to remove all traces of old gasket material and sealant from the cover and engine block. The cover is made of aluminum, so be careful not to nick or gouge it. Clean the gasket sealing surfaces with lacquer thinner or acetone.

33 Apply a thin layer of anaerobic sealant to both sides of the new gasket, then position the gasket on the engine block (the dowel pins should keep it in place). Apply sealant to the bottom of the gasket, where it meet the oil pan.

34 Attach the cover to the engine and install the bolts. Follow a criss-cross pattern when tightening the fasteners and work up to the torque listed in this Chapter's Specifications in three steps.

35 The remainder of installation is the reverse of removal. Refer to Section 13 for oil pan installation.

36 Add oil and coolant, start the engine and check for leaks.

13.5 Disconnect the oil level sensor connector (arrow)

---

13 Oil pan - removal and installation

Refer to illustrations 13.5, 13.15, 13.16a, 13.16b and 13.17

Removal

1 Disconnect the cable from the negative battery terminal. **Note:** *On models equipped with the Theftlock audio system, be sure the lockout feature is turned off before performing any procedure which requires disconnecting the battery.*

2 Remove the serpentine drivebelt (see Chapter 1) and the belt tensioner **(see illustration 12.5).**

3 Refer to Chapter 3 and unbolt the air conditioning compressor and set it aside without disconnecting the refrigerant lines.

4 Remove the electric cooling fan assemblies.

5 Raise the front of the vehicle and place it securely on jackstands. Apply the parking brake and block the rear wheels to keep it from rolling off the stands. Remove the lower splash pan and drain the engine oil (refer to Chapter 1 if necessary). Disconnect the oil-level sensor connector from the sensor **(see illustration).**

13.15 Remove these bolts (arrows) at the pan and transmission, then remove the transmission-to-engine brace

6 Remove the front exhaust pipe.

7 Remove the steering gear pinch bolt (see Chapter 10). **Caution:** *Be sure to separate the steering gear from the rack and pinion stub shaft to avoid damage to the steering gear and intermediate shaft.*

8 Remove the hood (see Chapter 11) and support the engine with a support fixture **(see illustration 12.13).**

9 Remove the nuts holding the transaxle mount to the frame, then remove the engine-to-frame mount retaining nuts (see Section 17).

10 Remove the flywheel/driveplate lower cover.

11 Remove the starter (see Chapter 5).

12 Place a floor jack under the frame front center crossmember.

13 Loosen the rear frame bolts **(see illustration 8.22a)** - DO NOT REMOVE THEM!

14 Remove the front frame bolts and lower the front of the frame **(see illustration 8.22b).**

15 At the rear side of the oil pan, remove the bolts from the transaxle-to-engine brace **(see illustration)**, then remove the brace.

16 Remove the three side bolts (connecting the sides of the cast oil pan to the main cap supports) on each side of the oil pan **(see illustrations).** Also remove the oil filter shield bolted to the top front of the pan.

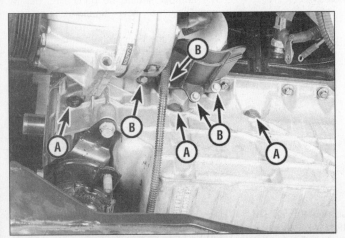

13.16a Remove the oil pan side bolts (arrows A indicate three on the radiator side) - also remove the oil filter shield bolts (B)

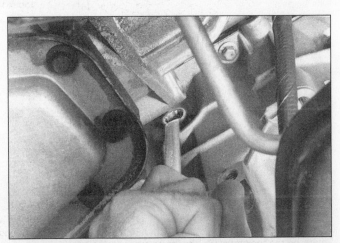

13.16b The side bolts on the rear side of the oil pan are more difficult to remove, but a box wrench with an offset bend in it can remove them

2A

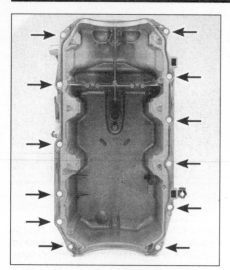

13.17 Remove the 12 oil pan-to-block bolts (arrows) - pan removed for clarity

13.19 Apply a bead of RTV sealant on either side of the rear main cap, where the pan gasket will meet it (arrow)

14.2 Oil pump mounting bolt location (arrow)

17   Remove the remaining 12 oil pan-to-block bolts, then carefully separate the oil pan from the block **(see illustration)**. Don't pry between the block and the pan or damage to the sealing surfaces could occur and oil leaks may develop. Instead, tap the pan with a soft-face hammer to break the gasket seal.

Installation

Refer to illustration 13.19

18   Clean the pan with solvent and remove all old sealant and gasket material from the block and pan mating surfaces. Clean the mating surfaces with lacquer thinner or acetone and make sure the bolt holes in the block are clear.

19   Apply a bead of RTV sealant to the front of the gasket, where it contacts the front cover, and a short bead (9/32-inch wide) to either side of the rear main cap where it meets the block, then install the new one-piece oil pan gasket **(see illustration)**.

20   Place the oil pan in position on the block and install the nuts/bolts.

21   After the pan-to-block fasteners are installed, tighten them to the torque listed in this Chapter's Specifications. Starting at the center, follow a criss-cross pattern and work up to the final torque in three steps.

22   After all the pan-to-block bolts have been torqued, install the oil pan side bolts and tighten them to Specifications.

23   The remaining steps are the reverse of the removal procedure.

24   Refill the engine with oil, run it until normal operating temperature is reached and check for leaks.

14   Oil pump - removal and installation

Refer to illustration 14.2

1   Remove the oil pan (see Section 13).

2   Unbolt the oil pump and lower it from the engine **(see illustration)**. **Note:** *The oil pump driveshaft will come out with the pump as you lower it. It's a rod with a hex-sided portion at each end.*

3   If the pump is defective, replace it with a new one - don't reuse the original or attempt to rebuild it. Inspect the hex ends of the oil

pump driveshaft. If there are signs that the corners of the hexes are rounding off, replace the shaft with a new one.

4   Prime the pump by pouring clean engine oil into the pick-up screen while turning the pump driveshaft.

5   To install the pump, turn the hexagonal driveshaft so it mates with the oil pump drive.

6   Install the pump mounting bolt and tighten it to the torque listed in this Chapter's Specifications.

7   The remainder of assembly is the reverse of the removal procedure.

15   Driveplate - removal and installation

Removal

Refer to illustrations 15.2a and 15.2b

1   Raise the vehicle and support it securely on jackstands, then refer to Chapter 7 and remove the transaxle. If it's leaking, now would be a very good time to replace the front pump seal/O-ring.

2   Remove the bolts that secure the drive-plate to the crankshaft **(see illustration)**. If the crankshaft turns, wedge a screwdriver in the ring gear teeth to jam the driveplate **(see illustration)**. **Note:** *There is a retaining ring*

15.2a Most driveplates have locating dowels (arrow) - if the one you're working on doesn't have one, make some marks to ensure proper alignment on reassembly

15.2b A large screwdriver wedged in one of the holes in the driveplate can be used to keep the driveplate from turning as the mounting bolts are removed

between the bolts and the driveplate, note which side faces the driveplate when removing it.

3　Remove the driveplate from the crankshaft. Since the driveplate is fairly heavy, be sure to support it while removing the last bolt. **Caution:** *When removing a flywheel, wear gloves to protect your fingers - the edges of the ring gear teeth may be sharp.*

4　Clean the driveplate to remove grease and oil. Inspect the surface for cracks, and check for cracked and broken ring gear teeth. Lay the driveplate on a flat surface to check for warpage.

5　Clean and inspect the mating surfaces of the driveplate and the crankshaft. If the crankshaft rear seal is leaking, replace it before reinstalling the driveplate (see Section 16).

Installation

6　Position the driveplate against the crankshaft. Be sure to align the marks made during removal. Note that some engines have an alignment dowel or staggered bolt holes to ensure correct installation. Before installing the bolts, apply thread locking compound to the threads and place the retaining ring in position on the driveplate.

7　Wedge a screwdriver through the ring gear teeth to keep the driveplate from turning as you tighten the bolts to the torque listed in this Chapter's Specifications.

8　The remainder of installation is the reverse of the removal procedure.

16　Rear main oil seal - replacement

Refer to illustration 16.4

1　Remove the transaxle (see Chapter 7).
2　Remove the driveplate (see Section 15).
3　Inspect the oil seal, as well as the oil pan and engine block surface for signs of leakage. Sometimes an oil pan gasket leak can appear to be a rear oil seal leak.
4　Pry the oil seal from the block with a screwdriver **(see illustration)**. Be careful not

to nick or scratch the crankshaft or the seal bore. Thoroughly clean the seal bore in the block with a shop towel. Remove all traces of oil and dirt.

5　Lubricate the lips of the new seal with engine oil or multi-purpose grease. Install the seal over the end of the crankshaft (make sure the lips of the seal point toward the engine) and carefully tap it into place. A special aftermarket tool may be available at your local auto parts store. The tool just fits the diameter of the seal and, used with a hammer, drives the seal in. **Note:** *Do not drive it in any further than the original seal was installed.*

6　Install the driveplate (see Section 15).
7　Install the transaxle (see Chapter 7).

17　Engine mounts - check and replacement

1　There are two mounts that connect the drivetrain to the chassis, one at the timing chain end and one at the transaxle end (see Chapter 7), and two upper mounts connecting the engine torque struts to the body near the top of the radiator. There is also a brace that connects the engine's oil pan to the transaxle **(see illustration 13.15)**.

2　Engine mounts seldom require attention, but broken or deteriorated mounts should be replaced immediately or the added strain placed on the driveline components may cause damage or wear.

Check

3　During the check, the engine must be raised slightly to remove the weight from the mounts.

4　Raise the vehicle and support it securely on jackstands, then position a jack under the engine oil pan. Place a large block of wood between the jack head and the oil pan, then carefully raise the engine just enough to take the weight off the mounts. **Warning:** *DO NOT place any part of your body under the engine when it's supported only by a jack!*

5　Check the mount insulators (the rubber

16.4　Carefully pry the old seal out

part between the engine and the chassis brackets) to see if the rubber is cracked, hardened or separated from the metal plates. Sometimes the rubber will split right down the center.

6　Check for relative movement between the mount plates and the engine or frame (use a large screwdriver or prybar to attempt to move the mounts). If movement is noted, lower the engine and tighten the mount fasteners.

7　Rubber preservative should be applied to the insulators to slow deterioration.

Replacement

Refer to illustrations 17.9a, 17.9b and 17.9c

8　Disconnect the negative battery cable from the battery, then raise the vehicle and support it securely on jackstands (if not already done). **Note:** *On models equipped with the Theftlock audio system, be sure the lockout feature is turned off before performing any procedure which requires disconnecting the battery.*

9　Raise the engine slightly with a jack or hoist. Remove the bolts/nuts holding the mount to the engine and to the chassis brackets, then raise the engine more until you can remove the mount **(see illustrations)**.

10　Installation is the reverse of removal. Use thread-locking compound on the mount bolts and be sure to tighten them securely to this Chapter's Specifications.

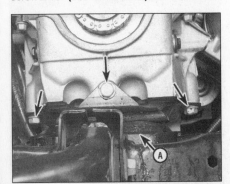

17.9a　The front engine mount (A) is between the front of the oil pan and the chassis - remove the bolts (arrows) holding the bracket to the oil pan . . .

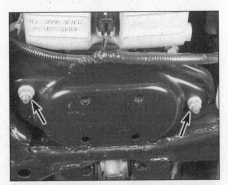

17.9b　. . . and from below remove the nuts (arrows) on the crossmember, then unbolt the mount from the engine bracket and install the new mount

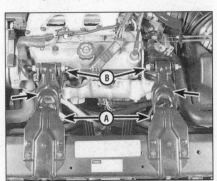

17.9c　The engine torque struts (arrows) control the front-to-rear movement of the engine - to replace them, remove the front (A) and rear (B) through-bolts

2A

Notes

Chapter 2 Part B
3.4L V6 engine

Contents

2B

Specifications

General

Cylinder numbers (drivebelt end-to-transaxle end)	
Front bank (radiator side)	2-4-6
Rear bank	1-3-5
Firing order	1-2-3-4-5-6

FRONT OF VEHICLE

Cylinder location and coil terminal identification diagram - 3.4L engine

24048-1-C HAYNES

Camshafts

Lobe lift	
Intake	0.370 inch (9.398 mm)
Exhaust	0.370 inch (9.398 mm)
Journal diameter	2.1643 to 2.1654 inches (54.973 to 55.001 mm)
Journal clearance	0.0019 to 0.0040 inch (0.049 to 0.102 mm)

Oil pump

Gear backlash	0.0037 to 0.00771 inch (0.094 to 0.195 mm)
Gear length	1.199 to 1.200 inches (30.45 to 30.48 mm)
Gear diameter	1.498 to 1.500 inches (38.05 to 38.10 mm)
Gear housing depth	1.202 to 1.205 inches (30.53 to 30.61 mm)
Gear housing inner diameter	1.504 to 1.506 inches (38.202 to 38.252 mm)
Gear side clearance	0.003 to 0.004 inch (0.08 to 0.10 mm)
Gear end clearance	0.002 to 0.006 inch (0.05 to 0.152 mm)
Pressure valve-to-bore clearance	0.0015 to 0.0035 inch (0.038 to 0.089 mm)

Torque specifications

Ft-lbs (unless otherwise indicated)

Camshaft carrier cover bolts	97 in-lbs
Camshaft carrier-to-cylinder head bolts	20
Camshaft sprocket bolts	96
Cylinder head bolts	
First step	44
Second step	Tighten an additional 90-degrees
Exhaust manifold-to-cylinder head	
Nut	
1995	18
1996 and 1997	116 in-lbs
Stud	13
Flywheel/driveplate-to-crankshaft bolts	60
Intake manifold-to-cylinder head bolts/nuts	30
Intermediate shaft belt sprocket bolt	96
Oil pan bolts/nuts	
Pan bolt (rear)	20
Others	97 in-lbs
Oil pump	
Mounting bolt	40
Drive bolt	27
Cover bolt	89 in-lbs
Engine front cover bolts	
Small	20
Large	35
Timing chain tensioner bolts	18
Crankshaft damper bolt	79
Crankshaft pulley-to-damper bolts	44

1   General information

Refer to illustration 1.4

Note: *On models equipped with the Theftlock audio system, be sure the lockout feature is turned off before performing any procedure which requires disconnecting the battery.*

This Part of Chapter 2 is devoted to in-vehicle repair procedures for the 3.4 liter V6 engine. This engine utilizes a cast-iron block with six cylinders arranged in a "V" shape at a 60-degree angle between the two banks.

The overhead camshaft aluminum cylinder heads have two exhaust valves and two intake valves for each cylinder, and have pressed-in valve guides and valve seats.

The camshafts are located inside aluminum camshaft carrier housings that are located on top of each cylinder head. Each camshaft carrier contains two camshafts, one for the exhaust valves and one for the intake valves. The camshaft thrust plates are at rear

1.4 3.4 liter Double Overhead Camshaft (DOHC) V6 engine

of the carriers. The aluminum of the carriers serves as the bearing surface for the camshafts.

The engine is easily identified by looking at the designation printed on the fuel rail cover **(see illustration)**.

All information concerning engine removal and installation and engine block and cylinder head overhaul can be found in Part D of this Chapter. The following repair procedures are based on the assumption the engine is installed in the vehicle. If the engine has been removed from the vehicle and mounted on a stand, many of the steps outlined in this Part of Chapter 2 will not apply.

The Specifications included in this Part of Chapter 2 apply only to the procedures contained in this Part. Part D of Chapter 2 contains the Specifications necessary for cylinder head and engine block rebuilding.

2   Repair operations possible with the engine in the vehicle

Many major repair operations can be accomplished without removing the engine from the vehicle.

Clean the engine compartment and the exterior of the engine with some type of degreaser before any work is done. It'll make the job easier and help keep dirt out of the internal areas of the engine.

Depending on the components involved, it may be helpful to remove the hood to improve access to the engine as repairs are performed (refer to Chapter 11 if necessary). Cover the fenders to prevent damage to the paint. Special pads are available, but an old bedspread or blanket will also work.

If vacuum, exhaust, oil or coolant leaks develop, indicating a need for gasket or seal replacement, the repairs can generally be done with the engine in the vehicle. The intake and exhaust manifold gaskets, timing chain cover gasket, oil pan gasket, crankshaft oil seals and cylinder head gaskets are all accessible with the engine in place.

Exterior engine components, such as the intake and exhaust manifolds, the oil pan (and the oil pump), the water pump, the starter motor, the alternator and the fuel system components can be removed for repair with the engine in place.

Since the cylinder heads can be removed without pulling the engine, valve component servicing can also be accomplished with the engine in the vehicle. Replacement of the camshaft timing belts and intermediate shaft chain and sprockets is also possible with the engine in the vehicle.

In extreme cases caused by a lack of necessary equipment, repair or replacement of piston rings, pistons, connecting rods and rod bearings is possible with the engine in the vehicle. However, this practice is not recommended because of the cleaning and preparation work that must be done to the components involved.

3   Top Dead Center (TDC) for number one position - locating

This procedure is essentially the same as that for the 3.1L V6 engine. Refer to Part A and follow the procedure outlined there.

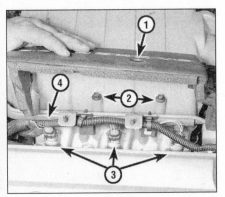

4.4 3.4L V6 plenum installation details

1 Engine identification cover
2 Plenum mounting bolts
  (front side shown)
3 Fuel injectors
4 Fuel rail

4 Intake manifold - removal and installation

Removal

Refer to illustrations 4.4 and 4.5

1 Disconnect the negative battery cable from the battery. **Caution:** *On models equipped with a Delco Theftlock audio system, be sure the lockout feature is turned off before performing any procedure which requires disconnecting the battery.*
2 Relieve the fuel system pressure (see Chapter 4).
3 Remove the fuel rail and disconnect any hoses or wires attached to the throttle body (see Chapter 4). **Note:** *When disconnecting fuel line fittings, be prepared to catch some fuel with a rag, then cap the fittings to prevent contamination.*
4 Raise the engine identification covers for access, then remove the plenum mounting bolts and lift off the plenum with the throttle body attached **(see illustration).**
5 Remove the radiator hose from the thermostat housing **(see illustration).**
6 Remove the connector from the coolant temperature sensor.
7 Remove the heater pipe nut at the throttle body.
8 Remove the manifold mounting bolts and nuts, then separate the manifold from the engine. Don't pry between the manifold and heads, as damage to the soft aluminum gasket sealing surfaces may result. If you're installing a new manifold, transfer all fittings and sensors to the new manifold.

Installation

Note: *The mating surfaces of the cylinder heads, block and manifold must be perfectly clean when the manifold is installed. Gasket removal solvents are available at most auto parts stores and may be helpful when removing old gasket material that's stuck to the heads and manifold (since the manifold is made of aluminum, aggressive scraping can*

4.5 Thermostat housing outlet (arrow)

cause damage). Be sure to follow the directions printed on the container.
9 Lift the old gaskets off. Use a gasket scraper to remove all traces of sealant and old gasket material, then clean the mating surfaces with lacquer thinner or acetone. If there's old sealant or oil on the mating surfaces when the manifold is installed, oil or vacuum leaks may develop. Use a vacuum cleaner to remove any gasket material that falls into the intake ports or the lifter valley.
10 Use a tap of the correct size to chase the threads in the bolt holes, if necessary, then use compressed air (if available) to remove the debris from the holes. **Warning:** *Wear safety glasses or a face shield to protect your eyes when using compressed air!*
11 Install the intake manifold gaskets.
12 Carefully lower the manifold into place and install the mounting bolts/nuts finger tight. **Note:** *To ease reassembly, you can temporarily install two M8 x 1.25 x 50 mm bolts, with washers, in the vertical holes in the intake manifold. This will help align the intake bolt grommet bores with the threaded holes in the cylinder heads.*
13 Tighten the mounting bolts/nuts in two steps, working from the center out, in a circular pattern, until they're all at the torque listed in this Chapter's Specifications. Then remove the two bolts from the vertical holes in the intake manifold.
14 Install the remaining components in the reverse order of removal. Use a new gasket between the lower intake manifold and the plenum.
15 Change the oil and filter and refill the cooling system (see Chapter 1). Start the engine and check for leaks.

5 Exhaust manifolds - removal and installation

Front Manifold

Refer to illustration 5.3

1 Disconnect the negative battery cable from the battery. **Caution:** *On models equipped with a Delco Theftlock audio system, be sure the lockout feature is turned off before performing any procedure which*

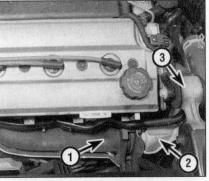

5.3 Remove the exhaust crossover pipe from the manifold

1 Front exhaust manifold
2 Exhaust crossover pipe
3 Engine torque strut

requires disconnecting the battery.
2 Remove the air cleaner assembly (see Chapter 4).
3 Remove the exhaust crossover pipe from the manifolds **(see illustration)**. **Note:** *The fasteners will be rusty; soak them with penetrating oil for 15 minutes before beginning removal.*
4 Remove the cooling fans (see Chapter 3).
5 Remove the mounting nuts, then remove the front exhaust manifold from the cylinder head. **Note:** *The heat shield will come off with the manifold.*
6 Clean the mating surfaces to remove all traces of old gasket material, then inspect the manifold for distortion and cracks. Warpage can be checked with a precision straightedge held against the mating flange. If a feeler gauge thicker than 0.030-inch can be inserted between the straightedge and flange surface, take the manifold to an automotive machine shop for resurfacing.
7 Place the manifold in position with a new gasket and install the mounting nuts finger tight. Make sure the heat shield is in its original position.
8 Starting in the middle and working out toward the ends, tighten the mounting nuts a little at a time until all of them are at the torque listed in this Chapter's Specifications.
9 Install the remaining components in the reverse order of removal.
10 Start the engine and check for exhaust leaks between the manifold and cylinder head and between the manifold and exhaust pipe.

Rear manifold

Refer to illustration 5.13

11 Disconnect the negative battery cable from the battery. **Caution:** *On models equipped with a Delco Theftlock audio system, be sure the lockout feature is turned off before performing any procedure which requires disconnecting the battery.*
12 Remove the air cleaner and duct assembly.

2B

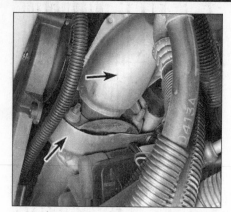

5.13 Remove the exhaust crossover pipe from the manifold (arrows)

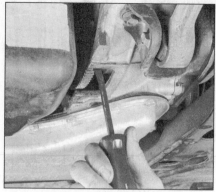

6.7 Have an assistant hold the ring gear with a large screwdriver as the damper-to-crankshaft bolt is loosened/tightened

6.9 Use a puller to remove the damper - use only the type that pulls on the hub of the damper (a puller that pulls on the outer circumference of the damper may cause damage)

13   Remove the exhaust crossover pipe from the manifold **(see illustration).**

14   Remove the EGR tube from the exhaust manifold (see Chapter 4).

15   Set the parking brake, block the rear wheels and raise the front of the vehicle supporting it securely on jackstands.

16   Remove the front exhaust pipe and catalytic converter assembly.

17   Remove the oxygen sensor.

18   If necessary, remove the rear alternator bracket.

19   Remove the transmission fluid dipstick tube.

20   Remove the steering gear intermediate shaft (see Chapter 10).

21   Remove the exhaust manifold nuts.

22   With the front of the vehicle on jackstands (not under the front engine/suspension "cradle")remove the rear cradle bolts, then lower the cradle with a hydraulic floorjack and remove the steering gear heat shield (see Chapter 10). **Warning:** *Make sure you have sturdy backup support materials (lengths of 4x4 or larger lumber, etc.) under the cradle just in case the hydraulic jack should fail.*

23   Remove the exhaust manifold heat shield, manifold and gasket.

24   Clean the mating surfaces to remove all traces of old gasket material, then inspect the manifold for distortion and cracks. Warpage can be checked with a precision straightedge held against the mating flange. If a feeler gauge thicker than 0.030-inch can be inserted between the straightedge and flange surface, take the manifold to an automotive machine shop for resurfacing.

25   Place the manifold in position with a new gasket and install the mounting nuts finger tight. Install the heat shield as it was installed originally.

26   Starting in the middle and working out toward the ends, tighten the mounting nuts a little at a time until all of them are at the torque listed in this Chapter's Specifications.

27   Install the remaining components in the reverse order of removal.

28   Start the engine and check for exhaust leaks between the manifold and cylinder head and between the manifold and exhaust pipe.

6   Crankshaft front oil seal - replacement

Refer to illustrations 6.7, 6.9, 6.10 and 6.11

1   Disconnect the negative battery cable from the battery. **Caution:** *On models equipped with a Delco Theftlock audio system, be sure the lockout feature is turned off before performing any procedure which requires disconnecting the battery.*

2   Loosen the lug nuts on the right front wheel.

3   Raise the vehicle and support it securely on jackstands.

4   Remove the right front wheel.

5   Remove the right front inner fender splash shield.

6   Remove the serpentine drivebelt (see Chapter 1).

7   Remove the driveplate cover and position a large screwdriver in the ring gear teeth to keep the crankshaft from turning while an assistant removes the crankshaft (center) bolt **(see illustration)**. **Note:** *The bolt is normally very tight, so use a large breaker bar and a six-point socket.*

8   Remove the pulley-to-damper bolts, then remove the pulley from the damper.

9   Pull the damper off the crankshaft with a bolt-type puller **(see illustration)**. Leave the Woodruff key in place in the end of the

crankshaft.

10   Note how the seal is installed - the new one must be installed to the same depth and facing the same way. Carefully pry the oil seal out of the cover with a seal puller **(see illustration)** or a large screwdriver. Be very careful not to distort the cover or scratch the crankshaft! Wrap electrician's tape around the tip of the screwdriver to avoid damage to the crankshaft.

11   Apply clean engine oil or multi-purpose grease to the outer edge of the new seal, then install it in the cover with the lip (spring side) facing IN. Drive the seal into place **(see illustration)** with a large socket and a hammer (if a large socket isn't available, a piece of pipe will also work). Make sure the seal enters the bore squarely; stop when the front face is at the proper depth.

12   Be sure to apply moly-base grease to the seal contact surface of the damper hub (if it isn't lubricated, the seal lip could be damaged and oil leakage would result). Apply a dab of RTV sealant to the keyway before tapping the damper in place with a block of wood, aligning the hub keyway with the Woodruff key in the crankshaft.

13   Install the pulley and tighten the bolts to the torque listed in this Chapter's Specifications.

14   Install and tighten the damper-to-

6.10 Carefully pry the old seal out with a seal removal tool (shown) or a large screwdriver

6.11 Drive the new seal into place with a large socket and hammer

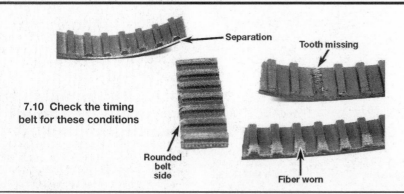

7.10 Check the timing belt for these conditions

7.11 To check the camshaft timing belt length, insert a small ruler between the tensioner pulley and the front cover flange (arrow), and measure the depth

crankshaft bolt to the torque listed in this Chapter's Specifications.

15   Reinstall the remaining parts in the reverse order of removal.

7   Timing belt, belt tensioner and pulleys - removal, inspection and installation

Note: This procedure is complicated, time-consuming and requires several special factory tools. Read through this entire section and acquire the necessary tools before beginning.

Timing belt cover removal

1   Disconnect the negative battery cable. **Caution:** *On models equipped with a Delco Theftlock audio system, be sure the lockout feature is turned off before performing any procedure which requires disconnecting the battery.*

2   Remove the bolts retaining the front cover to the camshaft carrier.

3   Remove the cover.

4   Refer to Chapter 5 and remove the ignition coil pack and its mounting bracket.

5   Remove the bolts and take off the rear cover.

6   Remove the ECM harness cover.

7   Remove the serpentine belt (see Chapter 1) and the serpentine belt tensioner.

8   Remove the clip holding the power steering line at the alternator stud.

9   Remove the cover bolts, then the center cover.

Timing belt inspection

Refer to illustrations 7.10a, 7.10b, 7.10c and 7.11

10   Inspect the timing belt for signs of wear, such as cracks or tears, and for oil contamination. Make sure the belt's teeth are in good condition. Check also for fraying or for wear around one edge of the belt, which would indicate misalignment of camshaft/belt drive components **(see illustrations)**. Replace the belt as necessary.

11   Check the timing belt length. Insert a very thin, narrow ruler under the tensioner pulley until it contacts the tensioner base **(see illustration)**. If the belt is too long, the ruler will drop into the groove in the tensioner bracket. Check this by recording the length

indicated on the ruler. If the depth from the edge of the pulley to the base of the tensioner measures 1.62 inches (41.1 mm) or less, the length of the belt is OK. If the ruler shows 1.75 inches (45.1 mm) or more, it means it dropped into the groove in the tensioner bracket, indicating that the belt is too long and must be replaced. **Note:** *If you are doing a repair procedure which requires you to remove the timing belts and you are close to the mileage or time schedule (see Chapter 1) for belt replacement, replace the belt.*

Timing belt removal

Refer to illustrations 7.20 and 7.22

12   Remove the upper intake manifold (plenum) (see Chapter 4).

13   Remove the serpentine belt (see Chapter 1), and the coolant recover tank (see Chapter 3).

14   If necessary, move the ECM aside, then remove its mounting bracket.

15   Remove the timing belt covers (see Steps 1 through 9).

16   Refer to Chapter 10 and unbolt the power steering pump and set it aside without disconnecting the fluid hoses.

17   Remove the camshaft carrier covers (see Section 8).

18   Remove the plastic cover over the wiring harness on the right strut tower.

19   Align the timing marks, by rotating the engine (clockwise only!) until the mark on the

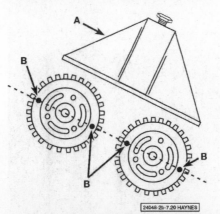

7.20 Align the original timing marks on the camshaft sprockets (B) or make new marks - the factory holding tool (A) locks the camshafts from turning

crankshaft damper is aligned with the arrow on the front cover.

20   Loosely clamp the two camshaft sprockets on each side of the engine together using clamping pliers or equivalent. The marks on the camshaft sprocket pairs should be aligned with a straight line through the center of the sprockets. If the old marks do not align, wipe the old marks off and make new marks **(see illustration)**. Do not allow the camshafts to move until after the tensioner and new timing belt are in place. If you have access to the factory camshaft-holding tools (Kent-Moore J-38613-A), insert one through the slot in each camshaft carrier (at the timing belt end of the front cylinder head, at the flywheel end of the rear cylinder head). Make sure the camshaft flats are aligned with the tool and bolt the tool in place to keep the camshafts from turning.

21   If the timing belt is not going to be removed (just the tensioner is going to be removed), use a C-clamp and a protective cloth to hold the belt in position on the rear exhaust camshaft sprocket. **Note:** *Make sure there is no deflection in the sprocket. If there is, set up your clamp again.*

22   Remove the retaining bolts from the tensioner side plate, then remove the side plate **(see illustration)**.

23   Remove the tensioner actuator from its base with a rotating motion. **Note:** *When you*

7.22 Timing belt tensioner side plate (arrow)

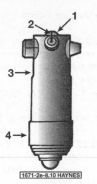

7.26 Timing belt tensioner actuator

1   *Rubber end plug*
2   *Paper clip (installation tool)*
3   *Rubber boot*
4   *Rod tip*

do this the tensioner will extend to its maximum travel. **Caution:** *A tapered bushing is positioned between the actuator and the mounting base; be careful not to lose it when removing the actuator.*

24   If you're going to reuse the belt, mark the direction of rotation on the belt.

25   Remove the belt by sliding it carefully off the sprockets and pulleys. **Caution:** *Do not kink, fold, twist or pry on the belt or you will cause damage.* **Note:** *If the sprockets are to be removed for replacement, see Camshaft timing Steps.*

Installation

Refer to illustration 7.26

26   Lightly clamp the body of the tensioner actuator in a vise with its rod tip facing down **(see illustration)**. **Caution:** *Do not position the actuator in a manner that will cause damage to the rod tip or the rubber boot.*

27   Leave the actuator in this position for at least five minutes to allow the oil to drain into the boot end.

28   Find a standard paper clip - one with no serrations - and straighten it out so that you have a straight length of about two inches. Form the remaining portion of the paper clip into a loop.

29   Remove the rubber end plug from the rear of the actuator **(see illustration 8.10)**. Do not remove the vent plug.

30   Push your paper clip through the center hole in the vent plug, and on into the pilot hole.

31   Retract the tensioner plunger by pushing the rod tip against a table top while turning the screw at the rear of the actuator clockwise.

32   When the tensioner plunger is fully retracted, align the screw slot with the vent hole and push the paper clip into the slot to retain the plunger.

33   If oil was lost from the tensioner, fill it to the bottom of the plug hole with a synthetic 5W-30 engine oil. **Note:** *Fill the tensioner only when it is fully retracted and the paper clip is installed.*

34   Install the rubber end plug; be sure it is snapped fully into place and fits flush against the body of the tensioner.

35   Check to be sure that all bushings and the holes they fit into are in good condition and properly installed, then fit the actuator onto its base. Be sure the actuator is free and can rotate under its own weight. **Note:** *Do not oil the bushings.* **Caution:** *Make sure the tensioner's tapered fulcrum is properly seated in its bushing.*

36   Install the tensioner plate assembly and tighten the bolts to the torque listed in this Chapter's Specifications.

37   Make sure the actuator rod tip is seated in the tensioner pulley socket, then remove the paper clip; this will allow the actuator to extend to its normal position.

38   Install the new timing belt by routing it counterclockwise around all the sprockets, staring with the intermediate shaft sprocket. Keep the belt firmly into the teeth of each sprocket and do not let slack develop.

39   Remove the clamps from the sprockets and rotate the tensioner pivot pulley (11 ft-lbs) to make sure the actuator engages the socket on the back of the pulley.

40   Seat the belt by rotating the engine three full turns clockwise (the direction of crankshaft rotation). **Caution:** *Do not rotate the engine counterclockwise.*

41   Align the timing marks on the crankshaft pulley and timing chain cover, then inspect the camshaft timing marks to be sure the camshaft timing is correct.

42   Reassembly is reverse of disassembly.

Camshaft timing adjustment and sprocket replacement

Refer to illustrations 7.47 and 7.49

43   Some special tools and procedures are required to adjust the camshaft timing or replace the sprockets. If you suspect that the camshaft timing is out of adjustment, check to see if the timing marks on the camshaft sprockets are properly aligned when the engine is at Top Dead Center (TDC) on the number 1 cylinder's exhaust stroke. When at #1 TDC exhaust, the timing marks should be aligned **(see illustration 7.20)**. If the timing marks are not aligned as shown, first try to determine if the cause is a slipped timing belt. If the belt has slipped, find the cause and replace the belt as required. If the belt is good (or new) and you suspect the camshafts are out of time, they will have to checked and/or adjusted as follows.

44   Turn the camshafts so the "flats" are facing up, then install the factory camshaft holders (refer to Step 20).

45   Loosen and remove the camshaft sprockets bolts so the sprockets can be pulled off for inspection or replacement. It might take a few light taps with a plastic hammer to free the sprockets. **Note:** *Do not lose the tapered lock rings for the sprocket bolts.*

46   Install the sprockets (new ones if they are being replaced) finger-tight.

47   Position the crankshaft timing mark at the TDC position **(see illustration)**.

48   Install the timing belt as in Step 38.

49   If necessary, scribe new timing marks on the camshaft sprockets using a straight-edge and a scribe, and remove the old timing marks. Slight movement of the camshaft sprockets may be necessary to align the marks **(see illustration)**.

50   Tighten the sprocket bolts at the rear bank camshafts and remove the timing clamp. **Note:** *The "running torque" (the torque required to turn the bolt before it is seated) should be 44 to 66 ft-lbs. If the running torque is either more or less than this specification, replace the shim ring and lock ring and inspect the camshaft for brinelling or damaged threads. The sprocket bolt is fully seated when the edge of the lock ring is flush with the sprocket.*

51   Turn the crankshaft 360 degrees and realign the crankshaft timing mark. **Note:** *The camshafts on the rear bank should now turn with the crankshaft, while the camshafts sprockets on the front bank should still freewheel.*

52   Repeat steps 49 and 50 on the front bank. **Note:** *When the camshaft timing procedure is complete, the position of the timing flats on the front bank of camshafts should differ from those of the rear bank camshafts by 180 degrees, i.e. the flats*

7.47 Align the crankshaft timing mark with the pointer on the front cover (A) - The mark on the intermediate shaft sprocket should align with the mark on the front cover (B)

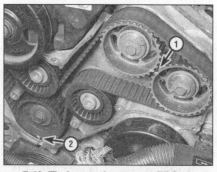

7.49 Timing marks at no. 1 TDC on exhaust stroke

1   *Camshaft sprocket timing marks (front bank shown). Make sure the camshafts are aligned this way.*
2   *Intermediate shaft sprocket timing mark*

8.3 Remove the camshaft carrier cover bolts with a socket, ratchet and extension

should be UP on one set while the flats on the other set are DOWN.

53 The remainder of the procedure is the reverse of the disassembly process. When installing a new belt, rotate the engine three turns clockwise to seat the belt and recheck the timing marks.

8 Camshaft carriers - removal and installation

Note: *This procedure is complicated, time-consuming and requires several special factory tools. Read through this entire section and acquire the necessary tools before beginning.*

Removal

Front carrier

Refer to illustrations 8.3, 8.12 and 8.13

1 Remove the breather hose from the front camshaft carrier cover.

2 Remove the spark plug wires from the spark plugs. **Note:** *Be sure each wire is labeled before removal to ensure correct reinstallation.*

3 Remove the carrier cover bolts **(see illustration)**, then remove the cover. **Note:** *If the cover sticks to the cylinder head, use a block of wood and a hammer to dislodge it. If the cover still won't come loose, pry on it carefully, but don't distort the sealing flange.*

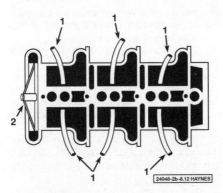

8.12 Install fuel line hoses under the camshafts and between the lifters to hold the lifters in place when the carrier is removed

1 Fuel hoses   2 Timing clamp

4 Remove the gasket and O-rings from the cover.

5 Remove the timing belt (see Section 7).

6 Remove the exhaust crossover pipe (see Section 5).

7 Drain the coolant and remove the upper radiator hose.

8 Remove the heater pipe hose at the plenum.

9 Remove the front exhaust manifold (see Section 5).

10 Remove the engine torque strut (see Section 19).

11 Remove the front engine coolant pipe and the front engine lift bracket from the cylinder head.

12 Install fuel line hoses under the camshafts and between the lifters to hold the lifters in place when the carrier is removed **(see illustration)**. **Note:** *You will need 6 lengths of hose. On the exhaust side the hose dimensions should be 6 x 3/16 inch. On the intake side the hose dimensions should be 3 x 5/32 inch.*

13 Remove the camshaft carrier mounting bolts, then remove the camshaft carrier **(see illustration)**.

Rear carrier

14 Remove the upper intake plenum (see Chapter 4).

15 Remove the rear timing belt cover (see Section 7).

16 Remove the spark plug wires from the spark plugs (see Chapter 1). **Note:** *Be sure each wire is labeled before removal to ensure correct reinstallation.*

17 Remove the breather hose from the cover.

18 Remove the carrier cover bolts, then remove the cover. **Note:** *If the cover sticks to the cylinder head, use a block of wood and a hammer to dislodge it. If the cover still won't come loose, pry on it carefully, but don't distort the sealing flange.*

19 Remove the gasket and O-rings from the cover.

20 Remove the timing belt (see Section 7).

21 Install fuel line hoses under the camshafts and between the lifters to hold the lifters in place when the carrier is removed **(see illustration 8.12)**. **Note:** *You will need 6 lengths of hose. On the exhaust side the hose dimensions should be 6 x 3/16 inch. On the intake side the hose dimensions should be 3 x 5/32 inch.*

22 Remove the camshaft carrier mounting bolts, then remove the camshaft carrier **(see illustration 8.13)**.

Installation

Refer to illustration 11.24

23 Installation is the reverse of removal, using new gaskets under the carriers and covers. **Note 1:** *Remove any accumulated oil from the lower (closest to exhaust) carrier-to-cylinder head bolt holes before installing the carriers.* **Note 2:** *The rubber hoses should keep the lifters in place, but while the carriers are off the engine, coat each lifter (bore surfaces) with petroleum jelly to further insure they stay in place during carrier installation. Remove the rubber hoses after carrier installation is complete.*

24 Refer to Section 7 for installation and timing of the camshaft timing belt. When installing the cover retaining bolts, be sure the bolt isolators **(see illustration)** are fully seated in the cover, then tighten the bolts to the torque listed in this Chapter's Specifications.

2B

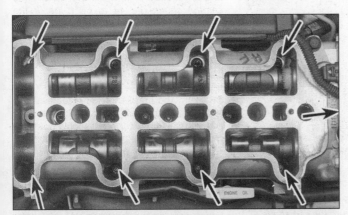

8.13 Camshaft carrier bolt locations (arrows) - arrow at right indicates location of the camshaft thrust plate cover

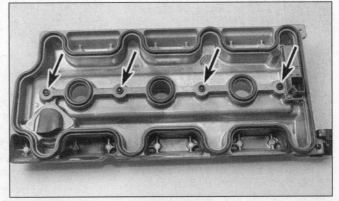

8.24 Make sure the bolt isolators (arrows) are fully seated before installing the cover

9   Camshafts, lifters, sprockets and oil seals - removal, inspection and installation

Note: *This procedure is complicated, time-consuming and requires several special factory tools. Read through this entire section and acquire the necessary tools before beginning.*

Removal

1   Remove the camshaft carriers (see Section 8).

2   Remove the lifters from the camshaft carrier housing. **Note:** *Keep the lifters in order so that they can be replaced in their original positions.*

3   Turn the camshafts so the "flats" are facing up, then lock the camshafts in position with the special tool, or equivalent (see Section 7).

4   Remove the camshaft sprocket bolts. Fabricate a special tool, to hold the sprockets while you loosen the bolts.

5   Using a soft-faced hammer, gently tap the sprockets off the camshafts or use a puller, if necessary. Remove the flat ring from the sprocket bore.

6   Remove the camshaft thrust plate cover and gasket (at the flywheel end of the carriers), then the thrust plate **(see illustration 8.13)**.

7   Remove the timing clamp, then remove the camshafts by carefully withdrawing them through the back of the camshaft carrier. **Caution:** *Be sure you don't damage the camshaft journals inside the carrier when you remove the camshafts.*

8   Remove the seals from the carrier by carefully prying them it out with a screwdriver. **Caution:** *The aluminum seal seating surface in the carrier is easily damaged.*

Inspection

Refer to illustration 9.9

9   Check for damage or pitting on the camshaft lobes. Check the nose of the camshaft for brinelling. Check the camshaft journals inside the carrier for wear or damage. For camshaft lobe lift inspection and journal diameter inspection, refer to Chapter 2 Part D. Visually inspect the lifters for wear, galling, score marks or discolorations from overheating **(see illustration)**.

Installation

10   Install the camshaft seal using a hammer and large socket or section of pipe the exact diameter of the seal. Make sure the seal enters the bore squarely; stop when the front face is at the same depth as the original seal. **Note:** *Coat the seal with clean engine oil or multi-purpose grease prior to installation.*

11   The remainder of installation is the reverse of removal paying particular attention to the following points:

a) *Coat the camshaft lobes and journals with moly-base grease or engine assembly lube prior to installation.*

b) *When installing the camshaft, exercise care to avoid damaging the seal.*

c) *When installing the thrust plate, be sure the arrow points up.*

d) *Be sure to check camshaft timing after reassembly and before starting the engine (see Sections 7 and 8).*

10   Valve springs, retainers and seals - replacement

This procedure is essentially the same as that described for the 3.1L engine. Refer to Part A of this Chapter and follow the procedure outlined there. The camshaft carriers must be removed for access to the valve springs (see Section 8).

11   Cylinder head - removal and installation

Caution: *Allow the engine to cool completely before loosening the cylinder head bolts.*

Note: *This procedure is complicated, time-consuming and requires several special factory tools. Read through this entire section and acquire the necessary tools before beginning.*

Removal

1   Remove the intake upper plenum (see Chapter 4) and lower intake manifold (see Section 4).

2   Remove the camshaft carrier (see Section 8).

3   If you're removing the front cylinder head, remove the oil dipstick tube mounting bolt and the electrical connector for the temperature sender. If you're removing the rear cylinder head, remove the electrical connector for the oxygen sensor.

4   If you're removing the front cylinder head, remove the exhaust manifold (see Section 5). If you're removing the rear cylinder head, remove the exhaust crossover

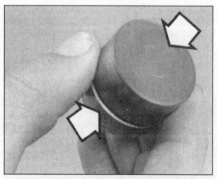

9.9 Check the lifters for signs of wear on the camshaft surface, valve surface and bore surface

pipe, separate the exhaust pipe at the exhaust manifold.

5   If you're removing the rear cylinder head, remove the timing belt tensioner bracket (see Section 7), and the rear exhaust manifold (see Section 5).

6   Lift the head off the engine. If resistance is felt, don't pry between the head and block as damage to the mating surfaces will result. Recheck for head bolts that may have been overlooked, then use a hammer and block of wood to tap up on the head and break the gasket seal. Be careful because there are locating dowels in the block which position each head. As a last resort, pry each head up at the rear corner only and be careful not to damage anything. After removal, place the head on blocks of wood to prevent damage to the gasket surfaces.

7   Refer to Part D for cylinder head disassembly, inspection and valve service procedures.

Installation

Refer to illustrations 11.12 and 11.14

8   The mating surfaces of each cylinder head and block must be perfectly clean when the head is installed.

9   Use a gasket scraper to remove all traces of carbon and old gasket material, then clean the mating surfaces with lacquer thinner or acetone. If there's oil on the mating surfaces when the head is installed, the gasket may not seal correctly and leaks may develop. When working on the block, it's a good idea to cover any holes with shop rags to keep debris out of the engine. Use a shop rag or vacuum cleaner to remove any debris that falls into the cylinders.

10   Check the block and head mating surfaces for nicks, deep scratches and other damage. If damage is slight, it can be removed with a file; if it's excessive, machining may be the only alternative.

11   Use a tap of the correct size to chase the threads in the head bolt holes. Dirt, corrosion, sealant and damaged threads will affect torque readings.

12   Position the new gasket over the dowel pins in the block **(see illustration)**. Be sure the metal tabs between the cylinders are facing up.

11.12 Position the new gasket over the dowel pins (arrows)

Tightening Sequence

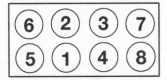

24048-2b-11.14 HAYNES

11.14 Cylinder head bolt tightening sequence

13 Carefully position the head on the block without disturbing the gasket.

14 Install the bolts and tighten them in the sequence shown **(see illustration)** to the torque listed in this Chapter's Specifications. Then, using the same sequence, further tighten each bolt the required angle listed in this Chapter's Specifications. Special torque-angle tools are available at most automotive parts stores. They are used with a standard torque wrench to achieve the desired angle and are highly recommended. If the tool is not available, mark the cylinder head bolt with paint to keep track of how far it has been turned.

15 The remaining installation steps are the reverse of removal.

16 Change the engine oil and filter (see Chapter 1).

12 Intermediate shaft belt sprocket and oil seal - removal and installation

Note: *This procedure is complicated, time-consuming and requires several special factory tools. Read through this entire section and acquire the necessary tools before beginning.*

Removal

Refer to illustration 12.4

1 Align the camshaft timing marks, then remove the timing belt (see Section 7).

2 Raise the car and support it on jackstands.

3 Remove the flywheel inspection cover.

4 Position a large screwdriver in the ring gear teeth to keep the crankshaft from turning while an assistant removes the intermediate shaft timing belt sprocket bolt **(see illustration)**. **Note:** *The intermediate shaft timing belt sprocket bolt is normally very tight, so use a large breaker bar and a six-point socket.*

5 Note the relationship of the sprocket's timing mark to the timing chain cover, then remove the sprocket with a puller. **Caution:** *Avoid pounding on the intermediate shaft or prying on the sprocket as these actions can damage the thrust bearing.*

6 Note how the oil seal is installed - the new one must be installed to the same depth and facing the same way. Carefully pry the oil seal out of the cover with a seal puller or a large screwdriver **(see illustration 6.10)**. Be very careful not to distort the cover or scratch the intermediate shaft! Wrap electrician's tape around the tip of the screwdriver to avoid damage to the intermediate shaft.

Installation

7 Apply clean engine oil or multi-purpose grease to the outer edge of the new seal, then install it in the cover with the lip (spring side) facing IN. Drive the seal into place with a hammer and large socket or section of pipe the exact diameter of the seal. **(see illustration 6.11)**. Make sure the seal enters the bore squarely and stop when the front face is at the proper depth.

8 Lubricate the seal "running surface" of the sprocket, then carefully fit the sprocket onto the intermediate shaft, through the seal and into the timing chain cover. **Note:** *Be sure the locating tangs of the intermediate shaft timing belt sprocket align with those on the timing chain sprocket (hidden behind the timing chain cover). To be sure the tangs are aligned, measure the distance from the front of the intermediate shaft sprocket to the timing chain cover. If the distance is more than 1.65 inches (42 mm), the tangs are not aligned.*

9 Check that the timing mark on the sprocket is aligned with the reference mark on the timing chain cover **(see illustration 7.49)**. If necessary, reposition the sprocket.

10 Lubricate the intermediate shaft O-ring with clean engine oil, then carefully place it into position on the end of the shaft.

11 Apply clean engine oil on the threads of the sprocket bolt, then install the sprocket bolt and washer. Tighten the bolt to the torque listed in this Chapter's Specifications while an assistant prevents the crankshaft from turning.

12 The remainder of installation is the reverse of removal.

13 Engine front cover - removal and installation

Note: *This procedure is complicated, time-consuming and requires several special factory tools. Read through this entire section and acquire the necessary tools before beginning.*

Removal

Refer to illustrations 13.5 and 13.15

1 Disconnect the negative battery cable, drain the engine oil and the coolant (see Chapter 1). **Caution:** *On models equipped with a Delco Theftlock audio system, be sure the lockout feature is turned off before performing any procedure which requires disconnecting the battery.*

2 Remove the serpentine drivebelt (see Chapter 1).

3 Remove the camshaft timing belt tensioner and it's bracket (see Section 7).

4 Remove the timing belt (see Section 7) and the timing belt idler pulleys. **Note:** *Mark the direction of rotation on the timing belt before removing it.*

5 Remove the front engine lift bracket **(see illustration)**.

6 Remove the cooling fans.

7 Disconnect the coolant hoses from the water pump.

8 Remove the heater pipe retaining screws from the frame.

9 Remove the starter (see Chapter 5).

10 Remove the crankshaft damper (see Section 6).

11 Remove the alternator (see Chapter 5).

12 Remove the oil filter.

13 Remove the oil cooler assembly, if equipped (see Chapter 3).

14 Remove the oil pan front nuts and bolts, and loosen the remaining oil pan fasteners.

15 Remove the air conditioning compressor and lay it aside without disconnecting the refrigerant lines **(see illustration)**.

12.4 Remove the bolt from the intermediate shaft sprocket (arrow)

13.5 Engine lift bracket (arrow)

13.15 Unbolt the air conditioning compressor and lay it aside, but DO NOT disconnect the refrigerant lines (arrow)

2B

16   Remove the lower front cover bolts.
17   Remove the intermediate shaft timing belt sprocket (see Section 12).
18   Remove the water pump pulley.
19   Remove any wiring or relays that will interfere with removal of the cover. Remove the screws and position the forward lamp relay center aside (see Chapter 12).
20   Remove the front cover-to-engine block bolts.
21   Separate the cover from the engine. If it's stuck, tap it with a soft-face hammer, but don't try to pry it off.
22   Use a gasket scraper to remove all traces of old gasket material and sealant from the cover and engine block. The cover is made of aluminum, so be careful not to nick or gouge it. Clean the gasket sealing surfaces with lacquer thinner or acetone.

Installation

23   Install the new gasket.
24   Apply a thin layer of RTV sealant to the lower edges of the timing chain cover, then install the cover.
25   Apply thread sealant to the upper timing chain cover bolts then install them. Draw the timing chain cover against the block by tightening the bolts in a criss-cross pattern. Tighten the bolts to the torque listed in this Chapter's Specifications.
26   The remainder of installation is the reverse of removal.
27   Add oil and coolant, start the engine and check for leaks.

14   Intermediate shaft chain and sprockets - removal, inspection and installation

Note: *This procedure is complicated, time-consuming and requires several special factory tools. Read through this entire section and acquire the necessary tools before beginning.*

Removal

1   Remove the engine front cover (see Section 13).
2   Mark the positions of the sprockets to the chain.
3   Remove the intermediate shaft chain tensioner bolts.
4   Remove the chain and sprockets as an assembly using a puller to pull the crankshaft sprocket off the crankshaft.
5   Remove the intermediate shaft chain tensioner. **Note:** *Replacement of the intermediate shaft itself requires engine removal, but this shaft is seldom replaced except during a complete engine overhaul.*

Inspection

6   The intermediate shaft chain should be replaced with a new one if the engine has high mileage, the chain has visible damage, or has too much freeplay. Failure to replace a worn intermediate shaft chain may result in erratic engine performance, loss of power and decreased fuel mileage. A worn, damaged or loose chain can break or "jump" time. In the worst case, chain breakage or "jumping" will result in severe engine damage.
7   The intermediate shaft chain tensioner should be replaced if it is worn, cracked, or displays other damage.

Installation

Refer to illustration 14.11

8   Install the tensioner on the block. **Note:** *Use the upper attaching bolt as the primary locator.*
9   Thread the remaining tensioner bolts into their holes finger tight.
10   Tighten the bolt in the slotted hole in the tensioner first., then tighten the remaining bolts to the torque listed in this Chapter's Specifications.
11   Fabricate a tool from a one-foot length of 1/8-inch welding rod or a coat hanger bent into a U-shape and formed into a hand grip at the end away from the bend. Retract the tensioner shoe using the special tool and insert an appropriately-sized drill bit or nail into the spring pin hole in the tensioner to hold it in position **(see illustration). Caution:** *Avoid using any type of tool that will damage the tensioner or mar the surface of the tensioner shoe.* **Note:** *Be sure the rivet or nail is stout enough to maintain the shoe in it's retracted position.*
12   Apply a light coating of clean engine oil to the tensioner's chain contact surfaces
13   Carefully install the intermediate shaft chain and sprockets assembly. **Note:** *Try to keep the two sprockets parallel as you install them on their respective shafts.* The crankshaft sprocket should be installed with it's large chamfer and counterbore toward the crankshaft. The intermediate shaft sprocket should be installed with it's splines facing away from the block. The crankshaft sprocket will need to be pressed on for the

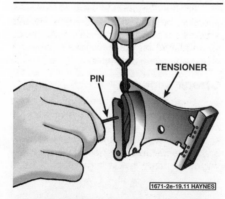

14.11 Retract the tensioner shoe using a special tool fabricated from a coat hanger or welding rod, and insert an appropriately-sized drill bit or nail into the spring pin hole in the tensioner

last 5/16-inch (8 mm) of it's travel; fabricate a special installer using a section of pipe and several washers and press it on using the crankshaft damper bolt. Finally, be sure the timing marks are aligned after installation. **Caution:** *Be sure the tensioner shoe and guide do not become dislodged or damaged during installation of the sprocket and chain assembly.*
14   When the sprockets and chain assembly are in place and properly timed, remove the retaining pin from the tensioner.
15   Install the intermediate shaft chain cover in the reverse order of removal (see Section 14).

15   Oil pan - removal and installation

Note: *On vehicles equipped with an automatic transaxle, it may be necessary to remove the transaxle (see Chapter 7) to provide additional clearance for the oil pan.*

Removal

Refer to illustrations 15.16a and 15.16b

1   Disconnect the cable from the negative battery terminal. Remove the air cleaner duct (see Chapter 4). **Caution:** *On models equipped with a Delco Theftlock audio system, be sure the lockout feature is turned off before performing any procedure which requires disconnecting the battery.*
2   Support the engine from above with a three-bar fixture hooked to the engine lifting brackets on the engine (see Chapter 2 Part A, Section 12).
3   Raise the front of the vehicle and place it securely on jackstands. Apply the parking brake and block the rear wheels to keep it from rolling off the stands.
4   Remove the front wheels and remove the lower splash pan.
5   Drain the engine oil (see Chapter 1) and remove the oil filter, the oil cooler assembly, and the oil level sensor.
6   Drain the coolant (see Chapter 1) and remove the coolant recovery tank.
7   Remove the steering gear mounting bolts and use a section of wire to hang the steering gear from the body (see Chapter 10).
8   Remove the right and left lower ball joint nuts, then separate the ball joints from the control arms (see Chapter 10).
9   Disconnect the power steering cooler line clamps at the frame.
10   Remove the engine mount nuts at the frame (see Section 19).
11   If necessary, remove the driveplate lower cover.
12   Remove the starter (see Chapter 5).
13   Place a floor jack under the frame front center crossmember.
14   Loosen the rear frame bolts - DO NOT REMOVE THEM!
15   Remove the front frame bolts and lower the front of the frame.
16   Remove the bolts and nuts, then carefully separate the oil pan from the block

15.16a Remove the bolts and nuts from around the perimeter of the oil pan, . . .

15.16b . . . then carefully separate the oil pan from the block

(see illustrations). Don't pry between the block and the pan or damage to the sealing surfaces could occur and oil leaks may develop. Instead, tap the pan with a soft-face hammer to break the gasket seal.

Installation

17   Clean the pan with solvent and remove all old sealant and gasket material from the block and pan mating surfaces. Clean the mating surfaces with lacquer thinner or acetone and make sure the bolt holes in the block are clear. Check the oil pan flange for distortion, particularly around the bolt holes. If necessary, place the pan on a block of wood and use a hammer to flatten and restore the gasket surface.

18   Always use a new gasket whenever the oil pan is installed. Apply a bead of RTV sealant to the front of the one-piece gasket, where it contacts the timing chain cover, and to the two tabs at the rear that fit where the rear main cap meets the block.

19   Place the oil pan in position on the block and install the nuts/bolts.

20   After the fasteners are installed, tighten them to the torque listed in this Chapter's Specifications. Starting at the center, follow a criss-cross pattern and work up to the final torque in three steps.

21   The remaining steps are the reverse of the removal procedure.

22   Refill the engine with oil, run it until normal operating temperature is reached and check for leaks.

16 Oil pump - removal, inspection and installation

This procedure is essentially the same as for the 3.1L V6 engine. Refer to Part A and follow the procedure outlined there.

However, use the bolt torque listed in this Chapter's Specifications.

17 Driveplate - removal and installation

This procedure is essentially the same as for the 3.1L V6 engine. Refer to Part A and follow the procedure outlined there. However, use the bolt torque listed in this Chapter's Specifications.

18 Rear main oil seal - replacement

This procedure is essentially the same as that for the 3.1L V6 engine. Refer to Part A and follow the procedure outlined there.

19 Engine mounts - check and replacement

1   There are four mounts that connect the drivetrain to the chassis, two at the timing chain end (a front and a rear), one at the transaxle end, and one upper mount connecting the engine torque strut to the body near the top of the radiator.

2   Engine mounts seldom require attention, but broken or deteriorated mounts should be replaced immediately or the added strain placed on the driveline components may cause damage or wear.

Check

3   During the check, the engine must be raised slightly to remove the weight from the mounts.

4   Raise the vehicle and support it securely on jackstands, then position a jack under the engine oil pan. Place a large block of wood

between the jack head and the oil pan, then carefully raise the engine just enough to take the weight off the mounts. **Warning:** *DO NOT place any part of your body under the engine when it's supported only by a jack!*

5   Check the mount insulators (the rubber part between the engine and the chassis brackets) to see if the rubber is cracked, hardened or separated from the metal plates. Sometimes the rubber will split right down the center.

6   Check for relative movement between the mount plates and the engine or frame (use a large screwdriver or prybar to attempt to move the mounts). If movement is noted, lower the engine and tighten the mount fasteners.

7   Rubber preservative should be applied to the insulators to slow deterioration.

Replacement

8   Disconnect the negative battery cable from the battery, then raise the vehicle and support it securely on jackstands (if not already done). **Caution:** *On models equipped with a Delco Theftlock audio system, be sure the lockout feature is turned off before performing any procedure which requires disconnecting the battery.*

All except the right (rear) engine mount

9   Raise the engine slightly with a jack or hoist. Remove the bolts/nuts holding the mount to the engine and to the chassis brackets, then raise the engine more until you can remove the mount nuts, remove the old mount and insert the new one, then lower the engine and tighten the nuts to Specifications.

Right (rear) engine mount

10   The procedure for replacing the rear engine mount is more involved. The hood must be removed and a three-bar engine support must be used to support the engine from above. Raise and support the front of the vehicle on jackstands.

11   Refer to Chapter 3 and remove the engine cooling fan.

12   Disconnect the engine torque strut from its mount.

13   Refer to Chapter 8 and remove the right driveaxle, then refer to Chapter 10 and disconnect the right balljoint at the control arm.

14   Remove the nuts from the right engine mount (it attaches the transaxle-to-engine brace to the front subframe), raise the engine and replace the mount.

15   Installation is the reverse of removal. Use thread-locking compound on the mount bolts and be sure to tighten them securely to this Chapter's Specifications.

2B

Notes

Chapter 2 Part C
3800 V6 Engine

Contents

Specifications

General

Cylinder numbers (drivebelt end-to-transaxle end)

Front bank (radiator side) 1-3-5
Rear bank 2-4-6
Firing order 1-6-5-4-3-2
Displacement .... 3.8 liters (231 cubic inches)

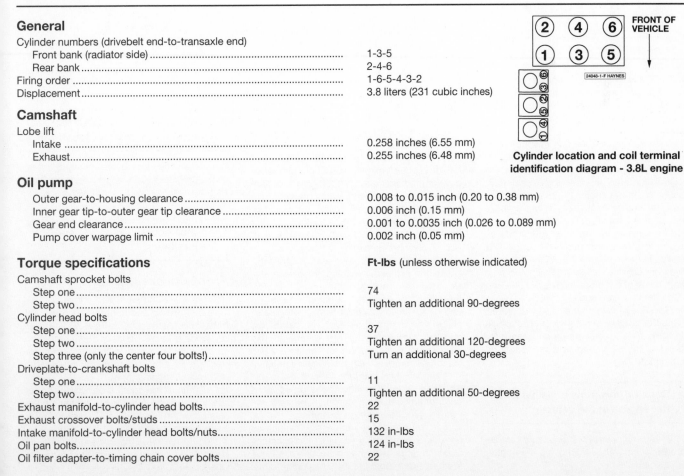

Cylinder location and coil terminal identification diagram - 3.8L engine

Camshaft

Lobe lift

Intake .... 0.258 inches (6.55 mm)
Exhaust .... 0.255 inches (6.48 mm)

Oil pump

Outer gear-to-housing clearance .... 0.008 to 0.015 inch (0.20 to 0.38 mm)
Inner gear tip-to-outer gear tip clearance .... 0.006 inch (0.15 mm)
Gear end clearance .... 0.001 to 0.0035 inch (0.026 to 0.089 mm)
Pump cover warpage limit .... 0.002 inch (0.05 mm)

Torque specifications

Ft-lbs (unless otherwise indicated)

Camshaft sprocket bolts

Step one 74
Step two .... Tighten an additional 90-degrees

Cylinder head bolts

Step one 37
Step two .... Tighten an additional 120-degrees
Step three (only the center four bolts!) .... Turn an additional 30-degrees

Driveplate-to-crankshaft bolts

Step one 11
Step two .... Tighten an additional 50-degrees

Exhaust manifold-to-cylinder head bolts 22
Exhaust crossover bolts/studs 15
Intake manifold-to-cylinder head bolts/nuts .... 132 in-lbs
Oil pan bolts .... 124 in-lbs
Oil filter adapter-to-timing chain cover bolts 22

Torque specifications (continued)

Ft-lbs (unless otherwise indicated)

Oil pump
    Cover-to-timing chain cover bolts .... 97 in-lbs
    Pickup tube and screen assembly bolts .... 132 in-lbs
Rocker arm pivot bolts
    Step one 11
    Step two .... Tighten an additional 90-degrees
Timing chain cover bolts
    1995 and 1996
        Large bolts 35
        Small bolts 15
    1997
        Large bolts 41
        Small bolts 18
    1998
        Step one .... 133 in-lbs
        Step two .... Tighten an additional 40 degrees
    1999
        Step one .... 177 in-lbs
        Step two .... Tighten an additional 40 degrees
Timing chain damper bolt 16
Valve cover nuts/bolts .... 88 in-lbs
Crankshaft balancer-to-crankshaft bolt
    Step one 111
    Step two .... Tighten an additional 76-degrees
Front engine mount
    Mount to engine bracket nuts 32
    Bracket to engine bolts 70
    Mount to frame nuts 50
Engine torque strut mount 37

1   General information

Caution: *On models equipped with the Theftlock audio system, be sure the lockout feature is turned off before performing any procedure which requires disconnecting the battery.*

This Part of Chapter 2 is devoted to in-vehicle repair procedures for the "3800" V6 engine (VIN code K).

Information concerning camshaft, balance shaft and engine removal and installation, as well as engine block and cylinder head overhaul, is in Part D of this Chapter.

The following repair procedures are based on the assumption the engine is installed in the vehicle. If the engine has been removed from the vehicle and mounted on a stand, many of the steps included in this Part of Chapter 2 will not apply.

The Specifications included in this Part of Chapter 2 apply only to the procedures in this Part. The Specifications necessary for rebuilding the block and cylinder heads are found in Part D.

2   Repair operations possible with the engine in the vehicle

Many major repair operations can be accomplished without removing the engine from the vehicle.

Clean the engine compartment and the exterior of the engine with some type of pressure washer before any work is done. A clean engine will make the job easier and will help keep dirt out of the internal areas of the engine.

Depending on the components involved, it may be a good idea to remove the hood to improve access to the engine as repairs are performed (refer to Chapter 11 if necessary).

If vacuum, exhaust, oil or coolant leaks develop, indicating a need for gasket or seal replacement, the repairs can generally be made with the engine in the vehicle. The intake and exhaust manifold gaskets, oil pan gasket and cylinder head gaskets are all accessible with the engine in place.

Exterior engine components such as the intake and exhaust manifolds, the oil pan, the oil pump, the water pump, the starter motor, the alternator and the fuel injection system can be removed for repair with the engine in place. The timing chain and sprockets can also be replaced with the engine in the vehicle, but the camshaft and balance shaft cannot be removed with the engine in place.

Since the cylinder heads can be removed without pulling the engine, valve component servicing can also be accomplished with the engine in the vehicle.

In extreme cases caused by a lack of necessary equipment, repair or replacement of piston rings, pistons, connecting rods and rod bearings is possible with the engine in the vehicle. However, this practice is not recommended because of the cleaning and preparation work that must be done to the components involved.

3   Top Dead Center (TDC) for number one piston - locating

This procedure is essentially the same as that for the 3.1L V6 engine. Refer to Part A and follow the procedure outlined there.

4   Valve covers - removal and installation

Front cover removal

Refer to illustrations 4.4, 4.7a and 4.7b

1   Disconnect the negative battery cable from the battery. **Caution:** *On models equipped with the Theftlock audio system, be sure the lockout feature is turned off before performing any procedure which requires disconnecting the battery.*

2   Remove the spark plug wires from the spark plugs and remove the harness cover. Number each wire before removal to ensure correct reinstallation.

3   Remove the serpentine drivebelt (see Chapter 1) and the alternator brace (see Chapter 5).

4.4 Remove the acoustic cover by twisting out the oil filler neck, then pulling up and forward on the cover

4.7a Remove the plastic cover (arrow) . . .

4.7b . . . then remove the valve cover bolts (arrows)

4   Remove the acoustic cover over the top of the intake plenum. Twist out the oil filler tube from the front valve cover, pull up the front of the acoustic cover and pull it forward (towards the radiator) to release it from the bracket at the rear of the plenum **(see illustration)**.

5   Remove the engine lift bracket from the front exhaust manifold (see Section 8).

6   Remove the fuel injector sight shield, if equipped.

7   Remove the valve cover mounting bolts/nuts **(see illustrations)**.

8   Detach the valve cover. **Note:** *If the cover sticks to the cylinder head, use a soft-face hammer to dislodge it.*

Rear cover removal

9   Disconnect the negative battery cable from the battery. **Caution:** *On models equipped with the Theftlock audio system, be sure the lockout feature is turned off before performing any procedure which requires disconnecting the battery.*

10   Remove the spark plug wires from the spark plugs and remove the wire holder. Be sure each wire is labeled before removal to ensure correct reinstallation.

11   Remove the serpentine drivebelt (see Chapter 1).

12   Remove the power steering pump, if necessary (see Chapter 10).

13   Refer to Chapter 3 and remove the coolant recovery tank.

14   Remove the engine lift brackets from the rear exhaust manifold studs.

15   Remove the fuel injector sight shield over the rear set of injectors.

16   Remove the valve cover mounting bolts/nuts.

17   Detach the valve cover. **Note:** *If the cover sticks to the cylinder head, use a soft-face hammer to dislodge it.*

Installation

18   The mating surfaces of the cylinder head and valve cover must be perfectly clean when the covers are installed. Use a gasket scraper to remove all traces of sealant or old gasket, then clean the mating surfaces with lacquer thinner or acetone (if there's sealant or oil on the mating surfaces when the cover is installed, oil leaks may develop). The valve

cover s are made of soft material, so be extra careful not to nick or gouge the mating surfaces with the scraper.

19   Apply thread locking compound to the mounting bolt threads. Place the valve cover and new gasket in position, then install the bolts.

20   Tighten the bolts/nuts in several steps to the torque listed in this Chapter's specifications.

21   Complete the installation by reversing the removal procedure. Be sure to add coolant if it was drained.

22   Start the engine and check for oil leaks at the valve cover -to-cylinder head joints.

---

5   Rocker arms and pushrods - removal, inspection and installation

Removal

Refer to illustration 5.3

1   Refer to Section 4 and detach the valve covers from the cylinder heads.

2   Loosen the rocker arm pivot bolts one at a time and detach the rocker arms, bolts, pivots and pivot retainers. Keep track of the rocker arm positions, since they must be returned to the same location. Store each set of rocker components separately in a marked plastic bag to ensure that they're reinstalled in their original locations.

3   Remove the pushrods and store them separately to make sure they don't get mixed up during installation **(see illustration)**.

Inspection

4   Check each rocker arm for wear, cracks and other damage, especially where the pushrods and valve stems contact the rocker arm.

5   Check the pivot seat in each rocker arm and the pivot faces. Look for galling, stress cracks and unusual wear patterns. If the rocker arms are worn or damaged, replace them with new ones and install new pivots or shafts as well.

6   Make sure the hole at the pushrod end of each rocker arm is open.

7   Inspect the pushrods for cracks and excessive wear at the ends. Roll each pushrod across a piece of plate glass to see if it's bent (if it wobbles, it's bent).

Installation

8   Lubricate the lower end of each pushrod with clean engine oil or moly-base grease and install them in their original locations. Make sure each pushrod seats completely in the lifter socket.

9   Apply moly-base grease to the ends of the valve stems, the upper ends of the pushrods and to the pivot faces to prevent damage to the mating surfaces before engine oil pressure builds up.

10   Coat the rocker arm pivot bolts with moly-base grease. Install the rocker arms, pivots and pivot retainers. Tighten the bolts to the torque listed in this Chapter's specifications. As the bolts are tightened, make sure the pushrods seat properly in the rocker arms.

11   Install the valve covers (see Section 4).

---

6   Valve springs, retainers and seals - replacement

This procedure is essentially the same as that described for the 3.1L engine. Refer to Part A of this Chapter and follow the procedure outlined there.

5.3 If more than one pushrod is being removed, store them in a perforated cardboard box to prevent mix-ups during installation - note the label indicating the front of the engine

2C (margin tab)

7.3 Remove the mounting bolts (not seen in this view) for the intake plenum (arrow) - there are 3 bolts on the front, 3 on the rear, one stud and one bolt at the throttle body end, and one bolt at the timing chain end

7.5 Carefully pry up on a casting boss - don't pry between gasket surfaces

7.6 Remove all traces of gasket material, but don't gouge the mating surfaces

7 Intake manifold - removal and installation

Removal

Refer to illustrations 7.3 and 7.5

1   Disconnect the negative battery cable from the battery. Remove the acoustic cover over the plenum **(see illustration 4.4)**. **Caution:** *On models equipped with the Theftlock audio system, be sure the lockout feature is turned off before performing any procedure which requires disconnecting the battery.*

2   Refer to Chapter 4 to relieve the fuel system pressure and disconnect any hoses or wires attached to the throttle body.

3   Remove the plenum-mounting bolts (and one stud) and remove the upper intake plenum **(see illustration)**. **Note:** *Two of the intake manifold bolts can't be accessed until the plenum has been removed.*

4   Refer to Chapter 6 and remove the EGR valve from the manifold. Refer to Chapter 5 and remove the alternator and bracket.

5   Remove the intake manifold mounting bolts and separate the manifold from the engine **(see illustration)**. Do not pry between the manifold and heads, as damage to the

gasket sealing surfaces may result. If you're installing a new manifold, transfer all fittings and sensors to the new manifold.

Installation

Refer to illustrations 7.6 and 7.10

Note: *The mating surfaces of the cylinder heads, block and manifold must be perfectly clean when the manifold is installed. Gasket removal solvents in aerosol cans are available at most auto parts stores and may be helpful when removing old gasket material that's stuck to the heads and manifold (since the manifold is made of aluminum, aggressive scraping can cause damage). Be sure to follow the directions printed on the container.*

6   Use a gasket scraper to remove all traces of sealant and old gasket material **(see illustration)**, then clean the mating surfaces with lacquer thinner or acetone. If there's old sealant or oil on the mating surfaces when the manifold is installed, oil or vacuum leaks may develop. Use shop towels to protect the lifter valley during gasket removal and a vacuum cleaner to remove any final debris.

7   Use a tap of the correct size to chase the threads in the bolt holes, then use compressed air (if available) to remove the debris from the holes. **Warning:** *Wear safety glasses or a face shield to protect your eyes when using compressed air.*

8   Install the new manifold gasket, applying RTV sealant to the four corners where the manifold, head and block come together.

9   Carefully lower the manifold into place. Apply thread locking compound to the mounting bolt threads and install the bolts finger tight.

10   Tighten the mounting bolts, following the recommended sequence **(see illustration)**, to the torque listed in this Chapter's specifications, including the two hidden bolts. Tighten the bolts again, in sequence.

11   Install the remaining components in the reverse order of removal. Install a new plenum-to-lower intake gasket when installing the plenum.

12   Change the oil and filter and fill the cooling system (see Chapter 1). Start the engine and check for oil and vacuum leaks.

8 Exhaust manifolds - removal and installation

Warning: *Allow the engine to cool completely before beginning this procedure.* **Note:** *Exhaust system fasteners are frequently difficult to remove - they get frozen in place because of the heating/cooling cycle to which they're constantly exposed. To ease removal, apply penetrating oil to the threads of all exhaust manifold and exhaust pipe fasteners and allow it to soak in.*

Removal

Front manifold

Refer to illustrations 8.5, 8.9 and 8.11

1   Disconnect the negative battery cable, and drain the cooling system (see Chapter 1). **Caution:** *On models equipped with the Theftlock audio system, be sure the lockout feature is turned off before performing any procedure which requires disconnecting the battery.*

2   Remove the cooling fan for access (see Chapter 3).

3   Remove the EGR valve adapter and pipe (see Chapter 5).

4   Remove the engine torque struts (see Section 17).

5   Remove the engine lifting bracket **(see illustration)**.

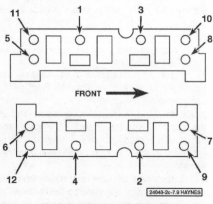

7.10 Intake manifold bolt tightening sequence

8.5 Remove the nuts and take off the engine lift bracket (arrow)

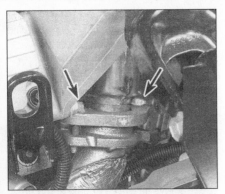

8.9 Remove the exhaust crossover pipe heat shield and remove the nuts (arrows) holding the crossover pipe to the manifold

8.11 Remove the front exhaust manifold bolts/studs (arrows indicate three)

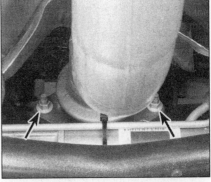

8.20 Remove the nuts (arrows) to separate the exhaust pipe from the rear manifold, just above the steering rack

6   Remove the acoustic cover over the intake manifold **(see illustration 4.4)**.

7   Remove the dipstick tube hold-down nut and work the dipstick tube out of the block.

8   Detach the spark plug wires from the front spark plugs, then remove the spark plugs (see Chapter 1).

9   Unbolt the crossover pipe and heat shield from the manifold **(see illustration)**.

10   Remove the manifold heat shield.

11   Unbolt and remove the exhaust manifold **(see illustration)**.

Rear manifold

Refer to illustration 8.20

12   Disconnect the negative battery cable. **Caution:** *On models equipped with the Theftlock audio system, be sure the lockout feature is turned off before performing any procedure which requires disconnecting the battery.*

13   Drain the coolant from the radiator (see Chapter 1).

14   Remove the two nuts attaching the crossover pipe to the rear exhaust manifold. On 1998 models, remove the heat shield at the brake booster.

15   Disconnect the spark plug wires from the rear spark plugs and remove the spark plugs (see Chapter 1).

16   Remove the EGR pipe and transaxle dipstick tube if it's in the way (see Chapters 6 and 7).

17   Remove the acoustic cover **(see illustration 4.4)** and the cover bracket. **Note:** *Disconnect the oxygen sensor electrical connector to allow the bracket to be removed.*

18   Remove the rear engine lifting bracket from the studs on the rear manifold.

19   Set the parking brake, block the rear wheels and raise the front of the vehicle, supporting it securely on jackstands.

20   Working under the vehicle, remove the two exhaust pipe-to-manifold nuts, then lower the vehicle **(see illustration)**. **Note:** *Soak the nuts with penetrating oil before attempting removal.*

21   Remove the right-rear engine mount-to-frame nuts (see Section 17) and raise the engine slightly with a floorjack to provide extra working room around the rear manifold.

22   Remove the bolts/studs and detach the manifold from the head. Note the location of the studs for later reference.

Installation

23   Clean the mating surfaces of the manifold and cylinder head to remove all traces of old gasket material, then check the manifold for warpage and cracks. If the

manifold gasket was blown, take the manifold to an automotive machine shop for resurfacing.

24   Place the manifold in position with a new gasket and install the bolts finger tight.

25   Starting in the middle and working out toward the ends, tighten the mounting bolts a little at a time until all of them are at the specified torque.

26   Install the remaining components in the reverse order of removal.

27   Start the engine and check for exhaust leaks between the manifold and cylinder head, between the manifold and exhaust pipe, between the manifolds and the crossover pipe, and at the EGR pipe connections.

9   Cylinder heads - removal and installation

Removal

Refer to illustrations 9.4a, 9.4b, 9.5 and 9.10

1   Disconnect the negative battery cable at the battery. Refer to Chapter 1 and drain the cooling system. **Caution:** *On models equipped with the Theftlock audio system, be sure the lockout feature is turned off before performing any procedure which requires disconnecting the battery.*

2   Disconnect the spark plug wires and remove the spark plugs (see Chapter 1). Be sure to label the plug wires to simplify reinstallation.

3   Remove the intake manifold as described in Section 7.

4   Refer to Chapter 5 and remove the ignition coil-pack, then refer to Section 17 and remove the torque struts from their brackets. One is mounted at each end of the front cylinder head. Remove the nuts/bolts holding the torque strut brackets to the cylinder head **(see illustrations)**.

5   Disconnect all wires and hoses from the cylinder head(s). Be sure to label them to simplify reinstallation. If removing the rear cylinder head, remove the alternator (see Chapter 5), then remove the water bypass

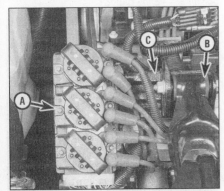

9.4a Remove the ignition coil-pack (A) and the torque strut (B) from the right torque strut mounting bracket (C) - left torque strut similar

9.4b Under the coil-pack, remove the alternator brace bolt (A) and the torque strut mount-to-head nut (B)

9.5 Remove the bolts holding the water bypass hoses to the belt tensioner (A indicates one of the hoses and its bolt), then remove the tensioner bolts (B indicates two)

9.10 Pry carefully - don't force a tool between the gasket surfaces

Installation

Refer to illustrations 9.13, 9.16 and 9.19

12 The mating surfaces of the cylinder heads and block must be perfectly clean when the heads are installed.

13 Use a gasket scraper to remove all traces of carbon and old gasket material **(see illustration)**, then clean the mating surfaces with lacquer thinner or acetone. If there's oil on the mating surfaces when the heads are installed, the gaskets may not seal correctly and leaks may develop. When working on the block, it's a good idea to cover the lifter valley with shop rags to keep debris out of the engine. Use a shop rag or vacuum cleaner to remove any debris that falls into the cylinders.

14 Check the block and head mating surfaces for nicks, deep scratches and other damage. If damage is slight, it can be removed with a file; if it's excessive, machining may be the only alternative.

15 Use a tap of the correct size to chase the threads in the head bolt holes. Dirt, corrosion, sealant and damaged threads will affect torque readings.

16 Position the new gaskets over the dowel pins in the block. Install "non-retorquing" type gaskets dry (no sealant), unless the manufacturer states otherwise. Most gaskets are marked UP or TOP **(see illustration)** because they must be installed a certain way and they have an arrow that must point to the front (timing chain end) of the engine. The left gasket may have an "L" near the arrow.

17 Carefully position the heads on the block without disturbing the gaskets.

18 Use NEW head bolts as these are a

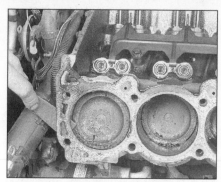

9.13 Carefully remove all traces of old gasket material

torque-to-yield design and the old ones must not be reused.

19 Tighten the bolts as directed in this Chapter's specifications in the sequence shown **(see illustration)**. This must be done in three steps, following the sequence each time.

20 The remaining installation steps are the reverse of removal.

21 Change the oil and filter (see Chapter 1).

---

10 Valve lifters - removal, inspection and installation

Refer to illustration 10.1

This procedure is essentially the same as that for the 3.1L V6 engine. Refer to Part A and follow the procedure outlined there. Refer to **illustration 10.1** for details of the roller lifter retainer plates on the 3800 engine.

---

11 Crankshaft front oil seal - replacement

Refer to illustrations 11.7a, 11.7b and 11.14
Caution: *The crankshaft balancer is serviced as an assembly. Do not attempt to separate the pulley from the balancer hub.*

1 Disconnect the negative cable from the battery. **Caution:** *On models equipped with the Theftlock audio system, be sure the lockout feature is turned off before performing any procedure which requires disconnecting the battery.*

hoses from the belt tensioner and remove the belt tensioner **(see illustration)**.

6 Detach the exhaust manifold(s) from the cylinder head(s) being removed (see Section 8).

7 Remove the valve cover(s) (see Section 4).

8 Remove the rocker arms and pushrods (see Section 5). **Caution:** *Keep the rocker arm components for each cylinder identified and together. They must go back in their original locations.*

9 Loosen the head bolts in 1/4-turn increments until they can be removed by hand. Work from the ends of the cylinder head to the center.

10 Lift the cylinder head off the engine. If resistance is felt, don't pry between the cylinder head and block as damage to the mating surfaces will result. Recheck for cylinder head bolts that may have been overlooked, then use a hammer and block of wood to tap the cylinder head and break the gasket seal. Be careful because there are locating dowels in the block which position each cylinder head. As a last resort, pry each cylinder head up at the rear corner only and be careful not to damage anything **(see illustration)**. After removal, place the cylinder head on blocks of wood to prevent damage to the gasket surfaces.

11 Refer to Chapter 2, Part D, for cylinder head disassembly, inspection and valve service procedures.

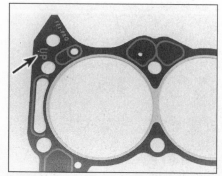

9.16 Look for gasket marks (arrow) to ensure correct installation

9.19 Cylinder head bolt TIGHTENING sequence

10.1 The roller lifters on the 3800 engine are retained by guides bolted to the sides of the lifter valley - remove the four bolts to take off the guides and remove the lifters

11.7a Wedge a large screwdriver in the teeth of the ring gear (flywheel) to keep it from turning while an assistant removes the balancer bolt

11.7b Remove the bolt in the center of the hub (arrow)

11.14 Be sure to align the keyway (arrow) with the key in the crankshaft

2   Loosen the lug nuts on the right front wheel.

3   Raise the vehicle and support it securely on jackstands.

4   Remove the right front wheel.

5   Remove the right front fender inner splash shield.

6   Remove the serpentine drivebelt (see Chapter 1).

7   Remove the lower bellhousing cover plate and hold the crankshaft with a special tool designed for this purpose (available at auto parts stores). If this tool is unavailable, position a large screwdriver in the ring gear teeth to keep the crankshaft from turning while an assistant removes the crankshaft balancer bolt **(see illustrations)**. The bolt is normally quite tight, so use a large breaker bar and a six-point socket.

8   The crankshaft balancer should pull off the crankshaft by hand. Leave the Woodruff key in place in the end of the crankshaft.

9   If there's a groove worn into the seal contact surface on the crankshaft balancer, sleeves are available that fit over the groove, restoring the contact surface to like-new condition. These sleeves are sometimes included with the seal kit. Check with your parts supplier for details.

10   Pry the old oil seal out with a seal removal tool or a screwdriver **(see Chapter 2 Part A)**. Be very careful not to nick or otherwise damage the crankshaft in the process.

11   Apply a thin coat of RTV sealant to the outer edge of the new seal. Lubricate the seal lip with moly-base grease or clean engine oil.

12   Place the seal squarely in position in the bore and press it into place with a special seal installer (available at auto parts stores). Make sure the seal enters the bore squarely and seats completely.

13   If the special tool is unavailable, carefully drive the seal into place with a hammer and large socket or section of pipe **(see Part A of this Chapter)**. The outer diameter of the socket or pipe should be the same size as the seal outer diameter.

14   Installation is the reverse of removal. Align the keyway with the key **(see illustration)** and avoid bending the metal tabs. Be sure to apply moly-base grease to the seal contact surface on the back side of the crankshaft balancer (if it isn't lubricated, the seal lip could be damaged and oil leakage would result).

15   Apply sealant to the threads and tighten the crankshaft bolt in two steps to the torque listed in this Chapter's Specifications.

16   Reinstall the remaining parts in the reverse order of removal.

17   Start the engine and check for oil leaks at the seal.

12   Timing chain cover, chain and sprockets - removal and installation

Removal

Refer to illustrations 12.11, 12.13, 12.14, 12.16, 12.17 and 12.19

1   Disconnect the negative battery cable from the battery. **Caution:** *On models equipped with the Theftlock audio system, be sure the lockout feature is turned off before performing any procedure which requires disconnecting the battery.*

2   Set the parking brake and put the transmission in Park. Raise the front of the vehicle and support it securely on jackstands. Remove the splash shield from the right inner fender.

3   Drain the oil and coolant (see Chapter 1).

4   Remove the coolant hoses from the timing chain cover and water pump, and loosen the water pump pulley (see Chapter 3).

5   Remove the serpentine drivebelt (see Chapter 1) and the drivebelt tensioner assembly **(see Section 9)**. Remove the water pump pulley.

6   Remove the crankshaft balancer (see Section 11).

7   Remove the large (8 mm) water pump-to-block bolts, leaving the smaller (6 mm) diameter bolts in place.

8   Unplug the connectors from the oil pressure, camshaft and crankshaft sensors (see Chapter 6). Remove the shield over the front of the crankshaft sensor.

9   Remove the oil pan bolts which attach to the front cover, then loosen the rest of the oil pan bolts (see Section 14).

10   Remove the engine oil cooler pipes from the oil filter adapter housing.

11   Remove the timing chain cover-to-engine block bolts **(see illustration)**. Note that two of the bolts also secure the crankshaft sensor. Lift the sensor off when removing these bolts.

12   Separate the cover from the front of the

12.11 Timing chain cover bolt locations (arrows)

2C

12.13 Remove all traces of old gasket material

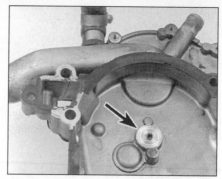

12.14 The camshaft thrust surface on this cover is worn away (arrow) which means that a new cover must be installed

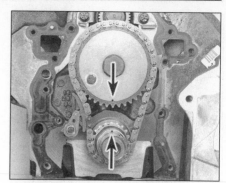

12.16 The marks on the crankshaft and camshaft sprockets (arrows) must be aligned adjacent to each other as shown

12.17 Remove the timing chain damper

engine, removing it with the water pump and oil filter adapter still attached.

13   Use a gasket scraper to remove all traces of old gasket material and sealant from the cover and engine block **(see illustration)**. The cover is made of aluminum, so be careful not to nick or gouge it. Clean the gasket sealing surfaces with lacquer thinner or acetone.

14   Check the camshaft thrust surface in the cover for excessive wear **(see illustration)**. If it's worn, a new cover will be required.

15   The timing chain should be replaced with a new one if the total free play midway between the sprockets exceeds one inch. Failure to replace the timing chain may result in erratic engine performance, loss of power and lowered fuel mileage.

16   Temporarily install the crankshaft balancer bolt and turn the crankshaft clockwise to align the timing marks on the crankshaft and camshaft sprockets directly opposite each other **(see illustration)**.

17   Detach the spring, then remove the bolt and separate the timing chain damper from the block **(see illustration)**.

18   Remove the camshaft sprocket bolt. Try not to turn the camshaft in the process (if you do, realign the timing marks after the bolts are loosened).

19   Alternately pull the camshaft sprocket and then the crankshaft sprocket forward and remove the sprockets and timing chain as an assembly **(see illustration)**.

20   Remove the camshaft gear.

21   Clean the timing chain components with solvent and dry them with compressed air (if available). **Warning:** *Wear eye protection.*

22   Inspect the components for wear and damage. Look for teeth that are deformed, chipped, pitted, polished or discolored.

Installation

Refer to illustration 12.24

23   If the crankshaft has been disturbed, install the crankshaft sprocket temporarily and turn the crankshaft until the mark on the sprocket is exactly at the top. If the camshaft was disturbed, install the camshaft sprocket temporarily and turn the camshaft until the timing mark is at the bottom, opposite the mark on the crankshaft sprocket **(see illustration 12.16)**.

24   Assemble the timing chain on the sprockets, then slide the sprocket and chain assembly onto the shafts with the timing marks aligned as shown in illustration 12.16. **Note:** *If it was removed for any reason, be sure to install the balance shaft drive gear, which is behind the camshaft sprocket. It drives the gear on the balance shaft and the two gears must be aligned before installing the timing chain with camshaft sprocket* **(see illustration)**.

25   Install the camshaft sprocket bolt and tighten to the torque listed in this Chapter's specifications.

26   Attach the timing chain damper assembly to the block and install the spring.

27   Lubricate the chain and sprocket with clean engine oil.

12.19 Remove the camshaft sprocket, timing chain and crankshaft sprocket as an assembly

28   Before the cover is installed, the oil pump cover must be removed and the cavity packed with petroleum jelly as described in Section 13.

29   Apply a thin layer of RTV sealant to both sides of the new gasket, then position the gasket on the engine block (the dowel pins should keep it in place). Attach the cover to the engine, making sure that the oil pump drive engages with the crankshaft.

30   Apply Teflon thread sealant to the bolt threads, then install them finger tight. Follow a criss-cross pattern when tightening the bolts and work up to the torque listed in this Chapter's specifications in three steps to avoid warping the cover.

31   The remainder of installation is the reverse of removal.

32   Add oil and coolant, start the engine and check for leaks.

13 Oil pump - removal, inspection and installation

Removal

Refer to illustrations 13.4 and 13.5

1   Remove the oil filter (see Chapter 1).

2   Remove the timing chain cover (see Section 12).

3   Remove the four bolts holding the oil

12.24 The balance shaft drive gear (A) must align with the balance shaft driven gear (B) before installing the timing chain and sprockets - note the dots on both gears are aligned

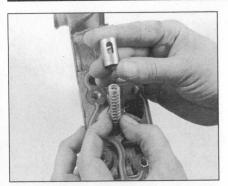

13.4 Remove the pressure regulator valve and spring, then check the valve for wear and damage

13.5 The oil pump cover is attached to the inside of the timing chain cover - a T-30 Torx driver is required for removal of the screws

13.10 Measuring the outer gear-to-housing clearance with a feeler gauge

filter adapter to the timing chain cover. The cover is spring loaded, so remove the bolts while keeping pressure on the cover, then release the spring pressure carefully.

4   Remove the pressure regulator valve and spring **(see illustration)**. Use a gasket scraper to remove all traces of the old gasket.

5   Remove the oil pump cover-to-timing chain cover bolts **(see illustration)**.

6   Lift out the cover and oil pump gears as an assembly.

Inspection

Refer to illustrations 13.10 and 13.11

7   Clean the parts with solvent and dry them with compressed air (if available). **Warning:** *Wear eye protection!*

8   Inspect all components for wear and score marks. Replace any worn out or damaged parts.

9   Reinstall the gears in the timing chain cover.

10   Measure the outer gear-to-housing clearance with a feeler gauge **(see illustration)**.

11   Measure the inner gear-to-outer gear clearance at several points **(see illustration)**.

12   Use a depth micrometer or a straightedge and feeler gauge to measure the gear end clearance (distance from the gear to the gasket surface of the cover).

13   Check for pump cover warpage by laying a precision straightedge across the cover and trying to slip a feeler gauge between the cover and straightedge.

14   Compare the measurements to this Chapter's Specifications. Replace all worn or damaged components with new ones.

Installation

15   Remove the gears and pack the pump cavity with petroleum jelly.

16   Install the gears - make sure petroleum jelly is forced into every cavity. Failure to do so could cause the pump to lose its prime when the engine is started, causing damage from lack of oil pressure.

17   Install the pump cover, using a new gasket - make sure you have the correct

gasket, its thickness is critical for maintaining the correct clearance.

18   Install the pressure regulator spring and valve and the oil filter adapter (with a new gasket).

19   Install the timing chain cover. Be sure to use a new gasket.

20   Install the oil filter and check the oil level. Start and run the engine and check for correct oil pressure, then look carefully for oil leaks at the timing chain cover.

21   Run the engine and check for oil leaks.

14   Oil pan - removal and installation

Removal

Refer to illustration 14.10

1   Disconnect the cable from the negative battery terminal. **Caution:** *On models equipped with the Theftlock audio system, be sure the lockout feature is turned off before performing any procedure which requires disconnecting the battery.*

2   Raise the vehicle and place it securely on jackstands. Drain the engine oil and replace the oil filter (refer to Chapter 1 if necessary).

3   Remove the driveplate inspection cover and starter, if necessary for access (refer to Chapter 5). Disconnect the electrical connector from the oil lever sensor, then remove the oil level sensor from the pan.

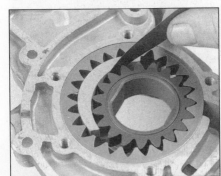

13.11 Measuring the inner gear tip-to-outer gear tip clearance with a feeler gauge

4   Disconnect the engine torque strut (see Section 17).

5   Disconnect the exhaust pipe and catalytic converter from the engine.

6   Disconnect the pipes leading from the engine oil cooler (see Chapter 3).

7   Refer to Section 17 and remove the frame-side nuts from the engine mount at the timing-chain-end of the engine.

8   Use a transmission jack or a floorjack with a block of wood to raise the engine/transaxle by raising under the transaxle, not the engine, to allow removal of the engine mount (see Section 17).

9   On 1999 models, remove the air conditioner compressor mounting bolt and move the compressor out of the way (see Chapter 3). Disconnect the power steering oil cooler pipe brackets from the frame.

10   Remove the oil pan mounting bolts **(see illustration)** and carefully lower the oil pan from the block. Don't pry between the block and the pan or damage to the sealing surfaces may result and oil leaks may develop. Instead, tap the pan with a soft-face hammer to break the gasket seal.

11   When the pan has been lowered enough, unbolt the oil pump pickup tube and screen assembly and let it drop down and come out with the pan.

Installation

12   Clean the screen and housing assembly with solvent and dry it with compressed air, if

14.10 The oil pan bolts (arrows indicate most in this view from below) are located around the perimeter of the oil pan

2C

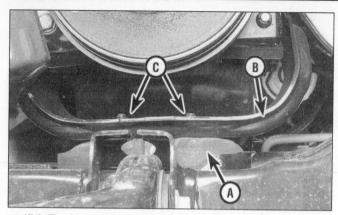

17.8 The front engine mount (A) is located between the front subframe and the engine front mount cradle (B) - remove the two nuts (C) at the cradle and two nuts below the subframe to remove the mount

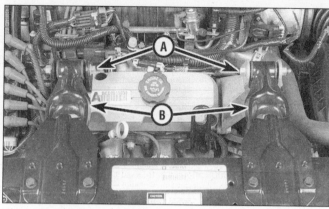

17.10 Remove the throughbolts (A) and the engine torque struts (B) for replacement

available. **Warning:** *Wear eye protection.*

13   If the oil screen is damaged or has metal chips in it, replace it. An abundance of metal chips indicates a major engine problem which must be corrected.

14   Make sure the mating surfaces of the pipe flange and the engine block are clean and free of nicks.

15   Clean the pan with solvent and remove all old sealant and gasket material from the block and pan mating surfaces. Clean the mating surfaces with lacquer thinner or acetone and make sure the bolt holes in the block are clear. Check the oil pan flange for distortion, particularly around the bolt holes. If necessary, place the pan on a block of wood and use a hammer to flatten and restore the gasket surface.

16   Always use a new gasket whenever the oil pan is installed. The one-piece gasket is not reusable. When installing the new gasket, apply a small amount of RTV sealant to the two tabs that fit next to the rear main cap (where the cap meets the block).

17   Place the oil pan in position under the block with the pump pickup tube and screen in the pan. When the pan is close enough, reach in and bolt the pickup tube (with a new gasket) to the block and put the pan up the rest of the way. Start all of the oil pan bolts finger-tight.

18   After the bolts are installed, tighten them to the torque listed in this Chapter's specifications. Starting at the center, follow a crisscross pattern and work up to the final torque in three steps.

19   The remaining steps are the reverse of the removal procedure.

20   Refill the engine with oil. Run the engine until normal operating temperature is reached and check for leaks.

15   Driveplate - removal and installation

This procedure is essentially the same as for the 3.1L engine. Refer to Section 15 in

Part A of this Chapter. Refer to this Chapter's Specifications for driveplate bolt torque for the 3.8L engine.

16   Rear main oil seal - replacement

This procedure is essentially the same as for the 3.1L V6 engine. Refer to Part A and follow the procedure outlined there. However, use the bolt torque listed in this Chapter's Specifications.

17   Engine mounts - check and replacement

Refer to illustrations 17.8 and 17.10
Note: *See Chapter 7 for transaxle mount information.*
Warning: *A special engine support fixture should be used to support the engine during repair operations. Similar fixtures are available from rental yards. Improper lifting methods or devices are hazardous and could result in severe injury or death. DO NOT place any part of your body under the engine/transaxle when it's supported only by a jack. Failure of the lifting device could result in serious injury or death.*

1   Engine mounts seldom require attention, but broken or deteriorated mounts should be replaced immediately or the added strain placed on the driveline components may cause damage or wear. The 3800 engine has a transaxle mount (see Chapter 7), two engine torque struts and a mount at the front (timing belt end) of the engine that attaches to a "cradle" type bracket under the front of the oil pan.

Check

2   During the check, the engine must be raised slightly to remove the weight from the mounts.

3   Raise the vehicle and support it securely on jackstands, then position a jack under the engine oil pan. Place a large block of wood

between the jack head and the oil pan, then carefully raise the engine just enough to take the weight off the mounts. **Warning:** *DO NOT place any part of your body under the engine when it's supported only by a jack!*

4   Check the mounts to see if the rubber is cracked, hardened or separated from the metal plates. Sometimes the rubber will split right down the center.

5   Check for relative movement between the mount plates and the engine or frame (use a large screwdriver or prybar to attempt to move the mounts). If movement is noted, lower the engine and tighten the mount fasteners.

6   Rubber preservative may be applied to the mounts to slow deterioration.

Replacement

7   Disconnect the negative battery cable from the battery, then raise the vehicle and support it securely on jackstands (if not already done). **Caution:** *On models equipped with the Theftlock audio system, be sure the lockout feature is turned off before performing any procedure which requires disconnecting the battery.*

8   Remove the right front wheel and loosen the inner fender splash panel.

8   Raise the engine slightly with a jack or hoist. Install an engine support as described in the **Warning** above. Remove the fasteners and detach the mount from the frame bracket **(see illustration)**.

9   Remove the mount-to-block bracket bolts/nuts and detach the mount.

10   The engine torque struts mount between the engine and the upper radiator support on the body **(see illustration)**. They can be replaced without jacking up the engine, by removing the throughbolts and the bolts attaching the struts to the mounts on the radiator support. **Note:** *When reinstalling the mounts, you may have to use a prybar to rotate the engine toward or away from the radiator to align the throughbolts.*

11   Installation is the reverse of removal. Use thread locking compound on the threads and be sure to tighten everything securely.

Chapter 2 Part D
General engine overhaul procedures

Contents

Specifications

General

VIN code
  3.1L .... M
  3.4L X
  3800 L
Displacement
  3.1L .... 192 cubic inches (3.1 liters)
  3.4L .... 204 cubic inches (3.4 liters)
  3800 .... 231 cubic inches (3.8 liters)
Cylinder compression pressure .... 100 psi minimum
Maximum variation between cylinders 30-percent
Firing order
  3.1L and 3.4L 1-2-3-4-5-6
  3800 1-6-5-4-3-2
Oil pressure .... 15 psi at 1100 rpm

Cylinder head

Warpage limit
  3.4L .... 0.004 inch (0.1 mm)*
  Others .... 0.005 inch (0.127 mm)*
*If more than 0.010 inch (0.25 mm) must be removed, replace the head

Engine block

Cylinder bore
  Diameter
    3.1L .... 3.5046 to 3.5053 inches (89.016 to 89.034 mm)
    3.4L .... 3.6228 to 3.6235 inches (92.020 to 92.038 mm)
    3800 .... 3.8 inches (96.5 mm)
  Out-of-round limit
    3.1L .... 0.0005 inch (0.014 mm)
    3.4L .... 0.0004 inch (0.010 mm)
    3800 .... 0.001 inch (0.0254 mm)
  Taper limit (thrust side)
    3.1L .... 0.0008 inch (0.020 mm)
    3.4L .... 0.00051 inch (0.013 mm)
    3800 .... 0.001 inch (0.0254 mm)
  Block deck warpage limit .... If more than 0.010 inch (0.25 mm) must be removed, replace the block

Valves and related components

Valve margin width, minimum
  3.1L
      Intake .... 0.083 inch (2.10 mm)
      Exhaust .... 0.106 inch (2.70 mm)
  3.4L .... 0.029 inch (0.75 mm)
  3800 .... 0.025 inch (0.635 mm)
Valve stem-to-guide clearance
  3.1L .... 0.0010 to 0.0027 inch (0.026 to 0.068 mm)
  3.4L
      Intake .... 0.0011 to 0.0026 inch (0.028 to 0.066 mm)
      Exhaust .... 0.0018 to 0.0033 inch (0.046 to 0.084 mm)
  3800 .... 0.0015 to 0.0032 inch (0.038 to 0.081 mm)
Valve spring free length (intake and exhaust)
  3.1L .... 1.89 inches (48.5 mm)
  3.4L .... 1.6551 inches (42.04 mm)
  3800
      1995 and 1996 .... 1.981 inches (50.32 mm)
      1998 .... 1.960 inches (49.78 mm)
Installed height
  3.1L .... 1.710 inches (43 mm)
  3.4L .... 1.400 inches (35.56 mm)
  3800 .... 1.690 to 1.720 inches (42.93 to 44.45 mm)

Crankshaft and connecting rods

Connecting rod journal
  Diameter
      3.4L and 3100 .... 1.9987 to 1.9994 inches (50.768 to 50.784 mm)
      3800 .... 2.2487 to 2.2499 inches (57.117 to 57.147 mm)
  Bearing oil clearance
      3.1L .... 0.0007 to 0.0024 inch (0.018 to 0.062 mm)
      3.4L .... 0.0011 to 0.0032 inch (0.028 to 0.082 mm)
      3800 .... 0.0005 to 0.0026 inch (0.0127 to 0.0660 mm)
Connecting rod side clearance (endplay)
  3.1L and 3.4L .... 0.007 to 0.017 inch (0.18 to 0.44 mm)
  3800 .... 0.004 to 0.020 inch (0.102 to 0.508 mm)
Main bearing journal
  Diameter
      3.1L .... 2.6473 to 2.6483 inches (67.239 to 67.257 mm)
      3.4L .... 2.6472 to 2.6479 inches (67.239 to 67.257 mm)
      3800 .... 2.4988 to 2.4998 inches (63.470 to 63.495 mm)
  Bearing oil clearance
      3.1L and 3.4L .... 0.0008 to 0.0025 inch (0.019 to 0.064 mm)
      3800 .... 0.0008 to 0.0022 inch (0.020 to 0.055 mm)
  Taper/out-of-round limit
      3.1L and 3.4L .... 0.0002 inch (0.005 mm)
      3800 .... 0.0003 inch (0.008 mm)
Crankshaft endplay (at thrust bearing)
  3.1L and 3.4L .... 0.002 to 0.008 inch (0.06 to 0.21 mm)
  3800 .... 0.003 to 0.011 inch (0.076 to 0.279 mm)

Camshaft

Bearing journal diameter
  3.1L .... 1.868 to 1.869 inches (47.45 to 47.48 mm)
  3.4L .... 2.1643 to 2.1654 inches (54.973 to 55.001 mm)
  3800 .... 1.8462 to 1.8448 inches (47.655 to 46.858 mm)
Bearing oil clearance
  3.1L .... 0.001 to 0.0039 inch (0.026 to 0.101 mm)
  3.4L .... 0.0019 to 0.0040 inch (0.049 to 0.102 mm)
  3800 .... 0.0016 to 0.0047 inch (0.041 to 0.119 mm)
Lobe lift
  3.1L .... 0.2727 inch (6.9263 mm)
  3.4L
      Intake .... 0.370 inch (9.398 mm)
      Exhaust .... 0.370 inch (9.398 mm)
  3800
      Intake .... 0.258 inch (6.55 mm)
      Exhaust .... 0.255 inch (6.48 mm)

Pistons and rings

Piston-to-bore clearance
  3.1L .... 0.0013 to 0.0027 inch (0.032 to 0.068 mm)
  3.4L .... 0.0008 to 0.0020 inch (0.020 to 0.052 mm)
  3800 .... 0.0004 to 0.0020 inch (0.010 to 0.051 mm)
Piston ring end gap
  Top compression ring
    3.1L .... 0.006 to 0.014 inch (0.15 to 0.36 mm)
    3.4L .... 0.008 to 0.018 inch (0.20 to 0.45 mm)
    3800
      1995 through 1998 .... 0.012 to 0.022 inch (0.305 to 0.559 mm)
      1999 .... 0.010 to 0.018 inch (0.25 to 0.46 mm)
  Second compression ring
    3.1L .... 0.0197 to 0.0280 inch (0.5 to 0.71 mm)
    3.4L .... 0.022 to 0.032 inch (0.56 to 0.81 mm)
    3800
      1995 through 1998 .... 0.030 to 0.040 inch (0.762 to 1.016 mm)
      1999 .... 0.023 to 0.033 inch (0.58 to 0.84 mm)
  Oil control ring
    3.1L and 3.4L .... 0.0098 to 0.0299 inch (0.25 to 0.76 mm)
    3800 .... 0.010 to 0.030 inch (0.254 to 0.762 mm)
Piston ring side clearance
  Compression ring
    3.1L .... 0.002 to 0.003 inch (0.05 to 0.085 mm)
    3.4L and 3800 .... 0.0013 to 0.0031 inch (0.033 to 0.079 mm)
  Oil control ring
    3.1L .... 0.008 to 0.0019 inch (0.20 to 0.048 mm)
    3.4L and 3800 .... 0.0011 to 0.0081 inch (0.028 to 0.206 mm)

Balance shaft (3800 only)

Endplay .... 0.0 to 0.0067 inch (0.0 to 0.171 mm)
Drive gear backlash .... 0.002 to 0.005 inch (0.050 to 0.127 mm)
Rear journal diameter .... 1.4994 to 1.5002 inch (38.085 to 38.105 mm)
Rear bearing oil clearance .... 0.0005 to 0.0043 inch (0.0127 to 0.109 mm)

Torque specifications***   **Ft-lbs** (unless otherwise indicated)

Main bearing caps, bolts/studs
  3.1L
    Step 1 37
    Step 2 .... Tighten an additional 77 degrees
  3.4L
    Step 1 37
    Step 2 .... Tighten an additional 75 degrees
  3800
    Step 1 30
    Step 2 .... Tighten an additional 110 degrees
    Side bolts
      Step 1 11
      Step 2 .... Tighten an additional 45 degrees
Connecting rod caps
  3.1L and 3.4L
    Step 1 15
    Step 2 .... Tighten an additional 75 degrees
  3800
    Step 1 20
    Step 2 .... Tighten an additional 50 degrees
Camshaft/intermediate shaft retainer bolts .... 89 in-lbs
Balance shaft retainer bolts 12
Balance shaft driven gear bolt
  Step 1 16
  Step 2 .... Tighten an additional 70 degrees

***Note: *Refer to Parts A, B or C for additional torque specifications.*

1 General information - engine overhaul

Included in this portion of Chapter 2 are the general overhaul procedures for the cylinder head and internal engine components.

The information ranges from advice concerning preparation for an overhaul and the purchase of replacement parts to detailed, step-by-step procedures covering removal and installation of internal engine components and the inspection of parts.

The following Sections have been written based on the assumption that the engine has been removed from the vehicle. For information concerning in-vehicle engine repair, as well as removal and installation of the external components necessary for the overhaul, see Chapter 2A (3.1L), 2B (3.4L), or 2C (3800) and Section 8 of this Chapter.

The Specifications included in this Part are only those necessary for the inspection

2D

and overhaul procedures which follow. Refer to Chapter 2, Part A, Part B or Part C for additional Specifications.

It's not always easy to determine when, or if, an engine should be completely overhauled, as a number of factors must be considered.

High mileage is not necessarily an indication that an overhaul is needed, while low mileage doesn't preclude the need for an overhaul. Frequency of servicing is probably the most important consideration. An engine that's had regular and frequent oil and filter changes, as well as other required maintenance, will most likely give many thousands of miles of reliable service. Conversely, a neglected engine may require an overhaul very early in its life.

Excessive oil consumption is an indication that piston rings, valve seals and/or valve guides are in need of attention. Make sure that oil leaks aren't responsible before deciding that the rings and/or guides are bad. Perform a cylinder compression check to determine the extent of the work required (see Section 3). Also check the vacuum readings under various conditions (see Section 4).

Loss of power, rough running, knocking or metallic engine noises, excessive valve train noise and high fuel consumption rates may also point to the need for an overhaul, especially if they're all present at the same time. If a complete tune-up doesn't remedy the situation, major mechanical work is the only solution.

An engine overhaul involves restoring the internal parts to the specifications of a new engine. During an overhaul, the piston rings are replaced and the cylinder walls are reconditioned (re-bored and/or honed). If a re-bore is done by an automotive machine shop, new oversize pistons will also be installed. The main bearings, connecting rod bearings and camshaft bearings are generally replaced with new ones and, if necessary, the crankshaft may be reground to restore the journals. Generally, the valves are serviced as well, since they're usually in less-than-perfect condition at this point. While the engine is being overhauled, other components, such as the distributor, starter and alternator, can be rebuilt as well. The end result should be a like new engine that will give many trouble free miles. **Note:** *Critical cooling system components such as the hoses, drivebelts, thermostat and water pump should be replaced with new parts when an engine is overhauled. The radiator should be checked carefully to ensure that it isn't clogged or leaking (see Chapter 3). If you purchase a rebuilt engine or short block, some rebuilders will not warranty their engines unless the radiator has been professionally flushed. Also, we don't recommend overhauling the oil pump - always install a new one when an engine is rebuilt.*

Before beginning the engine overhaul, read through the entire procedure to familiarize yourself with the scope and requirements of the job. Overhauling an engine isn't

difficult, but it is time-consuming. Plan on the vehicle being tied up for a minimum of two weeks, especially if parts must be taken to an automotive machine shop for repair or reconditioning. Check on availability of parts and make sure that any necessary special tools and equipment are obtained in advance. Most work can be done with typical hand tools, although a number of precision measuring tools are required for inspecting parts to determine if they must be replaced. Often an automotive machine shop will handle the inspection of parts and offer advice concerning reconditioning and replacement. **Note:** *Always wait until the engine has been completely disassembled and all components, especially the engine block, have been inspected before deciding what service and repair operations must be performed by an automotive machine shop.* Since the block's condition will be the major factor to consider when determining whether to overhaul the original engine or buy a rebuilt one, never purchase parts or have machine work done on other components until the block has been thoroughly inspected. As a general rule, time is the primary cost of an overhaul, so it doesn't pay to install worn or substandard parts.

As a final note, to ensure maximum life and minimum trouble from a rebuilt engine, everything must be assembled with care in a spotlessly-clean environment.

2 Oil Pressure check

Refer to illustration 2.2

1   Low engine oil pressure can be a sign of an engine in need of rebuilding. A "low oil pressure" indicator (often called an "idiot light") is not a test of the oiling system. Such indicators only come on when the oil pressure is dangerously low. Even a factory oil pressure gauge in the instrument panel is only a relative indication, although much better for driver information than a warning light. A better test is with a mechanical (not electrical) oil pressure gauge. When used in conjunction with an accurate tachometer, an engine's oil pressure performance can be compared to the manufacturers Specifications.

2   Find the oil pressure indicator sending unit **(see illustration)**.

3   Remove the oil pressure sending unit and install a fitting which will allow you to directly connect your hand-held, mechanical oil pressure gauge. Use Teflon tape or sealant on the threads of the adapter and the fitting on the end of your gauge's hose.

4   Connect an accurate tachometer to the engine, according to the tachometer manufacturer's instructions.

5   Check the oil pressure with the engine running (full operating temperature) at the specified engine speed, and compare it to this Chapter's Specifications. If it's extremely low, the bearings and/or oil pump are probably worn out.

2.2 The oil pressure sending unit is located near the oil filter

3 Cylinder compression check

Refer to illustration 3.6

1   A compression check will tell you what mechanical condition the upper end (pistons, rings, valves, head gaskets) of the engine is in. Specifically, it can tell you if the compression is down due to leakage caused by worn piston rings, defective valves and seats or a blown head gasket. **Note:** *The engine must be at normal operating temperature and the battery must be fully charged for this check.*

2   Begin by cleaning the area around the spark plugs before you remove them. Compressed air should be used, if available, otherwise a small brush or even a bicycle tire pump will work. The idea is to prevent dirt from getting into the cylinders as the compression check is being done.

3   Remove all of the spark plugs from the engine (see Chapter 1).

4   Block the throttle wide open.

5   Disable the fuel and ignition systems by removing the PCM IGN fuse from the instrument panel fuse block and the IGNITION fuse from the underhood fuse block (1995 models), or the PCM BATT fuse from the instrument panel fuse block and the IGNITION fuse from the underhood fuse block (1996 and later models).

6   Install the compression gauge in the number one spark plug hole **(see illustration)**.

7   Crank the engine over at least seven compression strokes and watch the gauge. The compression should build up quickly in a healthy engine. Low compression on the first stroke, followed by gradually increasing pressure on successive strokes, indicates worn piston rings. A low compression reading on the first stroke, which doesn't build up during successive strokes, indicates leaking valves or a blown head gasket (a cracked head could also be the cause). Deposits on the undersides of the valve heads can also cause low compression. Record the highest gauge reading obtained.

8   Repeat the procedure for the remaining cylinders, turning the engine over for the same length of time for each cylinder, and compare the results to this Chapter's Specifications.

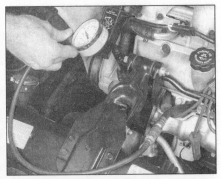

3.6 A compression gauge with a threaded fitting for the spark plug hole is preferred over the type that requires hand pressure to maintain the seal - be sure to open the throttle valve as far as possible during the compression check

9   If the readings are below normal, add some engine oil (about three squirts from a plunger-type oil can) to each cylinder, through the spark plug hole, and repeat the test.

10   If the compression increases after the oil is added, the piston rings are definitely worn. If the compression doesn't increase significantly, the leakage is occurring at the valves or head gasket. Leakage past the valves may be caused by burned valve seats and/or faces or warped, cracked or bent valves.

11   If two adjacent cylinders have equally low compression, there's a strong possibility the head gasket between them is blown. The appearance of coolant in the combustion chambers or the crankcase would verify this condition.

12   If one cylinder is about 20-percent lower than the others, and the engine has a slightly rough idle, a worn exhaust lobe on the camshaft could be the cause.

13   If the compression is unusually high, the combustion chambers are probably coated with carbon deposits. If that's the case, the cylinder heads should be removed and decarbonized.

14   If compression is way down or varies greatly between cylinders, it would be a good idea to have a leak-down test performed by an automotive repair shop. This test will pinpoint exactly where the leakage is occurring and how severe it is.

15   Install the fuses and drive the vehicle to restore the "block learn" memory.

4   Vacuum gauge diagnostic checks

A vacuum gauge provides valuable information about what is going on in the engine at a low cost. You can check for worn rings or cylinder walls, leaking head or intake manifold gaskets, incorrect carburetor adjustments, restricted exhaust, stuck or burned valves, weak valve springs, improper ignition or valve timing and ignition problems.

Unfortunately, vacuum gauge readings are easy to misinterpret, so they should be used in conjunction with other tests to confirm the diagnosis.

Both the gauge readings and the rate of needle movement are important for accurate interpretation. Most gauges measure vacuum in inches of mercury (in-Hg). As vacuum increases (or atmospheric pressure decreases), the reading will increase. Also, for every 1,000-foot increase in elevation above sea level, the gauge readings will decrease about one inch of mercury.

Connect the vacuum gauge directly to intake manifold vacuum, not to ported (carburetor) vacuum. Be sure no hoses are left disconnected during the test or false readings will result.

Before you begin the test, allow the engine to warm up completely. Block the wheels and set the parking brake. With the transmission in Park, start the engine and allow it to run at normal idle speed.

Read the vacuum gauge; an average, healthy engine should normally produce about 17 to 22 inches of vacuum with a fairly steady needle. Refer to the following vacuum gauge readings and what they indicate about the engine's condition:

1   A low, steady reading usually indicates a leaking gasket between the intake manifold and carburetor or throttle body, a leaky vacuum hose, late ignition timing or incorrect camshaft timing. Eliminate all other possible causes, utilizing the tests provided in this Chapter before you remove the timing chain cover to check the timing marks.

2   If the reading is three to eight inches below normal and it fluctuates at that low reading, suspect an intake manifold gasket leak at an intake port.

3   If the needle has regular drops of about two to four inches at a steady rate, the valves are probably leaking. Perform a compression or leak-down test to confirm this.

4   An irregular drop or down-flick of the needle can be caused by a sticking valve or an ignition misfire. Perform a compression or leak-down test and read the spark plugs.

5   A rapid vibration of about four inches-Hg vibration at idle combined with exhaust smoke indicates worn valve guides. Perform a leak-down test to confirm this. If the rapid vibration occurs with an increase in engine speed, check for a leaking intake manifold gasket or head gasket, weak valve springs, burned valves or ignition misfire.

6   A slight fluctuation, say one inch up and down, may mean ignition problems. Check all the usual tune-up items and, if necessary, run the engine on an ignition analyzer.

7   If there is a large fluctuation, perform a compression or leak-down test to look for a weak or dead cylinder or a blown head gasket.

8   If the needle moves slowly through a wide range, check for a clogged PCV system, incorrect idle fuel mixture, throttle body or intake manifold gasket leaks.

9   Check for a slow return after revving the engine by quickly snapping the throttle open until the engine reaches about 2,500 rpm and let it shut. Normally the reading should drop to near zero, rise above normal idle reading (about 5 in-Hg over) and then return to the previous idle reading. If the vacuum returns slowly and doesn't peak when the throttle is snapped shut, the rings may be worn. If there is a long delay, look for a restricted exhaust system (often the muffler or catalytic converter). An easy way to check this is to temporarily disconnect the exhaust ahead of the suspected part and re-test.

5   Engine removal - methods and precautions

If you've decided the engine must be removed for overhaul or major repair work, several preliminary steps should be taken. Locating a suitable place to work is extremely important. Adequate work space, along with storage space for the vehicle, will be needed.

Cleaning the engine compartment and engine before beginning the Removal procedure will help keep tools clean and organized. An engine hoist will also be necessary. Safety is of primary importance, considering the potential hazards involved in removing the engine from this vehicle.

If the engine is being removed by a novice, a helper should be available. Advice and aid from someone more experienced would also be helpful. There are many instances when one person cannot simultaneously perform all of the operations required when lifting the engine out of the vehicle.

Plan the operation ahead of time. Arrange for or obtain all of the tools and equipment you'll need prior to beginning the job. Some of the equipment necessary to perform engine removal and installation safely and with relative ease in addition to a hydraulic jack, jack stands and an engine hoist) are a complete sets of wrenches and sockets as described in the front of this manual, wooden blocks and plenty of rags and cleaning solvent for mopping up spilled oil, coolant and gasoline.

Plan for the vehicle to be out of use for quite a while. A machine shop will be required to perform some of the work which the do-it-yourselfer can't accomplish without special equipment. These shops often have a busy schedule, so it would be a good idea to consult them before removing the engine in order to accurately estimate the amount of time required to rebuild or repair components that may need work.

Always be extremely careful when removing and installing the engine. Serious injury can result from careless actions. Plan ahead, take your time and a job of this nature, although major, can be accomplished successfully. **Note:** *Because it may be some time before you reinstall the engine, it is very helpful to make sketches or take photos of various accessory mountings and wiring hookups before removing the engine.*

2D

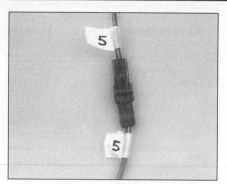

6.4 Label each wire before unplugging the connector

6.8 While the vehicle is raised, disconnect any wiring harnesses attached to the block

6.12 Paint or scribe alignment marks on the driveplate and the torque converter to ensure that the two components are still in balance when they're reassembled

6   Engine - removal and installation

Warning 1: *The models covered by this manual are equipped with airbags. Always disable the airbag system before working in the vicinity of the impact sensors, steering column or instrument panel to avoid the possibility of accidental deployment of the airbag(s), which could cause personal injury (see Chapter 12). The yellow wires and connectors routed through the instrument panel and, on 1995 and earlier models, to the front of the vehicle, are for this system. Do not use electrical test equipment on these yellow wires or tamper with them in any way.*

Warning 2: *Gasoline is extremely flammable, so take extra precautions when you work on any part of the fuel system. Don't smoke or allow open flames or bare light bulbs near the work area, and don't work in a garage where a natural gas-type appliance (such as a water heater or a clothes dryer) with a pilot light is present. Since gasoline is carcinogenic, wear latex gloves when there's a possibility of being exposed to fuel, and, if you spill any fuel on your skin, rinse it off immediately with soap and water. Mop up any spills immediately and do not store fuel-soaked rags where they could ignite. The fuel system is under constant pressure, so, if any fuel lines are to be disconnected, the fuel pressure in the system must be relieved first. When you perform any kind of work on the fuel system, wear safety glasses and have a Class B type fire extinguisher on hand.*

Warning 3: *The air conditioning system is under high pressure - have a dealer service department or service station evacuate the system and recapture the refrigerant before disconnecting any of the hoses or fittings.*

Removal

Refer to illustrations 6.4, 6.8, 6.12 and 6.21

Note 1: *The procedure outlined below illustrates the necessary steps to remove the engine traditionally, i.e. from above with an engine hoist.*

Note 2: *On 1999 models, always replace the accelerator cable whenever the engine is removed from the vehicle. Move the cruise control cable out of the way to avoid any damage. If the cruise control cable is kinked*

during engine removal, replace the cable.

1   Relieve the fuel system pressure (see Chapter 4), then disconnect the negative cable from the battery. **Caution:** *On models equipped with a Delco Theftlock audio system, be sure the lockout feature is turned off before performing any procedure which requires disconnecting the battery.*

2   Cover the fenders and cowl. Special pads are available to protect the fenders, but an old bedspread or blanket will also work. Remove the hood (see Chapter 11).

3   Remove the air intake duct assembly (see Chapter 4).

4   To ensure correct reassembly, label each vacuum line, emission system hose, electrical connector, ground strap and fuel line. Pieces of masking tape with numbers or letters written on them prevent confusion at assembly time **(see illustration)**. Or sketch the engine compartment routing of lines, hoses and wires.

5   Drain the cooling system (see Chapter 1) and label and detach all coolant hoses from the engine. Remove the coolant recovery tank (see Chapter 3).

6   Disconnect the throttle and cruise control cables (see Chapter 4) and TV cable (see Chapter 7).

7   Disconnect the air conditioning hoses from the compressor, hang them out of the way, detach the air conditioning compressor from its mounting bracket and remove it from the engine compartment (see Chapter 3).

8   Raise the vehicle and suitably support it on jackstands. While raised, perform the disassembly procedures that can be done only from underneath, such as disconnecting the exhaust, disconnecting the transmission cooler lines where they are held by a clip to one of the oil pan bolts and disconnecting wiring harnesses attached to the block **(see illustration)**.

9   Refer to the last section ("engine mounts") in Part A, B or C to remove the frame-side nuts from the engine mount (do not disconnect the transaxle mount). Support the transaxle with a suitable jack and block of wood, and remove the brace between the engine and transaxle.

10   Drain the engine oil and remove the filter (see Chapter 1).

11   Remove the starter (see Chapter 5). Remove the driveplate access cover.

12   Make an alignment mark between the driveplate and the torque converter **(see illustration)**, then rotate the crankshaft and remove the converter bolts.

13   Remove the lower bellhousing to-engine bolt.

14   Remove the transmission jack, lower the vehicle and replace the floor jack under the transaxle, then support the engine with an engine hoist from above.

15   Remove the heater hoses, radiator hoses, cooling fans and radiator (see Chapter 3).

16   Unbolt the power steering pump and bracket and tie them out of the way.

17   Remove the intake manifold plenum (see Chapter 4).

18   Raise the engine enough to take the weight off the engine mounts and remove the engine torque struts (see Part A, B or C of this Chapter).

19   Working at the back of the engine, remove the remaining bellhousing bolts.

20   Raise the engine and pull it forward to free it from the torque converter.

21   Tie the wiring harnesses out of the way, raise the engine with the hoist, and with a combination of tilting, twisting and raising, move the engine around any obstructions and pull it out of the vehicle, raising it high enough to clear the front of the body **(see illustration)**.

22   Remove the driveplate or flywheel (see Part A) while the engine is out of the vehicle

6.21 With the accessories tied out of the way and the engine mount through-bolts removed, raise the engine with the hoist

but still on the hoist, and mount the engine on an engine stand.

Installation

23 While the engine is out, check the engine mounts and the transmission mount (see Chapter 7). If they're worn or damaged, replace them.

24 Carefully lower the engine, twisting it to clear any harnesses or obstructions, until the converter snout lines up and the bellhousing-to-engine bolts can be inserted. **Caution:** *DO NOT use the transmission-to-engine bolts to force the transmission and engine together. Take great care when mating the torque converter to the driveplate, following the procedure outlined in Chapter 7. Make sure the alignment marks you made on the driveplate and the torque converter during removal are lined up.*

25 Install the driveplate-to-torque converter bolts and tighten them to the torque listed in Chapter 7 Specifications.

26 Reinstall the remaining components in the reverse order of removal. Double-check to make sure everything is hooked up right, using the sketches or photos taken earlier to go by.

27 Add coolant, oil, power steering and transmission fluid as needed.

28 Run the engine and check for leaks and proper operation of all accessories, then install the hood and test drive the vehicle.

7 Engine rebuilding alternatives

The home mechanic is faced with a number of options when performing an engine overhaul. The decision to replace the engine block, piston/connecting rod assemblies and crankshaft depends on a number of factors, with the number one consideration being the condition of the block. Other considerations are cost, access to machine shop facilities, parts availability, time required to complete the project and the extent of prior mechanical experience.

Some of the rebuilding alternatives include:

Individual parts - If the inspection procedures reveal the engine block and most engine components are in reusable condition, purchasing individual parts may be the most economical alternative. The block, crankshaft and piston/connecting rod assemblies should all be inspected carefully. Even if the block shows little wear, the cylinder bores should be surface-honed.

Short-block - A short-block consists of an engine block with a crankshaft and piston/connecting rod assemblies already installed. All new bearings are incorporated and all clearances will be correct. The existing camshaft, valve train components, cylinder heads and external parts can be bolted to the short block with little or no machine shop work necessary. Some rebuilding companies include a new timing chain, camshaft and lifters with their short-block assemblies.

Long-block - A long-block consists of a short block plus an oil pump, oil pan, cylinder heads, rocker arm covers, camshaft and valve train components, timing sprockets and chain and timing chain cover. All components are installed with new bearings, seals and gaskets incorporated throughout. The installation of manifolds and external parts is all that's necessary. Give careful thought to which alternative is best for you and discuss the situation with local automotive machine shops, auto parts dealers and experienced rebuilders before ordering or purchasing replacement parts.

8 Engine overhaul - disassembly sequence

1 It's much easier to disassemble and work on the engine if it's mounted on a portable engine stand. A stand can often be rented quite cheaply from an equipment rental yard. Before it's mounted on a stand, the flywheel/driveplate should be removed from the engine.

2 If a stand isn't available, it's possible to disassemble the engine with it blocked up on the floor. Be extra careful not to tip or drop the engine when working without a stand.

3 If you're going to obtain a rebuilt engine, all external components must come off first, to be transferred to the replacement engine, just as they will if you're doing a complete engine overhaul yourself. These include:

Alternator and brackets
Emissions control components
Ignition coil/module assembly, spark plug wires and spark plugs
Thermostat and housing cover
Water pump
Engine front cover
Fuel injection components
Intake/exhaust manifolds
Oil filter
Engine mounts
Flywheel/driveplate

Note: *When removing the external components from the engine, pay close attention to details that may be helpful or important during installation. Note the installed position of gaskets, seals, spacers, pins, brackets, washers, bolts and other small items.*

4 If you're obtaining a short-block, then the cylinder heads, oil pan and oil pump will have to be removed as well. See *Engine rebuilding alternatives* for additional information regarding the different possibilities to be considered.

5 If you're planning a complete overhaul, the engine must be disassembled and the internal components removed in the following general order:

Intake and exhaust manifolds
Valve covers
Rocker arms and pushrods
Valve lifters
Cylinder heads
Timing chain cover and oil pump
Timing chain and sprockets
Camshaft
Balance shaft (3800 engine only)

Oil pan
Piston/connecting rod assemblies
Crankshaft and main bearings

6 Before beginning the disassembly and overhaul procedures, make sure the following items are available. Also, refer to *Engine overhaul - reassembly sequence* for a list of tools and materials needed for engine reassembly.

Common hand tools
Small cardboard boxes or plastic bags for storing parts
Gasket scraper
Ridge reamer
Engine balancer puller
Micrometers
Telescoping gauges
Dial indicator set
Valve spring compressor
Cylinder surfacing hone
Piston ring groove-cleaning tool
Electric drill motor
Tap and die set
Wire brushes
Oil gallery brushes
Cleaning solvent

9 Cylinder head - disassembly

Refer to illustrations 9.2, 9.3 and 9.4

Note: *New and rebuilt cylinder heads are commonly available for most engines at dealerships and auto parts stores. Due to the fact that some specialized tools are necessary for the disassembly and inspection procedures, and replacement parts aren't always readily available, it may be more practical and economical for the home mechanic to purchase replacement heads rather than taking the time to disassemble, inspect and recondition the originals.*

1 Cylinder head disassembly involves removal of the intake and exhaust valves and related components. Remove the rocker arm bolts, pivots and rocker arms from the cylinder heads. Label the parts or store them separately so they can be reinstalled in their original locations.

2 Before the valves are removed, arrange to label and store them, along with their

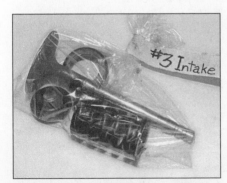

9.2 A small plastic bag, with an appropriate label, can be used to store the valve train components so they can be kept together and reinstalled in the original positions

2D

9.3 Use a valve spring compressor to compress the spring, then remove the keepers from the valve stem

9.4 If the valve won't pull through the guide, deburr the edge of the stem end and the area around the top of the keeper groove with a file or whetstone

related components, so they can be kept separate and reinstalled in their original locations **(see illustration)**.

3   Compress the springs on the first valve with a spring compressor and remove the keepers **(see illustration)**. Carefully release the valve spring compressor and remove the retainer, the spring and the spring seat (if used).

4   Pull the valve out of the head, then remove the oil seal from the guide. If the valve binds in the guide (won't pull through), push it back into the head and deburr the area around the keeper groove with a fine file or whetstone **(see illustration)**.

5   Repeat the procedure for the remaining valves. Remember to keep all the parts for each valve together so they can be reinstalled in the same locations.

6   Once the valves and related components have been removed and stored in an organized manner, the heads should be thoroughly cleaned and inspected. If a complete engine overhaul is being done, finish the engine disassembly procedures before beginning the cylinder head cleaning and inspection process.

10   Cylinder head - cleaning and inspection

1   Thorough cleaning of the cylinder heads and related valve train components, followed by a detailed inspection, will enable you to decide how much valve service work must be done during the engine overhaul. **Note:** *If the engine was severely overheated, the cylinder head is probably warped* (see Step 12).

Cleaning

2   Scrape all traces of old gasket material and sealant off the head gasket, intake manifold and exhaust manifold mating surfaces. Be very careful not to gouge the cylinder head. Special gasket-removal solvents that soften gaskets and make removal much easier are available at auto parts stores.

3   Remove all built-up scale from the coolant passages.

4   Run a stiff wire brush through the various holes to remove deposits that may have formed in them.

5   Run an appropriate-size tap into each of the threaded holes to remove corrosion and thread sealant that may be present. If compressed air is available, use it to clear the holes of debris produced by this operation. **Warning:** *Wear eye protection when using compressed air!*

6   Clean the rocker arm pivot stud or bolt threads with a wire brush.

7   Clean the cylinder head with solvent and dry it thoroughly. Compressed air will speed the drying process and ensure that all holes and recessed areas are clean. **Note:** *Decarbonizing chemicals are available and may prove very useful when cleaning cylinder heads and valve train components. They're very caustic and should be used with caution. Be sure to follow the instructions on the container.*

8   Clean the rocker arms, pivots, bolts and pushrods with solvent and dry them thoroughly (don't mix them up during the cleaning process). Compressed air will speed the drying process and can be used to clean out the oil passages.

9   Clean all the valve springs, keepers and retainers with solvent and dry them

thoroughly. Do the components from one valve at a time to avoid mixing up the parts.

10   Scrape off any heavy deposits that may have formed on the valves, then use a motorized wire brush to remove deposits from the valve heads and stems. Again, make sure the valves don't get mixed up.

Inspection

Note: *Be sure to perform all of the following inspection procedures before concluding machine shop work is required. Make a list of the items that need attention.*

Cylinder head
Refer to illustrations 10.12 and 10.14

11   Inspect the head very carefully for cracks, evidence of coolant leakage and other damage. If cracks are found, check with an automotive machine shop concerning repair. If repair isn't possible, a new cylinder head must be obtained.

12   Using a straightedge and feeler gauge, check the head gasket mating surface for warpage **(see illustration)**. If the warpage exceeds the limit in this Chapter's Specifications, it can be resurfaced at an automotive machine shop. **Note:** *If the heads are resurfaced, the intake manifold flanges will also require machining.*

13   Examine the valve seats in each of the combustion chambers. If they're pitted, cracked or burned, the head will require valve service that's beyond the scope of the home mechanic.

14   Check the valve stem-to-guide clearance by measuring the lateral movement of the valve stem with a dial indicator attached securely to the head **(see illustration)**. The valve must be in the guide and approximately 1/16-inch off the seat. The total valve stem movement indicated by the gauge needle must be divided by two to obtain the actual clearance. After this is done, if there's still some doubt regarding the condition of the valve guides, they should be checked by an automotive machine shop (the cost should be minimal).

10.12 Check the cylinder head gasket surface for warpage by trying to slip a feeler gauge under the straightedge (see this Chapter's Specifications for the maximum warpage allowed and use a feeler gauge of that thickness)

10.14 A dial indicator can be used to determine the valve stem-to-guide clearance (move the valve stem as indicated by the arrows)

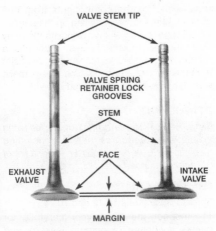

10.15 Check for valve wear at the points shown here

Valves

Refer to illustrations 10.15 and 10.16

15 Carefully inspect each valve face for uneven wear, deformation, cracks, pits and burned areas. Check the valve stem for scuffing and galling and the neck for cracks. Rotate the valve and check for any obvious indication that it's bent. Look for pits and excessive wear on the end of the stem. The presence of any of these conditions **(see illustration)** indicates the need for valve service by an automotive machine shop.

16 Measure the margin width on each valve **(see illustration)**. Any valve with a margin narrower than specified in this Chapter will have to be replaced with a new one.

Valve components

Refer to illustrations 10.17 and 10.18

17 Check each valve spring for wear (on the ends) and pits. Measure the free length and compare it to this Chapter's Specifications **(see illustration)**. Any springs that are shorter than specified have sagged and shouldn't be re-used. The tension of all springs should be checked with a special fixture before deciding they're suitable for use in a rebuilt engine (take the springs to an automotive machine shop for this check).

18 Stand each spring on a flat surface and

check it for squareness **(see illustration)**. If any of the springs are distorted or sagged, replace all of them with new parts.

19 Check the spring retainers and keepers for obvious wear and cracks. Any questionable parts should be replaced with new ones, as extensive damage will occur if they fail during engine operation.

Rocker arm components

20 Check the rocker arm faces (the areas that contact the pushrod ends and valve stems) for pits, wear, galling, score marks and rough spots. Check the rocker arm pivot contact areas and pivots as well. Look for cracks in each rocker arm and bolt.

21 Inspect the pushrod ends for scuffing and excessive wear. Roll each pushrod on a flat surface, like a piece of plate glass, to determine if it's bent.

22 Check the rocker arm bolt holes in the cylinder heads for damaged threads.

23 Any damaged or excessively worn parts must be replaced with new ones.

All components

24 If the inspection process indicates the valve components are in generally poor condition and worn beyond the limits specified, which is usually the case in an engine that's being overhauled, reassemble the valves in the cylinder head (see Section 11 for valve servicing recommendations).

11 Valves - servicing

1 Because of the complex nature of the job and the special tools and equipment needed, servicing of the valves, the valve seats and the valve guides, commonly known as a valve job, should be done by a professional.

2 The home mechanic can remove and disassemble the head, do the initial cleaning and inspection, then reassemble and deliver it to a dealer service department or an automotive machine shop for the actual service work. Doing the inspection will enable you to see what condition the head and valvetrain components are in and will ensure

that you know what work and new parts are required when dealing with an automotive machine shop.

3 The dealer service department, or automotive machine shop, will remove the valves and springs, recondition or replace the valves and valve seats, recondition the valve guides, check and replace the valve springs, spring retainers and keepers (as necessary), replace the valve seals with new ones, reassemble the valve components and make sure the installed spring height is correct. The cylinder head gasket surface will also be resurfaced if it's warped.

4 After the valve job has been performed by a professional, the head will be in like new condition. When the head is returned, be sure to clean it again before installation on the engine to remove any metal particles and abrasive grit that may still be present from the valve service or head resurfacing operations. Use compressed air, if available, to blow out all the oil holes and passages.

12 Cylinder head - reassembly

Refer to illustrations 12.6 and 12.7

1 Regardless of whether or not the head was sent to an automotive repair shop for valve servicing, make sure it's clean before beginning reassembly.

2 If the head was sent out for valve servicing, the valves and related components will already be in place. Begin the reassembly procedure with Step 8.

3 Beginning at one end of the head, lubricate and install the first valve. Apply moly-base grease or clean engine oil to the valve stem.

4 Install the shims, if originally installed, before the valve seals.

5 Install new seals on each of the valve guides. Gently tap each seal into place until it's completely seated on the guide. Many seal sets come with a plastic installer, but use hand pressure. Do not hammer on the seals or they could be driven down too far and subsequently leak. Don't twist or cock the seals during installation or they won't seal properly on the valve stems.

2D

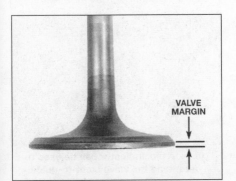

10.16 The margin width on the valve must be as specified (if no margin exists, the valve cannot be re-used)

10.17 Measure the free length of each valve spring with a dial or vernier caliper

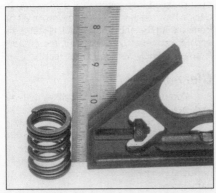

10.18 Check each valve spring for squareness

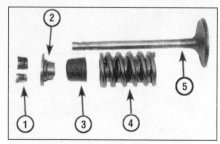

12.6 Typical valve components

1	Keepers	4	Spring
2	Retainer	5	Valve
3	Oil seal		

6   The V6 components may be installed in the following order **(see illustration):**

Shims
Seals (intake only)
Valves, followed by the stem O-rings
Spring dampers
Springs
Oil shedder shields (exhaust only)
Retainers
Keepers

7   Compress the springs with a valve spring compressor and carefully install the keepers in the groove, then slowly release the compressor and make sure the keepers seat properly. Apply a small dab of grease to each keeper to hold it in place if necessary **(see illustration)**. Tap the valve stem tips with a plastic hammer to seat the keepers, if necessary.

8   Repeat the procedure for the remaining valves. Be sure to return the components to their original locations - don't mix them up!

9   Check the installed valve spring height with a ruler graduated in 1/32-inch increments or a dial caliper. If the head was sent out for service work, the installed height should be correct (but don't automatically assume it is). The measurement is taken from the top of each spring seat or top shim to the bottom of the retainer. If the height is greater than specified in this Chapter, shims can be added under the springs to correct it. **Caution:** *Do not, under any circumstances, shim the springs to the point where the installed height is less than specified.*

10   Apply moly-base grease to the rocker arm faces and the pivots, then install the rocker arms and pivots on the cylinder heads. Tighten the bolts/nuts finger-tight.

13.3 Remove the retaining bolts and the camshaft thrust plate

12.7 Apply a small dab of grease to each keeper as shown here before Installation - it'll hold them in place on the valve stem as the spring is released

13 Camshaft (3.1L and 3800), intermediate shaft (3.4L) and balance shaft (3800) - removal and inspection

Removal

Camshaft (3.1L and 3800) and intermediate shaft (3.4L)

Refer to illustrations 13.1 and 13.3

Note: *The intermediate shaft on 3.4L engines is removed and installed much like a conventional camshaft, although it does not operate the lifters or valves.*

1   Remove the bolt and clamp holding the oil pump drive and pull the oil pump drive straight up and out of the block **(see illustration)**.

2   Refer to Chapter 2 Part A or Part B and remove the timing chain and sprockets (lifters should already be removed and stored in a marked container).

3   Remove the bolts holding the camshaft (or intermediate shaft) thrust plate to the block **(see illustration)**.

4   Slide the camshaft or intermediate shaft straight out of the engine, using a long bolt (with the same thread as the camshaft sprocket bolt) screwed into the front of the camshaft as a "handle". Support the shaft near the block and be careful not to scrape or nick the bearings.

Balance shaft (3800 only)

Refer to illustrations 13.8 and 13.9

5   Refer to Chapter 2 Part C and remove

13.8 Remove the retaining bolts and the balance shaft thrust plate

13.1 Remove the bolt (arrow) and pull out the oil pump drive

the timing chain and sprockets (lifters should already be removed and stored in marked plastic bags).

6   Check the gear backlash between the balance shaft drive gear (behind the camshaft sprocket) and the balance shaft driven gear. Set up a dial indicator against the top teeth of the balance shaft driven gear (the one on the front of the balance shaft) and rock the gear by hand. Compare the backlash to this Chapter's Specifications. The gears will have to be replaced if the backlash is greater than specified.

7   Remove the balance shaft drive gear (behind the camshaft sprocket). Set up a dial indicator on the nose of the balance shaft and zero it. Reaching inside the lifter valley, grab the balance shaft and move it forward and back in the block while watching the dial indicator. Compare this endplay measurement with this Chapter's Specifications. If it is incorrect, a new balance shaft thrust plate will have to be installed.

8   Remove the two balance shaft thrust plate bolts and take off the thrust plate **(see illustration)**.

9   The balance shaft's front bearing fits tightly into the front of the block, and a slide hammer must be used to remove the shaft and its bearing **(see illustration)**. Once the bearing is free of the block, withdraw the balance shaft straight out by hand, being careful to not cock it against its rear bearing.

Inspection

Refer to illustrations 13.11a and 13.11b

10   After the camshaft, intermediate shaft or

13.9 A slide hammer must be threaded into the front of the balance shaft to pull the balance shaft front bearing out of the block

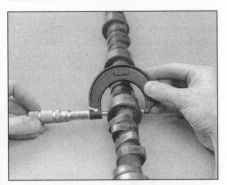

13.11a Measure the camshaft bearing journals with a micrometer

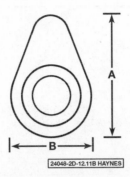

13.11b Measure the camshaft lobe maximum diameter (A) and the minimum (B) - subtract (B) from (A), the difference is the lobe lift

14.1 A ridge reamer is required to remove the ridge from the top of each cylinder - do this before removing the pistons!

balance shaft has been removed, clean it with solvent and dry it, then inspect the bearing journals for uneven wear, pitting and evidence of seizure. If the journals are damaged, the bearing inserts in the block are probably damaged as well. Both the shaft and bearings will have to be replaced.

11   Measure the bearing journals with a micrometer **(see illustration)** to determine whether they are excessively worn or out-of-round. Measure the camshaft lobes also to check for wear. Measure the camshaft lobes at their highest point, then subtract the measurement of the lobe at it's smallest diameter - the difference is the lobe lift **(see illustration)**.

12   Inspect the camshaft lobes for heat discoloration, score marks, chipped areas, pitting and uneven wear. If the lobes are in good condition and if the lobe lift measurements are as specified, you can reuse the camshaft.

13   Check the camshaft bearings in the block for wear and damage. Look for galling, pitting and discolored areas.

14   The inside diameter of each bearing can be determined with a small hole gauge and outside micrometer or an inside micrometer. Subtract the camshaft bearing journal diameter(s) from the corresponding bearing inside diameter(s) to obtain the bearing oil clearance. If it's excessive, new bearings will be required regardless of the condition of the originals.

15   Balance shaft and camshaft bearing replacement requires special tools and expertise that place it outside the scope of the home mechanic. Take the block to an automotive machine shop to ensure the job is done correctly.

14   Pistons and connecting rods - removal

Refer to illustrations 14.1, 14.3, 14.4 and 14.6
Note: *Prior to removing the piston/connecting rod assemblies, remove the cylinder heads, the oil pan and the oil pump by referring to the appropriate Sections in chapter 2 Part A, B or C.*

1   Use your fingernail to feel if a ridge has formed at the upper limit of ring travel (about 1/4-inch down from the top of each cylinder). If carbon deposits or cylinder wear have produced ridges, they must be completely removed with a special tool **(see illustration)**. Follow the manufacturer's instructions provided with the tool. Failure to remove the ridges before attempting to remove the piston/connecting rod assemblies may result in piston breakage.

2   After the cylinder ridges have been removed, turn the engine upside-down so the crankshaft is facing up. On 3.1L and 3.4L

engines, remove the oil baffle plate bolted to the main caps.

3   Before the connecting rods are removed, check the endplay with feeler gauges. Slide them between the first connecting rod and the crankshaft throw until the play is removed **(see illustration)**. The endplay is equal to the thickness of the feeler gauge(s). If the endplay exceeds the service limit, new connecting rods will be required. If new rods (or a new crankshaft) are installed, the endplay may fall under the minimum specified in this Chapter (if it does, the rods will have to be machined to restore it - consult an automotive machine shop for advice if necessary). Repeat the procedure for the remaining connecting rods.

4   Check the connecting rods and caps for identification marks. If they aren't plainly marked, use a small center-punch **(see illustration)** to make the appropriate number of indentations on each rod and cap (1, 2, 3, etc., depending on the cylinder they're associated with).

5   Loosen each of the connecting rod cap nuts 1/2-turn at a time until they can be removed by hand. Remove the number one connecting rod cap and bearing insert. Don't drop the bearing insert out of the cap.

6   Slip a short length of plastic or rubber hose over each connecting rod cap bolt to protect the crankshaft journal and cylinder wall as the piston is removed **(see illustration)**.

2D

14.3 Check the connecting rod side clearance with a feeler gauge as shown

14.4 Mark the rod bearing caps in order from the front of the engine to the rear (one mark for the front cap, two for the second one and so on)

14.6 To prevent damage to the crankshaft journals and cylinder walls, slip sections of rubber or plastic hose over the rod bolts before removing the pistons/rods

7 Remove the bearing insert and push the connecting rod/piston assembly out through the top of the engine. Use a wooden or plastic hammer handle to push on the upper bearing surface in the connecting rod. If resistance is felt, double-check to make sure all of the ridge was removed from the cylinder.

8 Repeat the procedure for the remaining cylinders.

9 After Removal, reassemble the connecting rod caps and bearing inserts in their respective connecting rods and install the cap nuts finger tight. Leaving the old bearing inserts in place until reassembly will help prevent the connecting rod bearing surfaces from being accidentally nicked or gouged.

10 Don't separate the pistons from the connecting rods.

15 Crankshaft - removal

Refer to illustrations 15.3 and 15.4

Note: *The crankshaft can be removed only after the engine has been removed from the vehicle. It's assumed the flywheel/driveplate, timing chain, oil pan, oil pump and piston/connecting rod assemblies have already been removed. The rear main oil seal retainer must also be removed first.*

1 Before the crankshaft is removed, check the endplay. Mount a dial indicator with the stem in line with the crankshaft and touching one of the crank throws.

2 Push the crankshaft all the way to the rear and zero the dial indicator. Next, pry the crankshaft to the front as far as possible and check the reading on the dial indicator. The distance it moves is the endplay. If it's greater than listed in this Chapter's Specifications, check the crankshaft thrust surfaces for wear. If no wear is evident, new main bearings should correct the endplay.

3 If a dial indicator isn't available, feeler gauges can be used. Gently pry or push the crankshaft all the way to the front of the engine. Slip feeler gauges between the crankshaft and the front face of the thrust main bearing to determine the clearance **(see illustration)**. **Note:** *The thrust bearing is located at the number three main bearing cap on 3.1L and 3.4L engines, and on the number two cap on 3800 engines.*

4 Check the main bearing caps to see if they're marked to indicate their locations. They should be numbered consecutively from the front of the engine to the rear. If they aren't, mark them with number stamping dies or a center-punch. Main bearing caps generally have a cast-in arrow, which points to the front of the engine **(see illustration)**. Loosen the main bearing cap bolts 1/4-turn at a time each, until they can be removed by hand. Note if any stud bolts are used and make sure they're returned to their original locations when the crankshaft is reinstalled.

5 Gently tap the caps with a soft-face

15.3 Checking crankshaft endplay with a feeler gauge

hammer, then separate them from the engine block. If necessary, use the bolts as levers to remove the caps. Try not to drop the bearing inserts if they come out with the caps.

6 Carefully lift the crankshaft straight out of the engine. It may be a good idea to have an assistant available, since the crankshaft is quite heavy. With the bearing inserts in place in the engine block and main bearing caps, return the caps to their respective locations on the engine block and tighten the bolts finger tight.

16 Engine block - cleaning

Refer to illustrations 16.4a, 16.4b, 16.8 and 16.10

1 Remove the main bearing caps and separate the bearing inserts from the caps and the engine block. Tag the bearings, indicating which cylinder they were removed from and whether they were in the cap or the block, then set them aside.

2 Using a gasket scraper, remove all traces of gasket material from the engine block. Be very careful not to nick or gouge the gasket sealing surfaces.

3 Remove all of the covers and threaded oil gallery plugs from the block. The plugs are usually very tight - they may have to be drilled out and the holes retapped. Use new plugs when the engine is reassembled.

4 Remove the core plugs from the engine

16.4a A hammer and large punch can be used to knock the core plugs sideways in their bores

15.4 The arrow on the main bearing cap indicates the front of the engine

block. To do this, knock one side of the plugs into the block with a hammer and punch, then grasp them with large pliers and pull them out **(see illustrations)**.

5 If the engine is extremely dirty, it should be taken to an automotive machine shop to be cleaned. **Note:** *If the block is cleaned in a caustic-solution hot tank, this will ruin any camshaft bearings left in the block. If the engine is being rebuilt, these bearings should be replaced anyway.*

6 After the block is returned, clean all oil holes and oil galleries one more time. Brushes specifically designed for this purpose are available at most auto parts stores. Flush the passages with warm water until the water runs clear, dry the block thoroughly and wipe all machined surfaces with a light, rust preventive oil. If you have access to compressed air, use it to speed the drying process and blow out all the oil holes and galleries. **Warning:** *Wear eye protection when using compressed air!*

7 If the block isn't extremely dirty or sludged up, you can do an adequate cleaning job with hot soapy water and a stiff brush. Take plenty of time and do a thorough job. Regardless of the cleaning method used, be sure to clean all oil holes and galleries very thoroughly, dry the block completely and coat all machined surfaces with light oil.

8 The threaded holes in the block must be clean to ensure accurate torque readings during reassembly. Run the proper size tap into each of the holes to remove rust,

16.4b Pull the core plugs from the block with pliers

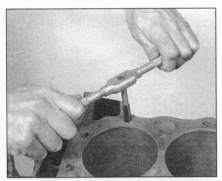

16.8 All bolt holes in the block - particularly the main bearing cap and head bolt holes - should be cleaned and restored with a tap (be sure to remove debris from the holes after this is done)

16.10 A large socket on an extension can be used to drive the new core plugs into the bores

corrosion, thread sealant or sludge and restore damaged threads **(see illustration)**. If possible, use compressed air to clear the holes of debris produced by this operation. Now is a good time to clean the threads on the head bolts and the main bearing cap bolts as well.

9 Reinstall the main bearing caps and tighten the bolts finger tight.

10 After coating the sealing surfaces of the new core plugs with a non-hardening sealant (such as Permatex no. 2), install them in the engine block **(see illustration)**. Make sure they're driven in straight and seated properly or leakage could result. Special tools are available for this purpose, but a large socket, with an outside diameter that will just slip into the core plug, a 1/2-inch drive extension and a hammer will work just as well.

11 Apply non-hardening sealant (such as Permatex no. 2 or Teflon pipe sealant) to the new oil gallery plugs and thread them into the holes in the block. Make sure they're tightened securely.

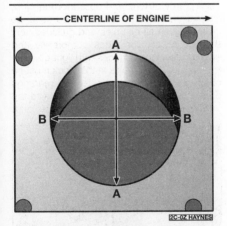

17.4a Measure the diameter of each cylinder at a right angle to the engine centerline (A), and parallel to the engine centerline (B) - out-of-round is the difference between A and B; taper is the difference between the diameter at the top of the cylinder and the diameter at the bottom of the cylinder

12 If the engine isn't going to be reassembled right away, cover it with a large plastic trash bag to keep it clean.

17 Engine block - inspection

Refer to illustrations 17.4a, 17.4b and 17.4c

Note: *The manufacturer recommends checking the block deck for warpage and the main bearing bore concentricity and alignment. Since special measuring tools are needed, the checks should be done by an automotive machine shop.*

1 Before the block is inspected, it should be cleaned as described in Section 16.

2 Visually check the block for cracks, rust and corrosion. Look for stripped threads in the threaded holes. It's also a good idea to have the block checked for hidden cracks by an automotive machine shop that has the special equipment to do this type of work. If defects are found, have the block repaired, if possible, or replaced.

3 Check the cylinder bores for scuffing and scoring.

4 Check the cylinders for taper and out-of-round conditions as follows **(see illustrations)**:

5 Measure the diameter of each cylinder at the top (just under the ridge area), center

17.4b The ability to "feel" when the telescoping gauge is at the correct point will be developed over time, so work slowly and repeat the check until you're satisfied the bore measurement is accurate

and bottom of the cylinder bore, parallel to the crankshaft axis.

6 Next, measure each cylinder's diameter at the same three locations perpendicular to the crankshaft axis.

7 The taper of each cylinder is the difference between the bore diameter at the top of the cylinder and the diameter at the bottom. The out-of-round specification of the cylinder bore is the difference between the parallel and perpendicular readings. Compare your results to this Chapter's Specifications.

8 If the cylinder walls are badly scuffed or scored, or if they're out-of-round or tapered beyond the limits given in this Chapter's Specifications, have the engine block rebored and honed at an automotive machine shop.

9 If a rebore is done, oversize pistons and rings will be required.

10 Using a precision straightedge and feeler gauge, check the block deck (the surface the cylinder heads mate with) for distortion as you did with the cylinder heads (see Section 10). If it's distorted beyond the specified limit, the block decks can be resurfaced by an automotive machine shop.

11 If the cylinders are in reasonably good condition and not worn to the outside of the limits, and if the piston-to-cylinder clearances can be maintained properly, they don't have to be rebored. Honing is all that's necessary (see Section 18).

2D

18 Cylinder honing

Refer to illustrations 18.3a and 18.3b

1 Prior to engine reassembly, the cylinder bores must be honed so the new piston rings will seat correctly and provide the best possible combustion chamber seal. **Note:** *If you don't have the tools or don't want to tackle the honing operation, most automotive machine shops will do it for a reasonable fee.*

2 Before honing the cylinders, install the main bearing caps and tighten the bolts to the torque listed in this Chapter's Specifications.

3 Two types of cylinder hones are commonly available - the flex hone or "bottle brush" type and the more traditional

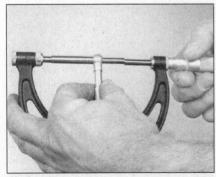

17.4c The gauge is then measured with a micrometer to determine the bore size

18.3a A "bottle brush" hone will produce better results if you've never honed cylinders before

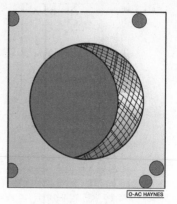

18.3b The cylinder hone should leave a smooth, crosshatch pattern with the lines intersecting at approximately a 60-degree angle

surfacing hone with spring-loaded stones. Both will do the job, but for the less experienced mechanic the "bottle brush" hone will probably be easier to use. You'll also need some honing oil (kerosene will work if honing oil isn't available), rags and an electric drill motor. Proceed as follows:

a) *Mount the hone in the drill motor, compress the stones and slip it into the first cylinder* **(see illustration)**. *Be sure to wear safety goggles or a face shield!*

b) *Lubricate the cylinder with plenty of honing oil, turn on the drill and move the hone up-and-down in the cylinder at a pace that will produce a fine crosshatch pattern on the cylinder walls, and with the drill square and centered with the bore. Ideally, the crosshatch lines should intersect at approximately a 45-60-degree angle* **(see illustration)**. *Be sure to use plenty of lubricant and don't take off any more material than is absolutely necessary to produce the desired finish.* **Note:** *Piston ring manufacturers may specify a different crosshatch angle - read and follow any instructions included with the new rings.*

c) *Don't withdraw the hone from the cylinder while it's running. Instead, shut off the drill and continue moving the hone up-and-down in the cylinder until it comes to a complete stop, then compress the stones and withdraw the hone. If you're using a "bottle brush" type hone, stop the drill motor, then turn the chuck in the normal direction of rotation while withdrawing the hone from the cylinder.*

d) *Wipe the oil out of the cylinder and repeat the procedure for the remaining cylinders.*

4   After the honing job is complete, chamfer the top edges of the cylinder bores with a small file so the rings won't catch when the pistons are installed. Be very careful not to nick the cylinder walls with the end of the file.

5   The entire engine block must be washed again very thoroughly with warm, soapy water to remove all traces of the abrasive grit produced during the honing operation. **Note:** *The bores can be considered clean when a lint-free white cloth - dampened with clean*

engine oil - used to wipe them out doesn't pick up any more honing residue, which will show up as gray areas on the cloth. Be sure to run a brush through all oil holes and galleries and flush them with running water.

6   After rinsing, dry the block and apply a coat of light rust preventive oil to all machined surfaces. Wrap the block in a plastic trash bag to keep it clean and set it aside until reassembly.

19 Pistons and connecting rods - inspection

Refer to illustrations 19.4a, 19.4b, 19.10 and 19.11

1   Before the inspection process can be carried out, the piston/connecting rod assemblies must be cleaned and the original piston rings removed from the pistons. **Note:** *Always use new piston rings when the engine is reassembled.*

2   Using a piston ring installation tool, carefully remove the rings from the pistons. Be careful not to nick or gouge the pistons in the process.

3   Scrape all traces of carbon from the top of the piston. A hand-held wire brush or a piece of fine emery cloth can be used once

19.4a The piston ring grooves can be cleaned with a special tool, as shown here . . .

the majority of the deposits have been scraped away. Do not, under any circumstances, use a wire brush mounted in a drill motor to remove deposits from the pistons. The piston material is soft and may be eroded away by the wire brush.

4   Use a piston ring groove-cleaning tool to remove carbon deposits from the ring grooves. If a tool isn't available, a piece broken off the old ring will do the job. Be very careful to remove only the carbon deposits - don't remove any metal and do not nick or scratch the sides of the ring grooves **(see illustrations)**.

5   Once the deposits have been removed, clean the piston/rod assemblies with solvent and dry them with compressed air (if available). **Warning:** *Wear eye protection. Make sure the oil return holes in the back sides of the ring grooves are clear.*

6   If the pistons and cylinder walls aren't damaged or worn excessively, and if the engine block isn't rebored, new pistons won't be necessary. Normal piston wear appears as even vertical wear on the piston thrust surfaces and slight looseness of the top ring in its groove. New piston rings, however, should always be used when an engine is rebuilt.

7   Carefully inspect each piston for cracks around the skirt, at the pin bosses and at the ring lands.

8   Look for scoring and scuffing on the thrust faces of the skirt, holes in the piston crown and burned areas at the edge of the crown. If the skirt is scored or scuffed, the engine may have been suffering from overheating and/or abnormal combustion, which caused excessively high operating temperatures. The cooling and lubrication systems should be checked thoroughly. A hole in the piston crown is an indication that abnormal combustion (preignition) was occurring. Burned areas at the edge of the piston crown are usually evidence of spark knock (detonation). If any of the above problems exist, the causes must be corrected or the damage will occur again. The causes may include intake air leaks, incorrect fuel/air mixture, low octane fuel, ignition timing and EGR system malfunctions.

9   Corrosion of the piston, in the form of

19.4b . . . or a section of broken ring

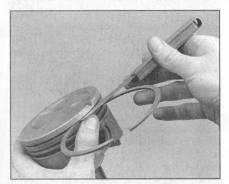

19.10 Check the ring side clearance with a feeler gauge at several points around the groove

19.11 Measure the piston diameter at a 90-degree angle to the piston pin and in line with it

small pits, indicates coolant is leaking into the combustion chamber and/or the crankcase. Again, the cause must be corrected or the problem may persist in the rebuilt engine.

10   Measure the piston ring side clearance by laying a new piston ring in each ring groove and slipping a feeler gauge in beside it **(see illustration)**. Check the clearance at three or four locations around each groove. Be sure to use the correct ring for each groove - they are different. If the side clearance is greater than specified in this Chapter, new pistons will have to be used.

11   Check the piston-to-bore clearance by measuring the bore (see Section 16) and the piston diameter. Make sure the pistons and bores are correctly matched. Measure the piston across the skirt, at a 90-degree angle to the piston pin **(see illustration)**. The measurement must be taken at a specific point to be accurate: The pistons are measured 0.45-inch from the bottom of the skirt, at right angles to the piston pin. Measure the cylinder bore 2.5-inches from the top for comparison with the piston measurement.

12   Subtract the piston diameter from the bore diameter to obtain the clearance. If it's greater than specified, the block will have to be rebored and new pistons and rings installed.

13   Check the piston-to-rod clearance by twisting the piston and rod in opposite directions. Any noticeable play indicates excessive wear, which must be corrected. The piston/connecting rod assemblies should be taken to an automotive machine shop to have the pistons and rods re-sized and new pins installed.

14   If the pistons must be removed from the connecting rods for any reason, they should be taken to an automotive machine shop. While they are there, have the connecting rods checked for bend and twist, since automotive machine shops have special equipment for this purpose. **Note:** *Unless new pistons and/or connecting rods must be installed, do not disassemble the pistons and connecting rods.*

15   Check the connecting rods for cracks and other damage. Temporarily remove the rod caps, lift out the old bearing inserts, wipe the rod and cap bearing surfaces clean and inspect them for nicks, gouges and scratches. After checking the rods, replace the old

bearings, slip the caps into place and tighten the nuts finger tight. **Note:** *If the engine is being rebuilt because of a connecting rod knock, be sure to install new rods.*

---

20 Crankshaft - inspection

Refer to illustrations 20.1, 20.2, 20.5 and 20.7

1   Remove all burrs from the crankshaft oil holes with a stone, file or scraper **(see illustration)**.

2   Clean the crankshaft with solvent and dry it with compressed air (if available). **Warning:** *Wear eye protection when using compressed air.* Be sure to clean the oil holes with a stiff brush **(see illustration)** and flush

20.1 The oil holes should be chamfered so sharp edges don't gouge or scratch the new bearings

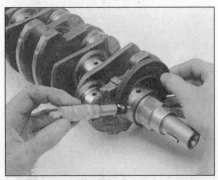

20.5 Measure the diameter of each crankshaft journal at several points to detect taper and out-of-round conditions

them with solvent.

3   Check the main and connecting rod bearing journals for uneven wear, scoring, pits and cracks.

4   Check the rest of the crankshaft for cracks and other damage. It should be Magnafluxed to reveal hidden cracks - an automotive machine shop will handle the procedure.

5   Using a micrometer, measure the diameter of the main and connecting rod journals and compare the results to this Chapter's Specifications **(see illustration)**. By measuring the diameter at a number of points around each journal's circumference, you'll be able to determine whether or not the journal is out-of-round. Take the measurement at each end of the journal, near the crank throws, to determine if the journal is tapered.

6   If the crankshaft journals are damaged, tapered, out-of-round or worn beyond the limits given in the Specifications, have the crankshaft reground by an automotive machine shop. Be sure to use the correct-size bearing inserts if the crankshaft is reconditioned.

7   Check the oil seal journals at each end of the crankshaft for wear and damage. If the seal has worn a groove in the journal, or if it's nicked or scratched **(see illustration)**, the new seal may leak when the engine is reassembled. In some cases, an automotive machine shop may be able to repair the journal by pressing on a thin sleeve. If repair

2D

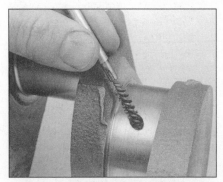

20.2 Use a wire or stiff plastic bristle brush to clean the oil passages in the crankshaft

20.7 If the seals have worn grooves in the crankshaft journals, or if the seal contact surfaces are nicked or scratched, the new seals will leak

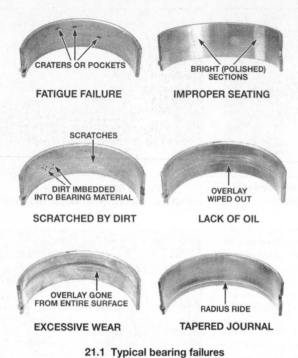

23.3 When checking piston ring end gap, the ring must be square in the cylinder bore (this is done by pushing the ring down with the top of a piston as shown)

23.4 With the ring square in the cylinder, measure the end gap with a feeler gauge

21.1 Typical bearing failures

isn't feasible, a new or different crankshaft should be installed.

8   Examine the main and rod bearing inserts (see Section 21).

21 Main and connecting rod bearings - inspection

Refer to illustration 21.1

1   Even though the main and connecting rod bearings should be replaced with new ones during the engine overhaul, the old bearings should be retained for close examination, as they may reveal valuable information about the condition of the engine **(see illustration)**.

2   Bearing failure occurs because of lack of lubrication, the presence of dirt or other foreign particles, overloading the engine and corrosion. Regardless of the cause of bearing failure, it must be corrected before the engine is reassembled to prevent it from happening again.

3   When examining the bearings, remove them from the engine block, the main bearing caps, the connecting rods and the rod caps and lay them out on a clean surface in the same general position as their location in the engine. This will enable you to match any bearing problems with the corresponding crankshaft journal.

4   Dirt and other foreign particles get into the engine in a variety of ways. It may be left in the engine during assembly, or it may pass through filters or the PCV system. It may get into the oil, and from there into the bearings. Metal chips from machining operations and normal engine wear are often present.

Abrasives are sometimes left in engine components after reconditioning, especially when parts aren't thoroughly cleaned using the proper cleaning methods. Whatever the source, these foreign objects often end up embedded in the soft bearing material and are easily recognized. Large particles won't embed in the bearing and will score or gouge the bearing and journal. The best prevention for this cause of bearing failure is to clean all parts thoroughly and keep everything spotlessly clean during engine assembly. Frequent and regular engine oil and filter changes are also recommended.

5   Lack of lubrication (or lubrication breakdown) has a number of interrelated causes. Excessive heat (which thins the oil), overloading (which squeezes the oil from the bearing face) and oil leakage or throw off (from excessive bearing clearances, worn oil pump or high engine speeds) all contribute to lubrication breakdown. Blocked oil passages, which usually are the result of misaligned oil holes in a bearing shell, will also oil starve a bearing and destroy it. When lack of lubrication is the cause of bearing failure, the bearing material is wiped or extruded from the steel backing of the bearing. Temperatures may increase to the point where the steel backing turns blue from overheating.

6   Driving habits can have a definite effect on bearing life. Low speed operation in too high a gear (lugging the engine) puts very high loads on bearings, which tends to squeeze out the oil film. These loads cause the bearings to flex, which produces fine cracks in the bearing face (fatigue failure). Eventually the bearing material will loosen in pieces and tear away from the steel backing. Short trip driving leads to corrosion of bearings because

insufficient engine heat is produced to drive off the condensed water and corrosive gases. These products collect in the engine oil, forming acid and sludge. As the oil is carried to the engine bearings, the acid attacks and corrodes the bearing material.

7   Incorrect bearing installation during engine assembly will lead to bearing failure as well. Tight-fitting bearings leave insufficient oil clearance and will result in oil starvation. Dirt or foreign particles trapped behind a bearing insert result in high spots on the bearing which lead to failure.

22 Engine overhaul - reassembly sequence

1   Before beginning engine reassembly, make sure you have all the necessary new parts, gaskets and seals as well as the following items on hand:

   Common hand tools
   Torque wrench (1/2-inch drive) with
      angle-torque gauge
   Piston ring Installation tool
   Piston ring compressor
   Crankshaft balancer Installation tool
   Short lengths of rubber or plastic hose
      to fit over connecting rod bolts
   Plastigage
   Feeler gauges
   Fine-tooth file
   New engine oil
   Engine assembly lube or moly-base
      grease
   Gasket sealant
   Thread locking compound

2   In order to save time and avoid

23.5 If the end gap is too small, clamp a file in a vise and file the ring ends (from the outside in only) to enlarge the gap slightly

23.9a Installing the spacer/expander in the oil control ring groove

23.9b DO NOT use a piston ring installation tool when installing the oil ring side rails

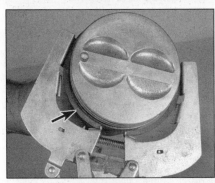

23.12 Installing the compression rings with a ring expander - the mark (arrow) must face up

problems, engine reassembly must be done in the following general order:

Crankshaft and main bearings
Piston/connecting rod assemblies
Balance shaft (3800 only)
Camshaft (intermediate shaft on 3.4L)
Oil pump drive assembly
Rear main oil seal
Timing chain and sprockets (intermediate shaft chain on 3.4L)
Timing chain cover (engine front cover on 3.4L)
Oil pump
Oil pan
Cylinder heads
Valve lifters
Camshaft carriers (3.4L)
Rocker arms and pushrods (3.1L and 3800)
Driveplate

Assembled after engine installation

Intake and exhaust manifolds
Valve covers

---

23 Piston rings - installation

Refer to illustrations 23.3, 23.4, 23.5, 23.9a, 23.9b and 23.12

1 Before installing the new piston rings, the ring end gaps must be checked. It's assumed the piston ring side clearance has been checked and verified correct (see Section 19).

2 Lay out the piston/connecting rod assemblies and the new ring sets so the ring sets will be matched with the same piston and cylinder during the end gap measurement and engine assembly.

3 Insert the top (number one) ring into the first cylinder and square it up with the cylinder walls by pushing it in with the top of the piston **(see illustration)**. The ring should be near the bottom of the cylinder, at the lower limit of ring travel.

4 To measure the end gap, slip feeler gauges between the ends of the ring until a gauge equal to the gap width is found **(see illustration)**. The feeler gauge should slide between the ring ends with a slight amount of drag. Compare the measurement to this

Chapter's Specifications. If the gap is larger or smaller than specified, double-check to make sure you have the correct rings before proceeding.

5 If the gap is too small, it must be enlarged or the ring ends may come in contact with each other during engine operation, which can cause serious engine damage. The end gap can be increased by filing the ring ends very carefully with a fine file. Mount the file in a vise equipped with soft jaws, slip the ring over the file with the ends contacting the file teeth and slowly move the ring to remove material from the ends. When performing this operation, file only from the outside in **(see illustration)**. **Note:** *When you have the end gap correct, remove any burrs from the filed ends of the rings with a whetstone.*

6 Excess end gap isn't critical unless it's greater than 0.040-inch. Again, double-check to make sure you have the correct rings for the engine. If the engine block has been bored oversize, necessitating oversize pistons, matching oversize rings are required.

7 Repeat the procedure for each ring that will be installed in the first cylinder and for each ring in the remaining cylinders. Remember to keep rings, pistons and cylinders matched up.

8 Once the ring end gaps have been checked/corrected, the rings can be installed on the pistons.

9 The oil control ring (lowest one on the piston) is usually installed first. It's composed of three separate components. Slip the spacer/expander into the groove **(see illustration)**. If an anti-rotation tang is used, make sure it's inserted into the drilled hole in the ring groove. Next, install the lower side rail. Don't use a piston ring installation tool on the oil ring side rails, as they may be damaged. Instead, place one end of the side rail into the groove between the spacer/expander and the ring land, hold it firmly in place and slide a finger around the piston while pushing the rail into the groove **(see illustration)**. Next, install the upper side rail in the same manner.

10 After the three oil ring components have been installed, check to make sure both the upper and lower side rails can be turned smoothly in the ring groove.

11 The number two (middle) ring is installed next. It's usually stamped with a mark, which

must face up, toward the top of the piston. **Note:** *Always follow the instructions printed on the ring package or box - different manufacturers may require different approaches. Don't mix up the top and middle rings, as they have different cross-sections.*

12 Use a piston ring installation tool and make sure the identification mark is facing the top of the piston, then slip the ring into the middle groove on the piston **(see illustration)**. Don't expand the ring any more than necessary to slide it over the piston.

13 Install the number one (top) ring in the same manner. Make sure the mark is facing up. Be careful not to confuse the number one and number two rings.

14 Repeat the procedure for the remaining pistons and rings.

---

24 Crankshaft - installation and main bearing oil clearance check

1 Crankshaft installation is the first step in engine reassembly. It's assumed at this point that the engine block and crankshaft have been cleaned, inspected and repaired or reconditioned.

2 Position the engine with the bottom facing up.

3 Remove the main bearing cap bolts and lift out the caps. Lay them out in the proper order to ensure correct installation.

4 If they're still in place, remove the original bearing inserts from the block and the

2D

24.11 Lay the Plastigage strips (arrow) on the main bearing journals, parallel to the crankshaft centerline

24.15 Measuring the width of the crushed Plastigage to determine the main bearing oil clearance (be sure to use the correct scale - standard and metric ones are included)

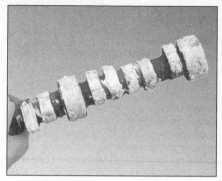

25.1 Coat the camshaft lobes and journals with assembly lube before installation

main bearing caps. Wipe the bearing surfaces of the block and caps with a clean, lint-free cloth. They must be kept spotlessly clean.

Main bearing oil clearance check

Refer to illustrations 24.11 and 24.15

Note: *Don't touch the faces of the new bearing inserts with your fingers. Oil and acids from your skin can etch the bearings.*

5   Clean the back sides of the new main bearing inserts and lay one in each main bearing saddle in the block. If one of the bearing inserts from each set has a large groove in it, make sure the grooved insert is installed in the block. Lay the other bearing from each set in the corresponding main bearing cap. Make sure the tab on the bearing insert fits into the recess in the block or cap, neither higher than the cap's edge nor lower. **Caution:** *The oil holes in the block must line up with the oil holes in the bearing inserts. Do not hammer the bearing into place and don't nick or gouge the bearing faces. No lubrication should be used at this time.*

6   The flanged thrust bearing must be installed in the last main cap. **Caution:** *Some engines have a 0.008-inch oversize rear main bearing. Check your crankshaft for a marking on the last counterweight, and check the backside of the old bearing insert for a similar marking. If they are marked oversize, an oversize rear bearing will be required.*

7   Clean the faces of the bearings in the block and the crankshaft main bearing journals with a clean, lint-free cloth.

8   Check or clean the oil holes in the crankshaft, as any dirt here can go only one way - straight through the new bearings.

9   Once you're certain the crankshaft is clean, carefully lay it in position in the main bearings.

10   Before the crankshaft can be permanently installed, the main bearing oil clearance must be checked.

11   Cut several pieces of the appropriate size Plastigage (they should be slightly shorter than the width of the main bearings) and place one piece on each crankshaft main bearing journal, parallel with the journal axis **(see illustration)**.

12   Clean the faces of the bearings in the caps and install the caps in their original locations (don't mix them up) with the arrows pointing toward the front of the engine. Don't disturb the Plastigage.

13   Starting with the center main and working out toward the ends, tighten the main bearing cap bolts to the torque listed in this Chapter's Specifications in three steps. Don't rotate the crankshaft at any time during this operation, and do not tighten one cap completely - tighten all caps equally. Before tightening, the main caps should be seated using light taps with a brass or plastic mallet.

14   Remove the bolts/studs and carefully lift off the main bearing caps. Keep them in order. Don't disturb the Plastigage or rotate the crankshaft. If any of the main bearing caps are difficult to remove, tap them gently from side-to-side with a soft-face hammer to loosen them.

15   Compare the width of the crushed Plastigage on each journal to the scale printed on the Plastigage envelope to obtain the main bearing oil clearance **(see illustration)**. Check the Specifications to make sure it's correct.

16   If the clearance is not as specified, the bearing inserts may be the wrong size (which means different ones will be required). Before deciding different inserts are needed, make sure no dirt or oil was between the bearing inserts and the caps or block when the clearance was measured. If the Plastigage was wider at one end than the other, the journal may be tapered (see Section 20).

17   Carefully scrape all traces of the Plastigage material off the main bearing journals and/or the bearing faces. Use your fingernail or the edge of a credit card - don't nick or scratch the bearing faces.

Final crankshaft installation

18   Carefully lift the crankshaft out of the engine.

19   Clean the bearing faces in the block, then apply a thin, uniform layer of moly-base grease or engine assembly lube to each of the bearing surfaces. Be sure to coat the thrust faces as well as the journal face of the thrust bearing.

20   Make sure the crankshaft journals are clean, then lay the crankshaft back in place in the block.

21   Clean the faces of the bearings in the caps, then apply lubricant to them.

22   Install the caps in their original locations with the arrows pointing toward the front of the engine. **Note:** *On 3800 engines, there are two side seals that must be placed in the side grooves of the rear main cap as it is installed. It wasn't necessary during the Plastigage check, but insert them now. They should be part of your engine overhaul gasket set. Also apply a thin coat of anaerobic sealant to the cap-to-block mating surfaces of the rear cap on the 3800.*

23   With all caps in place and bolts just started, tap the ends of the crankshaft forward and backward with a lead or brass hammer to line up the main bearing and crankshaft thrust surfaces.

24   Following the procedures outlined in Step 13, retighten all main bearing cap bolts to the torque listed in this Chapter's Specifications, starting with the center main and working out toward the ends.

25   Rotate the crankshaft a number of times by hand to check for any obvious binding.

26   The final step is to check the crankshaft endplay with feeler gauges or a dial indicator as described in Section 15. The endplay should be correct if the crankshaft thrust faces aren't worn or damaged and new bearings have been installed.

25   Camshaft (3.1L and 3800), intermediate shaft (3.4L) and balance shaft (3800) - installation

Camshaft (3.1L and 3800) and intermediate shaft (3.4L)

Refer to illustration 25.1

1   Lubricate the camshaft bearing journals and cam lobes with a special camshaft installation lubricant **(see illustration)**.

2   Slide the camshaft into the engine, using a long bolt (the same thread as the camshaft sprocket bolt) screwed into the front of the camshaft as a "handle." Support the cam near the block and be careful not to

25.5 Drive the front balance shaft bearing in (it's attached to the balance shaft) just until the retainer plate can be installed

25.8 The balance shaft gear mark (arrow) should point straight down

25.9 Align the marks (arrows) on both balance shaft gears as shown

scrape or nick the bearings. Install the camshaft retainer plate (3.1L) or intermediate shaft plate (3.4L) and tighten the bolts to the torque listed in this Chapter's Specifications.

3   On 3.1L and 3.4l engines, dip the gear portion of the oil pump drive in engine oil and insert it into the block. It should be flush with its mounting boss before inserting the retaining bolt. **Note:** *Position a new O-ring on the oil pump driveshaft before installation.*

4   Complete the installation of the timing chain and sprockets (3.1L engine: see Part A; 3.4L engine: see Part B; 3800 engine, Part C). On 3800 engines, perform the following procedure for balance shaft installation before installing the timing chain and sprockets.

Balance shaft (3800 only)

Refer to illustrations 25.5, 25.8 and 25.9

5   Lubricate the front bearing and rear journal of the balance shaft with engine oil and insert the balance shaft carefully into the block. When the front bearing approaches the insert in the front of the block, use a hammer and an appropriate-size socket to drive the front bearing into its insert. Drive it in just enough to allow installation of the balance shaft bearing retainer **(see illustration)**. Tighten the balance shaft retainer bolts to the torque listed in this Chapter's Specifications.

6   Install the balance shaft driven gear and its bolt.

7   Turn the camshaft so that with the camshaft sprocket temporarily installed, the timing mark is straight down.

8   With the camshaft sprocket and the camshaft gear removed, turn the balance shaft so the timing mark on the gear points straight down **(see illustration)**.

9   Install the camshaft gear (that drives the balance shaft) onto the cam, aligning it with the keyway and align the marks on the balance shaft gear and the camshaft gear **(see illustration)** by turning the balance shaft.

10   After the camshaft sprocket, crankshaft sprocket and timing chain have been installed (see Chapter 2 part C), tighten the balance shaft driven gear bolt to the torque listed in this Chapter's Specifications.

26   Rear main oil seal - replacement

Refer to part A of this Chapter for the rear main seal replacement procedure.

27   Pistons and connecting rods - installation and rod bearing oil clearance check

1   Before installing the piston/connecting rod assemblies, the cylinder walls must be perfectly clean, the top edge of each cylinder must be chamfered, and the crankshaft must be in place.

2   Remove the cap from the end of the number one connecting rod (check the marks made during removal). Remove the original bearing inserts and wipe the bearing surfaces of the connecting rod and cap with a clean, lint-free cloth. They must be kept spotlessly clean.

Piston Installation and rod bearing oil clearance check

Refer to illustrations 27.5, 27.11, 27.13 and 27.17

Note: *Don't touch the faces of the new bearing inserts with your fingers. Oil and acids from your skin can etch the bearings.*

3   Clean the back side of the new upper bearing insert, then lay it in place in the connecting rod. Make sure the tab on the bearing fits into the recess in the rod. Don't hammer the bearing insert into place and be very careful not to nick or gouge the bearing face. Don't lubricate the bearing at this time.

4   Clean the back side of the other bearing insert and install it in the rod cap. Again, make sure the tab on the bearing fits into the recess in the cap, and don't apply any lubricant. It's critically important that the mating surfaces of the bearing and connecting rod are perfectly clean and oil free when they're assembled.

5   Stagger the piston ring gaps around the piston **(see illustration)**.

6   Slip a section of plastic or rubber hose over each connecting rod cap bolt.

7   Lubricate the piston and rings with clean engine oil and attach a piston ring

compressor to the piston. Leave the skirt protruding about 1/4-inch to guide the piston into the cylinder. The rings must be compressed until they're flush with the piston.

8   Rotate the crankshaft until the number one connecting rod journal is at BDC (bottom dead center) and apply a coat of engine oil to the cylinder walls.

9   With the mark or notch on top of the piston facing the front of the engine, gently insert the piston/connecting rod assembly into the number one cylinder bore and rest the bottom edge of the ring compressor on the engine block.

10   Tap the top edge of the ring compressor to make sure it's contacting the block around its entire circumference.

11   Gently tap on the top of the piston with the end of a wooden or plastic hammer handle **(see illustration)** while guiding the end of the connecting rod into place on the crankshaft journal. The piston rings may try to pop out of the ring compressor just before entering the cylinder bore, so keep some pressure down on the ring compressor. Work slowly, and if any resistance is felt as the piston enters the cylinder, stop immediately. Find out what's hanging up and fix it before proceeding. Do not, for any reason, force the piston into the cylinder - you might break a ring and/or the piston.

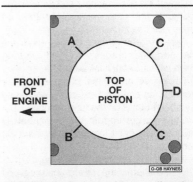

27.5 Ring end gap positions - align the oil ring spacer gap at D, the oil ring side rails at C (one inch either side of the pin centerline), and the compression rings at A and B, one inch either side of the pin centerline

2D

12 Once the piston/connecting rod assembly is installed, the connecting rod bearing oil clearance must be checked before the rod cap is permanently bolted in place.

13 Cut a piece of the appropriate size Plastigage slightly shorter than the width of the connecting rod bearing and lay it in place on the number one connecting rod journal, parallel with the journal axis **(see illustration)**.

14 Clean the connecting rod cap bearing face, remove the protective hoses from the connecting rod bolts and install the rod cap. Make sure the mating mark on the cap is on the same side as the mark on the connecting rod.

15 Install the nuts and tighten them to the torque listed in this Chapter's Specifications. Work up to it in three steps. **Note:** *Use a thin-wall socket to avoid erroneous torque readings that can result if the socket is wedged between the rod cap and nut. If the socket tends to wedge itself between the nut and the cap, lift up on it slightly until it no longer contacts the cap. Do not rotate the crankshaft at any time during this operation.*

16 Remove the nuts and detach the rod cap, being very careful not to disturb the Plastigage.

17 Compare the width of the crushed Plastigage to the scale printed on the Plastigage envelope to obtain the oil clearance **(see illustration)**. Compare it to this Chapter's Specifications to make sure the clearance is correct.

18 If the clearance is not as specified, the bearing inserts may be the wrong size (which means different ones will be required). Before deciding different inserts are needed, make sure no dirt or oil was between the bearing inserts and the connecting rod or cap when the clearance was measured. Also, recheck the journal diameter. If the Plastigage was wider at one end than the other, the journal may be tapered (see Section 20).

Final connecting rod installation

19 Carefully scrape all traces of the Plastigage material off the rod journal and/or bearing face. Be very careful not to scratch the bearing - use your fingernail or the edge of a credit card.

20 Make sure the bearing faces are perfectly clean, then apply a uniform layer of clean moly-base grease or engine assembly lube to both of them. You'll have to push the piston into the cylinder to expose the face of the bearing insert in the connecting rod - be sure to slip the protective hoses over the rod bolts first.

21 Slide the connecting rod back into place on the journal, remove the protective hoses from the rod cap bolts, install the rod cap and tighten the nuts to the torque listed in this Chapter's Specifications. Again, work up to the torque in three steps.

22 Repeat the entire procedure for the remaining pistons/connecting rods.

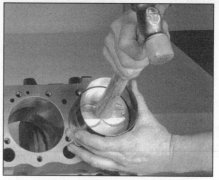

27.11 Drive the piston into the cylinder bore with the end of a wooden or plastic hammer handle

23 The important points to remember are:

a) *Keep the back sides of the bearing inserts and the insides of the connecting rods and caps perfectly clean when assembling them.*

b) *Make sure you have the correct piston/rod assembly for each cylinder.*

c) *The arrow or mark on the piston must face the front of the engine.*

d) *Lubricate the cylinder walls with clean oil.*

e) *Lubricate the bearing faces when installing the rod caps after the oil clearance has been checked.*

24 After all the piston/connecting rod assemblies have been properly installed, rotate the crankshaft a number of times by hand to check for any obvious binding.

25 As a final step, the connecting rod endplay must be checked (see Section 14).

26 Compare the measured endplay to this Chapter's Specifications to make sure it's correct. If it was correct before disassembly and the original crankshaft and rods were reinstalled, it should still be right. If new rods or a new crankshaft were installed, the endplay may be inadequate. If so, the rods will have to be removed and taken to an automotive machine shop for re-sizing.

28 Initial start-up and break-in after overhaul

Warning: *Have a fire extinguisher handy when starting the engine for the first time.*

1 Once the engine has been installed in the vehicle, double-check the oil and coolant levels.

2 With the spark plugs out of the engine, remove the PCM IGN fuse from the instrument panel fuse block and the IGNITION fuse from the underhood fuse block (1995 models), or the PCM BATT fuse from the instrument panel fuse block and the IGNITION fuse from the underhood fuse block (1996 and later models). Crank the engine until oil pressure registers on the gauge or the light goes out.

3 Install the spark plugs, hook up the plug wires and install the fuses.

4 Start the engine. It may take a few

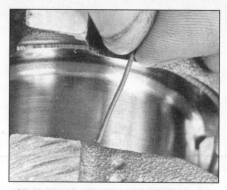

27.13 Lay the Plastigage strips on each rod bearing journal, parallel to the crankshaft centerline

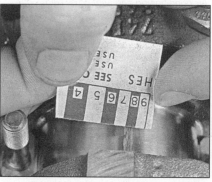

27.17 Measuring the width of the crushed Plastigage to determine the rod bearing oil clearance (be sure to use the correct scale - standard and metric ones are included)

moments for the fuel system to build up pressure, but the engine should start without a great deal of effort. **Note:** *If the engine keeps backfiring, recheck the valve timing and spark plug wire routing.*

5 After the engine starts, it should be allowed to warm up to normal operating temperature. While the engine is warming up, make a thorough check for fuel, oil and coolant leaks.

6 Shut the engine off and recheck the engine oil and coolant levels.

7 Drive the vehicle to an area with no traffic, accelerate from 30 to 50 mph, then allow the vehicle to slow to 30 mph with the throttle closed. Repeat the procedure 10 or 12 times. This will load the piston rings and cause them to seat properly against the cylinder walls. Check again for oil and coolant leaks.

8 Drive the vehicle gently for the first 500 miles (no sustained high speeds) and keep a constant check on the oil level. It isn't unusual for an engine to use oil during the break-in period.

9 At approximately 500 to 600 miles, change the oil and filter.

10 For the next few hundred miles, drive the vehicle normally. Don't pamper it or abuse it.

11 After 2000 miles, change the oil and filter again and consider the engine broken in.

Chapter 3
Cooling, heating and air conditioning systems

Contents

Specifications

General

Coolant capacity	See Chapter 1
Radiator pressure cap rating	15 psi
Thermostat opening temperature	188-degrees F
Refrigerant type	R-134a
Refrigerant capacity	
1995 and 1996	2.0 pounds
1997 and 1998	1.88 pounds

Torque specifications

	Ft-lbs (unless otherwise indicated)
Compressor mounting bolts	
3.1L	37
3.4L	
Front bolts	36
Rear bolts	19
3800	
Front nuts	74
Upper bolt	36
Lower bolt	59
Rear bracket bolts	23
Oil cooler connector	37
Thermostat housing bolts	
3.1L and 3.4L	18
3800	20
Water pump attaching bolts	
3.1L and 3.4L	89 in-lbs
3800	
Short bolts	
Step 1	132 in-lbs
Step 2	Tighten an additional 80-degrees
Long bolts	
Step 1	15
Step 2	Tighten an additional 40-degrees
Water pump pulley bolts	
3.1L and 3.4L	18
3800	115 in-lbs

3

1   General information

Engine cooling system

All vehicles covered by this manual employ a pressurized engine cooling system with thermostatically controlled coolant circulation. An impeller type water pump mounted on the engine block pumps coolant through the engine and radiator. The coolant flows around each cylinder and back to the radiator. Cast-in coolant passages direct coolant around the intake and exhaust ports, near the spark plug areas and the exhaust valve guides.

A wax-pellet type thermostat is located in a housing connected to the upper radiator hose. During warm up the closed thermostat prevents coolant from circulating through the radiator. As the engine nears normal operating temperature, the thermostat opens and allows hot coolant to travel through the radiator, where it's cooled before returning to the engine.

The cooling system is sealed by a pressure-type radiator cap, which raises the boiling point of the coolant and increases the cooling efficiency of the radiator. If the system pressure exceeds the cap pressure relief value, the excess pressure in the system forces the spring-loaded valve inside the cap off its seat and allows the coolant to escape through a hose into a coolant reservoir. When the system cools, the excess coolant is automatically drawn from the reservoir back into the radiator.

The coolant reservoir serves as both the point at which fresh coolant is added to the cooling system to maintain the proper level and as a holding tank for expelled coolant.

This type of cooling system is known as a closed design because coolant that escapes past the pressure cap is saved and reused.

Heating system

The heating system consists of a blower fan and heater core located under the instrument panel, the hoses connecting the heater core to the engine cooling system and the heater/air conditioning control assembly. Hot engine coolant is circulated through the heater core. When the heater mode is activated, a trap door opens to expose the heater box to the passenger compartment. A fan switch on the control head activates the blower motor, which forces air through the core, heating the air.

Air conditioning system

The air conditioning system consists of a condenser mounted in front of the radiator, an evaporator mounted adjacent to the heater core, a compressor mounted on the engine, a filter-drier (accumulator), which contains a high-pressure relief valve, and the hoses and lines connecting all of the above components.

A blower fan forces the warmer air of the passenger compartment through the evaporator core (sort of a radiator-in-reverse), transferring the heat from the air to the refrigerant. The liquid refrigerant boils off into low pressure vapor, taking the heat with it when it leaves the evaporator.

2   Antifreeze - general information

Refer to illustration 2.4

Warning: *Do not allow antifreeze to come in contact with your skin or painted surfaces of the vehicle. Rinse off spills immediately with plenty of water. Antifreeze is highly toxic if ingested. Never leave antifreeze lying around in an open container or in puddles on the floor; children and pets are attracted by it's sweet smell and may drink it. Check with local authorities about disposing of used antifreeze. Many communities have collection centers which will see that antifreeze is disposed of safely. Never dump used antifreeze on the ground or pour it into drains.*
Note: *Non-toxic antifreeze is now available at most auto parts stores, but even these types should be disposed of properly.*

The cooling system should be filled with a water/ethylene glycol-based antifreeze solution which will prevent freezing down to at least -20-degrees F (even lower in cold climates). It also provides protection against corrosion and increases the coolant boiling point.

The cooling system should be drained, flushed and refilled at least every other year (see Chapter 1). The use of antifreeze solutions for periods of longer than two years is likely to cause damage and encourage the formation of rust and scale in the system. However, 1996 and later models are filled with a new, long-life coolant called "DEX-COOL", with a manufacturer recommended maintenance interval of five years.

Before adding antifreeze to the system, check all hose connections. Antifreeze can leak through very minute openings.

The exact mixture of antifreeze to water which you should use depends on the relative weather conditions. The mixture should contain at least 50-percent antifreeze, but should never contain more than 70-percent antifreeze. Consult the mixture ratio chart on the antifreeze container before adding coolant. Hydrometers are available at most auto parts stores to test the coolant **(see illustration)**. Use antifreeze which meets the vehicle manufacturer's specifications.

3   Thermostat - check and replacement

Warning: *The engine must be completely cool when this procedure is performed.*
Note: *Don't drive the vehicle without a thermostat! The computer may stay in open loop mode and emissions and fuel economy will suffer.*

Check

1   Before assuming the thermostat is to blame for a cooling system problem, check the coolant level, drivebelt tension (see Chapter 1) and temperature gauge (or light) operation.

2   If the engine seems to be taking a long time to warm up (based on heater output or temperature gauge operation), the thermostat is probably stuck open. Replace the thermostat with a new one.

3   If the engine runs hot, use your hand to check the temperature of the upper radiator hose. If the hose isn't hot, but the engine is, the thermostat is probably stuck closed, preventing the coolant inside the engine from escaping to the radiator. Replace the thermostat. **Caution:** *Don't drive the vehicle without a thermostat. The computer may stay in open loop and emissions and fuel economy will suffer.*

4   If the upper radiator hose is hot, it means the coolant is flowing and the thermostat is open. Consult the *Troubleshooting* Section at the front of this manual for cooling system diagnosis.

Replacement

Refer to illustrations 3.8, 3.11a, 3.11b, 3.12a and 3.12b

5   Disconnect the negative battery cable from the battery and partially drain the cooling system (see Chapter 1). **Caution:** *On models equipped with a Theftlock audio system, be sure the lockout feature is turned off before performing any procedure which requires disconnecting the battery. If the coolant is relatively new or in good condition, save it and reuse it. If it is to be replaced, see Section 2 for cautions about proper handling of used antifreeze.*

6   Remove the air cleaner and duct (see Chapter 4).

7   On the 3800 engine, remove the fuel injector sight shield.

8   Follow the upper radiator hose to the engine to locate the thermostat cover **(see**

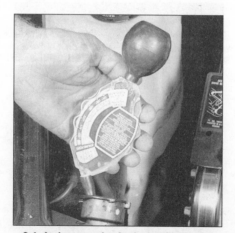

2.4 An inexpensive hydrometer can be used to test the condition of your coolant

3.8 Upper radiator hose clamp at the thermostat cover - 3.1L engine shown

A   *Radiator hose clamp*
B   *Coolant bleed screw*

3.11a Thermostat cover bolts (arrows) - 3.1L engine

3.11b Thermostat cover bolts (arrows) - 3800 engine

3.12a Note how it's installed, then remove the thermostat (the spring end points toward the engine)

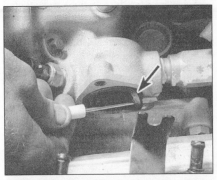

3.12b If the thermostat comes out without its rubber seal (arrow), pry it out of the housing with a small screwdriver

illustration). On all models, the thermostat is located at the top-center of the engine at the transaxle end. On the 3800 engine it is just ahead of the throttle body.

9   Loosen the hose clamp, then detach the hose from the thermostat cover. If the hose sticks, grasp it near the end with a pair of adjustable pliers and twist it to break the seal, then pull it off. If the hose is old or deteriorated, cut it off and install a new one.

10   If the outer surface of the large fitting that mates with the hose is deteriorated (corroded, pitted, etc.) it may be damaged further by hose removal. If it is, the thermostat cover will have to be replaced.

11   Remove the bolts/nuts and detach the thermostat cover **(see illustrations)**. If the cover is stuck, tap it with a soft-face hammer to jar it loose. Be prepared for some coolant to spill as the gasket seal is broken.

12   Note how it's installed (which end is facing up), then remove the thermostat **(see illustrations)**.

13   Remove all traces of old gasket material and sealant from the housing and cover with a gasket scraper. Clean the gasket mating surfaces with lacquer thinner or acetone.

14   Install the new thermostat in the housing. Make sure the correct end faces up

- the spring end is normally directed into the engine. A new rubber seal should be in place on the thermostat before installation.

15   Install the cover and bolts/nuts, using RTV sealant around the bolt threads. Tighten the bolts to the torque listed in this Chapter's Specifications.

16   The remaining steps are the reverse of removal.

17   Refill the cooling system (see Chapter 1). **Note:** *Be sure to bleed the system of air.*

18   Start the engine and allow it to reach normal operating temperature, then check for leaks and proper thermostat operation (as described in Steps 2 through 4).

4 Engine cooling fans and circuit - check and fan replacement

Warning: *Keep hands, tools and clothing away from the fan, even if the engine is not running. To avoid injury or damage DO NOT operate the engine with a damaged fan. Do not attempt to repair fan blades - replace a damaged fan with a new one.*

Check

Refer to illustrations 4.1 and 4.2

1   To test a fan motor, unplug the electrical connector at the motor and use fused jumper wires to connect the fan directly to the battery **(see illustration)**. If the fan still doesn't work, replace the motor.

2   If the motor tests OK, check the cooling fan relays, located in the underhood fuse/relay panel **(see illustration)**. There are three fan relays, number 1 and 2 are in the electrical box at the front of the right fenderwell, and number 3 is in the electrical box at the front of the left fenderwell.

3   Test the relays (see Chapter 12).

4   If the relays and the fan motor are good, check the wiring from the relays to the PCM (computer) for open or short circuits.

5   If the circuit checks OK but the fan(s) still don't come on, check the engine coolant temperature sensor (see Chapter 6).

Replacement

Refer to illustrations 4.8, 4.10 and 4.12
Note: *This procedure applies to either fan.*

3

4.1 Disconnect the electrical connector from the fan and apply fused battery power and ground to the terminals (arrows) - fan shown removed from vehicle for clarity

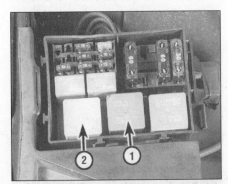

4.2 The cooling fan relays are easily identifiable by viewing the decal on the inside of the underhood fuse/relay box cover - relays no. 1 and no. 2 (shown) are in the electrical box on the right fenderwell

4.8 Unbolt the torque strut brackets (upper arrows) from the radiator support

4.10 Detach the bolts (arrows) securing the tops of the two fans (center arrows) and the sides - the bottom legs of the fan assemblies (not shown here) simply slip over tangs on the bottom of the radiator support

4.12 Remove the nut (arrow) to remove the fan blade from the motor

6   Disconnect the cable from the negative terminal of the battery. **Caution:** *On models equipped with a Theftlock audio system, be sure the lockout feature is turned off before performing any procedure which requires disconnecting the battery.*

7   Remove the air intake duct and air cleaner (see Chapter 4).

8   Remove the bolts and swing the engine torque strut(s) away from the radiator to allow room for fan removal **(see illustration)**. Loosen the through-bolts in the strut mounts first to avoid damage to the rubber bushings.

9   Disconnect the electrical connectors from the fan(s).

10   Detach the fan retaining bolts **(see illustration)**. **Note:** *It is extremely important to mark the installed position of each fan (left side or right side) because each fan motor*

5.6 Disconnect the transmission cooler lines (arrows) from the right side of the radiator

5.7 On the left side, disconnect the upper radiator hose (arrow) - lower radiator hose is at the bottom right of the radiator

has a different wattage rating and insufficient cooling could occur if they are not installed in their original positions.

11   Pull the fan assembly up slightly to dislodge its tabs from the radiator, then guide the fan assembly out from the engine compartment, making sure that all wiring clips are disconnected. Be careful not to contact the radiator cooling fins.

12   If a fan is damaged, remove the nut holding the fan blade to the motor **(see illustration)**. **Note:** *On some models, the fan motor can be separated from the plastic mount for replacement, on others it is sold only as an assembly.*

13   Installation is the reverse of removal.

5   Radiator and coolant reservoir - removal and installation

Warning: *The engine must be completely cool when this procedure is performed.*

Radiator

Removal
Refer to illustrations 5.6, 5.7, 5.8 and 5.9

1   Disconnect the negative battery cable from the battery. **Caution:** *On models equipped with a Theftlock audio system, be sure the lockout feature is turned off before*

5.8 Remove the upper radiator support bolts (A indicates right-side mount) and disconnect the coolant overflow hose (B)

performing any procedure which requires disconnecting the battery.

2   Drain the cooling system (see Chapter 1). If the coolant is relatively new or in good condition, save it and reuse it. Refer to the coolant **Warning** in Section 2.

3   Remove the air cleaner assembly (see Chapter 4).

4   Unbolt and swing away the engine torque strut mounts from the upper radiator support **(see illustration 4.8)**. Loosen the through-bolts in the strut mounts first to avoid damage to the rubber bushings.

5   Refer to Section 4 and remove the engine cooling fans. Disconnect the electrical connector from the low-coolant sensor in the right radiator tank **(see illustration 5.14)**.

6   Disconnect the cooler lines from the radiator **(see illustration)**, then cap the ends to prevent excessive fluid loss and contamination. Use a drip pan to catch spilled fluid.

7   Loosen the hose clamps, then detach the radiator hoses from the fittings **(see illustration)**. If they're stuck, grasp each hose near the end with a pair of adjustable pliers and twist it to break the seal, then pull it off - be careful not to distort the radiator fittings. If the hoses are old or deteriorated, cut them off and install new ones.

8   Disconnect the reservoir hose from the radiator neck and remove the bolts from the upper radiator mounting brackets fittings **(see illustration)**.

9   Remove the bolt holding the transmission cooler lines to the bottom of the radiator **(see illustration)**.

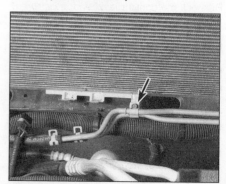

5.9 Remove the bolt (arrow) retaining the transmission lines to the radiator

5.13 The rubber insulators (arrows) must be in place before installing the radiator

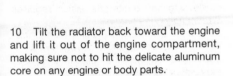

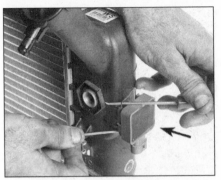

5.14 Remove the low coolant warning sensor (arrow) by prying back the two spring clips - use a new O-ring when reinstalling the sensor

5.19 Remove the screw (A), the nut (B) and the plastic retainer pin (C), then remove the coolant recovery tank

10   Tilt the radiator back toward the engine and lift it out of the engine compartment, making sure not to hit the delicate aluminum core on any engine or body parts.

11   With the radiator removed, it can be inspected for leaks and damage. If it needs repair, have a radiator shop or dealer service department perform the work, as special techniques are required.

12   Bugs and dirt can be removed from the radiator with compressed air and a soft brush. Don't bend the cooling fins as this is done.

Installation

Refer to illustrations 5.13 and 5.14

13   Installation is the reverse of the removal procedure. Be sure that the radiator mounting insulators are in place and in good condition before installing the radiator **(see illustration)**.

14   If the radiator is to be replaced, remove the low-coolant sensor from the old radiator and attach it with the clips to the new radiator, using a new O-ring lubricated with clean coolant **(see illustration)**.

15   After installation, fill the cooling system with the proper mixture of antifreeze and water. Be sure to bleed the system of air (see Chapter 1).

16   Start the engine and check for leaks. Allow the engine to reach normal operating temperature, indicated by the upper radiator hose becoming hot. Recheck the coolant level and add more if required.

17   Check and add automatic transmission fluid as needed.

Coolant reservoir

Refer to illustration 5.19

18   Disconnect the radiator overflow hose from the top of the radiator **(see illustration 5.8)**.

19   Remove the mounting fasteners from the right shock tower and lift the coolant reservoir from the vehicle **(see illustration)**.

20   Prior to installation make sure the reservoir is clean and free of debris which could be drawn into the radiator (wash it with

soapy water and a brush if necessary, then rinse thoroughly).

21   Installation is the reverse of removal.

6   Water pump - check

Refer to illustration 6.4

1   A failure in the water pump can cause serious engine damage due to overheating.

2   There are three ways to check the operation of the water pump while it's installed on the engine. If the pump is defective, it should be replaced with a new or rebuilt unit.

3   With the engine running at normal operating temperature, squeeze the upper radiator hose. If the water pump is working properly, a pressure surge should be felt as the hose is released. **Warning:** *Keep your hands away from the fan blades!*

4   Water pumps are equipped with weep or vent holes. If a failure occurs in the pump seal, coolant will leak from the hole **(see illustration)**. In most cases you'll need a flashlight and mirror to find the hole on the under side of the water pump to check for leaks.

5   If the water pump shaft bearings fail there may be a howling sound coming from the drivebelt area while the engine is running. Shaft wear can be felt if the water

6.4 The weep hole (arrow) is located on the top of the water pump (pump removed for clarity, 3.1L shown)

pump pulley is rocked up-and-down. Don't mistake drivebelt slippage, which causes a squealing sound, for water pump bearing failure.

7   Water pump - removal and installation

Warning: *Wait until the engine is completely cool before beginning this procedure.*

Removal

Refer to illustrations 7.3, 7.5a and 7.5b

1   Disconnect the negative battery cable from the battery. **Caution:** *On models equipped with a Theftlock audio system, be sure the lockout feature is turned off before performing any procedure which requires disconnecting the battery.*

2   Drain the cooling system (see Chapter 1). If the coolant is relatively new or in good condition, save it and reuse it. Refer to Section 5 and remove the coolant recovery tank.

3   Loosen the bolts on the water pump pulley, using belt tension and a prybar to hold it **(see illustration)**.

4   Remove the serpentine belt (see Chapter 1). On 3.1L engines, remove the small belt guard just above the water pump.

5   Remove the bolts/nuts and detach the

7.3 Use a prybar or long screwdriver to hold the pump pulley from turning while loosening the bolts

3

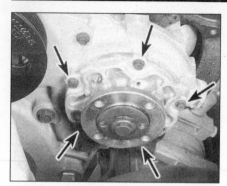

7.5a Unscrew the water pump retaining bolts and remove the water pump (3.1L shown, 3.4L similar)

7.5b Water pump mounting bolts - 3800 engine

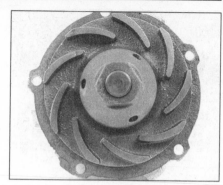

7.7 Inspect the impeller for damage or corrosion

water pump from the engine **(see illustrations)**. **Note:** *Most 3.1L and 3.4L models have a locating mark at the top of the pump. If yours doesn't have one, make a mark yourself for help in orienting the pump during reassembly (if the same pump is to be reinstalled).*

Installation

Refer to illustration 7.7

6   Clean the fastener threads and any threaded holes in the engine to remove corrosion and sealant.

7   Compare the new pump to the old one to make sure they're identical. If using the existing pump, inspect the back of the pump for a broken or corroded impeller **(see illustration)**.

8   Remove all traces of old gasket material from the engine with a gasket scraper.

9   Clean the engine and water pump mating surfaces with lacquer thinner or acetone.

10   Carefully attach the pump and new gasket to the engine and start the bolts/nuts finger tight. Make sure the alignment mark (3.1L and 3.4L models) is at the top.

11   Tighten the fasteners in 1/4-turn increments to the torque figure listed in this Chapter's Specifications. Don't overtighten them or the pump may be distorted.

12   Reinstall all parts removed for access to the pump.

13   Refill and bleed the cooling system (see Chapter 1). Run the engine and check for leaks.

8.1a Coolant temperature gauge sending unit (arrow) - 3.1L engine

8   Coolant temperature gauge sending unit - check and replacement

Warning: *Wait until the engine is completely cool before beginning this procedure.*

Check

Refer to illustrations 8.1a and 8.1b

1   The coolant temperature indicator system is composed of a temperature gauge or warning light mounted in the dash and a coolant temperature sending unit mounted on the engine **(see illustrations)**. On 3.4L engines, the sending unit is a single-wire sender mounted on the left cylinder head, below the hose connection on the thermostat cover.

2   If an overheating indication occurs, check the coolant level in the system and then make sure the wiring between the gauge and the sending unit is secure and all fuses are intact.

3   To check the circuit and gauge operation, disconnect the electrical connector to the sending unit and using a jumper wire, connect the dark green wire terminal in the harness connector to ground. Turn the ignition to On (engine NOT running). If the gauge deflects full scale, the circuit and gauge are OK. The problem lies in the sending unit.

4   To confirm the sending unit is defective, check the resistance of the unit when the engine is cool. Resistance should be high -

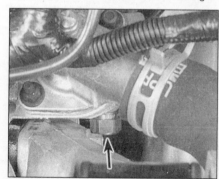

8.1b Coolant temperature gauge sending unit (arrow) - 3800 engine

approximately 1365 ohms at 100-degrees F. Next, run the engine until it is fully warmed up and check the resistance of the sending unit again. The resistance should now be low - approximately 44 ohms at 280-degrees F. If it doesn't respond, replace the sending unit.

Replacement

5   **Warning:** *Make sure the engine is cool before removing the defective sending unit.* There will be some coolant loss as the unit is removed, so be prepared to catch it. Refer to the coolant **Warning** in Section 2.

6   Prepare the new sending unit by lightly coating the threads with sealant. Disconnect the electrical connector and unscrew the sensor. Install the new sensor as quickly as possible to minimize coolant loss.

7   Check the coolant level after the replacement unit has been installed and fill up the system, if necessary (see Chapter 1). Check now for proper operation of the gauge and sending unit.

9   Engine oil cooler - general information and replacement

1   The engine oil cooler on 3.1L and 3.4L models is sandwiched between the oil filter and the engine. Coolant flows through the cooler from two hoses connected to pipes.

2   To replace the oil cooler, refer to Chapter 1 for removal of the oil filter and draining of the cooling system.

3   Disconnect the electrical connector from the oil pressure sending unit on the block.

4   Disconnect the electrical connector at the knock sensor (see Chapter 6).

5   Disconnect the hose clamps and two coolant hoses from the oil cooler.

6   Use a deep socket to remove the threaded adapter holding the oil cooler housing to the oil filter boss on the engine. Pull the oil cooler from the block.

7   Installation is the reverse of removal. Make sure the block mounting surface is clean before installation and that the seal on the engine-side of the cooler is intact and lightly oiled.

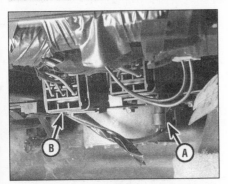

10.3 Blower motor connector location (A), and blower relay (B)

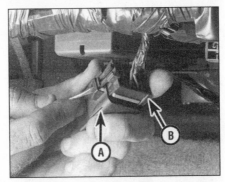

10.6 Use a small screwdriver to release the blower relay (A) from the harness connector (B)

10.7 Blower motor resistor location (arrow)

10 Blower motor and circuit - check

Refer to illustrations 10.3, 10.6, 10.7, 10.9 and 10.11

Warning: *The models covered by this manual are equipped with airbags. Always disable the airbag system before working in the vicinity of the impact sensors, steering column or instrument panel to avoid the possibility of accidental deployment of the airbag(s), which could cause personal injury (see Chapter 12). The yellow wires and connectors routed through the instrument panel are for this system. Do not use electrical test equipment on these yellow wires or tamper with them in any way while working under the instrument panel.*

1   Check the fuses and all connections in the circuit for looseness and corrosion. Make sure the battery is fully charged. Refer to the heating and air conditioning system wiring diagrams at the end of Chapter 12 when performing the following checks.
2   Remove the lower right dash insulator panel (below the glove box) for access to the blower motor.
3   Disconnect the electrical connector to the blower motor and connect a voltmeter or test light to the purple wire terminal in the harness connector **(see illustration)**.
4   Turn the ignition to On and place the blower switch on High, battery voltage should be indicated. Using an ohmmeter or self-powered continuity tester, check for

continuity to chassis ground on the black wire terminal.
5   If voltage is present and the ground continuity is good, but the blower motor does not operate when connected, the blower motor is faulty.
6   If no voltage was present at the High speed, place the blower switch on Medium and/or Low and check for voltage at the blower motor connector, the voltage will be lower due to the resistors. If voltage is indicated on Medium and/or Low but not on High, the blower relay or related circuit is faulty (don't forget to check the fuses). Remove the blower relay **(see illustration)** for further testing (see Chapter 12).
7   If no voltage is present at the Medium and/or Low positions, disconnect the electrical connector from the blower motor resistor **(see illustration)**.
8   Using an ohmmeter, check for continuity between the terminal on the resistor corresponding to the dark blue wire terminal in the harness connector and each of the other terminals. Continuity should be indicated across each terminal, although the actual resistance values will vary. If any resistor indicates an open circuit, replace the resistor assembly.
9   To replace the blower resistor, remove the mounting screws and withdraw the resistor assembly from the housing. Inspect the resistor coils for an open circuit condition **(see illustration)**.
10   If the resistors are good, check the

blower switch. Turn the ignition to On and check for battery voltage at the yellow, tan and light blue wire terminals in the blower resistor harness connector as the blower speed switch is moved to the different positions.
11   If voltage was not indicated on one or more of the terminals, the blower speed switch could have a fault at one or more of its switch positions. Remove the heater and air conditioning control assembly (see Section 13) and check for continuity between the terminal corresponding to the brown wire in the harness connector and each of the other terminals as the switch is moved to the different speed positions **(see illustration)**. If continuity is not indicated, replace the switch assembly.
12   If the switch is good, check for battery voltage at the brown wire terminal of the harness connector with the ignition On. If voltage is not present, check the circuit from the control panel harness connector to the fuse box. Also check the circuits from the control panel to the resistor and from the resistor to the blower relay, if necessary.

11 Blower motor - removal and installation

Refer to illustrations 11.2, 11.3 and 11.4
Warning: *The models covered by this manual are equipped with airbags. Always disable the airbag system before working in the vicinity of the impact sensors, steering column or instrument panel to avoid the possibility of accidental deployment of the airbag(s), which could cause personal injury (see Chapter 12). The yellow wires and connectors routed through the instrument panel are for this system. Do not use electrical test equipment on these yellow wires or tamper with them in any way while working under the instrument panel.*

1   Remove the lower right dash insulator panel (below the glove box) for access to the blower motor (see Chapter 11).
2   Disconnect the electrical connector from the blower motor and remove the three

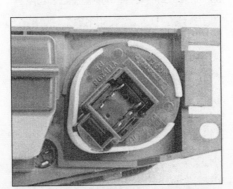

10.9 Inspect the backside of the blower resistor for burned or damaged coils

10.11 Check the terminals on the back of the blower speed switch for continuity

3

11.2 Remove the three screws (arrows) retaining the blower motor to the housing

11.3 Lower the blower motor and fan assembly straight down to remove it from the vehicle

11.4 The center (arrow) of the blower fan must be cut to remove a damaged fan

screws from the blower housing **(see illustration)**.

3   Pull the blower motor and fan straight down **(see illustration)**.

4   If the fan is damaged, it can be removed from the blower motor in several ways, as the fan is not simply retained by a nut or clip. The plastic is formed around the motor's shaft **(see illustration)**. The plastic in this area can be cut with a hot knife or a soldering iron. Then support the fan with wood or metal supports placed between the fan and the motor plate, and use a drill press or arbor press to push down on the motor shaft until it is released from the plastic. **Caution:** *Do not use a hammer or the motor shaft could be damaged*. The new fan can be pressed in

place, but it should have 0.30-inch clearance between it and the motor plate.

5   Blower motor installation is the reverse of the removal procedure.

12 Heater core - removal and installation

Warning: *The models covered by this manual are equipped with airbags. Always disable the airbag system before working in the vicinity of the impact sensors, steering column or instrument panel to avoid the possibility of accidental deployment of the airbag(s), which could cause personal injury (see Chapter 12). The yellow wires and connectors routed*

through the instrument panel are for this system. Do not use electrical test equipment on these yellow wires or tamper with them in any way while working under the instrument panel.

Removal

Refer to illustrations 12.4, 12.5a, 12.5b, 12.5c, 12.6, 12.7, 12.8a and 12.8b

1   Disconnect the battery cable at the negative battery terminal. **Caution:** *On models equipped with a Theftlock audio system, be sure the lockout feature is turned off before performing any procedure which requires disconnecting the battery.*

2   Drain the cooling system (see Chapter 1).

3   From the inside of the car, remove the lower left and right dash insulator panels (below the steering column and glove box, see Chapter 11).

4   Remove the two screws holding the rear floor duct adapter and remove the duct **(see illustration)**.

5   The heater core is located under the instrument panel behind a large plastic cover. Remove the screws around the perimeter of the cover and carefully work the cover off **(see illustrations)**.

6   Remove the screws retaining the two coolant pipe clamps **(see illustration)**

7   Remove the metal clips where the heater core pipes enter the core, then twist

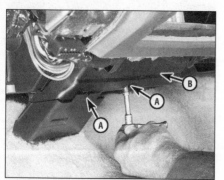

12.4 Remove the screws (A) and the rear floor duct adapter (B)

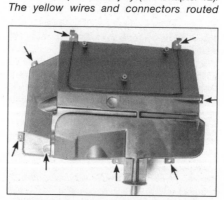

12.5a Heater core cover screw locations (arrows) (cover removed for clarity)

12.5b When you are ready to pull down the cover, fold this duct connector at the floor down against the carpet for clearance

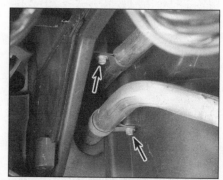

12.5c With all screws out, gently twist and pull the cover from the heater core housing

12.6 Remove these two screws (arrows) retaining the heater core pipe clamps near the firewall

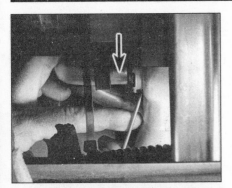

12.7 Use a small screwdriver to pry off the clips holding the pipes (arrow indicates one) to the heater core

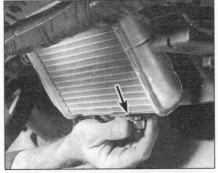

12.8a Remove the screw and take off the heater core retaining bracket (arrow)

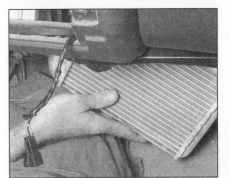

12.8b Since the pipe connections are on the left of the core, lower the core from the right first, to spill as little coolant as possible

and pull the two pipes out of the core **(see illustration)**.

8   Remove the screw and the clamp at the bottom center of the heater core and pull the core down and out **(see illustrations)**. **Caution:** *Have plenty of old towels on the floor to protect the carpet from spilled coolant.*

Installation

Refer to illustration 12.9

9   Installation is the reverse of removal. **Note:** *When reinstalling the heater core, make sure new O-rings are in place where the heater core pipes enter the core (see illustration)*.

10   Refill and bleed the cooling system (see Chapter 1).

11   Start the engine and check for leaks and proper heater operation.

13 Heater and air conditioning control assembly - removal and installation

Refer to illustrations 13.3a, 13.3b and 13.3c

Warning: *The models covered by this manual are equipped with airbags. Always disable the airbag system before working in the vicinity of the impact sensors, steering column or instrument panel to avoid the possibility of*

12.9 Replace the seals where the pipes enter the heater core (arrows)

accidental deployment of the airbag(s), which could cause personal injury (see Chapter 12). The yellow wires and connectors routed through the instrument panel are for this system. Do not use electrical test equipment on these yellow wires or tamper with them in any way while working under the instrument panel.

1   Disconnect the battery cable from the negative battery terminal. **Caution:** *On models equipped with a Theftlock audio system, be sure the lockout feature is turned off before performing any procedure which requires disconnecting the battery.*

2   Remove the main instrument panel bezel to allow access to the heater/air condi-

tioning control mounting screw (see Chapter 11).

3   Remove the control assembly retaining screw and pull the unit out and to your left to guide its tabs out of a slot-mount on the right side **(see illustration)**. Pull it out just far enough to allow disconnecting the electrical connectors from the control head **(see illustrations)**.

4   To install the control assembly, reverse the removal procedure.

14 Air conditioning and heating system - check and maintenance

Warning: *The air conditioning system is under high pressure. DO NOT loosen any fittings or remove any components until after the system has been discharged. Air conditioning refrigerant should be properly discharged into an EPA-approved recovery container at a dealership service department or an automotive air conditioning repair facility. Always wear eye protection when disconnecting air conditioning system fittings.*

1   The following maintenance steps should be performed on a regular basis to ensure that the air conditioner continues to operate at peak efficiency:

a) *Check the drivebelt (see Chapter 1).*
b) *Check the condition of the hoses. Look for cracks, hardening and deterioration.*

3

13.3a Remove the screw (arrow) on the left, then slide the panel out of its slot-mount on the right side

13.3b Pull the bezel forward, then detach the two electrical connectors by squeezing the tabs together and pulling the connectors off

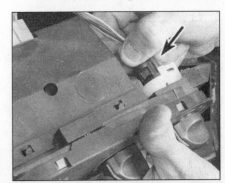

13.3c On some models, the blower speed switch connector (arrow) pulls straight out; this model has a tab that must be depressed while pulling

Look at potential leak areas (hoses and fittings) for signs of refrigerant oil leaking out. **Warning:** *Do not replace air conditioning hoses until the system has been discharged by a dealership or air conditioning repair facility.*

c) *Check the fins of the condenser for leaves, bugs and other foreign material. A soft brush and compressed air can be used to remove them.*

d) *Check the wire harness for correct routing, broken wires, damaged insulation, etc. Make sure the electrical connectors are clean and tight.*

e) *Maintain the correct refrigerant charge.*

2   The system should be run for about 10 minutes at least once a month. This is particularly important during the winter months because long-term non-use can cause hardening of the internal seals.

3   Because of the complexity of the air conditioning system and the special equipment required to effectively work on it, accurate troubleshooting of the system should be left to a certified air conditioning technician.

4   If the air conditioning system doesn't operate at all, check the fuse panel. Check the HVAC fuse and the air conditioning compressor relay.

5   Watch the air conditioning compressor while the system is on. The clutch at the front of the compressor should be engaged and turning. If it is not, connect a jumper wire with battery voltage to the clutch electrical connector. If it still doesn't operate, connect another jumper wire from the ground side of the clutch's electrical connector to an engine ground. If it still fails to engage, the clutch needs repair or replacement, both of which should be handled by a dealer service department or air conditioning repair shop.

6   If the compressor clutch did operate when the voltage was applied, check the low-pressure cycling switch (not on all models), located in the low-pressure line near or on the accumulator. Pull the electrical connector off and insert a short jumper wire (a paper clip formed into a U-shape will work) to connect both terminals. If the compressor clutch now engages, the refrigerant is probably low, see recharging procedure below.

7   The most common cause of poor cooling is simply a low system refrigerant charge. If a noticeable drop in cool air output occurs, the following quick check will help you determine if the refrigerant level is low. For more complete information on the air conditioning system, refer to the *Haynes Automotive Heating and Air Conditioning Manual.*

Checking the refrigerant charge

Refer to illustration 14.11

8   Warm the engine up to normal operating temperature.

9   Place the air conditioning temperature selector at the coldest setting and the blower at the highest setting. Open the doors (to make sure the air conditioning system doesn't cycle off as soon as it cools the passenger compartment).

10   With the compressor engaged - the clutch will make an audible click and the center of the clutch will rotate - feel the surface of the accumulator and the evaporator inlet pipe. **Note:** *The 3800 V6 uses a type of compressor that does not cycle; it changes its stroke to match system demand.* If the smaller diameter line feels warm and the receiver/drier feels cool, the system is properly charged. On 3800 V6 models, feel the pipe on either side of the expansion tube - there should be a noticeable difference in temperature.

11   Place a thermometer in the dashboard vent nearest the evaporator and add refrigerant to the system until the indicated temperature is around 40 to 45-degrees F **(see illustration)**. If the ambient (outside) air temperature is very high, say 110-degrees F, the duct air temperature will probably be higher, but generally the air conditioning is 30 to 40-degrees F cooler than the ambient air. **Note:** *Humidity of the ambient air also affects the cooling capacity of the system. Higher ambient humidity lowers the effectiveness of the air conditioning system.*

Adding refrigerant

Refer to illustrations 14.12 and 14.15

Note: *There are two types of refrigerant; R-12, used on earlier models, and the more environmentally friendly R-134a used on all* models covered by this book. These two refrigerants (and their appropriate refrigerant oils) are not compatible and must never be mixed or components will be damaged. Use only R-134a refrigerant and compatible oils when servicing your system.

12   Buy an R-134a automotive charging kit at an auto parts store. A charging kit includes a 14-ounce can of refrigerant, a tap valve and a short section of hose that can be attached between the tap valve and the system low side service valve **(see illustration)**. Because one can of refrigerant may not be sufficient to bring the system charge up to the proper level, it's a good idea to buy an extra can. Make sure that one of the cans contains red refrigerant dye. If the system is leaking, the red dye will leak out with the refrigerant and help you pinpoint the location of the leak.

13   Hook up the charging kit by following the manufacturer's instructions. **Warning:** *DO NOT hook the charging kit hose to the system high side! The fittings on the charging kit are designed to fit only on the low side of the system.*

14   Back off the valve handle on the charging kit and screw the kit onto the refrigerant can, making sure first that the O-ring or rubber seal inside the threaded portion of the kit is in place. **Warning:** *Wear protective eye wear when dealing with pressurized refrigerant cans.*

15   Remove the dust cap from the low-side charging connection and attach the quick-connect fitting on the kit hose **(see illustration)**.

16   Warm up the engine and turn on the air conditioner. Keep the charging kit hose away from the fan and other moving parts. **Note:** *The charging process requires the compressor to be running. Your compressor may cycle off if the pressure is low due to a low charge. If the clutch cycles off, you can pull the low-pressure cycling switch plug from the evaporator inlet line and attach a jumper wire across the terminals. This will keep the compressor ON.*

17   Turn the valve handle on the kit until the stem pierces the can, then back the handle out to release the refrigerant. You should be able to hear the rush of gas. Add refrigerant to the low side of the system until both the

14.11 Use a thermometer in the center dash vent while the air conditioning is ON to check for cooling efficiency

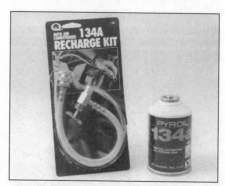

14.12 A basic charging kit for R-134a systems is available at most auto parts stores

14.15 Add refrigerant to the low-side port only (arrow) - the procedure is easier if you wrap the can with a warm, wet towel to prevent icing

accumulator surface and the evaporator inlet pipe feel about the same temperature. Allow stabilization time between each addition.

18 If you have an accurate thermometer, you can place it in the center air conditioning duct inside the vehicle and keep track of the "conditioned" air temperature. A charged system that is working properly should put out air that is 40-degrees F. If the ambient (outside) air temperature is very high, say 110-degrees F, the duct air temperature will probably be higher, but generally the air conditioning is 30 to 40-degrees-F cooler than the ambient air.

19 When the can is empty, turn the valve handle to the closed position and release the connection from the low-side port. Replace the dust cap. **Warning:** *Never add more than one can of refrigerant to the system (if more than one can is required, the system should be evacuated and leak tested).*

20 Remove the charging kit from the can and store the kit for future use with the piercing valve in the UP position, to prevent inadvertently piercing the can on the next use.

Heating systems

21 If the carpet under the heater core is damp, or if antifreeze vapor or steam is coming through the vents, the heater core is leaking. Remove it (see Section 12) and install a new unit (most radiator shops will not repair a leaking heater core).

22 If the air coming out of the heater vents isn't hot, the problem could stem from any of the following causes:

a) *The thermostat is stuck open, preventing the engine coolant from warming up enough to carry heat to the heater core. Replace the thermostat (see Section 3).*

b) *A heater hose is blocked, preventing the flow of coolant through the heater core. Feel both heater hoses at the firewall. They should be hot. If one of them is cold, there is an obstruction in one of the hoses or in the heater core, or the heater control valve is shut. Detach the hoses and back flush the heater core with a water hose. If the heater core is clear but circulation is impeded, remove the two hoses and flush them out with a water hose.*

c) *If flushing fails to remove the blockage*

from the heater core, the core must be replaced (see Section 12).

23 If the blower motor speed does not correspond to the setting selected on the blower switch, the problem could be a bad fuse, circuit, control panel or blower resistor (see Section 10).

24 If there isn't any air coming out of the vents:

a) *Turn the ignition ON and activate the fan control. Place your ear at the heating/air conditioning register (vent) and listen. Most motors are audible. Can you hear the motor running?*

b) *If you can't (and have already verified that the blower switch and the blower motor resistor are good), the blower motor itself is probably bad (see Section 11).*

25 Inspect the drain hose from the heater/evaporator assembly at the right-center of the firewall, make sure it is not clogged **(see illustration)**. If there is a humid mist coming from the system ducts, this hose may be plugged with leaves or road debris.

Eliminating air conditioning odors

26 Unpleasant odors that often develop in air conditioning systems are caused by the growth of a fungus, usually on the surface of the evaporator core. The warm, humid environment there is a perfect breeding ground for mildew to develop.

27 The evaporator core on most vehicles is difficult to access, and factory dealerships have a lengthy, expensive process for eliminating the fungus by opening up the evaporator case and using a powerful disinfectant and rinse on the core until the fungus is gone. You can service your own system at home, but it takes something much stronger than basic household germ-killers or deodorizers.

28 Aerosol disinfectants for automotive air conditioning systems are available in most auto parts stores, but remember when shopping for them that the most effective treatments are also the most expensive. The basic procedure for using these sprays is to start by running the system in the RECIRC mode for ten minutes with the blower on its highest speed. Use the highest heat mode to dry out the system and keep the compressor

from engaging by disconnecting the wiring connector at the compressor (see Section 16).

29 The disinfectant can usually comes with a long spray hose. Remove the blower motor resistor (see Section 11), point the nozzle inside the hole and spray, according to the manufacturer's recommendations. Try to cover the whole surface of the evaporator core, by aiming the spray up, down and sideways. Follow the manufacturer's recommendations for the length of spray and waiting time between applications.

30 Once the evaporator has been cleaned, the best way to prevent the mildew from coming back again is to make sure your evaporator housing drain tube is clear **(see illustration 14.25)**.

15 Air conditioning accumulator/drier - removal and installation

Warning: *The air conditioning system is under high pressure. DO NOT loosen any fittings or remove any components until after the system has been discharged. Air conditioning refrigerant should be properly discharged into an EPA-approved container at a dealership service department or an automotive air conditioning repair facility. Always wear eye protection when disconnecting air conditioning system fittings.*

Removal

Refer to illustrations 15.2 and 15.3

1 Have the air conditioning system discharged (see **Warning** above). Disconnect the cable from the negative terminal of the battery. **Caution:** *On models equipped with a Theftlock audio system, be sure the lockout feature is turned off before performing any procedure which requires disconnecting the battery.*

2 Disconnect the refrigerant inlet and outlet lines **(see illustration)**, using a back-up wrench. Cap or plug the open lines immediately to prevent the entry of dirt or moisture.

3 Loosen the clamp bolt on the mounting bracket and slide the accumulator/drier assembly up and out of the bracket **(see illustration)**.

14.25 Check that the evaporator drain tube (arrow) on the firewall is not plugged

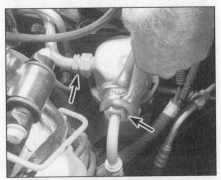

15.2 Disconnect the inlet and outlet lines (arrows) using a backup wrench so the line doesn't get twisted

15.3 Remove the accumulator clamp bolt (arrow)

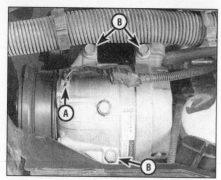

16.8 Disconnect the electrical connector (A) from the air conditioning compressor - on the 3.1L model there are three mounting bolts (B)

16.9 Remove the retaining bolt (arrow) securing the refrigerant lines to back of the compressor

17.2 The condenser lines (arrows) are located just to the left of the radiator

Installation

4   If you are replacing the accumulator/drier with a new one, drain the old oil out of the old drier into a measuring container. Add that amount of new oil, plus one ounce, to the new unit (oil must be R-134a compatible).

5   Place the new accumulator/drier into position in the bracket.

6   Install the inlet and outlet lines, using clean refrigerant oil on the new O-rings. Tighten the mounting bolt securely.

7   Connect the cable to the negative terminal of the battery.

8   Have the system evacuated, recharged and leak tested by a dealership service department or an automotive air conditioning repair facility.

16   Air conditioning compressor - removal and installation

Warning: *The air conditioning system is under high pressure. DO NOT loosen any fittings or remove any components until after the system has been discharged. Air conditioning refrigerant should be properly discharged into an EPA-approved container at a dealership service department or an automotive air conditioning repair facility. Always wear eye protection when disconnecting air conditioning system fittings.*
Note: *The accumulator/drier (see Section 15) and the expansion (orifice) tube (see Section 19) should be replaced whenever the compressor is replaced.*

Removal

Refer to illustrations 16.8 and 16.9

1   Have the air conditioning system discharged (see **Warning** above). Disconnect the cable from the negative terminal of the battery. **Caution:** *On models equipped with Theftlock audio system, be sure the lockout feature is turned off before performing any procedure which requires disconnecting the battery.*

2   Clean the compressor thoroughly around the refrigerant line fittings.

3   Remove the serpentine drivebelt (see Chapter 1).

4   Refer to Section 4 and remove the right-side electric cooling fan.

5   On 3.1L and 3800 engines, refer to Chapter 2 Part A or Part C and remove the right-side engine strut mount bracket.

6   On most models, a plastic splash shield must be removed from underneath for access to the compressor mounts.

7   Raise the vehicle and support it securely on jackstands.

8   Disconnect the electrical connector from the air conditioning compressor **(see illustration)**.

9   Disconnect the suction and discharge lines from the compressor. Both lines are mounted to the back of the compressor with a plate secured by one bolt **(see illustration)**. Plug the open fittings to prevent the entry of dirt and moisture, and discard the seals between the plate and compressor.

10   On 3.1L models, remove the three bolts **(see illustration 16.8)** and remove the compressor. On 3.4L and 3800 engines, unbolt and remove the rear compressor mount.

11   On 3.4L and 3800 models, remove the compressor-to-front-bracket bolts (3.4L) or nuts (3800) and remove the compressor from the engine compartment. **Note:** *On 3800 models, the compressor must be pulled forward off the three studs on its front mount. If there isn't room, the front engine mount may have to be removed (refer to Chapter 2, Part C).*

Installation

12   If a new compressor is being installed, drain the new compressor of oil. Drain the oil from the old compressor into a graduated container. If less than one ounce was drained, add two ounces of new oil to the new compressor. If more than one ounce was drained from the old compressor, add that exact amount of new oil to the new compressor. Also follow any directions included with the new compressor. **Note:** *Some replacement compressors come with refrigerant oil in them. Follow the directions*

with the compressor regarding the draining of excess oil prior to installation. **Caution:** *The oil used must be labeled as compatible with R-134a systems.*

13   Installation is the reverse of the disassembly. When installing the line fitting bolt to the compressor, use new seals lubricated with clean refrigerant oil, and tighten the bolt securely.

14   Reconnect the battery cable to the negative battery terminal.

15   Have the system evacuated, recharged and leak tested by a dealership service department or an automotive air conditioning repair facility.

17   Air conditioning condenser - removal and installation

Warning: *The air conditioning system is under high pressure. DO NOT loosen any fittings or remove any components until after the system has been discharged. Air conditioning refrigerant should be properly discharged into an EPA-approved container at a dealership service department or an automotive air conditioning repair facility. Always wear eye protection when disconnecting air conditioning system fittings.*

Removal

Refer to illustrations 17.2 and 17.4

1   Have the air conditioning system discharged and recovered (see **Warning** above). Disconnect the cable from the negative terminal of the battery. **Caution:** *On models equipped with a Theftlock audio system, be sure the lockout feature is turned off before performing any procedure which requires disconnecting the battery.*

2   Disconnect the refrigerant line fittings from the right side of the condenser and cap the open fittings to prevent the entry of dirt and moisture. **(see illustration)**.

3   Remove the cooling fans (see Section 4) and the radiator (see Section 5).

4   Pull the condenser toward the engine, wiggling it until it is free of the upper and lower rubber insulators, then withdraw it

17.4 Pull the condenser core carefully until it is free of the rubber insulators (arrows)

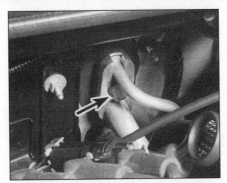

18.3 Remove the clamp bolt (arrow) and disconnect the two refrigerant lines at the firewall

18.5a Remove the screws and the evaporator core cover . . .

carefully from the vehicle **(see illustration)**. **Caution:** *The condenser is made of aluminum - be careful not to damage it during removal.*

Installation

5   Installation is the reverse of removal. Be sure to use new, compatible O-rings on the refrigerant line fittings lubricated the O-rings with clean refrigerant oil. If a new condenser is installed, add 1 ounce of new refrigerant oil to the system (R-134a compatible).

6   Have the system evacuated, recharged and leak tested by a dealership service department or an automotive air conditioning repair facility.

18 Air conditioning evaporator - removal and installation

Warning 1: *The models covered by this manual are equipped with airbags. Always disable the airbag system before working in the vicinity of the impact sensors, steering column or instrument panel to avoid the possibility of accidental deployment of the airbag(s), which could cause personal injury (see Chapter 12). The yellow wires and connectors routed through the instrument panel are for this system. Do not use electrical test equipment on these yellow*

wires or tamper with them in any way while working under the instrument panel.
Warning 2: *The air conditioning system is under high pressure. DO NOT loosen any fittings or remove any components until after the system has been discharged. Air conditioning refrigerant should be properly discharged into an EPA-approved container at a dealership service department or an automotive air conditioning repair facility. Always wear eye protection when disconnecting air conditioning system fittings.*

Removal

Refer to illustrations 18.3, 18.5a and 18.5b

1   Have the air conditioning system discharged and the refrigerant recovered (see **Warning** above). Disconnect the cable from the negative terminal of the battery. **Caution:** *On models equipped with a Theftlock audio system, be sure the lockout feature is turned off before performing any procedure which requires disconnecting the battery.*

2   Drain the cooling system (see Chapter 1).

3   Disconnect the air conditioning lines at the passenger side of the firewall **(see illustration)**.

4   Follow the procedures in Section 12 for removing the heater core.

5   Remove the evaporator core cover, then slide the evaporator core out carefully **(see illustrations)**.

6   Check the core over carefully for signs of leaks.

7   If a new evaporator core is to be installed, save all of the sealing gaskets from the original unit and transfer them.

Installation

8   Installation is the reverse of the removal procedure. Lubricate all O-rings with clean refrigerant oil.

9   If a new evaporator has been installed, add 3 ounces of new refrigerant oil (oil must be R-134a compatible). Have the system evacuated, recharged and leak tested by a dealership service department or an automotive air conditioning repair facility.

19 Air conditioning expansion (orifice) tube - removal and installation

Refer to illustrations 19.3 and 19.4
Warning: *The air conditioning system is under high pressure. DO NOT loosen any fittings or remove any components until after the system has been discharged. Air conditioning refrigerant should be properly discharged into an EPA-approved container at a dealership service department or an automotive air conditioning repair facility. Always wear eye protection when disconnecting air conditioning system fittings.*
Note: *Whenever the expansion tube is replaced, the accumulator-drier should also be replaced (see Section 15).*

1   Have the air conditioning system discharged and the refrigerant recovered (see **Warning** above). Disconnect the cable from the negative terminal of the battery. **Caution:** *On models equipped with a Theftlock audio system, be sure the lockout feature is turned off before performing any procedure which requires disconnecting the battery.*

2   Remove the air cleaner and duct (see Chapter 4).

3   Disconnect the refrigerant high-pressure line at the fitting right over the transaxle, about ten inches behind the accumulator/drier **(see illustration)**.

4   The expansion *(orifice)* tube is a tube

3

18.5b . . . then pull the evaporator core (arrow) down and out to remove it

19.3 Disconnect the high pressure line at this fitting (arrow) to replace the expansion (orifice) tube

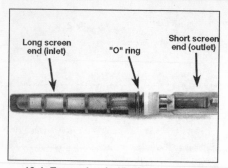

Long screen end (inlet)　"O" ring　Short screen end (outlet)

19.4 Expansion (orifice) tube details

with a fixed-diameter orifice and a mesh filter at each end **(see illustration)**. When you separate the pipe at the fitting you will see one end of the orifice tube inside the pipe leading to the evaporator. Use needle-nose pliers to remove the orifice tube.

5　The orifice tube acts to meter the refrigerant, changing it from high-pressure liquid to low-pressure liquid. It is possible to reuse the orifice tube if:

a) *The screens aren't plugged with grit or foreign material*

b) *Neither screen is torn*

c) *The plastic housing over the screens is intact*

d) *The brass orifice inside the plastic housing is unrestricted*

6　Installation is the reverse of removal. Be sure to insert the expansion tube with the shorter end in first, toward the evaporator. **Caution:** *Always use a new O-ring when installing the expansion tube.*

7　Retighten the fitting and refrigerant line, then have the system evacuated, recharged and leak-tested by the shop that discharged it.

Chapter 4
Fuel and exhaust systems

Contents

Specifications

General

Fuel pressure (key On, engine not running)

1995	41 to 47 psi
1996	48 to 55 psi
1997	41 to 47 psi
1998	
3.1L	41 to 47 psi
3.8L	48 to 55 psi

Fuel pressure at idle (with vacuum to fuel pressure regulator)

1995	31 to 44 psi
1996	38 to 52 psi
1997	31 to 44 psi
1998	
3.1L	31 to 44 psi
3.8L	38 to 52 psi
Injector resistance	11.4 to 12.6 ohms

Torque specifications

Ft-lbs (unless otherwise indicated)

Exhaust pipe-to-manifold nuts	15 to 22
Fuel pressure regulator mounting screw	80 in-lbs
Fuel pressure regulator to fuel pipe nut	156 in-lbs
Fuel rail mounting bolts	89 in-lbs
IAC valve screws	27 in-lbs
Throttle body bolts/nuts	18

1   General information

All models are equipped with Multiport Fuel Injection (MFI) system and OBD II self-diagnosis system except 1995 3.1L engines which are equipped with OBD I self-diagnosis system (see Chapter 6).

The fuel system consists of a fuel tank, an electric fuel pump and fuel pump relay, an air cleaner assembly and a fuel injection system.

Multiport Fuel Injection (MFI) system

This system utilizes injectors mounted above each intake port. The throttle body on the MFI system serves only to control the amount of air passing into the system. Because each cylinder is equipped with an injector mounted immediately adjacent to the intake valve, much better control of the fuel/air mixture ratio is possible.

Fuel pump and lines

Fuel is circulated from the fuel tank to the fuel injection system, and back to the fuel tank, through a pair of lines running along the underside of the vehicle. An electric fuel pump is attached to the fuel sending unit inside the fuel tank. A return system routes all vapors and excess fuel back to the fuel tank through separate return lines.

Exhaust system

The exhaust system includes an exhaust manifold fitted with an exhaust oxygen sensor, a catalytic converter, an exhaust pipe, and a muffler. The catalytic converter is an emission control device added to the exhaust system to reduce pollutants. A single-bed converter is used in combination with a three-way (reduction) catalyst. Refer to Chapter 6 for more information regarding the catalytic converter.

2   Fuel pressure relief procedure

Refer to illustrations 2.3a and 2.3b

Warning: *Gasoline is extremely flammable, so take extra precautions when you work on any part of the fuel system. Don't smoke or allow open flames or bare light bulbs near the work area, and don't work in a garage where a natural gas-type appliance (such as a water heater or a clothes dryer) with a pilot light is present. Since gasoline is carcinogenic, wear latex gloves when there's a possibility of being exposed to fuel, and, if you spill any* fuel on your skin, rinse it off immediately with soap and water. Mop up any spills immediately and do not store fuel-soaked rags where they could ignite. The fuel system is under constant pressure, so, if any fuel lines are to be disconnected, the fuel pressure in the system must be relieved first. When you perform any kind of work on the fuel system, wear safety glasses and have a Class B type fire extinguisher on hand.

Caution: After the fuel pressure has been relieved, it's a good idea to lay a shop towel over any fuel connection to be disassembled, to absorb the residual fuel that may leak out.

1   Before servicing any fuel system component, you must relieve the fuel pressure to minimize the risk of fire or personal injury.

2   Remove the fuel filler cap - this will relieve any pressure built up in the tank.

3   Locate the test port on the fuel rail and connect a fuel pressure gauge, equipped with a bleed-off valve and drain tube, to the test port. **Note:** On all 3.1L engines, the fuel pressure test port is located at the front (passenger side) of the engine on the end of the right (rear) fuel rail. On 1995 3.4L engines, the fuel pressure test port is located at the front (passenger side) of the engine in the crossover pipe between the fuel rails. On 1996 through 1997 3.4L engines, the fuel pressure test port is located on the left (front) fuel rail which requires removing the injector trim cover to access the test port (see Section 13). On 1998 3.8L engines, the fuel pressure test port is located at the fuel pressure regulator **(see illustration)** which also requires removing the injector trim cover to access the test port (see Section 13). Relieve the fuel pressure by bleeding the fuel through the bleed-off valve and into a metal can **(see illustration)**.

4   If the specialized fuel pressure gauge is not available, follow this alternate method that will easily bleed the fuel pressure. Disconnect the cable from the negative terminal of the battery. **Caution:** On models equipped with a Theftlock audio system, be sure the lockout feature is turned off before performing any procedure which requires disconnecting the battery. Place a bundle of

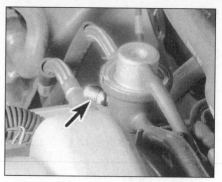

2.3a On 3.8L engines, the fuel pressure test port (arrow) is located on the fuel pressure regulator - unscrew the cap and install a fuel pump pressure gauge

rags under and around the fuel pressure test port. Cover the port with another rag and depress the core of the Schrader valve with a small screwdriver, allowing the fuel to bleed out into the rags. Dispose of the rags in a covered, marked container.

5   Unless this procedure is followed before servicing fuel lines or connections, fuel spray (and possible injury) may occur.

---

3   Fuel pump/fuel pressure - check

Warning: Gasoline is extremely flammable, so take extra precautions when you work on any part of the fuel system. See the **Warning** in Section 2.

Note: In order to perform the fuel pressure test, you will need to obtain a fuel pressure gauge capable of measuring high fuel pressure and an adapter set for the fuel injection system being tested.

Preliminary checks

1   Check that there is adequate fuel in the fuel tank.

2   Verify the fuel pump actually runs. Have an assistant turn the ignition switch to ON - you should hear a brief whirring noise (approximately two seconds) as the pump comes on and pressurizes the system. **Note:**

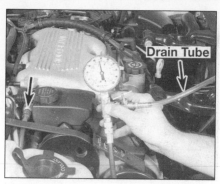

2.3b Attach a fuel pressure gauge to the test port (arrow) and open the valve to drain the excess fuel out of the drain tube (arrow) and into an approved fuel container (3.1L engine shown)

The fuel pump is easily heard through the gas tank filler neck. If there is no response from the fuel pump (makes no sound) proceed to Step 9 and check the fuel pump electrical circuit.

Fuel pump output and pressure check

Refer to illustrations 3.6 and 3.7

3   Connect a fuel pressure gauge to the fuel pressure test port (see Section 2 for test port location).

4   Turn the ignition switch ON (engine not running) with the air conditioning off. The fuel pump should run for about two seconds - note the reading on the gauge. After the pump stops running the pressure should hold steady. It should be within the range listed in this Chapter's Specifications.

5   Start the engine and let it idle at normal operating temperature. The pressure should be lower by 3 to 10 psi. If all the pressure readings are within the limits listed in this Chapter's Specifications, the system is operating properly.

6   If the pressure did not drop by 3 to 10 psi after starting the engine, apply 12 to 14 inches of vacuum to the pressure regulator, using a hand-held vacuum pump **(see illustration)**. If the pressure drops, repair the vacuum source to the regulator. If the pressure does not drop, replace the regulator.

7   If the fuel pressure is not within specifications, check the following:

a) If the pressure is higher than specified, check for vacuum to the fuel pressure regulator **(see illustration)**. Vacuum must fluctuate with the increase or decrease in the engine rpm. If vacuum is present, check for a pinched or clogged fuel return hose or pipe. If the return line is OK, replace the regulator.

b) If the pressure is lower than specified, change the fuel filter to rule out the possibility of a clogged filter. If the pressure is still low, install a fuel line shut-off adapter between the pressure regulator and the return line (this can be fabricated from fuel line, a shut off valve

3.6 Connect a vacuum pump to the fuel pressure regulator, apply vacuum to the fuel pressure regulator and check the fuel pressure - the fuel pressure should decrease as the vacuum increases

3.7 Disconnect the vacuum hose from the fuel pressure regulator (arrow) and check for vacuum - vacuum must fluctuate with the increase or decrease in engine rpm

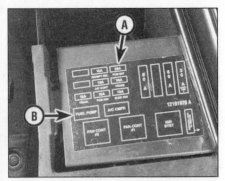

3.9 The ECM or PCM BAT fuse (A) and the fuel pump relay (B) locations are clearly marked on the cover of the passenger side fuse/relay control box in the engine compartment

3.10 Remove the fuel pump relay and check for voltage at the electrical connector (arrow) while the ignition key is cycled ON and OFF - one terminal should have battery voltage at all times with the ignition key ON, and another terminal should have voltage for about two seconds with the ignition key ON

and the necessary fittings to mate with the pressure regulator and the return line, or, instead of a shut-off valve, use fuel hose that can be pinched with a pair of pliers). With the valve open (or the hose not pinched), start the engine (if possible) and slowly close the valve or pinch the hose (only pinch the hose on the adapter you fabricated). If the pressure rises above 47 psi, replace the regulator (see Section 13). **Warning:** *Don't allow the fuel pressure to exceed 60 psi. Also, don't attempt to restrict the vehicle's return line by pinching it, as the nylon fuel line will be damaged.*

c) *If the pressure is still low with the fuel return line restricted, an injector (or injectors) may be leaking (see Section 13) or the in-tank fuel pump may be faulty.*

8   After the testing is done, relieve the fuel pressure (see Section 2) and remove the fuel pressure gauge.

Fuel pump electrical circuit check

Refer to illustrations 3.9 and 3.10

Note: *Refer to Chapter 12 for additional wiring schematics that detail the fuel pump relay and circuit.*

9   If the pump does not turn on (makes no sound) with the ignition switch in the ON position, check the ECM BAT (fuel pump) fuse **(see illustration)**. If the fuse is blown, replace the fuse and see if the pump works. If the pump now works, check for a short in the circuit between the fuel pump relay and the fuel pump.

10   If the pump still does not work, check the fuel pump relay circuit. With the help of an assistant cycle the ignition key ON and OFF (engine not running), while checking for battery voltage at the relay connector **(see illustration)**. If battery voltage does not exist, check the circuit from the PCM to the relay.

Note 1: *If oil pressure drops below the specified pressure level, the oil pressure switch will act as a fuel pressure cut-off device. Be sure to check the oil pressure*

switch and circuit in the event of a difficult problem diagnosing the fuel pump circuit (refer to the wiring diagrams at the end of Chapter 12).

Note 2: *The theft deterrent system (if equipped) is equipped with a fuel enable circuit. If this system is malfunctioning it will not allow the PCM to signal the fuel pump relay or the engine to crank over. Be sure to check the theft deterrent system and circuit in the event of a difficult problem diagnosing the fuel pump circuit.*

11   If battery voltage exists, check the relay (see Chapter 12) or replace the relay with a known good relay and retest. If necessary, have the relay checked by a qualified automotive electrical specialist.

12   If the fuel pump does not activate, check for power to the fuel pump at the fuel tank. Access to the fuel pump is difficult, but it is possible to check for battery voltage at the electrical connector near the tank. If voltage is present at the fuel pump connector, replace the fuel pump.

4   Fuel lines and fittings - repair and replacement

Warning: *Gasoline is extremely flammable, so take extra precautions when you work on any part of the fuel system. See the* **Warning** *in Section 2.*

1   Always relieve the fuel pressure before servicing fuel lines or fittings on fuel-injected vehicles (see Section 2).

2   The fuel feed, return and vapor lines extend from the fuel tank to the engine compartment. The lines are secured to the underbody with clip and screw assemblies. These lines must be occasionally inspected for leaks, kinks and dents.

3   If evidence of dirt is found in the system or fuel filter during disassembly, the line should be disconnected and blown out. Check the fuel strainer on the fuel level

sending unit (see Section 8) for damage and deterioration.

Steel and nylon tubing

4   Because fuel lines used on fuel-injected vehicles are under high pressure, they require special consideration.

5   If replacement of a metal fuel line or emission line is called for, use welded steel tubing meeting original equipment specifications. Don't use copper or aluminum tubing to replace steel tubing. These materials cannot withstand normal vehicle vibration.

6   If is becomes necessary to replace a section of nylon fuel line, replace it only with the correct part number - don't use any substitutes.

7   Some fuel lines have threaded fittings with O-rings. Any time the fittings are loosened to service or replace components:

a) *Use a back-up wrench while loosening and tightening the fittings.*

b) *Check all O-rings for cuts, cracks and deterioration. Replace any that appear worn or damaged.*

c) *If the lines are replaced, always use original equipment parts, or parts that meet the GM standards specified in this Section.*

d) *Use specialty fuel line disconnect tools to release the spring-lock mechanisms inside the quick-disconnect fuel line fittings particular to many of the components (fuel filter, fuel rail, fuel pressure regulator, etc.).*

Rubber hose

Warning: *These models are equipped with electronic fuel injection - use only original equipment replacement hoses or their equivalent. Others may fail from the high pressures of this system.*

8   When rubber hose is used to replace a metal line, use reinforced, fuel resistant hose. Hose other than this could fail prematurely and could fail to meet Federal emission standards. Hose inside diameter must match line outside diameter. **Warning:** *Don't substitute rubber hose for metal line on high-pressure systems. Use only genuine factory replacement lines or lines meeting factory specifications.*

9   Don't use rubber hose within four inches of any part of the exhaust system or within ten inches of the catalytic converter. Metal lines and rubber hoses must never be allowed to chafe against the frame. A minimum of 1/4-inch clearance must be maintained around a line or hose to prevent contact with the frame.

Removal and installation

Refer to illustrations 4.10, 4.12a, 4.12b and 4.13

Note: *The following procedure and accompanying illustrations are typical for vehicles covered by this manual. On quick-disconnect (non-threaded) fittings, clean off the fittings*

4

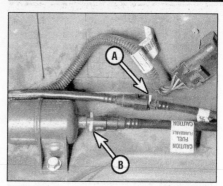

4.10 Some models are equipped with fuel lines that can be disconnected by pinching the tabs and separating each connector

A Fuel return line   B Fuel feed line

before disconnection to prevent dirt from getting in the fittings. After disconnection, clean the fittings with compressed air and apply a few drops of oil.

10   Relieve the fuel pressure (see Section 2) and disconnect the fuel feed, return or vapor line at the fuel tank **(see illustration)**. **Note:** *Some fuel line connections may be threaded. Be sure to use a back-up wrench when separating the connections.*

11   Remove all fasteners attaching the lines to the vehicle body.

12   Detach the fitting(s) that attach the fuel hoses to the engine compartment metal lines **(see illustrations)**. Twisting them back and forth will allow them to separate more easily.

13   Installation is the reverse of removal.

4.13 Always replace the fuel line O-rings (if equipped)

5.6 Loosen the clamps and remove the fuel filler and the vapor return hoses (arrows)

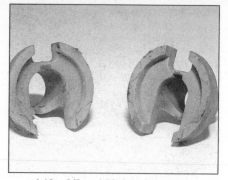

4.12a 3/8 and 5/16-inch fuel line disconnect tools

Be sure to use new O-rings at the threaded fittings, if equipped **(see illustration)**.

5   Fuel tank - removal and installation

Refer to illustrations 5.6, 5.7 and 5.9
Warning: *Gasoline is extremely flammable, so take extra precautions when you work on any part of the fuel system. See the* **Warning** *in Section 2.*
Note: *Don't begin this procedure until the fuel gauge indicates the tank is empty or nearly empty. If the tank must be removed when it isn't empty (for example, if the fuel pump malfunctions), siphon any remaining fuel from the tank prior to removal.*

1   Unless the vehicle has been driven far enough to completely empty the tank, it's a good idea to siphon the residual fuel out before removing the tank from the vehicle. **Warning:** *DO NOT start the siphoning action by mouth! Use a siphoning kit, available at most auto parts stores.*

2   Relieve the fuel system pressure (see Section 2).

3   Detach the cable from the negative terminal of the battery. **Caution:** *On models equipped with a Theftlock audio system, be sure the lockout feature is turned off before performing any procedure which requires disconnecting the battery.*

5.7 Use the special fuel line disconnect tools to disengage the fuel lines at the front of the fuel tank

4.12b On quick-connect fuel lines, use the special fuel line disconnect tools and push them into the connector (arrows) to separate the fuel lines

4   Raise the vehicle and support it securely on jackstands.

5   Disconnect the exhaust rubber hangers and allow the rear portion of the exhaust system to rest on the rear axle, then remove the exhaust pipe heat shields.

6   Disconnect the fuel filler hose and vapor lines from the fuel tank **(see illustration)**.

7   Disconnect the fuel feed and return lines and the vapor return line from the fuel pump **(see illustration)**. **Note:** *Use special fuel line disconnect tools (see Section 4) to separate the fuel lines from the harness assembly near the fuel tank supports.*

8   Support the fuel tank with a floor jack.

9   Disconnect both fuel tank retaining straps **(see illustration)**.

10   Lower the tank enough to disconnect the electrical connectors from the fuel pump/fuel level sending unit.

11   Remove the tank from the vehicle.

12   Installation is the reverse of removal.

6   Fuel tank cleaning and repair - general information

1   All repairs to the fuel tank or filler neck should be carried out by a professional who has experience in this critical and potentially dangerous work. Even after cleaning and flushing of the fuel system, explosive fumes can remain and ignite during repair of the tank.

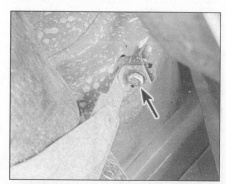

5.9 Support the fuel tank with a jack and remove the fuel tank strap bolts (arrow)

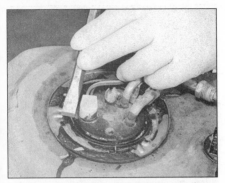

7.5 On early models, carefully tap the lock ring counterclockwise until the locking tabs align with the slots in the fuel tank

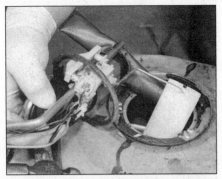

7.6 Lift the fuel pump assembly from the fuel tank and make sure the float and the strainer are not damaged by carefully angling the assembly out of the fuel tank opening

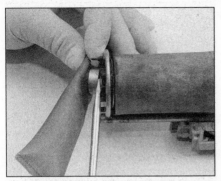

7.8 Pry on the collar to detach the strainer (filter) from the fuel pump

2   If the fuel tank is removed from the vehicle, it should not be placed in an area where sparks or open flames could ignite the fumes coming out of the tank. Be especially careful inside garages where a natural gas-type appliance is located, because the pilot light could cause an explosion.

7   Fuel pump - removal and installation

Warning: *Gasoline is extremely flammable, so take extra precautions when you work on any part of the fuel system. See the **Warning** in Section 2.*
1   Relieve the fuel system pressure (see Section 2).
2   Disconnect the cable from the negative battery terminal. **Caution:** *On models equipped with a Delco Loc II or Theftlock audio system, be sure the lockout feature is turned off before performing any procedure which requires disconnecting the battery.*
3   The fuel pump/sending unit assembly is located inside the fuel tank on all models covered by this manual. Remove the fuel tank from the vehicle (see Section 5).

1995 and 1996 models

Refer to illustrations 7.5, 7.6, 7.8, 7.9 and 7.10
4   The fuel pump/sending unit assembly on these models is held in place by a cam

lock ring mechanism consisting of an inner ring with three locking cams and a fixed outer ring with three retaining tangs.
5   To unlock the fuel pump/sending unit assembly, turn the inner ring counter-clockwise until the locking cams are free of the retaining tangs **(see illustration)**.
6   Lift the fuel pump/sending unit assembly out of the tank **(see illustration)**. **Caution:** *The fuel level float and sending unit are delicate. Don't bump them during removal or the accuracy of the sending unit may be affected.*
7   Inspect the condition of the O-ring around the opening of the tank. If it is dried, cracked or deteriorated, replace it.
8   Remove the strainer from the lower end of the fuel pump **(see illustration)**. If it's dirty, remove it, clean it with solvent and blow it out with compressed air. If it's too dirty to be cleaned, replace it.
9   Disconnect the electrical connector from the fuel pump **(see illustration)**.
10   Separate the fuel pump from the bracket **(see illustration)**.
11   Installation of a new fuel pump is the reverse of removal.
12   Position a new rubber O-ring around the opening in the fuel tank and guide the fuel pump/sending unit assembly into the tank.
13   Turn the inner lock ring clockwise until the locking cams are fully engaged by the retaining tangs. **Note:** *Since you've installed a new O-ring, it may be necessary to push*

down on the inner lock ring until the locking cams slide under the retaining tangs.
14   Install the fuel tank (see Section 5).

1997 and 1998 models

Refer to illustrations 7.15, 7.16, 7.18a, 7.18b and 7.21
15   The fuel pump/sending unit assembly on these models is held in place by a snap-ring. Using a pair of snap-ring pliers, expand the retaining collar and remove it from the top of the fuel pump assembly **(see illustration)**.
16   Lift the fuel pump/sending unit assembly from the fuel tank **(see illustration)**. **Caution:** *The fuel level float and sending unit are delicate. Do not bump them against the tank during removal or the accuracy of the sending unit may be affected.*

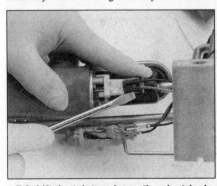

7.9 Lift the tab to release the electrical connector from the fuel pump

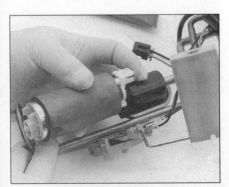

7.10 Remove the fuel pump from the bracket

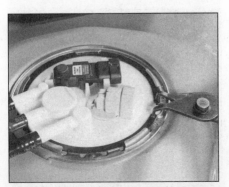

7.15 On later models, use a pair of snap-ring pliers to remove the retaining collar from the fuel pump assembly

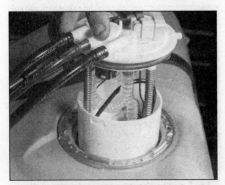

7.16 Lift the fuel pump/sending unit assembly from the fuel tank

4

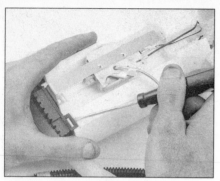

7.18a Pry on the plastic tab to remove the protective shield from the foot of the assembly

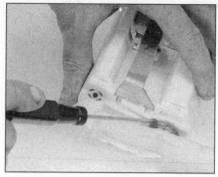

7.18b Carefully pry the fuel strainer from the inlet pipe

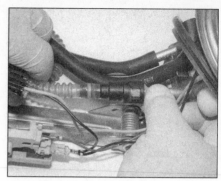

7.21 Squeeze the tabs to release the fuel line from the collar

17   Inspect the condition of the O-ring around the opening of the tank. If it is dried, cracked or deteriorated, replace it.

18   Remove the strainer from the lower end of the fuel pump **(see illustrations)**. If it is dirty, clean it with a suitable solvent and blow it out with compressed air. If it is too dirty to be cleaned, replace it.

19   Remove the fuel pressure sensor mounting bolts and separate the sensor from the top of the fuel pump assembly.

20   If it is necessary to separate the fuel pump and sending unit, disconnect the electrical connectors at the pump, noting

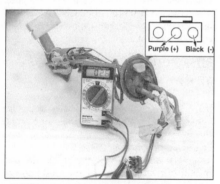

8.3 Connect the probes of an ohmmeter to the fuel level sending unit harness and check the resistance of the fuel level sending unit by moving the float from EMPTY (down) to FULL (up) and comparing the change in resistance

their position. Follow the procedure in Section 8.

21   Disconnect the fuel line from the pump **(see illustration)**.

22   Installation is the reverse of removal. Reassemble the fuel pump to the sending unit bracket and insert the assembly into the fuel tank.

23   Install the fuel tank (see Section 5).

8   Fuel level sending unit - check and replacement

Warning: *Gasoline is extremely flammable, so take extra precautions when you work on any part of the fuel system. See the* **Warning** *in Section 2.*

Check

Refer to illustration 8.3

1   Raise the vehicle and secure it on jackstands.

2   The fuel sending unit electrical connector is not accessible with the fuel tank in the vehicle. Remove the fuel tank (see Section 5) and the sending unit (see Section 8) from the fuel tank for testing.

3   Position the probes of an ohmmeter on the sending unit electrical connector terminals **(see illustration)** and check for resistance with the float at the top (full). The resistance of the sending unit should be about 90 ohms. Then check for resistance

with the float at the bottom (empty). The resistance should be about 2 ohms.

4   If the readings are incorrect or there is very little change in resistance as the float travels from full to empty, replace the fuel level sending unit assembly.

Replacement

Refer to illustration 8.6, 8.8a and 8.8b

5   Remove the fuel tank (see Section 5) and the fuel pump/sending unit (see Section 7) from the vehicle.

6   Disconnect the sending unit electrical connector from the assembly **(see illustration)**.

7   On 1995 and 1996 models, remove the screws securing the sending unit to the return tube.

8   On 1997 and 1998 models, carefully separate the sending unit bracket from the base of the fuel pump assembly **(see illustrations)**.

9   Installation is the reverse of removal.

9   Air cleaner assembly - removal and installation

Refer to illustrations 9.3 and 9.5

1   Detach the cable from the negative terminal of the battery. **Caution:** *On models equipped with a Delco Loc II or Theftlock audio system, be sure the lockout feature is*

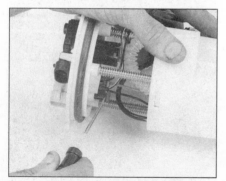

8.6 Detach the fuel level electrical connector from the fuel pump (1997 and 1998 model shown)

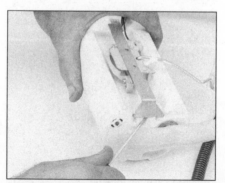

8.8a On 1997 and 1998 models, pry the bracket from the base of the fuel pump

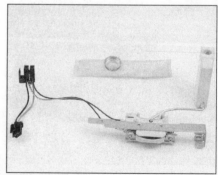

8.8b Exploded view of a 1997 and 1998 fuel level sending unit and related parts

9.3 Disconnect the electrical connectors (arrows), then loosen the clamps from the air intake duct and detach the air intake duct from the air cleaner assembly

9.5 Remove the screws (arrows) and lift out the air cleaner assembly

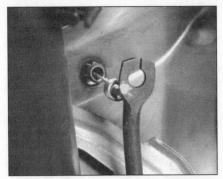

10.2 Slide the accelerator cable through the slot in the pedal arm

turned off before performing any procedure which requires disconnecting the battery.

2   Disconnect the electrical connector to the mass air flow (MAF) sensor on 3.1L and 3.4L engines and the air intake temperature (IAT) sensor connector on all engines.

3   Loosen the clamps and remove the air intake duct located between the throttle body and the air cleaner assembly (see illustration).

4   Unsnap the clips or remove the retaining screws from the air cleaner cover, then lift the air filter element and the air cleaner cover from the air cleaner housing (see Chapter 1).

5   Remove the retaining screws and lift the lower air cleaner housing from the engine compartment (see illustration).

6   Installation is the reverse of removal.

10   Accelerator cable - removal and installation

Refer to illustrations 10.2, 10.6, 10.7 and 10.8

Removal

1   Detach the screws and the clip retaining the lower instrument panel trim and lower the trim (if necessary) (see Chapter 11).

2   Detach the accelerator cable from the accelerator pedal (see illustration).

3   Squeeze the accelerator cable cover tangs and push the cable through the firewall into the engine compartment.

4   On 3.8L engines, remove the fuel injector trim cover from the top of the engine.

5   Remove the screws to the accelerator control splash shield (if equipped).

6   Detach any accelerator cable retaining clips (see illustration).

7   Squeeze the accelerator cable retaining tangs and push the cable through the accelerator cable bracket (see illustration).

8   Rotate the throttle lever and pass the cable through the slot in the lever (see illustration).

9   Pull the cable through the firewall and into the engine compartment.

Installation

10   Installation is the reverse of removal.

Note: To prevent possible interference, flexible components (hoses, wires, etc.) must not be routed within two inches of moving parts, unless routing is controlled.

11   Operate the accelerator pedal and check for any binding condition by completely opening and closing the throttle.

12   Apply sealant around the accelerator cable at the engine compartment side of the firewall.

11   Fuel injection system - general information

Refer to illustrations 11.3a and 11.3b

1   These models are equipped with the Multiport Fuel Injection (MFI) system. These modern fuel injection systems are equipped with the updated OBD II self-diagnosis system, except 1995 3.1L engines which are equipped with the OBD I self-diagnosis system.

2   The fuel system consists of a fuel tank, an electric fuel pump and fuel pump relay, an air cleaner assembly and an electronic fuel injection system.

Multiport Fuel Injection (MFI) system

3   Multiport Fuel Injection (MFI) consists of an air intake manifold, the throttle body, the injectors, the fuel rail assembly, an electric fuel pump and associated plumbing (see illustrations overleaf).

4   Air is drawn through the air cleaner and throttle body. A Mass Air Flow (MAF) sensor informs the PCM of volume and pressure variations.

5   While the engine is running, the fuel constantly circulates through the fuel rail, which removes vapors and keeps the fuel

4

10.6 Using a screwdriver detach the retaining clips securing the accelerator and the cruise control cables to the inner fenderwell

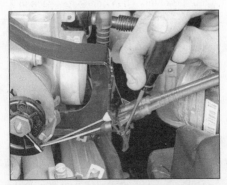

10.7 Release the locking tabs to separate the cable from the bracket

10.8 Pass the cable end through the slot in the throttle lever

11.3a Fuel injection component locations on a 3.1L engine

1	Fuel pump relay	4	Idle Air Control valve	7	Mass Air Flow sensor
2	Powertrain Control Module (PCM)	5	Throttle Position Sensor	8	Fuel pressure regulator
3	Upper intake manifold (plenum)	6	Intake Air Temperature sensor	9	Fuel rail (left bank)

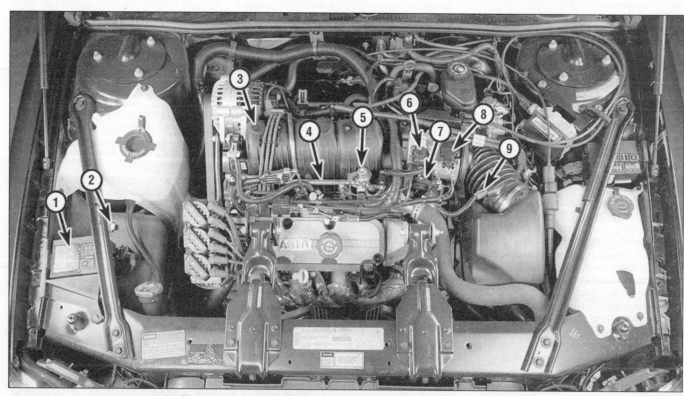

11.3b Fuel injection component locations on a 3.8L engine (trim cover removed)

1	Fuel pump relay	4	Fuel rail (left bank)	7	Throttle Position Sensor
2	Powertrain Control Module (PCM)	5	Fuel pressure regulator	8	Mass Air Flow sensor
3	Upper intake manifold (plenum)	6	Idle Air Control valve	9	Intake Air Temperature sensor

12.8 Use a stethoscope or screwdriver to listen and determine if the injectors are working properly - they should make a steady clicking sound that rises and falls with engine speed changes

12.9 Check the resistance of each injector and compare the readings to the Specifications

12.10 Install the "noid" light into each injector electrical connector and confirm that it blinks when the engine is cranking or running

cool while maintaining sufficient pressure to the injectors under all running conditions.

6   Operation of the MFI system is controlled by the PCM so that it works in conjunction with the rest of the vehicle functions to provide optimum driveability and emissions control.

7   Because the MFI system meters fuel and air precisely, it is important to the proper operation of the vehicle that the fuel and air filters be changed at the specified intervals.

12 Fuel injection system - check

Refer to illustrations 12.8, 12.9 and 12.10

Warning: *Gasoline is extremely flammable, so take extra precautions when you work on any part of the fuel system. See the* **Warning** *in Section 2.*

Note: *The following procedure is based on the assumption that the fuel pump is working and the fuel pressure is adequate (see Section 3).*

1   Check to see that the battery is fully charged, as the control unit and sensors depend on an accurate supply voltage in order to properly meter the fuel.

2   Check the air filter element - a dirty or partially blocked filter will severely impede performance and economy (see Chapter 1).

3   Check the fuel filter and replace it if necessary (see Chapter 1).

4   Check the ground wire connections on the intake manifold for tightness. Check all electrical connectors that are related to the system. Loose connectors and poor grounds can cause many problems that resemble more serious malfunctions.

5   If a blown fuse is found, replace it and see if it blows again. If it does, search for a grounded wire in the harness.

6   Check the air intake duct to the intake manifold for leaks, which will result in an excessively lean mixture. Also check the condition of all vacuum hoses connected to the intake manifold.

7   Remove the air intake duct from the throttle body and check for dirt, carbon or other residue build-up. If it's dirty,

clean it with aerosol carburetor cleaner and a rag.

8   With the engine running, place an automotive stethoscope against each injector, one at a time, and listen for a clicking sound, indicating operation **(see illustration)**. If you don't have a stethoscope, place the tip of a screwdriver against the injector and listen through the handle.

9   Unplug the injector electrical connector(s) and test the resistance of each injector. Compare the values to the Specifications listed in this Chapter **(see illustration)**.

10   Install an injector test light ("noid" light) into each injector electrical connector, one at a time **(see illustration)**. Crank the engine over. Confirm that the light flashes evenly on each connector. This will test for voltage to the injectors.

11   The remainder of the system checks can be found in the following Sections.

13 Fuel injection system - component check and replacement

Warning: *Gasoline is extremely flammable, so take extra precautions when you work on any part of the fuel system. See the* **Warning** *in Section 2.*

Throttle body

Check

Refer to illustration 13.2

1   Detach the air intake duct from the throttle body and move the duct out of the way.

2   Have an assistant depress the throttle pedal while you watch the throttle valve. Check that the throttle valve moves smoothly when the throttle is moved from closed (idle position) to fully open (wide open throttle). **Note:** *Spray carburetor cleaner into the throttle body, especially around the shaft area* **(see illustration)** *to free-up any binding caused by the accumulation of carbon deposits or sludge buildup.*

3   Wiggle the throttle lever while watching the throttle shaft inside the bore. If it appears worn (loose), replace the throttle body unit.

Replacement

Refer to illustrations 13.9 and 13.11

Warning: *Wait until the engine is completely cool before beginning this procedure.*

Note: *1995 3.4L engines are equipped with one piece intake plenum/throttle body assembly see Chapter 2 for the removal procedures.*

4   Disconnect the cable from the negative terminal of the battery. **Caution:** *On models equipped with a Theftlock audio system, be sure the lockout feature is turned off before performing any procedure which requires disconnecting the battery. On 3.4L and 3.8L engines, drain the engine coolant (see Chapter 1).*

5   Detach the air intake duct (see Section 9).

6   On 3.8L engines, remove the trim cover from the top of the engine.

7   Unplug the Idle Air Control (IAC) valve and the Throttle Position Sensor (TPS) electrical connectors (see Chapter 6). Unplug the Mass Air Flow sensor (MAF) electrical connector on 3.8L engines.

8   Mark and disconnect any vacuum hoses connected to the throttle body. Also detach the breather hose, if equipped.

4

13.2 Spray carburetor cleaner into the throttle body to break away any carbon deposits or sludge that may have collected around the throttle plate

13.9 On 3.1L and 3.4L engines, remove the accelerator cable bracket bolts (arrows) (3.1L engine shown)

13.11 Throttle body mounting details (3.1L engine)

1 *Throttle body mounting bolt*
2 *Coolant bypass hose*
3 *Throttle Position Sensor*
4 *Idle Air Control valve*

13.16 Measure the resistance across terminals D and C, then across terminals A and B

9   Disconnect the accelerator cable and the cruise control cable (see Section 10) from the throttle lever, then detach the cable retaining bracket on 3.1L and 3.4L engines (see illustration).

10   On 3.1L engines, loosen and detach the coolant bypass hoses from the intake manifold. Plug the hoses and fittings to prevent coolant loss. On 3.8L engines, detach the lower throttle body support bracket.

11   Remove the throttle body nuts and bolts and detach the throttle body (see illustration).

12   Clean off all traces of old gasket material from the throttle body and the plenum.

13   Install the throttle body and a new gasket and tighten the bolts to the torque listed in this Chapter's Specifications.

14   The rest of the procedure is the reverse of removal. Be sure to check the coolant level (see Chapter 1) and add, if necessary.

Idle Air Control (IAC) valve

Check

Refer to illustration 13.16

15   The Idle Air Control valve (IAC) controls the engine idle speed. This output actuator is mounted on the throttle body and is controlled by voltage pulses sent from the PCM (computer). The IAC valve pintle moves in or out allowing more or less intake air into the system according to the engine conditions. To increase idle speed, the PCM retracts the IAC valve pintle away from the seat and allows more air to bypass the throttle bore. To decrease idle speed, the PCM extends the IAC valve pintle towards the seat, reducing the air flow.

16   To check the IAC valve, unplug the electrical connector and, using an ohmmeter, measure the resistance across terminals A and B, then terminals C and D. Each resistance check should indicate 40 to 80 ohms (see illustration). If not, replace the IAC valve.

17   There is an alternate method for testing the IAC valve. Various SCAN tools are available from auto parts stores and specialty tool companies that can be plugged into the DLC (diagnostic connector) for the purpose of

monitoring the sensors. Connect the SCAN tool and switch to the Idle Air Motor Position mode and monitor the steps (motor winding position). The SCAN tool should indicate between 10 to 200 steps depending upon the rpm range. Allow the engine to idle for several minutes and while observing the count reading, snap the throttle to achieve high rpm (under 3,500). Repeat the procedure several times and observe the SCAN tool steps (counts) when the engine goes back to idle. The readings should be within 5 to 10 steps each time. If the readings fluctuate greatly, replace the IAC valve. The PCM will set Codes P0506 or P0507 in the event of IAC failure. **Note:** *When the IAC valve electrical connector is disconnected for testing, the PCM will have to "relearn" its idle mode. In other words, it will take a certain amount of time before the idle motor resets for the correct idle speed. Make sure the idle is smooth and not misfiring before plugging in the SCAN tool. Refer to Chapter 6 for additional information concerning SCAN tools.*

18   Next, remove the valve (see Step 19) and inspect it:

a) *Check the pintle for excessive carbon deposits. If necessary, clean it with aerosol carburetor cleaner. Also clean the IAC valve housing to remove any deposits.*

b) *Check the IAC valve electrical connections. Make sure the pins are not bent and make good contact with the connector terminals.*

Replacement

Refer to illustration 13.20

19   Unplug the electrical connector from the Idle Air Control (IAC) valve.

20   Unscrew the valve or remove the two IAC valve attaching screws and withdraw the valve (see illustration).

21   Check the condition of the rubber O-ring. If it's hardened or deteriorated, replace it. On models equipped with a gasket, remove the gasket.

22   Clean the sealing surface and the bore

of the idle air/vacuum signal housing assembly to ensure a good seal. **Caution:** *The IAC valve itself is an electrical component and must not be soaked in any liquid cleaner, as damage may result.*

23   Before installing the IAC valve, the position of the pintle must be checked. If the pintle is extended too far, damage to the assembly may occur.

24   Measure the distance from the flange or gasket mounting surface of the IAC valve to the tip of the pintle. If the distance is greater than 1-1/8 inch, reduce the distance by applying firm pressure onto the pintle to retract it. Try some side-to-side motion in the event the pintle binds.

25   Position the new O-ring or gasket on the IAC valve. Lubricate the O-ring with a light film of engine oil. Install the IAC valve and tighten the valve or the mounting screws securely.

26   Plug in the electrical connector at the IAC valve assembly. **Note:** *No adjustment is made to the IAC assembly after reinstallation. The IAC resetting is controlled by the PCM when the engine is started.*

Throttle Position Sensor (TPS)

Check

27   Check for stored trouble codes in the PCM using the On Board Diagnosis system (see Chapter 6).

28   For the checking and replacement procedures for the TPS, refer to *Information sensors* in Chapter 6.

13.20 Remove the IAC valve screws (arrows) and separate the IAC from the throttle body

13.31 Use a special fuel line disconnect tool to release the fuel line couplers (arrows) from the fuel rail (3.1L engine shown)

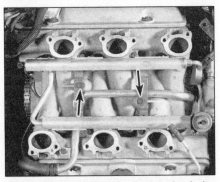

13.34 Remove the fuel rail mounting bolts (arrows) (3.1L engine shown)

13.35 It may be necessary to gently pry the fuel rail up to remove it

Fuel rail and injectors

Refer to illustrations 13.31, 13.34, 13.35, 13.36 and 13.37

Warning: *Before any work is performed on the fuel lines, fuel rail or injectors, the fuel system pressure must be relieved* (see Section 2). **Note:** *Refer to Section 12 for the injector checking procedure.*

29   Detach the cable from the negative terminal of the battery. **Caution:** *On models equipped with a Theftlock audio system, be sure the lockout feature is turned off before performing any procedure which requires disconnecting the battery.*

30   On 3.1L and 3.4L engines, remove the upper half of the intake manifold and the throttle body assembly as a unit (see Chapter 2). On 3.8L engines, remove the fuel injector trim cover.

31   Using a special fuel line removal tool, detach the fuel lines from the fuel rail **(see illustrations 4.12a, 4.12b and the accompanying illustration)**.

32   Detach the vacuum line at the fuel pressure regulator.

33   Label and unplug the injector electrical connectors.

34   Remove the fuel rail retaining bolts **(see illustration)**.

35   Carefully remove the fuel rail with the injectors **(see illustration)**. **Caution:** *Use care when handling the fuel rail assembly to avoid damaging the injectors.*

36   To remove the fuel injectors, spread the

injector retaining clip and pull the injector from the fuel rail **(see illustration)**.

37   Remove the injector O-ring seals **(see illustration)**.

38   Install the new O-ring seal(s), as required, on the injector(s) and lubricate them with a light film of engine oil. **Note:** *It is recommended that all of the O-rings be replaced whenever the fuel rail is removed.*

39   Install the injectors on the fuel rail.

40   Secure the injectors with the retaining clips.

41   Installation is the reverse of the removal procedure.

Fuel pressure regulator

Check

42   Refer to Section 3 for the fuel pressure regulator checking procedure.

Replacement

Refer to illustrations 13.46 and 13.47

43   Relieve the fuel system pressure (see Section 2).

44   Disconnect the cable from the negative terminal of the battery. **Caution:** *On models equipped with a Theftlock audio system, be sure the lockout feature is turned off before performing any procedure which requires disconnecting the battery.*

45   Remove the fuel rail following the procedure described earlier in this Section.

46   On all 3.1L and 1995 3.4L engines, remove the fuel return pipe from the bottom

of the regulator, then remove the pressure regulator mounting screw **(see illustration)** and separate the fuel pressure regulator assembly from the fuel rail while noting the installed position of the filter screen.

47   On 1996 and later 3.4L and 3.8L engines, compress the snap-ring with snap-ring pliers and lift the ring from the regulator **(see illustration)**. Lift the regulator while simultaneously twisting it and remove it from the housing. Remove the filter screen from the regulator housing and clean it with compressed air. Install new O-rings and lubricate them with a light coat of oil.

48   Reassembly is the reverse of disassembly. Be sure to replace all gaskets and

13.36 To remove an injector from the fuel rail, spread the retaining clip with a small screwdriver, then pull the injector from the fuel rail

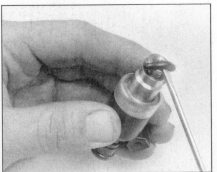

13.37 Carefully pry the seals off the injectors and replace them with new ones

13.46 On 3.1L and 1995 3.4L engines, remove the return line (A) and the mounting screw (B) from the fuel pressure regulator

13.47 On 1996 and later 3.4L engines and all 3.8L engines, remove the snap-ring (arrow) from the top of the pressure regulator

4

13.50 Remove the screws (arrows) from the MAF sensor on 3.8L models

Mass Air Flow (MAF) sensor (3.8L engine)

Refer to illustration 13.50

49   Disconnect the electrical connector.

50   Remove the MAF sensor bolts **(see illustration)** from the assembly.

51   Remove the MAF sensor. **Caution:** *The MAF sensor is delicate - if you plan to reinstall the existing unit, handle it carefully.*

52   Installation is the reverse of the removal procedure.

14   Exhaust system servicing - general information

Refer to illustrations 14.1a, 14.1b, and 14.1c
Warning: *The vehicle's exhaust system generates very high temperatures and must*

be allowed to cool down completely before any of the components are touched. Be especially careful around the catalytic converter, where the highest temperatures are generated.

Replacement of exhaust system components is basically a matter of removing the heat shields, disconnecting the component and installing a new one **(see illustrations)**. The heat shields and exhaust system hangers must be reinstalled in the original locations or damage could result. Due to the high temperatures and exposed locations of the exhaust system components, rust and corrosion can seize parts together. Penetrating oils are available to help loosen frozen fasteners. However, in some cases it may be necessary to cut the pieces apart with a hacksaw or cutting torch. The latter method should be employed only by persons experienced in this work.

seals, otherwise a dangerous fuel leak may develop. When installing the seals, lubricate them with a light film of engine oil.

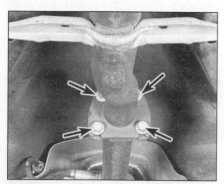

14.1a Be sure to spray penetrating lubricant onto the flange bolts (arrows) before removing them

14.1b Make sure all exhaust pipe brackets are not cracked or damaged

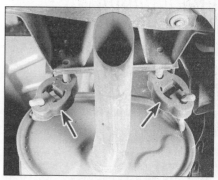

14.1c Check the rubber hangers (arrows) for deterioration or cracks that may cause the exhaust system to drop

Chapter 5
Engine electrical systems

Contents

Specifications

General

Ignition coil resistance (all engines)
    Primary resistance... 0.3 to 0.7 ohms
    Secondary resistance.. 5,000 to 6,500 ohms
Spark plug wire resistance .... Less than 30,000 ohms
Cylinder numbers .... See Chapter 2
Firing order .... See Chapter 2

Charging system

Alternator charging output.. 13 to 14.5 volts

1 General information

Warning: *Because of the very high voltage generated by the ignition system, extreme care should be taken whenever an operation involving ignition components is performed. This not only includes the ignition coil(s), module and spark plug wires, but related items that are connected to the systems as well, such as the electrical connections, tachometer and testing equipment.*

All engines covered by this manual are equipped with a distributorless Direct Ignition System (DIS) which mounts the coil pack on top of the ignition module with spark plug wires connecting the spark plugs to the coil packs.

The distributorless ignition system includes three coil packs, an ignition control module (ICM), two crankshaft position sensors, a camshaft position sensor and the PCM.

The charging system consists of a belt-driven alternator with an integral voltage regulator and the battery. These components work together to supply electrical power for the ignition system, the lights and all accessories.

1995 through 1997 models are equipped with the CS-130 (100 amp) alternator. 1998 models are equipped with either a CS-130 or the CS-144 (124 amp) alternator. All types use a conventional pulley and fan. The CS-130 alternators should be considered non-serviceable and, if found to be faulty, should be exchanged as cores for new or rebuilt units. CS-144 alternators can be rebuilt but it is recommended that the home mechanic exchange the alternator for a rebuilt unit. Because of the expense and the limited availability of parts, no alternator overhaul information is included in this manual.

2 Battery - emergency jump starting

Refer to the *Booster battery (jump) starting* procedure at the front of this manual.

3 Battery - removal and installation

Warning: *Hydrogen gas is produced by the battery, so keep open flames and lighted cigarettes away from it at all times. Always wear eye protection when working around a battery. Rinse off spilled electrolyte immediately with large amounts of water.*

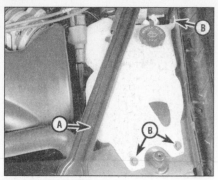

3.2a Remove the engine compartment support brace (A) and the windshield washer reservoir retaining bolts (B)

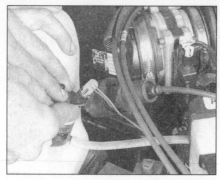

3.2b Turn the windshield washer reservoir over and disconnect the electrical connector and the washer hose - insert a vacuum plug over the reservoir outlet to avoid excessive spillage from the washer reservoir

3.4 Remove the battery hold-down bolts (arrows) from the battery carrier

Removal

Refer to illustrations 3.2a, 3.2b and 3.4

1   The battery is located at the left front corner of the engine compartment.

2   Remove the engine compartment left support brace and the windshield washer fluid reservoir **(see illustrations)**.

3   Detach the cables from the negative and positive terminals of the battery. **Warning:** *To prevent arcing, disconnect the negative (-) cable first, then remove the positive (+) cable.* **Caution:** *On models equipped with a Theftlock audio system, be sure the lockout feature is turned off before performing any procedure which requires disconnecting the battery.*

4   Remove the hold-down clamp bolts and the clamp from the battery carrier **(see illustration)**

5   Carefully lift the battery from the carrier. **Warning:** *Always keep the battery in an upright position to reduce the likelihood of electrolyte spillage. If you spill electrolyte on your skin, rinse it off immediately with large amounts of water.*

Installation

Note: *The battery carrier and hold-down clamp should be clean and free from corrosion before installing the battery. Make certain that there are no parts in the carrier before installing the battery.*

6   Set the battery in position in its carrier. Don't tilt it.

7   Install the hold-down clamp and bolts. The bolt should be snug, but overtightening it may damage the battery case.

8   Install both battery cables, positive first, then the negative. **Note:** *The battery terminals and cable ends should be cleaned prior to connection* (see Chapter 1).

4   Battery cables - check and replacement

1   Periodically inspect the entire length of each battery cable for damage, cracked or burned insulation and corrosion. Poor battery cable connections can cause starting

problems and decreased engine performance.

2   Check the cable-to-terminal connections at the ends of the cables for cracks, loose wire strands and corrosion. The presence of white, fluffy deposits under the insulation at the cable terminal connection is a sign the cable is corroded and should be replaced. Check the terminals for distortion, missing mounting bolts or nuts and corrosion.

3   When removing the cables, always disconnect the negative cable first and hook it up last or the battery may be shorted by the tool used to loosen the cable clamps. Even if only the positive cable is being replaced, be sure to disconnect the negative cable from the battery first. **Caution:** *On models equipped with a Theftlock audio system, be sure the lockout feature is turned off before performing any procedure which requires disconnecting the battery.*

4   Disconnect the old cables from the battery, then trace each of them to their opposite ends and detach them from the starter solenoid and ground terminals. Note the routing of each cable to ensure correct installation.

5   If you're replacing either or both cables, take the old ones with you when buying the new ones - the replacements must be identical. Cables have characteristics that make them easy to identify: Positive cables are normally red, larger in diameter and have a larger diameter battery post and clamp; ground cables are normally black, smaller in diameter and have a slightly smaller battery post and clamp.

6   Clean the threads of the solenoid or ground connection with a wire brush to remove rust and corrosion. Apply a light coat of petroleum jelly to the threads to prevent future corrosion.

7   Attach the cable to the solenoid or ground connection and tighten the mounting nut/bolt securely.

8   Before connecting a new cable to the battery, make sure it reaches the battery post without having to be stretched.

9   Connect the positive cable first, followed by the negative cable. Tighten the nuts and apply a thin coat of petroleum jelly to the terminal and cable connection.

5   Ignition system - general information

The engines covered in this manual are equipped with a distributorless Direct Ignition System (DIS) which is controlled by the PCM. This system offers no moving parts, less maintenance, more coil cool down time between spark plug firing and the elimination of mechanical timing adjustments.

DIS (Direct Ignition System)

The DIS ignition systems use a "waste spark" method of spark distribution. Each cylinder is paired with its opposing cylinder in the firing order (1-4, 2-5, 3-6) so one cylinder under compression fires simultaneously with its opposing cylinder, where the piston is on the exhaust stroke. Since the cylinder on the exhaust stroke requires very little of the available voltage to fire its plug, most of the voltage is used to fire the plug of the cylinder on the compression stroke.

The DIS system includes a three coil packs, an ignition module, two crankshaft position sensors, except 1998 3.8L engines which use a single (dual hall effect) sensor, a engine crankshaft balancer with crankshaft sensor interrupter rings, a camshaft position sensor, spark plugs, spark plug wires and the Powertrain Control Module (PCM).

Conventional ignition coils have one end of the secondary winding connected to the engine ground. On DIS, neither end of the secondary winding is grounded - instead, one end of the coils secondary winding is directly attached to the spark plug and the other end is attached the spark plug of the companion cylinder.

The crankshaft reluctor ring disrupts signal voltage from the crankshaft position sensors to indicate crankshaft position and crankshaft speed. These signals are used by the Ignition Control Module (ICM) during start up and passed on to the Powertrain

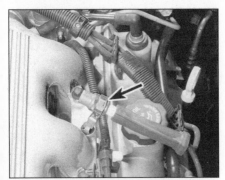

6.3a To use a calibrated ignition tester (available at most auto parts stores), simply disconnect a spark plug wire, attach the wire to the tester, clip the tester to a convenient ground and operate the starter - if there's enough power to fire the plug, sparks will be visible between the electrode tip and the tester body

6.3b Using an ohmmeter, check the resistance of each spark plug wire

6.6 Remove the coil pack from the module assembly and check for a trigger signal on the module terminals with a test light while an assistant cranks the engine over

Control Module (PCM) to adjust ignition timing.

The DIS system is also integrated with the Knock Sensor (KS) system which uses knock sensors in connection with the Powertrain Control Module (PCM) to control spark timing. The KS system allows the engine to have maximum spark advance without spark knock which also improves driveability and fuel economy.

Secondary (spark plug) wiring

The secondary (spark plug) wires are a carbon-impregnated cord conductor encased in an 8 mm (5/16-inch) diameter rubber jacket with an outer silicone covering. This type of wire will withstand very high temperatures and provides an excellent insulator for the high secondary ignition voltage. Silicone spark plug boots form a tight seal on the plug. The boot should be twisted 1/2-turn before removing (for more information on spark plug wiring refer to Chapter 1).

6 Ignition system - check

Warning: *Because of the very high voltage generated by the ignition system, extreme care should be taken whenever an operation is performed involving ignition components. This not only includes the coils, control module and spark plug wires, but related items connected to the system as well, such as the electrical connections, tachometer and any test equipment.*

Note: *All ignition system information sensors such as the crankshaft position sensor, camshaft position sensor and the knock sensors are covered in Chapter 6.*

General checks

Refer to illustrations 6.3a and 6.3b

1   Check all ignition wiring connections for tightness, cuts, corrosion or any other signs of a bad connection. A faulty or poor connection at a spark plug could also result in a misfire. Also check for carbon deposits inside the spark plug boots. Remove the spark plugs, if necessary, and check for fouling (see Chapter 1).

2   Check for ignition and battery supply to the PCM. Check the ignition fuses (see Chapter 12).

3   Use a calibrated ignition tester to verify adequate available secondary voltage (25,000 volts) at the spark plug **(see illustration)**. Using an ohmmeter, check the resistance of the spark plug wires **(see illustration)**. Each wire should measure less than 30,000 ohms.

4   Check to see if the fuel pump and relay are operating properly (see Chapter 4). The fuel pump should activate for two seconds when the ignition key is cycled ON.

Ignition module

Refer to illustration 6.6

5   Disconnect the ignition module harness connector and check for battery voltage to terminal L (pink wire) from the 15 amp IGN fuse with the ignition key ON (engine not running). If no battery voltage is present, replace the fuse and check again. Repair the circuit to the ignition system if necessary.

6   Next, check for a trigger signal from the ignition module. Remove the coil pack from the ignition module to expose the module terminals. Connect a test light between each of the module terminals and have an assistant crank the engine over **(see illustration)**. This test checks the triggering circuit in the ignition module. A blinking test light indicates the module is triggering. The test light should blink quickly and constantly as each coil pack is triggered to fire by the switching signal from the ignition module.

7   If there is no blinking light, the ignition module is most likely the problem but not always. The PCM should also relay reference signals to fire the fuel injectors if all the information is being received from the camshaft and crankshaft sensors. It is best to install a SCAN tool and monitor the PCM activity to differentiate the ignition system problems (see Chapter 6).

8   A slowly blinking light, at this point, indicates the PCM is not seeing a crank sensor signal (see Chapter 6). At this point, the problem is in the camshaft or crankshaft sensor(s), sensor circuits or the ignition module. **Note:** *Refer to Chapter 6 for additional information and testing procedures for the camshaft sensor and the crankshaft sensors. It will be necessary to verify that the crankshaft sensors and camshaft sensor is operating correctly before changing the ignition module. A defective ignition module can only be diagnosed by process of elimination.*

Ignition coil packs

Refer to illustrations 6.10 and 6.11

9   Refer to Steps 6 through 8 to determine if the coils are receiving the correct trigger signal from the ignition module.

10   Use an ohmmeter and check the secondary resistance for each coil pack **(see illustration)**. Refer to the Specifications listed at the beginning of this Chapter for the correct amount of resistance.

11   Next, remove each coil pack (see Section 7) and check the primary resistance

6.10 Check the coil secondary resistance by connecting the ohmmeter leads to the towers of each coil pack

5

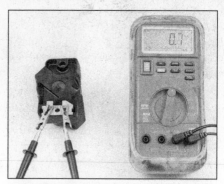

6.11 With the coil pack removed from the module assembly, check the coil primary resistance with an ohmmeter

7.2 Disconnect the electrical connectors (arrows) from the ignition module (3.1L engine shown, others similar)

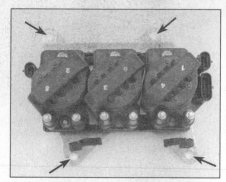

7.4 Remove the ignition module/coil pack bracket bolts (arrows) (3.1L engine shown, others similar) - module/coil pack removed for clarity

for each individual coil pack **(see illustration)**. Refer to the Specifications listed at the beginning of this Chapter for the correct amount of resistance.

12   If the indicated resistance is less than the resistance listed in this Chapter's Specifications, replace the coil pack.

7   Ignition coils and module - removal and installation

Refer to illustrations 7.2, 7.4, 7.5a and 7.5b

1   Detach the cable from the negative terminal of the battery. **Caution:** *On models equipped with a Theftlock audio system, be sure the lockout feature is turned off before performing any procedure which requires disconnecting the battery.*

2   Unplug the electrical connectors from the module **(see illustration)**.

3   If the plug wires are not numbered, label them and detach the plug wires at the coil assembly.

4   Remove the module/coil assembly mounting bolts and lift the assembly from the vehicle **(see illustration)**.

5   To remove the coils from the ignition module, simply remove the mounting screws and unplug the coil from the ignition module terminals **(see illustrations)**.

6   Installation is the reverse of removal.

Note: *When installing the coils, make sure they are properly seated on the ignition module.*

8   Charging system - general information and precautions

Caution: *On models equipped with a Theftlock audio system, be sure the lockout feature is turned off before performing any procedure which requires disconnecting the battery.*

The charging system consists of a belt-driven alternator with an integral voltage regulator and the battery. These components work together to supply electrical power for the ignition system, the lights and all accessories.

1995 through 1997 models are equipped with the CS-130 (100 amp) alternator. 1998 models are equipped with either the CS-130 or the CS-144 (124 amp) alternator. All types use a conventional pulley and fan. The CS-130 alternators should be considered non-serviceable and, if found to be faulty, should be exchanged as cores for new or rebuilt units. CS-144 alternators can be rebuilt but it is recommended that the home mechanic exchange the alternator for a rebuilt unit. Because of the expense and the limited availability of parts, no alternator overhaul information is included in this manual.

The purpose of the voltage regulator is to limit the alternator's output voltage to a preset value. This prevents power surges, circuit overloads, etc., during peak voltage output. On all models with which this manual is concerned, the voltage regulator is contained within the alternator housing.

The charging system does not ordinarily require periodic maintenance. The drivebelt, electrical wiring and connections should, however, be inspected at the intervals suggested in Chapter 1.

Take extreme care when making circuit connections to a vehicle equipped with an alternator and note the following. When making connections to the alternator from a battery, always match correct polarity. Before using arc welding equipment to repair any part of the vehicle, disconnect the wires from the alternator and the battery terminals. Never start the engine with a battery charger connected. Always disconnect both battery leads before using a battery charger.

The charging indicator light on the dash lights up when the ignition switch is turned on and goes out when the engine starts. If the light stays on or comes on once the engine is running, a charging system problem has occurred.

9   Charging system - check

1   If a malfunction occurs in the charging circuit, do not immediately assume that the alternator is causing the problem.

2   First, check the following items:

a) *Make sure the battery cable connections at the battery are clean and tight.*

b) *The battery electrolyte specific gravity (if possible). If it is low, charge the battery.*

c) *Check the external alternator wiring and connections. They must be in good condition.*

d) *Check the drivebelt condition and tension (Chapter 1).*

e) *Make sure the alternator mounting bolts are tight.*

f) *Run the engine and check the alternator for abnormal noise (may be caused by a*

7.5a To detach the coil packs from the ignition module, remove the screws (arrows) . . .

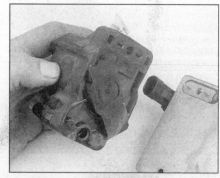

7.5b . . . and pull straight up - when installing a coil pack, line up the blade terminals and press downward - make sure it's fully seated before tightening the retaining screws

loose drive pulley, loose mounting bolts, worn or dirty bearings, defective diode or defective stator).

3   Check the charge light bulb and circuit. With the ignition key ON and the engine not running, the lamp should be ON. If not, detach the wiring harness at the alternator.

a) *Install a fused jumper wire (5 amp) to ground and connect the other end to the lead that was removed from the L terminal on the alternator.*

b) *If the charging lamp on the dash comes ON, the alternator is defective. Replace the alternator.*

c) *If the charging lamp on the dash remains OFF, locate the open circuit between the alternator and the bulb on the dash. First check the bulb to make sure it is not blown.*

d) *With the ignition key ON and the engine running, the lamp should be OFF. If it remains ON while running, stop the engine and remove the lead from the L terminal on the alternator.*

e) *If the lamp on the dash goes OFF, the alternator is defective.*

f) *If the lamp on the dash remains ON, there is a grounded L terminal in the wiring harness.*

4   Using a voltmeter, check the battery voltage with the engine off. It should be approximately 12 volts.

5   Start the engine and check the battery voltage again. It should now be approximately 14 to 15 volts.

10   Alternator - removal and installation

Removal

1   Detach the cable from the negative terminal of the battery. **Caution:** *On models equipped with a Theftlock audio system, be sure the lockout feature is turned off before performing any procedure which requires disconnecting the battery.*

2   Remove the drivebelt (see Chapter 1).

3.1L and 3.8L engines

Refer to illustrations 10.3 and 10.4

3   Label and detach the wires from the backside of the alternator **(see illustration)**.

4   Remove the mounting bolts and separate the alternator from the engine **(see illustration)**. **Note:** *It may be necessary to loosen or remove the front and rear alternator support brackets.*

3.4L engine

Note: *This procedure requires the removal of many parts and lowering of the engine to access the alternator.*

5   Detach the ignition coils/module from the engine and position them aside (see Section 7 if necessary).

6   Raise the vehicle, support it securely on

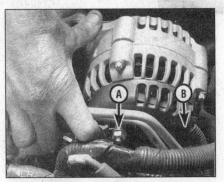

10.3 Disconnect the BAT terminal (A) and the voltage regulator connector (B) from the back of the alternator (3.1L engine shown)

jackstands and remove the right front wheel.

7   Remove the right inner fenderwell splash shield as described in the fender removal Section of Chapter 11.

8   Remove the exhaust pipe, exhaust pipe heat shield and the catalytic converter from the rear exhaust manifold.

9   Detach the steering (intermediate) shaft from the steering gear (see Chapter 10).

10   Place a floor jack under the engine crossmember and remove the rear crossmember mounting bolts, then lower the crossmember no more than four inches to access the alternator.

11   Detach the alternator cooling duct, then label and detach the wires from the backside of the alternator.

12   Remove the alternator mounting bolts and support brackets, then separate the alternator from the engine. **Note:** *It may be necessary to remove the power steering gear inlet hose to allow alternator to be removed.*

Installation

13   If you're replacing the alternator, take the old one with you when purchasing the new one. Make sure the new/rebuilt unit is identical to the old alternator. Look at the terminals - they should be the same in number, size and location as the terminals on the old alternator. Finally, look at the identification numbers - they'll be stamped into the housing or printed on a tag attached to the housing. Make sure the numbers are the same on both alternators.

14   Many new/rebuilt alternators DO NOT have a pulley installed, so you may have to switch the pulley from the old one to the new/rebuilt one.

15   Installation is the reverse of removal.

16   Check the charging voltage to verify proper operation of the alternator (see Section 8).

11   Starting system - general information and precautions

The function of the starting system is to crank the engine quickly enough to allow it to start. The starting system is composed of a

10.4 Remove the alternator mounting bolts (arrows) (3.1L engine shown)

starter motor, solenoid, ignition switch and battery. The battery supplies the electrical energy to the solenoid, which then completes the circuit to the starting motor, which does the actual work of cranking the engine.

The solenoid and starter motor are mounted together at the lower front side of the engine. No periodic lubrication or maintenance is required.

The electrical circuitry of the vehicle is arranged so that the starter motor can only be operated when the transmission selector lever is in Park or Neutral.

There are two types of starters used in these models. 1995 models and 1996 models with 3.1L engines are equipped with SD 205 series starters which have serviceable starter solenoids. All 1996 models with 3.4L engines and 1997 and later models are equipped with PG-260 series starters which are not serviceable and in the event of failure must be replaced as a complete unit.

Always observe the following precautions when working on the starting system:

a) *Excessive cranking of the starter motor can overheat it and cause serious damage. Never operate the starter motor for more than 15 seconds at a time without pausing to allow it to cool for at least two minutes.*

b) *The starter is connected directly to the battery and could arc or cause a fire if mishandled, overloaded or shorted out.*

c) *Always detach the cable from the negative terminal of the battery before working on the starting system.*

12   Starter motor - testing in vehicle

Note: *Before diagnosing starter problems, make sure the battery is fully charged.*

1   If the starter motor does not turn at all when the switch is operated, make sure that the shift lever is in Neutral or Park.

2   Make sure that the battery is charged and that all cables, both at the battery and starter solenoid terminals, are secure.

3   If the starter motor spins but the engine is not cranking, the overrunning clutch in the starter motor is slipping and the motor must

5

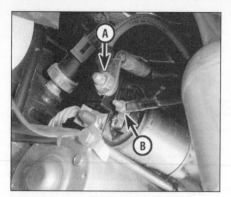

13.4 Disconnect the battery terminal (A) and the switch terminal (B) from the starter solenoid

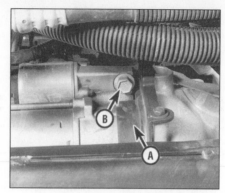

13.6 Remove the torque converter cover (A) and the starter motor bolts (one shown, B) to detach the starter from the engine block

3   On 3.1L engines, remove the air cleaner housing (if necessary).
4   Working under the vehicle, clearly label, then disconnect the wires from the terminals on the starter solenoid **(see illustration)**.
5   Remove the torque converter cover (see Chapter 7).
6   Remove the mounting bolts and detach the starter. Note the locations of the spacer shims (if used) - they must be reinstalled in the same positions **(see illustration)**.
7   Installation is the reverse of removal.

---

14   Starter solenoid - removal and installation

Refer to illustrations 14.3 and 14.5
Note: *This procedure applies to all 1995 models and 1996 models equipped with 3.1L engines only. All 1996 models with 3.4L engines and 1997 and later models are equipped with non-serviceable starters and in the event of failure must be replaced as a complete unit.*
1   Detach the cable from the negative terminal of the battery. **Caution:** *On models equipped with a Theftlock audio system, be sure the lockout feature is turned off before performing any procedure which requires disconnecting the battery.*
2   Remove the starter motor (Section 13).
3   Disconnect the strap from the solenoid to the starter motor terminal **(see illustration)**.
4   Remove the screws that secure the solenoid to the starter motor **(see illustration 14.3)**.
5   Twist the solenoid in a clockwise direction to disengage the flange from the starter body **(see illustration)**.
6   Installation is the reverse of removal.

be removed from the engine for replacement.
4   If, when the switch is actuated, the starter motor does not operate at all but the solenoid clicks, then the problem lies with either the battery, the main solenoid contacts or the starter motor itself.
5   If the solenoid plunger cannot be heard when the switch is actuated, the solenoid itself is defective or the solenoid circuit is open.
6   To check the solenoid, connect a jumper lead between the battery (+) and the "S" terminal on the solenoid. If the starter motor now operates, the solenoid is OK and the problem is in the ignition switch, neutral start switch or in the wiring.
7   If the starter motor still does not operate, remove the starter/solenoid assembly for disassembly, testing and repair.
8   If the starter motor cranks the engine at an abnormally slow speed, first make sure that the battery is charged and that all terminal connections are clean and tight. If the engine is partially seized, or has the wrong viscosity oil in it, it will crank slowly.
9   Run the engine until normal operating temperature is reached, then stop the engine, disconnect the electrical connectors from the ignition module/coil pack assembly.
10   Connect a voltmeter positive lead to the starter motor terminal of the solenoid and then connect the negative lead to ground.
11   Crank the engine and take the voltmeter readings as soon as a steady figure is indicated. Do not allow the starter motor to turn for more than 15 seconds at a time. A reading of 9 volts or more, with the starter motor turning at normal cranking speed, is normal. If the reading is 9 volts or more but the cranking speed is slow, the motor is faulty. If the reading is less than 9 volts and

the cranking speed is slow, the solenoid contacts are probably burned.

---

13   Starter motor - removal and installation

Refer to illustrations 13.4 and 13.6
Note: *On some vehicles, it may be necessary to remove the exhaust pipe(s) or frame crossmember to gain access to the starter motor. In extreme cases it may even be necessary to unbolt the mounts and raise the engine slightly to get the starter out.*
1   Detach the cable from the negative terminal of the battery. **Caution:** *On models equipped with a Theftlock audio system, be sure the lockout feature is turned off before performing any procedure which requires disconnecting the battery.*
2   Raise the front of the vehicle and support it securely on jackstands. Apply the parking brake and block the rear wheels to keep the vehicle from rolling off the jackstands.

14.3 Disconnect the starter field strap (A) from the solenoid, then remove the solenoid mounting screws (B)

14.5 Rotate the solenoid 1/4-turn clockwise and disengage it from the starter motor

Chapter 6
Emissions and engine control systems

Contents

Specifications

Torque specifications

Crankshaft sensor bolts
    3.1L and 3.4L engines .... 96 in-lbs
    3800 engine .... 14 to 28 ft-lbs
Camshaft sensor bolts
    3.1L and 3.4L engines .... 96 in-lbs
    3800 engine .... 35 to 53 in-lbs

1 General information

Refer to illustration 1.5

To prevent pollution of the atmosphere from burned and evaporating gases, a number of emissions control systems are incorporated on the vehicles covered by this manual. The combination of systems used depends on the year in which the vehicle was manufactured, the locality to which it was originally delivered and the engine type. The major systems incorporated on the vehicles with which this manual is concerned include the:

    Fuel Control System
    Exhaust Gas Recirculation (EGR) system
    Evaporative Emissions Control (EVAP) system
    Transmission Converter Clutch (TCC) system
    Positive Crankcase Ventilation (PCV) system
    Catalytic converter

All of these systems are linked, directly or indirectly, to the On Board Diagnostic (OBD) system. The Sections in this Chapter include general descriptions, checking procedures (where possible) and component replacement procedures (where applicable) for each of the systems listed above.

Before assuming that an emissions control system is malfunctioning, check the fuel and ignition systems carefully. In some cases special tools and equipment, as well as specialized training, are required to accurately diagnose the causes of a rough running or difficult to start engine. If checking and servicing become too difficult, or if a procedure is beyond the scope of the home mechanic, consult your dealer service department or other qualified repair shop. This does not necessarily mean, however, that the emissions control systems are particularly difficult to maintain and repair. You can quickly and easily perform many checks and do most (if not all) of the regular maintenance at home with common tune-up and hand tools. **Note:** *The most frequent cause of emissions system problems is simply a loose or broken vacuum hose or wiring connection. Therefore, always check the hose and wiring connections first.*

Pay close attention to any special precautions outlined in this Chapter. It should be noted that the illustrations of the various systems may not exactly match the system installed on your particular vehicle due to changes made by the manufacturer during production or from year to year.

A Vehicle Emissions Control Information (VECI) label is located in the engine compartment of all vehicles with which this manual is concerned **(see illustration)**. This label contains important emissions specifications and setting procedures, as well as a vacuum hose schematic with emissions components identified. When servicing the engine or emissions systems, the VECI label in your particular vehicle should always be checked for up-to-date information. **Note:** *Because of a federally mandated extended warranty which covers the emission control system components (and any components which have a primary purpose other than emission control but have significant effects on emissions), check with your dealer about warranty coverage before working on any emission related systems.*

The number of emissions control system components on later model fuel-injected vehicles has actually decreased due to the high efficiency of the new fuel injection and ignition systems. These models are equipped with a three way catalytic converter containing beads which are coated with a catalyst material containing platinum, palladium and rhodium to reduce the level of nitrogen oxides.

1.5 A Vehicle Emissions Control Information (VECI) label will be found in the engine compartment of all vehicles - if it's missing, obtain a new one from a dealer parts department (1997 3.1L model shown)

6

2   On Board Diagnostic (OBD) system and trouble codes

Note: *1995 3.1L models are equipped with OBD I self diagnosis system, while 1995 3.4L models and all 1996 and later models are equipped with OBD II self diagnosis system. Both systems require the use of a Scan tool to access trouble codes. However, many of the information sensor checks and replacement procedures do apply to both systems. Because OBD I and OBD II systems require a special SCAN tool to access the trouble codes, have the vehicle diagnosed by a dealer service department or other qualified automotive repair facility if the proper SCAN tool is not available. The codes indicated in the text are designed and mandated by the EPA for all 1995 OBD I and 1995 and later OBD II vehicles produced by automobile manufacturers. These generic trouble codes do not include the manufacturer's specific trouble codes. Consult a dealer service department or other qualified repair shop for additional information. Refer to the troubleshooting tips in the beginning of this manual to gain some insight to the most likely causes of a problem.*

Diagnostic tool information

Refer to illustrations 2.1, 2.2 and 2.4

1   A digital multimeter is a necessary tool for checking fuel injection and emission related components **(see illustration)**. A digital volt-ohmmeter is preferred over the older style analog multimeter for several reasons. The analog multimeter cannot display the volts-ohms or amps measurement in hundredths and thousandths increments. When working with electronic circuits which are often very low voltage, this accurate reading is most important. Another good reason for the digital multimeter is the high impedance circuit. The digital multimeter is equipped with a high resistance internal circuitry (10 million ohms). Because a voltmeter is hooked up in parallel with the circuit when testing, it is vital that none of the voltage being measured should be allowed to travel the parallel path set up by the meter itself. This dilemma does not show itself when measuring larger amounts of voltage (9 to 12 volt circuits) but if you are measuring a low voltage circuit such as the oxygen sensor signal voltage, a fraction of a volt may be a significant amount when diagnosing a problem.

2   Hand-held scanners are the most powerful and versatile tools for analyzing engine management systems used on later model vehicles **(see illustration)**. Early model scanners handle codes and some diagnostics for many OBD I systems. Each brand scan tool must be examined carefully to match the year, make and model of the vehicle you are working on. Often interchangeable cartridges are available to access the particular manufacturer; Ford, GM, Chrysler, etc.). Some manufacturers will specify by continent; Asia, Europe, USA, etc. Seek the advice of your local parts retailer.

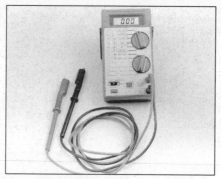

2.1 Digital multimeters can be used for testing all types of circuits; because of their high impedance, they are much more accurate than analog meters for measuring millivolts in low-voltage computer circuits

3   With the arrival of the federally mandated emission control system (OBD II), a specially designed scanner must also be developed. At this time, several manufacturers plan to release OBD II scan tools for the home mechanic. Ask the parts salesperson at a local auto parts store for additional information concerning dates and costs. **Note:** *Although OBD II codes cannot be accessed without a Scan tool, follow the simple component checks in Section 4.*

4   Another type of code reader and less expensive is available at parts stores **(see illustration)**. These tools simplify the procedure for extracting codes from the engine management computer by simply "plugging in" to the diagnostic connector on the vehicle wiring harness.

General description

Refer to illustrations 2.5a and 2.5b

5   The electronically controlled fuel and emissions system is linked with many other related engine management systems. It consists mainly of sensors, output actuators and a Powertrain Control Module (PCM) **(see illustrations)**. Completing the system are various other components which respond to commands from the PCM.

6   In many ways, this system can be compared to the central nervous system in the human body. The sensors (nerve endings) constantly gather information and send this

2.4 Trouble code tools simplify the task of extracting the trouble codes

2.2 Scanners like the Actron Scantool and the AutoXray XP240 are powerful diagnostic aids - programmed with comprehensive diagnostic information, they can tell you just about anything you want to know about your engine management system

data to the PCM (brain), which processes the data and, if necessary, sends out a command for some type of vehicle change (limbs).

7   Here's a specific example of how one portion of this system operates: An oxygen sensor, mounted in the exhaust manifold and protruding into the exhaust gas stream, constantly monitors the oxygen content of the exhaust gas as it travels through the exhaust pipe. If the percentage of oxygen in the exhaust gas is incorrect, an electrical signal is sent to the PCM. The PCM takes this information, processes it and then sends a command to the fuel injectors, telling it to change the fuel/air mixture. To be effective, all this happens in a fraction of a second, and it goes on continuously while the engine is running. The end result is a fuel/air mixture which is constantly kept at a predetermined ratio, regardless of driving conditions.

Obtaining trouble codes

Refer to illustrations 2.11a and 2.11b

8   One might think that a system which uses exotic electrical sensors and is controlled by an on-board computer would be difficult to diagnose. This is not necessarily the case.

9   The On Board Diagnostic (OBD) system has a built-in self-diagnostic system, which indicates a problem by turning on a "SERVICE ENGINE SOON" light on the instrument panel when a fault has been detected. **Note:** *Since some of the trouble codes do not set the 'SERVICE ENGINE SOON' light, it is a good idea to access the OBD system and look for any trouble codes that may have been recorded and need tending.*

10   Perhaps more importantly, the PCM will recognize this fault, in a particular system monitored by one of the various information sensors, and store it in its memory in the form of a trouble code. Although the trouble code cannot reveal the exact cause of the malfunction, it greatly facilitates diagnosis as you or a dealer mechanic can "tap into" the PCM's memory and be directed to the problem area.

2.5a Typical engine control components - 3.1L engine

1	Manifold Absolute Pressure sensor	
2	Digital EGR valve	
3	Idle Air Control valve	
4	Throttle Position Sensor (not visible)	

5	Intake Air Temperature sensor
6	Mass Air Flow sensor
7	Engine Coolant Temperature sensor (not visible)

8	PCV valve
9	Powertrain Control Module
10	Camshaft position sensor (not visible)

2.5b Typical engine control components - 3800 engine

1	Digital EGR valve
2	Idle Air Control valve
3	Mass Air Flow sensor
4	Intake Air Temperature sensor

5	Throttle Position Sensor
6	Engine Coolant Temperature sensor (not visible)

7	Powertrain Control Module
8	PCV valve (underneath MAP sensor)
9	Manifold Absolute Pressure sensor

6

2.11a The 12-pin Data Link Connector (DLC) found on models equipped with OBD I

A *Ground*
B *Diagnostic test terminal (not present on all models)*

11   To retrieve this information from the PCM on most OBD I and all OBD II systems, a SCAN tool must be connected to the Data Link Connector (DLC) **(see illustrations)**. The SCAN tool is a hand-held digital computer scanner that interfaces with the on-board computer. The SCAN tool is a very powerful tool; it not only reads the trouble codes but also displays the actual operating conditions of the sensors and actuators. SCAN tools are expensive, but they are necessary to accurately diagnose a modern computerized fuel-injected engine. SCAN tools are available from automotive parts stores and specialty tool companies. **Note:** *On some 1995 OBD I models with a 12-pin Data Link Connector, trouble codes can be access by connecting terminal B to terminal A with a jumper wire with the ignition key in the ON position, and the codes can be read by watching the flashes of the SERVICE ENGINE SOON light on the instrument panel (for example, one flash, pause, followed by four flashes would indicate a code 14). It should be noted, however, that some models with a 12-pin diagnostic connector do not have a terminal B present in the connector. On these models a scan tool is required to access trouble codes.* **Caution:** *Don't crank or start the engine when terminals A and B are connected by the jumper wire.*

2.11b The 16-pin Data Link Connector (DLC) found on models equipped with OBD II - the DLC (arrow) is located to the right of the steering column

12   The self-diagnosis feature built into this system does not detect all possible faults. If you suspect a problem with the On Board Diagnostic (OBD) system, but the SERVICE ENGINE SOON light has not come on and no trouble codes have been stored, take the vehicle to a dealer service department or other qualified repair shop for diagnosis.
13   Furthermore, when diagnosing an engine performance, fuel economy or exhaust emissions problem (which is not accompanied by a SERVICE ENGINE SOON light) do not automatically assume the fault lies in this system. Perform all standard troubleshooting procedures, as indicated elsewhere in this manual, before turning to the On Board Diagnostic (OBD) system.
14   Finally, since this is an electronic system, you should have a basic knowledge of automotive electronics before attempting any diagnosis. Damage to the PCM, Programmable Read Only Memory (PROM) calibration unit or related components can easily occur if care is not exercised.

Clearing trouble codes

15   To clear the codes from the PCM memory, install the SCAN tool, scroll the menu for the function that describes "CLEARING CODES' and follow the prescribed method for that particular SCAN tool or momentarily remove the PCM/IGN fuse from the fuse box for 30 seconds. Clearing codes may also be accomplished by removing the fusible link (main power fuse) located near the battery positive terminal (see Chapter 12) or by disconnecting the cable from the positive terminal (+) of the battery. **Caution:** *On models equipped with a Theftlock audio system, be sure the lockout feature is turned off before disconnecting the battery cable. Disconnecting the power to the PCM to clear the memory can be an important diagnostic tool, especially on intermittent problems.* **Caution:** *To prevent damage to the PCM, the ignition switch must be OFF when disconnecting or connecting power to the PCM.* **Note:** *Disconnecting the negative battery terminal will erase any radio preset codes that have been stored.*

Trouble Code Identification

16   Following is a list of the typical Trouble Codes which may be encountered while diagnosing the On Board Diagnostic (OBD I and OBD II) system. Also included are simplified troubleshooting procedures. If the problem persists after these checks have been made, the vehicle must be diagnosed by a professional mechanic who can use specialized diagnostic tools and advanced troubleshooting methods to check the system. Procedures marked with an asterisk (*) indicate component replacements which may not cure the problem in all cases. For this reason, you may want to seek professional advice before purchasing replacement parts.

OBD I Trouble Codes

Trouble Code	Circuit or system	Probable cause
13	Oxygen sensor circuit	Check the wiring and connectors from the oxygen sensor. Replace oxygen sensor (see Section 4).*
14	Coolant sensor circuit	If the engine is experiencing overheating problems, the problem must be rectified (high temperature indicated) before continuing (see Chapters 1 and 3). Check all wiring and connectors associated with the sensor. Replace the coolant sensor (see Section 4).*
15	Coolant sensor circuit	See above. Also, check the thermostat for proper operation (low temperature indicated).
16	System voltage low	Check the alternator and or voltage regulator and ignition feed circuit to PCM
17	Camshaft sensor circuit	Check the wiring and connectors from the camshaft position sensor. Replace camshaft position sensor (see Section 4).*
21	TPS circuit (signal voltage high)	Check for sticking or misadjusted TPS. Check all wiring and connections at the TPS and at the PCM. Replace the TPS* (see Section 4).
22	TPS circuit (signal voltage low)	See above.
23	Intake Air Temperature (IAT) sensor	Low temperature indicated (see Section 4).
24	Vehicle Speed Sensor (VSS)	A fault in this circuit should be indicated only while the vehicle is in motion. Disregard code 24 if set when drive wheels are not turning. Check connections at the PCM. Check the TPS setting (see Section 4).

OBD I Trouble Codes (continued)

Trouble Code	Circuit or system	Probable cause
25	Intake Air Temperature (IAT) sensor	High temperature indicated. Check the resistance of the IAT sensor. Check the wiring and connections to the sensor (see Section 4). Replace the (IAT) sensor.*
28	Transmission Range (TR) pressure switch	TR pressure switch in the valve body indicates a fault in the shift detection system between the 5 pressure switches and the TFT sensor. Have the vehicle diagnosed by a dealer service department or other qualified repair shop.
33	Manifold Absolute Pressure (MAP) signal voltage high	Check vacuum hose(s) from MAP sensor. Check electrical sensor or circuit connections at the PCM. Replace MAP sensor (see Section 4).*
34	Manifold Absolute Pressure (MAP) signal voltage low	Check vacuum hose(s) from MAP sensor. Check electrical sensor or circuit connections at the PCM. Replace MAP sensor (see Section 4).*
35	Idle Speed Error	Check the resistance of the IAC valve. Check the wiring and connections to the sensor (see Section 4).
36	24X signal Error	Check the wiring and connectors from the 24X crankshaft position sensor. Replace 24X crankshaft position sensor (see Section 4).*
37	Brake switch stuck "ON"	TCC brake switch indicates an open or short circuit. Have the TCC brake switch checked by a dealer service department or other qualified repair shop.
41	Ignition Control circuit	Timing circuit error. Check the wiring and connectors between the ignition module and the PCM. Check the ignition module (see Chapter 5). Replace the PCM.*
42	Ignition Control Circuit	Bypass error. Check the wiring and connectors between the ignition module and the PCM. Check the ignition module (see Chapter 5). Replace the PCM.*
43	Knock Sensor (KS) circuit	Check the PCM for an open or short to ground; if necessary, reroute the harness away from other wires such as spark plugs, etc. Replace the knock sensor (see Section 4).*
44	Lean exhaust	Check the wiring and connectors from the oxygen sensor to the PCM. Check the PCM ground terminal. Check the fuel pressure (Chapter 4). Replace the oxygen sensor (see Section 4).*
45	Rich exhaust	Check the evaporative charcoal canister and its components for the presence of fuel. Check for fuel or contaminated oil. Check the fuel pressure regulator. Check for a leaking fuel injector. Check for a sticking EGR valve. Replace the oxygen sensor (see Section 4).*
46	PASS-Key circuit	If engine will not start, have theft deterrent system diagnosed by a dealership service department or other qualified repair shop.
51	PROM Error	Faulty or incorrect PROM. Diagnosis should be performed by a dealer service department or other qualified repair shop
53	System voltage high	Code 53 will set if the voltage at the PCM is greater than 17.1-volts. Check the charging system (see Chapter 5).
54	Fuel pump relay low voltage	Check the fuel pump relay and circuit for shorts or damage (see Chapter 4).
58	Transmission Fluid Temperature (TFT) sensor	The TFT sensor located in the valve body indicates a low fluid temperature. Have the transmission diagnosed by a dealer service department or other qualified repair shop.
59	Transmission Fluid Temperature (TFT) sensor	The TFT sensor located in the valve body indicates a high fluid temperature. Have the transmission diagnosed by a dealer service department or other qualified repair shop.
66	A/C refrigerant pressure sensor circuit	Low pressure. signal voltage from the pressure sensor to the PCM is below .1 volt See Chapter 3.
70	A/C refrigerant pressure sensor circuit	High pressure. signal voltage from the pressure sensor to the PCM is above 4.9 volts See Chapter 3.
72	Vehicle speed sensor loss	Output speed remains undetected or inconsistent. Check the VSS (See Section 4).
75	Digital EGR valve	No #1 solenoid faulty or EGR passage obstructed. Have the EGR valve diagnosed by a dealer service department or other qualified repair shop.
76	Digital EGR valve	No #2 solenoid faulty or EGR passage obstructed. Have the EGR valve diagnosed by a dealer service department or other qualified repair shop.
77	Digital EGR valve	No #3 solenoids faulty or EGR passage obstructed. Have the EGR valve diagnosed by a dealer service department or other qualified repair shop.
79	Transmission fluid temperature sensor circuit	PCM detects high transmission temperature. Have the transmission fluid temp sensor and circuit diagnosed by a dealer service department or other qualified repair shop.
80	Transmission Component Error	Torque Converter Clutch (TCC) slippage above 150 RPM Have the transmission diagnosed by a dealer service department or other qualified repair shop.
82	3X signal Error	Check the wiring and connectors from the 3X crankshaft position sensor. Replace 3X crankshaft position sensor (see Section 4).*

6

OBD I Trouble Codes (continued)

Trouble Code	Circuit or system	Probable cause
85	PROM Error	Check connector at PCM. If OK, reprogram the PCM. Service should be performed by a dealer service department or other qualified repair shop.
86	Analog/Digital Error	Check for a short to B+ in all circuits leading to the A/D multiplexer in the PCM. Have the system diagnosed by a dealer service department or other qualified repair shop.
87	EEPROM Error	Check connector at PCM. If OK, reprogram the PCM. Service should be performed by a dealer service department or other qualified repair shop.
90	TCC solenoid circuit	PCM detects incorrect voltage values at the TCC solenoid. Have the TCC system diagnosed by a dealer service department or other qualified repair shop.
96	Transmission circuit	Low voltage. Check the charging system. Have the transmission circuit diagnosed by a dealer service department or other qualified repair shop.
98	PCM program	Invalid. reprogram the PCM. Service should be performed by a dealer service department or other qualified repair shop.
99	PCM program	Invalid. reprogram the PCM. Service should be performed by a dealer service department or other qualified repair shop.

Component replacement may not cure the problem in all cases. For this reason, you may want to seek professional advice before purchasing replacement parts.

OBD II Trouble Codes

Code	Code Definition	Location
P0101	Mass Air Flow (MAF) sensor error	See Section 4
P0102	Mass air flow (MAS) low frequency error	See Section 4
P0103	Mass air flow (MAS) high frequency error	See Section 4
P0107	Manifold Absolute Pressure (MAP) sensor circuit low input	See Section 4
P0108	Manifold Absolute Pressure (MAP) sensor circuit high input	See Section 4
P0112	Intake Air Temperature (IAT) sensor circuit low input	See Section 4
P0113	Intake Air Temperature (IAT) sensor circuit high input	See Section 4
P0117	Electronic Coolant Temperature (ECT) sensor circuit low input	See Section 4
P0118	Electronic Coolant Temperature (ECT) sensor circuit high input	See Section 4
P0121	Throttle Position Sensor (TPS) range/performance fault	See Section 4
P0122	Throttle Position Sensor (TPS) circuit low input	See Section 4
P0123	Throttle Position Sensor (TPS) circuit high input	See Section 4
P0125	Engine coolant temperature error	See Section 4
P0131	Upstream heated O_2 sensor circuit low voltage (Bank 1, Sensor 1)	See Section 4
P0132	Upstream heated O_2 sensor circuit high voltage (Bank 1, Sensor 1)	See Section 4
P0133	Upstream heated oxygen sensor circuit slow response sensor (Bank 1, Sensor 1)	See Section 4
P0137	Downstream heated O_2 sensor circuit low voltage (Bank 1, Sensor 2)	See Section 4
P0138	Downstream heated O_2 sensor circuit high voltage (Bank 1, Sensor 2)	See Section 4
P0140	Downstream heated oxygen sensor circuit insufficient sensor 2 activity	See Section 4
P0141	O_2 sensor heater circuit fault (Bank 1, Sensor 2)	See Section 4
P0171	System Adaptive fuel too lean	See Chapter 4
P0172	System Adaptive fuel too rich	See Chapter 4
P0191	Injector Pressure sensor system performance	See Chapter 4
P0192	Injector Pressure sensor circuit low input	See Chapter 4
P0193	Injector Pressure sensor circuit high input	See Chapter 4
P0201	Fuel injector No. 1 control circuit	See Chapter 4
P0202	Fuel injector No. 2 control circuit	See Chapter 4

OBD II Trouble Codes (continued)

Code	Code Definition	Location
P0203	Fuel injector No. 3 control circuit	See Chapter 4
P0204	Fuel injector No. 4 control circuit	See Chapter 4
P0205	Fuel injector No. 5 control circuit	See Chapter 4
P0206	Fuel injector No. 6 control circuit	See Chapter 4
P0218	Transmission fluid overtemperature	See Chapter 7
P0230	Fuel pump circuit fault	See Chapter 4
P0300	Engine misfire detected	See Chapter 5
P0301	Cylinder number 1 misfire detected	See Chapter 5
P0302	Cylinder number 2 misfire detected	See Chapter 5
P0303	Cylinder number 3 misfire detected	See Chapter 5
P0304	Cylinder number 4 misfire detected	See Chapter 5
P0325	Knock sensor circuit 1 fault	See Section 4
P0326	Knock sensor circuit performance	See Section 4
P0351	COP ignition coil 1 primary circuit fault	See Chapter 5
P0352	COP ignition coil 2 primary circuit fault	See Chapter 5
P0353	COP ignition coil 3 primary circuit fault	See Chapter 5
P0354	COP ignition coil 4 primary circuit fault	See Chapter 5
P0400	EGR flow fault	See Section 5
P0401	EGR insufficient flow detected	See Section 5
P0402	EGR excessive flow detected	See Section 5
P0420	Catalyst system efficiency below threshold (Bank 1)	See Section 8
P0421	Catalyst system efficiency below threshold (Bank 1)	See Section 8
P0430	Catalyst system efficiency below threshold (Bank 2)	See Section 8
P0431	Catalyst system efficiency below threshold (Bank 2)	See Section 8
P0441	EVAP incorrect purge flow	See Section 6
P0443	EVAP VMV circuit fault	See Section 6
P0452	EVAP fuel tank pressure sensor low input	See Section 4
P0453	EVAP fuel tank pressure sensor high input	See Section 4
P0502	VSS circuit low input	See Section 4
P0503	VSS circuit range performance	See Section 4
P0506	IAC system rpm lower than expected	See Chapter 4
P0507	IAC system rpm higher than expected	See Chapter 4
P0602	PCM control module programming error	See Section 4
P0705	Transaxle Range sensor circuit malfunction	See Section 4
P1171	Inadequate fuel flow	See Chapter 4

Component replacement may not cure the problem in all cases. For this reason, you may want to seek professional advice before purchasing replacement parts.

6

---

3 Powertrain Control Module (PCM) - check and replacement

Note 1: *1995 3.4L models are equipped with a replaceable PROM in the PCM that must be installed into the new PCM when exchanged. All other models are equipped with(non-replaceable) EEPROM that must be recalibrated with a special factory SCAN tool (TECH 1) after replacement of the PCM.*

Note 2: *1995 3.1L models and all 1996 and 1997 models are equipped with a replaceable Knock sensor (KS) module in the PCM that must be installed into the new PCM when exchanged.*

Check

1   The PCM on all models is located in the right front corner of the engine compartment. Remove the cover (see Step 7) for access to the PCM.

2   Using the tips of your fingers, tap vigorously on the side of the computer while the engine is running. If the computer is not functioning properly, the engine may stumble or stall and display glitches on the engine data stream obtained using a SCAN tool or other diagnostic equipment.

3   If the PCM fails this test, check the electrical connectors. Each connector is color coded to fit the respective slot in the computer body. If there are no obvious signs

of damage, have the unit checked at a dealer service department or other qualified repair shop.

Replacement

Refer to illustration 3.7

Caution: *To prevent damage to the PCM, the ignition switch must be turned Off when disconnecting or connecting in the PCM connectors.*

4   The PCM on all models is located in the right front corner of the engine compartment.

5   Disconnect the cable from the negative battery terminal. **Caution:** *On models equipped with a Theftlock audio system, be sure the lockout feature is turned off before*

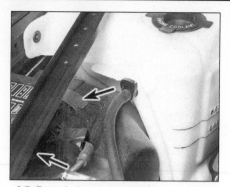

3.7 Detach the clasps (arrows) from the PCM housing cover

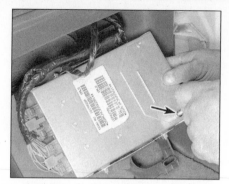

3.13 Remove the access cover from the PCM

3.14 Press the retaining tabs out to release the PROM

disconnecting the battery cable.

6   Remove the engine coolant reservoir (see Chapter 3).

7   Remove the PCM housing cover **(see illustration)**.

8   Carefully lift the PCM from the engine compartment without damaging the electrical connectors and wiring harness to the computer.

9   Unplug the electrical connectors from the PCM. Each connector is color coded to fit its respective receptacle in the PCM.

10   Installation is the reverse of removal.

PROM (1995 3.4L models)

Refer to illustrations 3.13 and 3.14

11   1995 3.4L models are equipped with a memory calibration chip called the PROM. New PCMs are not supplied with a PROM, therefore it is necessary to remove the original and install it into the new PCM. Use care not to damage the PROM when working with these delicate electrical components.

12   Remove the PCM from the engine compartment (see Step 4).

13   Remove the screws and detach the access cover from the PCM **(see illustration)**.

14   Using two fingers, carefully push both retaining clips back away from the PROM and lift the unit straight out of the PCM **(see illustration)**. **Note:** *There are two types of clips used on the PROM sockets; hollow type tabs or solid type tabs.*

15   Installation is the reverse of removal. Be sure to use the alignment notches in the seat

area of the PCM when sliding the PROM back in place. Press only on the ends of the PROM assembly until it snaps back into place.

Knock Sensor (KS) module (1995 3.1L and all 1996 and 1997 models)

Refer to illustrations 3.18 and 3.19

16   1995 3.1L engine, and all 1996 and 1997 models are equipped with a knock sensor (KS) module. New PCMs are not supplied with a KS module, therefore it is necessary to remove the original and install it into the new PCM. Use care not to damage the KS module when working with these delicate electrical components.

17   Remove the PCM from the engine compartment (see Step 4).

18   Remove the screws and detach the access cover from the PCM **(see illustration)**.

19   Using two fingers, carefully squeeze the retaining clips together and lift the KS module straight out of the PCM **(see illustration)**.

20   Installation is the reverse of removal. Be sure to use the alignment notches in the seat area of the PCM when sliding the KS module back in place. Press only on the end of the KS module assembly until it snaps back into place.

EEPROM reprogramming (1995 3.1L and all 1996 and later models)

21   The 1995 3.1L models and 1996 and later models are equipped with Electrical Erasable Programmable Read Only Memory (EEPROM) chip that is permanently soldered

to the PCM circuit board. The EEPROM can be reprogrammed using the GM TECH 1 scan tool. Do not attempt to remove this component from the PCM. Have the EEPROM reprogrammed at a dealer service department or other qualified repair shop.

---

4   Information sensors - general information and testing

Caution 1: *When performing the following tests, use only a high-impedance (10 mega ohms) digital multi-meter to prevent damage to the PCM.*

Caution 2: *On models equipped with a Theftlock audio system, be sure the lockout feature is turned off before disconnecting the battery cable.*

Note 1: *Because this system requires a special TECH 1 SCAN tool to access the self-diagnosis system, have the vehicle codes extracted by a dealer service department or other qualified repair facility if the SCAN tool is not available for diagnostic purposes. There are several checks the home mechanic can perform to test for a NO START condition but in the event the driveability symptoms are intermittent or varied, it will be necessary to monitor the operation of the sensor(s) with a SCAN tool or oscilloscope.*

Note 2: *Refer to Chapter 5 for additional information concerning the ignition system and the crankshaft sensor diagnostics.*

Thermistor (two-wire) sensors (coolant temperature, intake air temperature, etc.)

Refer to illustrations 4.1a and 4.1b

1   Thermistors are variable resistors that sense temperature level changes and convert them to a voltage signal. The engine coolant temperature sensor (ECT) and the intake air temperature sensor (IAT) are thermistor type sensors. As the sensor temperature DECREASES, the resistance will INCREASE. As the sensor temperature INCREASES, the resistance will DECREASE. To check thermistor-type sensors select the ohms range on the multi-meter, disconnect the harness connector at the sensor and connect

3.18 Remove the screws and lift the cover to expose the knock sensor module

3.19 Pinch the tabs and lift the knock sensor module from the PCM

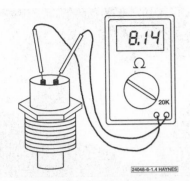

4.1a Be sure the ohmmeter probes make clean contact with the terminals of the sensor when checking the resistance (thermistor type sensor shown)

Temperature (degrees-F)	Resistance (ohms)
212	176
194	240
176	332
158	458
140	668
122	972
112	1182
104	1458
95	1800
86	2238
76	2795
68	3520
58	4450
50	5670
40	7280
32	9420

4.1b Coolant temperature and intake air temperature sensors approximate temperature vs. resistance relationships

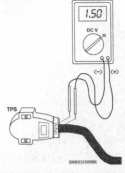

4.3 Carefully backprobe the GROUND (-) and the SIGNAL (+) terminals using straight pins to make contact without disconnecting the harness connector (potentiometer type sensor shown)

the test probes to the sensor terminals **(see illustration)**. The resistance reading (ohms) should be high when the sensor is cold, and low when the sensor is hot **(see illustration)**. Be sure the tips of the probe make clean contact with the terminals inside the sensor to insure an accurate reading.

2   After the resistance of the sensor has been checked, test the system for the proper reference voltage from the computer. Simply disconnect the harness connector at the sensor, select the voltage range on the multi-meter and probe the terminals on the harness for the voltage signal. Reference voltage should be approximately 5.0 volts. The ignition switch must be in the ON position (engine not running). If there is no reference voltage available to the sensor, then the circuit and the computer must be checked.

Potentiometers (three-wire) sensors (TPS, EGR valve position sensor)

Refer to illustration 4.3

3   The potentiometer is a variable resistor that converts the voltage signal by varying the resistance according to the driving situation. The signal the potentiometer generates is used by the computer to determine position and direction of the device within the component. Although it is possible to measure resistance changes of the sensor, it is best to measure voltage changes as the end result of the potentiometer's performance. Select the DC volts function on the multi-meter, carefully backprobe the harness connector using straight pins inserted into the correct terminals and connect the meter probes to the pins. Connect the negative probe (-) to the ground terminal and the positive probe to the SIGNAL terminal. It will be necessary to refer to the wiring diagrams at the end of this manual for the correct terminals. Observe the meter as the signal arm is moved through its complete range (sweep). The voltage should vary as the arm is moved through its range. These sensors are often used as the throttle position sensor or the EGR valve position sensor. Most of these type sensors will vary from as little as 0.2 volts, up to 5.0 volts (closed to open).

VOLTAGE RANGE	ALTITUDE
3.8 - 5.5V	Below 1,000
3.6 - 5.3V	1,000 - 2,000
3.5 - 5.1V	2.000 - 3,000
3.3 - 5.0V	3,000 - 4,000
3.2 - 4.8V	4,000 - 5,000
3.0 - 4.6V	5,000 - 6,000
2.9 - 4.5V	6,000 - 7,000
2.8 - 4.3V	7,000 - 8,000
2.6 - 4.2V	8,000 - 9,000
2.5 - 4.0V	9,000 - 10,000 FEET

LOW ALTITUDE = HIGH PRESSURE = HIGH VOLTAGE

4.5a Typical Manifold Absolute Pressure (MAP) sensor altitude (pressure) vs. voltage values

4   After the SIGNAL voltage has been checked, test the system for the proper reference voltage from the computer. Simply disconnect the harness connector at the sensor, select the voltage range on the rotary switch on the volt/ohmmeter and probe the correct terminals on the harness for the voltage signal. Reference voltage should be approximately 5.0 volts. The ignition switch must be in the ON position (engine not running). If there is no reference voltage available to the sensor, then the circuit and the computer must be checked.

Pressure/vacuum (three-wire) sensors (MAP, BARO, vacuum sensors, etc.)

Refer to illustrations 4.5a and 4.5b

5   The pressure/vacuum sensors monitor the intake manifold pressure changes resulting from changes in engine load and speed and converts the information into a voltage output. The PCM uses the sensor to control fuel delivery and ignition timing. The sensor SIGNAL voltage to the PCM varies from below 2.0 volts at idle (high vacuum) to above 4.0 volts with the ignition key ON (engine not running) or wide open throttle (WOT) (low vacuum). These values correspond with the altitude and pressure changes

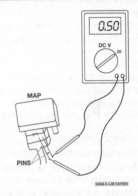

4.5b It will be necessary to run the engine to check for voltage fluctuations in order to create pressure and vacuum changes within the system (pressure/vacuum type sensor shown)

the vehicle experiences while driving **(see illustration)**. Select the DC volts function on the meter, carefully backprobe the harness connector terminals using straight pins and connect the voltmeter probes to the pins **(see illustration)**. Connect the negative probe (-) to the ground terminal and the positive probe to the SIGNAL terminal. It will be necessary to refer to the manufacturer's schematic or wiring diagram for the correct terminals. Observe the meter as the engine idles and then slowly raise the engine rpm to wide open throttle. The voltage should increase from approximately 0.5 to 1.5 volts (high vacuum) to 5.0 volts (low vacuum). If the engine stalls or runs roughly, it is possible to simulate conditions by attaching a hand-held vacuum pump to the pressure/vacuum sensor to simulate running conditions. Also, be sure the manufacturer specifies the type of pressure/vacuum sensor installed on the vehicle. Some manufacturers equip the fuel injection system with a voltage varying sensor while others use a frequency varying sensor. The latter type must be checked using the frequency (Hz) scale on the meter.

6   If SIGNAL voltage does not exist, test the system for the proper reference voltage

6

from the computer. Simply disconnect the harness connector at the sensor, select the voltage range on the meter and probe the correct terminals on the harness for the voltage signal. Reference voltage should be approximately 5.0 volts. The ignition switch must be in the ON position (engine not running). If there is no reference voltage available to the sensor, then the circuit and the computer must be checked.

Magnetic reluctance (two-wire) sensors (crankshaft, vehicle speed, etc.)

Refer to illustration 4.7

7   Magnetic reluctance type sensors consist of a permanent magnet with a coil wire wound around the assembly. Crankshaft sensors and vehicle speed sensors are common applications of this type sensor. A steel disk mounted on a gear (crankshaft, input shaft, etc.) has tabs that pass between the pole pieces of the magnet causing a break in the magnetic field when passed near the sensor. This break in the field causes a magnetic flux producing reluctance (resistance) thereby changing the voltage signal. This voltage signal is used to determine crankshaft position, vehicle speed, etc. Because magnetic energy is a free-standing source of energy and does not require battery power to produce voltage, this type of sensor must be checked by observing voltage fluctuations with an AC volt meter. Simply switch the voltmeter to the AC scale and connect the probes to the sensor. On vehicle speed sensors it will be necessary to place the transmission in neutral, then with the help of an assistant, hold one tire still while spinning the other tire (approximately 2 MPH or faster) and, observe the voltage fluctuations. This test can also be performed with the sensor removed from the vehicle, by turning the sensor's drive gear **(see illustration)**. **Note:** *Some vehicle speed sensors don't have a drive gear - this type of sensor will have to be checked in place.* On crankshaft position sensors it will be necessary to have an assistant crank the engine over in short bursts at the ignition key while you observe the voltage fluctuations. The meter should register slight voltage fluctuations that are constant and relatively the same range. These small voltage fluctuations indicate that the magnetic portion of the sensor is producing a magnetic field and "sensing" engine parameters for the computer.

Hall effect (three-wire) sensors (crankshaft, camshaft, etc.)

Refer to illustration 4.9

8   These sensors consist of a single hall effect switch, and a magnet which are separated by an air gap. The hall effect switch completes the ground circuit when a magnetic field is present. As the engine rotates, these sensors will produce ON OFF signals to the PCM to determine crankshaft and camshaft position and speed. Hall effect

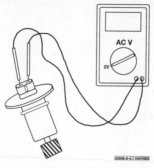

4.7 Connect the probes of the volt meter directly to the VSS and observe AC voltage fluctuations as the drive gear is slowly rotated

crankshaft sensors generally use an interrupter ring located on the back of the crankshaft balancer to disrupt the ground signal from the sensor. Always be sure to check the interrupter ring for damage while diagnosing a faulty crankshaft position sensor. Hall effect camshaft sensors typically use a rotating magnet on the camshaft sprocket or in the sensor housing to complete the hall effect switch ground signal. The PCM uses the sensors to control fuel delivery and ignition timing. The camshaft sensor typically produces only one ON OFF signal per camshaft revolution while the crankshaft sensor produces as many as thirty ON OFF signals per crankshaft revolution depending on the make and manufacturer of the vehicle.

9   To check Hall effect type sensors, select the DC volts function on the multi-meter, carefully backprobe the harness connector terminals using pins and connect the voltmeter probes to the pins **(see illustration)**. Connect the negative probe (-) to the ground connection and the positive probe to the SIGNAL terminal. It will be necessary to refer to the wiring diagrams at the back of this manual for the correct terminals. With the ignition key in the ON position and the engine OFF, rotate the engine crankshaft by hand (one full turn) and observe the voltmeter. If the sensor is operating properly it should trigger ON OFF voltage readings on the voltmeter while the engine is being rotated. Depending on the make and model of the vehicle, there should be 5.0 to 12 volts of signal voltage. **Note:** *When testing camshaft sensors it may be necessary to have an assistant crank the engine over in short bursts at the ignition key (detach the primary (low-voltage) wires from the coil to prevent the engine from starting) while observing the voltmeter. It could take as many as two complete crankshaft revolutions before a camshaft sensor signal is detected.*

10   If SIGNAL voltage does not exist, test the system for the proper reference voltage from the computer. Simply disconnect the harness connector at the sensor, select the voltage range on the rotary switch on the volt/ohmmeter and probe the correct terminals on the harness for the reference

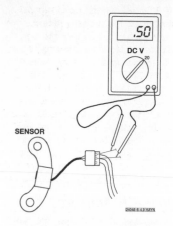

4.9 Carefully backprobe the GROUND (-) and the SIGNAL (+) terminals using sewing pins to make contact without disconnecting the harness connector (Hall effect type sensor shown)

signal. Depending on the make and model of the vehicle there should be 5.0 to 12 volts of reference voltage (5 volts is the most common). The ignition switch must be in the ON position (engine not running). If there is no reference voltage available to the sensor, the circuit and the computer must be checked.

Dual Hall effect (four-wire) sensors (crankshaft)

11   Dual Hall effect sensors consist of two hall-effect switches and a shared magnet mounted between them. The magnet and each Hall-effect switch are separated by an air gap. Each hall effect switch completes the ground circuit when a magnetic field is present. Dual hall effect sensors are often used as a crankshaft sensor in place of two single hall effect switches described above. Typically the crankshaft balancer is equipped with two "interrupter rings" (each having a different number of interrupter blades) which create two separate ON OFF signal patterns that can be used for the timing and the ignition sequence.

12   To check dual hall effect type sensors, select the DC volts function with the rotary switch, carefully backprobe the harness connector terminals using pins and position the voltmeter probes onto the pins **(see illustration 4.9)**. Connect the negative probe (-) to the ground connection and the positive probe to one SIGNAL terminal. It will be necessary to refer to the manufacturer's schematic or wiring diagram for the correct terminals. With the ignition key in the ON position and the engine OFF, rotate the engine crankshaft by hand (one full turn) and observe the volt meter. Next, connect the positive probe to the second SIGNAL terminal. If the sensor is operating properly it should trigger ON OFF voltage readings on the voltmeter from both SIGNAL terminals while the engine is being rotated. Depending on the make and model of the vehicle, there should be 5 to 12 volts of signal voltage at each terminal.

13 If SIGNAL voltage does not exist, test the system for the proper reference voltage from the computer. Simply disconnect the harness connector at the sensor, select the voltage range on the rotary switch on the volt/ohmmeter and probe the correct terminals on the harness for the reference signal. Depending on the make and model of the vehicle there should be 5.0 to 12 volts of reference voltage (5 volts is the most common). The ignition switch must be in the ON position (engine not running). If there is no reference voltage available to the sensor, the circuit and the computer must be checked.

Oxygen (O₂) sensors

14 The oxygen sensor(s) monitors the oxygen content of the exhaust gas stream. The oxygen content in the exhaust reacts with the oxygen sensor to produce a voltage output which varies from 0.1-volt (high oxygen, lean mixture) to 0.9-volts (low oxygen, rich mixture). The PCM constantly monitors this variable voltage output to determine the ratio of oxygen to fuel in the mixture. The PCM alters the air/fuel mixture ratio by controlling the pulse width (open time) of the fuel injectors. The PCM and the oxygen sensor(s) attempt to maintain a mixture ratio of 14.7 parts air to 1 part ratio of fuel at all times. The oxygen sensor produces no voltage when it is below its normal operating temperature of about 600-degrees F. During this initial period before warm-up, the PCM operates in OPEN LOOP mode. When checking the oxygen sensor system, it will be necessary to test all oxygen sensors. **Note:** *Because the oxygen sensor(s) are difficult to access, probing the harness electrical connectors for testing purposes will require patience. The exhaust manifolds and pipes are extremely hot and will melt stray electrical probes and leads that touch the surface during testing. If possible, use a SCAN tool that plugs into the DLC (diagnostic link). This tool will access the PCM data stream and indicates the millivolt changes for each individual oxygen sensor.*

15 Check the oxygen sensor millivolt signal. Locate the oxygen sensor electrical connector and carefully backprobe it using a long pin(s) into the appropriate wire terminals. In most models, connect the positive probe (+) of a voltmeter onto the SIGNAL wire and the negative probe (-) to the ground wire. Consult the wiring diagrams at the end of Chapter 12 for additional information on the oxygen sensor electrical connector wire color designations. **Note:** *Downstream oxygen sensors will produce much slower fluctuating voltage values to reflect the results of the catalyzed exhaust mixture from rich or lean to less presence of CO, HC and Nox molecules. Here the CO₂ and H₂O gaseous forms do not register or react with the oxygen sensors to such a large degree.* Monitor the SIGNAL voltage (millivolts) as the engine goes from cold to warm.

16 The oxygen sensor will produce a steady voltage signal of approximately 0.1 to 0.2 volts (100 to 200 millivolts) with the engine cold (open loop). After a period of approximately two minutes, the engine will reach operating temperature and the oxygen sensor will start to fluctuate between 0.1 to 0.9 volts (100 to 900 millivolts) (closed loop). If the oxygen sensor fails to reach the closed loop mode or there is a very long period of time until it does switch into closed loop mode, replace the oxygen sensor with a new part. **Note:** *Downstream oxygen sensors will not change voltage values as quickly as upstream oxygen sensors. Because the downstream oxygen sensors detect oxygen content after the exhaust has been catalyzed, voltage values should fluctuate much slower and deliberate.*

17 Also inspect the oxygen sensor heater. Disconnect the oxygen sensor electrical connector and working on the oxygen sensor side, connect an ohmmeter between the black wire (-) and brown wire (+). It should measure approximately 5 to 7 ohms. **Note:** *The wire colors often change from the harness connector to the oxygen sensor connector wires according to manufacturer's specifications. Follow the wire colors to the oxygen sensor electrical connector and determine the matching wires and their colors before testing the heater resistance.*

18 Check for proper supply voltage to the heater. Disconnect the oxygen sensor electrical connector and working on the engine side of the harness, measure the voltage between the black wire (-) and brown wire (+) on the oxygen sensor electrical connector. There should be battery voltage with the ignition key ON (engine not running). If there is no voltage, check the circuit between the main relay, the fuse and the sensor. **Note:** *It is important to remember that supply voltage will only reach the O₂ sensor with the ignition key ON (engine not running).*

19 If the oxygen sensor fails any of these tests, replace it with a new part.

Mass Air Flow (MAF) sensors

20 The MAF sensor measures the amount of air passing through the sensor body and ultimately entering the engine through the throttle body. The PCM uses this information to control fuel delivery - the more air entering the engine (acceleration), the more fuel needed.

21 A SCAN tool is necessary to check the output of the MAF sensor. The SCAN tool displays the sensor output in grams per second. With the engine idling at normal operating temperature, the display should read 4 to 7 grams per second. When the engine is accelerated the values should raise and remain steady at any given RPM. A failure in the MAF sensor or circuit will also set a diagnostic trouble code.

Knock sensors

22 Knock sensors detect abnormal vibration in the engine. The knock control system is designed to reduce spark knock during periods of heavy detonation. This allows the engine to use maximum spark advance to improve driveability. Knock sensors produce AC output voltage which increases with the severity of the knock. The signal is fed into the PCM and the timing is retarded to compensate for the severe detonation.

23 To check a knock sensor, disconnect the electrical connector and drain the engine coolant as described in Chapter 1. Remove the sensor from the engine block, then reconnect the wiring harness to it. **Note:** *Most knock sensors have a 1/4-inch pipe thread, use a pipe plug of the same size to thread into the engine block as the sensor is removed. This will relieve the task of draining the coolant with minimal coolant loss.* These type of sensors must be checked by observing voltage fluctuations with a voltmeter. Simply switch the voltmeter to the lowest voltage scale and connect the negative probe (-) to the sensor body (ground) and the positive probe to the sensor terminal. With the voltmeter connected to the sensor, gently tap on the bottom of the knock sensor with a hammer or similar device (this simulates the knock from the engine) and observe voltage fluctuations on the meter. If no voltage fluctuations can be detected, the sensor is bad and should be replaced with a new part.

Neutral Start switch

24 The Neutral Start switch or Transaxle range sensor, located on the rear upper part of the automatic transaxle, indicates to the PCM when the transaxle is in Park or Neutral. This information is used for Transaxle Converter Clutch (TCC), Exhaust Gas Recirculation (EGR) and Idle Air Control (IAC) valve operation. **Caution:** *The vehicle should not be driven with the Neutral Start switch disconnected because idle quality will be adversely affected.*

25 For more information regarding the Neutral Start switch, which is part of the Neutral start and back-up light switch assembly, see Chapter 7.

Air conditioning control

26 During air conditioning operation, the PCM controls the application of the air conditioning compressor clutch. The PCM controls the air conditioning clutch control relay to delay clutch engagement after the air conditioning is turned ON to allow the IAC valve to adjust the idle speed of the engine to compensate for the additional load. The PCM also controls the relay to disengage the clutch on WOT (wide open throttle) to prevent excessively high rpm on the compressor. Be sure to check the air conditioning system as detailed in Chapter 3 before attempting to diagnose the air conditioning clutch or electrical system.

Power steering pressure sensor

27 Turning the steering wheel increases power steering fluid pressure and engine

6

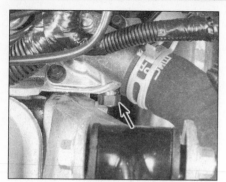

5.1 Location of the engine coolant temperature (ECT) sensor (arrow) (3800 engine shown, 3.1L similar)

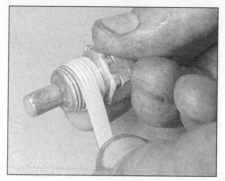

5.2 To prevent coolant leakage, be sure to wrap the temperature sensor threads with Teflon tape before installation

5.7 On 3.1L and 3.4L models, remove the clamps (arrows) securing the MAF sensor to the air cleaner housing and the air intake duct

load. The pressure switch will close before the load can cause an idle problem. A pressure switch that will not open or an open circuit from the PCM will cause timing to retard at idle and this will affect idle quality. A pressure switch that will not close or an open circuit may cause the engine to die when the power steering system is used heavily. Any problems with the power steering pressure switch or circuit should be repaired by a dealer service department or other qualified repair shop.

Fuel Tank Pressure (FTP) sensor

28   The fuel tank pressure (FTP) sensor is used to monitor the fuel tank pressure or vacuum during the OBD II test portion for emissions integrity. This test scans various sensors and output actuators to detect abnormal amounts of fuel vapors that may not be purging into the canister and/or the intake system for recycling. The FTP sensor helps the PCM monitor this pressure differential (pressure vs. vacuum) inside the fuel tank. Any problems with the fuel tank pressure (FTP) sensor or circuit should be repaired by a dealer service department or other qualified repair shop.

Transaxle Converter Clutch (TCC) system

29   The purpose of the Torque Converter Clutch (TCC) system, equipped in automatic transaxles, is to eliminate the power loss of the torque converter stage when the vehicle is in the cruising mode (usually above 35 mph). This economizes the automatic transaxle to the fuel economy of the manual transaxle. The lock-up mode is controlled by the PCM through the activation of the TCC apply solenoid which is built into the automatic transaxle. When the vehicle reaches a specified speed, the PCM energizes the solenoid and allows the torque converter to lock-up and mechanically couple the engine to the transaxle, under which conditions emissions are at their minimum. However, because of other operating condition demands (deceleration, passing, idle, etc.), the transaxle must also function in its normal, fluid-coupled mode.

When such latter conditions exist, the solenoid de-energizes, returning the torque converter to normal operation. The converter also returns to normal operation whenever the brake pedal is depressed.
30   Due to the requirement of special diagnostic equipment for the testing of this system, and the possible requirement for dismantling of the automatic transaxle to replace components of this system, Checking and replacing of the components should be handled by a dealer service department or other qualified repair facility.

5   Information sensors - replacement

Engine Coolant Temperature (ECT) sensor

Refer to illustrations 5.1 and 5.2
Warning: *Wait until the engine is completely cool before beginning this procedure.*
1   The coolant temperature sensor on 3.1L and 3800 models is located below the thermostat housing **(see illustration)**. On the 3.4L engine it is located on the lower intake manifold at the rear of the right cylinder head (facing the firewall). The coolant temperature sensor is a thermistor (a resistor which varies the value of its resistance in accordance with temperature changes). Refer to Section 4 for

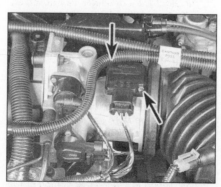

5.8 On the 3800 engine, remove the screws (arrows) securing the MAF sensor to the throttle body

the checking procedures.
2   Before installing the new sensor, wrap the threads with Teflon sealing tape to prevent leakage and thread corrosion **(see illustration)**.
3   To remove the sensor, release the locking tab, unplug the electrical connector, then carefully unscrew the sensor. **Caution:** *Handle the coolant sensor with care. Damage to this sensor will affect the operation of the entire fuel injection system.*
4   Installation is the reverse of removal. Check the coolant level and add some, if necessary (see Chapter 1).

Mass Airflow (MAF) sensor (1995 3.4L and all 1996 and later models)

Refer to illustrations 5.7 and 5.8
5   The Mass Airflow Sensor (MAF) is located on the air intake duct on 3.1L and 3.4L models and is located on the throttle body on the 3800 engine **(see illustration 2.5a and 2.5b)**. The MAF sensor is a hot-wire type sensor and is used to measure the amount of air entering the engine. Refer to Section 4 for the checking procedures.
6   Disconnect the electrical connector from the MAF sensor.
7   On 3.1L and 3.4L models, loosen the clamps securing the MAF sensor to the air intake duct and remove the sensor from the vehicle **(see illustration)**.

5.13 On the 3800 engine, squeeze the clips and disengage the MAP sensor from the PCV valve housing

5.15 Location of the Intake Air Temperature (IAT) sensor (arrow)

5.18 Location of the downstream oxygen sensor - some 1995 models may not be equipped with a downstream oxygen sensor

5.23 Use a special slotted socket to remove the oxygen sensor from the exhaust manifold or exhaust pipe

8   On the 3800 engine, remove the bolts and lift the MAF sensor from the throttle body **(see illustration)**.

9   Installation is the reverse of removal.

Manifold Absolute Pressure (MAP) sensor

Refer to illustration 5.13

10   The Manifold Absolute Pressure (MAP) sensor on 3.1L models is mounted to the upper intake manifold in front of the ignition coils, On 3.4L models, the MAP sensor is located on top of the intake plenum next to the throttle body and on the 3800 engine it is located at the front of the engine underneath the fuel injector trim cover **(see illustration 2.5a and 2.5b)**. This sensor is a pressure/vacuum type sensor which monitors the intake manifold pressure changes resulting from changes in engine load and speed. Refer to Section 4 for the checking procedures.

11   To replace the sensor on 3.1L models, detach the vacuum hose, unplug the electrical connector and remove the mounting screws.

12   To replace the sensor on 3.4L models, unplug the electrical connector and remove the sensor retaining bracket and bolt. Then pull straight up to remove it.

13   To replace the sensor on the 3800 engine, unplug the electrical connector and detach the retaining clips to remove it **(see illustration)**.

14   Installation is the reverse of removal.

Intake Air Temperature (IAT) sensor

Refer to illustration 5.15

15   The Intake Air Temperature (IAT) sensor is located inside the air duct directly downstream of the air filter housing on all models **(see illustration)**. Also refer to **illustrations 2.5a and 2.5b** if necessary. The IAT sensor is a thermistor (a resistor which varies the value of its resistance in accordance with temperature changes). Refer to Section 4 for the checking procedures.

16   To remove an IAT sensor, unplug the electrical connector and remove the sensor from the air intake duct. Carefully twist the sensor to release it from the rubber boot.

17   Installation is the reverse of removal.

Oxygen sensor(s)

Refer to illustrations 5.18 and 5.23

Note: *Because it is installed in the exhaust manifold or pipe, which contracts when cool, the oxygen sensor may be very difficult to loosen when the engine is cold. Rather than risk damage to the sensor (assuming you are planning to reuse it in another manifold or pipe) or the threads which it screws into, start and run the engine for a minute or two, then shut it off. Be careful not to burn yourself during the following procedure.*

18   1995 3.1L and 3800 models are equipped with a single heated oxygen sensor located in the rear exhaust manifold while 1995 3.4L and all 1996 and later models are equipped with an upstream O2 sensor (before the catalytic converter in the rear exhaust manifold) and a downstream O2 sensor (after the catalytic converter) **(see illustration)**. The oxygen sensor(s) monitors the oxygen content of the exhaust gas stream. Oxygen content in the exhaust reacts with the oxygen sensor to produce a voltage output which allows the PCM to change the air fuel ratio in the engine. Refer to Section 4 for the checking procedures.

19   The following is a list of special precautions which must be taken whenever the sensor is serviced.

a) *The oxygen sensor has a permanently attached pigtail and electrical connector which should not be removed from the sensor. Damage or removal of the pigtail or electrical connector can adversely affect operation of the sensor.*

b) *Grease, dirt and other contaminants should be kept away from the electrical connector and the louvered end of the sensor.*

c) *Do not use cleaning solvents of any kind on the oxygen sensor.*

d) *Do not drop or roughly handle the sensor.*

e) *The silicone boot must be installed in the correct position to prevent the boot from being melted and to allow the sensor to operate properly.*

f) *The sensor is designed to allow air circulation to the internal portion of the sensor. Whenever the sensor is removed and installed or replaced, make sure the air passages are not restricted.*

20   Disconnect the cable from the negative terminal of the battery. **Caution:** *On models equipped with a Theftlock audio system, be sure the lockout feature is turned off before disconnecting the battery cable.*

21   Raise the vehicle and place it securely on jackstands.

22   Remove any exhaust heat shields which would interfere with the removal of the oxygen sensor(s), then disconnect the electrical connector from the sensor.

23   Carefully unscrew the sensor from the exhaust manifold or the exhaust pipe **(see illustration)**.

24   Anti-seize compound must be used on the threads of the sensor to facilitate future removal. The threads of new sensors will already be coated with this compound, but if an old sensor is removed and reinstalled, recoat the threads.

25   Install the sensor and tighten it securely.

26   Reconnect the electrical connector of the pigtail lead to the main engine wiring harness.

27   Lower the vehicle, take it on a test drive and check to see that no trouble codes set.

Throttle Position Sensor (TPS)

Refer to illustrations 5.28 and 5.30

28   The Throttle Position Sensor (TPS) is located on the end of the throttle shaft on the throttle body **(see illustration)**. The TPS is a potentiometer type sensor and is used to

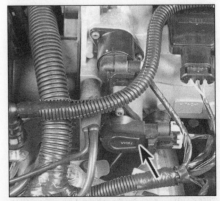

5.28 The Throttle Position Sensor (arrow) is located on the side of the throttle body (3800 engine shown)

6

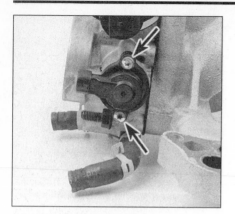

5.30 Remove the TPS mounting screws (arrows)

5.33a The 24x crankshaft sensor and dual hall effect crankshaft sensor (arrow) is mounted at the front of the engine behind the crankshaft balancer (3800 engine shown)

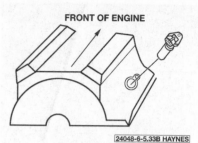

5.33b The 3X and 7X crankshaft sensor is mounted on the right side of the engine block (facing the firewall)

measure the throttle valve position and angle. Refer to Section 4 for the checking procedures.

29 Disconnect the electrical connector from the TPS. **Note:** *It may be necessary to remove the air inlet tube (air duct) to access the sensor connector.*

30 Remove the mounting screws from the TPS **(see illustration)** and remove the TPS from the throttle body.

31 When installing the TPS, be sure to align the socket locating tangs on the TPS with the throttle shaft in the throttle body.

32 Installation is the reverse of removal.

Crankshaft position sensor(s)

Refer to illustrations 5.33a, 5.33b and 5.39

33 3.1L and 3.4L models are equipped with two crankshaft position sensor(s), the first crankshaft sensor (24X sensor) is mounted at the front of the engine behind the crankshaft balancer **(see illustration)**. The 24X sensor is a hall effect type sensor that produces 24 ON/OFF signals per crankshaft revolution. This sensor monitors crankshaft position and speed to improve idle spark control below 1250 RPM. The second crankshaft sensor (3X sensor on 1995 models or a 7X sensor on 1996 and later models) is mounted on the side of the engine block **(see illustration)**. 3X and 7X sensors are hall effect type sensors that produce 7 ON/OFF signals per crankshaft revolution. This sensor

monitors crankshaft position and speed for the Ignition control module which then in turn sends a signal to the PCM to control the ignition and fuel systems. Refer to Section 4 for the checking procedures.

34 3800 models are equipped with a dual (18X and 3X) crankshaft position sensor which is mounted at the front of the engine behind the crankshaft balancer **(see illustration 5.33a)**. This sensor is a dual hall effect type sensor that can produce two signal patterns (outputs) at the same time. The 18X portion of the switch will produce 18 ON/OFF signals per crankshaft revolution while the 3X portion of the switch will produce 3 ON/OFF signals per crankshaft revolution. Refer to Section 4 for the checking procedures.

24X and dual hall effect sensor replacement

35 Disconnect the negative terminal from the battery. **Caution:** *On models equipped with a Theftlock audio system, be sure the lockout feature is turned off before disconnecting the battery cable.*

36 Disconnect the electrical connector from the crankshaft sensor.

37 Remove the crankshaft balancer (see Chapter 2).

38 On 3800 models, carefully pry off the sensor cover. On 3.1L and 3.4L models, remove the connector retaining bracket.

39 Remove the bolts securing the sensor to the front cover **(see illustration)**.

40 Installation is the reverse of removal. Tighten the bolts to the torque listed in this Chapter's Specifications.

3X and 7X sensor replacement

41 Disconnect the negative terminal from the battery. **Caution:** *On models equipped with a Theftlock audio system, be sure the lockout feature is turned off before disconnecting the battery cable.*

42 Disconnect the electrical connector from the crankshaft sensor.

43 Remove the bolt from the crankshaft sensor and remove the sensor.

44 Installation is the reverse of removal. Tighten the bolts to the torque listed in this Chapter's Specifications.

Camshaft position sensor

Refer to illustration 5.45a and 5.45b

45 The camshaft sensor on 3.1L models is mounted at the front of the engine block in between the cylinder heads **(see illustration)**. The camshaft sensor on 3.4L models is mounted to the top of the left cylinder head at the rear of the engine. The camshaft sensor on 3800 models is mounted in the front cover of the engine above the crankshaft sensor **(see illustration)**. The camshaft sensor is a

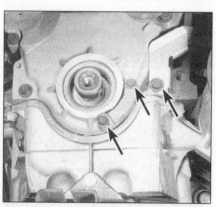

5.39 Remove the sensor retaining bolts (arrows) (3.1L engine shown)

5.45a On 3.1L models, follow the cam sensor wiring harness (arrows) to locate the cam sensor

5.45b On the 3800 engine, the camshaft sensor (arrow) is located on the front cover (view from below)

5.50 There are two knock sensors (arrow), one on each side of the engine block

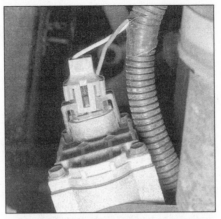

5.52a Typical Vehicle speed sensor (VSS) found on 1995 and 1996 models - the speed sensor is located at the rear of the transaxle housing near the right driveaxle

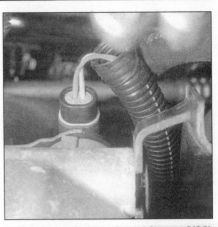

5.52b Typical Vehicle Speed Sensor (VSS) found on 1997 and 1998 models

hall effect type sensor which produces 1 ON/OFF signal for every two crankshaft revolutions. This signal tells the PCM that the No. 1 piston is on the intake stroke. Refer to Section 4 for the checking procedures.

46 Disconnect the negative terminal from the battery. **Caution:** *On models equipped with a Theftlock audio system, be sure the lockout feature is turned off before disconnecting the battery cable.*

47 Disconnect the electrical connector from the camshaft sensor. **Note:** *On 3.1L models it may be necessary remove the power steering pump to allow access to the camshaft sensor.*

48 Remove the bolt from the camshaft sensor and remove the sensor.

49 Installation is the reverse of removal. Tighten the bolts to the torque listed in this Chapter's Specifications.

Knock sensors

Refer to illustration 5.50

Warning: *Wait for the engine to cool completely before performing this procedure.*

50 The knock sensor(s) are located on each side of the engine block **(see illustration)**. This sensor is used to control spark knock by retarding ignition timing during periods of heavy detonation. Refer to Section 4 for the checking procedures.

51 The knock sensor is threaded into the engine block coolant passage, when it is removed, the coolant will drain from the engine block. Drain the cooling system (see Chapter 1). Place a drain pan under the sensor, disconnect the electrical connector and remove the knock sensor. A new sensor is pre-coated with thread sealant, do not apply any additional sealant or the operation of the sensor may be effected. Install the knock sensor and tighten it securely (approximately 14 ft-lbs). Don't overtighten the sensor or damage may occur. Plug in the electrical connector, refill the cooling system and check for leaks.

Vehicle Speed Sensor (VSS)

Refer to illustrations 5.52a and 5.52b

52 The Vehicle Speed Sensor (VSS) is located at the rear the transaxle housing near the right drive axle **(see illustrations)**. This sensor is a magnetic reluctance type sensor which sends a pulsing voltage signal to the PCM, which the PCM converts to miles per hour. The VSS is major component in the Transaxle Converter Clutch (TCC) system. Refer to Section 4 for the checking procedures.

53 To replace the VSS, detach the sensor retaining bolt(s) and or bracket, unplug the sensor and remove it from the transaxle.

54 Installation is the reverse of removal.

---

6 Exhaust Gas Recirculation (EGR) system

General description

1 The EGR system meters exhaust gases into the engine induction system through passages cast into the intake manifold. From there the exhaust gases pass into the fuel/air mixture for the purpose of lowering combustion temperatures, thereby reducing the amount of oxides of nitrogen (NOx) formed.

2 The linear EGR valve feeds small amounts of exhaust gas back into the intake manifold and then into the combustion chamber independent of intake manifold vacuum. The linear EGR valve operates without intake manifold vacuum thereby allowing accurate (finer) amounts of exhaust gas to be recirculated back into the intake system. A PCM controlled pintle within the linear EGR valve passes exhaust gasses through a small orifice upon command from the PCM. This EGR valve operates similar to the stepper motor type particular to IAC valves that control idle quality. By sending a 5 volt reference signal to the EGR valve, the PCM detects and sets the pintle

position with the feedback signal from the EGR valve.

3 Common engine problems associated with the EGR system are rough idling or stalling at idle, rough engine performance during light throttle application and stalling during deceleration.

4 If the EGR system will not allow the PCM to control the position of the EGR valve pintle, it will set a diagnostic trouble code. Have the EGR system checked by a dealer service department or qualified independent repair facility in the event of EGR system failure.

Check

5 Special electronic diagnostic equipment is needed to check this valve and should be left to a dealer service department or other qualified repair facility.

Replacement

Refer to illustration 6.7

6 Disconnect the electrical connector from the EGR valve.

7 Remove the two mounting bolts and remove the EGR valve from the intake manifold or EGR valve adapter **(see illustration)**.

8 Remove the EGR valve and gasket.

6

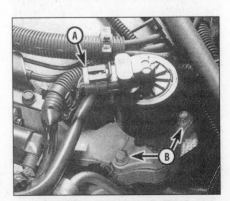

6.7 Disconnect the electrical connector (A) and remove the linear EGR valve mounting bolts (B)

9   Clean the mounting surface of the EGR valve. Remove all traces of gasket material from the intake manifold and from the valve if it is to be reinstalled. Clean both mating surfaces with a cloth dipped in lacquer thinner or acetone.

10   Install a new gasket and the EGR valve and tighten the bolts securely.

11   Connect the electrical connector onto the EGR valve.

7   Evaporative Emissions Control (EVAP) System

Note: *These models are equipped with an Enhanced Evaporative Emission (EVAP) system. This EVAP system will conduct up to eight different tests using the On Board Diagnostic system to detect leaks, pressure variations or electrical problems within this closed network. Because it is governed by the PCM and OBD II emissions regulations, have the system checked by a dealer service department in the event of malfunction.*

General description

Refer to illustration 7.1

1   This system is designed to trap and store fuel that evaporates from the throttle body and fuel tank which would normally enter the atmosphere and contribute to hydrocarbon (HC) emissions **(see illustration)**.

2   The system consists of a charcoal-filled canister and lines running to and from the canister. These lines include a vent line from the gas tank, a vent line from the throttle body, an EVAP vent solenoid (electronic), a charcoal canister and the intake manifold. In addition, there is an EVAP canister purge valve in the canister. The PCM controls the vacuum to the purge valve with an electrically operated solenoid. The fuel tank cap is also an integral part of the system. An indication that the system is not operating properly is a strong fuel odor.

3   The PCM monitors the vacuum level through the fuel tank pressure sensor signal (mounted on the tank). At the appropriate time, the EVAP canister purge valve and the EVAP vent solenoid are turned on which allows the engine to draw a small amount of vacuum on the entire EVAP system. Once the proper vacuum level is set, the PCM turns off the purge valve sealing the system closed. The PCM then monitors the system for leaks and sets a diagnostic code if trouble is detected.

Check

4   The EVAP canister is located behind the left rear wheel.

5   Check all lines in and out of the canister for kinks, leaks and breaks along their entire lengths. Repair or replace as necessary.

6   Check the gasket in the gas cap for

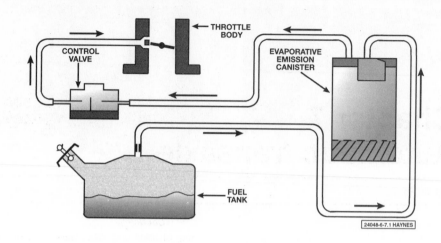

7.1 Details of a typical EVAP system

signs of drying, cracking or breaks. Replace the gas cap with a new one if defects are found.

7   On purge valve systems, the computer operates the purge valve and the vent solenoid by changing its frequency signal. The EVAP pressure sensor detects abnormal high pressure in the purge lines. Check for battery voltage to the purge control solenoid and the pressure sensor with the ignition key ON (engine not running). If no battery voltage is present, have the PCM and the EVAP system circuit checked at a dealer service department or other qualified repair shop. If battery voltage exists, connect the solenoid and the pressure sensor and if there is no obvious sounds from the EVAP vent solenoid (buzzing), have it checked by a dealer service department or other qualified repair shop. Remember, the purge valve will not be activated by the computer until fuel tank pressure exceeds 0.7 psi.

Replacement

9   Clearly label, then detach all vacuum lines from the canister.

10   Loosen the canister mounting clamp bolt and pull the canister out.

11   Installation is the reverse of removal.

8   Positive Crankcase Ventilation (PCV) system

General description

1   The positive crankcase ventilation system reduces hydrocarbon emissions by circulating fresh air through the crankcase to pick-up blow-by gases, which are then rerouted through the throttle body and burned in the engine.

2   The main components of this system are vacuum hoses and a PCV valve, which regulates the flow of gases according to engine speed and manifold vacuum.

Check and replacement

3   Checking the system and PCV valve replacement are covered in Chapter 1.

9   Catalytic converter

General description

1   The catalytic converter is an emission control device added to the exhaust system to reduce pollutants from the exhaust gas stream. These systems are equipped with a single bed monolith catalytic converter. This monolithic converter contains a honeycomb mesh which is also coated with two types of catalysts. One type is the oxidation catalyst while the other type is a three-way catalyst that contains platinum and palladium. The three-way catalyst lowers the levels of oxides of nitrogen (NOx) as well as hydrocarbons (HC) and carbon monoxide (CO) emissions. The oxidation catalyst lowers the levels of hydrocarbons and carbon monoxide.

Check

2   The test equipment for a catalytic converter is expensive and highly sophisticated. If you suspect the converter is malfunctioning, take it to a dealer service department or authorized emissions inspection facility for diagnosis and repair.

3   Whenever the vehicle is raised for service of underbody components, check the converter for leaks, corrosion and other damage. If damage is discovered, the converter should be replaced.

4   Because the converter is welded to the exhaust system, converter replacement requires removal of the exhaust pipe assembly (see Chapter 4). Take the vehicle, or the exhaust system, to a dealer service department or a muffler shop.

Chapter 7
Automatic transaxle

Contents

Specifications

General

Fluid type and capacity	See Chapter 1

Torque specifications

	Ft-lbs (unless otherwise indicated)
PNP switch-to-case bolts	18
Shift control assembly nuts	18
Shift cable bracket bolts (at transaxle)	18
Speed sensor bolt	71 to 124 in-lbs
Transaxle-to-engine bolts	55
Torque converter-to-driveplate bolts	46
Torque converter cover bolts	60 in-lbs
TV cable-to-transaxle case bolt	72 in-lbs

1 General information

Refer to illustration 1.1

The vehicles covered by this manual are equipped with either a three or four-speed Hydra-Matic automatic transaxle. Three models of Hydra-Matic automatic transaxles are used on these vehicles: the 3T40 three-speed, and the 4T60E and 4T65E electronic four-speeds.

Due to the complexity of the clutches and the hydraulic control system, and because of the special tools and expertise required to perform an automatic transaxle overhaul, it should not be undertaken by the home mechanic. Therefore, the procedures in this Chapter are limited to general diagnosis, routine maintenance, adjustment and transaxle removal and installation.

If the transaxle requires major repair work, it should be left to a dealer service department or an automotive or transmission repair shop. You can, however, remove and install the transaxle yourself and save the expense, even if the repair work is done by a transmission shop (but be sure a proper diagnosis has been made before removing the transaxle).

Replacement and adjustment procedures the home mechanic can perform include those involving the throttle valve (TV) cable and the shift linkage.

Caution 1: *On models equipped with a Theftlock audio system, be sure the lockout feature is turned off before performing any procedure which requires disconnecting the battery.*

Caution 2: *Never tow a disabled vehicle with an automatic transaxle at speeds greater than 35 mph or for distances over 50 miles if the front wheels are on the ground.*

2 Diagnosis - general

Note: *Automatic transmission malfunctions may be caused by five general conditions: poor engine performance, improper adjustments, hydraulic malfunctions, mechanical malfunctions or malfunctions in the computer or its signal network. Diagnosis of these problems should always begin with a check of the easily repaired items: fluid level and condition (see Chapter 1) and shift linkage adjustment. Next, perform a road test to determine if the problem has been corrected or if more diagnosis is necessary. If the problem persists after the preliminary tests and corrections are completed, additional diagnosis should be done by a dealer service department or transmission repair shop. Refer to the Troubleshooting section at the front of this manual for information on symptoms of transmission problems.*

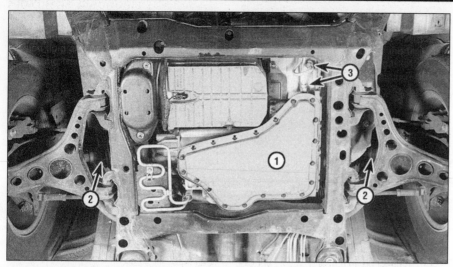

1.1 An underside view of an automatic transaxle and its related components

1 *Transaxle fluid pan*   2 *Driveaxles*   3 *Transaxle cooler lines*

Preliminary checks

1   Drive the vehicle to warm the transaxle to normal operating temperature.

2   Check the fluid level as described in Chapter 1:

   a) *If the fluid level is unusually low, add enough fluid to bring the level within the designated area of the dipstick, then check for external leaks (see below).*

   b) *If the fluid level is abnormally high, drain off the excess, then check the drained fluid for contamination by coolant. The presence of engine coolant in the automatic transmission fluid indicates that a failure has occurred in the internal radiator walls that separate the coolant from the transmission fluid (see Chapter 3).*

   c) *If the fluid is foaming, drain it and refill the transaxle, then check for coolant in the fluid or a high fluid level.*

3   Check the engine idle speed. **Note:** *If the engine is malfunctioning, do not proceed with the preliminary checks until it has been repaired and runs normally.*

4   Check the shift linkage or cable (see Section 6 or 7). Make sure it's properly adjusted and operates smoothly.

5   On models equipped with a 3T40 transaxle (some 1995 and 1996 models), check the throttle valve (TV) cable (see Section 6). Make sure it's properly adjusted and operates smoothly. On models equipped with a four-speed transaxle, check the vacuum modulator and its base for leaks (see Section 5).

Fluid leak diagnosis

6   Most fluid leaks are easy to locate visually. Repair usually consists of replacing a seal or gasket. If a leak is difficult to find, the following procedure may help.

7   Identify the fluid. Make sure it's transmission fluid and not engine oil or brake fluid (automatic transmission fluid is a deep red color).

8   Try to pinpoint the source of the leak. Drive the vehicle several miles, then park it over a large sheet of cardboard. After a minute or two, you should be able to locate the leak by determining the source of the fluid dripping onto the cardboard.

9   Make a careful visual inspection of the suspected component and the area immediately around it. Pay particular attention to gasket mating surfaces. A mirror is often helpful for finding leaks in areas that are hard to see.

10   If the leak still cannot be found, clean the suspected area thoroughly with a degreaser or solvent, then dry it.

11   Drive the vehicle for several miles at normal operating temperature and varying speeds. After driving the vehicle, visually inspect the suspected component again.

12   Once the leak has been located, the cause must be determined before it can be properly repaired. If a gasket is replaced but the sealing flange is bent, the new gasket will not stop the leak. The bent flange must be straightened.

13   Before attempting to repair a leak, check to make sure that the following conditions are corrected or they may cause another leak. **Note:** *Some of the following conditions cannot be fixed without highly specialized tools and expertise. Such problems must be referred to a transmission repair shop or a dealer service department.*

Gasket leaks

14   Check the pan periodically. Make sure the bolts are tight, no bolts are missing, the gasket is in good condition and the pan is flat (dents in the pan may indicate damage to the valve body inside).

15   If the pan gasket is leaking, the fluid level or the fluid pressure may be too high, the vent may be plugged, the pan bolts may be too tight, the pan sealing flange may be warped, the sealing surface of the transaxle housing may be damaged, the gasket may be damaged or the transaxle casting may be cracked or porous. If sealant instead of gasket material has been used to form a seal between the pan and the transaxle housing, it may be the wrong type of sealant.

Seal leaks

16   If a transaxle seal is leaking, the fluid level or pressure may be too high, the vent may be plugged, the seal bore may be damaged, the seal itself may be damaged or improperly installed, the surface of the shaft protruding through the seal may be damaged or a loose bearing may be causing excessive shaft movement.

17   Make sure the dipstick tube seal is in good condition and the tube is properly seated. Periodically check the area around the speedometer gear or sensor for leakage. If transmission fluid is evident, check the O-ring for damage.

Case leaks

18   If the case itself appears to be leaking, the casting is porous and will have to be repaired or replaced.

19   Make sure the oil cooler hose fittings are tight and in good condition.

Fluid comes out vent pipe or fill tube

20   If this condition occurs, the transaxle is overfilled, there is coolant in the fluid, the case is porous, the dipstick is incorrect, the vent is plugged or the drain-back holes are plugged.

---

3   Driveaxle oil seals - replacement

Refer to illustration 3.3

1   Raise the vehicle and support it securely on jackstands.

2   Remove the driveaxle(s) (see Chapter 8).

3   Use a hammer and chisel to pry up the outer lip of the seal to dislodge it so it can be pried out of the housing **(see illustration)**. **Note:** *The manufacturer recommends using a slide hammer to remove the metal-type seal.*

4   Compare the new seal to the old one to make sure they're the same.

5   Coat the lips of the new seal with transmission fluid.

6   Place the new seal in position and tap it into the bore with a hammer and a large

3.3 Dislodge the differential seal by working around the outer edge with a hammer and chisel

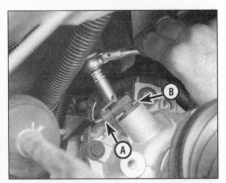

4.2 Disconnect the electrical connector (A) from the speed sensor (B), then remove the hold-down bolt and sensor (the socket here is on the bolt)

4.4 Before reinstalling the speed sensor, replace the O-ring with a new one

5.2 Vacuum modulator assembly

1 Vacuum connection   *2 Plunger*

socket or a piece of pipe that's the same diameter as the outside edge of the seal.

7   Reinstall the various components in the reverse order of removal.

4   Vehicle Speed Sensor (VSS) - removal and installation

Refer to illustrations 4.2 and 4.4

Note: *Any time the speed sensor is removed, you MUST install a new O-ring.*

1   The speed sensor is located on the right (passenger) side of the extension housing. To determine if the O-ring is leaking, look for transmission fluid around the sensor.

2   Unplug the sensor electrical connector **(see illustration)**.

3   Remove the sensor hold-down bolt and remove the sensor.

4   Remove the old O-ring **(see illustration)** and install a new O-ring on the sensor.

5   Installation is the reverse of removal. Tighten the sensor hold-down bolt securely.

5   Vacuum modulator (four-speed transaxles) - check and replacement

Check

Refer to illustration 5.2

1   The vacuum modulator is connected to engine manifold vacuum to rapidly respond to

changes in engine loading, and has an important effect on shift quality. If your vehicle exhibits shifting problems such as slipping or shifts that are either too soft or too harsh, check the vacuum supply to the modulator. With the engine running, connect a vacuum gauge to the modulator's vacuum line (at the modulator). Anything less than normal engine vacuum here of 13 to 17 inches (idling hot in Drive with the brakes applied) could cause shifting problems. If vacuum is too low, find the engine problem, hose kink or hose leak that is causing the low vacuum signal.

2   Connect a hand-held vacuum pump to the vacuum connection on the modulator (removed from vehicle) and apply 15 to 20 inches of vacuum while watching the plunger **(see illustration)**.

If the plunger isn't drawn in as vacuum is applied, the modulator should be replaced. The modulator should be able to hold this vacuum for at least half a minute.

3   When the modulator is withdrawn from the transaxle, turn it so the vacuum pipe is down. If any oil, water or other fluid drips out, the modulator should be replaced. **Note:** *A vehicle with a modulator whose diaphragm has a leak may exhibit excessive smoking at the tailpipe, due to transaxle fluid being drawn into the engine and burned.*

4   The body of the modulator can be checked for leaks by coating the outside with soapy water and blowing (by mouth, no more than 6 psi) into the vacuum connector, using a short length of vacuum hose. Bubbles on

the outside of the modulator or along the seam indicate a leak.

Replacement

Refer to illustrations 5.6, 5.7 and 5.8

5   The modulator is located on the front (radiator) side of the transaxle, below the exhaust crossover pipe.

6   Disconnect the vacuum line, and remove the mounting bolt or stud, then withdraw the modulator **(see illustration)**.

7   Remove the O-ring from the modulator cavity, using a small screwdriver or hook **(see illustration)**.

8   Use a small magnet to remove the modulator valve from the transaxle **(see illustration)**. Inspect the valve for signs of abnormal wear or scoring.

9   Installation is the reverse of the removal procedure. Always use a new O-ring and make sure the modulator valve is installed the same way it came out.

6   Throttle Valve (TV) cable (three-speed transaxles) - replacement and adjustment

Replacement

Refer to illustration 6.5

1   Disconnect the TV cable from the throttle by rotating the throttle until the cable eye can be pulled out of the throttle notch with needle-nose pliers.

7

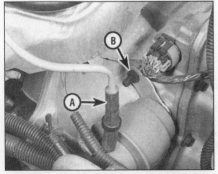

5.6 Disconnect the vacuum line (A) and remove the mounting bolt (B)

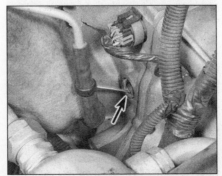

5.7 Remove the O-ring (arrow) from the transaxle case

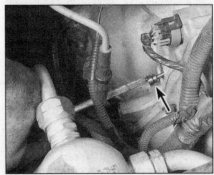

5.8 A magnet can be used to reach in and extract the modulator valve (arrow)

6.5 Hold the transaxle TV link with needle-nose pliers and slide the cable link off the pin

7.3 Pry up on the cable end (arrow) until it releases from the stud on the transaxle lever

7.4 Squeeze the sides of the cable housing grommet (A) to release it from the bracket (B)

2   Disconnect the TV cable housing from the throttle bracket by compressing the tangs and pushing the cable housing back through the bracket

3   Disconnect any clips or straps retaining the cable to the transaxle. Refer to Chapter 4 for removal of the air cleaner and duct.

4   Remove the bolt retaining the cable to the transaxle.

5   Pull up on the cover until the end of the cable can be seen, then disconnect it from the transaxle TV link **(see illustration)**. Remove the cable from the vehicle.

6   To install the cable, connect it to the transaxle TV link and push the cover securely over the cable. Route the cable to the top of the engine, push the housing through the throttle bracket until it clicks into place, place the connector over the throttle lever pin and pull back to lock it. Secure the cable with any retaining clips or straps.

Adjustment

7   The engine MUST NOT be running during this adjustment.

8   Depress the re-adjust button (located at the throttle lever end of the cable) and push the slider through the fitting (away from the throttle lever) as far as it will go.

9   Release the re-adjust button.

10   Manually turn the throttle lever to the "wide open throttle" position until the re-adjust tab makes audible clicks, then release the throttle lever. The cable is now adjusted.

Note: *Don't use excessive force at the*

throttle lever to adjust the TV cable. If great effort is required to adjust the cable, disconnect the cable at the transaxle end and check for free operation. If it's still difficult, replace the cable. If it's now free, suspect a bent TV link in the transaxle or a problem with the throttle lever.

7   Shift cable - replacement and adjustment

Warning: *The models covered by this manual are equipped with airbags. Always disable the airbag system before working in the vicinity of the impact sensors, steering column or instrument panel to avoid the possibility of accidental deployment of the airbag(s), which could cause personal injury (see Chapter 12). The yellow wires and connectors routed through the console are for this system. Do not use electrical test equipment on these yellow wires or tamper with them in any way while working around the console.*

Floor shift models

Refer to illustrations 7.3, 7.4, 7.6, 7.7a and 7.7b

1   Disconnect the cable from the negative battery terminal. **Caution:** *On models equipped with a Theftlock audio system, be sure the lockout feature is turned off before performing any procedure which requires disconnecting the battery.*

2   Refer to Chapter 4 and remove the air cleaner and duct.

3   Disconnect the shift cable from the shift lever on the transaxle **(see illustration)**.

4   To detach the shift cable from the transaxle bracket, remove the U-clip retainer (if used), then squeeze the tangs on the cable housing grommet and pull the cable and grommet through the bracket **(see illustration)**.

5   Pull the retaining clip from the front of the shift handle, just below the grip, slip the grip off, then remove the center console (see Chapter 11).

6   Disconnect the shift cable from the shift lever **(see illustration)**.

7   Remove the clip at the cable housing end, then pry out the grommet **(see illustrations)** from the front of the shift lever assembly and pull out the shift cable through the hole in the mount. You may have to pull back the carpeting to expose the cable. **Note:** *There may be one or two cable-ties holding the cable to the vehicle's wiring harness in the engine compartment. Cut the ties off to release the cable.*

8   Guide the new cable through the hole in the floor and install the grommet.

9   Connect the shift cable to the shift lever.

10   Install the center console trim panel (see Chapter 11).

11   Place the shift control lever (inside the vehicle) in Neutral. Make sure it remains in the Neutral position until the shift cable is installed.

12   Attach the shift cable to the transaxle bracket.

13   Place the shift lever on the transaxle in

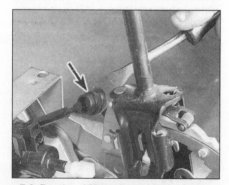

7.6 Pry the shift cable end (arrow) from the stud on the shifter

7.7a Pull off the retaining clip (arrow) from the shift cable

7.7b Squeeze the grommet (arrow) and pull the cable forward through the hole in the bracket

the Neutral position by rotating it counter-clockwise from Park through Reverse into Neutral.

14   Connect the shift cable end to the shift lever on the transaxle, and install new cable-ties where needed.

15   Reconnect the cable to the negative battery terminal.

Column shift models

16   Perform Steps 1 through 4.

17   Refer to Chapter 11 and remove the lower sound insulator panel and the lower steering column cover.

18   Disconnect the cable end from the shift control lever, and pry the cable grommet from the U-shaped mount on the steering column.

19   Pull the cable through the hole in the firewall to the engine side. Installation is the reverse of removal.

Adjustment

Refer to illustration 7.20

20   The shift control cable is in two sections, joined by a coupler retained by a metal spring clip **(see illustration)**. Do not remove this clip! If either section of the cable is damaged, replace the whole assembly as a unit. **Note:** *A new cable may come as two pieces, with instructions for the proper engagement of the two sections.*

21   Install the two sections of new cable to their respective end mountings at the transaxle and shift control. Push the adjuster clip into its first "notch" on the end of the shift control side of the coupling.

22   With both the transaxle and shift control set in the Neutral position, connect the two halves until you feel them lock together, then push the clip onto its last position. There is a smaller clip in the transaxle end of the coupler, and when fully assembled, this clip should be flush with the coupler (not sticking out at all). Pull the two halves of the cable away from each other to test that the connection is secure. Once engaged, do not remove the adjuster clip or another new cable set will have to be purchased.

8   Shift lever assembly - removal and installation

Refer to illustration 8.5

1   Disconnect the negative cable from the battery. **Caution:** *On models equipped with a Theftlock audio system, be sure the lockout feature is turned off before performing any procedure which requires disconnecting the battery.*

2   Remove the console (see Chapter 11).

3   Disconnect the shift cable from the gear shift lever (see Section 7).

4   Disconnect the interlock cable from the gear shift lever (see Section 10), then disconnect the shift indicator cable (see Section 9).

5   Remove the retaining nuts and lift the floor shift control assembly out of the vehicle **(see illustration)**.

7.20 The shift cable is in two halves, retained by an adjuster clip (A) and a horse-shoe clip (B) - do not remove either clip!

6   Place the floor shift control assembly in position on the mounting studs and install the nuts. Tighten the nuts to the specified torque.

7   Connect the shift cables.

8   Install the console.

9   Reconnect the negative battery cable.

9   Shift indicator cable (column shift) - replacement and adjustment

Warning: *The models covered by this manual are equipped with airbags. Always disable the airbag system before working in the vicinity of the impact sensors, steering column or instrument panel to avoid the possibility of accidental deployment of the airbag(s), which could cause personal injury (see Chapter 12). The yellow wires and connectors routed through the console are for this system. Do not use electrical test equipment on these yellow wires or tamper with them in any way while working around the console.*

Replacement

1   Refer to Chapter 10 and lower the steering column from the dashboard.

2   Remove the steering column covers.

3   The shift indicator cable attaches to the shift control lever on the top side of the steering column.

4   Disconnect the shift indicator cable on the column by pulling the end out of its square hole.

5   Follow the cable to the instrument panel, removing any retaining clips along the way, and disconnect the upper end from the shift indicator in the instrument panel.

6   Replacement is the reverse of the removal process.

Adjustment

7   Where the steering column meets the bottom of the instrument panel, remove the small filler panel that covers the shift indicator.

8   With the engine Off and the parking brake applied, put the shift lever in Neutral. **Note:** *Go by feel of the detents, rather than the shift indicator.*

9   By hand, move the indicator's pointer

8.5 Shift lever assembly mounting nuts (arrows)

until the orange portion of the indicator completely fills the slot under the letter N on the indicator panel. Once adjusted, the shift indicator should show all of the gear positions correctly throughout the shift range.

10   Brake/transmission shift interlock system - description, check and component replacement

Warning: *The models covered by this manual are equipped with airbags. Always disable the airbag system before working in the vicinity of the impact sensors, steering column or instrument panel to avoid the possibility of accidental deployment of the airbag(s), which could cause personal injury (see Chapter 12). The yellow wires and connectors routed through the console are for this system. Do not use electrical test equipment on these yellow wires or tamper with them in any way while working around the console.*

Description

1   The brake transmission interlock system prevents the (column or floor-mounted) shift lever from being moved out of Park unless the brake pedal is depressed simultaneously. When the car is started, a solenoid is energized, locking the shift lever in Park; when the brake pedal is depressed, the solenoid is de-energized, unlocking the shift lever so that it can be moved out of Park. **Note:** *Before making the following checks, refer to Chapter 9 and verify that the brake light switch is functioning properly because it is part of the interlock circuit.*

Check

Refer to illustration 10.3

2   On column-shift models, remove the trim panel under the dash, in front of the steering column and the metal plate above it. Using a flashlight, locate the brake/trans-mission shift interlock solenoid - it's mounted to the left of the column, just ahead of the column mount.

3   On console-shift models, remove the center console (see Chapter 11) and locate the brake/transmission shift interlock

7

10.3 On console-shift models, the solenoid (arrow) is mounted in the shift assembly in the console

10.11 To disengage the column-shift solenoid from the actuator rod, pry the fingers loose and pull the solenoid half of the actuator rod connector from the other half of the connector

10.17 Pry the solenoid's rod-end (arrow) from the shifter

solenoid, in front of the shift lever **(see illustration)**. **Note:** *For solenoid testing, reattach the wiring connector to the interlock solenoid.*

4   Verify that the brake/transmission shift interlock solenoid operates as follows:

a) *When the ignition key is in the Lock position, the solenoid plunger should be in and you should not be able to move the shift lever, even with the brake pedal applied.*

b) *With the ignition key is turned to the Off position, the solenoid plunger should be popped out and you should be able to move the shift lever to any gear position without applying the brake pedal.*

c) *When the ignition key is turned to the Run position, the solenoid should go back into the solenoid and you should not be able to move the shift lever; except with the brake pedal applied, the solenoid plunger should be released (pop out) and you should be able to move the shift lever out of Park into any gear.*

d) *Place the key in the Lock position, then turn the key to the Acc (accessory) position. The solenoid plunger should go in a little further than it does when the key is turned to Lock, and you should not be able to move the shift lever (even with the brake applied).*

5   If the solenoid doesn't operate as described above, unplug the electrical connector from the solenoid, apply battery voltage to the solenoid and verify that it "clicks" on, then open the circuit and verify that the solenoid clicks off.

a) *If the solenoid doesn't operate as described, replace it.*

b) *If the solenoid is operating properly, troubleshoot the circuit between the battery and the solenoid, and between the solenoid and ground.*

c) *If the solenoid circuit is okay, take the vehicle to a dealer service department.*

Component replacement

Solenoid

6   Disconnect the cable from the negative battery terminal. **Caution:** *On models equipped with a Theftlock audio system, be sure the lockout feature is turned off before performing any procedure which requires disconnecting the battery.*

Column-shift models

Refer to illustration 10.11

7   Disable the airbag system (see Chapter 12).

8   Remove the trim panel under the left side of the dash (see Chapter 11) and the metal plate above it.

9   Lower the steering column (see Chapter 10).

10   Unplug the electrical connector from the solenoid, and remove the solenoid mounting screw.

11   Disengage the solenoid from the actuator rod **(see illustration)**.

12   Remove the solenoid assembly, spring and solenoid-half of the actuator rod connector.

13   Remove the solenoid-half of the actuator rod connector and spring and install them on the new solenoid.

14   Connect the new solenoid assembly to the actuator rod. Installation is otherwise the reverse of removal.

Floor-shift models

Refer to illustration 10.17

15   Remove the center console (see Chapter 11).

16   Unplug the electrical connector from the solenoid.

17   Pry the end of the solenoid rod from its pin on the shift lever assembly, and detach the solenoid from the shift control base **(see illustration)**.

18   Installation is the reverse of removal.

Park/lock cable (floor-shift models only)

Refer to illustrations 10.20, 10.21a and 10.21b

19   Remove the center console, the left lower dash trim panel, the knee bolster and the knee bolster deflector (see Chapter 11).

20   Move the shifter to the Park position and detach the Park/lock cable from the shift lever **(see illustration)**. **Note:** *Pull rearward on the cable end to disengage it from the pin on the shifter assembly.*

21   Detach the Park/lock cable from the bracket on the shift lever assembly **(see illustrations)**.

22   Refer to Chapter 10 and lower the steering column from the dashboard. **Warning:** *The airbag system must be disabled* (see Chapter 12).

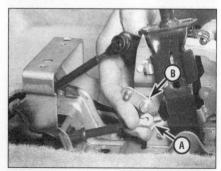

10.20 Pull rearward on the shift cable end (A) until it comes off the pin (B) on the shifter

10.21a Remove the clip (arrow) from the cable housing end . . .

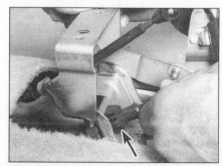

10.21b . . . then use pliers to squeeze the grommet (arrow) until the cable can be worked forward through the hole in the floor

23 Remove the covers from the lower steering column to expose the back of the ignition switch.

24 Turn the ignition key to the Run position. Insert a small screwdriver into the back of the ignition switch to depress the plastic latch and withdraw the cable from the ignition switch.

25 Remove the Park/lock cable.

26 Installation is the reverse of removal.

11 Park Neutral Position (PNP) switch - check and replacement

Refer to illustrations 11.6, 11.7 and 11.9

1 Disconnect the negative cable from the battery. **Caution:** *On models equipped with a Theftlock audio system, be sure the lockout feature is turned off before performing any procedure which requires disconnecting the battery.*

2 Shift the transaxle into Neutral.

3 Refer to Chapter 4 and remove the air cleaner and the duct to the throttle body.

4 Refer to Section 7 and remove the shift cable from the shift lever and the cable bracket.

5 Make a paint or scribe mark on the transaxle shift lever, relative to its position on the splined shaft from the transaxle when in Neutral, then remove the nut and take off the shift lever.

6 Disconnect the electrical connectors from the PNP (or Range Selector) switch **(see illustration)**.

7 Remove the bolts and detach the switch **(see illustration)**.

8 To install the switch (transmission shaft still in its Neutral position), line up the flats on the switch with the flats in the shaft and lower the switch onto the shaft.

9 Install the bolts. The alignment of the switch is made by moving the switch slightly when tightening the two mounting bolts. A factory tool makes this easier, but the tool isn't absolutely necessary. If you are reinstalling your original switch, the bolts will have made a scratched circle on the mounting bosses **(see illustration)**. If you bolt it down with the bolts aligned exactly over these circles, the switch be positioned correctly. If you are installing a new switch, the replacement switch comes with a plastic pin inside that locks it into the Neutral position. Just bolt it down. When you

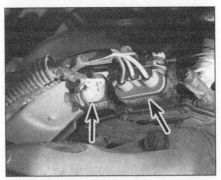

11.6 Electrical connectors (arrows) on the side of the PNP switch

attach the shift lever and cable and move the selector through its range, the plastic pin will shear off inside and the PNP switch will be perfectly adjusted.

10 The remainder of installation is the reverse of removal.

11 Connect the negative battery cable and verify that the engine will start only in Neutral or Park.

12 Auxiliary oil cooler - removal and installation

1 On some models, an auxiliary oil cooler is provided for the automatic transaxle fluid. The cooler looks like as small radiator and is mounted in front of the engine radiator and air-conditioning condenser, just behind the grille. Transaxle fluid flow comes from the transaxle to the auxiliary cooler through the transaxle fluid output line, and then from the auxiliary cooler to the standard cooler in the right-hand tank of the engine radiator.

2 To remove the cooler, place a suitable drain pan under the cooler to catch the fluid and use backup wrenches to remove the lower fluid line from the cooler.

3 When no more fluid comes out, remove the fitting on the upper fluid line.

4 Remove the four screws (two into the upper radiator support, two into the lower radiator support) and remove the cooler. **Caution:** *If transaxle fluid spills on painted body surfaces, clean it off immediately to avoid damaging the finish.*

5 Installation is the reverse of the removal

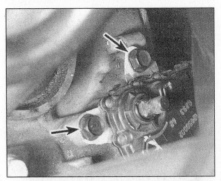

11.7 Remove the two mounting bolts (arrows) and take off the PNP switch

procedure. **Caution:** *Do not tighten the mounting bolts until you are sure the cooling lines are properly threaded into the cooler, with no cross-threading.*

13 Transaxle mount - check and replacement

Refer to illustrations 13.1, 13.3 and 13.5

1 Insert a large screwdriver or prybar into the space between the transaxle bracket and the mount and try to pry the transaxle up slightly **(see illustration)**. The transaxle bracket should not move away from the insulator much at all.

2 To replace the mount, raise and suitably support the front of the vehicle on jackstands.

3 Remove the left front wheel and the inner splash shield **(see illustration)**.

4 Support the engine with a floorjack and a block of wood, and raise the engine/transaxle enough to take some tension off the transaxle mount.

5 Remove the nuts attaching the insulator to the crossmember and the nuts attaching the insulator to the transaxle **(see illustration overleaf)**.

6 Raise the engine/transaxle slightly with the jack and remove the insulator, noting which holes are used in the support for proper alignment during installation.

7 Installation is the reverse of the removal procedure. Be sure to tighten the nuts/bolts securely.

7

11.9 Align your old switch on reinstallation by positioning the scratched circles (arrows) exactly under the bolts

13.1 Pry on the transaxle mount to check for a broken insulator

13.3 Remove the two screws (arrows) and take off the left inner splash shield for access to the transaxle mount

14 Automatic transaxle - removal and installation

Refer to illustrations 14.5, 14.18a and 14.18b
Warning: *This is a difficult procedure for the home mechanic, requiring the use of several specialized tools, including a transmission jack and a three-bar engine support fixture. Such tools can be rented, but the job is still difficult to do without a hydraulic lift. Safely raising the vehicle enough for the transaxle and subframe to be pulled out from underneath is a problem without a hoist.*

Removal

1   Disconnect the negative cable from the battery. **Caution:** *On models equipped with a Theftlock audio system, be sure the lockout feature is turned off before performing any procedure which requires disconnecting the battery.*
2   Raise the vehicle and support it securely on jackstands.
3   Drain the transaxle fluid (Chapter 1).
4   Remove the torque converter cover.
5   Mark the torque converter-to-driveplate relationship so they can be installed in the same position **(see illustration).**
6   Remove the torque converter-to-driveplate bolts. Turn the crankshaft pulley bolt for access to each bolt.
7   Remove the starter motor (see Chapter 5).
8   Remove the driveaxles (see Chapter 8).
9   Disconnect the speed sensor (see Section 4).
10   Disconnect the electrical connectors from the transaxle.
11   On models so equipped, disconnect the vacuum hose(s).
12   Remove any exhaust components which will interfere with transaxle removal (see Chapter 4).
13   If equipped, disconnect the TV cable from the transaxle (see Section 6).
14   Disconnect the shift linkage from the transaxle (see Section 7).
15   Support the engine using a three-bar support fixture to retain the engine in the body.
16   Support the transaxle with a jack - preferably a special jack made for this purpose. Safety chains will help steady the transaxle on the jack.
17   Remove the brace between the engine and transaxle (attached to the oil pan on the right side) and the bolts securing the transaxle to the flywheel end of the engine.
18   Lower the transaxle slightly and disconnect and plug the transaxle cooler lines **(see illustrations).** Make sure all of the fluid has drained out into a suitable container.
19   Remove the dipstick tube. Refer to Chapter 8 and remove the driveaxles.
20   Refer to Chapter 10 and disconnect the tie rod ends, then unbolt the steering rack and hold it to the body with heavy wire, away from the chassis.

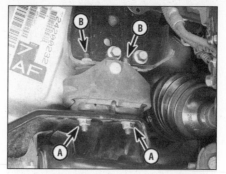

13.5 Remove the mount-to-chassis nuts (A), then the mount-to-transaxle-bracket nuts (B)

21   Refer to Chapter 2 and disconnect the engine mount nuts at the chassis, then support the front subframe assembly with a jack and remove the four bolts holding the subframe to the vehicle. **Warning:** *Never put any part of your body under the front subframe while it is unbolted from the vehicle.*
22   Move the transaxle back to disengage it from the engine block dowel pins and make sure the torque converter is detached from the driveplate. Secure the torque converter to the transaxle so it will not fall out during removal. Lower the front subframe and transaxle from the vehicle. Remove the transaxle mount from the subframe and separate the transaxle.

Installation

23   Prior to installation, make sure the torque converter is fully engaged in the transmission. To do this, rotate the converter while pushing it toward the transaxle. If it wasn't already fully in place, you'll feel it "clunk" into position as it engages with the input shaft and front pump. It may even "clunk" more than once. Lubricate the torque converter hub with multi-purpose grease.
24   With the transaxle and subframe secured to the jack, raise it evenly into position. Be sure to keep it level so the torque converter does not slide out. **Warning:** *Do not place any part of your body under the subframe until the four subframe bolts are back in place.*

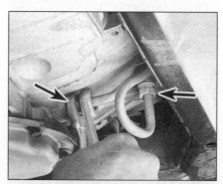

14.18a Use a flare nut wrench on the tube nut and an open end wrench on the fitting adapter when detaching the transaxle cooler lines (arrows) from the transaxle

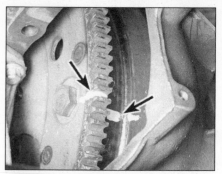

14.5 Make alignment marks (arrows) on the flywheel and torque converter so they can be reinstalled in the same relative positions

25   Turn the torque converter to line up the bolt holes with the holes in the driveplate. The mark on the torque converter and the driveplate made in Step 5 must line up.
26   Move the transaxle forward carefully until the dowel pins and the torque converter are engaged.
27   Install the transaxle housing-to-engine bolts. Tighten them securely.
28   Install the torque converter-to-driveplate bolts. Tighten the bolts to the specified torque.
29   Install the suspension and chassis components which were removed. Tighten the bolts and nuts to the specified torque.
30   Remove the jacks supporting the transaxle and the engine.
31   Install the dipstick tube.
32   Install the starter motor (Chapter 5).
33   Connect the vacuum hose(s) (if equipped).
34   Connect the shift and TV linkage.
35   Plug in the transaxle electrical connectors.
36   Install the torque converter cover.
37   Install the driveaxles (Chapter 8).
38   Connect the speedometer/speed sensor cable.
39   Adjust the shift linkage (Section 7).
40   Install any exhaust system components that were removed or disconnected.
41   Lower the vehicle.
42   Fill the transaxle (Chapter 1), run the vehicle and check for fluid leaks.

14.18b Remove the bolt (arrow) retaining the transaxle cooler lines to the side of the transaxle

Chapter 8 Driveaxles

Contents

Specifications

Torque specifications

	Ft-lbs
Driveaxle hub nut	159
Hub/bearing assembly-to-steering knuckle bolts	
1995	60
1996 on	52
Wheel lug nuts	See Chapter 1

1 Driveaxles - general information and inspection

Power is transmitted from the transaxle to the front wheels by two driveaxles, which consist of splined solid axles with constant velocity (CV) joints at each end.

There are two types of CV joints used. The outer joint is a double-offset design using ball bearings with an inner and outer race is used to allow angular movement. The inner CV joint is a tripot design, with a spider bearing assembly and tripot housing to allow angular movement and permit the driveaxle to slide in and out.

The CV joints are protected by rubber boots, which are retained by clamps so the joints are protected from water and dirt. The boots should be inspected periodically (see Chapter 1). Damaged CV joint boots must be replaced immediately or the joints can be damaged. Boot replacement involves removing the driveaxles (Section 2). It's a good idea to disassemble, clean, inspect and repack the CV joint whenever replacing a CV joint boot to make sure the joint isn't contaminated with moisture or dirt, which would cause premature failure of the CV joint (see Section 3).

The most common symptom of worn or damaged CV joints, besides lubricant leaks, are a clicking noise in turns, a clunk when accelerating from a coasting condition or vibration at highway speeds.

Some specialized tools and procedures are required to disassemble and overhaul the CV joints in a driveaxle. Once removed from the vehicle, a spindle removal tool or hydraulic press is required to separate the hub and bearing assembly from the outer end of the driveaxle. Because rebuilt driveaxles are commonly available at auto parts stores, we recommend that the home mechanic not rebuild the axles, but instead bring them to a shop for hub/bearing removal and replacement with a fully-rebuilt, guaranteed unit.

Warning: *Since many of the procedures covered in this Chapter involve working under*

2.1 Before raising the vehicle, remove the wheel center cap and use a breaker bar and socket to loosen the hub nut

the vehicle, make sure it's securely supported on sturdy jackstands or on a hoist where the vehicle can easily be raised and lowered.

2 Driveaxles - removal and installation

Removal

Refer to illustrations 2.1, 2.5a, 2.5b, 2.6, 2.7a and 2.7b

1   Remove the wheel cover and loosen the hub nut **(see illustration)**. **Note:** *This isn't necessary if you are only removing the driveaxle for access to other components.* Loosen the wheel lug nuts, raise the front of the vehicle and support it securely on jackstands. Apply the parking brake and block the rear wheels to keep the vehicle from rolling off the jackstands. Remove the front wheel.

2   Remove the driveaxle hub nut (again, this is only necessary if you plan to separate the hub/bearing assembly from the driveaxle). To prevent the hub from turning, insert a screwdriver through the caliper and into a disc cooling vane, then remove the nut.

3   Remove the brake caliper, disc and caliper mounting bracket (see Chapter 9). **Note:** *Support the caliper out of the way with a piece of wire.*

4   Refer to Chapter 9 and disconnect the

8

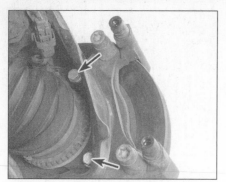

2.5a Remove the caliper bracket bolts and disc, then remove the two bolts (arrows) at the rear of the hub/ bearing assembly

2.5b Remove the remaining two front bolts (arrows) from the hub/ bearing assembly

2.6 A large prybar (arrow) can be used to pry the inner joint of the driveaxle outward from the transaxle

2.7a Carefully remove the driveaxle and hub/bearing assembly through the opening in the steering knuckle

2.7b Take care to avoid nicking the teeth of the ABS exciter ring (arrow) on the outer driveaxle ends

2.9 Use a large screwdriver (fitted into the ledge or groove on the inner joint) to seat the inner CV joint in the transaxle

electrical connector from the ABS wheel sensor, then remove the wheel sensor.

5   Remove the four bolts securing the hub/bearing assembly to the steering knuckle (**see illustrations**).

6   Using a large screwdriver or prybar, carefully pry the driveaxle out of the transaxle (**see illustration**). **Caution:** *Do not tear the inner joint's boot with the prybar.*

7   Support the CV joints and carefully remove the driveaxle through the opening in the steering knuckle (**see illustrations**). **Caution:** *Do not tear the inner or outer boots on any sharp components as you withdraw the axle. Do not nick the ABS exciter ring on the outer joint of each driveaxle.*

Installation

Refer to illustration 2.9

8   Lubricate the differential seal with multi-purpose grease. Install the driveaxle through the opening in the steering knuckle. While supporting the CV joints, insert the splined end of the inner CV joint into the differential side gear.

9   Seat the shaft in the side gear by positioning the end of a screwdriver in the groove in the CV joint and tapping it into position with a hammer (**see illustration**).

10   Grasp the inner CV joint housing (not the driveaxle) and pull out to make sure the axle has seated securely.

11   Install the hub/bearing assembly onto the steering knuckle. Tighten the mounting

bolts to the torque listed in this Chapter's Specifications.

12   If removed, install a NEW driveaxle hub nut and tighten it securely.

13   Install the brake disc, caliper mount and caliper (see Chapter 9).

14   Install the wheel and lower the vehicle. Tighten the driveaxle hub nut to the torque listed in this Chapter's Specifications.

15   Install the wheel cover.

3   Driveaxle boot - replacement

Note: *If the inner or outer joints exhibit wear indicating the need for an overhaul (usually due to torn boots), explore all options before beginning the job. Complete rebuilt driveaxles are available on an exchange basis, which eliminates a lot of time and work. Whatever is decided, check on the cost and availability of parts before disassembling the vehicle.*

1   Remove the driveaxle (see Section 2).

2   Place the driveaxle in a vise lined with rags to avoid damage to the shaft.

Inner tripot joint

Refer to illustrations 3.3, 3.4, 3.10 and 3.11

3   Cut off the boot retaining clamps and slide the boot towards the center of the driveaxle (**see illustration**). Mark the tripot housing and driveaxle so they can be reinstalled in the same relative positions, then slide the housing off the spider assembly.

4   Remove the spider assembly from the axle by first removing the inner retaining ring and sliding the spider assembly back to expose the outer retaining ring. Remove the outer retaining ring and slide the joint off the driveaxle (**see illustration**).

5   Use tape or a cloth wrapped around the spider bearing assembly to retain the bearings during removal and installation.

6   Remove the spider assembly from the axle, followed by the inner retaining ring.

7   Slide the boot off the axle.

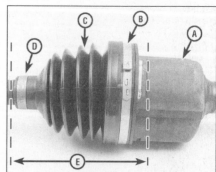

3.3 Inner tripot joint components

A   *Tripot housing*
B   *Inner clamp*
C   *Boot*
D   *Outer clamp*
E   *Adjust the length of the joint, from the small end of the boot to the groove on the tripot housing to 8-3/32 inches*

3.4 Snap-ring pliers should be used to remove both the inner and outer retaining rings

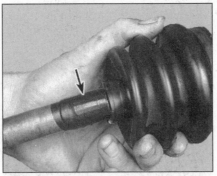

3.10 Before installing the boot, wrap the axle splines with electrical tape (arrow) to prevent damage to the boot

3.11 When installing the spider assembly on the driveaxle, make sure the recess in the counterbore (arrow) is facing the end of the driveaxle

8   Clean all of the old grease out of the housing and spider assembly. Carefully disassemble each section of the spider assembly, one at a time, and clean the needle bearings with solvent. Inspect the rollers, spider cross, bearings and housing for scoring, pitting and other signs of abnormal wear. Apply a coat of CV joint grease to the inner bearing surfaces to hold the needle bearings in place when reassembling the spider assembly.

9   Pack the housing with half of the grease furnished with the new boot and place the remainder in the boot.

10   Wrap the driveaxle splines with tape to avoid damaging the boot, then slide the new inner clamp and boot onto the axle **(see illustration)**. Remove the tape and install the inner retaining ring, sliding it past its groove.

11   Install the spider bearing with the recess in the counterbore facing the end of the driveaxle **(see illustration)**. Install the outer retaining ring, slide the spider to the end of the shaft, then seat the inner retaining ring in its groove.

12   Install the tripot housing.

13   Seat the boot in the housing and axle seal grooves, then adjust the length of the joint **(see illustration 3.3)**. Insert a small screwdriver between the boot and housing to equalize the pressure inside the boot, then install and tighten the retaining clamps. **Note:** *A special clamp crimping tool, available at most auto parts stores, is required to tighten*

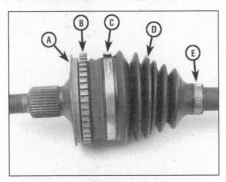

3.14 Outer CV joint components

A Outer deflector ring
B ABS exciter ring
C Outer boot clamp
D Boot
E Inner boot clamp

the clamps. Install the driveaxle as described in Section 2.

Outer CV joint

Refer to illustrations 3.14, 3.15, 3.18, 3.19, 3.20, 3.21, 3.22a, 3.22b, 3.25, and 3.26

14   Cut the two boot clamps with sharp side-cutter pliers and remove them, then slide the boot toward the center of the driveaxle **(see illustration)**.

15   Using snap-ring pliers, spread the retaining ring and slide the joint assembly off the axleshaft **(see illustration)**.

16   Slide the old boot off the driveaxle.

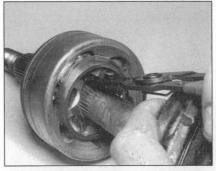

3.15 Use snap-ring pliers to spread the inner retaining ring, then pull the CV joint off the axleshaft

17   Place marks on the inner race and cage so they both can be installed facing out when reassembling the joint.

18   Press down on the inner race far enough to allow a ball bearing to be removed. If it's difficult to tilt, tap the inner race with a brass punch and hammer **(see illustration)**.

19   Pry the balls out of the cage, one at a time, with a blunt screwdriver or wooden tool **(see illustration)**.

20   With all of the balls removed from the cage and the cage/inner race assembly tilted 90-degrees, align the cage windows with the outer race lands and remove the assembly from the outer race **(see illustration)**.

3.18 Gently tap the inner race with a brass punch to tilt it enough to allow ball bearing removal

3.19 Using a dull screwdriver, carefully pry the balls out of the cage

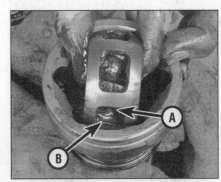

3.20 Tilt the inner race and cage 90-degrees, then align the windows in the cage (A) with the lands (B) and rotate the inner race up and out of the outer race

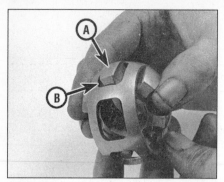

3.21 Align the inner race lands (A) with the cage windows (B) and rotate the inner race out of the cage

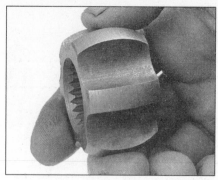

3.22a Check the inner race lands and grooves for pitting and score marks

3.22b Check the cage for cracks, pitting and score marks - shiny spots are normal and don't affect operation

21   Remove the inner race from the cage by turning the inner race 90-degrees in the cage, aligning the inner lands with the cage windows and rotating the inner race out of the cage **(see illustration).**

22   Clean the components with solvent to remove all traces of grease. Inspect the cage and races for pitting, score marks, cracks and other signs of wear and damage. Shiny, polished spots are normal and won't

adversely affect CV joint operation **(see illustrations).**

23   Install the inner race in the cage by reversing the technique described in Step 21.

24   Install the inner race and cage assembly in the outer race by reversing the procedure in Step 20. The marks that were previously applied to the inner race and cage must both be visible after the assembly is installed in the outer race.

25   Press the balls into the cage windows **(see illustration).**

26   Pack the CV joint assembly with lubricant through the inner splined hole. Force the grease into the bearing by inserting a wooden dowel through the splined hole and pushing it to the bottom of the joint. Repeat this procedure until the bearing is completely packed **(see illustration).**

27   Install the small clamp and the boot on the driveaxle as described in Step 10. Apply a liberal amount of grease to the inside of the axle boot. **Note:** *There are several grooves on the driveaxle at the point where the boot will be clamped. There are three large grooves. The lip on the boot should go in the large groove closest to the narrow groove.*

28   Position the CV joint assembly on the axleshaft, aligning the splines. Press the CV joint onto the axleshaft until the retaining ring is seated in the groove.

29   Seat the inner end of the boot in the seal groove and install and tighten the retaining clamps. **Note:** *A special clamp crimping tool, available at most auto parts stores, is required to tighten the clamps.*

30   Install the driveaxle as described in Section 2.

3.25 Align the cage windows and the inner and outer race grooves, then tilt the cage and inner race to insert the balls

3.26 Apply grease through the splined hole, then insert a wooden dowel (approximately 15/16-inch diameter) through the hole and push down - the dowel will force the grease into the joint

Chapter 9 Brakes

Contents

Specifications

General

Brake fluid type	See Chapter 1

Disc brakes

Brake pad lining minimum thickness	See Chapter 1
Disc (front and rear)	
Minimum thickness	Refer to the dimension stamped into the disc
Runout (maximum)	0.004 inch
Thickness variation limit	0.0005 inch

Drum brakes

Brake shoe lining minimum thickness	See Chapter 1
Brake drum	
Maximum diameter	Refer to the dimension stamped into the drum
Runout (maximum)	0.006 inch

Torque Specifications

Ft-lbs (unless otherwise indicated)

Bleeder valve	
Front	115 in-lbs
Rear	
Caliper	97 in-lbs
Wheel cylinder	62 in-lbs
Caliper mounting (slide) bolts (1995 through 1998)	
Front	80
Rear	20
Caliper mounting bolts (1999)	
Front	63
Rear	32
Caliper mounting bracket bolts	
Front	148
Rear	81
Brake hose-to-caliper bolt	
Front and rear (1995 through 1998)	32
Front (1999)	40
Rear (1999)	32
Proportioner valve caps	20
Wheel cylinder mounting bolts	15
Wheel lug nuts	See Chapter 1

1   General information

General

The vehicles covered by this manual are equipped with hydraulically operated front and rear brake systems. All front brake systems are disc type, while the rear brakes are either disc or drum. All brakes are self adjusting. Front and rear disc brakes automatically compensate for pad wear. Rear drum brakes incorporate an adjusting mechanism which is activated any time the service brakes are applied.

Hydraulic system

The hydraulic system consists of two separate circuits. The master cylinder has separate reservoirs for the two circuits and in the event of a leak or failure in one hydraulic circuit, the other circuit will remain operative. A visual warning of circuit failure or air in the system is given by a warning light activated on the dash.

Proportioner valves

The proportioner valves are designed to provide better front to rear braking balance

9

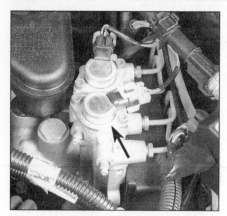

2.2 The ABS modulator/motor pack (arrow) is mounted on the side of the master cylinder

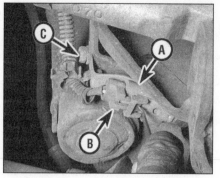

2.4a The front wheel ABS sensor (A) is mounted to the hub/bearing assembly - the electrical connector (B) snaps on and the sensor is retained by a bracket and bolt (C)

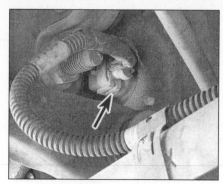

2.4b An ABS sensor (arrow) is also mounted at each rear wheel, behind the brake assembly

with heavy brake application. These valves allow more pressure to be applied to the front brakes (under certain braking operations) due to the fact the rear of the vehicle is lighter and does not require as much braking force.

Power brake booster

The power brake booster, utilizing engine manifold vacuum and atmospheric pressure to provide assistance to the hydraulically operated brakes, is mounted on the firewall in the engine compartment.

Parking brake

The parking brake operates the rear brakes only, through cable actuation. It's activated by a pedal mounted on the left side kick panel.

Service

After completing any operation involving disassembly of any part of the brake system, always test drive the vehicle to check for proper braking performance before resuming normal driving. When testing the brakes, perform the tests on a clean, dry flat surface. Conditions other than these can lead to inaccurate test results.

Test the brakes at various speeds with both light and heavy pedal pressure. The vehicle should stop evenly without pulling to one side or the other. Avoid locking the brakes because this slides the tires and diminishes braking efficiency and control of the vehicle.

Tires, vehicle load and front-end alignment are factors which also affect braking performance. **Caution:** *On models equipped with the "Theftlock" audio system, be sure the lockout feature is turned off before performing any procedure which requires disconnecting the battery.*

2　Anti-lock Brake System (ABS) - general information

Refer to illustrations 2.2, 2.4a and 2.4b

Anti-lock Brake Systems (ABS) maintain vehicle maneuverability, directional stability, and optimum deceleration under severe

braking conditions on most road surfaces. It does so by monitoring the rotational speed of the wheels and controlling the brake line pressure to the wheels during braking. This prevents the wheels from locking up on slippery roads or during hard braking.

Hydraulic modulator/motor pack assembly

The hydraulic modulator/motor pack assembly, mounted on the side of the master cylinder, controls hydraulic pressure to the front calipers and rear wheel cylinders or calipers by modulating hydraulic pressure to prevent wheel lock-up **(see illustration)**.

The Electronic Brake Control Module (EBCM) is located under the left side of the dash. The EBCM monitors the ABS system and controls the anti-lock valve solenoids. It accepts and processes information received from the brake switch and wheel speed sensors to control the hydraulic line pressure and avoid wheel lock up. It also monitors the system and stores fault codes which indicate specific problems.

Each sensor assembly consists of a variable reluctance sensor mounted adjacent to a "toothed ring" with an air gap between them **(see illustrations)**. A wheel speed sensor and toothed ring are mounted in the hub/bearing unit of each front wheel and each rear wheel. The air gap between the sensors and the rings is not adjustable, and the sensors themselves are not rebuildable. If a sensor malfunctions, the sensor must be replaced. If a ring malfunctions, it must be driven off the hub/bearing unit and a new one pressed on.

A wheel speed sensor measures wheel speed by monitoring the rotation of the toothed ring. As the teeth of the ring move through the magnetic field of the sensor, an AC voltage signal is generated. This signal frequency increases or decreases in proportion to the speed of the wheel. The EBCM monitors these three signals for changes in wheel speed; if it detects the sudden deceleration of a wheel, i.e. wheel lockup, the EBCM activates the ABS system.

Warning lights

The ABS system has self-diagnostic capabilities. Each time the vehicle is started, the EBCM runs a self-test. There are three warning lights on the instrument panel, a red BRAKE light, an amber ABS light and a blue LOW TRAC light, each with their own functions. During starting, the red BRAKE warning light should come on briefly then go out. If the red BRAKE light stays on, it indicates a problem with the main braking system, such as low fluid level detected or the parking brake is still on. If the lights stays on after the parking brake is released, check the brake fluid level in the master cylinder reservoir (see Chapter 1).

The amber ABS light indicates a problem with the ABS system, not the main or basic brake system. If the light stays on steadily, it indicates that there is a problem with the ABS system, but the main system is still working. If you have a steady ABS light, drive to a dealer service department or other qualified repair shop for diagnosis and repair. However, if the ABS light *flashes*, however, there is a more serious fault in the ABS system which may have affected the regular braking system. Pull over immediately and have the vehicle towed to a dealer or other qualified repair shop for service.

Checks

Although a special electronic tester is necessary to properly diagnose the system, the home mechanic can perform a few preliminary checks before taking the vehicle to a dealer service department which is equipped with this tester:

a) *Make sure the brake calipers are in good condition.*
b) *Check the electrical connector at the controller.*
c) *Check the fuses.*
d) *Follow the wiring harness to the speed sensors and brake light switch and make sure all connections are secure and the wiring isn't damaged.*

If the above preliminary checks don't rectify the problem, the vehicle should be diagnosed by a dealer service department.

3.5 Spray the caliper and disc with brake cleaner before beginning any repairs

3.6 Position a large C-clamp so that the solid end of the clamp is on the back of the caliper and the adjustable end is against the outer pad - tighten the clamp to push the pistons back

3.7 Mounting bolt locations for the front caliper (arrows)

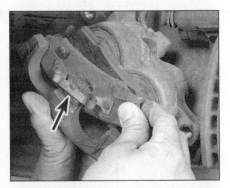

3.9 It may be necessary to pry the spring of the outer pad (arrow) away from the caliper while removing the outer pad

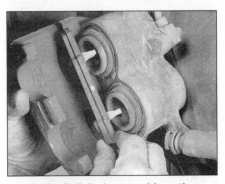

3.10a Pull the inner pad from the caliper and . . .

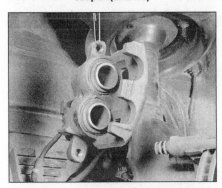

3.10b . . . then suspend the caliper by a wire

3.11 Apply some anti-squeal compound to the back of the pads

3   Disc brake pads - replacement

Warning: *Disc brake pads must be replaced on both front or rear wheels at the same time - never replace the pads on only one wheel. Also, the dust created by the brake system may contain asbestos, which is harmful to your health. Never blow it out with compressed air and don't inhale any of it. An approved filtering mask should be worn when working on the brakes. Do not, under any circumstances, use petroleum-based solvents to clean brake parts. Use brake cleaner or denatured alcohol only!*

1995 through 1998 models

Front

Removal
Refer to illustrations 3.5, 3.6, 3.7, 3.9, 3.10a and 3.10b

1   Remove and discard two-thirds of the brake fluid from the master cylinder.
2   Loosen the wheel lug nuts.
3   Raise the vehicle and support it securely on jackstands.
4   Remove the wheel and reinstall two lug nuts to hold the disc in position.
5   Clean the caliper, disc and other components with brake system cleaner before beginning any brake work **(see illustration).** This should remove traces of potentially hazardous brake dust. Collect the drippings in a plastic container.
6   Use a large C-clamp over the caliper to push the pistons back into the body of the

caliper **(see illustration).**
7   Remove the caliper mounting bolts **(see illustration).**
8   Pull the caliper straight up and off, but do not allow it to hang by the brake hose.
9   Remove the outer pad from the caliper **(see illustration).** If necessary, use a screwdriver to pry up on the retaining spring of the outer pad while sliding it out of the caliper.
10   Unclip the inner pad from the pistons and suspend the caliper by a wire to avoid damaging the brake hose **(see illustrations).**

Installation
Refer to illustrations 3.11, 3.12a, 3.12b, 3.13 and 3.14
11   Coat the back of the new brake pads with

an anti-squeal compound **(see illustration).**
12   Install the new inner and outer pads into the caliper **(see illustrations).**

3.12a Snap the new inner pad into the caliper pistons . . .

3.12b . . . then install the new outer pad (caliper shown removed for clarity)

9

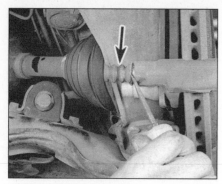

3.13 If the boots need replacing, pry them out

3.14 Lubricate the caliper mounting bolts before inserting and tightening them to Specifications

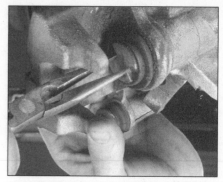

3.23 Use a pair of needle-nose pliers, with the tips engaged with the cutouts in the piston face, to turn the piston into the cylinder bore

3.25a Install the upper anti-rattle clip . . .

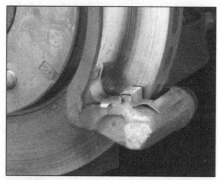

3.25b . . . and the lower anti-rattle clip in the caliper mounting bracket - make sure they're both fully seated

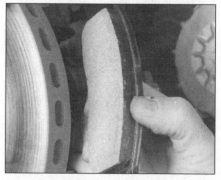

3.25c Install the inner pad . . .

13 If the boots for the caliper mounting bolts need replacing, pry them out with a small screwdriver **(see illustration)**.

14 Install the caliper over the disc and align the bolt holes. The rubber boots should be between the caliper and the mounting bracket. Lubricate the entire length of the mounting bolts with a thin film of silicone grease **(see illustration)**. Be sure to tighten the caliper mounting bolts to the torque listed in this Chapter's Specifications.

15 Lower the vehicle. Fill the reservoir with the recommended fluid (see Chapter 1) and pump the brake pedal several times to bring the pads into contact with discs.

16 Road test the vehicle carefully before returning it to normal service.

Rear

Removal

17 Remove and discard two-thirds of the brake fluid from the reservoir.

18 Loosen the wheel lug nuts, raise the vehicle and support it securely on jackstands. Remove the wheels.

19 Install two lug nuts to retain the disc when the caliper is removed.

20 Remove the bolt and washer attaching the cable support bracket to the caliper body, which allows enough cable slack to permit the caliper body to rotate enough for pad replacement. It isn't necessary to detach the cable or the brake hose.

21 Remove the lower caliper bolt, then pivot the caliper up.

22 Remove the pads and anti-rattle clips from the caliper mounting bracket.

Installation

Refer to illustrations 3.23, 3.25a, 3.25b, 3.25c and 3.25d

23 Using a two-pin spanner or a pair of needle-nose pliers, turn the piston to retract it into the caliper bore **(see illustration)**. Turn the piston as necessary so that a line drawn through the slots in the piston face would be exactly perpendicular to a line drawn through the caliper mounting bolt holes.

24 Using a small screwdriver, gently lift one edge of the piston boot to release any trapped air; the boot should lay flat.

25 Apply a coating of anti-squeal compound to the backing plates of the new pads. Install the anti-rattle clips and the pads in the caliper **(see illustrations)**. **Note:** *The pad with the wear sensor is the outer pad.*

26 Pivot the caliper down over the disc and pads. Lubricate the caliper mounting bolt with high-temperature grease and install it, tightening it to the torque listed in this Chapter's Specifications.

27 The remainder of reassembly is the opposite of disassembly. **Warning:** *Before driving the vehicle, pump the brakes several times to seat the pads against the disc. Road test the vehicle carefully before returning it to normal service.*

1999 models (front or rear)

Refer to illustrations 3.32a through 3.32m
Warning: *Disc brake pads must be replaced*

on both front or both rear wheels at the same time - never replace the pads on only one wheel. Also, the dust created by the brake system may contain asbestos, which is harmful to your health. Never blow it out with compressed air and don't inhale any of it. An approved filtering mask should be worn when working on the brakes. Do not, under any circumstances, use petroleum-based solvents to clean brake parts. Use brake system cleaner only!

Note: *This procedure applies to the front **and** rear brake pads.*

28 Remove the cap from the brake fluid reservoir. Remove about two-thirds of the fluid from the reservoir. **Caution:** *Brake fluid will damage paint. If any fluid is spilled, wash it off immediately with plenty of clean, cold water.*

29 Loosen the front or rear wheel lug nuts, raise the front or rear of the vehicle and support it securely on jackstands. Block the wheels at the opposite end.

30 Remove the wheels. Work on one brake assembly at a time, using the assembled brake for reference, if necessary.

31 Inspect the brake disc carefully as outlined in Section 5. If machining is necessary, follow the information in that Section to remove the disc.

32 Follow the accompanying photo sequence for the actual pad replacement procedure **(see illustrations 3.32a through 3.32m)**. Be sure to stay in order and read the caption under each illustration.

3.25d . . . and the outer pad in to the caliper mounting bracket, then swing the caliper down into place. Install the caliper mounting bolt and tighten it to the torque listed in this Chapter's Specifications

3.32a Before disassembling the brake, wash it thoroughly with brake system cleaner and allow it to dry - position a drain pan under the brake to catch the residue - DO NOT use compressed air to blow off brake dust!

3.32b To make room for the new pads, use a C-clamp to depress the piston into the caliper before removing the caliper and pads - do this a little at a time, keeping an eye on the fluid level in the master cylinder to make sure it doesn't overflow

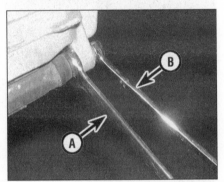

3.32c Hold the caliper slide pin with an open-end wrench (A) and loosen the lower mounting bolt with another wrench (B)

3.32d Pivot the caliper up and support it in this position for access to the brake pads

3.32e Remove the inner brake pad

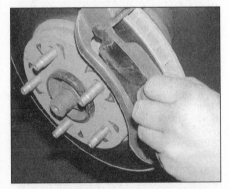

3.32f Remove the outer brake pad

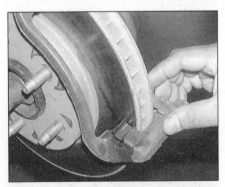

3.32g Remove the upper and lower pad retainers from the caliper mounting bracket

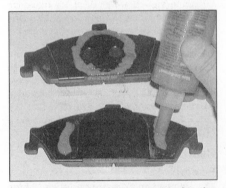

3.32h Apply anti-squeal compound to the back of both pads (let the compound "set up" a few minutes before installing them)

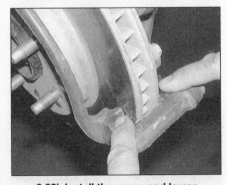

3.32i Install the upper and lower pad retainers

33   When reinstalling the caliper, be sure to tighten the mounting bolts to the torque listed in this Chapter's Specifications. Tighten the wheel lug nuts to the torque listed in the Chapter 1 Specifications.

34   After the job has been completed, firmly depress the brake pedal a few times to bring the pads into contact with the disc. Check the level of the brake fluid, adding some if necessary (see Chapter 1). Check the operation of the brakes carefully before placing the vehicle into normal service.

4   Brake caliper - removal and installation

Warning: *Dust created by the brake system may contain asbestos, which is harmful to your health. Never blow it out with compressed air and don't inhale any of it. An approved filtering mask should be worn when working on the brakes. Do not, under any circumstances, use petroleum-based solvents to clean brake parts. Use brake cleaner or denatured alcohol only!*

9

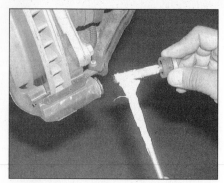

3.32j Clean the caliper slide pin and inspect it for scoring and corrosion; coat the pin with high-temperature grease

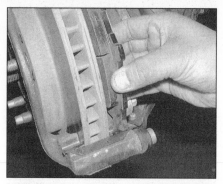

3.32k Install the inner brake pad; if you're replacing the front pads, it's the one with the wear indicator on it, which must be positioned at the top (on the rear brakes, the outer pad has the wear indicator)

3.32l Install the outer brake pad; if you're replacing the rear pads, it's the one with the wear indicator on it, which must be positioned at the bottom

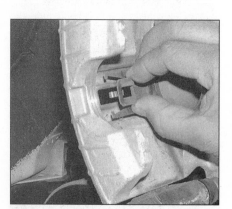

3.32m Check the condition of the anti-rattle spring in the center of the caliper, replacing it if necessary. Swing the caliper down over the pads and install the lower mounting bolt, tightening it to the torque listed in this Chapter's Specifications. Note: *If the caliper won't fit over the pads, use a C-clamp to push the piston into the caliper a little further*

Note : *If caliper replacement is indicated (usually because of fluid leakage) explore all options before beginning the job. New and factory-rebuilt calipers are available on an exchange basis, which makes this job quite easy.*

Removal

Refer to illustration 4.1

1   The removal procedure is the same as in Section 3 with the exception of disconnecting the hydraulic line from the caliper **(see illustration)**. On 1995 through 1998 rear calipers, the parking brake cable will have to be disconnected from the caliper.

Installation

2   The installation procedure is the same as in Section 3.

3   When attaching the hydraulic line to the caliper, use new copper washers at the line-to-caliper connection. Tighten the fitting bolt to the torque listed in this Chapter's Specifications.

4   Bleed the hydraulic system as described in Section 10.

4.1 Remove the bolt (arrow) to separate the hydraulic line from the caliper

---

5   Brake disc - inspection, removal and installation

Refer to illustrations 5.3, 5.4a, 5.4b, 5.5a, 5.5b and 5.6

Inspection

1   Loosen the wheel lug nuts, raise the vehicle and support it securely on jackstands. Apply the parking brake and block the wheels to keep the vehicle from rolling off the jackstands. Remove the wheel and install the lug nuts, flat side against the disc, to hold the disc in place. It may be necessary to install washers under the lug nuts to enable the nuts to apply pressure to the disc.

2   Remove the brake caliper as outlined in Section 3 (it's part of the pad replacement procedure). You don't have to disconnect the brake hose. After removing the caliper bolts, suspend the caliper out of the way with a piece of wire - DO NOT let it hang by the hose.

3   Visually inspect the disc surface for score marks and other damage. Light scratches and shallow grooves are normal and may not be detrimental to brake operation, but deep score marks - over 0.015-inch (0.38 mm) deep - require disc removal and refinishing by an automotive machine shop. Be sure to check both sides of the disc **(see**

5.3 The brake pads on this vehicle were obviously neglected, as they wore down to the rivets and cut deep grooves into the disc - wear this severe will require replacement of the disc

illustration). If pulsating has been felt during application of the brakes, suspect excessive disc runout.

4   To check disc runout, mount a dial indicator with the stem resting at a point about 1/2-inch from the outer edge of the disc **(see illustration)**. Set the indicator to zero and turn the disc. The indicator reading should not exceed the specified allowable runout limit. If it does, the disc should be refinished by an automotive machine shop. **Note:** *The discs should be resurfaced, regardless of the dial indicator reading, to impart a smooth finish and ensure perfectly flat brake pad surfaces which will eliminate pedal pulsations. At the very least, if you don't have the discs resurfaced, remove the glaze with sandpaper or emery cloth using a swirling motion* **(see illustration)**.

5   Never machine the disc to a thickness less than the specified minimum allowable refinish thickness. The minimum wear (or discard) thickness is cast into the disc **(see illustration)**. This shouldn't be confused with the minimum refinish thickness. The disc thickness can be checked with a micrometer **(see illustration)**.

Removal

6   Remove the lug nuts that were put on to hold the disc in place. Remove the caliper mounting bracket and remove the disc from

5.4a Check for runout with a dial indicator - mount it with the indicator needle about 1/2-inch from the outer edge of the disc

5.4b If you don't have the discs machined, at the very least be sure to remove the glaze from the disc surface with sandpaper or emery cloth (use a swirling motion as shown here)

5.5a The minimum wear (or discard) thickness is cast into the disc

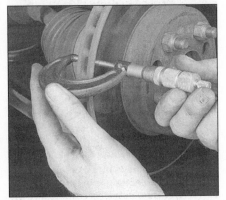

5.5b Measure the thickness of the disc at several points with a micrometer

the hub **(see illustration)**. **Note:** *The mounting bracket bolts require a Torx bit to remove.*

Installation

7   Install the caliper mounting bracket, using a non-hardening thread locking compound on the (cleaned) bolts and tighten them to the torque listed in this Chapter's Specifications. Place the disc in position over the threaded studs.

8   Install the caliper mounting bracket, brake pads and caliper (refer to Section 3, if necessary). Tighten the mounting bracket bolts and the caliper bolts to the torque values listed in this Chapter's Specifications.

9   Install the wheel, then lower the vehicle to the ground. Tighten the lug nuts to the torque listed in the Chapter 1 Specifications. Depress the brake pedal a few times to bring the brake pads into contact with the disc. Bleeding of the system won't be necessary unless the brake hose was disconnected from the caliper. Check the operation of the brakes carefully before driving the vehicle in traffic.

6   Drum brake shoes - replacement

Warning: *Drum brake shoes must be replaced on both rear wheels at the same*

5.6 Remove the two caliper mounting bracket bolts (arrows) - they are Torx-head bolts

time - never replace the shoes on only one wheel. Also, the dust created by the brake system contains asbestos, which is harmful to your health. Never blow it out with compressed air and don't inhale any of it. An approved filtering mask should be worn when working on the brakes. Do not, under any circumstances, use petroleum-based solvents to clean brake parts. Use brake cleaner or denatured alcohol only!

Removal

Refer to illustrations 6.3, 6.4, 6.5a, 6.5b, 6.5c, 6.5d and 6.5e

1   Loosen the wheel lug nuts, raise the rear of the vehicle and support it securely on jackstands. Block the front wheels to keep the vehicle from rolling off the jackstands.

2   Release the parking brake and remove the wheel. **Note:** *All four rear shoes must be replaced at the same time, but to avoid mixing up parts, work on only one brake assembly at a time.*

3   Remove the brake drum. If it's difficult to remove, back off the parking brake cable (see Section 12), remove the access hole plug from the backing plate, insert a screwdriver

6.3 Insert a screwdriver through the hole (arrow) in the backing plate and turn the adjuster screw star wheel to retract the brake shoes

through the hole and turn the adjuster screw star wheel **(see illustration)**. This will allow the brake shoes to retract. Use a rubber mallet to tap gently on the outer rim of the drum and/or around the inner drum diameter by the spindle. Avoid using excessive force.

4   Clean the brake assembly with brake system cleaner - DO NOT use compressed air to blow the dust out of the brake assembly **(see illustration)**.

6.4 Before doing any work on the rear brakes, wash down the whole assembly with brake cleaner

9

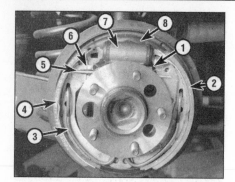

6.5a Drum brake components

1 *Actuator spring*   5 *Adjuster screw*
2 *Trailing shoe*   6 *Actuator lever*
3 *Retractor spring*   7 *Wheel cylinder*
4 *Leading shoe*   8 *Backing plate*

**6.5b Use a pair of needle-nose pliers to
remove the actuator spring**

**6.5c Wedge a flat-bladed screwdriver
under the spring and pry it out of the
leading brake shoe, then remove the
shoe, adjuster screw and actuator lever**

**6.5d Lift the retractor spring from the
trailing brake shoe and swing the shoe
out from the hub area to gain access to
the parking brake cable**

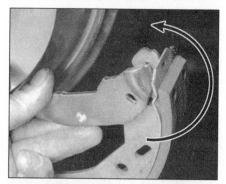

**6.5e Rotate the brake shoe to release the
parking brake lever from the shoe**

**6.6a Lubricate the contact surfaces of the
backing plate with high-
temperature grease**

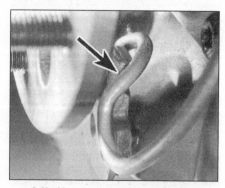

**6.6b Use a screwdriver to pry the
retractor spring over the alignment
peg (arrow)**

5   Refer to the accompanying photo
sequence and perform the brake shoe
removal procedure **(see illustrations)**. Be
sure to stay in order and to read the caption
under each illustration.

Installation

Refer to illustrations 6.6a, 6.6b, 6.6c and 6.8

6   Installation of the shoes is the reverse of
removal. Lubricate the components as
shown **(see illustrations overleaf)**.

7   Set the preliminary shoe adjustment by

**6.6c Lubricate the adjuster screw with
high-temperature grease prior
to installation**

turning the star wheel on the adjuster so that
the drum just slips over the shoes.

8   Before reinstalling the drum, check it for
cracks, score marks, deep scratches and
hard spots, which will appear as blue discolored areas. If the hard spots can't be
removed with fine emery cloth or if any of the
other conditions listed above exist, the drum
must be taken to an automotive machine
shop to have it turned. **Note:** *The drums
should be resurfaced, regardless of the surface appearance, to impart a smooth finish
and ensure a perfectly round drum (which will
eliminate brake pedal pulsations related to
out-of-round drums). At the very least, if you
don't have the drums resurfaced, remove the
glaze from the surface with sandpaper or
emery cloth using a swirling motion. If the
drum won't "clean up" before the maximum*

**6.8 The maximum permissible diameter is
cast into the drum**

*service limit is reached in the machining oper-
ation, install a new one. The maximum wear
diameter is cast into each brake drum* **(see
illustration)**.

9   Install the brake drum on the hub flange.
Using a screwdriver inserted through the
backing plate, adjust the shoes until they
drag on the drum as the drum is turned, then
back-off the star wheel until the shoes don't
drag.

10   Mount the wheel, install the lug nuts,
then lower the vehicle.

11   Apply and release the brake pedal 30 to
35 times using normal pedal force. Pause
about one second between pedal applications. After adjustment, make sure that both
wheels turn freely.

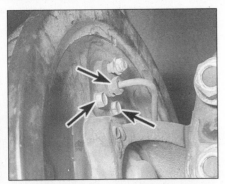

7.4 A flare-nut wrench should be used to unscrew the brake line fitting (upper arrow) - to remove the wheel cylinder, remove the two bolts (lower arrows)

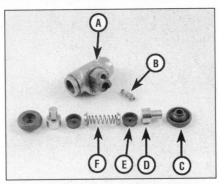

7.7 Wheel cylinder components - exploded view

A Wheel cylinder	D Piston
body	E Seal
B Bleeder screw	F Spring
C Boot	

8.2 Unplug the fluid level sensor connector (upper arrow) and unscrew the brake line fittings (lower arrows) (non-ABS master cylinder)

7 Wheel cylinder - removal, overhaul and installation

Refer to illustrations 7.4 and 7.7

Note: *If an overhaul is indicated (usually because of fluid leakage or sticking brakes) explore all options before beginning the job. New wheel cylinders are available, which makes this job quite easy. If you do rebuild the wheel cylinder, make sure rebuild kits are available before proceeding. If the vehicle has high mileage, new wheel cylinders are highly recommended.*

Warning: *Never rebuild or replace just one wheel cylinder. Replace or rebuild both rear wheel cylinders at the same time.*

Removal

1   Raise the rear of the vehicle and support it securely on jackstands. Block the front wheels to keep the vehicle from rolling off the jackstands.
2   Remove the brake shoe assembly (see Section 6).
3   Carefully clean the area around the wheel cylinder on both sides of the backing plate.
4   Unscrew the brake line fitting **(see illustration)**, but don't pull the line away from the wheel cylinder.
5   Remove the wheel cylinder retaining bolts.
6   Remove the wheel cylinder from the brake backing plate and place it on a clean workbench. Immediately plug the brake line on the vehicle to prevent fluid loss and contamination.

Overhaul

7   Remove the bleeder valve, seals, pistons, boots and spring assembly from the wheel cylinder body **(see illustration). Note:** *Take note of exactly how the seals and pistons were installed, and which direction the seals face.*
8   Clean the wheel cylinder with brake fluid, denatured alcohol or brake system cleaner. **Warning:** *Do not, under any circumstances, use petroleum-based solvents to clean brake parts.*
9   Use compressed air to dry the wheel

cylinder and blow out the passages.
10   Check the bore for corrosion and score marks. Crocus cloth may be used to remove light corrosion and stains, but the cylinder must be replaced with a new one if the defects can't be removed easily, or if the bore is scored.
11   Lubricate the new seals with brake fluid.
12   Install the spring in the cylinder first, making sure that the metal end caps are still attached at each end.
13   Install the seals. **Note:** *The flared sides of the seals must face the inside of the wheel cylinder, matching the flare on the metal cups at each end of the spring. The flat side of the seals must face the inner ends of the pistons.*
14   Lubricate the pistons with clean brake fluid, then install them with the larger diameter end toward the seals. Install the boots over the smaller diameter end of the pistons and seat the boots all around the groove at each end of wheel cylinder. Squeeze the two piston ends back and forth against the spring pressure to make sure neither piston is binding.

Installation

15   Place the wheel cylinder in position.
16   Connect the brake line, tightening the fitting by hand.
17   Install the wheel cylinder bolts and tighten them to the torque listed in this Chapter's Specifications.
18   Tighten the brake line fitting securely.
19   Install the brake shoes (see Section 6).
20   Bleed the brakes (see Section 10).

8 Master cylinder - removal, overhaul and installation

Warning: *On models with ABS brakes, the master cylinder is combined with the ABS hydraulic unit/modulator and employ a set of spring-loaded, precision gears. The alignment and tensioning of these is a critical safety concern. While the master cylinder and ABS hydraulic unit may be unbolted from the vehicle (such as for replacement of the power brake booster), they must not be separated*

from each other. Only a technician with a factory scan tool can relieve the tension on these gears and safely separate the master cylinder from the ABS hydraulic unit/modulator assembly. The gear tensioning relief procedure must be performed with the master cylinder assembly installed in the vehicle, not removed from the vehicle.

Removal

Refer to illustrations 8.2 and 8.6

1   Detach the cable from the negative battery terminal.
2   Unplug the electrical connector from the fluid level sensor switch **(see illustration)**. On models with ABS, also disconnect the two solenoid valve electrical connectors and the ABS motor pack six-terminal electrical connector.
3   Place rags under the line fittings and prepare caps or plastic bags to cover the ends of the lines once they're disconnected. **Caution:** *Brake fluid will damage paint. Cover all painted parts and be careful not to spill fluid during this procedure.*
4   Loosen the fittings at the ends of the brake lines where they enter the master cylinder. To prevent rounding off the flats on the fittings, use a flare-nut wrench, which wraps around the hex.
5   Pull the brake lines away from the master cylinder or hydraulic unit and plug the ends to prevent contamination.
6   Remove the two mounting nuts **(see illustration)** and detach the master cylinder

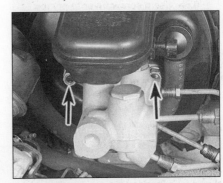

8.6 Remove the master cylinder mounting nuts (arrows)

9

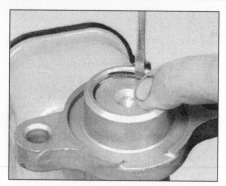

8.11 Press down on the piston and remove the primary piston lock ring

8.12 Remove the primary piston assembly

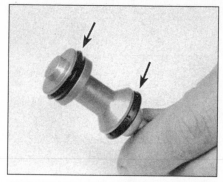

8.16 The secondary piston seals must be installed with the lips facing out as shown

8.18 Install the secondary piston assembly

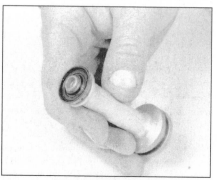

8.19a The primary piston seal must be installed with the lip facing away from the piston

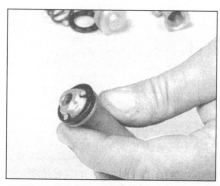

8.19b Install the seal guard over the seal

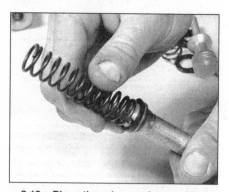

8.19c Place the primary piston spring in position

8.19d Insert the spring retainer into the spring

(or master cylinder/hydraulic unit assembly) from the vehicle.

7   Remove the reservoir cover and reservoir diaphragm, then discard any remaining fluid.

Overhaul (non-ABS models only)

Refer to illustrations 8.11, 8.12, 8.16, 8.18, 8.19a, 8.19b, 8.19c, 8.19d, 8.19e, 8.19f, 8.20 and 8.32

8   Mount the master cylinder in a vise. Be sure to line the vise jaws with rags or blocks of wood to prevent damage to the cylinder body.

9   The fluid reservoir is attached to the master cylinder body with two roll pins. Drive them out with a 1/8-inch punch. Pull straight up on the reservoir assembly and separate it

from the master cylinder body. Remove and discard the two O-rings.

10   Remove the proportioner valve caps, which are on top of the large bosses on the left side of the master cylinder (just above where the fluid lines attached). Using needlenose pliers, carefully remove the O-rings, the springs, the proportioner valve pistons and seals. Make sure you don't scratch or otherwise damage the piston stems or the bores. Set each proportioner valve assembly aside.

11   Remove the primary piston lock ring by depressing the piston and prying the ring out with a screwdriver **(see illustration)**.

12   Remove the primary piston assembly from the bore **(see illustration)**.

13   Remove the secondary piston assembly from the bore. It may be necessary to remove the master cylinder from the vise and invert it,

carefully tapping it against a block of wood to expel the piston.

14   Clean the master cylinder body, the primary and secondary piston assemblies, the proportioner valve assemblies and the reservoir in brake cleaner or denatured alcohol and dry them off with filtered, unlubricated compressed air or a clean (lint-free) shop rag. **Warning:** *DO NOT, under any circumstances, use petroleum-based solvents to clean brake parts.*

15   Inspect the master cylinder piston bore for corrosion and score marks. If any corrosion or damage in the bore is evident, replace the master cylinder body - don't use abrasives to try to clean it up.

16   Remove the old seals from the secondary piston assembly and install the new seals with the cup lips facing out **(see illustration)**.

17   Attach the spring retainer to the secondary piston assembly.

18   Lubricate the cylinder bore with clean brake fluid and install the spring and secondary piston assembly **(see illustration)**.

19   Disassemble the primary piston assembly, noting the locations of the parts, then lubricate the new seals with clean brake fluid and install them on the piston **(see illustrations)**.

20   Install the primary piston assembly in the cylinder bore **(see illustration)**, depress it and install the lock ring.

21   Inspect the proportioner valves for corrosion and score marks. Replace them if necessary.

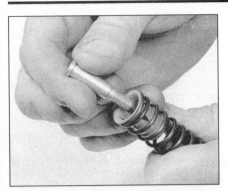

8.19e Insert the spring retaining bolt through the retainer and spring and thread it into the piston

8.19f Lubricate the O-ring with clean brake fluid, then install it on the piston

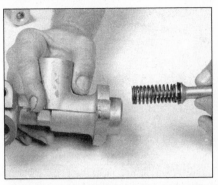

8.20 Insert the primary piston assembly into the bore

8.32 Install the reservoir diaphragm in the cover

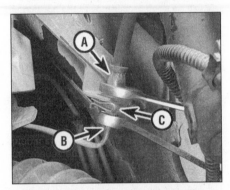

9.2 Using a back-up wrench on the flexible hose side of the fitting (A), loosen the tube nut (B) with a flare-nut wrench and remove the U-clip (C) from the hose fitting

22 Lubricate the new O-rings and proportioner valve seals with the silicone grease supplied with the rebuild kit. Also lubricate the stem of the proportioner valve pistons.

23 Install the new seals on the proportioner valve pistons with the seal lips facing toward the cap assembly.

24 Install the proportioner valve pistons and seals in the master cylinder body.

25 Install the springs in the master cylinder body.

26 Install the new O-rings in their respective grooves in the proportioner valve cap assemblies.

27 Install the proportioner valve caps in the master cylinder and tighten them to the torque listed in this Chapter's Specifications.

28 Inspect the reservoir for cracks and distortion. If any damage is evident, replace it.

29 Lubricate the new reservoir O-rings with clean brake fluid and press them into their respective grooves in the master cylinder body. Make sure they're properly seated.

30 Lubricate the reservoir fittings with clean brake fluid and install the reservoir on the master cylinder body by pressing it straight down.

31 Drive in new reservoir retaining (roll) pins. Make sure you don't damage the reservoir or master cylinder body.

32 Inspect the reservoir diaphragm and cover for cracks and deformation. Replace any damaged parts with new ones and attach the diaphragm to the cover (see illustration).
Note: Whenever the master cylinder is

removed, the complete hydraulic system must be bled (see Section 10). The time required to bleed the system can be reduced if the master cylinder is filled with fluid and bench bled (refer to Steps 33 through 36) before it's installed on the vehicle.

33 Insert threaded plugs of the correct size into the brake line outlet holes and fill the reservoirs with brake fluid. The master cylinder should be supported so brake fluid won't spill during the bench bleeding procedure.

34 Loosen one plug at a time and push the piston assembly into the bore to force air from the master cylinder. To prevent air from being drawn back in, the appropriate plug must be replaced before allowing the piston to return to its original position.

35 Stroke the piston three or four times for each outlet to ensure that all air has been expelled.

36 Since high pressure isn't involved in the bench bleeding procedure, there is an alternative to the removal and replacement of the plugs with each stroke of the piston assembly. Before pushing in on the piston assembly, remove one of the plugs completely. Before releasing the piston, however, instead of replacing the plug, simply put your finger tightly over the hole to keep air from being drawn back into the master cylinder. Wait several seconds for the brake fluid to be drawn from the reservoir into the piston bore,

then repeat the procedure. When you push down on the piston it'll force your finger off the hole, allowing the air inside to be expelled. When only brake fluid is being ejected from the hole, replace the plug and go on to the other port.

37 Refill the master cylinder reservoirs and install the diaphragm and cover assembly.
Note: The reservoirs should only be filled to the top of the reservoir divider to prevent overflowing when the cover is installed.

Installation

38 Carefully install the master cylinder by reversing the removal steps, fill the reservoir with the recommended fluid (see Chapter 1), then bleed the brakes at each wheel (see Section 10).

---

9 Brake hoses and lines - inspection and replacement

Refer to illustration 9.2
Warning: On ABS-equipped vehicles, do not replace any rubber brake hoses except with parts specifically designated for ABS models.

1 About every six months, raise the vehicle and support it securely on jackstands, then check the flexible hoses that connect the steel brake lines to the front and rear brake assemblies. Look for cracks, chafing of the outer cover, leaks, blisters and other damage. The hoses are important and vulnerable parts of the brake system and the inspection should be thorough. A light and mirror will be helpful to see into restricted areas. If a hose exhibits any of the above conditions, replace it with a new one.

Front brake hose

2 Using a back-up wrench, disconnect the brake line from the hose fitting, being careful not to bend the frame bracket or twist the brake line (see illustration).

3 Use pliers to remove the U-clip from the female fitting at the bracket, then remove the hose from the bracket.

4 At the caliper end of the hose, remove the bolt from the fitting block, then remove the hose and the copper washers on either side of the fitting block.

9

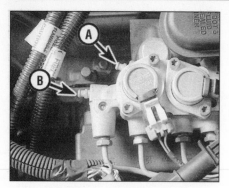

10.5 ABS hydraulic modulator assembly bleeder valves

A Rear bleeder   B Front bleeder

5   When installing the hose, always use new copper washers on either side of the fitting block and lubricate all bolt threads with clean brake fluid.

6   With the fitting flange engaged with the caliper locating ledge, attach the hose to the caliper.

7   Without twisting the hose, install the female fitting in the hose bracket. It'll fit the bracket in only one position.

8   Install the U-clip retaining the female fitting to the frame bracket.

9   Using a back-up wrench, attach the brake line to the hose fitting.

10   When the brake hose installation is complete, there shouldn't be any kinks in the hose. Make sure the hose doesn't contact any part of the suspension. Check it by turning the wheels to the extreme left and right positions. If the hose makes contact, remove the hose and correct the installation as necessary.

Rear brake hose

11   Using a back-up wrench, disconnect the hose at both ends, being careful not to bend the bracket or steel lines.

12   Remove the U-clip with pliers and separate the female fittings from the brackets.

13   Unbolt the hose retaining clip and remove the hose.

14   Without twisting the hose, install the female ends in the frame bracket. It'll fit the bracket in only one position.

15   Install the U-clip retaining the female end to the bracket.

16   Using a back-up wrench, attach the steel line fittings to the female fittings. Again, be careful not to bend the bracket or steel line.

17   Make sure the hose installation didn't loosen the frame bracket. Tighten the bracket if necessary.

18   Fill the master cylinder reservoir and bleed the system (refer to Section 10).

Metal brake lines

19   When replacing brake lines, be sure to buy the correct replacement parts. Don't use copper or any other tubing for brake lines.

20   Prefabricated brake lines, with the ends

10.13 When bleeding the brakes, a hose is connected to the bleeder valve at the caliper and then submerged in brake fluid - air will be seen as bubbles in the container and in the tube (all air must be expelled before continuing to the next wheel)

already flared and fittings installed, are available at auto parts stores and dealer service departments. If necessary, carefully bend the line to the proper shape. A tubing bender must be used for this. **Caution:** *Don't crimp or damage the line.*

21   When installing the new line, make sure it's securely supported in the brackets with plenty of clearance between moving or hot components.

22   After installation, check the master cylinder fluid level and add fluid as necessary. Bleed the brake system as outlined in the next Section and test the brakes carefully before driving the vehicle in traffic.

---

10   Brake hydraulic system - bleeding

Refer to illustrations 10.5 and 10.13
Note: *Bleeding the brakes is necessary to remove air that manages to find its way into the system when its been opened during removal and installation of a hose, line, caliper or master cylinder.*
Warning: *Wear eye protection when bleeding the brake system. If you get fluid in your eyes, rinse them immediately with water and seek medical attention.*

ABS-equipped models only

1   Do not touch the brake pedal at any time during this preliminary procedure, which must be performed before any bleeding operation.

2   Start the vehicle and watch the amber ABS warning light for at least ten seconds. If the warning light stays ON this long, your vehicle exhibits an ABS problem that can only be solved at a dealership or other qualified repair shop equipped with the proper scan tool.

3   If the warning light performed normally, i.e. it turned OFF after about three seconds, then turn the vehicle OFF. Repeat the procedure and if the ABS warning light turns OFF again after about three seconds, turn the

vehicle OFF and you can bleed the brake system as described below for non-ABS vehicles.

4   After the bleeding process is completed, if the pedal feels soft, perform the above warning light test five times, **without** touching the brake pedal, then repeat the bleeding procedure.

5   **Warning:** *If an ABS-equipped model has been allowed to run dry at the master cylinder, the hydraulic modulator assembly must be bled before bleeding the calipers/wheel cylinders.* Attach the bleeder hose to the rearmost bleeder valve on the modulator assembly **(see illustration)**. With the other end of the hose in a jar partially filled with clean brake fluid, crack the valve slowly and have an assistant depress the brake pedal. Keep the pedal down until fluid flows. Close the valve and release the brake pedal. Repeat this until no air is evident as the fluid enters the jar, then repeat the procedure for the forward bleeder valve. After bleeding the hydraulic modulator assembly, bleed the rest of the braking systems as described below.

All models

Note: *This procedure applies only to ABS models which have passed the test described in Steps 1 through 3.*
6   It'll probably be necessary to bleed the system at all four brakes if air has entered the system due to low fluid level, or if the brake lines have been disconnected at the master cylinder.

7   If a brake line was disconnected at only one wheel, then only that caliper or wheel cylinder must be bled.

8   If a brake line is disconnected at a fitting located between the master cylinder and any of the brakes, that part of the system served by the disconnected line must be bled.

9   Remove any residual vacuum from the power brake booster by applying the brake several times with the engine off.

10   Remove the master cylinder reservoir cover and fill the reservoir with brake fluid. Reinstall the cover. **Note:** *Check the fluid level often during the bleeding procedure and add fluid as necessary to prevent the level from falling low enough to allow air bubbles into the master cylinder.*

11   Have an assistant on hand, as well as a supply of new (DOT 3) brake fluid, an empty, clear plastic container, a length of inch plastic, rubber or vinyl tubing to fit over the bleeder valve and a wrench to open and close the bleeder valve.

12   Beginning at the right rear wheel, loosen the bleeder valve slightly, then tighten it to a point where it's snug but can still be loosened quickly and easily.

13   Place one end of the tubing over the bleeder valve and submerge the other end in brake fluid in the container **(see illustration)**.

14   Have your assistant depress the pedal to the floor, then hold the pedal down firmly.

15   While the pedal is held down, open the bleeder valve just enough to allow fluid to

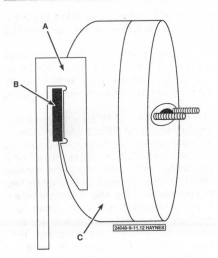

11.12 Booster "cam-lock" components

A   Firewall bracket with slot
B   Tab shown locked in bracket slot
C   Booster assembly

flow out of the valve. Watch for air bubbles to exit the submerged end of the tube. When the fluid slows after a couple of seconds, close the valve and have your assistant release the pedal.

16   Repeat Steps 14 and 15 until no more air is seen leaving the tube, then tighten the bleeder valve and proceed to the left front wheel, the left rear wheel and the right front wheel, in that order, and perform the same procedure. Be sure to check the fluid in the master cylinder reservoir frequently.

17   Never use old brake fluid. It contains moisture which will can boil, rendering the brakes useless.

18   Fill the master cylinder with fluid at the end of the operation.

19   Check the operation of the brakes. The pedal should feel firm when depressed. If necessary, repeat the procedure. On ABS-equipped models, see Step 4.

20   Do not operate the vehicle if you have any doubts as to the effectiveness of the brake system. Seek professional advice if you can't obtain a firm pedal.

11   Power brake booster - check, removal and installation

Refer to illustration 11.12

1   The power brake booster unit requires no special maintenance apart from periodic inspection of the vacuum hose and the case.

Operating check

2   Depress the brake pedal several times with the engine off and make sure there is no change in the pedal reserve distance (the minimum distance to the floor).

3   Depress the pedal and start the engine. If the pedal goes down slightly, operation is normal.

12.6 Parking brake pedal (A) and front end of parking brake cable (B)

Airtightness check

4   Start the engine and turn it off after one or two minutes. Depress the pedal several times slowly. If the pedal goes down farther the first time but gradually rises after the second or third depression, the booster is airtight.

5   Depress the brake pedal while the engine is running, then stop the engine with the brake pedal depressed. If there is no change in the pedal reserve travel after holding the pedal for 30 seconds, the booster is airtight.

Removal

6   Dismantling of the power unit requires special tools and is not ordinarily done by the home mechanic. If a problem develops, install a new or factory rebuilt unit.

7   Remove the nuts attaching the master cylinder to the booster and carefully pull the master cylinder forward until it clears the mounting studs. Be careful to avoid bending or kinking the brake lines. **Warning:** *On ABS-equipped models, do not disconnect the master cylinder from the hydraulic modulator assembly* (see Section 8).

8   Disconnect the vacuum hose where it attaches to the power brake booster.

9   On models with the 3.4L engine, Refer to Chapter 2, Part B for removal of the upper intake manifold.

10   On all models, remove the fuel injector trim cover on the rear bank (firewall side) of the engine.

11   From the passenger compartment, disconnect the brake pushrod from the top of the brake pedal. **Caution:** *Keep the pedal from moving while doing this, to avoid damage to the brake switch.*

12   The booster is mounted to the firewall with a "cam-lock" bracket. On the right side of the bracket, use a screwdriver to pry the booster's locking tab out of the notch on the bracket **(see illustration)**. Insert the screwdriver between the tab and the notch.

13   If you do not have access to the factory tool that holds the front of the booster for removal/installation, there are two other ways to do the job. If you have a large strap wrench, wrap it around the body of the booster. You can also install two short lengths of rubber fuel hose over the master-cylinder mounting studs at the front of the

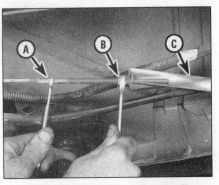

12.8 Hold the cable with a small wrench (A) while turning the adjuster nut (B) at the equalizer (C)

booster, and use a prybar between the two studs to turn the booster as described in the next Step.

14   While holding the tab out of the notch (toward the firewall), rotate the booster counterclockwise until it comes free of the bracket. **Caution:** *Be careful not to tear the boot (interior side of the firewall) around the booster pushrod as you remove the booster.*

Installation

15   Installation is the reverse of removal. Make sure the locking tab is completely seated in the firewall bracket slot.

16   Carefully test the operation of the brakes before driving the vehicle.

12   Parking brake - adjustment

Rear disc brakes

Refer to illustrations 12.6 and 12.8

1   Using heavy pedal pressure, depress the brake pedal three times.

2   **Note:** *The parking brake mechanism has no release lever. You step on the pedal to apply the parking brake, then the next time you step on the pedal, the parking brake is released.*

3   Raise the rear of the vehicle and support it securely on jackstands.

4   Make sure the parking brake is fully released.

5   Turn the ignition key to the On position.

6   If the brake warning light is on, pull down on the front parking brake cable to remove the slack from the pedal assembly **(see illustration)**.

7   At the rear caliper housings, the two parking brake levers should be against the lever stops. If they are not, check for binding in the rear cables and/or loosen the cables at the adjuster until both the left and the right levers are against the stops.

8   Tighten the parking brake cable at the equalizer **(see illustration)** until either the left or right lever just begins to move off the stop. There should be 0.020 to 0.040-inch clearance between the lever and the stop.

9   While holding down on the main (hydraulic) brake pedal, operate the parking

9

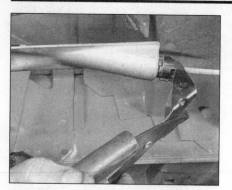

13.6 Special pliers like these can be used to release parking brake cables wherever cable retainers go through brackets (shown at equalizer) - regular plier or a hose clamp can also be used to depress the fingers of the retainer

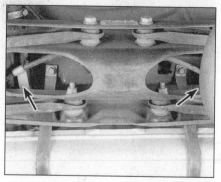

13.14 Detach the cable brackets (arrows, right bracket is behind exhaust pipe in photo) from the rear crossmember

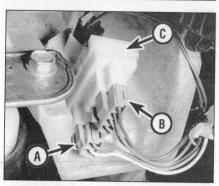

14.1 Disconnect the electrical connectors (A and B) from the brake light switch (C) - the wires at connector A are the ones to check for brake light operation

brake several times to check for a firm pedal. Lower the vehicle.

Rear drum brakes

10   Adjust the rear brake shoes (see Section 6).
11   Apply the parking brake 10 clicks, then release it. Repeat this five times.
12   Make sure the parking brake is fully released. Turn the ignition on. If the brake warning light is on, operate the manual brake release and pull down on the front parking brake cable to remove slack.
13   Raise the car and support it securely on jackstands.
14   Adjust the parking brake by turning the nut on the equalizer **(see illustration 12.8)** while spinning both rear wheels. When either wheel begins to drag, stop adjusting and back off the equalizer nut one full turn.
15   Apply the parking brake 4 clicks and check the rear wheel rotation. You should not be able to turn the wheel by hand in the direction of forward movement; the wheel should drag or not turn at all when spun in the direction of rearward rotation.
16   Release the parking brake and be sure the rear wheels spin freely, then lower the car.

---

13   Parking brake cables - replacement

Refer to illustrations 13.6 and 13.14

Front cable

1   Raise and support the vehicle.
2   Loosen the adjuster nut at the equalizer **(see illustration 12.8)**.
3   Detach the front cable from the parking brake lever assembly **(see illustration 12.6)**. **Note:** *Refer to Chapter 11 for removal of the left underdash sound insulator panel.*
4   Remove the nut at the underbody bracket.

5   Detach the clip from the underbody.
6   Release the cable end from the equalizer **(see illustration)**. Special tools (available at auto parts stores) are available and make disconnecting cable retainers much easier, but an ordinary pair of pliers or a small hose clamp tightened around the fingers of the retaining clip can be used.
7   Installation is the reverse of removal.

Rear cable, left or right

8   Raise the vehicle and support it.
9   Disconnect the spring from the equalizer, if necessary.
10   Detach the equalizer from the cable.
11   On models with rear drum brakes, detach the cable from the backing plate and parking brake lever (see Section 6). On models with rear disc brakes, detach the rear cable from the front cable at the retainer.
12   On rear disc models, detach the cable retainer from caliper lever.
13   On rear disc models, detach the cable from the parking brake lever at the caliper. Detach the cable from the caliper bracket **(see illustration 13.6)**.
14   Detach the clips holding the cable to the rear suspension crossmember **(see illustration)**.
15   Installation is the reverse of removal.

---

14   Brake light switch - check, replacement and adjustment

Check

Refer to illustration 14.1

1   The brake light switch **(see illustration)** is located on the brake pedal bracket, just to the right of the steering column mount). You'll need to remove the left underdash sound panel (the trim panel beneath the steering column) to get to the switch and connector (see Chapter 11).
2   With the brake pedal in the fully released position, the switch plunger is pressed into the switch housing. When the brake pedal is depressed, the plunger protrudes from the

switch, which closes the circuit and sends current to the brake lights.
3   If the brake lights are inoperative, check the fuse (see Chapter 12).
4   If the fuse is okay, verify that voltage is available at the switch (orange wire, **see illustration 14.1)**.
5   If there's no voltage to the switch, use a test light to find the open circuit condition between the fuse panel and the switch. If there is voltage to the switch, close the switch (depress the brake pedal) and verify that there's voltage on the other side of the switch.
6   If there's no voltage on the other side of the switch with the brake pedal depressed, replace the switch (see Step 7). If voltage is available, check for voltage at the brake lights. If the no power is present, look for an open circuit condition between the switch and the brake lights. Also check the brake light bulbs, even though it isn't likely that both of them would fail at the same time.

Replacement

7   Remove the left under-dash sound insulator panel (see Chapter 11).
8   Unplug the electrical connector from the switch **(see illustration 14.1)**.
9   Remove the switch from the bracket.
10   The switch must be adjusted as it's installed (see below).

Adjustment

11   Depress the brake pedal, insert the switch into its bracket and push it in until it's fully seated.
12   Slowly pull the brake pedal to the rear until you no longer hear any "clicking" sounds. The switch should now be adjusted.
13   You can check your work with an ohmmeter or continuity tester by verifying that the switch contacts are open at one inch or less of brake pedal travel, and closed thereafter.
14   Installation is otherwise the reverse of removal.

Chapter 10
Suspension and steering systems

Contents

Specifications

Torque specifications

Ft-lbs (unless otherwise stated)

Front suspension

Control arm pivot bolts	52
Subframe-to-body bolts	
Tighten in order: right rear, right front, left rear, left front	133
Lower balljoint nut	63
Stabilizer bar clamp nuts	35
Front hub and wheel bearing assembly bolts	See Chapter 8
Strut mount cover nuts	24
Strut damper shaft nut	59
Strut cartridge nut	82
Driveaxle hub nut	See Chapter 8

Rear suspension

Rear hub and wheel bearing assembly bolts	52
Strut-to-body nuts	37
Strut-to-knuckle nut	90
Trailing arm-to-body nut/bolt	
1995 through 1998	44 (then tighten an additional 90-degrees)
1999	70
Trailing arm-to-knuckle nut/bolt	
1995 through 1998	66 (then tighten an additional 75-degrees)
1999	
With bolt size 16 x 2 x 90	66 (then tighten an additional 75-degrees)
With bolt size 16 x 2 x 105	52 (then tighten an additional 65-degrees)
Suspension crossmember-to-body bolt	85
Stabilizer bar link bolt	52
Stabilizer bar clamp bolt	40
Lateral link rod	
To knuckle	90
To crossmember	34
Steering system	
Airbag module-to-steering wheel screws	25 in-lbs
Steering gear mounting bolts	59
Tie-rod end nut	40
Tie-rod jam nut	50
Intermediate shaft pinch-bolt	35
Power steering pump mounting bolts	25
Steering wheel hub nut	30
Wheel lug nuts	See Chapter 1

1.1 Front suspension components

1	Strut/knuckle assembly	3	Control arm	5	Control arm pivot bolt
2	Balljoint	4	Subframe bolts	6	Tie-rod end

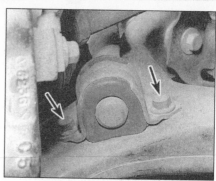

2.3 Remove the stabilizer bar bolts (arrows) on the control arm

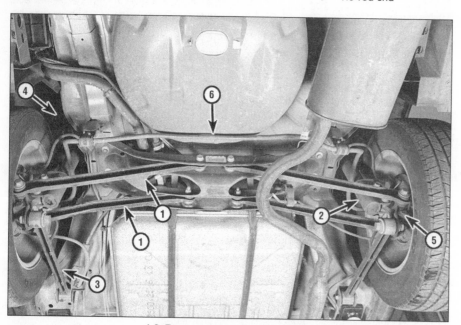

1.2 Rear suspension components

1	Lateral link rods	3	Trailing arm	5	Knuckle
2	Strut	4	Coil spring	6	Stabilizer bar

1   General information

Refer to illustrations 1.1 and 1.2

Warning: *Whenever any of the suspension or steering fasteners are loosened or removed, they must be inspected and, if necessary, replaced with new ones of the same part number or of original equipment quality and design. Torque specifications must be followed for proper reassembly and component retention. Never attempt to heat or straighten any suspension or steering components. Instead, replace any bent or damaged part with a new one.*

The front suspension is a strut design which is made up of a strut welded to a knuckle and supported by a coil spring. The strut/knuckle bearing is located under the lower spring seat, with the upper spring seat attaching to the chassis. Because of the location of the bearing, the strut cartridge can be removed from the engine compartment without disassembling the spring and strut/knuckle. The strut/knuckle assemblies are connected by balljoints to the lower control arms, which are mounted to the frame. The control arms are connected by a stabilizer bar, which reduces body lean during cornering **(see illustration)**.

The rear suspension is independent, with a coil spring/strut assembly on each side bolted to knuckle assemblies that are located by trailing arms, parallel lateral links, and a stabilizer bar **(see illustration)**.

The rack-and-pinion steering gear is located behind the engine/transaxle assembly on the subframe and actuates the steering arms which connect to the steering knuckles. All vehicles are equipped with power steering. The steering column is connected to the steering gear through an insulated coupler. The steering column is designed to collapse in the event of an accident.

Note: *On models equipped with the Theftlock audio system, be sure the lockout feature is turned off before performing any procedure which requires disconnecting the battery.*

2   Stabilizer bar and bushings (front) - removal and installation

Refer to illustrations 2.3 and 2.4

Removal

1   Loosen the lug nuts on both front wheels, raise the vehicle and support it securely on jackstands. Remove the front wheels.

2   Remove the steering shaft pinch bolt (see Section 17). **Warning:** *The wheels should be straight ahead and the steering column locked. On airbag-equipped models, don't allow the steering wheel to turn after the steering shaft is disconnected from the steering gear. Pass the seat belt through the steering wheel and clip it into place.*

3   Remove the stabilizer bar-to-control arm nuts/bolts **(see illustration)**.

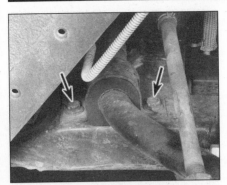

2.4 Remove the stabilizer bar bracket-to-frame bolts (arrows)

4   Remove the stabilizer bar bracket-to-frame nuts/bolts **(see illustration)**.

5   Place a jack under the rear of the subframe crossmember, then loosen the two front subframe-to-body bolts four turns. Remove the two rear subframe-to-body bolts **(see illustration 1.1)**. Slowly lower the jack and allow the rear of the subframe to drop down.

6   Pull the stabilizer bar to the rear, swing it down then remove it through the left side wheel well. **Warning:** *Do not place any part of your body under the subframe assembly when it is lowered from the vehicle, even though it is supported by a jack.*

7   Inspect the bushings for wear and damage and replace them if necessary. To remove them, pry the bushing clamp off with a screwdriver and pull the bushings off the bar. To ease installation, spray the inside and outside of the bushings with a silicone-based lubricant. Do not use petroleum-based lubricants on any rubber suspension part!

Installation

8   Assemble the shaft bushings and clamps on the bar, guide the bar through the wheel well, over the frame and into position.

9   Install the clamps loosely to the frame and control arm and install all of the bolts before tightening any of them. Tighten the bolts to the torque listed in this Chapter's Specifications.

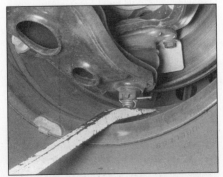

3.3a Check for movement between the balljoint and steering knuckle when prying up

10   Raise the subframe into place while guiding the steering shaft into position in the steering gear and install the rear bolts. Tighten the subframe bolts to the torque figures listed in this Chapter's Specifications.

11   Install the pinch bolt and tighten it to the torque listed in this Chapter's Specifications.

12   Install the wheels and lower the vehicle. Tighten the lug nuts to the torque listed in the Chapter 1 Specifications.

---

3   Balljoint - check and replacement

Refer to illustrations 3.3a and 3.3b

Check

1   Raise the front of the vehicle and support it securely on jackstands. Apply the parking brake and block the rear wheels to keep the vehicle from rolling off the jackstands.

2   Visually inspect the rubber seal for damage, deterioration and leaking grease. If any of these conditions are noticed, the balljoint should be replaced.

3   Place a large prybar under the balljoint and attempt to push the balljoint up. Next, position the prybar between the steering knuckle and control arm and pry down **(see illustrations)**. If any movement is seen or felt during either of these checks, a worn out balljoint is indicated.

4   Have an assistant grasp the tire at the top and bottom and move the top of the tire in-and-out. If you see any play in the balljoint, replace it.

5   Separate the control arm from the steering knuckle (see Section 4). Using your fingers (don't use pliers), try to twist the stud in the socket. If the stud turns, replace the balljoint.

Replacement

6   Loosen the wheel lug nuts, raise the front of the vehicle and support it securely on

3.3b With the prybar positioned between the steering knuckle boss and balljoint, pry down and check for play in the balljoint - if there is any play, replace the balljoint

jackstands. Apply the parking brake and block the rear wheels to keep the vehicle from rolling off the jackstands. Remove the wheel.

7   Separate the control arm from the steering knuckle (see Section 4).

8   Using a 1/8-inch drill bit, drill a pilot hole into the center of each balljoint-to-steering knuckle rivet **(see illustration 4.3)**. Be careful not to damage the CV joint boot in the process.

9   Using a 1/2-inch drill bit, drill the head off each rivet. Work slowly and carefully to avoid deforming the holes in the steering knuckle.

10   Loosen (but don't remove) the stabilizer bar-to-control arm bolts. Pull the control arm down and remove the balljoint from between the control arm and steering knuckle. **Note:** *You may have to chisel between the steering knuckle and the balljoint to shear off the remains of the rivets.*

11   Position the new balljoint on the steering knuckle and install the bolts (supplied in the balljoint kit). Tighten the bolts to the torque specified in the new balljoint instruction sheet.

12   Insert the balljoint into the control arm, install the castellated nut, tighten it to the torque listed in this Chapter's Specifications and install a new cotter pin. It may be necessary to tighten the nut some to align the cotter pin hole with an opening in the nut, which is acceptable. Never loosen the castellated nut to allow cotter pin insertion.

13   Tighten the stabilizer bar-to-control arm bolts to the torque listed in this Chapter's Specifications.

14   Install the wheel, lower the vehicle and tighten the lug nuts to the torque listed in the Chapter 1 Specifications. It's a good idea to take the vehicle to a dealer service department or alignment shop to have the front end alignment checked and, if necessary, adjusted.

---

4   Control arm - removal, and installation

Refer to illustrations 4.3, 4.4 and 4.5

Removal

1   Loosen the wheel lug nuts, raise the front of the vehicle and support it securely on jackstands. Apply the parking brake and block the rear wheels to keep the vehicle from rolling off the jackstands. Remove the wheel.

2   If only one control arm is being removed, disconnect only that end of the stabilizer bar. If both control arms are being removed, disconnect both ends (see Section 2 if necessary).

3   Remove the cotter pin and loosen the balljoint stud-to-control arm castellated nut

10

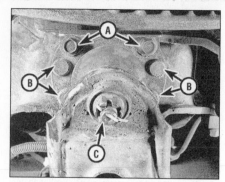

4.3 Balljoint components

A   *Balljoint heat shield bolts*
B   *Balljoint rivets*
C   *Castellated balljoint nut and cotter pin*

(see illustration). Note: *On 1997 and 1998 models, remove the two bolts and the balljoint heat shield.*

4   Separate the balljoint from the knuckle with a two-jaw puller, with the center bolt on the nut and stud **(see illustration)**. Remove the nut once the stud is free and pry the control arm down.

5   Remove the two control arm pivot bolts and detach the control arm **(see illustration)**.

6   The control arm bushings are replaceable, but special tools and expertise are necessary to do the job. Carefully inspect the bushings for hardening, excessive wear and cracks. If they appear to be worn or deteriorated, take the control arm to a dealer service department or other qualified repair shop.

Installation

7   Position the control arm in the subframe brackets and install the pivot bolts/nuts. Don't tighten the bolts completely yet.

8   Insert the balljoint stud into the control arm boss, install the castellated nut and tighten it to the torque listed in this Chapter's Specifications. If necessary, tighten the nut a little more (but not more than one flat of the nut) if the cotter pin hole doesn't line up with an opening on the nut. Install a new cotter pin.

9   Place a floor jack under the balljoint and raise the suspension to simulate normal ride

5.2 Mark the position of the strut mount cover (arrow) before loosening the three nuts

4.4 Use a two-jaw puller clamped over the control arm with the center bolt of the puller pushing on the balljoint nut

height. Tighten the control arm pivot bolts/nuts to the torque listed in this Chapter's Specifications.

10   Install the stabilizer bar-to-control arm clamp over the end bushing and tighten the bolts to the torque listed in this Chapter's Specifications (see Section 2).

11   Install the wheel and lower the vehicle. Tighten the lug nuts to the torque listed in the Chapter 1 Specifications.

12   Drive the vehicle to a dealer service department or an alignment shop to have the front wheel alignment checked and, if necessary, adjusted.

---

5   Strut and spring assembly (front) - removal and installation

Note: *On these models the strut cartridge can be replaced with the strut and spring assembly installed in the vehicle (see Section 7). Because it isn't necessary to remove and disassemble the strut and spring assembly for strut cartridge replacement, removal of the assembly should only be required to repair damage to the spring, seats and strut/knuckle components.*

Removal

Refer to illustration 5.2

1   Loosen the wheel lug nuts, raise the front of the vehicle and support it securely on jackstands. Apply the parking brake and block the rear wheels to keep the vehicle from rolling off the jackstands. Remove the wheel.

2   Mark the position of the strut mount cover to the strut tower **(see illustration)**.

3   Separate the tie-rod end from the steering knuckle as described in Section 15.

4   Refer to Chapter 9 and remove the brake caliper, mounting bracket and disc. Hang the caliper out of the way. On models so equipped, remove the bolt and secure the ABS sensor out of the way.

5   Remove the hub and wheel bearing bolts (see Section 8).

6   Remove the driveaxle (see Chapter 8).

7   Separate the balljoint from the lower control arm (see Section 4).

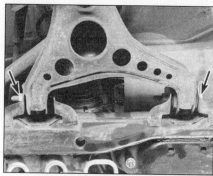

4.5 Remove the two control-arm-to-subframe bolts/nuts (arrows)

8   Support the strut and spring assembly with one hand and remove the three strut mount tower nuts **(see illustration 5.2)**. Lower the assembly and remove it from the vehicle.

Inspection

9   Check the strut body for leaking fluid, dents, cracks and other obvious damage which would warrant repair or replacement.

10   Check the coil spring for chips and cracks in the spring coating (this will cause premature spring failure due to corrosion). Inspect the spring seats for hardening, cracks and general deterioration.

11   Inspect the knuckle/strut for corrosion, bending or twisting.

Installation

12   Slide the strut assembly up into the fenderwell and insert the three upper mounting studs through the holes in the shock tower. Once the three studs protrude from the shock tower, install the strut cover to the marked position, then the nuts so the strut won't fall back through. This may require an assistant, since the strut is quite heavy and awkward.

13   Connect the lower balljoint to the control arm and install the nut. Tighten the nut to the torque listed in this Chapter's Specifications and install a new cotter pin. If the cotter pin won't pass through, tighten the nut a little more, but just enough to align the hole in the stud with a castellation on the nut (don't loosen the nut).

14   Install the driveaxle and hub/wheel bearing assembly (see Chapter 8).

15   Install the brake components (see Chapter 9).

16   Install the tie-rod end in the steering arm and tighten the castellated nut to the torque listed in this Chapter's Specifications. Install a new cotter pin. If the cotter pin won't pass through, tighten the nut a little more, but just enough to align the hole in the stud with a castellation on the nut (don't loosen the nut).

17   Install the wheel, lower the vehicle and tighten the lug nuts to the torque listed in the Chapter 1 Specifications.

18   Tighten the three upper mounting nuts to the torque listed in this Chapter's Specification.

6.2 Install the spring compressor and alternately tighten each clamp to evenly compress the spring

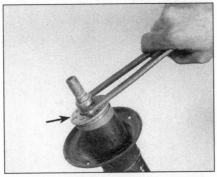

6.4 Remove the cartridge retaining nut (arrow) with a two-pin spanner

6.5 Slide the strut cartridge out of the strut body

6 Coil spring/strut body/steering knuckle - replacement

Refer to illustrations 6.2, 6.4, 6.5 and 6.6

1   Refer to Section 5 to remove the coil spring/strut body/steering knuckle assembly from the vehicle. Mount the assembly in a sturdy vise. **Warning:** *A compressed coil spring can be dangerous. Follow all instructions included with the spring compressor for safe operation, and if chains or safety clamps are included with the tool, use them.*

2   The strut body and the steering knuckle are serviced as an assembly (they are welded together). If either the spring or the strut/knuckle assembly must be replaced, rent or purchase a coil-spring compressor and attach it to the spring with the two clamps on opposite sides of the spring **(see illustration)**.

3   Refer to Section 7 and remove the nut from the strut cartridge, then remove the upper strut components to take the compressed spring off. **Warning:** *When releasing the compressor from the spring, release it just as evenly and slowly as you installed it.*

4   To replace the strut cartridge (out of vehicle), use a two-pin spanner to remove the cartridge nut **(see illustration)**. **Note:** *The special tool used in Section 7 isn't necessary when the spring is removed from the strut assembly.*

5   Remove the cartridge from the strut/knuckle assembly **(see illustration)**.

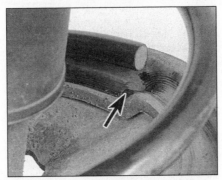

6.6 When installing the spring, place the end into the recessed portion of the lower seat (arrow)

6   Reassembly is the reverse of the removal process. **Note:** *When installing a new spring, make sure the end of the lowest coil fits snugly into the notch on he lower spring mount and stays there during the installation process* **(see illustration)**.

7 Strut cartridge - replacement in vehicle

Refer to illustrations 7.2, 7.3a, 7.3b, 7.4a, 7.4b and 7.5

1   Mark the position of the strut mount

7.2 Remove the strut shaft nut using this tool (arrow) with a wrench on it, and an extension with a Torx bit through the top to hold the strut shaft from turning

cover **(see illustration 5.2)** and remove the nuts and the cover. **Note:** *The vehicle should be on the ground with full weight on the suspension.*

2   Remove the strut shaft nut, using a special tool that grips the nut while allowing a Torx bit to be used to keep the shaft from turning **(see illustration)**.

3   Pry out the strut mount bushing and the upper strut bumper **(see illustrations)**. You may have to compress the strut shaft down into the cartridge using a length of pipe that just fits over the strut shaft.

4   Remove the strut cartridge nut using a special tool which engages with the slots in the nut (available at most auto parts stores) **(see illustrations)**.

7.3a Remove the strut mount bushing (arrow) . . .

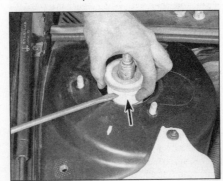

7.3b . . . and the upper strut bumper (arrow)

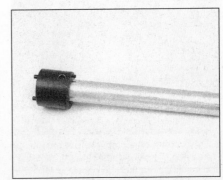

7.4a Strut cartridge nut removal tool - the lugs at the large end fit into the slots in the nut

10

7.4b In use, the tool fits down over the strut shaft and a breaker bar can be used to turn it

5   Grasp the strut cartridge and lift it out **(see illustration)**.
6   If the old cartridge had been leaking oil, use a suction pump to remove the damper fluid from the strut body and pour it into an approved oil container.
7   Insert the replacement strut cartridge, which is a self-contained unit, into position and install the nut. Tighten the cartridge nut to the torque listed in this Chapter's Specifications.
8   Install the bumper.
9   Temporarily install the strut shaft nut enough to grip it with locking pliers to raise the shaft if it doesn't come up by itself, then remove the nut and install the bushing.
10   Install the strut shaft nut. Tighten the nut to the torque listed in this Chapter's Specifications.
11   Install the strut mount cover and nuts. Tighten the nuts to the torque listed in this Chapter's Specifications.

8   Front hub and wheel bearing assembly - removal and installation

Note: *The front hub and wheel bearing assembly is sealed-for-life and must be replaced as a unit.*

9.2 Disconnect the stabilizer bar mounts by removing the pivot bolts/nuts (A), allowing the insulator brackets to come out with the bar, or remove the bracket bolts (B), spread the clamp and remove the bar from the clamp (C is the rubber insulator)

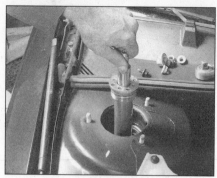

7.5 Lift the cartridge out

1   The hub/bearing assembly is pressed onto the front driveaxle. Refer to Chapter 8 for removal of the driveaxle.
2   Take the driveaxle to a dealership, driveline shop or other automotive repair facility to have the hub/bearing assembly pressed off the driveaxle.
3   Inspect the bearing assembly and if it is to be reused, grease the axle splines with multi-purpose grease and have the shop press it onto the driveaxle. **Note:** *Only a new driveaxle nut should be used. Do not reuse the old one.* Tighten the nut to the Specifications listed in Chapter 8.
4   Push the driveaxle and hub/bearing assembly into position and install the bolts. Tighten the bolts to the torque listed in the Chapter 8 Specifications.
5   Install the brake disc, caliper and (if equipped) the ABS sensor (see Chapter 9).
6   Install the wheel, lower the vehicle and tighten the lug nuts to the torque listed in Chapter 1 Specifications.

9   Stabilizer bar and bushings (rear) - removal and installation

Refer to illustrations 9.2 and 9.5
1   Raise the rear of the vehicle and support it securely on jackstands. Block the front wheels to keep the vehicle from rolling off the jackstands.
2   Remove the bolts and detach the two

9.5 Remove the two strut-to-knuckle nuts (arrows) and pull off the stabilizer bar end clamps and rubber insulators

stabilizer shaft insulators at the chassis **(see illustration)**.
3   Mark the strut-to-knuckle position by scribing or painting around the strut bolts and nuts.
5   Support the left knuckle with a jack and remove the nuts from the strut-to-knuckle bolts **(see illustration)**. **Warning:** *Do not remove the strut-to-knuckle bolts.*
6   The strut-to-knuckle nuts retain the end clamps on the stabilizer bar. Pry the clamps and insulators from the ends of the bar.
7   Remove the stabilizer bar through the left side. **Note:** *You may need a prybar or large screwdriver to pry the bar ends past the strut.*
8   Inspect the bushings for cracks, hardening and wear. Replace them if necessary.
9   Installation is the reverse of the removal procedure. Make sure the marks made in Step 3 line up before tightening the knuckle bolts.

10   Rear strut - removal, inspection and installation

Refer to illustrations 10.3 and 10.9
1   Loosen the wheel lug nuts, raise the rear of the vehicle and support it securely on jackstands. Block the front wheels to keep the vehicle from rolling off the jackstands. Remove the wheel.
2   Support the bottom of the knuckle with a floor jack.
3   Open the trunk and loosen the three strut-to-body nuts **(see illustration)**.
4   Detach the brake hose bracket from the strut housing.
5   Remove the brake caliper and hang it out of the way on a piece of wire (see Chapter 9).
6   Mark the relationship of the strut to the knuckle and outline the knuckle bolts/nuts.
7   Detach the stabilizer bar from the knuckle (see Section 9).
8   Remove the strut-to-body nuts **(see illustration 10.3)**, and lower the strut assembly until there is no more spring pressure on the knuckle.

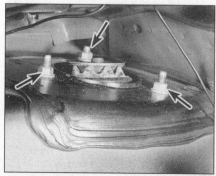

10.3 Location of the rear strut-to-body bolts (arrows)

10.9 Remove the rear strut-to-knuckle bolts (A) - B is the brake hose bracket bolt

11.2 Disconnect the rear-wheel ABS electrical connector (arrow), if equipped

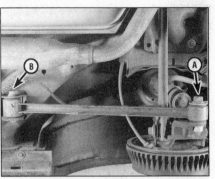

12.4 Remove the trailing arm-to-knuckle bolt and nut (A) and the trailing arm-to-chassis nut and bolt (B)

9   Remove the strut-to-knuckle nuts and knock the bolts out with a brass or plastic hammer **(see illustration).**
10   Separate the strut from the knuckle and remove the strut (with coil spring assembly in place) from the vehicle.
11   Refer to Section 6 for removal of the coil spring from the strut. If the strut is being replaced, install the coil spring and upper strut components from the old assembly to the new strut. **Note:** *There is no serviceable cartridge on the rear struts. The strut itself must be replaced.*
12   Installation is the reverse of the removal procedure. Make sure the strut-to-knuckle alignment marks made during Step 6 line up before tightening the bolts to the torque listed in this Chapter's Specifications.

---

11   Rear hub and wheel bearing assembly - removal and installation

Refer to illustration 11.2
Note: *The rear hub and wheel bearing assembly is sealed-for-life and must be replaced as a unit.*

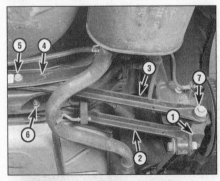

12.7 Lateral link rod details

1 Knuckle	*6 Front rod inner*
2 Front rod	*mounting bolt*
3 Rear rod	*7 Rear rod outer*
4 Crossmember	*mounting bolt*
5 Rear rod inner	*(front rod bolt*
mounting bolt	*similar)*

Removal

1   Loosen the wheel lug nuts, raise the rear of the vehicle and support it securely on jackstands. Block the front wheels to keep the vehicle from rolling off the jackstands. Remove the wheel.
2   Remove the brake drum or the brake caliper and disc (see Chapter 9). Support the caliper with a piece of wire. If equipped, unplug the ABS electrical connector **(see illustration).**
3   Remove the four hub-to-knuckle bolts.
4   Remove the hub and bearing assembly, maneuvering it out through the brake caliper bracket as necessary.

Installation

5   Position the hub and bearing assembly on the knuckle and align the holes. Install the bolts. After all four bolts have been installed, tighten them to the torque listed in this Chapter's Specifications.
6   Install the brake drum or the brake caliper and disc, tightening the caliper bolts to the torque listed in the Chapter 9 Specifications. Install the wheel. Lower the vehicle and tighten the wheel lug nuts to the torque listed in Chapter 1 Specifications.

12   Rear suspension arms - removal and installation

1   Loosen the wheel lug nuts, raise the rear of the vehicle and support it securely on jackstands. Block the front wheels to keep

12.8 Locations of the inner lateral link rod bolts/nuts (arrows)

the vehicle from rolling off the jackstands. Remove the wheels.
2   Remove the stabilizer bar as outlined in Section 9.
3   Remove the brake drums or calipers and discs from the hubs. See Chapter 9 if difficulty is encountered. If equipped, unplug the ABS electrical connectors **(see illustration 11.2).**

Trailing arms

Refer to illustration 12.4
4   Remove the trailing arm-to-knuckle nut and bolt and the trailing arm-to-chassis nut and bolt **(see illustration).**
5   Detach the trailing arm and lower it from the vehicle.
6   Installation is the reverse of removal. Do not tighten the nuts and bolts to the torque listed in this Chapters Specifications until the vehicle weight has been lowered onto the suspension (you can simulate normal ride height by raising the suspension with a floor jack). Reconnect the ABS electrical connector, if removed.

Lateral link rods

Refer to illustrations 12.7 and 12.8
7   Remove the nuts and bolts connecting the rods to the knuckle **(see illustration).**
8   Remove the rod inner bolts at the crossmember **(see illustration). Note:** *The bolts for the front rods are difficult to access. You will have to lower the rear of the fuel tank a few inches for better access* (see Chapter 4).
9   Installation is the reverse of removal. Don't tighten the bolts to the torque listed in this Chapter's Specifications until the vehicle weight has been lowered onto the suspension (you can simulate normal ride height by raising the suspension with a floor jack). After installation have the rear toe checked by a dealer service department or alignment shop.

---

13   Rear knuckle - removal and installation

1   Mark the strut-to-knuckle relationship and scribe or paint a line around the knuckle nuts.

10

14.2 use a Torx bit to remove the two airbag module screws from behind the steering wheel

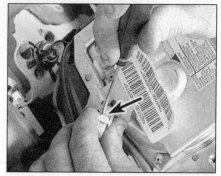

14.3a Use a small screwdriver to release the plastic locking clip (arrow) from the airbag module connector, then . . .

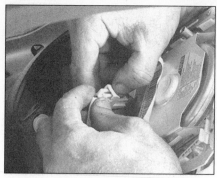

14.3b . . . squeeze the tab and separate the airbag connector

2   Refer to Section 11 and remove the rear hub/bearing assembly.

3   On models with rear drum brakes, remove the brake shoe assembly and the backing plate (see Chapter 9).

4   Remove the bolts/nuts and detach the trailing arm, lateral link rods and stabilizer bar from the knuckle (see Sections 9 and 12).

5   Remove the strut-to-knuckle nuts and knock the bolts out with a brass or plastic hammer.

7   Separate the knuckle from the strut.

8   To install the knuckle, slide it into the strut flange. Install the stabilizer bar bracket and insert the two bolts. Install the nuts finger tight. Connect the lateral link rods and trailing arm to the knuckle, but do not tighten at this

time. Align the marks made in Step 1 and tighten the strut-to-knuckle bolts to the torque listed in this Chapter's Specifications. The remainder of installation is the reverse of removal.

9   Don't tighten the trailing arm or lateral link rod bolts/nuts to the torque listed in this Chapter's Specifications until the vehicle weight has been lowered onto the suspension (you can simulate normal ride height by raising the suspension with a floor jack). After installation have the rear toe checked by a dealer service department or alignment shop.

14   Steering wheel - removal and installation

Refer to illustrations 14.2, 14.3a, 14.3b, 14.4, 14.5, 14.6, 14.7 and 14.8

Warning: *These models are equipped with airbags. Always turn the steering wheel to the straight ahead position, place the ignition switch in the Lock position and disable the airbag system (see Chapter 12) before working in the vicinity of the impact sensors, steering column or instrument panel to avoid the possibility of accidental deployment of the airbag, which could cause personal injury.*

1   Disconnect the negative battery cable.

Note: *On models equipped with the Theftlock audio system, be sure the lockout feature is*

turned off before performing any procedure which requires disconnecting the battery.

2   Using a number 30 Torx bit, remove the two screws that secure the airbag module to the steering wheel **(see illustration)**.

3   Lift the airbag module carefully away from the steering wheel and disconnect the yellow airbag electrical connector. This is a two-part disconnection, as there is a plastic clip that must be removed before the connector can be disconnected **(see illustrations)**. Remove the module. **Warning:** *When carrying the airbag module, keep the driver's side of it away from your body, and when you place it on the bench, have the driver's side facing up.*

4   Remove the steering wheel nut **(see illustration)**.

5   Mark the relationship of the steering wheel to the shaft **(see illustration)**.

6   Install a steering wheel puller (available at most auto parts stores) and turn the center bolt until the wheel is free **(see illustration)**.

7   Remove the puller and disconnect the horn and ground wire connector **(see illustration)**. Remove the steering wheel. **Warning:** *Don't allow the steering shaft to turn with the steering wheel removed. If the shaft turns, the airbag coil assembly (the mechanism which protects the airbag wiring when the steering wheel is turned) will become uncentered, which may cause the airbag harness to break when the vehicle is returned to service.*

14.4 Remove the steering wheel nut with a deep socket

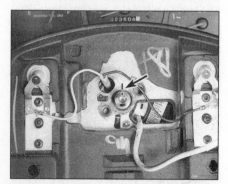

14.5 Make two paint marks (arrow) to show alignment of wheel before removal

14.6 A steering wheel puller threads into two holes in the steering wheel - tightening the center bolt removes the wheel

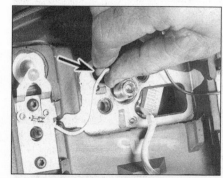

14.7 Disconnect the horn and ground wire connector

14.8 When properly aligned, the airbag coil will be centered with the marks aligned (in circle here) and the tab fitted between the projections on the top of the steering column (arrow)

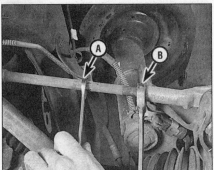

15.2 Hold the tie-rod with one wrench on the flats (A) while using another wrench to loosen the jam nut (B)

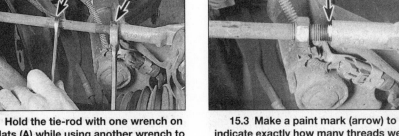

15.3 Make a paint mark (arrow) to indicate exactly how many threads were engaged in the tie-rod end (jam nut has been backed off)

8   Installation is the reverse of removal. Before installing the steering wheel, make sure the airbag coil assembly is centered **(see illustration)**. If it isn't, see Chapter 12, Section 8, Step 14 for the centering procedure. Connect the airbag connector to the back of the airbag module just as it was before steering wheel removal, i.e. with the plastic locking device in place. Be sure to tighten the steering wheel nut and airbag screws to the torque listed in this Chapter's Specifications.
9   Refer to Chapter 12 for the procedure to enable the airbag system.

15 Tie-rod ends - removal and installation

Refer to illustrations 15.2, 15.3, 15.4a and 15.4b

Removal

1   Loosen the wheel lug nuts, raise the front of the vehicle and support it securely on jackstands. Apply the parking brake and block the rear wheels to keep the vehicle from rolling off the jackstands. Remove the wheel.
2   Loosen the tie-rod end jam nut **(see illustration)**.
3   Mark the relationship of the tie-rod end

to the threaded portion of the tie-rod **(see illustration)**. This will ensure the toe-in setting is restored when reassembled.
4   Remove the cotter pin, loosen the nut and disconnect the tie-rod end from the steering knuckle arm with a puller **(see illustrations)**. **Note:** *Back the tie-rod end nut off until it is flush with the stud, apply the puller's center bolt against it until it breaks free, then remove the nut and detach the tie-rod end from the knuckle arm.*
5   Unscrew the tie-rod end from the tie-rod.

Installation

6   Thread the tie-rod end onto the tie-rod to the marked position and connect the tie-rod end to the steering arm. Install the castellated nut and tighten it to the torque listed in this Chapter's Specifications. Install a new cotter pin.
7   Tighten the jam nut securely and install the wheel. Lower the vehicle and tighten the lug nuts to the torque listed in the Chapter 1 Specifications.
8   Have the front end alignment checked by a dealer service department or an alignment shop.

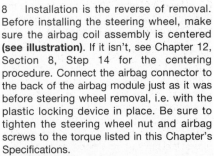

15.4b ...a "pickle fork" tool can also be used (hammered between the tie-rod end and the knuckle), but there's a good chance the boot will be ruined, which is OK if you are replacing the tie-rod end with a new one

16 Steering gear boots - replacement

Refer to illustration 16.8

1   Remove the steering gear from the vehicle (see Section 17).
2   Remove the tie-rod ends from the steering gear (see Section 15).
3   Remove the jam nuts and outer boot clamps.
4   Cut off both inner boot clamps and discard them.
5   Mark the location of the breather tube (if used) in relation to the rack assembly, then remove the boots and the tube.
6   Install a new clamp on the inner end of the boot.
7   Apply multi-purpose grease to groove on the tie-rod (where the outer boot clamp will ride) and the mounting grooves on the steering gear (where the inner boot end will be clamped).
8   Line up the breather tube with the marks made during removal and slide the new boot onto the steering gear housing **(see illustration)**.
9   Make sure the boot isn't twisted, then tighten the new inner clamp.
10   Install the outer clamps and tie-rod end jam nuts.
11   Install the tie-rod ends (see Section 15) and tighten the nuts securely.
12   Install the steering gear assembly.

10

15.4a It's best to use a puller to remove the tie-rod end, but ...

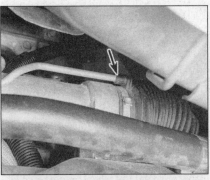

16.8 Align the connector on the boot with the breather tube (arrow)

17.6 Remove the pinch bolt (arrow) - this view is looking down on the steering gear below the brake master cylinder and booster

17.12 Disconnect the two fluid lines (arrows) from the rack - this view is looking forward from the rear of the subframe

17.13 Steering rack mounting bolt/nut (arrow) - left-side shown, right-side similar

17 Steering gear - removal and installation

Refer to illustrations 17.6, 17.12 and 17.13

Warning: *Make sure the steering shaft is not turned while the steering gear is removed or you could damage the airbag system. To prevent the shaft from turning, place the ignition key in the LOCK position or thread the seat belt through the steering wheel and clip it into place.*

Removal

1   Disconnect the cable from the negative battery terminal. **Note:** *On models equipped with the Theftlock audio system, be sure the lockout feature is turned off before performing any procedure which requires disconnecting the battery.*
2   On models equipped with the 3.4L engine, remove the air cleaner and duct assembly.
3   Loosen the front wheel lug nuts, raise the front of the vehicle and support it securely on jackstands. Apply the parking brake and block the rear wheels to keep the vehicle from rolling off the jackstands. Remove both front wheels. **Note:** *The jackstands must be behind the front suspension subframe, not supporting the vehicle by the subframe.*
4   On models equipped with the 3.4L engine, remove the right side engine splash shield.
5   Set the steering wheel straight ahead, check that the wide spline or "block tooth" on the upper steering shaft assembly is at the 12 o'clock position and that the ignition switch is set to "lock." **Warning:** *Failure to do this can result in damage to the airbag system's coil unit.*
6   Roll back the boot at the bottom of the steering column to expose the flange and steering coupler assembly. Mark the coupler and steering column shaft, remove the pinch bolt and separate the steering column from the power steering input shaft **(see illustration)**.

7   On models equipped with the 3.4L V6 engine, remove the exhaust pipe and catalytic converter assembly.
8   Separate the tie-rod ends from the steering arms (see Section 15).
9   Support the rear of the subframe assembly with a jack and remove the rear bolts. Loosen (but do not remove) the front bolts of the subframe and lower the rear approximately five inches (three inches on models equipped with the 3.4L V6 engine).
10   Remove the heat shield from the steering gear.
11   Remove the fluid pipe clip from the rack.
12   Place a drain pan or tray under the vehicle, positioned beneath the steering gear. Using a flare-nut wrench, disconnect the pressure and return lines from the steering gear. Plug the lines to prevent excessive fluid loss **(see illustration)**.
13   Remove the steering gear mounting bolts and nuts **(see illustration)**.
15   Lift the steering gear out of the mounts then move it forward and detach the coupler from the steering gear.
16   Support the steering gear and carefully maneuver the entire assembly out through the left side wheel opening.

Installation

17   Pass the steering gear assembly through the left wheel opening and place it in position in the mounts. Install the mounting bolts and nuts, tightening them to the torque listed in this Chapter's Specifications.
18   Attach the pressure and return lines to the steering gear. Connect the line retainer.
19   Install the heat shield.
20   Raise the subframe into position and install NEW bolts. Tighten the subframe bolts to the torque listed in this Chapter's Specifications.
21   Connect the tie-rod ends to the steering arms and tighten the nuts to the torque listed in this Chapter's Specifications. Install new cotter pins.
22   Install the exhaust system, if removed.

23   Center the steering gear and have an assistant guide the coupler onto the steering shaft, with the previously applied marks aligned. Install and tighten the pinch bolt to the torque listed in this Chapter's Specifications. **Warning:** *Be sure the shaft is seated before you install the pinch bolt or the shafts may disengage.*
24   Install the front wheels, lower the vehicle and tighten the lug nuts to the torque listed in the Chapter 1 Specifications.
25   Reconnect the negative battery cable.
26   Fill the power steering pump with the recommended fluid, bleed the system (see Section 19) and recheck the fluid level. Check for leaks.
27   Have the front end alignment checked by a dealer service department or an alignment shop.

18 Power steering pump - removal and installation

Refer to illustrations 18.6, 18.8, 18.9a and 18.9b

Removal

1   Disconnect the cable from the negative battery terminal. **Note:** *On models equipped with the Theftlock audio system, be sure the lockout feature is turned off before performing any procedure which requires disconnecting the battery.*
2   Remove the coolant recovery reservoir, if necessary.
3   On models equipped with the 3.4L V6 engine, remove the air cleaner and duct assembly.
4   On models equipped with the 3.1L engine, detach the ignition control wiring harness near the pump and position it aside.
5   Remove the drivebelt (see Chapter 1).
6   Position a drain pan under the vehicle. Remove as much fluid from the reservoir as possible with a suction pump, then remove the return line (rubber hose connection with

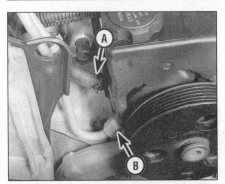

18.6 Disconnect the return line (A) and the pressure line (B)

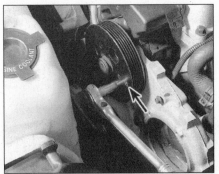

18.8 Using a socket and short extension inserted through one of the holes in the pulley (arrow), remove the three pump mounting bolts - rotate the pulley to access each bolt

18.9a Remove the pulley with the puller - the flanged collar (arrow) fits onto the groove on the front of the pulley

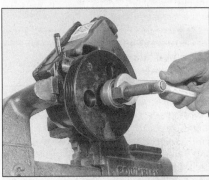

18.9b Press the pulley onto the shaft with the installation tool

clamp) from the rack to the reservoir **(see illustration)**.

7   Using a flare-nut wrench and a back-up wrench, disconnect the pressure hose from the pump.

8   Remove the pump mounting bolts and detach the pump from the engine, being careful not to spill the remaining fluid **(see illustration)**.

Installation

9   If a new pump is to be installed, the pulley will have to be transferred to the new pump. Use a power steering pulley puller (available at most auto parts stores) to remove the pulley and install it on the new pump **(see illustrations)**. **Note:** *Take note of how far the pulley was pressed onto the old pump's shaft before removing the pulley.*

10   If your new pump doesn't come with a reservoir, you can swap your old one to the new pump. Remove the reservoir by pulling on the two sliding clips that hold the reservoir to the pump. Install a new O-ring at the fluid connection and clip the reservoir onto the new pump.

11   Position the pump on the mounting bracket and install the bolts.

12   Connect the pressure and return lines to the pump.

13   Fill the reservoir with the recommended fluid and bleed the system, following the procedure described in the next Section.

19   Power steering system - bleeding

1   Following any operation in which the power steering fluid lines have been disconnected, the power steering system must be bled to remove air and obtain proper steering performance.

2   With the front wheels turned all the way to the left and the ignition key OFF, check the power steering fluid level and, if low, add fluid until it reaches the Cold mark on the dipstick.

3   Start the engine and allow it to run at fast idle. Recheck the fluid level and add more if necessary to reach the Cold mark on the dipstick.

4   Bleed the system by turning the wheels

from side-to-side, without hitting the stops. This will work the air out of the system. Don't allow the reservoir to run out of fluid.

5   When the air is worked out of the system, return the wheels to the straight ahead position and leave the engine running for several minutes before shutting it off. Recheck the fluid level.

6   Road test the vehicle to be sure the steering system is functioning normally with no noise.

7   Recheck the fluid level to be sure it's up to the Hot mark on the dipstick while the engine is at normal operating temperature. Add fluid if necessary.

20   Wheels and tires - general information

Refer to illustration 20.1

All vehicles covered by this manual are equipped with metric-size fiberglass or steel

belted radial tires **(see illustration)**. The use of other size or type tires may affect the ride and handling of the vehicle. Don't mix different types of tires, such as radials and bias belted, on the same vehicle, since handling may be seriously affected. Tires should be replaced in pairs on the same axle, but if only one tire is being replaced, be sure

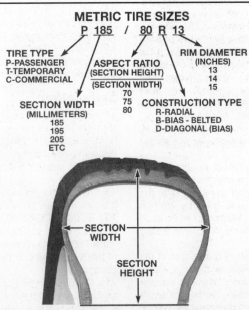

METRIC TIRE SIZES

P 185 / 80 R 13

TIRE TYPE
P-PASSENGER
T-TEMPORARY
C-COMMERCIAL

ASPECT RATIO
(SECTION HEIGHT)
(SECTION WIDTH)
70
75
80

RIM DIAMETER
(INCHES)
13
14
15

SECTION WIDTH
(MILLIMETERS)
185
195
205
ETC

CONSTRUCTION TYPE
R-RADIAL
B-BIAS - BELTED
D-DIAGONAL (BIAS)

SECTION WIDTH

SECTION HEIGHT

20.1 Metric size code

10

it's the same size, structure and tread design as the other.

Because tire pressure affects handling and wear, the tire pressures should be checked at least once a month or before any extended trips (see Chapter 1).

Wheels must be replaced if they're bent, dented, leak air, have elongated bolt holes, are heavily rusted, out of vertical symmetry or if the lug nuts won't stay tight. Wheel repairs by welding or peening aren't recommended.

Tire and wheel balance is important to the overall handling, braking and performance of the vehicle. Unbalanced wheels can adversely affect handling and ride characteristics as well as tire life. Whenever a tire is installed on a wheel, the tire and wheel should be balanced by a shop with the proper equipment.

21 Wheel alignment - general information

Refer to illustration 21.1

A wheel alignment refers to the adjustments made to the wheels so they're in proper angular relationship to the suspension and the ground. Wheels that are out of proper alignment not only affect steering control, but also increase tire wear. The adjustment most commonly required is the toe-in adjustment but camber adjustment is also possible **(see illustration)**.

Getting the proper wheel alignment is a very exacting process, one in which complicated and expensive machines are necessary to perform the job properly. Because of this, you should have a technician with the proper equipment perform these tasks. We will, however, attempt to give you a basic idea of what's involved with wheel alignment so you can better understand the process and deal intelligently with the shop that does the work.

Toe-in is the turning in of the wheels. The purpose of a toe specification is to ensure parallel rolling of the wheels. In a vehicle with zero toe-in, the distance between the front edges of the wheels will be the same as the distance between the rear edges of the wheels. The actual amount of toe-in is normally only a fraction of an inch. Incorrect toe-in will cause the tires to wear improperly by making them scrub against the road surface. On the front end, toe adjustment is controlled by the tie-rod end position on the tie-rod. On the rear, a special tool is required to adjust the position of the rear lateral link rod in its inner mount.

Camber is the tilting of the wheels from the vertical when viewed from the front or rear of the vehicle. When the wheels tilt out at the top, the camber is said to be positive (+). When the wheels tilt in at the top the camber is negative (-). The amount of tilt is measured in degrees from the vertical and this measurement is called the camber angle. This angle affects the amount of tire tread which contacts the road and compensates for changes in the suspension geometry when the vehicle is cornering or traveling over an undulating surface. Camber can be adjusted after the strut mounting holes have been elongated with a file. Camber adjustment, front or rear, must be done with the vehicle on the alignment rack, by an experienced technician.

Caster is not adjustable. If the caster angle is not to specification, the suspension components must be checked for damage.

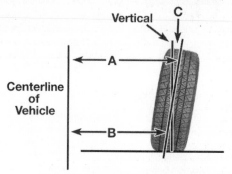

CAMBER ANGLE (FRONT VIEW)

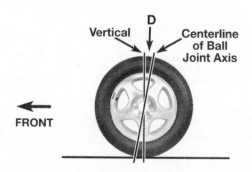

CASTER ANGLE (SIDE VIEW)

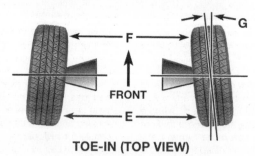

TOE-IN (TOP VIEW)

21.1 Front end alignment details

A minus B = C (degrees camber)
D = degrees caster
E minus F = toe-in (measured in inches)
G = toe-in (expressed in degrees)

Chapter 11   Body

Contents

1   General information

Warning: *The models covered by this manual are equipped with airbags. Always disable the airbag system (see Chapter 12) before working in the vicinity of the impact sensors, steering column or instrument panel. Failure to follow these procedures may cause accidental deployment of the airbag, which could cause personal injury. The airbag circuits are easily identified by yellow insulation covering the entire wiring harness. Do not use electrical test equipment on any of these wires or tamper with them in any way.*

Caution: *On models equipped with a Theftlock audio system, be sure the lockout feature is turned off before performing any procedure which requires disconnecting the battery.*

These models feature a "unibody" construction, using a floor pan with front and rear frame side rails which support the body components, front and rear suspension systems and other mechanical components.

Certain body components are particularly vulnerable to accident damage and can be unbolted and repaired or replaced. Among these parts are the body moldings, front fenders, doors, bumpers, the hood, trunk lid and all glass.

Only general body maintenance practices and body panel repair procedures within the scope of the do-it-yourselfer are included in this Chapter.

2   Body - maintenance

1   The condition of your vehicle's body is very important, because the resale value depends a great deal on it. It's much more difficult to repair a neglected or damaged body than it is to repair mechanical components. The hidden areas of the body, such as the wheel wells, the frame and the engine compartment, are equally important, although they don't require as frequent attention as the rest of the body.

2   Once a year, or every 12,000 miles, it's a good idea to have the underside of the body steam cleaned. All traces of dirt and oil will be removed and the area can then be inspected carefully for rust, damaged brake lines, frayed electrical wires, damaged cables and other problems. The front suspension components should be greased after completion of this job.

3   At the same time, clean the engine and the engine compartment with a steam cleaner or water-soluble degreaser.

4   The wheel wells should be given close attention, since undercoating can peel away and stones and dirt thrown up by the tires can cause the paint to chip and flake, allowing rust to set in. If rust is found, clean down to the bare metal and apply an anti-rust paint.

5   The body should be washed about once a week. Wet the vehicle thoroughly to soften the dirt, then wash it down with a soft sponge and plenty of clean soapy water. If the surplus dirt is not washed off very carefully, it can wear down the paint.

6   Spots of tar or asphalt thrown up from the road should be removed with a cloth soaked in solvent.

7   Once every six months, wax the body and chrome trim. If a chrome cleaner is used to remove rust from any of the vehicle's plated parts, remember that the cleaner also removes part of the chrome, so use it sparingly.

3   Vinyl trim - maintenance

Don't clean vinyl trim with detergents, caustic soap or petroleum-based cleaners. Plain soap and water works just fine, with a soft brush to clean dirt that may be ingrained. Wash the vinyl as frequently as the rest of the vehicle. After cleaning, application of a high-quality rubber and vinyl protectant will help prevent oxidation and cracks. The protectant can also be applied to weatherstripping, vacuum lines and rubber hoses, which often fail as a result of chemical degradation, and to the tires.

4   Upholstery and carpets - maintenance

1   Every three months, remove the floormats and clean the interior of the vehicle (more frequently if necessary). Use a stiff whisk broom to brush the carpeting and

11

loosen dirt and dust, then vacuum the upholstery and carpets thoroughly, especially along seams and crevices.

2   Dirt and stains can be removed from carpeting with basic household or automotive carpet shampoos available in spray cans. Follow the directions and vacuum again, then use a stiff brush to bring back the "nap" of the carpet.

3   Most interiors have cloth or vinyl upholstery, either of which can be cleaned and maintained with a number of material-specific cleaners or shampoos available in auto supply stores. Follow the directions on the product for usage, and always spot-test any upholstery cleaner on an inconspicuous area (bottom edge of a back seat cushion) to ensure that it doesn't cause a color shift in the material.

4   After cleaning, vinyl upholstery should be treated with a protectant. **Note:** *Make sure the protectant container indicates the product can be used on seats - some products may make a seat too slippery.* **Caution:** *Do not use protectant on vinyl-covered steering wheels.*

5   Leather upholstery requires special care. It should be cleaned regularly with saddlesoap or leather cleaner. Never use alcohol, gasoline, nail polish remover or thinner to clean leather upholstery.

6   After cleaning, regularly treat leather upholstery with a leather conditioner, rubbed in with a soft cotton cloth. Never use car wax on leather upholstery.

7   In areas where the interior of the vehicle is subject to bright sunlight, cover leather seating areas of the seats with a sheet if the vehicle is to be left out for any length of time.

5   Body repair - minor damage

Plastic body panels

The following repair procedures are for minor scratches and gouges. Repair of more serious damage should be left to a dealer service department or qualified auto body shop. Below is a list of the equipment and materials necessary to perform the following repair procedures on plastic body panels. Although a specific brand of material may be mentioned, it should be noted that equivalent products from other manufacturers may be used instead.

> *Wax, grease and silicone removing*
>> *solvent*
> *Cloth-backed body tape*
> *Sanding discs*
> *Drill motor with three-inch disc holder*
> *Hand sanding block*
> *Rubber squeegees*
> *Sandpaper*
> *Non-porous mixing palette*
> *Wood paddle or putty knife*
> *Curved tooth body file*
> *Plastic body panel repair compound*
>> *and material*

Flexible panels (front and rear bumper fascia)

1   Remove the damaged panel, if necessary or desirable. In most cases, repairs can be carried out with the panel installed.

2   Clean the area(s) to be repaired with a wax, grease and silicone removing solvent applied with a water-dampened cloth.

3   If the damage is structural, that is, if it extends through the panel, clean the backside of the panel area to be repaired as well. Wipe dry.

4   Sand the rear surface about 1-1/2 in beyond the break.

5   Cut two pieces of fiberglass cloth large enough to overlap the break by about 1-1/2 in. Cut only to the required length.

6   Mix the adhesive from the repair kit according to the instructions included with the kit, and apply a layer of the mixture approximately 1/8-inch thick on the backside of the panel. Overlap the break by at least 1-1/2 inches

7   Apply one piece of fiberglass cloth to the adhesive and cover the cloth with additional adhesive. Apply a second piece of fiberglass cloth to the adhesive and immediately cover the cloth with additional adhesive insufficient quantity to fill the weave.

8   Allow the repair to cure for 20 to 30 minutes at 60-degrees to 80-degrees F.

9   If necessary, trim the excess repair material at the edge.

10   Remove all of the paint film over and around the area(s) to be repaired. The repair material should not overlap the painted surface.

11   With a drill motor and a sanding disc (or a rotary file), cut a "V" along the break line approximately 1/2-inch wide. Remove all dust and loose particles from the repair area.

12   Mix and apply the repair material. Apply a light coat first over the damaged area; then continue applying material until it reaches a level slightly higher than the surrounding finish.

13   Cure the mixture for 20 to 30 minutes at 60-degrees to 80-degrees F.

14   Roughly establish the contour of the area being repaired with a body file. If low areas or pits remain, mix and apply additional adhesive.

15   Block sand the damaged area with sandpaper to establish the actual contour of the surrounding surface.

16   If desired, the repaired area can be temporarily protected with several light coats of primer. Because of the special paints and techniques required for flexible body panels, it is recommended that the vehicle be taken to a paint shop for completion of the body repair.

Steel body panels

See photo sequence

Repair of minor scratches

17   If the scratch is superficial and does not penetrate to the metal of the body, repair is very simple. Lightly rub the scratched area with a fine rubbing compound to remove loose paint and built-up wax. Rinse the area with clean water.

18   Apply touch-up paint to the scratch, using a small brush. Continue to apply thin layers of paint until the surface of the paint in the scratch is level with the surrounding paint. Allow the new paint at least two weeks to harden, then blend it into the surrounding paint by rubbing with a very fine rubbing compound. Finally, apply a coat of wax to the scratch area.

19   If the scratch has penetrated the paint and exposed the metal of the body, causing the metal to rust, a different repair technique is required. Remove all loose rust from the bottom of the scratch with a pocket knife, then apply rust inhibiting paint to prevent the formation of rust in the future. Using a rubber or nylon applicator, coat the scratched area with glaze-type filler. If required, the filler can be mixed with thinner to provide a very thin paste, which is ideal for filling narrow scratches. Before the glaze filler in the scratch hardens, wrap a piece of smooth cotton cloth around the tip of a finger. Dip the cloth in thinner and then quickly wipe it along the surface of the scratch. This will ensure that the surface of the filler is slightly hollow. The scratch can now be painted over as described earlier in this Section.

Repair of dents

20   When repairing dents, the first job is to pull the dent out until the affected area is as close as possible to its original shape. There is no point in trying to restore the original shape completely as the metal in the damaged area will have stretched on impact and cannot be restored to its original contours. It is better to bring the level of the dent up to a point which is about 1/8-inch below the level of the surrounding metal. In cases where the dent is very shallow, it is not worth trying to pull it out at all.

21   If the back side of the dent is accessible, it can be hammered out gently from behind using a soft-face hammer. While doing this, hold a block of wood firmly against the opposite side of the metal to absorb the hammer blows and prevent the metal from being stretched.

22   If the dent is in a section of the body which has double layers, or some other factor makes it inaccessible from behind, a different technique is required. Drill several small holes through the metal inside the damaged area, particularly in the deeper sections. Screw long, self-tapping screws into the holes just enough for them to get a good grip in the metal. Now the dent can be pulled out by pulling on the protruding heads of the screws with locking pliers.

23   The next stage of repair is the removal of paint from the damaged area and from an inch or so of the surrounding metal. This is done with a wire brush or sanding disk in a drill motor, although it can be done just as

effectively by hand with sandpaper. To complete the preparation for filling, score the surface of the bare metal with a screwdriver or the tang of a file, or drill small holes in the affected area. This will provide a good grip for the filler material. To complete the repair, see the subsection on filling and painting later in this Section.

Repair of rust holes or gashes

24 Remove all paint from the affected area and from an inch or so of the surrounding metal using a sanding disk or wire brush mounted in a drill motor. If these are not available, a few sheets of sandpaper will do the job just as effectively.

25 With the paint removed, you will be able to determine the severity of the corrosion and decide whether to replace the whole panel, if possible, or repair the affected area. New body panels are not as expensive as most people think and it is often quicker to install a new panel than to repair large areas of rust.

26 Remove all trim pieces from the affected area except those which will act as a guide to the original shape of the damaged body, such as headlight shells, etc. Using metal snips or a hacksaw blade, remove all loose metal and any other metal that is badly affected by rust. Hammer the edges of the hole in to create a slight depression for the filler material.

27 Wire brush the affected area to remove the powdery rust from the surface of the metal. If the back of the rusted area is accessible, treat it with rust inhibiting paint.

28 Before filling is done, block the hole in some way. This can be done with sheet metal riveted or screwed into place, or by stuffing the hole with wire mesh.

29 Once the hole is blocked off, the affected area can be filled and painted. See the following subsection on filling and painting.

Filling and painting

30 Many types of body fillers are available, but generally speaking, body repair kits which contain filler paste and a tube of resin hardener are best for this type of repair work. A wide, flexible plastic or nylon applicator will be necessary for imparting a smooth and contoured finish to the surface of the filler material. Mix up a small amount of filler on a clean piece of wood or cardboard (use the hardener sparingly). Follow the manufacturer's instructions on the package, otherwise the filler will set incorrectly.

31 Using the applicator, apply the filler paste to the prepared area. Draw the applicator across the surface of the filler to achieve the desired contour and to level the filler surface. As soon as a contour that approximates the original one is achieved, stop working the paste. If you continue, the paste will begin to stick to the applicator. Continue to add thin layers of paste at 20-minute intervals until the level of the filler is just above the surrounding metal.

32 Once the filler has hardened, the excess can be removed with a body file. From then on, progressively finer grades of sandpaper should be used, starting with a 180-grit paper and finishing with 600-grit wet-or-dry paper. Always wrap the sandpaper around a flat rubber or wooden block, otherwise the surface of the filler will not be completely flat. During the sanding of the filler surface, the wet-or-dry paper should be periodically rinsed in water. This will ensure that a very smooth finish is produced in the final stage.

33 At this point, the repair area should be surrounded by a ring of bare metal, which in turn should be encircled by the finely feathered edge of good paint. Rinse the repair area with clean water until all of the dust produced by the sanding operation is gone.

34 Spray the entire area with a light coat of primer. This will reveal any imperfections in the surface of the filler. Repair the imperfections with fresh filler paste or glaze filler and once more smooth the surface with sandpaper. Repeat this spray-and-repair procedure until you are satisfied that the surface of the filler and the feathered edge of the paint are perfect. Rinse the area with clean water and allow it to dry completely.

35 The repair area is now ready for painting. Spray painting must be carried out in a warm, dry, windless and dust free atmosphere. These conditions can be created if you have access to a large indoor work area, but if you are forced to work in the open, you will have to pick the day very carefully. If you are working indoors, dousing the floor in the work area with water will help settle the dust which would otherwise be in the air. If the repair area is confined to one body panel, mask off the surrounding panels. This will help minimize the effects of a slight mismatch in paint color. Trim pieces such as chrome strips, door handles, etc., will also need to be masked off or removed. Use masking tape and several thickness of newspaper for the masking operations.

36 Before spraying, shake the paint can thoroughly, then spray a test area until the spray painting technique is mastered. Cover the repair area with a thick coat of primer. The thickness should be built up using several thin layers of primer rather than one thick one. Using 600-grit wet-or-dry sandpaper, rub down the surface of the primer until it is very smooth. While doing this, the work area should be thoroughly rinsed with water and the wet-or-dry sandpaper periodically rinsed as well. Allow the primer to dry before spraying additional coats.

37 Spray on the top coat, again building up the thickness by using several thin layers of paint. Begin spraying in the center of the repair area and then, using a circular motion, work out until the whole repair area and about two inches of the surrounding original paint is covered. Remove all masking material 10 to 15 minutes after spraying on the final coat of paint. Allow the new paint at least two weeks to harden, then use a very

fine rubbing compound to blend the edges of the new paint into the existing paint. Finally, apply a coat of wax.

6 Body repair - major damage

1 Major damage must be repaired by an auto body/frame repair shop with the necessary welding and hydraulic straightening equipment.

2 If the damage has been serious, it is vital that the structure be checked for proper alignment or the vehicle's handling characteristics may be adversely affected. Other problems, such as excessive tire wear and wear in the driveline and steering may occur.

3 Due to the fact that all of the major body components (hood, fenders, etc.) are separate and replaceable units, any seriously damaged components should be replaced rather than repaired. Sometimes these components can be found in a wrecking yard that specializes in used vehicle components, often at considerable savings over the cost of new parts.

7 Hinges and locks - maintenance

Once every 3000 miles, or every three months, the hinges and latch assemblies on the doors, hood and trunk should be given a few drops of light oil or lock lubricant. The door latch strikers should also be lubricated with a thin coat of grease to reduce wear and ensure free movement. Lubricate the door and trunk locks with spray-on graphite lubricant.

8 Windshield and fixed glass - replacement

Replacement of the windshield and fixed glass requires the use of special fast setting adhesive/caulk materials. These operations should be left to a dealer or a shop specializing in glass work.

9 Hood - removal, installation and adjustment

Note: *The hood is somewhat awkward to remove and install, at least two people should perform this procedure.*

Removal and installation

Refer to illustrations 9.3 and 9.4

1 Open the hood, then place blankets or pads over the fenders and cowl area of the body. This will protect the body and paint as the hood is lifted off.

2 Disconnect any cables or wires that will interfere with removal.

3 Make marks or scribe a line around the

11

These photos illustrate a method of repairing simple dents. They are intended to supplement *Body repair - minor damage* in this Chapter and should not be used as the sole instructions for body repair on these vehicles.

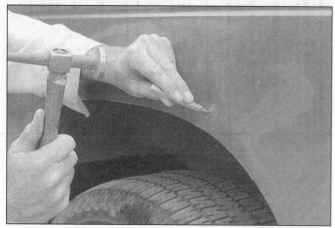

1   If you can't access the backside of the body panel to hammer out the dent, pull it out with a slide-hammer-type dent puller. In the deepest portion of the dent or along the crease line, drill or punch hole(s) at least one inch apart . . .

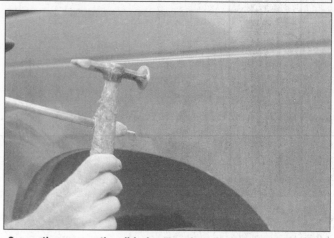

2   . . . then screw the slide-hammer into the hole and operate it. Tap with a hammer near the edge of the dent to help 'pop' the metal back to its original shape. When you're finished, the dent area should be close to its original contour and about 1/8-inch below the surface of the surrounding metal

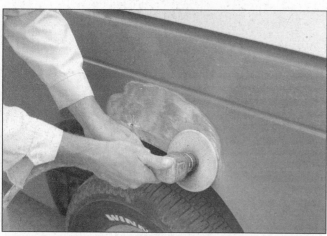

3   Using coarse-grit sandpaper, remove the paint down to the bare metal. Hand sanding works fine, but the disc sander shown here makes the job faster. Use finer (about 320-grit) sandpaper to feather-edge the paint at least one inch around the dent area

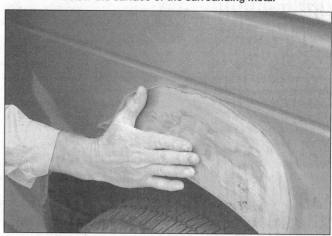

4   When the paint is removed, touch will probably be more helpful than sight for telling if the metal is straight. Hammer down the high spots or raise the low spots as necessary. Clean the repair area with wax/silicone remover

5   Following label instructions, mix up a batch of plastic filler and hardener. The ratio of filler to hardener is critical, and, if you mix it incorrectly, it will either not cure properly or cure too quickly (you won't have time to file and sand it into shape)

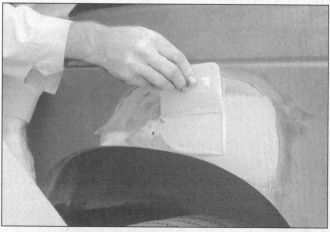

6   Working quickly so the filler doesn't harden, use a plastic applicator to press the body filler firmly into the metal, assuring it bonds completely. Work the filler until it matches the original contour and is slightly above the surrounding metal

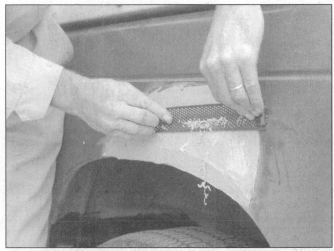

7 Let the filler harden until you can just dent it with your fingernail. Use a body file or Surform tool (shown here) to rough-shape the filler

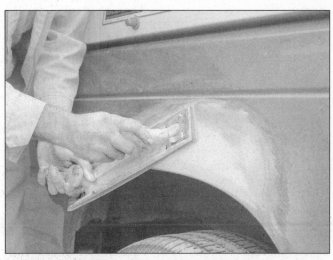

8 Use coarse-grit sandpaper and a sanding board or block to work the filler down until it's smooth and even. Work down to finer grits of sandpaper - always using a board or block - ending up with 360 or 400 grit

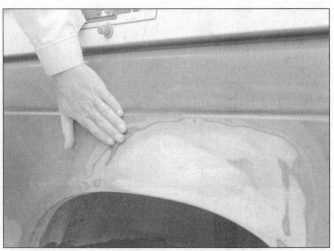

9 You shouldn't be able to feel any ridge at the transition from the filler to the bare metal or from the bare metal to the old paint. As soon as the repair is flat and uniform, remove the dust and mask off the adjacent panels or trim pieces

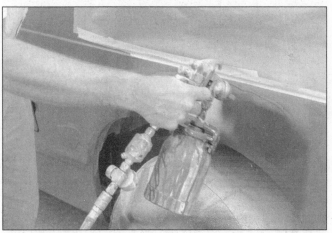

10 Apply several layers of primer to the area. Don't spray the primer on too heavy, so it sags or runs, and make sure each coat is dry before you spray on the next one. A professional-type spray gun is being used here, but aerosol spray primer is available inexpensively from auto parts stores

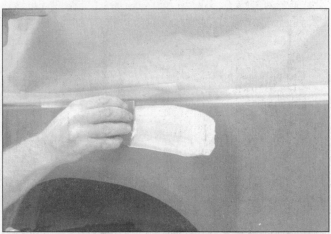

11 The primer will help reveal imperfections or scratches. Fill these with glazing compound. Follow the label instructions and sand it with 360 or 400-grit sandpaper until it's smooth. Repeat the glazing, sanding and respraying until the primer reveals a perfectly smooth surface

12 Finish sand the primer with very fine sandpaper (400 or 600-grit) to remove the primer overspray. Clean the area with water and allow it to dry. Use a tack rag to remove any dust, then apply the finish coat. Don't attempt to rub out or wax the repair area until the paint has dried completely (at least two weeks)

9.3 Before removing the hood, draw a mark around the hinge plate

9.4 Use a small screwdriver to pry the retaining clip out of its locking groove, then detach the end of the strut from the mounting stud

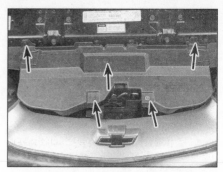

9.10a Remove the bolts and plastic retaining pins (arrows) securing the air deflector to access the hood latch assembly

9.10b Loosen the bolts (arrows) and move the hood latch to adjust the hood closed position

9.11 Screw the hood bumpers (arrow) in or out to adjust the hood flush with the fenders

hood hinge to ensure proper alignment during installation **(see illustration)**.
4   Have an assistant support the weight of the hood and detach the support struts **(see illustration)**.
5   Remove the hinge-to-hood bolts and lift off the hood.
6   Installation is the reverse of removal. Align the hinge bolts with the marks made in step 3.

Adjustment

Refer to illustrations 9.10a, 9.10b and 9.11
7   Fore-and-aft and side-to-side adjustment of the hood is done by moving the hinge plate slot after loosening the bolts or nuts.
8   Scribe a line around the entire hinge plate so you can determine the amount of movement.
9   Loosen the bolts or nuts and move the hood into correct alignment. Move it only a little at a time. Tighten the hinge bolts and carefully lower the hood to check the position.
10   If necessary after installation, the entire hood latch assembly can be adjusted up-and-down as well as from side-to-side on the radiator support so the hood closes securely and flush with the fenders. To make the adjustment, first remove the air deflector covering the hood latch **(see illustration)**. Scribe a line or mark around the hood latch mounting bolts to provide a reference point, then loosen them and reposition the latch assembly, as necessary **(see illustration)**. Following adjustment, retighten the mounting bolts.

11   Finally, adjust the hood bumpers on the radiator support so the hood, when closed, is flush with the fenders **(see illustration)**.
12   The hood latch assembly, as well as the hinges, should be periodically lubricated with white, lithium-base grease to prevent binding and wear.

10   Hood latch and release cable - removal and installation

Warning: *The models covered by this manual are equipped with airbags. Always disable the airbag system* (see Chapter 12) *before working in the vicinity of the impact sensors, steering column or instrument panel. Failure to follow these procedures may cause*

10.2 Pry out the cable retainer (arrow) from the backside of the hood latch assembly, then disengage the cable

accidental deployment of the airbag, which could cause personal injury. The airbag circuits are easily identified by yellow insulation covering the entire wiring harness. Do not use electrical test equipment on any of these wires or tamper with them in any way.

Latch

Refer to illustration 10.2
1   Scribe a line around the latch to aid alignment when installing, then remove the retaining bolts securing the hood latch to the radiator support **(see illustration 9.10b)**. Remove the latch.
2   Disconnect the hood release cable by disengaging the cable from the latch assembly **(see illustration)**.
3   Installation is the reverse of removal.
Note: *Adjust the latch so the hood engages securely when closed and the hood bumpers are slightly compressed.*

Cable

Refer to illustrations 10.6 and 10.7
4   Disconnect the hood release cable from the latch assembly as described in step 1.
5   Attach a piece of thin wire or string to the end of the cable and unclip all remaining cable retaining clips. **Note:** *It may be necessary on some vehicles to remove the air cleaner assembly* (see Chapter 4) *to allow access for release cable removal.*
6   Working in the passenger compartment, remove the driver's side lower insulating panel **(see illustration)**.

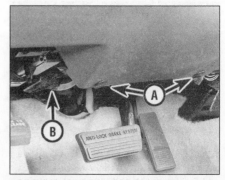

10.6 Detach the plastic clips (A) and remove the driver's side lower insulating panel (B) to access the hood release lever

7   Remove the two hood release lever mounting bolts and detach the hood release lever **(see illustration)**.

8   Pull the cable and grommet rearward into the passenger compartment until you can see the wire or string. Ensure that the new cable has a grommet attached then remove the wire or string from the old cable and fasten it to the new cable.

9   With the new cable attached to the wire or string, pull the wire or string back through the firewall until the new cable reaches the latch assembly.

10   Working in the passenger compartment, reinstall the new cable into the hood release lever. Use pliers to crimp the retaining clip which secures the cable to the release lever.

11   The remainder of the installation is the reverse of removal. **Note:** *Push on the grommet with your fingers from the passenger compartment to seat the grommet in the firewall correctly.*

11   Bumpers - removal and installation

Warning: *The models covered by this manual are equipped with airbags. Always disable the airbag system (see Chapter 12) before working in the vicinity of the impact sensors, steering column or instrument panel. Failure to follow these procedures may cause accidental deployment of the airbag, which could cause personal injury. The airbag circuits are easily identified by yellow insulation covering the entire wiring harness. Do not use electrical test equipment on any of these wires or tamper with them in any way.*

Caution: *On models equipped with a Theftlock audio system, be sure the lockout feature is turned off before performing any procedure which requires disconnecting the battery.*

Front bumper

Refer to illustrations 11.3, 11.4a,11.4b, 11.5, 11.6 and 11.7

1   Open the hood and disconnect the negative battery cable.

2   Raise the front of the vehicle and support it securely on jackstands.

10.7 Remove the hood release lever retaining screws (arrows) and pull the cable rearward into the passenger compartment

3   Working in the front wheel opening, detach the retaining screws securing the inner fenderwell extension panels to the bumper cover **(see illustration)**.

4   Remove the lower radiator air deflector and the lower bumper cover support panel **(see illustrations)**.

5   Remove the retaining screws securing the bumper cover to each fender **(see illustration)**. Disconnect the side marker lamp electrical connectors.

6   Working under the front of the vehicle, remove the retaining nuts securing the bumper to the bumper energy absorbers **(see illustration)**.

7   Remove the upper retaining pins

11.4a Detach the lower air deflector . . .

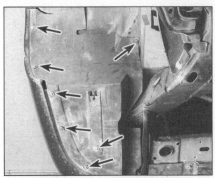

11.3 Remove the inner fenderwell extension panel screws (arrows) from inside the wheel opening and from the lower front corner(s) of the bumper cover

securing the bumper cover in the hood opening **(see illustration)**.

8   Separate the bumper cover from the fenders, then pull the bumper assembly straight out and away from the vehicle to remove it.

9   To remove the bumper cover from the bumper, simply detach the plastic clips securing the upper and lower edges of the bumper cover.

10   Installation is the reverse of removal.

Rear bumper

Refer to illustrations 11.12, 11.13, 11.15a, 11.15b, 11.16 and 11.17

11   Apply the parking brake, raise the rear of

11.4b . . . and the lower bumper cover support bolt (arrow)

11.5 Detach the bolts (arrows) securing the bumper cover to both fenders

11.6 Using a ratchet, long extension and a socket, remove the front bumper retaining bolts (arrows)

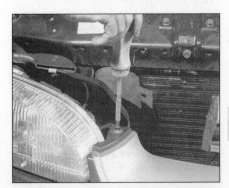

11.7 Remove the the center pin to release the clips securing the bumper cover in the hood opening

11

11.12 Detach the nuts, bolts and screws (arrows) and remove the rear wheel opening splash shield

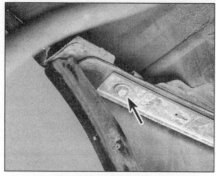

11.13 Working in the splash shield opening, remove the bolt (arrow) securing the bumper cover to the rear quarter panels

11.15a Working in the trunk compartment, remove the remaining fasteners (arrows) securing the bumper cover to the rear quarter panels

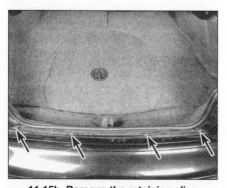

11.15b Remove the retaining clips securing the bumper in the trunk lid opening

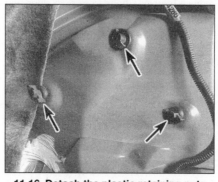

11.16 Detach the plastic retaining nuts (arrows) to release the tail light housing from the rear quarter panel

11.17 Using a ratchet, long extension and a socket, remove the rear bumper retaining bolts (arrows)

the vehicle, support it securely on jackstands and remove the rear wheels.

12 Working in the rear wheel opening, detach the splash shield located at the rear of the wheel opening from each side of the vehicle **(see illustration)**.

13 Working under the vehicle, remove the retaining bolts securing the bumper cover to the rear quarter panels **(see illustration)**.

14 Remove the rear side marker lights and the license plate lamp (see Chapter 12).

15 Working inside the trunk compartment, remove the plastic retaining nuts and clips securing the trunk finishing panels. Peel back the trunk finishing panels and remove the remaining nuts and bolts securing the

bumper cover to rear quarter panels and the trunk opening **(see illustrations)**.

16 Detach the rear tail light housings, disconnect the electrical connectors and remove both tail light housings from the vehicle **(see illustration)**.

17 Working back under the vehicle, remove the retaining nuts securing the bumper to the bumper energy absorbers **(see illustration)**. Pull the bumper assembly straight out and away from the vehicle to remove it.

18 To remove the bumper cover from the bumper, simply detach the plastic clips securing the upper and lower edges of the bumper cover.

19 Installation is the reverse of removal.

12   Front fender - removal and installation

Refer to illustrations 12.4, 12.6a, 12.6b, 12.6c and 12.6d

1 Remove the hood (see Section 9).

2 Raise the vehicle, support it securely on jackstands and remove the front wheel.

3 Remove the rocker panel finish moulding (if equipped) from the side of the vehicle that the fender is to be removed.

4 Remove the inner fenderwell splash shield **(see illustration)**.

5 Remove the front bumper assembly (see Section 11).

12.4 Detach the inner fenderwell retaining bolts (arrows) and remove the inner fenderwell

12.6a Remove the retaining bolt (arrow) securing the front of the fender

12.6b Remove the fender retaining bolt (arrow) located in the wheel opening

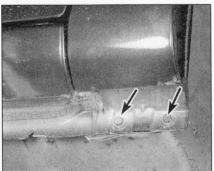

12.6c Remove the retaining bolts (arrows) securing the fender to the rocker panel

12.6d Detach the remaining bolts (arrows) in the hood opening, then remove the fender from the vehicle

13.3 Before removing the trunk lid, draw marks around the bolt heads to aid in the reinstallation process

6   Remove the remaining fender mounting bolts **(see illustrations)**.

7   Detach the fender. It's a good idea to have an assistant support the fender while it's being moved away from the vehicle to prevent damage to the surrounding body panels.

8   Installation is the reverse of removal.

---

13   Trunk lid and balance spring - removal, installation and adjustment

Note: *The trunk lid is heavy and somewhat awkward to remove and install - at least two people should perform this procedure.*

Removal and installation

Trunk lid

Refer to illustration 13.3

1   Open the trunk lid and cover the edges of the trunk compartment with pads or cloths to protect the painted surfaces when the lid is removed.

2   Disconnect any cables or wire harness connectors attached to the trunk lid that would interfere with removal.

3   Make alignment marks around the trunk lid hinge bolts **(see illustration)**.

4   While an assistant supports the lid,

remove the hinge bolts from both sides and lift the trunk lid off the vehicle.

5   Installation is the reverse of removal.
Note: *When reinstalling the trunk lid, align the hinge bolts with the marks made during removal.*

Balance spring

Refer to illustration 13.7

6   Open the trunk lid and have an assistant support the lid.

7   Use a long piece of pipe or similar tool to pry the balance spring end up and over its retaining bracket **(see illustration)**.

8   Slide the balance spring out from the hinged end and remove it from the vehicle.

9   Installation is the reverse of removal.

Adjustment

Refer to illustrations 13.13 and 13.14

10   Fore-and-aft   and   side-to-side adjustment of the trunk lid is done by moving the hood in relation to the hinge plate after loosening the bolts or nuts.

11   Scribe a line around the hinge bolt heads as described earlier in this Section so you can judge the amount of movement.

12   Loosen the bolts or nuts and move the trunk lid into correct alignment. Move it only a little at a time. Tighten the hinge bolts or nuts and carefully lower the trunk lid to check the alignment.

13   If necessary after installation, the entire

trunk lid latch assembly can be adjusted up and down as well as from side to side on the trunk lid so the lid closes securely and is flush with the rear quarter panels. To do this, scribe a line around the trunk lid latch mounting bolts to provide a reference point. Then loosen the bolts and reposition the latch assembly as necessary **(see illustration)**. Following adjustment, retighten the mounting bolts.

14   Adjust the bumpers on the trunk lid, so that the trunk lid is flush with the rear quarter panels when closed **(see illustration)**.

15   The trunk lid latch assembly, as well as the hinges, should be periodically lubricated with white lithium-base grease to prevent sticking and wear.

---

14   Trunk lid latch, latch striker and lock cylinder - removal and installation

---

Latch and latch striker

Refer to illustration 14.4

1   Unplug any electrical connectors and detach any cables from the latch assembly.

2   The trunk lid latch is retained by bolts which can readily be removed with a wrench **(see illustration 13.13)**. For adjustment procedures, see Section 13.

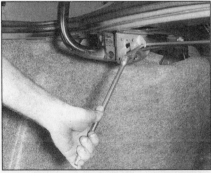

13.7 Pry the balance spring up and over the spring retaining bracket to release spring tension

13.13 Loosen the bolts (arrows) and move the latch assembly as necessary to adjust the trunk lid flush with the quarter panels in the closed position

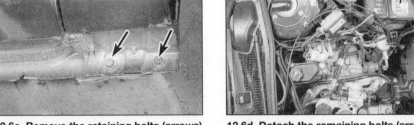

13.14 Adjust the bumpers so they're slightly compressed when the trunk lid is in the closed position

11

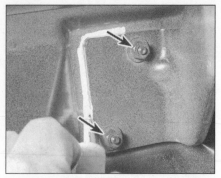

14.4 The latch striker is retained by nuts (arrows) - scribe a line around the striker before removal as a reference point

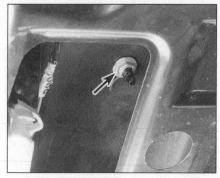

14.6a Remove the nuts (arrow) securing the center . . .

14.6b . . . and the outer edges (arrow) of the rear trim panel . . .

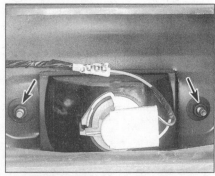

14.6c Disconnect the electrical connectors from the reverse lamps and remove the bolts (arrows), then detach the rear trim panel from the trunk lid and remove it from the vehicle

3   To access the striker, remove the plastic retaining nuts and clips securing the rear trunk finishing panel. Then scribe a line around the latch striker to provide a reference point.
4   Detach the striker retaining nuts and remove the striker from the vehicle **(see illustration)**.
5   Installation is the reverse of removal.

Lock cylinder

Refer to illustrations 14.6a, 14.6b, 14.6c and 14.7
6   Remove the trunk lid rear trim panel **(see illustrations)**.
7   Using a small drill bit, drill out the rivets

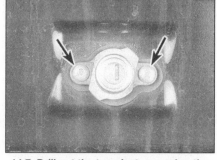

14.7 Drill out the two rivets securing the lock cylinder

securing the lock cylinder **(see illustration)**, then pull the lock cylinder out of the trunk lid and remove it from the vehicle.
8   Installation is the reverse of removal.

15 Door trim panel - removal and installation

Caution: *On models equipped with a Theftlock audio system, be sure the lockout feature is turned off before performing any procedure which requires disconnecting the battery.*

Removal

Refer to illustrations 15.1, 15.2, 15.3, 15.4, 15.5, 15.6a, 15.6b, 15.7 and 15.9

15.1 Detach the retaining screw (arrow) and pull the inside handle lever to remove the bezel

1   Disconnect the cable from the negative terminal of the battery. Remove the inside door handle trim bezel **(see illustration)**.
2   On manual window equipped models, remove the window crank, using a hooked tool to remove the retainer clip **(see illustration)**. A special tool is available for this purpose, but it's not essential. With the clip removed, pull off the handle.
3   On power window equipped models, pry out the armrest switch control plate **(see illustration)** and disconnect the electrical connections.
4   Remove the finishing panel from above the armrest pull handle **(see illustration)**.

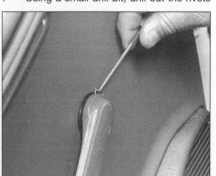

15.2 If your vehicle is equipped with manual windows, use a hooked tool like this to remove the window crank retaining clip

15.3 Use a small screwdriver to disengage the retaining clips securing the switch control plate

15.4 Use a small screwdriver or similar tool to pry out the armrest finishing panel

15.5 Remove the screws (arrow) securing the armrest pull handle

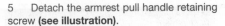

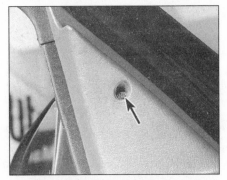

15.6a Remove the screws (arrow) securing the upper . . .

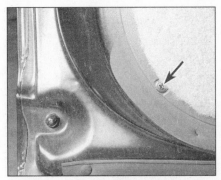

15.6b . . . and lower edges (arrow) of the door trim panel

5   Detach the armrest pull handle retaining screw **(see illustration)**.
6   Remove the remaining door panel retaining screws securing the outer edge of the door panel **(see illustrations)**.
7   Insert a wide putty knife or a special trim panel removal tool between the trim panel and the head of the retaining clip to disengage the door panel retaining clips **(see illustration)**. **Note:** *Door trim panel retaining clips are approximately six to ten inches apart. Pry at the clip location only. Prying in between clips will result in distorted or damaged door trim panels.*
8   Once all of the clips and screws are disengaged, detach the trim panel and remove the trim panel from the vehicle by gently pulling it up and out.
9   For access to the inner door remove the door panel support bracket **(see illustration)**. Then peel back the watershield, taking care not to tear it.
10   To install the door panel, work through the window opening and engage the hooks on the back of the trim panel onto the door and push down until they are seated, then press the door panel retaining clips into place. **Note:** *When installing door trim panel retaining clips, make sure the clips are lined up with their mating holes first, then gently tap inward with the palm of your hand.*
11   The remainder of the installation is the reverse of removal.

16   Door - removal, installation and adjustment

Caution: *On models equipped with a Theftlock audio system, be sure the lockout feature is turned off before performing any procedure which requires disconnecting the battery.*
Note: *The door is heavy and somewhat awkward to remove and install - at least two people should perform this procedure. This procedure applies to both front and rear doors.*

Removal and installation

Refer to illustrations 16.7a and 16.7b
1   Raise the window completely and

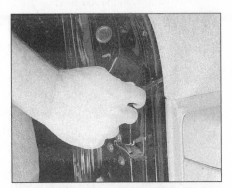

15.7 Insert a trim removal tool or a putty knife between the door and the trim panel to disengage the clips along the outer edge of the door trim panel

disconnect the negative cable from the battery if equipped with power windows.
2   Open the door all the way and support it on jacks or blocks covered with rags to prevent damaging the paint.
3   Remove the door trim panel and water deflector as described in (Section 15).
4   Unplug all electrical connections, ground wires and harness retaining clips from the door. **Note:** *It is a good idea to label all connections to aid the reassembly process.*
5   Working on the door side, detach the rubber conduit between the body and the door. Pull the wiring harness through the conduit hole and remove the wiring from the door.
6   Mark around the door hinges with a pen or a scribe to facilitate realignment during reassembly.

16.7a Front door retaining bolts (arrows)

15.9 To access the inner door, detach the door panel support bracket retaining clip

7   Have an assistant hold the door, remove the hinge-to-door bolts **(see illustrations)** and lift the door off.
8   Installation is the reverse of removal.

Adjustment

Refer to illustration 16.12
9   Having proper door-to-body alignment is a critical part of a well functioning door assembly. First check the door hinge pins and bushings for excessive play. **Note:** *If the door can be lifted (1/16-inch or more) without the car body lifting with it the hinge pins and bushings should be replaced.*
10   Door-to-body alignment adjustments are made by loosening the hinge-to-body bolts or hinge-to-door bolts and moving the door. Proper body alignment is achieved

11

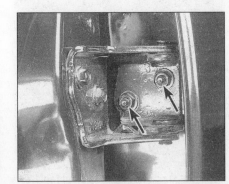

16.7b Open the front door to access the rear door retaining bolts (arrows)

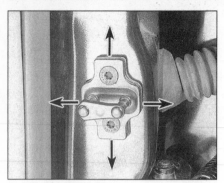

16.12 Adjust the door lock striker by loosening the mounting screws and gently tapping the striker in the desired direction

17.2 Remove the latch retaining screws (arrows) from the end of the door, then detach the actuating rods and pull the latch assembly through the access hole

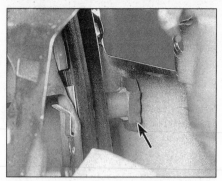

17.9 To remove the lock cylinder, detach the plastic clip securing the lock rod, then pry off the lock cylinder retaining clip (arrow)

when the top of the doors are parallel with the roof section, the front door is flush with the fender, the rear door is flush with the rear quarter panel and the bottom of the doors are aligned with the lower rocker panel. If these goals can't be reached by adjusting the hinge-to-body or hinge-to-door bolts, body alignment shims may have to be purchased and inserted behind the hinges to achieve correct alignment.

11   To adjust the door closed position, first check that the door latch is contacting the center of the latch striker bolt. If not, remove the striker bolt and add or subtract washers to achieve correct alignment.

12   Finally, adjust the latch striker bolt as necessary (up and down or sideways) to provide positive engagement with the latch mechanism **(see illustration)** and the door panel is flush with the center pillar or rear quarter panel.

---

17   Door latch, lock cylinder and handles - removal and installation

---

Door latch

Refer to illustration 17.2

1   Raise the window then remove the door trim panel and watershield as described in (Section 15).

2   Remove the screws securing the latch to the door **(see illustration)**.

3   Working through the large access hole, position the latch as necessary to disengage the outside door handle and outside lock cylinder to latch rods and the inside handle to latch rod.

4   All door locking rods are attached by plastic clips. The plastic clips can be removed by unsnapping the portion engaging the connecting rod and then by pulling the rod out of its locating hole.

5   Position the latch as necessary to disengage the door lock actuator rod. Then remove the latch assembly from the door.

6   Installation is the reverse of removal.

Door lock cylinder and outside handle

Refer to illustrations 17.9 and 17.11

7   To remove the lock cylinder, raise the window and remove the door trim panel and watershield as described in Section 15.

8   Working through the large access hole, disengage the plastic clip that secures the lock cylinder to the latch rod.

9   Using a pair of pliers, slide the lock cylinder retaining clip out of engagement and remove the lock cylinder from the door **(see illustration)**.

10   To remove the outside handle, work through the access hole and disengage the plastic clip that secures the outside handle-to-latch rod.

11   Drill out the rivets securing the outside handle **(see illustration),** then pull the handle out of the door and remove it from the vehicle.

12   Installation is the reverse of removal.

Inside handle

Refer to illustration 17.15

13   Remove the door trim panel as described in Section 15 and peel away the watershield.

14   Detach the actuating rods from the handle and position them aside.

15   Drill out the rivet securing the inside handle **(see illustration)**.

16   Remove the handle retaining bolt. Then pull forward on the handle to disengage it from the inner door panel.

17   Installation is the reverse of removal.

---

18   Door window glass - removal and installation

Refer to illustrations 18.4 and 18.5

1   Remove the door trim panel and the plastic watershield (see Section 15).

2   Lower the window glass all the way down into the door.

3   Carefully pry out the inner and outer weatherstripping from the door window opening.

4   Loosen the front guide channel **(see illustration)** and remove the window frame weatherstripping.

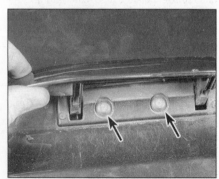

17.11 Lift the outside handle to access the retaining rivets (arrows)

17.15 Detach the actuating rods (A), drill out the handle retaining rivets (B), then remove the retaining bolt (C)

18.4 Remove the forward window guide channel retaining bolts (arrow)

18.5 Raise the window just enough to access the glass retaining rivets (arrow) through the hole in the door frame, then drill out the rivets securing the glass to the equalizer arm

19.4 Detach the window equalizer arm retaining bolt (arrow)

19.5 Remove the regulator retaining bolts (arrows) or drill out the window regulator rivets (if equipped)

5   Raise the window just enough to access the window retaining rivets through the hole in the door frame **(see illustration)**.
6   Place a rag over the glass to help prevent scratching the glass, then drill out the two glass mounting rivets.
7   Remove the glass by pulling it up and out.
8   Installation is the reverse of removal.

19   Door window glass regulator - removal and installation

Refer to illustrations 19.4 and 19.5
Warning: *The regulator arms are under extreme pressure and can cause serious injury if the motor or counter-balance spring is removed without locking the sector gear. This can be done by inserting a bolt and nut through the holes in the backing plate and sector gear to lock them together.*
Caution: *On models equipped with a Theftlock audio system, be sure the lockout feature is turned off before performing any procedure which requires disconnecting the battery.*
1   Remove the door trim panel and the plastic watershield (see Section 15).
2   Remove the window glass assembly (see Section 18).
3   On models with power windows,

disconnect the electrical connector from the window regulator motor.
4   Remove the equalizer arm retaining bolt **(see illustration)**.
5   Remove the retaining bolts or drill out the rivets that secure the window regulator to the door frame **(see illustration)**.
6   Pull the equalizer arm and regulator assemblies through the service hole in the door frame to remove it.
7   Installation is the reverse of removal.

20   Outside mirrors - removal and installation

Refer to illustrations 20.3 and 20.5
Caution: *On models equipped with a Theftlock audio system, be sure the lockout feature is turned off before performing any procedure which requires disconnecting the battery.*
1   Disconnect the negative cable from the battery.
2   Remove the door trim panel and the plastic watershield (see Section 15).
3   Remove the foam insulating pad from the door window frame **(see illustration)**.
4   Disconnect the electrical connector from the mirror.
5   Remove the three mirror retaining nuts

or bolts and detach the mirror from the vehicle **(see illustration)**.
6   Installation is the reverse of removal.

21   Center console - removal and installation

Refer to illustrations 21.3, 21.4, 21.5 and 21.6
Warning: *The models covered by this manual are equipped with airbags. Always disable the airbag system before working in the vicinity of the impact sensors, steering column or instrument panel to avoid the possibility of accidental deployment of the airbag(s), which could cause personal injury (see Chapter 12). The yellow wires and connectors routed through the console are for this system. Do not use electrical test equipment on these yellow wires or tamper with them in any way while working around the console.*
Caution: *On models equipped with a Theftlock audio system, be sure the lockout feature is turned off before performing any procedure which requires disconnecting the battery.*
1   Disconnect the negative cable from the battery.
2   Apply the parking brake lever and place the gear selector into the neutral position.
3   Pry out the shift lever knob retaining clip and remove the knob **(see illustration)**.

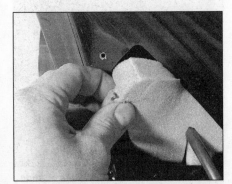

20.3 Peel out the foam insulating pad from the door window frame

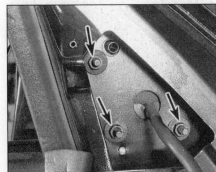

20.5 Outside mirror retaining nut locations (arrows)

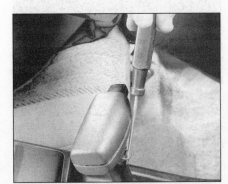

21.3 Pry out the retaining clip and remove the shift knob

11

21.4 Pry out the gear selector trim bezel

21.5 Remove the screws (arrows) located under the gear selector trim plate

21.6 Open the console glove box and remove the retaining screws (arrows), securing the rear half of the console

4   Pry out the gear selector trim bezel by disengaging the clips on the front edge **(see illustration)**. Then disconnect the electrical connectors and remove the bezel from the console assembly.

5   Remove the retaining screws securing the front half of the console **(see illustration)**.

6   Working in the console glove box, detach the retaining screws securing the rear half of the console **(see illustration)**.

7   Lift the console up and over the shift lever. Disconnect any electrical connections and remove the console from the vehicle.

8   Installation is the reverse of removal.

---

22 Dashboard trim panels - removal and installation

Warning: *The models covered by this manual are equipped with airbags. Always disable the air bag system before working in the vicinity of the impact sensors, steering column or instrument panel to avoid the possibility of accidental deployment of the airbag(s), which could cause personal injury (see Chapter 12). The yellow wires and connectors routed through the instrument panel are for this system. Do not use electrical test equipment on these yellow wires or tamper with them in any way while working around the instrument panel.*

Caution: *On models equipped with a Theftlock audio system, be sure the lockout feature is turned off before performing any procedure which requires disconnecting the battery.*

Instrument cluster bezel

Refer to illustration 22.2

1   Tilt the steering wheel down to the lowest position. **Note:** *If the vehicle is equipped with a column shift lever, place the gear selector in the L1 position.*

2   Grasp the bezel securely and pull back sharply to detach the clips from the instrument panel **(see illustration)**.

3   Unplug any electrical connectors that interfere with removal.

4   Installation is the reverse of removal.

Lower steering column trim cover

Refer to illustration 22.5

5   Remove the lower clips securing the sound insulator panel to the lower steering cover, then remove the steering column cover retaining screws **(see illustration)**.

6   Lift the lower edge of the steering column cover upward and detach the clips or fasteners on the upper edge.

7   Unplug any electrical connectors, then lower the trim panel from the instrument panel.

8   Installation is the reverse of removal.

Knee bolster

Refer to illustration 22.10

9   Remove the lower steering column trim cover as described above.

10   Detach the knee bolster retaining screws and remove it from the vehicle **(see illustration)**.

11   Installation is the reverse of removal.

Glove box

12   To remove the glove box, simply remove the screws from the hinge. Open the glove box door, squeeze the plastic sides in and lower the glove box from the instrument panel.

13   Installation is the reverse of the removal procedure.

---

23 Seats - removal and installation

Front seat

Refer to illustration 23.2

1   Position the seat all the way forward or all the way to the rear to access the front seat retaining bolts.

22.2 Grasp the Instrument cluster bezel and carefully pull outward to detach the retaining clips

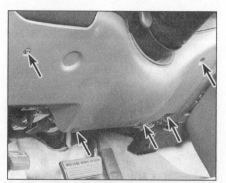

22.5 Lower steering column cover retaining screw and clip locations (arrows)

22.10 Knee bolster retaining bolt locations (arrows)

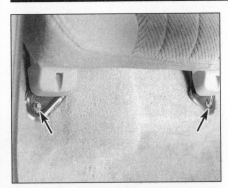

23.2 Detach the trim covers (if equipped) and remove the bolts (arrows) from the front and rear of the seat

23.5 Using a socket and ratchet, remove the rear seat cushion retaining bolts

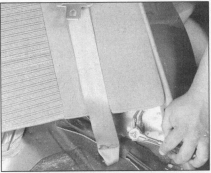

23.6 Detach the bolts securing the lower corners of the seat back, then lift upward and out to remove the seat back

2   Detach any bolt trim covers and remove the retaining bolts **(see illustration)**.

3   Tilt the seat upward to access the underside, then disconnect any electrical connectors and lift the seat from the vehicle.

4   Installation is the reverse of removal.

Rear seat

Refer to illustrations 23.5 and 23.6

5   Remove the seat cushion retaining bolts **(see illustration)**. Then lift up on the front edge and remove the cushion from the vehicle.

6   Detach the retaining bolts at the lower edge of the seat back **(see illustration)**, then lift up on the lower edge of the seat back and remove it from the vehicle.

7   Installation is the reverse of removal.

24 Seat belt check

1   Check the seat belts, buckles, latch plates and guide loops for obvious damage and signs of wear.

2   See if the seat belt reminder light comes on when the key is turned to the Run or Start position. A chime should also sound.

3   The seat belts are designed to lock up during a sudden stop or impact, yet allow free movement during normal driving. Make sure the retractors return the belt against your chest while driving and rewind the belt fully when the buckle is unlatched.

4   If any of the above checks reveal problems with the seat belt system, replace parts as necessary.

11

Notes

Chapter 12
Chassis electrical system

Contents

1 General information

The electrical system is a 12-volt, negative ground type. Power for the lights and all electrical accessories is supplied by a lead/acid-type battery which is charged by the alternator.

This Chapter covers repair and service procedures for the various electrical components not associated with the engine. Information on the battery, alternator, ignition system and starter motor can be found in Chapter 5. It should be noted that when portions of the electrical system are serviced, the negative battery cable should be disconnected from the battery to prevent electrical shorts and/or fires. **Caution:** *On models equipped with a Theftlock audio system, be sure the lockout feature is turned off before performing any procedure which requires disconnecting the battery.*

2 Electrical troubleshooting - general information

A typical electrical circuit consists of an electrical component, any switches, relays, motors, fuses, fusible links or circuit breakers related to that component and the wiring and electrical connectors that link the component to both the battery and the chassis. To help

you pinpoint an electrical circuit problem, wiring diagrams are included at the end of this Chapter.

Before tackling any troublesome electrical circuit, first study the appropriate wiring diagrams to get a complete understanding of what makes up that individual circuit. Trouble spots, for instance, can often be narrowed down by noting if other components related to the circuit are operating properly. If several components or circuits fail at one time, chances are the problem is in a fuse or ground connection, because several circuits are often routed through the same fuse and ground connections.

Electrical problems usually stem from simple causes, such as loose or corroded connections, a blown fuse, a melted fusible link or a bad relay. Visually inspect the condition of all fuses, wires and connections in a problem circuit before troubleshooting it.

If testing instruments are going to be utilized, use the diagrams to plan ahead of time where you will make the necessary connections in order to accurately pinpoint the trouble spot.

The basic tools needed for electrical troubleshooting include a circuit tester or voltmeter (a 12-volt bulb with a set of test leads can also be used), a continuity tester, which includes a bulb, battery and set of test leads, and a jumper wire, preferably with a circuit breaker incorporated, which can be used to bypass electrical components.

Before attempting to locate a problem with test instruments, use the wiring diagram(s) to decide where to make the connections.

Voltage checks

Voltage checks should be performed if a circuit is not functioning properly. Connect one lead of a circuit tester to either the negative battery terminal or a known good ground. Connect the other lead to an electrical connector in the circuit being tested, preferably nearest to the battery or fuse. If the bulb of the tester lights, voltage is present, which means that the part of the circuit between the electrical connector and the battery is problem free. Continue checking the rest of the circuit in the same fashion. When you reach a point at which no voltage is present, the problem lies between that point and the last test point with voltage. Most of the time the problem can be traced to a loose connection. **Note:** *Keep in mind that some circuits receive voltage only when the ignition key is in the Accessory or Run position.*

Finding a short

One method of finding shorts in a circuit is to remove the fuse and connect a test light or voltmeter in its place to the fuse terminals. There should be no voltage present in the circuit. Move the wiring harness from side-to-side while watching the test light. If the bulb

12

3.1a The passenger compartment fuse block is located on the right side of the instrument panel and becomes accessible after removing the cover

3.1b There are two engine compartment fuse blocks, one located on the right side by the coolant reservoir . . .

3.1c . . . and another is located on the left side next to the windshield washer fluid reservoir - both fuse blocks contain fuses and relays

goes on, there is a short to ground somewhere in that area, probably where the insulation has rubbed through. The same test can be performed on each component in the circuit, even a switch.

Ground check

Perform a ground test to check whether a component is properly grounded. Disconnect the battery and connect one lead of a self-powered test light, known as a continuity tester, to a known good ground. Connect the other lead to the wire or ground connection being tested. If the bulb goes on, the ground is good. If the bulb does not go on, the ground is not good.

Continuity check

A continuity check is done to determine if there are any breaks in a circuit - if it is passing electricity properly. With the circuit off (no power in the circuit), a self-powered continuity tester can be used to check the circuit. Connect the test leads to both ends of the circuit (or to the "power" end and a good ground), and if the test light comes on the circuit is passing current properly. If the light doesn't come on, there is a break somewhere in the circuit. The same procedure can be used to test a switch, by connecting the continuity tester to the switch terminals. With the switch turned On, the test light should come on.

Finding an open circuit

When diagnosing for possible open circuits, it is often difficult to locate them by sight because oxidation or terminal misalignment are hidden by the electrical connectors. Merely wiggling an electrical connector on a sensor or in the wiring harness may correct the open circuit condition. Remember this when an open circuit is indicated when troubleshooting a circuit. Intermittent problems may also be caused by oxidized or loose connections.

Electrical troubleshooting is simple if you keep in mind that all electrical circuits are basically electricity running from the battery, through the wires, switches, relays, fuses and fusible links to each electrical component

(light bulb, motor, etc.) and to ground, from which it is passed back to the battery. Any electrical problem is an interruption in the flow of electricity to and from the battery.

3   Fuses - general information

Refer to illustrations 3.1a, 3.1b, 3.1c and 3.3

1   The electrical circuits of the vehicle are protected by a combination of fuses, circuit breakers and fusible links. The fuse blocks are located under a cover on the right end of the instrument panel and in the engine compartment **(see illustrations)**.

2   Each of the fuses is designed to protect a specific circuit, and the various circuits are identified on the fuse panel itself.

3   Miniaturized fuses are employed in the fuse block. These compact fuses, with blade terminal design, allow fingertip removal and replacement. If an electrical component fails, always check the fuse first. The easiest way to check fuses is with a test light. Check for power at the exposed terminal tips of each fuse. If power is present on one side of the fuse but not the other, the fuse is blown. A blown fuse can also be confirmed by visually inspecting it **(see illustration)**.

4   Be sure to replace blown fuses with the correct type. Fuses of different ratings are physically interchangeable, but only fuses of

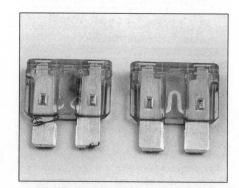

3.3 When a fuse blows, the element between the terminal melts - the fuse on the left is blown, the fuse on the right is good

the proper rating should be used. Replacing a fuse with one of a higher or lower value than specified is not recommended. Each electrical circuit needs a specific amount of protection. The amperage value of each fuse is molded into the fuse body.

If the replacement fuse immediately fails, don't replace it again until the cause of the problem is isolated and corrected. In most cases, the cause will be a short circuit in the wiring caused by a broken or deteriorated wire.

4   Fusible links - general information

Some circuits are protected by fusible links. Fusible links are circuit protection devices that are part of the wiring harness itself, that are designed to melt and open the circuit when a short causes excessive current flow. Fusible links are used in circuits which are not ordinarily fused, such as the ignition circuit.

Although the fusible links appear to be a heavier gauge than the wire they are protecting, the appearance is due to the thick insulation. All fusible links are several wire gauges smaller than the wire they are designed to protect.

Fusible links cannot be repaired, but a new link of the same size wire can be put in its place. The procedure is as follows:

a)   Disconnect the negative cable from the battery.

b)   Disconnect the fusible link from the wiring harness.

c)   Cut the damaged fusible link out of the wiring just behind the electrical connector.

d)   Strip the insulation back approximately 1/2-inch.

e)   Position the electrical connector on the new fusible link and crimp it into place.

f)   Use rosin core solder at each end of the new link to obtain a good solder joint.

g)   Use plenty of electrical tape around the soldered joint. No wires should be exposed.

h)   Connect the battery ground cable. Test the circuit for proper operation.

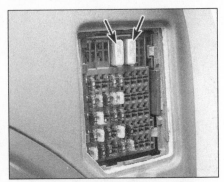

5.1 Circuit breakers for the power window and power seat circuits are located in the interior compartment fuse block

5.2 Perform a continuity test with an ohmmeter to check a circuit breaker - no reading (infinite resistance) indicates a bad circuit breaker

6.4 Most relays are marked on the outside to easily identify the control circuit and power circuits

5 Circuit breakers - general information

Refer to illustrations 5.1 and 5.2

Circuit breakers protect components such as power windows, power seats and headlights. Several circuit breakers are located in the interior fuse box **(see illustration)**. On some models the circuit breaker resets itself automatically, so an electrical overload in the circuit will cause it to fail momentarily, then come back on. If the circuit doesn't come back on, check it immediately. Once the condition is corrected, the circuit breaker will resume its normal function. Some circuit breakers have a button on top and must be reset manually.

To test a circuit breaker , simply use an ohmmeter to check continuity between the terminals. A reading of zero to 1.0 ohms indicates a good circuit breaker . No reading on the meter indicates a bad circuit breaker **(see illustration)**.

6 Relays - general information and testing

General information

1   Several electrical accessories in the vehicle, such as the fuel injection system, horns, starter, and fog lamps use relays to transmit the electrical signal to the component. Relays use a low-current circuit (the control circuit) to open and close a high-current circuit (the power circuit). If the relay is defective, that component will not operate properly. The various relays are mounted in engine compartment **(see illustration 3.1b)** and several locations throughout the vehicle. If a faulty relay is suspected, it can be removed and tested using the procedure below or by a dealer service department or a repair shop. Defective relays must be replaced as a unit.

Testing

Refer to illustration 6.4

2   It's best to refer to the wiring diagram for the circuit to determine the proper hook-ups for the relay you're testing. However, if you're not able to determine the correct hook-up from the wiring diagrams, you may be able to determine the test hook-ups from the information that follows.

3   On most relays, two of the terminals are the relay's control circuit (they connect to the relay coil which, when energized, closes the large contacts to complete the circuit). The other terminals are the power circuit (they are connected together within the relay when the control-circuit coil is energized).

4   Most relays are marked as an aid to help you determine which terminals are the control circuit and which are the power circuit **(see illustration)**.

5   Connect a fused jumper wire between one of the two control circuit terminals and the positive battery terminal. Connect another jumper wire between the other control circuit terminal and ground. When the connections are made, the relay should click. On some relays, polarity may be critical, so, if the relay doesn't click, try swapping the jumper wires on the control circuit terminals.

6   With the jumper wires connected, check for continuity between the power circuit terminals as indicated by the markings on the relay.

7   If the relay fails any of the above tests, replace it.

7 Turn signal/hazard flasher - check and replacement

Refer to illustration 7.1

Warning: *The models covered by this manual are equipped with airbags. Always disable the airbag system before working in the vicinity of the impact sensors, steering column or instrument panel to avoid the possibility of accidental deployment of the airbag(s), which could cause personal injury (see Section 26). The yellow wires and connectors routed through the instrument panel are for this system. Do not use electrical test equipment on these yellow wires or tamper with them in any way while working under the instrument panel.*

Caution: *On models equipped with a Theftlock audio system, be sure the lockout feature is turned off before performing any procedure which requires disconnecting the battery.*

Check

1   The models covered in this manual use a single combination turn signal and hazard flasher which is mounted in a junction block to the left of the steering column under the instrument panel **(see illustration)**.

2   When the flasher unit is functioning properly, an audible click can be heard during its operation. If the turn signals fail on one side or the other and the flasher unit does not make its characteristic clicking sound, a faulty turn signal bulb is indicated.

3   If both turn signals fail to blink, the problem may be due to a blown fuse, a faulty flasher unit, a broken switch or a loose or open connection. If a quick check of the fuse box indicates that the turn signal fuse has blown, check the wiring for a short before installing a new fuse.

Replacement

4   Remove the lower sound insulating panel (see Chapter 11 if necessary).

5   Disconnect the electrical connector and remove the flasher unit from the firewall.

6   Make sure that the replacement unit is identical to the original. Compare the old one to the new one before installing it.

7   Installation is the reverse of removal.

7.1 The combination turn signal and hazard flasher (arrow) is mounted to the firewall just to the left of the steering column under the instrument panel

12

8.2 Use a small screwdriver to pry off the steering column trim cover

8.3a Remove the snap-ring and lift the airbag coil off

8.3b Use a special tool (available at most auto parts stores) to compress the lock plate for access to the retaining ring

8   Steering column switches - removal and installation

Warning: *The models covered by this manual are equipped with airbags. Always disable the airbag system before working in the vicinity of the impact sensors, steering column or instrument panel to avoid the possibility of accidental deployment of the airbag(s), which could cause personal injury (see Section 26). The yellow wires and connectors routed through the instrument panel are for this system. Do not use electrical test equipment on these yellow wires or tamper with them in any way while working under the instrument panel.*

Caution: *On models equipped with a Theftlock audio system, be sure the lockout feature is turned off before performing any procedure which requires disconnecting the battery.*

Removal

Refer to illustrations 8.2, 8.3a, 8.3b, 8.4, 8.5, 8.6a, 8.6b, 8.6c and 8.8

1   Detach the cable from the negative battery terminal and disable the airbag system (see Section 26).
2   Remove the steering wheel (see Chapter 10) and the steering column trim cover **(see illustration)**.
3   Remove the airbag coil retaining snap-ring and remove the coil assembly; let the coil

hang by the wiring harness. Remove the wave washer. Using a lock plate removal tool, depress the lock plate for access to the retaining ring **(see illustrations)**. Use a small screwdriver to pry the retaining ring out of the groove in the steering shaft and remove the lock plate.
4   Use a small screwdriver to remove the hazard warning knob **(see illustration)**.
5   Remove the turn signal cancel cam **(see illustration)**.
6   Disconnect the electrical connector from the turn signal lever then pull the lever straight out to detach from the switch assembly. Detach the retaining screws securing the dimmer switch and position it to the side, then remove the turn signal switch mounting screws **(see illustrations)**.
7   Remove the lower steering column trim panel and the knee bolster as described in Chapter 11.
8   Locate the turn signal switch electrical connector and unplug it **(see illustration)**. Remove the wiring protector.
9   Pull the wiring harness and electrical connector up through the steering column and remove the switch assembly.

Installation

Refer to illustrations 8.14 and 8.15

10   Feed the turn signal switch connector and wiring harness down through the column. Use a section of mechanics wire to pull it through, if necessary.

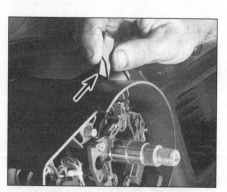

8.4 Remove the hazard warning knob (arrow)

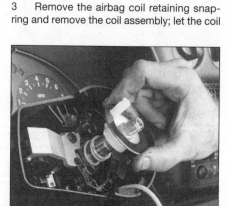

8.5 Remove the cancel cam assembly

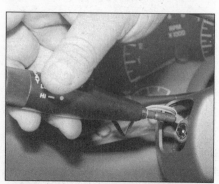

8.6a Grasp the turn signal lever securely and pull it straight out to detach it

8.6b Remove the dimmer switch retaining screws (arrows), then position it to the side

8.6c Place the switch in the right turn position to access all the switch retaining screws (arrows)

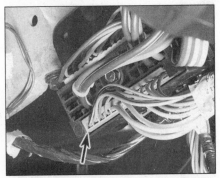

8.8 The turn signal switch electrical connector is located under the dash near the steering column

11 Plug in the connector and replace the wiring protector.

12 Seat the turn signal switch on the column and install the turn signal switch mounting screws and lever arm. Install the hazard knob and multi-function lever. Press the multi-function lever straight in until it snaps in place.

13 Install the cancel cam and the lock plate. Depress the lock plate and install the retaining ring.

14 If necessary, center the airbag coil as follows (it will only become uncentered if the spring lock is depressed and the hub rotated with the coil off the column) **(see illustration)**:

a) *Turn the coil over and depress the spring lock.*

b) *Rotate the hub in the direction of the arrow until it stops.*

c) *Rotate the hub in the opposite direction 2-1/2 turns and release the spring lock.*

15 Install the wave washer and the airbag coil **(see illustration)**. Pull the slack out of the airbag coil lower wiring harness to keep it tight through the steering column, or it may be cut when the steering wheel is turned. Install the airbag coil retaining snap-ring.

16 The remainder of installation is the reverse of removal.

---

9 **Ignition switch and key lock cylinder - removal and installation**

Warning: *The models covered by this manual are equipped with airbags. Always disable the airbag system before working in the vicinity of the impact sensors, steering column or instrument panel to avoid the possibility of accidental deployment of the airbag(s), which could cause personal injury (see Section 26). The yellow wires and connectors routed through the instrument panel are for this system. Do not use electrical test equipment on these yellow wires or tamper with them in any way while working under the instrument panel.*
Caution: *On models equipped with a Theftlock audio system, be sure the lockout feature is turned off before performing any*

8.14 To center the airbag coil, depress the spring lock (arrow); rotate the hub in the direction of the arrow until it stops; back the hub off 2-1/2 turns and release the spring lock

procedure which requires disconnecting the battery.

Lock cylinder

Refer to illustrations 9.3 and 9.4

1 The lock cylinder is located on the upper right-hand side of the steering column. It should be removed only in the Run position, otherwise damage to the warning buzzer switch may occur.

2 Remove the steering wheel (Chapter 10) and turn signal switch (see Section 8). **Note:** *The turn signal switch need not be fully removed provided that it is pushed to the rear far enough for it to be slipped over the end of the shaft. Do not pull the harness out of the column.*

3 Insert the key and place the lock cylinder in the Run position, then use needle-nose pliers or a small screwdriver to remove the buzzer switch **(see illustration)**.

4 Remove the lock cylinder retaining screw **(see illustration)**.

5 Remove the lock cylinder by turning the key to the Start position, then pulling the assembly straight out.

6 To install, rotate the lock cylinder and align the cylinder key with the keyway in the steering column housing.

7 Push the lock all the way in and install the retaining screw.

8 Install the remaining components, referring to the appropriate Sections.

9.4 The lock cylinder is held in place by a Torx-head screw (arrow)

8.15 When properly installed, the airbag coil will be centered with the marks aligned (circle) and the tab fitted between the projections on the top of steering column (arrow)

9.3 Lift off the buzzer switch and clip with needle-nose pliers or a small screwdriver

Ignition switch

Refer to illustrations 9.12a, 9.12b, 9.13a and 19.13b

9 Disconnect the negative cable at the battery and disable the airbag system as described in Section 26.

10 Place the ignition switch in the Lock position. If the key lock cylinder has been removed, pull the actuating rod up until a definite stop can be felt, then move it down one detent.

11 Remove the lower steering column trim panel from beneath the steering column.

12 Remove the bolts that secure the steering column to the dash assembly **(see illustrations)**, then carefully lower the

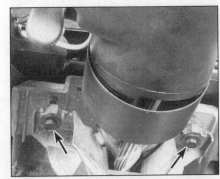

9.12a Remove the bolts (arrows) securing the steering column to the lower edge of the instrument panel

12

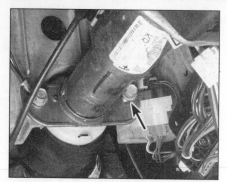

9.12b Detach one bolt (arrow) at the base of the steering column to help lower the column enough to access the ignition switch

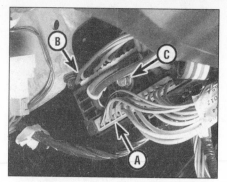

9.13a Disconnect the turn signal switch connector (A), the dimmer switch connector (B) and the ignition switch connector retaining bolt (C)

9.13b After the steering column has been lowered, remove the ignition switch retaining screws (arrows)

steering column down and rest the steering wheel on the seat. On column shift models, remove the shift indicator cable clip and detach the PRNDL adjuster bracket.

13   Disconnect the turn signal switch and the dimmer switch electrical connectors from the ignition switch connector at the base of the steering column, then remove the ignition switch connector **(see illustration)**. Remove the ignition switch retaining screws **(see illustration)** and lift the switch out of the steering column jacket. On floor shift models, detach the park lock cable from the ignition switch.

14   Prior to installation, make sure the ignition switch is in the Lock position.

15   Connect the actuating rod to the switch.

16   Press the switch into position and install the screws.

17   The remainder of the installation is the reverse of the removal. Raise the steering column into position and install and tighten the nuts to 20 ft-lbs. Make sure the switch is actuated when the ignition key is turned to the Start position. If it doesn't, loosen the switch screws and adjust the position of the switch on the steering column.

10   Headlight switch - removal and installation

Refer to illustrations 10.3 and 10.4
Warning: *The models covered by this manual*

are equipped with airbags. Always disable the airbag system before working in the vicinity of the impact sensors, steering column or instrument panel to avoid the possibility of accidental deployment of the airbag(s), which could cause personal injury (see Section 26). The yellow wires and connectors routed through the instrument panel are for this system. Do not use electrical test equipment on these yellow wires or tamper with them in any way while working under the instrument panel.*
Caution: *On models equipped with a Theftlock audio system, be sure the lockout feature is turned off before performing any procedure which requires disconnecting the battery.*
Note: *To remove the dimmer switch follow the steering column switch removal procedures (see Section 8).*

1   Detach the cable from the negative battery terminal and disable the airbag system (see Section 26).

2   Remove the instrument cluster bezel (see Chapter 11).

3   Pry out the defogger grille from the corner of the instrument panel **(see illustration)**.

4   Using a small screwdriver detach the retaining clips securing the switch **(see illustration)**.

5   Disconnect the electrical connector and remove the switch from the vehicle.

6   Installation is the reverse of removal.

11   Radio and speakers - removal and installation

Warning: *The models covered by this manual are equipped with airbags. Always disable the airbag system before working in the vicinity of the impact sensors, steering column or instrument panel to avoid the possibility of accidental deployment of the airbag(s), which could cause personal injury (see Section 26). The yellow wires and connectors routed through the instrument panel are for this system. Do not use electrical test equipment on these yellow wires or tamper with them in any way while working under the instrument panel.*
Caution: *On models equipped with a Theftlock audio system, be sure the lockout feature is turned off before performing any procedure which requires disconnecting the battery.*

Radio

Refer to illustrations 11.3a and 11.3b

1   Detach the cable from the negative battery terminal and disable the airbag system (see Section 26).

2   Remove the instrument cluster bezel (see Chapter 11).

3   Remove the screws, pull the radio out and disconnect the electrical connection and antenna lead **(see illustrations)**.

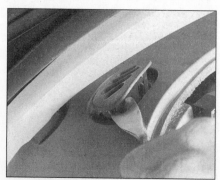

10.3 Using a small screwdriver or a trim removal tool pry out the defogger grille from the corner of the instrument panel

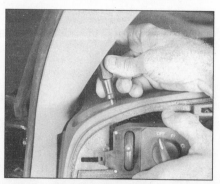

10.4 Depress the switch locking tabs and pull the switch outward to remove it

11.3a Remove the bolts (arrows) securing the radio

11.3b Pull the radio out, support it and unplug the connectors

11.7 Remove the screws (arrows), detach the speaker and unplug the electrical connector

12.2 Detach the antenna lead from the antenna base by pulling the cable straight out

4   Remove the radio from the instrument panel.
5   Installation is the reverse of removal.

Front speakers

Refer to illustration 11.7
6   Remove the front door trim panel (see Chapter 11).
7   Remove the speaker retaining bolts. Disconnect the electrical connector and remove the speaker from the vehicle (**see illustration**).
8   Installation is the reverse of removal.

Rear speakers

9   Remove the rear seat from the vehicle (see Chapter 11).
10   Detach the rear seat belts through the slot in the rear parcel shelf.
11   Pry up the plastic clips securing the rear parcel shelf. Then lift up and out to remove it from the vehicle.
12   Remove the speaker retaining screws. Disconnect the electrical connector and remove the speaker from the vehicle.
13   Installation is the reverse of removal.

12   Antenna - removal and installation

Caution: *On models equipped with a Theftlock audio system, be sure the lockout feature is turned off before performing any procedure which requires disconnecting the battery.*

Fixed antenna

Refer to illustrations 12.2, 12.3 and 12.4
1   Working in the trunk, pry out the plastic clips securing the passenger side trunk finishing panels to allow access to the backside of the antenna.
2   Disconnect the antenna lead from the antenna base (**see illustration**).
3   Use a small wrench and remove the antenna mast (**see illustration**).
4   Using a pair of snap-ring pliers or similar tool, detach the antenna base retaining nut

and remove the antenna base assembly from the vehicle (**see illustration**).
5   Installation is the reverse of removal.

Power antenna mast

Note: *At least two people should perform this task.*
6   Remove the antenna mast retaining nut (**see illustration 12.4**).
7   With one person controlling the ignition switch and the second person holding the antenna mast, turn the ignition key and the radio to the ON position. This will enable the antenna mast to unwind itself from the motor assembly.
8   When installing the antenna mast insert the antenna cable with the teeth facing the antenna motor. Then have your assistant turn the ignition key and the radio to the ON position. This will enable the antenna mast to wind itself back into the motor assembly.
9   The remainder of the installation is the reverse of removal.

Power antenna motor

10   Remove the antenna mast retaining nut (**see illustration 12.4**).
11   Working in the trunk, pry out the plastic clips securing the passenger side trunk finishing panels to allow access to the antenna motor.
12   Detach the motor retaining bolts.

12.3 Use a small wrench to remove the antenna mast

Disconnect the electrical connector, antenna lead and the antenna ground strap then remove the antenna motor from the vehicle.
13   Installation is the reverse of removal.

13   Rear window defogger - check and repair

1   The rear window defogger consists of a number of horizontal elements baked onto the glass surface.
2   Small breaks in the element can be repaired without removing the rear window.

Check

Refer to illustrations 13.5 and 13.6
3   Turn the ignition switch and defogger system switches to the ON position.
4   Using a voltmeter, place the positive probe against the battery feed terminal and the negative probe against the negative (ground) bus bar. The positive terminal is located on the drivers side and the negative terminal is located on the passengers side. If battery voltage is not indicated, check the fuse, defogger switch and related wiring.
5   When measuring voltage during the next two tests, wrap a piece of aluminum foil around the tip of the voltmeter positive

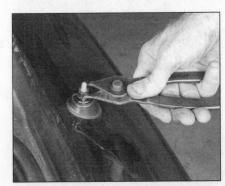

12.4 The antenna base retaining nut can be removed using a pair of snap-ring pliers or similar tool

13.5 When measuring the voltage at the rear window defogger grid, wrap a piece of aluminum foil around the positive probe of the voltmeter and press the foil against the wire with your finger

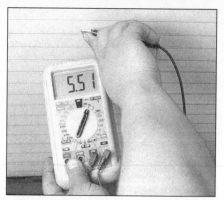

13.6 To determine if a heating element has broken, check the voltage at the center of each element - if the voltage is 6-volts, the element is unbroken

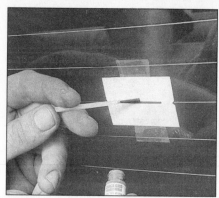

13.13 To use a defogger repair kit, apply masking tape to the inside of the window at the damaged area, then brush on the special conductive coating

probe and press the foil against the heating element with your finger **(see illustration)**.

6   Place the negative lead against the negative (ground) bus bar. Check the voltage at the center of each heating element **(see illustration)**. If the voltage is 6-volts, the element is okay (there is no break). If the voltage is 10-volts or more, the element is broken somewhere between the mid-point and ground. If the voltage is 0-volts the element is broken between the mid-point and the positive side.

7   To find the break, slide the probe toward the positive side. The point at which the voltmeter deflects from zero to several volts is the point at which the heating element is broken. **Note:** *If the heating element is not broken, the voltmeter will indicate 12-volts at the positive side and gradually decrease to 0-volts as you slide the positive probe toward the ground side.*

Repair

Refer to illustration 13.13

8   Repair the break in the element using a repair kit specifically recommended for this purpose, such as Dupont paste No. 4817 (or equivalent). Included in this kit is plastic conductive epoxy.

9   Prior to repairing a break, turn off the system and allow it to cool off for a few minutes.

10   Lightly buff the element area with fine steel wool, then clean it thoroughly with rubbing alcohol.

11   Use masking tape to mask off the area being repaired.

12   Thoroughly mix the epoxy, following the instructions provided with the repair kit.

13   Apply the epoxy material to the slit in the masking tape, overlapping the undamaged area about 3/4-inch on either end **(see illustration)**.

14   Allow the repair to cure for 24 hours before removing the tape and using the system.

14 Headlight bulb - replacement

Refer to illustration 14.3
Warning: *Halogen gas filled bulbs are under pressure and may shatter if the surface is scratched or the bulb is dropped. Wear eye protection and handle the bulbs carefully, grasping only the base whenever possible. Do not touch the surface of the bulb with your fingers because the oil from your skin could cause it to overheat and fail prematurely. If you do touch the bulb surface, clean it with rubbing alcohol.*

1   Open the hood.
2   Remove the headlight housing (see Section 15).
3   Rotate the headlight bulb holder counterclockwise as viewed from the rear **(see illustration)**.
4   Withdraw the bulb assembly from the headlight housing.
5   Remove the bulb from the bulb holder by pulling it straight out.
6   If its necessary to replace the bulb holder, simply unplug the electrical connector and replace it with a new one.
7   Without touching the glass with your

14.3 Rotate the headlight bulb holder counterclockwise and pull the bulb socket assembly out of the housing - when installing the new bulb, don't touch the surface (clean it with rubbing alcohol if you do)

bare fingers, insert the new bulb into the socket assembly and then lock the bulb holder into the place by aligning the tabs with the headlight housing and rotating the bulb holder clockwise until stops.

8   Reinstall the headlight housing and test the headlight operation, then close the hood.

15 Headlight housing - removal and installation

Refer to illustrations 15.1 and 15.2
Warning: *The models covered by this manual are equipped with airbags. Always disable the airbag system before working in the vicinity of the impact sensors, steering column or instrument panel to avoid the possibility of accidental deployment of the airbag(s), which could cause personal injury (see Section 26). The yellow wires and connectors routed through the instrument panel are for this system. Do not use electrical test equipment on these yellow wires or tamper with them in any way while working under the instrument panel.*

1   Remove the radiator baffle retaining clip and position the top of the baffle aside **(see illustration)**.

15.1 Detach the retaining clip securing the radiator air baffle

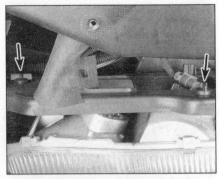

15.2 Working behind the headlight housing, detach the headlight housing retaining screws (arrows)

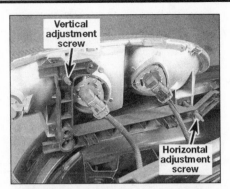

16.1 The headlight adjustment screws (arrows) can be accessed from behind the headlight housing - a Torx-head tool will be required for making headlight adjustments (headlight housing removed for clarity purposes only)

2   Remove the thumbscrews securing the headlight housing to the headlight housing support **(see illustration)**.

3   Pull the inboard end out slightly, then slide the headlight housing towards the center of the vehicle to dislodge the retaining clips from the outer edge.

4   Disconnect the headlight bulbs (see Section 14) and the turn signal bulb from the headlight housing and remove the housing from the vehicle.

5   The remainder of the installation is the reverse of removal.

16   Headlights - adjustment

Refer to illustrations 16.1 and 16.3
Caution: *The headlights must be aimed correctly. If adjusted incorrectly they could blind the driver of an oncoming vehicle and*

cause a serious accident or seriously reduce your ability to see the road. The headlights should be checked for proper aim every 12 months and any time a new headlight is installed or front end body work is performed. It should be emphasized that the following procedure is only an interim step which will provide temporary adjustment until the headlights can be adjusted by a properly equipped shop.

1   Headlights have two spring-loaded adjusting screws, one on the top controlling up-and-down movement and one on the side controlling left-and-right movement **(see illustration)**.

2   There are several methods of adjusting the headlights. The simplest method requires a blank wall 25 feet in front of the vehicle and a level floor.

3   Position masking tape vertically on the wall in reference to the vehicle centerline and the centerlines of both headlights **(see illustration)**.

4   Position a horizontal tape line in reference to the centerline of all the headlights. **Note:** *It may be easier to position the tape on the wall with the vehicle parked only a few inches away.*

5   Adjustment should be made with the vehicle sitting level, the gas tank half-full and no unusually heavy load in the vehicle.

6   Starting with the low beam adjustment, position the high intensity zone so it is two inches below the horizontal line and two inches to the right of the headlight vertical line. Adjustment is made by turning the top adjusting screw clockwise to raise the beam and counterclockwise to lower the beam. The adjusting screw on the side should be used in the same manner to move the beam left or right.

7   With the high beams on, the high intensity zone should be vertically centered with the exact center just below the horizontal line. **Note:** *It may not be possible to position the headlight aim exactly for both high and low beams. If a compromise must be made, keep in mind that the low beams are the most used and have the greatest effect on safety.*

8   Have the headlights adjusted by a dealer service department or service station at the earliest opportunity.

17   Bulb replacement

Front turn signal and parking lights

Refer to illustration 17.2

1   Remove the headlight housing as described in Section 15.

2   Depress the socket retaining clip and twist the bulb socket a quarter turn counterclockwise, then remove the bulb assembly from the housing **(see illustration)**.

3   The defective bulb can then be twisted out of the socket and replaced.

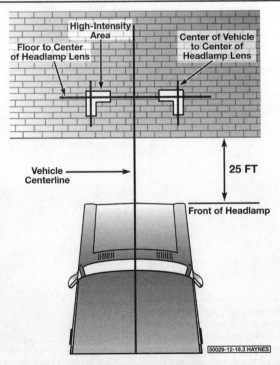

16.3 Headlight aiming details

High-Intensity Area

Floor to Center of Headlamp Lens

Center of Vehicle to Center of Headlamp Lens

Vehicle Centerline

25 FT

Front of Headlamp

50029-12-19.3 HAYNES

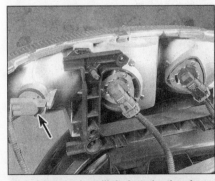

17.2 After the headlight housing has been removed, the front turn signal/parking light bulb can be replaced by depressing the socket retaining clip (arrow) and rotating it counterclockwise

12

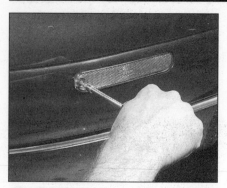

17.4 Remove the side marker/turn signal housing retaining screw (arrow) . . .

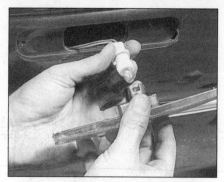

17.5 . . . then rotate the bulb socket counterclockwise to separate it from the lens

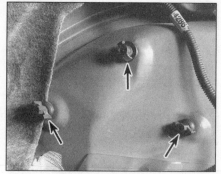

17.9 With the trunk compartment rear finishing panel removed, detach the plastic retaining nuts (arrow) securing the tail light housing

Front side marker lights

Refer to illustrations 17.4 and 17.5

4   Detach the side marker light retaining screw **(see illustration).**
5   Pull the side marker light outward. Then twist the bulb socket a quarter turn counterclockwise and remove the bulb assembly from the side marker light lens **(see illustration).**
6   The defective bulb can then be pulled straight out of the socket and replaced.
7   Installation of the lens is the reverse of removal.

Rear turn signal, brake, tail and back-up lights

Refer to illustrations 17.9 and 17.11

8   Detach the plastic clips securing the trunk compartment rear finishing panel, then remove the panel from the vehicle.
9   Working from the inside of the trunk detach the retaining nuts securing the rear tail light housing **(see illustration).**
10   Pull the tail light assembly outward to access the tail light bulbs.
11   Depress the socket retaining clip and twist the bulb socket a quarter turn counterclockwise, then remove the bulb assembly from the housing **(see illustration).**
12   The defective bulb can then be twisted out of the socket and replaced.
13   Installation of the tail light housing is the reverse of removal.

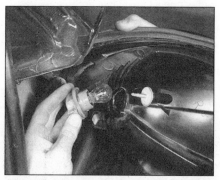

17.11 Squeeze the clip then rotate and lift the bulb holder out of the housing - push in and rotate the bulb to remove it

License plate light

Refer to illustration 17.14

14   Detach the retaining screws which secure the lens to the trunk lid **(see illustration).**
15   The defective bulb can then be pulled straight out of the socket and replaced.
16   Installation of the lens is the reverse of removal.

High-mounted brake light

Refer to illustration 17.18

17   The high-mounted brake light bulb can be accessed from the trunk compartment.
18   Reaching up under the high mounted brake light, depress the socket retaining clip and twist the bulb socket a quarter turn

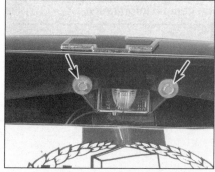

17.14 Remove the screws (arrows) to access the license plate light bulb

counterclockwise, then remove the bulb assembly from the housing **(see illustration).**
19   The defective bulb can then be twisted out of the socket and replaced.
20   Installation is the reverse of removal.

Interior light

Refer to illustration 17.21

21   Using a small screwdriver, remove the lens and replace the bulb **(see illustration).**

Instrument cluster illumination

Refer to illustration 17.22

22   To gain access to the instrument cluster illumination lights, the instrument cluster will have to be removed (see Section 19). The bulbs can then be removed and replaced from the rear of the cluster **(see illustration).**

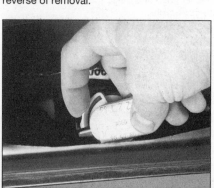

17.18 The high-mounted brake light bulb can be reached through the access hole in the trunk compartment

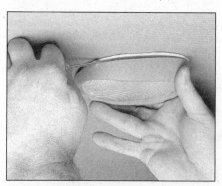

17.21 Pry off the interior light lens to access the bulb

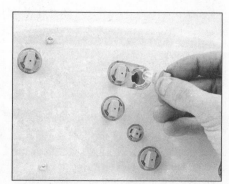

17.22 Rotate the bulb and lift it out of the cluster

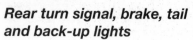

19.3 Remove the instrument cluster retaining screw (arrows)

18 Daytime Running Lights (DRL) - general information

The Daytime Running Lights (DRL) system used on all Canadian and later US models illuminates the headlights whenever the engine is running. The only exception is with the engine running and the parking brake engaged. Once the parking brake is released, the lights will remain on as long as the ignition switch is on, even if the parking brake is later applied.

The DRL system supplies reduced power to the headlights so they will be bright enough for daytime visibility while prolonging headlight life.

19 Instrument cluster - removal and installation

Refer to illustration 19.3

Warning: *The models covered by this manual are equipped with airbags. Always disable the airbag system before working in the vicinity of the impact sensors, steering column or instrument panel to avoid the possibility of accidental deployment of the airbag(s), which could cause personal injury (see Section 26). The yellow wires and connectors routed through the instrument panel are for this system. Do not use electrical test equipment on*

these yellow wires or tamper with them in any way while working under the instrument panel.

Caution: *On models equipped with a Theftlock audio system, be sure the lockout feature is turned off before performing any procedure which requires disconnecting the battery.*

1   Detach the cable from the negative battery terminal and disable the airbag system (see Section 26).
2   Remove instrument cluster bezel (see Chapter 11).
3   Remove the screws securing each side of the instrument cluster **(see illustration)**.
4   Tilt the top of the instrument cluster inward towards the center of the passenger compartment, then detach the electrical connector from the back of the cluster.
5   Disengage the instrument cluster lower locating pins from the instrument panel and remove it from the vehicle
6   Installation is the reverse of removal.

20 Wiper motor - check and replacement

Check

Note: *Refer to the wiring diagrams for wire colors and locations in the following checks. Keep in mind that power wires are generally larger in diameter and brighter colors, where ground wires are usually smaller in diameter and darker colors. When checking for voltage, probe a grounded 12-volt test light to each terminal at a connector until it lights; this verifies voltage (power) at the terminal.*

1   If the wipers work slowly, make sure the battery is in good condition and has a strong charge (see Chapter 1). If the battery is in good condition, remove the wiper motor (see below) and operate the wiper arms by hand. Check for binding linkage and pivots. Lubricate or repair the linkage or pivots as necessary. Reinstall the wiper motor. If the wipers still operate slowly, check for loose or corroded connections, especially the ground connection. If all connections look OK, replace the motor.
2   If the wipers fail to operate when activated, check the fuse. If the fuse is OK, connect a jumper wire between the wiper motor and ground, then retest. If the motor works

now, repair the ground connection. If the motor still doesn't work, turn the wiper switch to the HI position and check for voltage at the motor. If there's voltage at the motor, remove the motor and check it off the vehicle with fused jumper wires from the battery. If the motor now works, check for binding linkage (see Step 1 above). If the motor still doesn't work, replace it. If there's no voltage at the motor, check for voltage at the wiper control module. If there's voltage at the wiper control module and no voltage at the at the wiper motor, check the switch for continuity. If the switch is OK, the wiper control module is probably bad.
3   If the interval (delay) function is inoperative, check the continuity of all the wiring between the switch and wiper control module. If the wiring is OK, check the resistance of the delay control knob of the multi-function switch (see Section 8). If the delay control knob is within the specified resistance, replace the wiper control module.
4   If the wipers stop at the position they're in when the switch is turned off (fail to park), check for voltage at the park feed wire of the wiper motor connector when the wiper switch is OFF but the ignition is ON. If no voltage is present, check for an open circuit between the wiper motor and the fuse panel.
5   If the wipers won't shut off unless the ignition is OFF, disconnect the wiring from the wiper control switch. If the wipers stop, replace the switch. If the wipers keep running, there's a defective limit switch in the motor; replace the motor.
6   If the wipers won't retract below the hoodline, check for mechanical obstructions in the wiper linkage or on the vehicle's body which would prevent the wipers from parking. If there are no obstructions, check the wiring between the switch and motor for continuity. If the wiring is OK, replace the wiper motor.

Replacement

Refer to illustrations 20.7, 20.8a, 20.8b, 20.8c, 20.10a, 20.10b and 20.12

7   Pry off the cover from the wiper arm retaining nuts, unscrew the nuts, detach the washer hoses and remove both wiper arms **(see illustration)**.
8   Remove the retaining screws, the washer hose and detach the cowl cover **(see illustrations)**.

20.7 Use a small screwdriver to pry off the wiper arm retaining nut cover, then remove the washer hose and the nut (arrow) and pull the arm straight off its splined shaft

20.8a Remove the screws (arrows) securing the outer edges of the cowl cover . . .

20.8b . . . then remove the screws (arrows) securing the center of the cowl cover

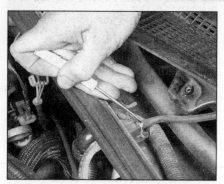

20.8c Lift the cowl cover up slightly and disconnect the washer hose

20.10a Remove the wiper motor linkage retaining bolts (arrows) from the drivers side of the cowl . . .

20.10b . . .and at the center of the cowl (arrow)

9   Disconnect the electrical connectors from the wiper motor.
10   Remove the wiper linkage bracket mounting bolts **(see illustrations)**.
11   Pull the linkage assembly out from the cowl, then turn it over to access the wiper motor retaining screws.
12   Remove the retaining screws and the wiper motor spindle nut **(see illustration)**. Separate the components.
13   Installation is the reverse of removal.

21 Horn - check and replacement

Check

Refer to illustration 21.4

Note: *Check the fuses before beginning electrical diagnosis.*

1   Remove the plastic air deflector surrounding the hood latch assembly and disconnect the electrical connector from the horn.
2   To test the horn(s), connect battery voltage to the horn terminal with a pair of jumper wires. If the horn doesn't sound, replace it.
3   If the horn does sound, check for voltage at the terminal when the horn button is depressed. If there's voltage at the

terminal, check for a bad ground at the horn.
4   If there's no voltage at the horn, check the relay (see Section 6). Note that most horn relays are either the four-terminal or externally grounded three-terminal type. The horn relay is located in the engine compartment fuse block on the drivers side of the vehicle **(see illustration)**.
5   If the relay is OK, check for voltage to the relay power and control circuits. If either of the circuits is not receiving voltage, inspect the wiring between the relay and the fuse panel.
6   If both relay circuits are receiving voltage, depress the horn button and check the circuit from the relay to the horn button for continuity to ground. If there's no continuity, check the circuit for an open. If there's no open circuit, replace the horn button.
7   If there's continuity to ground through the horn button, check for an open or short in the circuit from the relay to the horn.

Replacement

Refer to illustration 21.9

8   To access the horns remove the plastic air deflector surrounding the hood latch assembly.
9   Disconnect the electrical connectors and remove the bracket bolts **(see illustration)**.
10   Installation is the reverse of removal.

22 Cruise control system - description and check

Refer to illustration 22.5

1   The cruise control system maintains vehicle speed with an electronic servo motor located in the engine compartment, which is connected to the throttle linkage by a cable. The system consists of the electronic control module, brake switch, control switches, a relay, the vehicle speed sensor and associated wiring. Listed below are some general procedures that may be used to locate common cruise control problems.
2   Locate and check the fuse (see Section 3).
3   Have an assistant operate the brake lights while you check their operation (voltage from the brake light switch deactivates the cruise control).
4   If the brake lights don't come on or don't shut off, correct the problem and retest the cruise control.
5   Inspect the cable linkage between the cruise control module and the throttle linkage. The cruise control module is located on the left (drivers) inner fenderwell of the engine compartment **(see illustration)**.
6   Visually inspect the wires connected to the cruise control actuator and check for damage and broken wires.

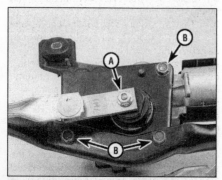

20.12 Turn the linkage assembly over to access the spindle nut (A) and the wiper motor retaining bolts (B)

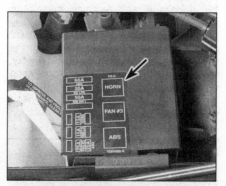

21.4 The horn relay (arrow) location is clearly marked on the engine compartment fuse block cover

21.9 Disconnect the electrical connector, remove the bolt(s) (arrows) and detach the horn(s)

22.5 The cruise control module (arrow) is located in the engine compartment on the (driver's side) inner fenderwell - check for damage to the connectors

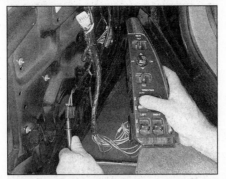

23.12 If no voltage is found at the motor with the switch depressed, check for voltage at the switch

24.6 Check for voltage at the lock solenoid while the switch is operated

7   The cruise control system uses a speed sensing device. The speed sensor is located in the transmission. To test the speed sensor see Chapter 6.

8   Test drive the vehicle to determine if the cruise control is now working. If it isn't, take it to a dealer service department · or an automotive electrical specialist for further diagnosis and repair.

23 Power window system - description and check

Refer to illustration 23.12

1   The power window system operates electric motors, mounted in the doors, which lower and raise the windows. The system consists of the control switches, the motors, regulators, glass mechanisms and associated wiring.

2   The power windows can be lowered and raised from the master control switch by the driver or by remote switches located at the individual windows. Each window has a separate motor which is reversible. The position of the control switch determines the polarity and therefore the direction of operation.

3   The circuit is protected by a fuse and a circuit breaker. Each motor is also equipped with an internal circuit breaker, this prevents one stuck window from disabling the whole system.

4   The power window system will only operate when the ignition switch is ON. In addition, many models have a window lockout switch at the master control switch which, when activated, disables the switches at the rear windows and, sometimes, the switch at the passenger's window also. Always check these items before troubleshooting a window problem.

5   These procedures are general in nature, so if you can't find the problem using them, take the vehicle to a dealer service department or other properly equipped repair facility.

6   If the power windows won't operate, always check the fuse and circuit breaker first.

7   If only the rear windows are inoperative, or if the windows only operate from the

master control switch, check the rear window lockout switch for continuity in the unlocked position. Replace it if it doesn't have continuity.

8   Check the wiring between the switches and fuse panel for continuity. Repair the wiring, if necessary.

9   If only one window is inoperative from the master control switch, try the other control switch at the window. **Note:** *This doesn't apply to the drivers door window.*

10   If the same window works from one switch, but not the other, check the switch for continuity.

11   If the switch tests OK, check for a short or open in the circuit between the affected switch and the window motor.

12   If one window is inoperative from both switches, remove the trim panel from the affected door and check for voltage at the switch and at the motor while the switch is operated **(see illustration).**

13   If voltage is reaching the motor, disconnect the glass from the regulator (see Chapter 11). Move the window up and down by hand while checking for binding and damage. Also check for binding and damage to the regulator. If the regulator is not damaged and the window moves up and down smoothly, replace the motor. If there's binding or damage, lubricate, repair or replace parts, as necessary. **Note:** *The window motor is an integral part of the window regulator assembly. See Chapter 11 for the removal procedures.*

14   If voltage isn't reaching the motor, check the wiring in the circuit for continuity between the switches and motors. You'll need to consult the wiring diagram for the vehicle. If the circuit is equipped with a relay, check that the relay is grounded properly and receiving voltage.

15   Test the windows after you are done to confirm proper repairs.

24 Power door lock system - description and check

Refer to illustration 24.6

The power door lock system operates the door lock actuators mounted in each

door. The system consists of the switches, actuators, a control unit and associated wiring. Diagnosis can usually be limited to simple checks of the wiring connections and actuators for minor faults which can be easily repaired. Since this system uses an electronic control unit, in-depth diagnosis should be left to a dealership service department. The door lock control unit is located behind the instrument panel, to the right of the fuse box.

Power door lock systems are operated by bi-directional solenoids located in the doors. The lock switches have two operating positions: Lock and Unlock. When activated, the switch sends a ground signal to the door lock control unit to lock or unlock the doors. Depending on which way the switch is activated, the control unit reverses polarity to the solenoids, allowing the two sides of the circuit to be used alternately as the feed (positive) and ground side.

Some vehicles may have an anti-theft systems incorporated into the power locks. If you are unable to locate the trouble using the following general Steps, consult your a dealer service department or other qualified repair shop.

1   Always check the circuit protection first. Some vehicles use a combination of circuit breakers and fuses.

2   Operate the door lock switches in both directions (Lock and Unlock) with the engine off. Listen for the click of the solenoids operating.

3   Test the switches for continuity. Replace the switch if there's not continuity in both switch positions.

4   Check the wiring between the switches, control unit and solenoids for continuity. Repair the wiring if there's no continuity.

5   Check for a bad ground at the switches or the control unit.

6   If all but one lock solenoids operate, remove the trim panel from the affected door (see Chapter 11) and check for voltage at the solenoid while the lock switch is operated One of the wires should have voltage in the Lock position; the other should have voltage in the Unlock position **(see illustration).**

7   If the inoperative solenoid is receiving voltage, replace the solenoid.

8   If the inoperative solenoid isn't receiving voltage, check for an open or short in the wire between the lock solenoid and the control unit. **Note:** *It's common for wires to break in the portion of the harness between the body and door (opening and closing the door fatigues and eventually breaks the wires).*

25 Electric rear view mirrors - description and check

1   Electric rear view mirrors use two motors to move the glass; one for up-and-down adjustments and one for left-to-right adjustments.

2   The control switch has a selector portion which sends voltage to the left or right side mirror. With the ignition ON, engine OFF, roll down the windows and operate the mirror control switch through all functions (left-right and up-down) for both the left and right side mirrors.

3   Listen carefully for the sound of the electric motors running in the mirrors.

4   If the motors can be heard but the mirror glass doesn't move, there's probably a problem with the drive mechanism inside the mirror. Remove and disassemble the mirror to locate the problem.

5   If the mirrors don't operate and no sound comes from the mirrors, check the fuse (see Section 3).

6   If the fuse is OK, remove the mirror control switch from its mounting without disconnecting the wires attached to it. Turn the ignition ON and check for voltage at the switch. There should be voltage at one terminal. If there's no voltage at the switch, check for an opening or short in the wiring between the fuse panel and the switch.

7   If there's voltage at the switch, disconnect it. Check the switch for continuity in all its operating positions. If the switch does not have continuity, replace it.

8   Re-connect the switch. Locate the wire going from the switch to ground. Leaving the switch connected, connect a jumper wire between this wire and ground. If the mirror works normally with this wire in place, repair the faulty ground connection.

9   If the mirror still doesn't work, remove the cover and check the wires at the mirror for voltage with a test light. Check with ignition ON and the mirror selector switch on the appropriate side. Operate the mirror switch in all its positions. There should be voltage at one of the switch-to-mirror wires in each switch position (except the neutral position).

10   If there's not voltage in each switch position, check the wiring between the mirror and control switch for opens and shorts.

11   If there's voltage, remove the mirror and test it off the vehicle with jumper wires. Replace the mirror if it fails this test (see Chapter 11).

26 Airbag - general information

Warning: *The models covered by this manual are equipped with airbags. Airbag system components are located in the steering wheel, steering column, instrument panel and under the front passenger seat. The airbag(s) could accidentally deploy if any of the system components or wiring harnesses are disturbed, so be extremely careful when working in these areas and don't disturb any airbag system components or wiring. You could be injured if an airbag accidentally deploys, or the airbag might not deploy correctly in a collision if any components or wiring in the system have been disturbed. The yellow wires and connectors routed through the instrument panel and below the passenger seat are for this system. Do not use electrical test equipment on these yellow wires or tamper with them in any way while working in their vicinity.*

Caution: *On models equipped with a Theftlock audio system, be sure the lockout feature is turned off before performing any procedure which requires disconnecting the battery.*

Description

Refer to illustration 26.2

1   The models covered by this manual are equipped with a Supplemental Inflatable Restraint (SIR) system, more commonly known as an airbag system. The SIR system is designed to protect the driver and passenger from serious injury in the event of a head-on or frontal collision.

2   The SIR system consists of a driver side airbag; located in the center of the steering wheel, a passenger side air bag located in the top of the dashboard above the glove box, an SIR coil assembly located in the steering column, an AIRBAG warning light located in the instrument cluster and a sensing and diagnostic module located under the front passenger seat **(see illustration)**.

Sensing and diagnostic module

3   The sensing and diagnostic module is designed to detect frontal crashes and deploy the air bags if a crash is severe

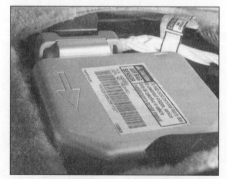

26.2 The airbag sensing and diagnostic module is located under the front passenger's seat

enough to warrant air bag deployment, record system data during a frontal crash and to supply back-up power to deploy the airbags in the event battery power is lost during a collision.

4   The sensing and diagnostic module also contains an on-board microprocessor which monitors the operation of the system. It performs a diagnostic check of the system every time the vehicle is started. If the system is operating properly, the AIRBAG warning light will blink on and off seven times. If there is a fault in the system, the light will remain on and the airbag control module will store fault codes indicating the nature of the fault. If the AIRBAG warning light remains on after staring, or comes on while driving, the vehicle should be taken to your dealer immediately for service.

Operation

5   For the airbag(s) to deploy, an impact of sufficient G force must occur within 30-degrees of the vehicle centerline. When this condition occurs, the circuit to the airbag inflator is closed and the airbag inflates. If the battery is destroyed by the impact, or is too low to power the inflators, a back-up power supply inside the diagnostic/energy reserve module supplies current to the airbags.

Self-diagnosis system

6   A self-diagnosis circuit in the module displays a light when the ignition switch is turned to the On position. If the system is operating normally, the light should go out after seven flashes. If the light doesn't come on, or doesn't go out after seven flashes, or if it comes on while you're driving the vehicle, there's a malfunction in the SIR system. Have it inspected and repaired as soon as possible. Do not attempt to troubleshoot or service the SIR system yourself. Even a small mistake could cause the SIR system to malfunction when you need it.

Servicing components near the SIR system

7   Nevertheless, there are times when you need to remove the steering wheel, radio or service other components on or near the instrument panel. At these times, you'll be working around components and wiring harnesses for the SIR system. SIR system wiring is easy to identify; they're all covered by a bright yellow conduit. Do not unplug the connectors for the SIR system wiring, except to disable the system. And do not use electrical test equipment on the SIR system wiring. **Always disable the SIR system before working near the SIR system components or related wiring.**

Disabling the SIR system

Refer to illustration 26.10

8   Turn the steering wheel to the straight ahead position, place the ignition switch in Lock and remove the key. Remove the airbag fuse from the fuse block (see Section 3). It's

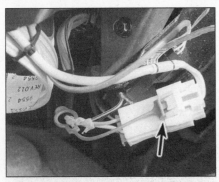

26.10 The driver's side airbag connector (arrow) is located at the base of the steering column; the passenger's side airbag connector is located behind the instrument panel glove box

also a good idea to disconnect the cable from the negative terminal of the battery, although this is not actually specified by the manufacturer. **Caution:** *On models equipped*

with a Theftlock audio system, be sure the lockout feature is turned off before performing any procedure which requires disconnecting the battery.

9   Remove the steering column lower trim panel and sound insulator panel below the instrument panel (see Chapter 11).

10   Unplug the yellow Connector Position Assurance (CPA) connector **(see illustration)** from the steering column harness. This step disables the driver side air bag.

11   Remove the glove box door assembly from the instrument panel (see Chapter 11).

12   Unplug the yellow Connector Position Assurance (CPA) connector located behind the instrument panel glove box. This step disables the passenger side air bag.

Enabling the SIR system

13   After you've disabled the airbags and performed the necessary service, plug in the steering column (driver's side) and passenger side CPA connectors. Reinstall the steering

column lower trim panel, the sound insulator panel and the glove box.

14   Install the airbag fuse. Reconnect the negative battery cable.

27   Wiring diagrams - general information

Since it isn't possible to include all wiring diagrams for every year covered by this manual, the following diagrams are those that are typical and most commonly needed.

Prior to troubleshooting any circuit, check the fuse and circuit breakers (if equipped) to make sure they're in good condition. Make sure the battery is properly charged and check the cable connections (see Chapter 1).

When checking a circuit, make sure that all electrical connectors are clean, with no broken or loose terminals. When unplugging an electrical connector, do not pull on the wires. Pull only on the connector housings themselves.

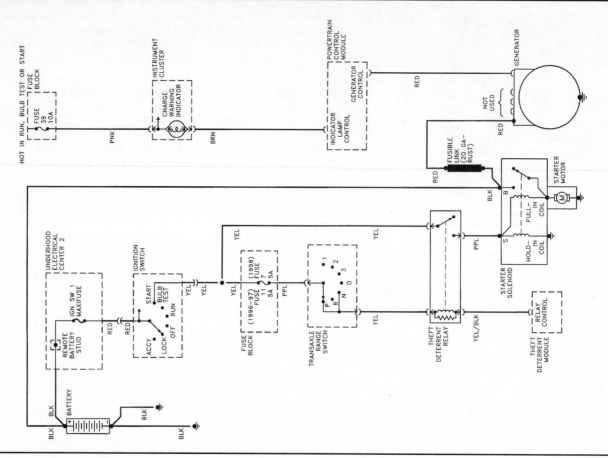

Typical 1996 and later starting and charging system

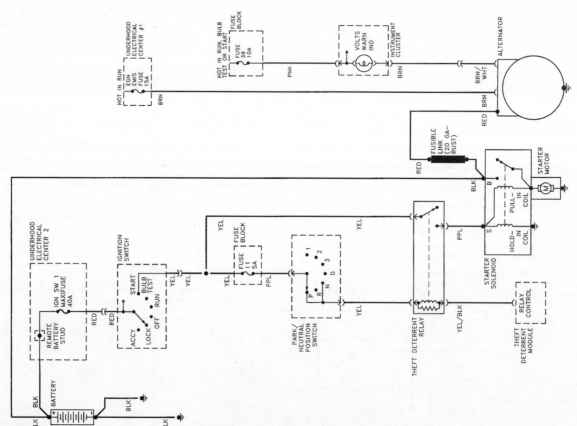

Typical 1995 starting and charging system

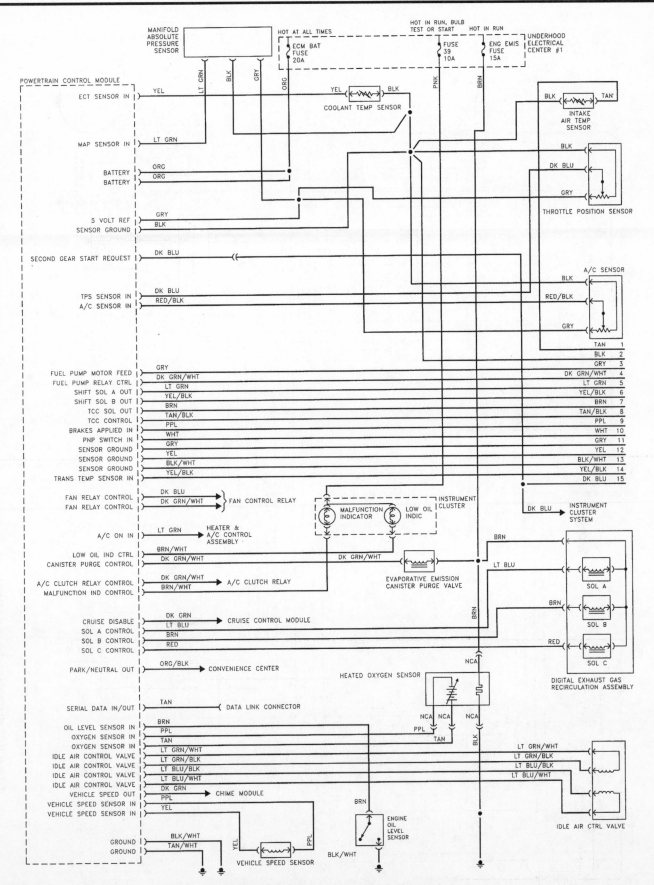

Typical 1995 3.1L engine control system (part 1 of 2)

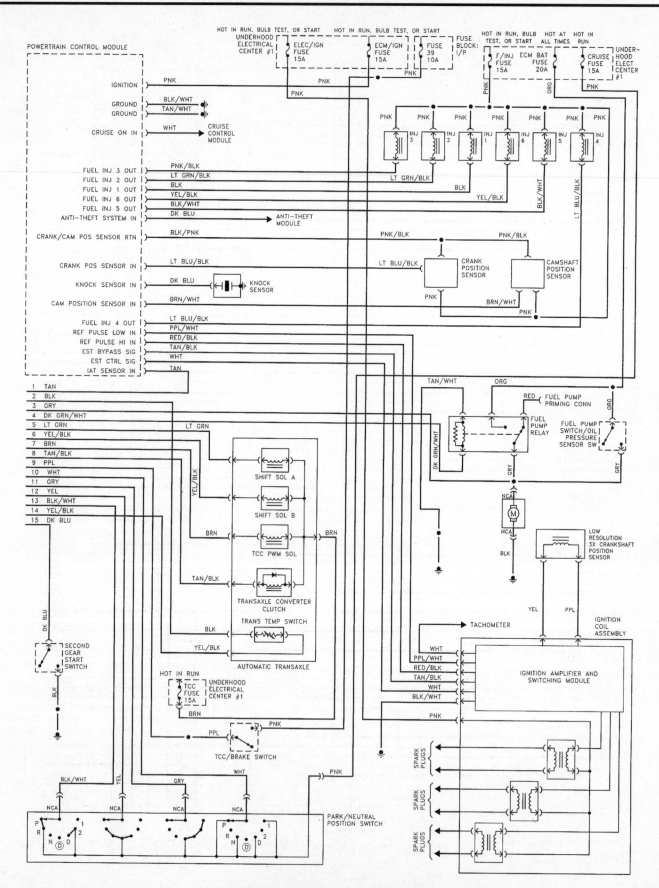

Typical 1995 3.1L engine control system (part 2 of 2)

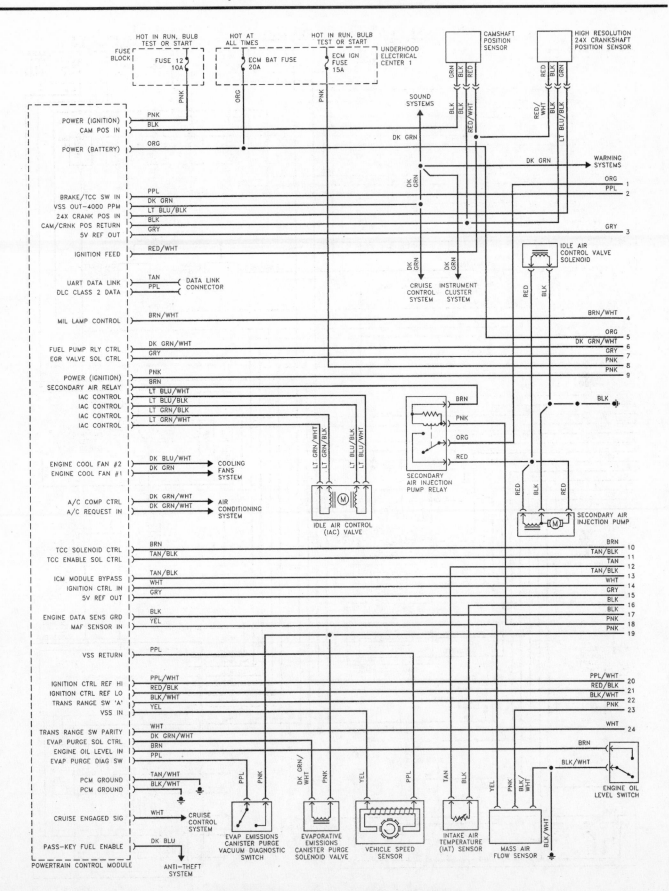

Typical 1995 3.4L engine control system (part 1 of 3)

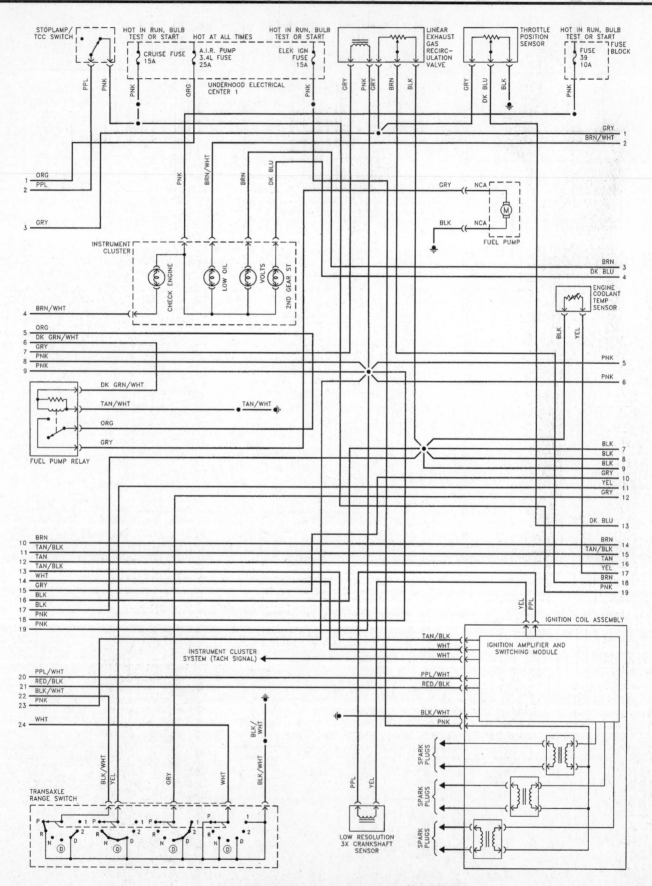

Typical 1995 3.4L engine control system (part 2 of 3)

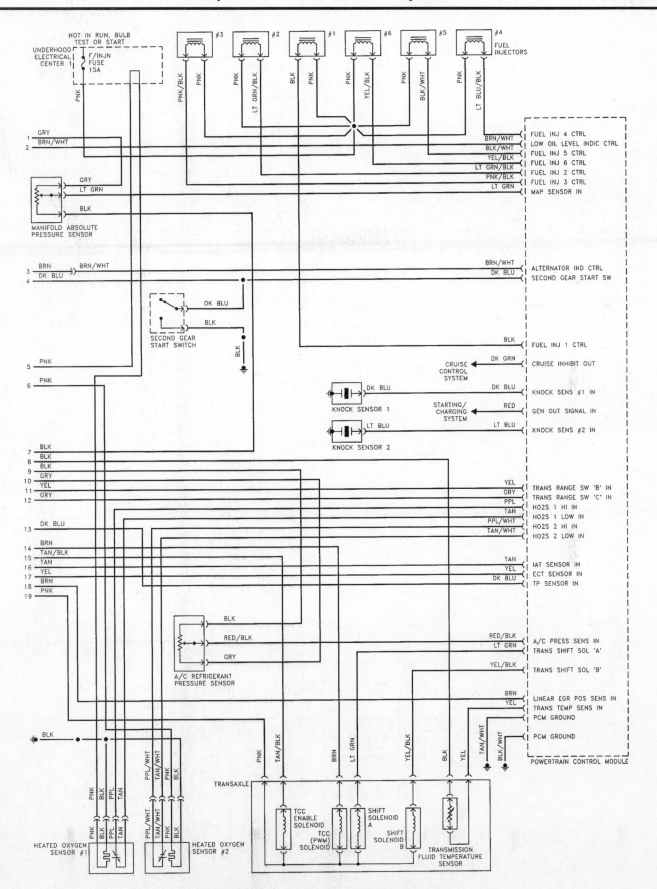

Typical 1995 3.4L engine control system (part 3 of 3)

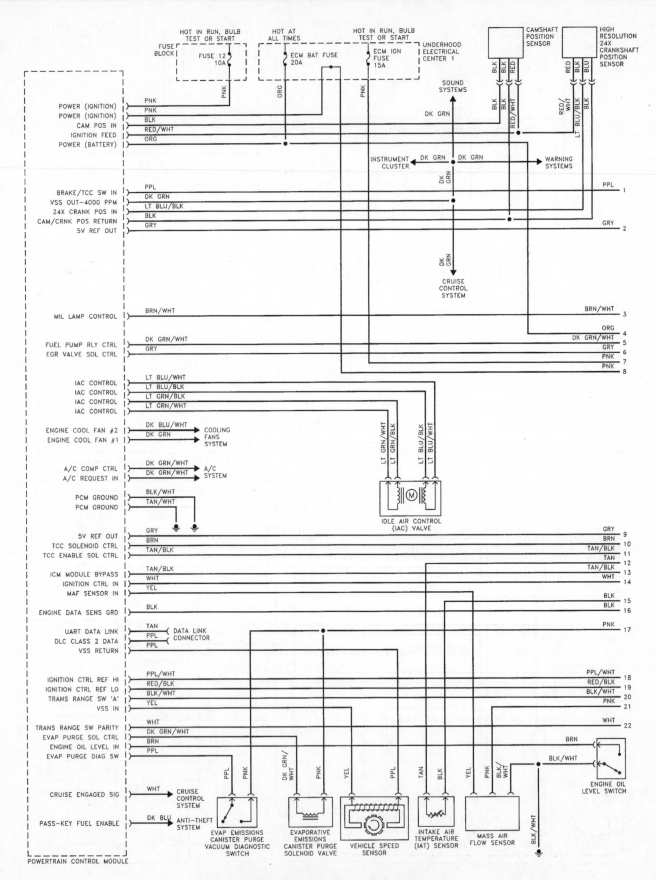

Typical 1996 3.1L engine control system (part 1 of 3)

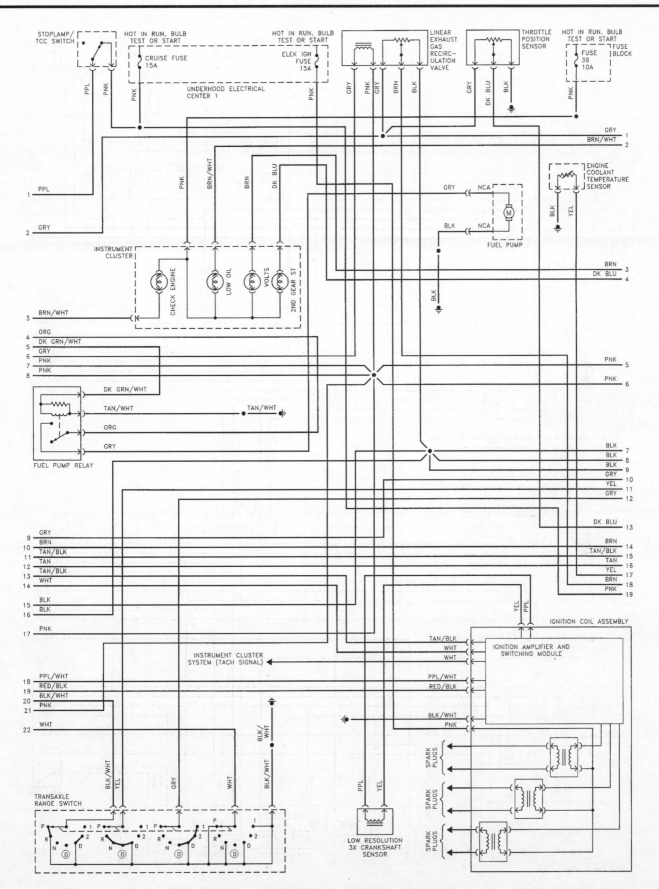

Typical 1996 3.1L engine control system (part 2 of 3)

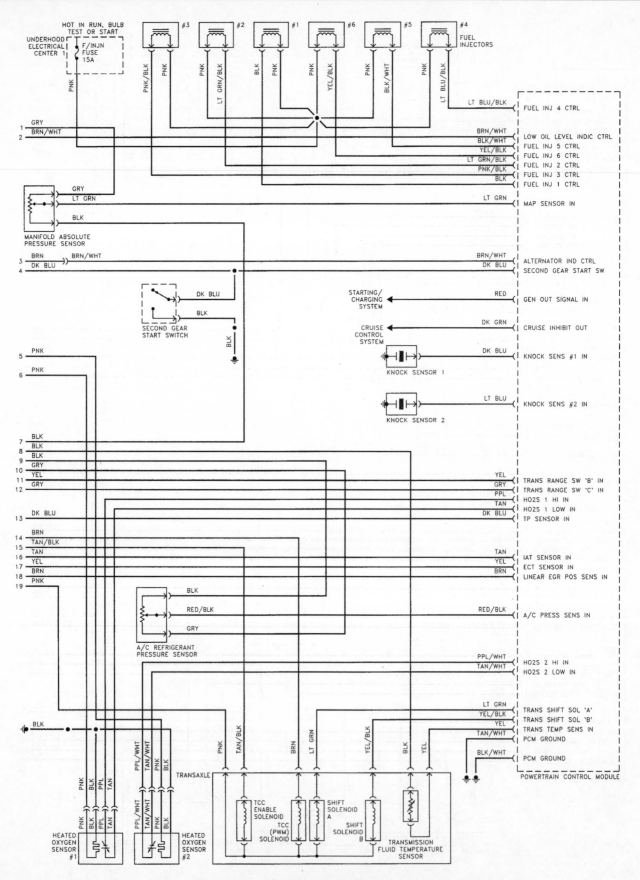

Typical 1996 3.1L engine control system (part 3 of 3)

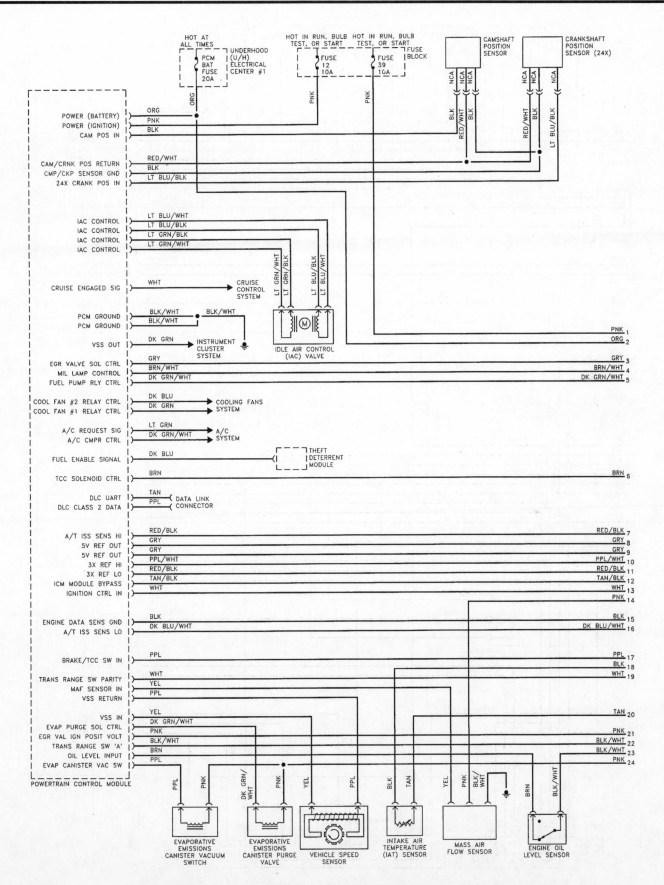

Typical 1996 and later 3.4L and 1997 and later 3.1L engine control system (part 1 of 3)

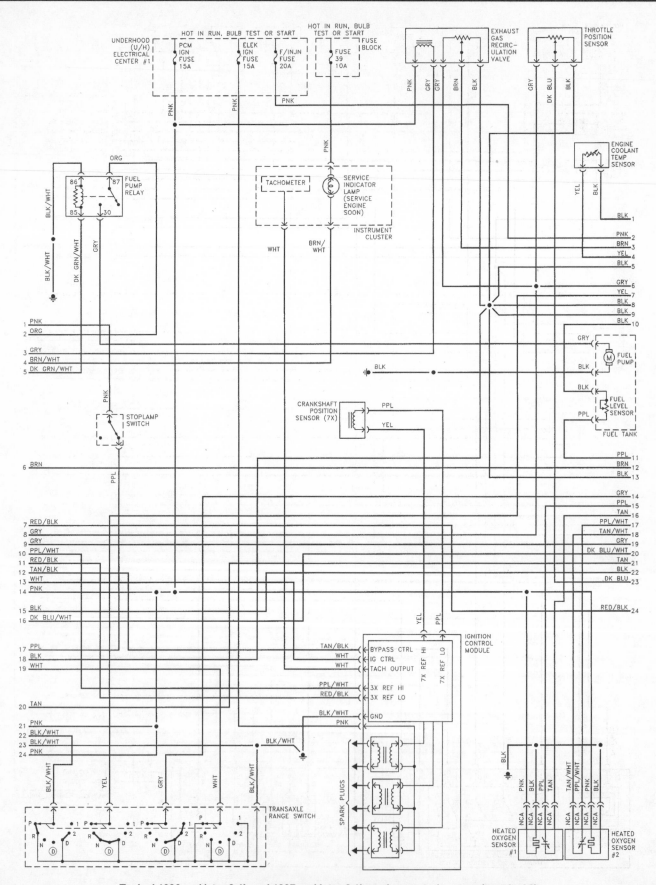

Typical 1996 and later 3.4L and 1997 and later 3.1L engine control system (part 2 of 3)

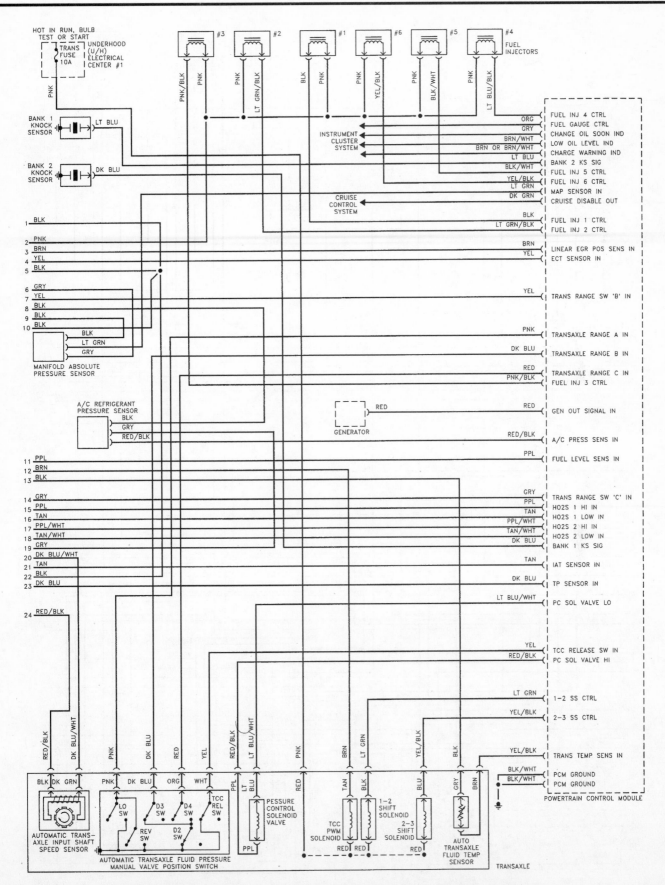

Typical 1996 and later 3.4L and 1997 and later 3.1L engine control system (part 3 of 3)

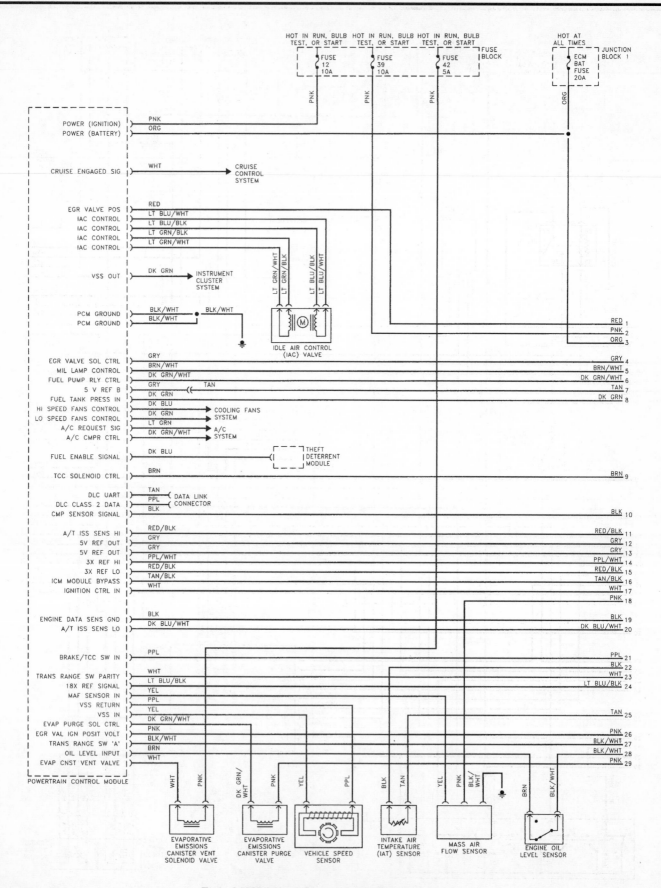

Typical 1998 3.8L engine control system (part 1 of 3)

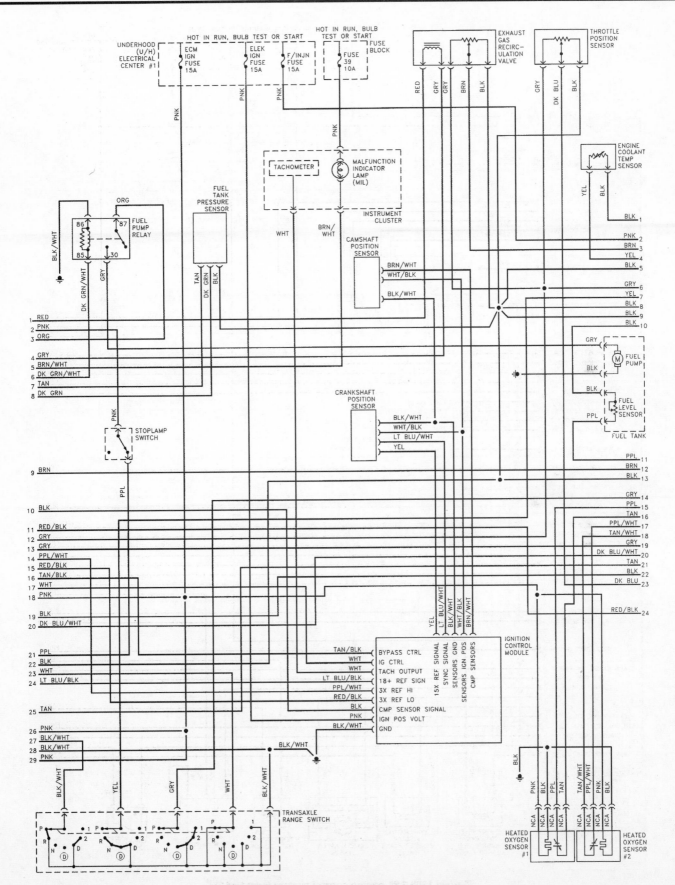

Typical 1998 3.8L engine control system (part 2 of 3)

12

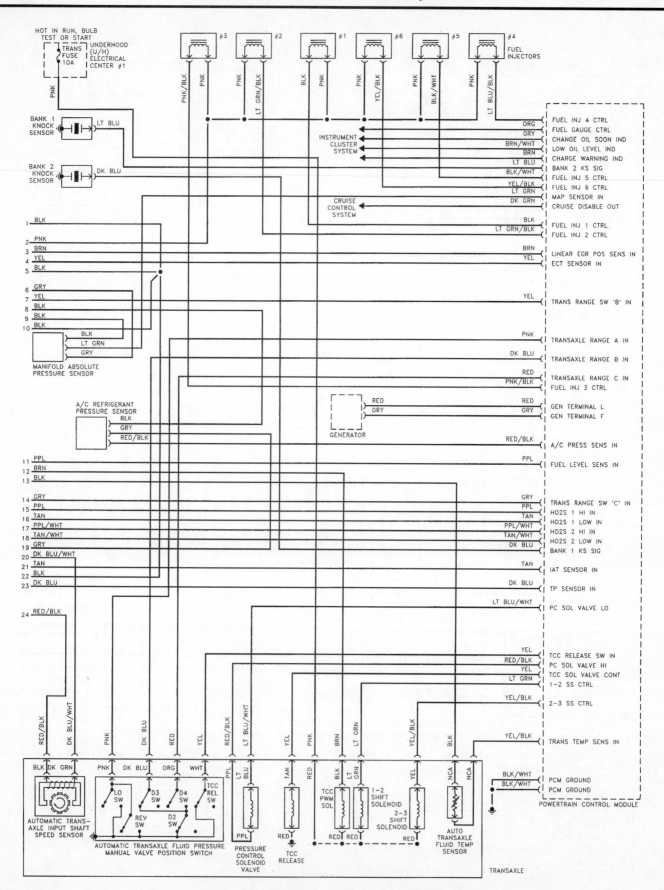

Typical 1998 3.8L engine control system (part 3 of 3)

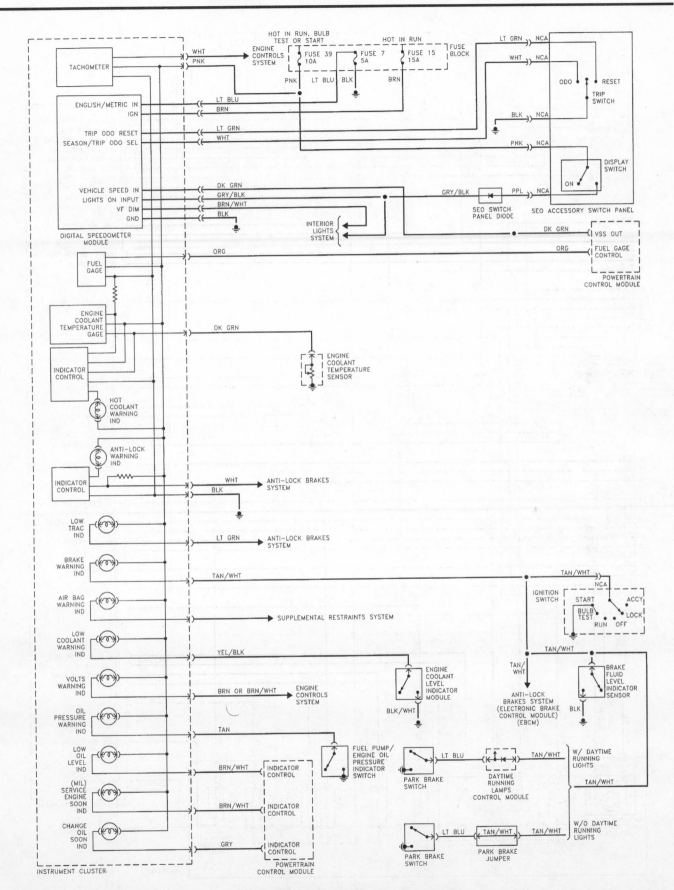

Typical 1995 and later engine warning system

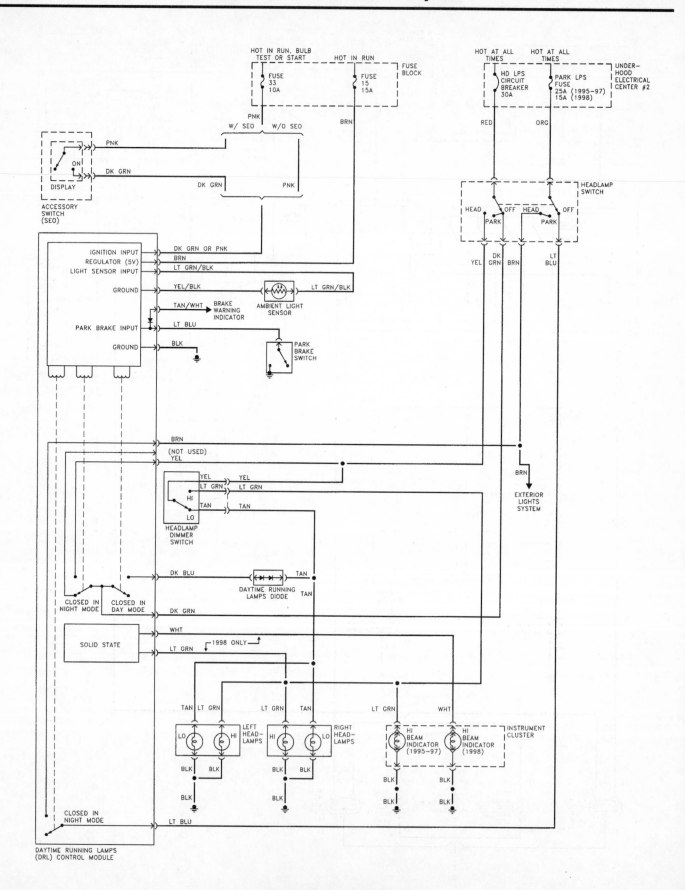

Typical 1995 and later headlight system

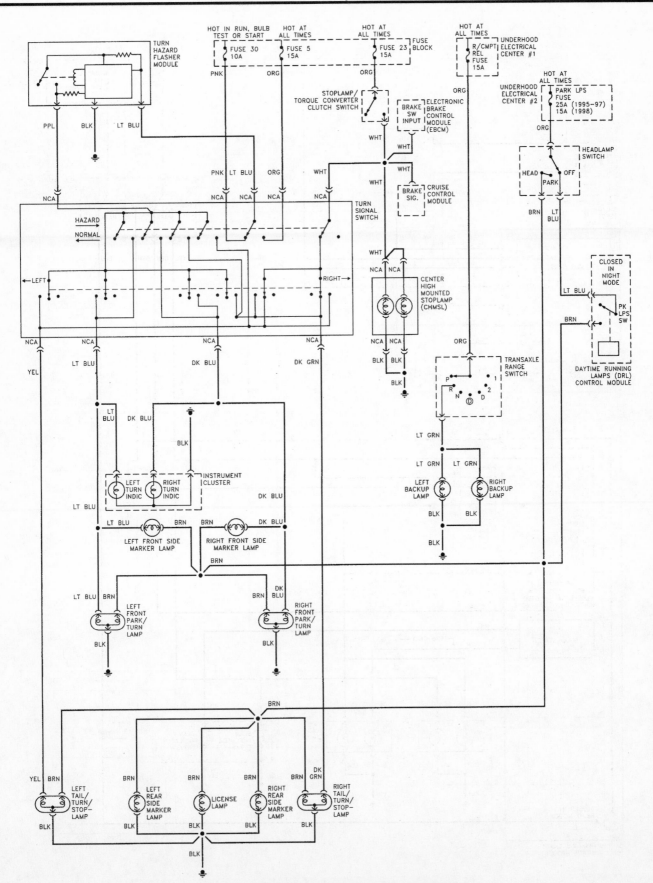

Typical exterior lighting system (except headlights)

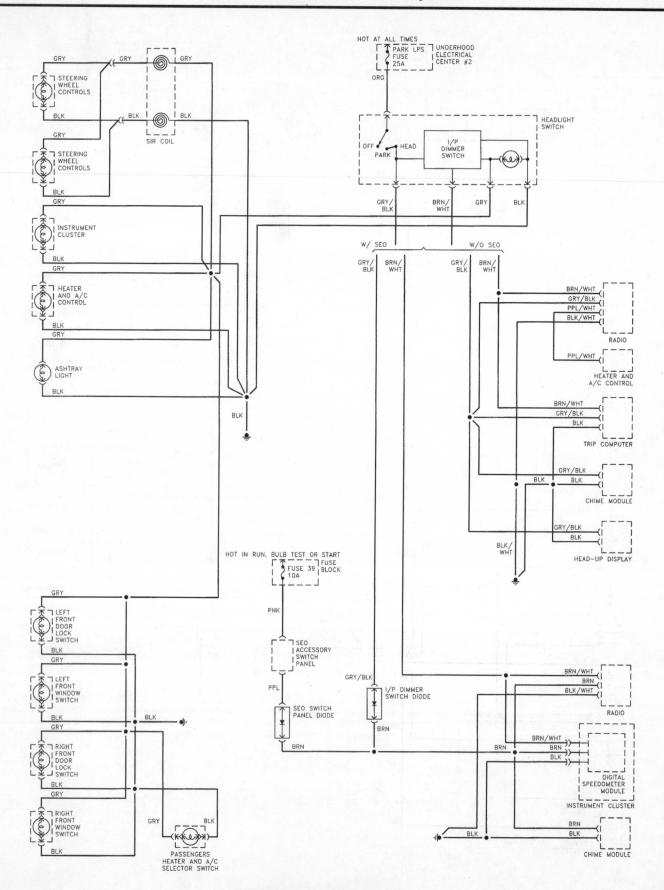

Typical 1995 interior illumination system

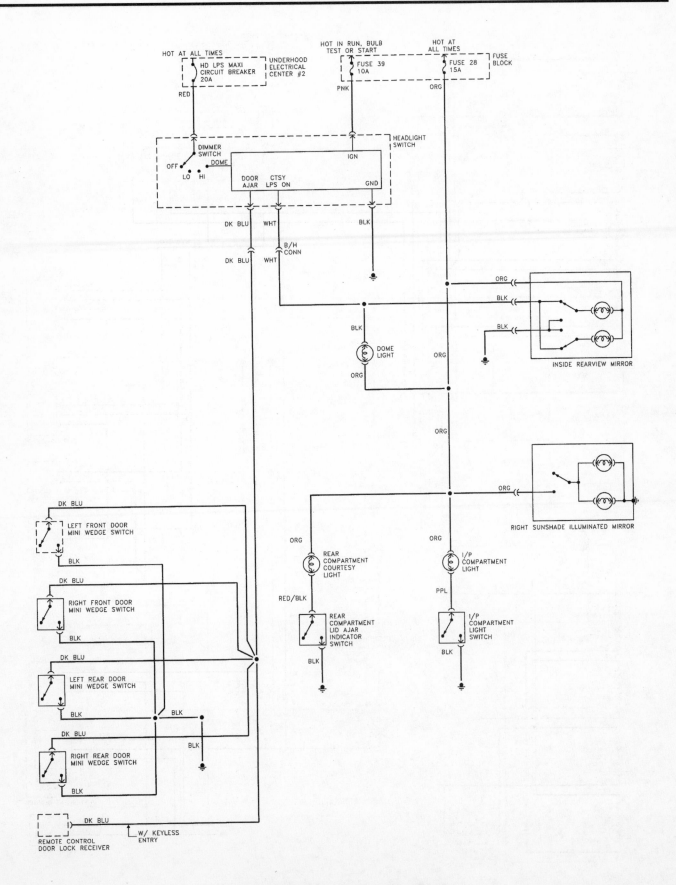

Typical 1995 interior courtesy light system

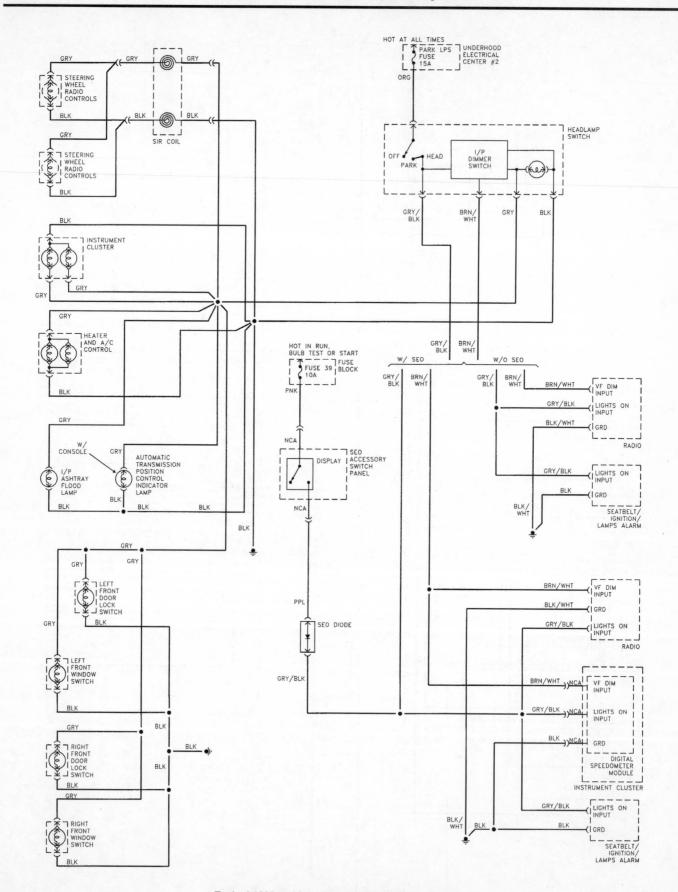

Typical 1996 and later interior illumination system

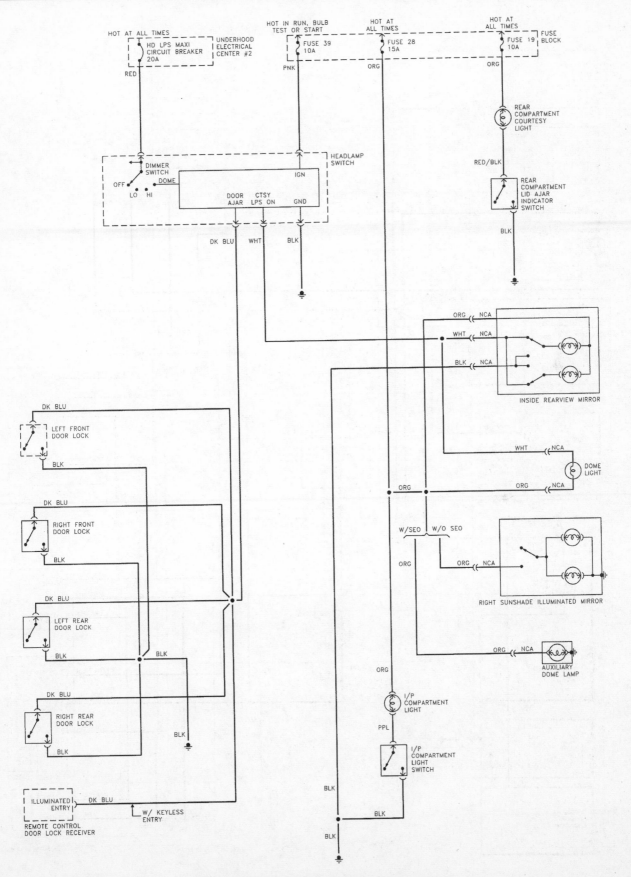

Typical 1996 and later interior courtesy light system

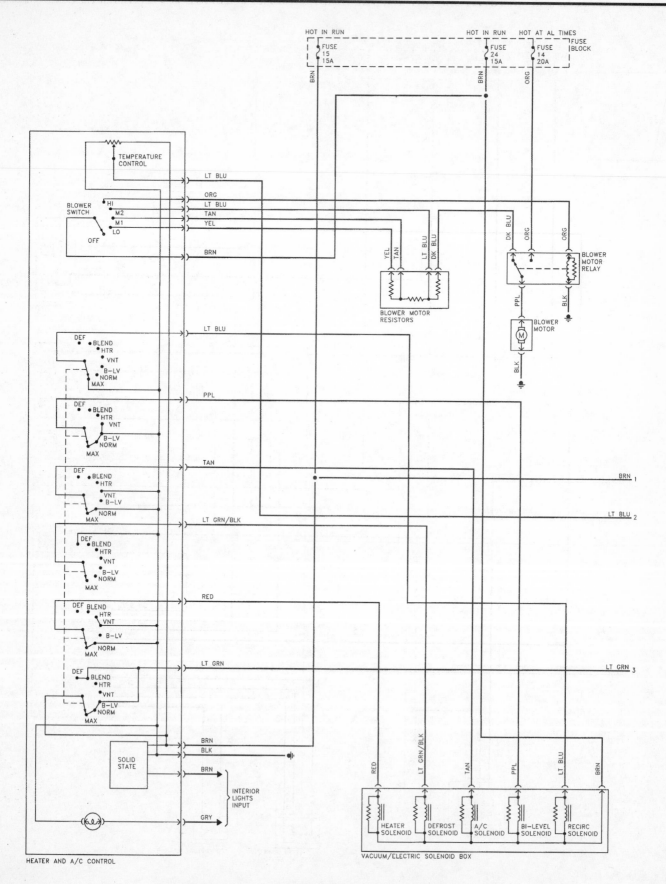

Typical 1995 heating, air conditioning and cooling system (part 1 of 2)

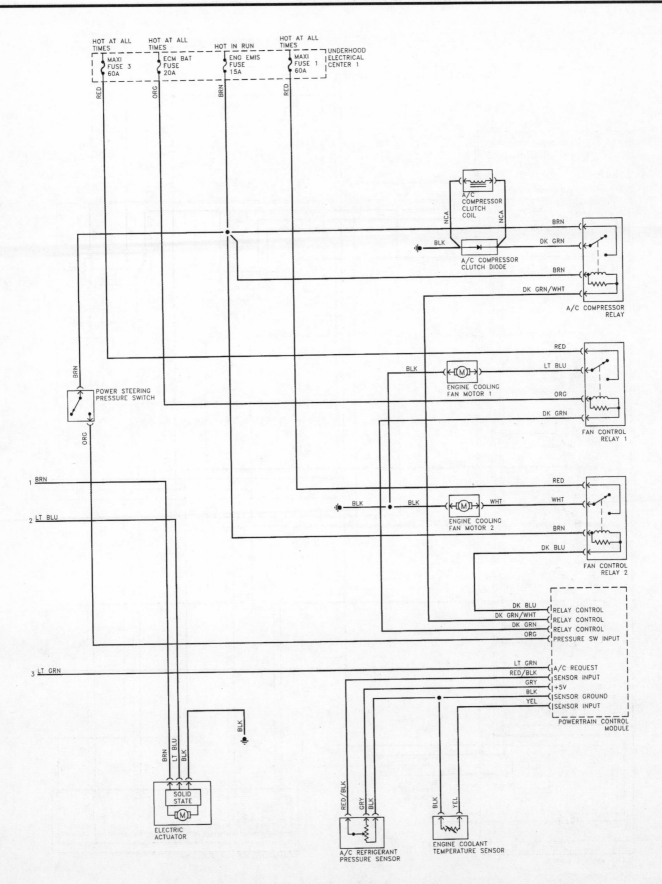

Typical 1995 heating, air conditioning and cooling system (part 2 of 2)

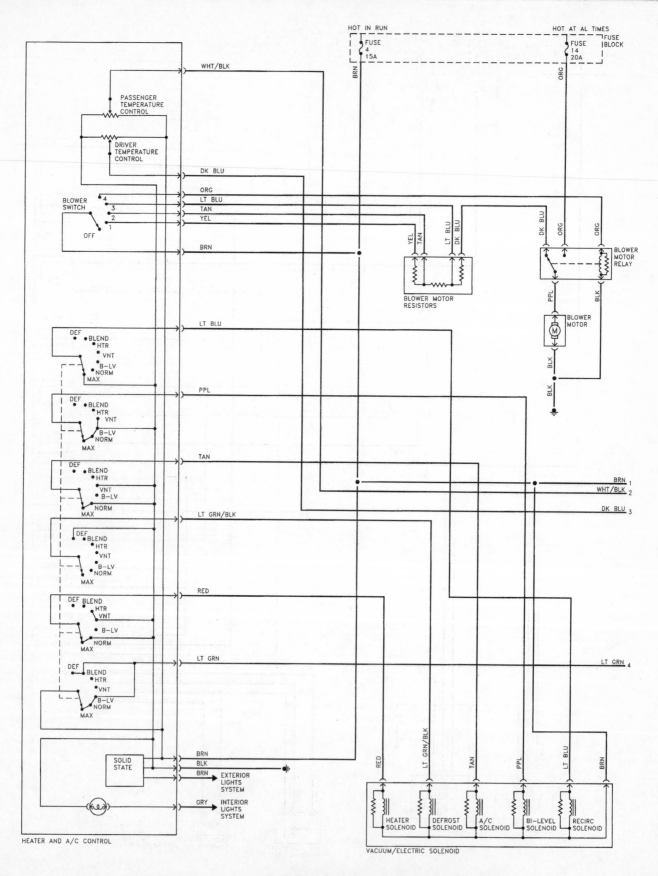

Typical 1996 and later heating, air conditioning and cooling system (part 1 of 2)

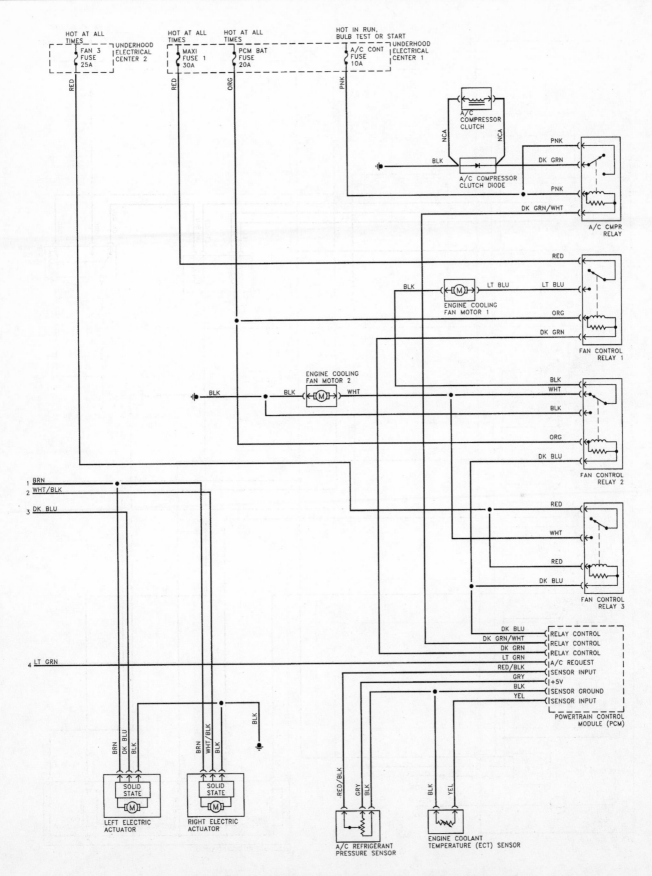

Typical 1996 and later heating, air conditioning and cooling system (part 2 of 2)

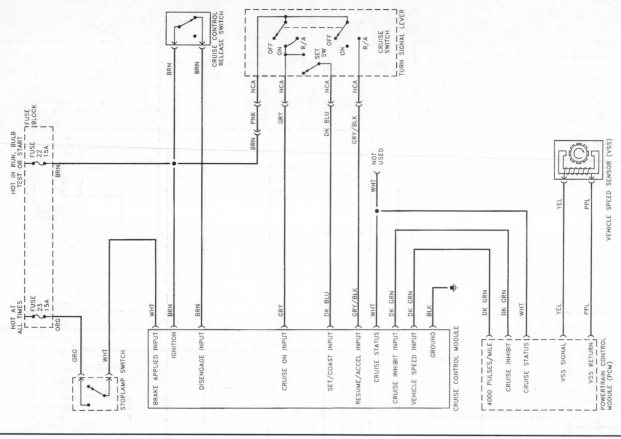

Typical 1996 and later cruise control system

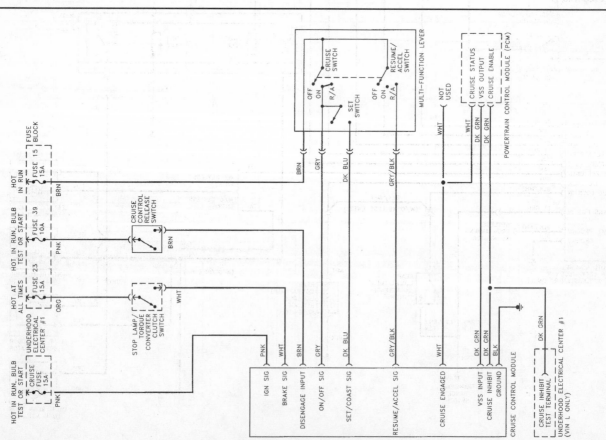

Typical 1995 cruise control system

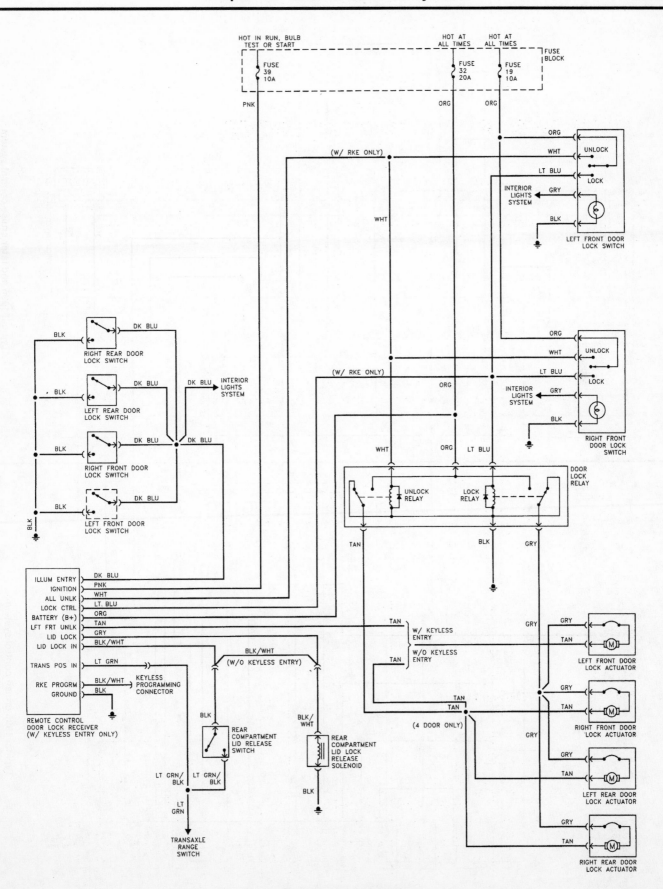

Typical power door lock system

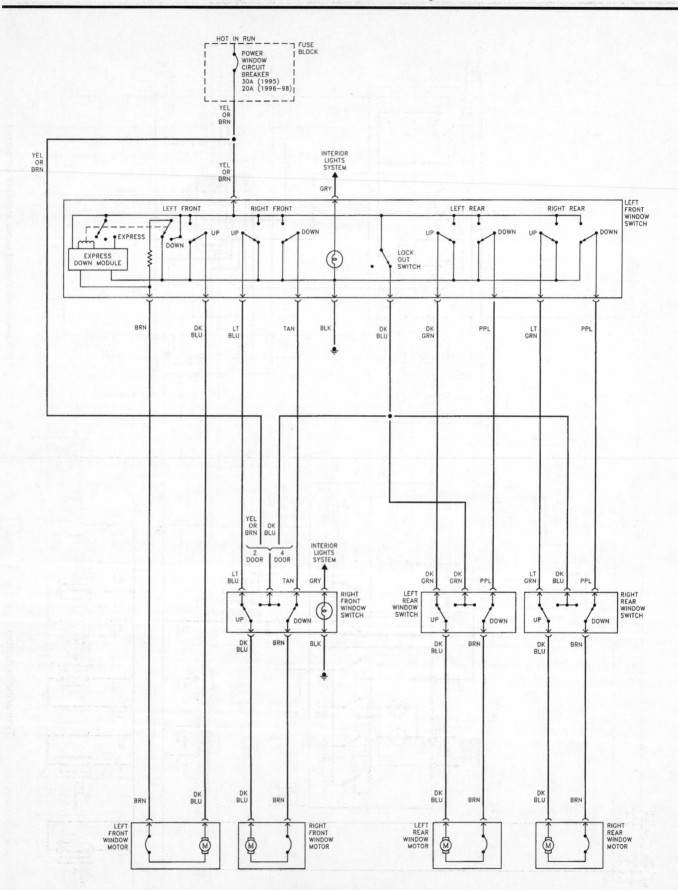

Typical power window system

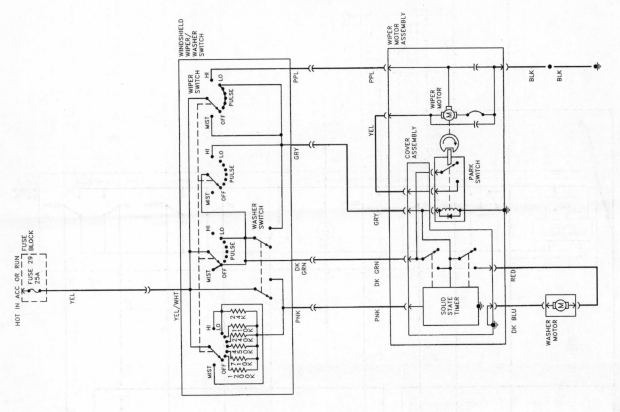

Typical windshield wiper and washer system

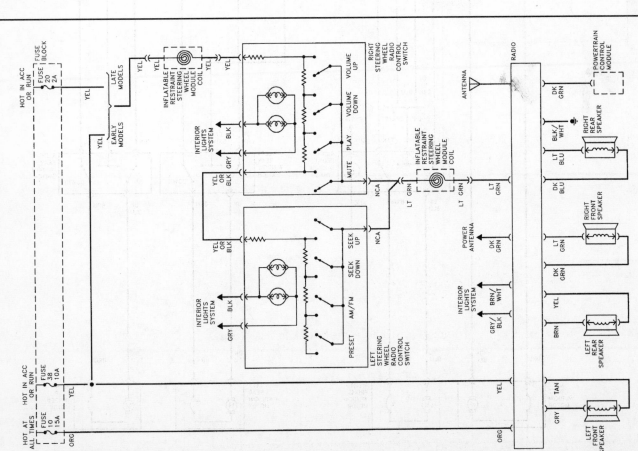

Typical audio system

12

Notes

Index

Haynes Automotive Manuals

NOTE: New manuals are added to this list on a periodic basis. If you do not see a listing for your vehicle, consult your local Haynes dealer for the latest product information.

ACURA
*12020 Integra '86 thru '89 & Legend '86 thru '90

AMC
Jeep CJ - see JEEP (50020)
14020 Mid-size models, Concord, Hornet, Gremlin & Spirit '70 thru '83
14025 (Renault) Alliance & Encore '83 thru '87

AUDI
15020 4000 all models '80 thru '87
15025 5000 all models '77 thru '83
15026 5000 all models '84 thru '88

AUSTIN-HEALEY
Sprite - see MG Midget (66015)

BMW
*18020 3/5 Series not including diesel or all-wheel drive models '82 thru '92
*18021 3 Series except 325iX models '92 thru '97
18025 320i all 4 cyl models '75 thru '83
18035 528i & 530i all models '75 thru '80
18050 1500 thru 2002 except Turbo '59 thru '77

BUICK
Century (front wheel drive) - see GM (829)
*19020 Buick, Oldsmobile & Pontiac Full-size (Front wheel drive) all models '85 thru '98
Buick Electra, LeSabre and Park Avenue;
Oldsmobile Delta 88 Royale, Ninety Eight and Regency; Pontiac Bonneville
19025 Buick Oldsmobile & Pontiac Full-size (Rear wheel drive)
Buick Estate '70 thru '90, Electra '70 thru '84, LeSabre '70 thru '85, Limited '74 thru '79
Oldsmobile Custom Cruiser '70 thru '90, Delta 88 '70 thru '85, Ninety-eight '70 thru '84
Pontiac Bonneville '70 thru '81, Catalina '70 thru '81, Grandville '70 thru '75, Parisienne '83 thru '86
19030 Mid-size Regal & Century all rear-drive models with V6, V8 and Turbo '74 thru '87
Regal - see GENERAL MOTORS (38010)
Riviera - see GENERAL MOTORS (38030)
Roadmaster - see CHEVROLET (24046)
Skyhawk - see GENERAL MOTORS (38015)
Skylark '80 thru '85 - see GM (38020)
Skylark '86 on - see GM (38025)
Somerset - see GENERAL MOTORS (38025)

CADILLAC
*21030 Cadillac Rear Wheel Drive all gasoline models '70 thru '93
Cimarron - see GENERAL MOTORS (38015)
Eldorado - see GENERAL MOTORS (38030)
Seville '80 thru '85 - see GM (38030)

CHEVROLET
*24010 Astro & GMC Safari Mini-vans '85 thru '93
24015 Camaro V8 all models '70 thru '81
24016 Camaro all models '82 thru '92
Cavalier - see GENERAL MOTORS (38015)
Celebrity - see GENERAL MOTORS (38005)
24017 Camaro & Firebird '93 thru '97
24020 Chevelle, Malibu & El Camino '69 thru '87
24024 Chevette & Pontiac T1000 '76 thru '87
Citation - see GENERAL MOTORS (38020)
*24032 Corsica/Beretta all models '87 thru '96
24040 Corvette all V8 models '68 thru '82
*24041 Corvette all models '84 thru '96
10305 Chevrolet Engine Overhaul Manual
24045 Full-size Sedans Caprice, Impala, Biscayne, Bel Air & Wagons '69 thru '90
24046 Impala SS & Caprice and Buick Roadmaster '91 thru '96
Lumina - see GENERAL MOTORS (38010)

24048 Lumina & Monte Carlo '95 thru '98
Lumina APV - see GM (38035)
24050 Luv Pick-up all 2WD & 4WD '72 thru '82
*24055 Monte Carlo all models '70 thru '88
Monte Carlo '95 thru '98 - see LUMINA (24048)
24059 Nova all V8 models '69 thru '79
*24060 Nova and Geo Prizm '85 thru '92
24064 Pick-ups '67 thru '87 - Chevrolet & GMC, all V8 & in-line 6 cyl, 2WD & 4WD '67 thru '87; Suburbans, Blazers & Jimmys '67 thru '91
*24065 Pick-ups '88 thru '98 - Chevrolet & GMC, all full-size pick-ups, '88 thru '98; Blazer & Jimmy '92 thru '94; Suburban '92 thru '98; Tahoe & Yukon '98
24070 S-10 & S-15 Pick-ups '82 thru '93, Blazer & Jimmy '83 thru '94,
*24071 S-10 & S-15 Pick-ups '94 thru '96 Blazer & Jimmy '95 thru '96
*24075 Sprint & Geo Metro '85 thru '94
*24080 Vans - Chevrolet & GMC, V8 & in-line 6 cylinder models '68 thru '96

CHRYSLER
25015 Chrysler Cirrus, Dodge Stratus, Plymouth Breeze '95 thru '98
25025 Chrysler Concorde, New Yorker & LHS, Dodge Intrepid, Eagle Vision, '93 thru '97
10310 Chrysler Engine Overhaul Manual
*25020 Full-size Front-Wheel Drive '88 thru '93
K-Cars - see DODGE Aries (30008)
Laser - see DODGE Daytona (30030)
*25030 Chrysler & Plymouth Mid-size front wheel drive '82 thru '95
Rear-wheel Drive - see Dodge (30050)

DATSUN
28005 200SX all models '80 thru '83
28007 B-210 all models '73 thru '78
28009 210 all models '79 thru '82
28012 240Z, 260Z & 280Z Coupe '70 thru '78
28014 280ZX Coupe & 2+2 '79 thru '83
300ZX - see NISSAN (72010)
28016 310 all models '78 thru '82
28018 510 & PL521 Pick-up '68 thru '73
28020 510 all models '78 thru '81
28022 620 Series Pick-up all models '73 thru '79
720 Series Pick-up - see NISSAN (72030)
28025 810/Maxima all gasoline models, '77 thru '84

DODGE
400 & 600 - see CHRYSLER (25030)
*30008 Aries & Plymouth Reliant '81 thru '89
30010 Caravan & Plymouth Voyager Mini-Vans all models '84 thru '95
*30011 Caravan & Plymouth Voyager Mini-Vans all models '96 thru '98
30012 Challenger/Plymouth Saporro '78 thru '83
30016 Colt & Plymouth Champ (front wheel drive) all models '78 thru '87
*30020 Dakota Pick-ups all models '87 thru '96
30025 Dart, Demon, Plymouth Barracuda, Duster & Valiant 6 cyl models '67 thru '76
*30030 Daytona & Chrysler Laser '84 thru '89
Intrepid - see CHRYSLER (25025)
*30034 Neon all models '95 thru '97
*30035 Omni & Plymouth Horizon '78 thru '90
*30040 Pick-ups all full-size models '74 thru '93
*30041 Pick-ups all full-size models '94 thru '96
*30045 Ram 50/D50 Pick-ups & Raider and Plymouth Arrow Pick-ups '79 thru '93
30050 Dodge/Plymouth/Chrysler rear wheel drive '71 thru '89
*30055 Shadow & Plymouth Sundance '87 thru '94
*30060 Spirit & Plymouth Acclaim '89 thru '95
*30065 Vans - Dodge & Plymouth '71 thru '96

EAGLE
Talon - see Mitsubishi Eclipse (68030)
Vision - see CHRYSLER (25025)

FIAT
34010 124 Sport Coupe & Spider '68 thru '78
34025 X1/9 all models '74 thru '80

FORD
10355 Ford Automatic Transmission Overhaul
*36004 Aerostar Mini-vans all models '86 thru '96
*36006 Contour & Mercury Mystique '95 thru '98
36008 Courier Pick-up all models '72 thru '82
36012 Crown Victoria & Mercury Grand Marquis '88 thru '96
10320 Ford Engine Overhaul Manual
36016 Escort/Mercury Lynx all models '81 thru '90
*36020 Escort/Mercury Tracer '91 thru '96
*36024 Explorer & Mazda Navajo '91 thru '95
36028 Fairmont & Mercury Zephyr '78 thru '83
36030 Festiva & Aspire '88 thru '97
36032 Fiesta all models '77 thru '80
36036 Ford & Mercury Full-size, Ford LTD & Mercury Marquis ('75 thru '82); Ford Custom 500, Country Squire, Crown Victoria & Mercury Colony Park ('75 thru '87); Ford LTD Crown Victoria & Mercury Gran Marquis ('83 thru '87)
36040 Granada & Mercury Monarch '75 thru '80
36044 Ford & Mercury Mid-size, Ford Thunderbird & Mercury Cougar ('75 thru '82); Ford LTD & Mercury Marquis ('83 thru '86); Ford Torino, Gran Torino, Elite, Ranchero pick-up, LTD II, Mercury Montego, Comet, XR-7 & Lincoln Versailles ('75 thru '86)
36048 Mustang V8 all models '64-1/2 thru '73
36049 Mustang II 4 cyl, V6 & V8 models '74 thru '78
36050 Mustang & Mercury Capri all models Mustang, '79 thru '93; Capri, '79 thru '86
*36051 Mustang all models '94 thru '97
36054 Pick-ups & Bronco '73 thru '79
36058 Pick-ups & Bronco '80 thru '96
36059 Pick-ups, Expedition & Mercury Navigator '97 thru '98
36062 Pinto & Mercury Bobcat '75 thru '80
36066 Probe all models '89 thru '92
36070 Ranger/Bronco II gasoline models '83 thru '92
*36071 Ranger '93 thru '97 & Mazda Pick-ups '94 thru '97
36074 Taurus & Mercury Sable '86 thru '95
*36075 Taurus & Mercury Sable '96 thru '98
*36078 Tempo & Mercury Topaz '84 thru '94
36082 Thunderbird/Mercury Cougar '83 thru '88
*36086 Thunderbird/Mercury Cougar '89 and '97
36090 Vans all V8 Econoline models '69 thru '91
*36094 Vans full size '92-'95
*36097 Windstar Mini-van '95-'98

GENERAL MOTORS
*10360 GM Automatic Transmission Overhaul
*38005 Buick Century, Chevrolet Celebrity, Oldsmobile Cutlass Ciera & Pontiac 6000 all models '82 thru '96
*38010 Buick Regal, Chevrolet Lumina, Oldsmobile Cutlass Supreme & Pontiac Grand Prix front-wheel drive models '88 thru '95
*38015 Buick Skyhawk, Cadillac Cimarron, Chevrolet Cavalier, Oldsmobile Firenza & Pontiac J-2000 & Sunbird '82 thru '94
*38016 Chevrolet Cavalier & Pontiac Sunfire '95 thru '98
38020 Buick Skylark, Chevrolet Citation, Olds Omega, Pontiac Phoenix '80 thru '85
38025 Buick Skylark & Somerset, Oldsmobile Achieva & Calais and Pontiac Grand Am all models '85 thru '95
38030 Cadillac Eldorado '71 thru '85, Seville '80 thru '85, Oldsmobile Toronado '71 thru '85 & Buick Riviera '79 thru '85
*38035 Chevrolet Lumina APV, Olds Silhouette & Pontiac Trans Sport all models '90 thru '95
General Motors Full-size Rear-wheel Drive - see BUICK (19025)

(Continued on other side)

* Listings shown with an asterisk (*) indicate model coverage as of this printing. These titles will be periodically updated to include later model years - consult your Haynes dealer for more information.

Haynes North America, Inc., 861 Lawrence Drive, Newbury Park, CA 91320-1514 • (805) 498-6703

Haynes Automotive Manuals (continued)

NOTE: New manuals are added to this list on a periodic basis. If you do not see a listing for your vehicle, consult your local Haynes dealer for the latest product information.

GEO
	Metro - *see CHEVROLET Sprint (24075)*
	Prizm - '85 thru '92 *see CHEVY (24060)*, '93 thru '96 *see TOYOTA Corolla (92036)*
*40030	**Storm** all models '90 thru '93
	Tracker - *see SUZUKI Samurai (90010)*

GMC
	Safari - *see CHEVROLET ASTRO (24010)*
	Vans & Pick-ups - *see CHEVROLET*

HONDA
42010	**Accord CVCC** all models '76 thru '83
42011	**Accord** all models '84 thru '89
42012	**Accord** all models '90 thru '93
42013	**Accord** all models '94 thru '95
42020	**Civic 1200** all models '73 thru '79
42021	**Civic 1300 & 1500 CVCC** '80 thru '83
42022	**Civic 1500 CVCC** all models '75 thru '79
42023	**Civic** all models '84 thru '91
*42024	**Civic & del Sol** '92 thru '95
*42040	**Prelude CVCC** all models '79 thru '89

HYUNDAI
*43015	**Excel** all models '86 thru '94

ISUZU
	Hombre - *see CHEVROLET S-10 (24071)*
*47017	**Rodeo** '91 thru '97; **Amigo** '89 thru '94; Honda Passport '95 thru '97
*47020	**Trooper & Pick-up**, all gasoline models Pick-up, '81 thru '93; Trooper, '84 thru '91

JAGUAR
*49010	**XJ6** all 6 cyl models '68 thru '86
*49011	**XJ6** all models '88 thru '94
*49015	**XJ12 & XJS** all 12 cyl models '72 thru '85

JEEP
*50010	**Cherokee, Comanche & Wagoneer Limited** all models '84 thru '96
50020	**CJ** all models '49 thru '86
*50025	**Grand Cherokee** all models '93 thru '98
50029	**Grand Wagoneer & Pick-up** '72 thru '91 Grand Wagoneer '84 thru '91, Cherokee & Wagoneer '72 thru '83, Pick-up '72 thru '88
*50030	**Wrangler** all models '87 thru '95

LINCOLN
	Navigator - *see FORD Pick-up (36059)*
59010	**Rear Wheel Drive** all models '70 thru '96

MAZDA
61010	**GLC Hatchback** (rear wheel drive) '77 thru '83
61011	**GLC** (front wheel drive) '81 thru '85
*61015	**323 & Protegé** '90 thru '97
*61016	**MX-5 Miata** '90 thru '97
*61020	**MPV** all models '89 thru '94
	Navajo - *see Ford Explorer (36024)*
61030	**Pick-ups** '72 thru '93 Pick-ups '94 thru '96 - *see Ford Ranger (36071)*
61035	**RX-7** all models '79 thru '85
*61036	**RX-7** all models '86 thru '91
61040	**626** (rear wheel drive) all models '79 thru '82
*61041	**626/MX-6** (front wheel drive) '83 thru '91

MERCEDES-BENZ
63012	**123 Series Diesel** '76 thru '85
*63015	**190 Series** four-cyl gas models, '84 thru '88
63020	**230/250/280** 6 cyl sohc models '68 thru '72
63025	**280 123 Series** gasoline models '77 thru '81
63030	**350 & 450** all models '71 thru '80

MERCURY
See FORD Listing.

MG
66010	**MGB** Roadster & GT Coupe '62 thru '80
66015	**MG Midget, Austin Healey Sprite** '58 thru '80

MITSUBISHI
*68020	**Cordia, Tredia, Galant, Precis & Mirage** '83 thru '93
*68030	**Eclipse, Eagle Talon & Ply. Laser** '90 thru '94
*68040	**Pick-up** '83 thru '96 & **Montero** '83 thru '93

NISSAN
72010	**300ZX** all models including Turbo '84 thru '89
*72015	**Altima** all models '93 thru '97
*72020	**Maxima** all models '85 thru '91
*72030	**Pick-ups** '80 thru '96 **Pathfinder** '87 thru '95
72040	**Pulsar** all models '83 thru '86
*72050	**Sentra** all models '82 thru '94
*72051	**Sentra & 200SX** all models '95 thru '98
*72060	**Stanza** all models '82 thru '90

OLDSMOBILE
*73015	**Cutlass** V6 & V8 gas models '74 thru '88

For other OLDSMOBILE titles, see BUICK, CHEVROLET or GENERAL MOTORS listing.

PLYMOUTH
For PLYMOUTH titles, see DODGE listing.

PONTIAC
79008	**Fiero** all models '84 thru '88
79018	**Firebird** V8 models except Turbo '70 thru '81
79019	**Firebird** all models '82 thru '92

For other PONTIAC titles, see BUICK, CHEVROLET or GENERAL MOTORS listing.

PORSCHE
*80020	**911** except Turbo & Carrera 4 '65 thru '89
80025	**914** all 4 cyl models '69 thru '76
80030	**924** all models including Turbo '76 thru '82
*80035	**944** all models including Turbo '83 thru '89

RENAULT
Alliance & Encore - *see AMC (14020)*

SAAB
*84010	**900** all models including Turbo '79 thru '88

SATURN
87010	**Saturn** all models '91 thru '96

SUBARU
89002	**1100, 1300, 1400 & 1600** '71 thru '79
*89003	**1600 & 1800** 2WD & 4WD '80 thru '94

SUZUKI
*90010	**Samurai/Sidekick & Geo Tracker** '86 thru '96

TOYOTA
92005	**Camry** all models '83 thru '91
92006	**Camry** all models '92 thru '96
92015	**Celica Rear Wheel Drive** '71 thru '85
*92020	**Celica Front Wheel Drive** '86 thru '93
92025	**Celica Supra** all models '79 thru '92
92030	**Corolla** all models '75 thru '79
92032	**Corolla** all rear wheel drive models '80 thru '87
92035	**Corolla** all front wheel drive models '84 thru '92
*92036	**Corolla & Geo Prizm** '93 thru '97
92040	**Corolla Tercel** all models '80 thru '82
92045	**Corona** all models '74 thru '82
92050	**Cressida** all models '78 thru '82
92055	**Land Cruiser** FJ40, 43, 45, 55 '68 thru '82
92056	**Land Cruiser** FJ60, 62, 80, FZJ80 '80 thru '96
*92065	**MR2** all models '85 thru '87
92070	**Pick-up** all models '69 thru '78
*92075	**Pick-up** all models '79 thru '95
*92076	**Tacoma** '95 thru '98, **4Runner** '96 thru '98, & **T100** '93 thru '98
*92080	**Previa** all models '91 thru '95
92085	**Tercel** all models '87 thru '94

TRIUMPH
94007	**Spitfire** all models '62 thru '81
94010	**TR7** all models '75 thru '81

VW
96008	**Beetle & Karmann Ghia** '54 thru '79
96012	**Dasher** all gasoline models '74 thru '81
*96016	**Rabbit, Jetta, Scirocco, & Pick-up** gas models '74 thru '91 & Convertible '80 thru '92
96017	**Golf & Jetta** all models '93 thru '97
96020	**Rabbit, Jetta & Pick-up** diesel '77 thru '84
96030	**Transporter 1600** all models '68 thru '79
96035	**Transporter 1700, 1800 & 2000** '72 thru '79
96040	**Type 3 1500 & 1600** all models '63 thru '73
96045	**Vanagon** all air-cooled models '80 thru '83

VOLVO
97010	**120, 130 Series & 1800 Sports** '61 thru '73
97015	**140 Series** all models '66 thru '74
*97020	**240 Series** all models '76 thru '93
97025	**260 Series** all models '75 thru '82
*97040	**740 & 760 Series** all models '82 thru '88

TECHBOOK MANUALS
10205	**Automotive Computer Codes**
10210	**Automotive Emissions Control Manual**
10215	**Fuel Injection Manual, 1978 thru 1985**
10220	**Fuel Injection Manual, 1986 thru 1996**
10225	**Holley Carburetor Manual**
10230	**Rochester Carburetor Manual**
10240	**Weber/Zenith/Stromberg/SU Carburetors**
10305	**Chevrolet Engine Overhaul Manual**
10310	**Chrysler Engine Overhaul Manual**
10320	**Ford Engine Overhaul Manual**
10330	**GM and Ford Diesel Engine Repair Manual**
10340	**Small Engine Repair Manual**
10345	**Suspension, Steering & Driveline Manual**
10355	**Ford Automatic Transmission Overhaul**
10360	**GM Automatic Transmission Overhaul**
10405	**Automotive Body Repair & Painting**
10410	**Automotive Brake Manual**
10415	**Automotive Detaiing Manual**
10420	**Automotive Eelectrical Manual**
10425	**Automotive Heating & Air Conditioning**
10430	**Automotive Reference Manual & Dictionary**
10435	**Automotive Tools Manual**
10440	**Used Car Buying Guide**
10445	**Welding Manual**
10450	**ATV Basics**

SPANISH MANUALS
98903	**Reparación de Carrocería & Pintura**
98905	**Códigos Automotrices de la Computadora**
98910	**Frenos Automotriz**
98915	**Inyección de Combustible 1986 al 1994**
99040	**Chevrolet & GMC Camionetas** '67 al '87 Incluye Suburban, Blazer & Jimmy '67 al '91
99041	**Chevrolet & GMC Camionetas** '88 al '95 Incluye Suburban '92 al '95, Blazer & Jimmy '92 al '94, Tahoe y Yukon '95
99042	**Chevrolet & GMC Camionetas Cerradas** '68 al '95
99055	**Dodge Caravan & Plymouth Voyager** '84 al '95
99075	**Ford Camionetas y Bronco** '80 al '94
99077	**Ford Camionetas Cerradas** '69 al '91
99083	**Ford Modelos de Tamaño Grande** '75 al '87
99088	**Ford Modelos de Tamaño Mediano** '75 al '86
99091	**Ford Taurus & Mercury Sable** '86 al '95
99095	**GM Modelos de Tamaño Grande** '70 al '90
99100	**GM Modelos de Tamaño Mediano** '70 al '88
99110	**Nissan Camionetas** '80 al '96, **Pathfinder** '87 al '95
99118	**Nissan Sentra** '82 al '94
99125	**Toyota Camionetas y 4Runner** '79 al '95

---

* Listings shown with an asterisk (*) indicate model coverage as of this printing. These titles will be periodically updated to include later model years - consult your Haynes dealer for more information.

Over 100 Haynes motorcycle manuals also available

5-98

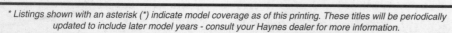

Haynes North America, Inc., 861 Lawrence Drive, Newbury Park, CA 91320-1514 • (805) 498-6703

THE WESTERN HERITAGE

Seventh Edition

VOLUME B
1300 TO 1815

DONALD KAGAN

YALE UNIVERSITY

STEVEN OZMENT

HARVARD UNIVERSITY

FRANK M. TURNER

YALE UNIVERSITY

Prentice
Hall

UPPER SADDLE RIVER, NEW JERSEY 07458

Library of Congress Cataloging–in–Publication Data

Kagan, Donald
    The Western heritage / Donald Kagan, Steven Ozment, Frank M. Turner.—
    Combined Volume, 7th ed.
        p.   cm.
    Includes bibliographical references and index.
    ISBN 0-13-027718-5
    1. Civilization, Western. I. Ozment, Steven E. II. Turner, Frank M. (Frank Miller), 1944-III. Title.
    CB245.K28 2001
    909′.09812—dc21   00-026148

Editorial Director: Charlyce Jones Owen
Editor-in-Chief, Development: Susanna Lesan
Development Editor: Roberta Meyer
Director of Production
   and Manufacturing: Barbara Kittle
Production Editor: Joseph Scordato
Prepress and Manufacturing Manager:
   Nick Sklitsis
Prepress and Manufacturing Buyer: Lynn Pearlman

Creative Design Director: Leslie Osher
Interior and Cover Designer: Nancy Wells
Electronic Page Layout: Scott Garrison, Joh Lisa,
   Thomas Benfatti
Photo Director: Beth Boyd
Photo Research: Barbara Salz
Cartographer: Carto-Graphics
Copy Editor: Write With, Inc.
Art Manager: Guy Ruggiero

Cover Art: "Scuola Olandese" (Dutch School), *Fiume gelato con pattinatori* (Frozen river with ice
   skaters). Galleria Sabauda, Torino/Art Resource, NY

This book was set in 10/12 Trump Mediaeval by the HSS in-house formatting
and production services group and was printed and bound by RR Donnelley & Sons.
The cover was printed by Phoenix Color Corp.

© 2001, 1998, 1991, 1987, 1983, 1979 by Prentice-Hall, Inc.
Pearson Education
Upper Saddle River, New Jersey 07458

Printed in the United States of America
10 9 8 7 6 5 4 3 2 1

ISBN 0-13-027283-3

Prentice-Hall International (UK) Limited, *London*
Prentice-Hall of Australia Pty. Limited, *Sydney*
Prentice-Hall Canada Inc., *Toronto*
Prentice-Hall Hispanoamericana, S.A., *Mexico*
Prentice-Hall of India Private Limited, *New Delhi*
Prentice-Hall of Japan, Inc. *Tokyo*
Pearson Education Asia Pte. Ltd., *Singapore*
Editora Prentice-Hall do Brasil, Ltda., *Rio de Janeiro*

TIME LINE PHOTO CREDITS:

Time Line 1: page 0, (left) Gary Cralle/The Image Bank;
(right) Winfield I. Parks Jr./National Geographic Image Collection; page 1, The Granger Collection; page 2, *Battle of
Alexander the Great at Issus.* Roman mosaic. Museo Arche-
ologico Nazionale, Naples, Italy. Scala/Art Resource; p. 3,
Robert Frerck/Woodfin Camp & Associates.

Time Line 2: page 192, Marvin Trachtenberg; page 193,
Bayeus, Musée de l'Eveche. "With special authorization
of the City of Bayeaux." Giraudon/Art Resource.

Time Line 3: page 288, *Elizabeth I, Armada Portrait,* c. 1588
(oil on panel) by George Gower (1540–96) (attr. to). Woburn
Abbey, Bedfordshire, UK/Bridgeman Art Library, Lon-
don/New York; p. 289, The Granger Collection.

Time Line 4: page 586, Philosopher, dramatist, poet, historian, and populizer of scientific ideas, Voltaire
(1694–1778). Bildarchiv Preussischer Kulterbesitz; page
587, By Permission of Musée de la Legion d'Honneur.

Time Line 5: page 778, Corbis; page 779, The Bridgeman
Art Library International.

Time Line 6: page 992, (left) Hulton Getty/Liaison
Agency, Inc.; (right) Franklin D. Roosevelt Library; page
993, (left) Corbis Sygma Photo News; (right, top) John
Launois/Black Star; (right, bottom) Reuters/Natalie
Behring/Archive Photos.

Brief Contents

Detailed Contents

PART 6 GLOBAL CONFLICT, COLD WAR, AND NEW DIRECTIONS 992

31   THE COLD WAR ERA
AND THE EMERGENCE OF
THE NEW EUROPE   1068

THE WEST & THE WORLD:
ENERGY AND THE MODERN WORLD   **1116**

Documents

Maps

Art & the West

The West & the World

Preface

As we enter the twenty-first century, the heritage of Western civilization is a major point of departure for understanding our own epoch. The unprecedented globalization of daily life has occurred in large measure through the spread of Western technological, economic, and political influences. From the sixteenth through the end of the twentieth century the West exerted vast influences throughout the globe for both good and ill, and the global citizens of this new century live in the wake of that impact. It is the goal of this book to introduce its readers to the Western heritage so that they may be better informed and more culturally sensitive citizens of the emerging global age.

Since *The Western Heritage* first appeared, we have sought to provide our readers with a work that does justice to the richness and variety of Western civilization. We hope that such an understanding of the West will foster lively debate on its character, values, institutions, and global influence. Indeed, we believe such a critical outlook on their own culture has characterized the peoples of the West since its earliest history. Through such debates we define ourselves and the values of our culture. Consequently, we welcome the debate and hope that *The Western Heritage*, seventh edition, can help to foster a genuinely informed discussion through its overview of Western civilization, its strengths, weaknesses, and the controversies surrounding it.

Human beings make, experience, and record their history. In this edition as in past editions, our goal has been to present Western civilization fairly, accurately, and in a way that does justice to that great variety of human enterprise. History has many facets, no one of which alone can account for the others. Any attempt to tell the story of the West from a single overarching perspective, no matter how timely, is bound to neglect or suppress some important part of that story. Like all authors, we have had to make selections for an introductory text, but we have attempted to provide the broadest possible coverage suitable to that task of introduction. To that end we hope that the vast array of documents included in this book will allow the widest possible spectrum of people over the course of the centuries to give personal voice to their experience and to allow our readers to enter into that experience.

We also believe that any book addressing the experience of the West must also look beyond its historical European borders. The students reading this book are drawn from a wide variety of cultures and experiences. They live in a world characterized by highly interconnected economies and instant communication between cultures. In this emerging multicultural society it seems both appropriate and necessary to recognize the ways in which Western civilization has throughout its history interacted with other cultures, influencing other societies and being influenced by them. Examples of this two-way interaction, such as that with Islam, appear throughout the text. To further highlight the theme of interaction, *The Western Heritage* includes a series of comparative essays, *The West & the World*. (For a fuller description, see below.)

Goals of the Text

Our primary goal has been to present a strong, clear narrative account of the central developments in Western history. We have also sought to call attention to certain critical themes:

- The capacity of Western civilization from the time of the Greeks to the present to generate transforming self-criticism.
- The development of political freedom, constitutional government, and concern for the rule of law and individual rights.
- The shifting relations among religion, society, and the state.
- The development of science and technology and their expanding impact on thought, social institutions, and everyday life.
- The major religious and intellectual currents that have shaped Western culture.

We believe that these themes have been fundamental in Western civilization, shaping the past and exerting a continuing influence on the present.

FLEXIBLE PRESENTATION   *The Western Heritage*, seventh edition, is designed to accommodate a variety of approaches to a course in Western civilization, allowing teachers to stress what is most important to them. Some teachers will ask students to read all the chapters. Others will select among them to reinforce assigned readings and lectures. We have reorganized and rewritten the last two chapters (30 and 31) to permit instructors to end their course by emphasizing either social or political factors in the twentieth-century experience.

INTEGRATED SOCIAL, CULTURAL, AND POLITICAL HISTORY   *The Western Heritage* provides one of the richest accounts of the social history of the West available today, with strong coverage of family life, the changing roles of women, and the place of the family in relation to broader economic, political, and social developments. This coverage reflects the explosive growth in social historical research in the past quarter century, which has enriched virtually all areas of historical study. In this edition we have again expanded both the breadth and depth of our coverage of social history through revisions of existing chapters, the addition of major new material, and the inclusion of new documents.

While strongly believing in the study of the social experience of the West, we also share the conviction that internal and external political events have shaped the Western experience in fundamental and powerful ways. The experiences of Europeans in the twentieth century under fascism, national socialism, and communism demonstrate that influence, as has, more recently, the collapse of communism in the former Soviet Union and eastern Europe. We have also been told repeatedly by teachers that no matter what their own historical specialization, they believe that a political narrative gives students an effective tool to begin to organize their understanding of the past. Consequently, we have made every effort to integrate the political with the social, cultural, and intellectual.

No other survey text presents so full an account of the religious and intellectual development of the West. People may be political and social beings, but they are also reasoning and spiritual beings. What they think and believe are among the most important things we can know about them. Their ideas about God, society, law, gender, human nature, and the physical world have changed over the centuries and continue to change. We cannot fully grasp our own approach to the world without understanding the intellectual currents of the past and their influence on our thoughts and conceptual categories.

CLARITY AND ACCESSIBILITY   Good narrative history requires clear, vigorous prose. As in earlier editions, we have paid careful attention to the quality of our writing, subjecting every paragraph to critical scrutiny. Our goal was to make our presentation fully accessible to students without compromising vocabulary or conceptual level. We hope this effort will benefit both teachers and students.

Changes in the Seventh Edition

INTRODUCING *ART & THE WEST*   A beautiful and important new feature enhances students' understanding of the artistic heritage of the West. In every chapter we highlight a work of art or architecture and discuss how the work illuminates and reflects the period in which it was created. In Chapter 5, for example, a portrait of a young woman on the wall of a house in Pompeii and the accompanying essay provide a glimpse into the life of well-to-do young women in the Roman Empire (p. 161). In Chapter 7, two views of Salisbury Cathedral illustrate an essay on Gothic architecture (p. 248). In Chapter 16, two paintings tell contrasting stories about domestic life in eighteenth-century France (p. 526), and in Part 4, works by Turner, Manet, and Seurat illustrate both the power of the new industrialism and its effects on European social life. Part 5 includes discussions of paintings by Grosz, Magritte, and Picasso. In Chapter 30, *Bread*, painted by the Soviet realist Tatjiana Yablonskaya, and Jackson Pollock's *One (Number 31, 1950)*, offer starkly contrasting views of twentieth-century culture (p. 1040). (See p. xxiv for a complete list of *Art & The West* essays.)

THE WEST & THE WORLD   In this feature, we focus on six subjects, comparing Western institutions with those of other parts of the world, or discussing the ways in which developments in the West have influenced cultures in other areas of the globe. In the seventh edition, the essays are:

Part 1: Ancient Warfare (new) (p. 186)

Part 2: The Invention of Printing in China and Europe (new) (p. 284)

Part 3: The Columbian Exchange (new) (p. 582)

Part 4: The Abolition of Slavery in the Transatlantic Economy (p. 736)

Part 5: Imperialism: Ancient and Modern (p. 928)

Part 6: Energy and the Modern World (new) (p. 1116)

RECENT SCHOLARSHIP   As in previous editions, changes in this edition reflect our determination to incorporate the most recent developments in historical scholarship and the concerns of professional historians. Of particular interest are expanded discussions of:

- **Women in the history of the West.**   Adding to our longstanding commitment to the inclusion of the experience of women in Western civilization, this edition presents new scholarship on women in the ancient world and the Middle Ages, women and the scientific revolution, and women under the authoritarian governments of the twentieth century. (See, especially, chapters 3, 4, 5, 7, 14, 30.)

- **The Scientific Revolution.** Chapter 14, which addresses the rise of the new science, has been wholly revised and rewritten to clarify the new scientific theory arising from the Copernican revolution, the new understanding of the Galileo case, the role of women in the new science, and the social institutions of the new science.
- **The Dutch Golden Age.** A new section in Chapter 15 discusses the United Netherlands during the seventeenth and eighteenth centuries.
- **Africa and the transatlantic economy.** An extensive section in Chapter 17 explores the relationship of Africa to the transatlantic economy of the sixteenth through eighteenth centuries. We examine the role of African society and politics in the slave trade, the experience of Africans forcibly transported to the Americas, and the incorporation of elements of African culture into the New World.
- **Jewish thinkers in the Enlightenment.** A new section in Chapter 18 discusses the thought of Spinoza and Moses Mendelsohn as they relate to the role of Jewish religion and society in the wider European culture.
- **The Holocaust.** The discussion of the Holocaust has been significantly expanded in two ways. Chapter 29 provides more analysis of the causes of the Holocaust, and Chapter 30 includes an extensive new narrative of the particular case of the destruction of the Jews of Poland.
- **Twentieth-century social history.** The seventh edition of *The Western Heritage* presents the most extensive treatment of twentieth-century social history available in a survey text. We examine, in Chapter 30, the experiences of women under authoritarian governments, the collectivization of Soviet agriculture, the destruction of the Polish Jewish community, and European migration. The chapter concludes with a new section on the coming of the computer and the impact of new technology on European life.
- **The history of the Cold War and Europe at the start of the twenty-first century.** Chapter 31, on the Soviet–American rivalry and the collapse of communism, has been wholly rewritten and includes the conflict in the former Yugoslavia. Instructors may close their course with either of the twentieth-century chapters, depending on the issues they wish to emphasize.

Chapter-by-Chapter Revisions

Chapter 1 The treatment of the origins of humankind has been completely rewritten to reflect the newest scholarship.

Chapters 3, 4, 5 contain new sections on Women in Homeric Society; Aspasia, Pericles' Common-law Wife; Greek Slavery; Women in Early Rome; Women of the Upper Classes in later Roman history.

Chapter 9 contains a discussion of medieval Russia.

Chapter 12 includes a shorter, rewritten discussion of The Thirty Years' War.

Chapter 14 has a wholly rewritten discussion of the Scientific Revolution and of the impact of the Scientific Revolution on philosophy, new or extensively rewritten sections on women and early modern science, the new institutions associated with the emerging scientific knowledge, religious faith and the new science, with an expanded discussion of the Galileo case.

Chapter 15 contains an extensive new section on the Dutch Golden Age, including the impact of its overseas empire on its prosperity.

Chapter 16 has a new section on The Impact of the Agricultural and Industrial Revolutions on Working Women.

Chapter 17 includes a much expanded and revised section on African Slavery, the experiences of Africans in the Americas, and the cultural institutions they brought with them.

Chapter 18 has a new section on Jewish Thinkers in the Age of Enlightenment with emphasis on Spinoza and Moses Mendelsohn.

Chapter 22 has a refocused discussion of Karl Marx's thought.

Chapter 25 expands the treatment of racial thinking and the non-Western world.

Chapter 28 includes a rewritten discussion of the Soviet Experience in the 1930s.

Chapter 29 expands the discussion of the Holocaust.

Chapter 30 is a largely new chapter on twentieth-century social history, with major new sections on state violence, women under authoritarian governments, the collectivization of Soviet agriculture, the destruction of the Polish Jews, and the impact of the computer.

Chapter 31 has been extensively rewritten and reorganized to reflect the latest scholarship on the Cold War through the collapse of communism. It ends with a discussion of Europe at the Opening of the Global Century.

The last two chapters are written so that instructors, though teaching both chapters, may choose to close their course with either, depending upon their personal emphasis. Those instructors wishing to emphasize social history might end the course with Chapter 30 and those wishing to emphasize political development and great power relations may choose to conclude with Chapter 31.

MAPS AND ILLUSTRATIONS   To help students understand the relationship between geography and history, we have added relief features to approximately one-half of the maps. All 90 maps have been carefully edited for accuracy. The text also contains close to 500 color and black and white illustrations, many of them new to the seventh edition.

PEDAGOGICAL FEATURES   This edition retains the pedagogical features of the last edition, including part-opening comparative timelines, a list of key topics at the beginning of each chapter, chapter review questions, and questions accompanying the more than 200 source documents in the text. Each of these features is designed to make the text more accessible to students and to reinforce key concepts.

- **Illustrated timelines** open each of the six parts of the book summarizing, side-by-side, the major events in politics and government, society and economy, and religion and culture.

- **Primary source documents**, more than one third new to this edition, acquaint students with the raw material of history and provide intimate contact with the people of the past and their concerns. Questions accompanying the source documents direct students toward important, thought-provoking issues and help them relate the documents to the material in the text. They can be used to stimulate class discussion or as topics for essays and study groups.

- Each chapter includes an **outline**, a **list of key topics**, and an **introduction**. Together these features provide a succinct overview of each chapter.

- **Chronologies** follow each major section in a chapter, listing significant events and their dates.

- *In Perspective* sections summarize the major themes of each chapter and provide a bridge to the next chapter.

- **Chapter review questions** help students review the material in a chapter and relate it to broader themes. They too can be used for class discussion and essay topics.

- **Suggested readings lists** following each chapter have been updated with new titles reflecting recent scholarship.

A NOTE ON DATES AND TRANSLITERATIONS   This edition of *The Western Heritage* continues the practice of using B.C.E. (before the common era) and C.E. (common era) instead of B.C. (before Christ) and A.D. (*anno domini*, the year of the Lord) to designate dates. We also follow the most accurate currently accepted English transliterations of Arabic words. For example, today Koran is being replaced by the more accurate Qur'an; similarly Muhammad is preferable to Mohammed and Muslim to Moslem.

Ancillary Instructional Materials

The ancillary instructional materials that accompany *The Western Heritage* include print and multimedia supplements that are designed to reinforce and enliven the richness of the past and inspire students with the excitement of studying the history of Western civilization.

Print Supplements for the Instructor

INSTRUCTOR'S MANUAL WITH TEST ITEMS   The Instructor's Manual contains chapter summaries, key points and vital concepts, and information on audio-visual resources that can be used in developing and preparing lecture presentations. Also included is a test item file that offers multiple-choice, identification, and essay test questions.

PRENTICE HALL CUSTOM TEST   This commercial-quality computerized test management program, for Windows and Macintosh environments, allows users to create their own tests using items from the printed Test Item File. The program allows users to edit the items in the Test Item File and to add their own questions. Online testing is also available.

TRANSPARENCY PACKAGE   This collection of full-color transparency acetates provides the maps, charts, and graphs from the text for use in classroom presentations.

ADMINISTRATIVE HANDBOOK by Jay Boggis provides instructors with resources for using *The Western Heritage* with Annenberg/CPB telecourse, *The Western Tradition*.

Print Supplements for the Student

STUDY GUIDE, VOLUMES I AND II The study guide includes commentaries, definitions, and a variety of exercises designed to reinforce the concepts in the chapter. These exercises include: identification, map exercises, and short-answer and essay questions.

DOCUMENTS SET, VOLUMES I AND II This carefully selected and edited set of documents provides over 100 additional primary source readings. Each document includes a brief introduction as well as questions to encourage critical analysis of the reading and to relate it to the content of the text.

MAP WORKBOOK This brief workbook gives students the opportunity to increase their knowledge of geography through identification and other map exercises. It is available free to students when shrink-wrapped with the text.

HISTORICAL ATLAS OF THE WORLD This four-color historical atlas provides additional map resources to reinforce concepts in the text. It is available for a nominal fee when shrink-wrapped with the text.

UNDERSTANDING AND ANSWERING ESSAY QUESTIONS Prepared by Mary L. Kelley, San Antonio College. This brief guide suggests helpful study techniques as well as specific analytical tools for understanding different types of essay questions and provides precise guidelines for preparing well-crafted essay answers. This guide is available free to students when shrink-wrapped with the text.

READING CRITICALLY ABOUT HISTORY: A GUIDE TO ACTIVE READING Prepared by Rose Wassman and Lee Ann Rinsky. This guide focuses on the skills needed to learn the essential information presented in college history textbooks. Material covered includes  vocabulary skills, recognizing organizational patterns, critical thinking skills, understanding visual aids, and practice sections. This guide is available free to students when shrink-wrapped with the text.

THEMES OF THE TIMES *The New York Times* and Prentice Hall are sponsoring *Themes of the Times*, a program designed to enhance student access to current information of relevance in the classroom. Through this program, the core subject matter provided in the text is supplemented by a collection of current articles from one of the world's most distinguished newspapers, *The New York Times*.

These articles demonstrate the vital, ongoing connection between what is learned in the classroom and what is happening in the world around us. To enjoy the wealth of information of *The New York Times* daily, a reduced subscription rate is available. For information call toll-free: 1-800-631-1222.

Prentice Hall and *The New York Times* are proud to co-sponsor *Themes of the Times*. We hope it will make the reading of both textbooks and newspapers a more dynamic, involving process.

TELECOURSE STUDY GUIDE, VOLUMES I AND II, by Jay Boggis correlates *The Western Heritage* with the Annenberg/CPB telecourse, *The Western Tradition*.

Multimedia Supplements

HISTORY ON THE INTERNET This guide focuses on developing the critical thinking skills necessary to evaluate and use online sources. The guide also provides a brief introduction to navigating the Internet, along with complete references related specifically to the History discipline and how to use the *Companion Website*™ available for *The Western Heritage*. This supplementary book is free to students when shrink-wrapped with the text.

COMPANION WEBSITE™
ADDRESS: WWW.PRENHALL.COM/KAGAN
Students can now take full advantage of the World Wide Web to enrich their study of Western Civilization through *The Western Heritage Companion Website*™. Features of the website include, for each chapter in the text, objectives, study questions, map labeling exercises, related links, and document exercises. A faculty module provides material from the Instructor's Manual and the maps and charts from the text in Powerpoint™ format.

POWERPOINT™ IMAGES CD ROM Available for Windows and Macintosh environments, this resource includes the maps, charts, and graphs from the text for use in Powerpoint™. Organized by chapters in the text, this collection of images is useful for classroom presentations and lectures.

IRC WESTERN CIVILIZATION CD ROM Available for Windows 95 and 3.1, this lecture and presentation resource includes a library of over 3000 images, each with a descriptive caption, plus film clips, maps, and sound recordings. A correlation guide lists the images as they correspond to the chapters of *The Western Heritage*. Contact your local Prentice Hall representative for information about the adoption requirements for this resource.

COURSE MANAGEMENT SYSTEMS   For instructors interested in distance learning, Prentice Hall offers fully customizable, online courses with enhanced content, www links, online testing, and many other course management features using the best available course management systems available, including WebCT, Blackboard, and ecollege online course architecture. Contact your local Prentice Hall representative or visit our special Demonstration Central Website at http://www.prenhall.com/demo for more information.

Acknowledgments

We are grateful to the scholars and teachers whose thoughtful and often detailed comments helped shape this revision:

Lenard R. Berlanstein, University of
  Virginia, Charlottesville
Stephanie Christelow, Idaho State University
Samuel Willard Crompton, Holyoke
  Community College
Robert L. Ervin, San Jacinto Community College
Benjamin Foster, Yale University
Joseph Gonzales, Moorpark College
Victor Davis Hanson, California State
  University, Fresno
William I. Hitchcock, Wellesley College

Pardaic Kenny, University of Colorado, Boulder
Raymond F. Kierstead, Reed College
David Lindberg, University of
  Wisconsin, Madison
Eleanor McCluskey, Palm Beach Atlantic College
  and Broward Community College
Robert J. Mueller, Hastings College
John Nicols, University of Oregon, Eugene
Sandra J. Peacock, State University of New York,
  Binghamton
John Powell, Pennsylvania State University
Robert A. Schneider, Catholic University
Hugo Schwyzer, Pasadena City College
Sidney R. Sherter, Long Island University
Roger P. Snow, College of Great Falls

Finally, we would like to thank the dedicated people who helped produce this revision. Our acquisitions editor, Charlyce Jones Owen; our development editor, Roberta Meyer; our production editor, Joe Scordato; Nancy Wells, who created the handsome new design of this edition; Scott Garrison, who formatted the pages; Lynn Pearlman, our manufacturing buyer; and Barbara Salz, photo researcher.

D.K.
S.O.
F.M.T.

About the Authors

DONALD KAGAN is Hillhouse Professor of History and Classics at Yale University, where he has taught since 1969. He received the A.B. degree in history from Brooklyn College, the M.A. in classics from Brown University, and the Ph.D. in history from Ohio State University. During 1958–1959 he studied at the American School of Classical Studies as a Fulbright Scholar. He has received three awards for undergraduate teaching at Cornell and Yale. He is the author of a history of Greek political thought, *The Great Dialogue* (1965); a four-volume history of the Peloponnesian war, *The Origins of the Peloponnesian War* (1969); *The Archidamian War* (1974); *The Peace of Nicias and the Sicilian Expedition* (1981); *The Fall of the Athenian Empire* (1987); and a biography of Pericles, *Pericles of Athens and the Birth of Democracy* (1991); and *On the Origins of War* (1995). He is coauthor, with Frederick W. Kagan of *While America Sleeps* (2000). With Brian Tierney and L. Pearce Williams, he is the editor of *Great Issues in Western Civilization*, a collection of readings.

STEVEN OZMENT is McLean Professor of Ancient and Modern History at Harvard University. He has taught Western Civilization at Yale, Stanford, and Harvard. He is the author of ten books. *The Age of Reform*, 1250–1550 (1980) won the Schaff Prize and was nominated for the 1981 American Book Award. *Magdalena and Balthasar: An Intimate Portrait of Life in Sixteenth Century Europe* (1986), *Three Behaim Boys: Growing Up in Early Modern Germany* (1990), *Protestants: The Birth of a Revolution* (1992), and *The Burgermeister's Daughter: Scandal in a Sixteenth Century German Town* (1996) were selections of the History Book Club, as is his most recent book, *Flesh and Spirit: Private Life in Early Modern Germany* (1999).

FRANK M. TURNER is John Hay Whitney Professor of History at Yale University, where he served as University Provost from 1988 to 1992. He received his B.A. degree at the College of William and Mary and his Ph.D. from Yale. He has received the Yale College Award for Distinguished Undergraduate Teaching. He has directed a National Endowment for the Humanities Summer Institute. His scholarly research has received the support of fellowships from the National Endowment for the Humanities and the Guggenheim Foundation and the Woodrow Wilson Center. He is the author of *Between Science and Religion: The Reaction to Scientific Naturalism in Late Victorian England* (1974), *The Greek Heritage in Victorian Britain* (1981), which received the British Council Prize of the Conference on British Studies and the Yale Press Governors Award, and *Contesting Cultural Authority: Essays in Victorian Intellectual Life* (1993). He has also contributed numerous articles to journals and has served on the editorial advisory boards of *The Journal of Modern History, Isis,* and *Victorian Studies*. He edited *The Idea of a University*, by John Henry Newman (1996). Since 1996 he has served as a Trustee of Connecticut College.

Part 3
1300–1750

POLITICS AND GOVERNMENT	SOCIETY AND ECONOMY	RELIGION AND CULTURE
1300–1400		
1309–1377 Pope resides in Avignon	1315–1317 Greatest famine of the Middle Ages	1300–1325 Dante Alighieri writes *Divine Comedy*
1337–1453 Hundred Years' War	1347–1350 Black Death peaks	1302 Boniface VIII issues bull *Unam Sanctam*
1356 *Golden Bull* creates German electoral college	1358 *Jacquerie* shakes France	1350 Boccaccio, *Decameron*
	1378 Ciompi Revolt in Florence	1375–1527 The Renaissance in Italy
	1381 English peasants' revolt	1378–1417 The Great Schism
		1380–1395 Chaucer writes *Canterbury Tales*
		1390–1430 Christine de Pisan writes in defense of women
1400–1500		1414–1417 The Council of Constance
1415–1433 Hussite revolt in Bohemia		
1428–1519 Aztecs expand in central Mexico		
1429 Joan of Arc leads French to victory in Orleans	1450 Johann Gutenberg invents printing with movable type	1425–1450 Lorenzo Valla exposes the *Donation of Constantine*
1434 Medici rule begins in Florence		1450 Thomas à Kempis, *Imitation of Christ*
1453–1471 Wars of the Roses in England		
1469 Marriage of Ferdinand and Isabella	1492 Christopher Columbus encounters the Americas	
1487 Henry Tudor creates Court of Star Chamber	1498 Vasco da Gama reaches India	1492 Expulsion of Jews from Spain
1500–1600		
1519 Charles V crowned Holy Roman emperor	1519 Hernan Cortes lands in Mexico	1513 Niccolo Machiavelli, *The Prince*
1530 *Augsburg Confession* defines Lutheranism	1519–1522 Ferdinand Magellan circumnavigates the Earth	1516 Erasmus compiles a Greek New Testament
	1525 German Peasants' Revolt	1516 Thomas More, *Utopia*
	1531–1533 Francisco Pizarro conquers the Incas	1517 Martin Luther's Ninety-five theses
1547 Ivan the Terrible becomes tsar of Russia	1540 Spanish open silver mines in Peru, Bolivia, and Mexico	1534 Henry VIII declared head of English Church
1555 *Peace of Augsburg* recognizes the legal principle, *cuius regio, eius religio*	1550–1600 The great witch panics	1540 Jesuit order founded
		1541 John Calvin becomes Geneva's reformer
1568–1603 Reign of Elizabeth I of England		1543 Copernicus, *On the Revolutions of the Heavenly Spheres*
1572 Saint Bartholomew's Day Massacre		1545–1563 Council of Trent
1588 English defeat of Spanish Armada		1549 English *Book of Common Prayer*
1598 Edict of Nantes gives Huguenots religious and civil rights		

Elizabeth I, The Armada Portrait

EUROPE IN TRANSITION

1300–1750

	POLITICS AND GOVERNMENT	SOCIETY AND ECONOMY	RELIGION AND CULTURE
1600–1700	1624–1642 Era of Richelieu in France 1629–1640 Charles I's years of personal rule 1640 Long Parliament convenes 1642 Outbreak of civil war in England 1643–1661 Cardinal Mazarin regent for Louis XIV 1648 Peace of Westphalia 1649–1652 The *Fronde* in France 1649 Charles I executed 1660 Charles II restored to the English throne 1661–1715 Louis XIV's years of personal rule 1682–1725 Reign of Peter the Great 1685 James II becomes king of England Louis XIV revokes Edict of Nantes 1688 "Glorious Revolution" in Britain	1600–1700 Period of greatest Dutch economic prosperity 1600–early 1700s Spain maintains commercial monopoly in Latin America 1607 English settle Jamestown, Virginia 1608 French settle Quebec 1618–1648 Thirty Years' War devastates German economy 1619 African slaves first bought at Jamestown, Virginia 1650s–1670s Commercial rivalry between Dutch and English 1661–1683 Colbert seeks to stimulate French economic growth 1690 Paris Foundling Hospital established	1605 Bacon, *The Advancement of Learning*; Shakespeare, *King Lear*, Cervantes, *Don Quixote* 1609 Kepler, *The New Astronomy* 1611 King James Version of the English Bible 1632 Galileo, *Dialogues on the Two Chief Systems of the World* 1637 Descartes, *Discourse on Method* 1651 Hobbes, *Leviathan* 1687 Newton, *Principia Mathematica* 1689 English Toleration Act 1690 Locke, *Essay Concerning Human Understanding*
1700–1789	1700–1721 Great Northern War between Sweden and Russia 1702–1714 War of Spanish Succession 1713 Peace of Utrecht 1720–1740 Age of Walpole in England and Fleury in France 1740 Maria Theresa succeeds to the Habsburg throne 1740–1748 War of the Austrian Succession 1756–1763 Seven Years' War 1767 Legislative Commission in Russia 1772 First Partition of Poland 1776 American Declaration of Independence  Declaration of Independence 1778 France aids the American colonies	1715–1763 Era of major colonial rivalry in the Caribbean 1719 Mississippi Bubble in France 1733 James Kay's flying shuttle 1750s Agricultural Revolution in Britain 1750–1840 Growth of new cities 1763 Britain becomes dominant in India 1763–1789 Enlightened absolutist rulers seek to spur economic growth 1765 James Hargreaves's spinning jenny 1769 Richard Arkwright's waterframe 1771–1775 Pugachev's Rebellion	1739 Wesley begins field preaching 1748 Montesquieu, *Spirit of the Laws* 1750 Rousseau, *Discourse on the Moral Effects of the Arts and Sciences* 1751 First volume Diderot's *Encyclopedia* 1762 Rousseau, *Social Contract* and *Émile* 1763 Voltaire, Treatise on Tolerance 1774 Goethe, *Sorrow of Young Werther* 1776 Smith, *Wealth of Nations* 1781 Kant, *Critique of Pure Reason* Joseph II adopts policy of toleration in Austria

The apparition of the Knight of Death, an allegory of the plague approaching a city, whose defenses against it are all too unsure. From the *Tres Riches Heures du Duc de Berry* (1284), Limbourg Brothers. Ms. 65/1284, fol. 90v. Musée Conde, Chantilly, France. Giraudon/Art Resource, N.Y.

The Late Middle Ages:
Social and Political Breakdown
(1300–1527)

The Hundred Years' War and the Rise of National Sentiment
The Causes of the War
Progress of the War

The Black Death
Preconditions and Causes
Popular Remedies
Social and Economic Consequences
New Conflicts and Opportunities

Ecclesiastical Breakdown and Revival: The Late Medieval Church
The Thirteenth-Century Papacy
Boniface VIII and Philip the Fair
The Avignon Papacy (1309–1377)
The Great Schism (1378–1417)
    and the Conciliar Movement to 1449

Medieval Russia
Politics and Society
Mongol Rule (1243–1480)
Liberation

KEY TOPICS

- The Hundred Years' War between England and France
- The effects of the bubonic plague on population and society
- The growing power of secular rulers over the papacy
- Schism, heresy, and reform of the church

The late Middle Ages saw almost unprecedented political, social, and ecclesiastical calamity. France and England grappled with each other in a bitter conflict known as the Hundred Years' War (1337–1453), an exercise in seemingly willful self-destruction that was made even more terrible in its later stages by the introduction of gunpowder and the invention of heavy artillery. Bubonic plague, known to contemporaries as the "Black Death," swept over almost all of Europe, killing as much as one-third of the population in many regions between 1348 and 1350 and transforming many pious Christians into believers in the omnipotence of death. A schism emerged within the church, which lasted thirty-nine years (1378–1417) and led, by 1409, to the election of no fewer than three competing popes and colleges of cardinals. In 1453, the Turks marched seemingly invincibly through Constantinople and toward the West. As their political and religious institutions buckled, as disease, bandits, and wolves ravaged their cities in the wake of war, and as Islamic armies gathered at their borders, Europeans beheld what seemed to be the imminent total collapse of Western civilization.

It was in this period that such scholars as Marsilius of Padua, William of Ockham, and Lorenzo Valla produced lasting criticisms of medieval assumptions about the nature of God, humankind, and society. Kings worked through parliaments and clergy through councils to place lasting limits on the pope's temporal power. The notion, derived from Roman law, that a secular ruler is accountable to the body of which he or she is head had already found expression in documents like the Magna Carta. It came increasingly to carry the force of accepted principle, and conciliarists (advocates of the judicial superiority of a church council over a pope) sought to extend it to establish papal accountability to the church.

✗ *But viewed in terms of their three great calamities—war, plague, and schism—the fourteenth and fifteenth centuries were years in which politics resisted wisdom, nature strained mercy, and the church was less than faithful to its mandate.*

The Hundred Years' War and the Rise of National Sentiment

Medieval governments were by no means all-powerful and secure. The rivalry of petty lords kept localities in turmoil, and dynastic rivalries could plunge entire lands into war, especially when power was being transferred to a new ruler, and woe to the ruling dynasty that failed to produce a male heir.

To field the armies and collect the revenues that made their existence possible, late medieval rulers depended on carefully negotiated alliances among a wide range of lesser powers. Like kings and queens in earlier centuries, they, too, practiced the art of feudal government, but on a grander scale and with greater sophistication. To maintain the order they required, the Norman kings of England and the Capetian kings of France finetuned traditional feudal relationships, stressing the duties of lesser to higher power and the unquestioning loyalty noble vassals owed the king. The result was a degree of centralized royal power unseen before in these lands and a nascent "national" consciousness that equipped both France and England for international warfare.

The Causes of the War

The conflict that came to be known as the Hundred Years' War began in May 1337 and lasted until October 1453. The English king Edward III (r. 1327–1377), the grandson of Philip the Fair of France (r. 1285–1314), may be said to have started the war by asserting a claim to the French throne when the French king Charles IV (r. 1322–1328), the last of Philip the Fair's surviving sons, died without a male heir. The French barons had no intention of placing the then fifteen-year-old Edward on the French throne, choosing instead the first cousin of Charles IV, Philip VI of Valois (r. 1328–1350), the first of a new French dynasty that ruled into the sixteenth century.

But there was more to the war than just an English king's assertion of a claim to the French throne. England and France were then emergent territorial powers in too close proximity to one another. Edward was actually a vassal of Philip's, holding several sizable French territories as fiefs from the king of France, a relationship that went back to the days of the Norman conquest. English possession of any French land was repugnant to the French because it threatened the royal policy of centralization. England and France also quarreled over control of Flanders, which, although a French fief, was subject to political influence from England because its principal industry, the manufacture of cloth, depended on supplies of imported English wool. Compounding these frictions was a long history of prejudice and animosity between the French and English people, who constantly confronted one another on the high seas and in port towns. Taken together, these various factors made the Hundred Years' War a struggle for national identity as well as for control of territory.

FRENCH WEAKNESS France had three times the population of England, was far the wealthier of the two countries, and fought on its own soil. Yet, for the greater part of the conflict, until after 1415, the major battles ended in often stunning English victories. (See Map 9–1.) The primary reason for these French failures was internal disunity caused by endemic social conflicts. Unlike England,

Edward III pays homage to his feudal lord Philip VI of France. Legally, Edward was a vassal of the king of France. Archives Snark International/Art Resource, N.Y.

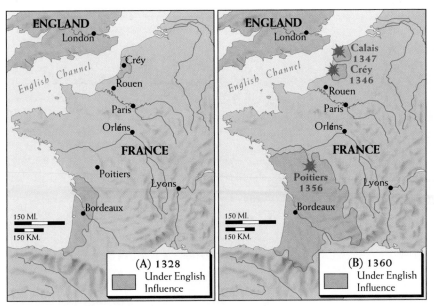

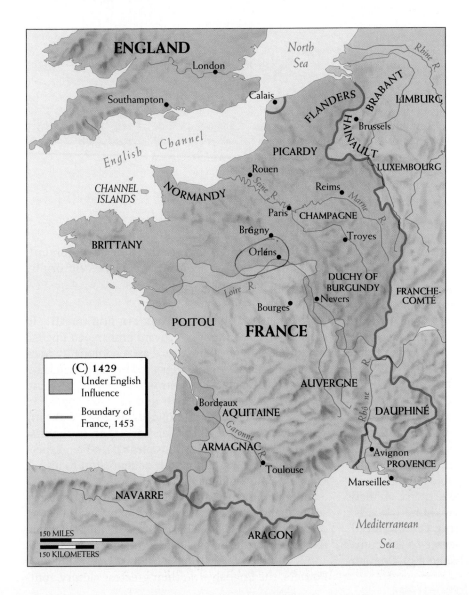

MAP 9–1 THE HUNDRED YEARS' WAR *The Hundred Years' War went on intermittently from the late 1330s until 1453. These maps show the remarkable English territorial gains up to the sudden and decisive turning of the tide of battle in favor of the French by the forces of Joan of Arc in 1429.*

Scene from an encamped army, surrounded by a barricade of wagons, some of which contain artillery pointed outward. 15th-century Germany. Kunstammlungen der Frusten zu Waldburg-Wolfegg, fol. 54r

France was still struggling in the fourteenth century to make the transition from a fragmented feudal society to a centralized "modern" state.

Desperate to raise money for the war, French kings resorted to such financial policies as depreciating the currency and borrowing heavily from Italian bankers, which aggravated internal conflicts. In 1355, in a bid to secure funds, the king convened a representative council of townspeople and nobles that came to be known as the Estates General. Although it levied taxes at the king's request, its members also used the king's plight to enhance their own regional rights and privileges, thereby deepening territorial divisions.

France's defeats also reflected English military superiority. The English infantry was more disciplined than the French, and English archers carried a formidable weapon, the longbow, capable of firing six arrows a minute with enough force to pierce an inch of wood or the armor of a knight at two hundred yards.

Finally, French weakness during the Hundred Years' War was due in no small degree to the comparative mediocrity of its royal leadership. English kings were far the shrewder.

Progress of the War

The war had three major stages of development, each ending with a seemingly decisive victory by one or the other side.

THE CONFLICT DURING THE REIGN OF EDWARD III In the first stage of the war, Edward embargoed English wool to Flanders, sparking urban rebellions by merchants and the trade guilds. Inspired by a rich merchant, Jacob van Artevelde, the Flemish cities, led by Ghent, revolted against the French and in 1340 signed an alliance with England acknowledging Edward as king of France. On June 23 of that same year, in the first great battle of the war, Edward defeated the French fleet in the Bay of Sluys, but his subsequent effort to invade France by way of Flanders failed.

In 1346 Edward attacked Normandy and, after a series of easy victories that culminated at the Battle of Crécy, seized Calais. Exhaustion of both sides and the onset of the Black Death forced a truce in late 1347, and the war entered a brief lull. In 1356, near Poitiers, the English won their greatest victory, rout-

This miniature illustrates two scenes from the English peasant revolt of 1381. On the left, Wat Tyler, one of the leaders of the revolt, is executed in the presence of King Richard II. On the right, King Richard urges armed peasants to end their rebellion. Arthur Hacker, *The Cloister of the World.* The Bridgeman Art Library.

ing France's noble cavalry and taking the French king, John II the Good (r. 1350–1364), captive back to England. The defeat brought a complete breakdown of political order to France.

Power in France now lay with the Estates General. Led by the powerful merchants of Paris under Étienne Marcel, that body took advantage of royal weakness, demanding and receiving rights similar to those granted the English privileged classes in the Magna Carta. But unlike the English Parliament, which represented the interests of a comparatively unified English nobility, the French Estates General was too divided to be an instrument for effective government.

To secure their rights, the French privileged classes forced the peasantry to pay ever-increasing taxes and to repair their war-damaged properties without compensation. This bullying became more than the peasants could bear, and they rose up in several regions in a series of bloody rebellions known as the *Jacquerie* in 1358 (after the peasant revolutionary popularly known as *Jacques Bonhomme,* or "simple Jack"). The nobility quickly put down the revolt, matching the rebels atrocity for atrocity.

On May 9, 1360, another milestone of the war was reached when England forced the Peace of Brétigny on the French. This agreement declared an end to Edward's vassalage to the king of France and affirmed his sovereignty over English territories in France (including Gascony, Guyenne, Poitou, and Calais). France also agreed to pay a ransom of three million gold crowns to win King John the Good's release. In return, Edward simply renounced his claim to the French throne.

Such a partition of French territorial control was completely unrealistic, and sober observers on both sides knew that it could not last long. France struck back in the late 1360s and by the time of Edward's death in 1377 had beaten the English back to coastal enclaves and the territory of Bordeaux.

FRENCH DEFEAT AND THE TREATY OF TROYES After Edward's death the English war effort lessened, partly because of domestic problems within England. During the reign of Richard II (r. 1377–1399), England had its own version of the *Jacquerie.* In June 1381, long-oppressed peasants and artisans joined in a great revolt of the unprivileged classes under the leadership of John Ball, a secular priest, and Wat Tyler, a journeyman. As in France, the revolt was brutally crushed within the year, but it left the country divided for decades.

The war intensified under Henry V (r. 1413–1422), who took advantage of internal French turmoil created by the rise to power of the duchy of Burgundy. With France deeply divided, Henry V struck hard in Normandy. Happy to see the rest of France besieged, the Burgundians foolishly watched from the sidelines while Henry's army routed the opposition led by the count of Armagnac, who had picked up the royal banner at Agincourt on October 25, 1415. In the years thereafter, belatedly recognizing that the defeat of

France would leave them easy prey for the English, the Burgundians closed ranks with French royal forces. The renewed French unity, loose as it was, promised to bring eventual victory over the English, but it was shattered in September 1419 when the duke of Burgundy was assassinated. In the aftermath of this shocking event, the duke's son and heir, determined to avenge his father's death, joined forces with the English.

France now became Henry V's for the taking—at least in the short run. The Treaty of Troyes in 1420 disinherited the legitimate heir to the French throne and proclaimed Henry V the successor to the French king, Charles VI. When Henry and Charles died within months of one another in 1422, the infant Henry VI of England was proclaimed in Paris to be king of both France and England. The dream of Edward III that had set the war in motion—to make the ruler of England the ruler also of France—had been realized, at least for the moment.

The son of Charles VI went into retreat in Bourges, where, on the death of his father, he became Charles VII to most of the French people, who ignored the Treaty of Troyes. Displaying unprecedented national feeling inspired by the remarkable Joan of Arc, they soon rallied to his cause and came together in an ultimately victorious coalition.

A contemporary portrait of Joan of Arc (1412–1431) in the National Archives in Paris. 15th c. Franco-Flemish miniature. Archives Nationales, Paris, France. Giraudon/Art Resource, N.Y.

The Hundred Years' War (1337–1443)	
1340	English victory at Bay of Sluys
1346	English victory at Crécy and seizure of Calais
1347	Black Death strikes
1356	English victory at Poitiers
1358	*Jacquerie* disrupts France
1360	Peace of Brétigny recognizes English holdings in France
1381	English peasants revolt
1415	English victory at Agincourt
1422	Treaty of Troyes proclaims Henry VI ruler of both England and France
1429	Joan of Arc leads French to victory at Orléans
1431	Joan of Arc executed as a heretic
1453	War ends; English retain only coastal town of Calais

JOAN OF ARC AND THE WAR'S CONCLUSION Joan of Arc (1412–1431), a peasant from Domrémy, presented herself to Charles VII in March 1429, declaring that the King of Heaven had called her to deliver besieged Orléans from the English. The king was understandably skeptical, but being in retreat from what seemed to be a hopeless war, he was willing to try anything to reverse French fortunes. And the deliverance of Orléans, a city strategic to the control of the territory south of the Loire, would be a godsend. Charles's desperation overcame his skepticism, and he gave Joan his leave.

Circumstances worked perfectly to her advantage. The English force, already exhausted by a six-month siege of Orléans, was at the point of withdrawal when Joan arrived with fresh French troops. After repulsing the English from Orléans, the French enjoyed a succession of victories they popularly attributed to Joan. She deserved much of this credit, but not because she was a military genius. She provided the French with something military experts could not: inspiration and a sense of national identity and self-confidence. Within a few months of the liberation of Orléans, Charles VII received his crown in Rheims and ended the nine-year "disinheritance" prescribed by the Treaty of Troyes.

Charles forgot his liberator as quickly as he had embraced her. When the Burgundians captured Joan in May 1430, he was in a position to secure her release, but did little for her. The Burgundians and the English wanted her publicly discredited, believing this would also discredit Charles VII and demoralize French resistance. She was turned

Joan of Arc Refuses to Recant Her Beliefs

Joan of Arc, threatened with torture, refused to recant her beliefs and instead defended the instructions she had received from the voices that spoke to her.

❖ *In the following excerpt from her self-defense, do you get the impression that the judges have made up their minds about Joan in advance? How does this judicial process, which was based on intensive interrogation of the accused, differ from a trial today? Why was Joan deemed heretical and not insane when she acknowledged hearing voices?*

On Wednesday, May 9th of the same year [1431], Joan was brought into the great tower of the castle of Rouen before us the said judges. And [she] was required and admonished to speak the truth on many different points contained in her trial which she had denied or to which she had given false replies, whereas we possessed certain information, proofs, and vehement presumptions upon them. Many of the points were read and explained to her, and she was told that if she did not confess them truthfully she would be put to the torture, the instruments of which were shown to her all ready in the tower. There were also present by our instruction men ready to put her to the torture in order to restore her to the way and knowledge of truth, and by this means to procure the salvation of her body and soul which by her lying inventions she exposed to such grave perils.

To which the said Joan answered in this manner: "Truly if you were to tear me limb from limb and separate my soul from my body, I would not tell you anything more: and if I did say anything, I should afterwards declare that you had compelled me to say it by force." Then she said that on Holy Cross Day last she received comfort from St. Gabriel; she firmly believes it was St. Gabriel. She knew by her voices whether she should submit to the Church, since the clergy were pressing her hard to submit. Her voices told her that if she desired Our Lord to aid her she must wait upon Him in all her doings. She said that Our Lord has always been the master of her doings, and the Enemy never had power over them. She asked her voices if she would be burned and they answered that she must wait upon God, and He would aid her.

From *The Trial of Jeanne D'Arc*, trans. by W. P. Barrett (New York: Gotham House, 1932), pp. 303–304.

over to the Inquisition in English-held Rouen. The inquisitors broke the courageous "Maid of Orléans" after ten weeks of interrogation, and she was executed as a relapsed heretic on May 30, 1431. (See "Joan of Arc Refuses to Recant Her Beliefs.") Twenty-five years later (1456) Charles reopened her trial, and she was declared innocent of all the charges. In 1920 the church declared her a saint.

In 1435, the duke of Burgundy made peace with Charles. France, now unified and at peace with Burgundy, continued progressively to force the English back. By 1453, the date of the war's end, the English held only their coastal enclave of Calais.

The Hundred Years' War, with sixty-eight years of at least nominal peace and forty-four of hot war, had lasting political and social consequences. It devastated France, but it also awakened French nationalism and hastened the transition there from a feudal monarchy to a centralized state. It saw Burgundy become a major European political power. And it

encouraged the English, in response to the seesawing allegiance of the Netherlands throughout the conflict, to develop their own clothing industry and foreign markets. In both France and England the burden of the on-again, off-again war fell most heavily on the peasantry, who were forced to support it with taxes and services.

The Black Death

Preconditions and Causes

In the late Middle Ages, nine-tenths of the population worked the land. The three-field system, in use in most areas since well before the fourteenth century, had increased the amount of arable land and thereby the food supply. The growth of cities and trade had also stimulated agricultural science and productivity. But as the food supply grew, so did the population. It is estimated that Europe's population

A Renaissance portrayal of the sixth-century (590) procession of St. Gregory to St. Peter's, an effort to end a plague. From the Soane Book of Hours *(c. 1500).*
Sir John Soane's Museum. E.T. Archive, London

rapidly through Spain and southern France and into northern Europe. Areas that lay outside the major trade routes, like Bohemia, appear to have remained virtually unaffected.

Bubonic plague made numerous reappearances in succeeding decades. By the early fifteenth century, it is estimated that western Europe as a whole had lost as much as two-fifths of its population. A full recovery did not occur until the sixteenth century. (See Map 9–2.)

Popular Remedies

The plague, transmitted by rat- or human-borne fleas, often reached a victim's lungs during the course of the disease. From the lungs, it could be spread from person to person by the victim's sneezing and wheezing. Contemporary physicians had no understanding of these processes, so even the most rudimentary prophylaxis against the disease was lacking. To the people of the time, the Black Death was a catastrophe with no apparent explanation and against which there was no known defense. Throughout much of western

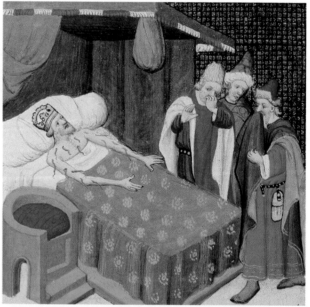

In this scene from an illustrated manuscript of Boccaccio's Decameron, *physicians apply leeches to an emperor. The text says he suffered from a disease that caused a terrible stench, which is why the physicians are holding their noses. Bleeding was the agreed-upon best way to prevent and cure illness and was practiced as late as the nineteenth century. Its popularity was rooted in the belief that a build-up of foul matter in the body caused illness by disrupting the body's four humors (blood, phlegm, yellow bile, and black bile). Bleeding released the foul matter and restored equilibrium among the humors, thus preserving good health by strengthening resistance to disease.*
Jean-Loup Charmet/Science Photo Library

doubled between the years 1000 and 1300 and by 1300 had begun to outstrip food production. There were now more people than there was food available to feed them or jobs to employ them, and the average European faced the probability of extreme hunger at least once during his or her expected thirty-five-year life span.

Between 1315 and 1317, crop failures produced the greatest famine of the Middle Ages. Densely populated urban areas such as the industrial towns of the Netherlands experienced great suffering. Decades of overpopulation, economic depression, famine, and bad health progressively weakened Europe's population and made it highly vulnerable to a virulent bubonic plague that struck with full force in 1348.

 This "Black Death," so called by contemporaries because of the way it discolored the body, was probably introduced by seaborne rats from Black Sea areas and followed the trade routes from Asia into Europe. Appearing in Sicily in late 1347, it entered Europe through the port cities of Venice, Genoa, and Pisa in 1348, and from there it swept

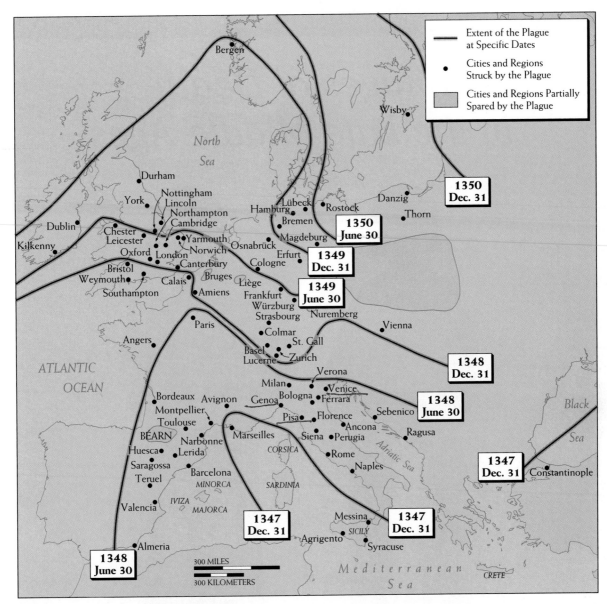

MAP 9–2   SPREAD OF THE BLACK DEATH   *Apparently introduced by seaborne rats from Black Sea areas where plague-infested rodents have long been known, the Black Death brought huge human, social, and economic consequences. One of the lower estimates of Europeans dying is 25,000,000. The map charts the plague's spread in the mid-fourteenth century. Generally following trade routes, the plague reached Scandinavia by 1350, and some believe it then went on to Iceland and even Greenland. Areas off the main trade routes were largely spared.*

Europe it inspired an obsession with death and dying and a deep pessimism that endured for decades after the plague years. (See "Art & the West.")

Popular wisdom held that a corruption in the atmosphere caused the disease. Some blamed poisonous fumes released by earthquakes. Many adopted aromatic amulets as a remedy. According to the contemporary observations of Boccaccio, who recorded the varied reactions to the plague in the *Decameron* (1353), some sought a remedy in moderation and a temperate life; others gave themselves over entirely to their passions (sexual promiscuity within the stricken areas apparently ran high); and still others, "the most sound, perhaps, in judgment," chose flight and seclusion as the best medicine. (See "Boccaccio Describes the Black Death in Florence.")

Among the most extreme social reactions were processions of flagellants. These religious fanatics beat themselves in ritual penance until they bled, believing that such action would bring divine intervention. The terror created by the flagellants (whose

Images of Death in the Late Middle Ages

The Prince of the World in the Church of St. Sebald, Nürnberg, 1320–1330. Germnisches Nationalmuseum, Nürnberg.

Throughout the Middle Ages, people perceived, and artists portrayed death both realistically and religiously: on the one hand, as a terrible, inescapable fate, and on the other, as the beginning of a new, eternal life, either in heaven or in hell. That life is death (transitory) and death is life (the afterlife) were two urgent and ironic teachings of the Christian Church. Many laity, finding the present world undesirable and death no sure release into a better one, understandably resisted. Graphic and sermonic instruction in the "Art of Dying" became the Church's response. Shown here, a sandstone sculpture, *The Prince of the World*, carries a vivid warning. When viewers looked behind this young, attractive prince, they discovered that beauty is only skin deep: His body, like everyone else's, is filled with worms and flesh-eating frogs. A serpent spirals up his left leg and enters his back—an allusion to the biblical teaching that the wages of sin are death. To drive home human mortality, the Church instructed laity to think often about the inevitability of death by visiting dying relatives and friends, watching them die and being buried, and thereafter visiting their graves often. This, in turn, would move them to resist the devil's temptations, obey the Church, avoid sin, and become eligible for heaven in the afterlife.

During the late Middle Ages, in both literature and art, the "Dance of Death" became a new reminder of human mortality and the need for Christian living and Church instruction. (It was first painted in 1424, on the wall of the Church of the Holy Innocents in Paris.) Death appeared as a living skeleton in lively conversation with mortal representatives—from pope to friar in the religious world, from emperor to laborer in the secular—none of whom, no matter how mighty, can elude Death's grasp. Even the Son of God, as an incarnate man, died a dreadful death. Although emerging in the late Middle Ages, the "Dance of Death" conveyed an old message, apparently urgently needed at the time because of the indiscipline and self-indulgence occasioned by the new horrors of the Black Death and the Hundred Years' War.

The Church's last word on death, however, was resplendently positive: Mortal men and women of true faith, like the crucified Son of God, might look forward to eternal life as shown in *The Resurrection*, from the *Isenheim Altarpiece*, 1509/10–1515.

Sources: Alberto Tenenti, "Death in History," in *Life and Death in Fifteenth Century Florence*, ed. M. Tetel et al. (Durham, NC: Duke University Press, 1989); Donald Weinstein, "The Art of Dying Well and Popular Piety in the Preaching and Thought of Girolamo Savonarola," in *ibid.*, 88–104; and James M. Clark, *The Dance of Death in the Middle Ages and the Renaissance* (Glasgow: Jackson, Son, and Col, 1950), pp. 1–4, 22–24, 106–110. Joseph L. Koerner, *The Moment of Self-Portraiture in German Renaissance Art* (Chicago, University of Chicago Press, 1993), pp. 199–200. H. W. Janson et al., *History of Art* (Upper Saddle River, NJ: Prentice Hall, 1997), p. 528.

Gruenwald, Mathias (1460–1528), *The Resurrection*. A panel from the Isenheim Altar. Limewood (around 1515), 250 × 650 cm. Musée d'Unterlinden, Colmar, France.

301

Boccaccio Describes the Ravages of the Black Death in Florence

The Black Death provided an excuse to the poet, humanist, and storyteller Giovanni Boccaccio (1313–1375) to assemble his great collection of tales, the Decameron. Ten congenial men and women flee Florence to escape the plague and while away the time telling stories. In one of the stories, Boccaccio embeds a fine clinical description of plague symptoms as seen in Florence in 1348 and of the powerlessness of physicians and the lack of remedies.

❖ *What did people do to escape the plague? Was any of it sound medical practice? What does the study of calamities like the Black Death tell us about the people of the past?*

In Florence, despite all that human wisdom and forethought could devise to avert it, even as the cleansing of the city from many impurities by officials appointed for the purpose, the refusal of entrance to all sick folk, and the adoption of many precautions for the preservation of health; despite also humble supplications addressed to God, and often repeated both in public procession and otherwise, by the devout; towards the beginning of the spring of the said year [1348] the doleful effects of the pestilence began to be horribly apparent by symptoms that [appeared] as if miraculous.

Not such were these symptoms as in the East, where an issue of blood from the nose was a manifest sign of inevitable death; but in men and women alike it first betrayed itself by the emergence of certain tumours in the groin or the armpits, some of which grew as large as a common apple, others as an egg, some more, some less, which the common folk called *gavoccioli*. From the two said parts of the body this deadly *gavoccioli* soon began to propagate and spread itself in all directions indifferently; after which the form of the malady began to change, spots black or livid making their appearance in many cases on the arm or the thigh or elsewhere, now few and large, now minute and numerous. And as the *gavoccioli* had been and still were an infallible token of approaching death, such also were these spots on whomsoever they shewed themselves. Which maladies seemed to set entirely at naught both the art of the physician and the virtues of physic; indeed, whether it was that the disorder was of a nature to defy such treatment, or that the physicians were at fault... and, being in ignorance of its source, failed to apply the proper remedies; in either case, not merely were those that recovered few, but almost all died within three days of the appearance of the said symptoms...and in most cases without any fever or other attendant malady.

From *The Decameron of Giovanni Boccaccio*, trans. by J. M. Rigg (London: J. M. Dent & Sons, 1930), p. 5.

---

dirty bodies may actually have served to transport the disease) became so socially disruptive and threatening even to established authority, that the church finally outlawed their processions.

Jews were cast as scapegoats for the plague. Centuries of Christian propaganda had bred hatred toward them, as had their role as society's moneylenders. Pogroms occurred in several cities, sometimes incited by the arrival of flagellants.

Social and Economic Consequences

Whole villages vanished in the wake of the plague. Among the social and economic conse-

quences of this depopulation were a shrunken labor supply and a decline in the value of the estates of the nobility.

FARMS DECLINE   As the number of farm laborers decreased, their wages increased and those of skilled artisans soared. Many serfs now chose to commute their labor services by money payments or to abandon the farm altogether and pursue more interesting and rewarding jobs in skilled craft industries in the cities. Agricultural prices fell because of lowered demand, and the price of luxury and manufactured goods—the work of skilled artisans—rose. The noble landholders suffered the greatest decline in power

A caricature of physicians (early sixteenth century). In the Middle Ages and later, people recognized the shortcomings of physicians and surgeons and visited them only as a last resort. Here a physician carries a uroscope (for collecting and examining urine); cloudy or discolored urine signaled an immediate need for bleeding. The physician/surgeon wears surgical shoes and his assistant carries a flail—a comment on the risks of medical services. Hacker Art Books Inc.

from this new state of affairs. They were forced to pay more for finished products and for farm labor, but received a smaller return on their agricultural produce. Everywhere their rents were in steady decline after the plague.

PEASANTS REVOLT To recoup their losses, some landowners converted arable land to sheep pasture, substituting more profitable wool production for labor-intensive grain crops. Others abandoned the effort to farm their land and simply leased it to the highest bidder. Landowners also sought simply to reverse their misfortune—to close off the new economic opportunities opened for the peasantry by the demographic crisis—through repressive legislation that forced peasants to stay on their farms and froze their wages at low levels. In France the direct tax on the peasantry, the *taille*, was increased, and opposition to it was prominent among the grievances behind the *Jacquerie*. In 1351, the English Parliament passed a Statute of Laborers,

which limited wages to preplague levels and restricted the ability of peasants to leave the land of their traditional masters. Opposition to such legislation was also a prominent factor in the English peasants' revolt in 1381.

CITIES REBOUND Although the plague hit urban populations especially hard, the cities and their skilled industries came, in time, to prosper from its effects. Cities had always been careful to protect their interests; as they grew, they passed legislation to regulate competition from rural areas and to control immigration. After the plague, the reach of such laws was progressively extended beyond the cities to include surrounding lands belonging to impoverished nobles and feudal landlords, many of whom were peacefully integrated into urban life.

The omnipresence of death whetted the appetite for goods that only skilled urban industries could produce. Expensive cloths and jewelry, furs from the north, and silks from the south were in great demand in the second half of the fourteenth century. Faced with life at its worst, people insisted on having the very best. Initially, this new demand could not be met. The basic unit of urban industry was the master and apprentices (usually one or two), whose numbers were purposely kept low and whose privileges were jealously guarded. The craft of the skilled artisan was passed from master to apprentice only very slowly. The first wave of plague transformed this already restricted supply of skilled artisans into a shortage almost overnight. As a result, the prices of manufactured and luxury items rose to new heights, and this in turn encouraged workers to migrate from the countryside to the city and learn the skills of artisans. Townspeople in effect profited coming and going from the forces that impoverished the landed nobility. As wealth poured into the cities and per capita income rose, the cost to urban dwellers of agricultural products from the countryside, now less in demand, declined.

There was also gain, as well as loss, for the church. Although it suffered losses as a great landholder and was politically weakened, it had received new revenues from the vastly increased demand for religious services for the dead and the dying and from the multiplication of gifts and bequests.

New Conflicts and Opportunities

By increasing the importance of skilled artisans, the plague contributed to new conflicts within the cities. The economic and political power of local artisans and trade guilds grew steadily in the late Middle Ages, along with the demand for their goods and services. The merchant and patrician classes found it increasingly difficult to maintain their traditional dominance and grudgingly gave guild masters a voice in city government. As the guilds won political power, they encouraged restrictive legislation to protect local industries. These restrictions, in turn, brought confrontations between master artisans, who wanted to keep their numbers low and expand their industries at a snail's pace, and the many journeymen, who were eager to rise to the rank of master. To the long-existing conflict between the guilds and the urban patriciate was now added a conflict within the guilds themselves.

After 1350 the two traditional "containers" of monarchy—the landed nobility and the church—were politically on the defensive, to no small degree as a consequence of the plague. Kings took full advantage of the new situation, drawing on growing national sentiment to centralize their governments and economies. As already noted, the plague reduced the economic power of the landed nobility. In the same period, the battles of the Hundred Years' War demonstrated the military superiority of paid professional armies over the traditional noble cavalry, thus bringing into question the role of the nobility. The plague also killed many members of the clergy—perhaps one-third of the German clergy fell victim to it as they dutifully ministered to the sick and dying. The reduction in clerical ranks occurred in the same century in which the residence of the pope in Avignon (1309–1377) and the Great Schism (1378–1415) were undermining much of the church's popular support.

Ecclesiastical Breakdown and Revival: The Late Medieval Church

At first glance, the popes may appear to have been in a very favorable position in the latter half of the thirteenth century. Frederick II had been vanquished and imperial pressure on Rome had been removed. The French king, Louis IX, was an enthusiastic supporter of the church, as evidenced by his two disastrous Crusades, which won him sainthood. Although it lasted only seven years, a reunion of the Eastern church with Rome was proclaimed by the Council of Lyons in 1274, when the Western church took advantage of Emperor Michael Palaeologus's request for aid against the Turks. But despite these positive events, the church was not really in as favorable a position as it appeared.

The Thirteenth-Century Papacy

As early as the reign of Pope Innocent III (r. 1198–1216), when papal power reached its height, there were ominous developments. Innocent had elaborated the doctrine of papal plenitude of power and on that authority had declared saints, disposed of *benefices*, and created a centralized papal monarchy with a clearly political mission. Innocent's transformation of the papacy into a great secular power weakened the church spiritually even as it strengthened it politically. Thereafter, the church as a papal monarchy and the church as the "body of the faithful" came increasingly to be differentiated. It was against the "papal church" and in the name of the "true Christian Church" that both reformers and heretics raised their voices in protest until the Protestant Reformation.

What Innocent began his successors perfected. Under Urban IV (r. 1261–1264), the papacy established its own law court, the *Rota Romana*, which tightened and centralized the church's legal proceedings. The latter half of the thirteenth century saw an elaboration of the system of clerical taxation; what had begun in the twelfth century as an emergency measure to raise funds for the Crusades became a fixed institution. In the same period, papal power to determine appointments to many major and minor church offices—the "reservation of *benefices*"—was greatly broadened. The thirteenth-century papacy became a powerful political institution governed by its own law and courts, serviced by an efficient international bureaucracy, and preoccupied with secular goals.

Papal centralization of the church undermined both diocesan authority and popular support. Rome's interests, not local needs, came to control church appointments, policies, and discipline. Discontented lower clergy appealed to the higher authority of Rome against the disciplinary measures of local bishops. In the second half of the thirteenth century, bishops and abbots protested such undercutting of their power. To its critics, the church in Rome was hardly more than a legalized, "fiscalized," bureaucratic institution. As early as the late twelfth century, heretical movements of Cathars and Waldensians had appealed to the biblical ideal of simplicity and separation from the world. Other reformers who were unquestionably loyal to the church, such as Saint Francis of Assisi, would also protest a perceived materialism in official religion.

POLITICAL FRAGMENTATION The church of the thirteenth century was being undermined by more than internal religious disunity. The demise of imperial power meant that the papacy in Rome was no longer the leader of anti-imperial (Guelf, or propapal) sentiment in Italy. Instead of being the center of Italian resistance to the emperor, popes now found themselves on the defensive against their old allies. That was the ironic price paid by the papacy to vanquish the Hohenstaufens.

Rulers with a stake in Italian politics now directed the intrigue formerly aimed at the emperor toward the College of Cardinals. For example, Charles of Anjou, king of Sicily, managed to create a French–Sicilian faction within the college. Such efforts to control the decisions of the college led Pope Gregory X (r. 1271– 1276) to establish the practice of sequestering the cardinals immediately on the death of the pope. The purpose of this so-called conclave of cardinals was to minimize extraneous political influence on the election of new popes, but the college had become so politicized that it proved to be of little avail.

In 1294 such a conclave, in frustration after a deadlock of more than two years, chose a saintly, but inept, Calabrian hermit as Pope Celestine V. Celestine abdicated under suspicious circumstances after only a few weeks in office. He also died under suspicious circumstances; his successor's critics later argued that he had been murdered for political reasons by the powers behind the papal throne to ensure the survival of the papal office. His tragicomic reign shocked a majority of the College of Cardinals into unified action. He was quickly replaced by his very opposite, Pope Boniface VIII (r. 1294–1303), a nobleman and a skilled politician. His pontificate, however, would augur the beginning of the end of papal pretensions to great-power status.

Boniface VIII and Philip the Fair

Boniface came to rule when England and France were maturing as nation–states. In England, a long tradition of consultation between the king and powerful members of English society evolved into formal "parliaments" during the reigns of Henry III (r. 1216–1272) and Edward I (r. 1272–1307), and these meetings helped to create a unified kingdom. The reign of the French king Philip IV the Fair (1285–1314) saw France become an efficient, centralized monarchy. Philip was no Saint Louis, but a ruthless politician. He was determined to end England's continental holdings, control wealthy Flanders, and establish French hegemony within the Holy Roman Empire.

Boniface had the further misfortune of bringing to the papal throne memories of the way earlier popes had brought kings and emperors to their knees. Very painfully he was to discover that the papal monarchy

Pope Boniface VIII (r. 1294–1303), depicted here, opposed the taxation of the clergy by the kings of France and England and issued one of the strongest declarations of papal authority over rulers, the bull Unam Sanctam. This statue is in the Museo Civico, Bologna, Italy. Scala/Art Resource, N.Y.

of the early thirteenth century was no match for the new political powers of the late thirteenth century.

THE ROYAL CHALLENGE TO PAPAL AUTHORITY France and England were on the brink of all-out war when Boniface became pope in 1294. Only Edward I's preoccupation with rebellion in Scotland, which the

Boniface VIII Reasserts the Church's Claim to Temporal Power

Defied by the French and the English, Pope Boniface VIII (r. 1294–1303) boldly reasserted the temporal power of the church in the bull Unam Sanctam *(November 1302). This document claimed that both spiritual and temporal power on earth were under the pope's jurisdiction, because in the hierarchy of the universe spiritual power both preceded and sat in judgment on temporal power.*

❖ *On what does the pope base his claims to supremacy? Is his argument logical, or does he beg the question? On what basis did secular rulers attack his arguments?*

We are taught by the words of the Gospel that in this church and in her power there are two swords, a spiritual one and a temporal one....Certainly anyone who denies that the temporal sword is in the power of Peter has not paid heed to the words of the Lord when he said, "Put up thy sword into its sheath" (Matthew 26:52). Both then are in the power of the church, the material sword and the spiritual. But the one is exercised for the church, the other by the church, the one by the hand of the priest, the other by the hand of kings and soldiers, though at the will and suffrance of the authority subject to the spiritual power....For, according to the blessed Dionysius, it is the law of divinity for the lowest to be led to the highest through intermediaries. In the order of the universe all things are not kept in order in the same fashion and immediately but the lowest are ordered by the intermediate and inferiors by superiors. But that the spiritual power excels any earthly one in dignity and nobility we ought the more openly to confess in proportion as spiritual things excel temporal ones. Moreover we clearly perceive this from the giving of tithes, from benediction and sanctification, from the acceptance of this power and from the very government of things. For, the truth bearing witness, the spiritual power has to institute the earthly power and to judge it if it has not been good. So it is verified the prophecy of Jeremiah (1:10) concerning the church and the power of the church, "Lo, I have set thee this day over the nations and over kingdoms."

Reprinted with the permission of Simon & Schuster from *The Crisis of Church and State, 1050–1300* by Brian Tierney. Copyright © 1964 by Prentice-Hall, Inc., renewed 1992 by Brian Tierney.

French encouraged, prevented him from invading France and starting the Hundred Years' War a half century earlier than it did start. As both countries mobilized for war, they used the pretext of preparing for a Crusade to tax the clergy heavily. In 1215 Pope Innocent III had decreed that the clergy were to pay no taxes to rulers without prior papal consent. Viewing English and French taxation of the clergy as an assault on traditional clerical rights, Boniface took a strong stand against it. On February 5, 1296, he issued a bull, *Clericis laicos*, which forbade lay taxation of the clergy without prior papal approval and took back all previous papal dispensations in this regard.

In England, Edward I retaliated by denying the clergy the right to be heard in royal court, in effect removing from them the protection of the king. But it was Philip the Fair who struck back with a vengeance: In August 1296 he forbade the exportation of money from France to Rome, thereby denying the papacy revenues it needed to operate. Boniface had no choice but to come quickly to terms

with Philip. He conceded Philip the right to tax the French clergy "during an emergency," and, not coincidentally, he canonized Louis IX in the same year.

Boniface was then also under siege by powerful Italian enemies, whom Philip did not fail to patronize. A noble family (the Colonnas), rivals of Boniface's family (the Gaetani) and radical followers of Saint Francis of Assisi (the Spiritual Franciscans), were at this time seeking to invalidate Boniface's election as pope on the grounds that Celestine V had resigned the office under coercion. Charges of heresy, simony, and even the murder of Celestine were hurled against Boniface.

Boniface's fortunes appeared to revive in 1300, a "Jubilee year." During such a year, all Catholics who visited Rome and fulfilled certain conditions had the penalties for their unrepented sins remitted. Tens of thousands of pilgrims flocked to Rome in that year, and Boniface, heady with this display of popular religiosity, reinserted himself into international politics. He championed Scottish resistance to England, for which he received a firm rebuke from an outraged Edward I and from Parliament.

Unam Sanctum = that Temporal authority was subject to the spiritual authority of the church.

Chapter 9 / Social and Political Breakdown (1300–1527) 307

But once again a confrontation with the king of France proved the more costly. Philip seemed to be eager for another fight with the pope. He arrested Boniface's Parisian legate, Bernard Saisset, the bishop of Pamiers and also a powerful secular lord, whose independence Philip had opposed. Accused of heresy and treason, Saisset was tried and convicted in the king's court. Thereafter, Philip demanded that Boniface recognize the process against Saisset, something that Boniface could do only if he was prepared to surrender his jurisdiction over the French episcopate. This challenge could not be sidestepped, and Boniface acted swiftly to champion Saisset as a defender of clerical political independence within France. He demanded Saisset's unconditional release, revoked all previous agreements with Philip in the matter of clerical taxation, and ordered the French bishops to convene in Rome within a year. A bull, *Ausculta fili*, or "Listen, My Son," was sent to Philip in December 1301, pointedly informing him that "God has set popes over kings and kingdoms."

***UNAM SANCTAM* (1302)**   Philip unleashed a ruthless antipapal campaign. Two royal apologists, Pierre Dubois and John of Paris, refuted papal claims to the right to intervene in temporal matters. Increasingly placed on the defensive, Boniface made a last-ditch stand against state control of national churches. On November 18, 1302, he issued the bull *Unam Sanctam*. This famous statement of papal power declared that temporal authority was "subject" to the spiritual power of the church. On its face a bold assertion, *Unam Sanctam* was in truth the desperate act of a besieged papacy. (See "Boniface VIII Reasserts the Church's Claim to Temporal Power.")

After *Unam Sanctam*, the French and the Colonnas moved against Boniface with force. Guillaume de Nogaret, Philip's chief minister, denounced Boniface to the French clergy as a common heretic and criminal. An army, led by Nogaret and Sciarra Colonna, surprised the pope in mid-August 1303 at his retreat in Anagni. Boniface was badly beaten and almost executed before an aroused populace liberated and returned him safely

Marsilius of Padua Denies Coercive Power to the Clergy

According to Marsilius, the Bible gave the pope no right to pronounce and execute sentences on any person. The clergy held a strictly moral and spiritual rule, their judgments to be executed only in the afterlife, not in the present one. Here, on earth, they should be obedient to secular authority. Marsilius argued this point by appealing to the example of Jesus.

❖ *How do Marsilius's arguments compare with those of Pope Boniface in the preceding document? Does Marsilius's argument, if accepted, destroy the worldly authority of the church? Why was his teaching condemned as heretical?*

We now wish...to adduce the truths of the holy Scripture...which explicitly command or counsel that neither the Roman bishop called pope, nor any other bishop or priest, or deacon, has or ought to have any rulership or coercive judgment or jurisdiction over any priest or nonpriest, ruler, community, group, or individual of whatever condition....Christ himself came into the world not to dominate men, nor to judge them [coercively]...not to wield temporal rule, but rather to be subject as regards the...present life; and moreover, he wanted to and did exclude himself, his apostles and disciples, and their successors, the bishops or priests, from all coercive authority or worldly rule, both by his example and by his word of counsel or command....When he was brought before Pontius Pilate...and accused of having called himself king of the Jews, and [Pilate] asked him whether he had said this...[his] reply included these words...."My kingdom is not of this world," that is, I have not come to reign by temporal rule or dominion, in the way...worldly kings reign.... This, then, is the kingdom concerning which he came to teach and order, a kingdom which consists in the acts whereby the eternal kingdom is attained, that is, the acts of faith and the other theological virtues; not however, by coercing anyone thereto.

A book illustration of the Palace of the Popes in Avignon in 1409, the year in which Christendom found itself confronted by three duly elected popes. The "keys" to the kingdom of God, which the pope held on earth as the vicar of Christ, decorate the three turret flags of the palace. In the foreground, the French poet Pierre Salmon, then journeying via Avignon to Rome, commiserates with a monk over the sad state of the Church and France, then at war with England. Book illustration, French, 1409. Paris, Bibliotheque Nationale. AKG Photo.

to Rome. But the ordeal proved too much for him and he died a few months later, in October 1303.

Boniface's immediate successor, Benedict XI (r. 1303–1304), excommunicated Nogaret for his deed, but there was to be no lasting papal retaliation. Benedict's successor, Clement V (r. 1305–1314), was forced into French subservience. A former archbishop of Bordeaux, Clement declared that *Unam Sanctam* should not be understood as in any way diminishing French royal authority. He released Nogaret from excommunication and pliantly condemned the Knights Templars, whose treasure Philip thereafter forcibly expropriated. In 1309 Clement moved the papal court to Avignon, an imperial city on the southeastern border of France. Situated on land that belonged to the pope, the city maintained its independence from the king. In 1311 Clement made it his permanent residence, to escape both a Rome ridden with strife after the confrontation between Boniface and Philip and

further pressure from Philip. There the papacy was to remain until 1377.

After Boniface's humiliation, popes never again seriously threatened kings and emperors, despite continuing papal excommunications and political intrigue. In the future, the relation between church and state would tilt in favor of the state and the control of religion by powerful monarchies. Ecclesiastical authority would become subordinate to larger secular political purposes.

The Avignon Papacy (1309–1377)

The Avignon papacy was in appearance, although not always in fact, under strong French influence. During Clement V's pontificate the French came to dominate the College of Cardinals, testing the papacy's agility both politically and economically. Finding itself cut off from its Roman estates, the papacy had to innovate to get needed funds. Clement expanded papal taxes, especially the practice of collecting annates, the first year's revenue of a church office, or *benefices* bestowed by the pope. Clement VI (r. 1342–1352) began the practice of selling indulgences, or pardons for unrepented sins. To make the purchase of indulgences more compelling, church doctrine on purgatory—a place of punishment where souls would atone for venial sins—also developed during this period. By the fifteenth century the church had extended indulgences to cover the souls of people already dead, allowing the living to buy a reduced sentence in purgatory for their deceased loved ones. Such practices contributed to the Avignon papacy's reputation for materialism and political scheming and gave reformers new ammunition.

POPE JOHN XXII　Pope John XXII (r. 1316–1334), the most powerful Avignon pope, tried to restore papal independence and to return to Italy. This goal led him into war with the Visconti, the most powerful ruling family of Milan, and a costly contest with Emperor Louis IV. John had challenged Louis's election as emperor in 1314 in favor of the rival Habsburg candidate. The result was a minor replay of the confrontation between Philip the Fair and Boniface VIII. When John obstinately and without legal justification refused to recognize Louis's election, the emperor retaliated by declaring John deposed and putting in his place an antipope. As Philip the Fair had also done, Louis enlisted the support of the Spiritual Franciscans, whose views on absolute poverty had been condemned by John as heretical. Two outstanding pamphleteers wrote lasting tracts for the royal cause: William of Ockham, whom John excommunicated in 1328, and Marsilius of Padua (ca. 1290–1342), whose teaching John declared heretical in 1327.

In his *Defender of Peace* (1324), Marsilius of Padua stressed the independent origins and autonomy of secular government. Clergy were subjected to the strictest apostolic ideals and confined to purely spiritual functions, and all power of coercive judgment was denied the pope. Marsilius argued that spiritual crimes must await an eternal punishment. Transgressions of divine law, over which the pope had jurisdiction, were to be punished in the next life, not in the present one, unless the secular ruler declared a divine law also a secular law. This assertion was a direct challenge to the power of the pope to excommunicate rulers and place countries under interdict. The *Defender of Peace* depicted the pope as a subordinate member of a society over which the emperor ruled supreme and in which temporal peace was the highest good. (See "Marsilius of Padua Denies Coercive Power to the Clergy.")

John XXII made the papacy a sophisticated international agency and adroitly adjusted it to the growing European money economy. The more the *Curia*, or papal court, mastered the latter, however, the more vulnerable it became to criticism. Under John's successor, Benedict XII (r. 1334–1342), the papacy became entrenched in Avignon. Seemingly forgetting Rome altogether, Benedict began construction of the great Palace of the Popes and attempted to reform both papal government and the religious life. His high-living French successor, Clement VI, placed papal policy in lockstep with the French. In this period the cardinals became barely more than lobbyists for policies favorable to their secular patrons.

NATIONAL OPPOSITION TO THE AVIGNON PAPACY As Avignon's fiscal tentacles probed new areas, monarchies took strong action to protect their interests. The latter half of the fourteenth century saw legislation restricting papal jurisdiction and taxation in France, England, and Germany. In England, where the Avignon papacy was identified with the French enemy after the outbreak of the Hundred Years' War, statutes that restricted payments and appeals to Rome and the pope's power to make high ecclesiastical appointments were passed by Parliament several times between 1351 and 1393.

In France, ecclesiastical appointments and taxation were regulated by the so-called Gallican liberties. These national rights over religion had long been exercised in fact and were legally acknowledged by the church in the *Pragmatic Sanction of Bourges*, published by Charles VII (r. 1422–1461) in 1438. This agreement recognized the right of the French church to elect its own clergy without papal

A portrayal of John Huss as he was led to the stake at Constance. After his execution, his bones and ashes were scattered in the Rhine River to prevent his followers from claiming them as relics. This pen-and-ink drawing is from Ulrich von Richenthal's Chronicle of the Council of Constance (ca. 1450). The Bettman Archive

interference, prohibited the payment of annates to Rome, and limited the right of appeals from French courts to the *Curia* in Rome. In German and Swiss cities in the fourteenth and fifteenth centuries, local governments also took the initiative to limit and even to overturn traditional clerical privileges and immunities.

JOHN WYCLIFFE AND JOHN HUSS [*England*] [*Czech*] The popular lay religious movements that most successfully assailed the late medieval church were the Lollards in England and the Hussites in Bohemia. The Lollards looked to the writings of John Wycliffe (d. 1384) to justify their demands, and both moderate and extreme Hussites to the writings of John Huss (d. 1415), although both Wycliffe and Huss would have disclaimed the extremists who revolted in their names.

Wycliffe was an Oxford theologian and a philosopher of high standing. His work initially served the anticlerical policies of the English government. He became within England what William of Ockham and Marsilius of Padua had been at the Bavarian court of Emperor Louis IV: a major intellectual spokesman for the rights of royalty against the secular pretensions of popes. After 1350 English kings greatly reduced the power of the Avignon papacy to make ecclesiastical appointments and collect taxes within England, a position that Wycliffe strongly

The Ruin of the Church during the Schism

Nicholas of Clamanges, a theologian writing around 1400, viewed the decades-long division of the papacy and the continuing growth of two separate papal courts, one in Avignon, another in Rome, as proof that the high clergy had become thoroughly corrupt. Popes and bishops had so lost face, that their threats of excommunication now fell on deaf ears. Only by ending the Schism could the church begin to restore its authority.

❖ *What incentive did either pope have to end the Schism? Did the loss of efficacy of papal disciplinary actions such as excommunication provide such an incentive? Which, if either, of the papal courts seemed to have greater validity?*

After the great increase of worldly goods...boundless avarice and blind ambition invaded the hearts of churchmen...Carried away by the glory of their position and the extent of their power [they] soon gave way to the[ir] degrading effects....Three most exacting and troublesome masters had now to be satisfied. *Luxury* demanded sundry gratifications—wine, sleep, banquets, music, debasing sports, and courtesans....*Display* required fine houses, castles, towers, palaces, rich and varied furniture, expensive clothes, horses, servants and the pomp of luxury....*Avarice*...carefully brought together vast treasures to supply the demands of the above vices....

For carrying on exactions and gathering their gains...the popes appointed their collectors in every province, those namely whom they knew to be most skillful in extracting money, owing to [their] energy, diligence, or harshness of temper....To these the popes granted the power of anathematizing anyone, even prelates, and of expelling from the communion of the faithful everyone who did not...satisfy their demands for money....Hence came suspensions from divine service, interdicts from entering a church, and anathemas a thousandfold intensified in severity.

Such things were resorted to in the rarest instances by the [Church] Fathers, and then only for the most horrible of crimes; for by these penalties a man is separated from the companionship of the faithful and turned over to Satan. But nowadays these inflictions have so fallen in esteem that they are used for the lightest offense, often for no offense at all, so that they no longer bring terror but are objects of contempt.

From James Harvey Robinson, ed., *Readings in European History*, Vol. I (Boston: Athenaeum, 1904), pp. 508–509.

supported. His views on clerical poverty followed original Franciscan ideals and, more by accident than by design, gave justification to government restriction and even confiscation of church properties within England. Wycliffe argued that the clergy "ought to be content with food and clothing."

Wycliffe also maintained that personal merit, not rank and office, was the only basis of religious authority. This was a dangerous teaching, because it raised allegedly pious laypeople above allegedly corrupt ecclesiastics, regardless of the latter's official stature. There was a threat in such teaching to secular as well as ecclesiastical dominion and jurisdiction. At his posthumous condemnation by the pope, Wycliffe was accused of the ancient heresy of Donatism—the teaching that the efficacy of the church's sacraments did not lie in their true performance, but also depended on the moral character of the clergy who administered them. Wycliffe also anticipated certain Protestant criticisms of the medieval church by challenging papal infallibility, the sale of indulgences, the authority of scripture, and the dogma of transubstantiation.

The Lollards, English advocates of Wycliffe's teaching, like the Waldensians, preached in the vernacular, disseminated translations of Holy Scripture, and championed clerical poverty. At first, they came from every social class. Lollards were especially prominent among the groups that had something tangible to gain from the confiscation of clerical properties (the nobility and the gentry) or that had suffered most under the current church system (the lower clergy and the poor people). After the English peasants' revolt in 1381, an uprising filled with egalitarian notions that could find support in Wycliffe's teaching, Lollardy was officially viewed as subversive. Opposed by an alliance of church and crown, it became a capital offense in England by 1401.

Heresy was not so easily brought to heel in Bohemia, where it coalesced with a strong national movement. The University of Prague, founded in 1348, became the center for both Czech nationalism and a native religious reform movement. The latter began within the bounds of orthodoxy. It was led by local intellectuals and preachers, the most famous of whom was John Huss, the rector of the university after 1403.

The Czech reformers supported vernacular translations of the Bible and were critical of traditional ceremonies and allegedly superstitious practices, particularly those relating to the sacrament of the Eucharist. They advocated lay communion with cup as well as bread, which was traditionally reserved only for the clergy as a sign of the clergy's spiritual superiority over the laity. Hussites taught that bread and wine remained bread and wine after priestly consecration, and they questioned the validity of sacraments performed by priests in mortal sin.

Wycliffe's teaching appears to have influenced the movement very early. Regular traffic between England and Bohemia had existed for decades, ever since the marriage in 1381 of Anne of Bohemia to King Richard II. Czech students studied at Oxford, and many returned with copies of Wycliffe's writings.

Huss became the leader of the pro-Wycliffe faction at the University of Prague. In 1410 his activities brought about his excommunication and the placement of Prague under papal interdict. In 1414 Huss won an audience with the newly assembled Council of Constance. He journeyed to the council eagerly, armed with a safe-conduct pass from Emperor Sigismund, naïvely believing that he would convince his strongest critics of the truth of his teaching. Within weeks of his arrival in early November 1414, he was formally accused of heresy and imprisoned. He died at the stake on July 6, 1415, and was followed there less than a year later by his colleague Jerome of Prague.

The reaction in Bohemia to the execution of these national heroes was fierce revolt. Militant Hussites, the Taborites, set out to transform Bohemia by force into a religious and social paradise under the military leadership of John Ziska. After a decade of belligerent protest, the Hussites won significant religious reforms and control over the Bohemian church from the Council of Basel.

The Great Schism (1378–1417) and the Conciliar Movement to 1449

Pope Gregory XI (r. 1370–1378) reestablished the papacy in Rome in January 1377, ending what had come to be known as the "Babylonian Captivity" of the church in Avignon, a reference to the biblical bondage of the Israelites. The return to Rome proved to be short lived, however.

URBAN VI AND CLEMENT VII On Gregory's death, the cardinals, in Rome, elected an Italian archbishop as Pope Urban VI (r. 1378–1389), who immediately announced his intention to reform the *Curia*. This was an unexpected challenge to the cardinals, most of whom were French, and they responded by calling for the return of the papacy to Avignon. The French king, Charles V, wanting to keep the papacy within the sphere of French influence, lent his support to a schism, which came to be known as the "Great Schism."

On September 20, 1378, five months after Urban's election, thirteen cardinals, all but one of whom was French, formed their own conclave and elected Pope Clement VII (r. 1378–1397), a cousin of the French king. They insisted that they had voted for Urban in fear of their lives, surrounded by a Roman mob demanding the election of an Italian pope. Be that as it may, the papacy now became a "two-headed thing" and a scandal to Christendom. (See "The Ruin of the Church during the Schism.") Allegiance to the two papal courts divided along political lines. England and its allies (the Holy Roman Empire, Hungary, Bohemia, and Poland) acknowledged Urban VI, whereas France and those in its orbit (Naples, Scotland, Castile, and Aragon) supported Clement VII. The Roman line of popes has, however, been recognized de facto in subsequent church history.

Two approaches were initially taken to end the schism. One tried to win the mutual cession of both popes, thereby clearing the way for the election of a new pope. The other sought to secure the resignation of the one in favor of the other. Both approaches proved completely fruitless. Each pope considered himself fully legitimate, and too much was at stake for a magnanimous concession on the part of either. One way remained: the forced deposition of both popes by a special council of the church.

CONCILIAR THEORY OF CHURCH GOVERNMENT Legally, a church council could be convened only by a pope, but the competing popes were not inclined to summon a council they knew would depose them. Also, the deposition of a legitimate pope against his will by a council of the church was as serious a matter then as the forced deposition of a monarch by a representative assembly.

The correctness of a conciliar deposition of a pope was thus debated a full thirty years before any direct action was taken. Advocates sought to fashion a church in which a representative council could effectively regulate the actions of the pope. The con-

Genghis Khan holding an audience. This Persian miniature shows the great conqueror and founder of the Mongol empire with members of his army and entourage as well as an apparent supplicant (lower right). E.T. Archive

ciliarists defined the church as the whole body of the faithful, of which the elected head, the pope, was only one part. And the pope's sole purpose was to maintain the unity and well-being of the church—something that the schismatic popes were far from doing. The conciliarists further argued that a council of the church acted with greater authority than the pope alone. In the eyes of the pope(s), such a concept of the church threatened both its political and its religious unity.

THE COUNCIL OF PISA (1409–1410)   On the basis of the arguments of the conciliarists, cardinals representing both popes convened a council on their own authority in Pisa in 1409, deposed both the Roman and the Avignon popes, and elected a new pope, Alexander V. To the council's consternation, neither pope accepted its action, and Christendom suddenly faced the spectacle of three contending popes. Although the vast majority of Latin Christendom accepted Alexander and his Pisan successor John XXIII (r. 1410–1415), the popes of Rome and Avignon refused to step down.

THE COUNCIL OF CONSTANCE (1414–1417)   The intolerable situation ended when Emperor Sigismund

prevailed on John XXIII to summon a new council in Constance in 1414, which the Roman pope Gregory XII also recognized. In a famous declaration entitled *Sacrosancta*, the council asserted its supremacy and proceeded to elect a new pope, Martin V (r. 1417–1431), after the three contending popes had either resigned or been deposed. The council then made provisions for regular meetings of church councils, within five, then seven, and thereafter every ten years.

Despite the role of the council of Constance in ending the Great Schism, in the official eyes of the church it was not a legitimate council. Nor have the schismatic popes of Avignon and Pisa been recognized as legitimate. (For this reason, another pope could take the name John XXIII in 1958.)

THE COUNCIL OF BASEL (R. 1431–1449)   Conciliar government of the church peaked at the Council of Basel, when the council negotiated church doctrine with heretics. In 1432 the Hussites of Bohemia presented the *Four Articles of Prague* to the council as a basis for the negotiations. This document contained requests for (1) giving the laity the Eucharist with cup as well as bread; (2) free, itinerant preaching; (3) the exclusion of the clergy from holding secular offices and owning property; and (4) just punishment of clergy who commit mortal sins.

In November 1433 an agreement was reached between the emperor, the council, and the Hussites, giving the Bohemians jurisdiction over their church similar to that held by the French and the English. Three of the four Prague articles were conceded: communion with cup, free preaching by ordained clergy, and like punishment of clergy and laity for mortal sins.

The end of the Hussite wars and the reform legislation curtailing the papal power of appointment and taxation were the high points of the Council of Basel. The exercise of such power by a council did not please the pope, and in 1438 he gained the opportunity to upstage the Council of Basel by negotiating a reunion with the Eastern Church. The agreement, signed in Florence in 1439, was short lived, but it restored papal prestige and signaled the demise of the Conciliar Movement. The Council of Basel collapsed in 1449. A decade later Pope Pius II (r. 1458–1464) issued the papal bull *Execrabilis* (1460) condemning appeals to councils as "erroneous and abominable" and "completely null and void."

Although many who had worked for reform now despaired of ever attaining it, the Conciliar Movement was not a total failure. It planted deep within the conscience of all Western peoples the conviction that the role of a leader of an institution is to provide for the well-being of its members, not just for that of the leader.

A second consequence of the Conciliar Movement was the devolving of religious responsibility onto the laity and secular government. Without papal leadership, secular control of national or territorial churches increased. Kings asserted power over the church in England and France. In German, Swiss, and Italian cities magistrates and city councils reformed and regulated religious life. This development could not be reversed by the powerful popes of the High Renaissance. On the contrary, as the papacy became a limited territorial regime, national control of the church ran apace. Perceived as just one among several Italian states, the Papal States could now be opposed as much on the grounds of "national" policy as for religious reasons.

Medieval Russia

In the late tenth century, Prince Vladimir of Kiev (972–1015), at that time Russia's dominant city, received delegations of Muslims, Roman Catholics, Jews, and Greek Orthodox Christians, each of which hoped to see Russians embrace their religion. Vladimir chose Greek Orthodoxy, which became the religion of Russia, adding strong cultural bonds to the close commercial ties that had long linked Russia to the Byzantine Empire.

Politics and Society

Vladimir's successor, Yaroslav the Wise (1016–1054), developed Kiev into a magnificent political and cultural center, with architecture rivaling that of Constantinople. He also sought contacts with the West in an unsuccessful effort to counter the political influence of the Byzantine emperors. After his death, rivalry among their princes slowly divided Russians into three cultural groups: the Great Russians, the White Russians, and the Little Russians (Ukrainians). Autonomous principalities also challenged Kiev's dominance, and it became just one of several national centers. Government in the principalities combined monarchy (the prince), aristocracy (the prince's council of noblemen), and democracy (a popular assembly of all adult males). The broadest social division was between freemen and slaves. Freemen included the clergy, army officers, *boyars* (wealthy landowners), townspeople, and peasants. Slaves were mostly prisoners of war. Debtors working off their debts made up a large, semifree, intermediate group.

Mongol Rule (1243–1480)

In the thirteenth century, Mongol, or Tatar, armies swept over China, much of the Islamic world, and Russia. Ghengis Khan (1155–1227) invaded Russia in 1223, and Kiev fell to Batu Khan in 1240. Russian cities became dependent, tribute-paying principalities of the segment of the Mongol Empire called the Golden Horde (a phrase derived from the Tatar words for the color of Batu Khan's tent), which included the steppe region of what is now southern Russia and had its capital at Sarai, on the lower Volga. The Golden Horde stationed officials in all the principal Russian towns to oversee taxation and the conscription of soldiers into Tatar armies. Mongol rule created further cultural divisions between Russia and the West. The Mongols intermarried with the Russians and also created harems filled with Russian women. Russians who resisted were sold into slavery in foreign lands. Russian women—under the influence of Islam, which had become the religion of the Golden Horde—began to wear veils and to lead more secluded lives. The Mongols, however, left Russian political and religious institutions largely intact and, thanks to their far-flung trade, brought most Russians greater peace and prosperity than they had enjoyed before.

Liberation

The princes of Moscow cooperated with their overlords in the collection of tribute and grew wealthy under the Mongols. As Mongol rule weakened, the princes took control of the territory surrounding the city. In a process that has come to be known as "the gathering of the Russian Land," they then gradually expanded the principality of Moscow through land purchases, colonization, and conquest. In 1380, Grand Duke Dimitri of Moscow (1350–1389) defeated Tatar forces at Kulikov Meadow in a victory that marks the beginning of the decline of Mongol hegemony. Another century would pass before Ivan III, called Ivan the Great (d. 1505), would bring all of northern Russia under Moscow's control and end Mongol rule (1480). By the last quarter of the fourteenth century, however, Moscow had become the political and religious center of Russia, replacing Kiev. In Russian eyes, it was destined to become the "third Rome" after the fall of Constantinople to the Turks in 1453.

In Perspective

War, plague, and schism convulsed much of late medieval Europe throughout the fourteenth and into the fifteenth century. Two-fifths of the population, particularly along the major trade routes, died from plague in the fourteenth century. War and famine continued to take untold numbers after the plague had passed. The introduction of gunpowder and heavy artillery during the long years of warfare between England and France resulted in new forms of human destruction. Periodic revolts erupted in town and countryside as ordinary people attempted to defend their traditional communal rights and privileges against the new autocratic territorial regimes. Even God's house seemed to be in shambles in 1409, when no fewer than three popes came to rule simultaneously.

There is, however, another side to the late Middle Ages. By the end of the fifteenth century the population losses were rapidly being made up. Between 1300 and 1500, education had become far more accessible, especially to laypeople. The number of universities increased 250 percent, from twenty to seventy, and the rise in the number of residential colleges was even more impressive, especially in France, where sixty-three were built. The fourteenth century saw the birth of humanism, and the fifteenth century gave us the printing press. Most impressive were the artistic and cultural achievements of the Italian Renaissance during the fifteenth century. The later Middle Ages were thus a period of growth and creativity, as well as one of waning and decline.

REVIEW QUESTIONS

1. What were the underlying and precipitating causes of the Hundred Years' War? What advantages did each side have? Why were the French finally able to drive the English almost entirely out of France?
2. What were the causes of the Black Death, and why did it spread so quickly throughout western Europe? Where was it most virulent? What were its effects on European society? How important do you think disease is in changing the course of history?
3. Discuss the struggle between Pope Boniface VIII and King Philip the Fair. Why was Boniface so impotent in the conflict? How had political conditions changed since the reign of Pope Innocent III in the late twelfth century, and what did that mean for the papacy?
4. Briefly trace the history of the church from 1200 to 1450. How did it respond to political threats from the growing power of monarchs? How great an influence did the church have on secular events?
5. What was the Avignon papacy, and why did it occur? What effect did it have on the state of the papacy? What relation does it have to the Great Schism? How did the church become divided and how was it reunited? Why was the Conciliar Movement a setback for the papacy?
6. Why were kings in the late thirteenth and early fourteenth centuries able to control the church more than the church could control the kings? How did kings attack the church during this period? Contrast these events with earlier ones in which the pope dominated rulers.

SUGGESTED READINGS

C. ALLMAND, *The Hundred Years' War: England and France at War, c. 1300–c. 1450* (1988). Good overview of the war's development and consequences.

P. ARIÈS, *The Hour of Our Death* (1983). People's familiarity with, and philosophy of, death in the Middle Ages.

R. Barber (Ed.), *The Pastons: Letters of a Family in the War of the Roses* (1984). Revelations of English family life in an age of crisis.

J. le Goff, *The Birth of Purgatory*, trans. by A. Goldhammer (1984). Cultural impact of the idea.

J. Huizinga, *The Waning of the Middle Ages: A Study of the Forms of Life, Thought, and Art in France and the Netherlands in the Dawn of the Renaissance* (1924). A classic study of "mentality" at the end of the Middle Ages; exaggerated, but engrossing.

W. H. McNeill, *Plagues and Peoples* (1976). The Black Death in a broader context.

D. N. Nicol, *The Byzantine Lady: Ten Portraits, 1250–1500* (1994)

F. Oakley, *The Western Church in the Later Middle Ages* (1979). Eloquent, sympathetic survey.

S. Ozment, *The Age of Reform, 1250–1550* (1980). Highlights of late medieval intellectual and religious history.

E. Perroy, *The Hundred Years' War*, trans. by W. B. Wells (1965). Still the most comprehensive one-volume account.

Y. Renovard, *The Avignon Papacy, 1305–1403*, trans. by D. Bethell (1970). The standard narrative account.

M. Spinka, *John Huss's Concept of the Church* (1966). Lucid and authoritative account of Hussite theology.

B. Tierney, *The Crisis of Church and State, 1050–1300* (1964). Part IV provides the major documents in the clash between Boniface VIII and Philip the Fair.

C. T. Wood, *Philip the Fair and Boniface VIII* (1967). Excerpts from the scholarly debate over the significance of this confrontation.

P. Ziegler, *The Black Death* (1969). Highly readable account.

Chapter 10

A map of America in 1596 with representations of the great Western explorers Columbus, Vespucci, Magellan, and Pizarro. Etching by Theodor de Bry, National Museum, Berlin. Bildarchiv Preussischer Kulturbesitz.

Renaissance and Discovery

KEY TOPICS

- The politics, culture, and art of the Italian Renaissance
- Political struggle and foreign intervention in Italy
- The powerful new monarchies of northern Europe
- The thought and culture of the northern Renaissance

If the late Middle Ages saw unprecedented chaos, it also witnessed a rebirth that would continue into the seventeenth century. Two modern Dutch scholars have employed the same word (Herfsttij, or "harvesttide") with different connotations to describe the period. Johan Huizinga has used the word to mean a "waning" or "decline," and Heiko Oberman has used it to mean "harvest." If something was dying away, some ripe fruit was being gathered and seed grain was sown. The late Middle Ages was a time of creative fragmentation.

By the late fifteenth century, Europe was recovering well from two of the three crises of the late Middle Ages: the demographic and the political. The great losses in population were being recaptured, and increasingly able monarchs and rulers were imposing a new political order. A solution to the religious crisis, however, would have to await the Reformation and Counter-Reformation of the sixteenth century.

Although the opposite would be true in the sixteenth and seventeenth centuries, the city–states of Italy survived the century and a half between 1300 and 1450 better than the territorial states of northern Europe. This was due to Italy's strategic location between East and West and its lucrative Eurasian trade. Great wealth gave rulers and merchants the ability to work their will on both society and culture. They became patrons of government, education, and the arts, always as much for self-aggrandizement as out of benevolence, for whether a patron was a family, a firm, a government, or the church, their endowments enhanced their reputation and power. The result of such patronage was a cultural Renaissance in Italian cities unmatched elsewhere.

With the fall of Constantinople to the Turks in 1453, the shrinkage of Italy's once unlimited trading empire began. City–state soon turned against city–state, and by the 1490s the armies of France invaded Italy. Within a quarter century, Italy's great Renaissance had peaked.

The fifteenth century also saw an unprecedented scholarly renaissance. Italian and northern humanists made a full recovery of classical knowledge and languages and set in motion educational reforms and cultural changes that would spread throughout Europe in the fifteenth and sixteenth centuries. In the process the Italian humanists invented, for all practical purposes, critical historical scholarship and exploited a new fifteenth-century invention, the "divine art" of printing with movable type.

In this period the vernacular—the local language—began to take its place alongside Latin, the international language, as a widely used literary and political means of communication. And European lands progressively superseded the universal Church as the community of highest allegiance, as patriotism and incipient nationalism seized hearts and minds as strongly as religion. Nations henceforth "transcended" themselves not by journeys to Rome, but by competitive voyages to the Far East and the Americas, as the age of global exploration opened.

For Europe, the late fifteenth and sixteenth centuries were a period of unprecedented territorial expansion and ideological experimentation. Permanent colonies were established within the Americas, and the exploitation of the New World's human and mineral resources was begun. Imported American gold and silver spurred scientific invention and a new weapons industry and touched off an inflationary spiral that produced an escalation in prices by the century's end. The new bullion also helped create an international traffic in African slaves as rival African tribes sold their captives to the Portuguese. These slaves were brought in ever-increasing numbers to work the mines and the plantations of the New World as replacements for faltering American natives. The period also saw social engineering and political planning on a large scale. Newly centralized governments began to put long-range economic policies into practice, a development that came to be known as mercantilism.

The Renaissance in Italy (1375–1527)

A historian has described the Renaissance as the "prototype of the modern world." In his *Civilization of the Renaissance in Italy* (1860), Jacob Burckhardt argues that in fourteenth- and fifteenth-century Italy, through the revival of ancient learning, new secular and scientific values began to supplant traditional religious beliefs. This was the period in which people began to adopt a rational, objective, and statistical approach to reality and to rediscover the importance of the individual and his or her artistic creativity. The result, in Burckhardt's words, was a release of the "full, whole nature of man."

Other scholars have found Burckhardt's description far too modernizing an interpretation of the Renaissance and have accused him of overlooking the continuity between the Middle Ages and the Renaissance. His critics especially stress the still strongly Christian character of Renaissance humanism. They point out that earlier "renaissances," especially that of the twelfth century, also saw the revival of the ancient classics, interest in the Latin language and Greek science, and an appreciation of the worth and creativity of individuals.

Despite the exaggeration and bias of Burckhardt's portrayal, most scholars agree that the Renaissance was a time of transition from the medieval to the modern world. Medieval Europe, especially before the twelfth century, had been a fragmented feudal society with an agricultural economy, and its thought and culture were largely dominated by the church. Renaissance Europe, especially after the fourteenth century, was characterized by growing national consciousness and political centralization, an urban economy based on organized commerce and capitalism, and ever-greater lay and secular control of thought and culture, including religion.

The distinctive features and achievements of the Renaissance are most strikingly revealed in Italy from roughly 1375 to 1527, the year of the infamous sack of Rome by imperial soldiers. What was achieved in Italy during the late fourteenth to the early sixteenth centuries also deeply influenced northern Europe. (See "Art & the West.")

The Italian City–State

Renaissance society was no simple cultural transformation. It first took distinctive shape within the cities of late medieval Italy. Italy had always had a cultural advantage over the rest of Europe because its geography made it the natural gateway between East and West. Venice, Genoa, and Pisa traded uninterruptedly with the Near East throughout the Middle Ages

An Unprecedented Self-Portrait

Albrecht Dürer (1471–1528), the greatest German painter of the Renaissance, was the son of a Nuremberg goldsmith and the apprentice of the city's then most famous painter, Michael Wolgemut. Naturally gifted and trained from childhood, Dürer at thirteen could draw so lifelike a reflection of himself in a mirror, that senior artists already then recognized his genius. A dowry from his marriage at twenty-two (his wife, Agnes Frey, was nineteen) permitted him to travel to Venice, where he acquired the skills of the great Italian artists. His ability to paint realistically led contemporaries to compare him to the legendary ancient Greek painter Apelles and won him many humanistic and princely patrons. According to one story, his dog, passing by a just finished painting his master had put outside to dry, mistook the work for the master himself and gave it a loving lick, leaving a permanent mark on the painting that Dürer proudly pointed out.

The *Self-Portrait* of 1500 was one of perhaps thirty self-portraits over Dürer's lifetime. (No previous artist painted himself as often or as provocatively.) For some scholars this painting signals a change from the medieval toward a more modern worldview. The individual becomes the primary focus, supplanting God and king. Exalting the power of art and the artist, Dürer presents himself as Christ-like and full faced, a pose traditionally reserved for members of the Holy Trinity. His own autograph, placed at eye level, backs up the portrait's bold proclamation: "I, Albrecht Dürer, divinely inspired artist."

The portrait's powerful effect is achieved by strict adherence to the rules of geometric proportionality (a subject on which Dürer wrote a major book) and by painstaking attention to detail. It is a work of perfect symmetry, and each hair of his head—even the fur on his coat—seems to have been drawn individually with great care. What the viewer beholds is neither Christ nor Everyman, but the gifted individual as many Renaissance thinkers dreamed him to be: a divinely endowed person capable of great achievement.

Dürer, Albrecht (1471–1528). *Self-portrait at Age 28 with Fur Coat.* 1500. Oil on wood, 67 × 49 cm. Alte Pinakothek, Munich, Germany. Scala/Art Resource, N.Y.

Sources: Jane Campbell Hutchison, *Albrecht Dürer: A Biography* (Princeton: Princeton University Press, 1990); Joseph Leo Koerner, *The Moment of Self-Portraiture in German Renaissance Art* (Chicago, 1993), esp. pp. xviii, 8–9, 40–42.

and maintained vibrant urban societies. When commerce revived on a large scale in the eleventh century, Italian merchants quickly mastered the business skills of organization, bookkeeping, scouting new markets, and securing monopolies. During the thirteenth and fourteenth centuries, trade-rich cities expanded to become powerful city–states, dominating the political and economic life of the surrounding countryside. By the fifteenth century, the great Italian cities had become the bankers of much of Europe.

GROWTH OF CITY–STATES   The growth of Italian cities and urban culture was assisted by the endemic warfare between the emperor and the pope and the Guelf (propapal) and Ghibelline (proimperial) factions that this warfare had created. Either of these might have successfully challenged the cities had they permitted each other to concentrate on that. Instead, they chose to weaken one another and thus strengthened the merchant oligarchies of the cities. Unlike those of northern Europe, which tended to be dominated by kings and territorial princes, the great Italian cities were left free to expand. They became independent states, absorbing the surrounding countryside and assimilating the area's nobility in a unique urban meld of old and new rich. There were five such major, competitive states in Italy: the duchy of Milan; the republics of Florence and Venice; the Papal States; and the kingdom of Naples. (See Map 10–1.)

Social strife and competition for political power were so intense within the cities that most had evolved into despotisms by the fifteenth century just to survive. Venice was a notable exception. It was ruled by a successful merchant oligarchy with power located in a patrician senate of 300 members and a ruthless judicial body, the Council of Ten, which anticipated and suppressed rival groups. Elsewhere, the new social classes and divisions within society produced by rapid urban growth fueled chronic, near-anarchic conflict.

SOCIAL CLASS AND CONFLICT   Florence was the most striking example. There were four distinguishable social groups within the city. The first was the old rich, or *grandi*, the nobles and merchants who traditionally ruled the city. The second group was the emergent newly rich merchant class—capitalists and bankers known as the *popolo grosso*, or "fat people." They began to challenge the old rich for political power in the late thirteenth and early fourteenth centuries. Then there were the middle-burgher ranks of guild masters, shop owners, and professionals—those smaller businesspeople who, in Florence as elsewhere, tended to take the side of the new rich against the conservative policies of the old rich. Finally, there was the *popolo minuto*, or the "little people," the lower economic classes. In 1457 one-third of the population of Florence, about 30,000 people, were officially listed as paupers, that is, having no wealth at all.

These social divisions produced conflict at every level of society, to which was added the ever-present fear of foreign intrigue. In 1378 there was a great revolt of the poor known as the Ciompi Revolt. It resulted from a combination of three factors that made life unbearable for those at the bottom of society: the feuding between the old and the new rich; the social anarchy that had resulted from the Black Death, which cut the city's population almost in half; and the collapse of the banking houses of Bardi and Peruzzi, which left the poor more economically vulnerable than ever. The successful revolt established a chaotic four-year reign of power by the lower Florentine classes. True stability did not return to Florence until the ascent to power of Cosimo de' Medici (1389–1464) in 1434.

Duchy of Milan	Republic of Venice
Republic of Genoa	Papal States
Republic of Florence	Kingdom of Naples

200 MILES
200 KILOMETERS

D. OF SAVOY — Milan
Turin   MANTUA
SALUZZO   FERRARA
Genoa   MODENA
LUCCA   Florence   ROMAGNA
CORSICA (GENOA)   Siena
SIENA
Rome
Adriatic Sea
Naples
SARDINIA (ARAGON)
Tyrrhenian Sea
Palermo
SICILY
Syracuse
Mediterranean Sea

MAP 10–1   RENAISSANCE ITALY   *The city–states of Renaissance Italy were self-contained principalities whose internal strife was monitored by their despots and whose external aggression was long successfully controlled by treaty.*

Florentine women doing needlework, spinning, and weaving. These activities took up much of a woman's time and contributed to the elegance of dress for which Florentine men and women were famed.
Alinari/Art Resource

DESPOTISM AND DIPLOMACY The wealthiest Florentine, Cosimo de' Medici, was an astute statesman. He controlled the city internally from behind the scenes, skillfully manipulating the constitution and influencing elections. Florence was governed by a council, first of six and later of eight members, known as the *Signoria*. These men were chosen from the most powerful guilds—those representing the major clothing industries (cloth, wool, fur, and silk) and such other groups as bankers, judges, and doctors. Through his informal, cordial relations with the electoral committee, Cosimo was able to keep councillors loyal to him in the *Signoria*. As head of the Office of Public Debt, he was able to favor congenial factions. His grandson Lorenzo the Magnificent (1449–1492, r. 1478–1492) ruled Florence in almost totalitarian fashion during the last quarter of the fifteenth century. The assassination of his brother in 1478 by a rival family, the Pazzi, who plotted with the pope against Medici rule, made Lorenzo a cautious and determined ruler.

Despotism was less subtle elsewhere. To prevent internal social conflict and foreign intrigue from paralyzing their cities, the dominant groups cooperated to install a hired strongman. Known as a *podestà*, his purpose was to maintain law and order. He was given executive, military, and judicial authority. His mandate was direct and simple: to permit, by whatever means required, the normal flow of business activity without which neither the old rich, the new rich, nor the poor of a city could long survive. Because these despots could not depend on the divided populace, they operated through mercenary armies, which they obtained through military brokers known as *condottieri*.

It was a hazardous job. Not only were despots subject to dismissal by the oligarchies that hired them, but they were also popular objects of assassination attempts. The spoils of success, however, were very great. In Milan, it was as despots that the Visconti family came to power in 1278 and the Sforza family in 1450. Both ruled without constitutional restraints or serious political competition. The latter produced one of Machiavelli's heroes, Ludovico il Moro.

Political turbulence and warfare gave birth to diplomacy. Consequently, the various city–states could stay abreast of foreign military developments and, if shrewd enough, gain power and advantage short of actually going to war. Most city–states established resident embassies in the fifteenth century. Their ambassadors not only represented them in ceremonies and as negotiators, but also became their watchful eyes and ears at rival courts.

Whether within the comparatively tranquil republic of Venice, the strong-arm democracy of Florence, or the undisguised despotism of Milan, the disciplined Italian city proved a most congenial climate for an unprecedented flowering of thought and culture. Italian Renaissance culture was promoted as vigorously by despots as by republicans and as enthusiastically by secularized popes as by the more spiritually minded.

Cosimo de' Medici (1389–1464), Florentine banker and statesman, in his lifetime the city's wealthiest man and most successful politician. This portrait is by Pontormo.
Erich Lessing, Art Resource, N.Y.

Such widespread support occurred because the main requirement for patronage of the arts and letters was the one thing that Italian cities of the High Renaissance had in abundance: great wealth.

Humanism

Several schools of thought exist on the meaning of "humanism." There are those who see the Italian Renaissance as the birth of modernity, characterized by an un-Christian philosophy that stressed the dignity of humankind and championed individualism and secular values. (These are the followers of the nineteenth-century historian Jacob Burckhardt.) Others argue that humanists were the very champions of authentic Catholic Christianity, who opposed the pagan teaching of Aristotle and the ineloquent Scholasticism that his writings nurtured. Still others see humanism as a form of scholarship consciously designed to promote a sense of civic responsibility and political liberty.

An authoritative modern commentator on humanism, Paul O. Kristeller, has accused all these views of dealing more with the secondary effects than

with the essence of humanism. Humanism, he believes, was no particular philosophy or value system, but simply an educational program that concentrated on rhetoric and sound scholarship for their own sake.

There is truth in each of these definitions. Humanism was the scholarly study of the Latin and Greek classics and of the ancient Church Fathers both for its own sake and in the hope of a rebirth of ancient norms and values. Humanists advocated the *studia humanitatis*, a liberal arts program of study that embraced grammar, rhetoric, poetry, history, politics, and moral philosophy. Not only were these subjects considered a joy in themselves, but they were also seen as celebrating the dignity of humankind and preparing people for a life of virtuous action. The Florentine Leonardo Bruni (ca. 1370–1444) first gave the name *humanitas*, or "humanity," to the learning that resulted from such scholarly pursuits. Bruni was a student of Manuel Chrysoloras, a Byzantine scholar who opened the world of Greek scholarship to a generation of young Italian humanists when he taught at Florence between 1397 and 1403.

The first humanists were orators and poets. They wrote original literature in both the classical and the vernacular languages, inspired by and modeled on the newly discovered works of the ancients. They also taught rhetoric within the universities. When humanists were not employed as teachers of rhetoric, their talents were sought as secretaries, speechwriters, and diplomats in princely and papal courts.

The study of classical and Christian antiquity existed before the Italian Renaissance. There were recoveries of ancient civilization during the Carolingian renaissance of the ninth century, within the cathedral school of Chartres in the twelfth century, during the great Aristotelian revival in Paris in the thirteenth century, and among the Augustinians in the early fourteenth century. These precedents, however, only partially compare with the grand achievements of the Italian Renaissance of the late Middle Ages. The latter was far more secular and lay dominated, had much broader interests, was blessed with far more recovered manuscripts, and possessed far superior technical skills than had been the case in the earlier "rebirths" of antiquity.

Unlike their Scholastic rivals, humanists were less bound to recent tradition; they did not focus all their attention on summarizing and comparing the views of recognized authorities on a text or question, but went directly to the original sources themselves. And their most respected sources were classical and biblical, not the medieval philosophers and theologians. Avidly searching out manuscript collections, Italian humanists made the full sources of Greek and Latin antiquity available to scholars during the fourteenth and fifteenth centuries. Mastery of Latin and Greek was the surgeon's tool of the humanist. There is a kernel of truth—but only a kernel—in the humanists' arrogant assertion that the period between themselves and classical civilization was a "dark middle age."

PETRARCH, DANTE, AND BOCCACCIO Francesco Petrarch (1304–1374) was the "father of humanism." (See "Petrarch's Letter to Posterity.") He left the legal profession to pursue letters and poetry. Most of his life was spent in and around Avignon. He was involved in Cola di Rienzo's popular revolt and two-year reign (1347–1349) in Rome as "tribune" of the Roman people. Petrarch also served the Visconti family in Milan in his later years.

Petrarch celebrated ancient Rome in his *Letters to the Ancient Dead*, fancied personal letters to Cicero, Livy, Vergil, and Horace. He also wrote a Latin epic poem (*Africa*, a poetic historical tribute to the Roman general Scipio Africanus) and a set of biographies of famous Roman men (*Lives of Illustrious Men*). Petrarch's most famous contemporary work was a collection of highly introspective love sonnets to a certain Laura, a married woman whom he romantically admired from a safe distance.

His critical textual studies, elitism, and contempt for the allegedly useless learning of the Scholastics were features that many later humanists also shared. Classical and Christian values coexist, not always harmoniously, in his work, an uneasy coexistence that is seen in many later humanists. Medieval Christian values can be seen in Petrarch's imagined dialogues with Saint Augustine and in tracts written to defend the personal immortality of the soul against the Aristotelians.

Petrarch was, however, far more secular in orientation than his famous near-contemporary Dante Alighieri (1265–1321), whose *Vita Nuova* and *Divine Comedy* form, with Petrarch's sonnets, the cornerstones of Italian vernacular literature. Petrarch's student and friend Giovanni Boccaccio (1313–1375) was also a pioneer of humanist studies. His *Decameron*—one hundred often bawdy tales told by three men and seven women in a country retreat from the plague that ravaged Florence in 1348—is both a stinging social commentary (especially in its exposé of sexual and economic misconduct) and a sympathetic look at human behavior. An avid collector of manuscripts, Boccaccio also assembled an encyclopedia of Greek and Roman mythology.

Petrarch's Letter to Posterity

In old age Petrarch wrote a highly personal letter to posterity in which he summarized the lessons he had learned during his lifetime. The letter also summarizes the original values of Renaissance humanists: their suspicion of purely materialistic pleasure, the importance they attached to friendship, and their utter devotion to and love of antiquity.

❖ *Does Petrarch's letter give equal weight to classical and Christian values? Why would he have preferred to live in another age?*

I have always possessed extreme contempt for wealth; not that riches are not desirable in themselves, but because I hate the anxiety and care which are invariably associated with them....I have, on the contrary, led a happier existence with plain living and ordinary fare....

The pleasure of dining with one's friends is so great that nothing has ever given me more delight than their unexpected arrival, nor have I ever willingly sat down to table without a companion....

The greatest kings of this age have loved and courted me....I have fled, however, from many...to whom I was greatly attached; and such was my innate longing for liberty that I studiously avoided those whose very name seemed incompatible with the freedom I loved.

I possess a well-balanced rather than a keen intellect—one prone to all kinds of good and wholesome study, but especially to moral philosophy and the art of poetry. The latter I neglected as time went on, and took delight in sacred literature....Among the many subjects that interested me, I dwelt especially upon antiquity, for our own age has always repelled me, so that, had it not been for the love of those dear to me, I should have preferred to have been born in any other period than our own. In order to forget my own time, I have constantly striven to place myself in spirit in other ages, and consequently I delighted in history....

If only I have lived well, it matter little to me how I have talked. Mere elegance of language can produce at best but an empty fame.

Frederick Austen Ogg, ed., *A Source Book of Mediaeval History: Documents Illustrative of European Life and Institutions from the German Invasions to the Renaissance* (New York: American Book Company, 1908), pp. 470–473.

Dante Alighieri (1265–1321) portrayed with scenes of hell, purgatory, and paradise from the Divine Comedy, *his classic epic poem.* Scala/Art Resource, N.Y.

EDUCATIONAL REFORMS AND GOALS Humanists were not bashful scholars. They delighted in going directly to primary sources and refused to be slaves to tradition. Such an attitude not only made them innovative educators, but also kept them constantly in search of new sources of information. Magnificent manuscript collections were assembled with great care, as if they were potent medicines for the ills of contemporary society.

The goal of humanist studies was to be wise and to speak eloquently, to know what is good, and to practice virtue. Learning was not to remain abstract and unpracticed. "It is better to will the good than to know the truth," Petrarch had taught, and this became a motto of many later humanists, who, like Petrarch, believed that learning ennobled people. Pietro Paolo Vergerio (1349–1420), the author of the most influential Renaissance tract on education, *On the Morals That Befit a Free Man*, left a classic summary of the humanist concept of a liberal education:

We call those studies liberal which are worthy of a free man; those studies by which we attain and practice virtue and wisdom; that education which calls forth, trains, and develops those highest gifts of body and mind which ennoble men and which are rightly judged to rank next in dignity to virtue only, for to a vulgar temper, gain and pleasure are the one aim of existence, to a lofty nature, moral worth and fame.[1]

The ideal of a useful education and well-rounded people inspired far-reaching reforms in traditional education. Quintilian's *Education of the Orator*, the

[1] Cited by De Lamar Jensen, *Renaissance Europe: Age of Recovery and Reconciliation* (Lexington, MA: D. C. Health, 1981), p. 111.

complete text of which was discovered in 1416, became the basic classical guide for the humanist revision of the traditional curriculum. Vittorino da Feltre (d. 1446) exemplified the ideals of humanist teaching. He not only had his students read the difficult works of Pliny, Ptolemy, Terence, Plautus, Livy, and Plutarch, but also subjected them to vigorous physical exercise and games. Another famous educator, Guarino da Verona (d. 1460), rector of the new University of Ferrara and a student of the age's most renowned Greek scholar, Manuel Chrysoloras, streamlined the study of classical languages and gave it systematic form.

Humanist learning was not confined to the classroom, as Baldassare Castiglione's (1478–1529) famous *Book of the Courtier* illustrates. Written as a practical guide for the nobility at the court of Urbino, it embodies the highest ideals of Italian humanism. It depicts the successful courtier as one who knew how to integrate knowledge of ancient languages and history with athletic, military, and musical skills, while practicing good manners and exhibiting a high moral character.

Noblewomen also played a role at court in education and culture, among them none more so than Christine de Pisan (1363?–1434). The Italian-born daughter of the physician and astrologer of the French king Charles V, she received as fine an education at the French court as anyone could have. She became expert in classical, French, and Italian languages and literature. Married at fifteen and the widowed mother of three at twenty-seven, she turned to writing lyric poetry to support herself. She soon became a well-known woman of letters who was much read throughout the courts of Europe. Her most famous work, *The City of Ladies*, is a chronicle of the accomplishments of the great women of history. (See "Christine de Pisan Instructs Women on How to Handle Their Husbands.")

THE FLORENTINE "ACADEMY" AND THE REVIVAL OF PLATONISM Of all the important recoveries of the past made during the Italian Renaissance, none stands out more than the revival of Greek studies, especially the works of Plato, in fifteenth-century Florence. Many factors combined to bring this revival about. An important foundation was laid in 1397 when the city invited Manuel Chrysoloras to come from Constantinople to promote Greek learning. A half century later (1439), the ecumenical Council of Ferrara–Florence, having convened to negotiate the reunion of the Eastern and Western churches, opened the door for many Greek scholars and manuscripts to enter the West.

After the fall of Constantinople to the Turks in 1453, Greek scholars fled to Florence for refuge. This was the background against which the Florentine Platonic Academy evolved under the patronage of Cosimo de' Medici and the supervision of Marsilio Ficino (1433–1499) and Pico della Mirandola (1463–1494).

The thinkers of the Renaissance were interested in every variety of ancient wisdom. They were especially attracted, however, to the Platonic tradition and to those Church Fathers who tried to synthesize Platonic philosophy with Christian teaching. The "Florentine Academy" was actually not a formal school, but an informal gathering of influential Florentine humanists devoted to the revival of the works of Plato and the Neoplatonists: Plotinus, Proclus, Porphyry, and Dionysius the Areopagite. To this end, Ficino edited and published the complete works of Plato.

Christine de Pisan Instructs Women on How to Handle Their Husbands

Renowned Renaissance noblewoman Christine de Pisan has the modern reputation of being perhaps the first feminist, and her book, The Treasure of the City of Ladies *(also known as* The Book of Three Virtues*), has been described as the Renaissance woman's survival manual. Here she gives advice to the wives of artisans.*

❖ *How does Christine de Pisan's image of husband and wife compare with other medieval views? Would the church take issue with her advice in any way? As a noblewoman commenting on the married life of artisans, does her high social standing influence her advice? Would she give similar advice to women of her own social class?*

All wives of artisans should be very painstaking and diligent if they wish to have the necessities of life. They should encourage their husbands or their workmen to get to work early in the morning and work until late....[And] the wife herself should [also] be involved in the work to the extent that she knows all about it, so that she may know how to oversee his workers if her husband is absent, and to reprove them if they do not do well....And when customers come to her husband and try to drive a hard bargain, she ought to warn him solicitously to take care that he does not make a bad deal. She should advise him to be chary of giving too much credit if he does not know precisely where and to whom it is going, for in this way many come to poverty....

In addition, she ought to keep her husband's love as much as she can, to this end: that he will stay at home more willingly and that he may not have any reason to join the foolish crowds of other young men in taverns and indulge in unnecessary and extravagant expense, as many tradesmen do, especially in Paris. By treating him kindly she should protect him as well as she can from this. It is said that three things drive a man from his home: a quarrelsome wife, a smoking fireplace, and a leaking roof. She too ought to stay at home gladly and not go off every day traipsing hither and yon gossiping with the neighbours and visiting her chums to find out what everyone is doing. That is done by slovenly housewives roaming about the town in groups. Nor should she go off on these pilgrimages got up for no good reason and involving a lot of needless expense.

Excerpt from *The Treasure of the City of Ladies* or *The Book of the Three Virtues*, by Christine de Pisan, trans. by Sarah Lawson (Penguin Classics, 1985), this translation copyright © Sarah Lawson, 1985. Reprinted by permission of Penguin Books Ltd.

The appeal of Platonism lay in its flattering view of human nature. It distinguished between an eternal sphere of being and the perishable world in which humans actually lived. Human reason was believed to belong to the former—indeed, to have preexisted in this pristine world and to continue to commune with it, to which the present knowledge of mathematical and moral truth bore witness.

Strong Platonic influence can be seen in Pico's *Oration on the Dignity of Man*, perhaps the most famous Renaissance statement on the nature of humankind. Pico wrote the *Oration* as an introduction to a pretentious collection of 900 theses. Published in Rome in December 1486, the theses were intended to serve as the basis for a public debate on all of life's important topics. The Oration drew on Platonic teaching to depict humans as the only creatures in the world who possessed the freedom to be whatever they chose, able at will to rise to the height of angels or to descend to the level of pigs.

CRITICAL WORK OF THE HUMANISTS: LORENZO VALLA

Because they were guided by a scholarly ideal of philological accuracy and historical truthfulness, the humanists could become critics of tradition even when that was not their intention. Dispassionate critical scholarship shook long-standing foundations, not the least of which were those of the medieval church.

The work of Lorenzo Valla (1406–1457), author of the standard Renaissance text on Latin philology, the *Elegances of the Latin Language* (1444), reveals the explosive character of the new learning. Although a good Catholic, Valla became a hero to later Protestants. His popularity among Protestants stemmed from his defense of predestination against the advocates of free will, and especially from his exposé of the *Donation of Constantine*. (See Chapter 6.)

The fraudulent *Donation*, written in the eighth century, purported to be a grant of vast territories made by the fourth-century Roman emperor Constantine to the pope. Valla did not intend the exposé of the *Donation* to have the devastating force that Protestants later attributed to it. He only proved in a careful, scholarly way what others had long suspected. Using the most rudimentary textual analysis and historical logic, Valla demonstrated that the document was filled with such anachronistic terms as *fief* and that it contained material that could not be in a genuine fourth-century document. In the same dispassionate way, Valla also pointed out errors in the Latin Vulgate, still the authorized version of the Bible for the Western church.

Such discoveries did not make Valla any less loyal to the church, nor did they prevent his faithful fulfillment of the office of apostolic secretary in Rome under Pope Nicholas V. Nonetheless, historical criticism of this type served those less loyal to the medieval church. It was no accident that young humanists formed the first identifiable group of Martin Luther's supporters.

CIVIC HUMANISM   Italian humanists were exponents of applied knowledge; their basic criticism of traditional education was that much of it was useless. Education, they believed, should promote individual virtue and public service. This ideal inspired what has been called civic humanism, by which is meant examples of humanist leadership of the political and cultural life. The most striking instance is to be found in Florence. There three humanists served as chancellors: Colluccio Salutati (1331–1406), Leonardo Bruni (ca. 1370–1444), and Poggio Bracciolini (1380–1459). Each used his rhetorical skills to rally the Florentines against the aggression of Naples and Milan. Bruni and Poggio also wrote adulatory histories of the city. Another accomplished humanist scholar, Leon Battista Alberti (1402–1472), was a noted architect and builder in the city. Whether it was humanism that accounted for such civic activity or just a desire to exercise great power remains a debated issue.

On the other hand, many humanists became cliquish and snobbish, an intellectual elite concerned only with pursuing narrow, antiquarian interests and writing pure, classical Latin in the quiet of their studies. It was in reaction to this elitist trend that the humanist historians Niccolò Machiavelli (1469–1527) and Francesco Guicciardini (1483–1540) adopted the vernacular and made contemporary history their primary source and subject matter.

Renaissance Art

In Renaissance Italy, as in Reformation Europe, the values and interests of the laity were no longer subordinated to those of the clergy. In education, culture, and religion, the laity assumed a leading role and established models for the clergy to imitate. This was a development due in part to the church's loss of international power during the great crises of the late Middle Ages. It was also encouraged by the rise of national sentiment, the creation of competent national bureaucracies staffed by the laity rather than by clerics, and the rapid growth of lay education during the fourteenth and fifteenth centuries. Medieval Christian values were adjusting to a more this-worldly spirit. Men and women began again to appreciate

Giotto's portrayal of the funeral of Saint Francis of Assisi. The saint is surrounded by his admiring brothers and a knight of Assisi (first on the right). Giotto's (1266–1336) work signals the evolution toward Renaissance art. The damaged areas on this fresco resulted from the removal of nineteenth-century restorations. Scala/Art Resource, N.Y.

and even glorify the secular world, secular learning, and purely human pursuits as ends in themselves.

This new perspective on life is prominent in the painting and sculpture of the High Renaissance—the late fifteenth and early sixteenth centuries, when Renaissance art reached its full maturity. Whereas medieval art tended to be abstract and formulaic, Renaissance art was emphatically concerned with the observation of the natural world and the communication of human emotions. Renaissance artists also tried to give their works a greater rational (chiefly mathematical) order—a symmetry and proportionality that reflected pictorially their deeply held belief in the harmony of the universe. The interest of Renaissance artists in ancient Roman art was closely allied to an independent interest in humanity and nature.

Renaissance artists had the advantage of new technical skills developed during the fifteenth century. In addition to the availability of oil paints, two special techniques were perfected: that of using shading to enhance naturalness (*chiaroscuro*) and that of adjusting the size of figures to give the viewer a feeling of continuity with the painting (linear perspective). These techniques permitted the artist to "rationalize" space and paint a more natural world. The result was that, compared to their flat Byzantine and Gothic counterparts, Renaissance paintings were filled with energy and life and stood out from the canvas in three dimensions.

The new direction was signaled by Giotto (1266–1336), the father of Renaissance painting. An admirer of Saint Francis of Assisi, whose love of nature he shared, Giotto painted a more natural world than his Byzantine and Gothic predecessors. Though still filled with religious seriousness, his work was no longer so abstract and unnatural a depiction of the world. The painter Masaccio (1401–1428) and the sculptor Donatello (1386–1466) continued to portray the world around them more literally and naturally. The heights were reached by the great masters of the High Renaissance: Leonardo da Vinci (1452–1519), Raphael (1483–1520), and Michelangelo Buonarroti (1475–1564).

LEONARDO DA VINCI More than any other person in the period, Leonardo exhibited the Renaissance ideal of the universal person. He was a true mas-

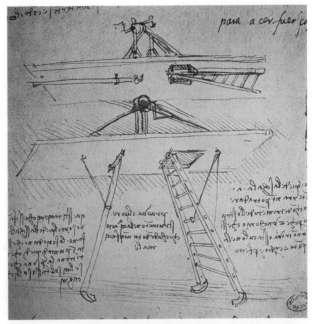

Aviation drawings by Leonardo da Vinci (1452–1519), who imagined a possible flying machine with a retractable ladder for boarding. David Forbert/SuperStock, Inc.

ter of many skills. One of the greatest painters of all time, he was also a military engineer for Ludovico il Moro in Milan, Cesare Borgia in Romagna, and the French king Francis I. Leonardo advocated scientific experimentation, dissected corpses to learn anatomy, and was an accomplished, self-taught botanist. His inventive mind foresaw such modern machines as airplanes and submarines. Indeed, the variety of his interests was so great that it could shorten his attention span, so that he was constantly moving from one activity to another. His great skill in conveying inner moods through complex facial features can be seen in the most famous of his paintings, the *Mona Lisa*, as well as in his self-portrait.

RAPHAEL   A man of great sensitivity and kindness, Raphael was apparently loved by contemporaries as much for his person as for his work. His premature death at thirty-seven cut short his artistic career. He is famous for his tender madonnas, the best known of which graced the monastery of San Sisto in Piacenza and is now in Dresden. Art historians praise his fresco *The School of Athens*,

a grandly conceived portrayal of the great masters of Western philosophy, as a virtually perfect example of Renaissance technique. It depicts Plato and Aristotle surrounded by the great philosophers and scientists of antiquity, who are portrayed with features of Raphael's famous contemporaries, including Leonardo and Michelangelo.

MICHELANGELO   The melancholy genius Michelangelo also excelled in a variety of arts and crafts. His eighteen-foot godlike sculpture David, which long stood majestically in the great square of Florence, is a perfect example of the Renaissance artist's devotion to harmony, symmetry, and proportion, as well as the extreme glorification of the human form. Four different popes commissioned works by Michelangelo. The most famous of these works are the frescoes for the Sistine Chapel, painted during the pontificate of Pope Julius II (r. 1503–1513), who

Commissioned in 1501, when the artist was 26, Michelangelo's David became the symbol of the Florentine republic and was displayed in front of the Palazzo Vecchio. The detail shown here highlights the restrained emotion and dignity for which the statue is famous. Michelangelo (1475–1564) David-p. (testa di profilo.) Accademia Firenze. Scala/Art Resource

Portrait by Raphael of Baldassare Castiglione (1748–1529), author of the Cortegiano. Portrait (c. 1515) now in the Louvre. Cliche des Musées Nationaux

These two works by Donatello, sculpted fifteen years apart, reveal the psychological complexity of Renaissance artists and their work. On the left is a youthful, sexy David, standing awkwardly and seemingly puzzled on the head of the slain Goliath. Created in 1440, it is the earliest free-standing nude made in the West since Roman times. Art Resource, N.Y *On the right, sculpted in 1454–1455 from poplar wood, is Mary Magdalen returned from her desert retreat; she is a frightful, toothless old woman, shorn of all dignity.* Scala/Art Resource, N.Y.

The frescoes of Michelangelo on the west wall ceiling of the Sistine Chapel in the Vatican Palace. Above the altar is his **Last Judgment.** Brett Froomer/The Image Bank

also set Michelangelo to work on the pope's own magnificent tomb. (See "Michaelangelo and Pope Julius II.") The Sistine frescoes originally covered 10,000 square feet and involved 343 figures, over half of which exceeded 10 feet in height. But it is their originality and perfection as works of art that impress most. This labor of love and piety took four years to complete. A person of incredible energy and endurance who lived to be almost ninety, Michelangelo insisted on doing almost everything himself and permitted his assistants only a few of the many chores involved in his work.

His later works are more complex and suggest deep personal changes. They mark, artistically and philosophically, the passing of High Renaissance painting and the advent of a new style known as mannerism, which reached its peak in the late sixteenth and early seventeenth centuries. A reaction against the simplicity and symmetry of High Renaissance art (which also found expression in music and literature), mannerism made room for the strange and even the abnormal and gave freer reign to the subjectivity of the artist. Mannerism acquired its name because the artist was permitted to express his or her own individual perceptions and feelings, to paint, compose, or write in a "mannered," or "affected," way. Tintoretto (d. 1594) and especially El Greco (d. 1614) became mannerism's supreme representatives.

Slavery in the Renaissance

Throughout Renaissance Italy, slavery flourished as extravagantly as art and culture. A thriving western slave market existed as early as the twelfth century, when the Spanish sold Muslim slaves captured in raids and war to wealthy Italians and other interested buyers. Contemporaries looked on such slavery as a merciful act, since these captives would otherwise have been killed. In addition to widespread household or domestic slavery, collective plantation slavery, following East Asian models, also developed during the High Middle Ages in the eastern Mediterranean. In the savannas of Sudan and on Venetian estates on the islands of Cyprus and Crete, gangs of slaves worked sugar cane plantations, the model for later western Mediterranean and New World slavery.

After the Black Death (1348–1350) had reduced the supply of laborers everywhere in western Europe, the demand for slaves soared. Slaves now began to be imported from Africa, the Balkans, Constantinople, Cyprus, Crete, and the lands surrounding the Black Sea. Because slaves were taken randomly from conquered people, they consisted of many races: Tatars, Circassians, Greeks, Russians, Georgians, and Iranians as well as Asians and Africans. According to one source, "By the end of the fourteenth century, there was hardly a well-to-do household in Tuscany without at least one slave: brides brought them [to their marriages] as part of their dowry, doctors accepted them from their patients in lieu of fees—and it was not unusual to find them even in the service of a priest."[2]

Owners had complete dominion over their slaves; in Italian law, this meant the "[power] to have, hold, sell, alienate, exchange, enjoy, rent or unrent, dispose of in [their] will[s], judge soul and body, and do with in perpetuity whatsoever may please [them] and [their] heirs and no man may gainsay [them]."[3] A strong, young, healthy slave cost the equivalent of the wages paid a free servant over several years. Considering the lifetime of free service thereafter, slaves could be well worth the cost.

The Tatars and Africans appear to have been the worst treated. But as in ancient Greece and Rome, slaves at this time were generally accepted as family members and were integrated into households. Not a few women slaves became mothers of their masters' children. Quite a few children of such

[2] Iris Origo, *The Merchant of Prato: Francesco di Marco Datini, 1335–1410* (New York: David Godine, 1986), pp. 90–91.

[3] *Ibid.*, p. 209.

Michelangelo and Pope Julius II

Vasari here describes how Pope Julius, the most fearsome and worldly of the Renaissance popes, forced Michelangelo to complete the Sistine Chapel before Michelangelo was ready to do so.

❖ *Did Michelangelo hold his own with the pope? What does this interchange suggest about the relationship of patrons and artists in the Renaissance? Were great artists like Michelangelo so revered that they could do virtually as they pleased?*

[The pope was very anxious to see the decoration of the Sistine Chapel completed and constantly inquired when it would be finished.] On one occasion, therefore, Michelangelo replied, "It will be finished when I shall have done all that I believe is required to satisfy Art." "And we command," rejoined the pontiff, "that you satisfy our wish to have it done quickly," adding that if it were not at once completed, he would have Michelangelo thrown headlong from the scaffolding. Hearing this, our artist, who feared the fury of the pope, and with good cause, without taking time to add what was wanting, took down the remainder of the scaffolding to the great satisfaction of the whole city on All Saints' day, when Pope Julius went into that chapel to sing mass. But Michelangelo had much desired to retouch some portions of the work *a secco* [that is, after the damp plaster upon which the paint had been originally laid *al fresco* had dried], as had

been done by the older masters who had painted the stories on the walls. He would also have gladly added a little ultramarine to the draperies and gilded other parts, to the end that the whole might have a richer and more striking effect.

The pope, too, hearing that these things were still wanting, and finding that all who beheld the chapel praised it highly, would now fain have had the additions made. But as Michelangelo thought reconstructing the scaffold too long an affair, the pictures remained as they were, although the pope, who often saw Michelangelo, would sometimes say, "Let the chapel be enriched with bright colors and gold; it looks poor." When Michelangelo would reply familiarly, "Holy Father, the men of those days did not adorn themselves with gold; those who are painted here less than any, for they were none too rich; besides which they were holy men, and must have despised riches and ornaments."

From James Harvey Robinson, ed., *Readings in European History*, Vol. 1 (Boston: Athenaeum, 1904), pp. 538–539.

This portrait of Katharina, by Albrecht Dürer, provides evidence of African slavery in Europe during the sixteenth century. Katharina was in the service of one João Bradao, a Portuguese economic minister living in Antwerp, then the financial center of Europe. Dürer became friends with Bradao during his stay in the Low Countries in the winter of 1520–1521. Albrecht Dürer, Portrait of the Moorish Woman Katharina. Uffizi Florence, Italy. Foto Marburg/Art Resource, NY

unions were adopted and raised as legitimate heirs of their fathers. It was clearly in the interest of their owners to keep slaves healthy and happy; otherwise they were of little use and could even become a threat. Still, slaves remained a foreign and suspected presence in Italian society; they were, as all knew, uprooted and resentful people.

Italy's Political Decline: The French Invasions (1494–1527)

The Treaty of Lodi

As a land of autonomous city–states, Italy had always relied on internal cooperation for its peace and safety from foreign invasion—especially by the Turks. Such cooperation had been maintained during the latter half of the fifteenth century thanks to a carefully constructed political alliance known as the Treaty of Lodi (1454–1455). The terms of the treaty brought Milan and Naples, long traditional enemies, into alliance with Florence. These three stood together for decades against Venice, which was frequently joined by the Papal States, to create an internal balance of power. When a foreign enemy threatened Italy, however, the five formed a united front.

Around 1490, following the rise to power of the Milanese despot Ludovico il Moro, hostilities between Milan and Naples resumed. The peace made possible by the Treaty of Lodi ended in 1494 when Naples, supported by Florence and the Borgia Pope Alexander VI (r. 1492–1503), prepared to attack Milan. Ludovico made what proved to be a fatal response in these new political alignments: He appealed for aid to the French. French kings had ruled Naples from 1266 to 1435, before they were driven out by Duke Alfonso of Sicily. Breaking a wise Italian rule, Ludovico invited the French to reenter Italy and revive their dynastic claim to Naples. In his haste to check his rival Naples, Ludovico did not recognize sufficiently that France also had dynastic claims to Milan. Nor did he foresee how insatiable the French appetite for Italian territory would become once French armies had crossed the Alps.

Charles VIII's March through Italy

The French king Louis XI had resisted the temptation to invade Italy, while nonetheless keeping French dynastic claims in Italy alive. His successor, Charles VIII (r. 1483–1498), an eager youth in his twenties, responded to Ludovico's call with lightning speed. Within five months, he had crossed the Alps (August 1495) and raced as conqueror through Florence and the Papal States into Naples. As Charles approached Florence, the Florentine ruler, Piero dé Medici, who had allied with Naples against Milan, tried to placate the French king by handing over Pisa and other Florentine possessions. Such appeasement only brought about Piero's forced exile by a population that was revolutionized then by the radical Dominican preacher Girolamo Savonarola (1452–1498). Savonarola convinced most of the fearful Florentines that the French king's arrival was a long-delayed and fully justified divine vengeance on their immorality.

Charles entered Florence without resistance. Thanks to Savonarola's flattery and the payment of a large ransom, the city was spared a threatened destruction. Savonarola continued to exercise virtual rule over Florence for four years after Charles's departure. The Florentines proved, however, not to be the stuff theocracies are made of. Savonarola's moral rigor and antipapal policies made it impossible for him to survive indefinitely. This became especially true after the Italian cities reunited and the ouster of the French invader, whom Savonarola had praised as a godsend, became national policy. Savonarola was imprisoned and executed in May 1498.

Charles's lightning march through Italy also struck terror in non-Italian hearts. Ferdinand of Aragon, who hoped to expand his own possessions in Italy from his kingdom of Sicily, now found himself vulnerable to a French–Italian axis. He took the initiative to create a counteralliance—the League of Venice, formed in March 1495—in which he joined with Venice, the Papal States, and Emperor Maximilian I against the French. The alliance set the stage for a conflict between France and Spain that would not end until 1559.

Ludovico il Moro meanwhile recognized that he had sown the wind; having desired a French invasion only so long as it weakened his enemies, he now saw Milan threatened by the whirlwind of events that he had himself created. In reaction, he joined the League of Venice, and this alliance was able to send Charles into retreat by May. Charles remained thereafter on the defensive until his death in April 1498.

Pope Alexander VI and the Borgia Family

The French returned to Italy under Charles's successor, Louis XII (r. 1498–1515). This time they were assisted by a new Italian ally, the Borgia pope, Alexander VI. Alexander was probably the most corrupt pope who ever sat on the papal throne. He openly promoted the political careers of Cesare and Lucrezia Borgia, the children he had had before he became pope, and he placed papal policy in tandem with the efforts of his powerful family to secure a political base in Romagna.

In Romagna, several principalities had fallen away from the church during the Avignon papacy. And Venice, the pope's ally within the League of Venice, continued to contest the Papal States for their loyalty. Seeing that a French alliance could give him the opportunity to reestablish control over the region, Alexander took steps to secure French favor. He annulled Louis XII's marriage to Charles VIII's sister so that Louis could marry Charles's widow, Anne of Brittany—a popular political move designed to keep Brittany French. The pope also bestowed a cardinal's hat on the archbishop of Rouen, Louis's favorite cleric. Most important, Alexander agreed to abandon the League of Venice; this withdrawal of support made the league too weak to resist a French reconquest of Milan. In exchange, Cesare Borgia received the sister of the king of

Navarre, Charlotte d'Albret, in marriage, a union that greatly enhanced Borgia military strength. Cesare also received land grants from Louis XII and the promise of French military aid in Romagna.

All in all it was a scandalous trade-off, but one that made it possible for both the French king and the pope to realize their ambitions within Italy. Louis successfully invaded Milan in August 1499. Ludovico il Moro, who had originally opened the Pandora's box of French invasion, spent his last years languishing in a French prison. In 1500 Louis and Ferdinand of Aragon divided Naples between them, while the pope and Cesare Borgia conquered the cities of Romagna without opposition. Alexander awarded his victorious son the title "duke of Romagna."

Pope Julius II

Cardinal Giuliano della Rovere, a strong opponent of the Borgia family, succeeded Alexander VI as Pope Julius II (r. 1503–1513). He suppressed the Borgias and placed their newly conquered lands in Romagna under papal jurisdiction. Julius came to be known as the "warrior pope," because he brought the Renaissance papacy to a peak of military prowess and diplomatic intrigue. Shocked, as were other contemporaries, by this thoroughly secular papacy, the

Major Political Events of the Italian Renaissance (1375–1527)	
1378–1382	The Ciompi Revolt in Florence
1434	Medici rule in Florence established by Cosimo de' Medici
1454–1455	Treaty of Lodi allies Milan, Naples, and Florence (in effect until 1494)
1494	Charles VIII of France invades Italy
1494–1498	Savonarola controls Florence
1495	League of Venice unites Venice, Milan, the Papal States, the Holy Roman Empire, and Spain against France
1499	Louis XII invades Milan (the second French invasion of Italy)
1500	The Borgias conquer Romagna
1512–1513	The Holy League (Pope Julius II, Ferdinand of Aragon, Emperor Maximilian, and Venice) defeats the French
1513	Machiavelli writes *The Prince*
1515	Francis I leads the third French invasion of Italy
1516	Concordat of Bologna between France and the papacy
1527	Sack of Rome by imperial soldiers

humanist Erasmus (1466?–1536), who had witnessed in disbelief a bullfight in the papal palace during a visit to Rome, wrote a popular anonymous satire entitled *Julius Excluded from Heaven*. This humorous account purported to describe the pope's unsuccessful efforts to convince Saint Peter that he was worthy of admission to heaven.

Assisted by his powerful allies, Pope Julius succeeded in driving the Venetians out of Romagna in 1509. Thus, he ended Venetian claims in the region and fully secured the Papal States. Having realized this long-sought papal goal, Julius turned to the second major undertaking of his pontificate: ridding Italy of his former ally, the French invader. Julius, Ferdinand of Aragon, and Venice formed a second Holy League in October 1511, and within a short period Emperor Maximilian I and the Swiss joined them. By 1512 the league had the French in full retreat, and they were soundly defeated by the Swiss in 1513 at Novara.

The French were nothing if not persistent. They invaded Italy a third time under Louis's successor, Francis I (r. 1515–1547). French armies massacred Swiss soldiers of the Holy League at Marignano in September 1515, avenging the earlier defeat at Novara. The victory won the Concordat of Bologna from the people in August 1516. The agreement gave the French king control over the French clergy in exchange for French recognition of the pope's superiority over church councils and his right to collect annates in France. This was an important compromise that helped keep France Catholic after the outbreak of the Protestant Reformation. But the new French entry into Italy also led to the first of four major wars with Spain in the first half of the sixteenth century: the Habsburg–Valois wars, none of which France won.

Niccolò Machiavelli

The period of foreign invasions made a shambles of Italy. The same period that saw Italy's cultural peak in the work of Leonardo, Raphael, and Michelangelo also witnessed Italy's political tragedy. One who watched as French, Spanish, and German armies wreaked havoc on Italy was Niccolò Machiavelli (1469–1527). The more he saw, the more convinced he became that Italian political unity and independence were ends that justified any means.

A humanist and a careful student of ancient Rome, Machiavelli was impressed by the way Roman rulers and citizens had then defended their homeland. They possessed *virtù*, the ability to act decisively and heroically for the good of their country. Stories of ancient Roman patriotism and self-sacrifice were Machiavelli's favorites, and he lamented the absence of such traits among his compatriots. Such romanticizing of the Roman past caused some exaggeration of both ancient virtue and contemporary failings. His Florentine contemporary, Francesco Guicciardini, a more sober historian less given to idealizing antiquity, wrote truer chronicles of Florentine and Italian history.

Machiavelli also held deep republican ideals, which he did not want to see vanish from Italy. He believed that a strong and determined people could struggle successfully with fortune. He scolded the Italian people for the self-destruction their own internal feuding was causing. He wanted an end to that behavior above all, so that a reunited Italy could drive all foreign armies out.

But were his fellow citizens up to such a challenge? The juxtaposition of what Machiavelli believed the ancient Romans had been with the failure of his contemporaries to attain such high ideals made him the famous cynic whose name—in the epithet "Machiavellian"—has become synonymous with ruthless political expediency. Only a strongman, he concluded in the end, could impose order on so divided and selfish a people; the salvation of Italy required, for the present, a cunning dictator. (See "Machiavelli Discusses the Most Important Trait for a Ruler.")

It has been argued that Machiavelli wrote *The Prince* in 1513 as a cynical satire on the way rulers actually did behave and not as a serious recommendation of unprincipled despotic rule. To take his advocacy of tyranny literally, it is argued, contradicts both his earlier works and his own strong family tradition of republican service. But Machiavelli seems to have been in earnest when he advised rulers to discover the advantages of fraud and brutality, at least as a temporary means to the higher end of a unified Italy. He apparently hoped to see a strong ruler emerge from the Medici family, which had captured the papacy in 1513 with the pontificate of Leo X (r. 1513–1521). At the same time, the Medici family retained control over the powerful territorial state of Florence. The situation was similar to that of Machiavelli's hero Cesare Borgia and his father Pope Alexander VI, who had earlier brought factious Romagna to heel by placing secular family goals and religious policy in tandem. The Prince was pointedly dedicated to Lorenzo de' Medici, duke of Urbino and grandson of Lorenzo the Magnificent.

Whatever Machiavelli's hopes may have been, the Medicis were not destined to be Italy's deliverers. The second Medici pope, Clement VII (r. 1523–1534), watched helplessly as Rome was sacked by the army of Emperor Charles V in 1527, also the year of Machiavelli's death.

machiavelli 1469–1527

Machiavelli Discusses the Most Important Trait for a Ruler

Machiavelli believed that the most important personality trait of a successful ruler was the ability to instill fear in his subjects.

❖ *Why did Machiavelli maintain that rulers must be feared? Do American politicians of today appear to embrace Machiavelli's theory?*

Here the question arises; whether it is better to be loved than feared or feared than loved. The answer is that it would be desirable to be both but, since that is difficult, it is much safer to be feared than to be loved, if one must choose. For on men in general this observation may be made: they are ungrateful, fickle, and deceitful, eager to avoid dangers, and avid for gain, and while you are useful to them they are all with you, offering you their blood, their property, their lives, and their sons so long as danger is remote, as we noted above, but when it approaches they turn on you. Any prince, trusting only in their words and having no other preparations made, will fall to his ruin, for friendships that are bought at a price and not by greatness and nobility of soul are paid for indeed, but they are not owned and cannot be called upon in time of need. Men have less hesitation in offending a man who is loved than one who is feared, for love is held by a bond of obligation which, as men are wicked, is broken whenever personal advantage suggests it, but fear is accompanied by the dread of punishment which never relaxes.

From Niccolò Machiavelli, *The Prince* (1513), trans. and ed. by Thomas G. Bergin (New York: Appleton-Century-Crofts, 1947), p. 48.

Revival of Monarchy in Northern Europe

After 1450, there was a progressive shift from divided feudal to unified national monarchies as "sovereign" rulers emerged. This is not to say that the dynastic and chivalric ideals of feudal monarchy vanished. Territorial princes did not pass from the scene; representative bodies persisted and in some areas even grew in influence. But in the late fifteenth and early sixteenth centuries, the old problem of the one and the many was decided in favor of the interests of monarchy.

The feudal monarchy of the High Middle Ages was characterized by the division of the basic powers of government between the king and his semiautonomous vassals. The nobility and the towns had acted with varying degrees of unity and success through evolving representative assemblies such as the English Parliament, the French Estates General, and the Spanish *Cortés* to thwart the centralization of royal power. Because of the Hundred Years' War and the Great Schism in the church, the nobility and the clergy were in decline by the late Middle Ages and less able to contain expanding monarchies. The increasingly important towns began to ally with the king. Loyal, business-wise townspeople, not the nobility and the clergy, increasingly staffed the royal offices and became the king's lawyers, bookkeepers, military tacticians, and foreign diplomats. This new alliance between king and town broke the bonds of feudal society and made possible the rise of sovereign states.

In a sovereign state, the powers of taxation, war making, and law enforcement no longer belong to semiautonomous vassals, but are concentrated in the monarch and are exercised by his or her chosen agents. Taxes, wars, and laws become national, rather than merely regional, matters. Only as monarchs became able to act independently of the nobility and representative assemblies could they overcome the decentralization that had been the basic obstacle to nation building. Ferdinand and Isabella of Spain rarely called the *Cortés* into session. The French Estates General did not meet at all from 1484 to 1560. Henry VII (r. 1485–1509) of England managed to raise revenues without going begging to Parliament after Parliament voted him customs revenues for life in 1485. Monarchs were also assisted by brilliant theorists, from Marsilius of Padua in the fourteenth century to Machiavelli to Jean Bodin in the sixteenth, who eloquently argued the sovereign rights of monarchy.

The many were, of course, never totally subjugated to the one. But in the last half of the fifteenth century, rulers demonstrated that the law was their creature. They appointed civil servants whose vision was no longer merely local or regional. In Castile they were the *corregidores*, in England the justices of the peace, and in France bailiffs operating through well-drilled lieutenants. These royal ministers and agents could become closely attached to the localities they administered in the ruler's name. And regions were able to secure congenial royal appointments. Throughout England, for example, local magnates served as representatives of the Tudors. Nonetheless, these new executives remained royal executives, bureaucrats whose outlook was "national" and whose loyalty was to the "state."

Monarchies also began to create standing national armies in the fifteenth century. The noble cavalry receded as the infantry and the artillery became the backbone of royal armies. Mercenary soldiers were recruited from Switzerland and Germany to form the major part of the "king's army." Professional soldiers who fought for pay and booty proved far more efficient than feudal vassals who fought simply for honor's sake. Monarchs who failed to meet their payrolls, however, faced a new danger of mutiny and banditry on the part of foreign troops.

The growing cost of warfare in the fifteenth and sixteenth centuries increased the need of monarchs for new national sources of income, but their efforts to expand royal revenues were hampered by the stubborn belief among the highest classes that they were immune from government taxation. The nobility guarded their properties and traditional rights and despised taxation as an insult and a humiliation. Royal revenues accordingly grew at the expense of those least able to resist and least able to pay.

The monarchs had several options when it came to raising money. As feudal lords, they could collect rents from their royal domains. They could also levy national taxes on basic food and clothing, such as the *gabelle*, or "salt tax," in France and the *alcabala*, or 10-percent sales tax on commercial transactions, in Spain. The rulers could also levy direct taxes on the peasantry, which they did through agreeable representative assemblies of the privileged classes in which the peasantry did not sit. The *taille*, which the French kings independently determined from year to year after the Estates General was suspended in 1484, was such a tax. Innovative fundraising devices in the fifteenth century included the sale of public offices and the issuance of high-interest government bonds. But rulers did not levy taxes on the powerful nobility. Rather, they borrowed from rich nobles and the great bankers of Italy and Germany. In money matters, the privileged classes remained as much the kings' creditors and competitors as their subjects.

France

Charles VII (r. 1422–1461) was a king made great by those who served him. His ministers created a permanent professional army, which—thanks initially to the inspiration of Joan of Arc—drove the English out of France. And largely because of the enterprise of an independent merchant banker named Jacques Coeur, the French also developed a strong economy, diplomatic corps, and national administration during Charles's reign. These were the sturdy tools with which Charles's son and successor, the ruthless Louis XI (r. 1461–1483), made France a great power.

There were two cornerstones of French nation building in the fifteenth century. The first was the collapse of the English Empire in France following the Hundred Years' War. The second was the defeat of Charles the Bold and his duchy of Burgundy. Perhaps Europe's strongest political power in the mid-fifteenth century, Burgundy aspired to dwarf both France and the Holy Roman Empire as the leader of a dominant middle kingdom. It might have done so had not the continental powers joined in opposition.

When Charles the Bold died in defeat in a battle at Nancy in 1477, the dream of Burgundian Empire died with him. Louis XI and Habsburg emperor Maximilian I divided the conquered Burgundian lands between them, with the treaty-wise Habsburgs getting the better part. The dissolution of Burgundy ended its constant intrigue against the French king and left Louis XI free to secure the monarchy. The newly acquired Burgundian lands and his own Angevin inheritance permitted the king to end his reign with a kingdom almost twice the size of that with which he had started. Louis successfully harnessed the nobility, expanded the trade and industry so carefully nurtured by Jacques Coeur, created a national postal system, and even established a lucrative silk industry at Lyons (later transferred to Tours).

A strong nation is a two-edged sword. Because Louis's successors inherited a secure and efficient government, they felt free to pursue what proved ultimately to be a debilitating foreign policy. Conquests in Italy in the 1490s and a long series of losing wars with the Habsburgs in the first half of the sixteenth century left France by the mid-sixteenth century again a defeated nation almost as divided internally as during the Hundred Years' War.

Spain

Spain, too, became a strong country in the late fifteenth century. Both Castile and Aragon had been poorly ruled and divided kingdoms in the mid-fifteenth century. The union of Isabella of Castile (r. 1474–1504) and Ferdinand of Aragon (r. 1479–1516) changed that situation. The two future sovereigns married in 1469, despite strong protests from neighboring Portugal and France, both of whom foresaw the formidable European power the marriage would create. Castile was by far the richer and more populous of the two, having an estimated five million inhabitants to Aragon's population of under one million. Castile was also distinguished by its lucrative sheep-farming industry, run by a government-backed organization called the *Mesta*, another example of a developing centralized economic planning. Although the marriage of Ferdinand and Isabella dynastically united the two kingdoms, they remained constitutionally separated. Each retained its respective government agencies—separate laws, armies, coinage, and taxation—and cultural traditions.

Ferdinand and Isabella could do together what neither was able to accomplish alone: subdue their realms, secure their borders, venture abroad militarily, and Christianize the whole of Spain. Between 1482 and 1492 they conquered the Moors in Granada. Naples became a Spanish possession in 1504. By 1512 Ferdinand had secured his northern borders by conquering the kingdom of Navarre. Internally, Ferdinand and Isabella won the allegiance of the *Hermandad*, a powerful league of cities and towns that served them against stubborn landowners. Townspeople allied themselves with the crown and progressively replaced the nobility within the royal administration. The crown also extended its authority over the wealthy chivalric orders, a further circumscription of the power of the nobility.

Spain had long been remarkable among European lands as a place where three religions—Islam, Judaism, and Christianity—coexisted with a certain degree of toleration. This toleration was to end dramatically under Ferdinand and Isabella, who made Spain the prime exemplar of state-controlled religion.

Ferdinand and Isabella exercised almost total control over the Spanish church as they placed religion in the service of national unity. They appointed the higher clergy and the officers of the Inquisition. The latter, run by Tomás de Torquemada (d. 1498), Isabella's confessor, was a key national agency established in 1479 to monitor the activity of converted Jews (*conversos*) and Muslims (*Moriscos*) in Spain. In 1492 the Jews were exiled and their properties were confiscated. In 1502 nonconverting Moors in Granada were driven into exile by Cardinal Francisco Jiménez de Cisneros (1437–1517), under whom Spanish spiritual life remained largely uniform and successfully controlled. This was a major reason Spain remained a loyal Catholic country throughout the sixteenth century and provided a base of operation for the European Counter-Reformation.

Despite a certain internal narrowness, Ferdinand and Isabella were rulers with wide horizons. They contracted anti-French marriage alliances that came to determine a large part of European history in the sixteenth century. In 1496 their eldest daughter, Joanna, later known as "the Mad," married Archduke Philip, the son of Emperor Maximilian I. The fruit of this union, Charles I, was the first ruler over a united Spain; by his inheritance and election as emperor in 1519, he came to rule over a European kingdom almost equal in size to that of Charlemagne. A second daughter, Catherine of Aragon, wed Arthur, the son of the English king Henry VII. After Arthur's premature death, she was betrothed to his brother, the future King Henry VIII (r. 1509–1547), whom she married eight years later, in 1509. The failure of this marriage became the key factor in the emergence of the Anglican church and the English Reformation.

The new power of Spain was also revealed in Ferdinand and Isabella's promotion of overseas exploration. They sponsored the Genoese adventurer Christopher Columbus (1451–1506), who arrived at the islands of the Caribbean while sailing west in search of a shorter route to the spice markets of the Far East. This patronage led to the creation of the Spanish Empire in Mexico and Peru, whose gold and silver mines helped to make Spain Europe's dominant power in the sixteenth century.

England

The latter half of the fifteenth century was a period of especially difficult political trial for the English. Following the Hundred Years' War, a defeated England was subjected to internal warfare between two rival branches of the royal family: the House of York and the House of Lancaster. This conflict, known to us today as the Wars of the Roses (because York's symbol, according to legend, was a white rose and Lancaster's a red rose), kept England in turmoil from 1455 to 1485.

The Lancastrian monarchy of Henry VI (r. 1422–1461) was consistently challenged by the duke of York and his supporters in the prosperous southern towns. In 1461 Edward IV (r. 1461–1483), son of the duke of York, successfully seized power and instituted a strong-arm rule that lasted more than twenty years; it was only briefly interrupted, in 1470–1471, by Henry VI's short-lived restoration. Assisted by loyal and able ministers, Edward effectively increased the power and finances of the monarchy.

His brother, Richard III (r. 1483–1485), usurped the throne from Edward's son, and after Richard's death, the new Tudor dynasty portrayed him as an unprincipled villain who had also murdered Edward's sons in the Tower of London to secure his hold on the throne. The best-known version of this characterization—unjust according to some—is found in Shakespeare's *Richard III*. Be that as it may, Richard's reign saw the growth of support for the exiled Lancastrian Henry Tudor, who returned to England to defeat Richard on Bosworth Field in August 1485.

Henry Tudor ruled as Henry VII (r. 1485–1509), the first of the new Tudor dynasty that would dominate England throughout the sixteenth century. To bring the rival royal families together and to make the hereditary claim of his offspring to the throne uncontestable, Henry married Edward IV's daughter, Elizabeth of York. He succeeded in disciplining the English nobility through a special instrument of the royal will known as the Court of Star Chamber. Created with the sanction of Parliament in 1487, the court was intended to end the perversion of English justice by "over-mighty subjects," that is, powerful nobles who used intimidation and bribery to win favorable verdicts in court cases. In the Court of Star Chamber, the king's councillors sat as judges and were not swayed by such tactics. The result was a more equitable court system.

It was also a court more amenable to the royal will. Henry shrewdly construed legal precedents to the advantage of the crown, using English law to further the ends of monarchy. He managed to confiscate lands and fortunes of nobles with such success that he was able to govern without dependence on Parliament for royal funds, always a cornerstone of strong monarchy. In these ways, Henry began to shape a monarchy that would develop into one of early modern Europe's most exemplary governments during the reign of his granddaughter, Elizabeth I.

The Holy Roman Empire

Germany and Italy were the striking exceptions to the steady development of politically centralized lands in the last half of the fifteenth century. Unlike England, France, and Spain, the Holy Roman Empire saw the many thoroughly repulse the one. In Germany, territorial rulers and cities resisted every effort at national consolidation and unity. As in Carolingian times, rulers continued to partition their kingdoms, however small, among their sons. By the late fifteenth century, Germany was hopelessly divided into some 300 autonomous political entities.

The princes and the cities did work together to create the machinery of law and order, if not of union, within the divided empire. The emperor and the major German territorial rulers reached an agreement in 1356, the *Golden Bull*. It established a seven-member electoral college consisting of the archbishops of Mainz, Trier, and Cologne; the duke of Saxony; the margrave of Brandenburg; the count Palatine; and the king of Bohemia. This group also functioned as an administrative body. They elected the emperor and, in cooperation with him, provided what transregional unity and administration existed.

The figure of the emperor gave the empire a single ruler in law if not in fact. The conditions of his rule and the extent of his powers over his subjects, especially the seven electors, were renegotiated with every imperial election. Therefore, the rights of the many (the princes) were always balanced against the power of the one (the emperor).

In the fifteenth century, an effort was made to control incessant feuding by the creation of an imperial diet known as the *Reichstag*. This was a national assembly of the seven electors, the nonelectoral princes, and representatives from the sixty-five imperial free cities. The cities were the weakest of the three bodies represented in the diet. During such an assembly in Worms in 1495, the members won from Emperor Maximilian I (r. 1493–1519) an imperial ban on private warfare, the creation of a Supreme Court of Justice to enforce internal peace, and an imperial Council of Regency to coordinate imperial and internal German policy. The latter was only grudgingly conceded by the emperor because it gave the princes a share in executive power.

Although important, these reforms were still a poor substitute for true national unity. In the sixteenth and seventeenth centuries, the territorial princes became virtually sovereign rulers in their various domains. Such disunity aided religious dissent and conflict. It was in the cities and territories of still-feudal, fractionalized, backward Germany that the Protestant Reformation broke out in the sixteenth century.

The Northern Renaissance

The scholarly works of northern humanists created a climate favorable to religious and educational reforms on the eve of the Reformation. Northern humanism was initially stimulated by the importation of Italian learning through such varied intermediaries as students who had studied in Italy, merchants who traded there, and the Brothers of the Common Life. This last was an influential lay religious movement that began in the Netherlands and permitted men and women to live a shared religious life without making formal vows of poverty, chastity, and obedience.

The northern humanists, however, developed their own distinctive culture. They tended to come from more diverse social backgrounds and to be more devoted to religious reforms than their Italian counterparts. They were also more willing to write for lay audiences as well as for a narrow intelligentsia. Thanks to the invention of printing with movable type, it became possible for humanists to convey their educational ideals to laypeople and clerics alike. Printing gave new power and influence to elites in both church and state, who now could popularize their viewpoints freely and widely.

The Printing Press

A variety of forces converged in the fourteenth and fifteenth centuries to give rise to the invention of the printing press. Since the days of Charlemagne, kings and princes had encouraged schools and literacy, to help provide educated bureaucrats to staff the offices of their kingdoms. Without people who could read, think critically, and write reliable reports, no kingdom, large or small, could be properly governed. By the fifteenth century, a new literate lay public had been created, thanks to the enormous expansion of schools and universities during the late Middle Ages. (The number of universities more than tripled between 1300 and 1500, growing from twenty to seventy.)

The invention of a cheap way to manufacture paper also helped to make books economical and to broaden their content. Manuscript books had been inscribed on vellum, a cumbersome and expensive medium. (It required 170 calfskins or 300 sheepskins to make a single vellum Bible.) Single-sheet woodcuts had long been printed. This involved carving a block of wood, inking it, and then stamping out as many copies as one could make before the wood deteriorated. The end product was much like a modern poster.

In response to the demand for books created by the expansion of lay literacy, Johann Gutenberg (d. 1468) invented printing with movable type in the mid-fifteenth century in the German city of Mainz, the center of printing for the whole of western Europe. Thereafter, books were rapidly and handsomely produced on topics both profound and practical and were intended for ordinary lay readers, scholars, and clerics alike. Especially popular in the early decades of print were books of piety and religion, calendars and almanacs, and "how-to" books (for example, on child rearing, making brandies and liquors, curing animals, and farming successfully).

The new technology proved enormously profitable to printers, whose numbers exploded. By 1500, within a scant fifty years of Gutenberg's press, printing presses operated in at least sixty German cities and in more than 200 cities throughout Europe. The printing press was a boon to the careers of humanists, who now gained international audiences.

Literacy deeply affected people everywhere, nurturing self-esteem and a critical frame of mind. By standardizing texts, the print revolution made anyone who could read an instant authority. Rulers in church and state now had to deal with a less credulous and less docile laity. Print was a powerful tool for political and religious propaganda as well. Kings could now indoctrinate people as never be-

The printing press made possible the diffusion of Renaissance learning. But no book stimulated thought more at this time than did the Bible. With Gutenberg's publication of a printed Bible in 1454, scholars gained access to a dependable, standardized text, so that Scripture could be discussed and debated as never before. Reproduced by permission of The Huntington Library, San Marino, California

fore, and clergymen found themselves able to mass-produce both indulgences and pamphlets. (See "The West & the World," p. 284.)

Erasmus

The far-reaching influence of Desiderius Erasmus (1466?–1536), the most famous of the northern humanists and the "prince of the humanists," illustrates the impact of the printing press. Erasmus gained fame both as an educational and as a religious reformer. His life and work make clear that many loyal Catholics wanted major reforms long before the Reformation made them a reality.

Erasmus earned his living by tutoring when patrons were scarce. He prepared short Latin dialogues for his students that were intended to teach them how to speak and live well, inculcating good manners and language by encouraging them to imitate what they read.

These dialogues were published under the title *Colloquies*; they grew in number and length in consecutive editions, coming also to embrace anticlerical dialogues and satires on popular religious superstition. Erasmus collected ancient and contemporary proverbs as well, which he published under the title *Adages*. Beginning with about 800 examples, he increased his collection to more than 5,000 in the final edition of the work. Among the locutions that the *Adages* popularized are the common modern expression "to leave no stone unturned" and the saying "Where there is smoke, there is fire."

Erasmus aspired to unite the classical ideals of humanity and civic virtue with the Christian ideals of love and piety. He believed that disciplined study of the classics and the Bible, if begun early enough, was the best way to reform both individuals and society. He summarized his own beliefs with the phrase *philosophia Christi*, a simple, ethical piety in imitation of Christ. He set this ideal in starkest contrast to what he believed to be the dogmatic, ceremonial, and factious religious practice of the later Middle Ages. What most offended him about the Scholastics, both those of the late Middle Ages and, increasingly, the new Lutheran ones, was their letting doctrine and disputation overshadow humble piety and Christian practice.

To promote his own religious beliefs, Erasmus labored to make the ancient Christian sources available in their original versions. He believed that only as people drank from the pure, unadulterated sources could moral and religious health result. He edited the works of the Church fathers and produced a Greek edition of the New Testament (1516), which became the basis for his new, more accurate Latin translation (1519).

These various enterprises did not please church authorities. They were unhappy with both Erasmus's "improvements" on the Vulgate, Christendom's Bible for over a thousand years, and his popular anticlerical satires. At one point in the mid-sixteenth century, all of Erasmus's works were placed on the *Index of Forbidden Books*. Erasmus also received Luther's unqualified condemnation for his views on the freedom of human will. Still, Erasmus's works became basic tools of reform in the hands of both Protestant and Catholic reformers.

Humanism and Reform

In Germany, England, France, and Spain, humanism stirred both educational and religious reform.

GERMANY   Rudolf Agricola (1443–1485), the "father of German humanism," spent ten years in Italy and introduced Italian learning to Germany when he returned. Conrad Celtis (d. 1508), the first German poet laureate, and Ulrich von Hutten (1488–1523), a fiery knight, gave German humanism a nationalist coloring hostile to non-German cultures, particularly Roman culture. Von Hutten especially illustrates the union of humanism, German nationalism, and Luther's religious reform. A poet who admired Erasmus, he attacked indulgences and published an edition of Valla's exposé of the Donation of Constantine. He died in 1523, the victim of a hopeless knights' revolt against the princes.

The *cause célèbre* that brought von Hutten onto the historical stage and unified reform-minded German humanists was the Reuchlin affair. Johann Reuchlin (1455–1522) was Europe's foremost Christian authority on Hebrew and Jewish learning. He wrote the first reliable Hebrew grammar by a Christian scholar and was personally attracted to Jewish mysticism. Around 1506, supported by the Dominican order in Cologne, a Christian who had converted from Judaism began a movement to suppress Jewish writings. When this man, whose name was Pfefferkorn, attacked Reuchlin, many German humanists, in the name of academic freedom and good scholarship—not for any pro-Jewish sentiment—rushed to Reuchlin's defense. The controversy lasted several years and produced one of the great satires of the period, the *Letters of Obscure Men* (1515), a merciless satire of monks and Scholastics to which von Hutten contributed. When Martin Luther came under attack in 1517 for his famous ninety-five theses against indulgences, many German humanists saw a repetition of the Scholastic attack on Reuchlin and rushed to his side.

ENGLAND   Italian learning came to England by way of English scholars and merchants and visiting Italian prelates. Lectures by William Grocyn (d. 1519) and Thomas Linacre (d. 1524) at Oxford

Thomas More (1478–1535), painted by Hans Holbein the Younger in 1527. The English statesman and author was beheaded by Henry VIII for his refusal to recognize the king's sovereignty over the English church.
The Frick Collection, New York

and those of Erasmus at Cambridge marked the scholarly maturation of English humanism. John Colet (1467–1519), dean of Saint Paul's Cathedral, patronized humanist studies for the young and promoted religious reform as well.

Thomas More (1478–1535), a close friend of Erasmus, is the best known English humanist. His *Utopia* (1516), a conservative criticism of contemporary society, rivals the plays of Shakespeare as the most-read sixteenth-century English work. *Utopia* depicted an imaginary society based on reason and tolerance that overcame social and political injustice by holding all property and goods in common and requiring everyone to earn their bread by their own work.

More became one of Henry VIII's most trusted diplomats. But his repudiation of the Act of Supremacy (1534), which made the king of England head of the English church in place of the pope (see Chapter 11), and his refusal to recognize the king's marriage to Anne Boleyn led to his execution in July 1535. Although More remained Catholic, humanism in England, as also in Germany, played an important role in preparing the way for the English Reformation.

FRANCE The French invasions of Italy made it possible for Italian learning to penetrate France, stirring both educational and religious reform. Guillaume Budé (1468–1540), an accomplished Greek scholar, and Jacques Lefèvre d'Étaples (1454–1536), a biblical authority, were the leaders of French humanism. Lefèvre's scholarly works exemplified the new critical scholarship and influenced Martin Luther. Guillaume Briçonnet (1470–1533), the bishop of Meaux, and Marguerite d'Angoulême (1492–1549), sister of King Francis I, the future queen of Navarre, and a successful spiritual writer in her own right, cultivated a generation of young reform-minded humanists. The future Protestant reformer John Calvin was a product of this native reform circle.

SPAIN Whereas in England, France, and Germany, humanism prepared the way for Protestant reforms, in Spain it entered the service of the Catholic Church. Here the key figure was Francisco Jiménez de Cisneros (1437–1517), a confessor to Queen Isabella and, after 1508, the "Grand Inquisitor"—a position that allowed him to enforce the strictest religious orthodoxy. Jiménez founded the University of Alcalá near Madrid in 1509, printed a Greek edition of the New Testament, and translated many religious tracts designed to reform clerical life and better direct lay piety. His great achievement, taking fifteen years to complete, was the *Complutensian Polyglot Bible*, a six-volume work that placed the Hebrew, Greek, and Latin versions of the Bible in parallel columns. Such scholarly projects and internal church reforms joined with the repressive measures of Ferdinand and Isabella to keep Spain strictly Catholic throughout the Age of Reformation.

Voyages of Discovery and the New Empire in the West

On the eve of the Reformation, the geographical as well as the intellectual horizons of Western people were changing. The fifteenth century saw the beginning of western Europe's global expansion and the transference of commercial supremacy from the Mediterranean and the Baltic to the Atlantic seaboard.

Gold and Spices

Mercenary motives, reinforced by traditional missionary ideals, inspired the Portuguese prince Henry the Navigator (1394–1460) to sponsor the Portuguese exploration of the African coast. His

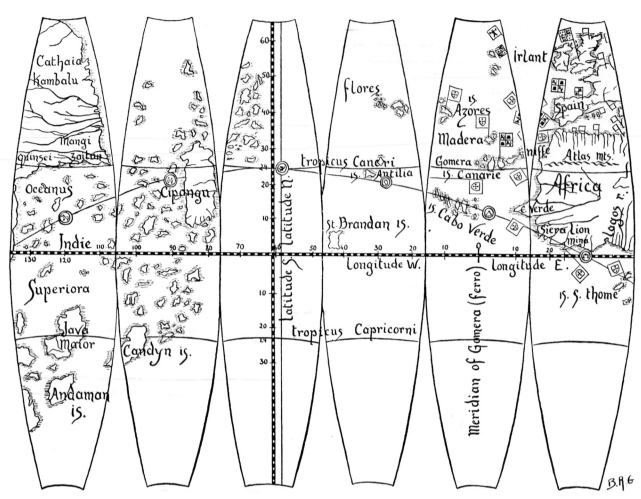

Labels on map: Cathaia, Kambalu, Mangi, quinsei, zaiton, Oceanus, Indie, Cipangu, Superiora, Java Maior, Candyn is., Andaman is., Latitude N., Latitude S., tropicus Canari, Antilia, St. Brandan is., Longitude W., tropicus Capricorni, Flores, Azores, Madera, Gomera, is. Canarie, is. Cabo Verde, C. Verde, Meridian of Gomera (Ferro), Longitude E., Irlant, Spain, Atlas mts., Africa, Sierra Lion mina, Lagos, is. S. thome, B.A.G.

What Columbus knew of the world in 1492 was contained in this map by the Nuremberg geographer Martin Behaim, creator of the first spherical globe of the Earth. The ocean section of Behaim's globe is reproduced here. Departing the Canary Islands (in the second section from the right), Columbus expected his first major landfall to be Japan (Cipangu, in the second section from the left). When he landed at San Salvador, he thought he was on the outer island of Japan. And when he arrived in Cuba, he thought he was in Japan. Reprinted from *Admiral of the Ocean Sea* by Samuel Eliot Morison. Copyright 1942 by Samuel Eliot Morison; renewed 1970 by Samuel Eliot Morison. By permission of Little, Brown and Company, Boston, Massachusetts

main object was the gold trade, which Muslims had monopolized for centuries. By the last decades of the fifteenth century, gold from Guinea was entering Europe by way of Portuguese ships calling at the port cities of Lisbon and Antwerp, rather than by the traditional Arab land routes. Antwerp became the financial center of Europe, a commercial crossroads where the enterprise and derring-do of the Portuguese, the Spanish, and especially the Flemish met the capital funds of the German banking houses of Fugger and Welser.

The rush for gold quickly expanded into a rush for the spice markets of India. In the fifteenth century the diet of most Europeans was a dull combination of bread and gruel, cabbage, turnips, peas, lentils, and onions, together with what meat became available during seasonal periods of slaughter. Spices, especially pepper and cloves, were in great demand, both to preserve and to enhance the taste of food.

Bartholomeu Dias (d. 1500) opened the Portuguese Empire in the East when he rounded the Cape of Good Hope at the tip of Africa in 1487. A decade later, in 1498, Vasco da Gama (d. 1524) reached the coast of India. When he returned to Portugal, he brought with him a cargo worth sixty times the cost of the voyage. Later, the Portuguese established themselves firmly on the Malabar Coast with colonies in Goa and Calcutta and successfully challenged the Arabs and the Venetians for control of the European spice trade.

While the Portuguese concentrated on the Indian Ocean, the Spanish set sail across the Atlantic. They did so in the hope of establishing a shorter route to the rich spice markets of the East Indies. But rather than beating the Portuguese at their own game, Christopher Columbus (1451–1506) came upon the Americas instead.

Amerigo Vespucci (1451–1512) and Ferdinand Magellan (1480–1521) showed that these new lands were not the outermost territory of the Far East, as Columbus died believing. Their travels proved the lands to be an entirely new continent that opened on the still greater Pacific Ocean. Magellan, in search of a westward route to the East Indies, died in the Philippines. (See Map 10–2.)

The Spanish Empire in the New World

Columbus's voyage of 1492 marked, unknowingly to those who undertook and financed it, the beginning of more than three centuries of Spanish conquest, exploitation, and administration of a vast American empire. That imperial venture produced important results for the cultures of both the European and the American continents. The gold and silver extracted from its American possessions financed Spain's major role in the religious and political conflicts of the age and contributed to European inflation in the sixteenth century.

In large expanses of both South and North America, Spanish government set an imprint of Roman Catholicism, economic dependence, and hierarchical social structure that has endured to the present day. Such influence was already clear with Columbus. On October 12, 1492, after a thirty-three day voyage from the Canary Islands, Columbus landed in San Salvador (Watlings Island) in the eastern Bahamas. He thought that he was on an outer island of Japan (or what he called Cipangu); he had undertaken his journey in the mistaken notion that the island of Japan would be the first land mass he would reach as he sailed west. This belief was based on Marco Polo's accounts of his years in China in the thirteenth century and the first globe map of the world, by Martin Behaim. That map, published in 1492, showed only ocean between the west coast of Europe and the east coast of Asia. Not until his third voyage to the Caribbean did Columbus realize that the island of Cuba was not Japan and that the South American continent beyond it was not China.

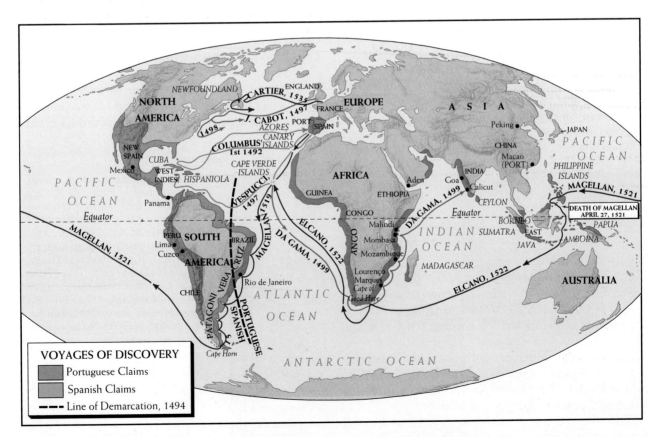

MAP 10–2   EUROPEAN VOYAGES OF DISCOVERY AND THE COLONIAL CLAIMS OF SPAIN AND PORTUGAL IN THE FIFTEENTH AND SIXTEENTH CENTURIES   *The map dramatizes Europe's global expansion in the fifteenth and sixteenth centuries.*

Taino Indians spoke Arawak

When Columbus landed in San Salvador, his three ships were met on the beach by naked and extremely friendly natives. Like all the natives Columbus met on his first voyage, they were Taino Indians, who spoke a variant of a language known as Arawak. From the start, the natives' generosity amazed Columbus. They freely gave his men all the corn and yams they desired and many sexual favors as well. "They never say no," Columbus marveled. At the same time Columbus observed how very easily they could be enslaved.

A Conquered World

Mistaking the islands where he landed for the East Indies, Columbus called the native peoples whom he encountered "Indians." That name persisted even after it had become clear that this was a new continent and not the East Indies. These native peoples had migrated across the Bering Straits from Asia onto the American landmass many thousands of years before the European voyages of discovery, creating communities all the way from Alaska to South America. The islands that Columbus mistakenly believed to be the East Indies came to be known as the West Indies.

Native Americans had established advanced civilizations going back to as early as the first millennium B.C.E. in two parts of what is today known as Latin America: Mesoamerica, which stretches from central Mexico into the Yucatan and Guatemala, and the Andean region of South America, primarily modern-day Peru and Bolivia. The earliest civilization in Mesoamerica, that of the Olmec, dates to about 1200 B.C.E. By the early centuries of the first millennium C.E. much of the region was dominated by the powerful city of Teotihuacán, which at the time was one of the largest urban centers in the world. The first millennium C.E. saw the flowering of the remarkable civilization of the Mayas in the Yucatan region. The Mayans built large cities with immense pyramids and achieved considerable skills in mathematics and astronomy.

The first great interregional civilization in Andean South America, that of Chavín, emerged during the first millennium B.C.E. Regional cultures of the succeeding Early Intermediate Period (100–600 C.E.) included the Nazca on the south coast of Peru and the Moche on the north coast. The Huari–Tiahuanco culture again imposed interregional conformity during the Middle Horizon (600–1000). In the Late Intermediate Period, the Chimu Empire (800–1400) dominated the valleys of the Peruvian north coast. These early Andean societies built major ceremonial centers throughout the Andes, constructed elaborate irrigation systems, canals, and highways, and created exquisite pottery, textiles, and metalwork.

At the time of the arrival of the first Spanish explorers, the Aztec Empire dominated Mesoamerica and the Inca Empire dominated Andean South America. (See Map 10–3.) Both were very rich, and their conquest promised the Spanish the possibility of acquiring large quantities of gold.

THE AZTECS IN MEXICO   The forebears of the Aztecs had arrived in the Valley of Mexico early in the twelfth century, where they lived as a sub-

Armored Spanish soldiers, under the command of Pedro de Alvarado (d. 1541) and bearing crossbows, engage unprotected and crudely armed Aztecs, who are nonetheless portrayed as larger than life by Spanish artist Diego Duran (16th century). Codex Duran: Pedro de Alvarado (c. 1485–1541), companion-at-arms of Hernando Cortes (1485–1547) besieged by Aztec warriors. Biblioteca Nacional, Madrid, Spain. The Bridgeman Art Library International Ltd.

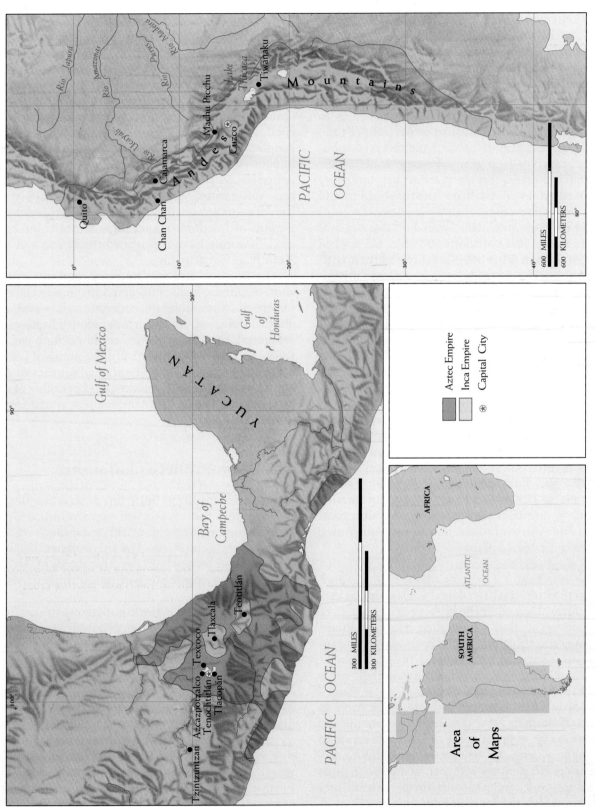

MAP 10–3 THE AZTEC AND INCA EMPIRES ON THE EVE OF THE SPANISH CONQUEST.

servient people. In 1428, under the leadership of Chief Itzcoatl, they rebelled against their rulers. That rebellion opened a period of Aztec conquest that reached its climax just after 1500. Their capital, Tenochtitlán (modern-day Mexico City), was located on an island in the center of a lake. By the time the Spanish conquerors arrived, the Aztecs governed many smaller tribes harshly, forcing labor and tribute from them. Believing that the gods must literally be fed with human bodies to guarantee continuing sunshine and fertility of the soil, the Aztecs also demanded and received thousands of captives each year to be sacrificed to their gods. Such policies left the Aztecs surrounded by terrorized tribes that felt no loyalty to them and longed for a liberator.

In 1519, Hernán Cortés landed on the coast of Mexico with a force of about 600 men. He opened communication with tribes nearby and then with Montezuma, the Aztec ruler. Montezuma initially believed Cortés to be a god. Aztec religion contained the legend of a priest named Quetzalcoatl who had been driven away four centuries earlier and had promised to return in the very year in which Cortés arrived. Montezuma initially attempted to appease Cortés with gifts of gold. The Indians had recently been ravaged by epidemic diseases of European origin, principally smallpox, and were in no position to oppose him. After several weeks of negotiations and the forging of alliances with subject tribes, Cortés's forces marched on Tenochtitlán, conquered it, and imprisoned Montezuma, who later died under unexplained circumstances. The Aztecs tried to drive the Spanish out, but by late 1521 they were defeated after great loss of life. Cortés proclaimed the former Aztec Empire to be New Spain.

THE INCAS IN PERU   The second great Native American civilization conquered by the Spanish was that of the Incas, located in the highlands of Peru. Like the Aztecs, they had vanquished many neighboring states and tribes and by the early sixteenth century ruled harshly over several million subject people, whom they compelled to build their roads and cities, farm their lands, and fight their wars.

In 1531, largely inspired by Cortés's example in Mexico, Francisco Pizarro sailed from Panama and landed on the western coast of South America to undertake a campaign against the Inca Empire. His force included perhaps 200 men armed with guns and swords and equipped with horses, the military power of which the Incas did not fathom.

In late 1531, Pizarro lured the Inca chief Atahualpa into a conference, where he captured him and killed many of his followers. Atahualpa attempted

to ransom himself by having a vast horde of gold transported from all over Peru to Pizarro. Discovering that he could not turn Atahualpa into a puppet ruler, Pizarro executed him in 1533. Division within the ranks of the Spanish conquerors prevented effective royal control of the sprawling Inca civilization until the late 1560s.

The conquests of Mexico and Peru stand among the most brutal episodes in modern Western history. One civilization armed with advanced weaponry subdued, in a remarkably brief time, two powerful peoples. Beyond the drama and bloodshed, the conquests made it very difficult for these Native American cultures to have a major impact on Western civilization. Some scholars believe, however, that the Iroquois tribes of North America set examples of freedom of speech, assembly, and religion that may have influenced the framers of the American Constitution.

The Spanish and the Native Americans made some accommodations to each other, but in the end European values, religion, economic goals, and language dominated. No group that retained indigenous religion, language, or values could become part of the new dominant culture or of the political power elite. In that sense, the Spanish conquests of the early sixteenth century marked the beginning of the process whereby South America was transformed into Latin America.

The Economy of Exploitation

From the beginning, both the native peoples of America and their lands were drawn into the Atlantic economy and the world of competitive European commercialism. For the Indians of Latin America and somewhat later, the blacks of Africa, that drive for gain meant various arrangements of forced labor.

There were three major components in the colonial economy of Latin America: mining, agriculture, and shipping. Each of them involved labor, servitude, or a relationship of dependence of the New World economy on that of Spain.

MINING   The early *conquistadores*, or "conquerors," were primarily interested in gold, but by the middle of the sixteenth century, silver mining provided the chief source of metallic wealth. The great mining centers were Potosí in Peru and somewhat smaller sites in northern Mexico. (See "Forced Indian Labor at Potosí".) The Spanish crown was particularly interested in mining because it received one-fifth (the *quinto*) of all mining revenues. For this reason, the

Forced Indian Labor at Potosí

The Potosí range in Peru was the site of the great silver-mining industry in the Spanish Empire. The vast amount of wealth contained in the region became legendary almost as soon as mining began there in the 1540s. Indians, most of whom were forced laborers working under the mita *system of conscription, did virtually all of the work underground. The description that follows, written by a Spanish friar in the early seventeenth century, portrays both the large size of the enterprise and the harsh conditions that the Indians endured. At any one time, only one-third of the 13,300 conscripted Indians were employed. The labor force was changed every four months.*

❖ *How efficient does the description suggest the mines were? What would have been the likely effect of working so long underground surrounded by burning candles?*

According to His Majesty's warrant, the mine owners on this massive range have a right to the *mita* [conscripted labor] of 13,300 Indians in the working and exploitation of the mines, both those which have been discovered, those now discovered, and those which shall be discovered. It is the duty of the *Corregidor* [municipal governor] of Potosí to have them rounded up and to see that they come in from all the provinces between Cuzco over the whole of El Collao and as far as the frontiers of Tarija and Tomina....

The *mita* Indians go up every Monday morning to the locality of Guayna Potosí which is at the foot of the range; the *Corregidor* arrives with all the provincial captains or chiefs who have charge of the Indians assigned him for his miner or smelter; that keeps him busy till 1 P.M., by which time the Indians are already turned over to these mine and smelter owners.

After each has eaten his ration, they climb up the hill, each to his mine, and go in, staying there from that hour until Saturday evening without coming out of the mine; their wives bring them food, but they stay constantly underground, excavating and carrying out the ore from which they get the silver. They all have tallow candles, lighted day and night; that is the light they work with, for as they are underground, they have need of it all the time....

These Indians have different functions in the handling of the silver ore; some break it up with bar or pick, and dig down in, following the vein in the mine; others bring it up; others up above keep separating the good and the poor in piles; others are occupied in taking it down from the range to the mills on herds of llamas; every day they bring up more than 8,000 of these native beasts of burden for this task. These teamsters who carry the metal do not belong to the *mita*, but are *mingados*—hired.

From Antonia Vázquez de Espinosa, *Compendium and Description of the Indies [ca. 1620]*, trans. by Charles Upson Clark (Washington, DC: Smithsonian Institution Press, 1968), p. 62. Reprinted by permission of the Smithsonian Institution Press.

crown maintained a monopoly over the production and sale of mercury, required in the silver-mining process. Exploring for silver never lost predominance during the colonial era. Its production by forced labor for the benefit of Spaniards and the Spanish crown epitomized the wholly extractive economy that stood at the foundation of colonial life.

AGRICULTURE The major rural and agricultural institution of the Spanish colonies was the *hacienda*, a large landed estate owned by persons originally born in Spain (*peninsulares*) or persons of Spanish descent born in America (*creoles*). Laborers on the *hacienda* usually stood in some relation of formal servitude to the owner and were rarely free to move from the services of one landowner to another.

The *hacienda* economy produced two major products: foodstuffs for mining areas and urban centers and leather goods used in mining machinery. Both farming and ranching were subordinate to the mining economy.

In the West Indies, the basic agricultural unit was the plantation. In Cuba, Hispaniola, Puerto Rico, and other islands, the labor of black slaves from Africa produced sugar to supply an almost insatiable demand for the product in Europe.

A final major area of economic activity in the Spanish colonies was urban service occupations, including government offices, the legal profession, and shipping. Practitioners of these occupations were either *peninsulares* or *creoles*, with the former dominating more often than not.

LABOR SERVITUDE All of this extractive and exploitive economic activity required labor, and the Spanish in the New World decided very early that the native population would supply that labor. A series of social devices was used to draw them into the new economic life imposed by the Spanish.

The first of these was the *encomienda*, a formal grant of the right to the labor of a specific number of Indians, usually a few hundred, but sometimes thousands, for a particular period of time. The institution stood in decline by the middle of the sixteenth century because the Spanish monarchs feared that the holders of *encomienda* might become a powerful independent nobility in the New World. They were also persuaded on humanitarian grounds against this particular kind of exploitation of the Indians.

The passing of the *encomienda* led to a new arrangement of labor servitude: the *repartimiento*. This device required adult male Indians to devote a certain number of days of labor annually to Spanish economic enterprises. In the mines of Peru, the *repartimiento* was known as the *mita*, the Inca term for their labor tax. *Repartimiento* service was often extremely harsh, and in some cases Indians did not survive their stint. The limitation on labor time led some Spanish managers to abuse their workers on the assumption that fresh workers would soon be appearing on the scene.

The eventual shortage of workers and the crown's pressure against extreme versions of forced labor led to the use of free labor. The freedom, however, was more in appearance than reality. Free Indian laborers were required to purchase goods from the landowner or mine owner, to whom they became forever indebted. This form of exploitation, known as *debt peonage*, continued in Latin America long after the nineteenth-century wars of liberation.

Black slavery was the final mode of forced or subservient labor in the New World. Both the Spanish and the Portuguese had earlier used African slaves in Europe. The sugar plantations of the West Indies now became the major center of black slavery. The conquest, the forced labor of the economy of exploitation, and the introduction of European diseases had devastating demographic consequences for the Native American population. For centuries, Europeans had lived in a far more complex human and animal environment than Native Americans did. They had frequent contact with different ethnic and racial groups and with a variety of domestic animals. Such interaction helped them develop strong immune systems that enabled them to survive the ravages of measles, smallpox, and typhoid. Native Americans, by contrast, grew up in a simpler and more sterile environment and were completely defenseless against these diseases. Within a generation, the native population of New Spain (Mexico) was reduced to an estimated 8 percent of its numbers, from 25,000,000 to 2,000,000.

The Impact on Europe

Among contemporary European intellectuals, Columbus's discovery increased skepticism about the wisdom of the ancients. If traditional knowledge about the world had been so wrong geographically, how could one trust it on other matters? For many, Columbus's discovery demonstrated the folly of relying on any fixed body of presumed authoritative knowledge. Both in Europe and in the New World, there were those who condemned the explorers' treatment of American natives, as more was learned about their cruelty. (See "Montaigne on 'Cannibals' in Foreign Lands.") Three centuries later, however, on the third anniversary of Columbus's discovery (1792), the great thinkers of the age lionized Columbus for having opened up new possibilities for civilization and morality. By establishing new commercial contacts among different peoples of the world, Columbus was said to have made cooperation, civility, and peace among them indispensible. Enlightenment thinkers drew parallels between the discovery of America and the invention of the printing press—both portrayed as world-historical events opening new eras in communication and globalization, an early multicultural experiment.[4]

On the material side, the influx of spices and precious metals into Europe from the new Spanish Empire was a mixed blessing. It contributed to a steady rise in prices during the sixteenth century that created an inflation rate estimated at 2 percent a year. The new supply of bullion from the Americas joined with enlarged European production to increase greatly the amount of coinage in circulation, and this increase in turn fed inflation. Fortunately, the increase in prices was by and large spread over a long period and was not sudden. Prices doubled in Spain by midcentury, quadrupled by 1600. In Luther's Wittenberg, the cost of

---

[4] Cf. Anthony Pagden, "The Impact of the New World on the Old: The History of an Idea," *Renaissance and Modern Studies* 30 (1986): 1–11.

Montaigne on "Cannibals" in Foreign Lands

The French philosopher Michel de Montaigne (1533–1592) had seen a Brazilian native in Rouen in 1562, an alleged cannibal brought to France by the explorer Villegagnon. The experience gave rise to an essay on the subject of what constitutes a "savage." Montaigne concluded that no people on earth were more barbarous than Europeans, who take natives of other lands captive.

❖ *Is Montaigne romanticizing New World natives? Is he being too hard on Europeans? Had the Aztecs or Incas had the ability to discover and occupy Europe, would they have enslaved and exploited Europeans?*

Now, to return to my subject, I think there is nothing barbarous and savage in that nation [Brazil], from what I have been told....Each man calls barbarism whatever is not his own practice; for indeed it seems we have no other test of truth and reason than the example and pattern of the opinions and customs of the country we live in. There [we] always [find] the perfect religion, the perfect government, the perfect and accomplished manners in all things. Those [foreign] people are wild, just as we call wild the fruits that Nature has produced by herself and in her normal course; where really it is those that we have changed artificially and led astray from the common order that we should rather call wild. The former retain alive and vigorous their genuine virtues and properties, which we have debased in the latter by adapting them to gratify our corrupted taste. And yet for all that, the savor and delicacy of some uncultivated fruits of those countries is quite as excellent, even to our taste, as that of our own. It is not reasonable that [our human] art should win the place of honor over our great and powerful mother Nature. We have so overloaded the beauty and richness of her works by our inventions that we have quite smothered her. Yet wherever her purity shines forth, she wonderfully puts to shame our vain and frivolous attempts: "Ivy comes readier without our care;/In lonely caves the arbutus grows more fair;/No art with artless bird song can compare."[1] All our efforts cannot even succeed in reproducing the nest of the tiniest little bird, its contexture, its beauty and convenience; or even the web of the puny spider. All things, says Plato,[2] are produced by nature, by fortune, or by art; the greatest and most beautiful by one or the other of the first two, the least and most imperfect by the last.

These nations, then, seem to me "barbarous" in this sense, that they have been fashioned very little by the human mind, and are still very close to their original naturalness. The laws of nature still rule them, very little corrupted by ours; and they are in such a state of purity that I am sometimes vexed that they were unknown earlier, in the days when there were men able to judge them better than we.

[1] Propertius, 1.11.10.

[2] Laws, 10.

From *The Complete Essays of Montaigne*, trans. by Donald M. Frame (Stanford: Stanford University Press, 1958), pp. 153–154.

basic food and clothing increased almost 100 percent between 1519 and 1540. Generally, wages and rents remained well behind the rise in prices.

The new wealth enabled governments and private entrepreneurs to sponsor basic research and expansion in the printing, shipping, mining, textile, and weapons industries. There is also evidence of large-scale government planning in such ventures as the French silk industry and the Habsburg–Fugger development of mines in Austria and Hungary.

In the thirteenth and fourteenth centuries capitalist institutions and practices had already begun to develop in the rich Italian cities. (One may point to the activities of the Florentine banking houses of Bardi and Peruzzi.) Those who owned the means of production, either privately or corporately, were clearly distinguished from the workers who operated them. Wherever possible, entrepreneurs created monopolies in basic goods. High interest was charged on loans—actual, if not legal, usury. And the "capitalist" virtues of thrift, industry, and orderly planning were everywhere in evidence—all intended to permit the free and efficient accumulation of wealth.

The late fifteenth and the sixteenth centuries saw the maturation of this type of capitalism together with its attendant social problems. The Medicis of Florence grew very rich as bankers of the pope, as did the Fuggers of Augsburg, who bankrolled Habsburg rulers. The Fuggers lent Charles I of Spain more than 500,000 florins to buy his election as Holy Roman Emperor in 1519 and boasted that they had created the emperor. The new wealth and industrial expansion also raised the expectations of the poor and the ambitious and heightened the reactionary tendencies of the wealthy. This effect, in turn, aggravated the traditional social divisions between the clergy and the laity, the urban patriciate and the guilds, and the landed nobility and the agrarian peasantry.

These divisions indirectly prepared the way for the Reformation as well, by making many people critical of traditional institutions and open to new ideas—especially those that seemed to promise greater freedom and a chance at a better life.

In Perspective

As it recovered from national wars during the late Middle Ages, Europe saw the establishment of permanent centralized states and regional governments. The foundations of modern France, Spain, England, Germany, and Italy were laid at this time. As rulers imposed their will on regions outside their immediate domains, the "one" progressively took control of the "many," and previously divided lands came together as nations.

Thanks to the work of Byzantine and Islamic scholars, ancient Greek science and scholarship found their way into the West in these centuries. Europeans had been separated from their classical cultural heritage for almost eight centuries. No other world civilization had experienced such a disjunction from its cultural past. The discovery of classical civilization occasioned a rebirth of intellectual and artistic activity in both southern and northern Europe. One result was the splendor of the Italian Renaissance, whose scholarship, painting, and sculpture remain among western Europe's most impressive achievements.

Ancient learning was not the only discovery of the era. New political unity spurred both royal greed and national ambition. By the late fifteenth centu-

ry, Europeans were in a position to venture far away to the shores of Africa, the southern and eastern coasts of Asia, and the New World of the Americas. European discovery was not the only outcome of these voyages: The exploitation of the peoples and lands of the New World revealed a dark side of Western civilization. Some penalties were paid even then. The influx of New World gold and silver created new human and economic problems on the European mainland. In some circles, Europeans even began to question their civilization's traditional values.

REVIEW QUESTIONS

1. Discuss Jacob Burkhardt's interpretation of the Renaissance. What criticisms have been leveled against it? How would you define the term "Renaissance" in the context of fifteenth- and sixteenth-century Italy?

2. How would you define Renaissance humanism? In what ways was the Renaissance a break with the Middle Ages, and in what ways did it owe its existence to medieval civilization?

3. Who were some of the famous literary and artistic figures of the Italian Renaissance? What did they have in common that might be described as "the spirit of the Renaissance"?

4. Why did the French invade Italy in 1494? How did this event trigger Italy's political decline? How do the actions of Pope Julius II and the ideas of Niccolò Machiavelli signify a new era in Italian civilization?

5. A common assumption is that creative work proceeds best in periods of calm and peace. Given the combination of political instability and cultural productivity in Renaissance Italy, do you think this assumption is valid?

6. How did the Renaissance in the north differ from the Italian Renaissance? In what ways was Erasmus the embodiment of the northern Renaissance?

7. What factors led to the voyages of discovery? How did the Spanish establish their empire in the Americas? Why was the conquest so violent? What was the experience of native peoples during and after the conquest?

SUGGESTED READINGS

L. B. Alberti, *The Family in Renaissance Florence*, trans. by R. N. Watkins (1962). A contemporary humanist, who never married, explains how a family should behave.

R. H. Bainton, *Erasmus of Christendom* (1960). Charming presentation.

H. BARON, *The Crisis of the Early Italian Renaissance*, vols. 1 and 2 (1966). A major work, setting forth the civic dimension of Italian humanism.

C. BOXER, *Four Centuries of Portuguese Expansion, 1415–1825* (1961). Comprehensive survey by the leading authority.

G. A. BRUCKER, *Renaissance Florence* (1969). Comprehensive survey of all facets of Florentine life.

G. A. BRUCKER, *Giovanni and Lusanna: Love and Marriage in Renaissance Florence* (1986). Love in the Renaissance shown to be more Bergman than Fellini.

J. BURCKHARDT, *The Civilization of the Renaissance in Italy* (1867). The old classic that still has as many defenders as detractors.

R. E. CONRAD, *Children of God's Fire: A Documentary History of Black Slavery in Brazil* (1983). Not for the squeamish.

A. W. CROSBY, *The Columbian Exchange: Biological and Cultural Consequences of 1492* (1973). A study of the epidemiological disaster that Columbus visited upon Native Americans.

E. L. EISENSTEIN, *The Printing Press as an Agent of Change: Communications and Cultural Transformations in Early Modern Europe*, 2 vols. (1979). Bold, stimulating account of the centrality of printing to all progress in the period.

W. K. FERGUSON, *Europe in Transition, 1300–1520* (1962). A major survey that deals with the transition from medieval society to Renaissance society.

F. GILBERT, *Machiavelli and Guicciardini* (1984). The two great Renaissance historians lucidly compared.

L. HANKE, *Bartholomé de Las Casas: An Interpretation of His Life and Writings* (1951). Biography of the great Dominican critic of Spanish exploitation of Native Americans.

J. HANKINS, *Plato in the Renaissance* (1992). A magisterial study of how Plato was read and interpreted by Renaissance scholars.

D. HERLIHY, *The Family in Renaissance Italy* (1974). Excellent on family structure and general features.

D. HERLIHY, *Women, Family, and Society in Medieval Europe: Historical Essays, 1978–1991*, ed. A. Molho (1998). A major medievalist's collected essays on medieval and Renaissance society.

D. HERLIHY AND C. KLAPISCH-ZUBER, *Tuscans and Their Families* (1985). Important work based on unique demographic data that give the reader a new appreciation of quantitative history.

D. L. JENSEN, *Renaissance Europe: Age of Recovery and Reconciliation* (1981). Up-to-date and comprehensive survey.

F. KATZ, *The Ancient American Civilizations* (1972). An excellent introduction.

R. KELSO, *Doctrine of the Lady of the Renaissance* (1978). Noblewomen in the Renaissance.

C. KLAPISCH-ZUBER, *Women, Family, and Ritual in Renaissance Italy* (1985). Provocative, wide-ranging essays documenting Renaissance Italy as very much a man's world.

P. O. KRISTELLER, *Renaissance Thought: The Classic, Scholastic, and Humanist Strains* (1961). A master shows the many sides of Renaissance thought.

I. MACLEAN, *The Renaissance Notion of Women* (1980). An account of the views of Renaissance intellectuals and their sources in antiquity.

L. MARTINES, *Power and Imagination: City States in Renaissance Italy* (1980). Stimulating account of cultural and political history.

S. E. MORRISON, *Admiral of the Ocean Sea: A Life of Christopher Columbus* (1946). Still the authoritative biography.

E. PANOFSKY, *Meaning in the Visual Arts* (1955). Eloquent treatment of Renaissance art.

J. H. PARRY, *The Age of Reconnaissance* (1964). A comprehensive account of exploration in the years 1450–1650.

P. PARTNER, *Renaissance Rome, 1500–1559: A Portrait of a Society* (1976). A description of the city from an insider's perspective.

J. B. A. POCOCK, *The Machiavellian Moment in Florentine Political Thought and the Atlantic Republican Tradition* (1975). Traces the influence of Florentine political thought in early modern Europe.

I. A. RICHTER (ED.), *The Notebooks of Leonardo da Vinci* (1985). The master in his own words.

Q. SKINNER, *The Foundations of Modern Political Thought; I: The Renaissance* (1978). Broad survey, including absolutely every known political theorist, major and minor.

Chapter 11

A Catholic Portrayal of Martin Luther Tempting Christ (1547). *Reformation propaganda often portrayed the pope as the Antichrist or the devil. Here Catholic propaganda turns the tables on the Protestant reformers by portraying a figure of Martin Luther as the Devil (note the monstrous feet and tail under his academic robes). Recreating the biblical scene of Christ being tempted by the Devil in the wilderness, the figure of Luther asks Christ to transform stone into bread, to which temptation Christ responds by saying that humans do not live by bread alone.* Versucung Christi, 1547, Gemälde, Bonn, Rheinisches Landesmuseum, Inv. Nr. 58.3.

The Age of Reformation

KEY TOPICS

- The social and religious background to the Reformation
- Martin Luther's challenge to the church and the course of the Reformation in Germany
- The Reformation in Switzerland, France, and England
- Transitions in family life between medieval and modern times

In the second decade of the sixteenth century, a powerful religious movement began in Saxony in Germany and spread rapidly throughout northern Europe, deeply affecting society and politics, as well as the spiritual lives of men and women. Attacking what they believed to be burdensome superstitions that robbed people of both their money and their peace of mind, Protestant reformers led a broad revolt against the medieval church. In a short span of time, hundreds of thousands of people from all social classes set aside the beliefs of centuries and adopted a more simplified religious practice.

The Protestant Reformation challenged aspects of the Renaissance, especially its tendency to follow classical sources in glorifying human nature and its loyalty to traditional religion. Protestants were more impressed by the human potential for evil than by the inclination to do good; they encouraged parents, teachers, and magistrates to be firm disciplinarians. On the other hand, Protestants also embraced many Renaissance values, especially in the sphere of educational reform and particularly with regard to training in ancient languages. Like the Italian humanists, the Protestant reformers prized the tools that allowed them to go directly to the original sources. For them, this meant the study of the Hebrew and Greek scriptures, enabling them to root their consequent challenges to traditional institutions in biblical authority.

Society and Religion

The Protestant Reformation occurred at a time of sharp conflict between the emerging nation–states of Europe, bent on conformity and centralization within their realms, and the self-governing small towns and regions, long accustomed to running their own affairs. Since the fourteenth century, the king's law and custom had progressively overridden local law and custom almost everywhere. Many towns and territories were keenly sensitive to the loss of traditional rights and freedoms. Many townspeople and village folk perceived in the religious revolt an ally in their struggle to remain politically free and independent. The Reformation came to be closely identified in the minds of its supporters with what we today might call states' rights or local control.

Social and Political Conflict

The Reformation broke out first in the free imperial cities of Germany and Switzerland. There were about sixty-five such cities, and each was in a certain sense a little kingdom unto itself. The great majority had Protestant movements, but with mixed success and duration. Some quickly turned Protestant and remained so. Some were Protestant only for a short time. Others developed mixed confessions, frowning on sectarianism and aggressive proselytizing, and letting Catholics and Protestants live side by side with appropriate barriers.

What seemed a life-and-death struggle with higher princely or royal authority was not the only conflict cities were experiencing. They also suffered deep internal social and political divisions. Certain groups favored the Reformation more than others. In many places, guilds whose members were economically prospering and socially rising were in the forefront of the Reformation. The printers' guild is a prominent example. Its members were literate, sophisticated about the world, in a rapidly growing industry, and economically very ambitious. They also

The Reformation broke out against a background of deep social and political divisions that bred resentment against authority. This early sixteenth-century woodcut by Georg Pencz presents a warning against tyranny. It shows a world turned upside down, with the hunted becoming the hunters. The rabbits capture the hunters and their dogs and subject them to the same brutal treatment—skinning, butchering, and cooking—that the hunters and dogs routinely inflict on rabbits. The message: tyranny eventually begets rebellion. From Max Geisberg, *The German Single-Leaf Woodcut, 1500–1550*, edited by Walter L. Strauss. Hacker Art Books, 1974. Used by permission of Hacker Art Books, Inc.

had an economic stake in fanning religious conflict with Protestant propaganda, which many, of course, also sincerely believed. Guilds with a history of opposition to reigning governmental authority also stand out among early Protestant supporters, regardless of whether their members were literate.

There is, in brief, evidence to suggest that people who felt pushed around and bullied by either local or distant authority—a guild by an autocratic local government, an entire city or region by a powerful prince or king—often perceived an ally in the Protestant movement, at least initially.

Social and political experience thus coalesced with the larger religious issues in both town and countryside. A Protestant sermon or pamphlet seemed directly relevant, for example, to the townspeople of German and Swiss cities who faced incorporation into the territory of a powerful local prince, who looked on them as obedient subjects rather than as free citizens. When Martin Luther and his comrades wrote, preached, and sang about a priesthood of all believers, scorned the authority of ecclesiastical landlords, and ridiculed papal laws as arbitrary human inventions, they touched political as well as religious nerves. And this was as true in the villages as in the towns. Like city dwellers, the peasants on the land also heard in the Protestant sermon and pamphlet a promise of political liberation and even a degree of social betterment. More than the townspeople, the peasants found their traditional liberties—from fishing and hunting rights to representation at local diets—progressively being chipped away by the great secular and ecclesiastical landlords who ruled over them.

Popular Religious Movements and Criticism of the Church

The Protestant Reformation could also not have occurred without the monumental crises of the medieval church during the "exile" in Avignon, the Great Schism, the Conciliar period, and the Renaissance papacy. For increasing numbers of people, the medieval church had ceased to provide a viable foundation for religious piety. Many intellectuals and laypeople felt a sense of crisis about the traditional teaching and spiritual practice of the church. Between the secular pretensions of the papacy and the dry teaching of Scholastic theologians, laity and clerics alike began to seek a more heartfelt, idealistic, and—often, in the eyes of the Pope—increasingly heretical religious piety. The late Middle Ages were marked by independent lay and clerical efforts to reform local religious practice and by widespread experimentation with new religious forms.

A variety of factors contributed to the growth of lay criticism of the church. The laity in the cities were becoming increasingly knowledgeable about the world and those who controlled their lives. They traveled widely—as soldiers, pilgrims, explorers, and traders. New postal systems and the printing press increased the information at their disposal. The new age of books and libraries raised literacy and heightened curiosity. Laypeople were increasingly able to take the initiative in shaping the cultural life of their communities.

From the Albigensians, Waldensians, Beguines, and Beghards in the thirteenth century to the Lollards and Hussites in the fifteenth, lay religious movements shared a common goal of religious simplicity in imitation of Jesus. Almost without exception, they were inspired by an ideal of apostolic poverty in religion; that is, all wanted a religion of true self-sacrifice like that of Jesus and the first disciples. The laity sought a more egalitarian church, one that gave the members as well as the head of the church a voice, and a more spiritual church, one that lived manifestly according to its New Testament model.

THE MODERN DEVOTION   One of the most constructive lay religious movements in northern Europe on the eve of the Reformation was that of the Brothers of the Common Life, or what came to be known as the Modern Devotion. The brothers fostered religious life outside formal ecclesiastical offices and apart from formal religious vows. Established by Gerard Groote (1340–1384), the Modern Devotion was centered at Zwolle and Deventer in the Netherlands. The brother and (less numerous) sister houses of the Modern Devotion, however, spread rapidly throughout northern Europe and influenced parts of southern Europe as well. In these houses clerics and laity came together to share a common life, stressing individual piety and practical religion. Lay members were not expected to take special religious vows or to wear special religious dress, nor did they abandon their ordinary secular vocations.

The brothers were also active in education. They worked as copyists, sponsored many religious and a few classical publications, ran hospices for poor students, and conducted schools for the young, especially boys preparing for the priesthood or a monastic vocation. As youths, Nicholas of Cusa, Johann Reuchlin, and Desiderius Erasmus were looked after by the brothers. Thomas à Kempis (d. 1471) summarized the philosophy of the brothers in what became the most popular religious book of the period, the *Imitation of Christ*. This semimystical guide to the inner life was intended primarily for monks and nuns, but was widely appropriated by laity who also wanted to pursue the ascetic life.

The Modern Devotion has been seen as the source of humanist, Protestant, and Catholic reform movements in the sixteenth century. Some scholars, how-

Injustice. This woodcut by an unknown artist compares the law, represented by the court scene in the center, to a spider's web, shown in the window on the right. Just as the web traps small, weak insects, the law ensnares the poor, seen hanging on the gallows and the wheel through the window on the left. And just as the large bee flies easily through the web, the rich and powerful escape punishment for their crimes. Hacker Art Books, Inc.

ever, believe that it represented an individualistic approach to religion, indifferent and even harmful to the sacramental piety of the church. It was actually a very conservative movement. The brothers retained the old clerical doctrines and values, while placing them within the new framework of an active common life. Their practices clearly met a need for a more personal piety and a more-informed religious life. Their movement appeared at a time when the laity was demanding good preaching in the vernacular and was even taking the initiative to endow special preacherships to ensure it. The Modern Devotion permitted laypeople to practice a full religious life without surrendering their life in the world.

LAY CONTROL OVER RELIGIOUS LIFE On the eve of the Reformation, Rome's international network of church offices, which had unified Europe religiously during the Middle Ages, began to fall apart in many areas. This collapse was hurried along by a growing sense of regional identity—incipient nationalism—and local secular administrative competence. The long-entrenched *benefice* system of the medieval church had permitted important ecclesiastical posts to be sold to the highest bidders and had left residency requirements in parishes unenforced. Such a system did not result in a vibrant local religious life. The substitutes hired by nonresident holders of *benefices* lived elsewhere, mostly in Rome. They milked the revenues of their offices, often performed their chores mechanically, and had neither firsthand knowledge of, nor much sympathy with, local needs and problems. Rare was the late medieval German town that did not have complaints about the maladministration, concubinage, or fiscalism of its clergy, especially the higher clergy (bishops, abbots, and prelates).

Communities had loudly protested the financial abuses of the medieval church long before Luther published his famous summary of economic grievances in 1520 in the *Address to the Christian Nobility of the German Nation*. The sale of indulgences in particular had been repeatedly attacked before Luther came on the scene. On the eve of the Reformation, this practice had expanded to permit people to buy release from time in purgatory for both themselves and their deceased loved ones. Rulers and magistrates had little objection to their sale and might even encourage it, so long as a generous portion of the income they generated remained in the local coffers. But when an indulgence was offered primarily for the benefit of distant interests, as with the Saint Peter's indulgence protested by Luther, resistance arose for strictly financial reasons, because their sale drained away local revenues.

The sale of indulgences would not end until rulers found new ways to profit from religion and the laity found a more effective popular remedy for religious anxiety. The Reformation provided the former by sanctioning the secular dissolution of monasteries and the confiscation of ecclesiastical properties. It held out the latter in its new theology of justification by faith.

City governments also undertook to improve local religious life on the eve of the Reformation by endowing preacherships. These positions, supported by *benefices*, provided for well-trained and dedicated pastors who could offer regular preaching and pastoral care that went beyond the routine performance of the mass and traditional religious functions. In many instances, these preacherships became platforms for Protestant preachers.

Magistrates also carefully restricted the growth of ecclesiastical properties and clerical privileges. During the Middle Ages, canon and civil law had come to recognize special clerical rights in both property and person. Because they were holy places, churches and monasteries had been exempted from the taxes and laws that affected others. They were treated as special places of "sacral peace" and asylum. It was considered inappropriate for holy persons (clergy) to be burdened with such "dirty jobs" as military service, compulsory labor, standing watch at city gates, and other obligations of citizenship. Nor was it thought right that the laity, of whatever rank, should sit in judgment on those who were their shepherds and intermediaries with God. The clergy, accordingly, came to enjoy an immunity of place (which exempted ecclesiastical properties from taxes and recognized their right of asylum) and an immunity of person (which exempted the clergy from the jurisdiction of civil courts).

On the eve of the Reformation, measures were passed to restrict these privileges and to end their abuses. Among them, we find efforts to regulate ecclesiastical acquisition of new property, to circumvent the right of asylum in churches and monasteries (a practice that posed a threat to the normal administration of justice), and to bring the clergy under the local tax code. Governments had understandably tired of ecclesiastical interference in what to them were strictly political spheres of competence and authority.

Martin Luther and German Reformation to 1525

Unlike France and England, late medieval Germany lacked the political unity to enforce "national" religious reforms during the late Middle Ages. There were no lasting Statutes of Provisors and Praemunire, as in England, nor a Pragmatic Sanction of Bourges, as in France, limiting papal jurisdiction and taxation on a national scale. What happened on a unified national level in England and France occurred only locally and piecemeal within German territories and towns. As popular resentment of clerical immunities and ecclesiastical abuses, especially over the selling of indulgences, spread among German cities and towns, an unorganized "national" opposition to Rome formed. German humanists had long given voice to such criticism, and by 1517 it was pervasive enough to provide a solid foundation for Martin Luther's reform.

Luther (1483–1546) was the son of a successful Thüringian miner. He was educated in Mansfeld, Magdeburg (where the Brothers of the Common Life were his teachers), and Eisenach. Between 1501 and 1505 he attended the University of Erfurt, where the nominalist teachings of William of Ockham and Gabriel Biel (d. 1495) prevailed. After receiving his master-of-arts degree in 1505, Luther registered with the law faculty, following his parents' wishes. But he never began the study of law. To the disappointment of his family, he instead entered the Order of the Hermits of Saint Augustine in Erfurt on July 17,

1505. This decision had apparently been building for some time and was resolved during a lightning storm in which Luther, terrified and crying out to Saint Anne for assistance (Saint Anne was the patron saint of travelers in distress), promised to enter a monastery if he escaped death.

Ordained in 1507, Luther pursued a traditional course of study. In 1510 he journeyed to Rome on the business of his order, finding there justification for the many criticisms of the church he had heard in Germany. In 1511 he moved to the Augustinian monastery in Wittenberg, where he earned his doctorate in theology in 1512. Thereafter, he became a leader within the monastery, the new university, and the spiritual life of the city.

Justification by Faith Alone

Reformation theology grew out of a problem then common to many of the clergy and the laity: the failure of traditional medieval religion to provide either full personal or intellectual satisfaction. Luther was especially plagued by the disproportion between his own sense of sinfulness and the perfect righteousness that medieval theology taught that God required for salvation. Traditional church teaching and the sacrament of penance proved to be of no consolation. Luther wrote that he came to despise the phrase "righteousness of God," for it seemed to demand of him a perfection he knew neither he nor any other human being could ever achieve. His insight into the meaning of "justification by faith alone" was a gradual process that extended between 1513 and 1518. The righteousness that God demands, he concluded, did not result from many religious works and ceremonies, but was given in full measure to those who believe and trust in Jesus Christ, who alone is the perfect righteousness satisfying to God. To believe in Christ meant to stand before God clothed in Christ's sure righteousness.

The Attack on Indulgences

An indulgence was a remission of the temporal penalty imposed by priests on penitents as a "work of satisfaction" for their mortal sins. According to medieval theology, after the priest absolved a penitent of guilt for the sins, the penitent remained under an eternal penalty, a punishment God justly imposed for sin. After absolution, however, this eternal penalty was said to be transformed into a temporal penalty, a manageable "work of satisfaction" that the penitent might perform here and now (for example, through prayers, fasting, almsgiving, retreats, and pilgrimages). Penitents who defaulted on such prescribed works of satisfaction could expect to suffer for them in purgatory.

A contemporary caricature depicts John Tetzel, the famous indulgence preacher. The last lines of the jingle read: "As soon as gold in the basin rings, right then the soul to Heaven springs." It was Tetzel's preaching that spurred Luther to publish his ninety-five theses. Courtesy Staatliche Lutherhalle

At this point, indulgences, which had earlier been given to Crusaders who did not complete their penances because they had fallen in battle, became an aid to laity, made genuinely anxious by their belief in a future suffering in purgatory for neglected penances or unrepented sins. In 1343 Pope Clement VI (r. 1342–1352) had proclaimed the existence of a "treasury of merit," an infinite reservoir of good works in the church's possession that could be dispensed at the pope's discretion. On the basis of this declared treasury, the church sold "letters of indulgence," which covered the works of satisfaction owed by penitents. In 1476, Pope Sixtus IV (r. 1471–1484) extended indulgences also to cover purgatory.

Originally, indulgences had been given only for the true self-sacrifice of going on a Crusade to the Holy Land. By Luther's time, they were regularly dispensed for small cash payments (very modest sums that were regarded as a good work of almsgiving). They were presented to the laity as remitting not only their own future punishments, but also those of their dead relatives presumed to be suffering in purgatory.

In 1517 Pope Leo X (r. 1513–1521) revived a plenary Jubilee Indulgence that had first been issued by Pope Julius II (r. 1503–1513), the proceeds from which were to be used to rebuild St. Peter's Basilica in Rome. Such an indulgence promised forgiveness of all outstanding unrepented sins upon the completion of certain acts. That kind of indulgence was subsequently preached on the borders of Saxony in the territories of Archbishop Albrecht of Mainz, who was much in need of revenues because of the large debts he had incurred in order to hold, contrary to church law, three ecclesiastical appointments. The selling of the indulgence was a joint venture by Albrecht, the Augsburg banking house of Fugger, and Pope Leo X, with half the proceeds going to the Pope and half to Albrecht and his creditors. The famous indulgence preacher John Tetzel (d. 1519) was enlisted to preach the indulgence in Albrecht's territories because he was a seasoned professional who knew how to stir ordinary people to action. As he exhorted on one occasion:

Don't you hear the voices of your dead parents and other relatives crying out, "Have mercy on us, for we suffer great punishment and pain. From this you could release us with a few alms.... We have created you, fed you, cared for you, and left you our temporal goods. Why do you treat us so cruelly and leave us to suffer in the flames, when it takes only a little to save us?"[1]

When, on October 31, 1517, Luther, according to tradition, posted his ninety-five theses against

[1]*Die Reformation in Augenzeugen berichten*, ed. by Helmar Junghaus (Düsseldorf: Karl Rauch Verlag, 1967), p. 44.

indulgences on the door of Castle Church in Wittenberg, he protested especially against the impression created by Tetzel that indulgences actually remitted sins and released the dead from punishment in purgatory. Luther believed that these claims went far beyond the traditional practice and seemed to make salvation something that could be bought and sold.

Election of Charles V

The ninety-five theses were embraced by humanists and other proponents of reform. The theses made Luther famous overnight and prompted official proceedings against him. In October, he was called before the general of the Dominican order in Augsburg. But as sanctions were being prepared against Luther, Emperor Maximilian I died (January 12, 1519), and this event, fortunate for the Reformation, turned attention away from heresy in Saxony to the contest for a new emperor.

The pope backed the French king, Francis I. However, Charles I of Spain, a youth of nineteen, succeeded his grandfather and became Emperor Charles V.

(See Map 11–1.) Charles was assisted by both a long tradition of Habsburg imperial rule and a massive Fugger campaign chest, which secured the votes of the seven electors. The electors, who traditionally enhanced their power at every opportunity, wrung new concessions from Charles for their votes. The emperor agreed to a revival of the Imperial Supreme Court and the Council of Regency and promised to consult with a diet of the empire on all major domestic and foreign affairs that affected the empire. These measures also helped the development of the Reformation by preventing unilateral imperial action against the Germans, something Luther could be thankful for in the early years of the Reformation.

Luther's Excommunication and the Diet of Worms

In the same month in which Charles was elected emperor, Luther entered a debate in Leipzig (June 27, 1519) with the Ingolstadt professor John Eck. During this contest, Luther challenged the infallibility of the Pope and the inerrancy of church coun-

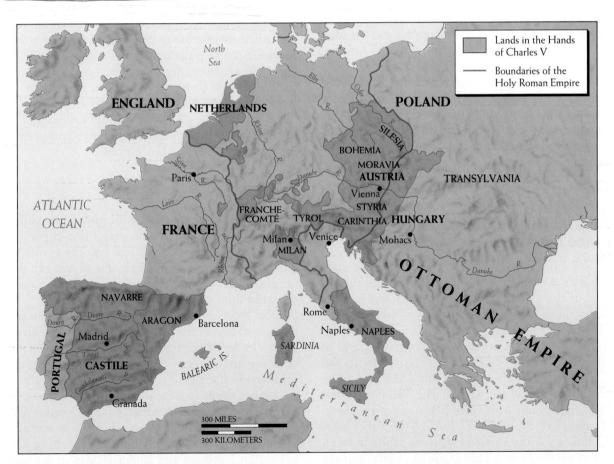

MAP 11–1 THE EMPIRE OF CHARLES V *Dynastic marriages and simple chance concentrated into Charles's hands rule over the lands shown here, plus Spain's overseas possessions. Crowns and titles rained down on him; his election in 1519 as emperor gave him new distractions and responsibilities.*

cils, appealing, for the first time, to the sovereign authority of Scripture alone. He burned all his bridges to the old church when he further defended certain teachings of John Huss that had been condemned by the Council of Constance.

In 1520, Luther signaled his new direction with three famous pamphlets. The *Address to the Christian Nobility of the German Nation* urged the German princes to force reforms on the Roman church, especially to curtail its political and economic power in Germany. The *Babylonian Captivity of the Church* attacked the traditional seven sacraments, arguing that only two, Baptism and the Eucharist, were biblical, and exalted the authority of Scripture, church councils, and secular princes over that of the pope. The eloquent *Freedom of a Christian* summarized the new teaching of salvation by faith alone.

On June 15, 1520, Leo's papal bull *Exsurge Domine* condemned Luther for heresy and gave him sixty days to retract. The final bull of excommunication, *Decet Pontificem Romanum*, was issued on January 3, 1521.

In April 1521 Luther presented his views before the empire's Diet of Worms, over which the newly elected Emperor Charles V presided. Ordered to recant, Luther declared that to do so would be to act against Scripture, reason, and his own conscience. On May 26, 1521, he was placed under the imperial ban and thereafter became an "outlaw" to secular as well as religious authority. For his own protection, friends hid him in a secluded castle, where he spent almost a year, from April 1521 to March 1522. During his stay, he translated the New Testament into German, using Erasmus's new Greek text and Latin translation, and he attempted, by correspondence, to oversee the first stages of the Reformation in Wittenberg.

Imperial Distractions: France and the Turks

The Reformation was greatly helped in these early years by the emperor's war with France and the advance of the Ottoman Turks into eastern Europe. Against both adversaries Charles V, who also remained a Spanish king with dynastic responsibilities outside the empire, needed German troops, and to that end he promoted friendly relations with the German princes. Between 1521 and 1559, Spain (the Habsburg dynasty) and France (the Valois dynasty) fought four major wars over disputed territories in Italy and along their borders. In 1526 the Turks overran Hungary at the Battle of Mohacs, while in western Europe the French-led League of Cognac formed against Charles for the second Habsburg–Valois war.

Thus preoccupied, the emperor agreed through his representatives at the German Diet of Speyer in 1526 that each German territory was free to enforce the

Edict of Worms (1521) against Luther "so as to be able to answer in good conscience to God and the emperor." That concession, in effect, gave the German princes territorial sovereignty in religious matters and the Reformation time to put down deep roots. Later (in 1555), the Peace of Augsburg would enshrine such local princely control over religion in imperial law.

How the Reformation Spread

In the late 1520s and on through the 1530s, the Reformation passed from the hands of the theologians and pamphleteers into those of the magistrates and princes. In many cities, the magistrates quickly followed the lead of the Protestant preachers and their sizable congregations in mandating the religious reforms they preached. In numerous instances, magistrates had themselves worked for decades to bring about basic church reforms and thus welcomed the preachers as new allies. Reform now ceased to be merely slogans and became laws that all townspeople had to obey.

The religious reform became a territorial political movement as well, led by the elector of Saxony and the prince of Hesse, the two most powerful German Protestant rulers. (See "Art & the West.") Like the urban magistrates, the German princes quickly recognized the political and economic opportunities offered them by the demise of the Roman Catholic Church in their regions. Soon they, too, were pushing Protestant faith and politics onto their neighbors. By the 1530s, Protestant cities and lands formed powerful defensive alliances and prepared for war with the Catholic emperor.

₀ The Peasants' Revolt ₀

In its first decade, the Protestant movement suffered more from internal division than from imperial interference. By 1525, Luther had become as much an object of protest within Germany as was the Pope. Original allies, sympathizers, and fellow travelers declared their independence from him.

Like the German humanists, the German peasantry also had at first believed Luther to be an ally. Since the late fifteenth century, the peasantry had been organized against efforts by territorial princes to override their traditional laws and customs and to subject them to new regulations and taxes. (See "German Peasants Protest Rising Feudal Exactions.") Peasant leaders, several of whom were convinced Lutherans, saw in Luther's teaching about Christian freedom and his criticism of monastic landowners a point of view close to their own. They openly solicited Luther's support of their political and economic rights, including their revolutionary request for release from serfdom.

A Royal Stag Hunt

Lucas Cranach, German, 1472–1553. *Hunting Near Hartenfels Castle*, 1540. Oil on wood, 116.8 × 170.2 cm. The Cleveland Art Museum, John L. Severance Fund, 1958.425.

In 1504, Lucas Cranach the Elder (1472-1553), the most famous sixteenth-century German painter after Albrecht Dürer, became court painter to the Elector of Saxony, who was one of seven German princes empowered to elect the Holy Roman Emperor. Cranach was also a close friend of Martin Luther, a best man at the reformer's wedding in 1525 and later godfather to his first son.

A court painter had many responsibilities: He painted the interiors and exteriors of his lord's residences, outfitted their rooms with portraits, tapestries, furniture, and utensils, and furnished the decorations for large celebrations—from coats of arms, flags, and tents to sketches for the court tailors of the clothing to be worn. Cranach's lord owned over a dozen residences, and Cranach worked in five of his castles.

Among the most popular of Cranach's works at the royal court were paintings of hunts, which were also social and political occasions for area royalty and nobility. In 1540, Cranach painted this major hunt, in the rich game reserve around Castle Torgau, which stands

in the background. Both hunt and painting were staged events and not the candid snapshot they appear. Before the hunt began, horsemen and dogs gathered the animals to be hunted into hedge pens bounded by a bend in the Elbe River. On the day of the hunt, the hunting party arranged itself in favorable positions to kill the stags, as they were released and crossed the river.

In the lower right, Princess Sybille stands armed and ready with her group, while Elector John Frederick, dressed in dark green hunting attire, cocks his crossbow as he waits for a stag to cross the river. To the left of the elector, a young hunter can be seen with three dogs and the Saxon motto initialed on his sleeves: "May the Word of God Remain into Eternity." The hunter in the blue-gray coat in the lower left foreground is the duke and future Elector of Saxony, Maurice. The scene also shows a bear hunt occurring in the upper left corner and a boar hunt in the upper right.

Source: *Lucas Cranach: Ein Maler-Unternehmer aus Franken*, ed. by Claus Grimm, et al. (Verlag Friedrich Pustet, Regensburg, 1994), pp. 311–313.

German Peasants Protest Rising Feudal Exactions

In the late fifteenth and early sixteenth centuries, German feudal lords, both secular and ecclesiastical, tried to increase the earnings from their lands by raising demands on their peasant tenants. As the personal freedoms of peasants were restricted, their properties confiscated, and their traditional laws and customs overridden, massive revolts occurred in southern Germany in 1525. Some historians see this uprising and the social and economic conditions that gave rise to it as the major historical force in early modern history. The list that follows is the most representative and well-known statement of peasant grievances.

❖ *Are the peasants' demands reasonable, given the circumstances of the sixteenth century? Are the peasants more interested in material than in spiritual freedom? Which of the demands are the most revolutionary?*

1. It is our humble petition and desire...that in the future...each community should choose and appoint a pastor, and that we should have the right to depose him should he conduct himself improperly....

2. We are ready and willing to pay the fair tithe of grain....The small tithes [of cattle], whether [to] ecclesiastical or lay lords, we will not pay at all, for the Lord God created cattle for the free use of man....

3. We...take it for granted that you will release us from serfdom as true Christians, unless it should be shown us from the Gospel that we are serfs.

4. It has been the custom heretofore that no poor man should be allowed to catch venison or wildfowl or fish in flowing water, which seems to us quite unseemly and unbrotherly as well as selfish and not agreeable to the Word of God....

5. We are aggrieved in the matter of woodcutting, for the noblemen have appropriated all the woods to themselves....

6. In regard to the excessive services demanded of us which are increased from day to day, we ask that this matter be properly looked into so that we shall not continue to be oppressed in this way....

7. We will not hereafter allow ourselves to be further oppressed by our lords, but will let them demand only what is just and proper according to the word of the agreement between the lord and the peasant. The lord should no longer try to force more services or other dues from the peasant without payment....

8. We are greatly burdened because our holdings cannot support the rent exacted from them.... We ask that the lords may appoint persons of honor to inspect these holdings and fix a rent in accordance with justice....

9. We are burdened with a great evil in the constant making of new laws....In our opinion we should be judged according to the old written law....

10. We are aggrieved by the appropriation...of meadows and fields which at one time belonged to a community as a whole. These we will take again into our own hands....

11. We will entirely abolish the due called *Todfall* [that is, heriot or death tax, by which the lord received the best horse, cow, or garment of a family upon the death of a serf] and will no longer endure it, nor allow widows and orphans to be thus shamefully robbed against God's will, and in violation of justice and right....

12. It is our conclusion and final resolution, that if any one or more of the articles here set forth should not be in agreement with the Word of God, as we think they are, such article we will willingly retract.

From *Translations and Reprints from the Original Sources of European History*, Vol. 2 (Philadelphia: Department of History, University of Pennsylvania, 1897).

Luther and his followers sympathized with the peasants. Indeed, for several years Lutheran pamphleteers made Karsthans, the burly, honest peasant who earned his bread by the sweat of his brow and sacrificed his own comfort and well-being for others, a symbol of the simple life that God desired all people to live. The Lutherans, however, were not social revolutionaries. When the peasants revolted against their masters in 1524–1525, Luther, not surprisingly, condemned them in the strongest possible

The punishment of a peasant leader in a village near Heilbronn. After the defeat of rebellious peasants in and around the city of Heilbronn, Jacob Rorbach, a well-to-do peasant leader from a nearby village, was tied to a stake and slowly roasted to death. © Badische Landesbibliothek

terms as "un-Christian" and urged the princes to crush their revolt without mercy. Tens of thousands of peasants (estimates run between 70,000 and 100,000) died by the time the revolt was put down.

For Luther, the freedom of the Christian was to be found in an inner release from guilt and anxiety, not in a right to restructure society by violent revolution. Had Luther supported the peasants' revolt, he would not only have contradicted his own teaching, but probably would also have ended any chance of the survival of his reform beyond the 1520s. Still, many believe that his decision ended the promise of the Reformation as a social revolution.

The Reformation Elsewhere

Although Luther's was the first, Switzerland and France had their own independent church reform movements almost simultaneously with Germany's. From these movements developed new churches as prominent and lasting as the Lutheran.

Zwingli and the Swiss Reformation

Switzerland was a loose confederacy of thirteen autonomous cantons, or states, and allied areas. (See Map 11–2.) Some cantons became Protestant, some remained Catholic, and a few other cantons and regions managed to effect a compromise. There were two main preconditions of the Swiss Reformation. First was the growth of national sentiment occasioned by popular opposition to foreign mercenary service. (Providing mercenaries for Europe's warring nations was a major source of Switzerland's livelihood.) Second was a desire for church reform that had persisted in Switzerland since the councils of Constance (1414–1417) and Basel (1431–1449).

THE REFORMATION IN ZURICH Ulrich Zwingli (1484–1531), the leader of the Swiss Reformation, had been humanistically educated in Bern, Vienna, and Basel. He was strongly influenced by Erasmus, whom he credited with having set him on the path to reform. He served as a chaplain with Swiss mercenaries during the disastrous Battle of Marignano in Italy in 1515 and thereafter became an eloquent critic of mercenary service. Zwingli believed that this service threatened both the political sovereignty and the moral well-being of the Swiss confederacy. By 1518, Zwingli was also widely known for opposition to the sale of indulgences and to religious superstition.

In 1519, he entered the competition for the post of people's priest in the main church of Zurich. His candidacy was contested because of his acknowledged fornication with a barber's daughter, an affair he successfully minimized in a forcefully written self-defense. Actually, his conduct was less scandalous to his contemporaries, who sympathized with the plight of the celibate clergy, than it may be to the modern reader. One of Zwingli's first acts as a reformer was to petition for an end to clerical celibacy and for the right of all clergy to marry, a practice that quickly became accepted in all Protestant lands.

From his new position as people's priest in Zurich, Zwingli engineered the Swiss Reformation. In March 1522, he was party to the breaking of the Lenten fast—an act of protest analogous to burning one's national flag today. Zwingli's reform guideline was very simple and very effective: Whatever lacked literal support in Scripture was to be neither believed nor practiced. As had also happened with Luther, that test soon raised questions about such honored traditional teachings and practices as fasting, transubstantiation, the worship of saints, pilgrimages, purgatory, clerical celibacy, and certain sacraments. A disputation held on January 29, 1523, concluded with the city government granting its sanction to Zwingli's Scripture test. Thereafter Zurich became, to all intents and purposes, the center of the Swiss Reformation. The new regime imposed a harsh discipline that made the city one of the first examples of puritanical Protestantism.

THE MARBURG COLLOQUY Landgrave Philip of Hesse (1504–1567) sought to unite Swiss and German Protestants in a mutual defense pact, a poten-

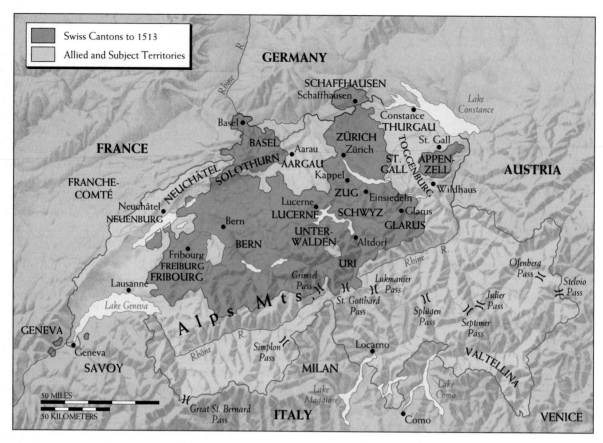

MAP 11–2   THE SWISS CONFEDERATION   *While nominally still a part of the Holy Roman Empire, Switzerland grew from a loose defensive union of the central "forest cantons" in the thirteenth century into a fiercely independent association of regions with different languages, histories, and, finally, religions.*

tially significant political alliance. His efforts were spoiled, however, by theological disagreements between Luther and Zwingli over the nature of Christ's presence in the Eucharist. Zwingli maintained a symbolic interpretation of Christ's words, "This is my body"; Christ, he argued, was only spiritually, not bodily, present in the bread and wine of the Eucharist. Luther, to the contrary, insisted that Christ's human nature could share the properties of his divine nature; hence, where Christ was spiritually present, he could also be bodily present, for his was a special nature. Luther wanted no part of an abstract, spiritualized Christ. Zwingli, on the other hand, feared that Luther had not broken sufficiently with medieval sacramental theology.

Philip of Hesse brought the two Protestant leaders together in his castle in Marburg in early October 1529, but they were unable to work out their differences on this issue. Luther left thinking Zwingli a dangerous fanatic. Although cooperation between the two sides did not cease, the disagreement splintered the Protestant movement theologically and politically. Separate defense leagues formed, and semi-Zwinglian theological

views came to be embodied in the *Tetrapolitan Confession*. This confession of faith was prepared by the Strasbourg reformers Martin Bucer and Caspar Hedio for presentation to the Diet of Augsburg (1530) as an alternative to the Lutheran Augsburg Confession.

SWISS CIVIL WARS   As the Swiss cantons divided between Protestantism and Catholicism, civil wars began. There were two major battles, both at Kappel, one in June 1529 and a second in October 1531. The first ended in a Protestant victory, which forced the Catholic cantons to break their foreign alliances and to recognize the rights of Swiss Protestants. During the second battle Zwingli was found wounded on the battlefield and was unceremoniously executed, his remains scattered to the four winds so his followers would have no relics to console and inspire them. The subsequent treaty confirmed the right of each canton to determine its own religion. Heinrich Bullinger (1504–1575), who was Zwingli's protégé and later married his daughter, became the new leader of the Swiss Reformation and guided its development into an established religion.

Anabaptists and Radical Protestants

The moderate pace and seemingly low ethical results of the Lutheran and Zwinglian reformations discontented many people, among them some of the original followers of Luther and Zwingli. They desired a more rapid and thorough implementation of apostolic Christianity—that is, a more visible moral transformation—and accused the major reformers of going only halfway. The most important of these radical groups were the Anabaptists, the sixteenth-century ancestors of the modern Mennonites and Amish. The Anabaptists were especially distinguished by their rejection of infant baptism and their insistence on only adult baptism. (The term "Anabaptism" derives from the Greek word meaning "to rebaptize.") They believed that baptism performed on a consenting adult conformed to Scripture and was more respectful of human freedom.

CONRAD GREBEL AND THE SWISS BRETHREN   Conrad Grebel (1498–1526), with whom Anabaptism originated, performed the first adult rebaptism in Zurich in January 1525. Initially a co-worker of Zwingli's and an even greater biblical literalist, Grebel broke openly with that reformer. In a religious disputation in October 1523, Zwingli supported the city government's plea for a very gradual removal of traditional religious practices.

The alternative of the Swiss Brethren, as Grebel's group came to be called, was embodied in the *Schleitheim Confession* of 1527. This document distinguished Anabaptists not only by their practice of adult baptism, but also by their refusal to go to war, to swear oaths, and to participate in the offices of secular government. Anabaptists physically separated from society to form a more perfect community in imitation of what they believed to be the example of the first Christians. Because of the close connection between religious and civic life in this period, the political authorities viewed such separatism as a threat to basic social bonds.

THE ANABAPTIST REIGN IN MÜNSTER   At first, Anabaptism drew its adherents from all social classes. But as Lutherans and Zwinglians joined with Catholics in opposition to the Anabaptists and persecuted them within the cities, a more rural, agrarian class came to make up the great majority. In 1529, rebaptism became a capital offense throughout the Holy Roman Empire. Estimates are that between 1525 and 1618 at least 1,000, and perhaps as many as 5,000, men and women were executed for rebaptizing themselves as adults. Brutal measures were universally applied against non-conformists after Anabaptist extremists came to power in the German city of Münster in 1534–1535.

Led by two Dutch emigrants, a baker, Jan Matthys of Haarlem, and a tailor, Jan Beukelsz of Leiden, the Anabaptist majority in Münster forced Lutherans and Catholics either to convert or to emigrate. The Lutherans and Catholics left, and the city was blockaded by besieging armies. Münster transformed itself into an Old Testament theocracy, replete with charismatic leaders and the practice of polygamy. The latter was undertaken as a measure of social control, because there were so many more women, recently widowed or deserted, than men in the city. Many women revolted against the practice and were allowed to leave the resented polygynous marriages.

The outside world was deeply shocked by such developments in Münster. Protestant and Catholic armies united to crush the radicals. The skeletons of their leaders long hung in public view as a warning to all who would so offend traditional Christian sensitivities. After this episode, moderate, pacifistic Anabaptism became the norm among most nonconformists. The moderate Anabaptist leader Menno Simons (1496–1561), the founder of the Mennonites, set the example for the future.

SPIRITUALISTS   Another radical movement, that of the Spiritualists, was made up mostly of isolated individuals distinguished by their disdain of all traditions and institutions. They believed that the only religious authority was God's spirit, which spoke here and now to every individual. Among them were several former Lutherans. Thomas Müntzer (d. 1525), who had close contacts with Anabaptist leaders in Germany and Switzerland, died as a leader of a peasants' revolt. Sebastian Franck (d. 1541), a freelance critic of all dogmatic religion, proclaimed the religious autonomy of every individual soul. Caspar Schwenckfeld (d. 1561) was a prolific writer and wanderer after whom the Schwenckfeldian Church is named.

ANTITRINITARIANS   A final group of radical Protestants was the Antitrinitarians, exponents of a commonsense, rational, and ethical religion. Chief among this group were the Spaniard Michael Servetus (1511–1553), executed in 1553 in Geneva for "blasphemies against the Holy Trinity," and the Italians Lelio (d. 1562) and Faustus Sozzini (d. 1604), the founders of Socinianism. These thinkers were the strongest opponents of Calvinism, especially its belief in original sin and predestination, and have a deserved reputation as defenders of religious toleration.

John Calvin and the Genevan Reformation

In the second half of the sixteenth century, Calvinism replaced Lutheranism as the dominant Protestant force in Europe. Calvinism was the religious ideology that inspired or accompanied massive political resistance in France, the Netherlands, and Scotland. It established itself within the geographical region of the Palatinate during the reign of Elector Frederick III (r. 1559–1576). Calvinists believed strongly in both divine predestination and the individual's responsibility to reorder society according to God's plan. They became zealous reformers determined to transform and order society so that men and women would act externally as they believed, or should believe, internally and were presumably destined to live eternally.

In his famous study, *The Protestant Ethic and the Spirit of Capitalism* (1904), the German sociologist Max Weber argues that this peculiar combination of religious confidence and self-disciplined activism produced an ethic that stimulated and reinforced the spirit of emergent capitalism. According to Weber's argument, there was thus a close association between Calvinism and other later forms of Puritanism and the development of modern capitalist societies.

The founder of Calvinism, John Calvin (1509–1564), was born into a well-to-do family, the son of the secretary to the bishop of Noyon in Picardy. He received church *benefices* at age twelve, which financed the best possible education at Parisian colleges and a law degree at Orléans. In the 1520s, he associated with the indigenous French reform party. Although he would finally reject this group as ineffectual, its members contributed to his preparation as a religious reformer.

It was probably in the spring of 1534 that Calvin experienced that conversion to Protestantism by which he said his "long stubborn heart" was "made teachable" by God. His own experience became a personal model of reform that he would later apply to the recalcitrant citizenry of Geneva. His mature theology stressed the sovereignty of God over all creation and the necessity of humankind's conformity to His will. In May 1534, Calvin dramatically surrendered the *benefices* he had held for so long and at such profit and joined the Reformation.

POLITICAL REVOLT AND RELIGIOUS REFORM IN GENEVA

Whereas in Saxony religious reform paved the way for a political revolution against the emperor, in Geneva a political revolution against the local prince–bishop laid the foundation for the religious change. Genevans successfully revolted against their resident prince–bishop in the late 1520s, and the city council assumed his legal and political powers in 1527.

In late 1533, the Protestant city of Bern dispatched two reformers to Geneva: Guillaume Farel (1489–1565) and Antoine Froment (1508–1581). In the summer of 1535, after much internal turmoil, the Protestants triumphed, and the traditional mass and other religious practices were removed. On May 21, 1536, the city voted officially to adopt the Reformation: "to live according to the Gospel and the Word of God...without...any more masses, statues, idols, or other papal abuses."

Calvin arrived in Geneva after these events, in July 1536. He was actually en route to a scholarly refuge in Strasbourg, in flight from the persecution of Protestants in France, when warring between France and Spain forced him to turn sharply south to Geneva. Farel successfully pleaded with him to stay in the city and assist the Reformation, threatening Calvin with divine vengeance if he turned away from this task.

Before a year had passed, Calvin had drawn up articles for the governance of the new church, as well as a catechism to guide and discipline the people. (See "Rules Governing Genevan Moral Behavior.") Both were presented for approval to the city councils in early 1537. Because of the strong measures they proposed to govern Geneva's moral life, many suspected that the reformers were intent upon creating a "new papacy." Opponents attacked Calvin and Farel, fearing that they were going too far too fast. Geneva's powerful Protestant ally, Bern, which had adopted a more moderate Protestant reform, pressured Geneva's magistrates to restore traditional

A portrait of the young John Calvin. Bibliotheque Publique et Universitaire, Geneva

religious ceremonies and holidays that Calvin and Farel had abolished. When the reformers opposed these actions, they were exiled from the city.

Calvin went to Strasbourg, a model Protestant city, where he became pastor to French exiles and wrote biblical commentaries. He also produced a second edition of his masterful *Institutes of the Christian Religion*, which many consider the definitive theological statement of the Protestant faith.

Most important, he learned from the Strasbourg reformer Martin Bucer how to achieve his goals.

CALVIN'S GENEVA   In 1540, Geneva elected syndics who were both favorable to Calvin and determined to establish full Genevan political and religious independence from Bern. They knew Calvin would be a valuable ally in this project and invited him to return. This he did in September 1540, never to leave

Rules Governing Genevan Moral Behavior

During Calvin's lifetime, Geneva gained the reputation of being a model evangelical city. Persecuted Protestants in the outside world considered it Europe's freest and most godly city. Strict moral enforcement made practice conform with faith. It also gave the city and the new church the order they needed to survive against their enemies. The following selections are from ordinances governing the village churches around Geneva.

❖ Are Calvin's rules designed primarily to protect the Reformation? What do these rules suggest that he fears most? Are the penalties heavy or slaps on the wrist? Is it a sign of the failure of his reform that the Genevan people never stopped doing these things?

Concerning the Time of Assembling at Church

That the temples be closed for the rest of the time [when religious services are not being held] in order that no one shall enter therein out of hours, impelled thereto by superstition; and if any one be found engaged in any special act of devotion therein or near by he shall be admonished for it: if it be found to be of a superstitious nature for which simple correction is inadequate, then he shall be chastised.

Blasphemy

Whoever shall have blasphemed, swearing by the body or by the blood of our Lord, or in similar manner, he shall be made to kiss the earth for the first offence; for the second to pay 5 sous, and for the third 6 sous, and for the last offence be put in the pillory for one hour.

Drunkenness

1. That no one shall invite another to drink under penalty of 3 sous.
2. That taverns shall be closed during the sermon, under penalty that the tavern-keeper shall pay 3 sous, and whoever may be found therein shall pay the same amount.

3. If any one be found intoxicated he shall pay for the first offence 3 sous and shall be remanded to the consistory; for the second offence he shall be held to pay the sum of 6 sous, and for the third 10 sous and be put in prison.
4. That no one shall make *roiaumes* [great feasts] under penalty of 10 sous.

Songs and Dances

If any one sing immoral, dissolute or outrageous songs, or dance the *virollet* or other dance, he shall be put in prison for three days and then sent to the consistory.

Usury

That no one shall take upon interest or profit more than five per cent upon penalty of confiscation of the principal and of being condemned to make restitution as the case may demand.

Games

That no one shall play at any dissolute game or at any game whatsoever it may be, neither for gold nor silver nor for any excessive stake, upon penalty of 5 sous and forfeiture of stake played for.

From *Translations and Reprints from the Original Sources of European History*, Vol. 3 (Philadelphia: Department of History, University of Pennsylvania, 1909), pp. 10-11.

the city again. Within months of his return, the city implemented new ecclesiastical ordinances that provided for cooperation between the magistrates and the clergy in matters of internal discipline.

Following the Strasbourg model, the Genevan Church was organized into four offices: (1) pastors, of whom there were five; (2) teachers or doctors to instruct the populace in, and to defend, true doctrine; (3) elders, a group of twelve laypeople chosen by and from the Genevan councils and empowered to "oversee the life of everybody"; and (4) deacons to dispense church goods and services to the poor and the sick.

Calvin and his followers were motivated above all by a desire to transform society morally. Faith, Calvin taught, did not sit idly in the mind, but conformed one's every action to God's law. The "elect" should live in a manifestly God-pleasing way if they were truly God's "elect." In the attempted realization of this goal, Calvin spared no effort. The consistory, or regulatory court, became his instrument of power. This body was composed of the elders and the pastors and was presided over by one of the four syndics. It enforced the strictest moral discipline.

Among the many personal conflicts in Geneva that gave Calvin his reputation as a stern moralist, none proved more damaging than his active role in the capture and execution of the Spanish physician and amateur theologian Michael Servetus in 1553. Earlier, Servetus had been condemned by the Inquisition. He died at the stake in Protestant Geneva for denying the doctrine of the Trinity, a subject on which he had written a scandalous book.

After 1555, the city's syndics were all devout Calvinists, greatly strengthening Calvin's position, and Geneva became home to thousands of exiled Protestants who had been driven out of France, England, and Scotland. Refugees (more than 5,000), most of them utterly loyal to Calvin, eventually made up more than one-third of the population of Geneva.

To the thousands of persecuted Protestants who flocked to Geneva in midcentury, the city was a beacon and a refuge, Europe's only free city. During Calvin's lifetime, Geneva also gained the reputation of being a "woman's paradise" because the laws there severely punished men who beat their wives.

Political Consolidation of the Lutheran Reformation

By 1530, the Reformation was in Europe to stay. It would, however, take several decades and major attempts to eradicate it, before all would recognize this fact. With the political triumph of Lutheranism in the empire by the 1550s, Protestant movements elsewhere gained a new lease on life.

The Diet of Augsburg

Emperor Charles V, who spent most of his time on politics and military maneuvers outside the empire, especially in Spain and Italy, returned to the empire in 1530 to direct the Diet of Augsburg. This meeting of Protestant and Catholic representatives assembled to impose a settlement of the religious divisions. With its terms dictated by the Catholic emperor, the diet adjourned with a blunt order to all Lutherans to revert to Catholicism.

The Reformation was by this time too firmly established for that to occur. In February 1531 the Lutherans responded with the formation of their own defensive alliance, the Schmalkaldic League. The league took as its banner the *Augsburg Confession*, a moderate statement of Protestant beliefs that had been spurned by the emperor at the Diet of Augsburg. In 1538, Luther drew up a more strongly worded Protestant confession known as the *Schmalkaldic Articles*. Under the leadership of Landgrave Philip of Hesse and Elector John Frederick of Saxony, the league achieved a stalemate with the emperor, who was again distracted by renewed war with France and the ever-resilient Turks.

The Expansion of the Reformation

In the 1530s German Lutherans formed regional consistories, judicial bodies composed of theologians and lawyers, which oversaw and administered the new Protestant churches. These consistories replaced the old Catholic episcopates. Philip Melanchthon, the "praeceptor of Germany," oversaw the enactment of educational reforms that provided for compulsory primary education, schools for girls, a humanist revision of the traditional curriculum, and catechetical instruction of the laity in the new religion.

The Reformation also entrenched itself elsewhere. Introduced into Denmark by Christian II (r. 1513–1523), Lutheranism thrived there under Frederick I (r. 1523–1533), who joined the Schmalkaldic League. Under Christian III (r. 1536–1559), Lutheranism became the official state religion.

In Sweden, King Gustavus Vasa (r. 1523–1560), supported by a Swedish nobility greedy for church lands, embraced Lutheranism, confiscated church property, and subjected the clergy to royal authority at the Diet of Vesteras (1527).

In politically splintered Poland, Lutherans, Anabaptists, Calvinists, and even Antitrinitarians found room to practice their beliefs. Primarily because of the absence of a central political authority, Poland became a model of religious pluralism and toleration in the second half of the sixteenth century.

Reaction against Protestants: The Interim

Charles V made abortive efforts in 1540–1541 to enforce a compromise between Protestants and Catholics. As these and other conciliar efforts failed, he turned to a military solution. In 1547 imperial armies crushed the Protestant Schmalkaldic League, defeating John Frederick of Saxony in April and taking Philip of Hesse captive shortly thereafter.

The emperor established puppet rulers in Saxony and Hesse and issued as imperial law the Augsburg Interim, a new order which mandated that Protestants everywhere readopt old Catholic beliefs and practices. Protestants were granted a few cosmetic concessions, for example, clerical marriage (with papal approval of individual cases) and communion in both kinds (that is, bread and wine). Although the Interim met only surface acceptance within Germany, it forced many Protestant leaders into exile. The Strasbourg reformer Martin Bucer, for example, departed to England, where he would play an important role in drafting the religious documents of the English Reformation during the reign of Edward VI. In Germany, the city of Magdeburg became a refuge for persecuted Protestants and the center of Lutheran resistance.

The Peace of Augsburg

The Reformation was too entrenched by 1547 to be ended even by brute force. Maurice of Saxony, handpicked by Charles V to rule Saxony, recognized the inevitable and shifted his allegiance to the Protestants. Confronted by fierce resistance and weary from three decades of war, the emperor was forced to relent. After suffering a defeat by Protestant armies in 1552, Charles reinstated the Protestant leaders and guaranteed Lutherans religious freedoms in the Peace of Passau (August 1552). With this declaration, he effectively surrendered his lifelong quest for European religious unity.

The Peace of Augsburg in September 1555 made the division of Christendom permanent. This agreement recognized in law what had already been well established in practice: *Cuius regio, eius religio*, meaning that the ruler of a land would determine the religion of the land. Lutherans were permitted to retain all church lands forcibly seized before 1552. An "ecclesiastical reservation" was added, however, that was intended to prevent high Catholic prelates who converted to Protestantism from taking their lands, titles, and privileges with them. Those discontented with the religion of their region were permitted to migrate to another.

The Peace of Augsburg did not extend official recognition to Calvinism and Anabaptism as legal forms of Christian belief and practice. Anabaptists had long adjusted to such exclusion by forming their own separatist communities. Calvinists, however, were not separatists and could not choose that route. They remained determined not only to secure the right to worship publicly as they pleased, but also to shape society according to their own religious convictions. While Anabaptists retreated and Lutherans enjoyed the security of an established religion, Calvinists organized to lead national revolutions throughout northern Europe in the second half of the sixteenth century.

The English Reformation to 1553

Late medieval England had a well-earned reputation for maintaining the rights of the crown against the pope. Edward I (r. 1272–1307) had rejected efforts by Pope Boniface VIII to prevent secular taxation of the clergy. Parliament passed the first Statutes of Provisors and *Praemunire* in the mid-fourteenth century, curtailing payments and judicial appeals to Rome as well as papal appointments in England. Lollardy, humanism, and widespread anticlerical sentiment prepared the way religiously and intellectually for Protestant ideas, which entered England in the early sixteenth century.

The Preconditions of Reform

In the early 1520s, future English reformers met at the White Horse Inn in Cambridge to discuss Lutheran writings smuggled into England by merchants and scholars. One of these future reformers was William Tyndale (ca. 1492–1536), who translated the New Testament into English in 1524–1525 while in Germany. Printed in Cologne and Worms, Tyndale's New Testament began to circulate in England in 1526.

Cardinal Thomas Wolsey (ca. 1475–1530), the chief minister of King Henry VIII (r. 1509–1547), and Sir Thomas More (1478–1535), Wolsey's successor, guided royal opposition to incipient English Protestantism. The king himself defended the seven sacraments against Luther, receiving as a reward the title "Defender of the Faith" from Pope Leo X. Following Luther's intemperate reply to Henry's amateur theological attack, More wrote a lengthy *Response to Luther* in 1523.

The King's Affair

While Lollardy and humanism may be said to have provided the native seeds for religious reform, it was Henry's unhappy marriage that broke the soil and allowed the seeds to take root. In 1509 Henry had married Catherine of Aragon (d. 1536), daughter of Ferdinand and Isabella of Spain, and the aunt of Emperor Charles V. By 1527 the union had produced no male heir to the throne and only one surviving child, a daughter, Mary. Henry was justifiably concerned about the political consequences of leaving only a female heir. In this period, people believed it unnatural for women to rule over men. At best a woman ruler meant a contested reign, at worst turmoil and revolution.

Henry even came to believe that his union with Catherine, who had many miscarriages and stillbirths, had been cursed by God, because Catherine had first been the wife of his brother, Arthur. Henry's father, King Henry VII, had betrothed Catherine to Henry after Arthur's untimely death in order to keep the English alliance with Spain intact. They were officially married in 1509, a few days before Henry VIII received his crown. Because marriage to the wife of one's brother was prohibited by both canon and biblical law (see Leviticus 18:16, 20:21), the marriage had required a special dispensation from Pope Julius II.

By 1527 Henry was thoroughly enamored of Anne Boleyn, one of Catherine's ladies in waiting. He determined to put Catherine aside and take Anne as his wife. This he could not do in Catholic England, however, without papal annulment of the marriage to Catherine. And therein lay a special problem. The year 1527 was also the year when soldiers of the Holy Roman Empire mutinied and sacked Rome. The reigning Pope Clement VII was at the time a prisoner of Charles V, who happened also to be Catherine's nephew. Even if this had not been the case, it would have been virtually impossible for the Pope to grant an annulment of a marriage that not only had survived for eighteen years, but had been made possible in the first place by a special papal dispensation.

Cardinal Wolsey, who aspired to become Pope, was placed in charge of securing the royal annulment. Lord Chancellor since 1515 and papal legate-at-large since 1518, Wolsey had long been Henry's "heavy" and the object of much popular resentment. When he failed to secure the annulment through no fault of his own, he was dismissed in disgrace in 1529. Thomas Cranmer (1489–1556) and Thomas Cromwell (1485–1540), both of whom harbored Lutheran sympathies, thereafter became the king's closest advisers. Finding the way to a papal annulment closed, Henry's new advisers struck a different course: Why not simply declare the king supreme in English spiritual affairs as he was in English temporal affairs? Then the king could settle the king's affair himself.

The "Reformation Parliament"

In 1529, Parliament convened for what would be a seven-year session that earned it the title the "Reformation Parliament." During this period, it passed a flood of legislation that harassed, and finally placed royal reins on, the clergy. In so doing, it established a precedent that would remain a feature of English government: Whenever fundamental changes are made in religion, the monarch must consult with and work through Parliament. In January 1531, the Convocation (a legislative assembly representing the English clergy) publicly recognized Henry as head of the church in England "as far as the law of Christ allows." In 1532 Parliament published official grievances against the church, ranging from alleged indifference to the needs of the laity to an excessive number of religious holidays. In the same year, Parliament passed the Submission of the Clergy, which effectively placed canon law under royal control and thereby the clergy under royal jurisdiction.

In January 1533 Henry wed the pregnant Anne Boleyn, with Thomas Cranmer officiating. In February 1533, Parliament made the king the highest court of appeal for all English subjects. In March 1533, Cranmer became archbishop of Canterbury and led the Convocation in invalidating the king's marriage to Catherine. In 1534, Parliament ended all payments by the English clergy and laity to Rome and gave Henry sole jurisdiction over high ecclesiastical appointments. The Act of Succession in the same year made Anne Boleyn's children legitimate heirs to the throne, and the Act of Supremacy declared Henry "the only supreme head in earth of the Church of England."

When Thomas More and John Fisher, bishop of Rochester, refused to recognize the Act of Succession and the Act of Supremacy, Henry had them executed, making clear his determination to have his way regardless of the cost. In 1536 and 1538, Parliament dissolved England's monasteries and nunneries.

Wives of Henry VIII

Henry's domestic life lacked the consistency of his political life. In 1536 Anne Boleyn was executed for alleged treason and adultery, and her daughter, Elizabeth, was declared illegitimate. Henry had four further marriages. His third wife, Jane Seymour, died in 1537 shortly after giving birth to the future Edward VI. Henry wed Anne of Cleves sight unseen on the advice of Cromwell, the purpose being to create by

An allegorical depiction of the Tudor succession by the painter Lucas de Heere (1534–1584). On Henry VIII's right stands his Catholic daughter Mary (1533–1558) and her husband Philip II of Spain. They are accompanied by Mars, the god of war. Henry's son, Edward VI (r. 1547–1553), kneels at the king's left. Elizabeth I (1558–1603) is shown standing in the foreground attended by Peace and Plenty, allegorical figures of what her reign brought to England. Sudeley Castle National Museums & Galleries of Wales

the marriage an alliance with the Protestant princes. Neither the alliance nor the marriage proved worth the trouble; the marriage was annulled by Parliament, and Cromwell was dismissed and eventually executed. Catherine Howard, Henry's fifth wife, was beheaded for adultery in 1542. His last wife, Catherine Parr, a patron of humanists and reformers, for whom Henry was the third husband, survived him to marry still a fourth time—obviously she was a match for the English king.

The King's Religious Conservatism

Henry's boldness in politics and his domestic affairs did not extend to religion. True, because of Henry's actions, the Pope had ceased to be head of the English Church and English Bibles were placed in English churches, but despite the break with Rome, Henry remained decidedly conservative in his religious beliefs. With the Ten Articles of 1536, he made only mild concessions to Protestant tenets, otherwise maintaining Catholic doctrine in a country filled with Protestant sentiment. Despite his many wives and amorous adventures, Henry absolutely forbade the English clergy to marry and threatened any clergy who were caught twice in concubinage with execution.

Angered by the growing popularity of Protestant views, even among his chief advisers, Henry struck directly at them in the Six Articles of 1539. These reaffirmed transubstantiation, denied the Eucharistic cup to the laity, declared celibate vows inviolable, provided for private masses, and ordered the continuation of auricular confession. (Protestants referred to the articles as the "whip with six stings.") Although William Tyndale's English New

Testament grew into the Coverdale Bible (1535) and the Great Bible (1539), and the latter was mandated for every English parish, England had to await Henry's death before it could become a genuinely Protestant country.

Main Events of the English Reformation

1529	Reformation Parliament convenes
1532	Parliament passes the Submission of the Clergy
1533	Henry VIII weds Anne Boleyn; Convocation proclaims marriage to Catherine of Aragon invalid
1534	Act of Succession makes Anne Boleyn's children legitimate heirs to the English throne
1534	Act of Supremacy declares Henry VIII "the only supreme head of the Church of England"
1535	Thomas More executed for opposition to Acts of Succession and Supremacy
1535	Publication of Coverdale Bible
1539	Henry VIII imposes the Six Articles
1547	Edward VI succeeds to the throne under protectorships of Somerset and Northumberland
1549	First Act of Uniformity imposes *Book of Common Prayer* on English churches
1553–1558	Mary Tudor restores Catholic doctrine
1558–1603	Elizabeth I fashions an Anglican religious settlement

The Protestant Reformation under Edward VI

[handwritten: son of Jane Seymour 3rd wife of Henry VIII]

When Henry died, his son and successor, Edward VI (r. 1547–1553), was only ten years old. Edward reigned under the successive regencies of Edward Seymour, who became the duke of Somerset (1547–1550), and the earl of Warwick, who became known as the duke of Northumberland (1550–1553). During this time, England fully enacted the Protestant Reformation. The new king and Somerset corresponded directly with John Calvin. During Somerset's regency, Henry's Six Articles and laws against heresy were repealed, and clerical marriage and communion with cup were sanctioned.

In 1547 the chantries, places where endowed masses had traditionally been said for the dead, were dissolved. In 1549, the Act of Uniformity imposed Thomas Cranmer's *Book of Common Prayer* on all English churches. Images and altars were removed from the churches in 1550. After Charles V's victory over the German princes in 1547, German Protestant leaders had fled to England for refuge. Several of these refugees, with Martin Bucer prominent among them, now directly assisted the completion of the English Reformation.

The Second Act of Uniformity, passed in 1552, imposed a revised edition of the *Book of Common Prayer* on all English churches. A forty-two-article confession of faith, also written by Thomas Cranmer, was adopted, setting forth a moderate Protestant doctrine. It taught justification by faith and the supremacy of Holy Scripture, denied transubstantiation (although not real presence), and recognized only two sacraments.

All these changes were short lived, however. In 1553, Catherine of Aragon's daughter succeeded Edward (who had died in his teens) to the English throne as Mary I (r. 1553–1558) and proceeded to restore Catholic doctrine and practice with a singlemindedness that rivaled that of her father. It was not until the reign of Anne Boleyn's daughter, Elizabeth I (r. 1558–1603), that a lasting religious settlement was worked out in England.

[handwritten left margin: Mary I dau. of Catherine of Aragon]

[handwritten left margin: Eliz. I dau. of Anne Boleyn]

Catholic Reform and Counter-Reformation

The Protestant Reformation did not take the medieval church completely by surprise. There were many internal criticisms and efforts at reform before there was a Counter-Reformation in reaction to Protestant successes.

Sources of Catholic Reform

Before the Reformation began, ambitious proposals had been made for church reform. But sixteenth-century Popes, ever mindful of how the councils of Constance and Basel had stripped the Pope of his traditional powers, quickly squelched such efforts to bring about basic changes in the laws and institutions of the church. They preferred the charge given to the Fifth Lateran Council (1513–1517) in the keynote address by the superior general of the Hermits of Saint Augustine: "Men are to be changed by, not to change, religion."

Despite such papal foot-dragging, the church was not without its reformers. Many new religious orders also sprang up in the sixteenth century to lead a broad revival of piety within the church. The first of these orders was the Theatines, founded in 1524 to groom devout and reform-minded leaders at the higher levels of the church hierarchy. One of the cofounders was Bishop Gian Pietro Carafa, who would be Pope Paul IV. Another new order, whose

The Ecstasy of Saint Teresa of Avila, *by Gianlorenzo Bernini (1598–1680). Mystics like Saint Teresa and Saint John of the Cross helped revive the traditional piety of medieval monasticism.* Scala/Art Resource, N.Y.

mission pointed in the opposite direction, was the Capuchins. Recognized by the Pope in 1528, they sought to return to the original ascetic and charitable ideals of Saint Francis and became very popular among the ordinary people to whom they directed their ministry. The Somaschi, who became active in the mid-1520s, and the Barnabites, founded in 1530, directed their efforts at repairing the moral, spiritual, and physical damage done to people in war-torn areas of Italy.

For women, there was the new order of Ursulines, founded in 1535. It established convents in Italy and France for the religious education of girls from all social classes and became very influential. Another new religious order, the Oratorians, officially recognized in 1575, was an elite group of secular clerics who devoted themselves to the promotion of religious literature and church music. Among their members was the great Catholic hymnist and musician Giovanni Perluigi da Palestrina (1526–1594).

In addition to these lay and clerical movements, the mystical piety of medieval monasticism was revived and popularized by the Spanish mystics Saint Teresa of Avila (1515–1582) and Saint John of the Cross (1542–1591).

Ignatius of Loyola and the Jesuits

Of the various reform groups, none was more instrumental in the success of the Counter-Reformation than the Society of Jesus, the new order of Jesuits. Organized by Ignatius of Loyola in the 1530s, it was officially recognized by the church in 1540. The society grew within the space of a century from its original 10 members to more than 15,000 members scattered throughout the world, with thriving missions in India, Japan, and the Americas.

The founder of the Jesuits, Ignatius of Loyola (1491–1556), was a heroic figure. A dashing courtier and *caballero* in his youth, he began his spiritual pilgrimage in 1521 after he had been seriously wounded in the legs during a battle with the French. During a lengthy and painful convalescence, he passed the time by reading Christian classics. So impressed was he with the heroic self-sacrifice of the church's saints and their methods of overcoming mental anguish and pain that he underwent a profound religious conversion. Henceforth, he, too, would serve the church as a soldier of Christ.

After recuperating, Ignatius applied the lessons he had learned during his convalescence to a program of religious and moral self-discipline that came to be embodied in the *Spiritual Exercises*. (See "Ignatius of Loyola's 'Rules for Thinking With the Church.'") This psychologically perceptive devotional guide contained mental and emotional

Protestant Reformation and Catholic Reform on the Continent	
1513–1517	Fifth Lateran Council fails to bring about reform in the church
1517	Luther posts ninety-five theses against indulgences
1519	Charles I of Spain elected Holy Roman Emperor (as Charles V)
1519	Luther challenges authority of Pope and inerrancy of church councils at Leipzig Debate
1521	Papal bull excommunicates Luther for heresy
1521	Diet of Worms condemns Luther
1521–1522	Luther translates the New Testament into German
1524–1525	Peasants' revolt in Germany
1527	The *Schleitheim Confession* of the Anabaptists
1529	Marburg Colloquy between Luther and Zwingli
1530	Diet of Augsburg fails to settle religious differences
1531	Formation of Protestant Schmalkaldic League
1534–1535	Anabaptists assume political power in city of Münster
1536	Calvin arrives in Geneva
1540	Jesuits, founded by Ignatius of Loyola, recognized as order by Pope
1546	Luther dies
1547	Armies of Charles V crush Schmalkaldic League
1548	Augsburg Interim outlaws Protestant practices
1555	Peace of Augsburg recognizes rights of Lutherans to worship as they please
1545–1563	Council of Trent institutes reforms and responds to the Reformation

exercises designed to teach one absolute spiritual self-mastery over one's feelings. It taught that a person could shape his or her own behavior—even create a new religious self—through disciplined study and regular practice.

Whereas in Jesuit eyes Protestants had distinguished themselves by disobedience to church authority and by religious innovation, the exercises of Ignatius were intended to teach good Catholics to deny themselves and submit without question to higher church authority and spiritual direction. Perfect discipline and self-control were the essential con-

Ignatius of Loyola's "Rules for Thinking With the Church"

As leaders of the Counter-Reformation, the Jesuits attempted to live by and instill in others the strictest obedience to Church authority. The following are some of the eighteen rules included by Ignatius in his Spiritual Exercises *to give Catholics positive direction. These rules also indicate the Catholic reformers' refusal to compromise with Protestants.*

❖ *Would Protestants find any of Ignatius's "rules" acceptable? Might any of them be controversial among Catholic laity as well as among Protestant laity?*

In order to have the proper attitude of mind in the Church Militant we should observe the following rules:

1. Putting aside all private judgment, we should keep our minds prepared and ready to obey promptly and in all things the true spouse of Christ our Lord, our Holy Mother, the hierarchical Church.
2. To praise sacramental confession and the reception of the Most Holy Sacrament once a year, and much better once a month, and better still every week....
3. To praise the frequent hearing of Mass....
4. To praise highly the religious life, virginity, and continence; and also matrimony, but not as highly....
5. To praise the vows of religion, obedience, poverty, chastity, and other works of perfection and supererogation....
6. To praise the relics of the saints...[and] the stations, pilgrimages, indulgences, jubilees, Crusade indulgences, and the lighting of candles in the churches.
7. To praise the precepts concerning fasts and abstinences...and acts of penance....
8. To praise the adornments and buildings of churches as well as sacred images....
9. To praise all the precepts of the church....
10. To approve and praise the directions and recommendations of our superiors as well as their personal behaviour....
11. To praise both the positive and scholastic theology....
12. We must be on our guard against making comparisons between the living and those who have already gone to their reward, for it is no small error to say, for example: "This man knows more than St. Augustine"; "He is another Saint Francis, or even greater."...
13. If we wish to be sure that we are right in all things, we should always be ready to accept this principle: I will believe that the white that I see is black, if the hierarchical Church so defines it. For I believe that between...Christ our Lord and...His Church, there is but one spirit, which governs and directs us for the salvation of our souls.

From *The Spiritual Exercises of St. Ignatius*, trans. by Anthony Mottola. Copyright © 1964 by Doubleday, a division of Bantam, Doubleday, Dell Publishing Group, Inc., pp. 139–141. Used by permission of Doubleday, a division of Random House, Inc.

ditions of such obedience. To these were added the enthusiasm of traditional spirituality and mysticism and uncompromising loyalty to the church's cause above all else. This was a potent combination that helped counter the Reformation and win many Protestants back to the Catholic fold, especially in Austria and Bavaria and along the Rhine. (See Map 11–3).

The Council of Trent (1545–1563)

The broad success of the Reformation and the insistence of the Emperor Charles V forced Pope Paul to call a general council of the church to reassert church doctrine. In anticipation, the Pope appointed a reform commission, chaired by Caspar Con-

tarini (1483–1542), a leading liberal theologian. His report, presented to the Pope in February 1537, bluntly criticized the fiscal practices and simony of the papal *Curia* as the primary source of the church's loss of esteem. The report was so critical, that Pope Paul attempted unsuccessfully to suppress its publication and Protestants reprinted and circulated it as justification of their criticism.

The long-delayed council of the church met in 1545 in the imperial city of Trent in northern Italy. There were three sessions, spread over eighteen years, with long interruptions due to war, plague, and imperial and papal politics. The council met from 1545 to 1547, from 1551 to 1552, and from 1562 to 1563, a period that spanned the careers of four different Popes.

Unlike the general councils of the fifteenth century, Trent was strictly under the Pope's control, with high Italian prelates prominent in the proceedings. Initially four of the five attending archbishops and twenty-one of the twenty-three attending bishops were Italian. Even at its final session in 1562, more than three-quarters of the council fathers were Italians. Voting was limited to the high levels of the clergy; university theologians, the lower clergy, and the laity were not permitted to share in the council's decisions.

The council's most important reforms concerned internal church discipline. Steps were taken to curtail the selling of church offices and other religious goods. Many bishops who resided in Rome rather than within their dioceses were forced to move to their appointed seats of authority. Trent strengthened the authority of local bishops so they could effectively discipline popular religious practice. The bishops were also subjected to new rules that required them not only to reside in their dioceses, but also to be highly visible by preaching regularly and conducting annual visitations. Trent also sought to give the parish priest a brighter image by requiring him to be neatly dressed, better educated, strictly celibate, and active among his parishioners. To this end, Trent also called for the construction of a seminary in every diocese.

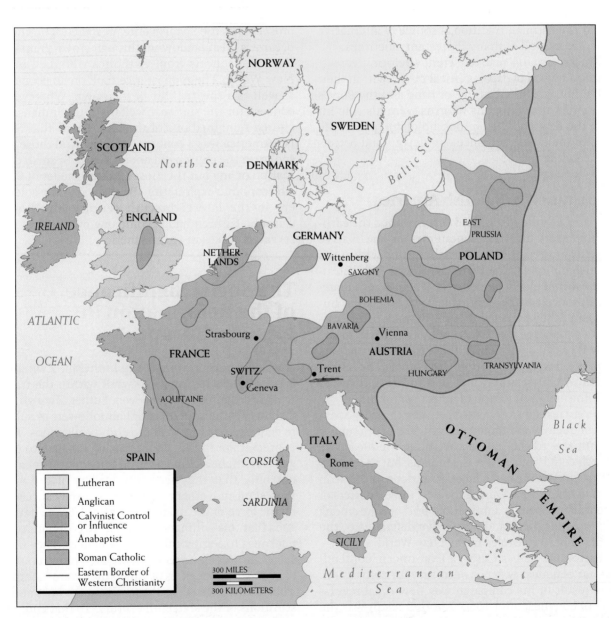

MAP 11–3   THE RELIGIOUS SITUATION ABOUT 1560   *By 1560 Luther, Zwingli, and Loyola were dead, Calvin was near the end of his life, the English break from Rome was complete, and the last session of the Council of Trent was about to assemble. This map shows "religious geography" of western Europe at the time.*

Not a single doctrinal concession was made to the Protestants, however. In the face of Protestant criticism, the Council of Trent gave a ringing reaffirmation to the traditional Scholastic education of the clergy; the role of good works in salvation; the authority of tradition; the seven sacraments; transubstantiation; the withholding of the Eucharistic cup from the laity; clerical celibacy; the reality of purgatory; the veneration of saints, relics, and sacred images; and the granting of letters of indulgence. The council resolved medieval Scholastic quarrels in favor of the theology of Saint Thomas Aquinas, further enhancing his authority within the church. Thereafter, the church offered its strongest resistance to groups like the Jansenists, who strongly endorsed the medieval Augustinian tradition, a source of alternative Catholic, as well as many Protestant, doctrines.

Rulers initially resisted Trent's reform decrees, fearing a revival of papal political power within their lands. But with the passage of time and the Pope's assurances that religious reforms were his sole intent, the new legislation took hold, and parish life revived under the guidance of a devout and better-trained clergy.

The Church in Spanish America

Roman Catholic priests had accompanied the earliest explorers and the conquerors of the Native Americans. Because of internal reforms within the Spanish church at the turn of the sixteenth century, these first clergy tended to be imbued with many of the social and religious ideals of Christian humanism. They believed that they could foster Erasmus's concept of the "philosophy of Christ" in the New World. Consequently, these missionary priests were filled with zeal not only to convert the inhabitants to Christianity, but also to bring to them learning and civilization of a European kind.

A very real tension existed between the early Spanish conquerors and the mendicant friars who sought to minister to the Indians. Without conquest, the church could not convert the Indians, but the priests often deplored the harsh labor conditions imposed on Native Americans. During the first three-quarters of a century of Spanish domination, priests were among the most eloquent and persuasive defenders of the rights of native peoples in the New World.

Bartolomé de Las Casas, a Dominican, contended that conquest was not necessary for conversion. One result of his campaign was new royal regulation of conquest after 1550. Another result was the "Black Legend," which portrayed all Spanish treatment of Indians as unprincipled and inhumane. Those who held this point of view drew heavily on Las Casas's writings. (See "A Defense of American Indians.") Although largely true, the "Black Legend" nonetheless exaggerated the case against Spain and has been exploited by Spanish critics. Many of the Indian rulers had also been exceedingly cruel, as witnessed by the Aztec demands for human sacrifice, and both the Aztecs and the Incas enslaved other peoples. Had the Aztecs discovered Spain and held the upper hand there, the persecution of native Europeans would likely have been as great as that of Native Americans at the hands of the Spanish.

By the end of the sixteenth century, the church in Spanish America had become largely an institution upholding the colonial status quo. On many occasions, individual priests did defend the communal rights of Indian tribes, but the colonial church also prospered as the Spanish elite prospered. The church became a great landowner through crown grants and through bequests from Catholics who died in the New World. The monasteries took on an economic as well as a spiritual life of their own. Whatever its concern for the spiritual welfare of the Indians, the church remained one of the indications that Spanish America was a conquered world. And those who spoke for the church did not challenge Spanish domination or any but the most extreme modes of Spanish economic exploitation. By the end of the colonial era in the late eighteenth century, the Roman Catholic Church had become one of the most conservative forces in Latin America.

The Social Significance of the Reformation in Western Europe

It was a common trait of the Lutheran, Zwinglian, and Calvinist reformers to work within the framework of reigning political power. Luther, Zwingli, and Calvin saw themselves and their followers as subject to definite civic responsibilities and obligations. Their conservatism in this regard has led scholars to characterize them as "magisterial reformers," meaning not only that they were the leaders of the major Protestant movements, but also that they succeeded by the force of the magistrate's sword. Some have argued that this willingness to resort to coercion led the reformers to compromise their principles. They themselves, however, never contemplated reform outside or against the societies of which they were members. They wanted it to take shape within the laws and institutions of the sixteenth century. To that end, they remained highly sensitive to what was politically and socially possible in their age. Some scholars believe that the reformers were too conscious of the historically possible, that their reforms went forward with

A Defense of American Natives

Bartolomé de Las Casas (1474–1566), a Dominican missionary to the New World, describes the native people of the islands of the Caribbean and their systematic slaughter by the Spanish.

❖ *Is Las Casas romanticizing the American natives? Does he truly respect their native culture and beliefs?*

This infinite multitude of people was so created by God that they were without fraud...or malice.... Toward the Spaniards whom they serve, patient, meek, and peaceful, [they] lay aside all contentious and tumultuous thoughts, and live without any hatred or desire of revenge. The people are most delicate and tender, enjoying such a feeble constitution of body as does not permit them to endure labour.... The[ir] nation [the West Indies] is very poor and indigent, possessing little, and by reason that they gape not after temporal goods, [being] neither proud nor ambitious. Their diet is such that the most holy hermit cannot feed more sparingly in the wildernesse. They go naked... and a poor shag mantle...is their greatest and their warmest covering. They lie upon mats; only those who have larger fortunes lie upon a kind of net which is tied at the four corners and so fasten'd to the roof, which the Indians in their natural language call *Hamecks* [hammocks]. They are of a very apprehensive and docile wit, and capable of all good learning, and very apt to receive our Religion, which when they have but once tasted [it], they are carried [off] with a very ardent and zealous desire to make further progress in it; so that I have heard divers Spaniards confess that they had nothing else to hinder them from enjoying heaven, but the ignorance of the true God.

To these quiet Lambs, endued with such blessed qualities, came the Spaniards like most cruel Tygres, Wolves, and Lions...for these forty years, minding nothing else but the slaughter of these unfortunate wretches...[whom] they have so cruelly and inhumanely butchered, [so] that of three millions of people which Hispaniola [modern Haiti and the Dominican Republic] itself did contain, there are left remaining alive scarce three hundred persons. And the island of Cuba...lies wholly desert, untilled and ruined. The islands of St. John and Jamaica lie waste and desolate. The Lycayan islands neighboring to the north upon Cuba and Hispaniola...are now totally unpeopled and destroyed; the inhabitants thereof amounting to above 500,000 souls, partly killed, and partly forced away to work in other places....Other islands there were near the island of St. John more than thirty in number, which were totally made desert. All which islands...lie now altogether solitary without any people or inhabitant.

Bartolomé de Las Casas, *The Tears of the Indians*, trans. by John Phillips (1656), from reprint of original edition (Stanford, CA: Academic Reprints, n.d.), pp. 2–4.

such caution that they changed late medieval society very little and actually encouraged acceptance of the sociopolitical status quo.

The Revolution in Religious Practices and Institutions

The Reformation may have been politically conservative, but by the end of the sixteenth century it had brought about radical changes in traditional religious practices and institutions in those lands where it succeeded.

RELIGION IN FIFTEENTH-CENTURY LIFE   In the fifteenth century, on the streets of the great cities of central Europe that later turned Protestant (for example,

Zurich, Strasbourg, Nuremberg, and Geneva), the clergy and the religious were everywhere. They made up six to eight percent of the total urban population, and they exercised considerable political as well as spiritual power. They legislated and taxed, they tried cases in special church courts, and they enforced their laws with threats of excommunication.

The church calendar regulated daily life. About one-third of the year was given over to some kind of religious observance or celebration. There were frequent periods of fasting. On almost a hundred days out of the year a pious Christian could not, without special dispensation, eat eggs, butter, fat, or meat.

Monasteries, and especially nunneries, were prominent and influential institutions. The children of society's most powerful citizens resided there.

Local aristocrats were closely identified with particular churches and chapels, whose walls recorded their lineage and proclaimed their generosity. On the streets, friars from near and far begged alms from passersby. In the churches the mass and liturgy were read entirely in Latin. Images of saints were regularly displayed, and on certain holidays their relics were paraded about and venerated.

There was a booming business at local religious shrines. Pilgrims gathered there by the hundreds—even thousands—many sick and dying, all in search of a cure or a miracle, but also for diversion and entertainment. Several times during the year, special preachers arrived in the city to sell letters of indulgence.

Many clergy walked the streets with concubines and children, although they were sworn to celibacy and forbidden to marry. The church tolerated such relationships upon payment of penitential fines.

People everywhere could be heard complaining about the clergy's exemption from taxation and, in many instances, also from the civil criminal code. People also grumbled about having to support church offices whose occupants actually lived and worked elsewhere. Townspeople also expressed concern that the church had too much influence over education and culture.

RELIGION IN SIXTEENTH-CENTURY LIFE   In these same cities, after the Reformation had firmly established itself, few changes in politics and society were evident. The same aristocratic families governed as before, and the rich generally got richer and the poor poorer. But overall numbers of clergy fell by two-thirds and religious holidays shrank by one-third. Cloisters were nearly gone, and many that remained were transformed into hospices for the sick and poor or into educational institutions, their endowments also turned over to these new purposes. A few cloisters remained for very devout old monks and nuns who could not be pensioned off or who lacked families and friends to care for them. But these remaining cloisters died out with their inhabitants.

In the churches, which had also been reduced in number by at least one-third, worship was conducted almost completely in the vernacular. In some, particularly those in Zwinglian cities, the walls were stripped bare and whitewashed to make sure that the congregation meditated only on God's word. The laity observed no obligatory fasts. Indulgence preachers no longer appeared. Local shrines were closed down, and anyone found openly venerating saints, relics, and images was subject to fine and punishment.

Copies of Luther's translation of the New Testament or, more often, excerpts from it could be found in private homes, and meditation on them was en-

couraged by the new clergy. The clergy could marry, and most did. They paid taxes and were punished for their crimes in civil courts. Domestic moral life was regulated by committees composed of roughly equal numbers of laity and clergy, over whose decisions secular magistrates had the last word.

Not all Protestant clergy remained enthusiastic about this new lay authority in religion. And the laity themselves were also ambivalent about certain aspects of the Reformation. Over half of the original converts returned to the Catholic fold before the end of the sixteenth century. Whereas one-half of Europe could be counted in the Protestant camp in the mid-sixteenth century, only one-fifth would be there by the mid-seventeenth century.[2]

The Reformation and Education

Another important cultural achievement of the Reformation was its implementation of many of the educational reforms of humanism in the new Protestant schools and universities. Many Protestant reformers in Germany, France, and England were humanists. And even when their views on Church doctrine and humankind separated them from the humanist movement, the Protestant reformers continued to share with the humanists a common opposition to Scholasticism and a belief in the unity of wisdom, eloquence, and action. The humanist program of studies, which provided the language skills to deal authoritatively with original sources, proved to be a more appropriate tool for the elaboration of Protestant doctrine than did scholastic dialectic, which remained ascendant in the Counter-Reformation.

The Catholic counterreformers recognized the close connections between humanism and the Reformation. Ignatius of Loyola observed the way in which the new learning had been embraced by and served the Protestant cause. In his *Spiritual Exercises*, he insisted that when the Bible and the Church Fathers were read directly, they be read under the guidance of the authoritative scholastic theologians: Peter Lombard, Bonaventure, and Thomas Aquinas. The last of these worthies, Ignatius argued, being "of more recent date," had the clearest understanding of what Scripture and the Fathers meant and therefore should guide the study of the past.

When, in August 1518, Philip Melanchthon (1497–1560), a young humanist and professor of Greek, arrived at the University of Wittenberg, his first act was to implement curricular reforms on the

[2]Geoffrey Parker, *Europe in Crisis, 1598–1648* (Ithaca, NY: Cornell University Press, 1979), p. 50.

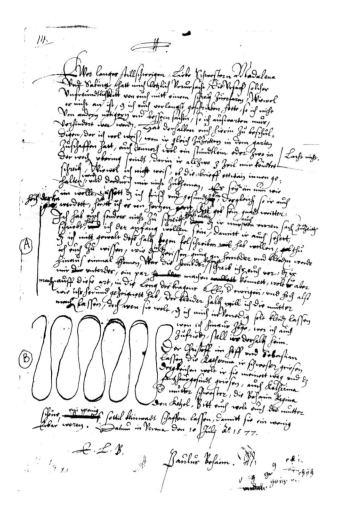

Brothers and sisters. While away from home at law school in Padua, Italy, nineteen-year-old Paul Behaim, Jr., the brother of Friedrich (see document on p. 381), wrote in July, 1577 to his older sisters Magdalena (22) and Sabina (21) to complain about the infrequency of their writing to him. Typical of sibling relations in every age, the letter is affectionate and joking. The sisters were then at home with their widowed mother and busy with the many chores of the self-sufficient sixteenth-century domestic household—especially, at this time of the year, gardening. Because of their alleged neglect Paul teasingly tells them that they must now do "penance" by making him two new shirts, as his were embarrassingly tattered. He indicated in the left margin the exact collar length (A) and style (B) he wishes the shirts to be. Sewing for the household was another regular domestic chore for burgher and patrician women not working in trades outside the home. But Magdalena and Sabina went even further to "cover" their brother: they also allowed him to receive income (to be repaid in the future) from their own paternal inheritances so that he might finish his legal education, on the successful completion of which the whole family depended for its future success. Geramnisches National Museum, Nuremberg, Germany, Behaim-Archiv Fasz. 106; Steven Ozment, Flesh and Spirit: Private Life in Early Modern Germany (Viking/Penguin, New York, 1999), pp. 174–176

humanist model. In his inaugural address, entitled *On Improving the Studies of the Young,* Melanchthon presented himself as a defender of good letters and classical studies against "barbarians who practice barbarous arts." By the latter, he meant the scholastic theologians of the later Middle Ages, whose methods of juxtaposing the views of conflicting authorities and seeking to reconcile them by disputation had, he believed, undermined both good letters and sound biblical doctrine. Scholastic dominance in the universities was seen by Melanchthon as having bred contempt for the Greek language and learning and as having encouraged neglect of the study of mathematics, sacred studies, and the art of oratory. Melanchthon urged the careful study of history, poetry, and other humanist disciplines.

Together, Luther and Melanchthon restructured the University of Wittenberg's curriculum. Commentaries on Lombard's *Sentences* were dropped, as was canon law. Straightforward historical study replaced old Scholastic lectures on Aristotle. Students read primary sources directly, not by way of accepted Scholastic commentators. Candidates for theological degrees defended the new doctrine on the basis of their own ex-

egesis of the Bible. New chairs of Greek and Hebrew were created. Luther and Melanchthon also pressed for universal compulsory education so that both boys and girls could reach vernacular literacy in the Bible.

In Geneva, John Calvin and his successor, Theodore Beza, founded the Genevan Academy, which later evolved into the University of Geneva. That institution, created primarily for training Calvinist ministers, pursued ideals similar to those set forth by Luther and Melanchthon. Calvinist refugees trained in the academy carried Protestant educational reforms to France, Scotland, England, and the New World. Through such efforts, a working knowledge of Greek and Hebrew became commonplace in educated circles in the sixteenth and seventeenth centuries.

Some contemporaries decried what they saw as a narrowing of the original humanist program as Protestants took it over. Erasmus, for example, came to fear the Reformation as a threat to the liberal arts and good learning. Sebastian Franck pointed to parallels between Luther's and Zwingli's debates over Christ's presence in the Eucharist and such old scholastic disputations as that over the Immaculate Conception of the Virgin.

Humanist culture and learning nonetheless remained indebted to the Reformation. The Protestant endorsement of the humanist program of studies remained as significant for the humanist movement as the latter had been for the Reformation. Protestant schools and universities consolidated and preserved for the modern world many of the basic pedagogical achievements of humanism. There, the *studia humanitatis*, although often as little more than a handmaiden to theological doctrine, found a permanent home, one that remained hospitable even in the heyday of conservative Protestantism.

The Reformation and the Changing Role of Women

The Protestant reformers took a positive stand on clerical marriage and strongly opposed monasticism and the celibate life. From this position, they challenged the medieval tendency alternately to degrade women as temptresses (following the model of Eve) and to exalt them as virgins (following the model of Mary). Protestants opposed the popular antiwoman and antimarriage literature of the Middle Ages. They praised woman in her own right, but especially in her biblical vocation as mother and housewife. Although from a modern perspective, women remained subject to men, new marriage laws gave them greater security and protection.

Relief of sexual frustration and a remedy for fornication were prominent in Protestant arguments for marriage. But the reformers also viewed their wives as indispensable companions in their work, and this not solely because they took domestic cares off their husbands' minds. Luther, who married in 1525 at the age of forty-two, wrote the following of women:

Imagine what it would be like without women. The home, cities, economic life, and government would virtually disappear. Men cannot do without women. Even if it were possible for men to beget and bear children, they still could not do without women.[3]

John Calvin wrote this at the death of his wife:

I have been bereaved of the best companion of my life, of one who, had it been so ordered, would not only have been the willing sharer of my indigence, but even of my death. During her life she was the faithful helper of my ministry.[4]

Such tributes were intended in part to overcome Catholic criticism that marriage distracted the cleric from his ministry. They were primarily the expression of a new value placed on the estate of marriage and family life. In opposition to the celibate ideal of the Middle Ages, Protestants stressed as no religious movement before them the sacredness of home and family. This attitude contributed to a more respectful and sharing relationship between husbands and wives and between parents and children. (See "A German Mother Advises Her Fifteen-Year-Old Son (1578).")

The ideal of the companionate marriage—that is, of husband and wife as co-workers in a special God-ordained community of the family, sharing authority equally within the household—led to an important expansion of the grounds for divorce in Protestant cities as early as the 1520s. Women now had an equal right with men to divorce and remarry in good conscience—unlike the situation in Catholicism, where only a separation from bed and table, not divorce and remarriage, was permitted a couple in a failed marriage. The reformers were actually more willing to permit divorce and remarriage on grounds of adultery and abandonment than were secular magistrates, who feared that liberal divorce laws would lead to social upheaval.

Protestant doctrines were as attractive to women as they were to men. Renegade nuns wrote exposés of the nunnery in the name of Christian freedom and justification by faith, declaring that the nunnery was no special woman's place at all and that supervisory male clergy (who alone could hear the nuns' confessions and administer sacraments to them) made their lives as unpleasant and burdensome as any abusive husband. Women in the higher classes, who enjoyed new social and political freedoms during the Renaissance, found in Protestant theology a religious complement to their greater independence in other walks of life. Some cloistered noblewomen, however, protested the closing of nunneries. They believed that the cloister provided them a more interesting and independent way of life than they would have known in the secular world.

Because they wanted women to become pious housewives, Protestants encouraged the education of girls to literacy in the vernacular, with the expectation that they would thereafter model their lives on the Bible. During their studies, however, women found biblical passages which suggested that they were equal to men in the presence of God. Education also gave some women a role as independent authors in the Reformation. From a modern perspective, these may seem like small advances, but they were significant, if indirect, steps in the direction of the emancipation of women.

---

[3]*Luther's Works, Vol. 54: Table Talk*, ed. and trans. by Theodore G. Tappert (Philadelphia: Fortress Press, 1967), p. 161.

[4]*Letters of John Calvin*, Vol. 2, trans. by J. Bonnet (Edinburgh: T. Constable, 1858), p. 216.

A German Mother Advises Her Fifteen-Year-Old Son (1578)

Although only fourteen miles away from his Nuremberg home, Friederich Behaim was fifteen and on his own for the first time at the Altdorf Academy, where he would spend the next three years of his life. As there was daily traffic back and forth, mother and son could correspond regularly, and Frau Behaim could give her son needed advice and articles of clothing.

❖ *What is the mother most concerned about? What do her concerns suggest about life in the sixteenth century? Does she appear to be more strict and demanding of her son than a modern mother would be? Is the son clueless, or skillfully manipulating the mother?*

Dear son Friederich...You write that you have been unable to get by on the money [I gave you]. I will let it pass this quarter, but see that you manage on it in the future. Enclosed is another gulden.

As for your clothes, I do not have Martin [a servant] here with me now (we are quarreling), but he has begun to work on your clothes. He has made stockings for your leather holiday trousers, which I am sending you with this letter. Since your everyday trousers are so bad, wear these for now until a new pair of woolen ones can be made and sent to you, which I will do as soon as I can. Send me your old trousers in the sack I sent you the pitcher in. As for the smock that you think should be lined [for the winter], I worry that the skirt may be too short and will not keep you warm. You can certainly wear it for another summer if it is not too small for you then and the weather not too warm. Just keep it clean and brushed. I will have a new coat made for you at the earliest.

You also write about [unhappiness with] your food. You must be patient for a while. You may not at the outset lodge a complaint against [your master], and especially while you are sitting at his table. [Only] he may speak out who eats his food and is also an authority in the house. So it would be better if the Inspector, who is there for a reason, reports it to him.

Will you once tell me who your table companions are! Also, let me know by All Saints what you have spent on beer and what you owe the tailor, so I may know how much to send you for the quarter.

As for your [sore] throat, there is nothing you can take for it but warm mead. Gargle often with it and keep your head warm. Put a muffler or scarf around your neck and wear your night coat when you are in your room. Avoid cold drinks and sit perhaps for a while by the fire. And do not forget to be bled on time [people then bled themselves once or twice a year as a health measure]...When you need paper, let me know....

I am sending some cleaning flakes for your leather pants. After you have worn them three times, put some on the knees...I will have your old coat patched and send it to you with the next carter [so that you can wear it] until the new one is made. Send me the two sacks with the next carter. You will find the [aforementioned] gulden in the trouser foot tied with a string.

Nothing more for now. God bless. 14 October, 1578.

Mrs. Paul Behaim

From *Three Behaim Boys: Growing Up in Early Modern Germany: A Chronicle of Their Lives*, ed. and trans. by Steven Ozment, pp. 107–108. Copyright © 1990 Yale University Press. Reprinted by permission of Yale University Press.

Family Life in Early Modern Europe

Changes in the timing and duration of marriage, in family size, and in infant and child care suggest that family life was under a variety of social and economic pressures in the sixteenth and seventeenth centuries. The Reformation was a factor in these changes, but not the only or even the major one.

A family has a certain force and logic of its own, regardless of the time and place in which it exists. The routine of family life conspires with basic instincts to establish characteristic patterns of behavior, reinforcing natural feelings and building expectations among family members. Time, place, and culture, however, are important. A person raised in a twelfth-century family would be different from one raised in a twentieth-century family, and growing up in Europe is not the same as growing up in China. But the differences do not lie in the ability of husbands and wives to love one another or of parents to make sacrifices for their children. They lie, rather, in the ways different cultures and religions infuse family life with values and influence the behavior of family members.

Later Marriages •

Between 1500 and 1800, men and women in western Europe and England married at later ages than they had in previous centuries. Men tended to be in their mid- to late twenties rather than in their late teens and early twenties, and women in their early to mid-twenties rather than in their teens. The canonical, or church-sanctioned, age for marriage remained fourteen for men and twelve for women, and engagements might occur at these young ages, especially among royalty and nobility. As it had done throughout the high and late Middle Ages, the church also recognized as valid free, private exchanges of vows between a man and a woman at these minimal ages. However, after the Reformation, which condemned such clandestine unions, the church increasingly required both parental agreement and public vows in church before a marriage could be recognized as fully licit—procedures it had always actually preferred.

Late marriage in the West reflected the difficulty couples had supporting themselves independently. The difficulty arose because of the population growth that occurred during the late fifteenth and early sixteenth centuries, when western Europe recovered much of the population loss incurred during the Great Plague. Larger families meant more heirs and hence a greater division of resources. In Germanic and Scandinavian countries, the custom of fair sharing of inheritance among all male children worked to delay marriages, for divided inheritances often meant small incomes for the recipients. It simply took the average couple a longer time than previously to prepare themselves materially for marriage. In the sixteenth century one in five women never married, and these, combined with the estimated 15 percent who were unmarried widows, constituted a sizable unmarried female population.

A later marriage meant a marriage of shorter duration, since couples who married in their thirties would not spend as much time together as couples who married in their twenties. Such marriages also contributed to more frequent remarriage for men because women who bore children for the first time at advanced ages had higher mortality rates than younger mothers. Moreover, as growing church condemnation and the rapid growth of orphanages and foundling homes between 1600 and 1800 confirm, delayed marriage increased premarital sex and raised the number of illegitimate children.

Arranged Marriages

Marriage tended to be "arranged" in the sense that the parents customarily met and discussed the terms of the marriage before the prospective bride and bridgegroom became party to the discussions. But the wealth and social standing of the bride and the bridegroom were not the only things condsidered when parents arrange a marriage. By the fifteenth century it was not unusual for the two involved people to have known each other in advance and even to have had some prior relationship. Also, emotional feeling for one another was increasingly respected by parents. Parents did not force total strangers to live together, and children had a legal right to protest and resist an unwanted marriage. A forced marriage was by definition invalid, and parents understood that unwanted marriages could fail. The best marriage was one desired by both parties and supported by their families.

Family Size

The western European family was conjugal, or nuclear; that is, it consisted of a father and a mother and two to four children who survived into adulthood. This nuclear family lived with a larger household, consisting of in-laws, servants, laborers, and boarders. The average husband and wife had seven or eight children—a birth about every two years. Of these, however, an estimated one third died by age five, and one half by their teens. Rare is the family, at any social level, that did not experience infant mortality and child death.

Birth Control

Artificial birth control has existed since antiquity. The ancient Egyptians used alligator dung and other acidic sperm killers, and sponges were also popular. In the West, the church's condemnation of *coitus interruptus* (male withdrawal before ejaculation) during the thirteenth and fourteenth centuries suggests that a contraceptive mentality—that is, a conscious and regular effort at birth control—may have been developing at this time. But early birth control measures, when applied, were not very effective, and for both historical and moral reasons the church firmly opposed them. During the eleventh century it suppressed an extreme ascetic sect, the Cathars, whom it accused of practicing birth control. The church also opposed (and still opposes) contraception on moral grounds. According to Saint Thomas Aquinas, a moral act must always aid and abet, never frustrate, the natural end of the being or thing in question, and he believed that the natural end of sex could be only the birth of children and their godly rearing within the bounds of holy matrimony and the community of the church.

Wet Nursing

The church allied with the physicians of early modern Europe on another intimate family matter: the condemnation of women who hired nurses to suckle their newborn children, sometimes for as long as a year and a half. The practice was popular among upper-class women, who looked on it as a symbol of their high rank. Wet nurses were women who had recently had a baby or were suckling a child of their own, and who, for a fee, agreed also to suckle another child. The practice appears to have increased the risk of infant mortality, exposing infants to a strange and shared milk supply from women who were usually not as healthy as the infants' own mothers and who often lived under less sanitary conditions. But nursing an infant was a chore some upper-class women found distasteful, and their husbands also preferred that they not do it. Among women, vanity and convenience appear to have been motives for turning to wet nurses. For husbands, more was at stake in the practice. Because the church forbade sexual intercourse while a women was lactating, and sexual intercourse was also believed to spoil a lactating woman's milk (pregnancy, of course, eventually ended her milk supply), a nursing wife often became a reluctant lover. In addition, nursing had a contraceptive effect (about 75 percent effective). Some women prolonged nursing their children precisely to delay a new pregnancy, and some husbands understood and cooperated in this form of family planning. For other husbands, however, especially noblemen and royalty who desired an abundance of male heirs, nursing seemed to rob them of offspring and to jeopardize the patrimony; hence, their support of wet nursing.

Loving Families?

The traditional western European family had features that may seem cold and unloving. When children were between the ages of eight and thirteen, parents routinely sent them out of their homes into apprenticeships, off to school, or into employment in the homes and businesses of relatives, friends, and even strangers. In addition, the emotional ties between spouses seem to have been a tenuous as those between parents and children. Widowers and widows often married again within a few months of their spouses' deaths, and marriages with extreme disparity in age between partners also suggest limited affection.

Portrait of two children from the Thenn family. Frankfurt, Stadelsch. Kunstinst

In response to modern-day criticism, an early modern parent would surely have asked, "What greater love can parents have for their children than to equip them to make their way vocationally in the world?" An apprenticed child was a self-supporting child, and hence a child with a future. Considering primitive living conditions, contemporaries could also appreciate the purely utilitarian and humane side of marriage and understand when widowers and widows quickly married again. On the other hand, marriages with extreme disparity in age were no more the norm in early modern Europe than the practice of wet nursing, and they received just as much criticism and ridicule.

Literary Imagination in Transition

Alongside the political and cultural changes brought about by the new religious systems of the Reformation (Lutheranism, Calvinism, and Puritanism) and Catholic reform, medieval outlooks and religious values continued into the seventeenth century. Major literary figures of the post-Reformation period had elements of both the old and the new in their own new transitional works. Two who stand out are Miguel de Cervantes Saavedra (1547–1616), writing in still deeply Catholic Spain, and William Shakespeare (1564–1616), who wrote in newly Anglican England.

Miguel de Cervantes Saavedra: Rejection of Idealism

Spanish literature of the sixteenth and seventeenth centuries reflects the peculiar religious and political history of Spain in this period. Traditional Catholic teaching was a major influence on all aspects of Spanish life. Since the joint reign of Ferdinand and Isabella (1479–1504), the church had received the unqualified support of the reigning political power. Although there was religious reform in Spain, and genuine Protestant groups were persecuted for "Lutheranism," a Protestant Reformation never occurred there, thanks largely to the entrenched power of the church and the Inquisition.

A second influence on Spanish literature was the aggressive piety of Spanish rulers. Their intertwining of Catholic piety and political power underlay a third influence: preoccupation with medieval chivalric virtues, in particular, questions of honor and loyalty. The novels and plays of the period almost invariably focus on a special test of character, bordering on the heroic, that

threatens honor and reputation. In this regard, Spanish literature remained more Catholic and medieval than that of England and France, where major Protestant movements had occurred. Two of the most important Spanish writers of this period became priests (Lope de Vega and Pedro Calderón de la Barca). The one generally acknowledged to be the greatest Spanish writer of all time, Cervantes, was preoccupied in his work with the strengths and weaknesses of traditional religious idealism.

Cervantes (1547–1616) had only a smattering of formal education. He educated himself by wide reading in popular literature and immersion in the "school of life." As a young man, he worked in Rome for a Spanish cardinal. As a soldier, he was decorated for gallantry in the Battle of Lepanto (1571). He also spent five years as a slave in Algiers after his ship was pirated in 1575. Later, while working as a tax collector, he was imprisoned several times for padding his accounts, and it was in prison that he began, in 1603, to write his most famous work, *Don Quixote*.

Miguel de Cervantes Saavedra (1547–1616), the author of Don Quixote, *considered by many to be Spain's greatest writer.* Art Resource, N.Y.

The first part of *Don Quixote* appeared in 1605. The intent of this work seems to have been to satirize the chivalric romances then popular in Spain. But Cervantes could not conceal his deep affection for the character he created as an object of ridicule. The work is satire only on the surface and has remained as much an object of study by philosophers and theologians as by students of Spanish literature. Cervantes presented Don Quixote as a none-too-stable middle-aged man. Driven mad by reading too many chivalric romances, he had come to believe he was an aspiring knight who had to prove his worthiness by brave deeds. To this end, he donned a rusty suit of armor and chose for his inspiration a quite unworthy peasant girl (Dulcinea), whom he fancied to be a noble lady to whom he could, with honor, dedicate his life.

Don Quixote's foil—Sancho Panza, a clever, worldly-wise peasant who serves as Quixote's squire—watches with bemused skepticism as his lord does battle with a windmill (which he has mistaken for a dragon) and repeatedly makes a fool of himself as he gallops across the countryside. The story ends tragically with Don Quixote's humiliating defeat by a well-meaning friend who, disguised as a knight, bests Quixote in combat and forces him to renounce his quest for knighthood. The humiliated Don Quixote does not, however, come to his senses as a result. He returns sadly to his village to die a shamed and brokenhearted old man.

Throughout the novel, Cervantes juxtaposes the down-to-earth realism of Sancho Panza with the old-fashioned religious idealism of Don Quixote. The reader perceives that Cervantes admired the one as much as the other and meant to portray both as representing attitudes necessary for a happy life.

William Shakespeare: Dramatist of the Age

There is much less factual knowledge about Shakespeare (1564–1616) than one would expect of the greatest playwright in the English language. He married at the early age of eighteen, in 1582, and he and his wife, Anne Hathaway, were the parents of three children (including twins) by 1585. He apparently worked as a schoolteacher for a time and in this capacity gained his broad knowledge of Renaissance learning and literature. His own reading and enthusiasm for the learning of his day are manifest in the many literary allusions that appear in his plays.

Shakespeare lived the life of a country gentleman. There is none of the Puritan distress over worldliness in his work. He took the new commercialism and the bawdy pleasures of the Elizabethan Age in stride and with amusement. He was a radical neither in politics nor religion. The few allusions in his works to the Puritans seem more critical than complimentary.

That Shakespeare was interested in politics is apparent from his historical plays and the references to contemporary political events that fill all his plays. He viewed government through the character of the individual ruler, whether Richard III or Elizabeth Tudor, not in terms of ideal systems or social goals. By modern standards, he was a political conservative, accepting the social rankings and the power structure of his day and demonstrating unquestioned patriotism.

Shakespeare knew the theater as one who participated in every phase of its life—as a playwright, an actor, and part owner of a theater. He was a member and principal writer of a famous company of actors known as the King's Men. Between 1590 and 1610, many of his plays were performed at court, where he moved with comfort and received both Queen Elizabeth's and King James's enthusiastic patronage.

Elizabethan drama was already a distinctive form when Shakespeare began writing. Unlike French drama of the seventeenth century, which was dominated by classical models, English drama developed in the sixteenth and seventeenth centuries as a blending of many forms: classical comedies and tragedies, medieval morality plays, and contemporary Italian short stories.

Two contemporaries, Thomas Kyd and Christopher Marlowe, influenced Shakespeare's tragedies. Kyd (1558–1594) wrote the first dramatic version of Hamlet. The tragedies of Marlowe (1564–1593) set a model for character, poetry, and style that only Shakespeare among the English playwrights of the period surpassed. Shakespeare synthesized the best past and current achievements. A keen student of human motivation and passion, he had a unique talent for getting into people's minds.

Shakespeare wrote histories, comedies, and tragedies. *Richard III* (1593), a very early play, stands out among the histories, although the picture it presents of Richard as an unprincipled villain is viewed by some scholars as "Tudor propaganda." Shakespeare's comedies, although not attaining the heights of his tragedies, surpass his history plays in originality.

Shakespeare's tragedies are considered his unique achievement. Four of these were written within a three-year period: *Hamlet* (1603), *Othello* (1604), *King Lear* (1605), and *Macbeth* (1606). The most original of the tragedies, *Romeo and Juliet* (1597), transformed an old popular story into a moving drama of "star-cross'd lovers." Both Romeo and Juliet, denied a marriage by their warring families, die tragic deaths. Romeo, believing Juliet to be dead when she has merely taken a sleeping potion, poisons himself. When Juliet awakes to find Romeo dead, she kills herself with his dagger.

Shakespeare's works struck universal human themes, many of which were deeply rooted in contemporary religious traditions. His plays were immensely popular with both the playgoers and the play readers of Elizabethan England. Still today, the works of no other dramatist from his age are performed in theaters or on film more regularly than his.

In Perspective

During the early Middle Ages, Christendom had been divided into Western and Eastern churches with irreconcilable theological differences. When, in 1517, Martin Luther posted ninety-five theses questioning the selling of indulgences and the traditional sacrament of penance that lay behind them, he created a division within Western Christendom itself—an internal division between Protestants and Catholics.

The Lutheran protest came at a time of political and social discontent with the church. Not only princes and magistrates, but many ordinary people as well, resented traditional clerical rights and privileges. In many instances the clergy were exempted from secular laws and taxes, while remaining powerful landowners whose personal lifestyles were not all that different from those of the laity. Spiritual and secular protest combined to make the Protestant Reformation a successful assault on the old church. In town after town and region after region within Protestant lands, the major institutions and practices of traditional piety were significantly transformed.

It soon became clear, however, that the division would not stop with the Lutherans. Making Scripture the only arbiter in religion had opened a Pandora's box. People proved to have very different ideas about what Scripture taught. Indeed, there seemed to be as many points of view as there were readers. Rapidly, the Reformation created Lutheran, Zwinglian, Anabaptist, Spiritualist, Calvinist, and Anglican versions of biblical religion—a splintering of Protestantism that has endured until today.

Catholics had been pursuing reform before the Reformation broke out in Germany, although without papal enthusiasm and certainly not along clear Protestant lines. When major reforms finally came in the Catholic Church around the mid-sixteenth century, they were doctrinally reactionary, but administratively and spiritually flexible. The church enforced strict obedience and conformity to its teaching, but it also provided the laity with a better educated and disciplined clergy. For laity who wanted a deeper and more individual piety, experimentation with proven spiritual practices was now

permitted. By century's end, such measures had successfully countered, and in some areas even spectacularly reversed, Protestant gains.

After the Reformation, pluralism steadily became a fact of Western religious life. It did so at first only by sheer force, since no one religious body was then prepared to concede the validity of alternative Christian beliefs and practices. During the sixteenth and seventeenth centuries, only those groups that fought doggedly for their faith gained the right to practice it freely. Despite these struggles, religious pluralism endured. Never again would there be only a Catholic Christian Church in Europe.

REVIEW QUESTIONS

1. What were the main problems of the church that contributed to the Protestant Reformation? Why was the church unable to suppress dissent as it had earlier?

2. What were the basic similarities and differences between the ideas of Luther and Zwingli? Between Luther and Calvin? Did the differences tend to split the Protestant ranks and thereby lessen the effectiveness of the movement?

3. Why did the Reformation begin in Germany? What political factors contributed to the success of the Reformation there as opposed to France or Italy?

4. What was the Catholic reformation, and what principal decisions and changes were instituted by the Council of Trent? Was the Protestant Reformation a healthy movement for the Catholic Church?

5. Why did Henry VIII finally break with the Catholic Church? Was the "new" religion he established really Protestant? What problems did his successors face as a result of Henry's move?

6. What impact did the Reformation have on women in the sixteenth and seventeenth centuries? What new factors and pressures affected relations between men and women, family size, and child care during this period?

SUGGESTED READINGS

Harold Bloom, *Shakespeare: The Invention of the Human* (1998). A modern master's complete analysis of the greatest writer in the English language.

W. Bouwsma, *John Calvin: A Sixteenth Century Portrait* (1988). Interpretation of Calvin against background of Renaissance intellectual history.

J. Delumeau, *Catholicism Between Luther and Voltaire: A New View of the Counter Reformation* (1977). Programmatic essay for a social history of the Counter-Reformation.

A. G. DICKENS, *The English Reformation* (1974). The best one-volume account.

G. DONALDSON, *The Scottish Reformation* (1960). Dependable, comprehensive narrative.

E. DUFFY, *The Stripping of the Altars: Traditional Religion in England, 1400–1580 (1992).* Strongest of recent arguments that popular piety survived the Reformation in England.

M. DURAN, *Cervantes* (1974). Detailed biography.

G. ELTON, *Reform and Reformation: England, 1509–1558* (1977). Standard political narrative.

H. O. EVENNETT, *The Spirit of the Counter Reformation* (1968). Essay on the continuity of Catholic reform and its independence from the Protestant Reformation.

B. GOTTLIEB, *The Family in the Western World* (1992). Accessible overview with up-to-date annotated bibliographies.

SCOTT HENDRIX, "Masculinity and Patriarchy in Reformation Germany," *Journal of the History of Ideas 56* (1995): 177–193. Caring males in the sixteenth century.

R. HOULBROOKE, *English Family Life, 1450–1716. An Anthology from Diaries* (1988). A rich collection of documents illustrating family relationships.

R. HOULBROOKE, *Death, Religion, and Family in England, 1480-1758)* (1998). How death was met in the early modern English family.

J. L. IRWIN (ed.), *Womanhood in Radical Protestantism, 1525–1675* (1979). Sources illustrating images of women in sectarian Protestant thought.

H. JEDIN, *A History of the Council of Trent,* vols. 1 and 2 (1957–1961). Comprehensive, detailed, and authoritative.

W. K. JORDAN, *Edward VI: The Young King* (1968). The basic biography.

A. MACFARLANE, *The Family Life of Ralph Josselin: A Seventeenth Century Clergyman* (1970). A model study of Puritan family life!

SHERRIN MARSHALL, ed., *Women in Reformation and Counter Reformation Europe: Private and Public Worlds* (1989). Lucid and authoritative presentations.

J. F. MCNEILL, *The History and Character of Calvinism* (1954). The most comprehensive account and very readable.

H. A. OBERMAN, *Luther: Man Between God and the Devil* (1989). Perhaps the best account of Luther's life, by a Dutch master.

J. O'MALLEY, *The First Jesuits* (1993). Extremely detailed account of the creation of the Society of Jesus and its original purposes.

S. OZMENT, *The Age of Reform, 1250–1550: An Intellectual and Religious History of Late Medieval and Reformation Europe* (1980). A broad survey of major religious ideas and beliefs.

S. OZMENT, *When Fathers Ruled: Family Life in Reformation Europe* (1983). A survey of sixteenth-century attitudes toward marriage and parenthood.

S. OZMENT, *Three Behaim Boys: Growing Up in Early Modern Germany* (1990). The lives of three boys in their late teens and early adulthood told in their own words.

S. OZMENT, *Flesh and Spirit: Private Life in Early Modern Germany* (1999)

R. R POST, *The Modern Devotion* (1968). Currently the authoritative interpretation.

J. G. RIDLEY, *Thomas Cranmer* (1962). The basic biography.

B. SCRIBNER, *Germany: A New Social and Economic History, 1450–1630* (1996). Collection of comprehensive essays presenting up-to-date research.

Q. SKINNER, *The Foundations of Modern Political Thought II: The Age of Reformation* (1978). A comprehensive survey that treats every political thinker and tract.

D. STARKEY, *The Reign of Henry VIII* (1985). Portrayal of the king as in control of neither his life nor his court.

L. STONE, *The Family, Sex and Marriage in England 1500–1800* (1977). Controversial but in many respects still the reigning view of English family history.

G. STRAUSS (ED. AND TRANS.), *Manifestations of Discontent in Germany on the Eve of the Reformation* (1971). Rich collection of sources of both rural and urban scenes.

G. STRAUSS, *Luther's House of Learning: The Indoctrination of the Young in the German Reformation* (1978). Account of Protestant efforts to rear children in the new faith, stressing the negative side.

MARTIN TREU, *Katherine von Bora* (1995). Short biography of Martin Luther's wife.

E. TROELTSCH, *The Social Teaching of the Christian Churches,* vols. 1 and 2, trans. by O. Wyon (1960). Old, liberal account of the Reformation and its critics, with fondness for the latter.

J. WITTE, JR., *From Sacrament to Contract: Marriage, Religion and Law in the Western Tradition* (1997). Five major legal–religious systems elucidated and compared

F. WENDEL, *Calvin: The Origins and Development of His Religious Thought,* trans. by P. Mairet (1963). The best treatment of Calvin's theology.

G. H. WILLIAMS, *The Radical Reformation* (1962). Broad survey of the varieties of dissent within Protestantism.

H. WUNDER, *He Is the Sun, She Is the Moon: A History of Women in Early Modern Germany* (1998). A model of gender history.

Chapter 12

The massacre of worshiping Protestants at Vassy, France (March 1, 1562), which began the French wars of religion. An engraving by an unidentified seventeenth-century artist. The Granger Collection

The Age of Religious Wars

KEY TOPICS

- The war between Calvinists and Catholics in France
- The Spanish occupation of the Netherlands
- The struggle for supremacy between England and Spain
- The devastation of central Europe during the Thirty Years' War

T*he late sixteenth century and the first half of the seventeenth century are described as the "age of religious wars" because of the bloody opposition of Protestants and Catholics across Europe. Both genuine religious conflict and bitter dynastic rivalries fueled the wars. In France, the Netherlands, England, and Scotland in the second half of the sixteenth century, Calvinists fought Catholic rulers for the right to govern their own territories and to practice their chosen religion openly. In the first half of the seventeenth century, Lutherans, Calvinists, and Catholics marched against one another in central and northern Europe during the Thirty Years' War. By the middle of the seventeenth century, English Puritans had successfully revolted against the Stuart monarchy and the Anglican Church.*

Renewed Religious Struggle

During the first half of the sixteenth century, religious conflict had been confined to central Europe and was primarily a struggle by Lutherans to secure rights and freedoms for themselves. In the second half of the sixteenth century, the focus shifted to western Europe—to France, the Netherlands,

England, and Scotland—and became a struggle by Calvinists for recognition. After the Peace of Augsburg (1555) and, with it, acceptance of the principle that a region's ruler would determine its religion (*cuius regio, eius religio*), Lutheranism became a legal religion in the Holy Roman Empire. The Peace of Augsburg did not, however, extend recognition to non-Lutheran Protestants. Both Catholics and Lutherans scorned Anabaptists and other sectarians as anarchists, and Calvinists were not yet strong enough to demand legal standing.

Outside the empire, the struggle for Protestant religious rights had intensified in most countries by the mid-sixteenth century. After the Council of Trent adjourned in 1563, Catholics began a Jesuit-led international counteroffensive against Protestants. At the time of John Calvin's death in 1564, Geneva had become both a refuge for Europe's persecuted Protestants and an international school for Protestant resistance, producing leaders fully equal to the new Catholic challenge.

Genevan Calvinism and Catholicism as revived by the Council of Trent were two equally dogmatic, aggressive, and irreconcilable church systems. Calvinists may have looked like "new papists" to critics when they dominated cities like Geneva. Yet when, as minorities, they found their civil and religious rights denied, they became true firebrands and revolutionaries. Calvinism adopted a presbyterian organization that magnified regional and local religious authority. Boards of presbyters, or elders, representing the many individual congregations of Calvinists, directly shaped the policy of the church at large.

By contrast, the Counter-Reformation sponsored a centralized episcopal church system, hierarchically arranged from pope to parish priest, that stressed absolute obedience to the person at the top. The high clergy—the pope and his bishops—not the synods of local churches, ruled supreme. Calvinism proved attractive to proponents of political decentralization who opposed totalitarian rulers, whereas Catholicism remained congenial to proponents of absolute monarchy determined to maintain, in the words of Louis XIV, "one king, one church, one law."

The opposition between the two religions can be seen even in the art and architecture that each came to embrace. The Catholic Counter-Reformation found the baroque style congenial. A successor to mannerism, baroque art is a grandiose, three-dimensional display of life and energy. Great baroque artists like Peter Paul Rubens (1571–1640) and Gianlorenzo Bernini (1598–1680) were Catholics. Protestants by contrast opted for a simpler and more restrained art and architecture, as can be seen in the English churches of Christopher Wren (1632–1723) and the gentle, searching portraits of the Dutch Mennonite, Rembrandt van Rijn (1606–1669). (See "Art & the West.")

As religious wars engulfed Europe, the intellectuals perceived the wisdom of religious pluralism and toleration more quickly than did the politicians. A new skepticism, relativism, and individualism in religion became respectable in the sixteenth and seventeenth centuries. (See Chapter 14.) Sebastian Castellio's (1515–1563) pithy censure of John Calvin for his role in the execution of the anti-Trinitarian Michael Servetus summarized a growing sentiment: "To kill a man is not to defend a doctrine, but to kill a man."[1] The French essayist Michel de Montaigne (1533–1592) asked in scorn of the dogmatic mind, "What do I know?" And the Lutheran Valentin Weigel (1533–1588), surveying a half century of religious strife in Germany, advised people to look within themselves for religious truth and no longer to churches and creeds.

Such skeptical views gained currency in larger political circles only at the cost of painful experience. Religious strife and civil war were best held in check where rulers tended to subordinate theological doctrine to political unity, urging tolerance, moderation, and compromise—even indifference—in religious matters. Rulers of this kind came to be known as *politiques*, and the most successful among them was Elizabeth I of England. By contrast, such rulers as Mary I of England, Philip II of Spain, and Oliver Cromwell, who took their religion with the utmost seriousness and refused every compromise, did not in the long run achieve their political goals.

As we shall see, the wars of religion were both internal national conflicts and truly international wars. Catholic and Protestant subjects struggled against one another for control of the crown of France, the Netherlands, and England. The Catholic governments of France and Spain conspired and finally sent armies against Protestant regimes in England and the Netherlands. The outbreak of the Thirty Years' War in 1618 made the international dimension of the religious conflict especially clear; before it ended in 1648, the war drew every major European nation directly or indirectly into its deadly net.

The French Wars of Religion (1562–1598)

Anti-Protestant Measures and the Struggle for Political Power

French Protestants are known as Huguenots, a term derived from Besançon Hugues, the leader of Geneva's political revolt against the House of Savoy in the 1520s, a prelude to that city's Calvinist

---

[1]*Contra libellum Calvini* (N.P., 1562), p. E2a.

Reformation. Huguenots were under surveillance in France already in the early 1520s when Lutheran writings and doctrines began to circulate in Paris. The capture of the French king Francis I by the forces of Emperor Charles V at the Battle of Pavia in 1525 provided a motive for the first wave of Protestant persecution in France. The French government hoped thereby to pacify their Habsburg conqueror, a fierce opponent of German Protestants, and to win their king's swift release.

A second major crackdown came a decade later. When Protestants plastered Paris and other cities with anti-Catholic placards on October 18, 1534, mass arrests of suspected Protestants followed. The government retaliation drove John Calvin and other members of the French reform party into exile. In 1540 the Edict of Fontainebleau subjected French Protestants to the Inquisition. Henry II (r. 1547–1559) established new measures against Protestants in the Edict of Chateaubriand in 1551. Save for a few brief interludes, the French monarchy remained a staunch foe of the Protestants until the ascension to the throne of Henry of Navarre in 1589.

The Habsburg–Valois wars (see Chapter 11) had ended with the Treaty of Cateau-Cambrésis in 1559, after which Europe experienced a moment of peace. But the same year marked the beginning of internal French conflict and a shift of the European balance of power away from France to Spain. The shift began with an accident. During a tournament held to celebrate the marriage of his thirteen-year-old daughter to Philip II, the son of Charles V and heir to the Spanish Habsburg lands, the French king, Henry II, was mortally wounded when a lance pierced his visor. This unforeseen event brought to the throne his sickly fifteen-year-old son, Francis II, under the regency of the queen mother, Catherine de Médicis. With the monarchy so weakened by Henry's death, three powerful families saw their chance to control France and began to compete for the young king's ear: the Bourbons, whose power lay in the south and west; the Montmorency-Chatillons, who controlled the center of France; and the Guises, who were dominant in eastern France.

The Guises were by far the strongest and had little trouble establishing firm control over the young king. Francis, duke of Guise, had been Henry II's general, and his brothers, Charles and Louis, were cardinals of the church. Mary Stuart, Queen of Scots and wife of Francis II, was their niece. Throughout the latter half of the sixteenth century, the name "Guise" remained interchangeable with militant, reactionary Catholicism.

The Bourbon and Montmorency-Chatillon families, in contrast, developed strong Huguenot sympathies, largely for political reasons. The Bourbon Louis I, prince of Condé (d. 1569), and the Montmorency-Chatillon Admiral Gaspard de Coligny (1519–1572) became the political leaders of the French Protestant resistance. They collaborated early in an abortive plot to kidnap Francis II from his Guise advisers in the Conspiracy of Amboise in 1560. This conspiracy was strongly condemned by John Calvin, who considered such tactics a disgrace to the Reformation.

Appeal of Calvinism

Often for quite different reasons, ambitious aristocrats and discontented townspeople joined Calvinist churches in opposition to the Guise-dominated French monarchy. In 1561 more than 2,000 Huguenot congregations existed throughout France. Yet Huguenots were a majority of the population in only two regions: Dauphiné and Languedoc. Although they made up only about one-fifteenth of the population, Huguenots were in important geographic areas and were heavily represented among the more powerful segments of French society. More than two-fifths of the French aristocracy became Huguenots. Many apparently hoped to establish within France a principle of territorial sovereignty akin to that secured within the Holy Roman Empire by the Peace of Augsburg. In this way, Calvinism indirectly served the forces of political decentralization.

John Calvin and Theodore Beza consciously sought to advance their cause by currying favor with powerful aristocrats. Beza converted Jeanne d'Albert, the mother of the future Henry IV. The prince of Condé was apparently converted in 1558 under the influence of his Calvinist wife. For many aristocrats—Condé probably among them—Calvinist religious convictions were attractive primarily as aids to long-sought political goals.

The military organization of Condé and Coligny progressively merged with the religious organization of the French Huguenot churches, creating a potent combination that benefited both political and religious dissidents. Calvinism gave political resistance justification and inspiration, and the forces of political resistance made Calvinism a viable religious alternative in Catholic France. Each side had much to gain from the other. The confluence of secular and religious motives, although beneficial to aristocratic resistance and the Calvinist religion alike, tended to cast suspicion on the religious appeal of Calvinism. Clearly, religious conviction was neither the only nor always the main reason for becoming a Calvinist in France in the second half of the sixteenth century.

Warring Architectural Styles: Baroque vs. Plain Churches

Art and architecture portrayed the beliefs of different religious systems as effectively as did the latter's creeds and laws. The Swiss, French, and English churches that grew out of the Reformed Protestant traditions of Ulrich Zwingli and John Calvin together with the non-conformist sectarian Protestants (Anabaptists, Puritans, Quakers) opposed both Catholic and Lutheran retention of traditional church art and architecture and of music in churches as a serious distraction from the Word of God. Although a gifted and much-praised musician, Zwingli could find no biblical basis for any ornamentation in a Christian service of worship. In this, he had the support not only of the sectarians who condemned the more flexible Luther, but also of the Humanist Erasmus. In Zwinglian, Calvinist, and sectarian churches across Europe, the walls were stripped bare, and the only music heard was a congregational recitation of the Psalms.

In Austria, southern Germany, and elsewhere, the Catholic Counter Reformation, led by the Jesuits, embraced the exuberant baroque style of art and architecture then popular in Italy. This style permitted the Catholic faith to be displayed grandly in three-dimensions, its impact magnified by choruses and musical instruments, an artistic and musical feast. The intent was to overwhelm the worshippers' senses and move them emotionally, leaving them filled with awe and wonder at the power and glory of their Church. The new style proved effective in reassuring the doubting faithful and bringing the many who had turned Protestant back into Catholic churches.

Baroque style was also a boon to the building trades and the careers of painters, sculpters, and musicians. Great baroque artists like Peter Paul Rubens (1571–1640) and Gianlorenzo Bernini (1598–1680) were Catholics. But Protestants also had their great plain church architects, such as the Englishman Christopher Wren (1632–1723), and popular artists, such as the Dutch Mennonite Rembrandt van Rijn (1606–1669), whose works were distinguished by their simplicity and restraint.

Interior of "Asamkirche," Asam Cosmas Damian (1686–1739). Saint Nepomit Church in Munich designed by the brothers Cosmas Damian and Egid Quirin Asam in 1733. The church stands next to the house the brothers built for themselves. Asamkirche (St. Johann-Nepomuk). Erich Lessing/Art Resource, N.Y.

Temple de Lyon. Bibliotheque Publique et Universitaire, Geneve

This eighteenth-century church, in Munich, is in the baroque style congenial to the Catholic Counter-Reformation. The interior explodes with energy and is filled with sculpture, paintings, and woodwork that dazzle the eyes. The intent was to give worshippers a keen sense of membership in the Church militant and move them to self-transcendence.

In stark contrast to the baroque style, this seventeenth-century Calvinist church in Lyon has no interior decoration to distract the worshipper from the Word of God. Here, the intent was to create an atmosphere of quiet introspection and reflection on one's own spiritual life in the presence of God's Word. For the Calvinists at worship in Lyon, the preacher is absolutely at center stage. There are no decorations, paintings, statuary, or elaborate stained glass. In Zwinglian churches the walls were even white-washed and no music or singing was permitted. Such simplicity contrasts dramatically with the Baroque style of contemporary Catholic churches.

393

Catherine de Médicis and the Guises

Following Francis II's death in 1560, Catherine de Médicis continued as regent for her minor son, Charles IX (r. 1560–1574). At a colloquy in Poissy, she tried unsuccessfully to reconcile the Protestant and Catholic factions. Fearing the power and guile of the Guises, Catherine, whose first concern was always to preserve the monarchy, sought allies among the Protestants. In 1562, after conversations with Beza and Coligny, she issued the January Edict, a measure that granted Protestants freedom to worship publicly outside towns—although only privately within them—and to hold synods. In March, this royal toleration came to an abrupt end when the duke of Guise surprised a Protestant congregation at Vassy in Champagne and proceeded to massacre several scores of worshipers. That event marked the beginning of the French wars of religion (March 1562).

Had Condé and the Huguenot armies rushed immediately to the queen's side after this attack, Protestants might well have secured an alliance with the crown. The queen mother's fear of Guise power was great at this time. But the hesitation of the Protestant leaders, due primarily to indecision on the part of Condé, placed the young king and the queen mother, against their deepest wishes, in firm Guise control. Cooperation with the Guises became the only alternative to capitulation to the Protestants.

Catherine de Médicis (1519–1589) exercised power in France during the reigns of her three sons Francis II (r. 1559–1560), Charles IX (r. 1560–1574), and Henry III (r. 1574–1589). Liaison Agency, Inc.

THE PEACE OF SAINT-GERMAIN-EN-LAYE During the first French war of religion, fought between April 1562 and March 1563, the duke of Guise was assassinated. It is a measure of the international character of the struggle in France that troops from Hesse and the Palatinate fought alongside the Huguenots. A brief resumption of hostilities in 1567–1568 was followed by the bloodiest of all the conflicts, between September 1568 and August 1570. In this period, Condé was killed and Huguenot leadership passed to Coligny. This was actually a blessing in disguise for the Protestants, because Coligny was far the better military strategist. In the Peace of Saint-Germain-en-Laye (1570), which ended the third war, the crown, acknowledging the power of the Protestant nobility, granted the Huguenots religious freedoms within their territories and the right to fortify their cities.

Perpetually caught between fanatical Huguenot and Guise extremes, Queen Catherine had always sought to balance one side against the other. Like the Guises, she wanted a Catholic France; she did not, however, desire a Guise-dominated monarchy. After the Peace of Saint-Germain-en-Laye the crown tilted manifestly toward the Bourbon faction and the Huguenots, and Coligny became Charles IX's most trusted adviser. Unknown to the king, Catherine began to plot with the

Guises against the ascendant Protestants. As she had earlier sought Protestant support when Guise power threatened to subdue the monarchy, she now sought Guise support as Protestant influence grew.

There was reason for Catherine to fear Coligny's hold on the king. Louis of Nassau, the leader of Protestant resistance to Philip II in the Netherlands, had gained Coligny's ear. Coligny used his position of influence to win the king of France over to a planned French invasion of the Netherlands in support of the Dutch Protestants. Such a course of action would have placed France squarely on a collision course with mighty Spain. Catherine recognized far better than her son that France stood little chance in such a contest. She and her advisers had been much sobered in this regard by news of the stunning Spanish victory over the Turks at Lepanto in October 1571 (to be discussed later).

THE SAINT BARTHOLOMEW'S DAY MASSACRE When Catherine lent her support to the infamous Saint Bartholomew's Day Massacre of Protestants, she did so out of a far less reasoned judgment. Her decision appears to have been made in a state of near panic. On August 22, 1572, four days after the Huguenot

Henry of Navarre had married the king's sister, Marguerite of Valois—still another sign of growing Protestant power—Coligny was struck down, although not killed, by an assassin's bullet. Catherine had apparently been party to this Guise plot to eliminate Coligny. After its failure, she feared both the king's reaction to her complicity with the Guises and the Huguenot response under a recovered Coligny. Catherine convinced Charles that a Huguenot coup was afoot, inspired by Coligny, and that only the swift execution of Protestant leaders could save the crown from a Protestant attack on Paris.

On Saint Bartholomew's Day, August 24, 1572, Coligny and 3,000 fellow Huguenots were butchered in Paris. Within three days an estimated 20,000 Huguenots were executed in coordinated attacks throughout France. It is a date that has ever since lived in infamy for Protestants.

Pope Gregory XIII and Philip II of Spain reportedly greeted the news of the Protestant massacre with special religious celebrations. Philip especially had good reason to rejoice. By throwing France into civil war, the massacre ended for the moment any planned French opposition to his efforts to subdue his rebellious subjects in the Netherlands. But the massacre of thousands of Protestants also gave the discerning Catholic world cause for new alarm. The event changed the nature of the struggle between Protestants and Catholics both within and beyond the borders of France. It was thereafter no longer an internal contest between Guise and Bourbon factions for French political influence, nor was it simply a Huguenot campaign to win basic religious freedoms. Henceforth, in Protestant eyes, it became an international struggle to the death for sheer survival against an adversary whose cruelty now justified any means of resistance.

PROTESTANT RESISTANCE THEORY   Only as Protestants faced suppression and sure defeat did they begin to sanction active political resistance. At first, they tried to practice the biblical precept of obedient subjection to worldly authority (Romans 13:1). Luther had only grudgingly approved resistance to the emperor after the Diet of Augsburg in 1530. In 1550 Lutherans in Magdeburg had published a highly influential defense of the right of lower authorities to oppose the emperor's order that all Lutherans return to the Catholic fold.

Calvin, who never faced the specter of total political defeat after his return to Geneva in September 1540, had always condemned willful disobedience and rebellion against lawfully constituted governments as un-Christian. But he also taught that lower magistrates, as part of the lawfully constituted government, had the right and duty to oppose tyrannical higher authority.

The exiled Scottish reformer John Knox, who had seen his cause crushed by Mary of Guise, the Regent of Scotland, and Mary I of England, laid the groundwork for later Calvinist resistance. In his famous *First Blast of the Trumpet Against the Terrible Regiment of Women* (1558), he declared that the removal of a heathen tyrant was not only permissible, but a Christian duty. He had the Catholic queen of England in mind.

After the great massacre of French Protestants on Saint Bartholomew's Day, 1572, Calvinists everywhere came to appreciate the need for an active defense of their religious rights. Classical Huguenot theories of resistance appeared in three major works of the 1570s. The first was the *Franco–Gallia* of François Hotman (1573), a humanist argument that the representative Estates General of France historically held higher authority than the French king. The second was Theodore Beza's *On the Right of Magistrates over Their Subjects* (1574), which, going beyond Calvin's views, justified the correction and even the overthrow of tyrannical rulers by lower authorities. (See "Theodore Beza Defends the Right to Resist Tyranny.") Finally, Philippe du Plessis Mornay's *Defense of Liberty Against Tyrants* (1579) admonished princes, nobles, and magistrates beneath the king, as guardians of the rights of the body politic, to take up arms against tyranny in other lands.

The Rise to Power of Henry of Navarre

Henry III (r. 1574–1589) was the last of Henry II's sons to wear the French crown. He found the monarchy wedged between a radical Catholic League, formed in 1576 by Henry of Guise, and vengeful Huguenots. Neither group would have been reluctant to assassinate a ruler whom they considered heretical and a tyrant. Like the queen mother, Henry sought to steer a middle course. In this effort, he received support from a growing body of neutral Catholics and Huguenots, who put the political survival of France above its religious unity. Such *politiques* were prepared to compromise religious creeds as might be required to save the nation.

The Peace of Beaulieu in May 1576 granted the Huguenots almost complete religious and civil freedom. France, however, was not ready then for such sweeping toleration. Within seven months of the Peace, the Catholic League forced Henry to return to the illusory quest for absolute religious unity in France. In October 1577, the king truncated the Peace of Beaulieu and once again circumscribed areas of permitted Huguenot worship. Thereafter, Huguenot and Catholic factions quickly returned to their accustomed anarchical military solutions. The Protestants were led by Henry of Navarre, now heir to the French throne by virtue of his marriage to Margaret of Valois, Henry III's sister.

Theodore Beza Defends the Right to Resist Tyranny

One of the oldest problems in political and social theory has been that of knowing when resistance to repression in matters of conscience is justified. Since Luther's day, Protestant reformers had urged their followers to obey established political authority. After the 1572 Saint Bartholomew's Day Massacre, however, pamphleteers urged Protestants to resist tyrants and persecutors with armed force. In 1574, Theodore Beza pointed out the obligation of rulers to act in the best interests of their subjects and the latter's right to resist them when they did not.

❖ *When does a ruler go too far, according to Beza? To whom may subjects appeal against a tyrant? Does Beza believe that individuals may take the law into their own hands?*

It is apparent that there is a mutual obligation between the king and the officers of a kingdom; that the government of the kingdom is not in the hands of the king in its entirety, but only the sovereign degree; that each of the officers has a share in accord with his degree; and that there are definite conditions on either side. If these conditions are not observed by the inferior officers, it is the part of the sovereign to dismiss and punish them....If the king, hereditary or elective, clearly goes back on the conditions without which he would not have been recognized and acknowledged, can there be any doubt that the lesser magistrates of the kingdom, of the cities, and of the provinces, the administration of which they have received from the sovereignty itself, are free of their oath, at least to the extent that they are entitled to resist flagrant oppression of the realm which they swore to defend and protect according to their office and their particular jurisdiction?...

We must now speak of the third class of subjects, which though admittedly subject to the sovereign in a certain respect, is, in another respect, and in cases of necessity the protector of the rights of the sovereignty itself, and is established to hold the sovereign to his duty, and even, if need be, constrain and punish him....The people is prior to all the magistrates, and does not exist for them, but they for it....Whenever law and equity prevailed, nations neither created nor accepted kings except upon definite conditions. From this it follows that when kings flagrantly violate these terms, those who have the power to give them their authority have no less power to deprive them of it.

From *Constitutionalism and Resistance in the Sixteenth Century: Three Treatises by Hotman, Beza, and Mornay*, trans. and ed. by Julian H. Franklin (New York: Pegasus, 1969), pp. 111–114.

In the mid-1580s the Catholic League, supported by the Spanish, became completely dominant in Paris. In what came to be known as the Day of the Barricades, Henry III attempted to rout the league with a surprise attack in 1588. The effort failed badly, and the king had to flee Paris. Forced by his weakened position into unkingly guerilla tactics, and also emboldened by news of the English victory over the Spanish Armada in 1588, Henry successfully plotted the assassinations of both the duke and the cardinal of Guise. These assassinations sent France reeling once again. Led by still another Guise brother, the Catholic League reacted with a fury that matched the earlier Huguenot response to the Massacre of Saint Bartholomew's Day. The king now had only one course of action: He struck an alliance with the Protestant Henry of Navarre in April 1589.

As the two Henrys prepared to attack the Guise stronghold of Paris, however, a fanatical Jacobin friar stabbed and killed Henry III. Thereupon, the Bourbon Huguenot Henry of Navarre succeeded the childless Valois king to the French throne as Henry IV (r. 1589–1610). Pope Sixtus V and Philip II stood aghast at the sudden prospect of a Protestant France. They had always wanted France to be religiously Catholic and politically weak, and they now acted to achieve that end. Spain rushed troops to support the besieged Catholic League. Philip II apparently even harbored hopes of placing his eldest daughter, Isabella, the granddaughter of Henry II and Catherine de Médicis, on the French throne.

Direct Spanish intervention in the affairs of France seemed only to strengthen Henry IV's grasp on the crown. The French people viewed his right to hereditary succession more seriously than his espoused

Protestant confession. Henry was also widely liked. Notoriously informal in dress and manner—a factor that made him especially popular with the soldiers—Henry also had the wit and charm to neutralize the strongest enemy in a face-to-face confrontation. He came to the throne as a *politique*, long weary with religious strife and fully prepared to place political peace above absolute religious unity. He believed that a royal policy of tolerant Catholicism would be the best way to achieve such peace. On July 25, 1593, he publicly abjured the Protestant faith and embraced the traditional and majority religion of his country. "Paris is worth a mass," he is reported to have said.

It was, in fact, a decision he had made only after a long period of personal agonizing. The Huguenots were understandably horrified by this turnabout, and Pope Clement VIII remained skeptical of Henry's sincerity. But most of the French church and people, having known internal strife too long, rallied to the king's side. By 1596, the Catholic League was dispersed, its ties with Spain were broken, and the wars of religion in France, to all intents, had ground to a close.

The Edict of Nantes

On April 13, 1598, Henry IV's famous Edict of Nantes proclaimed a formal religious settlement. The following month, on May 2, 1598, the Treaty of Vervins ended hostilities between France and Spain.

Henry IV Recognizes Huguenot Religious Freedom

By the Edict of Nantes (April 13, 1598), Henry IV recognized Huguenot religious freedoms and the rights of Protestants to participate in French public institutions. Here are some of its provisions.

❖ *Are Huguenots given equal religious standing with Catholics? Are there limitations on their freedoms?*

We have by this perpetual and irrevocable Edict pronounced, declared, and ordained and we pronounce, declare and ordain:

Art. I. Firstly, that the memory of everything done on both sides from the beginning of the month of March, 1585, until our accession to the Crown and during the other previous troubles, and at the outbreak of them, shall remain extinct and suppressed, as if it were something which had never occurred....

Art. II. We forbid all our subjects, of whatever rank and quality they may be, to renew the memory of these matters, to attack, be hostile to, injure or provoke each other in revenge for the past, whatever may be the reason and pretext...but let them restrain themselves and live peaceably together as brothers, friends, and fellow-citizens....

Art. III. We ordain that the Catholic, Apostolic, and Roman religion shall be restored and reestablished in all places and districts of this our kingdom and the countries under our rule, where its practice has been interrupted....

Art. VI. And we permit those of the so-called Reformed religion to live and dwell in all the towns and districts of this our kingdom and the countries under our rule, without being annoyed, disturbed, molested or constrained to do anything against their conscience, or for this cause to be sought out in their houses and districts where they wish to live, provided that they conduct themselves in other respects to the provisions of our present Edict....

Art. XXI. Books dealing with the matters of the aforesaid so-called Reformed religion shall not be printed and sold publicly, except in the towns and districts where the public exercise of the said religion is allowed....

Art. XXII. We ordain that there shall be no difference or distinction, because of the aforesaid religion, in the reception of students to be instructed in Universities, Colleges, and schools, or of the sick and poor into hospitals, infirmaries, and public charitable institutions....

Art. XXVII. In order to reunite more effectively the wills of our subjects, as is our intention, and to remove all future complaints, we declare that all those who profess or shall profess the aforesaid so-called Reformed religion are capable of holding and exercising all public positions, honours, offices, and duties whatsoever...in the towns of our kingdom...notwithstanding all contrary oaths.

From *Church and State Through the Centuries: A Collection of Historic Documents*, trans. and ed. by S. Z. Ehler and John B. Morrall (New York: Biblo and Tannen, 1967), pp. 185–187. Reprinted by permission of Biblo-Moser Book Publishers.

	Main Events of French Wars of Religion
1559	Treaty of Cateau-Cambrésis ends Habsburg–Valois wars
1559	Francis II succeeds to French throne under regency of his mother, Catherine de Médicis
1560	Conspiracy of Amboise fails
1562	Protestant worshipers massacred at Vassy in Champagne by the duke of Guise
1572	The Saint Bartholomew's Day Massacre leaves thousands of Protestants dead
1589	Assassination of Henry III brings the Huguenot Henry of Navarre to throne as Henry IV
1593	Henry IV embraces Catholicism
1598	Henry IV grants Huguenots religious and civil freedoms in the Edict of Nantes
1610	Henry IV assassinated

In 1591, Henry IV had already assured the Huguenots of at least qualified religious freedoms. The Edict of Nantes made good that promise. It recognized and sanctioned minority religious rights within what was to remain an officially Catholic country. This religious truce—and it was never more than that—granted the Huguenots, who by this time numbered well over one million, freedom of public worship, the right of assembly, admission to public offices and universities, and permission to maintain fortified towns. Most of the new freedoms, however, were to be exercised within their own towns and territories. Concession of the right to fortify their towns reveals the continuing distrust between French Protestants and Catholics. As significant as it was, the edict only transformed a long hot war between irreconcilable enemies into a long cold war. To its critics, it had only created a state within a state. (See "Henry IV Recognizes Huguenot Religious Freedom.")

A Catholic fanatic assassinated Henry IV in May 1610. Although he is best remembered for the Edict of Nantes, Henry IV put in place political and economic policies that were equally important. They laid the foundations for the transformation of France into the absolute state it would become under Cardinal Richelieu and Louis XIV. Ironically, in pursuit of the political and religious unity that had escaped Henry IV, Louis XIV, calling for "one king, one church, one law," would revoke the Edict of Nantes in 1685. (See Chapter 13.) This action would force France and Europe to learn again by bitter experience the hard lessons of the wars of religion. Rare is the politician who learns from the lessons of history rather than repeating its mistakes.

Imperial Spain and the Reign of Philip II (r. 1556–1598)

Pillars of Spanish Power

Until the English defeated the mighty Spanish Armada in 1588, no one person stood larger in the second half of the sixteenth century than Philip II of Spain. Philip was heir to the intensely Catholic and militarily supreme western Habsburg kingdom. The eastern Habsburg lands of Austria, Bohemia, and Hungary had been given over by his father, Charles V, to Philip's uncle, the emperor Ferdinand I. These lands, together with the imperial title, remained in the possession of the Austrian branch of the family.

NEW WORLD RICHES   Populous and wealthy Castile gave Philip a solid home base. The regular arrival in Seville of bullion from the Spanish colonies in the New World provided additional wealth. In the 1540s great silver mines had been opened in Potosí in present-day Bolivia and in Zacatecas in Mexico. These gave Philip the great sums needed to pay his bankers and mercenaries. He nonetheless never managed to erase the debts left by his father or to finance his own foreign adventures fully. He later contributed to the bankruptcy of the Fuggers when, at the end of his life, he defaulted on his enormous debts.

INCREASED POPULATION   The new American wealth brought dramatic social change to the peoples of Europe during the second half of the sixteenth century. As Europe became richer, it was also becoming more populous. In the economically and politically active towns of France, England, and the Netherlands, populations had tripled and quadrupled by the early seventeenth century. Europe's population exceeded 70 million by 1600.

The combination of increased wealth and population triggered inflation. A steady two-percent-a-year rise in prices in much of Europe had serious cumulative effects by midcentury. There were more people than before and greater coinage in circulation, but less food and fewer jobs; wages stagnated while prices doubled and tripled in much of Europe.

This was especially the case in Spain. Because the new wealth was concentrated in the hands of a few, the traditional gap between the "haves"—the propertied, privileged, and educated classes—and the "have-nots" greatly widened. Nowhere did the unprivileged suffer more than in Spain, where the Castilian peasantry, the backbone of Philip II's great empire, became the most heavily taxed people of Europe. Those whose labor contributed most to making possible Spanish hegemony in Europe in the second half of the sixteenth century prospered least from it.

EFFICIENT BUREAUCRACY AND MILITARY A subjugated peasantry and wealth from the New World were not the only pillars of Spanish strength. Philip II shrewdly organized the lesser nobility into a loyal and efficient national bureaucracy. A reclusive man, he managed his kingdom by pen and paper rather than by personal presence. He was also a learned and pious Catholic, although some popes suspected that he used religion as much for political as for devotional purposes. That he was a generous patron of the arts and culture is evident in his unique retreat outside Madrid, the Escorial, a combination palace, church, tomb, and monastery. Philip also knew personal sorrows: His mad and treacherous son, Don Carlos, died under suspicious circumstances in 1568—some contemporaries suspected that Philip had him quietly executed—only three months before the death of the queen.

SUPREMACY IN THE MEDITERRANEAN During the first half of Philip's reign, attention focused almost exclusively on the Mediterranean and the Turkish threat. By history, geography, and choice, Spain had traditionally been Catholic Europe's champion against Islam. During the 1560s the Turks advanced deep into Austria, while their fleets dominated the Mediterranean. Between 1568 and 1570, armies under Philip's half-brother, Don John of Austria, the illegitimate son of Charles V, suppressed and dispersed the Moors in Granada.

In May 1571 a Holy League of Spain, Venice, and the pope, again under Don John's command, formed to check Turkish belligerence in the Mediterranean. In what was the largest naval battle of the sixteenth century, Don John's fleet engaged the Ottoman navy under Ali Pasha off Lepanto in the Gulf of Corinth on October 7, 1571. Before the engagement ended, over one-third of the Turkish fleet had been sunk or captured and 30,000 Turks had died. The Mediterranean for the moment belonged to Spain, and the Europeans were left to fight each other. Philip's armies also succeeded in putting down resistance in neighboring Portugal, which Spain annexed in 1580. The conquest of Portugal not only added to Spanish sea power, but also brought the magnificent Portuguese overseas empire in Africa, India, and the Americas into the Spanish orbit.

The Revolt in the Netherlands

The spectacular Spanish military success in southern Europe was not repeated in northern Europe. When Philip attempted to impose his will within the Netherlands and on England and France, he learned the lessons of defeat. The resistance of the Netherlands especially proved the undoing of Spanish dreams of world empire. (See Map 12–1.)

CARDINAL GRANVELLE The Netherlands was the richest area not only of Philip's Habsburg kingdom, but of Europe as well. In 1559 Philip had departed the Netherlands for Spain, never again to return. His half-sister, Margaret of Parma, assisted by a special council of state, became regent in his absence. The council was headed by Philip's handpicked lieutenant, the extremely able Antoine Perrenot (1517–1586), known after 1561 as Cardinal Granvelle. Granvelle hoped to check Protestant gains by internal church reforms. He planned to

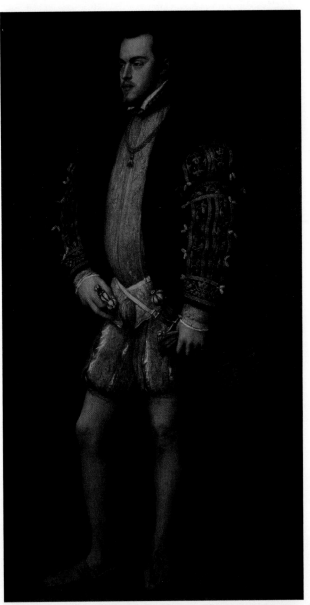

Titian's portrait of Philip II of Spain (r. 1556–1598), the most powerful ruler of his time. Alinari/Art Resource, N.Y.

MAP 12–1   THE NETHERLANDS
DURING THE REFORMATION   *The
northern and southern provinces
of the Netherlands. The former,
the United Provinces, were mostly
Protestant in the second half of the
sixteenth century, while the southern Spanish Netherlands made
peace with Spain and remained
largely Catholic.*

break down the traditional local autonomy of the seventeen Netherlands provinces by stages and establish in its place a centralized royal government directed from Madrid. A politically docile and religiously uniform country was the goal.

The merchant towns of the Netherlands were, however, Europe's most independent; many, like magnificent Antwerp, were also Calvinist strongholds. By tradition and habit, the people of the Netherlands inclined far more toward variety and toleration than toward obeisant conformity and hierarchical order. Two members of the council of state formed a stubborn opposition to the Spanish overlords, who now sought to reimpose their traditional rule with a vengeance. They were the Count of Egmont (1522–1568) and William of Nassau, the Prince of Orange (1533–1584), known as "the Silent" because of his extremely small circle of confidants.

Like other successful rulers in this period, William of Orange placed the Netherlands' political autonomy and well-being above religious creeds. He personally passed through successive Catholic, Lutheran, and Calvinist stages. In 1561, he married Anne of Saxony, the daughter of the Lutheran elector Maurice and the granddaughter of the late Landgrave Philip of Hesse. He maintained his Catholic practices until 1567, when he turned Lutheran. After

the Saint Bartholomew's Day Massacre (1572), Orange (as he was called) became an avowed Calvinist.

In 1561, Cardinal Granvelle proceeded with a planned ecclesiastical reorganization of the Netherlands. It was intended to tighten the control of the Catholic hierarchy over the country and to accelerate its consolidation as a Spanish ward. Orange and Egmont, organizing the Dutch nobility in opposition, succeeded in gaining Granvelle's removal from office in 1564. Aristocratic control of the country after Granvelle's departure, however, proved woefully inefficient. Popular unrest continued to grow, especially among urban artisans, who joined the congregations of radical Calvinist preachers in increasing numbers.

THE COMPROMISE   The year 1564 also saw the first fusion of political and religious opposition to Regent Margaret's government. This opposition resulted from Philip II's unwise insistence that the decrees of the Council of Trent be enforced throughout the Netherlands. William of Orange's younger brother, Louis of Nassau, who had been raised a Lutheran, led the opposition, and it received support from the Calvinist-inclined lesser nobility and townspeople. A national covenant called the *Compromise* was drawn up, a solemn pledge to resist the decrees of Trent and the Inquisition. Grievances were loudly and persistently voiced. When Regent Margaret's government spurned the protesters as "beggars" in 1566, Calvinists rioted through the country. Louis called on French Huguenots and German Lutherans to send aid to the Netherlands, and a full-scale rebellion against the Spanish regency appeared imminent.

THE DUKE OF ALBA The rebellion failed to materialize, however, because the Netherlands' higher nobility would not support it. Their shock at Calvinist iconoclasm and anarchy was as great as their resentment of Granvelle's more subtle repression. Philip, determined to make an example of the Protestant rebels, dispatched the duke of Alba to suppress the revolt. His army of 10,000 journeyed northward from Milan in 1567 in a show of combined Spanish and papal might. A special tribunal, known to the Spanish as the Council of Troubles and among the Netherlanders as the Council of Blood, reigned over the land. The counts of Egmont and Horn and several thousand suspected heretics were publicly executed before Alba's reign of terror ended.

The Spanish levied new taxes, forcing the Netherlands to pay for the suppression of its own revolt. One of these taxes, the "tenth penny," a ten-percent sales tax, met such resistance from merchants and artisans that it remained uncollectible in some areas even after a reduction to three percent. Combined persecution and taxation sent tens of thousands fleeing from the Netherlands during Alba's cruel six-year rule. Alba came to be more hated than Granvelle or the radical Calvinists had ever been.

RESISTANCE AND UNIFICATION William of Orange was an exile in Germany during these turbulent years. He now emerged as the leader of a broad movement for the Netherlands' independence from Spain. The northern, Calvinist-inclined provinces of Holland, Zeeland, and Utrecht, of which Orange was the *stadholder*, or governor, became his base. As in France, political resistance in the Netherlands gained both organization and inspiration by merging with Calvinism.

The early victories of the resistance attest to the popular character of the revolt. A case in point is the capture of the port city of Brill by the "Sea Beggars," an international group of anti-Spanish exiles and criminals, among them many Englishmen. William of Orange did not hesitate to enlist their services. Their brazen piracy, however, had forced Queen Elizabeth to disassociate herself from them and to bar their ships from English ports. In 1572, the Beggars captured Brill and other seaports in Zeeland and Holland. Mixing with the native population, they quickly sparked rebellions against Alba in town after town and spread the resistance southward. In 1574, the people of Leiden heroically resisted a long Spanish siege. The Dutch opened the dikes and flooded their country to repulse the hated Spanish. The faltering Alba had by that time ceded power to Don Luis de Requesens, who replaced him as commander of Spanish forces in the Netherlands in November 1573.

THE PACIFICATION OF GHENT The greatest atrocity of the war came after Requesens's death in 1576. Spanish mercenaries, leaderless and unpaid, ran

The Milch Cow, a sixteenth-century satirical painting depicting the Netherlands as a cow in whom all the great powers of Europe have an interest. Elizabeth of England is feeding her (England had longstanding commercial ties with Flanders); Philip II of Spain is attempting to ride her (Spain was trying to reassert its control over the entire area); William of Orange is trying to milk her (he was the leader of the anti-Spanish rebellion); and the king of France holds her tail (France hoped to profit from the rebellion at Spain's expense). Rijksmuseum, Amsterdam

amok in Antwerp on November 4, 1576, leaving 7,000 people dead in the streets. The event came to be known as the Spanish Fury.

These atrocities accomplished in four short days what neither religion nor patriotism had previously been able to do. The ten largely Catholic southern provinces (what is roughly modern Belgium) now came together with the seven largely Protestant northern provinces (what is roughly the modern Netherlands) in unified opposition to Spain. This union, known as the Pacification of Ghent, was accomplished on November 8, 1576. It declared internal regional sovereignty in matters of religion, a key clause that permitted political cooperation among the signatories, who were not agreed over religion. It was a Netherlands version of the territorial settlement of religious differences brought about in the Holy Roman Empire in 1555 by the Peace of Augsburg. Four provinces initially held out, but they soon made the resistance unanimous by joining the all-embracing Union of Brussels in January 1577. For the next two years, the Spanish faced a unified and determined Netherlands.

Don John, the victor over the Turks at Lepanto in 1571, had taken command of Spanish land forces in November 1576. He now experienced his first defeat. Confronted by unified Netherlandic resistance, he signed the humiliating Perpetual Edict in February 1577. This edict provided for the removal of all Spanish troops from the Netherlands within twenty days. The withdrawal of troops gave the country to William of Orange and effectively ended for the time being whatever plans Philip may have had for using the Netherlands as a staging area for an invasion of England.

William of Orange Defends Himself to the Dutch Estates

Branded an outlaw by Philip II of Spain, the Protestant Dutch Prince William of Orange defended himself to his countrymen in an eloquent address known as the Apology *(1581).*

❖ *Is this a rhetorical speech of the kind we still hear today—making an enemy's condemnation a badge of honor? Did being branded as an outlaw by the Spanish king put William in greater danger? If so, from whom? How did William's life end in 1584? Did the condemnation by the Spanish King have anything to do with it?*

What could be more gratifying in this world, especially to one engaged in the great and excellent task of securing liberty for a good people oppressed by evil men, than to be mortally hated by one's enemies, who are at the same time enemies of the fatherland, and from their mouths to receive a sweet testimony to one's fidelity to his people and to his obstinate opposition to tyrants and disturbers of the peace? Such is the pleasure that the Spaniards and their adherents have prepared for me in their anxiety to disturb me. They have but gratified me by that infamous proscription by which they sought to ruin me. Not only do I owe to them this favor, but also the occasion to make generally known the equity and justice of my enterprises....

My enemies object that I have "established liberty of conscience." I confess that the glow of fires in which so many poor Christians have been tormented is not an agreeable sight to me, although it may rejoice the eyes of the duke of Alba and the Spaniards; and that it has been my opinion that persecutions should cease in the Netherlands....

They denounce me as a hypocrite, which is absurd enough....As their friend, I told them quite frankly that they were twisting a rope to hang themselves when they began the barbarous policy of persecution....

As for me personally...it is my head that they are looking for, and they have vowed my death by offering such a great sum of money [25,000 crowns]. They say that the war can never come to an end so long as I am among you....

If, gentlemen, you believe that my exile, or even my death, may serve you, I am ready to obey your behests. Here is my head, over which no prince or monarch has authority save you. Dispose of it as you will for the safety and preservation of our commonwealth. But if you judge that such little experience and energy as I have acquired through long and assiduous labors, if you judge that the remainder of my possessions and of my life can be of service to you, I dedicate them to you and to the fatherland.

From James Harvey Robinson, *Readings in European History*, Vol. 2 (Boston: Ginn and Co., 1906), pp. 177–179.

THE UNION OF ARRAS AND THE UNION OF UTRECHT
The Spanish, however, were nothing if not persistent. Don John and Alessandro Farnese of Parma, the regent Margaret's son, revived Spanish power in the southern provinces, where constant fear of Calvinist extremism had moved the leaders to break the Union of Brussels. In January 1579 the southern provinces formed the Union of Arras, and within five months they made peace with Spain. These provinces later served the cause of the Counter-Reformation. The northern provinces responded with the formation of the Union of Utrecht.

NETHERLANDS INDEPENDENCE Seizing what now appeared to be a last opportunity to break the back of Netherlandic resistance, Philip II declared William of Orange an outlaw and placed a bounty of 25,000 crowns on his head. The act predictably stiffened the resistance of the northern provinces. In a famous defiant speech to the Estates General of Holland in December 1580, known as the Apology, Orange publicly denounced Philip as a heathen tyrant whom the Netherlands need no longer obey. (See "William of Orange Defends Himself to the Dutch Estates.")

On July 22, 1581, the member provinces of the Union of Utrecht met in The Hague and formally declared Philip no longer their ruler. They turned instead to the French duke of Alençon, Catherine de Médici's youngest son. The southern provinces had also earlier looked to him as a possible middle way between Spanish and Calvinist overlordship. All the northern provinces save Holland and Zeeland accepted Alençon as their "sovereign" (Holland and Zeeland distrusted him almost as much as they did Philip II), but with the understanding that he would be only a titular ruler. But Alençon, an ambitious failure, saw this as his one chance at greatness. When he rashly attempted to take actual control of the provinces in 1583, he was deposed and returned to France.

Spanish efforts to reconquer the Netherlands continued into the 1580s. William of Orange, assassinated in July 1584, was succeeded by his seventeen-year-old son, Maurice (1567–1625), who, with the assistance of England and France, continued Dutch resistance. Fortunately for the Netherlands, Philip II began now to meddle directly in French and English affairs. He signed a secret treaty with the Guises (the Treaty of Joinville in December 1584) and sent armies under Farnese into France in 1590. Hostilities with the English, who had openly aided the Dutch rebels, also increased. Gradually, they built toward a climax in 1588, when Philip's great Armada was defeated in the English Channel.

These new fronts overextended Spain's resources, strengthening the Netherlands. Spanish preoccupation with France and England permitted the northern provinces to drive out all Spanish soldiers by 1593. In 1596, France and England formally recognized the independence of these provinces. Peace was not, however, concluded with Spain until 1609, when the Twelve Years' Truce gave the northern provinces virtual independence. Full recognition came finally in the Peace of Westphalia in 1648.

England and Spain (1553–1603)

Mary I

Before Edward VI died in 1553, he agreed to a device to make Lady Jane Grey, the teenage daughter of a powerful Protestant nobleman and, more important, the granddaughter on her mother's side of Henry VIII's younger sister Mary, his successor in place of the Catholic Mary Tudor (r. 1553–1558). But popular support for the principle of hereditary monarchy was too strong to deprive Mary of her rightful rule. Popular uprisings in London and elsewhere led to Jane Grey's removal from the throne within days of her crowning, and she was eventually beheaded.

Portrait of Mary I (r. 1553–1558), Queen of England. By Sir Anthony Mor (Antonio Moro) (1517/20–76/7), Prado, Madrid. 1554 (panel). Prado, Madrid/Bridgeman Art Library, London/Index

Once enthroned, Mary proceeded to act even beyond the worst fears of the Protestants. In 1554 she entered a highly unpopular political marriage with Prince Philip (later Philip II) of Spain, a symbol of militant Catholicism to English Protestants. At his direction, she pursued a foreign policy that in 1558 cost England its last enclave on the Continent, Calais.

Mary's domestic measures were equally shocking to the English people and even more divisive. During her reign, Parliament repealed the Protestant statutes of Edward and reverted to the Catholic religious practice of her father, Henry VIII. The great Protestant leaders of the Edwardian Age—John Hooper, Hugh Latimer, and Thomas Cranmer—were executed for heresy. Hundreds of Protestants either joined them in martyrdom (282 were burned at the stake during Mary's reign) or took flight to the Continent. These "Marian exiles" settled in Germany and Switzerland, forming especially large communities in Frankfurt, Strasbourg, and Geneva. (John Knox, the future leader of the Reformation in Scotland, was prominent among them.) There they worshiped in their own congregations, wrote tracts justifying armed resistance, and waited for the time when a Protestant counteroffensive could be launched in their homelands. They were also exposed to religious beliefs more radical than any set forth during Edward VI's reign. Many of these exiles later held positions in the Church of England during Elizabeth I's reign.

Elizabeth I

Mary's successor was her half-sister, Elizabeth I (r. 1558–1603), the daughter of Henry VIII and Anne Boleyn. Elizabeth had remarkable and enduring successes in both domestic and foreign policy. Assisted by a shrewd adviser, Sir William Cecil (1520–1598), she built a true kingdom on the ruins of Mary's reign. Between 1559 and 1563, she and Cecil guided a religious settlement through Parliament that prevented England from being torn asunder by religious differences in the sixteenth century, as the Continent was. Another ruler who subordinated religious to political unity, Elizabeth merged a centralized episcopal system, which she firmly controlled, with broadly defined Protestant doctrine and traditional Catholic ritual. In the resulting Anglican Church, inflexible religious extremes were not permitted.

In 1559 an Act of Supremacy passed Parliament, repealing all the anti-Protestant legislation of Mary Tudor and asserting Elizabeth's right as "supreme governor" over both spiritual and temporal affairs. In the same year, the Act of Uniformity mandated a revised version of the second *Book of Common Prayer* (1552) for every English parish. In 1563, the issuance of the *Thirty-Nine Articles on Religion*, a revision of Thomas Cranmer's

Elizabeth I (r. 1558–1603) standing on a map of England in 1592. An astute politician in both foreign and domestic policy, Elizabeth was perhaps the most succesful ruler of the sixteenth century. National Portrait Gallery, London

original forty-two, made a moderate Protestantism the official religion within the Church of England.

CATHOLIC AND PROTESTANT EXTREMISTS   Elizabeth hoped to avoid both Catholic and Protestant extremism at the official level by pursuing a middle way. Her first archbishop of Canterbury, Matthew Parker (d. 1575), represented this ideal. But Elizabeth could not prevent the emergence of subversive Catholic and Protestant zealots. When she ascended the throne, Catholics were in the majority in England. The extremists among them, encouraged by the Jesuits, plotted against her. Catholic radicals were also encouraged and later directly assisted by the Spanish, who were piqued both by Elizabeth's Protestant sympathies and by her refusal to follow the example of her half-sister Mary and take Philip II's hand in marriage. Elizabeth remained unmarried throughout her reign, using the possibility of a marriage as a political alliance very much to her diplomatic advantage.

Catholic extremists hoped eventually to replace Elizabeth with Mary Stuart, Queen of Scots. Unlike

Elizabeth, who had been declared illegitimate during the reign of her father, Mary Stuart had an unblemished claim to the throne by way of her grandmother Margaret, the sister of Henry VIII. Elizabeth acted swiftly against Catholic assassination plots and rarely let emotion override her political instincts. Despite proven cases of Catholic treason and even attempted regicide, she executed fewer Catholics during her forty-five years on the throne than Mary Tudor had executed Protestants during her brief five-year reign. She showed little mercy, however, to separatists and others who threatened the unity of her rule.

Elizabeth dealt cautiously with the Puritans, who were Protestants working within the national church to "purify" it of every vestige of "popery" and to make its Protestant doctrine more precise. The Puritans had two special grievances:

1. the retention of Catholic ceremony and vestments within the Church of England, which made it appear to the casual observer that no Reformation had occurred, and

2. the continuation of the episcopal system of Church governance, which conceived of the English church theologically as the true successor to Rome, while placing it politically under the firm hand of the queen and her compliant archbishop.

Sixteenth-century Puritans were not separatists. They enjoyed wide popular support and were led by widely respected men like Thomas Cartwright (d. 1603). They worked through Parliament to create an alternative national church of semiautonomous congregations governed by representative presbyteries (hence, "Presbyterians"), following the model of Calvin and Geneva. Elizabeth dealt firmly, but subtly, with this group, conceding absolutely nothing that lessened the hierarchical unity of the Church of England and her control over it.

The more extreme Puritans wanted every congregation to be autonomous, a law unto itself, with neither higher episcopal nor presbyterian control. They came to be known as Congregationalists. Elizabeth and her second archbishop of Canterbury, John Whitgift (d. 1604), refused to tolerate this group, whose views on independence they found patently subversive. The Conventicle Act of 1593 gave such separatists the option of either conforming to the practices of the Church of England or facing exile or death.

DETERIORATION OF RELATIONS WITH SPAIN A series of events led inexorably to war between England and Spain, despite the sincerest desires on the part of both Philip II and Elizabeth to avoid a confrontation. In 1567 the Spanish duke of Alba marched his mighty army into the Netherlands, which was, from the English point of view, simply a convenient staging area for a Spanish invasion of England. Pope Pius V (r. 1566–1572), who favored a military conquest of Protestant England, "excommunicated" Elizabeth for heresy in 1570. This mischievous act only encouraged both internal resistance and international intrigue against the queen. Two years later, as noted earlier, the piratical Sea Beggars, many of whom were Englishmen, occupied the port city of Brill in the Netherlands and aroused the surrounding countryside against the Spanish.

Following Don John's demonstration of Spain's awesome sea power at the famous naval battle of Lepanto in 1571, England signed a mutual defense pact with France. Also in the 1570s, Elizabeth's famous seamen John Hawkins (1532–1595) and Sir Francis Drake (1545?–1596) began to prey regularly on Spanish shipping in the Americas. Drake's circumnavigation of the globe between 1577 and 1580

Elizabeth I before Parliament. The artist shows the Queen small and in the background, and places Parliament prominently in the foreground, suggesting that England, despite the enormous power of the Queen, is a land where parliamentary government reigns supreme.
The Folger Shakespeare Library

was one in a series of dramatic demonstrations of English ascendancy on the high seas.

After the Saint Bartholomew's Day Massacre, Elizabeth was the only protector of Protestants in France and the Netherlands. In 1585 she signed the Treaty of Nonsuch, which provided English soldiers and cavalry to the Netherlands. Funds that had previously been funneled covertly to support Henry of Navarre's army in France now flowed openly.

MARY, QUEEN OF SCOTS   These events made a tinderbox of English–Spanish relations. The spark that finally touched it off was Elizabeth's execution of Mary, Queen of Scots (1542–1587).

Mary Stuart was the daughter of King James V of Scotland and Mary of Guise and had resided in France from the time she was six years old. This thoroughly French and Catholic queen had returned to Scotland after the death of her husband, the French king Francis II, in 1561. There she found a successful, fervent Protestant Reformation that had won legal sanction the year before in the Treaty of Edinburgh (1560). As hereditary heir to the throne of Scotland, Mary remained queen by divine and human right. She was not intimidated by the Protestants who controlled her realm. She established an international French court culture, the gaiety and sophistication of which impressed many Protestant nobles whose religion often made their lives exceedingly dour.

Mary was closely watched by the ever-vigilant Scottish reformer John Knox. He fumed publicly and always with effect against the queen's private mass and Catholic practices, which Scottish law made a capital offense for everyone else. Knox won support in his role of watchdog from Elizabeth and Cecil. Elizabeth personally despised Knox and never forgave him for writing the *First Blast of the Trumpet Against the Terrible Regiment of Women*, a work aimed at provoking a revolt against Mary Tudor, but published in the year of Elizabeth's ascent to the throne. Elizabeth and Cecil tolerated Knox because he served their foreign policy, never permitting Scotland to succumb to the young Mary and her French and Catholic ways.

In 1568, a public scandal forced Mary's abdication and flight to her cousin Elizabeth in England. Mary's reputed lover, the earl of Bothwell, was, with cause, suspected of having killed her legal husband, Lord Darnley. When a packed court acquitted Bothwell, he subsequently married Mary. The outraged reaction from Protestant nobles forced Mary to surrender the throne to her one-year-old son, who became James VI of Scotland (and, later, Elizabeth's successor as King James I of England). Because of Mary's clear claim to the English throne, she remained an international symbol of a possible Catholic England, and she was consumed by the desire to be queen of England. Her presence in England, where she resided under house arrest for nineteen years, was a constant discomfort to Elizabeth.

In 1583 Elizabeth's vigilant secretary, Sir Francis Walsingham, uncovered a plot against Elizabeth involving the Spanish ambassador Bernardino de Mendoza. After Mendoza's deportation in January 1584, popular antipathy toward Spain and support for

A portrayal of the execution of Mary, Queen of Scots and the apparent subsequent burning (left) of her body, so that no relics might survive for her followers to revere.   Unknown Dutch artist. National Galleries of Scotland

An Unknown Contemporary Describes Queen Elizabeth

No sixteenth-century ruler governed more effectively than Elizabeth I of England (r. 1558–1603), who was both loved and feared by her subjects. An unknown contemporary has left the following description, revealing not only her intelligence and political cunning, but also something of her immense vanity.

❖ *How does this description compare with that of Mary I? How do the personal qualities and political skills of the two leaders differ?*

I will proceed with the description of the queen's disposition and natural gifts of mind and body, wherein she either matched or exceeded all the princes of her time, as being of a great spirit yet tempered with moderation, in adversity never dejected, in prosperity rather joyful than proud; affable to her subjects, but always with due regard to the greatness of her estate, by reason whereof she was both loved and feared.

In her later time, when she showed herself in public, she was always magnificent in apparel; supposing haply thereby that the eyes of her people (being dazzled by the glittering aspect of her outward ornaments) would not so easily discern the marks of age and decay of natural beauty; and she came abroad the more seldom, to make her presence the more grateful and applauded by the multitude, to whom things rarely seen are in manner as new.

She suffered not, at any time, any suitor to depart discontented from her, and though ofttimes he obtained not that he desired, yet he held himself satisfied with her manner of speech, which gave hope of success in the second attempt....

Latin, French, and Italian she could speak very elegantly, and she was able in all those languages to answer ambassadors on the sudden....Of the Greek tongue she was also not altogether ignorant. She took pleasure in reading of the best and wisest histories, and some part of Tacitus's *Annals* she herself turned into English for her private exercise. She also translated Boethius's *On the Consolation of Philosophy* and a treatise of Plutarch, *On Curiosity*, with divers others....

It is credibly reported that not long before her death, she had a great apprehension of her own age and declination by seeing her face (then lean and full of wrinkles) truly represented to her in a glass, which she a good while very earnestly beheld; perceiving thereby how often she had been abused by flatterers (whom she held in too great estimation) that had informed her the contrary.

From James Harvey Robinson, ed., *Readings in European History*, Vol. 2 (Boston: Athenaeum, 1906), pp. 191–193.

Protestant resistance in France and the Netherlands became massive throughout England.

In 1586 Walsingham uncovered still another plot against Elizabeth, the so-called Babington plot (after Anthony Babington, who was caught seeking Spanish support for an attempt on the queen's life). This time he had uncontestable proof of Mary's complicity. Elizabeth believed that the execution of a sovereign, even a dethroned sovereign, weakened royalty everywhere. She was also aware of the outcry that Mary's execution would create throughout the Catholic world, and Elizabeth sincerely wanted peace with English Catholics. But she really had no choice in the matter and consented to Mary's execution, which took place on February 18, 1587. This event dashed all Catholic hopes for a bloodless reconversion of Protestant England. After the execution of the Catholic queen of Scotland, Pope Sixtus V (r. 1585–1590), who feared Spanish domination almost as much as he abhorred English Protes-

tantism, could no longer withhold public support for a Spanish invasion of England. Philip II ordered his Armada to make ready.

THE ARMADA Spain's war preparations were interrupted in the spring of 1587 by Sir Francis Drake's successful shelling of the port city of Cádiz, an attack that inflicted heavy damage on Spanish ships and stores. After "singeing the beard of Spain's king," as he put it, Drake raided the coast of Portugal, further incapacitating the Spanish. The success of these strikes forced the Spanish to postpone their planned invasion of England until the spring of 1588.

On May 30 of that year, a mighty fleet of 130 ships bearing 25,000 sailors and soldiers under the command of the duke of Medina-Sidonia set sail for England. In the end, however, the English won a stunning victory. The invasion barges that were to transport Spanish soldiers from the galleons onto

English shores were prevented from leaving Calais and Dunkirk. The swifter English and Netherlandic ships, helped by what came to be known as an "English wind," dispersed the waiting Spanish fleet, over one-third of which never returned to Spain.

The news of the Armada's defeat gave heart to Protestant resistance everywhere. Although Spain continued to win impressive victories in the 1590s, it never fully recovered from that defeat. Spanish soldiers faced unified and inspired French, English, and Dutch armies. By the time of Philip's death on September 13, 1598, his forces had been successfully rebuffed on all fronts. His seventeenth-century successors were all inferior leaders who never knew responsibilities equal to his. Nor did Spain ever again know such imperial grandeur. The French soon dominated the Continent, while in the New World the Dutch and the English progressively whittled away Spain's once glorious overseas empire.

Elizabeth died on March 23, 1603, leaving behind her a strong nation poised to expand into a global empire. (See "An Unknown Contemporary Describes Queen Elizabeth.")

The Thirty Years' War (1618–1648)

The Thirty Years' War in the Holy Roman Empire was the last and most destructive of the wars of religion. Religious and political differences had long set Catholics against Protestants and Calvinists against Lutherans. What made the Thirty Years' War so devastating was the entrenched hatred of the various sides and their seeming determination to sacrifice all for their religious beliefs and extension of political power. As the conflicts multiplied, virtually every major European land became involved either directly or indirectly. When the hostilities ended in 1648, the peace terms shaped the map of northern Europe much as we know it today.

Preconditions for War

FRAGMENTED GERMANY In the second half of the sixteenth century, Germany was an almost ungovernable land of about 360 autonomous political entities. (See Map 12–2.) There were independent secular principalities (duchies, landgraviates, and marches); ecclesiastical principalities (archbishoprics, bishoprics, and abbeys); numerous free cities; and castle regions dominated by knights. The Peace of Augsburg (1555) had given each a significant degree of sovereignty within its own borders. Each levied its own tolls and tariffs and coined its own money, practices that made land travel and trade between the various regions dif-

ficult and sometimes impossible. In addition, many of these little lands were filled with great-power pretensions. Political decentralization and fragmentation characterized Germany as the seventeenth century opened; it was not a unified nation like Spain, England, or even strife-filled France.

Because of its central location, Germany had always been Europe's highway for merchants and traders going north, south, east and west. Europe's rulers pressed in on Germany both for reasons of trade and because some held lands or legal privileges within certain German principalities. German princes, in their turn, looked to import and export markets beyond German borders and opposed any efforts to consolidate the Holy Roman Empire, lest their territorial rights, confirmed by the Peace of Augsburg, be overturned. German princes were not loath to turn to Catholic France or to the kings of Denmark and Sweden for allies against the Habsburg emperor.

After the Council of Trent, Protestants in the empire suspected the existence of an imperial and papal conspiracy to re-create the Catholic Europe of pre-Reformation times. The imperial diet, which the German princes controlled, demanded strict observance of the constitutional rights of Germans, as set forth in agreements with the emperor since the mid-fourteenth century. In the late sixteenth century, the emperor ruled only to the degree to which he was prepared to use force of arms against his subjects.

RELIGIOUS DIVISION Religious conflict accentuated the international and internal political divisions. (See Map 12–3.) During this period, the population within the Holy Roman Empire was about equally divided between Catholics and Protestants, the latter having perhaps a slight numerical edge by 1600. The terms of the Peace of Augsburg had attempted to freeze the territorial holdings of the Lutherans and the Catholics (the so-called ecclesiastical reservation). In the intervening years, however, the Lutherans had gained and kept political control in some Catholic areas, as had the Catholics in a few previously Lutheran areas. Such territorial reversals, or the threat of them, only increased the suspicion and antipathy between the two sides.

The Lutherans had been far more successful in securing their rights to worship in Catholic lands than the Catholics had been in securing such rights in Lutheran lands. The Catholic rulers, who were in a weakened position after the Reformation, had made, but resented, concessions to Protestant communities within their territories. With the passage of time, they demanded that all ecclesiastical princes, electors, archbishops, bishops, and abbots who had deserted the Catholic for the Protestant side be immediately deprived of their religious offices and that their ecclesiastical holdings be promptly returned to Catholic

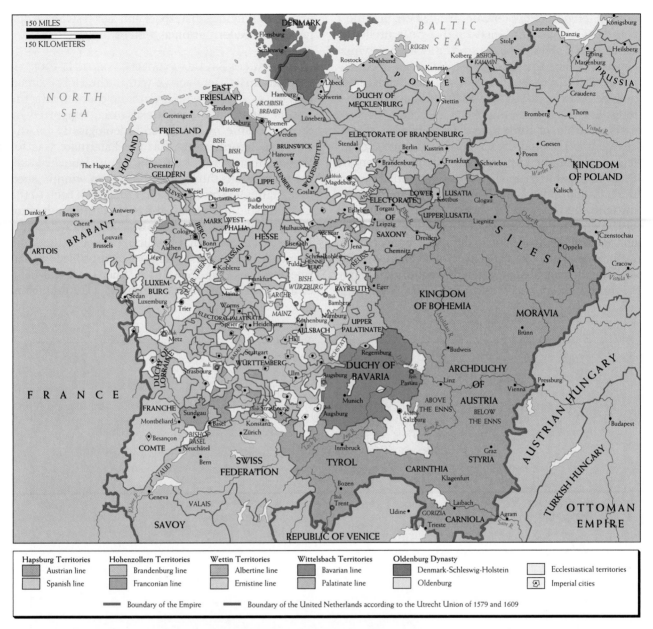

MAP 12–2   GERMANY IN 1547   *Mid-sixteenth-century Germany was an almost ungovernable land of about 360 autonomous political entities.* Originally "Map of Germany Showing It's Great Division/Fragmentation in the 16th Century" from Majo Holborn, *A History of Germany: The Reformation*, Copyright © 1982 by Princeton University Press. Reprinted by permission of Princeton University Press.

control in accordance with the ecclesiastical reservation. However, the Lutherans and, especially, the Calvinists in the Palatinate ignored this stipulation at every opportunity.

There was also religious strife in the empire between liberal and conservative Lutherans and between Lutherans and the growing numbers of Calvinists. The last half of the sixteenth century was a time of warring Protestant factions within German universities. And in addition to the heightened religious strife, a new scientific and material culture was becoming ascen-

dant in intellectual and political circles, increasing the anxiety of religious people of all persuasions.

CALVINISM AND THE PALATINATE   As elsewhere in Europe, Calvinism was the political and religious leaven within the Holy Roman Empire on the eve of the Thirty Years' War. Unrecognized as a legal religion by the Peace of Augsburg, it gained a strong foothold within the empire when Frederick III (r. 1559–1576), a devout convert to Calvinism, became elector Palatine (ruler within the Palatinate; see Map 12–3) and made it the official religion of his domain. Heidelberg became a German Geneva in the 1560s: both a great intellectual center of Calvinism and a staging area for Calvinist penetration into the empire. By 1609, Palatine Calvinists headed a Protestant defensive alliance that received outside support from Spain's sixteenth-century enemies: England, France, and the Netherlands.

The Lutherans came to fear the Calvinists almost as much as they did the Catholics. Palatine Calvinists seemed to the Lutherans directly to threaten the Peace of Augsburg—and hence the legal foundation of the Lutheran states—by their bold missionary forays into the empire. Also, outspoken Calvinist criticism of the doctrine of Christ's real presence in the Eucharist shocked the more religiously conservative Lutherans. The elector Palatine once expressed his disbelief in transubstantiation by publicly shredding the host and mocking it as a "fine God." To Luther-

ans, such religious disrespect and aggressiveness disgraced the Reformation as well as the elector.

Maximilian of Bavaria and the Catholic League If the Calvinists were active within the Holy Roman Empire, so also were their Catholic counterparts, the Jesuits. Staunchly Catholic Bavaria, supported by Spain, became militarily and ideologically for the Counter-Reformation what the Palatinate was for Protestantism. From there, the Jesuits launched successful missions throughout the empire, winning such major cities as Strasbourg and Osnabrück back to the Catholic fold by 1600. In 1609 Maximilian, duke of Bavaria, organized a Catholic League to counter a new Protestant alliance that had been formed in the same year under the leadership of the Calvinist Elector Palatine, Frederick IV (r. 1583–1610). When the league fielded a great army under the command of Count Johann

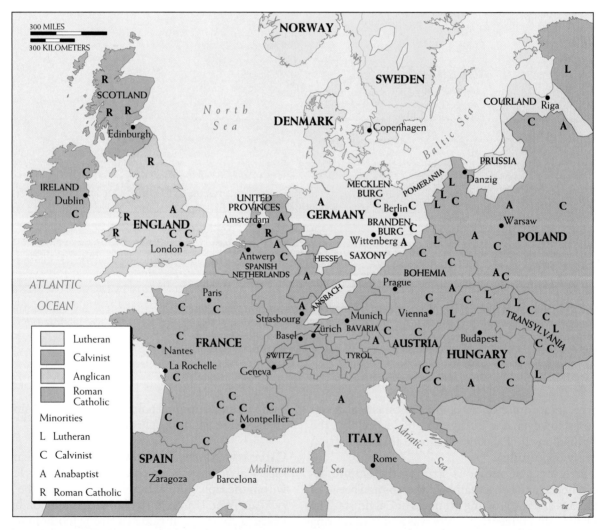

MAP 12–3 RELIGIOUS DIVISIONS ABOUT 1600 *By 1600, few could seriously expect Christians to return to a uniform religious allegiance. In Spain and southern Italy, Catholicism remained relatively unchallenged, but note the existence elsewhere of large religious minorities, both Catholic and Protestant.*

MAP 12–4 THE HOLY ROMAN EMPIRE ABOUT 1618 *On the eve of the Thirty Years' War, the Holy Roman Empire was politically and religiously fragmented, as revealed by this somewhat simplified map. Lutherans dominated the north and Catholics the south, while Calvinists controlled the United Provinces and the Palatinate and were important in Switzerland and Brandenburg.*

von Tilly, the stage was set, both internally and internationally, for the worst of the religious wars, the Thirty Years' War. (See Map 12–4.)

Four Periods of War

The war went through four distinguishable periods. During its course, it drew in every major western European nation—at least diplomatically and financially if not by direct military involvement. The four periods were the Bohemian (1618–1625); the Danish (1625–1629); the Swedish (1630–1635); and the Swedish–French (1635–1648).

THE BOHEMIAN PERIOD The war broke out in Bohemia after the ascent to the Bohemian throne in 1618 of the Habsburg Ferdinand, archduke of Styria, who was also in the line of succession to the imperial throne. Educated by the Jesuits and a fervent Catholic, Ferdinand was determined to restore the traditional faith to the eastern Habsburg lands (Austria, Bohemia, and Poland).

No sooner had Ferdinand become king of Bohemia than he revoked the religious freedoms of Bohemian Protestants. In force since 1575, these freedoms had even been recently broadened by Emperor Rudolf II (r. 1576–1612) in his Letter of Majesty in 1609. The Protestant nobility in Prague responded to Ferdinand's act in May 1618 by literally throwing his regents out the window. The event has ever since been known as the "defenestration of Prague." (The three officials fell fifty feet into a dry moat that, fortunately, was padded with manure, which cushioned their fall and spared their lives.) In the following year Ferdinand became Holy Roman Emperor as Ferdinand II, by the unanimous vote of the seven electors. The Bohemians, however, defiantly deposed him in Prague and declared the Calvinist elector Palatine, Frederick V (r. 1616–1623), their overlord.

What had begun as a revolt of the Protestant nobility against an unpopular king of Bohemia thereafter escalated into an international war. Spain sent troops to Ferdinand, who found more immediate allies in Maximilian of Bavaria and the opportunistic Lutheran elector John George I of Saxony (r. 1611–1656), who saw a sure route to territorial gain by joining in an easy victory over the weaker elector Palatine. This was not the only time politics and greed would overshadow religion during the long conflict, although Lutheran–Calvinist religious animosity also overrode a common Protestantism.

Ferdinand's army under Tilly routed Frederick V's troops at the Battle of White Mountain in 1620. By 1622, Ferdinand had managed not only to subdue and re-Catholicize Bohemia, but to conquer the

The horror of the Thirty Years' War is captured in this painting by Jan Brueghel (1568–1625) and Sebastien Vranx (1573–1647). During the breaks in fighting, marauding armies ravaged the countryside, destroying villages and massacring the rural population.
Kunsthistorisches Museum, Vienna

Palatinate as well. Meanwhile, the duke of Bavaria pressed the conflict into northwestern Germany, laying claim to land as he went.

THE DANISH PERIOD   These events raised new fears that a reconquest and re-Catholicization of the empire now loomed, which was precisely Ferdinand II's design. The Lutheran King Christian IV (r. 1588–1648) of Denmark, who already held territory within the empire as the duke of Holstein, was eager to extend Danish influence over the coastal towns of the North Sea. Encouraged by the English, the French, and the Dutch, he picked up the Protestant banner of resistance, opening the Danish period of the conflict (1625–1629). Entering Germany with his army in 1626, he was, however, quickly humiliated by Maximilian and forced to retreat into Denmark.

As military success made Maximilian stronger and an untrustworthy ally, emperor Ferdinand sought a more pliant tool for his policies in Albrecht of Wallenstein (1583–1634), a powerful mercenary. Another opportunistic Protestant, Wallenstein had gained a great deal of territory by joining Ferdinand during the conquest of Bohemia. A brilliant and ruthless military strategist, Wallenstein carried Fer-

dinand's campaign into Denmark. By 1628 he commanded a crack army of more than 100,000 and also became a law unto himself, completely outside the emperor's control.

Wallenstein, however, had broken Protestant resistance so successfully that Ferdinand could issue the Edict of Restitution in 1629, a proclamation that dramatically reasserted the Catholic safeguards of the Peace of Augsburg (1555). It reaffirmed the illegality of Calvinism—a completely unrealistic move by 1629—and ordered the return of all church lands acquired by the Lutherans since 1552, an equally unrealistic mandate despite its legal basis. Compliance would have involved the return of no less than sixteen bishoprics and twenty-eight cities and towns to Catholic allegiance. The new edict struck panic in the hearts of Protestants and Habsburg opponents everywhere.

THE SWEDISH PERIOD   Gustavus Adolphus of Sweden (r. 1611–1632), a deeply pious king of a unified Lutheran nation, became the new leader of Protestant forces within the empire, opening the Swedish period of the war (1630–1635). He was bankrolled by two very interested bystanders: the French minister Cardinal Richelieu, whose foreign policy was to protect French interests by keeping Habsburg armies tied down in Germany, and the Dutch, who had not forgotten Spanish Habsburg domination in the sixteenth century. In alliance with the electors of Brandenburg and Saxony, the Swedish king won a smashing victory at Breitenfeld in 1630, one that so dramatically reversed the course of the war that it has been regarded as the most decisive engagement of the long conflict.

One of the reasons for the overwhelming Swedish victory at Breitenfeld was the military genius of Gustavus Adolphus. The Swedish king brought a new mobility to warfare by having both his infantry and his cavalry employ fire-and-charge tactics. At six deep, his infantry squares were smaller than the traditional ones, and he filled them with equal numbers of musketeers and pikemen. His cavalry also alternated pistol shots with charges with the sword. His artillery was lighter and more mobile in battle. Each unit of his army—infantry, cavalry, and artillery—had both defensive and offensive capability and could quickly change from one to the other.

Gustavus Adolphus died at the hands of Wallenstein's forces during the Battle of Lützen (November 1632)—a very costly engagement for both sides that created a brief standstill. Ferdinand had long been resentful of Wallenstein's independence, although he was the major factor in imperial success. In 1634, Ferdinand had Wallenstein assassinated. By that time, not only had Wallenstein served his purpose for the emperor, but, ever opportunistic, he was even trying openly to strike bargains with the Protestants for his services. The Wallenstein episode is a telling commentary on this war without honor. Despite the deep religious motivations, greed and political gain were the real forces at work in the Thirty Years' War. Even allies that owed one another their success were not above treating each other as mortal enemies.

In the Peace of Prague in 1635 the German Protestant states, led by Saxony, reached a compromise with Ferdinand. The Swedes, however, received continued support from France and the Netherlands. Desiring to maximize their investment in the war, they refused to join the agreement. Their resistance to settlement plunged the war into its fourth and most devastating phase.

THE SWEDISH–FRENCH PERIOD The French openly entered the war in 1635, sending men and munitions as well as financial subsidies. After their entrance, the war dragged on for thirteen years, with French, Swedish, and Spanish soldiers looting the length and breadth of Germany—warring, it seemed, simply for the sake of warfare itself. The Germans, long weary of the devastation, were too disunited to repulse the foreign armies; they simply watched and suffered. By the time peace talks began in the Westphalian

cities of Münster and Osnabrück in 1644, an estimated one-third of the German population had died as a direct result of the war. It has been called the worst European catastrophe since the Black Death of the fourteenth century.

The Treaty of Westphalia

The Treaty of Westphalia in 1648 brought all hostilities within the Holy Roman Empire to an end. (See Map 12–5.) It rescinded Ferdinand's Edict of Restitution and firmly reasserted the major feature of the religious settlement of the Peace of Augsburg, with the ruler of each land again permitted to determine the religion there. The treaty also gave the Calvinists their long-sought legal recognition. The independence of the Swiss Confederacy and the United Provinces of Holland, long recognized in fact, was now proclaimed in law. And the treaty elevated Bavaria to the rank of an elector state. The provisions of the treaty made the German princes supreme over their principalities. Yet, as guarantors of the treaty, Sweden and France found many occasions to meddle in German affairs until the century's end, France to considerable territorial gain. Brandenburg–Prussia emerged as the most powerful northern German state. Because the treaty broadened the legal status of Protestantism, the pope opposed it altogether, but he had no power to prevent it.

France and Spain remained at war outside the empire until 1659, when French victories forced the humiliating Treaty of the Pyrenees on the Spanish. Thereafter France became Europe's dominant power, and the once vast Habsburg kingdom waned.

By confirming the territorial sovereignty of Germany's many political entities, the Treaty of Westphalia perpetuated German division and political weakness into the modern period. Only two German states attained any international significance during the seventeenth century: Austria and Brandenburg–Prussia. The petty regionalism within the empire also reflected on a small scale the drift of larger European politics. In the seventeenth century, distinctive nation–states, each with its own political, cultural, and religious identity, reached maturity and firmly established the competitive nationalism of the modern world.

In Perspective

Both religion and politics played major roles in each of the great conflicts of the Age of Religious Wars–the internal struggle in France, Spain's unsuccessful effort to subdue the Netherlands, England's successful

MAP 12–5   EUROPE IN 1648 *At the end of the Thirty Years' War, Spain still had extensive possessions. Austria and Brandenburg–Prussia were prominent, the independence of the United Provinces and Switzerland was recognized, and Sweden held important river mouths in northern Germany.*

resistance of Spain, and the steady march of virtually every major European power through the hapless Holy Roman Empire during the first half of the seventeenth century. Parties and armies of different religious persuasions are visible in each conflict, and in each we also find a life-or-death political struggle.

The wars ended with the recognition of minority religious rights and a guarantee of the traditional boundaries of political sovereignty. In France, the Edict of Nantes (1598) brought peace by granting Huguenots basic religious and civil freedoms and by recognizing their towns and territories. With the departure of the Spanish, peace and sovereignty also came to the Netherlands, guaranteed initially by the Twelve Years' Truce (1609) and secured fully by the Peace of Westphalia (1648). The conflict between England and Spain ended with the removal of the Spanish threat to English sovereignty in politics and religion, which resulted from the execution of Mary, Queen of Scots (1587) and the English victory over the Armada (1588). In the Holy Roman Empire, peace came with the reaffirmation of the political principle of the Peace of Augsburg (1555), as the Peace of Westphalia brought the Thirty Years' War to an end by again recognizing the sovereignty of rulers within their lands and their right to determine the religious beliefs of their subjects. Europe at midcentury had real, if brief, peace.

REVIEW QUESTIONS

1. What part did politics play in the religious positions of the French leaders? How did the king (or his regent) decide which side to favor? What led to the infamous Saint Bartholomew's Day Massacre, and what did it achieve?
2. How did Spain achieve a position of dominance in the sixteenth century? What were its strengths and weaknesses as a nation? What were Philip II's goals? Which was he unable to achieve and why?
3. Henry of Navarre (Henry IV of France), Elizabeth I, and William of Orange were all *politiques*. Define the term and explain why it applies to these three rulers.
4. Discuss the background to the establishment of the Anglican church in England. What were the politics of Mary I? What was Elizabeth I's settlement, and how difficult was it to impose on all of England? Who were her detractors and what were their criticisms?
5. Why was the Thirty Years' War fought? To what extent did politics determine the outcome of the war? Discuss the Treaty of Westphalia in 1648. Could matters have been resolved without war?

6. It has been said that the Thirty Years' War is the outstanding example in European history of meaningless conflict. Evaluate this statement and provide specific reasons for or against it.

SUGGESTED READINGS

F. BRAUDEL, *The Mediterranean and the Mediterranean World in the Age of Philip the Second*, vols. 1 and 2 (1976). Widely acclaimed work of a French master historian.

N. Z. DAVIS, *Society and Culture in Early Modern France* (1975). Essays on popular culture.

R. DUNN, *The Age of Religious Wars, 1559–1689* (1979). Excellent brief survey of every major conflict.

J. H. ELLIOTT, *Europe Divided 1559–1598* (1968). Direct, lucid narrative account.

G. R. ELTON, *England under the Tudors* (1955). Masterly treatment.

J. H. FRANKLIN (ED. AND TRANS.), *Constitutionalism and Resistance in the Sixteenth Century: Three Treatises by Hotman, Beza, and Mornay* (1969). Three defenders of the right of people to resist tyranny.

P. GEYL, *The Revolt of the Netherlands, 1555–1609* (1958). The authoritative survey.

J. GUY, *Tudor England* (1990). The standard history and good synthesis of recent scholarship.

C. HAIGH, *Elizabeth I* (1988). Elizabeth portrayed as a magnificent politician and propagandist.

D. LOADES, *Mary Tudor* (1989). Authoritative and good storytelling.

J. LYNCH, *Spain under the Habsburgs I: 1516–1598* (1964). Political narrative.

G. MATTINGLY, *The Armada* (1959). A masterpiece and novellike in style.

J. E. NEALE, *The Age of Catherine de Médicis* (1962). Short, concise summary.

G. PARKER, *Europe in Crisis, 1598–1648* (1979). The big picture at a gallop.

J. G. RIDLEY, *John Knox* (1968). Large, detailed biography.

J. H. M. SALMON, *Society in Crisis: France in the Sixteenth Century* (1976). Standard narrative account.

A. SOMAN (ED.), *The Massacre of St. Bartholomew's Day: Reappraisals and Documents* (1974). Results of an international symposium on the anniversary of the massacre.

K. THOMAS, *Religion and the Decline of Magic* (1971). Provocative, much-acclaimed work focused on popular culture.

C. V. WEDGWOOD, *William the Silent* (1944). Excellent political biography of William of Orange.

J. WORMALD, *Mary, Queen of Scots: A Study in Failure* (1991). Mary portrayed as a queen who did not understand her country and was out of touch with the times.

Chapter 13

Charles I governed England from 1625 to 1649. His attempts to establish an absolutist government in matters of both church and state provoked clashes with the English Parliament and the outbreak of the Civil War in 1642. He was executed in 1649. Daniel Mytens/The Granger Collection

Paths to Constitutionalism and Absolutism:
England and France in the Seventeenth Century

Two Models of European Political Development

Constitutional Crisis and Settlement in Stuart England
James I
Charles I
Oliver Cromwell and the Puritan Republic
Charles II and the Restoration of the Monarchy
James II and Renewed Fears of a Catholic England
The "Glorious Revolution"

Rise of Absolute Monarchy in France
Henry IV and Sully
Louis XIII and Richelieu
Young Louis XIV and Mazarin

The Years of Louis's Personal Rule
King by Divine Right
Versailles
Suppression of the Jansenists
Government Geared for Warfare
Louis's Early Wars
Revocation of the Edict of Nantes
Louis's Later Wars
Louis XIV's Legacy

KEY TOPICS

- The factors behind the divergent political paths of England and France in the seventeenth century

- The conflict between Parliament and the king over taxation and religion in early Stuart England, the English Civil War, and the abolition of the monarchy

- The Restoration and the development of Parliament's supremacy over the monarchy after the "Glorious Revolution"

- The establishment of an absolutist monarchy in France under Louis XIV

- Religious policies of Louis XIV

- The wars of Louis XIV

During the seventeenth century, England and France moved in two very different political directions. By the close of the century, after decades of fierce civil war and religious conflict that pitted Parliament and monarch against each other, England had developed into a parliamentary monarchy with a policy of religious toleration. Parliament, composed of the House of Lords and the House of Commons, shared responsibility for government with the monarch. It met regularly, and the Commons, composed primarily of wealthy landed gentry, had to stand for election every three years. By contrast, France developed an absolutist, centralized form of government dominated by a monarchy that shared little power with any other national institutions. Its authority resided rather in a complex set of relationships with local nobility, guilds, and towns and in its ability to support the largest standing army in Europe. In the seventeenth century France also abandoned Henry IV's policy of religious toleration and proscribed all but the Roman Catholic church.

[handwritten marginal note:] proscribe = to denounce or condemn as dangerous or harmful; prohibit; outlaw

These English and French forms of government became models for other nations. The French model, termed absolutism in the nineteenth century, would be imitated by other monarchies across the continent during the eighteenth century. The English model would later inspire the political creed known in the nineteenth century as liberalism. Like all such political labels, these terms, although useful, can conceal considerable complexity. English "parliamentary monarchs" did not share all power with Parliament; they controlled the army, foreign policy, and much patronage. Likewise the "absolute monarchs" of France and their later imitators elsewhere in Europe were not truly absolute: laws, traditions, and many local institutions and customs limited their power.

Two Models of European Political Development

In the second half of the sixteenth century, changes in military organization, weapons, and tactics sharply increased the cost of warfare. Because traditional sources of revenue were inadequate to finance these growing costs—as well as the costs of government—monarchs sought new sources. Only monarchies that built a secure financial base which was not deeply dependent on the support of estates, diets, or assemblies of nobles achieved absolute rule. The French monarchy succeeded in this effort after midcentury, whereas the English monarchy failed. The paths to that success and failure led to the two models of government—absolutism in France and parliamentary monarchy in England—that shaped subsequent political development in Europe.

In their pursuit of adequate income, English monarchs of the seventeenth century threatened the local political interests and economic well-being of the country's nobility and others of great landed and commercial wealth. These politically active groups, invoking traditional English liberties in their defense, effectively resisted the monarchs' attempted intrusions throughout the century.

The experience of Louis XIV, the French king, was different. During the second half of the seventeenth century, he would make the French nobility dependent upon his goodwill and patronage. In turn, he would support their local influence and their place in a firm social hierarchy. But even the French king's dominance of the nobility was not complete. Louis accepted the authority of the noble-dominated *Parlement* of Paris to register royal decrees before they officially became law, and he permitted regional *parlements* to exercise considerable authority over local administration and taxation. Funds from taxes levied by the central monarchy found their way into many local pockets.

Religious factors also affected the political destinies of England and France. A strong Protestant religious movement known as Puritanism arose in England and actively opposed the Stuart monarchy. Puritanism represented a nonpolitical force that sought at first to limit and eventually to overturn the English monarchy. Louis XIV, in contrast, crushed the Protestant communities of France. He was generally supported in these efforts by Roman Catholics, who saw religious uniformity enforced by the monarchy working to their advantage.

There were also major institutional differences between the two countries. In Parliament, England possessed a political institution that had long bargained with the monarch over political issues. In the early seventeenth century, to be sure, Parliament did not meet regularly and was not the strong institution it would become by the close of the century. Nor was there anything certain or inevitable about the transformation it underwent over the course of the century. The institutional basis for it, however, was in place. Parliament was there and expected to be consulted from time to time. Its members—nobility and gentry—had experience organizing and speaking, writing legislation, and criticizing royal policies. Furthermore, the English had a legal and political tradition based on concepts of liberty to which members of Parliament and their supporters throughout the country could and did appeal in their conflict with the monarchy.

For all intents, France lacked a similarly strong tradition of broad liberties, representation, and bargaining between the monarchy and other national institutions. The Estates General had met from time to time to grant certain revenues to the monarch, but it played no role after the early seventeenth century. It met in 1614, but thereafter the monarchy was able to find other sources of income, and the Estates General was not called again until the eve of the French Revolution in 1789. Consequently, whatever political forces might have wished to oppose or limit the monarchy lacked both an institutional base from which to operate and a tradition of meetings during which the necessary political skills might have been developed.

Finally, personalities played an important role. During the first half of the century, France profited from the guidance of two of its most able statesmen: Cardinals Richelieu and Mazarin. Mazarin trained Louis XIV to be a hardworking, if not always wise, monarch. Louis drew strong and capable ministers about himself. The four Stuart monarchs of England, on the other hand, had trouble simply making people trust them. They did not always keep their word.

This elegant painting portays a very quiet London of the mid-1630s. During the next sixty years it would suffer wrenching political turmoil and the devastation of a great fire. Claude de Jongh (fl. 1615–1663), *The Thames at Westminster Stairs*, signed and dated 163(?1 or 7). Oil on panel, 18-1/4 × 31-1/2 in. (46.4 × 80 cm). B1973.1.31. Yale Center for British Art, Paul Mellon Collection

They acted on whim. They often displayed faulty judgment. In a political situation that demanded compromise, they rarely offered any. They offended significant groups of their subjects unnecessarily. In a nation that saw itself as strongly Protestant, they were suspected, sometimes accurately, of Catholic sympathies. Many of Charles's opponents in Parliament, of course, had flaws of their own, but the nature of the situation focused attention and criticism on the king.

In both England and France, the nobility and large landowners stood at the top of the social hierarchy and sought to protect their privileges and local interests. Important segments of the British nobility and landed classes came to distrust the Stuart monarchs, whom they believed sought to undermine their local political control and social standing. Parliamentary government was the result of the efforts of these English landed classes to protect their concerns and limit the power of the monarchy to interfere with life on the local level. The French nobility under Louis XIV, in contrast, eventually concluded that the best way to secure its own interests was to support his monarchy. He provided nobles with many forms of patronage, and he protected their tax exemptions, their wealth, and their local social standing.

The divergent developments of England and France in the seventeenth century would have surprised most people in 1600. It was not inevitable that the English monarchy would have to govern through Parliament or that the French monarchy would avoid dealing with national political institutions that could significantly limit its authority. The Stuart kings of England certainly aspired to the autocracy Louis XIV achieved, and some English political philosophers eloquently defended the divine right of kings and absolute rule. At the beginning of the seventeenth century, the English monarchy was strong. Queen Elizabeth, after a reign of almost forty-five years, was much revered. Parliament met only when called to provide financial support to the monarch. France, on the other hand, was emerging from the turmoil of its religious wars. The strife of that conflict had torn the society asunder. The monarchy was relatively weak. Henry IV, who had become king in 1589, pursued a policy of religious toleration. The French nobles had significant military forces at their disposal and in the middle of the seventeenth century confronted the king with rebellion. These conditions would change dramatically in both nations by the late seventeenth century.

Constitutional Crisis and Settlement in Stuart England

James I

In 1603 without opposition or incident, James VI of Scotland (r. 1603–1625), the son of Mary Stuart, Queen of Scots, succeeded the childless Elizabeth as James I of England. His was a difficult situation. The elderly queen had been very popular and was totally identified with the nation. James was not well known, would never be popular, and, as a Scot, was an outsider. He inherited not only the crown, but also a large royal debt and a fiercely divided church—problems that his politically active subjects expected him to address. The new king strongly advocated the divine right of kings, a subject on which he had written a book—*A Trew Law of Free Monarchies*—in 1598. He expected to rule with a minimum of consultation beyond his own royal court.

James quickly managed to anger many of his new subjects, but he did not wholly alienate them. In this period, Parliament met only when the monarch summoned it, which James hoped to do rarely. Its chief business was to grant certain sources of income. The real value of these revenues, however, had been falling during the past half century, limiting their importance and thus the importance of Parliament to the king. To meet his needs, James developed other sources of income, largely by levying—solely on the authority of ill-defined privileges claimed to be attached to the office of king—new custom duties known as *impositions*. These were a version of the older customs duties known as *tonnage* and *poundage*. Members of Parliament resented these independent efforts to raise revenues as an affront to their authority over the royal purse, but they did not seek a serious confrontation. Rather, throughout James's reign, they wrangled and negotiated behind the scenes.

The religious problem also festered under James. Puritans within the Church of England had hoped that James's experience with the Scottish Presbyterian church and his own Protestant upbringing would incline him to favor their efforts to further the reformation of the English church. Since the days of Elizabeth, they had sought to eliminate elaborate religious ceremonies and replace the hierarchical episcopal system of church governance with a more representative Presbyterian form like that of the Calvinist churches on the Continent.

In January 1604, the Puritans had their first direct dealing with the new king. James responded in that month to a statement of Puritan grievances, the so-called Millenary Petition, at a special religious conference at Hampton Court. The political implications of the demands in this petition concerned him, and their tone offended him. To the dismay of the Puritans, he firmly declared his intention to maintain and even enhance the Anglican episcopacy. "A Scottish presbytery," he snorted, "agreeth as well with monarchy as God and the devil. No bishops, no king." James was not simply being arbitrary. Elizabeth also had not accommodated the Puritan demands. To have done so would have worsened the already existing strife within the Church of England.

Both sides left the conference with their suspicions of one another largely confirmed. The Hampton Court conference did, however, sow one fruitful seed: A commission was appointed to render a new translation of the Bible. That mission was fulfilled in 1611 with the publication of the eloquent authorized, or King James, version.

James also offended the Puritans with his opposition to their narrow view of human life and social activities. The Puritans believed that Sunday should be a day taken up largely with religious observances and little leisure or recreation. James believed that recreation and sports were innocent activities and good for his people. He also believed that Puritan narrowness discouraged Roman Catholics from converting to the Church of England. Consequently, in 1618 he issued the *Book of Sports*, which permitted games on Sunday for people who attended Church of England services. Many clergy refused to read his order from the pulpit, and he had to rescind it. (See "King James I Defends Popular Recreation Against the Puritans.")

It was during James's reign that some religious dissenters began to leave England. In 1620 Puritan separatists founded Plymouth Colony in Cape Cod Bay in North America, preferring flight from England to Anglican conformity. Later in the 1620s, a larger, better financed group of Puritans left England to found the Massachusetts Bay Colony. In each case, the colonists believed that reformation would or could not go far enough in England and that only in America could they worship freely and organize a truly reformed church.

Although James inherited a difficult situation, he also created special problems for himself. His court became a center of scandal and corruption. He governed by favorites, the most influential of whom was the duke of Buckingham, whom rumor made the king's homosexual lover. Buckingham controlled royal patronage and openly sold peerages and titles to the highest bidders—a practice that angered the nobility because it cheapened their rank. There had always been court favorites, but never before had a single person so controlled access to the monarch.

James's foreign policy also roused opposition. He regarded himself as a peacemaker. Peace reduced pressures on royal revenues and the need for larger debts. The less his demands for money, the less the king had to depend on the goodwill of Parliament. In 1604 he concluded a much-needed peace with Spain, England's chief adversary during the second half of the sixteenth century. His subjects viewed this peace as a sign of pro-Catholic sentiment. James further increased suspicions when he tried unsuccessfully to relax the penal laws against

King James I Defends Popular Recreation Against the Puritans

The English Puritans believed in strict observance of the Sabbath, disapproving any sports, games, or general social conviviality on Sunday. James I thought that these strictures prevented many Roman Catholics from joining the Church of England. In 1618, he ordered the clergy of the Church of England to read the Book of Sports *from their pulpits. In this declaration, he permitted people to engage in certain sports and games after church services. His hope was to allow innocent recreations on Sunday while encouraging people to attend the Church of England. Despite the king's good intentions, the order offended the Puritans. The clergy resisted his order and he had to withdraw it.*

❖ *What motives of state might have led James I to issue this declaration? How does he attempt to make it favorable to the Church of England? Why might so many clergy have refused to read this statement to their congregations?*

With our own ears we heard the general complaint of our people, that they were barred from all lawful recreation and exercise upon the Sunday's afternoon, after the ending of all divine service, which cannot but produce two evils: the one the hindering of the conversion of many [Roman Catholic subjects], whom their priests will take occasion hereby to vex, persuading them that no honest mirth or recreation is lawful or tolerable in our religion, which cannot but breed a great discontentment in our people's hearts, especially as such as are peradventure upon the point of turning [to the Church of England]: the other inconvenience is, that this prohibition barreth the common and meaner sort of people from using such exercises as may make their bodies more able for war, when we or our successors shall have occasion to use them; and in place thereof sets up filthy tipplings and drunkenness, and breeds a number of idle and discontented speeches in their ale-houses. For when shall the common people have leave to exercise, if not upon the Sundays and holy days, seeing they must apply their labor and win their living in all working days?...

[A]s for our good people's lawful recreation, our pleasure likewise is, that after the end of divine service our good people be not disturbed,...or discouraged from any lawful recreation, such as dancing, either men or women; archery for men, leaping, vaulting, or any other such harmless recreation, or from having of Hay-games, Whitsun-ales, and Morris-dances; and the setting up of May-poles and other sports therewith used;...but withal we do here account still as prohibited all unlawful games to be used upon Sundays only, as bear and bull-baitings...and at all times in the meaner sort of people by law prohibited, bowling.

And likewise we bar from this benefit and liberty all such known as recusants [Roman Catholics], either men or women, as will abstain from coming to church or divine service, being therefore unworthy of any lawful recreation after the said service, that will not first come to the church and serve God; prohibiting in like sort the said recreations to any that, though [they] conform in religion [i.e., members of the Church of England], are not present in the church at the service of God, before their going to the said recreations.

From Henry Bettenson, ed., *Documents of the Christian Church*, 2d ed. (London: Oxford University Press, 1963), pp. 400–403. By permission of Oxford University Press.

Catholics. The English had not forgotten the brutal reign of Mary Tudor and the acts of treason by Catholics during Elizabeth's reign. In 1618 James hesitated, not unwisely, to rush English troops to the aid of Protestants in Germany at the outbreak of the Thirty Years' War. This hesitation caused some to question his loyalty to the Anglican Church. These suspicions increased when he tried to arrange a marriage between his son Charles and

the Spanish *Infanta* (the daughter of the king of Spain). In the king's last years, as his health failed and the reins of government passed increasingly to his son Charles and to Buckingham, parliamentary opposition and Protestant sentiment combined to undo his pro-Spanish foreign policy. In 1624, shortly before James's death, England entered a continental war against Spain largely in response to the pressures of members of Parliament.

Parliament Presents Charles I with the Petition of Right

After becoming monarch in 1625, Charles I (1625–1649) imposed unparliamen-tary taxes, coerced freemen, and quartered troops in transit in private homes. These actions deeply offended Parliament, which, in 1628, refused to grant him any funds until he rescinded those practices by recognizing the Petition of Right (June 1628). The Petition constituted a general catalog of the offenses associated with the exercise of arbitrary royal authority.

❖ *What limits does the Petition attempt to place on royal taxation? How did the Petition criticize arbitrary arrest? Why was the quartering of soldiers in private homes so offensive?*

[The Lords Spirit and Temporal, and commons in Parliament assembled] do humbly pray your Most Excellent Majesty, that no man hereafter be compelled to make or yield any gift, loan, benevolence, tax, or such like charge, without common consent by Act of parliament; and that none be called to make answer, to take such oath, or to give attendance, or be confined, or other-wise molested or disquieted concerning the same, or for refusal thereof; and that no freeman, in any such manner as in before-mentioned, be impris-oned or detained; and that your Majesty will be pleased to remove the said soldiers and mariners [who have been quartered in private homes], and that your people may not be so burdened in time to come; and that the foresaid commissions for proceeding by martial law, may be revoked and annulled; and that hereafter no commissions of like nature may issue forth to any person or per-sons whatsoever, to be executed as aforesaid, lest by colour of them any of your Majesty's subjects be destroyed or put to death, contrary to the laws and franchise of the land.

All which they most humble pray of your Most Excellent Majesty, as their rights and liberties according to the laws and statues of this realm.

The King's Reply: The King willeth that right be done according to the laws and customs of the realm; and that the statues be put in due execu-tion, that his subjects may have no cause to com-plain of any wrong or oppressions, contrary to their just rights and liberties, to the preservation whereof he holds himself as well obliged as of his prerogative.

From *The Constitutional Documents of the Puritan Revolution*, ed. by Samuel R. Gardiner (Oxford: Clarendon Press, 1889), pp. 4–5.

Charles I

Parliament had favored the war with Spain, but would not adequately finance it because its members dis-trusted Buckingham. Unable to gain adequate funds from Parliament, Charles I (r. 1625– 1649), like his fa-ther, resorted to extraparliamentary measures. He levied new tariffs and duties and attempted to collect discontinued taxes. He even subjected the English peo-ple to a so-called forced loan (a tax theoretically to be repaid), imprisoning those who refused to pay. The gov-ernment quartered troops in transit to war zones in private homes. All these actions intruded on life at the local level and challenged the power of the local nobles and landowners to control their districts.

When Parliament met in 1628, its members were furious. Taxes were being illegally collected for a war that was going badly for England and that now, through royal blundering, involved France as well as Spain. Parliament expressed its displeasure by making the king's request for new funds conditional on his recognition of the Petition of Right. (See "Parliament Presents Charles I with the Petition of Right.") This important declaration of constitu-tional freedom required that henceforth there should be no forced loans or taxation without the consent of Parliament, that no freeman should be imprisoned without due cause, and that troops should not be billeted in private homes. It was thus an expression of resentment and resistance to the intrusion of the monarchy on the local level. Though Charles agreed to the petition, there was little confidence that he would keep his word.

YEARS OF PERSONAL RULE   In August 1628, Charles's chief minister, Buckingham, with whom Parliament had been in open dispute since 1626, was assassinated. His death, while sweet to many, did not resolve the hostility between the king and Parliament. In January 1629, Parliament further underscored its resolve to limit royal prerogative. It declared that religious innovations leading to "popery"—the term used to condemn Charles's high-church policies—and the levying of taxes without parliamentary consent were acts of treason. Perceiving that things were getting out of hand, Charles promptly dissolved Parliament and did not call it again until 1640, when war with Scotland forced him to do so.

To conserve his limited resources, Charles made peace with France in 1629 and Spain in 1630. This policy again roused fears among some of his subjects that he was too friendly to Roman Catholic powers. The French and Roman Catholic background of Charles's wife furthered these suspicions. Part of her marriage contract permitted her to hear mass daily at the English court. Charles's attitude toward the Church of England also raised suspicions. He supported a group within the church, known as Arminians, who rejected many Puritan doctrines and favored elaborate, high-church practices. The Puritans were convinced these practices would bring a return to Roman Catholicism.

To allow Charles to rule without renegotiating financial arrangements with Parliament, his chief minister, Thomas Wentworth (after 1640, earl of Strafford), instituted a policy known as *thorough*. This policy imposed strict efficiency and administrative centralization in government. Its goal was absolute royal control of England. Its success depended on the king's ability to operate independently of Parliament, which no law required him to summon.

Charles's ministers exploited every legal fundraising device. They enforced previously neglected laws and extended existing taxes into new areas. For example, starting in 1634, they gradually extended inland to the whole of England a tax called *ship money*, normally levied only on coastal areas to pay for naval protection. A great landowner named John Hampden mounted a legal challenge to the extension of this tax. Although the king prevailed in what was a close legal contest, his victory was costly. It deepened the animosity toward him among the powerful landowners, who would elect and sit in Parliament should he need to summon it.

During these years of personal rule, Charles surrounded himself with an elaborate court and patronized some of the greatest artists of the day. Like his father, he sold noble titles and knighthoods, lessening their value and the social exclusiveness conferred on those who already possessed them. Nobles and great landowners feared that the growth of the court, the king's relentless pursuit of revenue, and the inflation of titles and honors would reduce their local influence and social standing. They also feared that the monarch might actually succeed in governing without ever again calling Parliament into session.

Charles might very well have ruled indefinitely without Parliament had not his religious policies provoked war with Scotland. James I had allowed a wide variety of religious observances in England, Scotland, and Ireland. Charles, by contrast, hoped to impose religious conformity at least within England and Scotland. William Laud (1573–1645), who was first Charles's religious advisor and, after 1633, archbishop of Canterbury, held a high-church view of Anglicanism. He favored powerful bishops, elaborate liturgy, and personal religious observance and devotion rather than the preaching and listening favored by the Puritans. As a member of the Court of High Commission, Laud had already radicalized the English Puritans by denying them the right to publish and preach. In 1637 Charles and Laud, against the opposition of the English Puritans as well as the Scots, tried to impose on Scotland the English episcopal system and a prayerbook almost identical to the Anglican *Book of Common Prayer*.

The Scots rebelled, and Charles, with insufficient resources for a war, was forced to call Parliament. The members of Parliament opposed his policies almost as much as they wanted to crush the rebellion. Led by John Pym (1584–1643), they refused even to consider funds for war until the king agreed to redress a long list of political and religious grievances. The king, in response, immediately dissolved Parliament—hence its name, the Short Parliament (April–May 1640). When the Presbyterian Scots invaded England and defeated an English army at the Battle of Newburn in the summer of 1640, Charles reconvened Parliament, this time on its terms, for a long and most fateful duration.

THE LONG PARLIAMENT The landowners and the merchant classes represented by Parliament had resented the king's financial measures and paternalistic rule for some time. The Puritans in Parliament resented his religious policies and deeply distrusted the influence of the Roman Catholic queen. The Long Parliament (1640–1660) thus acted with widespread support and general unanimity when it convened in November 1640.

The House of Commons impeached both the earl of Strafford and Archbishop Laud. Disgraced and convicted by a parliamentary bill of attainder (a judgment of treason entailing loss of civil rights), Stafford was executed in 1641. Laud was imprisoned and also later executed (1645). Parliament abolished the Court of Star Chamber and the Court of High Commission, royal instruments of political and religious *thorough*, respectively. The levying of new taxes without the consent of Parliament and the inland extension of *ship money* now became illegal. Finally, Parliament resolved that no more than three years should elapse between its meetings and that it could not be dissolved without its own consent. Parliament was determined that neither Charles nor any future English king could again govern without consulting it.

Despite its cohesion on these initial actions, Parliament was divided over the precise direction to take on religious reform. Both moderate Puritans (the Presbyterians) and more extreme Puritans (the Independents) wanted the complete abolition of the episcopal system and the *Book of Common Prayer*. The majority Presbyterians sought to reshape England religiously along Calvinist lines, with local congregations subject to higher representative governing bodies (presbyteries). Independents wanted a much more fully decentralized church with every congregation as its own final authority. Finally, many conservatives in both houses of Parliament were determined to preserve the English church in its current form. Their numbers fell dramatically after 1642, however, when many of them left the House of Commons with the outbreak of civil war.

These divisions further intensified in October 1641, when a rebellion erupted in Ireland and Parliament was asked to raise funds for an army to suppress it. Pym and his followers, loudly reminding the House of Commons of the king's past behavior, argued that Charles could not be trusted with an army and that Parliament should become the commander-in-chief of English armed forces. Parliamentary conservatives, on the other hand, were appalled by such a bold departure from tradition.

ERUPTION OF CIVIL WAR Charles saw the division within Parliament as a chance to reassert his power. On December 1, 1641, Parliament presented him with the "Grand Remonstrance," a more-than-200-article summary of popular and parliamentary grievances against the crown. In January 1642, he invaded Parliament with his soldiers. He intended to arrest Pym and the other leaders, but they had been forewarned and managed to escape. The king then withdrew from London and began to raise an army. Shocked by his action, a majority of the House of Commons passed the Militia Ordinance, which gave Parliament authority to raise an army of its own. The die was now cast. For the next four years (1642–1646), civil war engulfed England.

Charles assembled his forces at Nottingham, and the war began in August. It was fought over two main issues:

- Would an absolute monarchy or a parliamentary government rule England?
- Would English religion be controlled by the king's bishops and conform to high Anglican practice or adopt a decentralized, Presbyterian system of church governance?

Charles's supporters, known as Cavaliers, were located in the northwestern half of England. The parliamentary opposition, known as Roundheads because of their close-cropped hair, had its stronghold in the southeastern half of the country. Supporters of both sides included nobility, gentry, and townspeople. The chief factor distinguishing them was religion; the Puritans tended to favor Parliament.

Oliver Cromwell and the Puritan Republic

Two factors led finally to Parliament's victory. The first was an alliance with Scotland consummated in 1643 when John Pym persuaded Parliament to accept the terms of the Solemn League and Covenant, an

Oliver Cromwell's New Model Army defeated the royalists in the English Civil War. After the execution of Charles I in 1649, Cromwell dominated the short-lived English republic, conquered Ireland and Scotland, and ruled as Lord Protector from 1653 until his death in 1658. Stock Montage, Inc./Historical Pictures Collection

agreement that committed Parliament, with the Scots, to a Presbyterian system of church government. For the Scots, this policy meant that they would never again be confronted with an attempt to impose the English prayerbook on their religious services. The second factor was the reorganization of the parliamentary army under Oliver Cromwell (1599–1658), a middle-aged country squire of iron discipline and strong Independent religious sentiment. Cromwell and his "godly men" favored neither the episcopal system of the king nor the pure Presbyterian system of the Solemn League and Covenant. They were willing to tolerate an established majority church, but only if it also permitted Protestant dissenters to worship outside it. (See "John Milton Defends Freedom to Print Books.")

The allies won the Battle of Marston Moor in 1644, the largest engagement of the war. In June 1645, Cromwell's newly reorganized forces, known as the New Model Army, fighting with disciplined fanaticism, won a decisive victory over the king at Naseby. (See Map 13–1.)

Defeated militarily, Charles tried again to take advantage of divisions within Parliament, this time seeking to win the Presbyterians and the Scots over to the royalist side. But Cromwell and his army firmly foiled him. In December 1648, Colonel Thomas Pride physically barred the Presbyterians, who made up a majority of Parliament, from taking their seats. After "Pride's Purge," only a "rump" of fewer than fifty members remained. Though small in numbers, this Independent Rump Parliament did not hesitate to use its power. On January 30, 1649, after a trial by a special court, the Rump Parliament executed Charles as a public criminal and thereafter abolished the monarchy, the House of Lords, and the Anglican Church. What had begun as a civil war had at this point become a revolution.

From 1649 to 1660, England became officially a Puritan republic, although for much of that time it was dominated by Cromwell. During this period, Cromwell's army conquered Ireland and Scotland, creating the single political entity of Great Britain. Cromwell, however, was a military man and no politician. He was increasingly frustrated by what seemed to him to be pettiness and dawdling on the part of Parliament. When, in 1653, the House of Commons entertained a motion to disband his expensive army of 50,000, Cromwell responded by marching in and disbanding Parliament. He ruled thereafter as Lord Protector.

This military dictatorship, however, proved no more effective than Charles's rule had been and became just as harsh and hated. Cromwell's great army and foreign adventures inflated his budget to

MAP 13–1   THE ENGLISH CIVIL WAR.   *This map shows the rapid deterioration of the royalist position in 1645.*

three times that of Charles's. Near chaos reigned in many places, and commerce suffered throughout England. Cromwell was as intolerant of Anglicans as Charles had been of Puritans. People deeply resented his Puritan prohibitions of drunkenness, theatergoing, and dancing. Political liberty vanished in the name of religious liberty.

Cromwell's challenge had been to devise a political structure to replace that of monarch and Parliament. He tried various arrangements, none of which worked. He quarreled with the various Parliaments that were elected while he was lord protector. By the time of his death in 1658, most of the English were ready to end the Puritan religious experiment and the republican political experiment and return to their traditional institutions of government. Negotiations between leaders of the

The bleeding head of Charles I is exhibited to the crowd after his execution on a cold day in January 1649. The contemporary Dutch artist also professed to see the immediate ascension of Charles's soul to heaven. In fact, many saw the king as a martyr.
An Eyewitness Representation of the Execution of King Charles I (1600–49) of England, 1649 (oil on canvas) by Weesop (fl. 1649–49). Private Collection/Bridgeman Art Library, London

army and the exiled Charles II (r. 1660–1685), son of Charles I, led to the restoration of the Stuart monarchy in 1660.

Charles II and the Restoration of the Monarchy

Charles II returned to England amid great rejoicing. A man of considerable charm and political skill, Charles set a refreshing new tone after eleven years of somber Puritanism. His restoration returned England to the status quo of 1642, with a hereditary monarch once again on the throne, no legal requirement that he summon Parliament regularly, and the Anglican Church, with its bishops and prayer book, supreme in religion.

The king, however, had secret Catholic sympathies and favored a policy of religious toleration. He wanted to allow all those outside the Church of England, Catholics as well as Puritans, to worship freely so long as they remained loyal to the throne. But in Parliament, even the ultraroyalist Anglicans did not believe that patriotism and religion could be separated. Between 1661 and 1665, through a series of laws known as the Clarendon Code, Parliament excluded Roman Catholics, Presbyterians, and Independents from the religious and political life of the nation. These laws imposed penalties for

attending non-Anglican worship services, required strict adherence to the *Book of Common Prayer* and the *Thirty-Nine Articles*, and demanded oaths of allegiance to the Church of England from all persons serving in local government.

At the time of the Restoration, England, again as under Cromwell in 1651, adopted navigation acts that required all imports to be carried either in English ships or in ships registered to the country from which the cargo originated. Dutch ships carried cargo from many nations, and such laws struck directly at Dutch dominance in the shipping industry. A series of naval wars between England and Holland ensued. Charles also attempted to tighten his grasp on the rich English colonies in North America and the Caribbean, many of which had been settled and developed by separatists who desired independence from English rule.

Although Parliament strongly supported the monarchy, Charles, following the pattern of his predecessors, required greater revenues than Parliament appropriated. These he obtained in part by increased customs duties. Because England and France were both at war with Holland, he also received aid from France. In 1670, England and France formally allied against the Dutch in the Treaty of Dover. In a secret portion of this treaty, Charles pledged to announce his conversion to Catholicism as soon as conditions in England permitted. In return for this announcement (which was never made), Louis XIV of France promised to pay a substantial subsidy to England.

In an attempt to unite the English people behind the war with Holland, and as a sign of good faith to Louis XIV, Charles issued the Declaration of Indulgence in 1672. This document suspended all laws against Roman Catholics and Protestant nonconformists. But again, the conservative Parliament proved less generous than the king and refused to grant money for the war until Charles rescinded the measure. After he did, Parliament passed the Test Act, which required all officials of the crown, civil and military, to swear an oath against the doctrine of transubstantiation—a requirement that no loyal Roman Catholic could honestly meet.

Parliament had aimed the Test Act largely at the king's brother, James, duke of York, heir to the throne and a recent devout convert to Catholicism. In 1678 a notorious liar named Titus Oates swore before a magistrate that Charles's Catholic wife, through her physician, was plotting with Jesuits and Irishmen to kill the king so that James could assume the throne. The matter was taken before Parliament, where Oates was believed. In the ensuing hysteria, known as the Popish Plot, several people were tried and executed. Riding the crest of anti-Catholic sentiment and led by the earl of Shaftesbury (1621–1683), opposition members of Parliament, called Whigs, made an impressive, but unsuccessful, effort to enact a bill excluding James from succession to the throne.

More suspicious than ever of Parliament, Charles II turned again to increased customs duties and the assistance of Louis XIV for extra income. By these means, he was able to rule from 1681 to 1685 without recalling Parliament. In those years, Charles suppressed much of his opposition. He drove the

John Milton Defends Freedom to Print Books

Certain Puritans were as concerned about resisting potential tyranny from Parliament as from the monarchy. During the English Civil War, the Parliament passed a very strict censorship measure. In "Areopagitica" (1644), John Milton, later the author of Paradise Lost (1667), attacked this law and contributed one of the major defenses of the freedom of the press in the history of Western culture. In the passage that follows, he compares the life of a book with the life of a human being.

❖ *Why does Milton think that it may be more dangerous and harmful to attack a book than to attack a person? Was life cheaper and intelligence rarer in his time? Does he have particular kinds of books in mind? What can a book do for society that people cannot?*

I deny not but that it is of greatest concern in the Church and Commonwealth to have a vigilant eye how books demean themselves as well as men; and thereafter to confine, imprison, and do sharpest justice on them as [if they were criminals]; for books are not absolutely dead things, but do contain a progeny of life in them to be as active as that soul was whose progeny they are; nay, they do preserve as in a vial the purest efficacy and extraction of that living intellect that bred them....He who kills a man kills a reasonable creature, God's Image; but he who destroys a good book, kills reason itself, kills the Image of God, as it were....Many a man lives [as] a burden to the Earth; but a good book is the precious lifeblood of a master spirit, embalmed and treasured up on purpose to a life beyond life. It is true, no age can restore a life, whereof, perhaps there is no great loss; and revolutions of ages do not oft recover the loss of a rejected truth, for the want of which whole nations fare the worse. We should be wary, therefore, what persecution we raise against the living labours of public men, how we spill that seasoned life of man preserved and stored up in books; since we see a kind of homicide may be thus committed, sometimes a martyrdom, and if it extends to the whole impression, a kind of massacre, whereof the execution ends not in the slaying of an elemental life, but strikes at that ethereal...essence, the breath of reason itself; slays an immortality rather than a life.

From J. A. St. John, ed., *The Prose Works of John Milton* (London: H. G. Bohn, 1843–1853), 2:8–9.

Charles II (r. 1660–1685) was a person of considerable charm and political skill. Here he is portrayed as the founder of the Royal Society. Robert Harding Picture Library

earl of Shaftesbury into exile, executed several Whig leaders for treason, and bullied local corporations into electing members of Parliament who were submissive to the royal will. When Charles died in 1685 (after a deathbed conversion to Catholicism), he left James the prospect of a Parliament filled with royal friends.

James II and Renewed Fears of a Catholic England

James II (r. 1685–1688) did not know how to make the most of a good thing. He alienated Parliament by insisting on the repeal of the Test Act. When Parliament balked, he dissolved it and proceeded openly to appoint known Catholics to high positions in both his court and the army. In 1687 he issued the Declaration of Indulgence, which suspended all religious tests and permitted free worship. Local candidates for Parliament who opposed the declaration were removed from their offices by the king's soldiers and were replaced by

Catholics. In June 1688, James went so far as to imprison seven Anglican bishops who had refused to publicize his suspension of laws against Catholics. Each of these actions represented a direct royal attack on the local power and authority of nobles, landowners, the church, and other corporate bodies whose members believed that they possessed particular legal privileges. James was attacking English liberty and challenging all manner of social privileges and influence.

Under the guise of a policy of enlightened toleration, James was actually seeking to subject all English institutions to the power of the monarchy. His goal was absolutism, and even conservative, loyalist Tories, as the royal supporters were called, could not abide this policy. The English feared, with reason, that James planned to imitate the religious intolerance of Louis XIV, who had, in 1685, revoked the Edict of Nantes (which had protected French Protestants for almost a century) and imposed Catholicism on the entire nation, using his dragoons against those who protested or resisted.

Test Act
an oath against
the doctrine
of Transub-
stantiation.

James soon faced united opposition. When his Catholic second wife gave birth to a son and Catholic male heir to the throne on June 20, 1688, opposition turned to action. The English had hoped that James would die without a male heir so that the throne would pass to Mary, his Protestant eldest daughter. Mary was the wife of William III of Orange, *stadtholder* of the Netherlands, great-grandson of William the Silent, and the leader of European opposition to Louis XIV's imperial designs. Within days of the birth of James's son, Whig and Tory members of Parliament formed a coalition and invited Orange to invade England to preserve "traditional liberties," that is, the Anglican Church and parliamentary government.

The "Glorious Revolution"

William of Orange arrived with his army in November 1688 and was received without opposition by the English people. In the face of sure defeat, James fled to France and the protection of Louis XIV. With James gone, Parliament declared the throne vacant and, on its own authority in 1689, proclaimed William and Mary the new monarchs, completing the successful bloodless "Glorious Revolution." William and Mary, in turn, recognized a Bill of Rights that limited the powers of the monarchy and guaranteed the civil liberties of the English privileged classes. Henceforth, England's monarchs would be subject to law and would rule by

William and Mary became the monarchs of England in 1689. Their accession brought England's economic and military resources into the balance against the France of Louis XIV. Robert Harding Picture Library

England in the Seventeenth Century	
1603	James VI of Scotland becomes James I of England
1604	Hampton Court conference
1611	Publication of the authorized, or King James, version of the English Bible
1625	Charles I becomes English monarch
1628	Petition of Right
1629	Charles I dissolves Parliament and embarks on eleven years of personal rule
1640	April–May, Short Parliament November, Long Parliament convenes
1641	Grand Remonstrance
1642	Outbreak of the Civil War
1645	Charles I defeated at Naseby
1648	Pride's Purge
1649	Charles I executed
1649–1660	Various attempts at a Puritan Commonwealth
1660	Charles II restored to the English throne
1670	Secret Treaty of Dover between France and England
1672	Parliament passes the Test Act
1678	Popish Plot
1685	James II becomes king of England
1688	"Glorious Revolution"
1689	William and Mary proclaimed English monarchs
1701	Acts of Settlement provides for Hanoverian succession
1702–1715	Reign of Queen Anne, the last of the Stuarts

the consent of Parliament, which was to be called into session every three years. The Bill of Rights also pointedly prohibited Roman Catholics from occupying the English throne. The Toleration Act of 1689 permitted worship by all Protestants but outlawed Roman Catholics and anti-Trinitarians (those who denied the Christian doctrine of the Trinity).

The measure closing this century of strife was the Act of Settlement in 1701. This bill provided for the English crown to go to the Protestant House of Hanover in Germany if none of the children of Queen Anne (r. 1702–1714), the second daughter of James II and the last of the Stuart monarchs, was alive at her death. She outlived all of her children, so in 1714, the elector of Hanover became King George I of England, the third foreign monarch to occupy the English throne in just over a century.

The Glorious Revolution of 1688 established a framework of government by and for the governed that seemed to bear out the arguments of John Locke's *Second Treatise of Government* (1690). In this work, Locke described the relationship of a king and his people as a bilateral contract. If the king broke that contract, the people, by whom Locke meant the privileged and powerful, had the right to depose him. Locke had written the essay before the revolution, but it came to be read as a justification for it. Although neither in fact nor in theory a "popular" revolution such as would occur in America and France a hundred years later, the Glorious Revolution did establish in England a permanent check on monarchical power by the classes represented in Parliament. At the same time, as will be seen in Chapter 15, in its wake the English government had achieved a secure financial base that would allow it to pursue a century of warfare.

Rise of Absolute Monarchy in France

Seventeenth-century France, in contrast to England, saw both discontent among the nobility and religious pluralism smothered by the absolute monarchy and the closed Catholic state of Louis XIV (r. 1643–1715). An aggressive ruler who sought glory (*la gloire*) in foreign wars, Louis XIV subjected his subjects at home to "one king, one law, one faith."

Historians once portrayed Louis XIV's reign as a time when the rising central monarchy exerted far-reaching, direct control of the nation at all levels. A somewhat different picture has now emerged. Louis's predecessors and their chief ministers, in the half century before his reign, had already tried to impose direct rule, arousing discontent and, at midcentury, a rebellion among the nobility. Louis's genius was to make the monarchy the most important and powerful political institution in France while also assuring the nobles and other wealthy groups of their social standing and political and social influence on the local level. Rather than destroying existing local social and political institutions, Louis largely worked through them. Once nobles understood that the king would support their local authority, they supported his central royal authority. In other words, the king and the nobles came to recognize that they needed each other. Nevertheless, Louis made it clear to all concerned that he was the senior partner in the relationship.

Louis's royal predecessors laid the institutional foundations for absolute monarchy and also taught him certain practices to avoid. Just as the emergence of a strong Parliament was not inevitable in England, neither was the emergence of an absolute monarchy in France.

Henry IV and Sully

Coming to the throne after the French wars of religion, Henry of Navarre who became Henry IV (r. 1589–1610; see Chapter 12) sought to curtail the privileges of the French nobility. His targets were the provincial governors and the regional *parlements*, especially the powerful *Parlement* of Paris, where a divisive spirit lived on. Here were to be found the old privileged groups, tax-exempt magnates who were largely preoccupied with protecting their self-interests. During the subsequent reign of Louis XIII (r. 1610–1643), royal civil servants known as *intendants* subjected these privileged groups to stricter supervision, implementing the king's will with some success in the provinces. An important function of the *intendants* was to prevent abuses from the sale of royal offices that conferred the right to collect revenues, sell licenses, or carry out other remunerative forms of administration. It was usually nobles who acquired these lucrative offices, which was one reason for their ongoing influence.

After decades of religious and civil war, an economy more amenable to governmental regulation emerged during Henry IV's reign. Henry and his finance minister, the duke of Sully (1560–1641), established government monopolies on gunpowder, mines, and salt, preparing the way for the mercantilist policies of Louis XIV and his minister, Colbert. They began a canal system to link the Atlantic and the Mediterranean by joining the Saône, the Loire, the Seine, and the Meuse rivers. They introduced the royal *corvée*, a labor tax that created a national force of drafted workers who were employed to improve roads and the conditions of internal travel. Sully even dreamed of organizing the whole of Europe politically and commercially into a kind of common market.

Louis XIII and Richelieu

Henry IV was assassinated in 1610, and the following year Sully retired. Because Henry's son and successor, Louis XIII, was only nine years old at his father's death, the task of governing fell to the queen mother, Marie de Médicis (d. 1642). Finding herself in a vulnerable position, she sought security abroad by signing a ten-year mutual defense pact with France's archrival Spain in the Treaty of Fontainebleau (1611). This alliance also arranged for the later marriage of Louis XIII to the Spanish *Infanta*, as well as for the marriage of the queen's daughter Elizabeth to the heir to the Spanish throne. The queen sought internal security against pressures from the French nobility by

Cardinal Richelieu laid the foundations for the political ascendancy of the French monarchy. Cardinal Richelieu by Philippe de Champaigne. The National Gallery, London

promoting the career of Cardinal Richelieu (1585–1642) as the king's chief adviser. Richelieu, loyal and shrewd, aspired to make France a supreme European power. He, more than any other person, was the secret of French success in the first half of the seventeenth century.

An apparently devout Catholic who also believed that the church best served both his own ambition and the welfare of France, Richelieu pursued a strongly anti-Habsburg policy. Although he supported the Spanish alliance of the queen and Catholic religious unity within France, he was determined to contain Spanish power and influence, even when that meant aiding and abetting Protestant Europe. It is an indication both of Richelieu's awkward political situation and of his diplomatic agility that he could, in 1631, pledge funds to the Protestant army of Gustavus Adolphus, the king of Sweden, while also insisting that Catholic Bavaria be spared from attack and that Catholics in conquered countries be permitted to practice their religion. One measure of the success of Richelieu's foreign policies can be seen in France's substantial gains in land and political influence when the Treaty of Westphalia (1648) ended hostilities in the Holy Roman Empire (see Chapter 12) and the Treaty of the Pyrenees (1659) sealed peace with Spain.

At home, Richelieu pursued centralizing policies utterly without qualm. Supported by the king, who let his chief minister make most decisions of state, Richelieu stepped up the campaign against separatist provincial governors and parlements. He made it clear that there was only one law, that of the king, and none could stand above it. When disobedient nobles defied his edicts, they were imprisoned and even executed. Such treatment of the nobility won Richelieu much enmity, even from the queen mother, who, unlike Richelieu, was not always willing to place the larger interests of the state above the pleasure of favorite nobles.

Richelieu started the campaign against the Huguenots that would end in 1685 with Louis XIV's revocation of the Edict of Nantes. Royal armies conquered major Huguenot cities in 1629. The subsequent Peace of Alais (1629) truncated the Edict of Nantes by denying Protestants the right to maintain garrisoned cities, separate political organizations, and independent law courts. Only Richelieu's foreign policy, which involved France in ties with Protestant powers, prevented the earlier implementation of the policy of extreme intolerance that marked the reign of Louis XIV. In the same year that Richelieu rescinded the independent political status of the Huguenots in the Peace of Alais, he also entered negotiations to make Gustavus Adolphus his counterweight to the expansion of Habsburg power within the Holy Roman Empire. By 1635, the Catholic soldiers of France were fighting openly with Swedish Lutherans against the emperor's army in the final phase of the Thirty Years' War. (See Chapter 12.)

Richelieu employed the arts and the printing press to defend his actions and to indoctrinate the French people in the meaning of *raison d'état* ("reason of state"). This also set a precedent for Louis XIV, who made elaborate use of royal propaganda and spectacle to assert and enhance his power.

Young Louis XIV and Mazarin

Although Richelieu helped lay the foundations for a much expanded royal authority, his immediate legacy was strong resentment of the monarchy among the French nobility and wealthy commercial groups. The crown's steady multiplication of royal offices, its replacement of local authorities by "state" agents, and its reduction of local sources of patronage undermined the traditional position of the privileged groups in French society. Among those affected were officers of the crown in the law courts and other royal institutions.

When Louis XIII died in 1643, Louis XIV was only five years old. During his minority, the queen mother, Anne of Austria (d. 1666), placed the reins of govern-

This medallion shows Anne of Austria, the wife of Louis XIII, with her son, Louis XIV. She wisely placed political authority in the hands of Cardinal Mazarin, who prepared Louis to govern France. Giraudon/Art Resource, N.Y.

ment in the hands of Cardinal Mazarin (1602–1661), who continued Richelieu's determined policy of centralization. During Mazarin's regency, long-building resentment produced a backlash: Between 1649 and 1652, in a series of widespread rebellions known as the *Fronde* (after the slingshot used by street boys), segments of the nobility and townspeople sought to reverse the drift toward absolute monarchy and to preserve local autonomy.

The *Parlement* of Paris initiated the revolt in 1649, and the nobility at large soon followed. Urging them on were the influential wives of princes whom Mazarin had imprisoned for treason. The many (the nobility) briefly triumphed over the one (the monarchy) when Mazarin released the imprisoned princes in February 1651. He and Louis XIV thereafter entered a short exile (Mazarin leaving France, Louis fleeing Paris). They returned in October 1652 after an interlude of inefficient and nearly anarchic rule by the nobility. The period of the *Fronde* convinced most French people that the rule of a strong king was preferable to the rule of many regional powers with competing and irreconcilable claims. At the same time, Louis XIV and his later advisors learned that heavy-handed policies like those of Richelieu and Mazarin could endanger the monarchy. Louis would ultimately concentrate unprecedented authority in the monarchy, but his means would be more clever than those of his predecessors.

The Years of Louis's Personal Rule

On the death of Mazarin, Louis XIV assumed personal control of the government. Unlike his royal predecessors, he appointed no single chief minister. One result was to make revolt more difficult. Rebellious nobles would now be challenging the king directly; they could not claim to be resisting only a bad minister.

Mazarin prepared Louis XIV well to rule France. The turbulent events of his youth also made an indelible impression on the king. Louis wrote in his memoirs that the *Fronde* caused him to loathe "kings of straw," and he followed two strategies to assure that he would never become one.

First, Louis and his advisors became masters of propaganda and the creation of a political image. Indoctrinated with a strong sense of the grandeur of his crown, Louis never missed an opportunity to impress it on the French people. When the *dauphin* (the heir to the French throne) was born in 1662, for example, Louis appeared for the celebration dressed as a Roman emperor.

Second, Louis made sure that the French nobles and other major social groups would benefit from the growth of his own authority. Although he maintained control over foreign affairs and limited the influence of noble institutions on the monarchy, he never tried to abolish those institutions or limit their authority at the local level. The crown, for example, usually conferred informally with regional *parlements* before making rulings that would affect them. Likewise, the crown would rarely enact economic regulations without consulting local opinion. Local *parlements* enjoyed considerable latitude in all regional matters. In an exception to this pattern, Louis did clash with the *Parlement* of Paris, with which he had to register laws, and eventually, in 1673, he curtailed much of its power. Many regional parlements and other regional authorities, however, had resented the power of that body.

Employing these strategies of propaganda and cooperation, Louis set out to anchor his rule in the principle of the divine right of kings, to domesticate the French nobility by binding them to the court rituals of Versailles, and to crush religious dissent. (See "Art & the West.")

King by Divine Right

Reverence for the king and the personification of government in his person had been nurtured in France since Capetian times. It was a maxim of French law and popular opinion that "the king of

Bishop Bossuet Defends the Divine Right of Kings

The revolutions of the seventeenth century caused many to fear anarchy far more than tyranny, among them the influential French bishop Jacques-Bénigne Bossuet (1627–1704), the leader of French Catholicism in the second half of the seventeenth century. Louis XIV made him court preacher and tutor to his son, for whom Bossuet wrote the celebrated Universal History. *In the following excerpt, Bossuet defends the divine right and absolute power of kings. He depicts kings as embracing in their person the whole body of the state and the will of the people they govern and, as such, as being immune from judgment by any mere mortal.*

❖ *Why might Bossuet have wished to make such extravagant claims for absolute royal power? How might these claims be transferred to any form of government? What are the religious bases of Bossuet's argument? How does this argument for absolute royal authority lead also to the need for a single uniform religion in France?*

The royal power is absolute....The prince need render account of his acts to no one. "I counsel thee to keep the king's commandment, and that in regard of the oath of God. Be not hasty to go out of his sight; stand not on an evil thing for he doeth whatsoever pleaseth him. Where the word of a king is, there is power; and who may say unto him, What doest thou? Whoso keepeth the commandment shall feel no evil thing" [Eccles. 8:2–5]. Without this absolute authority the king could neither do good nor repress evil. It is necessary that his power be such that no one can hope to escape him, and finally, the only protection of individuals against the public authority should be their innocence. This confirms the teaching of St. Paul: "Wilt thou then not be afraid of the power? Do that which is good" [Rom. 13:3].

God is infinite, God is all. The prince, as prince, is not regarded as a private person: he is a public personage, all the state is in him; the will of all the people is included in his. As all perfection and all strength are united in God, so all the power of individuals is united in the person of the prince. What grandeur that a single man should embody so much!...

Behold an immense people united in a single person; behold this holy power, paternal and absolute; behold the secret cause which governs the whole body of the state, contained in a single head: you see the image of God in the king, and you have the idea of royal majesty. God is holiness itself, goodness itself, and power itself. In these things lies the majesty of God. In the image of these things lies the majesty of the prince.

From *Politics Drawn from the Very Words of Holy Scripture*, as quoted in James Harvey Robinson, ed., *Readings in European History*, Vol. 2 (Boston: Athenaeum, 1906), pp. 275–276.

France is emperor in his realm" and the king's wish the law of the land. Building on this reverence, Louis XIV defended absolute royal authority on the grounds of divine right.

An important source for Louis's concept of royal authority was his devout tutor, the political theorist Bishop Jacques-Bénigne Bossuet (1627–1704). An ardent champion of the Gallican liberties—the traditional rights of the French king and church against the pope in matters of ecclesiastical appointments and taxation—Bossuet defended what he called the "divine right of kings." (See "Bishop Bossuet Defends the Divine Right of Kings.") In support of his claims, he cited examples of Old Testament rulers divinely appointed by, and answerable only to, God. As medieval popes had insisted that only God could judge a pope,

so Bossuet argued that none save God could judge the king. Kings may have remained duty-bound to reflect God's will in their rule—in this sense, Bossuet considered them always subject to a higher authority. Yet as God's regents on Earth, they could not be bound to the dictates of mere princes and parliaments. Such assumptions lay behind Louis XIV's alleged declaration, *"L'état, c'est moi"* ("I am the state").

Versailles

More than any other monarch of the day, Louis XIV used the physical setting of his royal court to exert political control. The palace court at Versailles on the outskirts of Paris became Louis's permanent residence after 1682. It was a true temple to royalty, architec-

Rigaud's Louis XIV: *The State Portrait*

Even if Louis XIV may never actually have said, "I am the state," the famous remark attributed to him, most of his subjects and the other crowned heads of Europe certainly saw him as such. Hyacinthe Rigaud painted Louis as the embodiment of official political power and authority, establishing the model for what became known for the rest of the century as "the state portrait."

Previously, most portraits or statues of Louis—and there were many—set him in an allegorical setting where he embodied qualities of mythical heroes or in a historical setting in which he resembled a Roman emperor. Rigaud's portrait (1701) is largely, though not entirely, a painting of royal majesty and royal symbols. A mature Louis appears in his coronation robes, decorated with *fleurs-de-lis*, which he would not have worn for decades. The robes, along with the crown and the throne which rests beside and behind him in the background, suggest that each day he is again crowned by his accomplishments, his justice, and his divine right to rule. He holds the scepter of state as a staff that steadies him, as he presumably saw himself steadying the French nation after the decades of turmoil that had preceded his reign. The sword of state hangs by his side partially covered, though he had led the nation in war through most of his reign and would do so throughout the next decade as well. On the base of the column at the rear of the painting in the shadows resides the figure of justice.

The Italian sculptor Bernini, who sculpted a bust of Louis taken from a portrait, once wrote, "The secret of portraits is to exaggerate what is fine, add a touch of grandeur, and diminish what is ugly or petty or even suppress it when this is possible without flattery."[1] Rigaud followed this advice in his portrait of Louis, which

Hyacinthe Rigaud, *Louis XIV*, 1701. Giraudon/Art Resource, N.Y.

[1]Quoted in Peter Burke, *The Fabrication of Louis XIV* (New Haven, CT: Yale University Press, 1992), p. 23.

displays many ironies about which both Louis and the artist must have been aware. The full, long wig suggests a more youthful figure than the now aged king of sixty-three years. Furthermore, through disease early in his reign, Louis had lost much of his hair. By the time the portrait was painted, he was often ill with gout and other diseases. The portrait hid these facts, but Rigaud, presumably with Louis's encouragement, did give his sitter a face reflecting maturity and perhaps a kind of worldly wisdom. Louis may have been comfortable with such a portrayal, because, from the middle of the 1680s, he had led a very restricted personal life after marrying his strictly devout mistress, Madame de Maintenon. The dancing monarch of the early years of the reign, suggested by the remarkably handsome, athletic legs and red shoes, had given way to a more restrained person and one so rigorously devout, that in 1685 he had undertaken a policy of persecuting French Protestants.

This portrait is of a single person and carries the name of a single artist. The majesty of the lone Louis XIV concealed a multilayered network of royal ministers and bureaucrats working, negotiating, and compromising with hundreds of local officials, councils, and courts that really constituted the royal government, later termed absolutism. The attribution of the portrait to Rigaud alone concealed the fact that this painting, as was the custom with many other portraits and large paintings of the late seventeenth and eighteenth centuries, was completed in an artist's workshop. The master of the workshop, Rigaud, in this case would have personally painted the face and usually the hands. Different artists would have completed other elements of the picture, with, for example, some specializing in drapery and others in clothing. These workshops allowed the master artist to preside over a commercialized artistic business serving the expanding demand for the luxury good of a personal portrait on the part of aristocrats and members of the expanding commercial and professional classes. The business of art extended beyond these workshops into the world of engravers and printers, who could disperse commercially more inexpensive paper copies of important works of art for their own profit and, in the case of political portraits, for purposes of establishing a popular image of persons in public life.

Louis deeply admired this portrait. Originally, he had intended to send it to Philip V of Spain, the grandson he installed on the Spanish throne, thus provoking the greatest European war of his reign. But he decided to keep it for himself and had several copies made and distributed. When various councils or other ministerial bodies met at Versailles in his absence after 1701, the portrait was carried into the room to remind all those present of the monarch whom they served and whose policies they carried out.

Peter Burke, *The Fabrication of Louis XIV* (New Haven, CT: Yale University Press, 1992); Daniel Roche, *France in the Age of the Enlightenment* (Cambridge, MA: Harvard University Press, 1998), pp. 273–277; Germain Bazin, *Baroque and Rococo Art* (New York: Praeger, 1966); Marilyn Stockstad, *Art History* (New York: Harry N. Abrams, Inc., and Prentice Hall, Inc., Publishers, 1999),pp. 750–751.

Versailles, as painted in 1668 by Pierre Patel the Elder (1605–1676). The central building is the hunting lodge built for Louis XII earlier in the century. The wings that appear here were some of Louis XIV's first expansions. Pierre Patel, *Perspective View of Versailles*, Chateau, Versailles, France. Giraudon/Art Resource, NY

turally designed and artistically decorated to proclaim the glory of the Sun King, as Louis was known. A spectacular estate with magnificent fountains and acres of orange groves, it became home to thousands of the more important nobles, royal officials, and servants. Although its physical maintenance and new additions, which continued throughout Louis's lifetime, consumed over half his annual revenues, Versailles paid significant political dividends.

Because Louis ruled personally, he was the chief source of favors and patronage in France. To emphasize his prominence, he organized life at court around every aspect of his own daily routine. He encouraged nobles to approach him directly, but required them to do so through elaborate court etiquette. Polite and fawning nobles sought his attention, entering their names on waiting lists to be in attendance at especially favored moments. The king's rising and dressing in particular were times of rare intimacy, when nobles could whisper their special requests in his ear. Fortunate nobles held his night candle as they accompanied him to his bed.

Although only five feet four inches tall, the king had presence and was always engaging in conversation. He turned his own sexuality to political ends and encouraged the belief at court that it was an honor to lie with him. Married to the Spanish *Infanta* Marie Thérèse for political reasons in 1660, he kept many mistresses. After Marie's death in 1683, he settled down in a secret marriage to Madame de Maintenon and apparently became much less the philanderer.

Court life was a carefully planned and successfully executed effort to domesticate and trivialize the nobility. Barred by law from high government positions, the ritual and play kept them busy and dependent, so they had little time to plot revolt. Dress codes and high-stakes gambling contributed to their indebtedness and dependency on the king. Members of the court spent the afternoons hunting, riding, or strolling about the lush gardens of Versailles. Evenings were given over to planned entertainment in the large salons (plays, concerts, gambling, and the like), followed by supper at 10:00 P.M. Even the king's retirement was part of the day's spectacle.

Moments near the king were important to most court nobles because they were effectively excluded from the real business of government. Louis ruled through powerful councils that controlled foreign affairs, domestic relations, and economic regulations. Each day after morning mass, which Louis always observed, he spent hours with the chief ministers of these councils, whom he chose from families long in royal service or from among people just beginning to rise in the social structure. Unlike the nobles at court, they had no real or potential power bases in the provinces and depended solely on the king for their standing in both government and society.

Some nobles, of course, did not attend Versailles. Some tended to their local estates and cultivated their local influence. Many others were simply too poor to cut a figure at court. All the nobility understood, however, that Louis, unlike Richelieu and Mazarin, would not threaten their local social standing. Louis supported France's traditional social structure and the social privileges of the nobility.

Suppression of the Jansenists

Like Richelieu before him, Louis believed that political unity and stability required religious conformity. His first move in this direction, which came early in his personal reign, was against the Roman Catholic Jansenists.

The French crown and the French church had by long tradition—originating with the so-called Gallican liberties in the fourteenth century—jealously guarded their independence from Rome. A great influx of Catholic religious orders, the Jesuits prominent among them, followed Henry IV's conversion to Catholicism. Because of their leadership at the Council of Trent and their close connections to Spain, the Jesuits had been banned from France by Catherine de Médicis. Henry IV, however, lifted the ban in 1603, with certain conditions: He required members of the order to swear an oath of allegiance to the king, he limited the number of new colleges they could open, and he required them to have special licenses for public activities.

The Jesuits were not, however, easily harnessed. They rapidly monopolized the education of the upper classes, and their devout students promoted the religious reforms and doctrine of the Council of Trent throughout France. In a measure of their success, Jesuits served as confessors to Henry IV, Louis XIII, and Louis XIV.

Jansenism arose in the 1630s as part of an intra-Catholic opposition to the theology and the political influence of the Jesuits. Jansenists adhered to the Augustinian tradition that had also spawned many Protestant teachings. Serious and uncompromising, they particularly opposed Jesuit teachings about free will. They believed with Saint Augustine that original sin so corrupted humankind that individuals could do nothing good nor secure their own salvation without divine grace. The namesake of the movement, Cornelius Jansen (d. 1638), was a Flemish theologian and the bishop of Ypres. His posthumously published *Augustinus* (1640) assailed Jesuit teaching on grace and salvation.

A prominent Parisian family, the Arnaulds, became Jansenist allies, adding a political element to the Jansenists' theological objections to the Jesuits.

Versailles was a palace of unprecedented luxury for the French monarch and his court. Even Louis XIV's bedroom was a scene of court ritual and political intrigue with specially favored nobles being allowed to awake him or to escort him to the room in the evening. Navlet Victor (1819–1886), *Vue de la chambre a coucher de Louis XIV a Versailles en 1861.* 0.63 x 0.95. Chateaux de Versailles et de Trianon © Photo RMN

Like many other French people, the Arnaulds believed that the Jesuits had been behind the assassination of Henry IV in 1610.

The Arnaulds dominated Jansenist communities at Port-Royal and Paris during the 1640s. In 1643, Antoine Arnauld published a work entitled *On Frequent Communion* in which he criticized the Jesuits for confessional practices that permitted the easy redress of almost any sin. The Jesuits, in turn, condemned the Jansenists as "crypto-Calvinists."

On May 31, 1653, Pope Innocent X declared heretical five Jansenist theological propositions on grace and salvation. In 1656, the pope banned Jansen's *Augustinus* and the Sorbonne censured Antoine Arnauld. In the same year, Antoine's friend, Blaise Pascal (1623–1662), the most famous of Jansen's followers, published the first of his *Provincial Letters* in defense of Jansenism. A deeply religious man, Pascal tried to reconcile the "reasons of the heart" with growing seventeenth-century reverence for the clear and distinct ideas of the mind. (See Chapter 14.) He objected to Jesuit moral theology not only as being lax and shallow, but also because he felt that its rationalism failed to do full justice to the religious experience.

In 1660 Louis permitted the papal bull *Ad Sacram Sedem* (1656) to be enforced in France, thus banning Jansenism. He also closed down the Port-Royal community. Thereafter, Jansenists either retracted their views or went underground. Much later, in 1710, Louis lent his support to a still more thorough purge of Jansenist sentiment.

Jansenism had offered the prospect of a Catholicism broad enough to appeal to France's Protestant Huguenots. By suppressing it, Louis also eliminated the best hope for bringing peaceful religious unity to his country.

Government Geared for Warfare

Louis's France was in many ways like much of the rest of contemporary Europe. It had a largely subsistence economy, and its cities enjoyed only limited commercial prosperity. It did not, in other words, achieve the economic strength of a modern industrial economy. By the 1660s, however, France was superior to any other European nation in administrative bureaucracy, armed forces, and national unity. Louis had sufficient resources at his disposal to raise and maintain a large and powerful army. His enemies and some later historians claimed that Louis wished to dominate all Europe, but it would appear that his chief military and foreign policy goal was to achieve secure international boundaries for France. He was particularly concerned to secure the northern borders of France along the Spanish Netherlands, the Franche-Comté, Alsace, and Lorraine. The geography of these lands provided potential avenues of invasion into France. Louis also assumed that he must frustrate Habsburg ambitions that endangered France and, as part of that goal, sought to secure his southern borders toward Spain. Furthermore, external events, particularly problems

Throughout the age of splendor at the court of Louis XIV, millions of French peasants lived lives of poverty and hardship, as depicted in this 1640 painting, Peasant Family *by Louis LeNain.*
Erich Lessing/Art Resource, N.Y.

raised by succession issues in other states, provided the occasion of Louis's wars as often as his own personal ambition did. Nonethless, he saw himself as a warrior king and on more than one occasion personally accompanied his armies on their campaigns. Whether reacting to external events or pursuing his own ambitions, Louis's pursuit of French interests raised among neighboring states the most profound fears of extensive French aggression and fostered the formation of major coalitions against France.

Three remarkable French ministers established and supported Louis XIV's great war machine: Colbert, Louvois, and Vauban.

COLBERT AND THE FRENCH ECONOMY Jean-Baptiste Colbert (1619–1683), controller general of finances and Louis's most brilliant minister, created the economic base Louis needed to finance his wars. Colbert worked to centralize the French economy with the same rigor that Louis had worked to centralize the French government. Colbert tried, with modest success, to organize much economic activity under state supervision and, through tariffs, carefully regulated the flow of imports and exports. He sought to create new national industries and organized factories around a tight regimen of work and ideology. He simplified the administrative bureaucracy, abolished unnecessary positions, and reduced the number of tax-exempt nobles. He also increased the *taille*, a direct tax on the peasantry and a major source of royal income.

This kind of close government control of the economy came to be known as *mercantilism* (a term invented by later critics of the policy). Its aim was to maximize foreign exports and internal reserves of bullion, the gold and silver necessary for making war. Modern scholars argue that Colbert overcontrolled the French economy and cite his "paternalism" as a major reason for the failure of French colonies in the New World. Be that as it may, his policies unquestionably transformed France into a major commercial power, with foreign bases in Africa, in India, and in the Americas, from Canada to the Caribbean.

LOUVOIS, VAUBAN, AND THE FRENCH MILITARY Louis's army, about a quarter of a million strong, was the creation of Michel Tellier and his more famous son, the marquis of Louvois (1641–1691). Louis's war minister from 1677 to 1691, Louvois was a superior military tactician.

Before Louvois, the French army had been an amalgam of local recruits and mercenaries, uncoordinated groups whose loyalty could not always be counted on. Without regular pay or a way to supply their every-day needs, troops often lived by pillage. Louvois instituted good salaries and improved discipline, making soldiering a respectable profession. He limited military commissions and introduced a system of promotion by merit, bringing dedicated fighters into the ranks. Enlistment was for four years and was restricted to single men. *Intendants*, the king's ubiquitous civil servants, monitored conduct at all levels.

Because it was well disciplined, this new, large, and powerful standing army had considerable public support. Unlike its undisciplined predecessor, the new army no longer threatened the lives, homes, or well-being of the people it was supposed to protect. It thus provides an excellent example of the kinds of benefits many saw in the growing authority of the central monarchy.

What Louvois was to military organization, Sebastien Vauban (1633–1707) was to military engineering. He perfected the arts of fortifying and besieging towns. He also devised the system of trench warfare and developed the concept of defensive frontiers that remained basic to military tactics through World War I.

Louis's Early Wars

THE WAR OF DEVOLUTION Louis's first great foreign adventure was the War of Devolution (1667–1668). It was fought, as would be the later and more devastating War of the Spanish Succession, over Louis's claim to the Spanish Belgian provinces through his wife, Marie Thérèse (1638–1683). According to the terms of the Treaty of the Pyrenees (1659), Marie had renounced her claim to the Spanish succession on condition that a 500,000-crown dowry be paid to Louis within eighteen months of the marriage, a condition that was not met. When Philip IV of Spain died in September 1665, he left all his lands to his sickly four-year-old son by a second marriage, Charles II (r. 1665–1700) and explicitly denied any lands to his daughter. Louis had always harbored the hope of turning the marriage to territorial gain and even before Philip's death had argued that Marie was entitled to a portion of the inheritance.

Louis had a legal argument on his side, which gave the war its name. He maintained that in certain regions of Brabant and Flanders, which were part of the Spanish inheritance, property "devolved" to the children of a first marriage rather than to those of a second. Therefore, Marie had a higher claim than Charles II to these regions. Although such regional laws could hardly bind the king of Spain, Louis was not deterred from sending his armies, under the viscount of Turenne, into Flanders and the Franche-Comté in 1667. In response to this aggression,

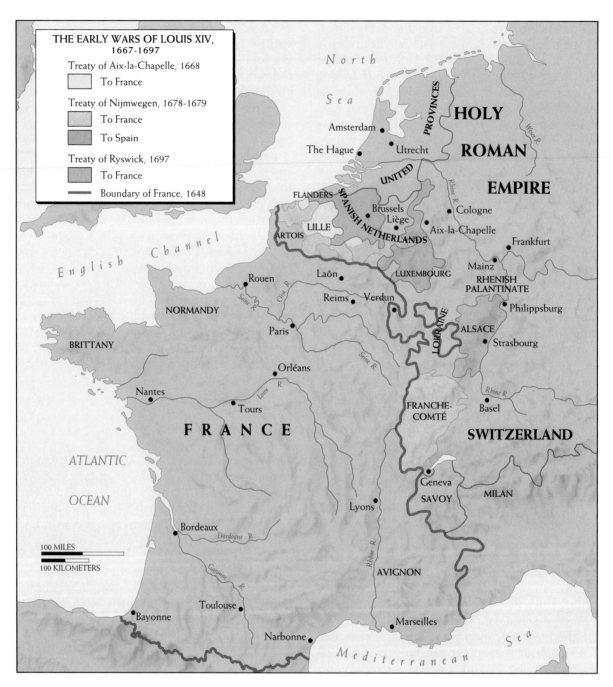

THE EARLY WARS OF LOUIS XIV,
1667-1697

Treaty of Aix-la-Chapelle, 1668

☐ To France

Treaty of Nijmwegen, 1678-1679

☐ To France

☐ To Spain

Treaty of Ryswick, 1697

☐ To France

— Boundary of France, 1648

MAP 13–2   THE WARS OF LOUIS XIV   *This map shows the territorial changes resulting from Louis XIV's first three major wars. The War of the Spanish Succession was yet to come.*

England, Sweden, and the United Provinces of Holland formed the Triple Alliance, a force sufficient to compel Louis to agree to peace under the terms in the Treaty of Aix-la-Chapelle (1668). The treaty gave him control of certain towns bordering the Spanish Netherlands. (See Map 13–2.)

INVASION OF THE NETHERLANDS   In 1670, with the signing of the Treaty of Dover, England and France became allies against the Dutch. Without the English,

the Triple Alliance crumbled. This left Louis in a stronger position to invade the Netherlands for a second time, which he did in 1672. This time he aimed directly at Holland, which had organized the Triple Alliance in 1667, foiling French designs in Flanders. Dutch gloating after the Treaty of Aix-la-Chapelle had offended Louis. Such cartoons as one depicting the sun (Louis was called the "Sun King") eclipsed by a great moon of Dutch cheese incensed him. Without neutralizing Holland, he knew he could never hope to acquire land in the Spanish Netherlands, much less fulfill his dreams of European hegemony.

Louis's invasion of the United Provinces in 1672 brought the downfall of the Dutch statesmen Jan and Cornelius De Witt. Replacing them was the twenty-seven-year-old Prince of Orange, destined after 1689 to become King William III of England. Orange was the great-grandson of William the Silent, who had repulsed Philip II and dashed Spanish hopes of dominating the Netherlands in the sixteenth century.

Orange, an unpretentious Calvinist who was in almost every way Louis's opposite, galvanized the seven provinces into a fierce fighting unit. In 1673 he united the Holy Roman Emperor, Spain, Lorraine, and Brandenburg in an alliance against Louis. His enemies now saw the French king as a "Christian Turk," a menace to the whole of western Europe, Catholic and Protestant alike. In the ensuing warfare, both sides experienced gains and losses. Louis lost his ablest generals, Turenne and Condé, in 1675, but a victory by Admiral Duquesne over the Dutch fleet in 1676 gave France control of the Mediterranean. The Peace of Nijmwegen, signed with different parties in successive years (1678 and 1679), ended the hostilities of this second war. There were various minor territorial adjustments, but no clear victor except the United Netherlands, which retained all of its territory.

Revocation of the Edict of Nantes

In the decade after his invasion of the Netherlands, Louis made his second major move to assure religious conformity. Following the proclamation of the Edict of Nantes in 1598, relations between the great Catholic majority (nine-tenths of the French population) and the Protestant minority remained hostile. There were about 1.75 million Huguenots in France in the 1660s, but their numbers were declining in the second half of the seventeenth century. The French Catholic Church had long denounced Calvinists as heretical and treasonous and had supported their persecution as both pious and patriotic.

Following the Peace of Nijmwegen in 1678–1679, which halted for the moment his aggression in Europe, Louis launched a methodical government campaign against the French Huguenots in a determined effort to unify France religiously. He hounded the Huguenots out of public life, banning them from government office and excluding them from such professions as printing and medicine. He used subsidies and selective taxation to encourage Huguenots to convert to Catholicism. And in 1681 he bullied them by quartering his troops in their towns. In the final stage of the persecution, Louis revoked the Edict of Nantes in October 1685. As a result, Protestant churches and schools were closed, Protestant ministers exiled, nonconverting laity forced to be galley slaves, and Protestant children ceremonially baptized by Catholic priests.

The revocation of the Edict of Nantes was a major blunder. Afterwards, Louis was viewed in Protestant countries as a new Philip II, intent on a Catholic reconquest of the whole of Europe, who must be resisted at all costs. The revocation prompted the voluntary emigration of more than a quarter million French people, who formed new communities and joined the resistance to France in England, Germany, Holland, and the New World. Thousands of French Huguenots served in the army of Louis's archfoe, William of Orange, later King William III of England. Many of those who remained in France became part of an uncompromising guerilla resistance to the king. Despite the many domestic and foreign liabilities it brought him, Louis, to his death, considered the revocation to be his most pious act, one that placed God in his debt.

Louis's Later Wars

THE LEAGUE OF AUGSBURG AND THE NINE YEARS' WAR
After the Treaty of Nijmwegen, Louis maintained his army at full strength and restlessly probed beyond his perimeters. In 1681 his forces conquered the free city of Strasbourg, prompting new defensive coalitions to form against him. One of these, the League of Augsburg, created in 1686 to resist French expansion into Germany, had grown by 1689 to include England, Spain, Sweden, the United Provinces, and the electorates of Bavaria, Saxony, and the Palatinate. It also had the support of the Austrian emperor Leopold. In 1688 Louis's armies invaded the Palatinate, ostensibly to claim on very weak ground its succession for his sister-in-law Charlotte Elisabeth. A long, extraordinarily destructive war resulted. Between 1689 and 1697, the league and France battled each other in the Nine Years' War. During the same period, England and France struggled for control of North America in what came to be known as King William's War.

The Nine Years' War ended when stalemate and exhaustion forced both sides to accept an interim settlement. The Peace of Ryswick, signed in September 1697, was a triumph for William of Orange, now William III of England, and Emperor Leopold. It secured Holland's borders and thwarted Louis's expansion into Germany. (See "Louis IV's Sister-in-Law Grieves for Her Homeland.")

Louis XIV's Sister-in-Law Grieves for Her Homeland

Charlotte Elisabeth, Duchesse d' Orléans (1652–1722), who was married to the brother of Louis XIV of France, had been born the daughter of the Elector of the Palatinate. After her marriage in 1671, she moved to the French court and was never permitted to revisit her homeland. She did, however, carry out an extensive correspondence with friends and family in Germany throughout her life. In August, 1688, Louis XIV invaded the Palatinate under the guise of restoring it to his sister-in-law. He had no real purpose except the conquest of the German region. This invasion was important for two reasons. First, it opened a war that continued until 1697. Second, at the onset of the original invasion, the French forces committed enormous atrocities against the civilian population, killing many civilians and destroying their homes. In these letters to her aunt and foster mother, Charlotte Elisabeth recounts her sadness and anger over the plight of these civilians and the difficulty of her own situation in the French court.

❖ *How do these letters reflect the plight of a woman who had been required to enter a dynastic marriage when war broke out? How does she report Louis XIV's using her name to further his own political and financial ends in the Palatinate? What kind of destruction was Charlotte Elisabeth aware of in her homeland?*

March 20, 1689

I had barely began to recover somewhat from poor Carllutz's death [her brother] when the horrendous and piteous calamity was visited upon the poor Palatinate, and what pains me most is that my name is being used to cast these poor people into utter misery. And when I cry about it, I am treated to great annoyance and sulking [by those in the French royal court at Versailles]. But to save my life I cannot stop lamenting and bemoaning the thought that I am as it were, my fatherland's ruin, especially when I see all of the Elector's, my late father's, hard work and care suddenly reduced to rubble in poor Mannheim. I am so horrified by all the destruction that has been wrought that every night when I have finally dozed off, I imagine that I am in Mannheim and Heidelberg amidst all the destruction, and then I wake up with a dreadful start and cannot go back to sleep for two whole hours. Then I see in my mind how everything was in my day and in what state it is now, indeed in what state I am myself, and then I cannot hold back a flood of tears. It also grieves me deeply that the King [Louis XIV] waited to inflict the ultimate devastation precisely until I had begged him to spare Mannheim and Heidelberg.

June 5, 1689

Although I should be accustomed by now to the thought of my poor fatherland in flames, having heard nothing else for so long, I still cannot help being regretful and grieved every time I am told that yet another place has been put to the torch.... Recently Monsieur [her husband] told me something that annoys me to the depth of my soul and which I had not known before, namely that the King [Louis XIV] has all taxes in the Palatinate levied in my name; now these poor people must think that I am profiting from their misery and that I am the cause of it, and that makes me deeply sad.

October 30, 1689

Yesterday I was told something that touched my heart very deeply, and I could not hear it without tears; namely that the poor people of Mannheim have all returned and are living in their cellars as if they were houses and even hold a daily market as if the town were still in its previous state.

From *Louis XIV's Sister-in-Law Grieves for Her Homeland*, Elborg Forster, ed., in Von der Pfalz, *A Woman's Life in the Court of the Sun King*, pp. 61, 64, 68, © 1984 The Johns Hopkins University Press. Reprinted by permission.

The foreign policy of Louis XIV brought warfare to all of Europe. This eighteenth century painting by Benjamin West memorializes the British victory over France in the battle of La Hogue in 1692. National Gallery of Art

WAR OF THE SPANISH SUCCESSION: TREATIES OF UTRECHT AND RASTADT After Ryswick, Louis, who seemed to thrive on partial success, made another attempt to secure and expand French interests against Habsburg influence. On November 1, 1700, Charles II of Spain, known as "the Sufferer" because of his genetic deformities and lingering illnesses, died.

Both Louis and the Austrian emperor Leopold had claims to the Spanish inheritance through their grandsons, Louis through his marriage to Marie Thérèse and Leopold through his marriage to her younger sister, Margaret Thérèse. Although Louis's grandson, Philip of Anjou, had the better claim (because Marie Thérèse was Margaret Thérèse's older sister), Marie Thérèse had renounced her right to the Spanish inheritance in the Treaty of the Pyrenees (1659), and the inheritance was expected to go to Leopold's grandson.

Louis nurtured fears that the Habsburgs would dominate Europe should they gain control of Spain as well as the Holy Roman Empire. Most of the nations of Europe, however, feared France more than the Habsburgs and determined to prevent a union of the French and Spanish crowns. As a result, before Charles II's death, negotiations began among the nations involved to partition his inheritance in a way that would preserve the existing balance of power.

Charles II upset these negotiations by leaving his entire inheritance to Philip of Anjou, Louis's grandson. At a stroke, Spain and its possessions had fallen to France. Although Louis had been party to the partition agreements that preceded Charles's death, he now saw God's hand in Charles's will; he chose to enforce its terms over those of the partition agreement. Philip of Anjou moved to Madrid and became Philip V of Spain. Louis, in what was interpreted as naked French aggression, sent his troops again into Flanders, this time to remove Dutch soldiers from Spanish territory in the name of the new French king of Spain. Louis also declared Spanish America open to French ships.

In September 1701, England, Holland, and the Holy Roman Empire formed the Grand Alliance to counter Louis. They sought to preserve the bal-

MAP 13–3 EUROPE IN 1714. *The War of the Spanish Succession ended in the year before the death of the aged Louis XIV. By then, France and Spain, although not united, were both ruled by members of the Bourbon family, and Spain had lost its non-Iberian possessions.*

ance of power by once and for all securing Flanders as a neutral barrier between Holland and France and by gaining for the emperor his fair share of the Spanish inheritance. After the formation of the Grand Alliance, Louis increased the stakes of battle by recognizing the claim of James Edward, the son of James II of England, to the English throne.

In 1701 the thirteen-year War of the Spanish Succession (1701–1714) began, and once again total war enveloped western Europe. France, for the first time, went to war with inadequate finances, a poorly equipped army, and mediocre military leadership. The English, in contrast, had

advanced weaponry (flintlock rifles, paper cartridges, and ring bayonets) and superior tactics (thin, maneuverable troop columns rather than the traditional deep ones). John Churchill, the duke of Marlborough, who succeeded William of Orange as military leader of the alliance, bested Louis's soldiers in every major engagement. He routed French armies at Blenheim in August 1704 and on the plain of Ramillies in 1706—two decisive battles of the war. In 1708–1709 famine, revolts, and uncollectible taxes tore France apart internally. Despair pervaded the French court. Louis wondered aloud how God could forsake one who had done so much for him.

Though ready to make peace in 1709, Louis could not bring himself to accept the stiff terms of the alliance. These included a demand that he transfer all Spanish possessions to the emperor's grandson Charles and remove Philip V from Madrid. Hostilities continued, and a clash of forces at Malplaquet (September 1709) left carnage on the battlefield unsurpassed until modern times.

France finally signed an armistice with England at Utrecht in July 1713 and concluded hostilities with Holland and the emperor in the Treaty of Rastadt in March 1714. This agreement confirmed Philip V as king of Spain, but gave Gibraltar and the island of Minona to England, making it a Mediterranean power. (See Map 13–3.) It also won Louis's recognition of the right of the House of Hanover to accede to the English throne.

Spanish power declined in the wake of the war. Philip should have tried to consolidate his internal power and protect Spanish overseas trade. However, his second wife, Elizabeth Farnese, used Spanish power to secure thrones for her two sons in Italy. Such diversions of government resources allowed the nobility and the provinces to continue to assert their privileges against the monarchy. Not until the reign of Charles III (r. 1759–1788) did Spain have a monarch concerned with efficient domestic and imperial administration and internal improvement. By the third quarter of the century, Spain was better governed, but it could no longer compete effectively in great-power politics.

Politically, the eighteenth century would belong to England as the sixteenth had belonged to Spain and the seventeenth to France. Although France remained intact and strong, the realization of Louis XIV's territorial ambitions had to await the rise of Napoleon Bonaparte. On his deathbed on September 1, 1715, Louis fittingly warned his heir, the *dauphin*, not to imitate his love of buildings and his liking for war.

Louis XIV's Legacy

Louis XIV left France a mixed legacy. His wars had brought widespread death and destruction and had sapped many of the nation's resources. Only a long period of peace could permit full economic recovery. Yet the years of war had established among both the army and much of the nobility a self-image of life in pursuit of military glory. Mid-eighteenth-century wars initiated in part from that outlook would undermine the recovering royal finances and cause an ongoing financial crisis that the monarchy never solved. Louis's policies of centralization would later make it difficult for France to develop effective institutions of representation and self-government The aristocracy, after its years of domestication at Versailles, would have difficulty providing the nation with effective leaders and ministers. Yet his reign had also laid the groundwork for a new French Empire by expanding trade into Asia and colonizing North America.

Despite his own ambitions for absolute rule and the association of the term "absolutism" with his mode of government, it is important to recognize that Louis's rule was not so absolute as to exert oppressive control over the daily lives of his subjects, as would be the case with police states of the nineteenth and twentieth centuries. His absolutism functioned primarily in the classic areas of European state action—the making of war and peace, the regulation of religion, and the oversight of economic activity. Even at the height of his power, local institutions, some controlled by townspeople and others by nobles, continued to exert administrative authority at the local level. The king and his ministers supported the high status and tax exemptions of these local elites. But in contrast to the Stuart kings of England, Louis firmly prevented them from capturing or significantly limiting his authority on the national level. Not until the French monarchy was so weakened by financial crisis at the end of the eighteenth century would it succumb to demands for a more representative form of government.

The Reign of Louis XIV (1643–1715)	
1643	Louis ascends the French throne at the age of five
1643–1661	Cardinal Mazarin directs the French government
1648	Peace of Westphalia
1649–1652	The *Fronde* revolt
1653	The pope declares Jansenism a heresy
1659	Treaty of Pyrenees between France and Spain
1660	Papal ban on Jansenists enforced in France
1661	Louis commences personal rule
1667–1668	War of Devolution
1670	Secret Treaty of Dover between France and Great Britain
1672–1679	French war against the Netherlands
1685	Louis revokes the Edict of Nantes
1689–1697	War of the League of Augsburg
1701	Outbreak of the War of the Spanish Succession
1713	Treaty of Utrecht between France and Great Britain
1714	Treaty of Rastatt between France and Spain
1715	Death of Louis XIV

In Perspective

In the seventeenth century, England and France developed divergent forms of government. England became the model for parliamentary monarchy, France for absolute monarchy.

The politically active English elite—the nobility, along with the wealthy landowning and commercial classes—struggled throughout the century to limit the authority of rulers—including Oliver Cromwell as well as the Stuart monarchs—over local interests. In the process, they articulated a political philosophy that stressed the need to prevent the central concentration of political power. The Bill of Rights of 1689 and the Toleration Act following the Glorious Revolution of William and Mary seemed to achieve the goals of this philosophy. These acts brought neither democracy nor full religious freedom in a modern sense; the Bill of Rights protected only the privileged, not all the English people, and the Toleration Act outlawed Catholics and Unitarians. Still, they firmly established representative government in England and extended legal recognition, at least in principle, to a variety of religious beliefs. The Bill of Rights required the monarch to call Parliament regularly.

In France, by contrast, the monarchy remained supreme. Although the king had to mollify privileged local elites by considering the interests of the nobility and the traditional rights of towns and regions, France had no national institution like Parliament through which he had to govern. Louis XIV was able, on his own authority, to fund the largest army in Europe. He could and did crush religious dissent. His own propaganda and the fear of his adversaries may have led to an exaggerated view of Louis's power, but his reign nonetheless provided a model of effective centralized power that later continental rulers tried to follow.

REVIEW QUESTIONS

1. By the end of the seventeenth century, England and France had different systems of government with different religious policies. What were the main differences? Similarities? Why did each nation develop as it did? How much did the particular personalities of the rulers of each nation determine the manner in which their political institutions emerged?
2. Why did the English king and Parliament come into conflict in the 1640s? What were the most important issues behind the war between them, and who bears more responsibility for it? What role did religion play in the conflict?
3. What was the Glorious Revolution and why did it take place? What were James II's mistakes, and what were the issues involved in the events of 1688? What kind of settlement emerged from the revolution? How did England in 1700 differ from England in 1600?
4. Discuss the development of absolutism in France. What policies of Henry IV and Louis XIII were essential in creating the absolute monarchy?
5. What were the chief ways Louis XIV consolidated his monarchy? What limits were there on his authority? What was Louis's religious policy?
6. Assess the success of Louis XIV's foreign policy. What were his aims? Were they realistic? To what extent did he attain them? To what extent did he forge events, and to what extent did he react to events outside France?

SUGGESTED READINGS

ROBERT ASHTON, *Counter-Revolution: The Second Civil War and Its Origins, 1646–1648* (1995). A major examination of the resumption of civil conflict in England that ended with the abolition of the monarchy, House of Lords, and established church.

W. BEIK, *Absolutism and Society in Seventeenth-Century France* (1985). An important study that questions the extent of royal power.

J. BERGIN, *Cardinal Richelieu: Power and the Pursuit of Wealth* (1985). Considers the role of finance and private wealth in the rise of Richelieu.

R. BONNEY, *Political Change in France under Richelieu and Mazarin, 1624–1661* (1978). A careful examination of how these two cardinals laid the foundation for Louis XIV's absolutism.

G. BURGESS, *Absolute Monarchy and the Stuart Constitution* (1996). A new study that challenges many of the traditional interpretive categories.

P. BURKE, *The Fabrication of Louis XIV* (1992). Examines the manner in which the public image of Louis XIV was forged in art.

P. COLLINSON, *The Religion of Protestants: The Church in English Society, 1559–1625* (1982). The best introduction to Puritanism.

J. H. ELLIOTT AND L. BROCKLISS, EDS., *The Age of the Favourite* (1999). Explores, in the European setting, the political impact of those figures who received extraordinary royal favor and patronage.

T. ERTMAN, *Birth of the Leviathan: Building States and Regimes in Medieval and Early Modern Europe* (1997). An extensive survey by a sociologist.

R. HUTTON, *Charles the Second, King of England, Scotland, and Ireland* (1989). Replaces all previous biographies.

M. KISHLANSKY, *A Monarchy Transformed: Britain, 1603–1714* (1996). The most recent overview.

J. R. MAJOR, *From Renaissance Monarchy to Absolute Monarchy: French Kings, Nobles and Estates* (1994). A major study by a leading scholar exploring the complexities of the relationship of the monarchy to other political and social groups.

R. METTAM, *Power and Faction in Louis XIV's France* (1988). Examines the political intricacies of the reign and suggests the limits to absolutism.

P. K. MONOD, *The Power of Kings: Monarchy and Religion in Europe, 1589–1715* (1999). An important and innovative examination of the roots of royal authority as early modern Europe became modern Europe.

G. PARKER, *The Military Revolution: Military Innovation and the Rise of the West, 1500–1800* (1988). Emphasizes the role of military organization and expenditures in the emergence of modern states.

H. PHILLIPS, *Church and Culture in Seventeenth-Century France* (1997). A clear examination of the major religious issues confronting France and their relationship to the larger culture.

O. RANUM, *The Fronde: A French Revolution, 1648–1652* (1993). The best recent work on the subject.

D. L. RUBIN (ED.), *The Sun King: The Ascendancy of French Culture During the Reign of Louis XIV* (1992). A collection of useful essays.

C. RUSSELL, *The Fall of the English Monarchies, 1637–1642* (1991). A major revisionist account.

K. SHARPE, *The Personal Rule of Charles I* (1992). An important narrative work.

J. SPUR, *The Restoration Church of England, 1646–1689* (1992). The standard work on this subject.

L. STONE, *The Causes of the English Revolution, 1529–1642* (1972). A classic survey stressing social history and ruminating over historians and historical method.

D. J. STURDY, *Louis XIV* (1998). A excellent brief overview with judicious comments on all major issues.

G. TREASURE, *Mazarin: The Crisis of Absolutism in France* (1996). An examination not only of Mazarin, but also of the larger national and international background.

R. D. TUMBLESON, *Catholicism in the English Protestant Imagination: Nationalism, Religion, and Literature, 1660–1745* (1998). Explores the impact of anti-Catholicism on English life during this critical period in the search for religious and political stability.

N. TYACKE, *Anti-Calvinists: The Rise of English Arminianism c. 1590–1640* (1987). The most important study of Archbishop Laud's policies and his predecessors.

D. UNDERDOWN, *Fire from Heaven: Life in an English Town in the Seventeenth Century* (1992). A lively account of a single English town.

J. B. WOLF, *Louis XIV* (1968). A very detailed political biography.

Chapter 14

Nicolaus Copernicus's transforming view of the universe, with the sun in the center, is summarized in this diagram from his De Revolutionibus Orbium Coelestium (On the Revolutions of Heavenly Spheres), published in 1543.
Library of the Collegium Maius, Cracow, Poland. Erich Lessing/Art Resource.

New Directions in Thought and Culture in the Sixteenth and Seventeenth Centuries

KEY TOPICS

- The astronomical theories of Copernicus, Brahe, Kepler, Galileo, and Newton and the emergence of the scientific worldview
- Impact of the new science on philosophy
- Social setting of early modern science
- Women and the scientific revolution
- Approaches to science and religion
- Witchcraft and witch hunts

The sixteenth and seventeenth centuries witnessed a sweeping change in the scientific view of the universe. An Earth-centered picture gave way to one in which the Earth was only another planet orbiting about the sun. The sun itself became one of millions of stars. This transformation of humankind's perception of its place in the larger scheme of things led to a profound rethinking of moral and religious matters, as well as of scientific theory. Faith and reason needed new modes of reconciliation, as did faith and science. The new ideas and methods of science, usually termed natural philosophy at the time, challenged those modes of thought associated with late medieval times: Scholasticism, and Aristotelian philosophy.

The impact of the new science that explored the realm of the stars through the newly invented telescope and the world of microorganisms through the newly invented microscope must be viewed in the context of two other factors that simultaneously challenged traditional modes of European *thought and culture in the sixteenth and seventeenth centuries. The first of these was the Reformation, which permanently divided the religious unity of central and western Europe and fostered decades of warfare and theological dispute. Although by no means a complete break with medieval thought, the theology of the Reformation did question many ideas associated with medieval Christianity and society. The second factor was the cultural impact of the encounter of Europe with the New World of the Americas. The interaction with the Americas meant that Europeans directly or indirectly acquired knowledge of new peoples, plants, and animals wholly different from their own and about which people in neither ancient nor medieval times had any information. Consequently, new uncertainties and unfamiliar vistas confronted many Europeans as they considered their souls, geographical knowledge, and physical nature.*

Side by side with this new knowledge and science, however, came a new wave of superstition and persecution. The changing world of religion, politics, and knowledge also created profound fear and anxiety among both the simple and the learned, resulting in Europe's worst witch hunts.

The Scientific Revolution

The process which established the new view of the universe is normally termed the *Scientific Revolution*. The revolution-in-science metaphor must be used carefully, however. Not everything associated with the "new" science was necessarily new. Sixteenth- and seventeenth-century natural philosophers were often re-examining and rethinking theories and data from the ancient world and the late middle ages. Moreover, the word *revolution* normally denotes rapid, collective political change involving large numbers of people. The Scientific Revolution was *not* rapid. It was a complex movement with many false starts and brilliant people suggesting wrong as well as useful ideas. Nor did it involve more than a few hundred people who labored in widely separated studies and crude laboratories located in Poland, Italy, Bohemia, France, and Great Britain. Furthermore, the achievements of the new science were not simply the function of isolated brilliant scientific minds. The leading figures of the Scientific Revolution often drew upon the aid of artisans and craftspeople to help them construct new instruments for experimentation and to carry out those experiments. Thus, the Scientific Revolution involved a reappropriation of older knowledge as well as new discoveries. Additionally, because the practice of science involves social ac-

tivity as well as knowledge, the revolution also saw the establishment of new social institutions to support the emerging scientific enterprise.

Science as we know it today was only in the process of becoming during the era of the Scientific Revolution. In fact the word *scientist*, invented in the 1830s, did not yet exist in the seventeenth century nor did anything resembling the modern scientific career. Individuals devoted to natural philosophy might work in universities or in the court of a prince or possibly in their own homes and workshops. Only in the second half of the seventeenth century did formal societies and academies devoted to the pursuit of natural philosophy come into existence. Even then the entire process of the pursuit of natural knowledge was a largely informal one.

Yet by the close of the seventeenth century the new scientific concepts and the methods of their construction were so impressive that they set the standard for assessing the validity of knowledge in the Western world. From the early seventeenth century through the end of the twentieth century science achieved greater cultural authority in the Western world than any other form of intellectual activity, and the authority and application of scientific knowledge became one of the defining characteristics of modern Western civilization.

Although new knowledge emerged in many areas during the sixteenth and seventeenth centuries, including medicine, chemistry, and natural history, the scientific achievements that most captured the learned imagination and persuaded people of the cultural power of natural knowledge were those that occurred in astronomy.

Nicolaus Copernicus Rejects an Earth-centered Universe

Nicolaus Copernicus (1473–1543) was a Polish astronomer who enjoyed a high reputation during his life. He had been educated first in Cracow and later in Italy. He led a largely isolated intellectual career and had not been known for strikingly original or unorthodox thought. In 1543, the year of his death, Copernicus published *On the Revolutions of the Heavenly Spheres*. Copernicus's book was "a revolution-making rather than a revolutionary text."[1] What Copernicus did was to provide an intellectual springboard for a complete criticism of the then-dominant view of the position of the Earth in the universe.

---

[1] Thomas S. Kuhn, *The Copernican Revolution: Planetary Astronomy in the Development of Western Thought* (New York: Vintage, 1959), p. 135.

Copernicus Ascribes Movement to the Earth

Copernicus published De Revolutionibus Orbium Caelestium (On the Revolutions of the Heavenly Spheres) *in 1543. In his preface, addressed to Pope Paul III, he explained what had led him to think that the Earth moved around the sun and what he thought were some of the scientific consequences of the new theory.*

❖ *How does Copernicus justify his argument to the Pope? How important was historical precedent and tradition to the Pope? Might Copernicus have thought that the Pope would be especially susceptible to such argument, even though what Copernicus proposed (the movement of the Earth) contradicted the Bible?*

I may well presume, most Holy Father, that certain people, as soon as they hear that in this book about the Revolutions of the Spheres of the Universe I ascribe movement to the Earthly globe, will cry out that, holding such views, I should at once be hissed off the stage....

So I should like your Holiness to know that I was induced to think of a method of computing the motions of the spheres by nothing else than the knowledge that the Mathematicians [who had previously considered the problem] are inconsistent in these investigations.

For, first, the mathematicians are so unsure of the movements of the Sun and Moon that they cannot even explain or observe the constant length of the seasonal year. Secondly, in determining the motions of these and of the other five planets, they use neither the same principles and hypotheses nor the same demonstrations of the apparent motions and revolutions....Nor have they been able thereby to discern or deduce the principal thing—namely the shape of the Universe and the unchangeable symmetry of its parts....

I pondered long upon this uncertainty of mathematical tradition in establishing the motions of the system of the spheres. At last I began to chafe

that philosophers could by no means agree on any one certain theory of the mechanism of the Universe, wrought for us by a supremely good and orderly Creator....I therefore took pains to read again the works of all the philosophers on whom I could lay hand to seek out whether any of them had ever supposed that the motions of the spheres were other than those demanded by the [Ptolemaic] mathematical schools. I found first in Cicero that Hicetas [of Syracuse, fifth century B.C.] had realized that the Earth moved. Afterwards I found in Plutarch that certain others had held the like opinion....

Thus assuming motions, which in my work I ascribe to the Earth, by long and frequent observations I have at last discovered that, if the motions of the rest of the planets be brought into relation with the circulation of the Earth and be reckoned in proportion to the circles of each planet, not only do their phenomena presently ensue, but the orders and magnitudes of all stars and spheres, nay the heavens themselves, become so bound together that nothing in any part thereof could be moved from its place without producing confusion of all the other parts of the Universe as a whole.

As quoted in Thomas S. Kuhn, *The Copernican Revolution: Planetary Astronomy in the Development of Western Thought* (New York: Vintage Books, 1959), pp. 137–139, 141–142.

THE PTOLEMAIC SYSTEM At the time of Copernicus, the standard explanation of the place of the Earth in the heavens combined the mathematical astronomy of Ptolemy, contained in his work entitled the *Almagest* (150 C.E.), with the physical cosmology of Aristotle. Over the centuries, commentators on Ptolemy's work had developed several alternative Ptolemaic systems, on the basis of which they made mathematical calculations relating to astronomy. Most of these writers assumed that the Earth was the center of the universe, an outlook known as *geocentricsm*. Drawing

upon Aristotle, these commentators assumed that above the Earth lay a series of concentric spheres, probably fluid in character, one of which contained the moon, another the sun, and still others the planets and the stars. At the outer regions of these spheres lay the realm of God and the angels. The Earth had to be the center because of its heaviness. The stars and the other heavenly bodies had to be enclosed in the spheres so that they could move, since nothing could move unless something was actually moving it. The state of rest was presumed natural; motion required explanation. This was the astronomy found in such works as Dante's *Divine Comedy*.

Numerous problems were associated with the Ptolemaic model, and these had long been recognized. The most important was the observed motions of the planets. At certain times the planets actually appeared to be going backwards. The Ptolemaic model accounted for these motions primarily through *epicycles*. The planet moved uniformly about a small circle (an epicyle), while the center of the epicyle moved uniformly about a larger circle (called a deferent), with the Earth at or near its center. The combination of these two motions, as viewed from the Earth, was meant to replicate the changing planetary positions among the fixed stars—and did so to a high degree of accuracy. The circles employed in Ptolemaic systems were not meant to represent the actual paths of anything; that is, they were not orbits. Rather, they were the components of purely mathematical models meant to predict planetary positions. Other intellectual, but nonobservational, difficulties related to the immense speed at which the spheres had to move around the Earth. To say the least, the Ptolemaic systems were cluttered. They were effective, however, as long as one assumed Aristotelian physics.

COPERNICUS'S UNIVERSE Copernicus's *On the Revolutions of the Heavenly Spheres* challenged the Ptolemaic picture in the most conservative manner possible. (See "Copernicus Ascribes Movement to the Earth.") Copernicus adopted many elements of the Ptolemaic model, but transferred them to a *heliocentric* (sun-centered) model which assumed that the Earth moved about the sun in a circle. Copernicus's model, which retained epicycles, was actually no more accurate than Ptolemy's. However, Copernicus could claim certain advantages over the ancient model. In particular, the epicycles were smaller. The retrograde motion of the planets now stood explained as a result of an optical illusion arising from an observer viewing the planets from a moving Earth. The order of the planets from the sun became more clearly intelligible when it was understood as a result of their increasing periods of revolution based on the planets' increasing distance from the sun.

The repositioning of the Earth had not been Copernicus's goal. Rather, Copernicus appears to have set out to achieve new intelligibility and mathematical elegance to astronomy. The means of doing so was to reject Aristotle's cosmology and to remove the Earth from the center of the universe. His system was no more accurate than the existing ones for predicting the location of the planets. He had used no new evidence. The major impact of his work was to provide another way of confronting some of the difficulties inherent in Ptolemaic astronomy. The Copernican system did not immediately replace the old astronomy, but it allowed other people who were also discontented with the Ptolemaic view to think in new directions. Indeed, for at least a century, the Copernican system was embraced by a distinct minority of natural philosophers and astronomers.

Tycho Brahe and Johannes Kepler Make New Scientific Observations

Tycho Brahe (1546–1601) took the next major step toward the conception of a sun-centered system. He did not embrace Copernicus's view of the universe and actually spent most of his life advocating an Earth-centered system. He suggested that the moon and the sun revolved around the Earth

Tycho Brahe in the Uranienburg observatory on the Danish island of Hven (1587). Brahe made the most important observations of the stars since antiquity. Kepler used his data to solve the problem of planetary motion in a way that supported Copernicus's sun-centered view of the universe. Ironically, Brahe himself had opposed Copernicus's view. Bildarchiv Preussischer Kulturbesitz

and that the other planets revolved around the sun. In pursuit of his own theory, Brahe constructed scientific instruments with which he made more extensive naked-eye observations of the planets than anyone previous to him. His labors produced a vastly expanded body of astronomical data from which his successors could work.

When Brahe died, these tables came into the possession of his assistant, Johannes Kepler (1571–1630), a German astronomer. Kepler was a convinced Copernican and a more consistently rigorous advocate of a heliocentric model than Copernicus himself. Deeply influenced by Renaissance Neoplatonism, which held the sun in special honor, Kepler was determined to find in Brahe's numbers mathematical harmonies that would support a sun-centered universe. After much work, Kepler discovered that to keep the sun at the center of things, he must abandon the circular components of Copernicus's model, particularly the epicycles. The mathematical relationships that emerged from his consideration of Brahe's observations suggested that the motions of the planets were elliptical. Then Kepler set forth the first astronomical model that actually portrayed motion—that is, the path of the planets—and those orbits were elliptical. Kepler published his findings in his 1609 book entitled *The New Astronomy*. He had solved the problem of planetary motion by using Copernicus's sun-centered universe and Brahe's empirical data.

Kepler had also defined a new problem. None of the available theories could explain why the planetary orbits were elliptical or, for that matter, why planetary motion was orbital at all rather than simply moving off along a tangent. That solution awaited the work of Sir Isaac Newton.

Galileo Galilei Argues for a Universe of Mathematical Laws

From Copernicus to Brahe to Kepler, there had been little new information about the heavens that might not have been known to Ptolemy. In 1609, however, the same year that Kepler published *The New Astronomy*, an Italian mathematician and natural philosopher named Galileo Galilei (1564–1642) first turned a telescope on the heavens. Using that recently-invented Dutch instrument, he saw stars where none had been known to exist, mountains on the moon, spots moving across the sun, and moons orbiting Jupiter. The heavens were far more complex than anyone had formerly suspected. These discoveries, with some work, could have been accommodated into the Ptolemaic model and even more

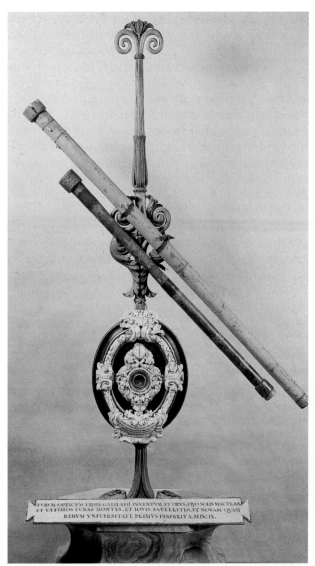

The telescope with which Galileo worked after 1609. He observed Earth's moon and the cyclical phases of the planet Venus and discovered the most prominent moons of Jupiter. *These observations had revolutionary intellectual and theological implications in the seventeenth century.* Muséo della Scienza, Florence, Italy. Scala/Art Resource, N.Y.

easily into Kepler's earth-centered model. Such accommodation would, however, have required a highly technical understanding of Ptolemaic astronomy. Galileo knew that few people who controlled patronage possessed such complex knowledge. Consequently, in the *Starry Messenger* (1610) and *Letters on Sunspots* (1613) he used his considerable rhetorical skills to argue that his newly observed physical evidence, most particularly the phases of Venus, required a Copernican interpretation of the heavens.

Galileo's career illustrates that the forging of the new science involved more than the presentation of arguments and evidence. In 1610 he had

telescope - recently invented Dutch instrument

left the University of Padua for Florence, where he became the philosopher and mathematician to the Grand Duke of Tuscany, who was a Medici. Galileo was now pursuing natural philosophy in a princely court and had become dependent upon princely patronage. To win such support for both his continued work and the theories he propounded, he named the moons of Saturn after the Medicis. As a natural philosopher working with the new telescope, he had literally presented recently discovered heavenly bodies to his patron. By both his political skills and his excellent prose, he had transformed himself into a high-profile advocate of Copernicanism. Galileo's problems with the Roman Catholic Church, which are discussed later in the chapter, arose from both his ideas and his flair for self-advertisement.

Galileo not only popularized the Copernican system, but also articulated the concept of a universe subject to mathematical laws. More than any other writer of the century, he argued that nature displayed mathematical regularity in its most minute details:

> Philosophy is written in that great book which ever lies before our eyes—I mean the universe—but we cannot understand it if we do not first learn the language and grasp the symbols in which it is written. This book is written in the mathematical language, and the symbols are triangles, circles, and other geometrical figures, without whose help it is impossible to comprehend a single word of it; without which one wanders through a dark labyrinth.[2]

The universe was rational; however, its rationality was not that of scholastic logic, but of mathematics. Copernicus had thought that the heavens conformed to mathematical regularity; Galileo saw this regularity throughout all physical nature.

A world of quantities was replacing one of qualities. All aspects of the world—including color, beauty, and taste—would increasingly be described in terms of the mathematical relationships among quantities. Mathematical models would eventually be applied even to social relations. The new natural philosophy portrayed nature as cold, rational, mathematical, and mechanistic. What was real and lasting was what was mathematically measurable. For many people, the power of the mathematical arguments that appeared irrefutable proved more persuasive than the new information from physical observation that produced so much controversy. Few intellectual shifts have wrought such momentous changes for Western civilization.

[2] Quoted in E. A. Burtt, *The Metaphysical Foundations of Modern Physical Science* (Garden City, NY: Anchor–Doubleday, 1954), p. 75.

Isaac Newton Discovers the Laws of Gravitation

The question that continued to perplex seventeenth-century scientists who accepted the theories of Copernicus, Kepler, and Galileo was how the planets and other heavenly bodies moved in an orderly fashion. The Ptolemaic and Aristotelian answer had been the spheres and a universe arranged in the order of the heaviness of its parts. Many unsatisfactory theories had been set forth to deal with the question. It was this issue of planetary motion that the Englishman Isaac Newton (1642–1727) addressed and, in so doing, established a basis for physics that endured for more than two centuries.

In 1687 Newton published *The Mathematical Principles of Natural Philosophy*, better known by its Latin title of *Principia Mathematica*. Much of the research and thinking for this great work had taken place more than fifteen years earlier. Galileo's mathematical bias permeated Newton's thought, as did his view that inertia applied to bodies both at

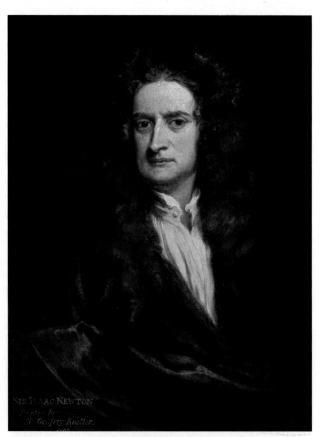

Sir Isaac Newton discovered the mathematical and physical laws governing the force of gravity. Newton believed that religion and science were compatible and mutually supportive, and that the study of nature gave one a better understanding of the Creator. This portrait of Newton is by Sir Godfrey Kneller. Sir Godfrey Kneller, *Sir Isaac Newton.* Bildarchiv Preussicher Kulturbesitz

empirical data = derived from experience or experiment

rest and in motion. Newton reasoned that the planets and all other physical objects in the universe moved through mutual attraction, or gravity. Every object in the universe affected every other object through gravity. The attraction of gravity explained why the planets moved in an orderly, rather than a chaotic, manner. Newton had found that "the force of gravity towards the whole planet did arise from and was compounded of the forces of gravity towards all its parts, and towards every one part was in the inverse proportion of the squares of the distances from the part."[3] Newton proved this relationship mathematically; he made no attempt to explain the nature of gravity itself.

Newton was a great mathematical genius, but he also upheld the importance of empirical data and observation. Like Francis Bacon (see below), he believed that one must observe phenomena before attempting to explain them. The final test of any theory or hypothesis for him was whether it described what was actually observed. Newton was a great opponent of the rationalism of the French philosopher Descartes (see below), which he believed included insufficient guards against error. Consequently, as Newton's own theory of universal gravitation became increasingly accepted, so, too, was Baconian empiricism.

Philosophy Responds to Changing Science

The revolution in scientific thought contributed directly to a major reexamination of Western philosophy. Several of the most important figures in the Scientific Revolution, such as Bacon and Descartes, were also philosophers discontented with the scholastic heritage. Bacon stressed the importance of empirical research. Descartes attempted to find certainty through the exploration of his own thinking processes. Newton's interests likewise extended to philosophy; he wrote broadly on many topics, including scientific method and theology.

If a single idea informed all of these philosophers, though in different ways, it was the idea of *mechanism*. The proponents of the new science sought to explain the world in terms of mechanical metaphors, or the language of machinery. The image to which many of them turned was that of the clock. Johannes Kepler once wrote, "I am much occupied with the investigation of the physical causes. My aim in this is to show that the machine of the universe is not similar to a divine animated being, but similar to a clock."[4] Nature conceived as machinery removed much of the mystery of the world and the previous assumption of the presence of divine purpose in nature. The qualities that seemed to inhere in matter came to be understood as the result of mechanical arrangement. Some writers came to understand God as a kind of divine watchmaker or mechanic who had arranged the world as a machine that would thereafter function automatically. The drive to a mechanical understanding of nature also meant that the language of science and of natural philosophy would become largely that of mathematics. The emphasis that Galileo had placed on mathematics spread to other areas of thought.

This new mode of thinking transformed physical nature from a realm in which Europeans looked for symbolic or sacramental meaning related to the divine into a realm where they looked for utility or usefulness. Previously, philosophers had often believed that a correct understanding of the natural order would reveal divine mysteries or knowledge relating to sacred history. Henceforth, they would tend to see knowledge of nature as revealing nothing beyond itself—nothing about divine purposes for the life of humankind on earth. Natural knowledge became the path toward the physical improvement of human beings through their ability to command the processes of nature. Many people associated with the new science also believed that such knowledge would strengthen the power of their monarchs.

Francis Bacon: The Empirical Method

Bacon (1561–1626) was an Englishman of almost universal accomplishment. He was a lawyer, a high royal official, and the author of histories, moral essays, and philosophical discourses. Traditionally, he has been regarded as the father of empiricism and of experimentation in science. Much of this reputation was actually unearned. Bacon was not a natural philosopher, except in the most amateur fashion. His real accomplishment was setting an intellectual tone and helping to create a climate conducive to scientific work.

In books such as *The Advancement of Learning* (1605), the *Novum Organum* (1620), and the *New Atlantis* (1627), Bacon attacked the scholastic belief that most truth had already been discovered and only required explanation, as well as the scholastic reverence for authority in intellectual life. (See "Bacon Attacks the Idols That Harm Human Understanding.") He believed that scholastic thinkers paid too much attention to tradition and to the knowledge of the ancients. He urged contemporaries to strike out on their own

[3] Quoted in A. Rupert Hall, *From Galileo to Newton, 1630–1720* (London: Fontana, 1970), p. 300.

[4] Quoted in Steven Shapin, *The Scientific Revolution* (Chicago: University of Chicago Press, 1996), p. 33.

Sir Francis Bacon (1561–1626), champion of the inductive method of gaining knowledge. By courtesy of the National Portrait Gallery, London

in search of a new understanding of nature. He wanted seventeenth-century Europeans to have confidence in themselves and their own abilities rather than in the people and methods of the past. Bacon was one of the first major European writers to champion the desirability of innovation and change.

Bacon believed that human knowledge should produce useful results—deeds rather than words. In particular, knowledge of nature should be brought to the aid of the human condition. These goals required the modification or abandonment of scholastic modes of learning and thinking. Bacon contended, "The [scholastic] logic now in use serves more to fix and give stability to the errors which have their foundation in commonly received notions than to help the search after truth."[5] Scholastic philosophers could not escape from their

syllogisms to examine the foundations of their thought and intellectual presuppositions. Bacon urged that philosophers and investigators of nature examine the evidence of their senses before constructing logical speculations. In a famous passage, he divided all philosophers into "men of experiment and men of dogmas" and then observed:

The men of experiment are like the ant, they only collect and use; the reasoners resemble spiders, who make cobwebs out of their own substance. But the bee takes a middle course: it gathers its material from the flowers of the garden and of the field, but transforms and digests it by a power of its own. Not unlike this is the true business of philosophy.[6]

By directing natural philosophy toward an examination of empirical evidence, Bacon hoped that it would achieve new knowledge and thus new capabilities for humankind.

Bacon boldly compared himself with Columbus, plotting a new route to intellectual discovery. The comparison is significant, because it displays the consciousness of a changing world that appears so often in writers of the late sixteenth and early seventeenth centuries. They were rejecting the past not from simple contempt or overweening pride, but rather from a firm understanding that the world was much more complicated than their medieval forebears had thought. Neither Europe nor European thought could remain self-contained. Like the new worlds on the globe, new worlds of the mind were also emerging.

Most of the people in Bacon's day, including the intellectuals, thought that the best era of human history lay in antiquity. Bacon dissented vigorously from that view. He looked to a future of material improvement achieved through the empirical examination of nature. His own theory of induction from empirical evidence was unsystematic, but his insistence on appealing to experience influenced others whose methods were more productive. He and others of his outlook received almost daily support from the reports not only of European explorers, but also of ordinary seamen who now sailed all over the world and could describe wondrous cultures, as well as plants and animals, unknown to the European ancients.

Bacon believed that science had a practical purpose and its goal was human improvement. Some scientific investigation does have this character. Much pure research does not. Bacon, however, linked science and material progress in the public mind. This was a powerful idea and has continued to influence Western civilization to the present day. It has made science and those who can appeal to the authority of science major forces for change and

[5] Quoted in Franklin Baumer, *Main Currents of Western Thought*, 4th ed. (New Haven, CT: Yale University Press, 1978), p. 281.

[6] Quoted in Baumer, p. 288.

Bacon Attacks the Idols That Harm Human Understanding

Francis Bacon wanted the men and women of his era to have the courage to change the way they thought about physical nature. In this famous passage from the Novum Organum *(1620), he attempted to explain why it is so difficult to ask new questions and seek new answers.*

❖ *Is Bacon's view of human nature pessimistic? Are people hopelessly trapped in overlapping worlds of self-interest and fantasy imposed by their nature and cultural traditions? How did Bacon expect people to overcome such formidable barriers?*

The idols and false notions which are now in possession of the human understanding and have taken deep root therein....so beset men's minds that truth can hardly find entrance....There are four classes of Idols which beset men's minds. To these for distinction's sake I have assigned names—calling the first class Idols of the Tribe; the second, Idols of the Cave; the third, Idols of the Marketplace; the fourth, Idols of the Theatre.

The Idols of the Tribe have their foundation in human nature itself; and in the tribe or race of men. For it is a false assertion that the sense of man is the measure of things. On the contrary, all perceptions as well as the sense as of the mind are according to the measure of the universe. And the human understanding is like a false mirror, which, receiving rays irregularly, distorts and discolours the nature of things by mingling its own nature with it.

The Idols of the Cave are the idols of the individual man. For every one (besides the errors common to human nature in general) has a cave or den of his own, which refracts and discolours the light of nature; owing either to his own proper and peculiar nature; or to his education and conversation with others; or to the reading of books, and the authority of those whom he esteems and admires....

There are also Idols formed by the intercourse and association of men with each other, which I call Idols of the Marketplace, on account of the commerce and consort of men there. For it is by discourse that men associate; and words are imposed according to the apprehension of the vulgar. And therefore the ill and unfit choice of words wonderfully obstructs the understanding....

Lastly, there are Idols which have immigrated into men's minds from the various dogmas of philosophies, and also from wrong laws of demonstration. These I call Idols of the Theatre; because in my judgment all the received systems are but so many stage plays, representing worlds of their own creation after an unreal and scenic fashion.

From Francis Bacon, *Essays, Advancement of Learning, New Atlantis, and Other Pieces*, ed. by Richard Foster Jones (New York: Odyssey, 1937), pp. 278–280.

innovation. Thus, though not making any major scientific contribution himself, Bacon directed investigators of nature to a new method and a new purpose. As a person actively associated with politics, Bacon also believed that the pursuit of new knowledge would increase the power of governments and monarchies. Again, his thought in this area opened the way for the eventual strong linkage between governments and the scientific enterprise.

René Descartes: The Method of Rational Deduction

Descartes (1596–1650) was a gifted mathematician who invented analytic geometry. His most important contribution, however, was to develop a scientific method that relied more on deduction than empirical observation and induction.

In 1637 he published his *Discourse on Method*, in which he rejected scholastic philosophy and education and advocated thought founded on a mathematical model. (See "Descartes Explores the Promise of Science.") The work appeared in French rather than in Latin, because Descartes wanted it to have wide circulation and application. In the *Discourse*, he began by saying that he would doubt everything except those propositions about which he could have clear and distinct ideas. This approach rejected all forms of intellectual authority, except the conviction of his own reason. Descartes concluded that he could not doubt his own act of thinking and his own exis-

René Descartes (1596–1650) believed that because the material world operated according to mathematical laws, it could be accurately understood by the exercise of human reason. Sebastian Bourdon, *Portrait of philosopher René Descartes.* Louvre, Paris, France. Erich Lessing/Art Resource, N.Y.

speculation. Reason was to be applied only to the mechanical realm of matter or to the exploration of itself.

Descartes's emphasis on deduction, rational speculation, and internal reflection by the mind, all of which he explored more fully in his *Meditations* of 1641, exercised broad influence among philosophers. His deductive methodology, however, eventually lost favor to scientific induction, whereby the scientist draws generalizations derived from empirical observations.

Thomas Hobbes: Apologist for Absolutism

Nowhere did the impact of the methods of the new science so deeply affect political thought as in the thought of Thomas Hobbes (1588–1679), the most original political philosopher of the seventeenth century. In his low view of human nature and his concept of a commonwealth based on convenant between the community and an all-powerful sovereign, Hobbes's thought contained echoes of Calvinism. Yet Hobbes presented these arguments in a materialistic philosophical framework that led many of his contemporaries rightly or wrongly to regard him as an atheist.

An urbane and much-traveled man, Hobbes enthusiastically supported the new scientific movement. During the 1630s he visited Paris, where he came to know Descartes, and he spent time with Galileo in Italy as well. He took special interest in the works of William Harvey (1578–1657), who was famous for his discovery of the circulation of blood through the body. Hobbes was also a superb classicist. His earliest published work was the first English translation of Thucydides' *History of the Peloponnesian War* and is still being reprinted today. Part of the darkness of Hobbes's view of human nature would appear to derive from Thucydides' historical analysis.

Hobbes had written works of political philosophy before the English civil war, but the turmoil of that struggle led him in 1651 to publish his *Leviathan*, a work of contemporaneous controversy and lasting influence. He was deeply concerned with the problem of how a strong central political authority might receive rigorous philosophical justification. In the *Leviathan*, Hobbes portrayed human beings and society in a thoroughly materialistic and mechanical way. He traced all psychological processes to bare sensation and regarded all human motivations as egoistical, intended to increase pleasure and minimize pain. According to his analysis, human reasoning penetrated to no deeper reality or wisdom than those physical sen-

tence. From this base, he proceeded to deduce the existence of God. The presence of God was important to Descartes because God guaranteed the correctness of clear and distinct ideas. Since God was not a deceiver, the ideas of God-given reason could not be false.

On the basis of such an analysis, Descartes concluded that human reason could fully comprehend the world. He divided existing things into two basic categories: thinking things and things occupying space—mind and body, respectively. Thinking was the defining quality of the mind, and extension (the property in virtue of which things occupy space) was the defining quality of material bodies. Human reason could grasp and understand the world of extension, which became the realm of the natural philosopher. That world had no place for spirits, divinity, or anything nonmaterial. Descartes separated mind from body to banish such things from the realm of scientific

Descartes Explores the Promise of Science

In 1637, Descartes published his Discourse on Method. *He wrote against what he believed to be the useless speculations of scholastic philosophy. He championed the careful investigation of physical nature on the grounds that it would expand the scope of human knowledge beyond anything previously achieved and in doing so make human beings the masters of nature. This passage contains much of the broad intellectual and cultural argument that led to the ever-growing influence and authority of science from the seventeenth century onward.*

❖ *How does Descartes compare the usefulness of science with previous speculative philosophy? How does he portray science as an instrument whereby human beings may master nature? What, if any, limits does he place on the extension of scientific knowledge? Why does he place so much emphasis on the promise of science to improve human health?*

My speculations were indeed truly pleasing to me; but I recognize that other men have theirs, which perhaps please them even more. As soon, however, as I had acquired some general notions regarding physics, and on beginning to make trial of them in various special difficulties had observed how far they can carry us and how much they differ from the principles hitherto employed, I believed that I could not keep them hidden without grievously sinning against the law which lays us under obligation to promote, as far as in us lies, the general good of all mankind. For they led me to see that it is possible to obtain knowledge highly useful in life, and that in place of the speculative philosophy taught in the Schools we can have a practical philosophy, by means of which, knowing the force and the actions of fire, water, air, and of the stars, of the heavens, and of all the bodies that surround us— knowing them as distinctly as we know the various crafts of the artisans—we may in the same fashion employ them in all the uses for which they are suited, thus rendering ourselves the mas-

ters and possessors of nature. This is to be desired, not only with a view to the invention of an infinity of arts by which we would be enabled to enjoy without heavy labor the fruits of the earth and all its conveniences, but above all for the preservation of health, which is, without doubt, of all blessings in this life, the first of all goods and the foundation on which the others rest. For the mind is so dependent on the temper and disposition of the bodily organisms that if any means can ever be found to render men wiser and more capable than they have hitherto been, I believe that it is in the science of medicine that the means must be sought....With no wish to depreciate it, I am yet sure there is no one, even of those engaged in the profession, who does not admit that all we know is almost nothing in comparison with what remains to be discovered; and that we could be freed from innumerable maladies, both of body and of mind, and even perhaps from the infirmities of age, if we had sufficient knowledge of their causes and of the remedies provided by nature.

From René Descartes, *Discourse on Method*, in Norman Kemp Smith, ed., *Descartes's Philosophical Writings* (New York: The Modern Library, 1958), pp. 130–131. Reprinted by permission of Macmillan Press Ltd.

sations. Consequently, for Hobbes, unlike both previous Christian and ancient philosophers, human beings exist for no higher spiritual ends or larger moral purpose than those of meeting the needs of daily life. In his view, human beings could fulfill even those limited goals only within the confines of a sovereign commonwealth established by contract that prevented the exercise of the natural human pursuit of self-interest with all its attendant potential for conflict.

Much of the persuasive power of Hobbes's political philosophy lay in his brilliant myth or political fiction about the original state of humankind. According to his account, human beings in their natural state are inclined to a "perpetual and restless desire" for power. Because all people want and, in their natural state, possess a natural right to everything, their equality breeds enmity, competition, diffidence, and perpetual quarreling—"a war of every man against every man." As Hobbes put it in a famous summary,

A portrait of Thomas Hobbes (1588–1679), whose political treatise, Leviathan, *portrayed rulers as absolute lords over their lands, incorporating in their persons the individual wills of all their people.* Bildarchiv Preussischer Kulturbesitz

In such condition there is no place for industry, because the fruit thereof is uncertain; and consequently no culture of the Earth; no navigation nor use of the commodities that may be imported by sea; no commodious building; no instruments of moving and removing such things as require much force; no knowledge of the face of the Earth; no account of time; no arts; no letters; no society; and, which is worst of all, continual fear and danger of violent death; and the life of man solitary, poor, nasty, brutish, and short.[7]

As seen in this passage, Hobbes, contrary to Aristotle and Christian thinkers like Thomas Aquinas, did not believe that human beings were naturally sociable. Rather, they were self-centered creatures lacking a master. Whereas earlier and later philosophers saw the original human state as a paradise from which humankind had fallen, Hobbes saw it as a state of natural, inevitable conflict in which neither safety, security, nor any final authority existed. Human beings in this state of nature were constantly haunted by fear of destruction and death.

Human beings escaped this terrible state of nature, according to Hobbes, only by entering into a particular kind of political contract according to which they agreed to live in a commonwealth tightly ruled by a recognized sovereign. This contract obliged every person, for the sake of peace and self-defense, to agree to set aside personal rights to all things and to be content with as much liberty against others as he or she would allow others against himself or herself. All agreed to live according to a secularized version of the golden rule, "Do not that to another which you would not have done to yourself."[8]

Because, however, words and promises are insufficient to guarantee this state, the contract also established the coercive use of force to compel compliance. Believing the dangers of anarchy to be always greater than those of tyranny, Hobbes thought that rulers should be absolute and unlimited in their power, once established as authority. Hobbes's political philosophy has no room for protest in the name of individual conscience or for individual resistance to some other legitimate authority beyond the sovereign. In a reply to critics of his position on sovereign authority, Hobbes pointed out the alternative:

The greatest [unhappiness] that in any form of government can possibly happen to the people in general is scarce sensible in respect of the miseries and horrible calamities that accompany a civil war or that dissolute condition of masterless men, without subjection to laws and a coercive power to tie their hands from rapine and revenge.[9]

The specific structure of this absolute government was not of enormous concern to Hobbes. He believed that absolute authority might be lodged in either a monarch or a legislative body. But once that person or body had been granted authority, there existed no argument for appeal. For all practical purposes, obedience to the Hobbesian sovereign was absolute.

Hobbes's argument for an absolute political authority that could assure order aroused sharp opposition. Monarchists objected to his willingness to assign sovereign authority to a legislature. Republicans rejected his willingness to accept a monarchical authority. Some religious writers, including those who supported the divine right of kings, furiously criticized his materialist arguments for an absolute political authority. Other religious writers attacked his refusal to recognize the authority of either God or the Church as standing beside or above his secular sovereign. The influence of Hobbes's political analysis would grow over the next three centuries as political and religious authority in the West became increasingly separated.

[7] Thomas Hobbes, *Leviathan*, Parts I and II, ed. by H. W. Schneider (Indianapolis: Bobbs-Merrill, 1958), p. 86, 106–107.

[8] Hobbes, p. 130.

[9] Hobbes, p. 152.

The famous title page illustration for Hobbes's Leviathan. *The ruler is pictured as absolute lord of his lands, but note that the ruler incorporates the mass of individuals whose self-interests are best served by their willing consent to accept him and cooperate with him.*
Rare Books Division, The New York Public Library. Astor, Lenox and Tilden Foundations.

John Locke: Defender of Moderate Liberty and Toleration

Locke (1632–1704) proved to be the most influential philosophical and political thinker of the seventeenth century. Although he was less original than Hobbes, his political writings became a major source of criticism of absolutism and provided a foundation for later liberal political philosophy in both Europe and America. His philosophical works dealing with human knowledge became the most important work of psychology for the eighteenth century.

Locke's family had Puritan sympathies, and during the English civil war his father had fought for the parliamentary forces against the Stuart monarchy. Although a highly cerebral person who was well read in all the major seventeenth-century natural philosophers, Locke became deeply involved with the tumultuous politics of the English Restoration period. He was a close associate of Anthony Ashley Cooper, the earl of Shaftesbury, considered by his contemporaries to be a radical in both religion and politics. Shaftesbury organized an unsuccessful rebellion against Charles II in 1682, after which both he and Locke, who lived with him, were forced to flee to Holland.

During his years of association with Shaftesbury and the opposition to Charles II, Locke wrote two treatises on government, which were published in 1690. In the first of these, he rejected arguments for absolute government that based political authority on the patriarchal model of fathers ruling over a family. After the publication of this treatise, no major political philosopher again appealed to the patriarchal model. In that regard, though not widely read today, Locke's *First Treatise of Government* proved enormously important by clearing the philosophical decks, so to speak, of a long-standing traditional argument that could not stand up to rigorous analysis.

John Locke (1632–1704), defender of the rights of the people against rulers who think their power absolute.
By courtesy of the National Portrait Gallery, London

thority. In this respect, government exists to protect the best achievements and liberty of the state of nature, not to overcome them. Thus, by its very foundation, Locke's government is one of limited authority.

The warfare that Hobbes believed characterized the state of nature emerged for Locke only when rulers failed to preserve people's natural freedom and attempted to enslave them by absolute rule. The relationship between rulers and the governed is that of trust, and if the rulers betray that trust, the governed have the right to replace them. In this regard, Locke's position resembled that of St. Thomas Aquinas, who also permitted rebellion against government when it violated laws of nature.

In his *Letter Concerning Toleration* (1689), Locke used the premises of the as yet unpublished *Second Treatise* to defend extensive religious toleration, which he saw as an answer to the destructive religious conflict of the past two centuries. To make his case for toleration, Locke claimed that each individual stood charged with working out his or her own religious salvation and that these efforts might lead various people to join different religious groups. For its part, government existed by its very nature to preserve property, not to make religious decisions for its citizens. Governments that attempted to impose religious uniformity thus misunderstood their real purpose. Moreover, government-imposed religious uniformity could not achieve real religious ends, because assent to religious truth must be freely given by the individual's conscience rather than by force. Consequently, Locke urged a wide degree of religious toleration among differing voluntary Christian groups. He did not, however, extend toleration to Roman Catholics, whom he believed to have given allegiance to a foreign prince (i.e., the Pope), or

In his *Second Treatise of Government,* Locke presented an extended argument for a government that must necessarily be both responsible for and responsive to the concerns of the governed. Locke portrayed the natural human state as one of perfect freedom and equality in which everyone enjoyed, in an unregulated fashion, the natural rights of life, liberty, and property. Locke, contrary to Hobbes, regarded human beings in their natural state as creatures of reason and basic goodwill rather than of uncontrolled passion and selfishness. For Locke, human beings possess a strong capacity for dwelling more or less peacefully in society before they enter a political contract. What they experience in the state of nature is not a state of war, but a condition of competition and modest conflict that requires a political authority to sort out problems rather than to impose sovereign authority. They enter into the contract to form political society to secure and preserve the rights, liberty, and property that they already possess prior to the existence of political au-

Major Works of the Scientific Revolution

1543	*On the Revolutions of the Heavenly Spheres* (Copernicus)
1605	*The Advancement of Learning* (Bacon)
1609	*The New Astronomy* (Kepler)
1620	*Novum Organum* (Bacon)
1632	*Dialogues on the Two Chief World Systems* (Galileo)
1637	*Discourse on Method* (Descartes)
1651	*Leviathan* (Hobbes)
1687	*Principia Mathematica* (Newton)
1689	*Letter Concerning Toleration* (Locke)
1690	*An Essay Concerning Human Understanding* (Locke)
1690	*Treatises of Government* (Locke)

John Locke Explores the Sources of Human Knowledge

An Essay Concerning Human Understanding (1690) was probably the most influential philosophical work ever written in English. Locke's fundamental idea, which is explicated in the passage that follows, was that human knowledge is grounded in the experiences of the senses and in the reflection of the mind on those experiences. He rejected any belief in innate ideas. His emphasis on experience led to the wider belief that human beings are creatures of their environment. After Locke, numerous writers argued that human beings could be improved if the political and social environments in which they lived were reformed.

❖ *How does Locke explain how the human mind comes to be furnished? What does Locke mean by experience? How does reflection deal with external sensations? What role does the external environment play in Locke's psychology?*

Let us then suppose the mind to be, as we say, white paper void of all characters, without any ideas. Whence comes it to be furnished? Whence comes it by that vast store which the busy and boundless fancy of man has painted on it with an almost endless variety? Whence has it all the materials of reason and knowledge? To this I answer, from experience; in that all our knowledge is founded, and from that it ultimately derives itself. Our observation, employed either about external sensible objects, or about the internal operations of our minds perceived and reflected on by ourselves, is that which supplies our understanding with all the materials of thinking. These two are the fountains of knowledge, from whence all the ideas we have, or can naturally have, do spring.

First, our senses, conversant about particular sensible objects, do convey into the mind several distinct perceptions of things, according to those various ways wherein those objects do affect them. And thus we come by those ideas we have of yellow, white, heat, cold, soft, hard, bitter, sweet, and all those which we call sensible qualities....This great source of most of the ideas we have, depending wholly upon our senses, and derived by them to the understanding, I call SENSATION.

Secondly, the other fountain from which experience furnisheth the understanding with ideas is the perception of the operations of our own mind within us, as it is employed about the ideas it has got...and such are perception, thinking, doubting, believing, reasoning, knowing, willing, and all the different actings of our own minds....I call this REFLECTION, the ideas it affords being such only as the mind gets by reflecting on its own operations within itself.... These two, I say, viz., external material things as the objects of SENSATION, and the operations of our own minds within as the objects of REFLECTION, are to me the only originals from whence all our ideas take their beginnings...

The understanding seems to me not to have the least glimmering of any ideas which it doth not receive from one of these two.

From John Locke, *An Essay Concerning Human Understanding*, Vol. 1 (London, Everyman's Library, 1961), pp. 77–78.

to atheists, whom he believed could not be trusted to keep their word. Despite these limitations, Locke's *Letter Concerning Toleration* established a powerful foundation for the future extension of toleration, religious liberty, and the separation of church and state. His vision of such expansive toleration was partially realized in England after 1688 and most fully in the United States after the American Revolution.

Finally, just as Newton had set forth laws of astronomy and gravitation, Locke hoped to elucidate the basic structures of human thought. He did so in the most immediately influential of his books, his *Essay Concerning Human Understanding* (1690), which became the major work of European psychology during the eighteenth century. There, Locke portrayed a person's mind at birth as a blank tablet whose content would be determined by sense experience. (See "John Locke Explores the Sources of Human Knowledge.") His vision of the mind has been aptly compared to an early version of behaviorism. It was a reformer's psychology which believed that the human condition could be improved by changing the environment.

Locke's view of psychology rejected the Christian understanding of original sin, yet he believed that his psychology had preserved religious knowledge. He thought that such knowledge came through divine revelation in scripture and also from the conclusions that human reason could draw from observing nature. He hoped that this interpretation of religious knowledge would prevent human beings from falling into what he regarded as fanaticism arising from the claims of alleged private revelations and irrationality arising from superstition. For Locke, reason and revelation were compatible and together could sustain a moderate religious faith that would avoid religious conflict.

The New Institutions of Expanding Natural Knowledge

One of the most fundamental features of the expansion of science was the emerging idea that *genuinely new knowledge* about nature and humankind could be discovered. In the late Middle Ages, the recovery of Aristotle and the rise of humanistic learning looked back to the ancients to rediscover the kind of knowledge that later Europeans needed. Luther and other Reformers had seen themselves as recovering a better understanding of the original Christian message. By contrast, the proponents of the new natural knowledge and the new philosophy sought to pursue what Bacon called the advancement of learning. New knowledge would be continuously created. This outlook required new institutions.

There were powerful social implications to the expansion of natural knowledge. Both the new science and the philosophical outlook associated with it opposed Scholasticism and Aristotelianism. These were not simply disembodied philosophical outlooks, but ways of approaching the world of knowledge still espoused by most scholars in the universities of the day. Such scholars had a clear vested interest in preserving those traditional outlooks. As they saw it, they were defending the Ancients against the Moderns. Not surprisingly, the advanced thinkers of the seventeenth century often criticized the universities. For example, in his *Discourse on Method*, Descartes was highly critical of the education he had received. Hobbes filled the *Leviathan* with caustic remarks about the kind of learning then dominating schools and universities, and Locke advocated educational reform.

Some of the criticism of universities was exaggerated. Medical faculties, on the whole, welcomed the advancement of learning in their fields of study. Most of the natural philosophers had themselves received their education at universities. Moreover, however slowly new ideas might penetrate universities, the expanding world of natural knowledge would be taught to future generations. And with that diffusion of science into the universities came new supporters of scientific knowledge beyond the small group of natural philosophers themselves. Universities also provided much of the physical and financial support for the teaching and investigation of natural philosophy and employed many scientists, the most important of whom was Newton himself. University support of science did, however, vary according to country, with the Italian universities being far more supportive than the French.

Yet because of the reluctance of universities to rapidly assimilate the new science, its pioneers quickly understood that they required a framework for cooperation and sharing of information that went beyond existing intellectual institutions. Consequently, they and their supporters established what have been termed "institutions of sharing" that allowed information and ideas associated with the new science to be gathered, exchanged, and debated.[10] The most famous of these institutions was the Royal Society of London, founded in 1660, whose members consciously saw themselves as following the path Bacon had laid out almost a half century earlier. The Royal Society had been preceded by the Academy of Experiments in Florence in 1657 and was followed by the French Academy of Science in 1666. Germany only slowly overcame the destruction of the Thirty Years' War, with the Berlin Academy of Science being founded in 1700. In addition to these major academies, there were many local societies and academies at which the new science was discussed and experiments were carried out.

These societies provided organizations that met regularly to hear papers and observe experiments. One of the reasons many early experiments achieved credibility was that they had been observed by persons of social respectability who belonged to one or more of the societies and who, because of their social standing, were presumed to be truthful witnesses of what they had observed. These groups also published information relating to natural philosophy and often organized libraries for their members. Perhaps most important, they attempted to separate the discussion and exploration of natural philosophy from the religious and political conflicts of the day. They intended science to exemplify an arena for the polite exchange of ideas and for civil disagreement and debate. This particular function of science as fostering civility became one of its major attractions.

The activities of the societies also constituted a kind of crossroads between their own members always drawn from the literate classes, and people outside the

[10] Lewis Pyenson and Susan Sheets-Pyenson, *Servants of Nature: A History of Scientific Institutions, Enterprises and Sensibilities* (New York: W. W. Norton & Company, 1999), p. 75.

The sixteenth and seventeenth centuries saw Europeans expanding their knowledge into the ancient past, into the New World, and into the starry heavens. In this painting, The Sciences and the Arts, *the artist depicts recent paintings that connect contemporary culture with the ancient world and the Bible. In the same room, he sets globes depicting the New World and astronomical instruments used by natural philosophers exploring the heavens according to the the theories of Copernicus, Kepler, and Galileo. Yet throughout all of the expansion of mind and geographical knowledge, women were generally excluded as they are in this painting. For example, only on the rarest occasion were women permitted to visit the Royal Society of London.* Adriaen Stalbent, *The Sciences and the Arts.* Wood, 93 × 114 cm. Inv. 1405. Museo del Prado, Madrid, Spain. Erich Lessing/Art Resource, N.Y.

elite classes, whose skills and practical knowledge might be important for advancing the new science. The latter included craftspeople who could manufacture scientific instruments, sailors whose travels had taken them to foreign parts and who might report upon the plants and animals they had seen there, and workers who had practical knowledge of problems in the countryside. In this respect, the expansion of the European economy and the drive toward empire contributed to the growth of the scientific endeavor by bringing back to Europe specimens and experiences that required classification, analysis, and observation.

In good Baconian fashion, the members of the societies presented science as an enterprise that could aid the goals of government and the growth of the economy. For example, mathematicians portrayed themselves as being useful for solving surveying and other engineering problems and for improving armaments. Furthermore, people who had ideas for improving production, navigation, or military artillery might seek the support of the associated societies. In the English context, these people became known as *projectors* and were satirized in Jonathan Swift's (1667–1745) *Gulliver's Travels.* (See "Jonathan Swift Satirizes Scientific Societies.")

The work, publications, and interaction of the scientific societies with both the government and private business established a distinct role and presence for scientific knowledge in European social life. By 1700 that presence was relatively modest, but it would grow steadily during the coming decades. The groups associated with the new science saw themselves as championing modern practical achievements of applied knowledge and urging religious toleration, mutual for-

Jonathan Swift Satirizes Scientific Societies

Swift was the greatest author of English satire in the eighteenth century. He was a deeply pessimistic person who thought that much of the promise held forth for the scientific enterprise would never be realized. In the "Third Voyage" of Gulliver's Travels, *published in 1726, Swift portrays Gulliver as visiting the land of Lagardo. In that country there exists a learned academy filled with scholars who pursue outlandish projects. Swift lists the efforts of a whole series of Projectors, each of whom is more impractical than the next. This passage in which Swift pillories the various people who hoped to receive patronage for projects from persons associated with the Royal Society of London remains one of the most famous satires of science in the English language. That Swift felt compelled to write it is a testimony to the cultural authority that science had achieved by the early eighteenth century.*

✤ *Why might Swift have so emphasized what he saw as the impracticality of science? How does this passage serve to refute the promise of science championed by Bacon and Descartes? How might Swift's presentation be seen as manifesting jealousy by a literary figure toward the growing influence of science?*

Gulliver reports a conversation he encountered while visiting Lagardo:

"The Sum of his Discourse was to this Effect. That about Forty Years ago, certain Persons went up to *Laputa*, either upon Business or Diversion; and after five Months Continuance, came back with a very little Smattering in Mathematics, but full of Volatile Spirits acquired in that Airy Region. That these Persons upon their Return, began to dislike the Management of every Thing below; and fell into Schemes of putting all Arts, Sciences, Languages, and Mechanics upon a new Foot. To this End they procured a Royal Patent for erecting an Academy of *Projectors* in *Lagado*; And the Humour prevailed so strongly among the People, that there is not a Town of any Consequence in the Kingdom without such an Academy. In these Colleges, the Professors contrive new Rules and Methods of Agriculture and Building, and new Instruments and Tools for all Trades and Manufactures, whereby, as they undertake, one Man shall do the Work of Ten; a Palace may be built in a Week, of Materials so durable as to last for ever without repairing. All the Fruits of the Earth shall come to Maturity at whatever Season we think fit to chuse; and increse an Hundred Fold more than they do at present; with innumerable other happy Proposals. The only Inconvenience is, that none of these Projects are yet brought to Perfection; and in the mean time, the whole Country lies miserably waste, the Houses in Ruins, and the People without Food or Cloaths. By all which, instead of

being discouraged they are Fifty Times more violently bent upon prosecuting their Schemes, driven equally on by Hope and Despair...."

Gulliver then reports what he found occurring in the rooms of an academy in Lagardo:

"The first Man I saw...had been Eight Years upon a Project for extracting Sun-Beams out of Cucumbers, which were to be put into Vials hermetically sealed, and let out to warm the Air in raw inclement Summers....

"I saw another at work to calcine ice into Gunpowder...

"There was another most ingenius Architect who had contrived a new Method for building Houses, by beginning at the Roof, and working downwards to the Foundation....

In another Apartment I was highly pleased with a Projector, who had found a Device of plowing the Ground with Hogs, to save the Charges of Plows, Cattle, and Labour. The Method is this: In an Acre of Ground you bury at six Inches Distance, and eight deep, a quantity of Acorns, Dates, Chesnuts, and other Masts or Vegatables whereof these Animals are fondest; then you drive six Hundred or more of them into the Field, where in a few Days they will root up the whole Ground in search of their Food, and make it fit for sowing, at the same time manuring it with their Dung. It is true, upon Experiment they found the Charge and Trouble very great, and they had little or no Crop. However, it is not doubted that this Invention may be capable of great Improvement."

From Jonathan Swift, *Gulliver's Travels*, Part III, chs. iv and v (New York: The Heritage Press, 1960), pp. 193–194, 197–199.)

bearance, and political liberty. Such people would form the social base for the eighteenth-century movement known as the Enlightenment.

Women in the World of the Scientific Revolution

The absence of women in the emergence of the new science of the seventeenth century has been a matter of much historical speculation. What characteristics of early modern European intellectual and cultural life worked against extensive contributions by women? Why have we heard so little of the activity by women that did actually occur in regard to the new science?

The same factors that had long excluded women from participating in most intellectual life continued to exclude them from working in the emerging natural philosophy. Traditionally, the institutions of European intellectual life had all but excluded women. Both monasteries and universities had been institutions associated with celibate male clerical culture. Except for a few exceptions in Italy, women had not been admitted to either medieval or early modern European universities; they would continue to be excluded from them until the end of the nineteenth century. Women could and did exercise much influence over princely courts where natural philosophers, such as Galileo, sought patronage, but they usually did not determine those patronage decisions or benefit from them. Queen Christina of Sweden was an exception by engaging René Descartes to provide the regulations for a new science academy. When various scientific societies were founded, women were not admitted to membership. In that regard, there were virtually no social spaces that might have permitted women easily to pursue science.

Yet a few isolated women from two different social settings did manage to engage in the new scientific activity—noblewomen and women from the artisan class. In both cases, they could do so only through their husbands or other men in their families.

The social standing of certain noblewomen allowed them to command the attention of ambitious natural philosophers who were part of their husband's social circle. Margaret Cavendish (1623–1673) actually made significant contributions to the scientific literature of the day. After she had been privately tutored and become widely read, her marriage to the duke of Newcastle introduced her into a circle of natural philosophers. She understood the new science, quarreled with the ideas of Descartes and Hobbes, and criticized the Royal Society for being more interested in novel scientific instruments than in solving practical problems. Her most important works were *Observations upon Experimental Philosophy* (1666) and *Grounds of Natural Philosophy* (1668). She was the only woman in the seventeenth century to be allowed to visit a meeting of the Royal Society of London. (See "Margaret Cavendish Questions the Fascination with Scientific Instruments.")

Women associated with artisan crafts actually achieved greater freedom in pursuing the new sciences than did noblewomen. Traditionally, women had worked in artisan workshops, often with their husbands, and might take over the business when their spouse died. In Germany, much astronomy occurred in these settings, with women assisting their fathers or husbands. One such German female astronomer, Maria Cunitz, published a book on astronomy that many people thought her husband had written until he added a preface supporting her sole authorship. Elisabetha and Johannes Hevelius constituted a wife-and-husband astronomical team, as did Maria Winkelmann and her husband Gottfried Kirch. In each case, the wife served as the assistant to an artisan astronomer. Although Winkelmann discovered a comet in 1702, not until 1930 was the discovery ascribed to her rather than to her husband. Nonetheless, contemporary philosophers did recognize her abilities and understanding of astronomy. Winkelmann had worked jointly with her husband who was the official astronomer of the Berlin Academy of Sciences and was responsible for establishing an official calendar published by the Academy. When her husband died in 1710, Winkelmann applied for permission to continue the work, basing her application for the post on the guild's tradition of allowing women to continue their husband's work, in this case the completion of observations required for creating an accurate calendar. After much debate, the Academy formally rejected her application on the grounds of her gender, although its members knew of her ability and previous accomplishments. Years later, she returned to the Berlin Academy as an assistant to her son, who had been appointed astronomer. Again, the Academy insisted that she leave, forcing her to abandon astronomy. She died in 1720.

Such policies of exclusion, however, did not altogether prevent women from aquiring knowledge about the scientific endeavors of the age. Margaret Cavendish had composed a *Description of a New World, called the Blazing World* (1666) to introduce women to the new science. Other examples of scientific writings for a female audience were Bernard de Fontenelle's *Conversations on the Plurality of Worlds* and Francesco Algarotti's *Newtonianism for Ladies* (1737). During the 1730s, Emilie du Châtelet aided Voltaire in his composition of an important French popularization of Newton's science. Her knowledge of mathematics was more extensive than his and crucial to his completing his book.

Margaret Cavendish Questions the Fascination with Scientific Instruments

Margaret Cavendish, Duchess of Newcastle, was the most scientifically informed woman of seventeenth-century England. She read widely in natural philosophy and had many acquaintances who were involved in the new science. While she was enthusiastic about the promise of science, she also frequently criticized some of its leading proponents, including Descartes and Hobbes. She was skeptical of the activities of the newly established Royal Society of London, which she was once permitted to visit. She believed that some of its members had become overly enthusiastic about experimentation and new scientific instruments for their own sakes and had begun to ignore the practical questions that she thought science should address. In this respect, her criticism of the Royal Society and its experiments is a Baconian one. She thought the Society had replaced scholastic speculation with experimental speculation and that both kinds of speculation ignored important problems of immediate utility.

❖ *Why might Margaret Cavendish think that the experiments which were reported about new optical instruments dealt with superficial wonders? Why does she contrast experimental philosophy with the beneficial arts? Do you find a feminist perspective in her comparison of the men of the Royal Society with boys playing with bubbles?*

Art has intoxicated so many men's brains, and wholly imployed their thoughts and bodily actions about phaenomena, or the exterior figure of objects, as all better Arts and Studies are laid aside;...But though there be numerous Books written of the wonder of these [experimental optical] Glasses, yet I cannot perceive any such; at best, they are but superficial wonders, as I may call them. But could Experimental Philosophers find out more beneficial Arts then our Forefathers have done, either for the better increase of Vegetables and brute Animals to nourish our bodies, or better and commodious contrivances in the Art of Architecture to build us houses, or for the advancing of trade and traffick...it would not only be worth their labour, but of as much praise as could be given to them: But, as Boys that play with watry Bubbles...are worthy of reproof rather than praise, for wasting their time with useless sports; so those that addict themselves to unprofitable Arts, spend more time than they reap benefit thereby.

From Margaret Cavendish, *Observations Upon Experimental Philosophy; to which is added, the Description of a New Blazing World* (London, 1666), pp. 10–11 as quoted in Anna Battigelli, *Margaret Cavendish and the Exiles of the Mind* (Lexington, KY: University of Kentucky Press, 1998), p. 94.

Still, with only a few exceptions, women were barred from science and medicine until the late nineteenth century, and not until the twentieth century did they enter these fields in any significant numbers. Not only did the institutions of science exclude them, but also, the ideas associated with medical practice, philosophy, and biology suggested that women and their minds were essentially different from, and inferior to, men and theirs. By the early eighteenth century, despite isolated precedents of women pursuing natural knowledge, reading scientific literature, and engaging socially with natural philosophers, it had become a fundamental assumption of European intellectual life that the pursuit of natural knowledge was a male vocation.

The New Science and Religious Faith

In the minds of many contemporaries, the new science posed a potential challenge to religion. Three major issues were at stake. First, certain theories and discoveries did not agree with biblical statements about the heavens. Second, the question arose, Would church authorities or the natural philosophers decide conflicts between religion and science. Finally, for many religious thinkers, the new science offered only a materialistic universe, replacing one of spiritual meaning and significance. Yet most of the natural philosophers genuinely saw their work as contributing to a deeper knowledge of the divine, thus supporting religious belief. Their efforts and those of their supporters to reconcile faith and the new science constituted a fundamental factor in the spread of science and its widespread acceptance in educated European circles. The process was not an easy one. (See "Art & the West.")

The Case of Galileo

The condemnation of Galileo by Roman Catholic authorities in 1633 is the single most famous incident of conflict between modern science and religious institutions. For centuries it was interpreted as exemplifying the forces of religion smothering scientific knowledge. More recent research has modified that picture.

The condemnation of Copernicanism and of Galileo occurred at a particularly difficult moment in the history of the Roman Catholic Church. In response to Protestant emphasis on private interpretation of scripture, the Council of Trent (1545–1563) had stated that only the church itself possessed the authority to interpret the Bible. Furthermore, after the Council, the Roman Catholic Church had adopted a more literalist mode of reading the Bible in response to the Protestant emphasis on the authority of scripture. Galileo's championing of Copernicanism took place in this particular climate of opinion and practice when the Roman Catholic Church, on the one hand, could not surrender the interpretation of the Bible to a layman and, on the other, had difficulty moving beyond a literal reading of the Bible for fear of being accused by the Protestants of abandoning scripture.

In a *Letter to the Grand Duchess Christina* (1615), Galileo, as a layman, had published his own views about how scripture should be interpreted to accommodate the new science. (See "Galileo Discussed the Relationship of Science to the Bible.") To certain Roman Catholic authorities, his actions resembled that of a Protestant who looked to himself rather than the church to understand the Bible. In 1615 and 1616, he visited Rome and discussed his views openly and aggressively. In early 1616, however, the Roman Catholic Inquisition formally censured Copernicus's views, placing *On the Revolutions of the Heavenly Spheres* on the Index of Prohibited Books. The ground for the condemnation was the disagreement of Copernicus with the literal word of the Bible and the biblical interpretations of the Church Fathers. It should be recalled that at the time there did not yet exist, even in Galileo's mind, fully satisfactory empirical evidence in support of Copernicus.

Galileo, who was not on trial in 1616, was formally informed of the condemnation of Copernicanism. It remains unclear exactly what agreement he and the Roman Catholic authorities reached as to what he would be permitted to write in regard to Copernicanism. It appears that he agreed not to advocate the physical truthfulness of Copernican astronomy, but to suggest only its theoretical possibility.

In 1623, however, a Florentine acquaintance of Galileo's was elected as Pope Urban VIII. He gave Galileo permission once again to discuss the Copernican system, which he did in *Dialogue on the Two Chief World Systems* (1632). The book clearly was designed to defend the physical truthfulness of Copernicanism. Moreover, the voices in the dialogue favoring the older system appeared slow-witted, and those voices presented the views of Pope Urban. Feeling both humiliated and personally betrayed, the Pope ordered an investigation of Galileo's book. The actual issue in Galileo's trial of 1633 was whether he had disobeyed the mandate of 1616, and it must have been clear to any observer that he had done so. Galileo was condemned, required to abjure his views, and placed under the equivalent of house arrest in his home near Florence for the last nine years of his life.

Although much more complicated than a simple case of a conflict between science and religion, the condemnation of Galileo cast a long and troubled shadow over the relationship of the emerging new science and the authority of the Roman Catholic Church. The controversy continued into the late twentieth century, when Pope John II formally ordered the reassessment of the Galileo case with the result that in 1992 the Roman Catholic Church admitted that errors had occurred, most particularly in the biblical interpretation of Pope Urban VIII's advisors.

Blaise Pascal: Reason and Faith

One of the most influential efforts to reconcile faith and the new science was presented by Pascal (1623–1662), a French mathematician and a physical scientist who surrendered his wealth to pursue an austere, self-disciplined life. He aspired to write a work that would refute both dogmatism (which he saw epitomized by the Jesuits) and skepticism. Pascal considered the Jesuits' casuistry (i.e., arguments designed to minimize and excuse sinful acts) a distortion of Christian teaching. He rejected the skeptics of his age be-

Art & the West

Vermeer's The Geographer and The Astronomer: Painting and The New Knowledge

During the sixteenth and seventeenth centuries, just as the theories and observations published by Copernicus, Kepler, and Galileo led to a new understanding of the heavens, the encounter with the Americas and the opening of new shipping lanes to Asia flooded Europe with new information about areas of the world previously unknown to Europeans. The Netherlands stood at a crucial juncture in both enterprises. Dutch opticians and metalworkers produced scientific instruments of the highest quality. Their boatyards constructed advanced ships that transported goods throughout the world as the Dutch established the first far-flung commercial empire. Religious toleration in the Netherlands permitted an active and open intellectual life, as did the Dutch policy of welcoming immigrants from everywhere. Dutch freedom of the press allowed the Netherlands to become a center for the publication of books that carried the new knowledge of astronomy, optics, geography and other sciences across Europe.

Two paintings of the late 1660s by the Dutch artist Jan Vermeer (1632–1675) reflect these developments: *The Astronomer* (1668) and *The Geographer* (1668–1669). Sales records suggest that Vermeer painted them as pendants; that is, they were meant to hang beside each other and to give meaning to each other. Astronomy and geography would have been closely related in the minds of a seventeenth-century Dutch artist and his contemporaries because the improved knowledge of the heavens was important for both navigation and calendars.

The geographer is shown consulting maps, which, over the course of the past two centuries, had seen the additions of new continents, islands, and rivers never recorded by the ancients. Used by Dutch fleets, those maps had opened the way for a worldwide trade that enriched the nation and led it into conflict with both France and England. Consequently, the geographer could look out through the window onto a wider world filled with more different kinds of goods and natural wonders than any Europeans had ever known. By placing on a map the regions where those goods originated and those wonders lay,

Vermeer van Delft, Jan, *The Geographer* (1668–69). Oil on canvas. Staedelsches Kunstinstitute, Frankfurt am Main. The Granger Collection

the geographer could make that expanding new world familiar to ordinary Europeans.

Vermeer's astronomer sits at his desk with his hand on a globe depicting the constellations of the night sky. On the side of the cabinet in the back of the room hangs a chart containing other astronomical information, and on the table is an instrument for making observations of the heavens. The scene portrays the kind of setting in which much theorizing about astronomy occurred. Clearly, science involved thinking and working through tables of observations as much as it did peering into the night sky. Through such mathematical theorizing, Newton would achieve the culmination of the Scientific Revolution about twenty years later with his publication of *Principia Mathematica* (1687). But the cultural fascination with astronomy predated that publication.

The Astronomer also depicts an important theme relating to science and religion. On the wall to the right, as a painting within the painting, hangs the *Finding of Moses*, an image artists often used to symbolize God's providential purposes. Because the *Finding of Moses* is at the side of the painting and the astronomer's back is to it, Vermeer might be suggesting that those practicing the new science must look to the light of nature alone, which streams in through the window. But as a Roman Catholic well aware of the fate of Galileo, Vermeer is probably suggesting that the new natural knowledge, like the life of Moses, did fulfill divine purposes. The presence of the astronomer with both the biblical painting and the astronomical globe thus appears to indicate that devout faith and the pursuit of rigorous science are compatible and mutually reinforcing.

Vermeer's method of painting as well as his content displays his fascination with optics, a subject that also interested many natural philosophers. In these and other paintings, Vermeer portrayed light illuminating interiors. He is believed to have used a *camera obscura*, a darkened box with a pinhole through which light projected the outside scene in precise detail and vibrant color. As one contemporary wrote, "I am certain that vision from these reflections in the dark can give no small light to the sight of the young artists; because besides gaining knowledge of nature, so one sees here what main or general [characteristics] should belong to a truly natural painting."[11] Vermeer's use of the *camera obscura* illustrates how the science and experiments of the new optics could influence the traditional craft of painting, expanding its capacity to portray the natural world.

Vermeer van Delft, Jan (1632–1675), *The Astronomer* (1668). Oil on canvas 31.5 × 45.5 cm. Louvre, Dep. des Peintures, Paris, France. Erich Lessing, Art Resource, NY

Mariet Westermann, *A Worldly Art: The Dutch Republic 1585–1718* (New York: Prentice Hall/ Abrams, 1996); Arthur K. Wheelock, Jr., *Vermeer and the Art of Painting* (New Haven: Yale University Press, 1995); J. M. Montias, *Vermeer and His Milieu: A Web of Social History* (Princeton: Princeton University Press, 1989); Arthur K. Wheelock, Jr., *Perspective, Optics, and Delft Artists Around 1650* (New York: Garland Press, 1977)

[11] Arthur K. Wheelock, Jr., *Vermeer and the Art of Painting* (New Haven, CT: Yale University Press, 1995), p. 18.

Galileo Discusses the Relationship of Science to the Bible

The religious authorities were often critical of the discoveries and theories of sixteenth- and seventeenth-century science. For years before his condemnation by the Roman Catholic Church in 1633, Galileo had contended that scientific theory and religious piety were compatible. In his Letter to the Grand Duchess Christiana *(of Tuscany), written in 1615, he argued that God had revealed truth in both the Bible and physical nature and that the truth of physical nature did not contradict the Bible if the latter were properly understood. Galileo encountered difficulties regarding this letter because it represented a layman telling church authorities how to read the Bible.*

❖ *Is Galileo's argument based on science or theology? Did the church believe that nature was as much a revelation of God as the Bible was? As Galileo describes them, which is the surer revelation of God, nature or the Bible? Why might the pope reject Galileo's argument?*

The reason produced for condemning the opinion that the Earth moves and the sun stands still is that in many places in the Bible one may read that the sun moves and the Earth stands still....

With regard to this argument, I think in the first place that it is very pious to say and prudent to affirm that the holy Bible can never speak untruth—whenever its true meaning is understood. But I believe nobody will deny that it is often very abstruse, and may say things which are quite different from what its bare words signify....

This being granted, I think that in discussions of physical problems we ought to begin not from the authority of scriptural passages, but from sense-experiences and necessary demonstrations; for the holy Bible and the phenomena of nature proceed alike from the divine Word, the former as the dictate of the Holy Ghost and the latter as the observant executrix of God's commands. It is necessary for the Bible, in order to be accommodated to the understanding of every man, to speak many things which appear to differ from the absolute truth so far as the bare meaning of the words is concerned. But Nature, on the other hand, is inexorable and immutable; she never transgresses the laws imposed upon her, or cares a whit whether her abstruse reasons and methods of operation are understandable to men. For that reason it appears that nothing physical which sense-expe-

rience sets before our eyes, or which necessary demonstrations prove to us, ought to be called in question (much less condemned) upon the testimony of biblical passages which may have some different meaning beneath their words. For the Bible is not chained in every expression to conditions as strict as those which govern all physical effects; nor is God any less excellently revealed in Nature's actions than in the sacred statements of the Bible....

From this I do not mean to infer that we need not have an extraordinary esteem for the passages of holy Scripture. On the contrary, having arrived at any certainties in physics, we ought to utilize these as the most appropriate aids in the true exposition of the Bible and in the investigation of those meanings which are necessarily contained therein for these must be concordant with demonstrated truths. I should judge the authority of the Bible was designed to persuade men of those articles and propositions which, surpassing all human reasoning, could not be made credible by science, or by any other means than through the very mouth of the Holy Spirit....

But I do not feel obliged to believe that the same God who has endowed us with senses, reason, and intellect has intended to forgo their use and by some other means to give us knowledge which we can attain by them.

cause they either denied religion altogether (atheists) or accepted it only as it conformed to reason (deists). He never produced a definitive refutation of the two sides. Rather, he formulated his views on these matters in piecemeal fashion in a provocative collection

of reflections on humankind and religion published posthumously under the title *Pensées*.

Pascal allied himself with the Jansenists, seventeenth-century Catholic opponents of the Jesuits. (See Chapter 13). His sister was a member of the Jansenist

Pascal invented this adding machine, the ancestor of mechanical calculators, around 1644. It has eight wheels with ten cogs each, corresponding to the numbers 0–9. The wheels move forward for addition, backward for subtraction. Bildarchiv Preussischer Kulturbesitz

convent of Port-Royal, near Paris. The Jansenists shared with the Calvinists Saint Augustine's belief in human beings' total sinfulness, their eternal predestination to heaven or hell by God, and their complete dependence on faith and grace for knowledge of God and salvation.

Pascal believed that in matters of religion, only the reasons of the heart and a "leap of faith" could prevail. For him, religion was not the domain of reason and science. He saw two essential truths in the Christian religion: that a loving God exists, and that human beings, because they are corrupt by nature, are utterly unworthy of God. He believed that the atheists and the deists of his age had overly estimated reason. To Pascal, reason itself was too weak to resolve the problems of human nature and destiny. Untimately, reason should drive those who truly heeded it to faith in God and reliance on divine grace.

Pascal made a famous wager with the skeptics. It is a better bet, he argued, to believe that God exists and to stake everything on his promised mercy than not to do so. This is because, if God does exist,

everything will be gained by the believer, whereas, should he prove not to exist, the loss incurred by having believed in him is by comparison slight.

Convinced that belief in God improved life psychologically and disciplined it morally (regardless of whether God proved in the end to exist), Pascal worked to strengthen traditional religious belief. He urged his contemporaries to seek self-understanding by "learned ignorance" and to discover humankind's greatness by recognizing its misery. He hoped thereby to counter what he believed to be the false optimism of the new rationalism and science.

The English Approach to Science and Religion

Francis Bacon established a key framework for reconciling science and religion that long influenced the English-speaking world. He had argued that there were two books of divine revelation: the Bible and nature. In studying nature, the natural philosopher could achieve a deeper knowledge of things divine, just as could the theologian studying the Bible. Because both books of revelation shared the same author, they must be compatible. Whatever discord might first appear between science and religion must eventually be reconciled. Natural theology based on a scientific understanding of the natural order would thus support theology derived from scripture.

Later in the seventeenth century, with the work of Newton, the natural universe became a realm of law and regularity. Many scientists were devout people who saw in the new picture of physical nature a new picture of God. The Creator of this rational, lawful nature must also be rational. To study nature was to come to a better understanding of that Creator. Science and religious faith were not only compatible, but mutually supportive. As Newton wrote, "The main Business of Natural Philosophy is to argue from Phaenomena without feigning Hypothesis, and to deduce Causes from Effects, till we come to the very first Cause, which certainly is not mechanical."[12]

The religious thought associated with such deducing of religious conclusions from nature became known as *physico-theology*. This reconciliation of faith and science allowed the new physics and astronomy to spread rapidly. At the very time when Europeans were finally tiring of the wars of religion, the new science provided the basis for a view of God that might lead away from irrational disputes and wars over religious doctrine. Faith in a rational God encouraged faith in the rationality of human beings and in their capacity to improve their lot once liberated from the traditions of the past. The Scientific Revolution provided the great model for the desirability of change and of criticism of inherited views.

Finally, the new science and the technological and economic innovations associated with its culture came again, especially among English thinkers, to be interpreted as part of a divine plan. By the late seventeenth century, natural philosophy and its practical achievements had become associated in the public mind with consumption and the market economy. Writers such as the Englishman John Ray in *The Wisdom of God Manifested in His Works of Creation* (1690) argued that it was evident that God had placed human beings in the world in order to understand it and then, having understood it, to turn it to productive practical use through rationality. Scientific advance and economic enterprise came to be interpreted in the public mind as the fulfillment of God's plan: Human beings were meant to improve

the world. This outlook provided a religious justification for the processes of economic improvement that would characterize much of eighteenth-century Western Europe.

Continuing Superstition

Despite the great optimism among certain European thinkers associated with the new ideas in science and philosophy, traditional beliefs and fears long retained their hold on the culture. During the sixteenth and seventeenth centuries, many Europeans remained preoccupied with sin, death, and the Devil. Religious people, including many among the learned and many who were sympathetic to the emerging scientific ideas, continued to believe in the power of magic and the occult. Until the end of the seventeenth century, almost all Europeans in one way or another believed in the power of demons.

Witch Hunts and Panic

Nowhere is the dark side of early modern thought and culture better seen than in the witch hunts and panics that erupted in almost every Western land. Between 1400 and 1700, courts sentenced an estimated 70,000–100,000 people to death for harmful magic (*maleficium*) and diabolical witchcraft. In addition to inflicting harm on their neighbors, these witches were said to attend mass meetings known as *sabbats*, to which they were believed to fly. They were also accused of indulging in sexual orgies with the Devil, who appeared at such gatherings in animal form, most often as a he-goat. Still other charges against them were cannibalism (they were alleged to be especially fond of small Christian children) and a variety of ritual acts and practices designed to insult every Christian belief and value.

Why did the great witch panics occur in the second half of the sixteenth and early seventeenth centuries? The misfortune created by religious division and warfare were major factors. Some argue that the Reformation was responsible for the witch panics. While the new theology portrayed demons and the Devil as still powerful, it weakened the traditional religious protections against them. Subsequently, the argument goes, people felt compelled to protect themselves by executing those perceived as witches. The new levels of violence exacerbated fears and hatreds and encouraged scapegoating, but political motives also played a role. As governments expanded control in their realms, they, like the church, wanted to eliminate all competition for the

[12] Quoted in Baumer, p. 323.

Three witches suspected of practicing harmful magic are burned alive on a pyre in Bade. On the left, two of them are shown feasting and cavorting with demons at a Sabbat. Bildarchiv Preussischer Kulturbesitz

loyalty of their subjects. Secular rulers, as well as the Pope, could pronounce their competitors "devilish." In fact, however, beliefs in witches and witch hunts had existed since the fifteenth century, well before the Reformation began.

Village Origins

The roots of the search for witches extended well beyond the world of the princes into both popular and elite cultures. In village societies, so-called cunning folk played a positive role in helping people cope with calamity. People turned to them for help when such natural disasters as plague and famine struck or when such physical disabilities as lameness or inability to conceive offspring be-

fell either humans or animals. The cunning folk provided consolation and gave people hope that such natural calamities might be averted or reversed through magic. In this way, they provided an important service and helped village life to keep functioning.

Possession of magical powers, for good or ill, made one an important person within village society. Not surprisingly, claims to such powers quite often were made by the people most in need of security and influence, namely, the old and the impoverished, especially single or widowed women. Belief in witches by village society may also have been a way of defying urban Christian society's attempts to impose its laws and institutions on the countryside. From this perspective, village Satanism became a fanciful substitute for an impossible social revolt, a way of spurning the values of one's new masters. It is also possible, although unlikely, that beliefs in witches among the rural population had a foundation in local fertility cults, whose semipagan practices, designed to ensure good harvests, may have acquired the features of diabolical witchcraft under church persecution.

Influence of the Clergy

Popular belief in magic was the essential foundation of the great witch hunts of the sixteenth and seventeenth centuries. Had ordinary people not believed that certain gifted individuals could aid or harm others by magical means, and had they not been willing to make accusations, the hunts could never have occurred. Yet the contribution of learned society was equally great. The Christian clergy also practiced magic, that of the holy sacraments, and the exorcism of demons had been one of its traditional functions within society. Fear of demons and the Devil, which the clergy actively encouraged, allowed clergymen to assert their moral authority over people and to enforce religious discipline and conformity.

In the late thirteenth century, the church declared that only its priests possessed legitimate magical power. Since such power was not human, theologians reasoned, it had to come either from God or from the Devil. If it came from God, then it was properly confined to, and exercised only on behalf of, the church. Those who practiced magic outside the church evidently derived their power from the Devil. From such reasoning grew accusations of "pacts" between non-Christian magicians and Satan. This made the witch hunts a life-and-death struggle against Christian society's worst heretics and foes: those who had directly sworn allegiance to the Devil himself.

The church based its intolerance of magic outside its walls on sincere belief in, and fear of, the Devil. But attacking witches was also a way for established Christian society to extend its power and influence into new areas. To accuse, try, and execute witches was a declaration of moral and political authority over a village or territory. As the cunning folk were local spiritual authorities, revered and feared by people, their removal became a major step in establishing a Christian beachhead in village society.

Why Women?

A good eighty percent of the victims of witch hunts were women, most between forty-five and sixty years of age and single. This suggests to some that misogyny fueled the witch hunts. Based on male hatred and sexual fear of women, and occurring at a time when women threatened to break out from under male control, witch hunts, it is argued, were simply woman hunts. Older single women may, however, have been vulnerable for a more basic social reason: They were a largely dependent social group in need of public assistance and hence became natural targets for the peculiar "social engineering" of the witch hunts. Some accused witches were women who sought to protect and empower themselves within their communities by claiming supernatural powers.

Gender, however, may have played a largely circumstantial role. Because of their economic straits, more women than men laid claim to the supernatural powers that made them influential in village society. For this reason, they found themselves on the front lines in disproportionate numbers when the church declared war against all who practiced magic without its blessing. Also, the involvement of many of these women in midwifery associated them with the deaths of beloved wives and infants and thus made them targets of local resentment and accusations. Both the church and midwives' neighbors were prepared to think and say the worst about these women. It was a deadly combination. (See "Why More Women than Men Are Witches.")

End of the Witch Hunts

Why did the witch hunts end in the seventeenth century? Many factors played a role. The emergence of a new, more scientific worldview made it difficult to believe in the powers of witches. When in the seventeenth century mind and matter came to be viewed as two independent realities, many people no longer believed that words and thoughts could affect the material world. A witch's curse was merely words. With advances in medicine and the beginning of insurance companies, people learned to rely on themselves when faced with natural calamity and physical affliction and no longer searched for supernatural causes and solutions. Witch hunts also tended to get out of hand. Accused witches sometimes alleged that important townspeople had also attended *sabbats*; even the judges could be so accused. At that point, the trials ceased to serve the purposes of those who were conducting them. They not only became dysfunctional, but threatened anarchy.

Although Protestants, like Catholics, hunted witches, the Reformation may also have contributed to an attitude of mind that put the Devil in a more manageable perspective. Protestants

Why More Women than Men Are Witches

A classic of misogyny, The Hammer of Witches *(1486), written by two Dominican monks, Heinrich Krämer and Jacob Sprenger, was sanctioned by Pope Innocent VIII as an official guide to the church's detection and punishment of witches. Here, Krämer and Sprenger explain why they believe that most witches are women rather than men.*

❖ *Why would two Dominican monks say such things about women? What are the biblical passages that they believe justify them? Do their descriptions have any basis in the actual behavior of women in that age? What is the rivalry between married and unmarried people that they refer to?*

Why are there more superstitious women than men? The first [reason] is that they are more credulous; and since the chief aim of the devil is to corrupt faith, therefore he rather attacks them....The second reason is that women are naturally more impressionable and ready to receive the influence of a disembodied spirit....The third reason is that they have slippery tongues and are unable to conceal from their fellow-women those things which by evil arts they know; and since they are weak, they find an easy and secret manner of vindicating themselves by witchcraft....[Therefore] since women are feebler both in mind and body, it is not surprising that they should come more under the spell of witchcraft. For as regards intellect, or the understanding of spiritual things, they seem to be of a different nature from men, a fact which is vouched for by the logic of the authorities, backed by various examples from the Scriptures....

But the natural reason [for woman's proclivity to witchcraft] is that she is more carnal than a man, as is clear from her many carnal abominations. And it should be noted that there was a defect in the formation of the first woman, since she was formed from a bent rib, that is, a rib of the breast, which is bent as it were in a contrary direction to a man. And since through this defect she is an imperfect animal, she always deceives....

As to her other mental quality, her natural will, when she hates someone whom she formerly loved, then she seethes with anger and impatience in her whole soul, just as the tides of the sea are always heaving and boiling....

Truly the most powerful cause which contributes to the increase of witches is the woeful rivalry between married folk and unmarried women and men. This [jealousy or rivalry exists] even among holy women, so what must it be among the others...?

Just as through the first defect in their intelligence women are more prone [than men] to abjure the faith, so through their second defect of inordinate affections and passions they search for, brood over, and inflict various vengeances, either by witchcraft or by some other means. Wherefore it is no wonder that so great a number of witches exist in this sex....[Indeed, witchcraft] is better called the heresy of witches than of wizards, since the name is taken from the more powerful party [that is, the greater number, who are women]. Blessed be the Highest who has so far preserved the male sex from so great a crime.

From *Malleus Maleficarum*, trans. by Montague Summers (Bungay, Suffolk, U.K.: John Rodker, 1928), pp. 41–47. Reprinted by permission.

ridiculed the sacramental magic of the old church as superstition and directed their faith to a sovereign God absolutely supreme over time and eternity. Even the Devil was believed to serve God's purposes and acted only with his permission. Ultimately, God was the only significant spiritual force in the universe. This belief made the Devil a less fearsome creature. "One little word can slay him," Luther wrote of the Devil in the great hymn of the Reformation, "A Mighty Fortress Is Our God."

Finally, the imaginative and philosophical literature of the sixteenth and seventeenth centuries, while continuing to display concern for religion and belief in the supernatural, also suggested that human beings have a significant degree of control over their own lives and need not be constantly fearing demons and resorting to supernatural aid.

In Perspective

The Scientific Revolution and the thought of writers whose work was contemporaneous with it mark a major turning point in the history of Western culture and eventually had a worldwide impact. The scientific and political ideas of the late sixteenth and seventeenth centuries gradually overturned many of the most fundamental premises of the medieval worldview. The sun replaced the Earth as the center of the solar system. The solar system itself came to be viewed as one of many possible systems in the universe. The new knowledge of the physical universe provided occasions for challenging the authority of the church and of scripture. Mathematics began to replace theology and metaphysics as the tool for understanding nature.

Parallel to these developments and sometimes related to them, political thought became much less concerned with religious issues. Hobbes generated a major theory of political obligation with virtually no reference to God. Locke theorized about politics with a recognition of God, but with little attention to scripture. He also championed greater freedom of religious and political expression. Locke produced a psychology that emphasized the influence of environment on human character and action. All of these new ideas gradually displaced or reshaped theological and religious modes of thought and placed humankind and life on Earth at the center of Western thinking. Intellectuals in the West consequently developed greater self-confidence in their own capacity to shape the world and their own lives.

None of this change came easily, however. The new science and enlightenment were accompanied by new anxieties that were reflected in a growing preoccupation with sin, death, and the Devil. The worst expression of this preoccupation was a succession of witch hunts and trials that took the lives of as many as 100,000 people between 1400 and 1700.

REVIEW QUESTIONS

1. Discuss the contributions of Copernicus, Brahe, Kepler, Galileo, and Newton to the Scientific Revolution. Which do you think made the most important contributions and why? What did Francis Bacon contribute to the foundation of scientific thought?
2. How would you define the term *Scientific Revolution*? In what ways was the event truly revolutionary? Which is more enduring, a political revolution or an intellectual one?
3. Compare and contrast the political philosophies of Thomas Hobbes and John Locke. How did each view human nature? Would you rather live under a government designed by Hobbes or by Locke? Why?
4. What factors prevented women from fully participating in the new science? How did family relationships help some women to become involved in the advance of natural philosophy?
5. What were the chief factors accounting for the condemnation of Galileo? How did Pascal seek to reconcile faith and reason? How did English natural theology support economic expansion?
6. How do you explain the phenomena of witchcraft and witch hunts in an age of scientific enlightenment? Why did the witch panics occur in the late sixteenth and early seventeenth centuries? How might the Reformation have contributed to them?

SUGGESTED READINGS

R. ASHCRAFT, *Revolutionary Politics and Locke's Two Treatises of Government* (1986). A major study emphasizing the radical side of Locke's thought.

J. BARRY, M. HESTER, AND G. ROBERTS, EDS. *Witchcraft in Early Modern Europe: Studies in Culture and Belief* (1998). A collection of recent essays.

M. BIAGIOLI, *Galileo Courtier: The Practice of Science in the Culture of Absolutism* (1993). A major revisionist work that emphasizes the role of the political setting on Galileo's career and thought.

H. BUTTERFIELD, *The Origins of Modern Science 1300–1800* (1949). A classic survey.

H. F. COHEN, *The Scientific Revolution: A Historiographical Inquiry* (1994). Supplants all previous discussions of the history of the concept of the Scientific Revolution.

J. DUNN, *The Political Thought of John Locke: An Historical Account of the "Two Treatises of Government"* (1969). Remains an excellent introduction.

M. A. FINOCCHIARO, *The Galileo Affair: A Documentary History* (1989). A collection of all the relevant documents and introductory commentary.

S. GAUKROGER, *Descartes: An Intellectual Biography* (1995). A major work that explores both the science and philosophy in Descartes's work.

A. GOLDGAR, *Impolite Learning: Conduct and Community in the Republic of Letters, 1680–1750* (1995). A lively survey of the structure of the European intellectual community.

I. HARRIS, *The Mind of John Locke: A Study of Political Theory in Its Intellectual Setting* (1994). The most comprehensive recent treatment.

P. HARRISON, *The Bible, Protestantism, and the Rise of Natural Science* (1998). Explores how the Protestant approach to the text of scripture contributed to the new scientific interpretation of nature.

E. HARTH, *Cartesian Women: Versions and Subversions of Rational Discourse in the Old Regime* (1992). A pioneering work on the relationship of educated French women to the new science.

A. JOHNS, *The Nature of the Book: Print and Knowledge in the Making* (1998). A brilliant study of the role of printing in the intellectual life of early modern Europe.

D. JOHNSTON, *The Rhetoric of* Leviathan: *Thomas Hobbes and the Politics of Cultural Transformation* (1986). An important study that links Hobbes's thought to the rhetoric of the Renaissance.

R. KIECKHEFER, *European Witch Trials: Their Foundations in Popular and Learned Culture 1300–1500* (1976). Excellent background for understanding the great witch panic.

A. KORS AND E. PETERS, EDS., *European Witchcraft, 1100–1700* (1972). Collection of major documents.

T. S. KUHN, *The Copernican Revolution* (1957). Remains the leading work on the subject.

C. LARNER, *Enemies of God: The Witchhunt in Scotland* (1981). Perhaps the most exemplary local study of the subject.

B. LEVACK, *The Witch Hunt in Early Modern Europe* (1986). Lucid survey.

D. LINDBERG AND R. L. NUMBERS, EDS., *God and Nature: Historical Essays on the Encounter Between Christianity and Science* (1986). An excellent collection of essays.

D. LINDBERG AND R. S. WESTMAN, EDS., *Reappraisals of the Scientific Revolution* (1990). Important essays pointing the way toward new understandings of the subject.

P. MACHAMER, ED., *The Cambridge Companion to Galileo* (1998). A wide-ranging collection of essays that aid the understanding of the entire spectrum of the new science.

O. MAYER, *Authority, Liberty, and Automatic Machinery in Early Modern Europe* (1986). A lively study that seeks to relate thought about machinery to thought about politics.

D. NOBLE, *A World Without Women: The Christian Clerical Culture of Western Science* (1992). A controversial account.

L. PYENSON AND S. SHEETS-PYENSON, *Servants of Nature: A History of Scientific Institutions, Enterprises, and Sensibilities* (1999). A history of the settings in which the creation and diffusion of scientific knowledge have occurred.

R. POPKIN, *The History of Scepticism from Erasmus to Spinoza* (1979). A classic study of the fear of loss of intellectual certainty.

R. PORTER AND M. TEICH, EDS., *The Scientific Revolution in National Context* (1992). Essays on the subject in each major European nation.

E. REEVES, *Painting the Heavens: Art and Science in the Age of Galileo* (1997). An exploration of the impact of Galileo's thought on the visual arts.

L. SCHIEBINGER, *The Mind Has No Sex? Women in the Origins of Modern Science* (1989). A major study of the subject.

S. SHAPIN, *The Scientific Revolution* (1996). The best brief introduction.

Q. SKINNER, *Reason and Rhetoric in the Philosophy of Hobbes* (1996). A major study by one of the leading scholars of Hobbes and early modern political thought.

L. STEWART, *The Rise of Public Science: Rhetoric, Technology, and Natural Philosophy in Newtonian Britain, 1660–1750* (1992). Examines how science became related to public life and economic development.

K. THOMAS, *Religion and the Decline of Magic* (1971). Provocative, much acclaimed work focused on popular culture.

R. TUCK, *Philosophy and Government 1572–1651* (1993). A continent-wide survey.

R. S. WESTFALL, *The Construction of Modern Science: Mechanisms and Mechanics* (1971). A classic work.

R. S. WESTFALL, *Never at Rest: A Biography of Isaac Newton* (1981). The major study.

N. WOLTERSTORFF, *John Locke and the Ethics of Belief* (1996). The best work on Locke's religious thought.

P. ZAGORIN, *Francis Bacon* (1998). A comprehensive treatment.

Chapter 15

***Peter the Great (r. 1682–1725) seeking to make Russia a military power, reorga-
nized the country's political and economic structures. His reign saw Russia enter
fully into European power politics.*** The Apotheosis of Tsar Peter the Great 1672–1725 by unknown artist, 1710. Historical Museum, Moscow, Russia/E.T. Archive

Successful and Unsuccessful Paths to Power (1686–1740)

The Maritime Powers
The Netherlands: Golden Age
  to Decline
France after Louis XIV
Great Britain: The Age of Walpole

Central and Eastern Europe
Sweden: The Ambitions of Charles XII
The Ottoman Empire

Poland: Absence of Strong Central Authority
The Habsburg Empire and the Pragmatic
  Sanction
Prussia and the Hohenzollerns

Russia Enters the European Political Arena
Birth of the Romanov Dynasty
Peter the Great

KEY TOPICS

- The Dutch Golden Age
- French aristocratic resistance to the monarchy
- Early eighteenth-century British political stability
- The efforts of the Habsburgs to secure their holdings
- The emergence of Prussia as a major power under the Hohenzollerns
- The efforts of Peter the Great to transform Russia into a powerful centralized nation along Western lines

T*he late seventeenth and early eighteenth centuries witnessed significant shifts of power and influence among the states of Europe. Nations that had been strong lost their status as significant military and economic units. Other countries that in some cases had figured only marginally in international relations came to the fore. Great Britain, France, Austria, Russia, and Prussia emerged during this period as the powers that would dominate Europe until at least World War I. Their political and economic dominance occurred at the expense of Spain, the United Netherlands, Poland, Sweden, and the Ottoman Empire. Equally essential to their rise was the weakness of the Holy Roman Empire after the Treaty of Westphalia (1648), which ended the Thirty Years' War.*

The successful competitors for international power were those states that created strong central political authorities. Farsighted observers in the late seventeenth century already understood that in the future those domains that would become or remain great powers must imitate the political and military organization of Louis XIV's France. Strong monarchy alone could impose unity of purpose on the state. The turmoil of seventeenth-century civil wars and aristocratic revolts had impressed people with the value of a firm centralized monarch as the guarantor of minimum domestic tranquility.

Imitation of French absolutism involved more than belief in a firm centralized monarchy; it usually also required building a standing army, organizing an efficient tax structure to support the army, and establishing a bureaucracy to collect the taxes. Moreover, the political classes of the country—especially the nobles—had to be converted to a sense of duty and loyalty to the central government that was more intense than their loyalty to other competing political and social institutions.

The waning powers were those that failed to achieve such effective organization. They were unable to employ their political, economic, and human resources to resist external aggression or to overcome the forces of domestic dissolution. Internal and external failures were closely related. If a state did not maintain or establish a central political authority with sufficient power over the nobility, the cities, the guilds, and the church, it could not raise a strong army to defend its borders or its economic interests. More often than not, the key element leading to success or failure was the character, personality, and energy of the monarch.

The Maritime Powers

In western Europe, Britain and France emerged as the dominant powers. This development represented a shift of influence away from Spain and the United Netherlands. Both of the latter countries had been strong and important during the sixteenth and seventeenth centuries, but they became politically and militarily marginal during the eighteenth century. Neither, however, disappeared from the map, and both retained considerable economic vitality and influence. Spanish power declined after the War of the Spanish Succession (see Chapter 13). The case of The Netherlands was more complicated.

The Netherlands: Golden Age to Decline

The seven provinces that became the United Provinces of the Netherlands were the single genuinely new state to appear on the European scene during the early modern period. They emerged as a nation after revolting against Spain in 1572. Spain acknowledged their autonomy only in a truce of 1609, though other European powers had recognized Dutch independence in the 1580s. The Netherlands won formal independence from Spain in the Treaty of Westphalia (1648). These eighty years of on-again, off-again warfare forged much of the national identity of the Netherlands. During the middle of the seventeenth century, the Dutch engaged in a series of naval wars with England. Then, in 1672, the armies of Louis XIV invaded the Netherlands. William III, the *stadtholder* of Holland, the most important of the provinces, rallied the Dutch and eventually led the entire European

coalition against France. As a part of that strategy, he answered the invitation of Protestant English aristocrats in 1688 to assume, along with his wife Mary, the English throne. (See Chapter 13.)

During both the seventeenth and eighteenth centuries, the political and economic life of the Netherlands differed from that of the rest of Europe. The other major nations pursued paths toward strong central government, generally under monarchies, as with France, or in the case of England, under a strong parliamentary system. By contrast, the Netherlands was formally a republic. Each of the provinces retained considerable authority, and the central government, embodied in the States General that met in the Hague, exercised its authority through a kind of ongoing negotiation with the provinces. Prosperous and populous Holland dominated the States General. The Dutch deeply distrusted monarchy and the ambitions of the House of Orange. Nonetheless, when confronted with major military challenges, the Dutch would permit the House of Orange and, most notably, William III to assume dominant leadership. These political arrangements proved highly resilient and allowed the republic to establish itself permanently in the European state system during the seventeenth century. When William died in 1702 and the wars with France ended in 1714, the Dutch reverted to their republican structures.

Although the provinces making up the Netherlands were traditionally identified with the Protestant cause in Europe during their revolt against Spain and the wars against Louis XIV, extensive toleration marked Dutch religious life. The Calvinist Reformed Church was the official church of the nation, and most of the political elite belonged to it, but it was not an established church. There were always a significant number of Roman Catholics and Protestants living in the Netherlands who did not belong to the Reformed Church. The country also became a haven for Jews driven out of other lands, particularly those who had been expelled from Spain. Consequently, while other European states attempted to impose a single religion on their people or tore themselves apart in religious conflict, in the Netherlands peoples of differing religious faiths lived together peacefully.

URBAN PROSPERITY   Beyond the climate of religious toleration, what most amazed seventeenth-century contemporaries about the Dutch Republic was its economic prosperity. While the rest of Europe fought over religion, the Dutch enriched themselves and attained a high standard of living. Their remarkable economic achievement was built on the foundations of high urban consolida-

In the mid-eighteenth century, when this picture of the Amsterdam Exchange was paint-ed, Amsterdam had replaced the cities of Italy and south Germany as the leading bank-ing center of Europe. Amsterdam retained this position until the late eighteenth century.
Painting by Hiob A. Berckheyde, "The Amsterdam Exchange". Canvas 85 x 105 cm. Coll. Museum Boijmans Van Beuningen, Rotterdam, The Netherlands

tion, transformed agriculture, extensive trade and finance, and an overseas commercial empire. (See "Art & the West.")

In the Netherlands, more people lived in cities than in any other area of Europe. By 1675, in Holland, the province where Amsterdam was located, at least sixty percent of the population were urban dwellers. Not until after the onset of industrialization in the late eighteenth century would such urban consolidation occur elsewhere, and then most notably in England. Trade, manufacture, shipbuilding, and finance were the engine of Dutch urban prosperity.

This urban concentration had been made possible by key transformations in Dutch farming that served as the model for the rest of Europe. During the seventeenth century, the Dutch drained and reclaimed much land from the sea. The Dutch were able to use this reclaimed terrain for highly profitable farming because their shipping interests dominated the Baltic trade, which provided them with a steady supply of grain. The availability of this cheap grain meant that Dutch farmers could use their land to produce more profitable dairy products and beef. Dutch farmers also diversified into the cultivation of cash products such as tulip bulbs. So successful was tulip cultivation, that for a few years in the late 1630s, market speculation led to the sale of tulip bulbs at astounding prices.

The Baltic grain trade was just one example of the Dutch acting as the chief trading nation of Europe. Their fishermen dominated the market for her-ring and supplied much of the continent's dried fish. The Dutch also supplied textiles to many parts of

Rachel Ruysch, Flower Still Life: *Flowers, Commerce, and Morality*

Rachel Ruysch, Dutch, 1664–1750, *Flower Still Life* (1956.57). The Toledo Museum of Art, Toledo, Ohio; Purchased with funds from the Libbey Endowment, Gift of Edward Drummond Libbey

Paintings often are intended to convey more than first meets the eye. Such is more or less obvious in allegorical scenes in which themes appear in the guise of ancient gods or other mythological figures. But a painting of objects of everyday life arranged on tables, known as a *still life*, can also hold deep symbolic and cultural meaning. From the Middle Ages onward, particular flowers had religious meaning, but during the seventeenth century flowers took on more worldly associations.

Rachel Ruysch (1664–1750) was a Dutch woman artist living in Amsterdam who specialized in depicting elaborate arrangements of flowers. These paintings stand as very beautiful images, but they are also much more. The floral still life portrayed flowers usually raised from bulbs, a major Dutch commercial enterprise. Several decades before Ruysch completed this particular painting, *Flower Still Life* (after 1700), a financial mania had gripped Holland, with speculation in rare tulip bulbs reaching enormous extravagance before the bubble burst. Consequently, a painting such as this one from the early eighteenth century—and there were hundreds of such still-life floral works executed in seventeenth and eighteenth-century Holland—would have recalled that event.

The flowers in this and other Dutch floral paintings represent work and commerce, not the natural bounty of the Dutch countryside. Commercial growers and traders brought such flowers to the Netherlands from its overseas empire and trading partners, and the flowers came to symbolize Dutch interaction with the most far-flung regions of the globe.

The variety of flowers in the bowl suggests wealth and abundance; these are valuable species, not humble objects of ordinary life. And never, except on canvas, would these flowers have bloomed at one time. Only the painter can gather them together in a single place at a single moment, in effect overcoming the cycle of nature.

Paintings such as this one have been called "a dialogue between this newly affluent society and its material possessions" and "an expression of how the phenomenon of plenty is to be viewed and understood."[1] These rich still life paintings allowed the Calvinist Dutch to accommodate a morality that emphasized frugality and abstinence with life in the single wealthiest society in Europe. The melancholy surrounding the images conveys a lesson in the vanity and transience of earthly beauty and richness. All of these beautiful, valuable, rare natural objects, whether flowers or food, will soon decay. The flowers in this bowl, so stunning at the peak of their blossoming, will in a matter of days wilt and eventually rot. The insects buzzing about the flowers will also disappear. Even the empty snail shells on the table suggest that earthly life is only temporary. Similarly, the shadows in so many of the floral arrangements suggest the shadows that surround human life and the transience of both light and life. Yet, by owning a painting of an exquisite, diverse collection of flowers, one could possess an object of great beauty that would itself not decay.

The amazing attention to detail in Ruysch's work reflects the growth in botanical observation and knowledge during the previous century. Van Leeuwenhoek, the inventor of the microscope, hired artists to draw the organisms he could see through the instrument. That invention, as well as other Dutch optical achievements, such as the magnifying glass, led many artists to paint with enormous attention to detail.

Many of the most important illustrators of botanical manuals and other works of natural history were women. Among the leading figures was Anna Maria Sibylla Merian (1647–1717), a German woman who moved to the Netherlands and traveled to the Dutch colony of Surinam to study both plants and insects. Her work would have been enormously helpful to Ruysch, who would only rarely have worked from an actual bowl of real flowers.

Sources: Norman Bryson, *Looking at the Overlooked: Four Essays on Still Life Painting* (Cambridge, MA: Harvard University Press, 1990); Mariët Westermann, *A Worldly Art: The Dutch Republic, 1585–1718* (Upper Saddle River, NJ and New York: Prentice Hall Publishers, Inc., and Harry N. Abrahms, Inc., 1990); Marilyn Stokstad, *Art History*, rev. ed. (Upper Saddle River, NJ and New York: Prentice Hall Publishers, Inc., and Harry N. Abrahms, Inc., 1999) pp. 798–801.

[1]Norman Bryson, *Looking at the Overlooked: Four Essays on Still Life Painting* (Cambridge, MA: Harvard University Press, 1990), p. 104.

Europe. Dutch ships appeared in harbors all over the continent, with their captains purchasing goods that they then transported and resold at a profit to other nations. Or such goods might be returned to the Netherlands, stored, and then sold later at more advantageous prices. Many of the handsome merchant houses lining the canals of Amsterdam had storage facilities on their upper floors. The overseas trades also supported a vast domestic industry of shipbuilding and ship supplies.

All of this trade, commerce, and manufacturing was supported by the most advanced financial system of the day. Capital could be more easily raised in Amsterdam than anyplace else in the seventeenth century. Shares traded easily and often speculatively in the Amsterdam bourse. Dutch capital financed economic life outside its own borders.

The final foundation of Dutch prosperity was the Dutch seaborne empire. During the late sixteenth and early seventeenth centuries, Dutch traders established a major presence in East Asia, particularly in spice-producing areas of Java, the Moluccas, and Sri Lanka. The vehicle for this penetration was the Dutch East Indies Company (chartered in 1602), shares of which traded on the Amsterdam bourse. The Dutch East Indies Company eventually displaced Portuguese dominance in the spice trade of East Asia and for many years prevented English traders from establishing a major presence there. Initially, the Dutch had only wanted commercial dominance of the spice trade, but in time, that goal led them to move toward producing the spices themselves, which required them to control many of the islands that now constitute Indonesia. The Netherlands remained the colonial master of this region until after World War II.

ECONOMIC DECLINE   The decline in political influence of the United Provinces of the Netherlands occurred within the eighteenth century. After the death of William III of Britain in 1702, the various local provinces prevented the emergence of another strong *stadtholder*. Unified political leadership therefore vanished. During the earlier long wars with Louis XIV and Britain, naval supremacy had slowly but steadily passed to the British. The fishing industry declined, and the Dutch lost their technological superiority in shipbuilding. Countries between which Dutch ships had once carried goods now traded directly with each other. For example, the British began to use their own vessels in the Baltic traffic with Russia.

Similar stagnation overtook the Dutch domestic industries, such as textile finishing, papermaking, and glassblowing. The disunity of the provinces and the absence of vigorous leadership hastened this economic decline and prevented action that might have slowed or halted it.

What saved the United Provinces from becoming completely insignificant in European affairs was their continued financial dominance. Well past the middle of the eighteenth century, their banks continued to finance European trade. Moreover, the Amsterdam bourse remained an important financial institution because, as will be seen later in this chapter, both France and England exprienced disastrously excessive and politically disruptive stock speculation in the early eighteenth century, which made them fearful of investment in shares.

France after Louis XIV

Despite its military reverses in the War of the Spanish Succession, France remained a great power. It was less strong in 1715 than in 1680, but it still possessed the largest European population, an advanced, if troubled, economy, and the administrative structure bequeathed it by Louis XIV. Moreover, even if France and its resources had been drained by the last of Louis's wars, the other major states of Europe were similarly debilitated. What France required was economic recovery and consolidation, wiser political leadership, and a less ambitious foreign policy. It did enjoy a period of recovery, but its leadership was at best indifferent. Louis XIV was succeeded by his five-year-old great-grandson Louis XV (r. 1715–1774). The young boy's uncle, the duke of Orléans, became regent and remained so until his death in 1720. The regency, marked by financial and moral scandals, further undermined the faltering prestige of the monarchy.

JOHN LAW AND THE MISSISSIPPI BUBBLE   The duke of Orléans was a gambler, and for a time he turned over the financial management of the kingdom to John Law (1671–1729), a Scottish mathematician and fellow gambler. Law believed that an increase in the paper-money supply would stimulate France's economic recovery. With the permission of the regent, he established a bank in Paris that issued paper money. Law then organized a monopoly, called the Mississippi Company, on trading privileges with the French colony of Louisiana in North America.

The Mississippi Company also took over the management of the French national debt. The company issued shares of its own stock in exchange for government bonds, which had fallen sharply in value. To redeem large quantities of bonds, Law encouraged speculation in Mississippi Company stock. In 1719, the price of the stock rose handsomely. Smart

The impending collapse of John Law's bank triggered a financial panic throughout France. Desperate investors, such as those shown here in the city of Rennes, sought to exchange their paper currency for gold and silver before the banks supply of precious metals was exhausted. Collection Musée de Bretagne, Rennes

investors, however, took their profits by selling their stock in exchange for paper money from Laws bank, which they then sought to exchange for gold. The bank, however, lacked enough gold to redeem all the paper money brought to it.

In February 1720, all gold payments were halted in France. Soon thereafter, Law himself fled the country. The Mississippi Bubble, as the affair was called, had burst. The fiasco brought disgrace on the government that had sponsored Law. The Mississippi Company was later reorganized and functioned profitably, but fear of paper money and speculation marked French economic life for decades.

RENEWED AUTHORITY OF THE *PARLEMENTS* The duke of Orléans made a second decision that also lessened the power of the monarchy: He attempted to draw the French nobility once again into the decision-making processes of the government. Louis XIV had filled his ministries and bureaucracies with persons from nonnoble families. The regent, under pressure from the nobility, tried to restore a balance. He set up a system of councils on which nobles were to serve along with bureaucrats. The years of idle noble domestication at Versailles, however, had worked too well, and the nobility seemed to lack both the talent and the desire to govern. The experiment failed.

Despite this failure, the great French nobles did not surrender their ancient ambition to assert their rights, privileges, and local influence over those of the monarchy. The chief feature of eighteenth-century French political life was the attempt of the nobility to use its authority to limit the power of the monarchy. The most effective instrument in this process was the *parlements*, or courts dominated by the nobility.

The French *parlements* were different from the English Parliament. These French courts, the most important of which was the *Parlement* of Paris, could not legislate. Rather, they had the power to recognize or not to recognize the legality of an act or law promulgated by the monarch. By long tradition, their formal approval had been required to make a royal law valid. Louis XIV had often restricted stubborn, uncooperative *parlements*. In another major political blunder, however, the duke of Orléans had formally approved the full reinstitution of the *parlements*' power to allow or disallow laws. Thereafter, the growing financial and moral weakness of the monarchy allowed these aristocratic judicial institutions to reassert their authority. This situation meant that until the revolution in 1789 the *parlements* became natural centers for aristocratic resistance to royal authority.

ADMINISTRATION OF CARDINAL FLEURY In 1726, Cardinal Fleury (1653–1743) became the chief minister of the French court. He was the last of the great clerics who loyally and effectively served the French monarchy. Like his seventeenth-century predecessors, the cardinals Richelieu and Mazarin, Fleury was a realist. He understood the political ambition and incapacity of the nobility and worked quietly to block their undue influence. He was also aware of the precarious financial situation of the royal treasury. The cardinal, who was seventy-three years old when he came to office, was determined to give the country a period of peace. He surrounded himself with able assistants who tried to solve France's financial problems. Part of the national debt was repudiated. New industries enjoying special privileges were established and roads and bridges built. On the whole, the nation prospered, but Fleury could never draw sufficient tax revenues from the nobles or the church to put the state on a stable financial footing.

Cardinal Fleury (1653–1743) was the tutor and chief minister of Louis XV from 1726 to 1743. Fleury gave France a period of peace and prosperity, but was unable to solve the state's long-term financial problems. This portrait is by Hyacinthe Rigaud

Madame de Pompadour (1721–1764) was the mistress of Louis XV. She exercised considerable political influence at the court and was a notable patron of artists, craftspeople, and writers. This 1763 portrait is by Hubert Drouais (1727–1775). Liaison Agency, Inc.

Fleury died in 1743, having unsuccessfully attempted to prevent France from intervening in the war that was then raging between Austria and Prussia. The cost of this intervention was to undo all his financial pruning and planning.

Another failure must also be attributed to this elderly cleric. Despite his best efforts, he had not trained Louis XV to become an effective monarch. Louis XV possessed most of the vices and almost none of the virtues of his great-grandfather Louis XIV. He wanted to hold on to absolute power, but was unwilling to work the long hours required. He did not choose many wise advisers after Fleury. He was tossed about by the gossip and intrigues of the court. His personal life was scandalous. Louis XV was not an evil person, but a mediocre one. And in a monarch, mediocrity was unfortunately often a greater fault than vice. Consequently, it was not a lack of resources or military strength that plagued France, but the absence of political leadership to organize, direct, and inspire its people.

Great Britain: The Age of Walpole

In 1713 Britain had emerged as a victor over Louis XIV, but the nation required a period of recovery. As an institution, the British monarchy was not in the degraded state of the French monarchy, yet its stability was not certain.

THE HANOVERIAN DYNASTY In 1714 the Hanoverian dynasty, as designated by the Act of Settlement (1701), came to the throne. Almost immediately, George I (r. 1714–1727) faced a challenge to his new title. The Stuart pretender James Edward (1688–1766), the son of James II, landed in Scotland in December 1715. His forces marched southward, but met defeat less than two months later. Although militarily successful against the pretender, the new dynasty and its supporters saw the need for consolidation.

WHIGS AND TORIES During the seventeenth century, England had been one of the most politically restive countries in Europe. The closing years of Queen Anne's reign (1702–1714) had seen sharp clashes between the political factions of Whigs and Tories over whether to end the war with France. The Tories had urged a rapid peace settlement and after 1710 had opened negotiations with France. During the same period, the Whigs were seeking favor from the elector of Hanover, the future George I, who would soon be their monarch. His concern for his domains in Hanover made him unsympathetic to the Tory peace policy. In the final months of Anne's reign, some Tories, fearing that they would lose power under the waiting Hanoverian dynasty, opened channels of communication with the Stuart pretender; a few even rallied to his cause. see p. 429 Queen Anne

Under these circumstances, George I, on his arrival in Britain, clearly favored the Whigs. Previously, the differences between the Whigs and the Tories had been vaguely related to principle. The Tories emphasized a strong monarchy, low taxes for landowners, and firm support of the Anglican Church. The Whigs supported monarchy, but wanted Parliament to retain final sovereignty. They favored urban commercial interests as well as the prosperity of the landowners. They encouraged a policy of religious toleration toward the Protestant nonconformists in England. Socially, both groups supported the status quo.

Neither group was organized like a modern political party. Outside Parliament, each party consisted of political networks based on local connections and economic influence. Each group acknowledged a few national spokespeople, who articulated positions and principles. After the

Sir Robert Walpole (1676–1745), far left, is shown talking with the Speaker of the House of Commons. Walpole, who dominated British political life from 1721 to 1742, is considered the first prime minister of Britain. Time/Life Syndication.

Hanoverian accession and the eventual Whig success in achieving the firm confidence of George I, the chief difference between the Whigs and the Tories for almost forty years was that one group had access to public office and patronage and the other did not. This early Hanoverian proscription of Tories from public life was one of the most prominent features of the age.

THE LEADERSHIP OF ROBERT WALPOLE The political situation after 1715 remained in flux, until Robert Walpole (1676–1745) took over the helm of government. Though previously active in the House of Commons since the reign of Queen Anne and a cabinet minister, what gave Walpole special prominence under the new dynasty was a British financial scandal similar to the French Mississippi Bubble.

Management of the British national debt had been assigned to the South Sea Company, which exchanged government bonds for company stock. As in the French case, the price of the stock soared, only to crash in 1720 when prudent investors sold their holdings and took their speculative profits.

Parliament intervened and, under Walpole's leadership, adopted measures to honor the national debt. To most contemporaries, Walpole had saved the financial integrity of the country and had thus proved himself a person of immense administrative capacity and political ability.

George I gave Walpole his full confidence. For this reason, Walpole has often been regarded as the first prime minister of Great Britain and the originator of the cabinet system of government. Walpole generally demanded that all the ministers in the cabinet agree on policy, but he could not prevent frequent public differences among them. Unlike a modern English prime minister, he was not chosen by the majority of the House of Commons. The real sources of his power were the personal support of the king, first George I and later George II (r. 1727–1760), his ability to handle the House of Commons, and his ironfisted control of government patronage, which bought support for himself and his policies from people who wanted jobs, appointments, favors, and government contracts. Such corruption supplied the glue of political loyalty.

Walpole's favorite slogan was *"Quieta non movere"* (roughly, "Let sleeping dogs lie"). To that end, he pursued peace abroad and supported the status quo at home. In this regard he much resembled Cardinal Fleury.

THE STRUCTURE OF PARLIAMENT   The structure of the eighteenth-century British House of Commons aided Walpole in his pacific policies. It was neither a democratic nor a representative body. Each of the counties into which Britain was divided elected two members. (See "Lady Mary Wortley Montagu Advises Her Husband on Election to Parliament.") But if the more powerful landed families in a county agreed on the candidates, there was no contest. Most members, however, were elected from a variety of units called *boroughs*. A few boroughs were large enough for

elections to be relatively democratic, but most had few electors. For example, a local municipal corporation or council of only a dozen members might have the right to elect a member of Parliament. In Old Sarum, one of the most famous corrupt, or "rotten," boroughs, the Pitt family simply bought up those pieces of property to which a vote was attached and thus in effect owned a seat in the House of Commons. Through proper electoral management, which involved favors to the electors, the House of Commons could be controlled.

The structure of Parliament and the manner in which the House of Commons was elected meant that the owners of property, especially wealthy nobles, dominated the government of England. They did not pretend to represent people and districts or to be responsive to what would later be called public opinion. They regarded themselves as representing various

Lady Mary Wortley Montagu (1689–1762) was a famous writer of letters and an extremely well-traveled woman of the eighteenth century. As the document on p. 494 suggests, she was also a shrewd and toughminded political advisor to her husband. National Portrait Gallery, London

This series of four Hogarth etchings satirizes the notoriously corrupt English electoral system. Hogarth shows the voters going to the polls after having been bribed and intoxicated with free gin. (Voting was then in public. The secret ballot was not introduced in England until 1872.) The fourth etching, "Chairing the Member," shows the triumphal procession of the victorious candidate, which is clearly turning into a brawl.

William Hogarth, *An Election Entertainment*, Print. The Metropolitan Museum of Art, Harris Brisbane Dick Fund, 1932. 32.35(212)

William Hogarth, *Canvassing for Votes*. Metropolitan Museum of Art, Harris Brisbane Dick Fund, 1932. 32.35 (213)

William Hogarth, *The Polling*, Print,
H. 16 1/2 in. W, 20 5/8 in. (clipped
impression). The Metropolitan Museum of Art, Gift of Sarah Lazarus,
1891. (91.1.75)

William Hogarth, *Chairing the Members*. Etching. Metropolitan Museum of Art, Harris Brisbane Dick Fund,
1932. 32.35 (214)

Lady Mary Wortley Montagu Advises Her Husband on Election to Parliament

In this letter of 1714, Lady Mary Wortley Montagu discussed with her husband the various paths that he might follow to gain election to the British House of Commons. Note her emphasis on knowing the right people and on having large amounts of money to spend on voters. Eventually, her husband was elected to Parliament in a borough that was controlled through government patronage.

❖ *What are the various ways in which candidates and their supporters used money to campaign? What role did friendships play in the campaigning? How important do the political ideas or positions of the candidates seem to be? Women could not vote in eighteenth-century parliamentary elections. Was there some other influence they exerted?*

You seem not to have received my letters, or not to have understood them: you had been chose undoubtedly at York, if you had declared in time; but there is not any gentleman or tradesman disengaged at this time; they are treating every night. Lord Carlisle and the Thompsons have given their interest to Mr. Jenkins. I agree with you of the necessity of your standing this Parliament, which, perhaps, may be more considerable than any that are to follow it; but, as you proceed, 'tis my opinion, you will spend your money and not be chose. I believe there is hardly a borough unengaged. I expect every letter should tell me you are sure of some place; and, as far as I can perceive you are sure of none. As it has been managed, perhaps it will be the best way to deposit a certain sum in some friend's hands, and buy some little Cornish borough: it would, undoubtedly, look better to be chose for a considerable town; but I take it to be now too late.

If you have any thoughts of Newark, it will be absolutely necessary for you to enquire after Lord Lexington's interest; and your best way to apply yourself to Lord Holdernesse, who is both a Whig and an honest man. He is now in town, and you may enquire of him if Brigadier Sutton stands there; and if not, try to engage him for you. Lord Lexington is so ill at the Bath, that it is a doubt if he will live 'till the elections; and if he dies, one of his heiresses, and the whole interest of his estate, will probably fall on Lord Holdernesse.

'Tis a surprize to me, that you cannot make sure of some borough, when a number of your friends bring in so many Parliament-men without trouble or expense. 'Tis too late to mention it now, but you might have applied to Lady Winchester, as Sir Joseph Jekyl did last year, and by her interest the Duke of Bolton brought him in for nothing; I am sure she would be more zealous to serve me, than Lady Jekyl.

From Lord Wharncliffe, ed., *Letters and Works of Lady Mary Wortley Montagu*, 3d ed., Vol. 1 (London: 1861), p. 211.

economic and social interests, such as the West Indian interest, the merchant interest, and the landed interest. These owners of property were suspicious of an administrative bureaucracy controlled by the crown or its ministers. To diminish royal influence, they or their agents served as local government administrators, judges, militia commanders, and tax collectors. In this sense, the British nobility and large landowners actually did govern the nation. And because they regarded the Parliament as the political sovereign, there was no absence of central political authority and direction. Consequently, the supremacy of Parliament gave Britain the unity that strong central monarchy provided elsewhere in Europe.

These parliamentary structures also helped to strengthen the financial position of the British government, which, under William III, had learned much about government finance from Dutch practices. The British monarch could not raise taxes the way his continental counterparts could, but the British government consisting of the monarch and Parliament could and did raise vast sums of tax revenue and loans to wage war throughout the eighteenth century. All Britons paid taxes; there were virtually no exemptions. The British credit market was secure through the regulation of the Bank of England, founded in 1693. This strong system of finance and tax collection was one of the cornerstones of eighteenth-century British power.

FREEDOM OF POLITICAL LIFE British political life was genuinely more free than that on the Continent. There were real limits on the power of Robert Walpole. Parliament could not wholly ignore popular political pressure. Even with the extensive use of patronage, many members of Parliament maintained independent views. Newspapers and public debate flourished. There was freedom of speech and association. There was no large standing army. Those Tories barred from political office and the Whig enemies of Walpole could and did openly oppose his policies—which would have been far more difficult on the Continent.

For example, in 1733 Walpole presented a scheme to the House of Commons to expand the scope of the excise tax, a tax that resembled a modern sales tax. The outcry in the press, on the public platform, and in the streets was so great that he eventually withdrew the measure. What the British regarded as their traditional political rights raised a real and potent barrier to the power of the government. Again, in 1739, the public outcry over the alleged Spanish treatment of British merchants in the Caribbean pushed Britain into a war that Walpole opposed and deplored.

Walpole's ascendancy, which lasted until 1742, did little to raise the level of British political morality, but it brought a kind of stability that Britain had not enjoyed for a century. The nation's foreign trade grew steadily and spread from New England to India. Agriculture, in many cases following Dutch models, became more productive. All forms of economic enterprise seemed to prosper. The navy became stronger. As a result of this political stability and economic growth, Great Britain became a European power of the first order and stood at the beginning of its era as a world power. Its government and economy during the next generation became a model for all progressive Europeans.

Central and Eastern Europe

The major factors in the shift of political influence among the maritime nations were naval strength, economic progress, foreign trade, and sound domestic administration. The conflicts among them occurred less in Europe than on the high seas and in their overseas empires. These nations existed in well-defined geographical areas with established borders. Their populations generally accepted the authority of the central government.

Central and eastern Europe were different. The entire region was economically much less advanced than western Europe. Except for the Baltic ports, the economy was agrarian. There were fewer cities and many more large estates populated by serfs. The states in this region did not possess overseas empires; nor did they engage in extensive overseas trade of any kind, except for the supply of grain to western Europe, grain more often than not carried on west European ships.

Changes in the power structure normally involved changes in borders or in the prince who ruled a particular area. Military conflicts took place at home rather than overseas. The political structure of this region, which lay largely east of the Elbe River, was very "soft." The almost constant warfare of the seventeenth century had led to a habit of temporary and shifting political loyalties. The princes and aristocracies of small states and principalities were unwilling to subordinate themselves to a central monarchical authority. Consequently, the political life of the region and the kind of state that emerged there were different from those of western Europe.

During the last half of the seventeenth century, central and eastern Europe began to assume the political and social contours that would characterize it for the next two centuries. After the Peace of Westphalia, the Austrian Habsburgs recognized the basic weakness of the position of the Holy Roman Emperor and started to consolidate their power outside Germany. At the same time, Prussia emerged as a factor in North German politics and as a major challenger to Habsburg domination of Germany. Most important, Russia at the opening of the eighteenth century became a military and naval power of the first order. These three states (Austria, Prussia, and Russia) achieved their new status largely as a result of the political decay or military defeat of Sweden, Poland, and the Ottoman Empire.

France and Great Britain in the Early Eighteenth Century	
1713	Treaty of Utrecht ends the War of the Spanish Succession
1714	George I becomes king of Great Britain and establishes the Hanoverian dynasty
1715	Louis XV becomes king of France
1715–1720	Regency of the duke of Orléans in France
1720	Mississippi Bubble bursts in France and South Sea Bubble bursts in Great Britain
1720–1742	Robert Walpole dominates British politics
1726–1743	Cardinal Fleury serves as Louis XV's chief minister
1727	George II becomes king of Great Britain
1733	Excise-tax crisis in Britain

Sweden: The Ambitions of Charles XII

Under Gustavus Adolphus II (r. 1611–1632), Sweden had played an important role as a Protestant combatant in the Thirty Years' War. During the rest of the seventeenth century, Sweden had consolidated its control of the Baltic, thus preventing Russian possession of a Baltic port and permitting Polish and German access to the sea only on Swedish terms. The Swedes also possessed one of the better armies in Europe. Sweden's economy, however, based primarily on the export of iron, was not strong enough to ensure continued political success.

In 1697 Charles XII (r. 1697–1718) came to the throne. He was headstrong, to say the least, and perhaps insane. In 1700, Russia began a drive to the west against Swedish territory. The Russian goal was a foothold on the Baltic. In the resulting Great Northern War (1700–1721), Charles XII led a vigorous and often brilliant campaign, but one that eventually resulted in the defeat of Sweden. In 1700 he defeated the Russians at the Battle of Narva, but then he turned south to invade Poland. The conflict dragged on, and the Russians were able to strengthen their forces.

In 1708 the Swedish monarch began a major invasion of Russia, but became bogged down in the harsh Russian winter. The next year, his army was decisively defeated at the Battle of Poltava. Thereafter, the Swedes could maintain only a holding action against their enemies. Charles himself sought refuge in Turkey and did not return to Sweden until 1714. He was killed under uncertain circumstances four years later while fighting the Danes in Norway.

The Great Northern War came to a close in 1721. Sweden had exhausted its military and economic resources and had lost its monopoly on the Baltic coast. Russia had conquered a large section of the eastern Baltic, and Prussia had gained a part of Pomerania. Internally, after the death of Charles XII, the Swedish nobles were determined to reassert their power over the monarchy. They did so, but then quarreled among themselves. Sweden played a very minor role in European affairs thereafter.

The Ottoman Empire

At the southeastern extreme of Europe, the Ottoman Empire was a barrier to the territorial ambitions of the Austrian Habsburgs, Poland, and Russia. The empire in the late seventeenth century still controlled most of the Balkan Peninsula and the entire coastline of the Black Sea. In theory, the empire existed to enhance the spread of Islam. Its population, however, was exceedingly diverse both ethnically and religiously. The empire ruled these people not on a territorial, but on a religious, basis. That is, it created units, called *millets*, that included all persons of a particular religious faith. Various laws and regulations applied to the persons who belonged to a particular millet rather than to a particular administrative territory. Non-Islamic persons in the empire were known as *zimmis*. They could practice their religion, but they were second-class citizens who could not rise in the service of the empire or profit much from its successes. This mode of government maintained the self-identity of these various peoples but allowed for little religious integration or interaction.

From the fifteenth century onward, the Ottoman Empire had tried to push further westward in Europe. The empire made its deepest military invasion into Europe in 1683, when it unsuccessfully besieged Vienna. In addition, numerous Christians in the Balkans and on the Aegean islands had converted to Islam. Many of these people had previously been forced to convert to Roman Catholicism by the Venetians and welcomed the Turks and their Islamic faith as vehicles for political liberation. Much of the Islamic presence in the Balkans today dates to these conversions.

By the last third of the seventeenth century, however, the Ottomans had overextended themselves politically, economically, and militarily. From the mid-sixteenth century, the Ottoman rulers spent so much time at war that they could not attend to meetings of governmental bodies in Constantinople. As time passed, political groups in the capital resisted any substantial strengthening of the central government or of the role of the sultan. Rivalries for power among army leaders and nobles, as well as their flagrant efforts to enrich themselves, weakened the effectiveness of the government. In the outer provinces, such as Transylvania, Wallachia, and Moldavia (all parts of modern Romania), the empire depended on the goodwill of local rulers, who paid tribute, but never submitted themselves fully to the imperial power. The empire's economy was weak, and its exports were primarily raw materials. Moreover, the actual conduct of most of its trade had been turned over to representatives of other nations.

By the early eighteenth century, the weakness of the Ottoman Empire meant that a political vacuum that would expand during the next two centuries had come into existence on the southeastern perimeter of Europe. The various European powers that had created strong armies and bureaucracies would begin to probe and eventually dismember the Ottoman Empire. In 1699, the Turks concluded a treaty with their longtime Habsburg enemy and surrendered all pretensions of control over, and consequent receipt of, revenues from Hungary, Transylvania, Croatia, and Slavonia. From this time onward, Russia also attempted to extend its territory and influence at the expense of the empire. By the early nineteenth century, many of the peoples who lived in the Balkans and around the Black Sea would seek to create their own national states. The retreat and decay of the Ottoman Empire and the scramble of other states and regional peoples to assume control of southeastern Europe would cause political and ethnic turmoil there from the eighteenth century to our own day.

Poland: Absence of Strong Central Authority

In no other part of Europe was the failure to maintain a competitive political position so complete as in Poland. In 1683, King John III Sobieski (r. 1674–1696) had led a Polish army to rescue Vienna from the Turkish siege. Following that spectacular effort, however, Poland became a byword for the dangers of aristocratic independence. In Poland as nowhere else on the Continent, the nobility became the single most powerful political factor in the country. Unlike the British nobility and landowners, the Polish nobility would not even submit to a central authority of their own making. There was no effective central authority in the form of either a king or a parliament.

The Polish monarchy was elective, but the deep distrust and divisions among the nobility prevented their electing a king from among themselves. Sobieski was a notable exception. Most of the Polish monarchs were foreigners and were the tools of foreign powers. The Polish nobles did have a central legislative body called the *Sejm*, or diet. It included only the nobles and specifically excluded representatives from corporate bodies, such as the towns. In the diet, however, there existed a practice known as the *liberum veto*, whereby the staunch opposition of any single member, who might have been bribed by a foreign power, could require the body to disband. Such opposition was termed "exploding the diet." This practice was most often the work of a group of dissatisfied nobles rather than of one person. Nonetheless, the requirement of unanimity was a major stumbling block to effective government. Localism reminiscent of the Middle Ages continued to hold sway as the nobles used all their energy to maintain their traditional "Polish liberties." There was no way to collect enough taxes to build up an army. The price of this noble liberty would eventually be the disappearance of Poland from the map of Europe during the latter half of the eighteenth century.

The Habsburg Empire and the Pragmatic Sanction

The close of the Thirty Years' War marked a fundamental turning point in the history of the Austrian Habsburgs. Previously, in alliance with the Spanish branch of the family, they had hoped to dominate all of Germany and to return it to the Catholic fold. They did not achieve either goal, and the decline of Spanish power meant that in future diplomatic relations the Austrian Habsburgs were on their own. The Treaty of Westphalia in 1648 permitted Protestantism within the Holy Roman Empire and also recognized the political autonomy of more than 300 corporate German political entities within the empire. These included large units (such as Saxony, Hanover, Bavaria, and Brandenburg) and scores of small cities, bishoprics, principalities, and petty territories of independent knights.

After 1648 the Habsburgs retained a firm hold on the title of Holy Roman Emperor, but the effectiveness of the title depended less on force of arms than on the cooperation that the emperor could elicit from the various political bodies in the empire. The diet of the empire sat at Regensburg from 1663 until the empire was dissolved in 1806. The diet and the emperor generally regulated the daily economic and political life of Germany. The post-Westphalian Holy Roman Empire resembled Poland in its lack of central authority. Unlike its Polish neighbor, however, the Holy Roman Empire was reorganized from within as the Habsburgs attempted to regain their authority. As will be seen shortly, Prussia set out on its course toward European power at the same time.

CONSOLIDATION OF AUSTRIAN POWER   While concentrating on their hereditary Austrian holdings among the German states, the Habsburgs also began to consolidate their power and influence within their other hereditary possessions. (See Map 15–1.) These included, first, the Crown of Saint Wenceslas, encompassing the kingdom of Bohemia (in the modern Czech Republic and Slovakia) and the duchies of Moravia and Silesia and, second, the Crown of Saint Stephen, which included Hungary, Croatia, and Transylvania. In the middle of the seventeenth century, much of Hungary remained occupied by the Turks and was liberated only at the end of the century.

In the early eighteenth century, the family extended its domains further, receiving the former Spanish (thereafter Austrian) Netherlands, Lombardy in northern Italy, and, briefly, the kingdom of Naples in southern Italy through the Treaty of Utrecht in 1713. During the eighteenth and nineteenth centuries, the

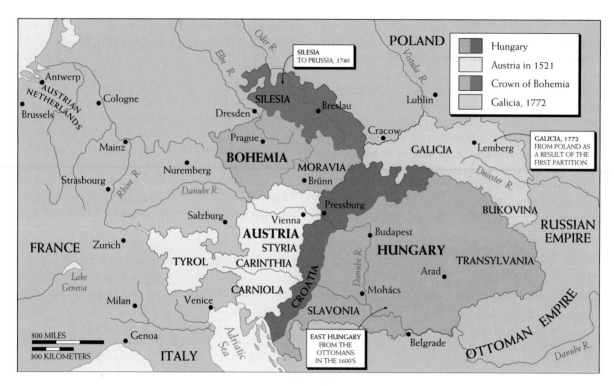

MAP 15–1   THE AUSTRIAN HABSBURG EMPIRE, 1521–1772   *The empire had three main units: Austria, Bohemia, and Hungary. Expansion was mainly eastward: East Hungary from the Ottomans (seventeenth century) and Galicia from Poland (1772). Meantime, Silesia was lost, but the Habsburgs retained German influences as Holy Roman emperors.*

Habsburgs' power and influence in Europe were based primarily on their territories outside Germany.

In the second half of the seventeenth century and later, the Habsburgs faced immense problems in these hereditary territories. In each, they ruled by virtue of a different title and had to gain the cooperation of the local nobility. The most difficult province was Hungary, where the Magyar nobility seemed ever ready to rebel. There was almost no common basis for political unity among peoples of such diverse languages, customs, and geography. Even the Habsburg zeal for Roman Catholicism no longer proved a bond for unity as they confronted the equally zealous Calvinism of many of the Magyar nobles. The Habsburgs established various central councils to chart common policies for their far-flung domains. Virtually all of these bodies dealt with only part of the Habsburgs' holdings. Repeatedly, the Habsburgs had to bargain with nobles in one part of of their empire to maintain their position in another.

Despite all these internal difficulties, Leopold I (r. 1657–1705) rallied his domains to resist the advances of the Turks and the aggression of Louis XIV. He achieved Ottoman recognition of his sovereignty over Hungary in 1699 and began the suppression of a long rebellion by his new Magyar subjects that lasted from 1703 to 1711. He also conquered much of the Balkan Peninsula and western Romania. These southeastward extensions allowed the Habsburgs to hope to develop Mediterranean trade through the port of Trieste. The expansion at the cost of the Ottoman Empire helped them to compensate for their loss of domination over the Holy Roman Empire. The new strength in the East gave them somewhat greater political leverage in Germany. Leopold I was succeeded by Joseph I (r. 1705–1711), who continued Leopold's policies.

THE HABSBURG DYNASTIC PROBLEM   When Charles VI (r. 1711–1740) succeeded Joseph, he had no male heir, and there was only the weakest of precedents for a female ruler of the Habsburg domains. Charles feared that on his death the Austrian Habsburg lands might fall prey to the surrounding powers, as had those of the Spanish Habsburgs in 1700. He was determined to prevent that disaster and to provide his domains with the semblance of legal unity. To those ends, he devoted much of his energy throughout his reign to seeking the approval of his family, the estates of his realms, and the major foreign powers for a document called the Pragmatic Sanction.

This instrument provided the legal basis for a single line of inheritance within the Habsburg dynasty through Charles VI's daughter Maria Theresa (r. 1740–

1780). Other members of the Habsburg family recognized her as the rightful heir. The nobles of the various Habsburg domains did likewise after extracting various concessions from Charles. So, when Charles VI died in October 1740, he believed that he had secured legal unity for the Habsburg Empire and a safe succession for his daughter.

Charles VI had indeed established a permanent line of succession and the basis for future legal bonds within the Habsburg holdings. He had failed, however, to protect his daughter from foreign aggression, either through the Pragmatic Sanction or, more importantly, by leaving her a strong army and a full treasury. Less than two months after his death, the fragility of the foreign agreements became apparent. In December 1740, Frederick II of Prussia invaded the Habsburg province of Silesia. Maria Theresa had to fight to defend her inheritance.

Prussia and the Hohenzollerns

The Habsburg achievement had been to draw together into an uncertain legal unity a collection of domains possessed through separate feudal titles. The achievement of the Hohenzollerns of Brandenburg–Prussia was to acquire a similar collection of titular holdings and then to forge them into a centrally administered unit. Despite the geographical separation of their territories and the paucity of their natural economic resources, they transformed feudal ties and structures into bureaucratic ones. They subordinated every social class and most economic pursuits to the strengthening of the institution that united their far-flung realms: the army. They thus made the term "Prussian" synonymous with administrative rigor and military discipline.

A STATE OF DISCONNECTED TERRITORIES   The rise of Prussia occurred within the German power vacuum created after 1648 by the Peace of Westphalia. It is the story of the extraordinary Hohenzollern family, which had ruled the German territory of Brandenburg since 1417. (See Map 15–2.) Through inheritance, the family had acquired the duchy of Cleves and the counties of Mark and Ravensburg in 1609, the duchy of East Prussia in 1618, and the duchy of Pomerania in 1637. Except for Pomerania, none of these lands

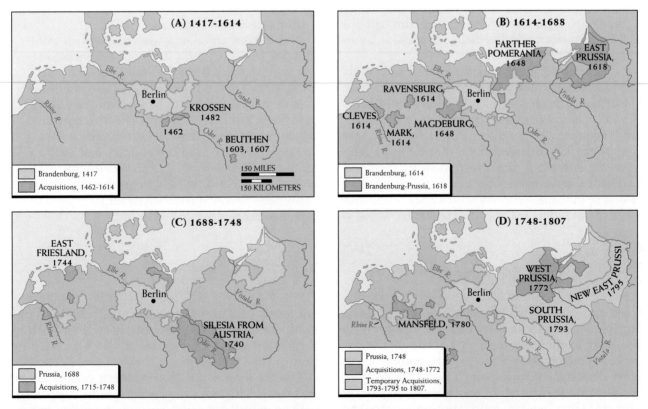

MAP 15–2   EXPANSION OF BRANDENBURG–PRUSSIA   *In the seventeenth century, Brandenburg–Prussia expanded mainly be acquiring dynastic titles in geographically separated lands. In the eighteenth century, it expanded through aggression to the east, seizing Silesia in 1740 and various parts of Poland in 1772, 1793, and 1795.*

The Great Elector Welcomes Protestant Refugees from France

The Hohenzollern dynasty of Brandenburg–Prussia pursued a policy of religious toleration. The family itself was Calvinist, whereas most of its subjects were Lutherans. When Louis XIV of France revoked the Edict of Nantes in 1685, Frederick William, the Great Elector, seized the opportunity to invite French Protestants into his realms. As his proclamation indicates, he wanted to attract persons with productive skills who could aid the economic development of his domains.

❖ *In reading this document, do you believe that religious or economic concerns more nearly led the elector of Brandenburg to welcome the French Protestants? What specific privileges did the elector extend to them? To what extent were these privileges a welcoming measure, and to what extent were they inducements to emigrate to Brandenburg? In what kind of economic activity does the elector expect the French refugees to engage?*

We, Friedrich Wilhelm, by Grace of God Margrave of Brandenburg...

Do hereby proclaim and make known to all and sundry that since the cruel persecutions and rigorous ill-treatment in which Our co-religionists of the Evangelical-Reformed faith have for some time past been subjected in the Kingdom of France, have caused many families to remove themselves and to betake themselves out of the said Kingdom into other lands, We now...have been moved graciously to offer them through this Edict...a secure and free refuge in all Our Lands and Provinces....

Since Our Lands are not only well and amply endowed with all things necessary to support life, but also very well-suited to the reestablishment of all kinds of manufactures and trade and traffic by land and water, We permit, indeed, to those settling therein free choice to establish themselves where it is most convenient for their profession and way of living....

The personal property which they bring with them, including merchandise and other wares, is to be totally exempt from any taxes, customs dues, licenses, or other imposts of any description, and not detained in any way....

As soon as these Our French co-religionists of the Evangelical-Reformed faith have settled in any town or village, they shall be admitted to the domiciliary rights and craft freedoms customary there, gratis and without payments of any fee; and shall be entitled to the benefits, rights, and privileges enjoyed by Our other, native, subjects, residing there....

Not only are those who wish to establish manufacture of cloth, stuffs, hats, or other objects in which they are skilled to enjoy all necessary freedoms, privileges and facilities, but also provision is to be made for them to be assisted and helped as far as possible with money and anything else which they need to realize their intention....

Those who settle in the country and wish to maintain themselves by agriculture are to be given a certain plot of land to bring under cultivation and provided with whatever they need to establish themselves initially....

From C. A. Macartney, ed., *The Habsburg and Hohenzollern Dynasties in the Seventeenth and Eighteenth Centuries* (New York: Walker, 1970), pp. 270–273.

was contiguous with Brandenburg. East Prussia lay inside Poland and outside the authority of the Holy Roman Emperor. All of the territories lacked good natural resources, and many of them were devastated during the Thirty Years' War. At Westphalia the Hohenzollerns lost part of Pomerania to Sweden, but were compensated by receiving three more bishoprics and the promise of the archbishopric of Magdeburg when it became vacant, as it did in 1680. By the late sev-

enteenth century, the scattered Hohenzollern holdings represented a block of territory within the Holy Roman Empire second in size only to that of the Habsburgs.

Despite its size, the Hohenzollern conglomerate was weak. The areas were geographically separate, with no mutual sympathy or common concern among them. In each, local noble estates limited the power of the Hohenzollern prince. The various areas were also exposed to foreign aggression.

FREDERICK WILLIAM, THE GREAT ELECTOR   The person who began to forge these separated regions and diverse nobles into a modern state was Frederick William (r. 1640–1688), who became known as the Great Elector. (The ruler of Brandenburg was called an Elector because he was one of the princes who elected the Holy Roman Emperor.) He established himself and his successors as the central uniting power by breaking the local noble estates, organizing a royal bureaucracy, and establishing a strong army. (See "The Great Elector Welcomes Protestant Refugees from France.")

Between 1655 and 1660, Sweden and Poland engaged in a war that endangered the Great Elector's holdings in Pomerania and East Prussia. Frederick William had neither the military nor the financial resources to confront this threat. In 1655, the Brandenburg estates refused to grant him new taxes; however, he proceeded to collect the required taxes by military force. In 1659 a different grant of taxes, originally made in 1653, elapsed; Frederick William continued to collect them, as well as those he had imposed by his own authority. He used the money to build up an army that allowed him to continue to enforce his will without the approval of the nobility. Similar threats and coercion took place against the nobles in his other territories.

There did occur, however, a political and social trade-off between the elector and his various nobles: In exchange for their obedience to the Hohenzollerns, the *Junkers* received the right to demand obedience from their serfs. Frederick William also tended to choose as the local administrators of the tax structure men who would normally have been members of the noble estates. He thus co-opted potential opponents into his service. His taxes fell most heavily on the backs of the peasants and the urban classes.

As the years passed, sons of *Junkers* increasingly dominated the army officer corps, and this practice became even more pronounced during the eighteenth century. All officials and army officers took an oath of loyalty directly to the elector. The army and the elector thus came to embody the otherwise absent unity of the state. The existence of the army made Prussia a valuable potential ally and a state with which other powers needed to curry favor.

FREDERICK WILLIAM I, KING OF PRUSSIA   Yet, even with the considerable accomplishments of the Great Elector, the house of Hohenzollern did not possess a crown. The achievement of a royal title was one of the few state-building accomplishments of Frederick I (r. 1688–1713). This son of the Great Elector was the least "Prussian" of his

family during these crucial years. He built palaces, founded Halle University (1694), patronized the arts, and lived luxuriously. In 1701, however, at the outbreak of the War of the Spanish Succession, he put his army at the disposal of the Habsburg Holy Roman Emperor. In exchange for this loyal service, the emperor permitted Frederick to assume the title of "King in Prussia." Thereafter Frederick became Frederick I, and he passed the much-desired royal title to his son Frederick William I in 1713.

Frederick William I (r. 1713–1740) was both the most eccentric and one of the most effective Hohenzollerns. After giving his father a funeral that matched the luxury of his life, Frederick William I immediately imposed strict austerity. Some jobs were abolished and some salaries lowered. His political aims seem to have been the consolidation of an obedient, compliant bureaucracy and the establishment of a bigger army. He initiated a policy of *Kabinett* government, which meant that lower officials submitted all relevant documents to him in his office, or *Kabinett*. Then he alone examined the papers, made his decisions, and issued his orders. He thus skirted the influence of ministers and ruled alone.

Frederick William I organized the bureaucracy along military lines. He united all departments under the *General-Ober-Finanz-Kriegs-und-Domänen-Direktorium*, more happily known to us as the General Directory. He imposed taxes on the nobility and changed most remaining feudal dues into monetary payments. He sought to transform feudal

Austria and Prussia in the Late-Seventeenth and Early-Eigheenth Centuries	
1640–1688	Reign of Frederick William, the Great Elector
1657–1705	Leopold I rules Austria and resists the Turkish invasions
1683	Turkish siege of Vienna
1688–1713	Reign of Frederick I of Prussia
1699	Peace treaty between Turks and Habsburgs
1711–1740	Charles VI rules Austria and secures agreement to the Pragmatic Sanction
1713–1740	Frederick William I builds up the military power of Prussia
1740	Maria Theresa succeeds to the Habsburg throne
1740	Frederick II violates the Pragmatic Sanction by invading Silesia

Though economically weak and with a small population, Prussia became an important state because it developed a large, well-trained army. Prussian troops were known for their discipline, the result of constant drill and harsh punishment. In this mid-eighteenth-century engraving one soldier is being whipped while another is about to run a gauntlet of other soldiers. Bildarchiv Preussischer Kulturbesitz

and administrative loyalties into a sense of duty to the monarch as a political institution rather than as a person. He once described the perfect royal servant as

an intelligent, assiduous, and alert person who after God values nothing higher than his king's pleasure and serves him out of love and for the sake of honor rather than money and who in his conduct solely seeks and constantly bears in mind his king's service and interests, who, moreover, abhors all intrigues and emotional deterrents.[2]

Service to the state and the monarch was to become impersonal, mechanical, and, in effect, unquestioning.

[2]Quoted in Hans Rosenberg, *Bureaucracy, Aristocracy, and Autocracy* (Boston: Beacon Press, 1958), p. 93.

THE PRUSSIAN ARMY   The discipline that Frederick William applied to the army was fanatical. During his reign, the size of the army grew from about 39,000 in 1713 to more than 80,000 in 1740. It was the third- or fourth-largest army in Europe, whereas Prussia ranked thirteenth in population. Rather than using recruiters, the king made each canton or local district responsible for supplying a quota of soldiers.

After 1725, Frederick William I always wore an officer's uniform. He formed one regiment from the tallest soldiers he could find in Europe. Separate laws applied to the army and to civilians. Laws, customs, and royal attention made the officer corps the highest social class of the state. Military service attracted the sons of *Junkers*. Thus, the army, the *Junker* nobility, and the monarchy were forged into a single political entity. Military priorities and values dominated Prussian government, society, and daily life as in no other state of Europe. It has often been said that whereas other nations possessed armies, the Prussian army possessed its nation.

Although Frederick William I built the best army in Europe, he avoided conflict. He wanted to drill his soldiers, but not to order them into battle. The army was for him a symbol of Prussian power and unity, not an instrument to be used for foreign adventures or aggression.

At his death in 1740, he passed to his son Frederick II, later known as "the Great" (r. 1740–1786), this superb military machine, but he could not also pass on the wisdom to refrain from using it. Almost immediately on coming to the throne, Frederick II upset the Pragmatic Sanction, invaded Silesia, and thus crystallized the Austrian–Prussian rivalry for control of Germany that would dominate central European affairs for over a century.

Russia Enters the European Political Arena

Though ripe with consequences for the future, the rise of Prussia and the new consolidation of the Austrian Habsburg domains seemed to many at the time only another shift in the long-troubled German scene. The emergence of Russia, however, as an active European power was a wholly new factor in European politics. Previously, Russia had been considered part of Europe only by courtesy, and before 1688 it did not even send minsters or ambassadors to western Europe. Geographically and politically, it lay on the periphery. Hemmed in by Sweden on the Baltic and by the Ottoman Empire on the Black Sea, Russia had no warm-water ports. Its chief outlet to the west was Archangel on the White Sea, which was ice free for only part of the year. There was little trade. What Russia did possess was a vast reserve of largely undeveloped natural and human resources.

Birth of the Romanov Dynasty

The reign of Ivan the Terrible, which had begun so well and closed so frighteningly, was followed by anarchy and civil war known as the "Time of Troubles." In 1613, hoping to restore stability, an assembly of nobles elected a seventeen-year-old boy named Michael Romanov (r. 1613–1654) as tsar. Thus began the dynasty that, despite palace revolutions, military conspiracies, assassinations, and family strife, ruled Russia until 1917.

Michael Romanov and his two successors, Alexis I (r. 1654–1676) and Theodore III (r. 1676–1682), brought stability and modest bureaucratic centralization to Russia. The country remained, however, weak and impoverished. After years of turmoil, the bureaucracy was still largely controlled by the *boyars*, the old nobility. This administrative apparatus could barely suppress a revolt of peasants and Cossacks (horsemen who lived on the steppe frontier) under Stepan Razin in 1670–1671. Furthermore, the government and the tsars faced the danger of mutiny from the *streltsy*, or guards of the Moscow garrison.

Peter the Great

In 1682, another boy—ten years old at the time—ascended the fragile Russian throne as co-ruler with his half brother. His name was Peter (r. 1682–1725), and Russia would never be the same after him. He and the sickly Ivan V had come to power on the shoulders of the *streltsy*, who expected to be rewarded for their support. Much vi-

Rise of Russian Power	
1533–1584	Reign of Ivan the Terrible
1584–1613	"Time of Troubles"
1613	Michael Romanov becomes tsar
1682	Peter the Great, age ten, becomes tsar
1689	Peter assumes personal rule
1696	Russia captures Azov on the Black Sea from the Turks
1697	European tour of Peter the Great
1698	Peter returns to Russia to put down the revolt of the *streltsy*
1700	The Great Northern War opens between Russia and Sweden; Russia defeated at Narva by Swedish Army of Charles XII
1703	Saint Petersburg founded
1709	Russia defeats Sweden at the Battle of Poltava
1718	Charles XII of Sweden dies
1718	Son of Peter the Great dies in prison under mysterious circumstances
1721	Peace of Nystad ends the Great Northern War
1721	Peter establishes a synod for the Russian church
1722	Peter issues the Table of Ranks
1725	Peter dies, leaving an uncertain succession

Peter the Great Issues a Table of Ranks

In 1722, after much consultation among his advisors and examination of how social and political ranks were established elsewhere in Europe, Peter the Great issued a Table of Ranks that became law in the vast Russian empire. This table indicated, with enormous precision, the hierarchy or official "pecking order" of the various offices among the military, the civilian bureaucracy, and the czarist court. In all cases, Peter declared that the military would take precedence over the other divisions. Note, significantly, that Peter omitted offices in the church from the ranks of state service.

The Table of Ranks was a cornerstone of Peter's effort to transform Russia into a modern European country. He was determined to establish a hierarchy of reward and social honor, as indicated in point 8 of the table, that would distinguish those people who served the state from those who possessed nobility merely by virtue of birth. Although he formally acknowledged that nobles by birth should receive all manner of formal courtesies, he reserved the highest honors to those serving the czar and the nation. Moreover, he made service to the state a formal path to ennoblement itself. Despite the precision of the listing of offices, there remained much confusion in the decades that followed about exactly which offices, degree of landholding, and the like permitted a person to receive a title of of nobility. Nonetheless, with later eighteenth- and nineteenth-century revisions, Peter's Table of Ranks essentially remained in force in Russia until the revolution in 1917.

These points listed from the Table of Ranks were intended to clarify the application and administration of the Table.

❖ *What steps did Peter take in these regulations to ensure that people did not attempt to go around the provisions of the Table of Ranks? How did he provide for the creation of new nobles through service to the state? How might the Table of Ranks and these provisions have fostered loyalty to the new social and political order that Peter sought to achieve?*

After announcing that all princes descended from himself and those married to such princes took precedence over all other ranks, these points of clarification followed:

3. Whoever shall demand honour higher than his rank or take a place higher than the rank given him, shall be fined two months pay for each offence...but this observance of each rank

olence and bloodshed had surrounded the disputed succession. Matters became even more confused when the boys' sister, Sophia, was named regent. Peter's followers overthrew her in 1689. From that date onward, Peter ruled personally, although in theory he shared the crown until Ivan died in 1696. The dangers and turmoil of his youth convinced Peter of two things: first, the power of the tsar must be made secure from the jealousy of the *boyars* and the greed of the *streltsy*; second, the military power of Russia must be increased. In both respects, he self-consciously resembled Louis XIV of France, who had experienced the turmoil of the *Fronde* during his youth and resolved to establish a strong monarchy safe from the noblity and defended by a powerful army.

Northwestern Europe, particularly the military resources of the maritime powers, fascinated Peter I, who eventually became known as Peter the Great. In 1697, he made a famous visit in transparent disguise to western Europe. There he dined and talked with the great and the powerful, who considered this almost seven-foot-tall ruler both crude and rude. His happiest moments on the trip were spent inspecting shipyards, docks, and the manufacture of military hardware in England and the Netherlands.

An imitator of the first order, Peter returned to Moscow determined to copy what he had seen abroad, for he knew that warfare would be necessary to make Russia a great power. He personally intervened in one project after anoth-

is not demanded on such occasions as when good friends or neighbors get together, or in public assemblies, but only in churches during Divine Service, in Court ceremonies such as ambassadorial audiences, formal dinners, official meetings, weddings, christenings, and suchlike public festivity and business...

* * * * *

7. All married women occupy ranks according to the grades of their husbands, and when they act in a manner contrary to this they must pay a fine such as their husbands would have paid for the same offence.

8. Although We allow free entry before others of lower grade in public assembly where the Court is to be found to the sons of the Russians State's Princes, Counts, Barons, distinguished Nobility, and servants of the highest rank, because of their aristocratic birth, or because of the outstanding grades of their fathers, and although We keenly desire to see that they are distinguished from others according to their dignity in all cases; however We do not allow anybody rank, until they have rendered service to Us and the fatherland, and have received a character reference to this effect.

* * * * *

11. All Russian or foreign servants who are or actually were in the first eight ranks, their law-

ful children and descendants in perpetuity are considered equal to the best ancient Nobility in all honours and advantages, even though they are of low birth, and have never been promoted to Noble rank by Crowned Heads or granted coats of arms.

* * * * *

15. To military men of commoner origin who serve up to Commissioned rank, when one of them receives the aforementioned grade, he is a Noble and so are the children born while he holds the Commission....

* * * * *

19. Since...the prominence of and worthiness of the grade of any individual is often diminished, when the dress and behavior are not consonant with them, similarly on the other hand many are ruined when they have accoutrements higher than their grade and property: We therefore graciously point out that everybody should have the dress, equipage and livery as his position and character reference demand. All must act in this manner, and must beware of the ordained penalty and greatest punishment.

From Paul Dukes, trans. and ed., *Russia under Catherine the Great: Select Documents on Government and Society.* Oriental Research Partners, 1978, pp. 10–12. Reprinted by permission of Oriental Research Partners

---

er, displaying enormous energy and determination tied to equally enormous impulsiveness. The tsar's drive toward westernization, though unsystematic, had five interrelated general goals: taming the *boyars* and the *streltsy*, achieving secular control of the church, reorganizing the internal administration, developing the economy, and constructing a major army and navy. Peter pursued each of these goals ruthlessly. His effort was unprecedented in Russian history in both its intensity and scope.

TAMING THE *BOYARS* AND *STRELTSY* Peter made a sustained attack on the *boyars* and their attachment to traditional Russian culture. In 1698, immediately on his return from abroad, he personally

shaved the long beards of the court *boyars* and sheared off the customary long, hand-covering sleeves of their shirts and coats, which had made them the butt of jokes throughout Europe. More important, he demanded that the nobles serve his state. He faced considerable opposition, but eventually imposed his will.

A Table of Ranks, published in 1722, embodied Peter's policy of drawing the nobility into state service. (See "Peter the Great Issues a Table of Ranks.") That table equated a person's social position and privileges with his rank in the bureaucracy or the military, rather than with his lineage among the traditional landed nobility. Peter thus made the social standing of individual *boyars* a function of their willingness to serve the central

After Peter the Great of Russia returned from his journey to western Europe, he personally cut off the traditional and highly prized long sleeves and beards of the Russian nobles. His action symbolized his desire to see Russia become more powerful and more modern.   The Granger Collection

state. Earlier tsars had created service nobles on the basis of merit, but none had envisioned drawing all nobles into state service. Unlike Prussian *Junkers*, however, the Russian nobility never became perfectly loyal to the state. They repeatedly sought to reassert their independence and their control of the Russian imperial court and to bargain with later tsars over local authority and the nobles' dominance of the serfs.

The *streltsy* fared less well than the *boyars*. In 1698, they had rebelled while Peter was on his European tour. On his return, he brutally suppressed the revolt. There were private tortures and public executions, in which Peter's own ministers took part. Almost 1,200 of the rebels were put to death, and their corpses remained on public display to discourage future disloyalty. The new military establishment that Peter built would serve the tsar and not itself.

ACHIEVING SECULAR CONTROL OF THE CHURCH
Peter quashed the potential independence of the Russian Orthodox Church with similar ruthlessness. Here again, he had to confront a problem that had arisen in the turbulent decades that had preceded his reign. The Russian church had long opposed the scientific, as well as the theological, thought of the West. In the mid-seventeenth century, a reformist movement led by Patriarch Nikon introduced changes into church texts and ritual. The Old Believers, a group of Russian Christians, strongly opposed these changes. Although condemned by the hierarchy, the Old Believers persisted in their opposition. Thousands of them committed suicide rather than submit to the new rituals. The Old Believers represented a rejection of change and innovation; their opposition discouraged the church hierarchy from making further substantial accommodations to modern thought.

In the future, Peter wanted to avoid two kinds of difficulties with the church: first, the clergy must not be able to oppose change and westernization; second, the hierarchy of the church must not be permitted to cause again the kind of controversy that had provoked the Old Believers. Consequently, in 1721, Peter simply abolished the position of patriarch. In its place he established a synod headed by a layman, called the procurator general, to rule the church in accordance with secular requirements. This action toward the church was the most radical transformation of a traditional institution in Peter's reign. It produced further futile opposition from the Old Believers, who saw the tsar as leading the church into new heresy.

REORGANIZING DOMESTIC ADMINISTRATION   In reorganizing his domestic administration, Peter looked to Swedish institutions called "colleges"—bureaus of several persons rather than departments headed by a single minister. These colleges, which he imposed on Russia, were to look after matters such as the collection of taxes, foreign relations, war, and economic affairs. This new organization was an attempt to breathe life into Russia's stagnant and inefficient administration.

In 1711, Peter created a central senate of nine members who were to direct the government when the tsar was away with the army. The purpose of these and other local administrative reforms was to establish a bureaucracy that could support an efficient army.

DEVELOPING THE ECONOMY AND WAGING WAR   The economic development advocated by Peter the Great was closely related to his military needs. He encouraged the establishment of an iron industry in the Ural Mountains, and by midcentury Russia had become the largest iron producer in Europe, although the industry later languished. He sent promising young Russians abroad to acquire technical and organizational skills. He tried to attract west European

Vüe des bords de la Neva en descendant la riviere entre le Palais d hyver de Sa Majesté Imperiale & les batimens de l'Academie des Sciences

Peter the Great built Saint Petersburg on the Gulf of Finland to provide Russia with better contact with western Europe. He moved Russia's capital there from Moscow in 1703. This is an eighteenth-century view of the city. The Granger Collection

Peter the Great Tells His Son to Acquire Military Skills

Enormous hostility existed between Peter the Great and his son Alexis. Peter believed that his son was not prepared to inherit the throne. In October 1715, he composed a long letter to Alexis in which he berated him for refusing to take military matters seriously. The letter indicates how an early eighteenth-century ruler saw the conduct of warfare as a fundamental part of the role of a monarch. Peter also points to Louis XIV of France as a role model. Peter and Alexis did not reach an agreement. Alexis died under mysterious circumstances in 1718, with Peter possibly responsible for his death.

❖ *How did Peter use the recent war with Sweden to argue for the necessity of his son acquiring military skills? What concept of leadership does Peter attempt to communicate to his son? Why did Peter see military prowess as the most important ability in a ruler?*

You cannot be ignorant of what is known to all the world, to what degree our people groaned under the oppression of the Swede before the beginning of the present war....

...You know what it has cost us in the beginning of this war...to make ourselves experienced in the art of war, and to put a stop to those advantages which our implacable enemies obtained over us....

But you even will not so much as hear warlike exercises mentioned: though it was by them that we broke through that obscurity in which we were involved, and that we make ourselves known to nations, whose esteem we share at present.

I do not exhort you to make war without lawful reasons: I only desire you to apply yourself to learn the art of it: for it is impossible well to govern without knowing the rules and discipline of it, was it for no other end than for the defense of the country.

...You mistake, if you think it is enough for a prince to have good generals to act under his order. Everyone looks upon the head; they study its inclinations and conform themselves to them: all the world own this....

You have no inclination to learn war. You do not apply yourself to it, and consequently you will never learn it: And how then can you command others, and judge of the reward which those deserve who do their duty, or punish others who fail of it? You will do nothing, nor judge of anything but by the assent and help of others, like a young bird that holds up his bill to be fed....

If you think there are some, whose affairs do not fail of success, though they do not go to war themselves; it is true: But if they do not go themselves, yet they have an inclination for it, and understand it.

For instance, the late King of France did not always take the field in person; but it is known to what degree he loved war, and what glorious exploits he performed in it, which make his campaigns to be called the theatre and school of the world. His inclinations were not confined solely to military affairs, he also loved mechanics, manufacture and other establishment, which rendered his kingdom more flourishing than any other whatsoever.

From Friedrich C. Weber, *The Present State of Russia* (London, 1722), 2:97-100; *The Global Experience*, 3/E, Vol. 2 by Riley, © 1999. Reprinted by permission of Prentice Hall, Inc., Upper Saddle River, NJ.

craftspeople to live and work in Russia. Except for the striking growth of the iron industry, these efforts had only marginal success.

But Peter did develop military support industries. What one historian has termed "Peter the Great's most revolutionary innovation" was his building of a Russian navy.[3] When Peter came to the throne, Russia had no real navy. In the mid-1690s, he oversaw the construction of ships to protect his interests in the Black Sea. Part of the reason for his subsequent trip to Western Europe was to learn how to build better warships. The construction of a Baltic fleet, largely built on the Finnish coast, was essential in the Great Northern War. By 1720, the Russian fleet was larger than that of either Sweden or Denmark. Only a decade earlier Russia had possessed no significant navy to launch against either Baltic power.

[3]Simon Dixon, *The Modernization of Russia, 1676–1825* (Cambridge: Cambridge University Press, 1999), p. 35.

The creation of a navy was one part of Peter's strategy to secure warm-water ports that would allow Russia to trade with the West and to influence European affairs. This ambition led him into wars with the Ottoman Empire and Sweden. His armies began fighting the Turks in 1695 and captured Azov on the Black Sea in 1696, though he was compelled to return the port in 1711.

Peter had more success against Sweden, where he profited from the inconsistency and irrationality of Charles XII. In 1700, Russia invaded the Swedish Baltic possessions. The Swedish king's failure to follow up his victory over the Russians at Narva in 1700 allowed Peter to regroup his forces and conserve his resources. In 1709, when Charles XII returned to fight Russia again, Peter was ready, and the Battle of Poltava sealed the fate of Sweden. In 1721 the Peace of Nystad, which ended the Great Northern War, confirmed the Russian conquest of Estonia, Livonia, and part of Finland. Henceforth, Russia possessed warm-water ports and a permanent influence on European affairs.

In the process of fighting these extensive wars, Peter reorganized the Russian army. He introduced effective and ruthless policies of conscription, drafting an unprecedented 130,000 soldiers during the first decade of the eighteenth century and almost 300,000 troops by the end of his reign. He had also adopted policies for the officer corps and general military discipline patterned on those of West European armies. In 1718–1719, he founded the College of War to administer the army. Such administration would be needed because, except for the 1720s, Russia was involved in war somewhere during every other decade of the eighteenth century.

At one point, the domestic and foreign policies of Peter the Great literally intersected. This was at the spot on the Gulf of Finland where he founded his new capital city of St. Petersburg in 1703. There he built government structures and compelled the *boyars* to construct town houses. He thus imitated those European monarchs who had copied Louis XIV by constructing smaller versions of Versailles. The founding of St. Petersburg went beyond establishing a central imperial court, however; it symbolized a new western orientation of Russia and Peter's determination to hold his position on the Baltic coast. He had begun the construction of the city and had moved the capital there even before his victory over Sweden was assured. Moreover, he and his successors employed architects from western Europe for many of the most prominent buildings in and around the city. Consequently, St. Petersburg looked different from other Russian cities. Both in Peter's day and later, many Russians saw St. Petersburg as a kind of illegitimate west European growth on Russian culture that symbolized Peter's autocracy and rejection of traditional Russian life and government.

Despite his notable successes, Peter's reign ended with a great question mark. He had long quarreled with his only son, Alexis. (See "Peter the Great Tells His Son to Acquire Military Skills.") Peter was jealous of the young man and feared that Alexis might undertake sedition. In 1718 Peter had his son imprisoned, and during this imprisonment Alexis died mysteriously. Thereafter Peter claimed the right to name a successor, but he could never bring himself to designate one. Consequently, when he died in 1725, there was no firm policy on the succession to the throne. For more than thirty years, soldiers and nobles again determined who ruled Russia. Peter had laid the foundations of a modern Russia, but he had failed to lay the foundations of a stable state.

In Perspective

By the second quarter of the eighteenth century, the major European powers were not nation–states in which the citizens felt themselves united by a shared sense of community, culture, language, and history. Rather, they were monarchies in which the personality of the ruler and the personal relationships of the great noble families exercised considerable influence over public affairs. The monarchs, except in Great Britain, had generally succeeded in making their power greater than the nobility's. The power of the aristocracy and its capacity to resist or obstruct the policies of the monarch were not destroyed, however. In Britain, of course, the nobility had tamed the monarchy, but even there tension between nobles and monarchs would continue throughout the rest of the century.

In foreign affairs, the new arrangement of military and diplomatic power established early in the century prepared the way for two long conflicts. The first was a commercial rivalry for trade and overseas empire between France and Great Britain. During the reign of Louis XIV, these two nations had collided over the French bid for dominance in Europe. During the eighteenth century, they dueled for control of commerce on other continents. The second arena of warfare was in central Europe, where Austria and Prussia fought for the leadership of the German states.

Behind these international conflicts and the domestic rivalry of monarchs and nobles, however, the society of eighteenth-century Europe began to change. The character and the structures of the societies over which the monarchs ruled were beginning to take on some features associated with the modern age. These economic and social developments would eventually transform the life of Europe to a degree beside which the state building of the early eighteenth-century monarchs paled.

REVIEW QUESTIONS

1. Explain why Britain and France remained leading powers in western Europe while the United Netherlands declined.

2. How did the structure of British government change under the political leadership of Robert Walpole? What were the chief sources of Walpole's political strength?

3. How was the Hohenzollern family able to forge a conglomerate of diverse landholdings into the state of Prussia? Who were the major personalities involved in this process, and what were their individual contributions? Why was the military so important in Prussia?

4. Compare and contrast the varying success with which the Hohenzollerns and Habsburgs each handled their problems. Which family was more successful and why? Why were Sweden, the Ottoman Empire, and Poland less successful?

5. How and why did Russia emerge as a great power? Discuss the character of Peter the Great. What were Russia's domestic problems before Peter came to power? What were his methods of reform? To what extent did he succeed? How were his reforms related to his military ambitions? Compare and contrast Peter the Great with Louis XIV of France.

6. Consider how between approximately 1685 and 1740 the problems and uncertainties of who would and could succeed to the thrones of the various states constutited one of the major political and diplomatic problems of European politics.

SUGGESTED READINGS

T. M. BARKER, *Army, Aristocracy, Monarchy: Essays in War, Society and Government in Austria, 1618–1780* (1982). Examines the intricate power relationships among these major institutions.

J. BLACK, *Eighteenth-Century Europe, 1700–1789* (1990). An excellent survey.

C. R. BOXER, *The Dutch Seaborne Empire* (1965). Remains the best treatment of the subject.

J. BREWER, *The Sinews of Power: War, Money and the English State, 1688–1783* (1989). An extremely important study of the financial basis of English power.

F. L. CARSTEN, *The Origins of Prussia* (1954). Discusses the groundwork laid by the Great Elector in the seventeenth century.

J. C. D. CLARK, *English Society: 1688–1832: Social Structure and Political Practice during the Ancien Régime* (1985). An important, controversial work that emphasizes the role of religion in English political life.

N. DAVIS, *God's Playground*, Vol. 1 (1991). Excellent on prepartition Poland.

W. DOYLE, *The Old European Order, 1660–1800* (1992). The most thoughtful treatment of the subject.

R. R. ERGANG, *The Potsdam Führer* (1941). The biography of Frederick William I.

R. J. W. EVANS, *The Making of the Habsburg Monarchy, 1550–1700: An Interpretation* (1979). Places much emphasis on intellectual factors and the role of religion.

F. FORD, *Robe and Sword: The Regrouping of the French Aristocracy after Louis XIV* (1953). An important book for political, social, and intellectual history.

L. HUGHES, *Russia in the Age of Peter the Great* (1998). Will likely stand for some time as the standard work.

C. J. INGRAO, *The Habsburg Monarchy, 1618–1815* (1994). The best recent survey.

J. I. ISRAEL, *The Dutch Republic, Its Rise, Greatness, and Fall, 1477–1806* (1995). The major survey of the subject.

R. A. KANN AND Z. V. DAVID, *The Peoples of the Eastern Habsburg Lands, 1526–1918* (1984). A helpful overview of the subject.

D. MCKAY AND H. M. SCOTT, *The Rise of the Great Powers, 1648–1815* (1983). Now the standard survey.

R. K. MASSIE, *Peter the Great: His Life and His World* (1980). A good popular biography.

G. PARKER, *The Military Revolution: Military Innovation and the Rise of the West (1500–1800)* (1988). A major work.

J. H. PLUMB, *The Growth of Political Stability in England, 1675–1725* (1969). Remains an important interpretive work.

J. L. PRICE, *The Dutch Republic in the Seventeenth Century* (1998). A sophisticated, concise introduction.

N. V. RIASANOVSKY, *The Image of Peter the Great in Russian History and Thought* (1985). Examines the legacy of Peter in Russian history.

S. SCHAMA, *An Embarrassment of Riches: An Interpretation of Dutch Culture in the Golden Age* (1987). Lively and controversial.

P. F. SUGAR, *Southeastern Europe under Ottoman Rule, 1354–1804* (1977). An extremely clear presentation.

Chapter 16

During the eighteenth century, with their employment opportunities tightly restricted, many unmarried women and widows served as governesses to children of the aristocracy and other wealthy groups in Europe. At the other end of the spectrum, many children born out of wedlock or to very poor parents might be left at foundling hospitals where many of them died quite young.

Chardin, Jean-Baptiste-Simeone: *The Governess* (#6432), National Gallery of Canada, Ottawa

Society and Economy Under the Old Regime in the Eighteenth Century

KEY TOPICS

- The varied privileges and powers of Europe's aristocracies in the Old Regime and their efforts to increase their wealth
- The plight of rural peasants
- Family structure and family economy
- The transformation of Europe's economy by the agricultural and industrial revolutions
- Urban growth and the social tensions that accompanied it
- The strains on the institutions of the Old Regime brought about by social change

During the French Revolution and the turmoil spawned by that upheaval, it became customary to refer to the patterns of social, political, and economic relationships that had existed in France before 1789 as the ancien régime, or the Old Regime. The term has come to be applied generally to the life and institutions of prerevolutionary Europe. Politically, it meant the rule of theoretically absolute monarchies with growing bureaucracies *and aristocratically led armies. Economically, a scarcity of food, the predominance of agriculture, slow transport, a low level of iron production, comparatively unsophisticated financial institutions, and, in some cases, competitive commercial overseas empires characterized the Old Regime. Socially, men and women living during the period saw themselves less as individuals than as members of distinct corporate bodies that possessed certain privileges or rights as a group.*

Tradition, hierarchy, a corporate feeling, and privilege were the chief social characteristics of the Old Regime. Yet it was by no means a static society. Change and innovation were fermenting in its midst. Farming became more commercialized, and both food production and the size of the population increased. The early stages of the Industrial Revolution made more consumer goods available, and domestic consumption expanded throughout the century. The colonies in the Americas provided strong demand for European goods and manufactures. Merchants in seaports and other cities were expanding their businesses. By preparing their states for war, European governments put new demands on the resources and the economic organizations of their nations. The spirit of rationality that had been so important to the Scientific Revolution of the seventeenth century continued to manifest itself in the economic life of the eighteenth century. The Old Regime itself fostered the changes that eventually transformed it into a different kind of society.

Major Features of Life in the Old Regime

Socially, prerevolutionary Europe was based on (1) aristocratic elites possessing a wide variety of inherited legal privileges; (2) established churches intimately related to the state and the aristocracy; (3) an urban labor force usually organized into guilds; and (4) a rural peasantry subject to high taxes and feudal dues. Of course, the men and women living during this period did not know it was the Old Regime. Most of them earned their livelihoods and passed their lives as their forebears had done for generations before them and as they expected their children to do after them.

Maintenance of Tradition

During the eighteenth century, the past weighed more heavily on people's minds than did the future. Few persons outside the government bureaucracies, the expanding merchant groups, and the movement for reform called the Enlightenment (see Chapter 18) considered change or innovation desirable. This was especially true of social relationships. Both nobles and peasants, for different reasons, repeatedly called for the restoration of traditional, or customary, rights. The nobles asserted what they considered their ancient rights against the intrusion of the expanding monarchical bureaucracies. The peasants, through petitions and revolts, called for the revival or the maintenance of the customary manorial rights that allowed them access to particular lands, courts, or grievance procedures.

Except for the early industrial development in Britain and the accompanying expansion of personal consumption, the eighteenth-century economy was also predominantly traditional. The quality and quantity of the grain harvest remained the most important fact of life for most of the population and the gravest concern for governments.

Hierarchy and Privilege

Closely related to this traditional social and economic outlook was the hierarchical structure of the society. The medieval sense of rank and degree not only persisted, but became more rigid during the century. In several continental cities, sumptuary laws regulating the dress of the different classes remained on the books. These laws forbade persons in one class or occupation from wearing clothes like those worn by their social superiors. The laws, which sought to make the social hierarchy easily visible, were largely ineffective by this time. What really enforced the hierarchy was the corporate nature of social relationships.

Each state or society was considered a community composed of numerous smaller communities. Eighteenth-century Europeans did not enjoy what Americans regard as "individual rights." Instead, a person enjoyed such rights and privileges as were guaranteed to the particular communities or groups of which she or he was a part. The "community" might include the village, the municipality, the nobility, the church, the guild, a university, or the parish. In turn, each of these bodies enjoyed certain privileges, some great and some small. The privileges might involve exemption from taxation or from some especially humiliating punishment, the right to practice a trade or craft, the right of one's children to pursue a particular occupation, or, for the church, the right to collect the tithe.

The Aristocracy

The eighteenth century was the great age of the aristocracy. The nobility constituted approximately 1 to 5 percent of the population of any given country. Yet in every country, the nobility was the single wealthiest sector of the population, had the widest degree of social, political, and economic power, and set the tone

The foundation of aristocratic life was the possession of land. English aristocrats and large landowners controlled local government as well as the English Parliament. This painting of Robert Andrews and his wife by Thomas Gainsborough (1728–1788) shows an aristocratic couple on their estate. The gun and the hunting dog in this portrait suggest the importance landowners assigned to the virtually exclusive hunting privileges they enjoyed on their land. © National Gallery, London

of polite society. In most countries, the nobility had their own separate house in the parliament, estates, or diet. Only nobles had any kind of representation in Hungary and Poland. Land continued to provide the aristocracy with its largest source of income, but aristocrats did not merely own estates: Their influence was felt throughout social and economic life. In much of Europe, however, it was felt that manual labor was regarded as beneath a noble. In Spain, it was assumed that even the poorer nobles would lead lives of idleness. In other nations, however, the nobility often fostered economic innovation and embraced the commercial spirit. Such willingness to change helped protect the nobility's wealth.

Varieties of Aristocratic Privilege

To be an aristocrat was a matter of birth and legal privilege. This much the aristocracy had in common across the Continent. In almost every other respect, they differed markedly from country to country.

BRITISH NOBILITY   The smallest, wealthiest, best-defined, and most socially responsible aristocracy resided in Great Britain. It consisted of about 400 families, and the eldest male members of each family sat in the House of Lords. Through the corruptions of the electoral system, these families also controlled many seats in the House of Commons. The estates of the British nobility ranged from a few thousand to fifty thousand acres, from which they received rents. The nobles owned about one-fourth of all the arable land in the country. Increasingly, the British aristocracy invested its wealth in commerce, canals, urban real estate, mines, and even industrial ventures. Because only the eldest son inherited the title and the land, younger sons moved into commerce, the army, the professions, and the church. British landowners in both houses of Parliament levied taxes and also paid them. They had few significant legal privileges, but their direct or indirect control of local government gave them immense political power and social influence. The aristocracy dominated the society and politics of the English counties. Their country houses, many of which were built in the eighteenth century, were centers for local society.

FRENCH NOBILITY   The situation of the continental nobilities was less clear cut. In France, the approximately 400,000 nobles were divided between nobles "of the sword," or those whose nobility was derived from military service, and those "of the robe," or those who had acquired their titles either by serving in the bureaucracy or by having purchased them. The two groups had quarreled in the past, but often cooperated during the eighteenth century to defend their common privileges.

The French nobles were also divided between those who held office or favor with the royal court at Versailles and those who did not. The court nobility reaped the immense wealth that could be gained from holding high office. The nobles' hold on such offices intensified during the century. By the late 1780s, appointments to the church, the army, and the bureaucracy, as well as other profitable positions, tended to go to the nobles already established in court circles. Whereas these well-connected aristocrats were rich, the provincial nobility, called *hobereaux*, were often little better off than wealthy peasants.

Despite differences in rank, origin, and wealth, certain hereditary privileges set all French aristocrats apart from the rest of society. They were exempt from many taxes. For example, most French nobles did not pay the *taille*, or land tax, the basic tax of the Old Regime. The nobles were technically liable for payment of the *vingtième*, or the "twentieth," which resembled an income tax, but they rarely had to pay it in full. The nobles were not liable for the royal *corvées*, or forced labor on public works, which fell on the peasants. In addition to these exemptions, French nobles could collect feudal dues from their tenants and enjoyed exclusive hunting and fishing privileges.

EASTERN EUROPEAN NOBILITIES East of the Elbe River, the character of the nobility became even more complicated and repressive. Throughout the area, the military traditions of the aristocracy remained important. In Poland, there were thousands of nobles, or *szlachta*, who were entirely exempt from taxes after 1741. Until 1768, these Polish aristocrats possessed the right of life and death over their serfs. Most of the Polish nobility were relatively poor. A few rich nobles who had immense estates exercised political power in the fragile Polish state.

In Austria and Hungary, the nobility continued to possess broad judicial powers over the peasantry through their manorial courts. They also enjoyed various degrees of exemption from taxation. The wealthiest of them, Prince Esterhazy of Hungary, owned ten million acres of land.

In Prussia, after the accession of Frederick the Great in 1740, the position of the Junker nobles became much stronger. Frederick's various wars required their full support. He drew his officers almost wholly from the Junker class. Nobles also increasingly made up the bureaucracy. As in other parts of eastern Europe, the Prussian nobles had extensive judicial authority over the serfs.

In Russia, the eighteenth century saw what amounted to the creation of the nobility. Peter the Great's (r. 1682–1725) linking of state service and noble social status through the Table of Ranks (1722) established among Russian nobles a self-conscious class identity that had not previously existed. Thereafter, they were determined to resist compulsory state service. In 1736, Empress Anna (r. 1730–1740) reduced such service to twenty-five years. In 1762, Peter III (r. 1762) exempted the greatest nobles entirely from compulsory service. In 1785, in the Charter of the Nobility, Catherine the Great (r. 1762–1796) legally defined the rights and privileges of noble men and women in exchange for the assurance that the nobility would serve the state voluntarily. Noble privileges included the right of transmitting noble status to a nobleman's wife and children, the judicial protection of noble rights and property, considerable power over the serfs, and exemption from personal taxes.

Aristocratic Resurgence

The Russian Charter of the Nobility constituted one aspect of the broader European-wide development termed the "aristocratic resurgence." This was the nobility's reaction to the threat to their social position and privileges that they felt from the expanding power of the monarchies. This resurgence took several forms in the eighteenth century. First, all nobilities tried to preserve their exclusiveness by making it more difficult to become a noble. Second, they pushed to reserve appointments to the officer corps of the armies, the bureaucracies, the government ministries, and the church exclusively for nobles. By doing this, they hoped to resist the encroaching power of the monarchies.

Third, the nobles attempted to use the authority of existing aristocratically controlled institutions against the power of the monarchies. These institutions included the British Parliament, the French courts, or *parlements*, and the local aristocratic estates and provincial diets in Germany and the Habsburg Empire.

Fourth, the nobility sought to improve its financial position by gaining further exemptions from taxation or by collecting higher rents or long-forgotten feudal dues from the peasantry. The nobility tried to shore up its position by various appeals to traditional and often ancient privileges that had lapsed over time. This aristocratic challenge to the monarchies was a fundamental political fact of the day and potentially a very disruptive one.

The Land and Its Tillers

Land was the economic basis of eighteenth-century life and the foundation of the status and power of the nobility. Well over three-fourths of all Europeans lived in the country, and few of them ever traveled more than a few miles from their birthplace. Except for the nobility and the wealthier nonaristocratic landowners, most people who dwelled on the land were poor—in many regions, desparately poor. They lived in various states of economic and social dependency, exploitation, and vulnerability.

Peasants and Serfs

Rural social dependency related directly to the land. The nature of the dependency differed sharply for free peasants, such as English tenants and most French cultivators, and for the serfs of Germany, Austria, and Russia, who were legally bound to a particular plot of land and a particular lord. But everywhere, the class that owned most of the land also controlled the local government and the courts. For example, in Great Britain, all farmers and smaller tenants had the legal rights of English citizens. The justices of the peace, however, who presided over the county courts and who could call out the local militia, were always substantial landowners, as were the members of Parliament, who made the laws. In eastern Europe, the landowners presided over the manorial courts. On the Continent, the burden of taxation fell on the tillers of the soil.

OBLIGATIONS OF PEASANTS   The power of the landlord increased as one moved across Europe from west to east. Most French peasants owned some land, but there were a few serfs in eastern France. Nearly all French peasants were subject to certain feudal dues, called *banalités*. These included the required use-for-payment of the lord's, or *seigneur's*, mill to grind grain and his oven to bake bread. The *seigneur* could also require a certain number of days each year of the peasant's labor. This practice of forced labor was termed the *corvée*. Because even landowning French peasants rarely possessed enough land to support their families, they had to rent more land from the *seigneur* and were also subject to feudal dues attached to those plots. In Prussia and Austria, despite attempts by the monar-

Eighteen-century France had some of the best roads in the world, but they were often built with forced labor. French peasants were required to work part of each year on such projects. This system, called the corvée, *was not abolished until the French Revolution in 1789.*   Claude Joseph Vernet, *Construction of a Road.* Louvre, Paris, France. Giraudon/Art Resource, NY

Russian Serfs Lament Their Condition

As with other illiterate groups in European history, it is difficult to recapture the voices of Russians serfs. The following verses from "The Slaves' Lament," a popular ballad from the era of the Pugachev Rebellion (1773–1775), indicate that the serfs were aware of how the legislation of that era which favored the landowning classes affected their lives. The verses embody the resentment that Pugachev's Rebellion ignited. Note how the verses suggest that the Tsar may be more favorable to serfs than their landowners are. Pugachev claimed to be Tsar Peter III, and many Russian serfs believed him and thus considered him a liberator from landlord tyranny. Throughout this ballad, serfs present themselves as slaves.

❖ *What specific complaints about landlords are expressed in these verses? What charges indicate that serfs may believe that their situation has worsened? What hope do they seem to place in the Tsar? What idealized picture of the world do the serfs believe they would themselves create?*

O woe to us slaves living for the masters!
We do not know how to serve their ferocity!
Service is like a sharp scythe;
And kindness is like the morning dew.

* * * * *

Brothers, how annoying it is to us
And how shameful and insulting
That another who is not worthy to be equal
   with us
Has so many of us in his power.

* * * * *

And if we steal from the lord one half
   kopeck,
The law commands us to be killed like a
   louse.
And if the master steals ten thousand,
Nobody will judge who should be hanged.
The injustice of the Russian sheriffs has
   increased:
Whoever brings a present is right beyond
   argument.
They have stopped putting their trust in the
   Creator for authority,
And have become accustomed to own us like
   cattle.
All nations rebuke us and wonder at our
   stupidity,
That such stupid people are born in Russia.
And indeed, stupidity was rooted in us long ago,
as each honour here has been given to vagrants.
The master can kill the servant like a gelding;
The denunciation by a slave cannot be believed.
Unjust judges have composed a decree

That we should be tyrannically whipped with a
   knout for that.

* * * * *

Better that we should agree to serve the tsar.
Better to live in dark woods
Than to be before the eyes of these tyrants;
They look on us cruelly with their eyes
And eat us as iron eats rye. No one wants to
   serve the tsar
But only to grind us down to the end.
And they try to collect unjust bribes,
And they are not frightened that people die cruelly.

* * * * *

Ah brothers, if we got our freedom,
We would not take the lands or the fields for
   ourselves.
We would go into service as soldiers, brothers,
And would be friendly among ourselves,
Would destroy all injustice
And remove the root of evil lords.

* * * * *

They [the landlords] sell all the good rye to
   the merchants,
And give us like pigs the bad.
The greedy lords eat meat at fast time,
And even when meat is allowed, the slaves
   must cook meatless cabbage soup.
O brothers, it is our misfortune
always to have rye kasha.
The lords drink and make merry,
And do not allow the slaves even to burst
   out laughing.

From Paul Dukes, trans. and ed., *Russia under Catherine the Great: Select Documents on Government and Society* (Oriental Research Partners, 1978), pp. 115–117. Reprinted by permission of Oriental Research Partners.

chies late in the century to improve the lot of the serfs, the landlords continued to exercise almost complete control over them. In many of the Habsburg lands, law and custom required the serfs to provide service, or *robot*, to the lords.

Serfs were worst off in Russia. There, nobles reckoned their wealth by the number of "souls," or male serfs, owned rather than by the acreage the landlord possessed. Russian landlords, in effect, regarded serfs merely as economic commodities. They could demand as many as six days a week of labor, known as *barshchina*, from the serfs. Like Prussian and Austrian landlords, they enjoyed the right to punish their serfs. On their own authority, Russian landlords could even exile a serf to Siberia. Serfs had no legal recourse against the orders and whims of their lords. There was little difference between Russian serfdom and slavery.

In southeastern Europe, where the Ottoman Empire held sway, peasants were free, though landlords tried to exert authority in every way. The domain of the landlords was termed a *çift*. The landlord was often an absentee who managed the estate through an overseer. During the seventeenth and eighteenth centuries, these landlords, like those elsewhere in Europe, often became more commercially oriented and turned to the production of crops, such as cotton, vegetables, potatoes, and maize, that could be sold in the market.

A scarcity of labor rather than the recognition of their legal rights supported the independence of the southeastern European peasants. A peasant might migrate from one landlord to another. Because the second landlord needed the peasant's labor, he had no reason to return him to the original landlord. During the seventeenth and eighteenth centuries, however, disorder originating in the capital of Constantinople (now Istanbul) spilled over into the Balkan Peninsula. In this climate, landlords increased their authority by offering their peasants protection from bandits or rebels who might destroy peasant villages. As in medieval times, the manor house or armed enclosure of a local landlord became the peasants' refuge. These landlords also owned all the housing and tools required by the peasants and furnished their seed grain. Consequently, despite legal independence, Balkan peasants under the Ottoman Empire became largely dependent upon the landlords, though never to the extent of serfs in eastern Europe or Russia.

PEASANT REBELLIONS   The Russian monarchy itself contributed to the further degradation of the serfs. Peter the Great gave whole villages to favored nobles. Later in the century, Catherine the Great confirmed the authority of the nobles over their serfs in exchange for the landowners' political cooperation. Russia experienced vast peasant unrest, with well over fifty

Emelyan Pugachev (1726–1775) led the largest peasant revolt in Russian history. In this contemporary propaganda picture he is shown in chains. An inscription in Russian and German was printed below the picture decrying the evils of revolution and insurrection.
Bildarchiv Preussischer Kulturbesitz

peasant revolts occurring between 1762 and 1769. These culminated in Pugachev's Rebellion between 1773 and 1775, when Emelyan Pugachev (1726–1775) promised the serfs land of their own and freedom from their lords. (See "Russian Serfs Lament Their Condition.") All of southern Russia was in turmoil until the government brutally suppressed the rebellion. Thereafter, any thought of liberalizing or improving the condition of the serfs was set aside for a generation.

Pugachev's was the largest peasant uprising of the eighteenth century, but smaller peasant revolts or disturbances took place in Bohemia in 1775, in Transylvania in 1784, in Moravia in 1786, and in Austria in 1789. There were almost no revolts in western Europe, but England experienced many rural riots. Rural rebellions were violent, but the peasants and serfs normally directed their wrath against property rather than persons. The rebels usually sought to reassert traditional or customary rights against practices that they perceived as innovations. Their targets were carefully chosen and included unfair pricing, onerous new or increased feudal dues, changes in methods of payment or land use, unjust officials, or extraordinarily brutal overseers and landlords. Peasant revolts were thus conservative in nature.

Aristocratic Domination of the Countryside: The English Game Laws

One of the clearest examples of aristocratic domination of the countryside and of aristocratic manipulation of the law to its own advantage was English legislation on hunting.

Between 1671 and 1831, English landowners had the exclusive legal right to hunt game animals, including, in particular, hares, partridges, pheasants, and moor fowl. Similar legislation covered other animals such as deer, the killing of which by an unauthorized person became a capital offense in the eighteenth century. By law, only persons owning a particular amount of landed property could hunt these animals. Excluded from the right to hunt were all persons renting land, wealthy city merchants who did not own land, and poor people in cities, villages, and the countryside. The poor were excluded because the elite believed that allowing the poor to enjoy the sport of hunting would undermine their work habits. The city merchants were excluded because the landed gentry in Parliament wanted to demonstrate visibly and legally the superiority of landed wealth over commercial wealth. Thus, the various game laws upheld the superior status of the aristocracy and the landed gentry.

The game laws represent a prime example of legislation related directly to economic and social status. The gentry who benefitted from the laws and whose parliamentary representatives had passed them also served as the local justices of the peace who administered the laws and punished their violation. The justices of the peace could levy fines and even have poachers impressed into the army. Gentry could also take civil legal action against wealthier poachers, such as rich farmers who rented land, and thus saddle them with immense legal fees. The gentry also employed gamekeepers to protect game from poachers. The gamekeepers were known to kill the dogs belonging to people suspected of poaching. By the middle of the century, gamekeepers had devised guns to shoot poachers who tripped their hidden levers.

A small industry arose to circumvent the game laws, however. Many poor people living either on an estate or in a nearby village would kill game for food. They believed that the game actually belonged to the community, and this poaching increased during hard times. Poaching was thus one way for the poor to find food.

Even more important was the black market in game animals sustained by the demand of urban people for this kind of luxury meat. Here arose the possibility of poaching for profit, and indeed, poaching technically meant the stealing or killing of game for sale. Local people from both the countryside and the villages would steal the game and then sell it to intermediaries called *higglers*. Later, coachmen took over this function. The higglers and the coachmen would smuggle the game into the cities, where poulterers would sell it at a premium price. Everyone involved made a bit of money along the way. During the second half of the century, English aristocrats began to construct large game preserves. The rural poor, who had lost their rights to communal land as a result of its enclosure by the large landowners, deeply resented these preserves, which soon became hunting grounds to organized gangs of poachers.

Penalties against poaching increased in the 1790s after the outbreak of the French Revolution, but so did the amount of poaching as the economic hardships caused by Britain's participation in the wars of the era put a greater burden on poor people and as the demand for food in English cities grew along with their population. By the 1820s, both landowners and reformers called for a change in the law. In 1831 Parliament rewrote the game laws, retaining the landowners' possession of the game, but permitting them to allow other people to hunt it. Poaching continued, but the exclusive right of the landed classes to hunt game had ended.

Family Structures and the Family Economy

In preindustrial Europe, the household was the basic unit of production and consumption. Few productive establishments employed more than a handful of people not belonging to the family of the owner, and those rare exceptions were in cities. The overwhelming majority of Europeans, however, lived in rural areas. There, as well as in small towns and cities, the household mode of organization predominated on farms, in artisans' workshops, and in small merchants' shops. With that mode of economic organization, there developed what is known as the family economy. Its structure as described here had prevailed over most of Europe for centuries.

Households

What was a household in the preindustrial Europe of the Old Regime? There were two basic models, one characterizing northwestern Europe and the other eastern Europe.

NORTHWESTERN EUROPE   In northwestern Europe, the household almost invariably consisted of a married couple, their children through their early teenage years, and their servants. Except for the few wealthy people, households were small, usu-

During the eighteenth century, most goods were produced in small workshops such as this iron forge painted by Joseph Wright of Derby (1734–1797), or in the homes of artisans. Not until very late in the century, with the early stages of industrialization, did a few factories appear. In the small early workshops, it would not have been uncommon for the family of the owner to visit, as portrayed in this painting. The Iron Forge, 1772 (oil on canvas) by Joseph Wright of Derby (1734–97). Broadlands Trust, Hants/Bridgeman Art Library, London.

ally consisting of not more than five or six members. Furthermore, in these households, more than two generations of a family rarely lived under the same roof. High mortality and late marriage prevented formation of families of three generations. In other words, grandparents rarely lived in the same household as their grandchildren, and families consisted of parents and children. The family structure of northwestern Europe was thus nuclear rather than extended.

Prior to recent research into family structures, historians had assumed that before industrialization Europeans lived in extended familial settings, with several generations living together in a household. Demographic investigation has now sharply reversed this picture. Children lived with their parents only until their early teens. Then they normally left home, usually to enter the work force of young servants who lived and worked in another household. A child of a skilled artisan might remain with his or her parents to learn a valuable skill; but only rarely would more than one child do so, because children's labor was more remunerative outside the home.

Those young men and women who had left home would eventually marry and form an independent household of their own. This practice of moving away from home is known as *neolocalism*. These young people married relatively late. Men were usually over twenty-six, and women over twenty-three. The new couple usually had children as soon after marriage as possible. Frequently, the woman was already pregnant at marriage. Family and community pressure often compelled the man to marry her. In any case, premarital sexual relations were common, though illegitimate births were rare. The new couple would soon employ a servant, who, together with their growing children, would undertake whatever form of livelihood the household used to support itself.

The word *servant* in this context may be confusing. It does not refer to someone looking after the needs of wealthy people. Rather, in preindustrial Europe, a servant was a person—either male or female—who was hired, often under a clear contract, to work for the head of the household in exchange for room, board, and wages. The servant was usually young and by no means always socially inferior to his or her employer. Normally, the servant was an integral part of the household and ate with the family.

Young men and women became servants when their labor was no longer needed in their parents' household or when they could earn more money for their family outside the parental household. Being a servant for several years—often as many as eight or ten—allowed young people to acquire the productive skills and the monetary savings necessary to begin their own household. These years spent as servants largely account for the late age of marriage in northwestern Europe.

EASTERN EUROPE As one moved eastward across the continent, the structure of the household and the pattern of marriage changed. In eastern Europe, both men and women usually married before the age of twenty. Consequently, children were born to much younger parents. Often—especially among Russian serfs—wives were older than their husbands. Eastern European households were generally larger than those in the West. Frequently a rural Russian household consisted of more than nine, and possibly more than twenty, members, with three or perhaps even four generations of the same family living together. Early marriage made this situation more likely. In Russia, marrying involved not starting a new household, but remaining in and expanding one already established.

The landholding structure in eastern Europe accounts, at least in part, for these patterns of marriage and the family. The lords of the manor who owned land wanted to ensure that it would be cultivated so they could receive their rents. Thus, in Poland, for example, landlords might forbid marriage between their own serfs and those from another estate. They might also require widows and widowers to remarry to assure adequate labor for a particular plot of land. Polish landlords also frowned on the hiring of free laborers—the equivalent of servants in the west—to help cultivate land. The landlords preferred to use other serfs. This practice inhibited the formation of independent households. In Russia, landlords ordered the families of young people in their villages to arrange marriages within a short, set time. These lords discouraged single-generation family households because the death or serious illness of one person in such a household might mean that the land assigned to it would go out of cultivation.

The Family Economy

Throughout Europe, most people worked within the family economy. That is to say, the household was the basic unit of production and consumption. Almost everyone lived within a household of some kind because it was virtually impossible for ordinary people to support themselves independently. Indeed, except for members of religious orders, people living outside a household were viewed with great suspicion. They were considered potentially criminal, disruptive, or at least dependent on the charity of others. Everywhere beggars met deep hostility. (See "Rules for the Berlin Poor House.")

Depending on their ages and skills, everyone in the household worked. The need to survive poor harvests or economic slumps meant that no one could be idle. Within this family economy, all goods and income produced went to the benefit of the household rather than to the individual family member. On a farm, much of the effort went directly into raising food or producing other agricultural goods that could be exchanged for food. Few western Europeans, however, had enough land to support their household from farming alone. Thus, one or more family members might work elsewhere and send wages home. For example, the father and older children might work as harvesters or might fish or might engage in other labor, either in the neighborhood or farther from home. If the father was such a migrant worker, the burden of farmwork would fall on his wife and their younger children. This was not an uncommon pattern.

The family economy also dominated the life of skilled urban artisans. The father was usually the chief artisan. He normally employed one or more servants, but would expect his children to work in the enterprise also. His eldest child was usually trained in the trade. His wife often sold his wares or opened a small shop of her own. Wives of merchants also frequently ran their husbands' businesses, especially when the husband traveled to purchase new goods. In any case, everyone in the family was involved. If business was poor, family members would look for employment elsewhere—not to support themselves as individuals, but to ensure the survival of the family unit.

In western Europe, the death of a father often brought disaster to the economy of the household. The continuing economic life of the family usually depended on his land or skills. The widow might take on the farm or the business, or his children might do so. The widow usually sought to remarry quickly to restore the labor and skills of a male to the household and to prevent herself from becoming dependent on relatives or charity.

The high mortality rate of the time meant that many households were reconstituted second-family groups that included stepchildren. Because of the advanced age of the widow or economic hard times, however, some households might simply dissolve. The widow became dependent on charity or relatives. The children became similarly dependent or entered the work force of servants earlier than they

Rules for the Berlin Poor House

Poverty was an enormous problem in eighteenth-century Europe, often forcing family members to work away from home and creating thousands of migrant workers and beggars. Governments were hostile to beggars and sometimes migrant workers, whom they regarded as a potential source of crime and disorder. Many of these concerns are evident in the regulations for the Berlin Poor House.

❖ *What were the distinctions made between the poor who deserved sympathy and those who did not? How would such a distinction affect social policy? Why might beggars have been regarded as dangers to public order? What attitudes toward work are displayed in these regulations?*

Whereas His Majesty...has renewed the prohibition of begging in the streets and in houses and has made all giving of alms punishable; it is decided to inform the public of the present measures for the relief of the poor, and to acquaint it with the main outlines of the above order:

1. In the new workhouse,...the genuinely needy and the poor deserving sympathy shall be cared for better than hitherto, but the deliberate beggars shall more resolutely be made to work.

2. The past organization of this house has therefore been totally altered, so that all persons to be received in it shall be divided into two entirely separate main classes, differentiated both in the status of their work and its location, in their dormitory and in their board.

3. The first class is meant for the old and for other persons deserving help and sympathy, who cannot entirely live by their work and do not wish to beg. Those report to the Poor's Chest in the Town Hall of Berlin, with a certificate from the Minister of their Church, showing their hitherto unblemished character, and after their references have been checked, they shall be accepted. They spin in the house as much wool as their age and health permits, and if they spin more than the cost of their keep, the surplus shall be paid out to them....

5. The second main class is destined for those who do not wish to make use of this benefaction, but would rather live by begging. These deliberate beggars will be arrested by the Poor Law Constables, if necessary with the assistance of the Police, irrespective of age or status, whether they be vagabonds, journeymen, citizens, discharged soldiers, their wives or children, and will be sent to the workhouse.

6. Those who are caught begging for the first time shall be put into this class for three months at least, for the second time, for a year, and for the third and later times for several years, according to circumstances, for life.

7. Similarly, this class is destined for those who after due process of law have been sent for punishment as runaway servants and apprentices, for a period of time determined by the Court.

8. All the persons under numbers 5, 6, and 7 shall be forced to spin and prepare wool, and shall be kept on a minimum standard, clearly differentiated from the first class, both in the status and quantity of their work in their board and their lodging.

9. The children shall be cared for separately,...and shall receive education for several hours a day....

10. Before a beggar is discharged, he must, in order that he shall not again become a public nuisance, prove an occupation in prospect or the existence of relations or of other persons, who will look after him and will put him up at once....

Kruegeger, *Geschichte der Manufacturen...*, as quoted and translated in S. Pollard and C. Holmes, eds., *Documents of European Economic History*, Vol. I (London: Edward Arnold, 1968), pp. 166–167. Reprinted by Permission of Edward Arnold Ltd.

would otherwise. In other cases, the situation could be so desperate that they would resort to crime or to begging. The personal, emotional, and economic vulnerability of the family cannot be overemphasized.

In eastern Europe, the family economy functioned in the context of serfdom and landlord domination. Peasants clearly thought in terms of their families and expanding the land available for cultivation. The village structure may have mitigated the pressures of the family economy, as did the multigenerational family. Dependence on the available land was the chief fact of life. There were many fewer artisan and merchant households, and there was far less geographical mobility than in western Europe.

Women and the Family Economy

The family economy established many of the chief constraints on the lives and personal experiences of women in preindustrial society. Most of the historical research that has been undertaken on this subject relates to western Europe. There, a woman's life experience was largely the function of her capacity to establish and maintain a household. For women, marriage was an economic necessity, as well as an institution that fulfilled sexual and psychological needs. Outside a household, a woman's life was vulnerable and precarious. Some women succeeded in becoming economically independent. They were the exception. Normally, unless she were an aristocrat or a member of a religious order, a woman probably could not support herself solely by her own efforts. Consequently, a woman devoted much of her life first to maintaining her parents' household and then to devising some means of getting her own household to live in as an adult. Bearing and rearing children were usually subordinate to these goals.

By the age of seven, a girl would have begun to help with the household work. On a farm, this might mean looking after chickens, watering the animals, or carrying food to adults working the land. In an urban artisan's household, she would do light work, perhaps cleaning or carrying and later sewing or weaving. The girl would remain in her parents' home as long as she made a real contribution to the family enterprise or as long as her labor elsewhere was not more remunerative to the family.

An artisan's daughter might not leave home until marriage, because at home she could learn increasingly valuable skills associated with the trade. The situation was different for the much larger number of girls growing up on farms. Their parents and brothers could often do all the necessary farmwork, and a girl's labor at home quickly became of little value to her family. She would then leave home, usually between the ages of twelve and fourteen. She might take up residence on another farm, but more likely she would migrate to a nearby town or city. She would rarely travel more than thirty miles from her parents' household. She would then normally become a servant, once again living in a household, but this time in the household of an employer. (See "Art & the West.")

Having migrated from home, the young woman's chief goal was to accumulate enough capital for a dowry. Her savings would make her eligible for marriage, because they would allow her to make the necessary contribution to form a household with her husband. Marriage within the family economy was a joint economic undertaking, and the wife was expected to make an immediate contribution of capital for establishing the household. A young woman might well work for ten years or more to accumulate a dowry. This practice meant that marriage was usually postponed until her mid- to late twenties.

Within marriage, earning enough money or producing enough farm goods to ensure an adequate food supply dominated women's concerns. Domestic duties, childbearing, and child rearing were subordinate to economic pressures. Consequently, couples tried to limit the number of children they had, usually through the practice of *coitus interruptus*, the withdrawal of the male before ejaculation. Parents often placed young children with wet nurses so the mother could continue to make her economic contribution to the household. The wet nurse, in turn, contributed to the economic welfare of her own household. The child would be fully reintegrated into its own family when it was weaned and would then be expected to aid the family at an early age.

The work of married women differed markedly between city and country and was in many ways a function of their husbands' occupations. If the peasant household had enough land to support itself, the wife spent much of her time quite literally carrying things for her husband—water, food, seed, harvested grain, and the like. There were few such adequate landholdings, however. If the husband had to do work besides farming, such as fishing or migrant labor, the wife might actually be in charge of the farm and do the ploughing, planting, and harvesting. In the city, the wife of an artisan or a merchant might well be in charge of the household finances and actively participate in managing the trade or manufacturing enterprise. When her husband died, she might take over the business and perhaps hire an artisan. Finally, if economic disaster struck the family, it was usually the wife who organized what Olwen Hufton has called the "economy of expedients,"[1] within which family members might be sent off to find work elsewhere or even to beg in the streets.

Despite all this economic activity, women found many occupations and professions closed to them because they were women. They labored with less education than men, because in such a society women at all levels of life consistently found fewer opportunities for education than men. They often received lower wages than men for the same work. As will be discussed later in the chapter, all of these disabilities worsened as a result of the mechanization of agriculture and the textile industries.

[1]Olwen Hufton, "Women and the Family Economy in Eighteenth-Century France," *French Historical Studies*, 9 (1976): 19.

Children and the World of the Family Economy

For women of all social ranks, childbirth was a time of fear and personal vulnerability. Contagious diseases endangered both mother and child. Puerperal fever was frequent, as were other infections from unsterilized medical instruments. (See "An Edinburgh Physician Describe the Dangers of Childbirth.") Not all midwives were skillful practitioners. Furthermore, most mothers and children immediately encountered immense poverty and wretched housing. Assuming that both mother and child survived, the mother might nurse the infant, but often the child would be sent to a wet nurse. Convenience may have led to this practice among the wealthy, but economic necessity dictated it for the poor. The structures and customs of the family economy did not permit a woman to devote herself entirely to rearing a child. The wet-nursing industry was well organized, with urban children being frequently transported to wet nurses in the country, where they would remain for months or even years.

Throughout Europe, the birth of a child was not always welcome. The child might represent another economic burden on an already hard-pressed household. Or it might be illegitimate.

The number of illegitimate births seems to have increased during the eighteenth century, possibly because increased migration of the population led to fleeting romances.

Through at least the end of the seventeenth century, unwanted or illegitimate births could lead to infanticide, especially among the poor. The parents might smother the infant or expose it to the elements. These practices were one result of both the ignorance and the prejudice surrounding contraception.

The late seventeenth and the early eighteenth centuries saw a new interest in preserving the lives of abandoned children. Although foundling hospitals established to care for abandoned children had existed before, their size and number expanded during these years. Two of the most famous were the Paris Foundling Hospital (1670) and the London Foundling Hospital (1739). Such hospitals cared for thousands of European children, and the demand for their services increased during the eighteenth century. For example, early in the century, an average of 1,700 children a year were admitted to the Paris Foundling Hospital. In the peak year of 1772, however, that number rose to 7,676 children. Not all of those children came from Paris. Many had been brought to the city from the provinces, where local foundling homes and hospitals were overburdened. The London Foundling Hos-

---

An Edinburgh Physician Describes the Dangers of Childbirth

Death in childbirth was a common occurrence throughout Europe until the twentieth century. This brief letter from an Edinburgh physician illustrates how devastating infectious diseases could be to women at the time of childbirth.

❖ *How does the passage illustrate a health danger that only women confronted? How might the likelihood of the death of oneself or a spouse in childbirth have affected one's attitudes toward children? How does the passage illustrate limitations on knowledge about disease in the eighteenth century?*

We had puerperal fever in the infirmary last winter. It began about the end of February, when almost every woman, as soon as she was delivered, or perhaps about twenty-four hours after, was seized with it; and all of them died, though every method was tried to cure the disorder. What was singular, the women were in good health before they were brought to bed, though some of them had been long in the hospital before delivery. One woman had been dismissed from the ward before she was brought to bed; came into it some days after with her labor upon her; was easily delivered, and remained perfectly well for twenty-four hours, when she was seized with a shivering and the other symptoms of the fever. I caused her to be removed to another ward; yet notwithstanding all the care that was taken of her she died in the same manner as the others.

From a letter to Mr. White from a Dr. Young of Edinburgh, 21 November, 1774, cited in C. White, *Treatise on the Management of Pregnant and Lying-In Women* (London, 1777), pp. 45–46, as quoted in Bridget Hill, ed., *Eighteenth-Century Women: An Anthology* (London: George Allen & Unwin, 1984), p. 102.

The Breakfast *and* Return from Market: *Two Scenes of Domestic Life*

What are known as *genre* paintings depict scenes of everyday life. Largely pioneered by the Dutch, such paintings became widespread throughout Europe during the eighteenth century. Genre painting made no claim to convey a message of universal importance. Furthermore, because the subject matter was domestic, people could enjoy these paintings without an extensive knowledge of history, classical literature, or the Bible.

French genre painters focused mostly on what would become known as the "woman's sphere" in the home. But that female domestic sphere, as illustrated in these works of Boucher and Chardin, was a complex world with numerous compartments. The home might be the feminine empire, but it was an empire of many provinces, just as there were different kinds of homes among the various social classes.

Boucher's *The Breakfast* (1739) portrays the breakfast room of a wealthy, probably nonaristocratic, family, filled with the expensive consumer goods available in Paris shops drawn from around the world. (Note, for example, the Chinese porcelain figure sitting on the shelf.) This domestic interior lacks any suggestion of political awareness or engagement in economic productivity. It is a scene of domestic, feminine consumption and child rearing

such as Rousseau would advocate in *Emile* (1762). (See Chapter 18.)

Chardin's *The Return from the Market* (1738) presents another level of the domestic sphere: that of

F. Boucher. *The Breakfast*. 1739. Paris. Louvre. Scala/Art Resource, NY

the servant. The woman in the painting appears to work in the home of a person of moderate means, perhaps a merchant. In this and other of his paintings, Chardin avoids the world of domestic consumption that appears in Boucher's painting. His interiors are worlds of domestic order and tranquillity, set aside from the bustle of an eighteenth-century city street. Domestic servants in the eight-eenth and nineteenth century were overwhelmingly women. Yet even among them, there existed a clear social hierarchy. This woman would have held a lower status than that of a governess who looked after the family's children. (See p. 512.)

Chardin was known for his remarkable ability to bring quiet dignity and warmth to the work of servants. He also suggests a certain dynamic element in the life of the family: The servant putting down the bread appears to be listening to the conversation in the other room. Later genre painters, such as the English artist Hogarth, would often suggest a strong moralizing tone, but Chardin is willing to portray his scenes without comment. He does not intrude upon the scene, which assumes a kind of timeless quality in the sense that households have needed to secure bread each day from time immemorial; this return from market is simply the most recent example. There is as much of a relaxed quality to Chardin's portrayal of this scene as there is a sense of energized arrangement in Boucher's. Chardin described his own painting as a kind of craft rather than a work of inspiration or academic rules. He seems to see his own painting as a kind of dignified everyday work, akin to the work performed by the woman returning from market.

Jean Baptiste Chardin, 1699–1799. *The Return from the Market* (*La Pourvoyeyse*). (1738). French. Musée Du Louvre, Paris/SuperStock

Albert Boime, *Art in an Age of Revolution, 1750–1800* (Chicago: University of Chicago Press, 1987); Norman Bryson, *Looking at the Overlooked: Four Essays on Still Life Painting* (Cambridge, MA.: Harvard University Press, 1990); Richard Rand, *Intimate Encounters: Love and Domesticity in Eighteenth-Century France* (Princeton, NJ: Princeton University Press, 1997).

Few children in the eighteenth century were as privileged as these in this landed English family. Most began working to help support their families as soon as they were physically able. It was during the eighteenth century, however, that Europeans apparently began to view childhood as a distinct period in human development. Even though Arthur Devis has painted these children to look something like little adults, he has included various toys associated with childhood. Arthur Devis (© 1711–1787), *Children in an Interior,* © 1742–1743, oil on canvas, 39 x 49 in. (99.0 x 125.5 cm), Yale Center for British Art, Paul Mellon Collection, B1978.43.5

pital lacked the income to deal with all the children brought to it. In the middle of the eighteenth century, the hospital found itself compelled to choose children for admission by a lottery system.

Sadness and tragedy surrounded abandoned children. Most of them were illegitimate infants from across the social spectrum. Many, however, were left with the foundling hospitals because their parents could not support them. There was a close relationship between rising food prices and increasing numbers of abandoned children in Paris. Parents would sometimes leave personal tokens or saints' medals on the abandoned baby in the vain hope that they might one day be able to reclaim the child. Few children were reclaimed. Leaving a child at a foundling hospital did not guarantee its survival. In Paris, only about 10 percent of all abandoned children lived to the age of ten.

Despite all of these perils of early childhood, children did grow up and come of age across Europe. The world of the child may not have received the kind of attention that it does today, but during the eighteenth century the seeds of that modern sensibility were sown. Particularly among the upper classes, new interest arose in the education of children. In most areas, education remained firmly in the hands of the churches. As economic skills became more demanding, literacy became more valuable, and literacy rates rose during the century. Yet most Europeans remained illiterate. Not until the late nineteenth century was the world of childhood inextricably linked to the process of education. Then children would be reared to become members of a national citizenry. In

the Old Regime, they were reared to make their contribution to the economy of their parents' family and then to set up their own households.

The Revolution in Agriculture

Thus far, this chapter has examined those groups that sought stability and that, except for certain members of the nobility, resisted change. Other groups, however, wished to pursue significant new directions in social and economic life. The remainder of the chapter will consider those forces and developments that would transform European life during the next century. These developments first appeared in agriculture.

The main goal of traditional peasant society was a stability that would ensure the local food supply. Despite differences in rural customs throughout Europe, the tillers resisted changes that might endanger the sure supply of food, which they generally believed that traditional cultivation would provide. The food supply was never certain, and the farther east one traveled, the more uncertain it became. Failure of the harvest meant not only hardship, but death from either outright starvation or protracted debility. Often, people living in the countryside had more difficulty finding food than did city dwellers, whose local government usually stored reserve supplies of grain.

Poor harvests also played havoc with prices. Smaller supplies or larger demand raised grain prices. Even small increases in the cost of food could exert heavy pressure on peasant or artisan families. If prices increased sharply, many of those families fell back on poor relief from their local municipality or county or the church.

Historians now believe that during the eighteenth century bread prices slowly but steadily rose, spurred largely by population growth. Since bread was their main food, this inflation put pressure on all of the poor. Prices rose faster than urban wages and brought no appreciable advantage to the small peasant producer. On the other hand, the rise in grain prices benefitted landowners and those wealthier peasants who had surplus grain to sell.

The rising grain prices gave landlords an opportunity to improve their incomes and lifestyle. To achieve those ends, landlords in western Europe began a series of innovations in farm production that became known as the Agricultural Revolution. Landlords commercialized agriculture and thereby challenged the traditional peasant ways of production. Peasant revolts and disturbances often resulted. The governments of Europe, hungry for new taxes and dependent on the goodwill of the nobility, used their armies and militias to smash peasants who defended the past.

NEW CROPS AND NEW METHODS The drive to improve agricultural production began during the sixteenth and seventeenth centuries in the Low Countries, where the pressures of the growing population and the shortage of land required changes in cultivation. Dutch landlords and farmers devised better ways to build dikes and drain land, so that they could farm more extensive areas. They also experimented with new crops, such as clover and turnips, that would increase the supply of animal fodder and restore the soil. These improvements became so famous that early in the seventeenth century English landlords hired Cornelius Vermuyden, a Dutch drainage engineer, to drain thousands of acres of land around Cambridge.

English landlords provided the most striking examples of eighteenth-century agricultural improvement. They originated almost no genuinely new farming methods, but they popularized ideas developed in the previous century either in the Low Countries or in England. Some of these landlords and agricultural innovators became famous. For example, Jethro Tull (1674–1741) was willing to conduct experiments himself and to finance the experiments of others. Many of his ideas, such as the rejection of manure as fertilizer, were wrong. Others, however, such as using iron plows to turn the earth more deeply and planting wheat by a drill rather than by casting, were excellent. His methods permitted land to be cultivated for longer periods without having to be left fallow.

Charles "Turnip" Townsend (1674–1738) encouraged other important innovations. He learned from the Dutch how to cultivate sandy soil with fertilizers. He also instituted crop rotation, using wheat, turnips, barley, and clover. This new system of rotation replaced the fallow field with one sown with a crop that both restored nutrients to the soil and supplied animal fodder. The additional fodder meant that more livestock could be raised. These fodders allowed animals to be fed during the winter and assured a year-round supply of meat. The larger number of animals increased the quantity of manure available as fertilizer for the grain crops. Consequently, in the long run, there was more food for both animals and human beings.

A third British agricultural improver was Robert Bakewell (1725–1795), who pioneered new methods of animal breeding that produced more and better animals and more milk and meat.

These and other innovations received widespread discussion in the works of Arthur Young (1741–1820), who edited the *Annals of Agriculture*. In 1793 he became secretary of the British Board of Agriculture. Young traveled widely across Europe, and his books are among the most important documents of life during the second half of the eighteenth century.

ENCLOSURE REPLACES OPEN-FIELD METHOD Many of the agricultural innovations, which were adopted only slowly, were incompatible with the existing organization of land in England. Small cultivators who lived in village communities still farmed most of the soil. Each farmer tilled an assortment of unconnected strips. The two- or three-field systems of rotation left large portions of land fallow and unproductive each year. Animals grazed on the common land in the summer and on the stubble of the harvest in the winter. Until at least the middle of the eighteenth century, the decisions about what crops would be planted were made communally. The entire system discouraged improvement and favored the poorer farmers, who needed the common land and stubble fields for their animals. The village method precluded expanding pastureland to raise more animals that would, in turn, produce more manure, which could be used for fertilizer. Thus, the methods of traditional production aimed at a steady, but not a growing, supply of food.

In 1700, approximately half the arable land in England was farmed by this open-field method. By the second half of the century, the rising price of wheat encouraged landlords to consolidate or enclose their lands to increase production. The enclosures were intended to use land more rationally and to achieve greater commercial profits. The process involved the fencing of common lands, the reclamation of previously untilled waste, and the transfor-

Grain production lay at the heart of eighteenth-century farming. In this engraving, farm workers can be seen threshing wheat, winnowing the grain, and finally putting the grain in bags so it can be carried to a mill and ground into flour. In many cases, the mill would be owned by the local landlord, who would charge peasants for its use.
Bildarchiv Preussicher Kulturbesitz

mation of strips into block fields. These procedures brought turmoil to the economic and social life of the countryside. Riots often ensued.

Because many English farmers either owned their strips or rented them in a manner that amounted to ownership, the larger landlords usually resorted to parliamentary acts to legalize the enclosure of the land, which they owned but rented to the farmers. Because the large landowners controlled Parliament, such measures passed easily. Between 1761 and 1792, almost 500,000 acres were enclosed through acts of parliament, compared with 75,000 acres between 1727 and 1760. In 1801, a general enclosure act streamlined the process.

The enclosures were controversial at the time and have remained so among historians. They permitted the extension of both farming and innovation and thus increased food production on larger agricultural units. They also disrupted small traditional communities; they forced off the land independent farmers, who had needed the common pasturage, and

poor cottage dwellers, who had lived on the reclaimed wasteland. The enclosures, however, did not depopulate the countryside. In some counties where the enclosures took place, the population increased. New soil had come into production, and services subsidiary to farming also expanded.

The enclosures did not create the labor force for the British Industrial Revolution. What the enclosures most conspicuously displayed was the introduction of the entrepreneurial or capitalistic attitude of the urban merchant into the countryside. This commercialization of agriculture, which spread from Britain slowly across the Continent during the next century, strained the paternal relationship between the governing and governed classes. Previously, landlords often had looked after the welfare of the lower orders through price controls or waivers of rent during depressed periods. As the landlords became increasingly concerned about profits, they began to leave the peasants to the mercy of the marketplace.

LIMITED IMPROVEMENTS IN EASTERN EUROPE   Improving agriculture tended to characterize farm production west of the Elbe. Dutch farming was quite efficient. In France, despite the efforts of the government to improve agriculture, enclosures were restricted. Yet there was much discussion in France about improving agricultural methods. These new procedures benefitted the ruling classes because better agriculture increased their incomes and assured a larger food supply, which discouraged social unrest.

In Prussia, Austria, Poland, and Russia, agricultural improvement was limited. Nothing in the relationship of the serfs to their lords encouraged innovation. In eastern Europe, the chief method of increasing production was to bring previously untilled lands under the plow. The landlords or their agents, and not the villages, normally directed farm management. By extending tillage, the great landlords sought to squeeze more labor from their serfs, rather than greater productivity from the soil. Eastern European landlords, like their western counterparts, sought to increase their profits, but they were much less ambitious and successful. The only significant nutritional gain achieved through their efforts was the introduction of maize and the potato. Livestock production did not increase significantly.

Expansion of the Population

The population explosion with which the entire world must contend today had its origins in the eighteenth century. Before that time, Europe's population had experienced dramatic increases, but plagues, wars, or famine had redressed the balance. Beginning in the second quarter of the eighteenth century, the population began to increase steadily. The need to feed this population caused food prices to rise, which spurred agricultural innovation. The need to provide everyday consumer goods for the expanding numbers of people fueled the demand side of the Industrial Revolution.

Our best estimates are that in 1700 Europe's population, excluding the European provinces of the Ottoman Empire, was between 100 million and 120 million people. By 1800 the figures had risen to almost 190 million and by 1850 to 260 million. The population of England and Wales rose from 6 million in 1750 to more than 10 million in 1800. France grew from 18 million in 1715 to about 26 million in 1789. Russia's population increased from 19 million in 1722 to 29 million in 1766. Such extraordinary sustained growth put new demands on all resources and considerable pressure on the existing social organization.

The population expansion occurred across the Continent in both the country and the cities. Only a limited consensus exists among scholars about the causes of this growth. There was a clear decline in the death rate. There were fewer wars and somewhat fewer epidemics in the eighteenth century. Hygiene and sanitation also improved. Better medical knowledge and techniques were once thought to have contributed to the decline in deaths. This factor is now discounted, because the more important medical advances came after the initial population explosion or would not have contributed directly to it.

Rather, changes in the food supply itself may have allowed population growth to be sustained. Improved and expanding grain production made one contribution. Another and even more important change was the cultivation of the potato. This tuber was a product of the New World and came into widespread European production during the eighteenth century. (See "The West & The World," p. 582.) On a single acre, enough potatoes could be raised to feed one peasant's family for an entire year. This more certain food supply enabled more children to survive to adulthood and rear children of their own.

The impact of the population explosion can hardly be overestimated. It created new demands for food, goods, jobs, and services. It provided a new pool of labor. Traditional modes of production and living had to be revised. More people lived in the countryside than could find employment there. Migration increased. There were also more people who might become socially and politically discontented. And because the population growth fed on itself, these pressures and demands continued to increase. The society and the social practices of the Old Regime literally outgrew their traditional bounds.

The Industrial Revolution of the Eighteenth Century

The second half of the eighteenth century witnessed the beginning of the industrialization of the European economy. That achievement of sustained economic growth is termed the *Industrial Revolution.* Previously, the economy of a province or a country might grow, but growth soon reached a plateau. Since the late eighteenth century, however, the economy of Europe has managed to expand at an almost uninterrupted pace. Depressions and recessions have been temporary, and even during such economic downturns, the Western economy has continued to grow.

At considerable social cost, industrialization made possible the production of more goods and more services than ever before in human history. Industrialization in Europe eventually overcame the economy of scarcity. The new means of production demanded new kinds of skills, new discipline in work, and a large labor force. The goods produced met immediate consumer demand and also created new demands. In the long run, industrialization clearly raised the standard of living and overcame the poverty that most Europeans, who lived during the eighteenth century and earlier, had taken for granted. It gave human beings greater control over the forces of nature than they had ever known before; yet by the middle of the nineteenth century, industrialism would also cause new and unanticipated problems with the environment.

During the eighteenth century, people did not call these economic developments a revolution. That term came to be applied to the British economic phenomena only after the French Revolution. Then continental writers observed that what had taken place in Britain was the economic equivalent of the political events in France, hence an *Industrial Revolution*. It was revolutionary less in its speed, which was on the whole rather slow, than in its implications for the future of European society.

A Revolution in Consumption

The most familiar side of the Industrial Revolution was the invention of new machinery, the establishment of factories, and the creation of a new kind of work force. Recent studies, however, have emphasized the demand side of the process and the vast increase in both the desire and the possibility of consuming goods and services that arose in the early eighteenth century.

The inventions of the Industrial Revolution increased the supply of consumer goods as never before in history. The supply of goods was only one side of the economic equation, however. The supply had been called forth by an unprecedented demand for humble goods of everyday life. Those goods included everyday consumer items such as clothing of all kinds, buttons, toys, china, furniture, rugs, kitchen utensils, candlesticks, brassware, silverware, pewterware, glassware, watches, jewelry, soap, beer, wines, and foodstuffs. It was the ever-increasing demand for these goods that sparked the ingenuity of designers and inventors. Furthermore, there seemed to be no limits to consumer demand.

Many social factors came into play to establish the markets for these consumer goods. During the seventeenth century, the Dutch had enjoyed enormous prosperity and had led the way in new forms of both everyday consumption and that of luxury goods. For reasons that are still not clear, during the eighteenth century, increasing numbers first of the English and then of people living on the Continent came to have more disposable income. This wealth may have resulted from the improvements in agriculture. Those incomes allowed people to buy consumer goods that previous generations had inherited or did not possess. What is key to this change in consumption is that it depended primarily upon expanding the various domestic markets in Europe.

This revolution, if that is not too strong a term, in consumption was not automatic. People became persuaded that they needed or wanted new consumer goods. Often, entrepreneurs caused it to happen by developing new methods of marketing. An enterprising manufacturer such as the porcelain manufacturer Josiah Wedgwood (1730–1795) first attempted to find customers among the royal family and the aristocracy. Once he had gained their business with luxury goods, he would then produce a somewhat less expensive version of the chinaware for middle-class customers. He also used advertising. He opened showrooms in London and had salespeople traveling all over England with samples and catalogs of his wares. On the Continent, he equipped salespeople with bilingual catalogs. There seemed to be no limit to the markets for different kinds of consumer goods that could be stimulated by social emulation on the one hand and advertising on the other.

Furthermore, the process of change in style itself became institutionalized. New fashions and inventions were always better than old ones. If new kinds of goods could be produced, there usually was a market for them. If one product did not find a market, its failure provided a lesson for the development of a different new product.

This expansion of consumption quietly, but steadily, challenged the social assumptions of the day. Fashion publications made all levels of society aware of new styles. Clothing fashions could be copied. Servants could begin to dress well if not luxuriously. There were changes in the consumption of food and drink that also called forth demand for new kinds of dishware for the home. Tea and coffee became staples. The brewing industry became fully commercialized. Those developments entailed the need for new kinds of cups and mugs and many more of them.

There would always be critics of this consumer economy. The vision of luxury and comfort it offered contrasted with the asceticism of ancient Sparta and contemporary Christian ethics. Yet ever-increasing consumption and production of the goods of everyday life became a hallmark of modern Western society from the eighteenth century to our own day. It would be difficult to overestimate the importance of the desire for consumer goods and the increasing material standard of living that they made possible in Western history after the eighteenth century. The presence and

Consumption of all forms of consumer goods increased greatly in the eighteenth century. This engraving illustrates a shop, probably in Paris. Here women, working apparently for a woman manager, are making dresses and hats to meet the demads of the fashion trade. As the document on page 540 demonstrates, some women writers urged more such employment opportunities for women. Bildarchiv Preussischer Kulturbesitz

accessibility of such goods became the hallmark of a nation's prosperity. It is perhaps relevant to note that it was the absence of such consumer goods, as well as of civil liberties, that during the 1980s led to such deep discontent with the communist regimes in Eastern Europe and the former Soviet Union.

Industrial Leadership of Great Britain

Great Britain was the home of the Industrial Revolution and, until the middle of the nineteenth century, maintained the industrial leadership of Europe. Several factors contributed to the early start in Britain.

Great Britain took the lead in the consumer revolution that expanded the demand for goods that could be efficiently supplied. London was by far the largest city in Europe. It was the center of a world of fashion and taste to which hundreds of thousands,

if not millions, of British citizens were exposed each year. In London, these people learned to want the consumer goods they saw on visits for business and pleasure. Newspapers thrived in Britain during the eighteenth century, allowing for advertising that increased consumer wants. The social structure of Britain allowed and even encouraged people to imitate the lifestyles of their social superiors. It seems to have been in Britain that a world of fashion first developed that led people to want to accumulate goods. In addition to the domestic consumer demand, the British economy benefitted from demand from the colonies in North America.

Britain was also the single largest free-trade area in Europe. The British had good roads and waterways without internal tolls or other trade barriers. The country was endowed with rich deposits of coal and iron ore. Its political structure was stable, and property was absolutely secure. The sound systems of banking and public credit established a stable climate for investment. Taxation in Britain was heavy, but it was efficiently and fairly collected, largely from indirect taxes. Furthermore, British taxes received legal approval through Parliament, with all social classes and all regions of the nation paying the same taxes. In contrast to the Continent, there was no pattern of privileged tax exemptions.

Finally, British society was mobile by the standards of the time. Persons who had money or could earn money could rise socially. The British aristocracy would receive into its midst people who had amassed large fortunes. Even persons of wealth not admitted to the aristocracy could enjoy their riches, receive social prominence, and exert political influence. No one of these factors preordained the British advance toward industrialism. Together, however, when added to the progressive state of British agriculture, they provided the nation with the marginal advantage to create a new mode of economic production.

New Methods of Textile Production

The industry that pioneered the Industrial Revolution and met growing consumer demand was the production of textiles for clothing. This industry provides the key example of industrialism emerging to supply the demands of an ever-growing market for everyday goods. Furthermore, it illustrates the surprising fact that much of the earliest industrial change took place not in cities, but in the countryside.

Although the eighteenth-century economy was primarily agricultural, manufacturing also permeated rural areas. The peasant family living in a one- or two-room cottage, rather than the factory, was the basic unit of production. The same peasants who tilled the land in spring and summer often spun thread or wove textiles in the winter.

Under what is termed the domestic, or putting-out, system, agents of urban textile merchants took wool or other unfinished fibers to the homes of peasants, who spun it into thread. The agent then transported the thread to other peasants, who wove it into the finished product. The merchant sold the wares. In thousands of peasant cottages from Ireland to Austria, there stood a spinning wheel or a handloom. Sometimes the spinners or weavers owned their own equipment, but more often than not by the middle of the century, the merchant capitalist owned the machinery as well as the raw material.

The domestic system of textile production was a basic feature of this family economy and would continue to be so in Britain and on the Continent well into the nineteenth century. By the mid-eighteenth century, however, a series of production bottlenecks had developed within the domestic system. The demand for cotton textiles was growing more rapidly than production, especially in Great Britain, which had a large domestic and North American market for cotton textiles. Inventors devised some of the most famous machines of the early Industrial Revolution in response to this consumer demand for cotton textiles.

THE SPINNING JENNY   Cotton textile weavers had the technical capacity to produce the quantity of fabric demanded. The spinners, however, did not have the equipment to produce as much thread as the weavers needed. James Kay's invention of the flying shuttle, which increased the productivity of the weavers, had created this imbalance during the 1730s. Thereafter, various groups of manufacturers and merchants offered prizes for the invention of a machine to eliminate this bottleneck.

About 1765, James Hargreaves (d. 1778) invented the spinning jenny. Initially, this machine allowed 16 spindles of thread to be spun, but by the close of the century its capacity had been increased to as many as 120 spindles.

THE WATER FRAME   The spinning jenny broke the bottleneck between the productive capacity of the spinners and the weavers, but it was still a piece of machinery used in the cottage. The invention that took cotton textile manufacture out of the home and put it into the factory was Richard Arkwright's (1732–1792) water frame, patented in 1769. This was a water-powered device designed to permit the production of a purely cotton fabric, rather than a cotton fabric containing linen fiber for durability. Eventually Arkwright lost his patent rights, and other manufacturers could use his invention freely. As a result, many factories sprang up in the countryside near streams that provided the necessary water power. From the 1780s onward, the cotton industry could meet an ever-expanding demand. Cotton output increased by 800 percent between 1780 and 1800. By 1815 cotton composed 40 percent of the value of British domestic exports and by 1830 just over 50 percent.

The Industrial Revolution had commenced in earnest by the 1780s, but the full economic and social ramifications of this unleashing of human productive capacity were not really felt until the early nineteenth century. The expansion of industry and the incorporation of new inventions often occurred rather slowly. For example, Edmund Cartwright (1743–1822) invented the power loom for machine weaving in the late 1780s. Yet not until the 1830s were there more power-loom weavers than handloom weavers in Britain. Nor did all the social ramifications of industrialism appear immediately. The first cotton mills used water power, were located in the country, and rarely employed more than two dozen workers. Not until the late-century application of the steam engine, perfected by James Watt (1736–1819) in 1769, to the running of textile machinery could factories easily be located in or near existing urban centers. The steam engine not only vastly increased and regularized the available energy, but also made possible the combination of urbanization and industrialization.

The Steam Engine

More than any other invention, the steam engine permitted industrialization to grow on itself and to expand into one area of production after another. This machine provided for the first time in human history a steady and essentially unlimited source of inanimate power. Unlike engines powered by water or the wind, the steam engine, driven by the burning of coal, provided a portable source of industrial power that did not fail or falter as the seasons of the year changed. Unlike human or animal power, the steam engine depended on mineral energy that did not tire during a day. Finally, the steam engine could be applied to many industrial and, eventually, transportation uses.

The first practical engine using steam power had been the invention of Thomas Newcomen (1663–1729) in the early eighteenth century. The piston of this device was moved when the steam that had been induced into the cylinder condensed, causing the piston to fall. The Newcomen machine was large, inefficient in its use of energy because both the condenser and the cylinder were heated, and practically untransportable. Despite these problems, English mine operators used the Newcomen machines to pump water out of coal and tin mines. By the third quarter of the eighteenth century, almost 100 Newcomen machines were operating in the mining districts of England.

During the 1760s, James Watt, a Scottish engineer and machine maker, began to experiment with a model of a Newcomen machine at the University of Glasgow. He gradually understood that separating the condenser from the piston and the cylinder would achieve much greater efficiency.

This painting shows the pithead of an eighteenth-century coal mine in England. The machinery on the left includes a steam engine that powered equipment to bring mined coal to the surface or to pump water from the mine. Britain's rich veins of coal were one of the factors contributing to its early industrialization. British School—A Pithead. Board of Trustees of the National Museums and Galleries on Merseyside, Walker Art Galley, Liverpool

In 1769 he patented his new invention, but transforming his idea into a practical application presented difficulties. His design required precise metalwork. Watt soon found a partner in Matthew Boulton (1728– 1809), a successful toy and button manufacturer in Birmingham, the city with the most skilled metalworkers in Britain. Watt and Boulton, in turn, consulted with John Wilkinson (1728–1808), a cannon manufacturer, to find ways to drill the precise metal cylinders required by Watt's design. In 1776, the Watt steam engine found its first commercial application pumping water from mines in Cornwall.

The use of the steam engine spread slowly because until 1800 Watt retained the exclusive patent rights. He was also reluctant to make further changes in his invention that would permit the engine to operate more rapidly. Boulton eventually persuaded him to make modifications and improvements that allowed the engines to be used not only for pumping, but also for running cotton mills. By the early nineteenth century, the steam engine had become the prime mover for all industry. With its application to ships and then to wagons on iron rails, the steam engine also revolutionized transportation.

Iron Production

The manufacture of high-quality iron has been basic to modern industrial development. Iron is the chief element of all heavy industry and land or sea transport. It has also been the material out of which most productive machinery itself has been manufactured. During the early eighteenth century, British ironmakers produced somewhat less than 25,000 tons annually. Three factors held back the production of the metal. First, charcoal rather than coke was used to smelt the ore. Charcoal, derived from wood, was becoming scarce and does not burn at as high a temperature as coke, derived from coal. Second, until the perfection of the steam engine, insufficient blasts could be achieved in the furnaces. Finally, the demand for iron was limited. The elimination of the first two problems also eliminated the third.

Eventually, British ironmakers began to use coke, and the steam engine provided new power for the blast furnaces. Coke was an abundant fuel because of Britain's large coal deposits. The existence of the steam engine both improved iron production and increased the demand for iron.

In 1784 Henry Cort (1740–1800) introduced a new puddling process, that is, a new method for melting and stirring the molten ore. Cort's process allowed

Major Inventions in the Textile-Manufacturing Revolution	
1733	James Kay's flying shuttle
1765	James Hargreaves's spinning jenny (patented 1770)
1769	James Watt's steam engine patent
1769	Richard Arkwright's water frame patent
1787	Edmund Cartwright's power loom

more slag (the impurities that bubbled to the top of the molten metal) to be removed and a purer iron to be produced. Cort also developed a rolling mill that continuously shaped the still-molten metal into bars, rails, or other forms. Previously, the metal had to be pounded into these forms.

All these innovations achieved a better, more versatile product at a lower cost. The demand for iron grew as its price became lower. By the early nineteenth century, the British produced over a million tons annually. The lower cost of iron, in turn, lowered the cost of steam engines and allowed them to be used more widely.

The Impact of the Agricultural and Industrial Revolutions on Working Women

The transformation of agriculture and industry, led to a series of seemingly modest changes that, taken collectively, diminshed the importance and the role of those women already in the work force.

Women had been an important part of traditional European agriculture. They worked in the fields and often were permitted to glean the grain left over after the general harvest. Some women also managed industries like milking and cheese production. However, primarily in western Europe, increasing commercialization and mechanization eroded these traditional roles. Machinery operated by men displaced the work of women in the field and their industry skills in dairying and home industry, particularly in Britain. Even nonmechanized labor came to favor men. For example, during the late eighteenth century, heavy scythes wielded by men replaced the lighter sickles that women had used to harvest grain. Moreover, the drive to maximize profits led landlords to enclose lands and curtail customary rights like gleaning.

This transformation of farming constricted women's ability to earn their living from the land. Women in farming regions came to be viewed as opponents of agricultural improvement because of its negative impact on their economic life. As a result, proponents of the new agriculture often demeaned the role of women in farming and its related work. Indeed, the vast literature on agricultural improvement specifically advocated removing women from the agricultural work force.

A similar process took place in textile manufacturing, where mechanization deprived many women of one of their most traditional means of earning income. Before mechanization thousands of women worked at spinning wheels to produce thread that handloom weavers, who were often their husbands, then wove. The earlier, small spinning jennies did not immediately disrupt this situation because women could use them in the loft of a home, but the larger ones required a factory setting where men often ran the machinery. As a result, most women spinners were put out of work, and those women who did move into the factory labor force performed less skilled work than men. But in the long run, the mechanization of spinning left many other women without one of their most traditional means of earning income.

Many working women, displaced from spinning thread or from farming, slowly turned to cottage industries, such as knitting, button making, straw plaiting, bonnet making, or glove stitching, that invariably earned them less than their former occupations. In later generations, women who earlier would have been spinners or farm workers moved directly into cottage industries. The work and skills involved in these occupations were considered inferior; and because it paid so poorly, women who did this work might become prostitutes or engage in other criminal activity. Consequently, the reputations and social standing of many such working women suffered.

Among women who did not work in the cottage industries, thousands became domestic servants in the homes of landed or commercial families. During the nineteenth century, such domestic service became the largest area of female employment. It was far more respectable than the cottage industries, but was separate from the technologically advanced world of factory manufacture or transport.

By the end of the eighteenth century, the work and workplaces of men and women were becoming increasingly separate and distinct. In this respect, many people, such as the English writer Priscilla Wakefield, believed that the kinds of employment open to women had narrowed. Wakefield called for new occupations for women. (See "Priscilla Wakefield Demands More Occupations for Women.")

This shift in female employment, or what one historian has termed "this defamation of women workers,"[2] produced several long term results. First, women's work, whether in cottage industries or domestic service, became associated with the home rather than with places where men worked. Second, the laboring life of most women was removed from the new technologies present in the new farming, transportation, and manufacturing. Woman's work thus appeared traditional, and people assumed that women could do only such work. Third, during the nineteenth and early twentieth centuries, Europeans also assumed that most women worked only to supplement a spouse's income. Finally, because the work women did was considered marginal and only as supplementing a male income, men were paid much more than women. Most people associate the Industrial Revolution with factories, but for many working women, the result of these revolutions was a life located more in homes than ever before. Indeed, in the nineteenth century, one, though only one, motive behind efforts to restrict the hours and improve the conditions of women in factories was the belief that it was bad for them to be there in the first place. We will address the larger picture of the relationship of the new industrial workplace to family life in Chapter 21.

The Growth of Cities

Remarkable changes occurred in the pattern of city growth between 1500 and 1800. In 1500, within Europe (excluding Hungary and Russia) there were 156 cities with a population greater than 10,000. Only four of those cities—Paris, Milan, Venice, and Naples—had populations larger than 100,000. By 1800, 363 cities had 10,000 or more inhabitants, and 17 of them had populations larger than 100,000. The percentage of the European population living in urban areas had risen from just over 5 percent to just over 9 percent. There had also occurred a major shift in urban concentration from southern, Mediterranean Europe to the north.

Patterns of Preindustrial Urbanization

The eighteenth century witnessed a considerable growth of towns, closely related to the tumult of the day and the revolutions with which the cen-

[2]Deborah Valenze, *The First Industrial Woman* (New York: Oxford University Press, 1995), p. 183.

(a)

(b)

Francis Wheatley (1747–1801), an English artist, painted these and many other scenes of late eighteenth-century rural life. These four paintings portray a very idealized view of the farming family. Had Wheatley painted this family a half-century or more earlier, the women might have appeared with the father and husband in the fields, as workers or as gleaners picking up grain left by the harvesters.

After the mid-century changes in agricultural production, women worked in the home and men in the fields. Wheatley illustrates this division in the paintings shown here: Women work at home, or look after the needs of men and children. Men work in the fields and return home in the evening. During the early nineteenth century, much of the dairy work shown in the first painting would also have become mechanized, performed largely by male workers. Francis Wheatley (RA) (1747–1801) (a) *Morning,* (b) *Noon,* (c) *Evening,* (d) *Night,* signed and dated 1799, oil on canvas, each 17½ x 21½ in. (44.5 x 54.5 cm), Yale Center for British Art, Paul Mellon Collection B1977.14.120, B1977.14.119, B1977.14.118, B1977.14.121.

(c)

(d)

Priscilla Wakefield Demands More Occupations for Women

At the end of the eighteenth century, Priscilla Walkefield was one several English women writers who began to demand a wider life for women. She was concerned that women found themselves able to pursue only occupations that paid poorly. Often, they were excluded from work on the grounds of their alleged physical weakness. She also believed that women should receive equal wages for equal work. These issues reflected a narrowing of opportunities for women that had occurred in England during the second half of the eighteenth century. As a result of the mechanization of both agriculture and the textile industry, many women found traditional occupations closing to them. Wakefield is thus addressing a general question of opportunities available to women and more recent developments. Many of the issues she raised have yet to be adequately addressed on behalf of women.

❖ *From reading this passage, what do you understand to have been the arguments at the end of the eighteenth century to limit the kinds of employment that women might enter? Why did women receive lower wages for work similar to or the same as that done by men? What occupations traditionally filled by men does Wakefield believe women might also pursue?*

Another heavy discouragement to the industry of women, is the inequality of the reward of their labor, compared with that of men; an injustice which pervades every species of employment performed by both sexes.

In employments which depend on bodily strength, the distinction is just; for it cannot be pretended that the generality of women can earn as much as men, when the produce of their labor is the result of corporeal exertion; but it is a subject of great regret, that this inequality should prevail even where an equal share of skill and application is exerted. Male stay-makers, mantua-makers, and hair-dressers, are better paid than female artists of the same professions; but surely it will never be urged as an apology for this disproportion, that women are not as capable of making stays, gowns, dressing hair, and similar arts, as men; if they are not superior to them, it can only be accounted for upon this principle, that the prices they receive for their labor are not sufficient to repay them for the expense of qualifying themselves for their business; and that they sink under the mortification of being regarded as artisans of inferior estimation....

Besides these employments which are commonly performed by women, and those already shown to be suitable for such persons as are above the condition of hard labor, there are some professions and trades customarily in the hands of men, which might be conveniently exercised by either sex.—Watchmaking requiring more ingenuity than strength, seems peculiarly adapted to women; as do many parts of the business of stationer, particularly, ruling account books or making pens. The compounding of medicines in an apothecary's shop, requires no other talents than care and exactness; and if opening a vein occasionally be an indispensable requisite, a woman may acquire the capacity of doing it, for those of her own sex at least, without any reasonable objection.... Pastry and confectionery appear particularly consonant to the habits of women, though generally performed by men; perhaps the heat of the ovens, and the strength requisite to fill and empty them, may render male assistants necessary; but certain women are most eligible to mix up the ingredients, and prepare the various kinds of cakes for baking.—Light turnery and toy-making depend more upon dexterity and invention than force, and are therefore suitable work for women and children....

Farming, as far as respects the theory, is commensurate with the powers of the female mind: nor is the practice of inspecting agricultural processes incompatible with the delicacy of their frames if their constitution be good.

Priscilla Wakefield, *Reflections on the Present Condition of the Female Sex* (1798) (London, 1817), pp. 125–127, as quoted in Bridget Hill, ed., *Eighteenth-Century Women: An Anthology* (London: George Allen & Unwin, 1984), pp. 227–228.

tury closed. London grew from about 700,000 inhabitants in 1700 to almost 1 million in 1800. By the time of the French Revolution, Paris had more than 500,000 inhabitants. Berlin's population tripled during the century, reaching 170,000 in 1800. Warsaw had 30,000 inhabitants in 1730, but almost 120,000 in 1794. Saint Petersburg, founded in 1703, numbered more than 250,000 inhabitants a century later. In addition to the growth of these capitals, the number of smaller cities of 20,000–50,000 people increased considerably. This urban growth must, however, be kept in perspective. Even in France and Great Britain, probably somewhat less than 20 percent of the population lived in cities. And the town of 10,000 inhabitants was much more common than the giant urban center.

These raw figures conceal significant changes that took place in how cities grew and how the population distributed itself. The major urban development of the sixteenth century had been followed by a leveling off, and even a decline, in the seventeenth. New growth began in the early eighteenth century and accelerated during the late eighteenth and the early nineteenth centuries. Between 1500 and 1750, major urban expansion took place within already established and generally already large cities. After 1750, the pattern changed with the birth of new cities and the rapid growth of older smaller cities.

GROWTH OF CAPITALS AND PORTS   In particular, between 1600 and 1750, the cities that grew most vigorously were capitals and ports. This situation reflects the success of monarchical state building during those years and the consequent burgeoning of bureaucracies, armies, courts, and other groups who lived in the capitals. The growth of port cities, in turn, reflects the expansion of European overseas trade—most especially, that of the Atlantic routes. Except for Manchester in England and Lyons in France, the new urban conglomerates were nonindustrial cities.

Furthermore, between 1600 and 1750, cities with populations of fewer than 40,000 inhabitants declined. These included older landlocked trading centers, medieval industrial cities, and ecclesiastical centers. They contributed less to the new political regimes, and the expansion of the putting-out system transferred to the countryside much production that had once occurred in medieval cities. Rural labor was cheaper than urban labor, and cities with concentrations of labor declined as production was moved from the urban workshop into the country.

EMERGENCE OF NEW CITIES AND GROWTH OF SMALL TOWNS   In the middle of the eighteenth century, a new pattern emerged. The rate of growth of existing large cities declined, while new cities began to emerge and existing smaller cities began to grow. Several factors were at work in the process, which Jan De Vries has termed "an urban growth from below."[3] First, there was the general overall population increase. Second, the early stages of the Industrial Revolution, particularly in Britain, occurred in the countryside and fostered the growth of smaller towns and cities located near factories. Factory organization itself led to new concentrations of population.

Cities also grew as a result of the new prosperity of European agriculture, even where there was little industrialization. Improved agricultural production promoted the growth of nearby market towns and other urban centers that served agriculture or allowed more prosperous farmers to have access to the consumer goods and recreation they wanted. This new pattern of urban growth—new cities and the expansion of smaller existing ones—would continue into the nineteenth century.

Urban Classes

Social divisions were as marked in the cities of the eighteenth century as they were in the industrial centers of the nineteenth. Visible segregation often existed between the urban rich and the urban poor. The nobles and the upper-middle class lived in fashionable town houses, often constructed around newly laid-out green squares. The poorest town dwellers usually congregated along the rivers. Small merchants and artisans lived above their shops. Whole families might live in a single room. Modern sanitary facilities were still unknown. There was little pure water. Cattle, pigs, goats, and other animals walked the streets with the people. All reports on the cities of Europe during this period emphasize both the striking grace and beauty of the dwellings of the wealthy and the dirt, filth, and stench that filled the streets.

Poverty was not just an urban problem; it was usually worse in the countryside. In the city, however, poverty was more visible in the form of crime, prostitution, vagrancy, begging, and alcoholism. Many a young man or woman from the

[3]Jan De Vries, "Patterns of Urbanization in Pre-Industrial Europe, 1500–1800," in H. Schmal, ed., *Patterns of Urbanization Since 1500* (London: Croom Helm, 1981), p. 103.

countryside migrated to the nearest city to seek a better life, only to discover poor housing, little food, disease, degradation, and finally death. It did not require the Industrial Revolution and the urban factories to make the cities into hellholes for the poor and the dispossessed. The full darkness of London life during the midcentury "gin age," when consumption of that liquor blinded and killed many poor people, is evident in the engravings of William Hogarth (1697–1764).

Also contrasting with the serenity of the aristocratic and upper-commercial-class lifestyle were the public executions that took place all over Europe, the breaking of men and women on instruments of torture in Paris, and the public floggings in Russia. Brutality condoned and carried out by the ruling classes was simply a fact of everyday life.

THE UPPER CLASSES

At the top of the urban social structure stood a generally small group of nobles, large merchants, bankers, financiers, clergy, and government officials. These upper-class men controlled the political and economic affairs of the town. Normally, they constituted a self-appointed and self-electing oligarchy that governed the city through its corporation or city council. These rights of self-government had usually been granted by some form of royal charter that gave the city corporation its authority and the power to select its own members. In a few cities on the Continent, artisan guilds controlled the corporations, but more generally, the councils were under the influence of the local nobility and the wealthiest commercial people.

THE MIDDLE CLASS

Another group in the city was the prosperous, but not always immensely wealthy, merchants, tradespeople, bankers, and professional people. They were the most dynamic element of the urban population and constituted the persons traditionally regarded as the middle class, or bourgeoisie. The concept of the middle class was much less clear cut than that of the nobility. The middle class itself was and would remain diverse and divided, with persons employed in the professions often resentful of those who drew their incomes from commerce. Less wealthy members of the middle class of whatever occupation resented wealthier members who might be connected to the nobility through social or business relationships.

The middle class had less wealth than most nobles, but more than urban artisans. Middle-class people lived in the cities and towns, and their sources of income had little or nothing to do with the land. In one way or another, they all benefitted from expanding trade and commerce, whether as merchants, as lawyers, or as small-factory owners. Theirs was a world in which the earning and saving of money allowed for rapid social mobility and change in lifestyle. They saw themselves as people willing to put their capital and energy to work, while they portrayed the nobility as idle. The members of the middle class tended to be economically aggressive and socially ambitious. People often made fun of them for these characteristics and were jealous of their success. The middle class normally supported reform, change, and economic growth. The bourgeoisie also wanted more rational regulations for trade and commerce, as did some of the more progressive aristocrats.

The middle class was made up of people whose lives fostered the revolution in consumption. On one hand, as owners of factories and of wholesale and retail businesses, they produced and sold goods for the expanding consumer market; on the other hand, members of the middle class were among the chief consumers. It was to their homes that the vast array of new consumer goods made their way. They were also the people whose social values clearly embraced the commercial spirit most fully. They might not enjoy the titles or privileges of the nobility, but they could enjoy considerable material comfort and prosperity. It was this style of life that less well-off people could still emulate as they sought to acquire consumer goods for themselves.

During the eighteenth century, the relationship between the middle class and the aristocracy was complicated. On one hand, the nobles, especially in England and France, increasingly embraced the commercial spirit associated with the middle class by improving their estates and investing in cities. On the other hand, wealthy members of the middle class often tried to imitate the lifestyle of the nobility by purchasing landed estates. The aspirations of the middle class for social mobility, however, conflicted with the determination of the nobles to maintain and reassert their own privileges and to protect their own wealth. The middle-class commercial figures—traders, bankers, manufacturers, and lawyers—often found their pursuit of both profit and prestige blocked by the privileges of the nobility and its social exclusiveness, by the inefficiency of monarchical bureaucracies dominated by the nobility, or by aristocrats who controlled patronage and government contracts.

The bourgeoisie was not rising to challenge the nobility; rather, both were seeking to add new dimensions to their existing political power and social prestige. The tensions that arose between the nobles and the middle class during the eighteenth century normally involved issues of power sharing or access to political influence, rather than clashes over values or goals associated with class.

The middle class in the cities also feared the lower-urban classes as much as they envied the nobility. The lower orders were a potentially violent element in society, a potential threat to property, and, in their poverty, a drain on national resources. The lower classes, however, were much more varied than either the city aristocracy or the middle class cared to admit.

ARTISANS   Shopkeepers, artisans, and wage earners were the single largest group in any city. They were grocers, butchers, fishmongers, carpenters, cabinetmakers, smiths, printers, handloom weavers, and tailors, to give a few examples. They had their own culture, values, and institutions. Like the peasants of the countryside, they were in many respects conservative. Their economic position was highly vulnerable. If a poor harvest raised the price of food, their own businesses suffered. These urban classes also contributed to the revolution in consumption, however. They could buy more goods than ever before, and, to the extent their incomes permitted, many of them sought to copy the domestic consumption of the middle class.

The lives of these artisans and shopkeepers centered on their work and their neighborhoods. They usually lived near or at their place of employment. Most of them worked in shops with fewer than a half dozen other artisans. Their primary institution had historically been the guild, but by the eighteenth century, the guilds rarely exercised the influence of their predecessors in medieval or early modern Europe.

Nevertheless, the guilds were not to be ignored. They played a conservative role. Rather than seeking economic growth or innovation, they tried to preserve the jobs and skills of their members. In many countries, the guilds were still able to determine who could pursue a particular craft. To lessen competition, they attempted to prevent too many people from learning a particular skill.

The guilds also provided a framework for social and economic advancement. At an early age, a boy might become an apprentice to learn a craft or trade. After several years, he would be made a journeyman. Still later, if successful and sufficiently competent, he might become a master. The artisan could also receive certain social benefits from the guilds, including aid for his family during sick-

This engraving illustrates a metalworking shop such as might have been found in almost any town of significance in Europe. Most of the people employed in the shop probably belonged to the same family. Note that two women are also working. The wife may very well have been the person in charge of keeping the accounts of the business. The two younger boys might be children of the owner or apprentices in the trade, or both.
Bildarchiv Preussischer Kulturbesitz

Manchester's Calico Printers Protest the New Machinery

The introduction of the new machines associated with the Industrial Revolution stirred much protest. With machines able to duplicate the skills of laborers, workers feared the loss of jobs and the resulting loss of status when their chief means of livelihood lay in their possession of those displaced and now mechanized skills. The following letter was sent anonymously to a Manchester manufacturer by English workers. It shows the outrage of those workers, the intimidation they were willing to use as threats, and their own economic fears.

❖ *How might new machines adversely affect the livelihood of workers? Did the workers have other complaints against Mr. Taylor in addition to the introduction of new machinery? How have these workers reached an agreement to protect the interests of James Hobson? How do the workers combine the threat of violent actions with claims that other actions they have taken are legal?*

Mr. Taylor, If you dont discharge James Hobson from the House of Correction we will burn your House about your Ears for we have sworn to stand by one another and you must immediately give over any more Mashen Work for we are determined there shall be no more of them made use of in the Trade and it will be madness for you to contend with the Trade as we are combined by Oath to fix Prices we can afford to pay him a Guinea Week and not hurt the fund if you was to keep him there till Dumsday therefore mind you comply with the above or by God we will keep our Words with you we will make some rare Bunfires in this Countey and at your Peril to call any more

Meetings mind that we will make the Mosney Pepel shake in their Shoes we are determined to destroy all Sorts of Masheens for Printing in the Kingdom for there is more hands then is work for so no more from the ingerd Gurnemen Rember we are a great number sworn nor you must not advertise the Men that you say run away from you when your il Usage was the Cause of their going we will punish you for that our Meetings are legal for we want nothing but what is honest and to work for selvs and familers and you want to starve us but it is better for you and a few more which we have marked to die then such a Number of Pore Men and their famerles to be starved.

From the *London Gazette*, 1786, p. 36, as reprinted in Douglas Hay, ed., *Albion's Fatal Tree* (New York: Pantheon Books, 1975), p. 318.

ness or the promise of admission for his son. The guilds were the chief protection for artisans against the operation of the commercial market. They were particularly strong in central Europe.

The Urban Riot

The artisan class, with its generally conservative outlook, maintained a rather fine sense of social and economic justice. These ideals were based largely on traditional practices. If the collective sense of what was economically "just" was offended, artisans frequently manifested their displeasure by rioting. (See "Manchester's Calico Printers Protest the New Machinery.") The most sensitive area was the price of bread, the staple food of the poor. If a baker or a grain merchant announced a price that was considered unjustly high, a bread riot might well ensue. Artisan leaders

would confiscate the bread or grain and sell it for what the urban crowd considered a "just price." They would then give the money paid for the grain or bread to the baker or merchant.

The potential for bread riots restrained the greed of merchants. Such disturbances represented a collective method of imposing the "just price" in place of the price set by the commercial marketplace. Thus, bread and food riots, which occurred throughout Europe, were not irrational acts of screaming, hungry people, but highly ritualized social phenomena of the Old Regime and its economy of scarcity.

Other kinds of riots also characterized eighteenth-century society and politics. The riot was a way in which people who were excluded in every other way from the political processes could make their will known. Sometimes urban rioters were incited by religious bigotry. For example, in 1753,

London Protestant mobs compelled the government ministry to withdraw an act to legalize Jewish naturalization. In 1780, the same rabidly Protestant spirit manifested itself in the Gordon riots. Lord George Gordon (1751–1793) had raised the specter of an imaginary Catholic plot after the government relieved military recruits from having to take specifically anti-Catholic oaths.

In these riots and in food riots, violence was normally directed against property rather than against people. The rioters themselves were not "riffraff," but usually small shopkeepers, freeholders, artisans, and wage earners. They usually wanted only to restore a traditional right or practice that seemed endangered. Nevertheless, considerable turmoil and destruction could result from their actions.

During the last half of the century, urban riots increasingly involved political ends. Though often simultaneous with economic disturbances, the political riot always had nonartisan leadership or instigators. In fact, the "crowd" of the eighteenth century was often the tool of the upper classes. In Paris, the aristocratic *Parlement* often urged crowd action in its disputes with the monarchy. In Geneva, middle-class citizens supported artisan riots against the local urban oligarchy. In Great Britain in 1792, the government incited mobs to attack English sympathizers of the French Revolution. Such outbursts of popular unrest indicate that the crowd or mob first entered the European political and social arena well before the revolution in France.

The Jewish Population: The Age of the Ghetto

Although the small Jewish communities of Amsterdam and other western European cities became famous for their intellectual life and financial institutions, the vast majority of European Jews lived in eastern Europe. In the eighteenth century and thereafter, the Jewish population of Europe was concentrated in Poland, Lithuania, and the Ukraine, where no fewer than three million Jews dwelled. There were perhaps as many as 150,000 Jews in the Habsburg lands, primarily Bohemia, around 1760. Fewer than 100,000 Jews lived in Germany. There were approximately 40,000 Jews in France. Much smaller Jewish populations resided in England and Holland, each of which had a Jewish population of fewer than 10,000. There were even smaller groups of Jews elsewhere.

In 1762, Catherine the Great of Russia specifically excluded Jews from a manifesto that welcomed foreigners to settle in Russia. She somewhat relaxed the exclusion a few years later, but Jews incorporated into the Russian Empire during her reign often felt that they needed to receive specific assurances of imperial protection for their livelihoods and religious practices against the ordinances of local officials. (See "Belorussian Jews Petition Catherine the Great.") After the first partition of Poland of 1772, to be discussed in Chapter 18, Russia included a large Jewish population. There were also larger Jewish communities in Prussia and under Austrian rule.

During the Old Regime, European Jews were separated from non-Jews, typically in districts known as ghettos. Relegated to the least desirable section of a city or to rural villages, most lived in poverty. This watercolor painting depicts a street in Kazimlesz, the Jewish quarter of Cracow, Poland. Judaica Collection, Max Berger, Vienna, Austria

Belorussian Jews Petition Catherine the Great

In the 1780s, through military expansion, Empress Catherine the Great of Russia (see Chapter 18) annexed Belorussia, bringing a new Jewish minority under her imperial government. In response to her decree, governing many aspects of the region's law and economy, Belorussian Jews petitioned the Empress to protect certain of their traditional rights regarding distillation and sale of spirits. They also petitioned for protection in court and for the right to retain their own traditional practices and courts for matters relating to their own community. The petition indicates how in Russia, as elsewhere in Europe, Jews were treated as a people apart. It also illustrates how Jews, like other minorities in Old Regime Europe, sought both to receive the protection of monarchies against arbitrary local officials and to maintain the integrity of long-standing social practices. The document also illustrates the Jews' dependence on the goodwill of the surrounding non-Jewish community.

❖ *In the first part of the petition, how do the petitioners attempt to appeal to long-standing custom to defend their interests? How do both parts of the petition suggest that Jewish law and practice distinct from the rest of the society governed Jewish social life? In the context of this petition, which non-Jewish authorities may actually or potentially influence Jewish life?*

...2. According to an ancient custom, when the squires built a new village, they summoned the Jews to reside there and gave them certain privileges for several years and then permanent liberty to distill spirits, brew beer and mead, and sell these drinks. On this basis, the Jews built houses and distillation plants at considerable expense....A new decree of Her Imperial Majesty...reserved [this right] to the squires....But a decree of the governor-general of Belorussia has now forbidden the squires to farm out distillation in their villages to Jews, even if the squires want to do this. As a result, the poor Jews who built houses in small villages and promoted both this trade and distillation have been deprived of these and left completely impoverished. But until all the Jewish people are totally ruined, the Jewish merchants suffer restraints equally with the poor rural Jews, since their law obliges them to assist all who share their religious faith. They therefore request an imperial decree authorizing the squire, if he wishes, to farm out distillation to Jews in rural areas.

3. Although, with Her Imperial Majesty's permission, Jews may be elected as officials..., Jews are allotted fewer votes than other people and hence no Jew can ever attain office. Consequently, Jews have no one to defend them in courts and find themselves in a desperate situation—given their fear and ignorance of Russian—in case of misfortune, even if innocent. To consummate all the good already bestowed, Jews dare to petition that an equal number of electors be required from Jews as from others (or, at least, that in matters involving Jews and non-Jews, a representative from the Jewish community hold equal rights with non-Jews, be present to accompany Jews in court, and attend the interrogation of Jews). But cases involving only Jews (except for promissory notes and debts) should be handled solely in Jewish courts, because Jews assume obligations among themselves, make agreements and conclude all kinds of deals in the Jewish language and in accordance with Jewish rites and laws (which are not known to others). Moreover, those who transgress their laws and order should be judged in Jewish courts. Similarly, preserve intact all their customs and holidays in the spirit of their faith, as is mercifully assured in the imperial manifesto.

Jews dwelled in most nations without enjoying the rights and privileges of other subjects of the monarchs, unless such rights were specifically granted to them. They were regarded as a kind of resident alien whose residence might well be temporary or changed at the whim of local rulers or the monarchical government.

No matter where they dwelled, the Jews of Europe under the Old Regime lived apart in separate communities from non-Jewish Europeans. These communities might be distinct districts of cities known as ghettos or in primarily Jewish villages in the countryside. Jews were also treated as a distinct people religiously and legally. In Poland for much of the century, they were virtually self-governing. In other areas, they lived under the burden of discriminatory legislation. Except in England, Jews could not and did not mix in the mainstream of the societies in which they dwelled. This period, which really may be said to have begun with the expulsion of the Jews from Spain at the end of the fifteenth century, is known as the age of the ghetto, or separate community.

During the seventeenth century, a few Jews had helped finance the wars of major rulers. These financiers often became close to the rulers and were known as "court Jews." Perhaps the most famous was Samuel Oppenheimer (1630–1703), who helped the Habsburgs finance their struggle against the Turks and the defense of Vienna. Even these privileged Jews, including Oppenheimer, however, often failed to have their loans repaid. The court Jews and their financial abilities became famous. They tended to marry among themselves.

The overwhelming majority of the Jewish population of Europe, however, lived in poverty. They occupied the most undesirable sections of cities or poor rural villages. They pursued moneylending in some cases, but often worked at the lowest occupations. Their religious beliefs, rituals, and community set them apart. Virtually all laws and social institutions kept them apart from their Christian neighbors in situations of social inferiority.

Under the Old Regime, it is important to emphasize, all of this discrimination was based on religious separateness. Jews who converted to Christianity were welcomed, even if not always warmly, into the major political and social institutions of gentile European society. Until the last two decades of the eighteenth century, in every part of Europe, however, those Jews who remained loyal to their faith were subject to various religious, civil, and social disabilities. They could not pursue the professions freely, they often could not change residence freely, and they stood outside the political structures of the nations in which they lived. Jews could be expelled from the cities in which they resided, and their property could be confiscated. They were regarded as socially and religiously inferior. They could be required to listen to sermons that insulted them and their religion. Jews might find their children taken away from them and given Christian instruction. They knew that their non-Jewish neighbors might suddenly turn against them and kill them or their fellow religious believers.

As will be seen in subsequent chapters, the end of the Old Regime brought major changes in the lives of these Jews and in their relationship to the larger culture.

In Perspective

Near the close of the eighteenth century, European society was on the brink of a new era. That society had remained traditional and corporate largely because of an economy of scarcity. Beginning in the eighteenth century, the commercial spirit and the values of the marketplace, although not new, were permitted fuller play than ever before in European history. The newly unleashed commercial spirit led increasingly to a conception of human beings as individuals rather than as members of communities. In particular, that spirit manifested itself in agricultural and industrial revolutions, as well as in the drive toward greater consumption. Together, those two vast changes in production overcame most of the scarcity that had haunted Europe and the West generally. The accompanying changes in landholding and production would bring major changes to the European social structure.

The expansion of population provided a further stimulus for change. More people meant more labor, more energy, and more minds contributing to the creation and solution of social difficulties. Cities had to accommodate themselves to expanding populations. Corporate groups, such as the guilds, had to confront the existence of a larger labor force. New wealth meant that birth would eventually become less and less a determining factor in social relationships, except in regard to the social roles assigned to the two sexes. Class structure and social hierarchy remained, but the boundaries became somewhat blurred.

Finally, the conflicting ambitions of monarchs, the nobility, and the middle class generated innovation. In the pursuit of new revenues, the monarchs interfered with the privileges of the nobles. In the name of ancient rights, the nobles attempted to secure and expand their existing social privileges. The middle class, in all of its diversity, was growing wealthier from trade, commerce, and the practice of the professions. Its members wanted social prestige and influence equal to their wealth. They resented privileges, frowned on hierarchy, and rejected tradition.

All these factors meant that the society of the eighteenth century stood at the close of one era in European history and at the opening of another.

REVIEW QUESTIONS

1. Describe the life of an English aristocrat at the beginning of the eighteenth century and toward its close. How did the English aristocrat differ

from the French aristocrat in this regard? What kind of privileges separated European aristocrats from other social groups?

2. How would you define the term *family economy*? What were some of the particular characteristics of the northwestern European household as opposed to that in eastern Europe? In what ways were the lives of women constrained by the family economy in pre-industrial Europe?

3. What caused the Agricultural Revolution? How did technological innovations help change European agriculture? To what extent did the English aristocracy contribute to the Agricultural Revolution? What were some of the reasons for peasant revolts in Europe in the eighteenth century?

4. What factors explain the increase in Europe's population in the eighteenth century? What were the effects of the population explosion? How did population growth contribute to changes in consumption?

5. What caused the Industrial Revolution of the eighteenth century? What were some of the technological innovations and why were they important? Why did Great Britain take the lead in the Industrial Revolution? How did the consumer contribute to the Industrial Revolution?

6. Describe city life during the eighteenth century. Were all European cities of the same character? What changes had taken place in the distribution of population in cities and towns? Compare the lifestyle of the upper class with that of the middle and lower classes. What were some of the causes of urban riots?

SUGGESTED READINGS

I. T. BERND AND G. RANKI, *The European Periphery and Industrialization, 1780–1914* (1982). Examines the experience of eastern and Mediterranean Europe.

J. BLUM, *Lord and Peasant in Russia from the Ninth to the Nineteenth Century* (1961). A classic wide-ranging discussion.

J. BLUM, *The End of the Old Order in Rural Europe* (1978). Comprehensive treatment of rural Europe, especially in central and eastern Europe.

F. BRAUDEL, *The Structures of Everyday Life: The Limits of the Possible*, trans. by M. Kochan (1982). A magisterial survey.

J. BREWER AND R. PORTER, *Consumption and the World of Goods* (1993). A large, wide-ranging collection of essays.

J. CANON, *Aristocratic Century: The Peerage of Eighteenth-Century England* (1985). A useful treatment.

A. CLARKE, *The Struggle for the Breeches: Gender and the Making of the British Working Class* (1995). A major, deeply researched exploration of the subject.

P. DEANE, *The First Industrial Revolution*, 2d ed. (1979). A well-balanced and systematic treatment.

J. DE VRIES, *European Urbanization, 1500–1800* (1984). An important and far-ranging treatment.

W. DOYLE, *The Old European Order: 1660–1800* (1992). The best and most accessible one-volume study.

P. EARLE, *The Making of the English Middle Class: Business, Community, and Family Life in London, 1660–1730* (1989). The most careful study of the subject.

M. W. FLINN, *The European Demographic System, 1500–1820* (1981). A major summary.

P. GOUBERT, *The* Ancien Régime: *French Society, 1600–1750*, trans. by S. Cox (1974). A superb account of the peasant social order.

D. HAY (ED.), *Albion's Fatal Tree: Crime and Society in Eighteenth-Century England* (1975). Separate essays on a previously little explored subject.

O. H. HUFTON, *The Poor of Eighteenth-Century France, 1750–1789* (1975). A brilliant study of poverty and the family economy.

E. L. JONES, *Agriculture and Economic Growth in England, 1650–1815* (1968). A good introduction.

A. KAHAN, *The Plow, the Hammer, and the Knout: An Economic History of Eighteenth-Century Russia* (1985). An extensive and detailed treatment.

D. LANDES, *The Wealth and Poverty of Nations: Why Some Are So Rich and Some So Poor* (1998). A lively, opinionated overview of economic development.

F. E. MANUEL, *The Broken Staff: Judaism Through Christian Eyes* (1992). An important discussion of Christian interpretations of Judaism.

M. A. MEYER, *The Origins of the Modern Jew: Jewish Identity and European Culture in Germany, 1749–1824* (1967). Organized around individual case studies.

P. B. MUNSENE, *Gentlemen and Poachers: The English Game Laws, 1671–1831* (1981). An excellent analysis of these laws.

S. POLLARD, *Peaceful Conquest: The Industrialization of Europe, 1760–1970* (1981). A useful survey.

G. RUDÉ, *The Crowd in History, 1730–1848* (1964). A pioneering study.

H. SCHMAL, (ED.), *Patterns of European Urbanization Since 1500* (1981). Major revisionist essays.

L. STONE, *An Open Elite?* (1985). Raises important questions about the traditional view of open access to social mobility in England.

T. TACKETT, *Priest and Parish in Eighteenth-Century France: A Social and Political Study of the Curés in a Diocese of Dauphiné, 1750–1791* (1977). An important local study that displays the role of the church in the fabric of social life in the Old Regime.

D. VALENZE, *The First Industrial Woman* (1995). An elegant, penetrating volume

A. VICKERY, *The Gentleman's Daughter: Women's Lives in Georgian England* (1998). A richly documented study.

E. A. WRIGLEY, *Continuity, Chance and Change: The Character of the Industrial Revolution in England* (1988). A major conceptual reassessment.

Chapter 17

During the seventeenth and eighteenth centuries, European maritime nations established overseas empires, and set up trading monopolies within them, in an effort to magnify their economic strength. As this painting of the Old Custom House Quay in London suggests, trade from these empires and the tariffs imposed on it were expected to generate revenue for the home country. But behind many of the goods carried in the great sailing ships in the harbor and landed on these docks lay the labor of African slaves working on the plantations of North and South America. Samuel Scott *Old Custom House Quay* Collection. By Courtesy of the Trustees of the Victoria & Albert Museum

The Transatlantic Economy, Trade Wars, and Colonial Rebellion

Periods of European Overseas Empires

Mercantile Empires
Mercantilist Goals
French–British Rivalry

The Spanish Colonial System
Colonial Government
Trade Regulation
Colonial Reform under the Spanish
   Bourbon Monarchs

Black African Slavery, the Plantation System, and the Atlantic Economy
The African Presence in the Americas
Slavery and the Transatlantic Economy
The Experience of Slavery

Mid-Eighteenth-Century Wars
The War of Jenkins's Ear
The War of the Austrian Succession
   (1740–1748)
The "Diplomatic Revolution" of 1756
The Seven Years' War (1756–1763)

The American Revolution and Europe
Resistance to the Imperial Search
   for Revenue
The Crisis and Independence
American Political Ideas
Events in Great Britain
Broader Impact of the American
   Revolution

KEY TOPICS

- Europe's mercantilist empires
- Spain's vast colonial empire in the Americas
- Africa, slavery, and the transatlantic plantation economies
- The wars of the mid-eighteenth century in Europe and the colonies
- The struggle for independence in Britain's North American colonies

The middle of the eighteenth century witnessed a renewal of European warfare on a worldwide scale. The conflict involved two separate, but interrelated, rivalries. Austria and Prussia fought for dominance in central Europe, while Great Britain and France dueled for commercial and colonial supremacy. The wars were long, extensive, and costly in both effort and money. They resulted in a new balance of power on the Continent and on the high seas. Prussia emerged as a great power, and Great Britain gained a world empire.

The expense of these wars led every major European government after the Peace of Paris of 1763 to reconstruct its policies of taxation and finance. The revised fiscal programs produced internal conditions for the monarchies of Europe that had significant effects lasting the rest of the century, including the American Revolution, enlightened absolutism on the Continent, a continuing financial crisis for the French monarchy, and reform of the Spanish Empire in South America.

Periods of European Overseas Empires

Since the Renaissance, European contacts with the rest of the world have gone through four distinct stages. The first was that of the European discovery, exploration, initial conquest, and settlement of the New World. This phase also witnessed the penetration of southeast Asian markets by Portugal and the Netherlands, which established major imperial outposts and influence in the region. The period closed by the end of the seventeenth century.

The second era—that of the mercantile empires, which are largely the concern of this chapter—was one of colonial trade rivalry among Spain, France, and Great Britain. Although during the sixteenth and seventeenth centuries differing motives had led to the establishment of overseas European empires, by the eighteenth century they generally existed to foster trade and commerce. Those commerical goals, however, often led to intense rivalry and conflict in key imperial trouble spots. As a result, the various imperial ventures led to the creation of large navies and fostered a series of major naval wars at the mid-century—wars that in turn became linked to warfare on the European continent. The Anglo-French side of the contest has often been compared to a second Hundred Years' War, with theaters of conflict in Europe, the Americas, and India.

A fundamental element of these first two periods of European imperial ventures in the Americas was the presence of slavery. By the eighteenth century, the slave population of the New World consisted almost entirely of a black population either recently forcibly imported from Africa or born to slaves whose forebears had been forcibly imported from Africa. There existed no precedent in human history for so large a forced migration of peoples from one continent to another or for the mid-Atlantic plantation economies supported by such slave labor. The creation in the Americas of this slave-based plantation economy led directly to over three centuries of extensive involvement in the slave trade by Europeans and white Americans with Africa—most particularly, the societies of West Africa. In turn, the slave trade created on the American continent extensive communities of Africans from the Chesapeake region of Maryland and Virginia south to Brazil. The Africans brought to the American experience not only their labor, but their languages, customs, and ethnic associations. The Atlantic economy and the societies that arose in the Americas were consequently very much the creation of both Europeans and Africans, while, as a result of the Spanish conquest, native Americans were pressed toward the margins of those societies.

Finally, during the second period, both the British colonies of the North American seaboard and the Spanish colonies of Mexico and Central and South America emancipated themselves from European control. This era of independence, part of which is discussed in this chapter and part in Chapter 21, may be said to have closed during the 1820s.

The third stage of European contact with the non-European world occurred in the nineteenth century. During that period, European governments carved new formal empires involving the direct European administration of indigenous peoples in Africa and Asia. Those nineteenth-century empires also included new areas of European settlement, such as Australia, New Zealand, and South Africa. The bases of these empires were trade, national honor, Christian missionary enterprise, and military strategy.

The last period of European empire occurred during the mid- and late twentieth century, with the decolonization of peoples who had previously lived under European colonial rule.

During the four-and-one-half centuries before decolonization, Europeans exerted political dominance over much of the rest of the world that was far disproportional to the geographical size or population of Europe. Europeans frequently treated other peoples as social, intellectual, and economic inferiors. They ravaged existing cultures because of greed, religious zeal, or political ambition. These actions are major facts of both European and world history and remain significant factors in the contemporary relationship between Europe and its former colonies. What allowed the Europeans to exert such influence and domination for so long over so much of the world was not any innate cultural superiority, but a technological supremacy related to naval power and gunpowder. Ships and guns allowed the Europeans to exercise their will almost wherever they chose.

Mercantile Empires

Navies and merchant shipping were the keystones of the mercantile empires that were meant to bring profit to a nation rather than to provide areas for settlement. The Treaty of Utrecht (1713) established the boundaries of empire during the first half of the century.

Except for Brazil, which was governed by Portugal, Spain controlled all of mainland South America. In North America, it ruled Florida, Mexico, California, and the Southwest. The Spanish also governed Central America and the islands of Cuba, Puerto Rico, and half of Hispaniola.

The British Empire consisted of the colonies along the North Atlantic seaboard, Nova Scotia, Newfoundland, Jamaica, and Barbados. Britain also possessed a few trading stations on the Indian subcontinent.

The French domains covered the Saint Lawrence River valley and the Ohio and Mississippi River valleys. They included the West Indian islands of Saint Domingue (Hispaniola), Guadeloupe, and Martinique and also stations in India. To the French and British merchant communities, India appeared as a vast potential market for European goods, as well as the source of calicos and spices that were in much demand in Europe.

The Dutch controlled Surinam, or Dutch Guiana, in South America, and various trading stations in Ceylon and Bengal. Most important, they controlled the trade with Java in what is now Indonesia. The Dutch had opened these markets largely in the seventeenth century and had created a vast trading empire far larger in extent, wealth, and importance than the geographical size of the United Netherlands would have led one to expect. The Dutch had been daring sailors and made important technological innovations in sailing.

All of these powers also possessed numerous smaller islands in the Caribbean. So far as eighteenth-century developments were concerned, the major rivalries existed among the Spanish, the French, and the British.

Mercantilist Goals

Where any formal economic theory lay behind the conduct of eighteenth-century empires, it was mercantilism, that practical creed of hard-headed businesspeople. The terms *mercantilism* and *mercantile system* were invented by later opponents and critics of the system whereby governments heavily regulated trade and commerce in hope of increasing national wealth. Economic writers believed it necessary for a nation to gain a favorable trade balance of gold and silver bullion. They regarded bullion as the measure of a country's wealth, and a nation was truly wealthy only if it amassed more bullion than its rivals. (See "Jacques Savary Praises Trade.")

The mercantilist statesmen and traders regarded the world as an arena of scarce resources and economic limitation. The attitudes associated with mercantilist thinking assumed very modest levels of economic growth. Such thinking predated the expansion of agricultural and later industrial productivity discussed in the previous chapter. Prior to the beginning of such sustained economic growth, the wealth of one nation was assumed to grow or to be increased largely at the direct cost of another nation. That is to say, the wealth of one state might expand only if its armies or navies conquered the domestic or colonial territory of another state and thus gained the productive capacity of that area, or if a state expanded its trading monopoly over new territory, or if, by smuggling, it could intrude upon the trading monopoly of another state.

From beginning to end, the economic well-being of the home country was the primary concern of mercantilist writers. Colonies were to provide markets and natural resources for the industries of the home country. In turn, the home country was to furnish military security and political administration for the colonies. For decades,

The Dutch established a major trading base at Batavia in the East Indies. The city they called Batavia is now Djakarta, Indonesia.
Bildarchiv Preussicher Kulturbesitz

Jacques Savary Praises Trade

During the seventeenth century, certain writers believed it necessary to justify trade and commerce. At the time, many people associated wealth and social prestige with the aristocracy and with landed estates. Wealth in land appeared more certain and less likely to disappear through speculation than commercial wealth did. Jacques Savary was a Frenchman who in the 1670s wrote a treatise on merchants. He sought to explain why trade and commerce were part of the divine plan for humankind. He also explained how such trade could expand the wealth and power of monarchs. In writing for a French audience, Savary would appear to have in mind the commercial achievements of the Dutch, with whom France was then at war, as well as of the English.

❖ *How does Savary justify trade as part of God's plan for human society? How does he relate trade to the prosperity of kingdoms and to parts of the economy not directly engaging in overseas trade? How does he see commerce enriching monarchs?*

By the manner in which Divine Providence has dispersed things throughout the world, it is clear that God wished to create unity and love among all men, because He imposed upon them the state of always having need one of another. He did not choose to permit necessities of existence to be found in one place, but rather spread out his gifts, in order that men might have to trade together....it is this endless exchange of the commodities of life which gives birth to Trade, and it is also Trade which adds sweetness to life....

It was not enough that Trade be necessary; it was also essential that it be profitable, in order to compel some men to devote their energies to it; for there are a number of provinces, in which the plentiful supply of most of the goods needed for everyday life would have given rise to laziness, had not the desire for profit and social advancement been a goad which forced them to enter Trade.

One cannot question its usefulness; firstly, with reference to the individuals who practise commerce, because the largest part of the population makes an honest living by this occupation....

The usefulness of Trade extends also to kingdoms and to the princes who rule them; the more Trade there is within a country, the greater its wealth. There have been states which have gained immense wealth in a short time, but when war has disrupted Trade, their provinces have suffered, have sometimes been unable to pay their taxes, and in the end their fields have lain uncultivated.

The kings can also derive great benefit from Trade; because, apart from the dues which are paid to them on goods entering or leaving the kingdom, it is indeed true that all the ready money which is in he hands of the merchants and business men draw the immense sums of which the kings sometimes have need for financing great enterprises.

From Jacques Savary, *The Compleat Merchant* (first published 1675), as quoted in Roger Mettam, ed., *Government and Society in Louis XIV's France* (London: The Macmillan Press Ltd., 1977), pp. 172–173.

both sides assumed that the colonies were the inferior partner in the relationship. The home country and its colonies were to trade exclusively with each other. To that end, they tried to forge trade-tight systems of national commerce through navigation laws, tariffs, bounties to encourage production, and prohibitions against trading with the subjects of other monarchs. National monopoly was the ruling principle.

Mercantilist ideas had always been neater on paper than in practice. By the early eighteenth century, mercantilist assumptions were far removed

from the economic realities of the colonies. The colonial and home markets simply did not mesh. Spain could not produce enough goods for South America. Economic production in the British North American colonies challenged English manufacturing and led to British attempts to limit certain colonial industries, such as iron and hat making.

Colonists of different countries wished to trade with each other. English colonists could buy sugar more cheaply from the French West Indies than from English suppliers. The traders and merchants of one nation always hoped to break the monopoly of another. For all these reasons, the eighteenth century became what one historian many years ago termed the "golden age of smugglers."[1] The governments could not control the activities of all their subjects. Clashes among colonists could and did bring about conflict between governments.

French–British Rivalry

Major flash points existed between France and Britain in North America. Their colonists quarreled endlessly with each other. Both groups of settlers coveted the lower Saint Lawrence River valley, upper New England, and, later, the Ohio River valley. There were other rivalries over fishing rights, the fur trade, and alliances with Native American tribes.

The heart of the eighteenth-century colonial rivalry in the Americas, however, lay in the West Indies. These islands, close to the American continents, were the jewels of empire. The West Indies raised tobacco, cotton, indigo, coffee, and, above all, sugar, for which there existed strong markets in Europe. These commodities were becoming part of daily life, especially in western Europe. They represented one aspect of those major changes in consumption that marked eighteenth-century European culture. Sugar in particular had become a staple rather than a luxury. It was used in coffee, tea, and cocoa, for making candy and preserving fruits, and in the brewing industry. There seemed no limit to its uses, no limit to consumer demand for it, and, for a time, almost no limit to the riches that it might bring to plantation owners. Only slave labor allowed the profitable cultivation of these products during the seventeenth and eighteen centuries.

India was another area of French–British rivalry. On the Indian subcontinent, both France and Britain traded through privileged, chartered companies that enjoyed a legal monopoly. The East India Company was the English institution; the French equivalent was the *Compagnie des Indes*. The trade of India and Asia figured only marginally in the economics of empire. Nevertheless, enterprising Europeans always hoped to develop profitable commerce with India. Others regarded India as a springboard into the even larger potential market of China. The original European footholds in India were trading posts called *factories*. They existed through privileges granted by various Indian governments.

Two circumstances in the middle of the eighteenth century changed this situation in India. First, the indigenous administration and government of several Indian states had decayed. Second, Joseph

Dupleix (1697–1763) for the French and Robert Clive (1725–1774) for the British saw the developing power vacuum as opportunities for expanding the control of their respective companies. To maintain their own security and to expand their privileges, each of the two companies began in effect to take over the government of some regions. Each group of Europeans hoped to checkmate the other.

The Dutch maintained their extensive commercial empire futher to the east in what today is Indonesia. By the eighteenth century, the other European powers more or less acknowledged Dutch predominance in that region.

The Spanish Colonial System

Spanish control of its American Empire involved a system of government and a system of monopolistic trade regulation. Both were more rigid in appearance than in practice. Actual government was often informal, and the trade monopoly was frequently breached. Until the middle of the eighteenth century, the primary purpose of the Spanish Emire was to supply Spain with the precious metals mined in the New World.

Colonial Government

Because Queen Isabella of Castile (r. 1474–1504) had commissioned Columbus, the technical legal link between the New World and Spain was the crown of Castile. Its powers both at home and in America were subject to few limitations. The Castilian monarch assigned the government of America to the Council of the Indies, which, with the monarch, nominated the viceroys of New Spain (Mexico) and Peru. These viceroys served as the chief executives in the New World and carried out the laws promulgated by the Council of the Indies.

Each of the viceroyalties was divided into several subordinate judicial councils, known as *audiencias*. There was also a variety of local officers, the most important of which were the *corregidores*, who presided over municipal councils. All of these offices provided the monarchy with a vast array of patronage, usually bestowed on persons born in Spain. Virtually all power flowed from the top of this political structure downward; in effect, local initiative or self-government scarcely existed.

Trade Regulation

The colonial political structures functioned largely to support Spanish commercial self-interest. The *Casa de Contratación* (House of Trade) in Seville reg-

[1]Walter Dorn, *Competition for Empire, 1740–1763* (New York: Harper, 1940), p. 266.

Visitors Describe the Portobello Fair

The Spanish tried to restrict all trade within their Latin American empire to a few designated ports. Each year, a fair was held in certain of these ports. The most famous such port was Portobello on the Isthmus of Panama. In the 1730s, two visitors saw the event and described it. This fair was the chief means of facilitating trade between the western coast of South America and Spain.

❖ *What products were sold at the fair? How does this passage illustrate the inefficiency of monopoly trade in the Spanish empire and the many chances for smuggling?*

The town of Portobello, so thinly inhabited, by reason of its noxious air, the scarcity of provisions, and the soil, becomes, at the time of the [Spanish] galleons one of the most populous places in all South America....

The ships are no sooner moored in the harbour, than the first work is, to erect, in the square, a tent made of the ship's sails, for receiving its cargo; at which the proprietors of the goods are present, in order to find their bales, by the marks which distinguish them. These bales are drawn on sledges, to their respective places by the crew of every ship, and the money given them is proportionally divided.

Whilst the seamen and European traders are thus employed, the land is covered with droves of mules from Panama, each drove consisting of above an hundred, loaded with chests of gold and silver, on account of the merchants of Peru. Some unload them at the exchange, others in the middle of the square; yet, amidst the hurry and confusion of such crowds, no theft, loss, or disturbance, is ever known. He who has seen this place during the *tiempo muerto*, or dead time, solitary, poor, and a perpetual silence reigning everywhere; the harbour quite empty, and every place wearing a melancholy aspect; must be filled with astonishment at the sudden change, to see the bustling multitudes, every house crowded, the square and streets encumbered with bales and chests of gold and silver of all kinds; the harbour full of ships and vessels, some bringing by the way of Rio de Chape the goods of Peru, such as *cacao*, *quinquina*, or Jesuit's bark, Vicuña wool, and bezoar stones; others coming from Carthagena, loaded with provisions; and thus a spot, at all times detested for its deleterious qualities, becomes the staple of the riches of the old and new world, and the scene of one of the most considerable branches of commerce in the whole earth.

The ships being unloaded, and the merchants of Peru, together with the president of Panama, arrived, the fair comes under deliberation. And for this purpose the deputies of the several parties repair on board the commodore of the galleons, where, in the presence of the commodore, and the president of Panama, ...the prices of the several kinds of merchandizes are settled.... The purchases and sales, as likewise the exchanges of money, are transacted by brokers, both from Spain and Peru. After this, every one begins to dispose of his goods; the Spanish brokers embarking their chests of money, and those of Peru sending away the goods they have purchased, in vessels called *chatas* and *bongos*, up the river Chagres. And thus the fair of Portobello ends.

From George Juan and Antonio de Ulloa, *A Voyage to South America*, Vol. 1 (London, 1772), pp. 103–110, as quoted in Benjamin Keen, ed., *Readings in Latin-American Civilization, 1492 to the Present* (New York: Houghton Mifflin, 1955), pp. 107–108.

ulated all trade with the New World. Cádiz was the only port authorized for use in the American trade. The *Casa* was the most influential institution of the Spanish Empire. Its members worked closely with the *Consulado* (Merchant Guild) of Seville and other groups involved with American commerce in Cádiz.

A complicated system of trade and bullion fleets administered from Seville was the key to maintaining Spain's trade monopoly. Each year, a fleet of commercial vessels (the *flota*) controlled by Seville merchants and escorted by warships carried merchandise from Spain to a few specified ports in America, including Portobello, Veracruz, and Cartagena on the Atlantic coast. (See "Visitors Describe the Portobello Fair.") There were no authorized ports on the Pacific Coast. Areas far to the south, such as Buenos Aires on the Rio de la Plata, received goods only after the shipments had been unloaded at one of the authorized ports. After selling their wares, the ships were loaded with silver and gold bullion, usually wintered in heavily fortified Caribbean ports, and then sailed back to Spain. The *flota* system always worked imperfectly, but trade outside it was illegal. Regulations prohibited the Spanish colonists within the American Empire from establishing direct trade with each other and from building their own shipping and commercial industry. Foreign merchants were also forbidden to breach the Spanish monopoly.

Colonial Reform under the Spanish Bourbon Monarchs

A crucial change occurred in the Spanish colonial system in the early eighteenth century. The War of the Spanish Succession (1701–1714) and the Treaty of Utrecht (1713) replaced the Spanish Habsburgs with the Bourbons of France on the Spanish throne. Philip V (r. 1700–1746) and his successors tried to use French administrative skills to reassert the imperial trade monopoly, which had decayed under the last Spanish Habsburgs and thus attempted to improve the domestic economy and revive Spanish power in European affairs.

Under Philip V, Spanish coastal patrol vessels tried to suppress smuggling in American waters. (See "Buccaneers Prowl the High Seas.") An incident arising from this policy (to be discussed later in the chapter) led to war with England in 1739, the year in which Philip established the viceroyalty of New Granada in the area that today includes Venezuela, Colombia, and Ecuador. The goal was to increase direct royal government in the area.

During the reign of Ferdinand VI (r. 1746–1759), the great midcentury wars exposed the vulnerability of the empire to naval attack and economic penetration. As an ally of France, Spain emerged as one of the defeated powers in 1763. Government circles became convinced that further changes in the colonial system had to be undertaken.

Charles III (r. 1759–1788), the most important of the royal imperial reformers, attempted to reassert Spain's control of the empire. Like his two Bourbon predecessors, Charles emphasized royal ministers rather than councils. Thus, the role of both the Council of the Indies and the *Casa de Contratación* diminished. After 1765, Charles abolished the monopolies of Seville and Cádiz and permitted other Spanish cities to trade with America. He also opened more South American and Caribbean ports to trade and authorized some commerce between Spanish ports in America. In 1776 he organized a fourth viceroyalty in the region of Rio de la Plata, which included much of present-day Argentina, Uruguay, Paraguay, and Bolivia. (See Map 17–1.)

While relaxing Spanish trade with and in America, Charles III attempted to increase the efficiency of tax collection and to end bureaucratic corruption. To achieve those ends, he introduced the institu-

tion of the *intendant* into the Spanish Empire. These loyal, royal bureaucrats were patterned on the French *intendants* made so famous and effective as agents of the absolutism of Louis XIV.

The late-eighteenth-century Bourbon reforms did stimulate the imperial economy. Trade expanded and became more varied. These reforms, however, also brought the empire more fully under direct Spanish control. Many *peninsulares* (persons born in Spain) entered the New World to fill new posts, which were often the most profitable jobs in the region. Expanding trade brought more Spanish merchants to Latin America. The economy remained export oriented, and economic life was still organized to benefit Spain. As a result of these policies, the *creoles* (persons of European descent born in the Spanish colonies) came to feel that they were second-class subjects. In time, their resentment would provide a major source of the discontent leading to the wars of independence in the early nineteenth century. The imperial reforms of Charles III were the Spanish equivalent of the new colonial measures undertaken by the British government after 1763, which led to the American Revolution.

Black African Slavery, the Plantation System, and the Atlantic Economy

Within various parts of Europe itself, slavery had existed since ancient times. Before the eighteenth century, little or no moral or religious stigma attached to slave owning or slave trading. It had a continuous existence in the Mediterranean world, where only the sources of slaves changed over the centuries. After the conquest of Constantinople in the mid-fifteenth century, the Ottoman Empire forbade the exportation of white slaves from regions under its control. The Portuguese then began to import African slaves into the Iberian Peninsula from the Canary Islands and West Africa. Black slaves from Africa were also not uncommon in other parts of the Mediterranean, and a few found their way into northern Europe. There they might be used as personal servants or displayed because of the novelty of their color in the courts of royalty or homes of the wealthy.

But from the sixteenth century onward, first within the West Indies and the Spanish and Portuguese settlements in South America and then in the British colonies on the South Atlantic seaboard of North America, slave labor became a fundamental social and economic factor. The development of those plantation economies based on slave labor led to an unprecedented interaction between the peoples of Europe and Africa and between the European settlers

Buccaneers Prowl the High Seas

By no means all of the trade in the Caribbean Sea occurred at the Portobello fair described in the previous document. Piracy was a major problem for transatlantic trade. There was often a fine line between freewheeling, buccaneering pirates operating for their own gain and privateers who in effect worked for various European governments that wanted to penetrate the commercial monopoly of the Spanish Empire. Alexander Exquemelin was a ship's surgeon who for a time plied his trade on board a pirate ship and then later settled in Holland. He wrote an account of those days in which he emphasizes the careful code of conduct among the pirates themselves and the harshness of their behavior toward both those on ships they captured and poor farmers and fishermen whom they robbed and virtually enslaved.

❖ *How did the restrictive commercial policy of the Spanish Empire encourage piracy and privateering? Was there a code of honor among the pirates? What kinds of people may have suffered most from piracy? To what extent did pirates have any respect for individual freedom? How romantic was the real world of pirates?*

When a buccaneer is going to sea he sends word to all who wish to sail with him. When all are ready, they go on board, each bringing what he needs in the way of weapons, powder and shot.

On the ship, they first discuss where to go and get food supplies....The meat is either [salted] pork or turtle...Sometimes they go and plunder the Spaniards' *corrales*, which are pens where they keep perhaps a thousand head of tame hogs. The rovers...find the house of the farmer...[whom] unless he gives them as many hogs as they demand, they hang...without mercy....

When a ship has been captured, the men decide whether the captain should keep it or not: if the prize is better than their own vessel, they take it and set fire to the other. When a ship is robbed, nobody must plunder and keep the loot to himself. Everything taken... must be shared..., without any man enjoying a penny more than his faire share. To prevent deceit, before the booty is distributed everyone has to swear an oath on the Bible that he has not kept for himself so much as the value of a sixpence... And should any man be found to have made a false

oath, he would be banished from the rovers, and never be allowed in their company....

When they have captured a ship, the buccaneers set the prisoners on shore as soon as possible, apart from two or three whom they keep to do the cooking and other work they themselves do not care for, releasing these men after two or three years.

The rovers frequently put in for fresh supplies at some island or other, often...lying off the south coast of Cuba.... Everyone goes ashore and sets up his tent, and they take turns to go on marauding expeditions in their canoes. They take prisoner...poor men who catch and set turtles for a living, to provide for their wives and children. Once captured, these men have to catch turtle for the rovers as long as they remain on the island. Should the rovers intend to cruise along a coast where turtle abound, they take the fishermen along with them. The poor fellows may be compelled to stay away from their wives and families four or five years, with no news whether they are alive or dead.

Alexander O. Exquemelin, *The Buccaneers of America*, Alexis Brown, tr. (Baltimore, Penguin Books, 1969) pp. 70–72.

in the Americas and Africa. It was from that point onward that Africa and Africans became drawn into the Western experience as never before in history.

The African Presence in the Americas

Once they had encountered and begun to settle the New World, the conquering Spanish and Portuguese faced a severe shortage of labor. They and

most of the French and English settlers who came later had no intention of undertaking manual work themselves. At first, they used Native Americans as laborers, but during the sixteenth century as well as afterwards, disease killed hundreds of thousands of the native population. As a result, labor soon became scarce. The Spanish and Portuguese then turned to the labor of imported African slaves. Settlers in the English colonies of

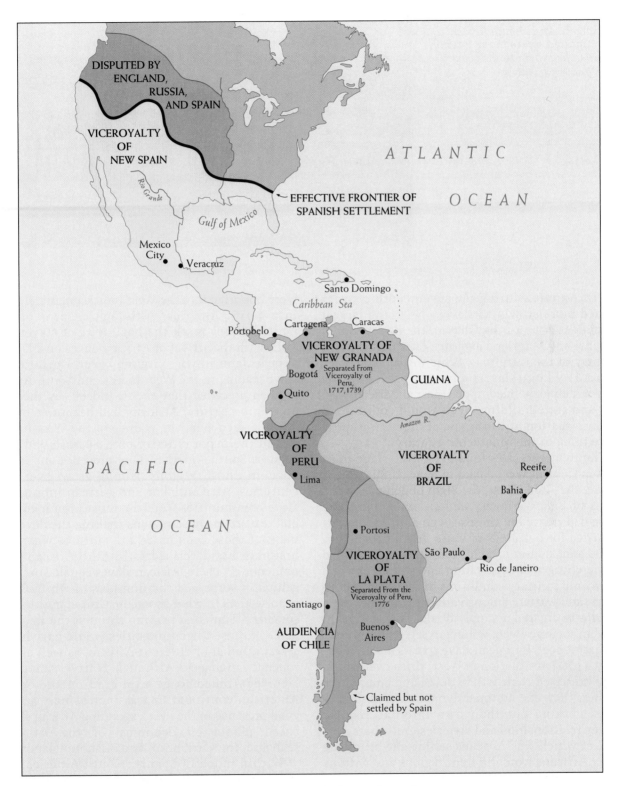

MAP 17–1   VICEROYALTIES IN LATIN AMERICA IN 1780   *The late-eighteenth-century viceroyalties in Latin America display the effort of the Spanish Bourbon monarchy to establish more direct conrol of the continent. They sought this control through the introductions of more royal officials and by establishing more governmental districts.*

This eighteenth-century print shows bound African captives being forced to a slaving port. It was largely African middlemen who captured slaves in the interior and marched them to the coast.
North Wind Picture Archives

North America during the seventeenth century turned more slowly to slavery, with the largest number coming to the Chesapeake Bay region of Virginia and Maryland and then later into the low country of the Carolinas. Which African peoples became sold into slavery during any given decade very largely depended upon internal African warfare and state-building. Such would continue to be the situation until the end of the transatlantic slave trade in the nineteenth century.

The major sources for slaves were slave markets in Central West Africa in Senegambia, Sierra Leone, the Gold Coast, the Bight of Benin, and the Bight of Biafra. Slavery and an extensive slave trade had existed in these as well as other regions of Africa for hundreds of years. Just as particular social and economic conditions in Europe had led to the voyages of exploration and settlement, political and military conditions in the African continent and warfare among various African nations similiarly created a supply of slaves that certain African societies were willing to sell to Europeans. In that respect, European slave traders did not confront a passive situation in West Africa over which they exercised their will by force and commerce. Rather, they encountered dynamic African societies working out their own internal historic power relationships and rivalries, one characteristic of which was Africans selling and acquiring other Africans from different regions and nations as slaves.

The West Indies, Brazil, and Sugar To grasp the full impact of the forced immigration of Africans on the Americas, it is necessary to take into account both continents and the entire picture of the transatlantic economy. Far more slaves were imported into the West Indies and Brazil than into North America. Although citizens of the United States mark the beginning of slavery in 1619 with the arrival of African slaves on a Dutch ship in Jamestown, Virginia, over a century of slave trading in the West Indies and South America had preceded that event. Indeed, by the late sixteenth century, Africans had become a major social presence on the islands of the West Indies and in the major cities of both Spanish and Portuguese South America. That presence and influence in those regions would grow over the centuries. African labor and African immigrant slave communities were the most prominent social feature of those regions making the development of those economies and cultures what one historian has described as "a Euro-African phenomenon."[2] There, African slaves equaled or more generally surpassed the numbers of white European settlers in what soon constituted multiracial societies. Someone passing through the marketplace of those towns and cities would have heard a vast number of different African, as well as European, languages. Although Native American labor continued to be exploited on the South American continent, it was increasingly a marginal presence in the ever-expanding African slave-based plantation economy of the Atlantic seaboard, the Caribbean, and offshore islands.

Within much of Spanish South America, the numbers of slaves declined during the late seventeenth century, and slavery became somewhat

[2]John Thornton, *Africa and the Africans in the Making of the Atlantic World, 1400–1800*, 2d ed. (Cambridge, U.K.: Cambridge University Press, 1998), p. 140

In the American South, the islands of the Caribbean, and in Brazil, the slaves labored on sugar plantations under the authority of overseers. The Granger Collection

A vast increase in the number of Africans brought as slaves to the Americas occurred during the eighteenth century, with the majority arriving in the Caribbean or Brazil. Early in the century, as many as 20,000 new Africans a year arrived in the West Indies as slaves. By 1725, it has been estimated, almost 90 percent of the population of Jamaica was black slaves. After the middle of the century, for some time the numbers were even larger. The influx of new Africans in most areas—even in the British colonies—meant that the numbers of new forced immigrants outnumbered the slaves of African descent already present.

Newly imported African slaves were needed because the fertility rate of the earlier slave population was low and the death rate high from disease, overwork, and malnutrition. The West Indies proved a particularly difficult region in which to secure a stable, self-reproducing slave population. The conditions for slaves there simply led to very high rates of mortality with new slaves coming primarily from the ongoing slave trade. A similar situation prevailed in Brazil. Restocking through the slave trade meant that the slave population of those areas consisted of African-born persons rather than of persons of African descent. Consequently, one of the key factors in the social life of many of the areas of American slavery during the eighteenth century was the presence of persons newly arrived from Africa, carrying with them African languages, religion, culture, and local African ethnic identities that they would infuse into the already existing slave communities. Thus, the eighteenth century witnessed an enormous impact of a new African presence throughout the Americas.

Slavery and the Transatlantic Economy

Different nations dominated the slave trade in different periods. During the sixteenth century, the Portuguese and the Spanish were most involved. The Dutch supplanted them during most of the seventeenth century. Thereafter, during the late seventeenth and eighteenth century, the English constituted the chief slave traders. French traders also participated.

Slavery touched most of the economy of the transatlantic world. Colonial trade followed roughly a geographic triangle. European goods—quite often guns—were carried to Africa to be exchanged for slaves, who were then taken to the West Indies, where they were traded for sugar and other tropical products, which were then shipped

less fundamental there than elsewhere. Slavery continued to expand its influence, however, in Brazil and in the Caribbean through the spreading cultivation of sugar to meet the demand of the European market. By the close of the seventeenth century, the Caribbean islands were the world center for the production of sugar and the chief supplier for the ever-growing consumer demand for the product. The opening of new areas of cultivation and other economic enterprises required additional slaves during the eighteenth century, a period of major slave importation. The growing prosperity of sugar islands that had begun to be exploited in the late seventeenth century, as well as new sugar, coffee, and tobacco regions of Brazil, where gold mining also required additional slaves, accounts for this increase in slave commerce and allowed higher prices to be paid for slaves. In Brazil, the West Indies, and the southern British colonies, prosperity and slavery went hand in hand.

to Europe. Not all ships covered all three legs of the triangle. Another major trade pattern existed between New England and the West Indies with New England fish or ship stores being traded for sugar. At various moments, the prosperity of such cities as Amsterdam, Liverpool, England, and Nantes, France, rested very largely on the slave trade. Cities in the British North American colonies, such as Newport, Rhode Island, profited from slavery sometimes by trading in slaves, but more often by supplying other goods to the West Indian market. All the shippers who handled cotton, tobacco, and sugar depended on slavery, though they might not have had direct contact with the institution, as did all the manufacturers and merchants who produced the finished products for the consumer market. (See "Art & the West.")

As had been the case during previous centuries, eighteenth-century political turmoil in Africa, such as the Kongo civil wars, made possible the increasing supply of slaves during that period. These Kongo wars had originated in a dispute over succession in the late seventeenth century and con-tinued into the eighteenth. In some cases, captives were simply sold to European slave traders calling at ports along the West African coast. In other cases, African leaders conducted slave raids so their captives could be sold to further finance the purchase of weapons for warfare. Similar political unrest and turmoil in the Gold Coast during the eighteenth century led to an increased supply of African captives to be sold into American slavery. Consequently, there existed a close relationship between warfare in West Africa, often far into the interior, and the economic development of the American Atlantic seaboard.

The Experience of Slavery

The Portuguese, Spanish, Dutch, French, and English slave traders forcibly transported several million (perhaps more than nine million, the exact numbers being in much dispute) Africans to the New World—the largest example of forced intercontinental migration in human history. During the first four centuries of settlement, far more black slaves came involuntarily to the New World

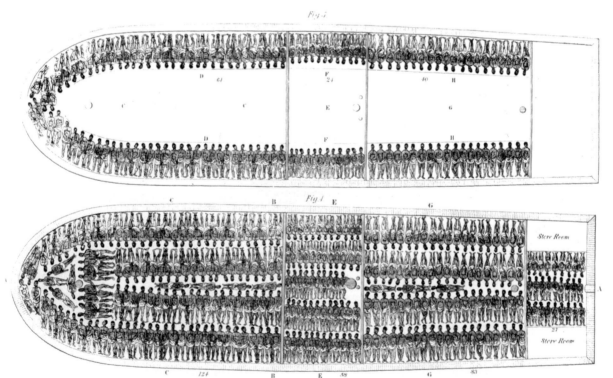

Loading plan for the main decks of the 320-ton slave ship Brookes. *The* Brookes *was only 25 feet wide and 100 feet long, but as many as 609 slaves were crammed on board for the nightmarish passage to the Americas. The average space allowed each person was only about 78 inches by 16 inches. The document from Thomas Phillips's journal describes the voyage across the Atlantic. (See "A Slave Trader Describes the Atlantic Passage.")* Photographs and Prints Division, Schomburg Center for Research in Black Culture, The New York Public Library, Astor, Lenox and Tilden Foundations

A Slave Trader Describes the Atlantic Passage

During 1693 and 1694, Captain Thomas Phillips carried slaves from Africa to Barbados on the ship Hannibal. *The financial backer of the voyage was the Royal African Company of London, which held an English crown monopoly on slave trading. Phillips sailed to the west coast of Africa, where he purchased the Africans who were sold into slavery by an African king. Then he set sail westward.*

❖ *Who are the various people described in this document who in one way or another were involved in or profited from the slave trade? What dangers did the Africans face on the voyage? What contemporary attitudes could have led this ship captain to treat and think of his human cargo simply as goods to be transported? What are the grounds of his self-pity for the difficulties he met?*

Having bought my complement of 700 slaves, 480 men and 220 women, and finish'd all my business at Whidaw [on the Gold Coast of Africa], I took my leave of the old king and his *cappasheirs* [attendants], and parted, with many affectionate expressions on both sides, being forced to promise him that I would return again the next year, with several things he desired me to bring from England.... I set sail the 27th of July in the morning, accompany'd with the East-India Merchant, who had bought 650 slaves, for the Island of St. Thomas...from which we took our departure on August 25th and set sail for Barbadoes.

We spent in our passage from St. Thomas to Barbadoes two months eleven days, from the 25th of August to the 4th of November following: in which time there happened such sickness and mortality among my poor men and Negroes. Of the first we buried 14, and of the last 320, which was a great detriment to our voyage, the Royal African Company losing ten pounds by every slave that died, and the owners of the ship ten pounds ten shillings, being the freight agreed on to be paid by the charter-party for every Negro delivered alive ashore to the African Company's agents at Barbadoes....The loss in all amounted to near 6500 pounds sterling.

The distemper which my men as well as the blacks mostly died of was the white flux, which was so violent and inveterate that no medicine would in the least check it, so that when any of our men were seized with it, we esteemed him a dead man, as he generally proved....

The Negroes are so incident to the small-pox that few ships that carry them escape without it, and sometimes it makes vast havock and destruction among them. But tho' we had 100 at a time sick of it, and that it went thro' the ship, yet we lost not above a dozen by it. All the assistance we gave the diseased was only as much water as they desir'd to drink, and some palm-oil to annoint their sores, and they would generally recover without any other helps but what kind nature gave them....

But what the small pox spar'd, the flux swept off, to our great regret, after all our pains and care to give them their messes in due order and season, keeping their lodgings as clean and sweet as possible, and enduring so much misery and stench so long among a parcel of creatures nastier than swine, and after all our expectations to be defeated by their mortality....

No gold-finders can endure so much noisome slavery as they do who carry Negroes; for those have some respite and satisfaction, but we endure twice the misery; and yet by their mortality our voyages are ruin'd, and we pine and fret ourselves to death, and take so much pains to so little purpose.

From Thomas Phillips, *"Journal," A Collection of Voyages and Travels*, Vol. VI, ed. by Awnsham and John Churchill (London, 1746), as quoted in Thomas Howard, ed., *Black Voyage: Eyewitness Accounts of the Atlantic Slave Trade* (Boston: Little, Brown and Company, 1971), pp. 85–87.

than did free European settlers or European indentured servants. The conditions of slaves' passage across the Atlantic were wretched. (See "A Slave Trader Describes the Atlantic Passage.") Quarters were unspeakably cramped, food was bad, disease was rampant. Many Africans died

during the crossing. There were always more African men than women transported, so it was difficult to keep any form of traditional African extended family structures in place. During the passage and later, many Africans attempted to recreate such structures among themselves, even if

A Dramatic Moment in the Transatlantic World: Copley's Watson and the Shark

John Singleton Copley, American, 1738–1815. *Watson and the Shark*, 1778. Oil on canvas, 72 1/4 × 90 3/8 in. Gift of Mrs. George von Lengerke Meyer. Courtesy, Museum of Fine Arts, Boston. Reproduced with permission. © 1999 Museum of Fine Arts, Boston. All Rights Reserved.

*B*oth the career of the North American born painter John Singleton Copley (1738–1815) and his monumental painting, *Watson and the Shark* (1778) illustrate the economic and cultural interconnections of the eighteenth-century transatlantic world. Copley was born in Massachusetts and became an accomplished portrait painter of the Boston elite. When hostilities erupted between Britain and the colonies, Copley moved to London in 1774, where his reputation had preceded him. He never returned to America.

In Britain, he undertook commissions for *history painting*, then considered the most prestigious subject for artists. Traditionally, history painting drew its subject matter from mythology, biblical narratives, or ancient history, but Copley was interested in portraying contemporary events. His figures were modern people, dressed in modern clothing but striking poses taken from classical and Renaissance art.

History painting claimed to convey a moral message usually of heroism, patriotism, or self-sacrifice. In 1778 Copley completed *Watson and the Shark*, recounting the experience of Brook Watson's rescue, as a boy of 14 in 1749, from the jaws of a shark in the harbor of Havana, Cuba. Watson, who later became Lord Mayor of London, lost most of his leg in the attack, but regarded his rescue and subsequent success as a merchant as an inspiring example to others who had encountered adversity.

In portraying the terrifying moment just before Watson's rescue, Copley presents the event as a profound drama, which he invites the viewer to attend. By seeking to evoke a powerful emotional response from the viewer, Copley was working in the category of art known at the time as the *sublime*. Yet Copley also used his power as a portraitist to depict each man in the painting as a real person, not as some allegorical figure.

Watson and the Shark is also one of the first paintings to prominently depict an African American. The black man in the middle of the painting holds the rope that will soon be used to rescue Watson. His presence also places the action in the world of the plantation economy and transatlantic trade. It is not clear whether he is a slave or whether, like Olaudah Equiano in the following document, a former slave now working as a sailor in the commercial shipping trade.

In several respects, this painting illustrates the interconnectedness of the eighteenth-century transatlantic world. Copley is an American artist working in London. The action occurs in a Spanish colony during a commercial venture. The person being rescued is an English subject who will become a rich merchant. The boat holds a cross section of races and cultures from Africa, Europe, and the Americas that characterized the world of the plantation economies.

Watson and the Shark is also important in art history for another reason. Through the contrasts of light and dark, Copley set out to achieve a dramatic painting of human beings in combat with powerful natural forces—the sea, the wind, and the shark. This would become a major theme of the late eighteenth- and early nineteenth-century artistic and literary movement known as Romanticism. *Watson and the Shark* stands as a major forerunner of this new direction of painting and taste.

Sources: Jules Prown, *John Singleton Copley* (Cambridge, Mass.: Harvard University Press, 1966]: John Wilmerding, *American Art* (New York: Penguin Books, 1976); Theodore Stebbins, Jr. et al., *A New World: Masterpieces of American Painting 1760–1910* (Boston: Museum of Fine Arts, 1983), pp. 210–211; Hugh Honour, *The Image of the Black in Western Art*, Vol 4, Part I., *From the American Revolution to World War I: Slave and Liberators* (Cambridge, Mass.: Harvard University Press, 1989).

they were not actually related by direct family ties. (See Olaudah Equiano Recalls His Experience at the Slave Market in Barbados.")

In the Americas, the slave population stood divided among new Africans recently arrived, old Africans who had lived there for some years, and creoles who were the descendants of earlier generations of African slaves. Plantation owners preferred the two latter groups, who were accustomed to the life of slavery. They sold for higher prices. The newly arrived Africans were subjected to a process known as *seasoning* whereby they were prepared for the laborious discipline of slavery and made to understand that they were no longer free. The process might involve receiving new names, acquiring new work skills, and learning, to an extent, the local European language. In some cases, newly arrived Africans would work in a kind of apprentice relationship to an older African slave of similar ethnic background. Other slaves were broken into slave labor through work on field gangs. Occasionally, plantation owners would prefer to buy younger Africans, whom they thought might be more easily acculturated to the labor conditions of the Americas. Generally, it was only such recently arrived Africans, seasoned in the West Indies, whom North American plantation owners were willing to purchase.

LANGUAGE AND CULTURE   The plantation to which the slaves eventually arrived always lay in a more or less isolated rural setting, but its inhabitants usually could visit their counterparts on other plantations or in nearby towns on market days. Within the sharply restricted confines of slavery, the recently arrived Africans were able at least for a time to sustain elements of their own culture and social structures. From the West Indies southward throughout the eighteenth century, there were more people whose first language was African rather than European. For example, Coromantee was the predominant language on Jamaica. In South Carolina and on St. Domingue, Kikongo was the language most commonly spoken among African slaves. It would take more than two generations for the colonial language to dominate, and even then what often resulted was a dialect combining an African and a European language.

Through these languages, Africans on plantation estates could organize themselves into *nations* with similar, though not necessarily identical, ethnic ties to regions of West Africa. The loyalty achieved through a shared African language in the American setting created a solidarity among African slaves that was wider than what in Africa had probably been a primary loyalty to a village. These nations

organized and sustained by the plantation experience might also become the basis for a wide variety of religious communities among African slaves that might have some kind of roots in their African experience. In this manner, some Africans maintained a loyalty to the Islamic faith of their homeland.

Many of the African nations on plantations, such as those of Brazil, organized lay brotherhoods that carried out various kinds of charitable work within the slave communities. In the Americas, the various African nations would elect their own kings and queens, who might preside over gatherings of the members of the nation drawn from various plantations.

The shared language of a particular African nation in an American setting provided a means for exclusive communication among slaves on the occasions of revolts such as that in South Carolina in 1739, in Jamaica in the early 1760s, and, most successfully, during the Haitian Revolution of the 1790s. In the South Carolina revolt, the slave owners believed that their slaves had communicated among themselves by playing African drums. In the aftermath of the revolt, the owners attempted to suppress the presence of such drum playing in the slave community.

DAILY LIFE   The life conditions of plantation slaves differed from colony to colony. Black slaves living in Portuguese areas had the fewest legal protections. In the Spanish colonies, the church attempted to provide some protection for black slaves, but devoted more effort toward protecting the Native Americans. Slave codes were developed in the British and the French colonies during the seventeenth century, but they provided only the most limited protection to slaves while assuring dominance to owners. Virtually all slave owners feared a revolt, and legislation and other regulations were intended to prevent one. All slave laws favored the master rather than the slave. Slave masters were permitted to whip slaves and inflict other exceedingly harsh corporal punishment. Furthermore, slaves were often forbidden to gather in large groups lest they plan a revolt. In most of these slave societies, the marriages of slaves were not recognized by law. Legally, the children of slaves continued to be slaves and were owned by the owner of their parents.

The daily life of most slaves during these centuries was one of hard agricultural labor, poor diet, and inadequate housing. Slave families could be separated by the owner during his life or sold separately after his death. Their welfare and their lives were sacrificed to the continuing expansion of the sugar, rice, and tobacco plantations that

Olaudah Equiano Recalls His Experience at the Slave Market in Barbados

Olaudah Equiano composed one of the most popular and influential slave narratives of the late eighteenth and early nineteenth centuries. He had led a remarkable life. Born in West Africa in what is today Nigeria, he spent his early life among the Ibo. He was captured and sold into slavery, making the dreaded Atlantic crossing described in the previous document. In the passage that follows, he recounts his arrival in Barbados and the experience of cultural disorientation, sale into slavery, and seeing Africans separated from their families. Equiano's life did not end in slavery, the most destructive aspects of which he also described in vivid detail. He achieved his freedom and then undertook an adventuresome life on various commercial and military ships plying the Caribbean, the Atlantic, and the Mediterranean. He also made a trip to the Arctic Ocean. Equiano's account consequently describes not only the life of a person taken from Africa and sold into American slavery, but also the life of a person who, once free, explored the entire transatlantic world. His autobiographical narrative, which first appeared in 1789 and displayed Equiano's wide reading, served two purposes for the antislavery campaign that commenced in the second half of the eighteenth century. (See "The West & the World," pp. 736–737.) First, it provided a firsthand report of the slave experience in crossing from Africa to America. Second, his powerful rhetoric and clear arguments demonstrated that, if free, Africans could achieve real personal independence. Many defenders of slavery had denied that Africans possessed the character and intelligence to be free persons.

❖ *What were the fears of the Africans on the slave ship as they approached the port? How were older slaves in Barbados used to calm their fears? How did the sale of slaves proceed? What happened to African families in the process of the sale?*

At last, we came in sight...of Barbados,...and we soon anchored...off Bridgetown. Many merchants and planters now came on board... They put us in separate parcels, and examined us attentively. They also made us jump, and pointed to the land, signifying we were to go there. We thought by this we should be eaten by these ugly men, as they appeared to us; and when, soon after we were all put down under the deck again, there was much dread and trembling among us, and nothing but bitter cries to be heard all the night from these apprehension, insomuch that at last the white people got some old slaves from the land to pacify us. They told us we were not to be eaten, but to work, and were soon to go on land, where were should see many of our country people. This report eased us much....We were conducted immediately to the merchant's yard, where we were all pent up together like so many sheep in a fold, without regard to sex or age. As every object was new to me, everything filled me with surprise...and indeed I thought these people were full of nothing but magical arts....We were not many days in the merchant's custody before we were sold after their usual manner which was this: On a signal given (as the beat of a drum), the buyers rush at once into the yard where the slaves are confined, and make choice of that parcel they like best. The noise and clamour with which this is attended, and the eagerness visible in the countenances of the buyers, serve not a little to increase the apprehension of the terrified Africans, who may well be supposed to consider them as the ministers of that destruction to which they think themselves devoted. In this manner, without scruple, relations and friends separate, most of them never to see each other again. I remember in the vessel in which I was brought over, in the men's apartment, there were several brothers who, in the sale, were sold in different lots; and it was very moving on this occasion to see and hear their cries at parting.... Surely this is a new refinement in cruelty, which, while it has no advantage to atone for it, thus aggravates distress, and adds fresh horrors even to the wretchedness of slavery.

From *The Interesting Narrative of the Life of Olaudah Equiano or Gustavus Vassa, The African, Written by Himself* (first published 1789), as quoted in Henry Louis Gates, Jr., and William L., Andrews, eds., *Pioneers of the Black Atalantic: Five Slave Narratives from the Enlightenment, 1772–1815* (Washington, DC: Counterpoint, 1998), pp. 221–223.

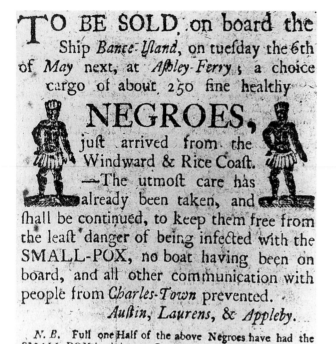

TO BE SOLD on board the Ship *Bance-Island*, on tuesday the 6th of *May* next, at *Aßley-Ferry*; a choice cargo of about 250 fine healthy **NEGROES**, juſt arrived from the Windward & Rice Coaſt. —The utmoſt care has already been taken, and ſhall be continued, to keep them free from the leaſt danger of being infected with the SMALL-POX, no boat having been on board, and all other communication with people from *Charles-Town* prevented. *Auſtin, Laurens, & Appleby.*

N. B. Full one Half of the above Negroes have had the SMALL-POX in their own Country.

Those Africans who survived the voyage across the Atlantic were immediately sold into slavery in the Americas. This slave-auction notice relates to a group of slaves whose ship had stopped at Charleston, South Carolina, and then landed elsewhere in the region to auction its human cargo. Notice the concern to assure potential buyers that the slaves were healthy. Corbis

made their owners wealthy and that produced goods for European consumers. Scholars have sometimes concluded that slaves in one area lived better than in another. Today, it is generally accepted that all the slaves in plantation societies led exposed and difficult lives with little variation among them.

CONVERSION TO CHRISTIANITY   The African slaves who were transported to the Americas, were, like the Native Americans, eventually converted in most cases to Christianity. In the Spanish, French, and Portuguese domains, they became Roman Catholics, and in the English colonies they became Protestants of one denomination or another. Both forms of Christianity preached to slaves the acceptance of their situation and a natural social hierarchy with masters at the top.

While African religion of a systematic character eventually disappeared, especially in the British colonies, some African religious practices survived in muted forms, gradually separated from African religious belief. These included an African understanding of nature and the cosmos and the belief in witches and other people with special spiritual powers, such as conjurers, healers, and practitioners of voodoo. Although slaves did manage to mix Christianity with their previous African religions, their conversion to Christianity was nonetheless another example, like that of the Native Americans, of the crushing of a set of non-European cultural values in the context of the New World economies and social structures.

EUROPEAN RACIAL ATTITUDES   The European settlers in the Americas and the slave traders also carried with them prejudices against black Africans. Many Europeans considered Africans to be savages or less than civilized. Still others looked down on them simply because they were slaves. Both Christians and Muslims had shared these attitudes in the Mediterranean world, where slavery had for so long existed. Furthermore, many European languages and cultures attached negative connotations to the idea and image of blackness. In virtually all these plantation societies, race was an important element in keeping black slaves in a position of marked subservience. Although racial thinking in regard to slavery became important primarily in the nineteenth century, the fact of slaves being differentiated from the rest of the population by race, as well as by their being chattel property, was fundamental to the system. All of these factors formed the racial prejudice that continues to plague society today in the former slave-owning regions.

The plantations that stretched from the middle Atlantic colonies of North America through the West Indies and into Brazil constituted a vast corridor of slave societies in which social and economic subordination was based on both involuntary servitude and race. These societies had not existed before the European discovery and exploitation of the resources of the Americas. In its extent and totality of dependence on slave labor and racial differences, this kind of society was novel in both European and world history. As already noted, its social and economic influence touched not only the plantation societies themselves, but West Africa, western Europe, and New England. It existed from the sixteenth century through the second half of the nineteenth century, when the emancipation of slaves had been completed through the slave revolt of Saint Domingue (1794), British outlawing of the slave trade (1807), the Latin American wars of independence, the Emancipation Proclamation of 1863 in the United States, and the Brazilian emancipation of 1888. To the present day, every society in which plantation slavery once existed still contends with the long-term effects of that institution.

Mid-Eighteenth-Century Wars

From the standpoint of international relations, the state system of the middle of the eighteenth century was quite unstable and tended to lead the major states of Europe into periods of prolonged warfare. The statesmen of the period generally assumed that warfare could be used to further national interests. There were essentially no forces or powers who saw it in their interest to prevent war or to maintain peace. Because eighteenth-century wars before the French Revolution were fought by professional armies and navies, civilian populations were rarely drawn deeply into the conflicts. Wars were not associated with domestic political or social upheaval, and peace was not associated with the achievement of international stability. Consequently, periods of peace at the conclusion of a war were often viewed simply as times when a nation might become strong enough to recommence warfare at a later period for the purpose of seizing another nation's territory or of invading another empire's area of trading monopoly.

There were two fundamental areas of great power rivalry: the overseas empires and central and eastern Europe. Alliances and general strategic concerns repeatedly interrelated these regions of conflict.

The War of Jenkins's Ear

In the middle of the eighteenth century, the West Indies had become a hotbed of trade rivalry. Spain attempted to tighten its monopoly, and English smugglers, shippers, and pirates attempted to pierce it. Matters came to a climax in the late 1730s.

The Treaty of Utrecht (1713) gave two special privileges to Great Britain in the Spanish Empire. The British received a thirty-year *asiento*, or contract, to furnish slaves to the Spanish. Britain also gained the right to send one ship each year to the trading fair at Portobello, a major Caribbean seaport on the Panamanian coast. These two privileges allowed British traders and smugglers potential inroads into the Spanish market. Little but friction arose from those rights. During the night, offshore, British ships often resupplied the annual legal Portobello ship with additional goods as it lay in port. Much to the chagrin of the British, the Spanish government took its own alleged trading monopoly seriously and maintained coastal patrols, which boarded and searched English vessels to look for contraband.

In 1731, during one such boarding operation, there was a fight, and the Spaniards cut off the ear of an English captain named Robert Jenkins. Thereafter he carried about his severed ear preserved in a jar of brandy. This incident was of little importance until 1738, when Jenkins appeared before the British Parliament, reportedly brandishing his ear as an example of Spanish atrocities to British merchants in the West Indies. The British merchant and West Indies interests put great pressure on Parliament to relieve Spanish intervention in their trade. Sir Robert Walpole (1676–1745), the British prime minister, could not resist these pressures. In late 1739, Great Britain went to war with Spain. This war might have been a relatively minor incident, but because of developments in continental European politics, it became the opening encounter to a series of European wars fought across the world until 1815.

The War of the Austrian Succession (1740–1748)

In December 1740, after being king of Prussia for less than seven months, Frederick II seized the Austrian province of Silesia in eastern Germany. The invasion shattered the provisions of the Pragmatic Sanction (see Chapter 15) and upset the continental balance of power as established by the Treaty of Utrecht. The young king of Prussia had treated the House of Habsburg simply as another German state rather than as the leading power in the region. Silesia itself rounded out Prussia's possessions, and Frederick was determined to keep his ill-gotten prize.

MARIA THERESA PRESERVES THE HABSBURG EMPIRE The Prussian seizure of Silesia could have marked the opening of a general hunting season on Habsburg holdings and the beginning of revolts by Habsburg subjects. Instead, it led to new political allegiances. Maria Theresa's great achievement was not the reconquest of Silesia, which eluded her, but the preservation of the Habsburg Empire as a major political power.

Maria Theresa was then only twenty-three and had succeeded to the Habsburg realms only two months before the invasion. She won loyalty and support from her various subjects not merely through her heroism, but, more specifically, by granting new privileges to the nobility. Most significant, the empress recognized Hungary as the most important of her crowns and promised the Magyars considerable local autonomy. She thus preserved the Habsburg state, but at considerable cost to the power of the central monarchy.

Hungary would continue to be, as it had been in the past, a particularly troublesome area in the Habsburg Empire. When the monarchy enjoyed periods of strength and security, guarantees made to Hun-

gary could be ignored. At times of weakness or when the Magyars could stir enough opposition, the monarchy promised new concessions.

FRANCE DRAWS GREAT BRITAIN INTO THE WAR   The war over the Austrian succession and the British–Spanish commercial conflict could have remained separate disputes. What quickly united them was the role of France. Just as British merchant interests had pushed Sir Robert Walpole into war, a group of aggressive court aristocrats compelled the elderly Cardinal Fleury (1653–1743), first minister of Louis XV, to abandon his planned naval attack on British trade and instead to support the Prussian aggression against Austria, the traditional enemy of France. This was among the more fateful decisions in French history.

In the first place, aid to Prussia consolidated a new and powerful state in Germany. That new power could, and indeed later did, endanger France. Second, the French move against Austria brought Great Britain into the Continental war, as Britain sought to make sure that the Low Countries remained in the friendly hands of Austria, not France. In 1744 the

British–French conflict expanded beyond the Continent, as France decided to support Spain against Britain in the New World. As a result, French military and economic resources were badly divided. France could not bring sufficient strength to the colonial struggle. Having chosen to continue the old struggle with Austria, France lost the struggle for the future against Great Britain. The war ended in stalemate in 1748 with the Treaty of Aix-la-Chapelle. Prussia retained Silesia, and Spain renewed the *asiento* agreement with Great Britain. Most observers rightly thought the treaty was a truce rather than a permanent peace.

The "Diplomatic Revolution" of 1756

Before the rivalries again erupted into war, a dramatic shift of alliances took place. In January 1756 Prussia and Great Britain signed the Convention of Westminster, a defensive alliance aimed at preventing the entry of foreign troops into the Germanies. Frederick II feared invasions by both Russia and France. The convention meant that Great

Britain, the ally of Austria since the wars of Louis XIV, had now joined forces with Austria's major eighteenth-century enemy.

Maria Theresa was despondent over this development. It delighted her foreign minister, Prince Wenzel Anton Kaunitz (1711–1794), however. He had long hoped for an alliance with France to help dismember Prussia. The Convention of Westminster made possible this alliance, which would have been unthinkable a few years earlier. France was agreeable because Frederick had not consulted with its ministers before coming to his understanding with Britain. So, later in May 1756, France and Austria signed a defensive alliance. Kaunitz had succeeded in completely reversing the direction that French foreign policy had followed since the sixteenth century. France would now fight to restore Austrian supremacy in central Europe.

The Seven Years' War (1756–1763)

Although the Treaty of Aix-la-Chapelle had brought peace in Europe, France and Great Britain continued to struggle unofficially on the colonial front. There were constant clashes between their settlers in the Ohio River valley and in upper New England. These were the prelude to what is known in American history as the French and Indian War. Once again, however, Frederick II precipitated a European war that extended into a colonial theater.

FREDERICK THE GREAT OPENS HOSTILITIES   In August 1756, Frederick II opened what would become the Seven Years' War by invading Saxony. Frederick considered this to be a preemptive strike against a conspiracy by Saxony, Austria, and France to destroy Prussian power. He regarded the invasion as a continuation of the defensive strategy of the Convention of Westminster. The invasion itself, however, created the very destructive alliance that Frederick feared. In the spring of 1757, France and Austria made a new alliance dedicated to the destruction of Prussia. They were eventually joined by Sweden, Russia, and many of the smaller German states.

Two factors in addition to Frederick's stubborn leadership (it was after this war that he came to be called Frederick the Great) saved Prussia. First, Britain furnished considerable financial aid. Second, in 1762 Empress Elizabeth of Russia died. Her successor was Tsar Peter III (he was murdered the same year), whose admiration for Frederick was boundless. He immediately made peace with Prussia, thus relieving Frederick of one enemy and allowing him to hold off Austria

and France. The Treaty of Hubertusburg of 1763 ended the continental conflict with no significant changes in prewar borders. Silesia remained Prussian, and Prussia clearly stood among the ranks of the great powers.

WILLIAM PITT'S STRATEGY FOR WINNING NORTH AMERICA   The survival of Prussia was less impressive to the rest of Europe than were the victories of Great Britain in every theater of conflict. The architect of these victories was William Pitt the Elder (1708–1778). Pitt was a person of colossal ego and administrative genius who had grown up in a commercial family. Although he had previously criticized British involvement with the Continent, once he became secretary of state in charge of the war in 1757, he reversed himself and pumped huge financial subsidies into the coffers of Frederick the Great. He regarded the German conflict as a way to divert French resources and attention from the colonial struggle. He later boasted of having won America on the plains of Germany.

North America was the center of Pitt's real concern. Put quite simply, he wanted all of North America east of the Mississippi for Great Britain, and that was exactly what he won. He sent more than 40,000 regular English and colonial troops

William Pitt the Elder guided Great Britain to a stunning victory in the Seven Years' War. National Portrait Gallery, London

against the French in Canada. Never had so many soldiers been devoted to a field of colonial warfare. He achieved unprecedented cooperation with the American colonies, whose leaders realized that they might finally defeat their French neighbors.

The French government was unwilling and unable to direct similar resources against the English in America. Their military administration was corrupt, the military and political commands in Canada were divided, and France could not adequately provision its North American forces. In September 1759, on the Plains of Abraham, overlooking the valley of the Saint Lawrence River at Quebec City, the British army under General James Wolfe defeated the French under Lieutenant General Louis Joseph de Montcalm. The French Empire in Canada was ending.

Pitt's colonial vision, however, extended beyond the Saint Lawrence Valley and the Great Lakes Basin. The major islands of the French West Indies fell to British fleets. Income from the sale of captured sugar helped finance the British war effort. British slave interests captured the bulk of the French slave trade. Between 1755 and 1760, the value of the French colonial trade fell by more than 80 percent. In India, the British forces under the command of Robert Clive defeated the French in 1757 at the Battle of Plassey. This victory opened the way for the eventual conquest of Bengal in northeast India and later of all India by the British East India Company. Never had Great Britain or any other European power experienced such a complete worldwide military victory.

THE TREATY OF PARIS OF 1763 The Treaty of Paris of 1763 reflected somewhat less of a victory than Britain had won on the battlefield. Pitt was no longer in office.

Conflicts of the Mid-Eighteenth Century

1713	Treaty of Utrecht
1739	Outbreak of War of Jenkins's Ear between England and Spain
1740	War of the Austrian Succession commences
1748	Treaty of Aix-la-Chapelle
1756	Convention of Westminster between England and Prussia
1756	Seven Years' War opens
1757	Battle of Plassey
1759	British forces capture Quebec
1763	Treaty of Hubertusburg
1763	Treaty of Paris

George III (r. 1760–1820) and Pitt had quarreled over policy, and the minister had departed. His replacement was the earl of Bute (1713–1792), a favorite of the new monarch. Bute was responsible for the peace settlement. Britain received all of Canada, the Ohio River valley, and the eastern half of the Mississippi River valley. Britain returned Pondicherry and Chandernagore in India and the West Indian sugar islands of Guadeloupe and Martinique to the French.

The Seven Years' War had been a vast conflict. Tens of thousands of soldiers and sailors had been killed or wounded. Major battles had been fought around the globe. At great internal sacrifice, Prussia had permanently wrested Silesia from Austria and had turned the Holy Roman Empire into an empty shell. Habsburg power now depended largely on the Hungarian domains. France, though still having sources of colonial income, was no longer a great colonial power. The Spanish Empire remained largely intact, but the British were still determined to penetrate its markets.

On the Indian subcontinent, the British East India Company was able to continue to impose its own authority on the decaying indigenous governments. The ramifications of that situation would extend until the middle of the twentieth century. In North America, the British government faced the task of organizing its new territories. From this time until World War II, Great Britain was a world power, not just a European one.

The quarter century of warfare also caused a long series of domestic crises among the European powers. The French defeat convinced many people in that nation of the necessity for political and administrative reform. The financial burdens of the wars had astounded all contemporaries. Every power had to begin to find ways to increase revenues to pay its war debt and to finance its preparation for the next combat. Nowhere did this search for revenue lead to more far-ranging consequences than in the British colonies in North America.

The American Revolution and Europe

The revolt of the British colonies in North America was an event in both transatlantic and European history. It erupted from problems of revenue collection common to all the major powers after the Seven Years' War. The War of the American Revolution also continued the conflict between France and Great Britain. The French support of the Americans deepened the existing financial and administrative difficulties of the French monarchy.

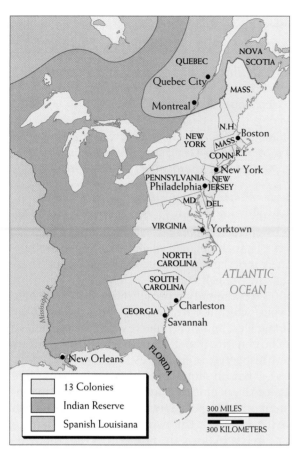

MAP 17–2   NORTH AMERICA IN 1763   *In the year of the victory over France, the English colonies lay along the Atlantic seaboard. The difficulties of organizing authority over the previous French territory in Canada and west of the Appalachian Mountains would contribute to the coming of the American Revolution.*

Resistance to the Imperial Search for Revenue

After the Treaty of Paris of 1763, the British government faced two imperial problems. The first was the sheer cost of empire, which the British felt they could no longer carry alone. The national debt had risen considerably, as had domestic taxation. Since the American colonies had been the chief beneficiaries of the conflict, the British felt that it was rational for the colonies henceforth to bear part of the cost of their protection and administration. The second problem was the vast expanse of new territory in North America that the British had to organize. This included all the land from the mouth of the Saint Lawrence River to the Mississippi River, with its French settlers and, more importantly, its Native American possessors. (See Map 17–2.)

The British drive for revenue began in 1764 with the passage of the Sugar Act under the ministry of George Grenville (1712–1770). The measure attempt-

ed to produce more revenue from imports into the colonies by the rigorous collection of what was actually a lower tax. Smugglers who violated the law were to be tried in admiralty courts without juries. The next year, Parliament passed the Stamp Act, which put a tax on legal documents and certain other items such as newspapers. The British considered these taxes legal because the decision to collect them had been approved by Parliament. They regarded them as just because the money was to be spent in the colonies.

The Americans responded that they alone, through their assemblies, had the right to tax themselves and that they were not represented in Parliament. Furthermore, the expenditure in the colonies of the revenue levied by Parliament did not reassure the colonists. They feared that if colonial government were financed from outside, they would lose control over it. In October 1765, the Stamp Act Congress met in America and drew up a protest to the crown. (See "The Stamp Act Congress Addresses George III.") There was much disorder in the colonies, particularly in Massachusetts, roused by groups known as the Sons of Liberty. The colonists agreed to refuse to import British goods. In 1766 Parliament repealed the Stamp Act, but through the Declaratory Act said that it had the power to legislate for the colonies.

This view of the "Boston Massacre" of March 5, 1770 by Paul Revere owes more to propaganda than fact. There was no order to fire and the innocent citizens portrayed here were really an angry, violent mob.
© Collection of The New-York Historical Society, New York City

The Stamp Act Congress Addresses George III

In 1765, the Stamp Act Congress met to protest the British imposition of taxes on the colonies. The resolutions of the Congress made it very clear that American leaders believed that Great Britain had no right to impose such taxation.

❖ *What are the rights of English citizens that the Americans claim? How has the Stamp Act violated them? Why do they believe that the British Parliament has no right to tax them? Do the colonists believe it possible for themselves to be represented in Parliament?*

The Members of this Congress, sincerely devoted, with the warmest sentiments of affection and duty to His Majesty's person and government...and with minds deeply impressed by a sense of the present and impending misfortunes of the British colonies on this continent; having considered as maturely as time will permit, the circumstances of the said colonies, esteem it our indispensable duty to make the following declarations of our humble opinion, respecting the most essential rights and liberties of the colonists, and of the grievances under which they labor, by reason of several late acts of Parliament.

I. That His Majesty's subjects in these colonies, own the same allegiance to the crown of Great Britain, that is owing from his subjects born within the realm, and all due subordination to that august body the Parliament of Great Britain.   *loyal & faithful*

II. That His Majesty's liege subjects in these colonies are entitled to all the inherent rights and liberties of his natural born subjects, within the kingdom of Great Britain.

III. That it is inseparably essential to the freedom of a people, and the undoubted right of Englishmen, that no taxes be imposed on them but with their own consent, given personally, or by their representatives.

IV. That the people of these colonies are not, and cannot, be represented in the House of Commons in Great Britain.

V. That the only representatives of the people of these colonies are persons chosen therein by themselves, and that no taxes ever have been, or can be constitutionally imposed on them, but by their respective legislatures.

VI. That all supplies to the crown being free gifts of the people, it is unreasonable and inconsistent with the principles and spirit of the British constitution, for the people of Great Britain to grant to His Majesty the property of the colonists.

VII. That trial by jury, is the inherent and invaluable right of every British subject in these colonies.

VIII. That the late act of Parliament entitled, An act for granting and supplying certain stamp duties, and other duties, in the British colonies and plantations, in America, etc. by imposing taxes on the inhabitants of these colonies, and the said act, and several other acts, by extending the jurisdiction of the courts of admiralty beyond its ancient limits, have a manifest tendency to subvert the rights and liberties of the colonists.

From the *Journal of the First Congress of the American Colonies...1765* (New York, 1845), pp. 27–29, as quoted in Oscar Handlin, ed., *Readings in American History* (New York: Alfred A. Knopf, 1957), pp. 116–117.

The Stamp Act crisis set the pattern for the next ten years. Parliament, under the leadership of a royal minister, would approve revenue or administrative legislation. The Americans would then resist by reasoned argument, economic pressure, and violence. Then the British would repeal the legislation, and the process would begin again. Each time, tempers on both sides became more frayed and positions more irreconcilable. With each clash, the Americans more fully developed their own thinking about political liberty.

The Crisis and Independence

In 1767 Charles Townshend (1725–1767), as Chancellor of the Exchequer, the British finance minister, led Parliament to pass a series of revenue acts relating to colonial imports. The colonists again resisted. The ministry sent over its own customs agents to administer the laws. To protect these new officers, the British sent troops to Boston in 1768. The obvious tensions resulted. In March 1770, the Boston Massacre, in which British troops killed

Thomas Paine was the author of Common Sense, *a political pamphlet published early in 1776 that helped galvanize American opinion in favor of independence.*
Bildarchiv Preussischer Kulturbesitz

five citizens, took place. That same year, Parliament repealed all of the Townshend duties except the one on tea.

In May 1773, Parliament passed a new law relating to the sale of tea by the East India Company. The measure permitted the direct importation of tea into the American colonies. It actually lowered the price of tea while retaining the tax imposed without the colonists' consent. In some cities, the colonists refused to permit the unloading of the tea; in Boston, a shipload of tea was thrown into the harbor.

The British ministry of Lord North (1732–1792) was determined to assert the authority of Parliament over the resistant colonies. During 1774, Parliament passed a series of laws known in American history as the Intolerable Acts. These measures closed the port of Boston, reorganized the government of Massachusetts, allowed troops to be quartered in private homes, and removed the trials of royal customs officials to England. The same year, Parliament approved the Quebec Act for the future administration of Canada. It extended the boundaries of Quebec to include the Ohio River valley. The Americans regarded the

Quebec Act as an attempt to prevent the extension of their mode of self-government westward beyond the Appalachian Mountains.

During these years, citizens critical of British policy had established committees of correspondence throughout the colonies. They made the various sections of the eastern seaboard aware of common problems and aided united action. In September 1774, these committees organized the gathering of the First Continental Congress in Philadelphia. This body hoped to persuade Parliament to restore self-government in the colonies and to abandon its attempt at direct supervision of colonial affairs. Conciliation, however, was not forthcoming. By April 1775, the Battles of Lexington and Concord had been fought. In June, the colonists suffered defeat at the Battle of Bunker Hill. Despite that defeat, the colonial assemblies soon began to meet under their own authority rather than under that of the king.

The Second Continental Congress gathered in May 1775. It still sought conciliation with Britain, but the pressure of events led it to begin to conduct the government of the colonies. By August 1775, George III had declared the colonies in rebellion. During the winter, Thomas Paine's (1737–1809) pamphlet *Common Sense* galvanized public opinion in favor of separation from Great Britain. A colonial army and navy were organized. In April 1776, the Continental Congress opened American ports to the trade of all nations. And on July 4, 1776, the Continental Congress adopted the Declaration of Independence. Thereafter, the War of the American Revolution continued until 1781, when the forces of George Washington defeated those of Lord Cornwallis at Yorktown. Early in 1778, however, the war had widened into a European conflict when Benjamin Franklin (1706–1790) persuaded the French government to support the rebellion. In 1779, the Spanish also came to the aid of the colonies. The 1783 Treaty of Paris concluded the conflict, and the thirteen American colonies had established their independence.

American Political Ideas

The political ideas of the American colonists had largely arisen out of the struggle of seventeenth-century English aristocrats and gentry against the absolutism of the Stuart monarchs. The American colonists looked to the English Revolution of 1688 as having established many of their own fundamental political liberties, as well as those of the English. The colonists claimed that, through the measures imposed from

The Horse America throwing his Master, an eighteenth-century cartoon (1779) mock-ing George III about the rebellion of the American colonies. Although he tried to re-assert some of the monarchical influence on Britain's politics that had eroded under George I and George II, the first two Hanoverian kings, George III never sought to make himself a tyrant as his critics charged.   The Granger Collection

1763 to 1776, George III and the British Parlia-ment were attacking those liberties and dissolv-ing the bonds of moral and political allegiance that had formerly united the two peoples. Con-sequently, the colonists employed a theory that had developed to justify an aristocratic rebellion to support their own popular revolution.

These Whig political ideas, largely derived from the writings of John Locke, were, however, only a part of the English ideological heritage that affect-ed the Americans. Throughout the eighteenth cen-tury, they had become familiar with a series of British political writers called the Common-wealthmen, who held republican political ideas that had their intellectual roots in the most radical thought of the Puritan revolution. During the early eighteenth century, these writers, the most influ-ential of whom were John Trenchard (1662–1723) and Thomas Gordon (d. 1750) in *Cato's Letters* (1720–1723), had relentlessly criticized the gov-ernment patronage and parliamentary management of Sir Robert Walpole and his successors. They ar-gued that such government was corrupt and that it undermined liberty. They regarded much parlia-mentary taxation as simply a means of financing political corruption. They also considered standing armies instruments of tyranny. In Great Britain, this republican political tradition had only a mar-ginal impact. The writers were largely ignored be-cause most British subjects regarded themselves as the freest people in the world. Three thousand miles away, however, colonists read the radical books and pamphlets and often accepted them at face value. The policy of Great Britain toward America following the Treaty of Paris of 1763 and certain political events in Britain had made many colonists believe that the worst fears of the Com-monwealthmen were coming true. All of these events coincided with the accession of George III to the throne.

Events in Great Britain

George III (r. 1760–1820) believed that a few powerful Whig families and the ministries that they controlled had bullied and dominated his two immediate royal predecessors. George III also believed that he should have ministers of his own choice and that Parliament should function under royal rather than aristocratic management. When William Pitt resigned after a disagreement with George over war policy, the king appointed the earl of Bute as his first minister. In doing so, he ignored the great Whig families that had run the country since 1715. The king sought the aid of politicians whom the Whigs hated. Moreover, he tried to use the same kind of patronage techniques developed by Walpole to achieve royal control of the House of Commons.

Between 1761 and 1770, George tried one minister after another, but each in turn failed to gain enough support from the various factions in the House of Commons. Finally, in 1770 he turned to Lord North, who remained the king's first minister until 1782. The Whig families and other political spokespersons claimed that George III was attempting to impose a tyranny. What they meant was that the king was attempting to curb the power of a particular group of the aristocracy. George III certainly was seeking to restore more royal influence to the government of Great Britain, but he was not attempting to make himself a tyrant.

THE CHALLENGE OF JOHN WILKES   Then, in 1763 began the affair of John Wilkes (1725–1797). This London political radical and member of Parliament published a newspaper called *The North Briton*. In issue number 45 of this paper, Wilkes strongly criticized Lord Bute's handling of the peace negotiations with France. Wilkes was arrested under the authority of a general warrant issued by the secretary of state. He pleaded the privileges of a member of Parliament and was released. The courts also later ruled that the vague kind of general warrant by which he had been arrested was illegal. The House of Commons, however, ruled that issue number 45 of *The North Briton* constituted libel, and expelled Wilkes. He soon fled the country and was outlawed. Throughout these procedures there was widespread support for Wilkes, and many popular demonstrations were held in his cause.

In 1768, Wilkes returned to England and again stood for election to Parliament. He won the election, but the House of Commons, under the influence of George III's friends, refused to seat him. He was elected three more times. After the fourth election, the House of Commons simply ignored the results and seated the government-supported candidate. As had happened earlier in the decade, large, popular, unruly demonstrations of shopkeepers, artisans, and small-property owners supported Wilkes. He also received aid from some aristocratic politicians who wished to humiliate George III. Wilkes himself contended during all his troubles that his was the cause of English liberty. "Wilkes and Liberty" became the slogan of all political radicals and many noble opponents of the monarch. Wilkes was finally seated in 1774, after having become the lord mayor of London.

The American colonists followed these developments closely. Events in Britain confirmed their fears about a monarchical and parliamentary conspiracy against liberty. The king, as their Whig friends told them, was behaving like a tyrant. The Wilkes affair displayed the arbitrary power of the monarch, the corruption of the House of Commons, and the contempt of both for popular electors. That same monarch and Parliament were attempting to overturn the traditional relationship of Great Britain to its colonies by imposing parliamentary taxes. The

Events in Britain and America Relating to the American Revolution	
1760	George III becomes king
1763	Treaty of Paris concludes the Seven Years' War
1763	John Wilkes publishes issue number 45 of *The North Briton*
1764	Sugar Act
1765	Stamp Act
1766	Sugar Act repealed and Declaratory Act passed
1767	Townshend Acts
1768	Parliament refuses to seat John Wilkes after his election
1770	Lord North becomes George III's chief minister
1770	Boston Massacre
1773	Boston Tea Party
1774	Intolerable Acts
1774	First Continental Congress
1775	Second Continental Congress
1776	Declaration of Independence
1778	France enters the war on the side of America
1778	Yorkshire Association Movement founded
1781	British forces surrender at Yorktown
1783	Treaty of Paris concludes War of the American Revolution

same government had then landed troops in Boston, changed the government of Massachusetts, and undermined the traditional right of jury trial. All of these events fulfilled too exactly the portrait of political tyranny that had developed over the years in the minds of articulate colonists.

MOVEMENT FOR PARLIAMENTARY REFORM   The political influences between America and Britain operated both ways. The colonial demand for no taxation without representation and the criticism of the adequacy of the British system of representation struck at the core of the eighteenth-century British political structure. British subjects at home who were no more directly represented in the House of Commons than were the Americans could adopt the colonial arguments. The colonial questioning of the tax-levying authority of the House of Commons was related to the protest of John Wilkes. Both the Americans and Wilkes were challenging the power of the monarch and the authority of Parliament. Moreover, both the colonial leaders and Wilkes appealed over the head of legally constituted political authorities to popular opinion and popular demonstrations. Both were protesting the power of a largely self-selected aristocratic political body. The British ministry was fully aware of these broader political implications of the American troubles.

The American colonists also demonstrated to Europe how a politically restive people in the Old Regime could fight tyranny and protect political liberty. They established revolutionary, but orderly, political bodies that could function outside the existing political framework: the congress and the convention. These began with the Stamp Act Congress of 1765 and culminated in the Constitutional Convention of 1787. The legitimacy of those congresses and conventions lay not in existing law, but in the alleged consent of the governed. This approach represented a new way to found a government.

Toward the end of the War of the American Revolution, calls for parliamentary reform arose in Britain itself. The method proposed for changing the system was the extralegal Association Movement.

THE YORKSHIRE ASSOCIATION MOVEMENT   By the close of the 1770s, many in Britain resented the mismanagement of the American war, the high taxes, and Lord North's ministry. In northern England in 1778, Christopher Wyvil (1740–1822), a landowner and retired clergyman, organized the Yorkshire Association Movement. Property owners, or freeholders, of Yorkshire met in a mass meeting to demand rather moderate changes in the corrupt system of parliamentary elections. They organized corresponding societies elsewhere. They intended that the association examine—and suggest reforms for—the entire government. The Association Movement was thus a popular attempt to establish an extralegal institution to reform the government.

The movement collapsed during the early 1780s because its supporters, unlike Wilkes and the American rebels, were not willing to appeal for broad popular support. Nonetheless, the agitation of the Association Movement provided many people with experience in political protest. Several of its younger figures lived to raise the issue of parliamentary reform after 1815.

Parliament was not insensitive to the demands of the Association Movement. In April 1780, the Commons passed a resolution that called for lessening the power of the crown. In 1782 Parliament adopted a measure for "economical" reform, which abolished some patronage at the disposal of the monarch. These actions, however, did not prevent George III from appointing a minister of his own choice. In 1783 shifts in Parliament obliged Lord North to form a ministry with Charles James Fox (1749–1806), a long-time critic of George III. The monarch was most unhappy with the arrangement.

In 1783 the king approached William Pitt the Younger (1759–1806), son of the victorious war minister, to manage the House of Commons. During the election of 1784, Pitt received immense patronage support from the crown and constructed a House of Commons favorable to the monarch. Thereafter, Pitt sought to formulate trade policies that would give his ministry broad popularity. In 1785, he attempted one measure of modest parliamentary reform. When it failed, the young prime minister, who had been only twenty-four at the time of his appointment, abandoned the cause of reform.

By the mid-1780s, George III had achieved a part of what he had sought since 1761. He had reasserted the influence of the monarchy in political affairs. It proved a temporary victory, because his own mental illness, which would eventually require a regency, weakened the royal power. The cost of his years of dominance had been high, however. On both sides of the Atlantic, the issue of popular sovereignty had been raised and widely discussed. The American colonies had been lost. Economically, this loss did not prove disastrous. British trade with America after independence actually increased.

Broader Impact of the American Revolution

The Americans—through their state constitutions, the Articles of Confederation, and the federal Constitution adopted in 1788—had demonstrated to

regency = the control of a regent or body of regents exercising the ruling power during the minority, absence or disability of a sovereign

Europe the possibility of government without kings and hereditary nobilities. They had established the example of a nation in which written documents based on popular consent and popular sovereignty—rather than on divine law, natural law, tradition, or the will of kings—were the highest political and legal authority. The political novelty of these assertions should not be ignored.

As the crisis with Britain unfolded during the 1760s and 1770s, the American colonists had come to see themselves first as preserving traditional English liberties against the tyrannical crown and corrupt Parliament and then as developing a whole new sense of liberty. By the mid-1770s, the colonists had rejected monarchical government and embraced republican political ideals. They would govern themselves through elected assemblies without any presence of a monarchical authority. Once a constitution was adopted, they would insist on a Bill of Rights specifically protecting a whole series of civil liberties. The Americans would reject the aristocratic social hierarchy that had existed in the colonies. They would embrace democratic ideals—even if the franchise remained limited. They would assert the equality of white male citizens not only before the law, but in ordinary social relations. They would reject social status based on birth and inheritance and assert the necessity of the liberty for all citizens to improve their social standing and economic lot by engaging in free commercial activity. They did not free their slaves, nor did they address issues of the rights of women or of Native Americans. Yet in making their revolution, the American colonists of the eighteenth century produced a society more free than any the world had seen and one that would eventually expand the circle of political and social liberty. In all these respects, the American Revolution was a genuinely radical movement, whose influence would widen as Americans moved across the continent and as other peoples began to question traditional modes of European government.

In Perspective

During the sixteenth and seventeenth centuries the west European maritime powers established extensive commercial, mercantile empires in North and South America. The point of these empires was to extract wealth and to establish com-

mercial advantage for the colonial power. The largest of these empires was that of Spain, but by the end of the seventeenth century Britain and France had also each established a major American presence. As a vast plantation economy emerged from the Chesapeake Bay through the southern North American Atlantic seaboard and the Caribbean south to Brazil, significant portions of these American empires became economically dependent upon slave labor, drawn from the forced immigration of Africans. Through this large slave labor force, African linguistic, social, and religious influences became major cultural factors in these regions.

During the eighteenth century, the great European powers engaged in warfare over their American empires and over their power in India. These colonial wars became entangled in dynastic wars in central and eastern Europe and resulted in worldwide mid century European conflict.

In the New World, Britain, France, and Spain battled for commercial dominance. France and Britain also clashed over their spheres of influence in India. By the third quarter of the century, Britain had succeeded in ousting France from most of its major holdings in North America and from any significant presence in India. Spain, though no longer a military power of the first order, had managed to maintain its vast colonial empire in Latin America and a large measure of its monopoly over the region's trade.

On the Continent, France, Austria, and Prussia collided over conflicting territorial and dynastic ambitions. Britain became involved to protect its continental interests and to use the continental wars to divert France from the colonial arena. With British aid, Prussia had emerged in 1763 as a major continental power. Austria had lost considerable territory to Prussia. France had accumulated a vast debt.

The midcentury conflicts in turn led to major changes in all the European states. Each of the monarchies needed more money and tried to govern itself more efficiently. This problem led Britain to attempt to tax the North American colonies, which led to a revolution and the colonies' independence. Already deeply in debt, the French monarchy aided the Americans, fell into a deeper financial crisis, and soon clashed sharply with the nobility as royal ministers tried to find new revenues. That clash eventually unleashed the French Revolution. Spain moved to administer its Latin American empire more efficiently, which increased revolutionary discontent in the early nineteenth century. In preparation for future wars, the rulers of Prussia, Austria, and Russia pursued a mode of activist government known as Enlightened Absolutism. This will be examined in the next chapter. In that regard, the mid-eighteenth-century wars set in motion most of the major political developments of the next half century.

REVIEW QUESTIONS

1. What were the fundamental ideas associated with mercantile theory? Did they work? Which European country was most successful in establishing a mercantile empire? Least successful? Why?
2. What were the main points of conflict between Britain and France in North America, the West Indies, and India? How did the triangles of trade function between the Americas, Europe, and Africa?
3. How was the Spanish colonial empire in the Americas organized and managed? What changes did the Bourbon monarchs institute in the Spanish Empire?
4. What was the nature of slavery in the Americas? How was it linked to the economies of the Americas, Europe, and Africa? In what respects was the plantation system unprecedented? What was the plantation system, and how did it contribute to the inhumane treatment of slaves?
5. The Seven Years' War was a major conflict, with battles fought around the globe. What were the results of this war? Which countries emerged in a stronger position and why?
6. Discuss the American Revolution in the context of European history. To what extent were the colonists influenced by European ideas and political developments? To what extent did their actions in turn influence Europe?

SUGGESTED READINGS

B. BAILYN, *The Ideological Origins of the American Revolution* (1967). Remains an important work illustrating the role of English radical thought in the perceptions of the American colonists.

B. BAILYN, *The Peopling of British North America: An Introduction* (1988). A study of the immigrants to the British colonies on the eve of the Revolution.

C. A. BAYLY, *Imperial Meridian: The British Empire and the World, 1780–1830* (1989). A major study of the empire after the loss of America.

I. BERLIN, *Many Thousands Gone: The First Two Centuries of Slavery in North America* (1998). The most extensive recent treatment emphasizing the differences in the slave economy during different decades.

L. BETHELL (ED.), *The Cambridge History of Latin America*, vols. 1 and 2 (1984). Excellent essays on the colonial era.

J. BLACK, *European Warfare, 1660–1815* (1994). A major, wide-ranging synthesis.

R. BLACKBURN, *The Making of New World Slavery from the Baroque to the Modern, 1492–1800* (1997). An extraordinary work.

D. BRADING, *The First America* (1991). A major study of colonial Latin America.

J. BREWER, *The Sinews of Power: War, Money, and the English State, 1688–1783* (1989). A study that emphasizes the financial power behind British military success.

J. BROOKE, *King George III* (1972). The best biography.

K. N. CHAUDHURI, *The Trading World of Asia and the English East India Company* (1978). Examines the impact of trade on both Asians and Europeans.

L. COLLEY, *Britons: Forging the Nation, 1707–1837* (1992). A major work with important discussions of the recovery from the loss of America.

P. CURTIN, *The Atlantic Slave Trade, a Census* (1969). Remains a major contribution.

D. B. DAVIS, *The Problem of Slavery in Western Culture* (1966). A brilliant and far-ranging discussion.

D. B. DAVIS, *The Problem of Slavery in the Age of Revolution, 1770–1823* (1975). A major work on both European and American history.

R. DAVIS, *The Rise of the Atlantic Economies* (1973). A major synthesis.

W. DORN, *Competition for Empire, 1740–1763* (1940). Still one of the best accounts of the mid-century struggle.

H. KLEIN, *The Middle Passage: Comparative Studies in the African Slave Trade* (1978). An overview of the movement of slaves from Africa to the Americas.

P. LANGFORD, *A Polite and Commercial People: England 1717–1783* (1989). An excellent survey covering social history, politics, the overseas wars, and the American Revolution.

J. LOCKHARDT AND S. B. SCHWARTZ, *Early Latin America: A History of Colonial Spanish America and Brazil* (1983). The standard work.

J. R. McNEIL, *Atlantic Empires of France and Spain: Louisbourg and Havana, 1700–1763* (1985). An examination of imperial policies for two key overseas outposts.

P. MAIER, *American Scripture: Making the Declaration of Independence* (1997). Replaces previous works on the subject.

S. W. MINTZ, *Sweetness and Power: The Place of Sugar in Modern History* (1985). Traces the role of sugar in the world economy and how sugar has had an impact on world culture.

A. PAGDEN, *Lords of All the World: Ideologies of Empire in Spain, Britain, and France, 1492–1830* (1995). One of the few comparative studies of empire during this period.

J. H. PARRY, *Trade and Dominion: The European Overseas Empires in the Eighteenth Century* (1971). A comprehensive account with attention to the European impact on the rest of the world.

J. C. RILEY, *The Seven Years' War and the Old Regime in France: The Economic and Financial Toll* (1986). A useful analysis of pressures that would undermine the French monarchy.

G. RUDÉ, *Wilkes and Political Liberty* (1962). A close analysis of popular political behavior.

K. W. SCHWEIZER, *Frederick the Great, William Pitt, and Lord Bute: The Anglo–Prussian Alliance, 1756–1763* (1991). The most recent study of this complex diplomacy.

I. K. STEELE, *The English Atlantic, 1675–1740: An Exploration of Communication and Community* (1986). An exploration of culture and commerce in the transatlantic world.

R. L. STEIN, *The French Sugar Business in the Eighteenth Century* (1988). A study that covers all aspects of the French sugar trade.

J. THORNTON, *Africa and Africans in the Making of the Atlantic World, 1400–1800* (1998). A discussion of the role of Africans in the emergence of the transatlantic economy.

J. WEST, *Gunpower, Government, and War in the Mid-Eighteenth Century* (1991). A study of how warfare touched much of government.

G. S. WOOD, *The Creation of the American Republic, 1776–1787* (1969). A far-ranging work dealing with Anglo–American political thought.

G. S. WOOD, *The Radicalism of the American Revolution* (1991). A major interpretation.

The Columbian Exchange: Disease, Animals, and Agriculture

The European encounter with the Americas produced remarkable ecological transformations that have shaped the world to the present moment. The same ships that carried Europeans and Africans to the New World also transported animals, plants, and germs that had never before appeared in the Americas. There was a similar transport back to Europe and Africa. Alfred Crosby, the leading historian of the process, has named this cross-continental flow "the Columbian exchange."

Diseases Enter the Americas

With the exception of a few ships that had gone astray or, in the case of the Vikings, that had gone in search of new lands, the American continents had been biologically separated from Europe, Africa, and Asia for tens of thousands of years. In the Americas no native animals could serve as major beasts of burden except for the llama, which could not transport more than about 100 pounds. Nor did animals constitute a major source of protein for native Americans, whose diets consisted largely of maize, beans, peppers, yams, and potatoes. At the same time, the American continents included areas of vast grassland without grazing animals that would have transformed those plants into animal protein. Moreover, it also appears that native peoples had lived on the long-isolated American continents without experiencing major epidemics.

By the second voyage of Columbus (1493), that picture began to change in remarkable ways. On his return voyage to Hispaniola and other islands of the Caribbean, Columbus brought a number of animals and plants that were previously unknown to the New World. The men on all his voyages and those on subsequent European voyages also carried diseases novel to the Americas.

The diseases thus transported by Europeans ultimately accounted for the conquest of the people of the Americas as did much as the advanced European weaponry. Much controversy surrounds the question of the actual size of the populations of Native Americans in the Caribbean islands, Mexico, Peru and the North Atlantic coast. All accounts present those populations as quite significant, with those of Mexico in particular numbering many millions. Yet in the first two centuries after the encounter, wherever Europeans went either as settlers or as conquerors, extremely large numbers of Native Americans died from diseases they had never before encountered. The most deadly such disease was smallpox, which destroyed millions of people. Beyond the devastation wrought by that disease, bubonic plague, typhoid, typhus, influenza, measles, chicken pox, whooping cough, malaria, and diphtheria produced deadly results in more localized epidemics. For example, an unknown disease, but quite possibly typhus, caused major losses among the Native Americans of New England between approximately 1616 and 1619.

Native Americans appear to have been highly susceptible to these diseases because, with no earlier exposure, they lacked immunity. Wherever such outbreaks are recorded, Europeans either contracted or died from them at a much lower rate than the Native Americans. These diseases would continue to victimize Native Americans at a higher rate than Americans of European descent through the end of the nineteenth century when smallpox and measles still killed large numbers of the Plains Indian peoples of North America.

Although many historical and medical questions still surround the subject, it appears almost certain that syphilis, which became a rampant venereal dis-

Within one year of Columbus' encounter with the Americas, the event had been captured in a woodcut published in Giuliano Dati's Narrative of Columbus *(1493). Columbus' several voyages, and those of later Europeans as well, introduced not only European warfare but began a vast ecological exchange of plants, animals, and diseases between the Old and New Worlds.* The Granger Collection

ease in Europe at the close of the fifteenth century and eventually spread around the globe, originated in the New World. It seems to have been an entirely new disease, spawned through a mutation when the causal agent for yaws migrated from the Americas to new climatic settings in Europe. Until the discovery of penicillin in the 1940s, syphilis remained a major concern of public health throughout the world.

Animals and Agriculture

The introduction of European livestock to the Americas quite simply revolutionized the agriculture of two continents. The most important new animals were pigs, cattle, horses, goats, and sheep. Once transported to the New World, these animals multiplied at unprecedented rates. The

place where this first occurred was in the islands of the Caribbean, during the first forty years of Spanish settlement and exploitation. This situation established the foundation for the later Spanish conquest of both Mexico and Peru by providing the Spanish with strong breeds of animals, especially horses, acclimated to the Americas when they set out to conquer the mainland of South America.

The horse became first the animal of the conquest and then the animal of colonial Latin American culture. Native Americans had no experience with such large animals who would obey the will of a human rider. The mounted Spanish horseman struck fear into these people, and for good reason. After the conquest, however, the Americas from Mexico southward became the largest horse-breeding region of the

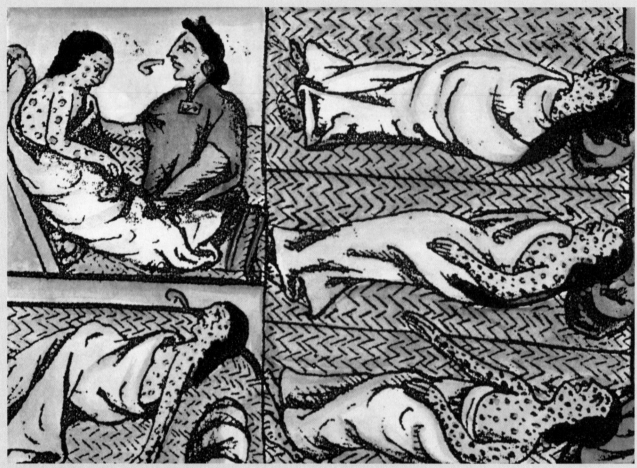

Nothing so destroyed the life of the Native Americans whom the Spanish encountered as the introduction of smallpox. With no immune defenses to this new disease, millions of Native Americans died of smallpox during the sixteenth and seventeenth centuries.
The Granger Collection.

world, with ranches raising thousands of animals. Horses became relatively cheap, and even Native Americans could acquire them. By the nineteenth century, the possession of horses would allow the Plains Indians of North America to resist the advance of their white conquerors.

The flourishing of pigs, cattle, and sheep allowed a vast economic exploitation of the Americas. These animals produced enormous quantities of hides and wool. Their presence in such large numbers also meant that the Americas from the sixteenth century through the present would support a diet more plentiful in animal protein than anywhere else in the world.

Europeans also brought their own plants to the New World, including peaches, oranges, grapes, melons, bananas, rice, onions, radishes, and various green vegetables. Socially, for three centuries the most significant of these was sugar cane, the cultivation of which created the major demand for slavery throughout the transatlantic plantation economy. Nutritionally, European wheat would, over the course of time, allow the Americas not only to feed themselves, but also to export large amount of grain throughout the world. This American production of wheat on the vast plains of the two continents contrasted sharply with the difficulty Europeans faced raising grain in the northern and northeastern parts of the continent, particularly in Russia.

No significant animals from the Americas, except the turkey, actually came to be raised in Europe. But the Americas did send to Europe a series of plants that eventually changed the European diet: maize, the potato, the sweet potato, the pepper, beans, manioc (tapioca), the peanut, squash, the pumpkin, pineapple, cocoa, and the tomato. All of these, to a greater or lesser degree, eventually entered the diet of Europeans and of European settlers and their descendants in the Americas. Maize and the potato, however, had the most transforming impact. Each of these two crops became a major staple in European farming, as well as the European diet. Both crops grow rapidly, supplying food quickly and steadily if not attacked by disease. Tobacco, we should note, originated in the Americas, too.

Maize was established as a crop in Spain within thirty years of the country's encounter with the New World. A century and a half later it was a commonplace in the Spanish diet, and its cultivation had spread to Italy and France. Maize produced more grain for the seed and farming effort than wheat did. Throughout Europe, maize was associated primarily with fodder for animals. But as early as the eighteenth-century travelers noted the presence of polenta in the peasant diet, and other forms of maize dishes, such as fried mush, spread.

The potato established its European presence more slowly than maize. The Spanish encountered the potato only when Pizarro conquered Peru, where it was a major part of the Native American food supply. It was adopted slowly by Europeans because it needed to be raised in climates more temperate than that of Spain and the Mediterranean. It appears to have become a major peasant food in Scotland, Ireland, and parts of Germany during the eighteenth century. It became more widely cultivated elsewhere in Europe only after new strains of the plant were imported from Chile in the late nineteenth century. In the middle of the seventeenth century, Irish peasants were urged to cultivate the potato as a major source of cheap nutrition that could grow in quantity on a small plot. The food shortages arising from the wars of Louis XIV and then during the eighteenth century led farmers in northern Europe to adopt the potato for similar reasons. It was nutrient insurance against failure of the grain harvest. There is good reason to believe that the cultivation of the potato was one of the major causes of the population increase in eighteenth- and nineteenth-century Europe. It was the quintessential food of the poor.

Many tragedies arose from the encounter between the people of the Americas and those of Europe, as well as the forging of new nations and civilizations in the Americas. But one of the last chapters of those tragedies to arise as a direct fallout of the Columbian exchange three centuries earlier was the Irish famine of the 1840s. Irish peasants had become almost wholly dependent upon the potato as a source of food. In the middle of the 1840s, an American parasite infected the Irish potato crop. The result of the failure of the crop was the death of hundreds of thousand of Irish peasants and the migration of still more hundreds of thousands to the Americas and elsewhere in the world.

❖ *Define the Columbian Exchange. What was the impact of European diseases on the Americas? Why was the impact so profound? Why could so many European crops grow well in the Americas? What was the cultural impact of animals taken from Europe to the Americas? How did food from the Americas change the diet of Europe and then later, as Europeans immigrated, the diet of the entire world?*

Part 4

1700–1850

	POLITICS AND GOVERNMENT	SOCIETY AND ECONOMY	RELIGION AND CULTURE
1700–1789	1713 **Peace of Utrecht**	1715–1763 **Colonial rivalry in the Caribbean**	1721 **Montesquieu,** *Persian Letters*
	1713–1740 **Frederick William I builds Prussian military**	1733 **James Kay's flying shuttle**	1733 **Voltaire,** *Letters on the English*
	1720–1740 **Walpole in England, Fleury in France**		1738 **Voltaire,** *Elements of the Philosophy of Newton*
	1739 **War of Jenkins's Ear**		
	1740 **Maria Theresa succeeds to Habsburg throne**		
	1740–1748 **War of the Austrian Succession**		
			Voltaire
			1739 **Wesley begins field preaching**
		1750s **Agricultural Revolution in Britain**	1748 **Hume,** *Inquiry into Human Nature*
	1756–1763 **Seven Years' War**	1750–1840 **Growth of new cities**	1748 **Montesquieu,** *Spirit of the Laws*
	1767 **Legislative Commission in Russia**	1763 **British establish dominance in India**	1750 **Rousseau,** *Discourse on the Moral Effects of the Arts and Sciences*
	1772 **First Partition of Poland**	1763–1789 **Enlightened absolutist rulers seek to spur economic growth**	
	1775–1783 **American Revolution**		1751 **First volume of Diderot's** *Encyclopedia*
	1785 **Catherine the Great of Russia issues Charter of Nobility**	1765 **James Hargreaves's spinning jenny**	1762 **Rousseau,** *Social Contract and Émile*
		1769 **Richard Arkwright's waterframe**	1763 **Voltaire,** *Treatise on Tolerance*
		1771–1775 **Pugachev's Rebellion**	1774 **Goethe,** *Sorrows of Young Werther*
		1780 **Gordon riots in London**	
		1787 **Edmund Cartwright's power loom**	1776 **Smith,** *Wealth of Nations*
			1779 **Lessing,** *Nathan the Wise*
1789–1815	1789 **Gathering of the Estates General at Versailles; fall of the Bastille; Declaration of the Rights of Man and Citizen**	1789–1802 **Revolutionary legislation restructures French political and economic life**	1781 **Joseph II adopts toleration in Austria**
			1781 **Kant,** *Critique of Pure Reason*
	1791 **French monarchy abolished**		1789 **Blake,** *Songs of Innocence*
	1793 **Louis XVI executed; Second Partition of Poland**		1790 **Civil Constitution of the Clergy; Burke,** *Reflections on the Revolution in France*
	1793–1794 **Reign of Terror**		1792 **Wollstonecraft,** *Vindication of the Rights of Woman*
	1795 **Third Partition of Poland**		1793 **France proclaims Cult of Reason**

ENLIGHTENMENT AND REVOLUTION

1700–1850

	POLITICS AND GOVERNMENT	SOCIETY AND ECONOMY	RELIGION AND CULTURE

1789–1815 (cont.)

1815–1850

POLITICS AND GOVERNMENT

1795 The Directory established in France

1799 Napoleon named First Consul in France

1803 War resumes between Britain and France

1804 Napoleonic Code; Napoleon crowned emperor

1805 Third Coalition formed against France; battles of Trafalgar and Austerlitz

1806 Napoleon establishes the Continental System

1807 Treaty of Tilsit between France and Russia

1808 Spanish resistance to Napoleon stiffens

1812 Napoleon invades Russia; meets defeat

1814 Napoleon abdicates; Congress of Vienna opens; Louis XVIII restored in France

1815 Napoleon defeated at Waterloo

1819 Carlsbad Decrees in Germanies; Peterloo Massacre and the Six Acts, Britain

1820 Spanish Revolution begins

1821 Greek Revolution begins

1823 France intervenes in Spanish Revolution

1825 Decembrist Revolt in Russia

1829 Catholic Emancipation Act in Great Britain

1830 Revolution in France, Belgium, and Poland; Serbia gains independence

1832 Great Reform Bill in Britain

1848 Revolutions sweep across Europe

SOCIETY AND ECONOMY

1794–1824 Wars of independence in Latin America break the colonial system

Napoleon Bonaparte

1810 Abolition of serfdom in Prussia

1800–1850 British industrial dominance

1825 Stockton and Darlington Railway opens

1828–1850 First European police departments

1830–1850 Railway building in western Europe

1833 English Factory Act to protect children

1834 German *Zollverein* established

1842 Chadwick, *Report on the Sanitary Condition of the Labouring Population*

1846 Corn Laws repealed in Britain

1847 Ten Hour Act passed in Britain

1848 Serfdom abolished in Austria and Hungary

RELIGION AND CULTURE

1794 France proclaims Cult of the Supreme Being

1798 Wordsworth and Coleridge, *Lyrical Ballads*; Malthus, *Essay on the Principle of Population*

1799 Schleiermacher, *Speeches on Religion to Its Cultured Despisers*

1802 Chateaubriand, *Genius of Christianity*

1802 Napoleon, Concordat with the Papacy

1806 Hegel, *Phenomenology of Mind*

1807 Fichte, *Addresses to the German Nation*

1808 Goethe, *Faust*, Part I

1812 Byron, *Childe Harold's Pilgrimage*

1817 Ricardo, *Principles of Political Economy*

1819 Byron, *Don Juan*

1829 Catholic Emancipation Act in Great Britain

1830–1842 Comte, *The Positive Philosophy*

1830 Lyell, *Principles of Geology*

1833 Russia begins "Official Nationality" policy

1835 Strauss, *Life of Jesus*

1840 Villermé, *Catalogue of the Physical and Moral State of Workers*

1843 Kierkegaard, *Fear and Trembling*

1848 Marx and Engels, *Communist Manifesto*

Chapter 18

Philosopher, dramatist, poet, historian, and popularizer of scientific ideas, Voltaire (1694–1778) was the most famous and influential of the eighteenth-century philosophes. His sharp satire and criticism of religious institutions opened the way for a more general critique of the European political and social status quo.

Nicolas de Largilliere. Portrait of Voltaire at age 23, bust length, 1728. Private Collection, Musée de la Ville de Paris, Musée Carnavalet, Paris, France. Giraudon/Art Resource, NY.

The Age of Enlightenment:
Eighteenth-Century Thought

The *Philosophes*

Formative Influences on the Enlightenment
Ideas of Newton and Locke
The Example of British Toleration and Stability
Need for Reform in France
The Emergence of a Print Culture

The *Encyclopedia*

The Enlightenment and Religion
Deism
Toleration
Radical Enlightenment Criticism of Religion
Jewish Thinkers in the Age of Enlightenement

The Enlightenment and Society
Beccaria and Reform of Criminal Law
The Physiocrats and Economic Freedom
Adam Smith on Economic Growth and Social Progress

Political Thought of the *Philosophes*
Montesquieu and *Spirit of the Laws*
Rousseau: A Radical Critique of Modern Society

Women in the Thought and Practice of the Enlightenment

Enlightened Absolutism
Frederick the Great of Prussia
Joseph II of Austria
Catherine the Great of Russia
The Partition of Poland
The End of the Eighteenth Century in Central and Eastern Europe

KEY TOPICS

- The intellectual and social background of the Enlightenment
- The *philosophes* of the Enlightenment and their agenda of intellectual and political reform
- Efforts of "enlightened" monarchs in central and eastern Europe to increase the economic and military strength of their domains
- The partition of Poland by Prussia, Russia, and Austria

economic change & political reform – the Enlightenment

During the eighteenth century, the conviction began to spread throughout the literate sectors of European society that economic change and political reform were both possible and desirable. This attitude is now commonplace, but it came into its own only after 1700. It represents one of the primary intellectual inheritances from that age. The movement of people and ideas that fostered such thinking is called the Enlightenment.

Its leading voices combined confidence in the human mind and human enterprise inspired by the Scientific Revolution and faith in the power of rational criticism to challenge the intellectual authority of tradition and the Christian past. These writers stood convinced that human beings could comprehend the operation of physical nature and mold it to the ends of material and moral improvement, economic growth, and political reform. They advocated agricultural improvement, commercial society, expanding consumption, and the application of innovative rational methods to traditional social and economic practices. *The rationality of the physical universe became a standard against which the customs and traditions of society could be measured and criticized. Such criticism penetrated every corner of contemporary society, politics, and religious opinion. As a result, the spirit of innovation and improvement came to characterize modern Europe and Western society.*

Some of the ideas and outlooks of the Enlightenment had a direct impact on several rulers in central and eastern Europe. These rulers, whose policies became known by the term "Enlightened Absolutism," sought to centralize their authority so as to reform their countries. They often attempted to restructure religious institutions and to sponsor economic growth. Although they frequently associated themselves with the Enlightenment, many of their military and foreign policies were in direct opposition to enlightened ideals. Nonetheless, both the Enlightenment writers and these monarchs were forces for modernization in European life.

The *Philosophes*

The writers and critics who forged the new attitudes favorable to change, who championed reform, and who flourished in the emerging print culture were the *philosophes*. Not usually philosophers in a formal sense, they sought rather to apply the rules of reason and common sense to nearly all the major institutions and social practices of the day. The most famous of their number included Voltaire, Montesquieu, Diderot, D'Alembert, Rousseau, Hume, Gibbon, Smith, Lessing, and Kant.

A few of these *philosophes* occupied professorships in universities. Most, however, were free agents who might be found in London coffeehouses, Edinburgh drinking spots, the salons of fashionable Parisian ladies, the country houses of reform-minded nobles, or the courts of the most powerful monarchs on the Continent. In eastern Europe, they were often to be found in the royal bureaucracies. They were not an organized group; they disagreed on many issues. Their relationship with each other and with lesser figures of the same turn of mind has quite appropriately been compared with that of a family, in which, despite quarrels and tensions, a basic unity remains.[1]

The chief bond among the *philosophes* was their common desire to reform thought, society, and government for the sake of human liberty. As Peter Gay

once suggested, this goal included "freedom from arbitrary power, freedom of speech, freedom of trade, freedom to realize one's talents, freedom of aesthetic response, freedom, in a word, of moral man to make his way in the world."[2] Though challenged over the last three centuries, no other single set of ideas has done so much to shape the modern world.

While expanding the realm of human action, much that the *philosophes* understood as freedom or improvement challenged traditional ideas, usually ideas associated with religion, a topic to be discussed shortly. Their call to rational improvement also embraced many of the economic changes of the day already considered in Chapter 16. In that regard, most of the advocates of agricultural improvement who sought to overturn so many of the customary practices also embodied the spirit of the Enlightenment. The same could be said of the inventors of the new textile machinery, the organizers of the early factory system, and the sponsors of the invention and spread of the steam engine and other improved means of transportation. The Enlightenment was a movement of intellectuals, but intellectuals deeply in touch with everyday life and intellectuals read by people who wished to transform everyday life.

The literary vehicles through which the *philosophes* delivered their message included books, pamphlets, plays, novels, philosophical treatises, encyclopedias, newspapers, and magazines. During the Reformation and the religious wars, writers had used the printed word to debate the proper mode of faith in God. The *philosophes* of the Enlightenment employed the printed word to proclaim a new faith in the capacity of humankind to improve itself without the aid of God.

The bulk of the readership of the *philosphes* was drawn from the prosperous commercial and professional people of the eighteenth-century towns and cities. These people discussed the reformers' writings and ideas in local philosophical societies, Freemason lodges, and clubs. They had enough income and leisure time to buy and read the *philosophes'* works. Although the writers of the Enlightenment did not consciously champion the goals or causes of the middle class, they did provide an intellectual ferment and a major source of ideas that could be used to undermine existing social practices and political structures. They taught their contemporaries how to pose pointed, critical questions. Moreover, the *philosophes* generally supported the growth, the expansion of trade, and the improvement of trans-

---

[1] Peter Gay, *The Enlightenment: An Interpretation*, vol. 1 (New York: Knopf, 1967), p. 4.

[2] Gay, p. 3.

port, which were transforming the society and the economy of the eighteenth century and enlarging the business and commerical classes.

The Enlightenment evolved over the course of the century and involved writers living at different times in various countries. Its early exponents popularized the rationalism and scientific ideas of the seventeenth century. (See Chapter 14.) They worked to expose contemporary social and political abuses and argued that reform was necessary and possible. Their progress in this cause was anything but steady. Among the obstacles they met were vested interests, political oppression, and religious condemnation. Yet, by midcentury, they had brought enlightened ideas to the European public in a variety of formats. They corresponded with each other, wrote for each other as well as for the public, and defended each other against the political and religious authorities.

By the second half of the century, they were sufficiently safe to quarrel among themselves on occasion. They had stopped talking in generalities, and their major advocates were addressing specific abuses. Their books and articles had become more specialized and more practical. They had become more concerned with politics than with religion. Having convinced Europeans that change was a good idea, they began to suggest exactly what changes were most desirable. They had become honored figures.

The *philosophes* believed that human society needed to and could be improved. But they were never certain that reform, if achieved, would be permanent. The optimism of the Enlightenment was a tempered hopefulness rather than a glib certainty. An undercurrent of pessimism characterized most of the works of the period. As D'Alembert wrote, "Barbarism lasts for centuries; it seems that it is our natural element; reason and good taste are only passing."[3]

What had been the forces in European life that gave rise to this group and their ideas?

Formative Influences on the Enlightenment

The Newtonian worldview, the stability and commerical prosperity of Great Britain after 1688, the need for administrative and economic reform in France after the wars of Louis XIV, and the consolidation of what is known as a print culture were the chief factors that fostered the ideas of the Enlightenment and the call for reform throughout Europe.

Ideas of Newton and Locke

Isaac Newton (1642–1727) and John Locke (1632–1704) were the major intellectual forerunners of the Enlightenment. Newton's formulation of the law of universal gravitation exemplified the power of the human mind. By example and in his writing, he encouraged Europeans to approach the study of nature directly and to avoid metaphysics and supernaturalism. Newton had always insisted on empirical support for his general laws and constantly used empirical experience to check his rational speculations. This emphasis on concrete experience became a key feature of Enlightenment thought. (See Art & the West.)

Newton also seemed to have revealed a pattern of rationality in the physical world. During the eighteenth century, thinkers began to apply this insight to society. If nature was rational, they reasoned, society, too, should be organized rationally.

As explained in Chapter 14, Newton's success in physics inspired his countryman John Locke to explain human psychology in terms of experience. In *An Essay Concerning Human Understanding* (1690), Locke argued that all humans

empirical = derived from or guided by experience or experiment

This elaborate eighteenth-century engraving pays homage to Isaac Newton, who was a major intellectual influence on the Enlightenment. This engraving is in the collection of the British Museum. Corbis

[3]Jean Le Rond d'Alembert, *Preliminary Discourse to the Encylopedia of Diderot*, Richard N. Schwab, tr. (Indianapolis: ITT Bobbs-Merrill Educational Publishing Company Inc., 1985), p. 103.

Joseph Wright, An Experiment on a Bird in the Air-Pump: Science in the Drawing Room

Joseph Wright of Derby, *An Experiment on a Bird in the Air-Pump* (1768). National Gallery, London, Great Britain. The Bridgeman Art Library.

The air-pump, devised by the pioneering English natural philosopher Robert Boyle in the 1650s, stood for over a century as major symbol of the new experimental science championed by the Royal Society of London. The instrument permitted air to be pumped out of a spherical glass jar to create a vacuum for the purpose of demonstrating the qualities of air and air pressure. The early air-pumps often functioned quite poorly because air would seep in through leaky seals, invading the vacuum. By the middle of the eighteenth century, however, many provincial English scientific societies possessed effective models such as the one portrayed in Joseph Wright's *An Experiment on a Bird in the Air-Pump* (1768).

Wright, who lived near Derby in an early industrial region of England, was a close friend of manufacturers and other persons interested in science several of whom belonged to the Lunar Society. In this dramatically lit painting, Wright portrays the excited interest of fashionable upper-class audiences in experimental science. At the same time, though, he suggests genuine apprehension about the practice of science.

Wright presents the central figure, who is operating the pump, as a natural philosopher about to demonstrate his superior knowledge and scientific skill through an experiment meant to indicate the necessity of air for the life of an animal. The experimenter holds the life and death of the bird in his hands as he moves to turn the switch that will create the vacuum. One figure observes the experiment with a sense of amazement, while another looks on with an expression of stoic acceptance. The man speaking to the young women, one of whom appears fearful and the other cautiously curious, may be explaining the need to place rationality above feelings in the pursuit of knowledge. Sacrificing the bird would advance the progress of science.

In his depiction of women (including one more interested in her male companion than in the experiment), Wright seems to be suggesting the commonly-held view of the day that women may approach science and experiments as observers, but may lack the intellectual qualities required for active participation in the experimental method.

In art historical terms, Wright, an English artist, has taken a genre of painting known as the *conversation piece* and made a scientific experiment the center of attention. Wright has also made another important substitution of a scientific subject for a more traditional one. The painting dramatically contrasts light and dark, a technique originally devised to highlight elements in paintings of religious scenes. Here the drama of the light highlights a secular scientific experiment on a natural subject that, especially in England, many people believed might lead to a new understanding of the divine. Thus, Wright could see the reverence once reserved for religious subjects now being evoked by a scientific one.

His painting, though coming a century after the first air pump experiments, demonstrates the manner in which, by the mid-eighteenth century, experimental science had established its cultural presence within polite society and its ability to foster civil conversation in place of political and religious disputes. Rather than discussing the Bible or politics, this group is observing a scientific experiment that will provide them with the opportunity for polite and presumably noncontroversial conversation, or at least conversation that will not lead to destructive quarrels.

Although, as an artist, Wright explored the challenges of painting light, the setting of this experiment would also seem to suggest that even in the eighteenth century he and others saw science as an uncertain and possibly temporary light surrounded by darkness and potential superstition.

Sources: David H. Solkin, *Painting for Money: The Visual Arts and the Public Sphere in Eighteenth-Century England* (New Haven, CT: Yale University Press, 1993); Steven Shapin and Simon Schaffer, *Leviathan and the Air-Pump: Hobbes, Boyle, and the Experimental Life* (Princeton, NJ: Princeton University Press, 1985).

enter the world a *tabula rasa,* or blank page. (See p. 463.) Personality is the product of the sensations that impinge on an individual from the external world throughout his or her life. Thus, experience, and only experience, shapes character. The implication of this theory was that human nature is changeable and can be molded by modifying the surrounding physical and social environment. Locke's was a reformer's psychology. It suggested the possibility of improving the human condition. Locke's psychology also, in effect, rejected the Christian doctrine that human beings are permanently flawed by sin. Human beings need not wait for the grace of God or other divine aid to better their lives. They could take charge of their own destiny.

The Example of British Toleration and Stability

Newton's physics and Locke's psychology provided the theoretical basis for a reformist approach to society. The domestic stability of Great Britain after the Revolution of 1688 furnished a living example of a society in which, to many contemporaries, enlightened reforms appeared to function for the benefit of all. England permitted religious toleration to all except Unitarians and Roman Catholics, and even they were not actually persecuted. Relative freedom of the press and free speech prevailed. The authority of the monarchy was limited, and political sovereignty resided in Parliament. The courts protected citizens from arbitrary government action. The army was small. Furthermore, the domestic economic life of Great Britain displayed far less regulation than that of France or other continental nations. In the view of reformist observers on the Continent, these liberal policies had produced not disorder and instability, but prosperity, stability, and a loyal citizenry. This view may have been idealized, but England was nonetheless significantly freer than any other European nation at the time.

Need for Reform in France

If the example of Great Britain suggested that change and freedom need not be disastrous, France seemed to illustrate those aspects of European politics and society that most demanded reform. Its legacy from Louis XIV was absolute monarchy, a large standing army, heavy taxation, and religious persecution of Protestants and dissident Roman Catholic Jansenists. His successors continued to curb liberties. The regime restricted freedom of worship and censored the press and

literary expression. Authors often had their works printed in Switzerland to avoid these restraints. Critics of the regime were subject to arbitrary arrest, although some of them reached accommodations with the authorities. State regulations hampered economic growth. Many aristocrats, regarding themselves as part of a military class, upheld traditional militaristic values.

Yet France, because it confronted its political thinkers so sharply with the need for reform, became a major center for the Enlightenment. There one of the earliest and by far the most influential voice of Enlightenment was François Marie Arouet, known to posterity as Voltaire (1694–1778). His career embodied both the conviction of the need for change in France and the admiration of Britain.

During the 1720s, Voltaire had offended the French authorities by certain of his writings. He was arrested and put in prison for a brief time. Later Voltaire went to England, visiting its best literary circles, observing its tolerant intellectual and religious climate, relishing the freedom he felt in its moderate political atmosphere, and admiring its science and economic prosperity. In 1733 he published *Letters on the English*, which appeared in French the next year. The book praised the virtues of the English and indirectly criticized the abuses of French society. In 1738 he published *Elements of the Philosophy of Newton*, which popularized the thought of the great scientist. Both works were well received and gave Voltaire a reputation as an important writer.

Thereafter Voltaire lived part of the time in France and part near Geneva, just across the French border, where the royal authorities could not bother him. He wrote essays, history, plays, stories, and letters that made him the "literary dictator" of Europe. He used the bitter venom of his satire and sarcasm against one evil after another in French and European life. In his most famous satire, *Candide* (1759), he attacked war, religious persecution, and what he regarded as unwarranted optimism about the human condition.

The Emergence of a Print Culture

The Enlightenment was the first major intellectual movement of European history to flourish in a print culture, that is, a culture in which books, journals, newspapers, and pamphlets had achieved a status of their own. Although printed books and pamphlets played a significant role during the Reformation and Counter-Reformation, the powerful messages of those movements were spread mostly by preaching. During the eighteenth century, the volume of printed material—books, jour-

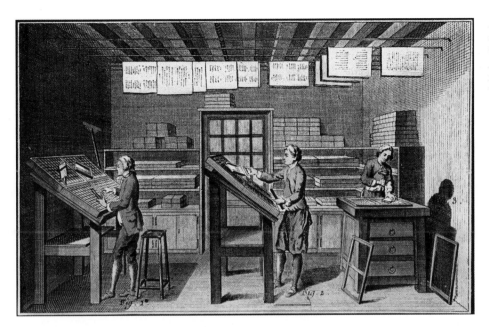

Printing shops were the productive centers for the book trade and newspaper publishing which spread the ideas of the Enlightenment.
The Granger Collection

nals, magazines, and daily newspapers—increased sharply throughout Europe, most notably in Britain. Prose came to be valued as highly as poetry, and the novel emerged as a distinct genre. The printed word had become the chief vehicle for the communication of ideas and would remain so until the electronic revolution of our own day.

A growing concern with everyday life and material concerns—with secular as opposed to religious issues—accompanied this expansion of printed forms. Toward the end of the seventeenth century, half the books published in Paris were religious; by the 1780s, only about 10 percent were.

Books were not inexpensive in this era, but they, and the ideas they conveyed, circulated in a variety of ways to reach a broad public. Private and public libraries grew in number, allowing single copies to reach many readers. Authors might also publish the same material in different formats. The English essayist, critic, and dictionary author Samuel Johnson (1709–1784), for example, published as books collections of essays that had first appeared in newspapers or journals.

Familiarity with books and secular ideas came increasingly to be expected within aristocratic and middle-class society. Popular publications, such as *The Spectator*, begun in 1711 by Joseph Addison (1672–1719) and Richard Steele (1672–1729), fostered the value of polite conversation and the reading of books. Coffeehouses became centers for the discussion of writing and ideas. The lodges of Freemasons, the meeting places for members of a movement that began in Britain and spread to the Continent, provided another site for the consideration of secular ideas in secular books.

The expanding market for printed matter allowed writers to earn a living from their work for the first time, making authorship an occupation. Parisian ladies sought out popular writers for their fashionable salons. Some writers, notably Alexander Pope (1688–1744) and Voltaire, grew wealthy, providing an example for their aspiring young colleagues. In a challenge to older aristocratic values, status for authors in this new print culture was based on merit and commercial competition, not heredity and patronage.

A division, however, soon emerged between high and low literary culture. Successful authors of the Enlightenment addressed themselves to monarchs, nobles, the upper middle classes, and professional groups and were read and accepted in these upper levels of society. Other authors found social and economic disappointment. They lived marginally, writing professionally for whatever newspaper or journal would pay for their pages. Many of these lesser writers grew resentful, blaming a corrupt society for their lack of success. From their anger, they often espoused radical ideas or carried Enlightenment ideas to radical extremes, transmitting them in this embittered form to their often lower class audience. The new print culture thus circulated the ideas of the Enlightenment to virtually all literate groups in society.

An expanding literate public and the growing influence of secular printed materials created a new and increasingly influential social force called public opinion. This force—the collective effect on political and social life of views circulated in print and discussed in the home, the workplace, and centers of leisure—seems not to have existed before the middle of the eighteenth century. Books and newspapers could have thousands of readers, who in effect supported the writers whose works they bought, discussing their ideas and circulating them widely. The writers, in turn, had to answer only to their readers. The result changed the cultural and political climate in Europe. In 1775 a new member of the French Academy declared that

A tribunal has arisen independent of all powers and that all powers respect, that appreciates all talents, that pronounces on all people of merit. And in an enlightened century, in a century in which each citizen can speak to the entire nation by way of print, those who have a talent for instructing men and a gift for moving them—in a word, men of letters—are, amid the public dispersed, what the orators of Rome and Athens were in the middle of the public assembled.[4]

Governments could no longer operate wholly in secret or with disregard to the larger public sphere. They, as well as their critics, had to explain and discuss their views and policies openly.

Continental European governments sensed the political power of the new print culture. They regulated the book trade, censored books and newspapers, confiscated offending titles, and imprisoned offending authors. The eventual expansion of freedom of the press represented also an expansion of the print culture—with its independent readers, authors, and publishers—and the challenge it posed to traditional intellectual, social, and political authorities.

The *Encyclopedia*

The midcentury witnessed the publication of the *Encyclopedia*, one the greatest monuments of the Enlightenment and its most monumental undertaking in the realm of print culture. Under the heroic leadership of Denis Diderot (1713–1784), and Jean le Rond d'Alembert (1717–1783), the first volume appeared in 1751. Eventually, numbering seventeen volumes of text and eleven of plates (illustrations), the project was completed in 1772.

The *Encyclopedia*, in part a collective plea for freedom of expression, reached fruition only after many attempts to censor it and to halt its publication. It was the product of the collective effort of more than 100 authors, and its editors had at one time or another solicited articles from all the major French *philosophes*. It included the most advanced critical ideas of the time on religion, government, and philosophy. To avoid official

censure, these ideas often had to be hidden in obscure articles or under the cover of irony. The *Encyclopedia* also included important articles and illustrations on manufacturing, canal building, ship construction, and improved agriculture, making it an important source of knowledge about eighteenth-century social and economic life. (See "The *Encyclopedia* Praises Mechanical Arts and Artisans.")

Between 14,000 and 16,000 copies of various editions of the *Encyclopedia* were sold before 1789. The project had been designed to secularize learning and to undermine intellectual assumptions that lingered from the Middle Ages and the Reformation. The articles on politics, ethics, and society ignored divine law and concentrated on humanity and its immediate well-being. The Encyclopedists looked to antiquity rather than to the Christian centuries for their intellectual and ethical models. For them, the future welfare of humankind lay not in pleasing God or following divine commandments, but rather in harnessing the power and resources of the Earth and in living at peace with one's fellow human beings. The good life lay here and now and was to be achieved through the application of reason to human relationships. With the publication of the *Encyclopedia*, Enlightenment thought became more fully diffused over the Continent, penetrating German and Russian intellectual and political circles.

The Enlightenment and Religion

For many, but not all, *philosophes* of the eighteenth century, ecclesiastical institutions were the chief impediment to human improvement and happiness. Voltaire's cry, "Crush the Infamous Thing," summed up the attitude of a number of *philosophes* toward the church and Christianity. Almost all varieties of Christianity, but especially Roman Catholicism, felt their criticism.

The critical *philosophes* complained that the churches hindered the pursuit of a rational life and the scientific study of humanity and nature. The clergy taught that humans were basically depraved, becoming worthy only through divine grace. According to the doctrine of original sin—either Protestant or Catholic—meaningful improvement in human nature on Earth was impossible. Religion thus turned attention away from this world to the world to come. For example, the *philosophes* argued that the Calvinist doctrine of predestination denied a relationship between virtuous actions in this life and the fate of the soul after death.

[4]Chrétien-Guillaume Malesherbes, as quoted in Roger Chartier, *The Cultural Origins of the French Revolution*, trans. by Lydia G. Cochran (Durham, NC: Duke University Press, 1991), pp. 30–31.

The *Encyclopedia* Praises Mechanical Arts and Artisans

The leading intellectuals and men of letters of the day wrote *the articles of the Encyclopedia. Yet the concrete reality of contemporaneous economic life in towns and the countryside fill its pages. Two of the most remarkable features of the* Encyclopedia *are the vast quantity of information it included in numerous articles about the mechanical arts and, in these articles, engravings that portrayed eighteenth-century French artisans in their workplace. The editors of the* Encyclopedia *believed that disseminating such information was necessary to aid the spirit of improvement and to promote economic growth. In the "Preliminary Discourse," which served as a general introduction to the* Encyclopedia, *D'Alembert explained the importance of the mechanical arts and the way the authors had explored these arts and the workshops where they were practiced.*

❖ *How does D'Alembert defend the importance of the mechanical arts? Why does he think they have not always received proper attention and appreciation? How did the authors of the* Encyclopedia *familiarize themselves with such work? What kind of conversation might have occurred between one of those authors and a skilled artisan operating his machinery?*

The mechanical arts, which are dependent upon manual operation and are subjugated...to a sort of routine, have been left to those among men whom prejudices have placed in the lowest class. Poverty has forced these men to turn to such work more often than taste and genius have attracted them to it. Subsequently it became a reason for holding them in contempt... However, the advantage that the liberal arts have over the mechanical arts...is sufficiently counterbalanced by the quite superior usefulness which the latter for the most part have for us. It is this very usefulness which reduced them perforce to purely mechanical operations in order to make them accessible to a larger number of men. But while justly respecting great geniuses for their enlightenment, society ought not to degrade the hands by which it is saved....

Too much has been written on the sciences; not enough has been written well on the mechanical arts....Thus everything impelled us to go directly to the workers.

We approached the most capable of them....We took the trouble of going into their shops, of questioning them, of writing at their dictation, of developing their thoughts and of drawing therefrom the terms peculiar to their professions, of setting up tables of these terms and of working out definitions for them, of conversing with those from whom we obtained memoranda, and (an almost indispensable precaution) of correcting through long and frequent conversations with others what some of them imperfectly, obscurely, and sometimes unreliably had explained. There are some artisans who are also men of letters, and we would be able to cite them here; but their numbers are very small. Most of those who engage in the mechanical arts have embraced them only by necessity and work only by instinct....

But there are some trades so unusual and some operations so subtle that unless one does the work oneself, unless one operates a machine with one's own hands, and sees the work being created under one's own eyes, it is difficult to speak of it with precision. Thus several times we had to get possession of the machines, to construct them, and to put a hand to the work. It was necessary to become apprentices, so to speak, and to manufacture some poor object ourselves in order to learn how to teach others the way good specimens are made.

From Jean Le Rond d'Alembert, *Preliminary Discourse to the Encyclopedia of Diderot*, Richard N. Schwab, trans. (Indianapolis: ITT Bobbs-Merrill Educational Publishing Company, Inc., 1985), pp. 41–42, 122–123.

Mired in conflicts over obscure doctrinal differences, the churches promoted intolerance and bigotry, inciting torture, war, and other forms of human suffering.

With this attack, the *philosophes* were challenging not only a set of ideas, but also some of Europe's most powerful institutions. The churches were deeply enmeshed in the power structure of the old regime. They owned large amounts of land and collected tithes from peasants before any secular authority collected its taxes. Most clergy were legally exempt from taxes and made only annual voluntary grants to the government. The upper clergy in most countries were relatives of aristocrats. Clerics were actively involved in politics, serving in the British House of Lords and advising princes on the Continent. In Protestant countries, the leading local landowner usually appointed the clergyman of a particular parish. Across the Continent, membership in the predominant denomination of the kingdom gave certain subjects political advantages. Nonmembership often excluded other subjects from political participation. Clergy frequently provided intellectual justification for the social and political status quo, and they were active agents of religious and literary censorship.

Deism

The *philosophes*, although critical of many religious institutions and frequently anticlerical, were not opposed to all religion. In Scotland, for example, the enlightened historian William Robertson (1721– 1793) was the head of the Scottish Kirk. In England, clergy of the established church did much to popularize the thought of Newton. What the *philosophes* sought, however, was religion without fanaticism and intolerance, a religious life that would largley substitute the authority of human reason for the authority of churches. The Newtonian worldview had convinced many writers that nature was rational. Therefore, the God who had created nature must also be rational, and the religion through which that God was worshiped should be rational. Most of them believed that the life of religion and of reason could be combined, giving rise to a movement known as *deism*.

The title of one of the earliest deist works, *Christianity Not Mysterious* (1696) by John Toland (1670–1722), indicates the general tenor of this religious outlook. Toland and later deist writers promoted religion as a natural and rational, rather than a supernatural and mystical, phenomenon. In this respect they differed from Newton and Locke, both of whom regarded themselves as distinctly Christian. Newton believed that God could interfere with the natural order, whereas the deists regarded God as a kind of divine watchmaker who had created the mechanism of nature, set it in motion, and then departed. Most of the deist writers were also strongly anticlerical and for that reason regarded as radical.

There were two major points in the deists' creed. The first was a belief in the existence of God, which they thought could be empirically justified by the contemplation of nature. Joseph Addison's poem on the spacious firmament (1712) illustrates this idea:

The spacious firmament on high,
With all the blue ethereal sky,
And spangled heav'n, a shining frame,
Their great Original proclaim:
Th' unwearied Sun, from day to day,
Does his Creator's power display,
And publishes to every land
The work of an Almighty hand.

Because nature provided evidence of a rational God, that deity must also favor rational morality. So the second point in the deists' creed was a belief in life after death, when rewards and punishments would be meted out according to the virtue of the lives people led on this Earth.

Deism was empirical, tolerant, reasonable, and capable of encouraging virtuous living. Voltaire wrote:

The great name of Deist, which is not sufficiently revered, is the only name one ought to take. The only gospel one ought to read is the great book of Nature, written by the hand of God and sealed with his seal. The only religion that ought to be professed is the religion of worshiping God and being a good man.[5]

Deists hoped that wide acceptance of their faith would end rivalry among the various Christian sects and with it religious fanaticism, conflict, and persecution. They also felt deism would remove the need for priests and ministers, who, in their view, were often responsible for fomenting religious differences and denominational hatred. Deistic thought led some contempraries to believe that God had revealed himself in various ways and that many religions might embody divine truth.

Toleration

According to the *philosophes*, religious toleration was a primary social condition for the virtuous life. Again Voltaire took the polemical lead in championing this cause. In 1762, the Roman Catholic political authorities in Toulouse ordered the execution of a Huguenot named Jean Calas. He stood accused of having murdered his son to prevent him from converting to Roman Catholicism. Calas was viciously tortured and publicly strangled without ever confessing his guilt. The confession would not have saved his life, but it would have given the Catholics good propaganda to use against Protestants.

Voltaire learned of the case only after Calas's death. He made the dead man's cause his own. In 1763, he published his *Treatise on Tolerance* and hounded the authorities for a new investigation. Finally, in 1765,

---

[5]Quoted in J. H. Randall, *The Making of the Modern Mind*, rev. ed. (New York: Houghton Mifflin, 1940), p. 292.

Voltaire Attacks Religious Fanaticism

The chief complaint of the philosophes against Christianity was that it bred a fanaticism that led people to commit crimes in the name of religion. In this passage from Voltaire's Philosophical Dictionary (1764), he directly reminds his readers of the intolerance of the Reformation era and indirectly refers to examples of contemporary religious excesses. He argues that the philosophical spirit can overcome fanaticism and foster toleration and more humane religious behavior. Shocking many of his contemporaries, he praises the virtues of Confucianism over those of Christianity.

❖ *What concrete examples of religious fanaticism might Voltaire have had in mind? Why does Voltaire contend that neither religion nor laws can contain religious fanaticism? Why does Voltaire admire the Chinese?*

Fanaticism is to superstition what delirium is to fever and rage to anger. The man visited by ecstasies and visions, who takes dreams for realities and his fancies for prophecies, is an enthusiast; the man who supports his madness with murder is a fanatic....

The most detestable example of fanaticism was that of the burghers of Paris who on St. Bartholomew's Night [1572] went about assassinating and butchering all their fellow citizens who did not go to mass, throwing them out of windows, cutting them in pieces.

Once fanaticism has corrupted a mind, the malady is almost incurable....

The only remedy for this epidemic malady is the philosophical spirit which, spread gradually, at last tames men's habits and prevents the disease from starting; for once the disease has made any progress, one must flee and wait for the air to clear itself. Laws and religion are not strong enough against the spiritual pest; religion, far from being healthy food for infected brains, turns to poison in them....

Even the law is impotent against these attacks of rage; it is like reading a court decree to a raving maniac. These fellows are certain that the holy spirit with which they are filled is above the law, that their enthusiasm is the only law they must obey.

What can we say to a man who tells you that he would rather obey God than men, and that therefore he is sure to go to heaven for butchering you?

Ordinarily fanatics are guided by rascals, who put the dagger into their hands; these latter resemble that Old Man of the Mountain who is supposed to have made imbeciles taste the joys of paradise and who promised them an eternity of the pleasures of which he had given them a foretaste, on condition that they assassinated all those he would name to them. There is only one religion in the world that has never been sullied by fanaticism, that of the Chinese men of letters. The schools of philosophy were not only free from this pest, they were its remedy; for the effect of philosophy is to make the soul tranquil, and fanaticism is incompatible with tranquility. If our holy religion has so often been corrupted by this infernal delirium, it is the madness of men which is at fault.

From Voltaire, *Philosophical Dictionary*, trans. by P. Gay (New York: Basic Books, 1962), pp. 267–269.

the judicial decision against the unfortunate man was reversed. For Voltaire, the case illustrated the fruits of religious fanaticism and the need for rational reform of judicial processes. (See "Voltaire Attacks Religious Fanaticism.") Somewhat later in the century, the German playwright and critic Gotthold Lessing (1729–1781) wrote *Nathan the Wise* (1779), a plea for toleration not only of different Christian sects, but also of religious faiths other than Christianity.

The premise behind all of these calls for toleration was, in effect, that life on Earth and human relationships should not be subordinated to religion. Secular values and considerations were more important than religious ones.

Radical Enlightenment Criticism of Religion

Some *philosophes* went beyond the formulation of a rational religious alternative to Christianity and the advocacy of toleration to attack the churches and the clergy with great vehemence. Voltaire repeatedly questioned the truthfulness of priests and the morality of the Bible. In his *Philosophical Dictionary* (1764), he humorously pointed out inconsistencies in biblical narratives and immoral acts of the biblical heroes. The Scottish philosopher David Hume (1711–1776), in "Of Miracles," a chapter in his *Inquiry into Human Nature* (1748), argued that no empirical evidence supported the belief in divine miracles central to much of Christianity. For Hume, the greatest miracle was that people believed in miracles. In *The Decline and Fall of the Roman Empire* (1776), Edward Gibbon (1737–1794), the English historian, explained the rise of Christianity in terms of natural causes rather than the influence of miracles and piety.

A few *philosophes* went further. Baron d'Holbach (1723–1789) and Julien Offray de La Mettrie (1709–1751) embraced positions very near to atheism and materialism. Theirs was distinctly a minority position, however. Most of the *philosophes* sought not the abolition of religion, but its transformation into a humane force that would encourage virtuous living. In the words of the title of a work by the German philosopher Immanuel Kant, they sought to pursue *Religion within the Limits of Reason Alone* (1793).

Jewish Thinkers in the Age of Enlightenment

Despite their emphasis on toleration, the *philosophes'* criticisms of traditional religion often reflected an implicit contempt not only for Christianity but also, and sometimes more vehemently, for Judaism. Their attack on the veracity of biblical miracles and biblical history undermined the authority of the Hebrew scriptures as well as the Christian. They often aimed their satirical barbs at personalities from the Hebrew scriptures. Some *philosophes* characterized Judaism as a more primitive faith than Christianity and one from which philosophical rationalism provided a path of escape. The Enlightenment view of religion thus served in some ways to further stigmatize Jews and Judaism in the eyes of non-Jewish Europeans.

Enlightenment values also, however, allowed certain Jewish intellectuals to rethink the relationship of their communities to wider European culture from which they had largely lived apart. Two major Jewish writers—one a few decades before the opening of the Enlightenment and one toward the close—entered the larger debate over religion and the place of Jews in European life. These were Baruch Spinoza (1632–1677) who lived in the Netherlands and Moses Mendelssohn (1729–1786) who lived in Germany. Spinoza set the example for a secularized ver-

sion of Judaism while Mendelssohn established the main outlines of an assimilationist position. While their approaches to the problem displayed certain similarities, there were also important differences.

Spinoza, the son of a Jewish merchant of Amsterdam, was deeply influenced by the new science of the mid-seventeenth century. Like his contemporaries, Hobbes and Descartes, he looked to the power of human reason to reconceptualize traditional thought. In that regard his thinking reflected the age of scientific revolution and looked toward the later Enlightenment.

In his *Ethics*, the most famous of his works, Spinoza so closely identified God and nature, or the spiritual and material worlds, that contemporaries condemned him. Many thought that he drew God and nature too intimately into a single divine substance, leaving little room for the possibility of a distinctly divine revelation to humankind in scripture. Both Christians and Jews also believed Spinoza's near pantheistic position meant that human beings might not be personally responsible for their actions and that there could be no personal, individual immortality of the human soul after death. During his lifetime the controversial character of his writings led both Jews and Protestants to criticize him as an athe-

The Dutch Jewish philosopher Baruch Spinoza was deeply influenced by the new science of the mid-seventeenth century. In his writings, Spinoza argued for rationality over traditional spiritual beliefs. Library of Congress

ist. At the age of 24, he was excommunicated by his own synagogue and thereafter lived apart from the Amsterdam Jewish community.

In his *Theologico-Political Treatise* (1670), Spinoza directly anticipated much of the religious criticism of the Enlightenment and its attacks on the power of superstition in human life. Spinoza described the origins of religion in thoroughly naturalistic terms. He believed the Hebrew Bible provided Jews with divine legislation but not with specially revealed theological knowledge. In this respect, he was calling upon both Jews and Christians to use their own reason in religious matters and to read the Bible like other ancient books. Spinoza's extensive rational and historical criticism of the biblical narratives disturbed Christian and Jewish contemporaries who saw him as a writer seeking to lead people away from all religion. He actually argued, however, that the formally organized religious institutions of both Christianity and Judaism led people away from the original teaching of scripture and encouraged them to persecute those who disagreed with the leaders of their respective churches and synagogues.

Because of Spinoza's excommunication from his synagogue, the later *philosophes* viewed him as a martyr for rationality against superstition. He also symbolized a Jew who, through the use of his critical reason, had separated himself from traditional Jewish religion and practices and attempted to enter the mainstream society. In that regard, he left Judaism to pursue a secular existence with little or no regard for his original faith. Consequently, his life and his writings as one commentator has stated "made it possible for defenders of the Enlightenment to advocate toleration of Jews while simultaneously holding Judaism in contempt."[6] This stance of championing toleration while condemning Judaism itself would later characterize the outlook of many non-Jewish Europeans to the assimilation of Jews into European civic life. It was, however, an outlook that could not without much modification be welcomed by Jewish communities themselves.

Moses Mendelsohn, the leading Jewish philosopher of the eighteenth century and a person known as the "Jewish Socrates," writing almost a century later also advocated the entry of Jews into modern European life. In contrast to Spinoza, however, Mendelsohn argued for the possibility of loyalty to Judaism combined with adherence to rational, enlightenment values. Mendelsohn could hold this position in part because of the influence of Lessing's arguments for toleration. Indeed, Mendelsohn

had been the person on whose life Lessing had modeled the chief character of *Nathan the Wise.*

Mendelsohn's most infuential work was *Jerusalem; or, On Ecclesiastical Power and Judaism* (1783) where he argued both for advancing extensive religious toleration and for maintaining the religious distinction of Jewish communities. Mendelsohn urged that religious diversity within a nation did not harm loyalty to the government; therefore, governments should be religiously neutral and Jews should enjoy the same civil rights as other subjects. Then in the spirit of the deists, he presented Judaism as one of many religious paths revealed by God. Jewish law and practice were intended for the moral benefit of Jewish communities; other religions similarly served other people. Consequently, various communities should be permitted to practice their religious faith alongside other religious groups.

Unlike Spinoza, Mendelsohn wished to advocate religious toleration while genuinely sustaining the traditional religious practices and faith of Judaism. Nevertheless, Mendelsohn believed that Jewish communities should *not* have the right to excommunicate their members over differences in theological opinions, but should tolerate within themselves a wide spectrum of outlooks. In this respect, Mendelsohn set forth a far more extensive vision of religious toleration than John Locke almost a century earlier, who had contended that numerous religious communities should be tolerated but that each should retain the right of excommunication (see Chapter 14.) Mendelsohn advocated broad toleration within the Jewish communities so that their members, if they wished, could embrace modern secular ideas without danger of excommunication. He thus sought both toleration *of* Jews within the broader non-Jewish European society and toleration *by* Jews of a wider spectrum of opinion within their own communities and congregations. His hope was that the rationalism of the Enlightenment would provide the foundation for both modes of toleration.

The Enlightenment and Society

Although the *philosophes* wrote much on religion, humanity was the center of their interest. As one writer in the *Encyclopedia* observed, "Man is the unique point to which we must refer everything, if we wish to interest and please amongst considerations the most arid and details the most dry."[7]

[6]Steven B. Smith, *Spinoza, Liberalism, and the Question of Jewish Identity* (New Haven, CT: Yale University Press, 1997), p. 166.

[7]Quoted in F. L. Baumer, *Main Currents of Western Thought*, 4th ed. (New Haven, CT.: Yale University Press, 1978), p. 374.

The *philosophes* believed that the application of human reason to society would reveal laws in human relationships similar to those found in physical nature. At the same time, the use of the word "man" in this passage was not simply an accident of language. Most *philosophes* were thinking primarily of men, not women, when they framed their reformist ideas. With a few exceptions, as will be seen later in the chapter, they had little interest in expanding women's intellectual and social opportunities.

Although the term did not appear until later, the idea of *social science* originated with the Enlightenment. *Philosophes* hoped to end human cruelty by discovering social laws and making people aware of them. These concerns are most evident in the *philosophes'* work on law and prisons.

Beccaria and Reform of Criminal Law

In 1764 Cesare Beccaria (1738–1794), an Italian *philosophe*, published *On Crimes and Punishments*, in which he applied critical analysis to the problem of making punishments both effective and just. He wanted the laws of monarchs and legislatures—that is, positive law—to conform with the rational laws of nature. He rigorously and eloquently attacked both torture and capital punishment. He thought that the criminal justice system should ensure a speedy trial and certain punishment and that the intent of punishment should be to deter further crime. The purpose of laws was not to impose the will of God or some other ideal of perfection; their purpose was to secure the greatest good or happiness for the greatest number of human beings. This utilitarian philosophy based on happiness in this life permeated most Enlightenment writing on practical reforms.

The Physiocrats and Economic Freedom

Economic policy was another area in which the *philosophes* saw existing legislation and administration preventing the operation of natural social laws. They believed that mercantilist legislation (designed to protect a country's trade from external competition) and the regulation of labor by governments and guilds actually hampered the expansion of trade, manufacture, and agriculture. In France, these economic reformers were called the *physiocrats*. Their leading spokespeople were François Quesnay (1694–1774) and Pierre Dupont de Nemours (1739–1817).

The physiocrats believed that the primary role of government was to protect property and to permit its owners to use it freely. They particularly felt that

all economic production depended on sound agriculture. They favored the consolidation of small peasant holdings into larger, more efficient farms. Here as elsewhere, there was a close relationship between the rationalism of the Enlightenment and the spirit of improvement at work in eighteenth-century European economic life.

Adam Smith on Economic Growth and Social Progress

The most important economic work of the Enlightenment was Adam Smith's (1723–1790) *Inquiry into the Nature and Causes of the Wealth of Nations* (1776). Smith, who was for a time a professor at Glasgow, believed that economic liberty was the foundation of a natural economic system. As a result, he urged that the mercantile system of England—including the navigation acts, the bounties, most tariffs, special trading monopolies, and the domestic regulation of labor and manufacture—be abolished. These regulations were intended to preserve the wealth of the nation, to capture wealth from other nations, and to maximize the work available for the nation's laborers. Smith argued, however, that they hindered the expansion of wealth and production. The best way to encourage economic growth, he maintained, was to unleash individuals to pursue their own selfish economic interests. As self-interested individuals sought to enrich themselves by meeting the needs of others in the marketplace, the economy would expand. Consumers would find their wants met as manufacturers and merchants competed for their business.

It was a basic assumption of mercantilism that the earth's resources are limited and scarce, so that one nation can acquire wealth only at the expense of others. Smith's book challenged this assumption. He saw the resources of nature—water, air, soil, and minerals—as boundless. To him, they demanded exploitation for the enrichment and comfort of humankind. In effect, Smith was saying that the nations and peoples of Europe need not be poor.

Smith is usually regarded as the founder of *laissez-faire* economic thought and policy, which favors a limited role for the government in economic life. *The Wealth of Nations* was, however, a complex book. Smith was no simple dogmatist. For example, he did not oppose all government activity touching the economy. The state, he argued, should provide schools, armies, navies, and roads. It should also undertake certain commercial ventures, such as the opening of dangerous new trade routes that were economically desirable, but too expensive or risky for private enterprise.

Within *The Wealth of Nations*, Smith, like other Scottish thinkers of the day, embraced an important theory of human social and economic development, known as the *four-stage theory*. According to this theory, human societies can be classified as hunting and gathering, pastoral or herding, agricultural, and commercial. The hunters and gatherers have little or no settled life. Pastoral societies are groups of nomads who tend their herds and develop some private property. Agricultural or farming societies are settled and have clear-cut property arrangements. Finally, in the commercial state there exist advanced cities, the manufacture of numerous items for wide consumption, extensive trade between cities and the countryside, as well as elaborate forms of property and financial arrangements. Smith and other Scottish writers described the passage of human society through these stages as a movement from barbarism to civilization.

The four-stage theory implicitly evaluated the later stages of economic development and the people dwelling in them as higher, more progressive, and more civilized than the earlier ones. A social theorist using this theory could thus very quickly look at a society and, on the basis of the state of its economic development and organizations, rank it in terms of the stage it had achieved. In point of fact, the commercial stage, the highest rank in the theory, described society as it appeared in northwestern Europe. Thus, Smith's theory allowed Europeans to look about the world and always find themselves dwelling at the highest level of human achievement. This outlook served as one of the major justifications in the minds of Europeans for their economic and imperial domination of the world during the next century. They repeatedly portrayed themselves as bringing a higher level of civilization to people elsewhere who, according to the four-stage theory, lived in lower stages of human social and economic development. Europeans thus imbued with the spirit of the Enlightenment presented themselves as carrying out a civilizing mission to the rest of the world.

Political Thought of the *Philosophes*

Nowhere was the *philosophes'* reformist agenda, as well as tensions among themselves, so apparent as in their political thought. Most *philosophes* were discontented with certain political features of their countries, but they were especially discontented in France. There the corruptness of the royal court, the blundering of the administrative bureaucracy, the less-than-glorious midcentury wars, and the power of the church compounded all problems. Consequently, the most important political thought of the Enlightenment occurred in France. The French *philosophes*, however, stood quite divided as to the proper solution to their country's problems. Their attitudes spanned a wide political spectrum, from aristocratic reform to democracy to absolute monarchy.

Montesquieu and *Spirit of the Laws*

Charles Louis de Secondat, Baron de Montesquieu (1689–1755), was a lawyer, a noble of the robe, and a member of a provincial *parlement*. He also belonged to the Bordeaux Academy of Science, before which he presented papers on scientific topics.

Although living comfortably within the bosom of French society, he saw the need for reform. In 1721, he published *The Persian Letters* to satirize contemporary institutions. The book consisted of letters purportedly written by two Persians visiting Europe. They explained to friends at home how European behavior contrasted with Persian life and customs. Behind the humor lay the cutting edge of criticism and an exposition of the cruelty and irrationality of much contemporaneous European life.

Charles de Secondat, Baron de Montesquieu (1689–1755), was the author of Spirit of the Laws, *possibly the most influential work of political thought of the eighteenth century.* Corbis

Montesquieu Defends the Separation of Powers

Spirit of the Laws (1748) was probably the most influential political work of the Enlightenment. In this passage Montesquieu explains how the division of powers within a government would make that government more moderate and would protect the liberty of its subjects. This idea was adopted by the writers of the United States Constitution when they devised the checks and balances of the three branches of government.

❖ *What did Montesquieu mean by "moderate governments," and why did he associate political liberty with such governments? What might he have seen as such a government in his own day? How does Montesquieu define the liberty of a subject? Why does he regard a situation where the power of government is not divided as one where there can be no liberty?*

Democratic and aristocratic states are not in their own nature free. Political liberty is to be found only in moderate governments; and even in these it is not always found. It is there only when there is no abuse of power. But constant experience shows us that every man invested with power is apt to abuse it, and to carry his authority as far as it will go....

To prevent this abuse, it is necessary from the very nature of things that power should be a check to power....

In every government there are three sorts of power: the legislative; the executive in respect to things dependent on the law of nations; and the executive in regard to matters that depend on the civil law [the realm of the judiciary]....

The political liberty of the subject is a tranquillity of mind arising from the opinion each person has of his safety. In order to have this liberty, it is requisite that government be so constituted as one man need not be afraid of another.

When the legislative and executive powers are united in the same person, or in the same body of magistrates, there can be no liberty; because apprehensions may arise, lest the same monarch or senate should enact tyrannical laws, to execute them in a tyrannical manner.

Again, there is no liberty, if the judiciary power be not separated from the legislative and executive. Were it joined with the legislative, the life and liberty of the subject would be exposed to arbitrary control; for the judge would be then the legislator. Were it joined to the executive power, the judge might behave with violence and oppression.

There would be an end of everything, were the same man or the same body, whether of the nobles or of the people, to exercise those three powers, that of enacting laws, that of executing the public resolutions, and of trying the causes of individuals.

In his most enduring work, *Spirit of the Laws* (1748), Montesquieu held up the example of the British constitution as the wisest model for regulating the power of government. With his interest in science, his hope for reform, and his admiration for Britain, he embodied all the major elements of the Enlightenment mind. (See "Montesquieu Defends the Separation of Powers.")

Montesquieu's *Spirit of the Laws*, perhaps the single most influential book of the century, exhibits the internal tensions of the Enlightenment. In it, Montesquieu pursued an empirical method, taking illustrative examples from the political experience of both ancient and modern nations. From these, he concluded there could be no single set of political laws that applied to all peoples at all times and in all places. The good political life depended rather on the relationship among many political variables. Whether the best form of government for a country was a monarchy or a republic, for example, depended on that country's size, population, social and religious customs, economic structure, traditions, and climate. Only a careful examination and evaluation of these elements could reveal what mode of government would prove most beneficial to a particular people.

So far as France was concerned, Montesquieu had some definite ideas. He believed in a monarchical government tempered and limited by various sets of intermediary institutions, including the aristocracy, the towns, and the other corporate bodies that enjoyed liberties the monarch had to respect. These corporate bodies might be said to represent various segments of the general population and thus of public opinion. In France, he regarded the aristocratic courts, or *parlements*, as the major example of an intermediary association. Their role was to limit the power of the monarchy and thus to preserve the liberty of its subjects.

In championing these aristocratic bodies and the general role of the aristocracy, Montesquieu was a political conservative. He adopted this conservatism in the hope of achieving reform, however, for he believed that the oppressive and inefficient absolutism of the monarchy accounted for the degradation of French life.

One of Montesquieu's most influential ideas was that of the division of power in government. For his model of a government with authority wisely separated among different branches, he took contemporary Great Britain. There, he believed, executive power resided in the king, legislative power in the Parliament, and judicial power in the courts. He thought any two branches could check and balance the power of the other. His perception of the eighteenth-century British constitution was incorrect because he failed to see how patronage and electoral corruption allowed a handful of powerful aristocrats to dominate the government. Moreover, he was also unaware of the emerging cabinet system, which was slowly making the executive power a creature of the Parliament.

Nevertheless, Montesquieu's analysis illustrated his strong sense that monarchs should be subject to constitutional limits on their power and that a separate legislature, not the monarch, should formulate laws. For this reason, although he set out to defend the political privileges of the French aristocracy, Montesquieu's ideas had a profound and still-lasting effect on the constitutional form of liberal democracies for more than two centuries.

Rousseau: A Radical Critique of Modern Society

Jean-Jacques Rousseau (1712–1778) held a view of the exercise and reform of political power that was quite different from Montesquieu's. Rousseau was a strange, isolated genius who never felt particularly comfortable with the other *philosophes*. His own life was troubled. He could form few close friendships. He sired numerous children, whom he abandoned to foundling hospitals. Yet perhaps more than any other writer of the mid-eighteenth century, he transcended the political

thought and values of his own time. Rousseau had a deep antipathy toward the world and the society in which he lived. It seemed to him impossible for human beings living according to the commercial values of his time to achieve moral, virtuous, or sincere lives. In 1750, in his *Discourse on the Moral Effects of the Arts and Sciences*, he contended that the process of civilization and enlightenment had corrupted human nature. In 1755, in his *Discourse on the Origin of Inequality*, Rousseau blamed much of the evil in the world on the uneven distribution of property.

In both works, Rousseau brilliantly and directly challenged the social fabric of the day. He drew into question the concepts of material and intellectual progress and the morality of a society in which commerce and industry were regarded as the most important human activities. The other *philosophes* generally believed that life would improve if people could enjoy more of the fruits of the Earth or could produce more goods. Rousseau raised the more fundamental question of what constitutes the good life. This question has haunted European social thought ever since the eighteenth century.

Jean-Jacques Rousseau (1712–1778) raised some of the most profound social and ethical questions of the Enlightenment. This portrait is by Maurice Quentin.
Maurice Quentin de la Tour, Jean Jacques Rousseau, ca. 1740. Original: Genf, Musèe d'Art et d'Histoire. Bildarchiv Preussischer Kulturbesitz

Rousseau carried these same concerns into his political thought. His most extensive discussion of politics appeared in *The Social Contract* (1762). Although the book attracted rather little immediate attention, by the end of the century it was widely read in France. Compared with Montesquieu's *Spirit of the Laws*, *The Social Contract* is a very abstract book. It does not propose specific reforms, but outlines the kind of political structure that Rousseau believed would overcome the evils of contemporary politics and society.

In the tradition of John Locke, most eighteenth-century political thinkers regarded human beings as individuals and society as a collection of individuals pursuing personal, selfish goals. These writers wished to liberate individuals from the undue bonds of government. Rousseau picked up the stick from the other end. His book opens with the declaration, "All men are born free, but everywhere they are in chains."[8] The rest of the volume is a defense of the chains of a properly organized society over its members.

Rousseau suggested that society is more important than its individual members, because they are what they are only by virtue of their relationship to the larger community. Independent human beings living alone can achieve very little. Through their relationship to the larger community, they become moral creatures capable of significant action. The question then becomes, What kind of community allows people to behave morally? In his two previous discourses, Rousseau had explained that the contemporaneous European society was not such a community; it was merely an aggregate of competing individuals whose chief social goal was to preserve selfish independence in spite of all potential social bonds and obligations.

Rousseau envisioned a society in which each person could maintain personal freedom while behaving as a loyal member of the larger community. Drawing on the traditions of Plato and Calvin, he defined freedom as obedience to law. In his case, the law to be obeyed was that created by the general will. In a society with virtuous customs and morals in which citizens have adequate information on important issues, the concept of the general will is normally equivalent to the will of a majority of voting citizens. Democratic participation in decision-making would bind the individual citizen to the community. Rousseau believed that the general will, thus understood, must always be right and that to obey the general will is to be free. This argument led him to the notorious conclusion that under certain circumstances some people must be forced to

be free. Rousseau's politics thus constituted a justification for radical direct democracy and for collective action against individual citizens.

Rousseau had in effect launched an assault on the eighteenth-century cult of the individual and the fruits of selfishness. He stood at odds with the commercial spirit that was transforming the society in which he lived. Rousseau would have disapproved of the main thrust of Adam Smith's *Wealth of Nations*, which he may or may not have read, and would no doubt have preferred a study on the *virtue* of nations. Smith wanted people to be prosperous; Rousseau wanted them to be good even if being good meant that they might remain poor. He saw human beings not as independent individuals, but as creatures enmeshed in necessary social relationships. He believed that loyalty to the community should be encouraged. As one device to that end, he suggested that a properly governed society should decree a civic religion based on the creed of deism. Such a shared religion, the observance of which he thought should be enforced by repressive legislation, could, he argued, help unify a society.

Rousseau had only a marginal impact on his own time. The other *philosophes* questioned his critique of material improvement. Aristocrats and royal ministers could hardly be expected to welcome his proposal for radical democracy. Too many people were either making or hoping to make money to appreciate his criticism of commercial values. He proved, however, to be a figure to whom later generations returned. Many leaders in the French Revolution were familiar with his writing, and he influenced many writers in the nineteenth and twentieth centuries who were critical of the general tenor and direction of Western culture. Rousseau hated much about the emerging modern society in Europe, but he contributed much to modernity by exemplifying for later generations the critic who dared to call into question the very foundations of social thought and action.

Women in the Thought and Practice of the Enlightenment

Women, especially in France, helped significantly to promote the careers of the *philosophes*. In Paris, the salons of women such as Marie-Thérèse Geoffrin (1699–1777), Julie de Lespinasse (1733–1776), and Claudine de Tencin (1689–1749) gave the *philosophes* access to useful social and political contacts and a receptive environment in which to circulate their ideas. Association with a fashionable salon brought *philosophes* increased social status and added luster and respectability to their

[8]Jean-Jacques Rousseau, *The Social Contract and Discourses*, trans. by G. D. H. Cole (New York: Dutton, 1950), p. 3.

ideas. They clearly enjoyed the opportunity to be the center of attention that a salon provided, and their presence at them could boost the sales of their works. The women who organized the salons were well connected to major political figures who could help protect the *philosophes* and secure them pensions. The marquise de Pompadour, the mistress of Louis XV (1721–1764), played a key role in overcoming efforts to censor the *Encyclopedia*. She also helped block the circulation of works attacking the *philosophes*. Other salon hostesses purchased the writings of the *philosophes* and distributed them among their friends. Madame de Tencin was responsible for promoting Montesquieu's *Spirit of the Laws* in this way.

Despite this help and support from the learned women of Paris, the *philosophes* were on the whole not strong feminists. Many urged better and broader education for women. They criticized the education women did receive as overly religious, and they tended to reject ascetic views of sexual relations. But in general, they displayed rather traditional views toward women and advocated no radical changes in the social condition of women.

Montesquieu, for example, illustrates some of these tensions in the views of Enlightenment writers toward women. He maintained in general that the status of women in a society was the result of climate, the political regime, culture, and women's physiological nature. He believed that women were not naturally inferior to men and should have a wider role in society. He showed himself well aware of the kinds of personal, emotional, and sexual repression European women endured in his day. He sympathetically observed the value placed on women's appearance and the prejudice women met as they aged. In *The Persian Letters*, he included a long exchange about the repression of women in a Persian harem, condemning by implication the restrictions on women in European society. Yet there were limits to Montesquieu's willingness to consider social change in regard to the role of women in European life. Although in the *Spirit of the Laws* he indicated a belief in the equality of the sexes, he still retained a traditional view of marriage and family and expected men to dominate those institutions. Furthermore, although he supported the right of women to divorce and opposed laws directly oppressive of women, he upheld the ideal of female chastity.

The views about women expressed in the *Encyclopedia* were less generous than those of Montesquieu. It suggested some ways to improve women's lives, but in general, it did not include the condition of women as a focus of reform. The editors, Diderot and d'Alembert, recruited men almost exclusively as contributors, and there is no indication that they saw a need to include many articles by women. Most of the articles that dealt with women specifically or that discussed women in connection with other subjects often emphasized their physical weakness and inferiority, usually attributed to menstruation or childbearing. Contributors disagreed on the social equality of women. Some favored it, others opposed it, and still others were indifferent. The articles conveyed a general sense that women were reared to be frivolous and unconcerned with important issues. The Encyclopedists discussed women primarily in a family context—as daughters, wives, and mothers—and presented

The salon of Mme. Marie Thérèse Geoffrin (1699–1777) was one of the most important gathering spots for Enlightenment writers during the middle of the eighteenth century. Well-connected women such as Mme. Geoffrin were instrumental in helping the philosophes *they patronized to bring their ideas to the attention of influential people in French society and politics.*
Giraudon/Art Resource, N.Y.

Rousseau Argues for Separate Spheres for Men and Women

Rousseau published Émile, *a novel about education, in 1762. In it, he made one of the strongest and most influential arguments of the eighteenth century for distinct social roles for men and women. Furthermore, he portrayed women as fundamentally subordinate to men. In the next document, Mary Wollstonecraft, a contemporary, presents a rebuttal.*

❖ *How does Rousseau move from the physical differences between men and women to an argument for distinct social roles and social spheres? What would be the proper kinds of social activities for women in Rousseau's vision? What kind of education would he think appropriate for women?*

There is no parity between the two sexes in regard to the consequences of sex. The male is male only at certain moments. The female is female her whole life or at least during her whole youth. Everything constantly recalls her sex to her; and, to fulfill its functions well, she needs a constitution which corresponds to it. She needs care during her pregnancy; she needs rest at the time of childbirth; she needs a soft and sedentary life to suckle her children; she needs patience and gentleness, a zeal and an affection that nothing can rebuff in order to raise her children. She serves as the link between them and their father; she alone makes him love them and gives him the confidence to call them his own. How much tenderness and care is required to maintain the union of the whole family! And, finally, all this must come not from virtues but from tastes, or else the human species would soon be extinguished.

The strictness of the relative duties of the two sexes is not and cannot be the same. When woman complains on this score about unjust man-made inequality, she is wrong. This inequality is not a human institution—or, at least, it is the work not of prejudice but of reason. It is up to the sex that nature has charged with the bearing of children to be responsible for them to the other sex. Doubtless it is not permitted to any one to violate his faith, and every unfaithful husband who deprives his wife of the only reward of the austere duties of her sex is an unjust and barbarous man. But the unfaithful woman does more; she dissolves the family and breaks all the bonds of nature....

Once it is demonstrated that man and woman are not and ought not be constituted in the same way in either character or temperament, it follows that they ought not to have the same education. In following nature's directions, man and woman ought to act in concert, but they ought not to do the same things. The goal of their labors is common, but their labors themselves are different, and consequently so are the tastes directing them....

The good constitution of children initially depends on that of their mothers. The first education of men depends on the care of women. Men's morals, their passions, their tastes, their pleasures, their very happiness also depend on women. Thus the whole education of women ought to relate to men. To please men, to be useful to them, to make herself loved and honored by them, to raise them when young, to care for them when grown, to counsel them, to console them, to make their lives agreeable and sweet—these are the duties of women at all times, and they ought to be taught from childhood. So long as one does not return to this principle, one will deviate from the goal, and all the precepts taught to women will be of no use for their happiness or for ours.

motherhood as their most important occupation. And on sexual behavior, the Encyclopedists upheld an unquestioned double standard.

In contrast to the articles, however, illustrations in the *Encyclopedia* showed women deeply involved in the economic activities of the day. The illustra-tions also showed the activities of lower class and working-class women, about whom the articles had little to say.

One of the most surprising and influential analyses of the position of women came from Jean-Jacques Rousseau. This most radical of all Enlightenment political theorists urged a very traditional and conservative role for women. In his novel *Émile* (1762) (discussed again in Chapter 20), he set forth a radical version of the view that men and women occupy separate spheres. He declared that women should be educated for a position subordinate to men, emphasizing especially women's function in bearing and rearing children. In his vision, there was little else for women to do but make themselves pleasing to men. He portrayed them as weaker and inferior to men in virtually all respects, except perhaps for their capacity for feeling and giving love. He excluded them from political life. The world of citizenship, political action, and civic virtue was to be populated by men. Women were assigned the domestic sphere alone. (See "Rousseau Argues for Separate Spheres for Men and Women.") Many of these attitudes were not new—some have roots as ancient as Roman law—but Rousseau's powerful presentation and the influence of his other writings gave them new life in the late eighteenth century. Rousseau deeply influenced many leaders of the French Revolution, who, as will be seen in the next chapter, often incorporated his view on gender roles in the policies they implemented.

Paradoxically, in spite of these views and in spite of his own ill treatment of the woman who bore his many children, Rousseau achieved a vast following among women in the eighteenth century. He is credited with persuading thousands of upper-class women to breast-feed their own children rather than putting them out to wet nurses. One explanation for this influence is that his writings, although they did not advocate liberating women or expanding their social or economic roles, did stress the importance of their emotions and subjective feelings. He portrayed the domestic life and the role of wife and mother as a noble and fulfilling vocation, giving middle- and upper-class women a sense that their daily occupations had purpose. He assigned them a degree of influence in the domestic sphere that they could not have competing with men outside it.

In 1792, in *A Vindication of the Rights of Woman*, Mary Wollstonecraft (1759–1797) brought Rousseau before the judgment of the rational Enlightenment ideal of progressive knowledge. The immediate incentive for this essay was her opposition to certain policies of the French Revolution, unfavorable to women, which were inspired by Rousseau. Wollstonecraft (who, like so many women of her day, died of puerperal fever shortly after childbirth) accused Rousseau and others after him who upheld traditional roles for women of attempting to narrow women's vision and limit their experience. She argued that to confine women to the separate domestic sphere because of supposed limitations of their physiological nature was to make them the sensual slaves of men. Confined in this separate sphere, they were the victims of male tyranny, their obedience was blind, and they could never achieve their own moral or intellectual identity. Denying good education to women would impede the progress of all humanity. (See "Mary Wollstonecraft Criticizes Rousseau's View of Women.") With these arguments, Wollstonecraft was demanding for women the kind of liberty that male writers of the Enlightenment had been championing for men for more than a century. In doing so, she placed herself among the *philosophes* and broadened the agenda of the Enlightenment to include the rights of women as well as those of men.

Major Works of the Enlightenment and Their Publication Dates

1670	Spinoza's *Theologico-Political Treatise*
1677	Spinoza's *Ethics* (published pothumously)
1687	Newton's *Principia Mathematica*
1690	Locke's *Essay Concerning Human Understanding*
1696	Toland's *Christianity Not Mysterious*
1721	Montesquieu's *Persian Letters*
1733	Voltaire's *Letters on the English*
1738	Voltaire's *Elements of the Philosophy of Newton*
1748	Montesquieu's *Spirit of the Laws*
1748	Hume's *Inquiry into Human Nature*, with the chapter "Of Miracles"
1750	Rousseau's *Discourse on the Moral Effects of the Arts and Sciences*
1751	First volume of the *Encyclopedia*, edited by Diderot
1755	Rousseau's *Discourse on the Origin of Inequality*
1759	Voltaire's *Candide*
1762	Rousseau's *Social Contract* and *Émile*
1763	Voltaire's *Treatise on Tolerance*
1764	Voltaire's *Philosophical Dictionary*
1764	Beccaria's *On Crimes and Punishments*
1776	Gibbon's *Decline and Fall of the Roman Empire*
1776	Smith's *Wealth of Nations*
1779	Lessing's *Nathan the Wise*
1783	Mendelsohn's *Jerusalem; or, On Ecclesiastical Power and Judaism*
1792	Wollstonecraft's *Vindication of the Rights of Woman*
1793	Kant's *Religion within the Limits of Reason Alone*

Mary Wollstonecraft Criticizes Rousseau's View of Women

Mary Wollstonecraft published A Vindication of the Rights of Woman *in 1792, thirty years after Rousseau's* Émile *had appeared. In this pioneering feminist work, she criticizes and rejects Rousseau's argument for distinct and separate spheres for men and women. She portrays that argument as defending the continued bondage of women to men and as hindering the wider education of the entire human race.*

❖ *What specific criticisms does Wollstonecraft direct against Rousseau's views? Why does Wollstonecraft put so much emphasis on a new kind of education for women?*

The most perfect education...is such an exercise of the understanding as is best calculated to strengthen the body and form the heart. Or, in other words, to enable the individual to attain such habits of virtue as will render it independent. In fact, it is a farce to call any being virtuous whose virtues do not result from the exercise of its own reason. This was Rousseau's opinion respecting men: I extend it to women....

I may be accused of arrogance; still I must declare what I firmly believe, that all the writers who have written on the subject of female education and manners from Rousseau to Dr. Gregory [a Scottish physician], have contributed to render women more artificial, weak characters, than they would otherwise have been; and, consequently, more useless members of society....

...Strengthen the female mind by enlarging it, and there will be an end to blind obedience; but, as blind obedience is ever sought for by power, tyrants and sensualists are in the right when they endeavour to keep women in the dark, because the former only wants slaves, and the latter a play-thing. The sensualist, indeed, has been the most dangerous of tyrants, and women have been duped by their lovers, as princes by their ministers, whilst dreaming that they reigned over them.

...Rousseau declares that a woman should never, for a moment, feel herself independent, that she should be governed by fear to exercise her natural cunning, and made a coquettish slave in order to render her a more alluring object of desire, a sweeter companion to man, whenever he chooses to relax himself. He carries the arguments, which he pretends to draw from the indications of nature, still further, and insinuates that truth and fortitude, the corner stones of all human virtue, should be cultivated with certain restrictions, because, with respect to the female character, obedience is the grand lesson which ought to be impressed with unrelenting rigour.

What nonsense! when will a great man arise with sufficient strength of mind to put away the fumes which pride and sensuality have thus spread over the subject! If women are by nature inferior to men, their virtues must be the same in quality, if not in degree, or virtue is a relative idea; consequently, their conduct should be founded on the same principles, and have the same aim.

Connected with man as daughters, wives, and mothers, their moral character may be estimated by their manner of fulfilling those simple duties; but the end, the grand end of their exertions should be to unfold their own faculties and acquire the dignity of conscious virtue....

But avoiding...any direct comparison of the two sexes collectively, or frankly acknowledging the inferiority of women, according to the present appearance of things, I shall only insist that men have increased that inferiority till women are almost sunk below the standard of rational creatures. Let their faculties have room to unfold, and their virtues to gain strength, and then determine where the whole sex must stand in the intellectual scale....

...I...will venture to assert, that till women are more rationally educated, the progress of human virtue and improvement in knowledge must receive continual checks....

The mother, who wishes to give true dignity of character to her daughter, must, regardless of the sneers of ignorance, proceed on a plan diametrically opposite to that which Rousseau has recommended with all the deluding charms of eloquence and philosophical sophistry: for his eloquence renders absurdities plausible, and his dogmatic conclusions puzzle, without convincing, those who have not ability to refute them.

From Mary Wollstonecraft, *A Vindication of the Rights of Woman*, ed. by Carol H. Poston (New York: W. W. Norton & Co., Inc., 1975), pp. 21, 22, 24–26, 35, 40, 41.

Enlightened Absolutism

Most of the *philosophes* favored neither Montesquieu's reformed and revived aristocracy nor Rousseau's democracy as a solution to contemporary political problems. Like other thoughtful people of the day in other stations and occupations, they looked to the existing monarchies. Voltaire was a very strong monarchist. In 1759 he published a *History of the Russian Empire Under Peter the Great*, which declared, "Peter was born, and Russia was formed."[9] Voltaire and other *philosophes*, such as Diderot, who visited Catherine II of Russia, and the physiocrats, some of whom were ministers to the French kings, did not wish to limit the power of monarchs. Rather, they sought to redirect that power toward the rationalization of economic and political structures and the liberation of intellectual life. Most *philosophes* were not opposed to power if they could find a way of using it for their own purposes or if they could profit in one way or another from their personal relationships to strong monarchs.

During the last third of the century, it seemed to some observers that several European rulers had actually embraced many of the reforms set forth by the *philosophes*. "Enlightened Absolutism" is the term used to describe this phenomenon. It indicates monarchical government dedicated to the rational strengthening of the central absolutist administration at the cost of other lesser centers of political power. The monarchs most closely associated with it are Frederick II of Prussia, Joseph II of Austria, and Catherine II of Russia. Each had complicated relationships to the community of enlightened writers.

Frederick II corresponded with the *philosophes*, provided Voltaire with a place at his court for a time, and even wrote history and political tracts. Catherine II, adept at what would later be called public relations, consciously sought to create the image of being enlightened. She read and cited the works of the *philosophes*, provided financial subsidies to Diderot, and corresponded extensively with Voltaire, lavishing compliments on him, all in the hope that she would receive favorable comments from them, as she indeed did. Joseph II continued numerous initiatives begun by his mother, Maria Theresa. He imposed a series of religious, legal, and social reforms that contemporaries believed he had derived from suggestions of the *philosophes*.

The relationship between these rulers and the writers of the Enlightenment was, however, more complicated than these appearances suggest. The humanitarian and liberating zeal of the Enlightenment writers was only part of what motivated the policies of the rulers. Frederick II, Joseph II, and Catherine II were also determined that their nations would play major diplomatic and military roles in Europe. In no small measure, they adopted Enlightenment policies favoring the rational economic and social integration of their realms because these policies also increased their military strength. As explained in Chapter 17, all the states of Europe had emerged from the Seven Years' War knowing that they would need stronger armies for future wars and increased revenues to finance those armies. The search for new revenues and internal political support was one of the incentives prompting the "enlightened" reforms of the monarchs of Russia, Prussia, and Austria. Consequently, they and their advisers used rationality to pursue many goals admired by most *philosophes*, but also to further what some among the *philosophes* considered irrational militarism. The flattery of monarchs could bend the opinions of a *philososphe*. For example, Voltaire, who had written against war, could praise the military expansion of Catherine's Russia because it appeared in his mind to bring civilization to peoples he regarded as uncivilized and because he enjoyed being known as a literary confidant of the empress.

Frederick the Great of Prussia

Frederick II, the Great (r. 1740–1786), sought the recovery and consolidation of Prussia in the wake of its suffering and near defeat in the midcentury wars. He succeeded, at great military and financial cost, in retaining Silesia, which he had seized from Austria in 1740, and worked to promote it as a manufacturing district. Like his Hohenzollern forebears, he continued to import workers from outside Prussia. He directed new attention to Prussian agriculture. Under state supervision, swamps were drained, new crops introduced, and peasants encouraged and sometimes compelled to migrate where they were needed. For the first time in Prussia, potatoes and turnips came into general production. Frederick also established a land-mortgage credit association to help landowners raise money for agricultural improvements.

The impetus for these economic policies came from the state. The monarchy and its bureaucracy were the engine for change. Most Prussians, however, did not prosper under Frederick's reign. The burden of taxation continued to fall disproportionately on peasants and townspeople.

Frederick's noneconomic policies met with somewhat more success. Continuing the Hohenzollern policy of toleration, he allowed Catholics and Jews to settle in his predominantly Lutheran country, and he protected the Catholics living in Silesia. This policy

---

[9]Quoted in Larry Wolff, *Inventing Eastern Europe: The Map of Civilization on the Mind of the Enlightenment* (Palo Alto, CA: Stanford University Press, 1994), p. 200.

Frederick II, the Great (r. 1740–1786), sought to create prosperity for all parts of the Prussian economy and would make personal visits to factories and shops to inspect the goods being made and sold in his kingdom. Here, as portrayed in a late nineteenth-century painting, he visits a fashionable shop. Gemalde von Albert Baur, ca. 1901. *Frederick II, the Great, the house von der Leyen in Krefeld, on June 10, 1763.* Bildarchiv Preussischer Kulturbesitz

permitted the state to benefit from the economic contribution of foreign workers. Frederick, however, virtually always appointed Protestants to major positions in the government and army.

Frederick also ordered a new codification of Prussian law, completed after his death. His objective was to rationalize the existing legal system, making it more efficient, eliminating regional peculiarities, and reducing aristocratic influence. Frederick shared this concern for legal reform with the other enlightened monarchs, who saw it as a means of extending and strengthening royal power.

Reflecting an important change in the European view of the ruler, Frederick liked to describe himself as "the first servant of the State." The impersonal state was beginning to replace the personal monarchy. Kings might come and go, but the apparatus of government—the bureaucracy, the armies, the laws, the courts, and the combination of power, service, and protection that compelled citizens' loyalty—remained. The state as an entity separate from the personality of the ruler came into its own after the French Revolution, but it was born in the monarchies of the old regime.

Joseph II of Austria

No eighteenth-century ruler so embodied rational, impersonal force as the emperor Joseph II of Austria. He was the son of Maria Theresa and co-ruler with her from 1765 to 1780. During the next ten years he ruled alone. He was an austere and humorless person. During much of his life, he slept on straw and ate little but beef. He prided himself on a narrow,

passionless rationality, which he sought to impose by his own will on the various Habsburg domains. Despite his eccentricities and the coldness of his personality, Joseph II sincerely wished to improve the lot of his people. He was much less a political opportunist and cynic than either Frederick the Great of Prussia or Catherine the Great of Russia. The ultimate result of his well-intentioned efforts was a series of aristocratic and peasant rebellions extending from Hungary to the Austrian Netherlands.

CENTRALIZATION OF AUTHORITY   As explained in Chapter 15, of all the rising states of the eighteenth century, Austria was the most diverse in its people and problems. Robert Palmer likened it to "a vast holding company."[10] The Habsburgs never succeeded in creating either a unified administrative structure or a strong aristocratic loyalty. To preserve the monarchy during the War of the Austrian Succession (1740–1748), Maria Theresa had guaranteed the aristocracy considerable independence, especially in Hungary.

During and after the conflict, however, Maria Theresa took steps to strengthen the power of the crown outside of Hungary, building more of a bureaucracy than had previous Habsburg rulers. In Austria and Bohemia, through major administrative reorganization, she imposed a much more efficient system of tax collection that extracted funds even from the clergy and the nobles. She also established several central councils to deal with governmental problems. To assure her government a sufficient supply of educated offi-

[10]Robert R. Palmer, *The Age of Democratic Revolution*, vol. 1 (Princeton, NJ: Princeton University Press, 1959), p. 103.

cials, she sought to bring all educational institutions into the service of the crown. She also expanded primary education on the local level.

Maria Theresa was concerned about the welfare of the peasants and serfs. She brought them some assistance by extending the authority of the royal bureaucracy over local nobles and decreeing limits on the amount of labor, or *robot*, landowners could demand from peasants. Her concern was not particularly humanitarian; rather, it arose from her desire to assure a good pool from which to draw military recruits. In all these policies and in her general desire to stimulate prosperity and military strength by royal initiative, Maria Theresa anticipated the policies of her son.

Joseph II was more determined than his mother, and his projected reforms were more wide ranging. He aimed to extend the borders of his territories in the direction of Poland, Bavaria, and the Ottoman Empire. His greatest ambition, however, was to increase the authority of the Habsburg emperor over his various realms. He sought to overcome the pluralism of the Habsburg holdings by imposing central authority in areas of political and social life in which Maria Theresa had wisely chosen not to exert authority.

In particular, Joseph sought to reduce Hungarian autonomy. To avoid having to guarantee Hungary's existing privileges or extend new ones at the time of his coronation, he refused to have himself crowned king of Hungary and even had the Crown of Saint Stephen sent to the Imperial Treasury in Vienna. He reorganized local government in Hungary to increase the authority of his own officials. He also required the use of German in all governmental matters. The Magyar nobility resisted these measures, and in 1790 Joseph had to rescind most of them.

ECCLESIASTICAL POLICIES   Another target of Joseph's assertion of royal absolutism was the church. From the reign of Charles V in the sixteenth century to that of Maria Theresa, the Habsburgs had been the most important dynastic champion of Roman Catholicism. Maria Theresa was devout, but she had not allowed the church to limit her authority. Although she had attempted to discourage certain of the more extreme modes of Roman Catholic popular religious piety, such as public flagellation, she adamantly opposed toleration. (See "Maria Theresa and Joseph II of Austria Debate Toleration.")

Joseph II was also a practicing Catholic, but from the standpoint of both enlightenment and pragmatic politics, he favored a policy of toleration. In October 1781, Joseph issued a toleration patent or decree that extended freedom of worship to Lutherans, Calvinists, and the Greek Orthodox. They were permitted to have their own places of worship, to sponsor schools, to enter skilled trades, and to hold academic appointments and positions in the public service. From 1781 through 1789, Joseph issued a series of patents and other enactments that relieved the Jews in his realms of certain taxes and signs of personal degradation. He also extended to them the right of private worship. Although these actions benefitted the Jews, they did not grant them full equality with other Habsburg subjects.

Joseph also sought to bring the various institutions of the Roman Catholic Church directly under royal control. He forbade direct communication between the bishops of his realms and the pope. Viewing religious orders as unproductive, he dissolved more than 600 monasteries and confiscated their lands. He excepted, however, certain orders that ran schools or hospitals. He dissolved the traditional Roman Catholic seminaries, which instilled in priests too great a loyalty to the papacy and too little concern for their future parishioners. In their place, he sponsored eight general

Joseph II of Austria (r. 1765–1790), shown here in the center, with his brother Leopold (later Leopold II) on his right, attempted to impose exceedingly rational policies on the Habsburg Empire. Joseph urged religious toleration and confiscated church lands. His attempts to tax the nobility stirred up a revolt that Leopold settled after Joseph's death by rescinding his policies. Pompeo Batoni (1708–1787). Kunsthistorisches Museum, Vienna

Maria Theresa and Joseph II of Austria Debate Toleration

In 1765 Joseph, the eldest son of the Empress Maria Theresa, had become co-regent with his mother. He began to believe that some measure of religious toleration should be introduced into the Habsburg realms. Maria Theresa, whose opinions on many political issues were quite advanced, adamantly refused to consider adopting a policy of toleration. This exchange of letters sets forth their sharply differing positions. The toleration of Protestants that is in dispute related only to Lutherans and Calvinists. Maria Theresa died in 1780; the next year Joseph issued an edict of toleration.

❖ *How does Joseph define toleration, and why does Maria Theresa believe that it is the same as religious indifference? Why does Maria Theresa fear that toleration will bring about political as well as religious turmoil? Why does Maria Theresa think that Joseph's belief in toleration has come from Joseph's acquaintance with wicked books?*

Joseph to Maria Theresa, July 20, 1777

It is only the word "toleration" which has caused the misunderstanding. You have taken it in quite a different meaning [from mine expressed in an earlier letter]. God preserve me from thinking it a matter of indifference whether the citizens turn Protestant or remain Catholic, still less, whether they cleave to, or at least observe, the cult which they have inherited from their fathers! I would give all I possess if all the Protestants of your states would go over to Catholicism.

The word "toleration," as I understand it, means only that I would employ any persons, without distinction of religion, in purely temporal matters, allow them to own property, practice trades, be citizens, if they were qualified and if this would be of advantage to the State and its industry. Those who, unfortunately, adhere to a false faith, are far further from being converted if they remain in their own country than if they migrate into another, in which they can hear and see the convincing truths of the Catholic faith. Similarly, the undisturbed practice of their religion makes them far better subjects and causes them to avoid irreligion, which is a far greater danger to our Catholics than if one lets them see others practice their religion unimpeded.

Maria Theresa to Joseph, Late July, 1777

Without a dominant religion? Toleration, indifference are precisely the true means of undermining everything, taking away every foundation; we others will then be the greatest losers.... He is no friend of humanity, as the popular phrase is, who allows everyone his own thoughts. I am speaking only in the political sense, not as a Christian; nothing is so necessary and salutary as religion. Will you allow everyone to fashion his own religion as he pleases? No fixed cult, no subordination to the Church—what will then become of us? The result will not be quiet and contentment; its outcome will be the rule of the stronger and more unhappy times like those which we have already seen. A manifesto by you to this effect can produce the utmost distress and make you responsible for many thousands of souls. And what are my own sufferings, when I see you entangled in opinions so erroneous? What is at stake is not only the welfare of the State but your own salvation....Turning your eyes and ears everywhere, mingling your spirit of contradiction with the simultaneous desire to create something, you are ruining yourself and dragging the Monarchy down with you into the abyss....I only wish to live so long as I can hope to descend to my ancestors with the consolation that my son will be as great, as religious as his forebears, that he will return from his erroneous views, from those wicked books whose authors parade their cleverness at the expense of all that is most holy and most worthy of respect in the world, who want to introduce an imaginary freedom which can never exist and which degenerates into license and into complete revolution.

As quoted in C. A. Macartney, ed., *The Habsburg and Hohenzollern Dynasties in the Seventeenth and Eighteenth Centuries* (New York: Walker, 1970), pp. 151–153. Reprinted by permission of Walker and Co.

seminaries whose training emphasized parish duties. He also issued decrees creating new parishes in areas with a shortage of priests, funding them with money from the confiscated monasteries. In effect, Joseph's policies made Roman Catholic priests the employees of the state, ending the influence of the Roman Catholic Church as an independent institution in Habsburg lands. In many respects, the ecclesiastical policies of Joseph II, known as *Josephinism*, prefigured those of the French Revolution.

ECONOMIC AND AGRARIAN REFORM   Like Frederick of Prussia, Joseph sought to improve the economic life of his domains. He abolished many internal tariffs and encouraged road building and the improvement of river transport. He went on personal inspection tours of farms and manufacturing districts. Joseph also reconstructed the judicial system to make laws more uniform and rational and to lessen the influence of local landlords. National courts with power over the landlord courts were established. All of these improvements were expected to bring new unity to the state and more taxes into the imperial coffers in Vienna.

Joseph's policies toward serfdom and the land were a far-reaching extension of those Maria Theresa had initiated. Over the course of his reign, he introduced a series of reforms that touched the very heart of the rural social structure. He did not seek to abolish the authority of landlords over their peasants, but he did seek to make that authority more moderate and subject to the oversight of royal officials. He abolished serfdom as a legally sanctioned state of servitude. He granted peasants a wide array of personal freedoms, including the right to marry, to engage in skilled work, and to have their children trained in skilled work without the landlord's permission.

Joseph reformed the procedures of the manorial courts and opened avenues of appeal to royal officials. He also encouraged landlords to change land leases so it would be easier for peasants to inherit them or to transfer them to other peasants. His goal in all of these efforts to reduce traditional burdens on peasants was to make them more productive and industrious farmers.

Near the end of his reign, Joseph proposed a new and daring system of land taxation. He decreed in 1789 that all proprietors of the land were to be taxed regardless of social status. No longer were the peasants alone to bear the burden of taxation. He abolished *robot* and commuted it into a monetary tax, only part of which was to go to the landlord, the rest reverting to the state. Resistant nobles blocked the implementation of this decree, and after Joseph died in 1790 it did not go into effect. This and other of Joseph's earlier measures, however, brought turmoil throughout the Habsburg realms. Peasants revolted

over disagreements about the interpretation of their newly granted rights. The nobles of the various realms protested the taxation scheme. The Hungarian Magyars resisted Joseph's centralization measures and forced him to rescind them.

On Joseph's death, the crown went to his brother Leopold II (r. 1790–1792). Although sympathetic to Joseph's goals, Leopold found himself forced to repeal many of the most controversial decrees, such as that on taxation. In other areas, Leopold thought his brother's policies simply wrong. For example, he returned much political and administrative power to local nobles because he thought it expedient for them to have a voice in government. Still, he did not repudiate his brother's policies wholesale. He retained, in particular, Joseph's religious policies and maintained political centralization to the extent he thought possible.

Catherine the Great of Russia

Joseph II never grasped the practical necessity of forging political constituencies to support his policies. Catherine II (r. 1762–1796), who had been born

Catherine the Great ascended to the Russian throne after the murder of her husband. She tried initially to enact major reforms, but she never intended to abandon absolutism. She assured nobles of their rights and by the end of her reign had imposed press censorship.
The Granger Collection

Russia from Peter the Great Through Catherine the Great

1725	Death of Peter the Great
1725–1727	Catherine I
1727–1730	Peter II
1730–1741	Anna
1740–1741	Ivan VI
1741–1762	Elizabeth
1762	Peter III
1762	Catherine II (the Great) becomes empress
1767	Legislative Commission summoned
1769	War with Turkey begins
1771–1775	Pugachev's Rebellion
1772	First Partition of Poland
1774	Treaty of Kuchuk-Kainardji ends war with Turkey
1775	Reorganization of local government
1783	Russia annexes the Crimea
1785	Catherine issues the Charter of the Nobility
1793	Second Partition of Poland
1795	Third Partition of Poland
1796	Death of Catherine the Great

a German princess, but who became empress of Russia, understood only too well the fragility of the Romanov dynasty's base of power.

After the death of Peter the Great in 1725, the court nobles and the army repeatedly determined the Russian succession. As a result, the crown fell primarily into the hands of people with little talent. Peter's wife, Catherine I, ruled for two years (1725–1727) and was succeeded for three years by Peter's grandson, Peter II. In 1730, the crown devolved on Anna, a niece of Peter the Great. During 1740 and 1741, a child named Ivan VI, who was less than a year old, was the nominal ruler. Finally, in 1741, Peter the Great's daughter Elizabeth came to the throne. She held the title of empress until 1762, but her reign was not notable for new political departures or sound administration. Her court was a shambles of political and romantic intrigue. Much of the power possessed by the tsar at the opening of the century had vanished.

At her death in 1762, Elizabeth was succeeded by Peter III, one of her nephews. He was a weak ruler whom many contemporaries considered mad. He immediately exempted the nobles from compulsory military service and then rapidly made peace with Frederick the Great, for whom he held unbounded admiration. That decision probably saved Prussia from military defeat in the Seven

Years' War. The one positive feature of this unbalanced creature's life was his marriage in 1745 to a young German princess born in Anhalt Zerbst. This was the future Catherine the Great.

For almost twenty years, Catherine lived in misery and frequent danger at the court of Elizabeth. During that time, she befriended important nobles and read widely in the books of the *philosophes*. She was a shrewd person whose experience in a court crawling with rumors, intrigue, and conspiracy had taught her how to survive. She exhibited neither love nor fidelity toward her demented husband. A few months after his accession as tsar, Peter was deposed and murdered with Catherine's approval, if not her aid, and she was immediately proclaimed empress.

Catherine's familiarity with the Enlightenment and the general culture of western Europe convinced her that Russia was very backward and that it must make major reforms if it was to remain a great power. She understood that any major reform must have a wide base of political and social support, especially since she had assumed the throne through a palace coup. In 1767, she summoned a legislative commission to advise her on revisions in the law and government of Russia. There were more than 500 delegates, drawn from all sectors of Russian life. Before the commission convened, Catherine issued a set of instructions, partly written by herself. They contained many ideas drawn from the political writings of the *philosophes*. The commission considered the instructions as well as other ideas and complaints raised by its members. (See "Catherine the Great Issues an Instruction to the Legislative Commission.")

The revision of Russian law, however, did not occur for more than half a century. In 1768, Catherine dismissed the commission before several of its key committees had reported. Yet the meeting had not been useless, for a vast amount of information had been gathered about the conditions of local administration and economic life throughout the realm. The inconclusive debates and the absence of programs from the delegates themselves suggested that most Russians saw no alternative to an autocratic monarchy. For her part, Catherine had no intention of departing from absolutism.

LIMITED ADMINISTRATIVE REFORM   Catherine proceeded to carry out limited reforms on her own authority. She gave strong support to the rights and local power of the nobility. In 1777, she reorganized local government to solve problems brought to light by the legislative commission. She put most local offices in the hands of nobles rather than creating a royal bureaucracy. In 1785 Catherine issued the Charter of the Nobility, which guaranteed nobles many rights and privileges. In part, the empress had no choice but to favor the nobles. They had the capacity to topple her from the throne. There were too few educated subjects in her realm to establish an independent bureaucracy, and the treasury could not afford an army strictly loyal to the crown. So Catherine wisely made a virtue of necessity. She strengthened the stability of her crown by making convenient friends with her nobles.

ECONOMIC GROWTH   Part of Catherine's program was to continue the economic development begun under Peter the Great. She attempted to suppress internal barriers to trade. Exports of grain, flax, furs, and naval stores grew dramatically. She also favored the expansion of the small Russian urban middle class that was so vital to trade. And through all of these departures Catherine tried to maintain ties of friendship and correspondence with the *philosophes*.

MAP 18–1   EXPANSION OF RUSSIA, 1689–1796   *The overriding territorial aim of Peter the Great in the first quarter, and of Catherine the Great in the latter half, of the eighteenth century was to secure year-round navigable outlets to the sea for the vast Russian Empire— hence Peter's push to the Baltic Sea and Catherine's to the Black Sea. Catherine also managed to acquire large areas of Poland through the partitions of that country.*

She knew that if she treated them kindly, they would be sufficiently flattered to give her a progressive reputation throughout Europe.

TERRITORIAL EXPANSION   Catherine's limited administrative reforms and her policy of economic growth had a counterpart in the diplomatic sphere. The Russian drive for warm-water ports continued. (See Map 18–1.) This goal required warfare with the Turks. In 1769, as a result of a minor Russian incursion, the Ottoman Empire declared war on Russia. The Russians responded in a series of strikingly successful military moves.

During 1769 and 1770, the Russian fleet sailed all the way from the Baltic Sea into the eastern Mediterranean. The Russian army won several major victories that by 1771 gave Russia control of Ottoman provinces on the Danube River and the Crimean coast of the Black Sea. The conflict dragged on until 1774, when it was closed by the Treaty of Kuchuk-Kainardji. The treaty gave Russia a direct outlet on the Black Sea, free navigation rights in its waters, and free access through the Bosporus. Moreover, the province of the Crimea became an independent state, which Catherine painlessly annexed in 1783.

The Partition of Poland

The Russian military successes obviously brought Catherine much domestic political support, but they made the other states of eastern Europe uneasy. These anxieties were overcome by an extraordinary division of Polish territory known as the First Partition of Poland.

The Russian victories along the Danube River were most unwelcome to Austria, which also harbored ambitions of territorial expansion in that direction. At the same time, the Ottoman Empire was pressing Prussia for aid against Russia. Frederick the Great made a proposal to Russia and Austria that would give each something it wanted, prevent conflict among the powers, and save appearances. After long, complicated, secret negotiations, the three powers agreed that Russia would abandon the conquered Danubian provinces. In compensation, Russia received a large portion of Polish territory with almost two million inhabitants. As a reward for remaining neutral, Prussia annexed most of the territory between East Prussia and Prussia proper. This land allowed Frederick to unite two previously separate sections of his realm. Finally, Austria took Galicia, with its important salt mines, and other Polish territory with more than two and one-half million inhabitants. (See Map 18–2.)

In September 1772, the helpless Polish aristocracy, paying the price for maintaining internal liberties at the expense of developing a strong central government,

Catherine the Great Issues an Instruction to the Legislative Commission

Catherine the Great hoped to reform the laws of Russia along the lines of political theory associated with the Enlightenment. To that end, during the 1760s she and her advisors planned for a Legislative Commission, which eventually met in 1767. Catherine issued a set of broad instructions to the commission outlining the principles she expected it to follow in its deliberations. She personally wrote and edited significant portions of the Instruction. *The commission did meet but, ultimately accomplished very little. Nonetheless, Catherine's* Instruction *went through a number of printings and translations during the second half of the eighteenth century. Occasionally, ministers and other administrators pointed to them as justifying certain of their decisions. Catherine took them very seriously throughout her reign. Even though the commission for which they were intended produced nothing lasting, Catherine's* Instruction *is the most important national document of broad political and legal principles written by a woman in the eighteenth century. Yet, the experience of most of Catherine's subjects in no manner reflected this* Instruction, *as during her reign Russian peasants were subjected to horrific punishment for rebelling and to complicated legal procedures governing most aspects of their life. The denunciation of Catherine by Alexander Radishchev toward the end of her reign (see next document) reflects the disillusionment created by the idealistic hopes she raised and the political reality of the government she pursued.*

❖ *Why does Catherine insist that Russia must have an absolutist government? How do these instructions define liberty and attempt to reconcile it with strong monarchical authority? How does the concept of liberty included in the* Instruction *compare and contrast with those protests that the American colonists made to King George III during the Stamp Act Crisis? (See Chapter 17.) Why do Catherine's instructions emphasize the necessity of simplicity in the law.*

ratified this seizure of nearly one-third of Polish territory. The loss was not necessarily fatal to Poland's continued existence, and it inspired a revival of national feeling. Real attempts were made to adjust the Polish political structures to the realities of the time. These proved, however, to be too little and too late. The political and military strength of Poland could not match that of its stronger, more ambitious neighbors. The partition of Poland clearly demonstrated that any nation that had not established a strong monarchy, bureaucracy, and army could no longer compete within the European state system. It also demonstrated that the major powers in eastern Europe were prepared to settle their own rivalries at the expense of such a weak state. If such territory from a weaker state had not been available, the tendency of the international rivalries would have been to warfare.

Russia and Prussia partitioned Poland again in 1793, and Russia, Prussia, and Austria partitioned it a third time in 1795, removing it from the map of Europe for more than a century. Each time, the great powers contended that they were saving themselves, and by implication the rest of Europe, from Polish anarchy. The fact of the matter was that Poland's political weakness left it vulnerable to plunderous aggression. The partitions of 1793 and 1795 took place in the shadow of the French Revolution, which left the absolute monarchies of eastern Europe concerned for their own stability. As a result, they reacted harshly even to minor attempts at reform by the Polish nobles, fearing that they might infect their own domains.

The End of the Eighteenth Century in Central and Eastern Europe

During the last two decades of the eighteenth century, all three regimes based on Enlightened Absolutism became more conservative and politically repressive. In Prussia and Austria, the

6. Russia is a European power....

9. The Sovereign is absolute, for no other than absolute Powers vested in one Person, can be suitable to the Extent of so vast an Empire.

10. An extensive Empire demands absolute Power in the person who rules it....

11. Any other than absolute Government, would not only be detrimental, but in the End destructive to Russia.

12. Another Reason is, that it is better to obey the Laws under the direction of one Master, than to be subject to the Wills of many.

13. What is the Object of absolute Government? Certainly not to deprive the People of their natural Liberty, but to direct their Conduct in such manner that the greatest good may be derived from all their Operations.

34. The Equality of Citizens consists in their being all subject to the same Laws.

35. This Equality requires a good Establishment which may prevent the Rich from oppressing the Poor, and from converting to their own private Advantage those Employments and Offices entrusted to them only for the benefit of the State.

36. Social or civil Liberty consists not in doing every one as he pleases.

37. In a State, that is in a Collection of People living in Society where Laws are established, Liberty can consist only in the Ability of doing what every one ought to desire, and in not being forced to do what should not be desired.

38. .....Liberty is the right of doing whatever is permitted by the Laws....

39. Civil Liberty is a Tranquillity of Mind arising from the Opinion that every individual of the whole Society enjoys his personal Security, and that People may possess this Liberty, the Laws must be such as that no one Citizen need be in fear of another, but that all alike should fear the Laws only.

...448. Every Law must be wrote in words intelligible to all, and at the same time Concise....

...450. When in any Law Exceptions, Limitations and Modifications are unnecessary, it is much better not to use them....

...452. Laws must not be filled up with Subtleties arising from quickness of parts; they are made equally for People of moderate as well as of quick Understanding....

453. Sincerity must be observed throughout all the Laws, they are given to punish Vice and evil Doings, so that they themselves must include great Virtue and Innocence.

From Paul Dukes, trans. and ed., *Russia Under Catherine the Great, Volume II, Catherine the Great's Instruction* (Nakaz) *to the Legislative Commission, 1767* (Newtonville, MA: Oriental Research Partners, 1977), pp. 43–44, 46, 99.

innovations of the rulers stirred resistance among the nobility. In Russia, fear of peasant unrest was the chief factor.

Frederick the Great of Prussia grew remote during his old age, leaving the aristocracy to fill important military and administrative posts. A reaction to Enlightenment ideas also set in among Prussian Lutheran writers.

In Austria, Joseph II's plans to restructure society and administration in his realms provoked growing frustration and political unrest, with the nobility calling for an end to innovation. In response, Joseph turned increasingly to censorship and his secret police.

Russia faced a peasant uprising, the Pugachev Rebellion, between 1773 and 1775, and Catherine the Great never fully recovered from the fears of social and political upheaval that it raised. Once the French Revolution broke out in 1789, the Russian empress censored books based on Enlightenment thought and sent offensive authors into Siberian exile. (See "Alexander Radishchev Attacks Russian Censorship.")

By the close of the century, fear of, and hostility to, change permeated the ruling classes of central and eastern Europe. This reaction had begun before 1789, but the events in France bolstered and sustained it for almost half a century. Paradoxically, nowhere did the humanity and liberalism of the Enlightenment encounter greater rejection than in those states that had been governed by "enlightened" rulers.

The enlightened absolute monarchs had embraced the Enlightenment spirit of innovation that pressed in all directions against tradition. They wanted to change the political, social, and economic structures of their realms. From the close of the Seven Years' War (1763) until the opening of the French Revolution in 1789, the monarchies of both western and eastern Europe had been the major agents of insti-

Alexander Radishchev Attacks Russian Censorship

Alexander Radishchev (1749–1802) was an enlightened Russian landowner who published A Journey from Saint Petersburg to Moscow *in 1790. The book criticized many aspects of Russian political and social life, including the treatment of serfs. Shortly after its publication, Catherine the Great, fearing that the kind of unrest associated with the French Revolution might spread to Russia, had Radishchev arrested. He was tried and sentenced to death, but Catherine commuted the sentence to a period of Siberian exile. All but eighteen copies of his book were destroyed. It was not published in Russia again until 1905. These passages criticizing censorship illustrate how a writer filled with the ideas of the Enlightenment could question some of the fundamental ways in which an enlightened absolutist ruler, such as Catherine, governed.*

❖ *How does Radishchev satirize censorship and the censors? Why does he contend that public opinion rather than the government will act as an adequate censor? Would work censored by public opinion be truly free from censorship? Why might Catherine the Great or other enlightened absolutist rulers have feared opinions like these?*

Having recognized the usefulness of printing, the government has made it open to all; having further recognized that control of thought might invalidate its good intention in granting freedom to set up presses, it turned over the censorship or inspection of printed works to the Department of Public Morals. Its duty in this matter can only be the prohibition of the sale of objectionable works. But even this censorship is superfluous. A single stupid official in the Department of Public Morals may do the greatest harm to enlightenment and may for years hold back the progress of reason: he may prohibit a useful discovery, a new idea, and may rob everyone of something great. Here is an example on a small scale. A translation of a novel is brought to the Department of Public Morals for its imprimatur. The translator, following the author in speaking of love calls it "the tricky god." The censor in uniform and in the fullness of piety strikes out the expression saying, "It is improper to call a divinity tricky." He who does not understand should not interfere....

Let anyone print anything that enters his head. If anyone finds himself insulted in print, let him get his redress at law. I am not speaking in jest. Words are not always deeds, thoughts are not crimes. These are the rules in the *Instruction for a New Code of Laws*. But an offense in words or in print is always an offense. Under the law no one is allowed to libel another, and everyone has the right to bring suit. But if one tells the truth about another, that cannot, according to the law, be considered a libel. What harm can there be if books are printed without a police stamp? Not only will there be no harm; there will be an advantage, an advantage from the first to the last, from the least to the greatest, from the Tsar to the last citizen....

I will close with this: the censorship of what is printed belongs properly to society, which gives the author a laurel wreath or uses his sheets for wrapping paper. Just so, it is the public that gives its approval to a theatrical production, and not the director of the theater. Similarly the Censor can give neither glory nor dishonor to the publication of a work. The curtain rises, and every one eagerly watches the performance. If they like it, they applaud; if not, they stamp and hiss. Leave what is stupid to the judgment of public opinion, stupidity will find a thousand censors. The most vigilant policy cannot check worthless ideas as well as a disgusted public. They will be heard just once; they will die, never to rise again. But once we have recognized the uselessness of the censorship, or, rather, its harmfulness in the realm of knowledge, we must also recognize the vast and boundless usefulness of freedom of the press.

From Alexander Radishchev, *A Journey from Saint Petersburg to Moscow* (Cambridge, MA: Harvard University Press, 1958), pp. 9–19. Copyright © 1958 by the President and Fellows of Harvard College. Reprinted by permission of Harvard University Press. As quoted in Thomas Riha, ed., *Readings in Russian Civilization*, 2d ed., rev., Vol II (Chicago: University of Chicago Press, 1969), pp. 269–271.

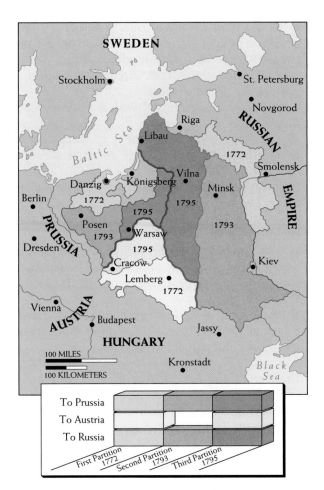

MAP 18–2 PARTITIONS OF POLAND, 1772, 1793 AND 1795 *The callous eradication of Poland from the map displayed eighteenth-century power politics at its most extreme. Poland, without strong central governmental institutions, fell victim to those states in central and eastern Europe that had developed such institutions.*

tutional change. In every case they provoked aristocratic, and sometimes popular, resistance and resentment. George III of Britain fought for years with Parliament and lost the colonies of North America in the process. Frederick II of Prussia succeeded with his program of reform only because he accepted new aristocratic influence over the bureaucracy and the army. Catherine II of Russia had to come to terms with Russia's nobility. Joseph II, who did not consult with the nobility of his domains, left those domains in turmoil.

These monarchs pushed for innovations from a desire for increased revenue. In France also, the royal drive for adequate fiscal resources led to aristocratic resistance. In France, however, neither the monarchy nor the aristocracy could control the social and political forces their quarrel unleashed.

In Perspective

The writers of the Enlightenment, known as philosophes, *charted a major new path in modern European and Western thought. They operated within a print culture that made public opinion into a distinct cultural force. Admiring Newton and the achievements of physical science, they tried to apply reason and the principles of science to the cause of social reform. They believed also that passions and feelings were essential parts of human nature. Throughout their writings they championed reasonable moderation in social life. More than any other previous group of Western thinkers, they strongly opposed the authority of the established churches and especially of Roman Catholicism. Most of them championed some form of religious toleration. They also sought to achieve a science of society that could discover how to maximize human productivity and material happiness. The great dissenter among them was Rousseau, who also wished to reform society, but in the name of virtue rather than material happiness.*

The political influence of these writers went in several directions. The founding fathers of the American republic looked to them for political guidance, as did moderate liberal reformers throughout Europe, especially within royal bureaucracies. The autocratic rulers of eastern Europe consulted the philosophes *in the hope that Enlightenment ideas might allow them to rule more efficiently. The revolutionaries in France would honor them. This diverse assortment of followers illustrates the diverse character of the* philosophes *themselves. It also shows that Enlightenment thought cannot be reduced to a single formula. Rather, it should be seen as an outlook that championed change and reform, giving central place to humans and their welfare on earth rather than to God and the hereafter.*

REVIEW QUESTIONS

1. How did the Enlightenment change basic Western attitudes toward reform, faith, and reason? What were the major formative influences on the *philosophes*? How important were Voltaire and the *Encyclopedia* in the success of the Enlightenment?
2. Why did the *philosophes* consider organized religion to be their greatest enemy? Discuss the basic tenets of deism. How did Jewish writers contribute to Enlightenment thinking about religion?

3. What were the attitudes of the *philosophes* toward women? What was Rousseau's view of women? What were the separate spheres he imagined men and women occupying? What were Mary Wollstonecraft's criticisms of Rousseau's view?

4. Compare the arguments of the mercantilists with those of Adam Smith in his book, *The Wealth of Nations*. How did both sides view the Earth's resources? Why might Smith be regarded as an advocate of the consumer? How did his theory of history work to the deteriment of less economically advanced non-European peoples.

5. Discuss the political views of Montesquieu and Rousseau. Was Montesquieu's view of England accurate? Was Rousseau a child of the Enlightenment or its enemy? Which did Rousseau value more, the individual or society?

6. Were the enlightened monarchs true believers in the ideal of the *philosophes*, or was their enlightenment a mere veneer? Were they really absolute in power? What motivated their reforms? What does the partition of Poland indicate about the spirit of enlightened absolutism?

SUGGESTED READINGS

G. J. BARKER-BENFIELD, *The Culture of Sensibility: Sex and Society in Eighteenth-Century Britain* (1992). A broad exploration of the role of women in society and literature in the age of Enlightenment.

R. P. BARTLETT, *Human Capital: The Settlement of Foreigners in Russia, 1762–1804* (1979). Examines Catherine's policy of attracting farmers and skilled workers to Russia.

D. BEALES, *Joseph II: In the Shadow of Maria Theresa, 1741–1780 (1987)*. The best treatment in English of the early political life of Joseph II.

C. B. A. BEHRENS, *Society, Government, and the Enlightenment: The Experiences of Eighteenth-Century France and Prussia* (1985). A wide-ranging comparative study.

D. D. BIEN, *The Calas Affair: Persecution, Toleration, and Heresy in Eighteenth-Century Toulouse* (1960). The standard treatment of the famous case.

R. CHARTIER, *The Cultural Origins of the French Revolution* (1991). A wide-ranging discussion of the emergence of the public sphere and the role of books and the book trade during the Enlightenment.

R. DARNTON, *The Literary Underground of the Old Regime* (1982). Essays on the world of printers, publishers, and booksellers.

R. DARNTON, *The Forbidden Best-Sellers of Pre-Revolutionary France* (1995). An exploration of what books the French read and the efforts of the government to control the book trade.

T. S. DOCK, *Women in the* Encyclopédie: *A Compendium* (1983). An analysis of the articles from the *Encyclopedia* that deal with women.

P. GAY, *The Enlightenment: An Interpretation*, 2 vols. (1966, 1969). A classic.

P. GAY, *Voltaire's Politics* (1988). A wide-ranging discussion.

C. C. GILLISPIE, *Science and Polity in France at the End of the Old Regime* (1980). A major survey.

D. GOODMAN, *The Republic of Letters: A Cultural History of the French Enlightenment* (1994). Concentrates on the role of salons.

N. HAMPSON, *A Cultural History of the Enlightenment* (1969). A useful introduction.

M. C. JACOB, *Living the Enlightenment: Freemasonry and Politics in Eighteenth-Century Europe* (1991). The best treatment in English of Freemasonry.

A. KERNAN, *Printing Technology, Letters, and Samuel Johnson* (1987). A discussion of print culture and its impact on English letters.

J. B. LANDES, *Women and the Public Sphere in the Age of the French Revolution* (1988). An extended essay on the role of women in public life during the eighteenth century.

J. P. LEDONNE, *The Russian Empire and the World, 1700–1917* (1996). An exploration of the major determinants in Russian expansion from the eighteenth to the early twentieth century.

C. A. MACARTNEY, *The Habsburg Empire, 1790–1918* (1971). Provides useful coverage of major mid-eighteenth century developments.

I. DE MADARIAGA, *Russia in the Age of Catherine the Great* (1981). The best discussion in English.

J. M. MCMANNERS, *Death and the Enlightenment: Changing Attitudes to Death among Christians and Unbelievers in Eighteenth-Century France* (1982). Explores a wide spectrum of religious beliefs.

M. A. MEYER, *The Origins of the Modern Jew: Jewish Identity and European Culture in Germany, 1749–1824* (1967). Remains a clear introduction.

S. NADLER, *Spinoza: A Life* (1999) The best recent biography.

C. ORWIN AND N. TARCOV, EDS., *The Legacy of Rousseau* (1997). Essays on the major themes of Rousseau's work.

D. ROCHE, *France in the Enlightenment* (1998). A brilliant work relating the society and government of eighteenth-century France to the Enlightenment agenda.

J. SCHWARTZ, *The Sexual Politics of Jean-Jacques Rousseau* (1984). A controversial reading of Rousseau's political thought organized around gender issues.

R. B. SHER, *Church and University in the Scottish Enlightenment: The Moderate Literati of Edinburgh* (1985). Examines the role of religious moderates in aiding the goals of the Enlightenment.

J. N. SHKLAR, *Men and Citizens, a Study of Rousseau's Social Theory* (1969). A thoughtful and provocative overview of Rousseau's political thought.

S. B. SMITH, *Spinoza, Liberalism, and the Question of Jewish Identity* (1997). A brilliant work.

D. SPADAFORA, *The Idea of Progress in Eighteenth Century Britain* (1990). A major study that covers many aspects of the Enlightenment in Britain.

S. I. SPENCER, *French Women and the Age of Enlightenment* (1984). An outstanding collection of essays that cover the political, economic, and cultural roles of women.

J. STAROBINSKI, *Jean-Jacques Rousseau: Transparency and Obstruction* (1971). A powerful analysis of Rousseau.

R. E. SULLIVAN, *John Toland and the Deist Controversy: A Study in Adaptation* (1982). An important and informative discussion.

A. M. WILSON, *Diderot* (1972). A splendid biography of the person behind the *Encyclopedia* and other major Enlightenment publications.

L. WOLFF, *Inventing Eastern Europe: The Map of Civilization on the Mind of the Enlightenment* (1994). A remarkable study of the manner in which Enlightenment writers recast the understanding of this part of the continent.

J. YOLTON, ED., *The Blackwell Companion to the Enlightenment* (1995). An excellent collection of essays.

Chapter 19

To symbolize the beginning of a new era in human history, French revolutionary legislators established a new calendar. The year 1793 became Year One in this new calendar and all the months of the year were given new names. This calendar for Year Two proclaims the indivisible unity of the revolution and the goals of Liberty, Equality, and Fraternity. Bildarchiv Preussischer Kulturbesitz

The French Revolution

The Crisis of the French Monarchy
The Monarchy Seeks New Taxes
The Aristocracy and the Clergy
Resist Taxation

The Revolution of 1789
The Estates General Becomes the National
Assembly
Fall of the Bastille
The "Great Fear" and the Surrender of
Feudal Privileges
The Declaration of the Rights of Man
and Citizen
The Royal Family Forced to Return to Paris

The Reconstruction of France
Political Reorganization
Economic Policy
The Civil Constitution of the Clergy
Counterrevolutionary Activity

A Second Revolution
End of the Monarchy
The Convention and the Role of
the *Sans-culottes*

Europe at War with the Revolution
Edmund Burke Attacks the Revolution
Suppression of Reform in Britain
The End of Enlightened Absolutism
in Eastern Europe
War with Europe

The Reign of Terror
The Republic Defended
The "Republic of Virtue"
Progress of the Terror

The Thermidorian Reaction
The End of the Terror
Establishment of the Directory
Removal of the *Sans-culottes* from
Political Life

KEY TOPICS

- The financial crisis that impelled the French monarchy to call the Estates General

- The transformation of the Estates General into the National Assembly, the Declaration of the Rights of Man and Citizen, and the reconstruction of the political and ecclesiastical institutions of France

- The second revolution, the end of the monarchy, and the turn to more radical reforms

- The war between France and the rest of Europe

- The Reign of Terror, the Thermidorian Reaction, and the establishment of the Directory

I n the spring of 1789, the long-festering conflict between the French monarchy and the aristocracy erupted into a new political crisis. This dispute, unlike earlier ones, quickly outgrew the issues of its origins and produced the wider disruption known as the French Revolution. Before the turmoil settled, small-town provincial lawyers and Parisian street or-

ators exercised more influence over the fate of the Continent than did aristocrats, royal ministers, or monarchs. Armies commanded by people of low birth and filled by conscripted village youths emerged victorious over forces composed of professional soldiers led by officers of noble birth. The very existence of the Roman Catholic faith in France was challenged. Politically and socially, neither France nor Europe would ever be the same after these events.

The Crisis of the French Monarchy

Although the French Revolution was a turning point in modern European history, it grew out of the tensions and problems that characterized practically all late-eighteenth-century states. The French monarchy emerged from the Seven Years' War (1756–1763) both defeated and in debt and was unable afterward to put its finances on a sound basis. French support of the American revolt against Great Britain further deepened the financial difficulties of the government. On the eve of the revolution, the interest and payments on the royal debt amounted to just over one-half of the entire budget. Given the economic vitality of the nation, the debt was neither overly large nor disproportionate to the debts of other European powers. The problem lay with the inability of the royal government to tap the wealth of the French nation through taxes to service and repay the debt. Paradoxically, France was a rich nation with an impoverished government.

The Monarchy Seeks New Taxes

The debt was symptomatic of the failure of the late eighteenth-century French monarchy to come to terms with the resurgent social and political power of aristocratic institutions and, in particular, the *parlements*. For twenty-five years after the Seven Years' War, there was a standoff between them as one royal minister after another attempted to devise new tax schemes that would tap the wealth of the nobility, only to be confronted by the opposition of both the *Parlement* of Paris and provincial *parlements*. Both Louis XV (r. 1715–1774) and Louis XVI (r. 1774–1792) lacked the character and the resolution to carry the dispute to a successful conclusion. The moral and political corruption of their courts and the indecision of Louis XVI meant that the monarchy could not rally the French public to its side. In place of a consistent policy for dealing with the

growing debt and aristocratic resistance to change, the monarchy gave way to hesitancy, retreat, and even duplicity.

In 1770, Louis XV appointed René Maupeou (1714–1792) as chancellor. The new minister was determined to break the *parlements* and increase taxes on the nobility. He abolished the *parlements* and exiled their members to different parts of the country. He then began an ambitious program of reform and efficiency. What ultimately doomed Maupeou's policy was less the resistance of the nobility than the death of Louis XV in 1774. His successor, Louis XVI, in an attempt to regain what he conceived to be popular support, restored all the *parlements* and confirmed their old powers.

France's successful intervention on behalf of the American colonists against the British did nothing to relieve the government's financial difficulties. By 1781, as a result of the aid to America, its debt was larger and its sources of revenues were unchanged. The new director-general of finances, Jacques Necker (1732–1804), a Swiss banker, then produced a public report which suggested that the situation was not so bad as had been feared. He argued that if the expenditures for the American war were removed, the budget was in surplus. Necker's report also revealed that a large portion of royal expenditures went to pensions for aristocrats and other royal court favorites. This revelation angered court aristocratic circles, and Necker soon left office. His financial sleight of hand, nonetheless, made it more difficult for later government officials to claim a real need to raise new taxes.

The monarchy hobbled along until 1786. By this time, Charles Alexandre de Calonne (1734–1802) was the minister of finance. Calonne proposed to encourage internal trade, to lower some taxes, such as the *gabelle* on salt, and to transform peasants' services to money payments. More important, Calonne urged the introduction of a new land tax that would require payments from all landowners regardless of their social status. If this tax had been imposed, the monarchy could have abandoned other indirect taxes. The government would also have had less need to seek additional taxes that required approval from the aristocratically dominated *parlements*. Calonne also intended to establish new local assemblies to approve land taxes; in these assemblies the voting power would have depended on the amount of land owned rather than on the social status of the owner. All these proposals would have undermined both the political and the social power of the French aristocracy.

This late eighteenth-century cartoon satirizes the French social structure. It shows a poor man in chains, who represents the vast majority of the population, supporting an aristocrat, a bishop, and a noble of the robe. The aristocrat is claiming feudal rights, the bishop holds papers associating the church with religious persecution and clerical privileges, and the noble of the robe holds a document listing the rights of the noble-dominated parlements. Corbis

The Aristocracy and the Clergy Resist Taxation

Calonne's policies and the country's fiscal crisis made a new clash with the nobility unavoidable, and the monarchy had very little room to maneuver. The creditors were at the door; the treasury was nearly empty. In 1787, Calonne met with an Assembly of Notables drawn from the upper ranks of the aristocracy and the church to seek support and approval for his plan. The assembly adamantly refused any such action; rather, it demanded that the aristocracy be allowed a greater share in the direct government of the kingdom. The notables called for the reappointment of Necker, who they believed had left the country in sound fiscal condition. Finally, they claimed that they had no right to consent to new taxes and that such a right was vested only in the medieval institution of the Estates General of France, which had not met since 1614. The notables believed that calling the Estates General, which had been traditionally organized to allow aristocratic and church dominance, would produce a victory for the nobility over the monarchy.

Again, Louis XVI backed off. He dismissed Calonne and replaced him with Étienne Charles Loménie de Brienne (1727–1794), archbishop of Toulouse and the chief opponent of Calonne at the Assembly of Notables. Once in office, Brienne found, to his astonishment, that the situation was as bad as his predecessor had asserted. Brienne himself now sought to impose the land tax. The *Parlement* of Paris, however, took the new position that it lacked authority to authorize the tax and said that only the Estates General could do so. Shortly thereafter, Brienne appealed to the Assembly of the Clergy to approve a large subsidy to allow funding of that part of the debt then coming due for payment. The clergy, like the *Parlement* dominated by aristocrats, not only refused the subsidy, but also reduced its existing contribution, or *don gratuit*, to the government.

As these unfruitful negotiations were taking place at the center of political life, local aristocratic *parlements* and estates in the provinces were making their own demands. They wanted a restoration of the privileges they had enjoyed during the early seventeenth century, before Richelieu and

Louis XIV had crushed their independence. Consequently, in July 1788, the king, through Brienne, agreed to convoke the Estates General the next year. Brienne resigned and Necker replaced him. The institutions of the aristocracy—and to a lesser degree, of the church—had brought the French monarchy to its knees. In the country of its origin, royal absolutism had been defeated.

The Revolution of 1789

The year 1789 proved to be one of the most remarkable in the history of both France and Europe. The French aristocracy had forced Louis XVI to call the Estates General into session. Yet the aristocrats' triumph proved to be quite brief. From the moment the monarch summoned the Estates General, the political situation in France changed drastically. Social and political forces that neither the nobles nor the king could control were immediately unleashed.

From that calling of the Estates General to the present, historians have heatedly debated the meaning of the event and the turmoil that followed over the next decade. Many historians long believed that the calling and gathering of the Estates General unleashed a clash between the bourgeoisie and the aristocracy that had been building in the decades before 1789. More recently, other historians have countered that the two groups actually had much in common by 1789 and that many members of both the bourgeoisie and the aristocracy resented and opposed the clumsy absolutism of the late-eighteenth-century monarchy. This second group of historians contends that the fundamental issue of 1789 was the determination of various social groups to reorganize the French government to assure the future political influence of all forms of wealth.

As this complicated process was being worked out, the argument goes, distrust arose between the aristocracy and increasingly radical middle-class leaders. The latter then turned to the tradespeople of Paris, building alliances with them to achieve their goals. That alliance radicalized the revolution. When, in the mid-1790s, revolutionary policies and actions became too radical, aristocratic and middle-class leaders once again cooperated to reassert the security of all forms of private wealth

Well-meaning but weak and vacillating, Louis XVI (r. 1774–1792) stumbled from concession to concession until he finally lost all power to save his throne. Joseph Siffred Duplessis, *Louis XVI.* Versailles, France. Giraudon/Art Resource, NY

and property. According to this view, conflict did exist among different social groups during the years of the revolution, but its causes were immediate, not hidden in the depths of French economic and social development.

Other historians also look to the influence of immediate rather than long-term causes. They believe that the faltering of the monarchy and the confusion following the calling, election, and organization of the Estates General created a political vacuum. Various leaders and social groups, often using the political vocabulary of the Enlightenment, stepped into that vacuum, challenging each other for dominance. The precedent for such public debate had been set during the years of conflict between the monarchy and the *parlements* when the latter had begun to challenge the former as the true representative of the nation. These debates and conflicts over the language, and hence values, of political life and activity had been made possible by the emergence of the new print culture with its reading public and numerous channels for the circulation of books, pamphlets, and newspapers. Emerging from this culture were a large number of often-unemployed authors who were resentful of their situation and ready to use their skills to radicalize the discussion. The result was a political debate wider than any before in European history. The events of the era represented a continuing effort to dominate public opinion about the future course of the nation. The French Revolution, according to this view, thus illustrates the character of a new political culture created by changes in the technology and distribution of print communication.

Yet another group of historians maintains that the events of 1789 through 1795 are only one chapter in a longer-term political reorganization of France following the paralysis of monarchical government, a process that was not concluded until the establishment of the Third Republic in the 1870s. According to this interpretation, the core accomplishment of the revolution of the 1790s was to lay the foundations for a republic that could assure both individual liberty and the safety of property. It was not until the last quarter of the nineteenth century, however, that such a republic actually came into existence.

To some extent, how convincing one finds each of these interpretations depends on which years or even months of the revolution one examines. The various interpretations are not, in any case, always mutually exclusive. Certainly, the weakness and ultimate collapse of the monarchy influenced events more than was once acknowledged. All

sides did indeed make use of the new formats and institutions of the print culture. Individual leaders shifted their positions and alliances quite frequently, sometimes out of principle, more often for political expediency. Furthermore, the actual political situation differed from city to city and from region to region. The controversial and divisive religious policies of the revolutionary government itself were often determining factors in the attitudes that French citizens assumed toward the revolution. What does seem clear is that much of the earlier consensus—that the revolution arose almost entirely from conflict between the aristocracy and bourgeoisie—no longer stands, except with many qualifications. The interpretive situation is now much more complicated, and a new consensus has yet to emerge.

The Estates General Becomes the National Assembly

Almost immediately after the Estates General was called, the three groups, or Estates, represented within it clashed with each other. The First Estate was the clergy, the Second Estate the nobility, and the Third Estate theoretically everyone else in the kingdom, although its representatives were drawn primarily from wealthy members of the commercial and professional middle classes. All the representatives in the Estates General were men. During the widespread public discussions preceding the meeting of the Estates General, representatives of the Third Estate made it clear that they would not permit the monarchy and the aristocracy to decide the future of the nation.

A comment by the Abbé Siéyès (1748–1836) in a pamphlet published in 1789 captures the spirit of the Third Estate's representatives: "What is the Third Estate? Everything. What has it been in the political order up to the present? Nothing. What does it ask? To become something."[1] (See Abbé Siéyès Presents the Cause of the Third Estate.)

DEBATE OVER ORGANIZATION AND VOTING The initial split between the aristocracy and the Third Estate occurred before the Estates General gathered. The public debate over the proper organization of the body drew the lines of basic disagreement. The aristocracy made two moves to limit the influence of the Third Estate. First, they demanded an equal number of representatives for each estate. Second,

---

[1]Quoted in Leo Gershoy, *The French Revolution and Napoleon* (New York: Appleton-Century-Crofts, 1964), p. 102.

Abbé Siéyès Presents the Cause of the Third Estate

Among the many pamphlets that appeared after the calling of the Estates General, one of the most famous was **What Is the Third Estate?** *by Abbé Emmanuel Siéyès. In this pamphlet Siéyès contrasted the vital contributions of the Third Estate to the nation with its exclusion from political and social privilege. He presents an image of the Third Estate in direct conflict with the aristocracy rather than with the monarchy. On the basis of this pamphlet many later observers and historians argued that the revolution was a conflict between the middle class and the aristocracy. The social structure of France, however, and the interactions of those two groups was much more complicated than Siéyès suggests. Both groups were discontented with monarchical government.*

❖ *How does Siéyès define the Third Estate? What injustices does he claim it suffers? What are the complaints that he makes on behalf of the Third Estate against the aristocracy? Why does Siéyès make a distinction between the court and the monarchy?*

Who, then would dare to say that the third estate has not within itself all that is necessary to constitute a complete nation? It is the strong and robust man whose one arm remains enchained. If the privileged order were abolished, the nation would be not something less but something more. Thus, what is the third estate? Everything; but an everything shackled and oppressed....

The third estate must be understood to mean the mass of the citizens belonging to the common order. Legalized privilege in any form deviates from the common order, constitutes an exception to the common law, and, consequently, does not appertain to the third estate at all. We repeat, a common law and a common representation are what constitute ONE nation. It is only too true that one is NOTHING in France when one has only the protection of the common law; if one does not possess some privilege, one must resign oneself to enduring contempt, injury, and vexations of every sort....

But here we have to consider the order of the third estate less in its civil status than in its relation with the constitution. Let us examine its position in the Estates General.

Who have been its so-called representatives? The ennobled or those privileged for a period of years. These false deputies have not even been always freely elected by the people....

Add to this appalling truth that, in one manner or another, all branches of the executive power also have fallen to the case which furnishes the Church, the robe, and the Sword. A sort of spirit of brotherhood causes the nobles to prefer themselves...to the rest of the nation. Usurpation is complete; in truth they reign.

...it is a great error to believe that France is subject to a monarchical regime.

...it is the court, and not the monarch, that has reigned. It is the court that makes and unmakes, appoints and discharges ministers, creates and dispenses positions, etc. And what is the court if not the head of this immense aristocracy which overruns all parts of France; which though its members attains all and everywhere does whatever is essential in all parts of the commonwealth?

From *A Documentary Survey of the French Revolution*, by Stewart, John Hall, © 1951. Reprinted by permission of Prentice Hall, Inc., Upper Saddle River, NJ

in September 1788, the *Parlement* of Paris ruled that voting in the Estates General should be conducted by order rather than by head—that is, each estate, or order, rather than each member, should have one vote. This procedure would ensure that the aristocratic First and Second Estates could always outvote the Third. Both moves exposed the hollowness of the aristocracy's alleged concern for French liberty and revealed it as a group determined to maintain its privileges. Spokespeople for the Third Estate de-

nounced the arrogant claims of the aristocracy. Although the aristocracy and the Third Estate shared many economic interests and goals, and some intermarriage had occurred throughout the country between nobles and the elite of the Third Estate, a fundamental social distance separated the members of the two orders. There were far more examples of enormous wealth and military experience among the nobility than among the Third Estate; the latter also had experienced various forms of political and social

The Estates General opened at Versailles in 1789 with much pomp and splendor. This print shows the representatives of the three estates seated in the hall and Louis XVI on a throne at its far end. Convocation of the Estates General at Versailles. Bibliotheque Nationale, Paris, France. Giraudon/Art Resource, NY

discrimination from the nobility. The resistance of the nobility to voting by head simply confirmed the suspicions and resentments of the members of the Third Estate, who were overwhelmingly lawyers of substantial, but not enormous, economic means.

The royal council eventually decided that the cause of the monarchy and fiscal reform would best be served by a strengthening of the Third Estate. In December 1788, the council announced that the Third Estate would elect twice as many representatives as either the nobles or the clergy. This so-called doubling of the Third Estate meant that it could easily dominate the Estates General if voting were allowed by head rather than by order. It was correctly assumed that liberal nobles and clergy would support the Third Estate, confirming that, despite social differences, these groups shared important interests and reform goals. The method of voting was settled by the king only after the Estates General had gathered at Versailles in May 1789.

THE *CAHIERS DE DOLÉANCES* When the representatives came to the royal palace, they brought with them *cahiers de doléances,* or lists of grievances, registered by the local electors, to be presented to the king. Many of these lists have survived and provide considerable information about the state of the country on the eve of the revolution. The documents recorded criticisms of government waste, indirect taxes, church taxes and corruption, and the hunting rights of the aristocracy. They included calls for periodic meetings of the Estates General, more equitable taxes, more local control of administration, unified weights and measures to facilitate trade and commerce, and a free press. The overwhelming demand of the *cahiers* was for equality of rights among the king's subjects. (See "The Third Estate of a French City Petitions the King.")

These complaints and demands could not, however, be discussed until the questions of organization and voting had been decided. From the beginning, the Third Estate, whose members consisted largely of local officials, professionals, and other persons of property, refused to sit as a separate order as the king desired. For several weeks there was a standoff. Then, on June 1, the Third Estate invited the clergy and the nobles to join them in organizing a new legislative body. A few members of the lower clergy did so. On June 17, that body declared itself the National Assembly.

The Third Estate of a French City Petitions the King

The cahiers de doléances *were the lists of grievances brought to Versailles in 1789 by members of the Estates General. The particular* cahier *that follows originated in Dourdan, a city of central France, and reflects the complaints of the Third Estate. The first two articles refer to the organization of the Estates General. The other articles ask that the king grant various forms of equality before the law and in matters of taxation. These demands for equality appeared in practically all the* cahiers *of the Third Estate.*

❖ *Which of the following petitions relate to political rights and which to economic equality? The slogan most associated with the French Revolution was "liberty, equality, fraternity." Which of these petitions represents each of those values?*

The order of the third estate of the City...of Dourdan...supplicates [the king] to accept the grievances, complaints, and remonstrances which it is permitted to bring to the foot of the throne, and to see therein only the expression of its zeal and the homage of its obedience.

It wishes:

1. That his subjects of the third estate, equal by such status to all other citizens, present themselves before the common father without other distinction which might degrade them.

2. That all the orders, already united by duty and common desire contribute equally to the needs of the State, also deliberate in common concerning its needs.

3. That no citizen lose his liberty except according to law: that, consequently, no one be arrested by virtue of special orders, or, if imperative circumstances necessitate such orders, that the prisoner be handed over to regular courts of justice within forty-eight hours at the latest.

12. That every tax, direct or indirect, be granted only for a limited time, and that every collection beyond such term be regarded as peculation, and punished as such....

15. That every personal tax be abolished; that thus the *capitation* [a poll tax] and the *taille* [tax from which nobility and clergy were exempt] and its accessories be merged with the *vingtièmes* [an income tax] in a tax on land and real or nominal property.

16. That such tax be borne equally, without distinction, by all classes of citizens and by all kinds of property, even feudal...rights.

17. That the tax substituted for the *corvée* be borne by all classes of citizens equally and without distinction. That said tax, at present beyond the capacity of those who pay it and the needs to which it is destined, be reduced by at least one-half.

From *A Documentary Survey of the French Revolution*, by Stewart, John Hall, © 1951. Reprinted by permission of Prentice Hall, Inc., Upper Saddle River, NJ

THE TENNIS COURT OATH Three days later, finding themselves accidentally locked out of their usual meeting place, the National Assembly moved to a nearby tennis court. There its members took an oath to continue to sit until they had given France a constitution. This was the famous Tennis Court Oath. Louis XVI ordered the National Assembly to desist from its actions, but shortly afterward a majority of the clergy and a large group of nobles joined the assembly.

On June 27, the king capitulated and formally requested the First and Second Estates to meet with the National Assembly, where voting would occur by head rather than by order. Had nothing further occurred, the government of France would have been transformed. Government by privileged orders had ended. The National Assembly, which renamed itself the National Constituent Assembly, was composed of people from all three orders, who shared liberal goals for the administrative, constitutional, and economic reform of the country. The revolution in France against government by privileged hereditary orders had begun.

Fall of the Bastille

Two new forces soon intruded on the scene. The first was Louis XVI himself, who attempted to regain the political initiative by mustering royal troops near Versailles and Paris. It appeared that he might, following the advice of Queen Marie Antoinette (1755–1793), his brothers, and the most conservative nobles, be contemplating disruption of the National Constituent Assembly. On July 11, without consulting assembly leaders, Louis abrupt-

This painting of the Tennis Court Oath, June 20, is by Jacques-Louis David (1748–1825). In the center foreground are members of different Estates joining hands in cooperation as equals. The presiding officer is Jean-Sylvain Bailly, soon to become mayor of Paris. Jacques-Louis David, *Oath of the Tennis Court.* Chateau, Versailles, France. Giraudon/Art Resource, NY

ly dismissed his minister of finance, Necker. These actions marked the beginning of a steady, but consistently poorly executed, royal attempt to undermine the assembly and halt the revolution. Most of the National Constituent Assembly wished to establish some form of constitutional monarchy, but from the start Louis's refusal to cooperate thwarted that effort. The king fatally decided to throw his lot in with the conservative aristocracy against the emerging forces of reform drawn from across the social and political spectrum.

The second new factor to impose itself on the events at Versailles was the populace of Paris. The mustering of royal troops created anxiety in the city, where throughout the winter and spring of 1789 there had been several bread riots. The Parisians who had elected their representatives to the Third Estate had continued to meet after the elections. By June they were organizing a citizen militia and collecting arms. They regarded the dismissal of Necker as the opening of a royal offensive against the National Constituent Assembly and the city.

On July 14, somewhat more than 800 people, most of them small shopkeepers, tradespeople, artisans, and wage earners, marched to the Bastille in search of weapons for the militia. This great fortress, with ten-foot-thick walls, had once held political prisoners. Through miscalculations and ineptitude on the part of the governor of the fortress, the troops in the Bastille fired into the crowd, killing ninety-eight people and wounding many others. Thereafter, the crowd stormed the fortress and eventually gained entrance. They released the seven prisoners inside, none of whom was there for political reasons, and killed several troops and the governor. They found no weapons.

On July 15, the militia of Paris, by then called the National Guard, offered its command to the Marquis de Lafayette (1757–1834). This hero of the American Revolution gave the guard a new insignia: the red and blue stripes of Paris, separated by the white stripe of the king. The emblem became the revolutionary cockade (badge) and eventually the flag of revolutionary France.

On July 14, 1789, crowds stormed the Bastille, a prison in Paris. This event, whose only practical effect was to free a few prisoners, marked the first time the populace of Paris redirected the course of the revolution. France, 18th c., *Siege of the Bastille, 14 July, 1789.* Musée de la Ville de Paris, Musée Carnavalet, Paris, France. Giraudon/Art Resource, N.Y.

The attack on the Bastille marked the first of many crucial *journées,* days on which the populace of Paris redirected the course of the revolution. The fall of the fortress signaled that the National Constituent Assembly alone would not decide the political future of the nation. As the news of the taking of the Bastille spread, similar disturbances took place in provincial cities. A few days later, Louis XVI again bowed to the force of events and personally visited Paris, where he wore the revolutionary cockade and recognized the organized electors as the legitimate government of the city. The king also recognized the National Guard. The citizens of Paris were, for the time being, satisfied. They also had established themselves as an independent political force with which other political groups might ally for their own purposes.

The "Great Fear" and the Surrender of Feudal Privileges

Simultaneous with the popular urban disturbances, a movement known as the "Great Fear" swept across much of the French countryside. Rumors had spread that royal troops would be sent into the rural districts. The result was an intensification of the peasant disturbances that had begun during the spring. The Great Fear saw the burning of *châteaux,* the destruction of records and documents, and the refusal to pay feudal dues. The peasants were determined to take possession of food supplies and land that they considered rightfully theirs. They were reclaiming rights and property that they had lost through the aristocratic resurgence of the last quarter century, as well as venting their general anger against the injustices of rural life.

On the night of August 4, 1789, aristocrats in the National Constituent Assembly attempted to halt the spreading disorder in the countryside. By pre-arrangement, several liberal nobles and clerics rose in the assembly and renounced their feudal rights, dues, and tithes. In a scene of great emotion, hunting and fishing rights, judicial authority, and special exemptions were surrendered. These nobles gave up what they had already lost and what they could not have regained without civil war in the rural areas. Later they would also, in many cases, receive compensation for their losses. Nonetheless, after the night of August 4, all French citizens were subject to the same and equal laws. That dramatic session of the assembly paved the way for the legal and social reconstruction of the nation. Without those renunciations, the constructive work of the National Constituent Assembly would have been much more difficult. (See "The National Assembly Decrees Civic Equality in France.")

Both the attack on the Bastille and the Great Fear displayed characteristics of the rural and urban riots that had occurred often in eighteenth-century France.

Louis XVI first thought that the turmoil over the Bastille was simply another bread riot. Indeed, the popular disturbances were only partly related to the events at Versailles. A deep economic downturn had struck France in 1787 and continued into 1788. The harvests for both years had been poor, and food prices in 1789 were higher than at any time since 1703. Wages had not kept up with the rise in prices. Throughout the winter of 1788–1789, an unusually cold one, many people suffered from hunger. Several cities had experienced wage and food riots. These economic problems helped the revolution reach the vast proportions it did.

The political, social, and economic grievances of many sections of the country became combined. The National Constituent Assembly could look to the popular forces as a source of strength against the king and the conservative aristocrats. When the various elements of the assembly later fell into quarrels among themselves, the resulting factions appealed for support to the politically sophisticated and well-organized shopkeeping and artisan classes. They, in turn, would demand a price for their cooperation.

The National Assembly Decrees Civic Equality in France

These famous decrees of August 4, 1789, in effect created civic equality in France. The special privileges previously possessed or controlled by the nobility were removed.

❖ *What institutions and privileges are included in "the feudal regime"? How do these decrees recognize that the abolition of some privileges and former tax arrangements will require new kinds of taxes and government financing to support religious, educational, and other institutions?*

1. The National Assembly completely abolishes the feudal regime. It decrees that, among the rights and dues...all those originating in real or personal serfdom, personal servitude, and those which represent them, are abolished without indemnification; all others are declared redeemable, and that the price and mode of redemption shall be fixed by the National Assembly....

2. The exclusive right to maintain pigeon-houses and dove-cotes is abolished....

3. The exclusive right to hunt and to maintain unenclosed warrens is likewise abolished....

4. All manorial courts are suppressed without indemnification.

5. Tithes of every description and the dues which have been substituted for them...are abol-

ished, on condition, however, that some other method be devised to provide for the expenses of divine worship, the support of the officiating clergy, the relief of the poor, repairs and rebuilding of churches and parsonages, and for all establishments, seminaries, schools, academies, asylums, communities, and other institutions, for the maintenance of which they are actually devoted....

7. The sale of judicial and municipal offices shall be suppressed forthwith....

8. Pecuniary privileges, personal or real, in the payment of taxes are abolished forever....

11. All citizens, without distinction of birth, are eligible to any office or dignity, whether ecclesiastical, civil or military....

From Frank Maloy Anderson, ed. and trans., *The Constitutions and Other Select Documents Illustrative of the History of France, 1789–1907*, 2d. ed., rev. and enl. (Minneapolis: H. W. Wilson, 1908), pp. 11–13.

The Declaration of the Rights of Man and Citizen

In late August 1789, the National Constituent Assembly decided that before writing a new constitution, it should set forth a statement of broad political principles. On August 27, the assembly issued the Declaration of the Rights of Man and Citizen. This declaration drew upon much of the political language of the Enlightenment and was also influenced by the Declaration of Rights adopted by Virginia in America in June 1776.

The French declaration proclaimed that all men were "born and remain free and equal in rights." The natural rights so proclaimed were "liberty, property, security, and resistance to oppression." Governments existed to protect those rights. All political sovereignty resided in the nation and its representatives. All citizens were to be equal before the law and were to be "equally admissible to all public dignities, offices, and employments, according to their capacity, and with no other distinction than that of their virtues and talents." There were to be due process of law and presumption of innocence until proof of guilt. Freedom of religion was affirmed. Taxation was to be apportioned equally according to capacity to pay. Property constituted "an inviolable and sacred right."[2]

[2]Quoted in Georges Lefebvre, *The Coming of the French Revolution*, trans. by R. R. Palmer (Princeton, NJ: Princeton University Press, 1967), pp. 221–223.

Civic equality was one of the hallmarks of the revolutionary era. This figure of Equality holds in her hand a copy of the Declaration of the Rights of Man and Citizen. Corbis

Although these statements were rather abstract, almost all of them were directed against specific abuses of the old aristocratic and absolutist regime. If any two principles of the future governed the declaration, they were civic equality and protection of property. The Declaration of the Rights of Man and Citizen has often been considered the death certificate of the Old Regime.

It was not accidental that the Declaration of the Rights of Man and Citizen specifically applied to men and not to women. As discussed in the previous chapter, much of the political language of the Enlightenment, and most especially that associated with Rousseau, separated men and women into distinct gender spheres. According to this view, which influenced the legislation of the revolutionary era, men were suited for citizenship, women for motherhood and the domestic life. Nonetheless, in the charged atmosphere of the summer of 1789, many politically active and informed Frenchwomen hoped that the guarantees of the declaration would be extended to them. Their issues of particular concern related to property, inheritance, family, and divorce. Some

people saw in the declaration a framework within which women might eventually enjoy the rights and protection of citizenship.

The Royal Family Forced to Return to Paris

Louis XVI stalled before ratifying both the declaration and the aristocratic renunciation of feudalism. The longer he hesitated, the stronger grew suspicions that he might again try to resort to the use of troops. Moreover, bread continued to be scarce. On October 5, a crowd of as many as 7,000 Parisian women armed with pikes, guns, swords, and knives marched to Versailles demanding more bread. They milled about the palace, and many stayed the night. Intimidated by these Parisian women, the king agreed to sanction the decrees of the assembly. The next day he and his family appeared on a balcony before the crowd. The Parisians, however, were deeply suspicious of the monarch and believed that he must be kept under the watchful eye of the people. They demanded that Louis and his family return to Paris. The monarch had no real choice in

The women of Paris marched to Versailles on October 5, 1789. The following day the royal family was forced to return to Paris with them. Henceforth, the French government would function under the constant threat of mob violence. France, 18th c., *To Versailles, to Versailles. The Women of Paris going to Versailles, 7 October, 1789.* Musée de la Ville de Paris, Musée Carnavalet, Paris, France. Giraudon/Art Resource, NY

the matter. On October 6, 1789, his carriage followed the crowd into the city, where he and his family settled in the palace of the Tuileries.

The march of the women of Paris was the first example of a popular insurrection employing the language of popular sovereignty directed against the monarch. The National Constituent Assembly also soon moved into Paris. Thereafter, both Paris and France remained relatively stable and peaceful until the summer of 1792. (See "Art & the West.")

The Reconstruction of France

Once established in Paris, the National Constituent Assembly set about reorganizing France. In government, it pursued a policy of constitutional monarchy; in administration, rationalism; in economics, unregulated freedom; and in religion, anticlericalism. Throughout its proceedings the assembly was determined to protect property in all its forms. In those policies, the aristocracy and the middle-class elite stood united. The assembly also sought to limit the impact on national life of the unpropertied elements of the nation and even of possessors of small amounts of property. Although championing civic equality before the law, the assembly spurned social equality and extensive democracy. In all these ways, the assembly charted a general course that, to a greater or lesser degree, nineteenth-century liberals across Europe would follow.

Political Reorganization

The Constitution of 1791, the product of the National Constituent Assembly's deliberations, established a constitutional monarchy. The major political authority of the nation would be a unicameral Legislative Assembly, in which all laws would originate. The monarch was allowed a suspensive veto that could delay, but not halt, legislation. Powers of war and peace were vested in the assembly.

ACTIVE AND PASSIVE CITIZENS   The constitution provided for an elaborate system of indirect elections intended to thwart direct popular pressure on the government. The citizens of France were divided into active and passive categories. Only active citizens—that is, men paying annual taxes equal to three days of local labor wages—could vote. They chose electors, who then in turn voted for the members of the legislature. At the level of electors or members, still further property qualifications were imposed. Only about fifty thousand citizens of a population of about twenty-five million could qualify as electors or members of the Legislative Assembly. Women could neither vote nor hold office.

These constitutional arrangements effectively transferred political power from aristocratic wealth to all forms of propertied wealth in the nation. Political authority would no longer be achieved through hereditary privilege or through purchase of titles, but through the accumulation of land and commercial property. These new political arrangements based on property rather than birth recognized the new complexities of French society that had developed over the past century and allowed more social and economic interests to have a voice in the governing of the nation.

The laws that excluded women from both voting and holding office did not pass unnoticed. In 1791 Olympe de Gouges (d. 1793), a butcher's daughter from Montauban who became a major revolutionary radical in Paris, composed a *Declaration of the Rights of Woman*, which she ironically addressed to Queen Marie Antoinette. Much of the document reprinted the Declaration of the Rights of Man and Citizen adding the word "woman" to the various original clauses. That strategy demanded that women be regarded as citizens and not merely as daughters, sisters, wives, and mothers of citizens. Olympe de Gouges further outlined rights that would permit women to own property and require men to recognize the paternity of their children. She called for equality of the sexes in marriage and improved education for women. She declared, "Women, wake up; the tocsin of reason is being heard throughout the whole universe; discover your rights."[3] Her declaration illustrated how the simple listing of rights in the Declaration of the Rights of Man and Citizen created a structure of universal civic expectations even for those it did not cover. The National Assembly had established a set of values against which it could itself be measured. It provided criteria for liberty, and those to whom it had not extended full liberties could demand to know why and could claim that the revolution was incomplete until they enjoyed those freedoms.

DEPARTMENTS REPLACE PROVINCES   In reconstructing the local and judicial administration, the National Constituent Assembly applied the rational spirit of the Enlightenment. It abolished the ancient French provinces, such as Burgundy and Brittany, and established in their place eighty-three departments, or *départements*, of generally equal size named after rivers, mountains, and other geographical features. (See Map 19–1.) The departments in turn were subdivided into districts, cantons, and communes. Most local elections

---

[3]Quoted in Sara E. Melzer and Leslie W. Rabine, eds., *Rebel Daughters: Women and the French Revolution* (New York: Oxford University Press, 1992), p. 88.

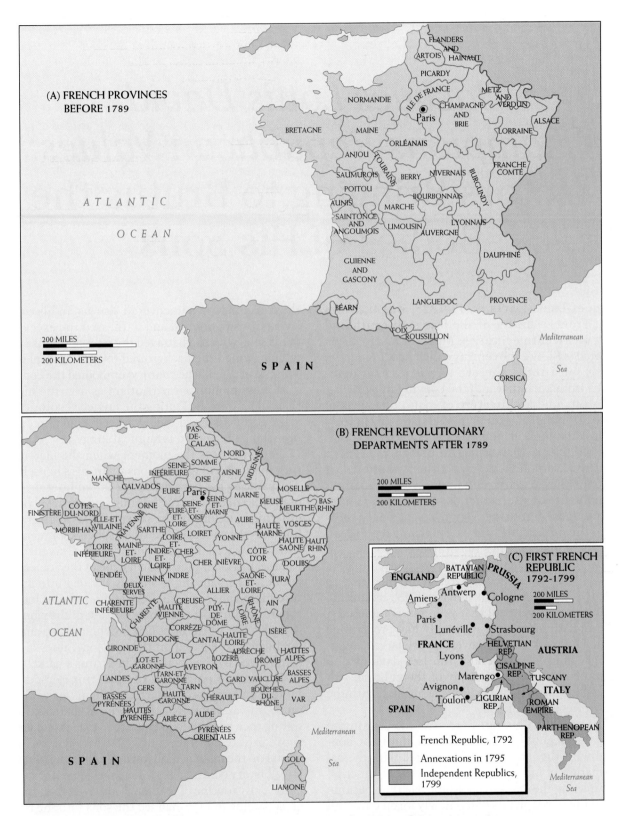

MAP 19–1   FRENCH PROVINCES AND THE REPUBLIC   *In 1789, the National Constituent Assembly redrew the map of France. The ancient provinces (A) were replaced with a larger
number of new, smaller departments (B). This redrawing of the map was part of the assembly's effort to impose greater administrative rationality in France. The borders of the
republic (C) changed as the French army conquered new territory.*

Jacques-Louis David Champions Republican Values: Lictors Bringing to Brutus the Bodies of His Sons

Jacques-Louis David (1748–1825) was the foremost French painter of the late eighteenth and early nineteenth centuries. Much of his art is associated with the movement called *neoclassicism*, which constituted a return to themes and topics drawn from antiquity and the copying in painting, sculpture, and architecture of major elements of classical models. Figures in such paintings rarely suggest movement and often seem to stand in a kind of tableau illustrating a moral theme. These paintings were didactic rather than emotional or playful. They usually pertained in some manner to public life or public morals, rather than to family life or daily routine. David was strongly critical of the old regime and used ancient republican themes in his paintings to point to the corruption of the current monarchical government.

David began the painting of *Lictors Bringing to Brutus the Bodies of His Sons* in 1789, before the revolutionary events of that year, but completed it only after the National Assembly had proclaimed itself. The work, which covers a very large canvas, though painted in literally the last days of old-regime France, conveys many of the political values and implies a social critique associated with the French Revolution itself.

The painting illustrates a famous incident in the history of republican Rome. Brutus, not to be confused with the later Brutus associated with the assassination of Julius Ceasar, had been instrumental in banishing the last king of Rome. He then became one of the two Consuls of the newly formed Roman Republic. Shortly thereafter, his two sons, Titus and Tiberius, became involved in an effort to restore the exiled king, who was a relative of their mother. Once the conspiracy was uncovered, Brutus, in his capacity as Consul, ordered and witnessed the execution of his sons who had betrayed the republic. This story, which formed the background for a famous play by Voltaire earlier in the century, embodied the concept of selfless republican patriotism as a virtue higher than ties to family. During the French revolution itself, Brutus assumed the status of a kind of cult figure who had opposed tyrannical kings.

David portrays the moment when the Lictors return the bodies of the two sons to Brutus's household. The painting has been described as "an interrogation of the idea of civic virtue" through its portrayal of the differing reactions of the parents.[4] David clearly illustrates the concept of separate spheres for men and women, which he may well have derived from Rousseau, a champion of the virtue of the ancient republics. The painting is sharply divided into an active male sphere on the left and a passive female sphere on the right. The male portion of the painting includes the world of politics, civic action, and republican virtue based on the rational values of law symbolized by the document in Brutus's hand.

The female portion of the painting depicts the mother and sisters of the executed sons, as well as a nurse, in various states of emotional distress, illustrating their presumed incapacity to place civic virtue above private family feelings. The basket, wool, and shears on the table, which form a still life within this large history painting, represent the domestic sphere of the daily routine of women. Moreover, their mother, according to Livy, had led the sons into the royal-

[4]Thomas Crow, *Emulation: Making Artists for Revolutionary France* (New Haven, CT: Yale University Press 1995), p. 108.

Jacques-Louis David (1748–1825), *Lictors bringing to Brutus the bodies of his sons.* 1789. Oil on canvas, 323 × 422 cm - Inv. 3693. Louvre, Paris, France. Erich Lessing/Art Resource, NY.

ist conspiracy. It has been suggested that a royalist *fleur-de-lis* appears in the cloth in the basket.

Brutus appears alone, separated from his family and from all other human emotions except dedication to the Roman Republic itself. The presence of the statue portraying the legend of Romulus and Remus suckled by the wolf symbolizes the manner in which the Roman Republic, at its origin, stood distinct from family life. Through this symbolism, David suggests that family loyalties and female influence stand in opposition to republican virtue. Indeed, loyalty to abstract political principles separated from human sympathies mark the years of the Terror, when revolutionary leaders often appealed directly to the experience of the ancient republics.

David himself was one of the great political survivors of the revolutionary era. He painted many of its events, became a strong Jacobin, was imprisoned for a time, and then emerged into public life to portray most of the major events of Napoleon's career. Under the restoration, he spent the end of his life in exile.

Robert Rosenblum and H. W. Janson, *Nineteenth-Century Art* (Englewood Cliffs, NJ and New York: Prentice Hall: Harry N. Abrams, Inc., 1984), pp. 24–50; Albert Boime, *Art in an Age of Revolution, 1750–1800* (Chicago: University of Chicago Press, 1987, pp. 417–421); Norman Bryson, *Looking at the Overlooked: Four Essays on Still Life Painting* (Cambridge, MA: Harvard University Press, 1900), pp. 156–158; and Thomas Crow, *Emulation: Making Artists for Revolutionary France* (New Haven, CT: Yale University Press, 1995).

Jacobin = (in the French Revolution) a member of a radical society or club of revolutionaries that promoted the Reign of Terror, & other extreme measures, active chiefly from 1789 – 1794: so called from the Dominican convent in Paris where they originally met.

were also indirect. The departmental reconstruction proved to be a permanent achievement of the assembly. The departments exist to the present day.

All the ancient judicial courts, including the seigneurial courts and the *parlements*, were also abolished. Uniform courts with elected judges and prosecutors were organized in their place. Procedures were simplified, and the most degrading punishments were removed from the books.

Economic Policy

In economic matters, the National Constituent Assembly continued the policies formerly advocated by Louis XVI's reformist ministers. It suppressed the guilds and liberated the grain trade. The assembly established the metric system to provide the nation with uniform weights and measures.

WORKERS' ORGANIZATIONS FORBIDDEN The new policies of economic freedom and uniformity disappointed both peasants and urban workers caught in the cycle of inflation. By decrees in 1789, the assembly placed the burden of proof on the peasants to rid themselves of the residual feudal dues for which compensation was to be paid. On June 14, 1791, the assembly crushed the attempts of urban workers to protect their wages by enacting the Chapelier Law, which forbade workers' associations. Peasants and workers were henceforth to be left to the freedom and mercy of the marketplace. (See "The Revolutionary Government Forbids Workers' Organizations.")

The Revolutionary Government Forbids Workers' Organizations

The Chapelier Law of June 14, 1791, was one of the most important pieces of revolutionary legislation. It abolished the kinds of labor organizations that had protected skilled workers under the Old Regime. The principles of this legislation prevented effective labor organization in France for well over half a century.

❖ *Why are workers' organizations declared to be contrary to the principles of liberty? Why were guilds seen as one of the undesirable elements of the Old Regime? What are the coercive powers that are to be brought to bear against workers' organizations? In light of this legislation, what courses of actions were left open to workers as they confronted the operation of the market economy?*

1. Since the abolition of all kinds of corporations of citizens of the same occupation and profession is one of the fundamental bases of the French Constitution, reestablishment thereof under any pretext or form whatsoever is forbidden.

2. Citizens of the same occupation or profession, entrepreneurs, those who maintain open shop, workers, and journeymen of any craft whatsoever may not, when they are together, name either president, secretaries, or trustees, keep accounts, pass decrees or resolutions, or draft regulations concerning their alleged common interests....

...4. If, contrary to the principles of liberty and the Constitution, some citizens associated in the same professions, arts, and crafts hold deliberations or make agreements among themselves tending to refuse by mutual consent or to grant only at a determined price the assistance of their industry or their labor, such deliberations and agreements, whether accompanied by oath or not, are declared unconstitutional, in contempt of liberty and the Declaration of the Rights of Man, and noneffective; administrative and municipal bodies shall be required so to declare them....

8. All assemblies composed of artisans, workers, journeymen, day laborers, or those incited by them against the free exercise of industry and labor appertaining to every kind of person and under all circumstances arranged by private contract, or against the action of police and the execution of judgments rendered in such connection, as well as against public bids and auctions of divers enterprises, shall be considered as seditious assemblies, and as such shall be dispersed by the depositories of the public force, upon legal requisitions made thereupon, and shall be punished according to all the rigor of the laws concerning authors, instigators, and leaders of the said assemblies, and all those who have committed assaults and acts of violence.

From *A Documentary Survey of the French Revolution*, by Stewart, John Hall, © 1951. Reprinted by permission of Prentice-Hall, Inc., Upper Saddle River, NJ.

CONFISCATION OF CHURCH LANDS   While these various reforms were being put into effect, the original financial crisis that had occasioned the calling of the Estates General persisted. The assembly did not repudiate the royal debt, because it was owed to the bankers, the merchants, and the commercial traders of the Third Estate. The National Constituent Assembly had suppressed many of the old, hated indirect taxes and had substituted new land taxes, but these proved insufficient. Moreover, there were not enough officials to collect them. The continuing financial problem led the assembly to take what may well have been, for the future of French life and society, its most decisive action. The assembly decided to finance the debt by confiscating and then selling the land and property of the Roman Catholic Church in France. The results were further inflation, religious schism, and civil war. In effect, the National Constituent Assembly had opened a new chapter in the relations of church and state in Europe.

THE *ASSIGNATS*   Having chosen to plunder the land of the church, the assembly authorized the issuance of *assignats*, or government bonds in December 1789. Their value was guaranteed by the revenue to be generated from the sale of church property. Initially, a limit was set on the quantity of *assignats* to be issued. The bonds, however, proved so acceptable to the public that they began to circulate as currency. The assembly decided to issue an ever-larger number of them to liquidate the national debt and to create a large body of new property owners with a direct stake in the revolution. Within a few months, however, the value of the *assignats* began to fall and inflation increased, putting new stress on the lives of the urban poor.

The Civil Constitution of the Clergy

The confiscation of church lands required an ecclesiastical reconstruction. In July 1790, the National Constituent Assembly issued the Civil Constitution of the Clergy, which transformed the Roman Catholic Church in France into a branch of the secular state. This legislation reduced the number of bishoprics from 135 to 83 and brought the borders of the dioceses into conformity with those of the new departments. It also provided for the election of priests and bishops, who henceforth became salaried employees of the state. The assembly consulted neither the Pope nor the French clergy about these broad changes. The king approved the measure only with the greatest reluctance.

The Civil Constitution of the Clergy was the major blunder of the National Constituent Assembly. It created embittered relations between the French church and state that have persisted to the present day. The measure immediately created immense opposition within the French church, even from bishops who had long championed Gallican liberties over papal domination. In the face of this resistance, the assembly unwisely ruled that all clergy must take an oath to support the Civil Constitution. Only seven bishops and about half the clergy did so. In reprisal, the assembly designated those clergy who had not taken the oath as "refractory" and removed them from their clerical functions.

Further reaction was swift. Refractory priests attempted to celebrate mass. In February 1791, the Pope condemned not only the Civil Constitution of the Clergy, but also the Declaration of the Rights of Man and Citizen. That condemnation marked the opening of a Roman Catholic offensive against liberalism and the revolution that continued throughout the nine-

The assignats were government bonds that were backed by confiscated church lands. They circulated as money. When the government printed too many of them, inflation resulted and their value fell.
Bildarchiv Preussischer Kulturbesitz

teenth century. Within France itself, the pope's action created a crisis of conscience and political loyalty for all sincere Catholics. Religious devotion and revolutionary loyalty became incompatible for many people. French citizens were divided between those who supported the constitutional priests and those who resorted to the refractory clergy. Louis XVI and his family favored the refractory clergy.

Counterrevolutionary Activity

The revolution had other enemies besides the Pope and the devout Catholics. As it became clear that the old political and social order was undergoing fundamental and probably permanent change, many aristocrats left France. Known as the *émigrés*, they settled in countries near the French border, where they sought to foment counterrevolution. Among the most important of their number was the king's younger brother, the count of Artois (1757–1836). In the summer of 1791, his agents and the queen persuaded Louis XVI to attempt to flee the country.

FLIGHT TO VARENNES On the night of June 20, 1791, Louis and his immediate family, disguised as servants, left Paris. They traveled as far as Varennes on their way to Metz. At Varennes the king was recognized, and his flight was halted. On June 24, a company of soldiers escorted the royal family back to Paris. The leaders of the National Constituent Assembly, determined to save the constitutional monarchy, announced that the king had been abducted from the capital. Such a convenient public fiction could not cloak the realities that the chief counterrevolutionary in France now sat on the throne and that the constitutional monarchy might not last long.

DECLARATION OF PILLNITZ Two months later, on August 27, 1791, under pressure from a group of *émigrés*, Emperor Leopold II of Austria, who was the brother of Marie Antoinette, and Frederick William II (r. 1786–1797), the king of Prussia, issued the Declaration of Pillnitz. The two monarchs promised to intervene in France to protect the royal family and to preserve the monarchy *if the other*

In June 1791, Louis XVI and his family attempted to flee France. They were recognized in the town of Varennes, where their flight was halted and they were returned to Paris. This ended any realistic hope for a constitutional monarchy. Corbis

major European powers agreed. This provision rendered the declaration meaningless because, at the time, Great Britain would not have given its consent. The declaration was not, however, so read in France, where the revolutionaries saw the nation surrounded by aristocratic and monarchical foes.

The National Constituent Assembly drew to a close in September 1791. Its task of reconstructing the government and the administration of France had been completed. One of its last acts was the passage of a measure that forbade any of its own members to sit in the Legislative Assembly then being elected. The new body met on October 1 and had to confront the immense problems that had emerged during the earlier part of the year. Within the Legislative Assembly, major political divisions also soon developed over the future course of the nation and the revolution. Those groups whose members had been assigned to passive citizenship began to demand full political participation in the nation.

A Second Revolution

By the autumn of 1791, the government of France had been transformed into a constitutional monarchy. Virtually all the other administrative and religious structures of the nation had also been reformed. The situation both inside and outside France, however, remained unstable. Louis XVI had reluctantly accepted the constitution on July 14, 1790. French aristocrats resented their loss of position and plotted to overthrow the new order. In the west of France, peasants resisted the revolutionary changes, especially as they affected the church. In Paris, many groups of workers believed that the revolution had not gone far enough. Furthermore, during these same months, women's groups in Paris began to organize both to support the revolution and to demand a wider civic role and civic protection for women. Radical members of the new Legislative Assembly also believed that the revolution should go further. The major foreign powers saw the French Revolution as dangerous to their own domestic political order. By the spring of 1792, all these unstable elements had begun to overturn the first revolutionary settlement and led to a second series of revolutionary changes far more radical and democratically extensive than the first.

End of the Monarchy

The issues raised by the Civil Constitution of the Clergy and Louis XVI's uncertain trustworthiness undermined the unity of the newly organized nation. Factionalism plagued the Legislative Assembly throughout its short life (1791–1792). Ever since the

original gathering of the Estates General, deputies from the Third Estate had organized themselves into clubs composed of politically like-minded persons. The most famous and best organized of these clubs were the Jacobins, whose name derived from the fact that Dominican friars were called Jacobins and the group met in a Dominican monastery in Paris. The Jacobins had also established a network of local clubs throughout the provinces. They had been the most advanced political group in the National Constituent Assembly and had pressed for a republic rather than a constitutional monarchy. Their political language and rhetoric were drawn from the most radical thought of the Enlightenment. That thought and language became all the more effective because the events of 1789–1791 had destroyed the old political framework and the old monarchical political vocabulary was less and less relevant. The political language and rhetoric of a republic filled that vacuum and for a time supplied the political values of the day. The events of the summer of 1791 led to the reassertion of demands for establishing a republic.

In the Legislative Assembly, a group of Jacobins known as the Girondists (because many of them came from the department of the Gironde) assumed leadership.[5] They were determined to oppose the forces of counterrevolution. They passed one measure ordering the *émigrés* to return or suffer loss of property and another requiring the refractory clergy to support the Civil Constitution or lose their state pensions. The king vetoed both acts.

Furthermore, on April 20, 1792, the Girondists led the Legislative Assembly in declaring war on Austria, by this time governed by Francis II (r. 1792–1835) and allied to Prussia. The Girondists believed that the pursuit of the war would preserve the revolution from domestic enemies and bring the most advanced revolutionaries to power. Paradoxically, Louis XVI and other monarchists also favored the war. They thought that the conflict would strengthen the executive power (the monarchy). The king also entertained the hope that foreign armies might defeat French forces and restore the Old Regime. Both sides were playing dangerously foolish politics.

The war radicalized the revolution and led to what is usually called the second revolution, which overthrew the constitutional monarchy and established a republic. Both the country and the revolution seemed in danger. As early as March 1791, a group of women led by Pauline Léon had petitioned the Legislative Assembly for the right to bear arms and to fight for

---

[5]The Girondists are also frequently called the Brissotins after Jacques-Pierre Brissot (1754–1793), their chief spokesperson in early 1792.

[margin note: Jacobins pressed for a republic rather than a const. monarchy]

French Women Petition to Bear Arms

The issue of women serving in the revolutionary French military appeared early in the revolution. In March 1791, Pauline Léon presented a petition to the National Assembly on behalf of more than 300 Parisian women asking the right to bear arms and train for military service for the revolution. Similar requests were made during the next two years. Some women did serve in the military, but in 1793 legislation specifically forbade women from participating in military service. The ground for that refusal was the argument that women belonged in the domestic sphere and military service would lead them to abandon family duties.

❖ Citoyenne *is the feminine form of the French word for citizen. How does this petition seek to challenge the concept of citizenship in the Declaration of the Rights of Man and Citizen? How do these petitioners relate their demand to bear arms to their role as women in French society? How do the petitioners relate their demands to the use of all national resources against the enemies of the revolution?*

Patriotic women come before you to claim the right which any individual has to defend his life and liberty.

...We are *citoyennes* [female citizens], and we cannot be indifferent to the fate of the fatherland.

...Yes, Gentlemen, we need arms, and we come to ask your permission to procure them. May our weakness be no obstacle; courage and intrepidity will supplant it, and the love of the fatherland and hatred of tyrants will allow us to brave all dangers with ease....

No, Gentlemen, We will [use arms] only to defend ourselves the same as you; you cannot refuse us, and society cannot deny the right nature gives us, unless you pretend the Declaration of Rights does not apply to women and that they should let their throats be cut like lambs, without the right to defend themselves. For can you believe the tyrants would spare us?...Why then not terrorize aristocracy and tyranny with all the resources of civic effort and the pure zeal, zeal which cold men can well call fanaticism and exaggeration, but which is only the natural result of a heart burning with love for the public weal?...

...If, for reasons we cannot guess, you refuse our just demands, these women you have raised to the ranks of *citoyennes* by granting that to their husbands, these women who have sampled the promises of liberty, who have conceived the hope of placing free men in the world, and who have sworn to live free or die—such women, I say, will never consent to concede the day to slaves; they will die first. They will uphold their oath, and a dagger aimed at their breasts will deliver them from the misfortunes of slavery! They will die, regretting not life, but the uselessness of their death; regretting moreover, not having been able to drench their hands in the impure blood of the enemies of the fatherland and to avenge some of their own!

But, Gentlemen, let us cast our eyes away from these cruel extremes. Whatever the rages and plots of aristocrats, they will not succeed in vanquishing a whole people of united brothers armed to defend their rights. We also demand only the honor of sharing their exhaustion and glorious labors and of making tyrants see that women also have blood to shed for the service of the fatherland in danger.

Gentlemen, here is what we hope to obtain from your justice and equity:

1. Permission to procure pikes, pistols, and sabres (even muskets for those who are strong enough to use them), within police regulations.

2. Permission to assemble on festival days and Sundays on the Champ de la Fédération, or in other suitable places, to practice maneuvers with these arms.

3. Permission to name the former French Guards to command us, always in conformity with the rules which the mayor's wisdom prescribes for good order and public calm.

Excerpts from Leon, "Petition to the National Assembly on Woman's Rights to Bear Arms" in *Women in Revolutionary Paris 1789–1795,* edited and translated by Darline Gay Levy, Harriet Branson Applewhite, and Mary Durham Johnson. Copyright © 1979, by the Board of Trustees of the University of Illinois. Used with permission of the University of Illinois Press.

On August 10, 1792, the Swiss Guards of Louis XVI fought Parisians who attacked the Tuileries Palace. Several hundred troops and citizens were killed, and Louis XVI and his family were forced to take refuge with the Legislative Assembly. After this event, the monarch virtually ceased to influence events in France. Jean Duplessi–Bertaux, *The Siege of the Palais des Tuileries, August 10, 1792.* Chateau, Versailles, France. Giraudon/Art Resource, NY

the protection of the revolution. (See "French Women Petition to Bear Arms.") Even before that, Léon had led an effort to allow women to serve in the National Guard. These demands to serve, voiced in the universal language of citizenship, illustrated how the words and rhetoric of the revolution could be used to challenge traditional social roles and the concept of separate social spheres for men and women. Furthermore, the pressure of war raised the possibility that the military needs of the nation could not be met if the ideal of separate spheres were honored. Once the war began, some Frenchwomen did enlist in the army and served with distinction.

Initially, the war effort went quite poorly. In July 1792, the duke of Brunswick, commander of the Prussian forces, issued a manifesto promising the destruction of Paris if harm came to the French royal family. This statement stiffened support for the war and increased the already significant distrust of the king.

Late in July, under radical working-class pressure, the government of Paris passed from the elected council to a committee, or commune, of representatives from the sections (municipal wards) of the city. On August 10, 1792, a very large Parisian crowd invaded the Tuileries palace and forced Louis XVI and Marie Antoinette to take refuge in the Legislative Assembly itself. The crowd fought with the royal Swiss guards. When Louis was finally able to call off the troops, several hundred of them and many Parisian citizens lay dead. The monarchy itself was also a casualty of that melee. Thereafter the royal family was imprisoned in comfortable quarters, but the king was allowed to perform none of his political functions. The recently established constitutional monarchy no longer had a monarch.

The Convention and the Role of the *Sans-culottes*

Early in September, the Parisian crowd again made its will felt. During the first week of the month, in what are known as the September Massacres, the Paris Commune summarily executed or murdered about 1,200 people who were in the city jails. Many of these people were aristocrats or priests, but the majority were

A Pamphleteer Describes a *Sans-culotte*

This document is a 1793 description of a sans-culotte *written either by one or by a sympathizer. It describes the* sans-culotte *as a hardworking, useful, patriotic citizen who bravely sacrifices himself to the war effort. It contrasts those virtues with the lazy and unproductive luxury of the noble and the personally self-interested plottings of the politician.*

❖ *What social resentments appear in this description? How could these resentments be used to create solidarity among the* sans-culottes *to defend the revolution? How does this document relate civic virtue to work? Do you see any relationship between the social views expressed in the document and the abolition of workers' organizations in a previous document? Where does this document suggest that the* sans-culotte *may need to confront enemies of the republic?*

A *sans-culotte* you rogues? He is someone who always goes on foot, who has no millions as you would all like to have, no chateaux, no valets to serve him, and who lives simply with his wife and children, if he has any, on a fourth or fifth story.

He is useful, because he knows how to work in the field, to forge iron, to use a saw, to use a file, to roof a house, to make shoes, and to shed his last drop of blood for the safety of the Republic.

And because he works, you are sure not to meet his person in the Café de Chartres, or in the gaming houses where others conspire and game; nor at the National theatre...nor in the literary clubs....

In the evening he goes to his section, not powdered or perfumed, or smartly booted in the hope of catching the eye of the citizenesses in the galleries, but ready to support good proposals with all his might, and to crush those which come from the abominable faction of politicians.

Finally, a *sans-culotte* always has his sabre sharp, to cut off the ears of all enemies of the Revolution; sometimes he even goes out with his pike; but at the first sound of the drum he is ready to leave for the Vendée, for the army of the Alps or for the army of the North....

From "Reply to an Impertinent Question: What is a Sans-culotte?" April 1793. Reprinted in Walter Markov and Albert Soboul, eds., *Die Sansculotten von Paris,* and republished trans. by Clive Emsley in Merryn Williams, ed., *Revolutions: 1775–1830* (Baltimore: Penguin Books, in association with the Open University, 1971), pp. 100–101.

simply common criminals. The crowd had assumed that the prisoners were all counterrevolutionaries.

The Paris Commune then compelled the Legislative Assembly to call for the election by universal male suffrage of a new assembly to write a democratic constitution. That body, called the Convention after its American counterpart of 1787, met on September 21, 1792. The previous day, the French army had halted the Prussian advance at the Battle of Valmy in eastern France. The victory of democratic forces at home had been confirmed by victory on the battlefield. As its first act, the Convention declared France a republic—that is, a nation governed by an elected assembly without a monarch.

GOALS OF THE *SANS-CULOTTES* The second revolution had been the work of Jacobins more radical than the Girondists and of the people of Paris known as the *sans-culottes*. The name of this group means "without breeches" and derived from the long trousers that, as

working people, they wore instead of aristocratic knee breeches. The *sans-culottes* were shopkeepers, artisans, wage earners, and, in a few cases, factory workers. The persistent food shortages and the revolutionary inflation had made their difficult lives even more burdensome. The politics of the Old Regime had ignored them, and the policies of the National Constituent Assembly had left them victims of unregulated economic liberty. The government, however, required their labor and their lives if the war was to succeed. From the summer of 1792 until the summer of 1794, their attitudes, desires, and ideals were the primary factors in the internal development of the revolution. (See "A Pamphleteer Describes a *Sans-culotte*.")

The *sans-culottes* generally knew what they wanted. The Parisian tradespeople and artisans sought immediate relief from food shortages and rising prices through price controls. They believed that all people had a right to subsistence and profoundly resented most forms of social inequality. This attitude made them intensely hostile to the aristocracy and the original leaders of the revolution of 1789, who they believed simply wanted to share political power, social prestige, and economic security with the aristocracy. The *sans-culottes'* hatred of inequality did not take them so far as to demand the abolition of property. Rather, they advocated a community of small property owners who would also participate in the political nation.

In politics they were antimonarchical, strongly republican, and suspicious even of representative government. They believed that the people should make the decisions of government to as great an extent as possible. In Paris, where their influence was most important, the *sans-culottes* had gained their political experience in meetings of the Paris sections. Those gatherings exemplified direct community democracy and were not unlike a New England town meeting. The economic hardship of their lives made them impatient to see their demands met.

THE POLICIES OF THE JACOBINS The goals of the *sans-culottes* were not wholly compatible with those of the Jacobins, republicans who sought representative government. Jacobin hatred of the aristocracy and hereditary privilege did not extend to a general suspicion of wealth. Basically, the Jacobins

favored an unregulated economy. From the time of Louis XVI's flight to Varennes onward, however, the more extreme Jacobins began to cooperate with leaders of the Parisian *sans-culottes* and the Paris Commune for the overthrow of the monarchy. Once the Convention began its deliberations, these Jacobins, known as the Mountain because of their seats high in the assembly hall, worked with the *sans-culottes* to carry the revolution forward and to win the war. This willingness to cooperate with the forces of the popular revolution separated the Mountain from the Girondists, who were also members of the Jacobin Club.

EXECUTION OF LOUIS XVI By the spring of 1793, several issues had brought the Mountain and its *sans-culottes* allies to domination of the Convention and the revolution. In December 1792, Louis XVI was put on trial as mere "Citizen Capet," the family name of extremely distant forebears of the royal family. The Girondists looked for some way to spare his life, but the Mountain defeated the effort. Louis was convicted, by a very narrow majority, of conspiring against the liberty of the people and the security of the state. He was condemned to death and was beheaded on January 21, 1793.

Louis XVI was executed on January 21, 1793. Execution of Louis XVI. Aquatint. French, 18th century.
Musée de la Ville de Paris, Musée Carnavalet, Paris. France. Giraudon/Art Resource, NY

The next month, the Convention declared war on Great Britain, Holland, and Spain. Soon thereafter, the Prussians renewed their offensive and drove the French out of Belgium. To make matters worse, General Dumouriez (1739–1823), the Girondist victor of Valmy, deserted to the enemy. Finally, in March 1793, a royalist revolt led by aristocratic officers and priests erupted in the Vendée in western France and roused much popular support. Thus, the revolution found itself at war with most of Europe and much of the French nation. The Girondists had led the country into the war, but had proved themselves incapable either of winning it or of suppressing the enemies of the revolution at home. The Mountain stood ready to take up the task. Every major European power was now hostile to the revolution.

Europe at War with the Revolution

Initially, the rest of Europe had been ambivalent toward the revolutionary events in France. Those people who favored political reform regarded the revolution as wisely and rationally reorganizing a corrupt and inefficient government. The major foreign governments thought that the revolution meant that France would cease to be an important factor in European affairs for several years.

Edmund Burke Attacks the Revolution

In 1790, however, the Irish-born writer and British statesman Edmund Burke (1729–1799) argued a different position in *Reflections on the Revolution in France*. Burke regarded the reconstruction of French administration as the application of a blind rationalism that ignored the historical realities of political development and the complexities of social relations. He also forecast further turmoil as people without political experience tried to govern France. As the revolutionaries proceeded to attack the church, the monarchy, and finally the rest of Europe, Burke's ideas came to have many admirers. His *Reflections* and later works became the handbook of European conservatives for decades. (See "Burke Denounces the Extreme Measures of the French Revolution.")

By the outbreak of the war with Austria in April 1792, the other European monarchies recognized the danger of both the ideas and the aggression of

Edmund Burke (1729–1799) published Reflections on the Revolution in France *in 1790. It became the most famous of all conservative denunciations of the revolution.* National Portrait Gallery, London

Burke Denounces the Extreme Measures of the French Revolution

Edmund Burke was undoubtedly the most important and articulate foreign critic of the French Revolution. His first critique, Reflections on the Revolution in France, *appeared in 1790. He continued to attack the revolution in later years. In 1796 he composed* Letters on a Regicide Peace, *which opposed a peace treaty between Great Britain and revolutionary France. In that work, he summarized what he regarded as the most fundamental evils of the revolutionary government: the execution of the king, the confiscation of property of the church and nobles, and the policy of de-Christianization.*

❖ *To which of the major events in the French Revolution does Burke make reference? Why, by 1796, would Burke and others have attached so much importance to the religious policies of the revolution? Did Burke exaggerate the evils of the revolution? Who might have been persuaded by Burke's condemnation?*

A government of the nature of that set up at our very door has never been hitherto seen, or even imagined in Europe....France, since her revolution, is under the sway of a sect, whose leaders have deliberately, at one stroke, demolished the whole body of that jurisprudence which France had pretty nearly in common with other civilized countries....

Its foundation is laid in regicide, in Jacobinism, and in atheism, and it has joined to those principles a body of systematic manners, which secures their operation....

I call a commonwealth regicide, which lays it down as a fixed law of nature, and a fundamental right of man, that all government, not being a democracy, is an usurpation. That all kings, as such, are usurpers; and for being kings may and ought to be put to death, with their wives, families, and adherents. That commonwealth which acts uniformly upon those principles...—this I call regicide by establishment.

Jacobinism is the revolt of the enterprising talents of a country against its property. When private men form themselves into associations for the purpose of destroying the pre-existing laws and institutions of their country; when they secure to themselves an army, by dividing amongst the people of no property the estates of the ancient and lawful proprietors, when a state recognizes those acts; when it does not make confiscations for crimes, but makes crimes for confiscations; when it has its

principal strength, and all its resources, in such a violation of property...—I call this Jacobinism by establishment.

I call it atheism by establishment, when any state, as such, shall not acknowledge the existence of God as a moral governor of the world;...—when it shall abolish the Christian religion by a regular decree;—when it shall persecute with a cold, unrelenting, steady cruelty, by every mode of confiscation, imprisonment, exile, and death, all its ministers; —when it shall generally shut up or pull down churches; when the few buildings which remain of this kind shall be opened only for the purpose of making a profane apotheosis of monsters, whose vices and crimes have no parallel amongst men...When, in the place of that religion of social benevolence, and of individual self-denial, in mockery of all religion, they institute impious, blasphemous, indecent theatric rites, in honour of their vitiated, perverted reason, and erect altars to the personification of their own corrupted and bloody republic;...when wearied out with incessant martyrdom, and the cries of a people hungering and thirsting for religion, they permit it, only as a tolerated evil—I call this atheism by establishment.

When to these establishments of regicide, of Jacobinism, and of atheism, you add the correspondent system of manners, no doubt can be left on the mind of a thinking man concerning their determined hostility to the human race.

From *The Works of the Right Honourable Edmund Burke* (London: Henry G. Bohn, 1856), 5: 206–208.

apotheosis = the elevation or exaltation of a person to the rank of a god; = the ideal example, epitome; quintessence

revolutionary France. The ideals of the Rights of Man and Citizen were highly exportable and applicable to the rest of Europe. In response, one government after another turned to repressive domestic policies.

Suppression of Reform in Britain

In Great Britain, William Pitt the Younger (1759–1806), the prime minister, who had unsuccessfully supported moderate reform of Parliament during the 1780s, turned against both reform and popular movements. The government suppressed the London Corresponding Society, founded in 1792 as a working-class reform group. In Birmingham, the government sponsored mob action to drive Joseph Priestley (1733–1804), a famous chemist and a radical political thinker, out of the country. In early 1793, Pitt secured parliamentary approval for acts suspending *habeas corpus* and making it possible to commit treason in writing. With less success, Pitt attempted to curb freedom of the press. All political groups who dared oppose the government faced being associated with sedition.

The End of Enlightened Absolutism in Eastern Europe

In eastern Europe, the revolution brought an end to enlightened absolutism. The aristocratic resistance to the reforms of Joseph II in the Habsburg lands led his brother, Leopold II, to come to terms with the landowners. Leopold's successor, Francis II (r. 1792–1835), became a major leader of the counterrevolution. In Prussia, Frederick William II (r. 1786–1797), the nephew of Frederick the Great, looked to the leaders of the Lutheran church and the aristocracy to discourage any potential popular uprisings, such as those of the downtrodden Silesian weavers. In Russia, Catherine the Great burned the works of her one-time friend Voltaire. She also exiled Alexander Radishchev (1749–1802) to Siberia for publishing his *Journey from Saint Petersburg to Moscow*, a work critical of Russian social conditions. (See the document "Alexander Radishchev Attacks Russian Censorship" in Chapter 18.)

In 1793 and 1795, the eastern powers once again combined against Poland. In that unhappy land, aristocratic reformers had finally achieved the abolition of the *liberum veto* and had organized a new constitutional monarchy in 1791. Russia and Prussia, which already had designs on Polish territory, saw or pretended to see a threat of revolution in the new Polish constitution. In 1793, they annexed large sections of the country. In 1795, Austria joined the two other powers in a final partition that removed Poland from the map of Europe until after World War I. The governments of eastern Europe had used the widely shared fear of further revolutionary disorder to justify old-fashioned eighteenth-century aggression.

War with Europe

In a paradoxical fashion, the very success of the revolution in France brought a rapid close to reform movements in the rest of Europe. The French invasion of the Austrian Netherlands and the revolutionary reorganization of that territory roused the rest of Europe to the point of active hostility. In November 1792, the Convention declared that it would aid all peoples who wished to cast off the burdens of aristocratic and monarchical oppression. The Convention had also proclaimed the Scheldt River in the Netherlands open to the commerce of all nations and thus had violated a treaty that Great Britain had made with Austria and Holland. The British were on the point of declaring war on France over this issue when the Convention issued its own declaration of hostilities in February 1793.

By April 1793, when the Mountain began to direct the French government, the nation was at war with Austria, Prussia, Great Britain, Spain, Sardinia, and Holland. The governments of those nations, allied in what is known as the First Coalition, were attempting to protect their social structures, political systems, and economic interests against the aggression of the revolution.

The Reign of Terror

The outbreak of war in the winter and spring of 1793 brought new, radical political actions within France. The government mobilized both itself and the nation for conflict. Throughout the nation, there was the sense that a new kind of war had erupted. In this war the major issue was not protection of national borders as such, but rather the defense of the bold new republican political and social order that had emerged during the past four years. The French people understood that the achievements of the revolution were in danger. To protect those achievements the government took extraordinary actions that touched almost every aspect of national life. (See "The Paris Jacobin Club Alerts the Nation to Internal Enemies of the Revolution.")

The Paris Jacobin Club Alerts the Nation to Internal Enemies of the Revolution

By early 1793, the revolutionary groups in Paris stood sharply divided amongst themselves. The Girondists (also known as Brissotins), who had led the nation into war, faced military reversals. General Dumouriez, a former revolutionary commander, had changed sides and was leading an army against France. At this point, on April 5, the radical Jacobin Club of Paris sent a circular to its provincial clubs, painting a dire picture of the fate of the revolution. While Dumouriez was marching against Paris, they accused members of the government and its administrators of conspiring to betray the revolution. The circular suggested that some people were cooperating with England in the war against France. The Jacobins also portrayed as counterrevolutionaries all those political figures who had opposed the execution of Louis XVI. The Paris Jacobins then called on their allies in the provinces to defend the revolution and to take vengeance against its internal enemies. The distortion of the motives of political enemies, the appeal to a possible reversal of the revolution, and the accusations of internal conspiracy served to justify the demand for justice against enemies of the revolution. The accusations embodied in this circular and the fears it sought to arouse represented the kind of thinking that informed the suspension of legal rights and due process associated with the Reign of Terror.

❖ *How did the Jacobins use the war to call for actions against their own domestic political enemies? What real and imagined forces did they see threatening the revolution? How did this circular constitute a smear campaign by one group of revolutionaries against other groups? What actions did the Jacobins seek?*

Friends, we are betrayed! To arms! To arms! The terrible hour is at hand when the defenders of the *Patrie* must vanquish or bury themselves under the bloody ruins of the Republic. Frenchmen, never was your liberty in such great peril! At last our enemies have put the finishing touch to their foul perfidy, and to complete it their accomplice Dumouriez is marching on Paris....

But Brothers, not all your dangers are to be found there!...You must be convinced of a grievous truth! Your greatest enemies are in your midst, they direct your operations. O Vengeance !!!....

Yes, brothers and friends, yes, it is in the Senate that parricidal hands tear at your vitals! Yes, the counter-revolution is in the Government..., in the National Convention! It is there, at the center of your security and your hope, that criminal delegates hold the threads of the web that they have woven with the horde of despots who come to butcher us!...It is there that a sacrilegious cabal is directed by the English court...and others....

Let us rise! Yes, let us rise! Let us arrest all the enemies of our revolution, and all suspected persons. Let us exterminate, without pity, all conspirators, unless we wish to be exterminated ourselves....

Let the departments, the districts, the municipalities, and all the popular societies unite and concur in protesting to the Convention, by dispatching thereto a veritable rain of petitions manifesting the formal wish for the immediate recall of all unfaithful members who have betrayed their duty by not wishing the death of the tyrant, and, above all, against those who have led astray so many of their colleagues. Such delegates are traitors, royalists, or fatuous men. The Republic condemns the friends of kings!...

Let us all unite equally to demand that the thunder of indictments be loosed against generals who are traitors to the Republic, against prevaricating ministers, against postal administrators, and against all unfaithful agents of the government. Therein lies our most salutary means of defence; but let us repel the traitors and tyrants.

The center of their conspiracy is here: it is in Paris that our perfidious enemies wish to consummate their crime. Paris, the cradle, the bulwark of liberty, is, without doubt, the place where they have sworn to annihilate the holy cause of humanity under the corpses of patriots.

From *A Documentary Survey of the French Revolution* by John Hall Stewart, © 1951. Reprinted by permission of Prentice-Hall, Inc., Upper Saddle River, NJ 07458.

cabal = secret plotters as against a gov. or a person in authority

The Republic Defended

To mobilize for war, the revolutionary government organized a collective executive in the form of powerful committees. These in turn sought to organize all French national life on a wartime footing. The result was an immense military effort dedicated to both the protection and the advancement of revolutionary ideals. Ironically, this war effort brought the suppression of many liberties within France itself and led ultimately to a destructive search for internal enemies of the revolution.

THE COMMITTEE OF PUBLIC SAFETY In April 1793, the Convention established a Committee of General Security and a Committee of Public Safety to carry out the executive duties of the government. The latter committee became more important and eventually enjoyed almost dictatorial power. The most prominent leaders of the Committee of Public Safety were Jaques Danton (1759–1794), who had provided heroic leadership in September 1792; Maximilien Robespierre (1758–1794), who became for a time the single most powerful member of the committee; and Lazare Carnot (1753–1823), who was in charge of the military. All of these men and the other figures on the committee were strong republicans who had opposed the weak policies of the Girondists. They conceived of their task as saving the revolution from mortal enemies at home and abroad. They enjoyed a working political relationship with the *sans-culottes* of Paris, but this was an alliance of expediency on the part of the committee.

THE *LEVÉE EN MASSE* The major problem for the Convention was to wage the war and at the same time to secure domestic support for the effort. In early June 1793, the Parisian *sans-culottes* invaded the Convention and successfully demanded the expulsion of the Girondist members. That action further radicalized the Convention and gave the Mountain complete control. On June 22, the Convention approved a fully democratic constitution, but delayed its implementation until the conclusion of the war. In point of fact, it was never implemented. On August 23, Carnot began a mobilization for victory by issuing a *levée en masse*, a military requisition on the entire population, conscripting males into the army and directing economic production to military purposes. On September 17, a ceiling on prices was established in accord with *sans-culotte* demands. During these same months, the armies of the revolution also successfully crushed many of the counterrevolutionary disturbances in the provinces.

Never before had Europe seen a nation organized in this way, nor one defended by a citizen army. Other events within France astounded Europeans even more. The Reign of Terror had begun. Those months of quasi-judicial executions and murders stretching from the autumn of 1793 to the midsummer of 1794 are probably the most famous or infamous period of the revolution. They can be understood only in the context of the war on one hand and the revolutionary expectations of the Convention and the *sans-culottes* on the other.

The "Republic of Virtue"

The presence of armies closing in on the nation made it easy to dispense with legal due process. The people who sat in the Convention and composed the Committee of Public Safety, however, did not see their actions simply in terms of expediency made necessary by war. They also believed they had created something new in world history, a "republic of virtue." In this republic, civic virtue would flourish in place of aristocratic and monarchical corruption. The republic of virtue manifested itself in many ways: in the renaming of streets from the egalitarian vocabulary of the revolution; in republican dress copied from that of the *sans-culottes* or the Roman Republic; in the absence of powdered wigs; in the suppression of plays that were insufficiently republican; and in a general attack against crimes, such as prostitution, that were supposedly characteristic of aristocratic society.

THE SOCIETY OF REVOLUTIONARY REPUBLICAN WOMEN Revolutionary women established their own distinct institutions during these months. In May 1793, Pauline Léon and Claire Lacombe founded the Society of Revolutionary Republican Women. Their purpose was to fight the internal enemies of the revolution. They saw themselves as militant citizens. Initially, the Jacobin leaders welcomed the organization. Its members and other women filled the galleries of the Convention to hear the debates and cheer their favorite speakers. The Society became increasingly radical, however. Its members sought stricter controls on the price of food and other commodities, worked to ferret out food hoarders, and brawled with working market women thought to be insufficiently revolutionary. The women of the Society also demanded the right to wear the revolutionary cockade usually worn only by male citizens. By October 1793, the Jacobins in the Convention had begun to fear the turmoil the Society was causing and banned all women's clubs and societies. The debates over these decrees show that the Jacobins believed that the Society opposed many of their economic policies, but the deputies used the Rousseauian language of separate spheres for men and women to justify their exclusion of women from active political life.

There were other examples of repression of women in 1793. Olympe de Gouges, author of the *Declaration of the Rights of Woman*, opposed the Terror and accused certain Jacobins of corruption. She was tried and guillotined in November 1793. The same year, women were formally excluded from serving in the French army. They were also excluded from the galleries of the Convention. In a very real sense, the exclusion of women from public political life was a part of the establishment of the Jacobin republic of virtue, because in such a republic men would be active citizens in the military and political sphere and women would be active in the domestic sphere.

DE-CHRISTIANIZATION The most dramatic departure of the republic of virtue, and one that illustrates the imposition of political values that would justify the Terror, was an attempt by the Convention to de-Christianize France. In November 1793, the Convention proclaimed a new calendar dating from the first day of the French Republic. There were twelve months of thirty days each, with names associated with the seasons and climate. Every tenth day, rather than every seventh, was a holiday. Many of the most important events of the next few years became known by their dates on the revolutionary calendar.[6] In November 1793, the Convention decreed the Cathedral of Notre Dame to be a "Temple of Reason." The legislature then sent trusted members, known as deputies on mission, into the provinces to enforce de-Christianization by closing churches, persecuting clergy and believers, and occasionally forcing priests to marry. This religious policy roused much opposition and deeply separated the French provinces from the revolutionary government in Paris.

ROBESPIERRE During the crucial months of late 1793 and early 1794, the person who emerged as the chief figure on the Committee of Public Safety

[6]From summer to spring, the months of the revolutionary calendar were *Messidor, Thermidor, Fructidor, Vendémiaire, Brumaire, Frimaire, Nivose, Pluviose, Ventose, Germinal, Floreal,* and *Prairial.*

Maximilien Robespierre (1785–1794) emerged as the most powerful revolutionary figure in 1793 and 1794, dominating the Committee of Public Safety. He considered the Terror essential for the success of the revolution. Giraudon/Art Resource, NY

was Robespierre. This complex Frenchman has remained controversial to the present day. He was utterly selfless and from the earliest days of the revolution had favored a republic. The Jacobin Club provided his primary forum and base of power. A shrewd and sensitive politician, Robespierre had opposed the war in 1792 because he feared it might aid the monarchy. He depended largely on the support of the *sans-culottes* of Paris, but he continued to dress as he had before the revolution and opposed de-Christianization as a political blunder. For him, the republic of virtue meant wholehearted support of republican government and the renunciation of selfish gains from political life. He once told the Convention:

If the mainspring of popular government in peacetime is virtue, amid revolution it is at the same time virtue and terror: virtue, without which terror is fatal; terror, without which virtue is impotent. Terror is nothing but prompt, severe, inflexible justice; it is therefore an emanation of virtue.[7]

[7]Quoted in Richard T. Bienvenu, *The Ninth of Thermidor: The Fall of Robespierre* (New York: Oxford University Press, 1968), p. 38.

Robespierre and those who supported his policies were among the first of a succession of secular ideologues of the left and the right who, in the name of humanity, would bring so much suffering to Europe in the following two centuries.

Progress of the Terror

The Reign of Terror manifested itself through a series of revolutionary tribunals established by the Convention during the summer of 1793. The mandate of these tribunals was to try the enemies of the republic, but the definition of "enemy" was uncertain and shifted as the months passed. It included those who might aid other European powers, those who endangered republican virtue, and, finally, good republicans who opposed the policies of the dominant faction of the government. In a very real sense, the Terror of the revolutionary tribunals systematized and channeled the popular resentment that had manifested itself in the September Massacres of 1792.

The first victims of the Terror were Marie Antoinette, other members of the royal family, and some aristocrats, who were executed in October 1793. They

On the way to her execution in 1793, Marie Antoinette was sketched from life by Jacques-Louis David as she passed his window. Jacques-Louis David, *Marie-Antoinette Taken to Her Execution*. Drawing. Bibliotheque Nationale, Paris, France. Giraudon/Art Resource, NY

were followed by certain Girondist politicians who had been prominent in the Legislative Assembly. These executions took place in the same weeks that the Convention had moved against the Society of Revolutionary Republican Women, whom it had also seen as endangering Jacobin control.

By the early months of 1794, the Terror had moved to the provinces, where the deputies on mission presided over the summary execution of thousands of people who had allegedly supported internal opposition to the revolution. One of the most infamous incidents occurred in Nantes, where several hundred people were simply tied to rafts and drowned in the river. The victims of the Terror were now coming from every social class, including the *sans-culottes*.

REVOLUTIONARIES TURN AGAINST THEMSELVES In Paris during the late winter of 1794, Robespierre began to orchestrate the Terror against republican political figures of the left and right. On March 24, he secured the execution of certain extreme *sans-culottes* leaders known as the *enragés*. They had wanted further measures regulating prices, securing social equality, and pressing de-Christianization. Robespierre then turned against more conservative republicans, including Danton. They were accused of being insufficiently militant on the war, profiting monetarily from the revolution, and rejecting any link between politics and moral virtue. Danton was executed during the first week in April. In this fashion, Robespierre exterminated the leadership from both groups that might have threatened his position.

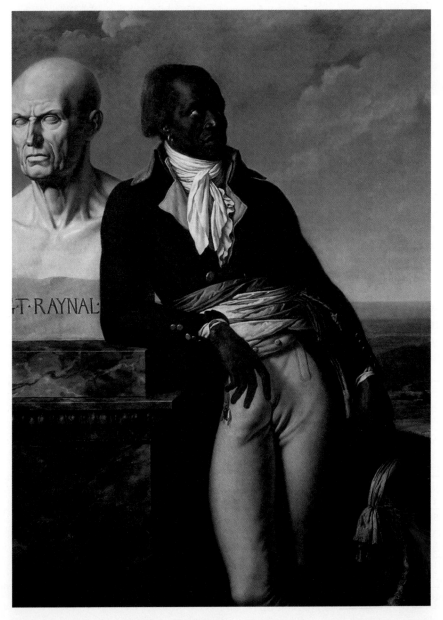

Jean-Baptiste Belley was a Senegalese African born in Gorée in 1747 and later taken to Saint-Domingue as a slave. In February, 1794, he was seated in the Convention along with two other people as representatives of citizens of Saint-Domingue. He had joined the French army there to resist counter-revolutionary forces, and once the representatives from Saint Domingue were seated, the Convention abolished slavery in the French colonies. Belley remained active in French revolutionary politics at least as late as 1797. He was one of several people of color from the Caribbean who served in either the Convention or the institutions of the Directory. Girodet de Roussy-Trioson Anne-Louis (1767–1824). *Portrait de Jean-Baptiste Belley*, depute de Saint Dominique a la Convention (1747–1805). Chateaux de Versailles et de Tranon. © Photo RMN

The Festival of the Supreme Being, which took place in June 1794, inaugurated Robespierre's new civic religion. Its climax occurred when a statue of Atheism was burned and another statue of Wisdom rose from the ashes. Pierre-Antoine Demachy, *Festival of the Supreme Being at the Champ de Mars on June 8, 1794.* Musée de la Ville de Paris, Musée Carnavalet, Paris, France. Giraudon/Art Resource, NY

Finally, on June 10, he secured passage of the Law of 22 *Prairial*, which permitted the revolutionary tribunal to convict suspects without hearing substantial evidence. The number of executions was growing steadily.

FALL OF ROBESPIERRE   In May 1794, at the height of his power, Robespierre, considering the worship of "Reason" too abstract for most citizens, abolished it and established the "Cult of the Supreme Being." This deistic cult reflected Rousseau's vision of a civic religion that would induce morality among citizens. Robespierre, however, did not long preside over his new religion. (See "The Convention Establishes the Worship of the Supreme Being.")

On July 26, Robespierre made an ill-tempered speech in the Convention, declaring that other leaders of the government were conspiring against himself and the revolution. Usually, such accusations against unnamed persons had preceded his earlier attacks. On July 27—the Ninth of *Thermidor*—members of the Convention, by prearrangement, shouted him down when he rose to make another speech. That night Robespierre was arrested, and the next

day he was executed. The revolutionary *sans-culottes* of Paris would not save him because he had deprived them of their chief leaders. The other Jacobins turned against him because, after Danton's death, they feared becoming the next victims. Robespierre had destroyed rivals for leadership without creating supporters for himself. In that regard, he was the selfless creator of his own destruction.

The fall of Robespierre might simply have been one more shift in the turbulent politics of the revolution. Instincts of self-preservation rather than major policy differences motivated those who brought about his demise. They had generally supported the Terror and the executions. Yet within a short time, the Reign of Terror, which ultimately claimed more than 25,000 victims, came to a close. The largest number of executions had involved peasants and *sans-culottes* who had joined rebellions against the revolutionary government. By the late summer of 1794, those provincial uprisings had been crushed, and the war against foreign enemies was also going well. These factors, combined with the feeling in Paris that the revolution had consumed enough of its own children, brought the Terror to an end.

The Convention Establishes the Worship of the Supreme Being

On May 7, 1794, the Convention passed an extraordinary piece of revolutionary legislation. It established the worship of the Supreme Being as a state cult. Although the law drew on the religious ideas of deism, the point of the legislation was to provide a religious basis for the new secular French state. The reader should pay particular attention to Article 7, which outlines the political and civic values that the Cult of the Supreme Being was supposed to nurture.

❖ *How does this declaration reflect the ideas of the Enlightenment? Why has it been seen as establishing a civil religion? What personal and social values was this religion supposed to nurture?*

1. The French people recognize the existence of the Supreme Being and the immortality of the soul.

2. They recognize that the worship worthy of the Supreme Being is the observance of the duties of man.

3. They place in the forefront of such duties detestation of bad faith and tyranny, punishment of tyrants and traitors, succoring of unfortunates, respect of weak persons, defence of the oppressed, doing to others all the good that one can, and being just towards everyone.

4. Festivals shall be instituted to remind man of the concept of the Divinity and of the dignity of his being.

5. They shall take their names from the glorious events of our Revolution, or from the virtues most dear and most useful to man, or from the greatest benefits of nature....

7. On the days of *décade* [the name given to a particular day in each month of the revolutionary calendar] it shall celebrate the following festivals:

To the Supreme Being and to nature; to the human race; to the French people; to the benefactors of humanity; to the martyrs of liberty; to liberty and equality; to the Republic; to the liberty of the world; to the love of the *Patrie* [Fatherland]; to the hatred of tyrants and traitors; to truth; to justice; to modesty; to glory and immortality; to friendship; to frugality; to courage; to good faith; to heroism; to disinterestedness; to stoicism; to love; to conjugal love; to paternal love; to maternal tenderness; to filial piety; to infancy; to youth; to manhood; to old age; to misfortune; to agriculture; to industry; to our forefathers; to posterity; to happiness.

From *A Documentary Survey of the French Revolution* by John Hall Stewart, © 1951. Reprinted by permission of Prentice-Hall, Inc., Upper Saddle River, NJ 07458.

The Thermidorian Reaction

This tempering of the revolution, called the Thermidorian Reaction, began in July 1794. It consisted of the destruction of the machinery of terror and the institution of a new constitutional regime. It was the result of a widespread feeling that the revolution had become too radical. In particular, it displayed a weariness of the Terror and a fear that the *sans-culottes* were exerting far too much political influence.

The End of the Terror

The influence of generally wealthy middle-class and professional people soon replaced that of the *sans-culottes*. Within days and weeks of Robespierre's execution, the Convention allowed the Girondists who had been in prison or hiding to return to their seats. There was a general amnesty for political prisoners. The Convention restructured the Committee of Public Safety, giving it much less power, and also repealed the notorious Law of 22 *Prairial*. Some, though by no means all, of the people responsible for the Terror were removed from public life. Leaders of the Paris Commune and certain deputies on mission were executed. The Paris Commune itself was outlawed. The Paris Jacobin Club was closed, and Jacobin clubs in the provinces were forbidden to correspond with each other.

The executions of former terrorists marked the beginning of "the white terror." Throughout the country, people who had been involved in the Reign

The closing of the Jacobin Club in November 1794 was a major event in the Thermidorean Reaction that began with the fall of Robespierre. Roger-Viollet, © Collection Violett/Liaison Agency, Inc.

of Terror were attacked and often murdered. Jacobins were executed with little more due process than they had extended to their victims a few months earlier. The Convention itself approved some of these trials. In other cases, gangs of youths who had aristocratic connections or who had avoided serving in the army roamed the streets, beating known Jacobins. In Lyons, Toulon, and Marseilles, these "bands of Jesus" dragged suspected terrorists from prisons and murdered them much as alleged royalists had been murdered during the September Massacres of 1792.

The republic of virtue gave way, if not to one of vice, at least to one of frivolous pleasures. The dress of the *sans-culottes* and the Roman Republic disappeared among the middle class and the aristocracy. New plays appeared in the theaters, and prostitutes again roamed the streets of Paris. Families of victims of the Reign of Terror gave parties in which they appeared with shaved necks, like the victims of the guillotine, and with

red ribbons tied about them. Although the Convention continued to favor the Cult of the Supreme Being, it allowed Catholic services to be held. Many refractory priests returned to the country. One of the unanticipated results of the Thermidorian Reaction was a genuine revival of Catholic worship.

The Thermidorian Reaction also saw the repeal of legislation that had been passed in 1792 making divorce more equitable for women. As this suggests, the reaction did not result in any extension of women's rights or improvement in women's education. The Thermidorians and their successors had seen enough attempts at political and social change. They sought to return family life to its status before the outbreak of the revolution. Political authorities and the church articulated a firm determination to reestablish separate spheres for men and women and to reinforce traditional gender roles. As a result, Frenchwomen may have had somewhat less freedom after 1795 than before 1789.

Establishment of the Directory

The Thermidorian Reaction involved further political reconstruction. The fully democratic constitution of 1793, which had never gone into effect, was abandoned. In its place, the Convention issued the Constitution of the Year III, which reflected the Thermidorian determination to reject both constitutional monarchy and democracy. The new document provided for a legislature of two houses. Members of the upper body, or Council of Elders, were to be men over forty years of age who were either husbands or widowers. The lower Council of Five Hundred was to consist of men of at least thirty who were either married or single. The executive body was to be a five-person Directory chosen by the Elders from a list submitted by the Council of Five Hundred. Property qualifications limited the franchise, except for soldiers, who, though without property, were permitted to vote.

The term *Thermidor* has come to be associated with political reaction. If the French Revolution had originated in political conflicts characteristic of the eighteenth century, by 1795 it had become something very different. A political structure and a society based on rank and birth had given way to a political system based on civic equality and social status based on property ownership. People who had never been allowed direct, formal access to political power had, to different degrees, been granted it. Their entrance into political life had given rise to questions of property distribution and economic regulations that could not again be ignored. Representation had been established as a principle of politics. Henceforth, the question before France and eventually before all of Europe would be which new groups would be permitted representation. In the *levée en masse*, the French had demonstrated to Europe the power of the secular ideal of nationhood.

The post-Thermidorian course of the French Revolution did not void these stunning changes in the political and social contours of Europe. What triumphed in the Constitution of the Year III was the revolution of the holders of property. For this reason the French Revolution has often been considered a victory of the bourgeoisie, or middle class. The property that won the day, however, was not industrial wealth, but the wealth stemming from commerce, the professions, and land. The largest new propertied class to emerge from the revolutionary turmoil was the peasantry, who, as a result of the destruction of aristocratic privileges, now owned their land.

And unlike peasants liberated from traditional landholding in other parts of Europe during the next century, French peasants had to pay no monetary compensation.

Removal of the *Sans-culottes* from Political Life

The most decisively reactionary element in the Thermidorian Reaction and the new constitution was the removal of the *sans-culottes* from political life. With the war effort succeeding, the Convention severed its ties with the *sans-culottes*. True to their belief in an unregulated economy, the Thermidorians repealed the ceiling on prices. As a result, the winter of 1794–1795 brought the worst food shortages of the period. There were many food riots, which the Convention put down with force to prove that the era of the *sans-culottes journées* had come to a close. Royalist agents, who aimed to restore the monarchy, tried to take advantage of their discontent. On October 5, 1795–13 *Vendémiaire*—the sections of Paris led by the royalists rose up against the Convention. The government turned the artillery against the royalist rebels. A general named Napoleon Bonaparte (1769–1821) commanded the cannon, and with a "whiff of grapeshot" he dispersed the crowd.

By the Treaty of Basel in March 1795, the Convention concluded peace with Prussia and Spain. The legislators, however, feared a resurgence of both radical democrats and royalists in the upcoming elections for the Council of Five Hundred. Consequently, the Convention ruled that at least two-thirds of the new legislature must have been members of the older body. The Thermidorians did not even trust the property owners as voters.

The newly established Directory again faced social unrest. In Paris, Gracchus Babeuf (1760–1797) led the Conspiracy of Equals. He and his followers called for more radical democracy and for more equality of property. They declared at one point, "The aim of the French Revolution is to destroy inequality and to re-establish the general welfare.... The Revolution is not complete, because the rich monopolize all the property and govern exclusively, while the poor toil like slaves, languish in misery, and count for nothing in the *state*."[8] In a sense, they were correct. The Directory fully intended to resist any further social changes in France that

---

[8]Quoted in John Hall Stewart, *A Documentary Survey of the French Revolution* (New York: Macmillan, 1966), pp. 656–657.

The French Revolution

1789

May 5	The Estates General opens at Versailles
June 17	The Third Estate declares itself the National Assembly
June 20	The National Assembly takes the Tennis Court Oath
July 14	Fall of the Bastille in the city of Paris
Late July	The Great Fear spreads in the countryside
August 4	The nobles surrender their feudal rights at a meeting of the National Constituent Assembly
August 27	Declaration of the Rights of Man and Citizen
October 5–6	Parisian women march to Versailles and force Louis XVI and his family to return to Paris

1790

July 12	Civil Constitution of the Clergy adopted
July 14	A new political constitution is accepted by the king

1791

June 14	Chapelier Law
June 20–24	Louis XVI and his family attempt to flee France and are stopped at Varennes
August 27	The Declaration of Pillnitz
October 1	The Legislative Assembly meets

1792

April 20	France declares war on Austria
August 10	The Tuileries palace is stormed, and Louis XVI takes refuge with the Legislative Assembly
September 2–7	The September Massacres
September 20	France wins the Battle of Valmy
September 21	The Convention meets, and the monarchy is abolished

1793

January 21	King Louis XVI is executed
February 1	France declares war on Great Britain
March	Counterrevolution breaks out in the Vendée
April	The Committee of Public Safety is formed
June 22	The Constitution of 1793 is adopted, but not implemented
July	Robespierre enters the Committee of Public Safety
August 23	*Levée en masse* proclaimed
September 17	Maximum prices set on food and other commodities
October 16	Queen Marie Antoinette is executed
October 30	Women's societies and clubs banned
November 10	The Cult of Reason is proclaimed; the revolutionary calendar, beginning on September 22, 1792, is adopted

1794

March 24	Execution of the leaders of the *sans-culottes* known as the *enragés*
April 6	Execution of Danton
May 7	Cult of the Supreme Being proclaimed
June 8	Robespierre leads the celebration of the Festival of the Supreme Being
June 10	The Law of 22 *Prairial* is adopted
July 27	The Ninth of *Thermidor* and the fall of Robespierre
July 28	Robespierre is executed

1795

August 22	The Constitution of the Year III is adopted, establishing the Directory

might endanger property. Babeuf was arrested, tried, and executed. This minor plot became famous many decades later, when European socialists attempted to find their historical roots in the French Revolution.

The suppression of the *sans-culottes*, the narrow franchise of the constitution, the rule of the two-thirds, and the Catholic royalist revival presented the Directory with problems that it never succeeded in overcoming. It lacked any broad base of meaningful political support. It particularly required active loyalty because France remained at war with Austria and Great Britain. Consequently, the Directory came to depend on the power of the army, rather than on constitutional processes, for governing the country. All the soldiers could vote. Moreover, within the army, created and sustained by the revolution, were officers who were eager for power and ambitious for political conquest. The results of the instability of the Directory and the growing role of the army held profound consequences not only for France but for the entire Western world.

In Perspective

The French Revolution is the central political event of modern European history. It unleashed political and social forces that shaped events in Europe and much of the rest of the world for the next two centuries. The revolution began with a clash between the monarchy and the nobility. Once the Estates General gathered, however, discontent could not be contained within the traditional boundaries of eighteenth-century political life. The Third Estate, in all of its diversity, demanded real influence in government. Initially, that meant the participation of middle-class members of the Estates General, but quite soon the people of Paris and the peasants of the countryside made their demands known. Thereafter, popular nationalism exerted itself on French political life and the destiny of Europe.

Revolutionary legislation and popular uprisings in Paris, the countryside, and other cities transformed the social as well as the political life of the nation. Nobles surrendered traditional social privileges. The church saw its property confiscated and its operations brought under state control. For a time, there was an attempt to de-Christianize the nation. Vast amounts of landed property changed hands, and France became a nation of peasant landowners. Urban workers lost much of the protection they had enjoyed under the guilds and became much more subject to the forces of the marketplace.

Great violence accompanied many of the revolutionary changes. The Reign of Terror took the lives of thousands. France also found itself at war with virtually all of the rest of Europe. Resentment, fear, and a new desire for stability brought the Terror to an end. That desire for stability, combined with a determination to defeat the foreign enemies of the revolution and to carry it abroad, would in turn work to the advantage of the army. Eventually, Napoleon Bonaparte would claim leadership in the name of stability and national glory.

REVIEW QUESTIONS

1. It has been said that France was a rich nation with an impoverished government. Explain this statement. How did the financial weaknesses of the French monarchy lay the foundations of the revolution of 1789?

2. Discuss the role of Louis in the French Revolution. What were some of Louis XVI's most serious mistakes? Had Louis been a more able ruler, could the French Revolution have been avoided? Might a constitutional monarchy have succeeded? Or did the revolution ultimately have little to do with the competence of the monarch?

3. How was the Estates General transformed into the National Assembly? How does the Declaration of the Rights of Man and Citizen reflect the social and political values of the eighteenth-century Enlightenment? What were the chief ways in which France and its government were reorganized in the early years of the revolution? Why has the Civil Constitution of the Clergy been called the greatest blunder of the National Assembly?

4. Why were some political factions dissatisfied with the constitutional settlement of 1791? What was the revolution of 1792 and why did it occur? Who were the *sans-culottes* and how did they become a factor in the politics of the period? How influential were they during the Terror in particular? Why did the *sans-culottes* and the Jacobins cooperate at first? Why did that cooperation end?

5. Why did France go to war with Austria in 1792? What were the benefits and drawbacks for France of fighting an external war while in the midst of a domestic political revolution? What were the causes of the Terror? How did the rest of Europe react to the French Revolution and the Terror?

6. A motto of the French Revolution was "equality, liberty and fraternity." How did the revolution both support and violate this motto? Did French women benefit from the revolution? Did French peasants benefit from it?

SUGGESTED READINGS

K. M. BAKER AND C. LUCAS (EDS.), *The French Revolution and the Creation of Modern Political Culture*, 3 vols. (1987). A splendid collection of important original articles on all aspects of politics during the revolution.

K. M. BAKER, *Inventing the French Revolution: Essays on French Political Culture in the Eighteenth Century* (1990). Influential essays on political thought before and during the revolution.

T. C. W. BLANNING (ED.), *The Rise and Fall of the French Revolution* (1996). A wide-ranging collection of essays illustrating the recent interpretive debates.

C. BLUM, *Rousseau and the Republic of Virtue: The Language of Politics in the French Revolution* (1986). An exploration of the role of Rousseau's political ideals in the debates of the French Revolution.

R. COBB, *The People's Armies* (1987). The best treatment in English of the revolutionary army.

K. EPSTEIN, *The Genesis of German Conservatism* (1966). A major study of antiliberal forces in Germany before and during the revolution.

F. FEHÉR, *The French Revolution and the Birth of Modernity* (1990). A wide-ranging collection of essays on political and cultural facets of the revolution.

A. FORREST, *The French Revolution and the Poor* (1981). A study that expands consideration of the revolution beyond the standard social boundaries.

F. FURET, *Revolutionary France, 1770–1880* (1988). An important survey by a historian who argues the revolution must be seen in the perspective of an entire century.

J. GODECHOT, *The Taking of the Bastille, July 14, 1789* (1970). Places the fall of the Bastille in the context of crowd behavior in the eighteenth century.

J. GODECHOT, *The Counter-Revolution: Doctrine and Action, 1789–1803* (1971). An examination of opposition to the revolution.

C. HESSE, *Publishing and Cultural Politics in Revolutionary Paris* (1991). Probes the world of print culture during the French Revolution.

P. HIGONNET, *Goodness beyond Virtue: Jacobins during the French Revolution* (1998). An outstanding work that clearly relates political values to political actions.

E. KENNEDY, *A Cultural History of the French Revolution* (1989). An important examination of the role of the arts, schools, clubs, and intellectual institutions.

M. KENNEDY, *The Jacobin Clubs in the French Revolution: The First Years* (1982). A careful scrutiny of the organizations chiefly responsible for the radicalizing of the revolution.

M. KENNEDY, *The Jacobin Clubs in the French Revolution: The Middle Years* (1988). A continuation of the previously listed study.

G. LEFEBVRE, *The French Revolution*, 2 vols. (1962–1964). The leading study of the scholar noted for his subtle class interpretation of the revolution.

D. G. LEVY, H. B. APPLEWHITE, AND M. D. JOHNSON (EDS. AND TRANS.), *Women in Revolutionary Paris, 1789–1795* (1979). A remarkable collection of documents on the subject.

G. LEWIS AND C. LUCAS (EDS.), *Beyond the Terror: Essays in French Regional and Social History, 1794–1815* (1983). Explorations of the counter-terror that followed in the wake of the Thermidorian Reaction.

H.-J. LÜSEBRINK AND R. REICHARDT, *The Bastille: A History of a Symbol of Despotism and Freedom*, N. Schürer, trans. (1997). A fascinating treatment of the Bastille as a political symbol in French and European political life.

T. W. MARGADANT, *Urban Rivalries in the French Revolution* (1992). Examines the political tensions between the central government in Paris and the cities and towns of the provinces.

S. E. MELZER AND L. W. RABINE (EDS.), *Rebel Daughters: Women and the French Revolution* (1992). A collection of essays exploring various aspects of the role and image of women in the French Revolution.

C. C. O'BRIEN, *The Great Melody: A Thematic Biography of Edmund Burke* (1992). The best recent biography.

M. OZOUF, *Festivals and the French Revolution* (1988). A pioneering study of the role of public festivals in the revolution.

R. R. PALMER, *Twelve Who Ruled: The Committee of Public Safety During the Terror* (1941). Classic analysis of the policies and problems of the committee.

R. R. PALMER, *The Age of Democratic Revolution: A Political History of Europe and America, 1760–1800*, 2 vols. (1959, 1964). An impressive survey of the political turmoil in the transatlantic world.

C. PROCTOR, *Women, Equality, and the French Revolution* (1990). An examination of how the ideas of the Enlightenment and the attitudes of revolutionaries affected the legal status of women.

W. J. SEWELL, JR., *A Rhetoric of Bourgeois Revolution: The Abbé Siéyès and What is the Third Estate* (1994). An important study of the political thought of Siéyès.

A. SOBOUL, *The Parisian* Sans-Culottes *and the French Revolution, 1793–94* (1964). Remains the best work on the subject.

B. S. STONE, *The French* Parlements *and the Crisis of the Old Regime* (1988). A study that considers the role of the aristocratic courts in bringing on the collapse of monarchical government.

D. G. SUTHERLAND, *France, 1789–1815: Revolution and Counterrevolution* (1986). A major synthesis based on recent scholarship in social history.

T. TACKETT, *Religion, Revolution, and Regional Culture in Eighteenth-Century France: The Ecclesiastical Oath of 1791* (1986). The most important study of this topic.

T. Tackett, *Becoming a Revolutionary: The Deputies of the French National Assembly and the Emergence of a Revolutionary Culture (1789–1790)* (1996). The best study of the early months of the revolution.

D. K. Van Kley, *The Religious Origins of the French Revolution: From Calvin to the Civil Constitution, 1560–1791* (1996). Examines the manner in which debates within French Catholicism influenced the coming of the revolution.

M. Walzer (Ed.), *Regicide and Revolution: Speeches at the Trial of Louis XVI* (1974). An important and exceedingly interesting collection of documents with a useful introduction.

Chapter 20

Napoleon Bonaparte used his military successes to consolidate his political leadership as First Consul and later as Emperor of France. In this heroic image, Jacques-Louis David portrays Napoleon as a force of nature conquering not only the armies of the enemies of France but also the Alps. On the rocks in the foreground his name follows those of Hannibal and Charlemagne, other great generals who had led armies over the Alps. Bildarchiv Preussischer Kulturbesitz

The Age of Napoleon and the Triumph of Romanticism

KEY TOPICS

- Napoleon's rise, his coronation as emperor, and his administrative reforms
- Napoleon's conquests, the creation of a French Empire, and Britain's enduring resistance
- The invasion of Russia and Napoleon's decline
- The reestablishment of a European order at the Congress of Vienna
- Romanticism and the reaction to the Enlightenment

By the late 1790s, there existed a general wish for stability in France, especially among property owners, who now included the peasants. The government of the Directory was not providing this stability. The one force that was able to take charge of the nation as a symbol of both order and popular national will was the army. The most politically astute of the army generals was Napoleon Bonaparte, who had been a radical during the early revo-

lution, a victorious general in Italy, and a supporter of the attempt to suppress revolutionary disturbances after Thermidor. *Furthermore, as a general, he was a leader in the French army, the institution seen most clearly to embody the popular values of the nation and the revolution.*

Once in power, Napoleon consolidated many of the achievements of the revolution. He also repudiated much of it by establishing an empire. Thereafter, his ambitions drew France into wars of conquest and liberation throughout the continent. For over a decade Europe was at war, with only brief periods of armed truce. In leading the French armies across the Continent, Napoleon spread many of the ideas and institutions of the revolution and overturned much of the old political and social order. He also provoked popular nationalism in opposition to his conquest. This new force and the great diplomatic alliances that arose against France eventually defeated Napoleon.

Throughout these Napoleonic years, new ideas and sensibilities, known by the term romanticism, grew across Europe. Many of the ideas had originated in the eighteenth century, but they flourished in the turmoil of the French Revolution and the Napoleonic Wars. The events and values of the revolution spurred the imagination of poets, painters, and philosophers. Some romantic ideas, such as romantic nationalism, supported the revolution; others, such as the emphasis on history and religion, opposed the values of the revolution.

The Rise of Napoleon Bonaparte

The chief danger to the Directory came from the royalists, who hoped to restore the Bourbon monarchy by legal means. Many of the *émigrés* had returned to France. Their plans for a restoration drew support from devout Catholics and from those citizens disgusted by the excesses of the revolution. Monarchy seemed to promise stability. The spring elections of 1797 replaced most incumbents with constitutional monarchists and their sympathizers, thus giving them a majority.

To preserve the republic and prevent a peaceful restoration of the Bourbons, the antimonarchist Directory staged a coup d'état on 18 *Fructidor* (September 4, 1797). They put their own supporters into the legislative seats won by their opponents. They then imposed censorship and exiled some of their enemies. At the request of the Directors,

Napoleon Bonaparte, the general in charge of the Italian campaign, had sent one of his subordinates to Paris to guarantee the success of the coup. In 1797, as in 1795, the army and Bonaparte had saved the day for the government installed in the wake of the Thermidorian Reaction.

Napoleon Bonaparte was born in 1769 to a poor family of lesser nobles at Ajaccio, Corsica. Because France had annexed Corsica in 1768, he went to French schools, pursued a military career, and in 1785 obtained a commission as a French artillery officer. He strongly favored the revolution and was a fiery Jacobin. In 1793, he played a leading role in recovering the port of Toulon from the British. As a reward for his service, he was appointed a brigadier general. His previous radical associations threatened his career during the Thermidorian Reaction, but his defense of the new regime on 13 *Vendémiaire* won him another promotion and a command in Italy.

Early Military Victories

By 1795, French arms and diplomacy had shattered the enemy coalition, but France's annexation of Belgium guaranteed continued fighting with Britain and Austria. The attack on Italy aimed at depriving Austria of the provinces of Lombardy and Venetia. In a series of lightning victories, Bonaparte crushed the Austrian and Sardinian armies. On his own initiative, and in many ways against the wishes of the government in Paris, he concluded the Treaty of Campo Formio in October 1797. The treaty took Austria out of the war and crowned Napoleon's campaign and independent policy with success. Before long, all of Italy and Switzerland had fallen under French domination.

In November 1797, the triumphant Bonaparte returned to Paris to be hailed as a hero and to confront France's only remaining enemy, Britain. He judged it impossible to cross the channel and invade England at that time. Instead, he chose to attack British interests through the eastern Mediterranean. He set out to capture Egypt from the Ottoman Empire. By this strategy, he hoped to drive the British fleet from the Mediterranean, cut off British communications with India, damage British trade, and threaten the British Empire.

Even though Napoleon overran Egypt, the invasion was a failure. Admiral Horatio Nelson (1758–1805) destroyed the French fleet at Abukir on August 1, 1798. Cut off from France, the French army could then neither accomplish anything of importance in the Near East nor get home. To make matters worse, the situation in Europe was deteriorating. The invasion of Egypt had alarmed Russia, which had its own ambitions in the Near East. The Russians, the Austrians, and the Ottomans soon joined Britain to form the Second Coalition. In 1799, the Russian and Austrian armies defeated the French in Italy and Switzerland and threatened to invade France.

The Constitution of the Year VIII

Economic troubles and the dangerous international situation eroded the already fragile support of the Directory. One of the Directors, the Abbé Siéyès, proposed a new constitution. The author of the pamphlet *What Is the Third Estate?* (1789) wanted to establish a vigorous executive body independent of the whims of electoral politics, a government based on the principle of "confidence from below, power from above." The change would require another coup d'état with military support. News of France's diplomatic misfortunes had reached Napoleon in Egypt. Without orders and leaving his doomed army behind, he returned to France in October 1799. Although some people thought that he deserved a court-martial for desertion, he received much popular acclaim. Soon he joined Siéyès. On 19 *Brumaire* (November 10, 1799), his troops drove out the legislators and ensured the success of the coup.

Siéyès appears to have thought that Napoleon could be used and then dismissed, but if so, he badly misjudged his man. The proposed constitution divided executive authority among three consuls. Bonaparte quickly pushed it aside, as he did Siéyès, and in December 1799, he issued the Constitution of the Year VIII. Behind a screen of universal male suffrage that suggested democratic principles, a complicated system of checks and balances that appealed to republican theory, and a Council of State that evoked memories of Louis XIV, the new constitution in fact established the rule of one man—the First Consul, Bonaparte. To find an appropriate historical analogy, one must go back to Caesar and Augustus and the earlier Greek tyrants. The career of Bonaparte, however, pointed forward to the dictators of the twentieth century. He was the first modern political figure to use the rhetoric of revolution and nationalism, to back it with military force, and to combine those elements into a mighty weapon of imperial expansion in the service of his own power and ambition.

The Consulate in France (1799–1804)

Establishing the Consulate in effect closed the revolution in France. The leading elements of the Third Estate—that is, officials, landowners, doctors, lawyers, and financiers—had achieved most of their goals by 1799. They had abolished hereditary privilege, and the careers thus opened to talent allowed them to achieve the wealth, status,

In this early nineteenth-century cartoon, England, personified by a caricature of Williams Pitt, and France, personified by a caricature of Napoleon, are carving out their areas of interest around the globe. Bildarchiv Preussischer Kulturbesitz

Napoleon Describes Conditions Leading to the Consulate

In late 1799 various political groups in France became convinced that the constitution that had established the Directory could not allow France to achieve military victory. They also feared domestic unrest and new outbreaks of the radicalism that had characterized the French Revolution during the mid-1790s. With the aid of such groups Napoleon Bonaparte seized power in Paris in November, 1799. Thereafter, under various political arrangements he governed France until 1814. He later gave his own version of the situation that brought him to power.

❖ *What are the factors that Napoleon outlines as having created a situation in which the government of France required change? In his narration how does he justify the use of military force? How does he portray himself as a savior of political order and liberty?*

On my return to Paris I found division among all authorities, and agreement upon only one point, namely, that the Constitution was half destroyed and was unable to save liberty.

All parties came to me, confided to me their designs, disclosed their secrets, and requested my support; I refused to be the man of a party.

The Council of Elders summoned me; I answered its appeal. A plan of general restoration had been devised by men whom the nation has been accustomed to regard as defenders of liberty, equality, and property; this plan required an examination, calm, free, exempt from all influence and all fear. Accordingly, the Council of Elders resolved upon the removal of the Legislative Body to Saint-Cloud; it gave me the responsibility of disposing the force necessary for its independence. I believed it my duty to my fellow citizens, to the soldiers perishing in our armies, to the national glory acquired at the cost of their blood, to accept the command....

I presented myself to the Council of Five Hundred, alone, unarmed, my head uncovered, just as the Elders had received and applauded me; I came to remind the majority of its wishes, and to assure it of its power.

The stilettos which menaced the deputies were instantly raised against their liberator; twenty assassins threw themselves upon me and aimed at my breast. The grenadiers of the Legislative Body whom I had left at the door of the hall ran forward, placed themselves between the assassins and myself. One of these brave grenadiers had his clothes pieced by a stiletto. They bore me out.

At the same moment cries of "Outlaw" were raised against the defender of the law. It was the fierce cry of assassins against the power destined to repress them.

They crowded around the president, uttering threats, arms in their hands; they commanded him to outlaw me. I was informed of this; I ordered him to be rescued from their fury, and six grenadiers of the Legislative Body secured him. Immediately afterwards some grenadiers of the Legislative Body charged into the hall and cleared it.

The factions, intimidated, dispersed and fled....

Frenchmen, you will doubtless recognize in this conduct the zeal of a soldier of liberty, a citizen devoted to the Republic. Conservative, tutelary, and liberal ideas have been restored to their rights through the dispersal of the rebels who oppressed the Councils....

From *A Documentary Survey of the French Revolution* by Stewart, John Hall, © 1951. Reprinted by permission of Prentice-Hall, Inc., Upper Saddle River, N.J.

and security for their property that they sought. The peasants were also satisfied. They had gained the land they had always wanted and had destroyed oppressive feudal privileges as well. The newly established dominant classes were profoundly conservative. They had little or no desire to share their new privileges with the lower social orders. Bonaparte seemed just the person to give them security. When he submitted his constitution to the voters in a plebiscite, they overwhelmingly approved it. (See "Napolean Describes Conditions Leading to the Consulate.")

Suppressing Foreign Enemies and Domestic Opposition

Bonaparte quickly justified the public's confidence by making peace with France's enemies. Russia had already quarreled with its allies and left the Second Coalition. A campaign in Italy brought another victory over Austria at Marengo in 1800. The Treaty of Luneville early in 1801 took Austria out of the war and confirmed the earlier settlement of Campo Formio. Britain was now alone and, in 1802, concluded the Treaty of Amiens, which brought peace to Europe.

Bonaparte also restored peace and order at home. He used generosity, flattery, and bribery to win over some of his enemies. He issued a general amnesty and employed in his own service persons from all political factions. He required only that they be loyal to him. Some of the highest offices were occupied by persons who had been extreme radicals during the Reign of Terror, others by persons who had fled the Terror and favored constitutional monarchy, and still others by former high officials of the old monarchical government.

On the other hand, Bonaparte was ruthless and efficient in suppressing opposition. He established a highly centralized administration in which prefects directly responsible to the central government in Paris managed all departments. He employed secret police. He stamped out once and for all the royalist rebellion in the west and made the rule of Paris effective in Brittany and the Vendée for the first time in many years.

Napoleon also used and invented opportunities to destroy his enemies. When a bomb plot on his life surfaced in 1804, the event provided an excuse to attack the Jacobins, though the bombing was the work of the royalists. Also in 1804, his forces violated the sovereignty of the German state of Baden to seize the Bourbon duke of Enghien (1772–1804). The duke was accused of participation in a royalist plot and put to death, though Bonaparte knew him to be innocent. The action was a flagrant violation of international law and of due process. Charles Maurice de Talleyrand-Périgord (1754–1838), Bonaparte's foreign minister, later termed the act "worse than a crime—a blunder," because it helped to provoke foreign opposition. On the other hand, it was popular with the former Jacobins, for it seemed to preclude the possibility of a Bourbon restoration. The executioner of a Bourbon was hardly likely to restore the royal family. The execution also seems to have put an end to royalist plots.

Concordat with the Roman Catholic Church

A major obstacle to internal peace was the steady hostility of French Catholics. Refractory clergy continued to advocate counterrevolution. The religious revival that dated from the Thermidorian Reaction increased discontent with the secular state created by the revolution. Bonaparte regarded religion as a political matter. He approved its role in preserving an orderly society, but was suspicious of any such power independent of the state.

In 1801, to the shock and dismay of his anticlerical supporters, Napoleon concluded a concordat with Pope Pius VII (r. 1800–1823). The settlement gave Napoleon what he most wanted. The agreement required both the refractory clergy and those who had accepted the revolution to resign. Their replacements received their spiritual investiture from the Pope, but the state named the bishops and paid their salaries and the salary of one priest in each parish. In return, the church gave up its claims on its confiscated property.

The concordat declared, "Catholicism is the religion of the great majority of French citizens." This was merely a statement of fact and fell far short of what the Pope had wanted: religious dominance for the Roman Catholic Church. The clergy had to swear an oath of loyalty to the state. The Organic Articles of 1802, which were actually distinct from the concordat, established the supremacy of state over church. Similar laws were applied to the Protestant and Jewish communities as well, reducing still further the privileged position of the Catholic Church. (See "Napoleon Makes Peace with the Papacy.")

The Napoleonic Code

In 1802 a plebiscite ratified Napoleon as consul for life, and he soon produced another constitution that granted him what amounted to full power. He thereafter set about reforming and codifying French law. The result was the Civil Code of 1804, usually known as the *Napoleonic Code*.

The Napoleonic Code safeguarded all forms of property and tried to make French society secure against internal challenges. All the privileges based on birth that had marked the Old Regime and that had been overthrown during the revolution remained abolished. Employment of salaried officials chosen on the basis of merit replaced the purchase of offices.

The conservative attitudes toward labor and women that had emerged during the revolutionary years also received full support. Workers' organizations remained forbidden, and workers had fewer rights than their employers. Within families, fathers were granted extensive control over their children and husbands over their wives. At the same time, laws of primogeniture remained abolished, and property was distributed among

Napoleon Makes Peace with the Papacy

In 1801, Napoleon concluded a concordat with Pope Pius VII. This document was the cornerstone of Napoleonic religious policy. The concordat, which was announced on April 8, 1802, allowed the Roman Catholic church to function freely in France only within the limits of Church support for the government as indicated in the oath included in Article 6.

❖ *Why was it to Napoleon's political advantage to make this agreement with the papacy? What privileges or advantages does the Church achieve in the document? Would the highest loyalty of a bishop who took the oath in Article 6 reside with the Church or the French state?*

The Government of the French Republic recognizes that the Roman, catholic and apostolic religion is the religion of the great majority of French citizens.

His Holiness likewise recognizes that this same religion has derived and in this moment again expects the greatest benefit and grandeur from the establishment of the catholic worship in France and from the personal profession of it which the consuls of the Republic make.

In consequence, after this mutual recognition, as well for the benefit of religion as for the maintenance of internal tranquility, they have agreed as follows:

1. The catholic, apostolic and Roman religion shall be freely exercised in France: its worship shall be public, and in conformity with the police regulations which the government shall deem necessary for the public tranquility....

4. The First Consul of the Republic shall make appointments, within the three months which shall follow the publication of the bull of His Holiness, to the archbishoprics and bishoprics of the new circumscription. His Holiness shall confer the canonical institution, following the forms established in relation to France before the change of government.

6. Before entering upon their functions, the bishops shall take directly, at the hands of the First Consul, the oath of fidelity which was in use before the change of government, expressed in the following terms:

"I swear and promise to God, upon the holy scriptures, to remain in obedience and fidelity to the government established by the constitution of the French Republic. I also promise not to have any intercourse, nor to assist by any counsel, nor to support any league, either within or without, which is inimical to the public tranquility; and if, within my diocese or elsewhere, I learn that anything to the prejudice of the state is being contrived, I will make it known to the government."

From Maloy Anderson, ed. and trans., *The Constitutions and Other Select Documents Illustrative of the History of France, 1789–1907,* 2d ed., rev. and enl. (Minneapolis: H. W. Wilson, 1908), pp. 296–297.

all children, males and females. Married women, however, could dispose of their own property only with the consent of their husbands. Divorce remained more difficult for women than for men. Before this code, French law had been a patchwork that differed from region to region. Within that confused set of laws, women had had opportunities to assert and protect their interests. The universality of the Napoleonic Code ended those possibilities.

Establishing a Dynasty

In 1804, Bonaparte seized on the bomb attack on his life to make himself emperor. He argued that establishing a dynasty would make the new regime secure and make further attempts on his life useless. Another new constitution was promulgated in which Napoleon Bonaparte was called Emperor of the French, instead of First Consul of the Republic. This constitution was also overwhelmingly ratified in a plebiscite.

To conclude the drama, Napoleon invited the Pope to Notre Dame to take part in the coronation. At the last minute, however, the Pope agreed that Napoleon should place the crown on his own head. The emperor had no intention of allowing anyone to think that his power and authority depended on the approval of the church. Henceforth, he was called Napoleon I.

The coronation of Napoleon, December 2, 1804, as painted by Jacques-Louis David. Having first crowned himself, the emperor is shown about to place the crown on the head of Josephine. Napoleon instructed David to paint Pope Pius VII with his hand raised in blessing. Giraudon/Art Resource, NY

Napoleon's Empire (1804–1814)

Between his coronation as emperor and his final defeat at Waterloo (1815), Napoleon conquered most of Europe in a series of military campaigns that astonished the world. France's victories changed the map of the continent. The wars put an end to the Old Regime and its feudal trappings throughout western Europe and forced the eastern European states to reorganize themselves to resist Napoleon's armies.

Everywhere, Napoleon's advance unleashed the powerful force of nationalism. His weapon was the militarily mobilized French nation, one of the achievements of the revolution. Napoleon could put as many as 700,000 men under arms at one time, risk as many as 100,000 troops in a single battle, endure heavy losses, and return to fight again. He could conscript citizen soldiers in unprecedented numbers, thanks to their loyalty to the nation and to their remarkable leader. No single enemy could match such resources. Even coali-

tions were unsuccessful, until Napoleon finally overreached himself and made mistakes that led to his own defeat.

Conquering an Empire

The Peace of Amiens (1802) between France and Great Britain was merely a truce. Napoleon's unlimited ambitions shattered any hope that it might last. He sent an army to restore the rebellious colony of Haiti to French rule. This move aroused British fears that he was planning the renewal of a French empire in America, because Spain had restored Louisiana to France in 1800. More serious were his interventions in the Dutch Republic, Italy, and Switzerland and his role in the reorganization of Germany. The Treaty of Campo Formio had required a redistribution of territories along the Rhine River, and the petty princes of the region engaged in a shameful scramble to enlarge their holdings. Among the results were the reduction of Austrian influence in Germany and the emergence of a smaller number of larger German states in the west, all dependent on Napoleon.

and soon occupied Vienna. On December 2, 1805, in perhaps his greatest victory, Napoleon defeated the combined Austrian and Russian forces at Austerlitz. The Treaty of Pressburg that followed won major concessions from Austria. The Austrians withdrew from Italy and left Napoleon in control of everything north of Rome. He was recognized as king of Italy.

Napoleon also made extensive political changes in Germany. In July 1806, he organized the Confederation of the Rhine, which included most of the western German princes. The withdrawal of these princes from the Holy Roman Empire led Francis II of Austria to dissolve that ancient political body and henceforth to call himself Emperor of Austria.

Prussia, which had carefully remained neutral up to this point, was now provoked into war against France. Napoleon's forces quickly crushed the famous Prussian army at the battles of Jena and Auerstädt on October 14, 1806. Two weeks later, Napoleon was in Berlin. There, on November 21, he issued the Berlin Decrees, forbidding his allies from importing British goods. On June 13, 1807, Napoleon defeated the Russians at Friedland and went on to occupy Königsberg, the capital of East Prussia. The French emperor was master of all Germany.

TREATY OF TILSIT   Unable to fight another battle and unwilling to retreat into Russia, Tsar Alexander I (r. 1801–1825) was ready to make peace. He and Napoleon met on a raft in the middle of the Niemen River while the two armies and the nervous king of Prussia watched from the bank. On July 7, 1807, they signed the Treaty of Tilsit, which confirmed France's gains. Moreover, the treaty reduced the Prussian state to half its previous size, and only the support of Alexander saved it from extinction. Prussia openly and Russia secretly became allies of Napoleon in his war against Britain.

Napoleon organized conquered Europe much like the domain of a Corsican family. The great French Empire was ruled directly by the head of the clan, Napoleon. On its borders lay several satellite states carved out as the portions of the several family members. His stepson ruled Italy for him, and three of his brothers and his brother-in-law were made kings of other conquered states. Napoleon denied a kingdom only to his brother Lucien, of whose wife he disapproved. The French emperor expected his relatives to take orders without question. When they failed to do so, he rebuked and even punished them. This establishment of the Napoleonic family as the col-

Admiral Viscount Horatio Nelson (1758–1805) was the greatest naval commander of his age. From the battle of Abukir in 1798 to his death at the battle of Trafalgar in 1805, he won a series of brilliant victories that gave Britain mastery of the seas.   Corbis

BRITISH NAVAL SUPREMACY   The British found these developments alarming enough to justify an ultimatum. When Napoleon ignored it, Britain declared war in May 1803. William Pitt the Younger returned to office as prime minister in 1804 and began to construct the Third Coalition. By August 1805, he had persuaded Russia and Austria to move once more against French aggression. A great naval victory soon raised the fortunes of the allies. On October 21, 1805, the British admiral Horatio, Lord Nelson, destroyed the combined French and Spanish fleets at the Battle of Trafalgar just off the Spanish coast. Nelson died in the battle, but the British lost no ships. The victory of Trafalgar put an end to all French hope of invading Britain and guaranteed British control of the sea for the rest of the war.

NAPOLEONIC VICTORIES IN CENTRAL EUROPE   On land the story was different. Even before Trafalgar, Napoleon had marched to the Danube River to attack his continental enemies. In mid-October he forced a large Austrian army to surrender at Ulm

Napoleon's victory at the battle of Austerlitz is considered his most brilliant. A French army of 73,000 crushed an Austro-Russian army of 86,000 under the command of the tsar and the emperor of Austria. Giraudon/Art Resource, NY

lective sovereigns of Europe was unpopular and provoked political opposition that needed only encouragement and assistance to flare up into serious resistance. (See "Napoleon Advises His Brother to Rule Constitutionally.")

The Continental System

After the Treaty of Tilsit, such assistance could come only from Britain, and Napoleon knew that he must defeat the British before he could feel safe. Unable to compete with the British navy, he continued the economic warfare begun by the Berlin Decrees. He planned to cut off all British trade with the European continent and thus to cripple British commercial and financial power. He hoped to cause domestic unrest and revolution, and thus to drive the British from the war. The Milan Decree of 1807 went further and attempted to stop neutral nations from trading with Britain.

Napoleon and the Continental System

1806	Napoleon establishes the Continental System prohibiting all trade with England
1807	The peace conference at Tilsit results in Russia joining the Continental System and becoming an ally of Napoleon
1809 and 1810	Napoleon at the peak of his power
1810	Russia withdraws from the Continental System and resumes relations with Britain; Napoleon plans to crush Russia militarily
1812	Napoleon invades Russia; the Russians adopt a scorched-earth policy and burn Moscow; the thwarted Napoleon deserts his dwindling army and rushes back to Paris

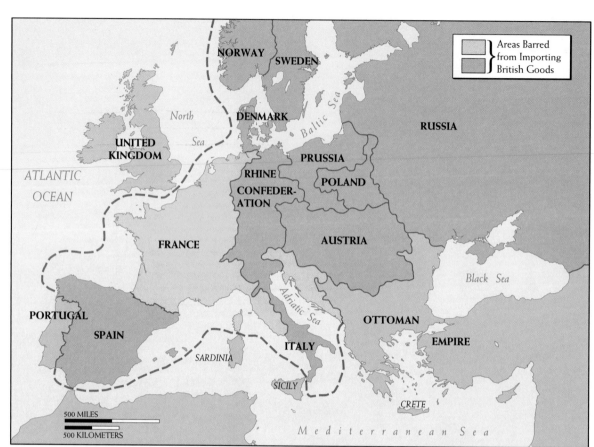

MAP 20–1   THE CONTINENTAL SYSTEM, 1806–1810   *Napoleon hoped to cut off all British trade with the European continent and thereby drive the British from the war.*

Despite initial drops in exports and domestic unrest, the British economy survived. British control of the seas assured access to the growing markets of North and South America and of the eastern Mediterranean. At the same time, the Continental System badly hurt the European economies. (See Map 20–1.) Napoleon rejected advice to turn his empire into a free-trade area. Such a policy would have been both popular and helpful. Instead, his tariff policies favored France, increased the resentment of foreign merchants, and made them less willing to enforce the system and more ready to engage in smuggling. It was in part to prevent smuggling that Napoleon invaded Spain in 1808. The resulting peninsular campaign in Spain and Portugal helped to bring on his ruin.

European Response to the Empire

Napoleon's conquests stimulated the two most powerful political forces in nineteenth-century Europe: liberalism and nationalism. The export of his version of the French Revolution directly and indirectly spread the ideas and values of the Enlightenment and the principles of 1789. Wherever Napoleon ruled, the Napoleonic Code was imposed, and hereditary social distinctions were abolished. Feudal privileges disappeared, and the peasants were freed from serfdom and manorial dues. In the towns, the guilds and the local oligarchies that had been dominant for centuries were dissolved or deprived of their power. New freedom thus came to serfs, artisans, workers, and entrepreneurs outside the privileged circles. The established churches lost their traditional independence and were made subordinate to the state. Church monopoly of religion was replaced by general toleration.

These reforms were not undone by the fall of Napoleon. Along with the demand for representative, constitutional government, they remained the basis of later liberal reforms. It also became clear, however, that Napoleon's policies were intended first for his own glory and that of France. The Continental System demonstrated that France, rather than Europe generally, was to be enriched by Napoleon's rule. Consequently, before long, the conquered states and peoples grew restive.

Napoleon Advises His Brother to Rule Constitutionally

As Napoleon swept through Europe, he set his relatives on the thrones of various conquered kingdoms and then imposed written constitutions on them. In this letter of November 1807, Napoleon sent his brother Jerome (1784–1860) a constitution for the Kingdom of Westphalia in Germany. The letter provides a good description of how Napoleon spread the political ideas and institutions of the French Revolution across Europe. Napoleon ignored, however, the possibility of nationalistic resentment that French conquest aroused, even when that conquest brought more liberal political institutions. Such nationalism would be one of the causes of his downfall.

❖ *What are the benefits that Napoleon believes his conquest and subsequent rule by his brother will bring to their new subjects? How does he believe that these, rather than military victory, will achieve new loyalty? How does Napoleon suggest playing off the resentment of the upper classes to consolidate power? What is the relationship between having a written constitution such as Napoleon is sending his brother and the power of public opinion that he mentions toward the close of the letter?*

I enclose the constitution for your Kingdom. You must faithfully observe it. I am concerned for the happiness of your subjects, not only as it affects your reputation, and my own, but also for its influence on the whole European situation.

Don't listen to those who say that your subjects are so accustomed to slavery that they will feel no gratitude for the benefits you give them. There is more intelligence in the Kingdom of Westphalia than they would have you believe; and your throne will never be firmly established except upon the trust and affection of the common people. What German opinion impatiently demands is that men of no rank, but of marked ability, shall have an equal claim upon your favour and your employment, and that every trace of serfdom, or of a feudal hierarchy between the sovereign and the lowest class of his subjects shall be done away with. The benefits of the Code Napoleon, public trial, and the introduction of juries, will be the leading features of your Government. And to tell you the truth, I count more upon their effects, for the extension and consolidation of your rule, than upon the most resounding victories. I want your subjects to enjoy a degree of liberty, equality, and prosperity hitherto unknown to the German people.... Such a method of government will be a stronger barrier between you and Prussia than the Elbe, the fortresses, and the protection of France. What people will want to return under the arbitrary Prussian rule, once it has tasted the benefits of a wise and liberal administration? In Germany, as in France, Italy, and Spain, people long for equality and liberalism. I have been managing the affairs of Europe long enough now to know that the burden of the privileged classes was resented everywhere. Rule constitutionally. Even if reason, and the enlightenment of the age, were not sufficient cause, it would be good policy for one in your position; and you will find that the backing of public opinion gives you a great natural advantage over the absolute kings who are your neighbors.

From J. M. Thompson, ed., *Napoleon's Letters* (London: Dent, 1954), pp. 190–191, as quoted in Maurice Hutt, ed., *Napoleon* (Englewood Cliffs, NJ: Prentice Hall, 1972), p. 34.

German Nationalism and Prussian Reform

The German response to Napoleon's success was particularly interesting and important. There had never been a unified German state. The great German writers of the Enlightenment, such as Immanuel Kant, Friedrich von Schiller, and Gotthold Lessing, were neither deeply politically engaged nor nationalistic.

At the beginning of the nineteenth century, the romantic movement had begun to take hold. One of its basic features in Germany was the emergence of nationalism, which went through two distinct stages there. Initially, nationalistic writers emphasized the unique and admirable qualities of

German culture, which, they argued, arose from the peculiar history of the German people. Such cultural nationalism prevailed until Napoleon's humiliation of Prussia at Jena in 1806.

At that point many German intellectuals began to urge resistance to Napoleon on the basis of German nationalism. The French conquest endangered the independence and achievements of all German-speaking people. Many nationalists were also critical of the German princes, who ruled selfishly and inefficiently and who seemed ever ready to lick the boots of Napoleon. Only a people united through its language and culture could resist the French onslaught. No less important in forging a German national sentiment was the example of France itself, which had attained greatness by enlisting the active support of the entire people in the patriotic cause. Henceforth, many Germans sought to solve their internal political problems by attempting to establish a unified German state, reformed to harness the energies of the entire people.

After Tilsit, only Prussia could arouse such patriotic feelings. Elsewhere German rulers were either under Napoleon's thumb or actively collaborating with him. Defeated, humiliated, and diminished, Prussia continued to resist, however feebly. To Prussia fled German nationalists from other states, calling for reforms and unification that were, in fact, feared and hated by Frederick William III (r. 1797–1840) and the Junker nobility. Reforms came about despite such opposition because the defeat at Jena had made clear the necessity of new departures for the Prussian state.

The Prussian administrative and social reforms were the work of Baron vom Stein (1757–1831) and Count von Hardenberg (1750–1822). Neither of these reformers intended to reduce the autocratic power of the Prussian monarch or to put an end to the dominance of the Junkers, who formed the bulwark of the state and of the army officer corps. Rather, they aimed at fighting French power with their own version of the French weapons. As Hardenberg declared,

Our objective, our guiding principle, must be a revolution in the better sense, a revolution leading directly to the great goal, the elevation of humanity through the wisdom of those in authority....Democratic rules of conduct in a monarchical administration, such is the formula...which will conform most comfortably with the spirit of the age.[1]

Although the reforms came from the top, they wrought important changes in Prussian society.

Stein's reforms broke the Junker monopoly of landholding. Serfdom was abolished. The power of the Prussian Junkers, however, did not permit the total end of the system in Prussia, as was occurring in the western principalities of Germany. In Prussia, peasants remaining on the land were forced to continue manorial labor, although they were free to leave the land if they chose. They could obtain the ownership of the land they worked only if they forfeited a third of it to the lord. The result was that Junker holdings grew larger. Some peasants went to the cities to find work, others became agricultural laborers, and some did actually become small freeholding farmers. In Prussia and elsewhere, serfdom had ended, but new social problems had been created as a landless labor force was enlarged by the population explosion.

Military reforms sought to increase the supply of soldiers and to improve their quality. Jena had shown that an army of free patriots commanded by officers chosen on merit rather than by birth could defeat an army of serfs and mercenaries commanded by incompetent nobles. To remedy the situation, the Prussian reformers abolished inhumane military punishments, sought to inspire patriotic feelings in the soldiers, opened the officer corps to commoners, gave promotions on the basis of merit, and organized war colleges that developed new theories of strategy and tactics.

These reforms soon enabled Prussia to regain its former power. Because Napoleon strictly limited the size of the Prussian army to 42,000 men, however, universal conscription could not be introduced until 1813. Before that date, the Prussians evaded the limit by training one group each year, putting them into the reserves, and then training a new group the same size. Prussia could thus boast an army of 270,000 by 1814.

The Wars of Liberation

SPAIN   In Spain more than elsewhere in Europe, national resistance to France had deep social roots. Spain had achieved political unity as early as the sixteenth century. The Spanish peasants were devoted to the ruling dynasty and especially to the Roman Catholic Church. France and Spain had been allies since 1796. In 1807, however, a French army came into the Iberian Peninsula to force Portugal to abandon its traditional alliance with Britain. The army stayed in Spain to protect lines of supply and communication. When a revolt broke out in Madrid in 1808, Napoleon used it as a pretext to depose the Spanish Bourbons and to place his brother Joseph (1768–1844) on the Spanish throne. Attacks on the privileges of the church increased public outrage. Many members of the upper classes were prepared to collaborate with Napoleon, but the peasants, urged on by the lower clergy and the monks, rose in a general rebellion. (See "Art & the West.")

---

[1]Quoted in Geoffrey Brunn, *Europe and the French Imperium* (New York: Harper & Row, 1938), p. 174.

A Commander Recalls an Incident in Spain

William Napier was a British officer during the Napoleonic Wars and later a distinguished leader in the British army. In the passage that follows, he describes his experiences in a battle that took place in 1811 during which he had difficulty leading his troops into battle and received a serious injury himself.

❖ *What were Napier's expectations of his men? of his officers? How does he explain the difficulties that his troops had in responding to his orders? How does he indicate his contempt for bad officers and yet a certain understanding that in war a person's character may display different faces?*

I arrived [with two companies] just in time to save Captain Dobbs, 52nd, and two men who were cut off from their regiment. The French were gathering fast about us, we could scarcely retreat, and Dobbs agreed with me that boldness would be our best chance; so we called upon the men to follow, and, jumping over a wall which had given us cover, charged the enemy with a shout which sent the nearest back....

Only the two men of the 52nd followed us, and we four arrived unsupported at a second wall, close to a considerable body of French, who rallied and began to close upon us. Their fire was very violent, but the wall gave cover. I was, however, stung by the backwardness of my men, and told Dobbs I would save him or lose my life by bringing up the two companies; he entreated me not, saying I could not make two paces from the wall and live. Yet I did go back to the first wall, escaped the fire, and, reproaching the men gave them the word again, and returned to Dobbs, who was now upon the point of being taken; but again I returned alone! The soldiers had indeed crossed the wall in their front, but kept edging away to the right to avoid the heavy fire. Being now maddened by this second failure, I made another attempt, but I had not made ten paces when a shot struck my spine, and the enemy very ungenerously continued to fire at me when I was down. I escaped death by dragging myself by my hands—for my lower extremities were paralyzed—towards a small heap of stones which was in the midst of

the field, and thus covering my head and shoulders....However, Captain Lloyd and my company, and some of the 52nd, came up at that moment, and the French were driven away.

The excuses for the soldiers were—1st That I had not made allowance for their exertions in climbing from the ravine up the hill-side with their heavy packs, and they were very much blown. 2nd Their own captains had not been with them for a long time, and they were commanded by two lieutenants, remarkable for their harsh, vulgar, tyrannical dispositions, and very dull bad officers withall; and one of them exhibited on this occasion such miserable cowardice as would be incredible if I had not witnessed it. I am sure he ordered the men not to advance, and I saw him leading them the second time to the right. This man was lying down with his face on the ground; I called to him, reproached him, bad him remember his uniform; nothing would stir him; until losing all patience I threw a large stone at his head. This made him get up, but when he got over the wall he was wild, his eyes staring and his hand spread out. He was a duellist, and had wounded one of the officers some time before. I would have broken him, but before I recovered my wound sufficiently to join, he had received a cannon-shot in the leg, and died at the old, desolate, melancholy mill below Sabugal. Everything combined to render death appalling, yet he showed no signs of weakness. Such is human nature, and so hard it is to form correct opinions of character!

Quoted in H. A. Bruce, *Life of Sir William Napier* (London: John Murray, 1864), 1:55–57.

In Spain, Napoleon faced a new kind of warfare. Guerrilla bands cut lines of communication, killed stragglers, destroyed isolated units, and then disappeared into the mountains. The British landed an army under Sir Arthur Wellesley (1769–1852), later the duke

of Wellington, to support the Spanish insurgents. Thus began the long peninsular campaign that would drain French strength from elsewhere in Europe and play a critical role in Napoleon's eventual defeat. (See "A Commander Recalls an Incident in Spain.")

Francisco Goya Memorializes a Night of Executions: The Third of May, 1808

Goya y Lucientes, Francisco de Goya. *The Third of May, 1808.* 1814–1815. Oil painting on canvas. Museo del Prado, Madrid, Spain. Scala/Art Resource, NY

$\mathcal{N}$apoleon had begun to send troops into Spain in 1807 after the king of Spain had agreed to aid France against Portugal, which was assisting Britain. By early 1808 Spain had essentially become an occupied nation. On May 2 riots took place in Madrid between French troops, including many soldiers whom Napoleon had recruited in Egypt, and Spanish civilians. The Spaniards were attempting to prevent the departure of members of the Spanish royal family whom they considered to be French prisoners. In response to the riots, the French marshall Joachim Murat ordered numerous executions, especially of artisans and clergy, during the night of May 2 and 3. The events of these two days marked the opening of five years of the Spanish effort to free their country from French rule.

After the restoration of the Spanish monarchy, Francisco Goya (1745–1828) depicted the savagery of those executions in the most memorable war painting of the Napoleonic era, *The Third of May, 1808*. Because the executions had taken place at night, and the French chose their victims at random, Goya portrays a mechanical process of execution. One group has already been shot; another is being killed; and a third group, some of whom are covering their eyes, will be next. None of these people were necessarily heroes of the insurgency of the previous day. They were ordinary people being executed by troops of a nation that considered itself the champion of popular sovereignty. Goya's painting is one of the first works of art to illustrate victims of modern ideological wars.

In portraying these modern political executions, Goya recalled the traditional portrayal of Christian martyrdom–the pose of the central figure suggests a crucifixion. But more important, he drew on popular political prints of military firing squads, such as Paul Revere's famous print of the Boston Mas-

sacre. The painting thus presents the French as both infidels violating Christian Spaniards, and as a mechanical killing force picking out hapless civilians, as if in prophesy of the summary executions of civilians in modern warfare.

Goya's painting also illustrates two forces of modern warfare confronting each other: the professional solider and the guerilla (a term coined during this era). The guerilla is a civilian who must fight with what he finds. By contrast, the soldiers in this painting appear well disciplined and have modern rifles. They carry out the executions by the light of the large technologically advanced gas or oil lanterns with which Napoleon equipped his troops.

The Napoleonic conquest of Europe awakened the force of nationalism as ordinary people in the conquered nations resisted French domination. In *The Third of May*, Goya succeeds in making ordinary people, rather than elite officers, the symbolic heroes of the national war of liberation. But once the French were defeated and the royal family restored to the Spanish throne, the interpretation of the May 1808 events became more complicated.

In fact, Goya prepared this painting to please the royal family upon its return to Madrid in 1815. The conservative monarchy could not tolerate the insurgency as a popular uprising. It had to be seen as loyal humble citizens protecting the monarchy and the Church against Napoleon and an infidel France. The victims portrayed in his painting thus appeared in 1815 to be less martyrs for liberty than defenders of the evicted royal family.

Sources: Alfonso E. Perez Sanchez and Eleanor A. Sayre, *Goya and the Spirit of Enlightenment* (Boston: Museum of Fine Arts, 1989); Albert Boime, *Art in an Age of Bonapartism 1800–1815* (Chicago: University of Chicago Press, 1990), pp. 210–212, 297–300; Janis A. Tomlinson, *Goya in the Twilight of Enlightenment* (New Haven: Yale University Press, 1992), pp. 131–149; Robet Rosenblum and H. W. Janson, *19th-Century Art* (Englewood Cliffs, New Jersey: Prentice-Hall, Inc. and New York: Harry N. Abrams, Inc, Publishers: 1984), pp. 55–56.

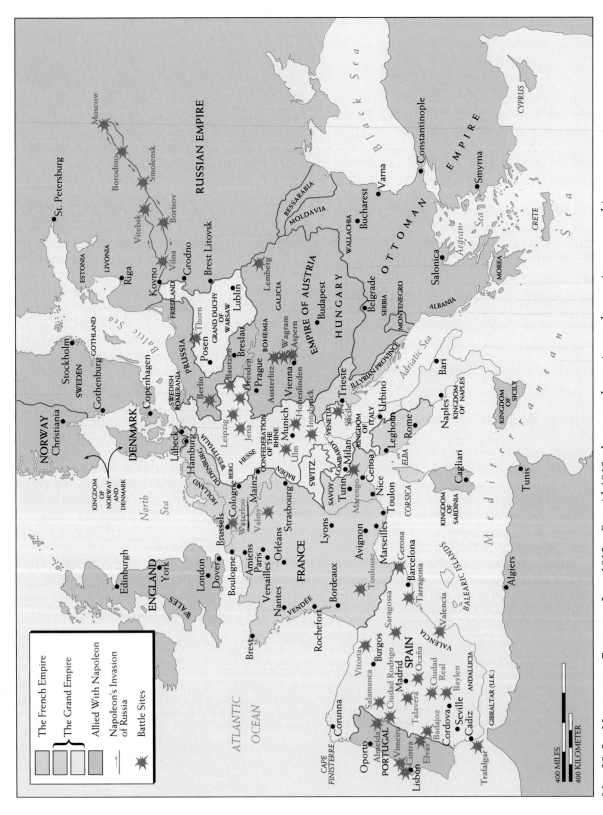

MAP 20–2   NAPOLEONIC EUROPE IN LATE 1812   *By mid-1812, the areas shown in peach were incorporated into France, and most of the rest of Europe was directly controlled by or allied with Napoleon. But Russia had withdrawn from the failing Continental System, and the decline of Napoleon was about to begin.*

AUSTRIA The French troubles in Spain encouraged the Austrians to renew the war in 1809. Since their defeat at Austerlitz, they had sought a war of revenge. The Austrians counted on Napoleon's distraction in Spain, French war weariness, and aid from other German princes. Napoleon was fully in command in France, however; and the German princes did not move. The French army marched swiftly into Austria and won the Battle of Wagram. The resulting Peace of Schönbrunn deprived Austria of much territory and $3^{1}/_{2}$ million subjects.

Another spoil of victory was the Austrian archduchess Marie Louise (1791–1847), daughter of the emperor. Napoleon's wife, Josephine de Beauharnais (1763–1814), was forty-six and had borne him no children. His dynastic ambitions, as well as the desire for a marriage matching his new position as master of Europe, led him to divorce his wife and to marry the eighteen-year-old Austrian princess. Napoleon had also considered marrying the sister of Tsar Alexander, but had received a polite rebuff.

The Invasion of Russia

The failure of Napoleon's marriage negotiations with Russia emphasized the shakiness of the Franco–Russian alliance concluded at Tilsit. The alliance was unpopular with Russian nobles because of the liberal politics of France and because the Continental System prohibited timber sales to Britain. Only French aid in gaining Constantinople could justify the alliance in their eyes, but Napoleon gave them no help against the Ottoman Empire. The organization of the Grand Duchy of Warsaw as a Napoleonic satellite on the Russian doorstep and its enlargement in 1809 after the Battle of Wagram angered Alexander. Napoleon's annexation of Holland in violation of the Treaty of Tilsit, his recognition of the French Marshal Bernadotte (1763–1844) as the future King Charles XIV of Sweden, and his marriage to an Austrian princess further disturbed the tsar. At the end of 1810, Russia withdrew from the Continental System and began to prepare for war. (See Map 20–2.)

Napoleon was determined to end the Russian military threat. He amassed an army of more than 600,000 men, including a core of Frenchmen and more than 400,000 other soldiers drawn from the rest of his empire. He intended the usual short campaign crowned by a decisive battle, but the Russians disappointed him by retreating before his advance. His vast superiority in numbers—the Russians had only about 160,000 troops—made it foolish for them to risk a battle. Instead they followed a "scorched-

When their marriage failed to produce a male heir, Napoleon divorced his first wife, Josephine de Beauharnais (1763–1814). Many considered the action one aspect of Napoleon's betrayal of the Revolution, especially because he then married a daughter of the Habsburg emperor. This portrait is by F. P. Gerard.
Gerard Francois, *The Empress Josephine.* Chateau, Fontainebleau, France. 1808. Giraudon/Art Resource, NY

earth" policy, destroying all food and supplies as they retreated. The so-called Grand Army of Napoleon could not live off the country, and the expanse of Russia made supply lines too long to maintain. Terrible rains, fierce heat, shortages of food and water, and the courage of the Russian rear guard eroded the morale of Napoleon's army. Napoleon's advisers urged him to abandon the venture, but he feared that an unsuccessful campaign would undermine his position in the empire and in France. He pinned his faith on the Russians' unwillingness to abandon Moscow without a fight.

In September 1812, Russian public opinion forced the army to give Napoleon the battle he wanted despite the canny Russian General Kutuzov's (1745–1813) wish to avoid the fight and to let the Russian winter defeat the invader. At Borodino, not far west of Moscow, the bloodiest battle of the Napoleonic era

Napoleon's second wife, Marie Louise (1791–1847), bore him a son. It was clear that Napoleon hoped to establish a new imperial dynasty in France. This portrait is by J. B. Isabey. Marie Louise (1791–1847) and the King of Rome (1811–73) (oil on canvas) by Francois Pascal Simon Gerard, Baron (1770–1837). Chateau de Versailles, France/Bridgeman Art Library, London/Giraudon

cost the French 30,000 casualties and the Russians almost twice as many. Yet the Russian army was not destroyed. Napoleon won nothing substantial, and the battle was regarded as a defeat for him.

Fires set by the Russians soon engulfed Moscow and left Napoleon far from home with a badly diminished army lacking adequate supplies as winter came to a vast and unfriendly country. After capturing the burned city, Napoleon addressed several peace offers to Alexander, but the tsar ignored them. By October, what was left of the Grand Army was forced to retreat. By December, Napoleon realized that the Russian fiasco would encourage plots against him at home. He returned to Paris, leaving the remnants of his army to struggle westward. Perhaps only as many as 100,000 of the original army of more than 600,000 lived to tell the tale of their terrible ordeal.

European Coalition

Even as the news of the disaster reached the West, the final defeat of Napoleon was far from certain. He was able to put down his opponents in Paris and raise another 350,000 men. Neither the Prussians nor the Austrians were eager to risk another bout with Napoleon, and even the Russians hesitated. The Austrian foreign minister, Prince Klemens von Metternich (1773–1859), would have been glad to make a negotiated peace that would leave Napoleon on the throne of a shrunken and chastened France rather than see Europe dominated by Russia. Napoleon might have won a reasonable settlement by negotiation had he been willing to make concessions that would have split his jealous opponents. He would not consider that solution, however. As he explained to Metternich,

Your sovereigns born on the throne can let themselves be beaten twenty times and return to their capitals. I cannot do this because I am an upstart soldier. My domination will not survive the day when I cease to be strong, and therefore feared.[2]

In 1813, patriotic pressure and national ambition brought together the last and most powerful coalition against Napoleon. The Russians drove westward, and Prussia and then Austria joined them. All were assisted by vast amounts of British money. From the west, Wellington marched his peninsular army into France. Napoleon's new army was inexperienced and poorly equipped. His generals had lost confidence and were tired. The emperor himself was worn out and sick. Still, he waged a skillful campaign in central Europe and defeated the allies at Dresden. In October, however, he was decisively defeated by the combined armies of the enemy at Leipzig in what the Germans called the Battle of the Nations. At the end of March 1814, the allied army marched into Paris. A few days later, Napoleon abdicated and went into exile on the island of Elba, off the coast of northern Italy.

The Congress of Vienna and the European Settlement

Fear of Napoleon and hostility to his ambitions had held the victorious coalition together. As soon as he was removed, the allies pursued their separate ambitions. The key person in achieving

---

[2]Quoted in Felix Markham, *Napoleon and the Awakening of Europe* (New York: Macmillan, 1965), pp. 115–116.

eventual agreement among them was Robert Stewart, Viscount Castlereagh (1769–1822), the British foreign secretary. Even before the victorious armies had entered Paris, he brought about the signing of the Treaty of Chaumont on March 9, 1814. It provided for the restoration of the Bourbons to the French throne and the contraction of France to its frontiers of 1792. Even more important was the agreement by Britain, Austria, Russia, and Prussia to form a Quadruple Alliance for twenty years to guarantee the peace terms and to act together to preserve whatever settlement they later agreed on. Remaining problems—and there were many—and final details were left for a conference to be held at Vienna.

Territorial Adjustments

The Congress of Vienna assembled in September 1814, but did not conclude its work until November 1815. Although a glittering array of heads of state attended the gathering, the four great powers conducted the important work of the conference. The only full session of the congress met to ratify the arrangements made by the big four. The easiest problem facing the great powers was France. All the victors agreed that no single state should be allowed to dominate Europe, and all were determined to see that France should be prevented from doing so again. The restoration of the French Bourbon monarchy, which was temporarily popular, and a nonvindictive boundary settlement were designed to keep France calm and satisfied.

The powers also built up a series of states to serve as barriers to any new French expansion. They established the kingdom of the Netherlands, including Belgium, in the north and added Genoa to Piedmont in the south. Prussia, whose power was increased by accessions in eastern Europe, was given important new territories along the Rhine River to deter French aggression in the west. Austria was given full control of northern Italy to prevent a repetition of Napoleon's conquests there. As for the rest of Germany, most of Napoleon's arrangements were left untouched. The venerable Holy Roman Empire, which had been dissolved in 1806, was not revived. (See Map 20–3.) In all these areas, the congress established the rule of legitimate monarchs and rejected any hint of the republican and democratic politics that had flowed from the French Revolution.

On these matters agreement was not difficult, but the settlement of eastern Europe sharply divided the victors. Alexander I of Russia wanted all Poland under his rule. Prussia was willing to give it to him in return for all of Saxony. Austria, however, was unwilling to surrender its share of Poland or to see Prussian power grow or Russia penetrate deeper into central Europe. The Polish–Saxon question brought the congress to a standstill and almost caused a new war among the victors. But defeated France provided a way out. The wily Talleyrand, now representing France at Vienna, suggested that the weight of France added to that of Britain and Austria might bring Alexander to his senses. When news of a secret treaty among the three leaked out, the tsar agreed to become ruler of a smaller Poland, and Frederick William III of Prussia accepted only part of Saxony. Thereafter, France was included as a fifth great power in all deliberations.

The Hundred Days and the Quadruple Alliance

Unity among the victors was further restored by Napoleon's return from Elba on March 1, 1815. The French army was still loyal to the former emperor, and many of the French people thought that their fortunes might be safer under his rule than under that of the restored Bourbons. The coalition seemed to be dissolving in Vienna. Napoleon seized the opportunity, escaped to France, and was soon restored

MAP 20–3   THE GERMAN STATES AFTER 1815   *As noted, the German states were also recognized.*

Arthur Wellesley, the duke of Wellington, first led troops against Napoleon in Spain and later defeated him at the battle of Waterloo, June 18, 1815. Unlike his great naval contemporary, Nelson, he survived to become an elder statesman of Britian. Bildarchiv Preussischer Kulturbesitz

Napoleonic Europe	
1797	Napoleon concludes the Treaty of Campo Formio
1798	Nelson defeats the French navy in the harbor of Abukir in Egypt
1799	Consulate established in France
1801	Concordat between France and the papacy
1802	Treaty of Amiens
1803	War renewed between France and Britain
1804	Execution of Duke of Enghien
1804	Napoleonic Civil Code issued
1804	Napoleon crowned as emperor
1805 (October 21)	Nelson defeats French fleet at Trafalgar
1805 (December 2)	Austerlitz
1806	Jena
1806	Continental System established by Berlin Decrees
1807	Friedland
1807	Treaty of Tilsit
1808	Beginning of Spanish resistance to Napoleonic domination
1809	Wagram
1809	Napoleon marries Archduchess Marie Louise of Austria
1812	Invasion of Russia and French defeat at Borodino
1813	Leipzig (Battle of the Nations)
1814	Treaty of Chaumont (March) establishes Quadruple Alliance
1814 (September)	Congress of Vienna convenes
1815 (March 1)	Napoleon returns from Elba
1815 (June 18)	Waterloo
1815 (September 26)	Holy Alliance formed at Congress of Vienna
1815 (November 20)	Quadruple Alliance renewed at Congress of Vienna
1821	Napoleon dies on Saint Helena

to power. He promised a liberal constitution and a peaceful foreign policy. The allies were not convinced. They declared Napoleon an outlaw (a new device under international law) and sent their armies to crush him. Wellington, with the crucial help of the Prussians under Field Marshal von Blücher (1742–1819), defeated Napoleon at Waterloo in Belgium on June 18, 1815. Napoleon again abdicated and was sent into exile on Saint Helena, a tiny Atlantic island off the coast of Africa, where he died in 1821.

The Hundred Days, as the period of Napoleon's return is called, frightened the great powers and made the peace settlement harsher for France. In addition to some minor territorial adjustments, the victors imposed a war indemnity and an army of occupation on France. Alexander proposed a Holy Alliance, whereby the monarchs promised to act together in accordance with Christian principles. Austria and Prussia signed; but Castlereagh thought it absurd and England abstained. The tsar, who was then embracing mysticism, believed his proposal a valuable tool for international relations. The Holy Alliance soon became a symbol of extreme political reaction.

The Quadruple Alliance among England, Austria, Prussia, and Russia was renewed on November 20, 1815. Henceforth, it was as much a coalition for the maintenance of peace as for the pursuit of victory over France. A coalition with such a purpose had not previously existed in European international relations. Its existence and later operation represented an important new departure in European affairs. Unlike the situation in the eighteenth century, certain powers were de-

LE CONGRÈS.

In this political cartoon of the Congress of Vienna, Tallyrand simply watches which way the wind is blowing, Castlereagh hesitates, while the monarchs of Russia, Prussia, and Austria form the dance of the Holy Alliance. The king of saxony holds onto his crown and the republic of Geneva pays homage to the Kingdom of Sardinia. Bildarchiv Preussischer Kulturbesitz

termined to prevent the outbreak of future war. The experiences of the statesmen at Vienna were very different from those of their eighteenth-century counterparts. They had seen the armies of the French Revolution change major frontiers of the European states. They had witnessed Napoleon overturning the political and social order of much of the continent. They had seen their nations experience unprecedented military organization and destruction. They knew that war affected not a relatively few people in professional armies and navies, but civilian populations and the entire social and political life of the continent. They were determined to prevent such upheaval and destruction from repeating itself.

Consequently, the chief aims of the Congress of Vienna were to prevent a recurrence of the Napoleonic nightmare and to arrange an acceptable settlement for Europe that might produce lasting peace. The leaders of Europe had learned that the previous peace treaties of the revolutionary era had failed and that the purpose of a treaty should be not to secure victory, but to secure future peace. The shared purpose of the diplomats was to establish a framework for future

stability, not to punish a defeated France. Through the Vienna Settlement, the great powers framed international relations in such a manner that the major powers would respect that settlement and not, as in the eighteenth century, use military force to change it.

The Congress of Vienna succeeded remarkably in achieving its goals. France accepted the new situation without undue resentment, in part because it was recognized not just as the defeated enemy of the revolutionary and Napoleonic eras, but also as a great power in the new international order. The victorious powers settled difficult problems among themselves and lesser states reasonably. They established a new legal framework whereby treaties were made between states rather than between monarchs. The treaties remained in place when a monarch died. Furthermore, during the quarter century of warfare, European leaders had come to calculate the nature of political and economic power in new ways that went beyond the simple vision of gaining a favorable balance of trade that had caused so many eighteenth-century wars. They took into account their natural resources, the technological structure of their

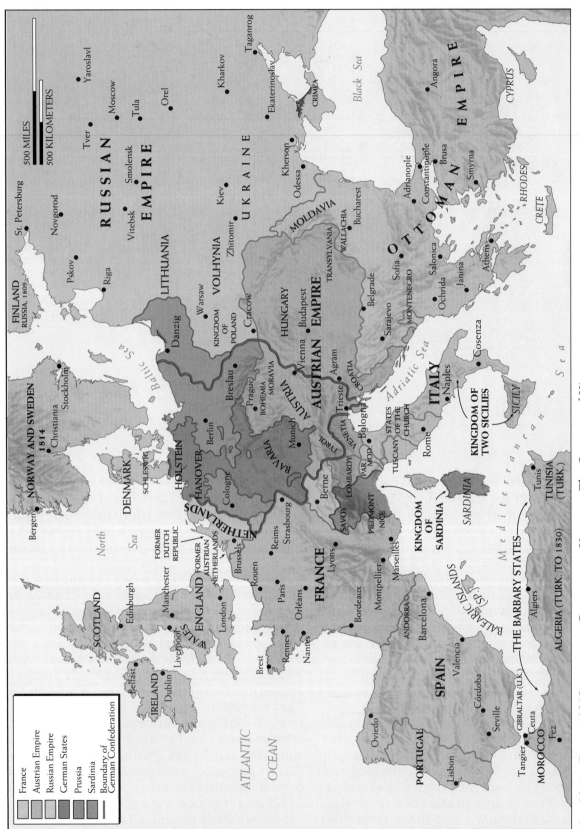

MAP 20-4 EUROPE 1815, AFTER THE CONGRESS OF VIENNA *The Congress of Vienna achieved the post-Napoleonic territorial adjustments shown on the map. The most notable arrangements dealt with areas along France's borders (the Netherlands, Prussia, Switzerland, and Piedmont) and in Poland and northern Italy.*

economies, their systems of education, and the possibility of a general growth in agriculture, commerce, and industry whereby all states could prosper economically and not one at the expense of others.

The congress has been criticized for failing to recognize and provide for the great forces that would stir the nineteenth century—nationalism and democracy. Such criticism is inappropriate, however. At the time there were relatively few nationalist pressures; the general desire across the continent was for peace. The settlement, like all such agreements, was aimed at solving past ills, and in that it succeeded. The powers would have had to have been more than human to have anticipated future problems or to have yielded to forces of which they disapproved and which they believed threatened international peace and stability. It was unusual enough—indeed, virtually unprecedented—to produce an international settlement that remained essentially intact for almost half a century and that allowed Europe to suffer no general war for a hundred years. (See Map 20-4.)

The Romantic Movement

The years of the French Revolution and the conquests of Napoleon saw the emergence of a new and important intellectual movement throughout Europe. *Romanticism*, in its various manifestations, was a reaction against much of the thought of the Enlightenment. Romantic writers opposed what they considered the excessive scientific narrowness of the eighteenth-century *philosophes*. They accused the latter of subjecting everything to geometrical and mathematical models and thereby demeaning feelings and imagination. Romantic thinkers refused to conceive of human nature as primarily rational. They wanted to interpret both physical nature and human society in organic rather than mechanical terms and categories. The Enlightenment *philosophes* had often criticized religion and faith; the romantics, in contrast, saw religion as basic to human nature and faith as a means to knowledge.

Some historians, most notably Arthur O. Lovejoy, have warned against speaking of a single European-wide romantic movement. They have pointed out that a variety of such movements—occurring almost simultaneously in Germany, England, and France—arose independently and had their own particular courses of development. Such considerations have not, however, prevented the

designation of a specific historical period, dated roughly from 1780 to 1830, as the *Age of Romanticism*, or the *romantic movement*.

Despite national differences, a shared reaction to the Enlightenment marked all of these writers and artists. They saw the imagination or some such intuitive intellectual faculty supplementing reason as a means of perceiving and understanding the world. Many of these writers urged a revival of Christianity, such as had permeated Europe during the Middle Ages. And unlike the *philosophes*, the romantics liked the art, literature, and architecture of medieval times. They were also deeply interested in folklore, folk songs, and fairy tales. The romantics were fascinated by dreams, hallucinations, sleepwalking, and other phenomena that suggested the existence of a world beyond that of empirical observation, sensory data, and discursive reasoning.

Romantic Questioning of the Supremacy of Reason

Several historical streams fed the romantic movement, including the individualism of the Renaissance and the Reformation, the pietism of the seventeenth century, and the eighteenth-century English Methodist movement. The influence of the last of these encouraged a heartfelt, practical religion in place of dogmatism, rationalism, and deism. The sentimental novels of the eighteenth century, such as Samuel Richardson's (1689–1761) *Clarissa* (1747), also paved the way for thinkers who would emphasize feeling and emotion. The so-called *Sturm und Drang*, "storm and stress," period of German literature and German idealist philosophy were important to the romantics. Two writers who were also closely related to the Enlightenment, however, provided the immediate intellectual foundations for romanticism: Jean-Jacques Rousseau and Immanuel Kant raised questions about the sufficiency of the rationalism so dear to the *philosophes*.

Rousseau and Education

It has already been pointed out in Chapter 18 that Jean-Jacques Rousseau, though sharing in the reformist spirit of the Enlightenment, opposed many of its other facets. What romantic writers especially drew from Rousseau was his conviction that society and material prosperity had corrupted human nature. In his works, Rousseau had portrayed humankind as happy and innocent by

In A Philosopher in a Moonlit Churchyard, *the British artist Philip James de Loutherbourg captured many of the themes of the Romantic movement. The painting suggests a sense of history, a love of Gothic architecture, a sense of the importance of religion, and a belief that the world is essentially mysterious.* Philip James de Loutherbourg (RA) (1740–1812), *A Philosopher in a Moonlit Churchyard*, signed and dated 1790. Oil on canvas, 34 × 27 in. (86.3 × 68.5 cm). B1974.3.4 Yale Center for British Art, Paul Mellon Collection.

nature and originally living in a state of equilibrium, able to do what it desired and desiring only what it was able to do. To become happy again, humankind must remain true to its natural being while still attempting to realize the new moral possibilities of life in society. In his *Social Contract* (1762), Rousseau had provided his prescription for the reorganization of political life which might achieve that goal.

Rousseau set forth his view on the individual's development toward the good and happy life in his novel *Émile* (1762). (See Chapter 18.) Initially, this treatise on education was far more influential than the *Social Contract*. In *Émile*, Rousseau stressed the difference between children and adults. He distinguished the stages of human maturation and urged that children be raised with maximum individual freedom. Each child should be allowed to grow freely, like a plant, and to learn by trial and error what reality is and how best to deal with it. The parent or teacher would help most by providing the basic necessities of life and warding off what was manifestly harmful. Beyond that, the adult should

stay completely out of the way, like a gardener who waters and weeds a garden but otherwise lets nature take its course. As noted in Chapter 18, Rousseau thought that, because of their physical differences, men and women would naturally grow into social roles with different spheres of activity.

Rousseau also thought that the child's sentiments, as well as its reason, should be permitted to flourish. To romantic writers, this concept of human development vindicated the rights of nature over those of artificial society. They thought that such a form of open education would eventually lead to a natural society. In its fully developed form, this view of life led the romantics to value the uniqueness of each individual and to explore childhood in great detail. Like Rousseau, the romantics saw humankind, nature, and society as organically interrelated.

Kant and Reason

Immanuel Kant (1724–1804) wrote the two greatest philosophical works of the late eighteenth century: *The Critique of Pure Reason* (1781) and *The*

Critique of Practical Reason (1788). He sought to accept the rationalism of the Enlightenment and still to preserve a belief in human freedom, immortality, and the existence of God. Against Locke and other philosophers who saw knowledge rooted in sensory experience alone, Kant argued for the subjective character of human knowledge. For Kant, the human mind did not simply reflect the world around it like a passive mirror; rather, the mind actively imposed on the world of sensory experience "forms of sensibility" and "categories of understanding." The mind itself generated these categories. In other words, the human mind perceives the world as it does because of its own internal mental categories. This meant that human perceptions were as much the product of the mind's own activity as of sensory experience.

Kant found the sphere of reality that was accessible to pure reason to be quite limited. He believed, however, that beyond the phenomenal world of sensory experience, over which "pure reason" was master, there existed what he called the "noumenal" world. This world was a sphere of moral and aesthetic reality known by "practical reason" and conscience. Kant thought that all human beings possessed an innate sense of moral duty or an awareness of what he called a *categorical imperative*. This term referred to an inner command to act in every situation as one would have all other people always act in the same situation. Kant regarded the existence of this imperative of conscience as incontrovertible proof of humankind's natural freedom. On the basis of humankind's moral sense, Kant postulated the existence of God, eternal life, and future rewards and punishments. He believed that these transcendental truths could not be proved by discursive reasoning. Still, he was convinced that they were realities to which every reasonable person could attest.

To many romantic writers, Kantian philosophy constituted a decisive refutation of the narrow rationality of the Enlightenment. Whether they called it "practical reason," "fancy," "imagination," "intuition," or simply "feeling," the romantics believed in the presence of a special power in the human mind that could penetrate beyond the limits of largely passive human understanding as set forth by Hobbes, Locke, and Hume. Most of them also believed that poets and artists possessed these powers in abundance. Other romantic writers appealed to the limits of human reason to set forth new religious ideas or political thought that was often at odds with Enlightenment writers.

Romantic Literature

The term *romantic* appeared in English and French literature as early as the seventeenth century. Neoclassical writers then used the word to describe literature that they considered unreal, sentimental, or excessively fanciful. In the eighteenth century, the English writer Thomas Warton (1728–1790) associated romantic literature with medieval romances. In Germany, a major center of the romantic literary movement, Johann Gottfried Herder (1744–1803) used the terms *romantic* and *Gothic* interchangeably. In both England and Germany, the term came to be applied to all literature that did not observe classical forms and rules and that gave free play to the imagination.

As an alternative to such dependence on the classical forms, August Wilhelm von Schlegel (1767– 1845) praised the "romantic" literature of Dante, Petrarch, Boccaccio, Shakespeare, the Arthurian legends, Cervantes, and Calderón. According to Schlegel, romantic literature was to classical literature what the organic and living were to the merely mechanical. He set forth his views in *Lectures on Dramatic Art and Literature* (1809–1811).

The romantic movement had peaked in Germany and England before it became a major force in France under the leadership of Madame de Staël (1766–1817) and Victor Hugo (1802–1885). (See "Madame de Staël Describes the New Romantic Literature of Germany.") So influential was the classical tradition in France that not until 1816 did a French writer openly declare himself a romantic. That was Henri Beyle (1783–1842), who wrote under the pseudonym Stendhal. He praised Shakespeare and Lord Byron and criticized his own countryman, the seventeenth-century classical dramatist Jean Racine (1639–1699).

The English Romantic Writers

The English romantics believed that poetry was enhanced by freely following the creative impulses of the mind. In this belief, they directly opposed Lockean psychology, which regarded the mind as a passive receptor and poetry as a mechanical exercise of "wit" following prescribed rules. For William Blake and Samuel Taylor Coleridge, the artist's imagination was God at work in the mind. As Coleridge expressed his views, the imagination was "a repetition in the finite mind of the eternal act of creation in the infinite I AM." So conceived of, poetry could not be con-

Madame de Staël Describes the New Romantic Literature of Germany

Anne Louise Germaine de Staël, known generally as Madame de Staël, was the daughter of the Jacques Necker, the finance minister of Louis XVI. In the years following the French Revolution, she was the friend of major French political liberals and was a firm critic of Napoleonic absolutism. More important for European literary life, Madame de Staël visited Germany, read widely in the emerging German romantic literature, and introduced it to both French and English-speaking Europe. Her book Concerning Germany *(1813) constituted a broad exploration of contemporary German culture. In the passage that follows, she gives a strong endorsement to the new literature then emerging in Germany. She points to the novelty of this Romantic poetry and then relates it to a new appreciation of Christianity and the Middle Ages. The Christian features which she associates with the poetry represent one strain among many of the religious revival that followed upon the de-Christianizing religious policies of the French Revolution.*

❖ *How does Madam de Staël characterize the new romantic school of poetry? Why does she contrast it with the literature that had its roots in ancient Greece and Rome? Why does she believe that the new literature will continue to grow? What is the relationship of the Middle Ages to the new poetry and other examples of the fine arts touched by romantic sensibilities?*

The word *romantic* has been lately introduced in Germany, to designate that kind of poetry which is derived from the songs of the Troubadours; that which owes its birth to the union of chivalry and Christianity. If we do not admit that the empire of literature has been divided between paganism and Christianity, the north and the south, antiquity and the middle ages, chivalry and the institutions of Greece and Rome, we shall never succeed in forming a philosophical judgment of ancient and of modern taste.

Some French critics have asserted that German literature is still in its infancy; this opinion is entirely false: men who are best skilled in the knowledge of languages, and the works of the ancients, are certainly not ignorant of the defects and advantages attached to the species of literature which they either adopt or reject; but their character, their habits, and their modes of reasoning, have led them to prefer that which is founded on the recollection of chivalry, on the wonders of the middle ages, to that which has for its basis the mythology of the Greeks. The literature of romance is alone capable of further improvement, because,

being rooted in our own soil, that alone can continue to grow and acquire fresh life: it expresses our religion; it recalls our history; its origin is ancient, although not of classical antiquity. Classic poetry, before it comes home to us, must pass through our recollections of paganism; that of the Germans is the Christian era of the fine arts; it employs our personal impressions to excite strong and vivid emotions; the genius by which it is inspired addresses itself immediately to our hearts; of all phantoms at once the most powerful and the most terrible....

The new school maintains the same system in the fine arts as in literature, and affirms that Christianity is the source of all modern genius; the writers of this school also characterize, in a new manner, all that in Gothic architecture agrees with the religious sentiments of Christians. It does not follow however from this, that the moderns can and ought to construct Gothic churches;...it is only of consequence to us, in the present silence of genius, to lay aside the contempt which has been thrown on all the conceptions of the middle ages.

From Madame De Staël, *Concerning Germany* (London, John Murray, 1814) as quoted in Howard E. Hugo, ed., *The Romantic Reader* (New York: Viking, 1957), pp. 64–66.

sidered idle play. Rather, it was the highest of human acts, humankind's self-fulfillment in a transcendental world.

BLAKE William Blake (1757–1827) considered the poet a seer and poetry to be translated vision. He thought it a great tragedy that so many people understood the world only rationally and could perceive no innocence or beauty in it. In the 1790s, he went through a deep personal depression that seems to have been related to his own inability to perceive the world as he believed it to be. The better one got to know the world, the more the life of the imagination and its spiritual values seemed to recede. Blake saw this problem as evidence of the materialism and injustice of English society. He was deeply impressed by the strong sense of contradiction between a true childlike vision of the world and conceptions of it based on experience.

COLERIDGE Samuel Taylor Coleridge (1772–1834) was the master of Gothic poems of the supernatural, such as "Christabel," and "The Rime of the Ancient Mariner." The latter relates the story of a sailor cursed for killing an albatross. The poem treats the subject as a crime against nature and God and raises the issues of guilt, punishment, and the redemptive possibilities of humility and penance. At the end of the poem, the mariner discovers the unity and beauty of all things. Having repented, he is delivered from his awful curse, which has been symbolized by the dead albatross hung around his neck:

O happy living things! no tongue
Their beauty might declare:
A spring of love gushed from my heart,
And I blessed them unaware...
The self-same moment I could pray;
And from my neck so free
The Albatross fell off, and sank
Like lead into the sea.

Coleridge also made major contributions to romantic literary criticism in his lectures on Shakespeare and in *Biographia Literaria* (1817), which presents his theories of poetry.

WORDSWORTH William Wordsworth (1770–1850) was Coleridge's closest friend. Together they published *Lyrical Ballads* in 1798 as a manifesto of a new poetry that rejected the rules of eighteenth-century criticism. Among Wordsworth's most important later poems is his "Ode on Intimations of Immortality" (1803), written in part to console Coleridge, who was suffering a deep personal cri-

sis. Its subject is the loss of poetic vision, something Wordsworth also keenly felt then in himself. Nature, which he had worshipped, no longer spoke freely to him, and he feared that it might never speak to him again:

There was a time when meadow, grove, and
    stream,
The earth, and every common sight,
To me did seem
Appareled in celestial light,
The glory and the freshness of a dream.
It is not now as it hath been of yore—
Turn whereso'er I may,
By night or day,
The things which I have seen I now can
see no more.

He had lost what he believed that all human beings lose in the necessary process of maturation: their childlike vision and closeness to spiritual reality. For both Wordsworth and Coleridge, childhood was the bright period of creative imagination. Wordsworth held a theory of the soul's preexistence in a celestial state before its creation. The child, being closer in time to its eternal origin and undistracted by worldly experience, recollects the supernatural world much more easily. Aging and urban living corrupt and deaden the imagination, making one's inner feelings and the beauty of nature less important. In his book-length

---

Publication Dates of Major Romantic Works

1762	Rousseau's *Émile*
1774	Goethe's *Sorrows of Young Werther*
1781	Kant's *Critique of Pure Reason*
1788	Kant's *Critique of Practical Reason**
1789	Blake's *Songs of Innocence*
1794	Blake's *Songs of Experience*
1798	Wordsworth and Coleridge's *Lyrical Ballads*
1799	Schlegel's *Lucinde*
1799	Schleiermacher's *Speeches on Religion to Its Cultured Despisers*
1802	Chateaubriand's *Genius of Christianity*
1806	Hegel's *Phenomenology of Mind*
1808	Goethe's *Faust*, Part I
1812	Byron's *Childe Harold's Pilgrimage*
1819	Byron's *Don Juan*

*Kant's books were not themselves part of the romantic movement, but they were fundamental to later romantic writers.

Lord Byron may well have been the most famous European poet of the first quarter of the nineteenth century. This portrait by the contemporary artist Géricault captures the poet in a brooding, introspective mood. Bildarchiv Preussischer Kulturbesitz

poem *The Prelude* (1850), Wordsworth presented a long autobiographical account of the growth of the poet's mind.

LORD BYRON   A true rebel among the romantic poets was Lord Byron (1788–1824). In Britain, even most of the other romantic writers distrusted and disliked him. He had little sympathy for their views of the imagination. Outside England, however, Byron was regarded as the embodiment of the new person of the French Revolution. He rejected the old traditions (he was divorced and famous for his paramours) and championed the cause of personal liberty. Byron was outrageously skeptical and mocking, even of his own beliefs. In *Childe Harold's Pilgrimage* (1812), he created a brooding, melancholy romantic hero. In *Don Juan* (1819), he wrote with ribald humor, acknowledged nature's cruelty as well as its beauty, and even expressed admiration for urban life.

The German Romantic Writers

Much romantic poetry was also written on the Continent, but almost all major German romantics wrote at least one novel. Romantic novels often were highly sentimental and borrowed material from medieval romances. The characters of romantic novels were treated as symbols of the larger truth of life. Purely realistic description was avoided. The first German romantic novel was Ludwig Tieck's (1773–1853) *William Lovell* (1793–1795). It contrasts the young Lovell, whose life is built on love and imagination, with those who live by cold reason alone and who thus become an easy prey to unbelief, misanthropy, and egoism. As the novel rambles to its conclusion, Lovell is ruined by a mixture of philosophy, materialism, and skepticism, administered to him by two women whom he naively loves.

Johann Wolfgang von Goethe (1749–1832), perhaps the greatest German writer of modern times, is portrayed here in the garb of a pilgrim against a Romantic background of classical ruins in the fields outside Rome. Tischbein, Johann Heinr. Wilh. 1751–1821. *Goethe in der romischen Campagna.* Stadelisches Kunstinstitut, Frankfurt/Artothek

SCHLEGEL Friedrich Schlegel (1767–1845) wrote a progressive early romantic novel, *Lucinde* (1799), which attacked contemporaneous prejudices against women as capable of being little more than lovers and domestics. Schlegel's novel reveals the ability of the romantics to become involved in the social issues of their day. He depicted Lucinde as the perfect friend and companion, as well as the unsurpassed lover, of the hero. Like other early romantic novels, the work shocked contemporary morals by frankly discussing sexual activity and by describing *Lucinde* as equal in all ways to the male hero.

GOETHE Towering above all of these German writers stood the figure of Johann Wolfgang von Goethe (1749–1832). Perhaps the greatest German writer of modern times, Goethe defies any easy classification. Part of his literary production fits into the romantic mold, and part of it was a condemnation of romantic excesses. The book that made his early reputation was *The Sorrows of Young Werther*, published in 1774. This novel, like many others in the eighteenth century, is composed of a series of letters. The hero falls in love with Lotte, who is married to another man. The letters explore their relationship and display the emotional sentimentalism that was characteristic of the age. Eventually Werther and Lotte part, but in his grief over his abandoned love, Werther takes his own life. This novel became popular through-

out Europe. Virtually all later romantic authors, and especially those in Germany, admired it because of its emphasis on feeling and on living outside the bounds of polite society.

Much of Goethe's early poetry was also erotic in nature. As he became older, however, Goethe became much more serious and self-consciously moral. He published many other works, including *Iphigenia at Tauris* (1787) and *Wilhelm Meister's Apprenticeship* (1792–1800), which explored how human beings come to live moral lives while still acknowledging the life of the senses.

Goethe's greatest masterpiece was *Faust*, a long dramatic work of poetry in two parts. Part I was published in 1808. It tells the story of Faust, who, weary of life, makes a pact with the Devil—he will exchange his soul for greater knowledge than other human beings possess. As the story progresses, Faust seduces a young woman named Gretchen. She dies, but is received into heaven as the grief-stricken Faust realizes that he must continue to live.

In Part II, completed in the year of Goethe's death (1832), Faust is taken through a series of strange adventures involving witches and various mythological characters. This portion of the work has never been admired so much as Part I. At the conclusion, however, Faust dedicates his life, or what remains of it, to the improvement of humankind. In his dedication, he feels that he has found a goal

Friedrich Schleiermacher (1768–1834) was the most important protestant theologian of the first half of the nineteenth century. He stressed the importance of feeling in religious experience. Bildarchiv Preussischer Kulturbesitz

that will allow him to overcome the restless striving that first induced him to make the pact with the Devil. That new knowledge breaks the pact. Faust then dies and is received by angels.

In this great work, Goethe obviously was criticizing much of his earlier thought and that of contemporary romantic writers. He was also attempting to portray the deep spiritual problems that Europeans would encounter as the traditional moral and religious values of Christianity were abandoned. Yet Goethe himself could not reaffirm those values. In that respect, both he and his characters symbolized the spiritual struggle of the nineteenth century.

Religion in the Romantic Period

During the Middle Ages, the foundation of religion had been the church. The Reformation leaders had appealed to the authority of the Bible. Then, later Enlightenment writers had attempted to derive religion from the rational nature revealed by Newtonian physics. Romantic religious thinkers, on the other hand, appealed to the inner emotions of humankind for the foundation of religion. Their forerunners were the mystics of Western Christianity. One of the first great examples of a religion characterized by romantic impulses—Methodism—arose in England.

Methodism

Methodism originated in the middle of the eighteenth century as a revolt against deism and rationalism in the Church of England. The Methodist revival formed an important part of the background of English romanticism. The leader of the Methodist movement was John Wesley (1703–1791). His education and religious development had been carefully supervised by his remarkable mother, Susannah Wesley, who bore eighteen children in addition to John.

While at Oxford, Wesley organized a religious group known as the "Holy Club." He soon left England for missionary work in Georgia in America, where he arrived in 1735. While he was crossing the Atlantic, a group of German Moravians on the ship had deeply impressed him. These German pietists exhibited unshakable faith and confidence during a violent storm at sea, while Wesley despaired of his life. Wesley concluded that they knew far better than he the meaning of justification by faith. When he returned to England in 1738 after an unhappy missionary career, Wesley began to worship with Moravians in London. There, in 1739, he underwent a conversion experience that he described in the words, "My heart felt strangely warmed." From that point on, he felt assured of his own salvation.

John Wesley (1703–1791) was the founder of Methodism. He emphasized the role of emotional experience in Christian conversion. Corbis

Chateaubriand Describes the Appeal of a Gothic Church

Throughout most of the eighteenth century, writers had harshly criticized virtually all aspects of the Middle Ages, then considered an unenlightened time. One of the key elements of romanticism was a new appreciation of all things medieval. In this passage from The Genius of Christianity, *Chateaubriand praises the beauty of the Middle Ages and the strong religious feelings produced by stepping into a Gothic church. The description exemplifies the typically romantic emphasis on feelings as the chief foundation of religion.*

❖ *Why does the capacity of a Gothic church to carry Chateaubriand back in time add to its power of inducing a religious feeling? How does Chateaubriand unite the church with nature to emphasize its religious character? Is this vision of religion dependent upon the authority of an organized church or of sacred writings, such as the Bible?*

You could not enter a Gothic church without feeling a kind of awe and a vague sentiment of the Divinity. You were all at once carried back to those times when a fraternity of cenobites [a particular order of monks], after having meditated in the woods of their monasteries, met to prostrate themselves before the altar and to chant the praises of the Lord, amid the tranquility and the silence of the night....

Everything in a Gothic church reminds you of the labyrinths of a wood; everything excites a feeling of religious awe, of mystery, and of the Divinity.

The two lofty towers erected at the entrance of the edifice overtop the elms and yew trees of the church yard, and produce the most picturesque effect on the azure of heaven. Sometimes their twin heads are illumined by the first rays of dawn; at others they appear crowned with a cap-ital of clouds or magnified in a foggy atmosphere. The birds themselves seem to make a mistake in regard to them, and to take them for the trees of the forests; they hover over their summits, and perch upon their pinnacles. But, lo! confused noises suddenly issue from the tops of these towers and scare away the affrighted birds. The Christian architect, not content with building forests, has been desirous to retain their murmurs; and, by means of the organ and of bells, he has attached to the Gothic temple the very winds and thunders that roar in the recesses of the woods. Past ages, conjured up by these religious sounds, raise their venerable voices from the bosom of the stones, and are heard in every corner of the vast cathedral. The sanctuary reechoes like the cavern of the ancient Sibyl; loud-tongued bells swing over your head, while the vaults of death under your feet are profoundly silent.

Viscount François René de Chateaubriand, *The Genius of Christianity*, trans. by C. I. White (Baltimore: J. Murphy, 1862), as quoted in Howard E. Hugo, ed., The Romantic Reader (New York: Viking, 1957), pp. 341–342.

Wesley discovered that he could not preach his version of Christian conversion and practical piety in Anglican Church pulpits. Therefore, late in 1739, he began to preach in the open fields near the cities and towns of western England. Thousands of humble people responded to his message of repentance and good works. Soon he and his brother Charles (1707–1788), who became famous for his hymns, began to organize Methodist societies. By the late eighteenth century, the Methodists had become a separate church. They ordained their own clergy and sent missionaries to America, where they eventually achieved their greatest success and most widespread influence.

Methodism stressed inward, heartfelt religion and the possibility of Christian perfection in this life. John Wesley described Christianity as "an inward principle...the image of God impressed on a created spirit, a fountain of peace and love springing up into everlasting life."[3] True Christians were those who were "saved in this world from all sin, from all unrighteousness...and now in such a sense perfect as not to commit sin and...freed from evil thoughts and evil tempers."[4]

[3]Quoted in Albert C. Outler, ed., *John Wesley: A Representative Collection of His Writings* (New York: Oxford University Press, 1964), p. 220.

[4]*Ibid.*

Many people, weary of the dry rationalism that derived from deism, found Wesley's ideal relevant to their own lives. The Methodist preachers emphasized the role of enthusiastic emotional experience as part of Christian conversion. After Wesley, religious revivals became highly emotional in style and content.

New Directions in Continental Religion

Similar religious developments based on feeling appeared on the Continent. After the Thermidorian Reaction, a strong Roman Catholic revival took place in France. Its followers disapproved of both the religious policy of the revolution and the anticlericalism of the Enlightenment. The most impor-

tant book to express these sentiments was *The Genius of Christianity* (1802), by Viscount François René de Chateaubriand (1768–1848). In this work, which became known as the "Bible of romanticism," Chateaubriand argued that the essence of religion was "passion." The foundation of faith in the church was the emotion that its teachings and sacraments inspired in the heart of the Christian. (See "Chateaubriand Describes the Appeal of a Gothic Church.")

Against the Newtonian view of the world and of a rational God, the romantics found God immanent in nature. No one stated the romantic religious ideal more eloquently or with greater impact on the modern world than Friedrich Schleiermacher (1768–1834). In 1799, he published *Speeches on Religion to Its Cultured De-*

The philosopher J. G. Fichte (1762–1814), shown here in the uniform of a Berlin home guard. Fichte glorified the role of the great individual in history. Bildarchiv Preussischer Kulturbesitz

spisers. It was a response to Lutheran orthodoxy, on the one hand, and to Enlightenment rationalism, on the other. The advocates of both were the "cultured despisers" of real, or heartfelt, religion. According to Schleiermacher, religion was neither dogma nor a system of ethics. It was an intuition or feeling of absolute dependence on an infinite reality. Religious institutions, doctrines, and moral activity expressed that primal religious feeling only in a secondary, or indirect, way.

Although Schleiermacher considered Christianity the "religion of religions," he also believed that every world religion was unique in its expression of the primal intuition of the infinite in the finite. He thus turned against the universal natural religion of the Enlightenment, which he termed "a name applied to loose, unconnected im-

pulses," and defended the meaningfulness of the numerous world religions. Every such religion was seen to be a unique version of the emotional experience of dependence on an infinite being. In so arguing, Schleiermacher interpreted the religions of the world in the same way that other romantic writers interpreted the variety of unique peoples and cultures.

Romantic Views of Nationalism and History

A distinctive feature of romanticism, especially in Germany, was its glorification of both the individual person and individual cultures. Behind these

This colored lithograph of G. W. F. Hegel shows him attired in robes of a university professor. Hegel was the most important philosopher of history in the Romantic period.
Bildarchiv Preussischer Kulturbesitz

Hegel Explains the Role of Great Men in History

Hegel believed that behind the development of human history from one period to the next lay the mind and purpose of what he termed the "World-Spirit," a concept somewhat resembling the Christian God. Hegel thought particular heroes from the past (such as Caesar) and in the present (such as Napoleon) were the unconscious instruments of that Spirit. In this passage from his lectures on the philosophy of history, Hegel explained how these heroes could change history. All these concepts are characteristic of the romantic belief that human beings and human history are always intimately connected with larger, spiritual forces at work in the world. The passage also reflects the widespread belief of the time that the world of civic or political action pertained to men and that of the domestic sphere belonged to women.

❖ *How might the career of Napoleon have inspired this passage? What are the antidemocratic implications of this passage? In this passage, do great men make history or do historical developments make great men? Why do you think Hegel does not associate this power of shaping history with women as well as men? In that regard, note how he relates history with political developments rather than with those of the private social sphere.*

Such are all great historical men—whose own particular aims involve those large issues which are the will of the World-Spirit. They may be called Heroes, inasmuch as they have derived their purposes and their vocation, not from the calm, regular course of things, sanctioned by the existing order, but from a concealed fount—one which has not attained to phenomenal, present existence—from that inner Spirit, still hidden beneath the surface, which, impinging on the outer world as on a shell, bursts it in pieces, because it is another kernel than that which belonged to the shell in question. They are men, therefore, who appear to draw the impulse of their life from themselves; and whose deeds have produced a condition of things and a complex of historical relations which appear to be only their interest, and their work.

Such individuals had no consciousness of the general Idea they were unfolding, while prosecuting those aims of theirs; on the contrary, they were practical, political men. But at the same time they were thinking men, who had an insight into the requirements of the time—what was ripe for development. This was the very Truth for their age, for their world; the species next in order, so to speak, and which was already formed in the womb of time. It was theirs to know this nascent principle; the necessary, directly sequent step in progress, which their world was to take; to make this their aim, and to expend their energy in promoting it. World-historical men—the Heroes of an epoch—must, therefore, be recognized as its clear-sighted ones; their deeds, their words are the best of that time.

From G. W. F. Hegel, *The Philosophy of History*, trans. by J. Sibree (New York: Dover, 1956), pp. 30–31. Reprinted by permission.

views lay the philosophy of German idealism, which understood the world as the creation of subjective egos. J. G. Fichte (1762–1814), an important German philosopher and nationalist, identified the individual ego with the Absolute that underlies all existing things. According to him and similar philosophers, the world is truly the creation of humankind. The world is as it is because especially strong persons conceive of it in a particular way and impose their wills on the world and other people. Napoleon served as the contemporary example of such a great person. This philosophy has ever

since served to justify the glorification of great persons and their actions in overriding all opposition to their will and desires.

Herder and Culture

In addition to this philosophy, the influence of new historical studies lay behind the German glorification of individual cultures. German romantic writers went in search of their own past in reaction to the copying of French manners in eighteenth-century Germany, the impact of the French Revolution, and the imperialism of Napoleon. An early leader in this effort was Johann Gottfried Herder (1744–1803). Herder had early resented the French cultural preponderance in Germany. In 1778, he published an influential essay entitled "On the Knowing and Feelings of the Human Soul." In it, he vigorously rejected the mechanical explanation of nature so popular with Enlightenment writers. He saw human beings and societies as developing organically, like plants, over time. Human beings were different at different times and places.

Herder revived German folk culture by urging the collection and preservation of distinctive German songs and sayings. His most important followers in this work were the Grimm brothers, Jakob (1785–1863) and Wilhelm (1786–1859), famous for their collection of fairy tales. Believing that each language and culture were the unique expression of a people, Herder opposed both the concept and the use of a "common" language, such as French, and "universal" institutions, such as those imposed on Europe by Napoleon. These, he believed, were forms of tyranny over the individuality of a people. Herder's writings led to a broad revival of interest in history and philosophy. Although initially directed toward the identification of German origins, such work soon expanded to embrace other world cultures as well. Eventually the ability of the romantic imagination to be at home in any age or culture spurred the study of non-Western religion, comparative literature, and philology.

Hegel and History

The most important philosopher of history in the romantic period was the German, Georg Wilhelm Friedrich Hegel (1770–1831). He is one of the most complicated and significant philosophers in the history of Western civilization.

Hegel believed that ideas develop in an evolutionary fashion that involves conflict. At any given time, a predominant set of ideas, which he termed the *thesis*, holds sway. The thesis is challenged by other conflicting ideas, which Hegel termed the *antithesis*. As these patterns of thought clash, a *synthesis* emerges that eventually becomes the new thesis. Then the process begins all over again. Periods of world history receive their character from the patterns of thought predominating during them. (See "Hegel Explains the Role of Great Men in History.")

Several important philosophical conclusions followed from this analysis. One of the most significant was the belief that all periods of history have been of almost equal value because each was, by definition, necessary to the achievements of those that came later. Also, all cultures are valuable because each contributes to the necessary clash of values and ideas that allows humankind to develop. Hegel discussed these concepts in *The Phenomenology of Mind* (1806), *Lectures on the Philosophy of History* (1822–1831), and other works, many of which were published only after his death. During his lifetime, his ideas became widely known through his university lectures at Berlin.

In Perspective

The various romantic ideas made a major contribution to the emergence of nationalism, which proved to be one of the strongest motivating forces of the nineteenth and twentieth centuries. The writers of the Enlightenment had generally championed a cosmopolitan outlook on the world. By contrast, the romantic thinkers emphasized the individuality and worth of each separate people and culture. A people or a nation was defined by a common language, a common history, a homeland that possessed historical associations, and common customs. This cultural nationalism gradually became transformed into a political creed. It came to be widely believed that every people, ethnic group, or nation should constitute a separate political entity and that only when it so existed could the nation be secure in its own character.

The example of France under the revolutionary government and then Napoleon had demonstrated the power of nationhood. Other peoples came to desire similar strength and confidence. Napoleon's toppling of ancient political structures, such as the Holy Roman Empire, proved the need for new political organization in Europe. By 1815 these were the aspirations of only a few Europeans, but as time passed, such yearnings came to be shared by scores of peoples from Ireland to Ukraine. The Congress of Vienna could ignore such feelings, but for the rest of the nineteenth century, as will be seen in subsequent chapters, statesmen had to confront the growing reality of the power these feelings unleashed.

REVIEW QUESTIONS

1. How did Napoleon rise to power? What groups supported him? What were the stages by which he eventually made himself emperor? What were his major domestic achievements? Did his rule more nearly fulfill or betray the ideals of the French Revolution?

2. What regions made up Napoleon's realm and what status did each region have within it? How did Napoleon rule his empire? Did his administration show foresight, or did the empire ultimately become a burden he could not afford?

3. Why did Napoleon decide to invade Russia? Why did the operation fail? Can Napoleon be considered a "military genius"? Why or why not? To what extent was his brilliance dependent on the ineptitude of his enemies?

4. Who were the principal personalities, and what were the most significant problems, of the Congress of Vienna? What were the results of the Congress and why were they significant?

5. Compare the role of feelings for romantic writers with the role of reason for Enlightenment writers. What questions did Rousseau and Kant raise about reason?

6. Why did poetry become important to romantic writers? How did the romantic concept of religion differ from Reformation Protestantism and Enlightenment deism? How did romantic writers use the idea of history?

SUGGESTED READINGS

M. H. ABRAMS, *The Mirror and the Lamp: Romantic Theory and the Critical Tradition* (1958). A standard text on romantic literary theory that looks at English romanticism in the context of German romantic idealism.

M. H. ABRAMS, *Natural Supernaturalism: Tradition and Revolution in Romantic Literature* (1971). A brilliant survey of romanticism across western European literature.

J. S. ALLEN, *Popular French Romanticism: Authors, Readers, and Books in the Nineteenth Century* (1981). Relates romanticism to popular culture.

F. C. BEISER, *Enlightenment, Revolution, and Romanticism: The Genesis of Modern German Political Thought, 1790–1800* (1992). The best recent study of the subject.

L. BERGERON, *France under Napoleon* (1981). An in-depth examination of Napoleonic administration.

J. F. BERNARD, *Talleyrand: A Biography* (1973). A useful account.

E. CASSIRER, *Kant's Life and Thought* (1981). A brilliant work by one of the major philosophers of this century.

D. G. CHANDLER, *The Campaigns of Napoleon* (1966). A good military study.

D. G. CHARLTON, *New Images of the Natural in France* (1984). An examination of the chang-ing attitude toward nature in France during the romantic era.

K. CLARK, *The Romantic Rebellion* (1973). A useful discussion that combines both art and literature.

O. CONNELLY, *Napoleon's Satellite Kingdoms* (1965). The rule of Napoleon and his family in Europe.

A. D. CULLER, *The Victorian Mirror of History* (1985). Studies in the writing of the nineteenth century with emphasis on romantic influences.

J. ENGELL, *The Creative Imagination: Enlightenment to Romanticism* (1981). An important book on the role of the imagination in romantic literary theory.

M. GLOVER, *The Peninsular War, 1807–1814: A Concise Military History* (1974). An interesting account of the military campaign that so drained Napoleon's resources in western Europe.

F. W. J. HEMMINGS, *Culture and Society in France: 1789–1848* (1987). Discusses French romantic literature, theater, and art.

H. HONOUR, *Romanticism* (1979). The best introduction to the subject in terms of the fine arts.

G. N. IZENBERG, *Impossible Individuality: Romanticism, Revolution, and the Origins of Modern Selfhood, 1787–1802* (1992). Explores the concepts of individualism in Germany, England, and France.

H. KISSINGER, *A World Restored: Metternich, Castlereagh and the Problems of Peace, 1812–1822* (1957). A provocative study by an author who became an American secretary of state.

S. KÖRNER, *Kant* (1955). A clear introduction to a brilliant thinker.

M. LEBRIS, *Romantics and Romanticism* (1981). A lavishly illustrated work that relates politics and romantic art.

G. LEFEBVRE, *Napoleon*, 2 vols., trans. by H. Stockhold (1969). The fullest and finest biography of the man.

F. MARKHAM, *Napoleon and the Awakening of Europe* (1954). Emphasizes the growth of nationalism.

R. MUIR, *Tactics and the Experience of Battle in the Age of Napoleon* (1998). A splendid account of the experience of troops in battle.

H. NICOLSON, *The Congress of Vienna* (1946). A good, readable account.

Z. A. PELCZYNSKI, *The State and Civil Society: Studies in Hegel's Political Philosophy* (1984). An important series of essays.

R. PLANT, *Hegel: An Introduction* (1983). Emphasis on his political thought.

R. PORTER AND M. TEICH (EDS.), *Romanticism in National Context* (1988). Essays on the phenomenon of romanticism in the major European nations.

B. M. G. REARDON, *Religion in the Age of Romanticism: Studies in Early Nineteenth-Century Thought* (1985). The best introduction to this important subject.

P. W. SCHROEDER, *The Transformation of European Politics, 1763–1848* (1994). A major synthesis of the diplomatic history of the period, emphasizing the new departures of the Congress of Vienna.

S. B. SMITH, *Hegel's Critique of Liberalism: Rights in Context* (1989). An excellent introduction to Hegelian political thought.

C. TAYLOR, *Hegel* (1975). The best one-volume introduction.

J. M. THOMPSON, *Napoleon Bonaparte: His Rise and Fall* (1952). A sound biography.

A. WALICKI, *Philosophy and Romantic Nationalism: The Case of Poland* (1982). Examines how philosophy influenced the character of Polish nationalism.

W. R. WARD, *The Protestant Evangelical Awakening* (1992). Examines the religious revivals of the eighteenth and nineteenth century from a transatlantic perspective.

B. YACK, *The Longing for Total Revolution: Philosophic Sources of Social Discontent from Rousseau to Marx and Nietzsche* (1986). A major exploration of the political philosophy associated with romanticism.

T. ZIOLKOWSKI, *German Romanticism and Its Institutions* (1990). An exploration of how institutions of intellectual life influenced creative literature.

Glossary

absolutism   Term applied to strong centralized continental monarchies that attempted to make royal power dominant over aristocracies and other regional authorities.

Acropolis (ACK-row-po-lis)   The religious and civic center of Athens. It is the site of the Parthenon.

Act of Supremacy   The declaration by Parliament in 1534 that Henry VIII, not the Pope, was the head of the Church in England.

agape (AG-a-pay)   Meaning "love feast." A common meal that was part of the central ritual of early Christian worship.

agora (AG-o-rah)   The Greek marketplace and civic center. It was the heart of the social life of the polis.

Agricultural Revolution   The innovations in farm production that began in the eighteenth century and led to a scientific and mechanized agriculture.

Albigensians (Al-bi-GEN-see-uns)   Thirteenth-century advocates of a dualist religion. They took their name from the city of Albi in southern France. Also called Cathars.

Anabaptists   Protestants who insisted that only adult baptism conformed to Scripture.

anarchism   The theory that government and social institutions are oppressive and unnecessary and that society should be based on voluntary cooperation among individuals.

Anschluss (AHN-shluz)   Meaning "union." The annexation of Austria by Germany in March 1938.

anti-Semitism   Prejudice, hostility, or legal discrimination against Jews.

apostolic primacy   The doctrine that the Popes are the direct successors to the Apostle Peter and as such heads of the Church.

Apostolic Succession   The Christian doctrine that the powers given by Jesus to his original disciples have been handed down from bishop to bishop through ordination.

appeasement   The Anglo–French policy of making concessions to Germany in the 1930s to avoid a crisis that would lead to war. It assumed that Germany had real grievances and that Hitler's aims were limited and ultimately acceptable.

Areopagus   The governing council of Athens, originally open only to the nobility. It was named after the hill on which it met.

Arete (AH-ray-tay)   Manliness, courage, and the excellence appropriate to a hero. It was considered the highest virtue of Homeric society.

Arianism (AIR-ee-an-ism)   The belief formulated by Arius of Alexandria (ca. 280–336 C.E.) that Jesus was a created being, neither fully man nor fully God, but something in between. It did away with the doctrine of the Trinity.

aristocratic resurgence   Term applied to the eighteenth-century aristocratic efforts to resist the expanding power of European monarchies.

Arminians (are-MIN-ee-ans)   A group within the Church of England who rejected Puritanism and the Calvinist doctrine of predestination in favor of free will and an elaborate liturgy.

Asia Minor   Modern Turkey. Also called Anatolia.

asiento (ah-SEE-ehn-tow)   The contract to furnish slaves to the Spanish colonies.

assignants (as-seen-YAHNTS)   Government bonds based on the value of confiscated Church lands issued during the early French Revolution.

Atomists   School of ancient Greek philosophy founded in the fifth century B.C.E. by Leucippus of Miletus and Democritus of Abdera. It held that the world consists of innumerable, tiny, solid, indivisible, and unchangeable particles called atoms.

Attica (AT-tick-a)   The region of Greece where Athens is located.

Augsburg (AWGS-berg) **Confession**   The definitive statement of Lutheran belief made in 1530.

Augustus (AW-gust-us)   The title given to Octavian in 27 B.C.E. and borne thereafter by all Roman emperors. It was a semireligious title that implied veneration, majesty, and holiness.

Ausgleich (AWS-glike)   Meaning "compromise." The agreement between the Habsburg Emperor and the Hungarians to give Hungary considerable administrative autonomy in 1867. It created the Dual Monarchy or Austria–Hungary.

autocracy (AW-to-kra-see)   Government in which the ruler has absolute power.

Axis   The alliance between Nazi Germany and Fascist Italy. Also called the Pact of Steel.

banalities   Exactions that the lord of a manor could make on his tenants.

baroque (bah-ROWK)   A style of art marked by heavy and dramatic ornamentation and curved rather than straight lines that flourished between 1550 and 1750. It was especially associated with the Catholic Counter-Reformation.

beguines (bi-GEENS)   Lay sisterhoods not bound by the rules of a religious order.

benefice   Church offices granted by the ruler of a state or the Pope to an individual. It also meant "fief" in the Middle Ages.

bishop   Originally a person elected by early Christian congregations to lead them in worship and supervise their funds. In time bishops became the religious and even political authorities for Christian communities within large geographical areas.

Black Death   The bubonic plague that killed millions of Europeans in the fourteenth century.

blitzkrieg (BLITZ-kreeg)   Meaning "lightning war." The German tactic early in World War II of employing fast-moving, massed armored columns supported by airpower to overwhelm the enemy.

Bolsheviks   Meaning the "majority." Term Lenin applied to his faction of the Russian Social Democratic Party. It became the Communist Party of the Soviet Union after the Russian Revolution.

boyars   The Russian nobility.

Bronze Age   The name given to the earliest civilized era, c. 4000 to 1000 B.C.E. The term reflects the importance of the metal bronze, a mixture of tin and copper, for the peoples of this age for use as weapons and tools.

Bund   A secular Jewish socialist organization of Polish Jews.

Caesaro-papism (SEE-zer-o-PAY-pi-zim)   The direct involvement of the ruler in religious doctrine and practice as if he were the head of the Church as well as the state.

cahiers de doleances (KAH-hee-ay de dough-LAY-ahnce)   Meaning "lists of grievances." Petitions for reforms submitted to the French Crown when the Estates General met in 1789.

caliphate (KAH-li-fate)   The true line of succession to Muhammad.

capital goods   Machines and tools used to produce other goods.

carbonari (car-buh-NAH-ree)   Meaning "charcoal burners." The most famous of the secret republican societies seeking to unify Italy in the 1820s.

categorical imperative   According to Emmanuel Kant (1724–1804), the internal sense of moral duty or awareness possessed by all human beings.

Catholic Emancipation   The grant of full political rights to Roman Catholics in Britain in 1829.

catholic   Meaning "universal." The body of belief held by most Christians enshrined within the Church.

censor   Official of the Roman republic charged with conducting the census and compiling the lists of citizens and members of the Senate. They could expel senators for financial or moral reasons. Two censors were elected every five years.

Chartism   The first large-scale European working-class political movement. It sought political reforms that would favor the interests of skilled British workers in the 1830s and 1840s.

chiaroscuro (kyar-eh-SKEW-row)   The use of shading to enhance naturalness in painting and drawing.

civic humanism   Education designed to promote humanist leadership of political and cultural life.

civilization   A form of human culture marked by urbanism, metallurgy, and writing.

classical economics   The theory that economies grow through the free enterprise of individuals competing in a largely self-regulating marketplace with government intervention held to a minimum.

clientage (KLI-ent-age)   The custom in ancient Rome whereby men became supporters of more powerful men in return for legal and physical protection and economic benefits.

Cold War   The ideological and geographical struggle between the U.S. and its allies and the U.S.S.R. and its allies that began after World War II and lasted until the dissolution of the U.S.S.R. in 1989.

Collectivization   The bedrock of Stalinist agriculture, which forced Russian peasants to give up their private farms and work as members of collectives, large agricultural units controlled by the state.

coloni (CO-loan-ee)   Farmers or sharecroppers on the estates of wealthy Romans.

Commonwealthmen   British political writers whose radical republican ideas influenced the American revolutionaries.

Concert of Europe   Term applied to the European great powers acting together (in "concert") to resolve international disputes between 1815 and the 1850s.

Conciliar Theory   The argument that General Councils were superior in authority to the Pope and represented the whole body of the faithful.

condottieri (con-da-TEE-AIR-ee)   Military brokers who furnished mercenary forces to the Italian states during the Renaissance.

Congress System   A series of international meetings among the European great powers to promote mutual cooperation between 1818 and 1822.

conquistadores (kahn-KWIS-teh-door-hez)   Meaning "conquerors." The Spanish conquerors of the New World.

conservatism   Support for the established order in Church and state. In the nineteenth century it implied support for legitimate monarchies, landed aristocracies, and established Churches. Conservatives favored only gradual, or "organic," change.

Consulate   French government dominated by Napoleon from 1799 to 1804.

consuls (CON-suls)   The two chief magistrates of the Roman state.

Consumer Revolution The vast increase in both the desire and the possibility of consuming goods and services that began in the early eighteenth century and created the demand for sustaining the Industrial Revolution.

Containment The U.S. policy during the Cold War of resisting Soviet expansion and influence in the expectation that the U.S.S.R. would eventually collapse.

Convention French radical legislative body from 1792 to 1794.

Corn Laws British tariffs on imported grain that protected the price of grain grown within the British Isles.

corporatism The planned economy of Fascist Italy that combined private ownership of capital with government direction of Italy's economic life and arbitration of labor disputes. All major areas of production were organized into state-controlled bodies called corporations, which were represented in the Chamber of Corporations that replaced the Chamber of Deputies. The state, not consumers and owners, determined what the economy produced.

corvee (cor-VAY) A French labor tax requiring peasants to work on roads, bridges, and canals.

Council of Nicaea (NIGH-see-a) The council of Christian bishops at Nicaea in 325 C.E. that formulated the Nicene Creed, a statement of Christian belief that rejected Arianism in favor of the doctrine that Christ is both fully human and fully divine.

Counter-Reformation The sixteenth-century reform movement in the Roman Catholic Church in reaction to the Protestant Reformation.

coup d'état (COO DAY-ta) The sudden violent overthrow of a government by its own army.

creed A brief statement of faith to which true Christians should adhere.

creoles (KRAY-ol-ez) Persons of Spanish descent born in the Spanish colonies.

Crusades Religious wars directed by the Church against infidels and heretics.

culture The ways of living built up by a group and passed on from one generation to another.

cuneiform (Q-nee-i-form) A writing system invented by the Sumerians that used a wedge-shaped stylus, or pointed tool, to write on wet clay tablets that were then baked or dried ("cuneus" means wedge in Latin). The writing was also cut into stone.

Curia (CURE-ee-a) The papal government.

Cynic (SIN-ick) **School, The** A fourth-century philosophical movement that ridiculed all religious observances and turned away from involvement in the affairs of the polis. Its most famous exemplar was Diogenes of Sinope (ca. 400-325 B.C.E.).

deacon Meaning "those who serve." In early Christian congregations, deacons assisted the presbyters, or elders.

deism A belief in a rational God who had created the universe, but then allowed it to function without his interference according to the mechanisms of nature and a belief in rewards and punishments after death for human action.

Delian (DEE-li-an) An alliance of Greek states under the leadership of Athens that was formed in 478–477 B.C.E. to resist the Persians. In time the league was transformed into the Athenian Empire.

deme (DEEM) A small town in Attica or a ward in Athens that became the basic unit of Athenian civic life under the democratic reforms of Clisthenes in 508 B.C.E.

demesne (di-MAIN) The part of a manor that was cultivated directly for the lord of the manor.

divine right of kings The theory that monarchs are appointed by and answerable only to God.

Domesday (DOOMS-day) **Book** A detailed survey of the wealth of England undertaken by William the Conqueror between 1080 and 1086.

domestic system of textile production Method of producing textiles in which agents furnished raw materials to households whose members spun them into thread and then wove cloth, which the agents then sold as finished products.

Donatism The heresy that taught that the efficacy of the sacraments depended on the moral character of the clergy who administered them.

Duce (DO-chay) Meaning "leader." Mussolini's title as head of the Fascist Party.

Duma (DOO-ma) The Russian parliament, after the Revolution of 1905.

Electors Nine German princes who had the right to elect the Holy Roman Emperor.

emigrés (em-ee-GRAYS) French aristocrats who fled France during the Revolution.

empiricism (em-PEER-ih-cism) The use of experiment and observation derived from sensory evidence to construct scientific theory or philosophy of knowledge.

enclosure The consolidation or fencing in of common lands by British landlords to increase production and achieve greater commercial profits. It also involved the reclamation of waste land and the consolidation of strips into block fields.

encomienda (en-co-mee-EN-da) The grant by the Spanish Crown to a colonist of the labor of a specific number of Indians for a set period of time.

ENIAC The Electronic Numerical Integrator and Computer. The first genuine modern digital computer, developed in the 1940s.

Enlightenment The eighteenth-century movement led by the philosophies that held that change and reform were both desirable through the application of reason and science.

Epicureans (EP-i-cure-ee-ans) School of philosophy founded by Epicurus of Athens (342–371 B.C.E.). It sought to liberate people from fear of death and the supernatural by teaching that the gods took no interest in human affairs and that true happiness consisted in pleasure, which was defined as the absence of pain. This could be achieved by attaining ataraxia, freedom from trouble, pain, and responsibility by withdrawing from business and public life.

equestrians (EE-quest-ree-ans) Literally "cavalrymen" or "knights." In the earliest years of the Roman Republic those who could afford to serve as mounted warriors. The equestrians evolved into a social rank of well-to-do businessmen and middle-ranking officials. Many of them supported the Gracchi.

Estates General The medieval French parliament. It consisted of three separate groups, or "estates:" clergy, nobility, and commoners. It last met in 1789 at the outbreak of the French Revolution.

Etruscans (EE-trus-cans) A people of central Italy who exerted the most powerful external influence on the early Romans. Etruscan kings ruled Rome until 509 B.C.E.

Eucharist (YOU-ka-rist) Meaning "thanksgiving." The celebration of the Lord's Supper. Considered the central ritual of worship by most Christians. Also called Holy Communion.

Euro The common currency created by the EEC in the late 1990s.

European Economic Community (EEC) The economic association formed by France, Germany, Italy, Belgium, the Netherlands, and Luxembourg in 1957. Also known as the Common Market.

European Union The new name given to the EEC in 1993. It included most of the states of Western Europe.

excommunication Denial by the Church of the right to receive the sacraments.

Existentialism The post-World War II Western philosophy that holds that human beings are totally responsible for their acts and that this responsibility causes them dread and anguish.

Führer (FYOOR-er) Meaning "leader." The title taken by Hitler when he became dictator of Germany.

Fabians British socialists in the late 19th and early 20th century who sought to achieve socialism through gradual, peaceful, and democratic means.

family economy The basic structure of production and consumption in preindustrial Europe.

fascism Political movements that tend to be antidemocratic, anti-Marxist, antiparliamentary, and often anti-Semitic. Fascists were invariably nationalists and exhalted the nation over the individual. They supported the interests of the middle class and rejected the ideas of the French Revolution and nineteenth-century liberalism. The first fascist regime was founded by Benito Mussolini (1883–1945) in Italy in the 1920s.

fealty An oath of loyalty by a vassal to a lord, promising to perform specified services.

feudal (FEW-dull) **society** The social, political, military, and economic system that prevailed in the Middle Ages and beyond in some parts of Europe.

fief Land granted to a vassal in exchange for services, usually military.

foederati (FAY-der-ah-tee) Barbarian tribes enlisted as special allies of the Roman Empire.

folk culture The distinctive songs, sayings, legends, and crafts of a people.

Fourteen Points President Woodrow Wilson's (1856–1924) idealistic war aims.

Fronde (FROHND) A series of rebellions against royal authority in France between 1649 and 1652.

gabelle (gah-BELL) The royal tax on salt in France.

Gaul (GAWL) Modern France.

German Confederation Association of German states established at the Congress of Vienna that replaced the Holy Roman Empire from 1815 to 1866.

ghetto Separate communities in which Jews were required by law to live.

Glasnost (GLAZ-nohst) Meaning "openness." The policy initiated by Mikhail Gorbachev (MEEK-hail GORE-buh-choff) in the 1980s of permitting open criticism of the policies of the Soviet Communist Party.

Glorious Revolution The largely peaceful replacement of James II by William and Mary as English monarchs in 1688. It marked the beginning of constitutional monarchy in Britain.

gold standard A monetary system in which the value of a unit of a nation's currency is related to a fixed amount of gold.

Golden Bull The agreement in 1356 to establish a seven-member electoral college of German princes to choose the Holy Roman Emperor.

Great Depression A prolonged worldwide economic downturn that began in 1929 with the collapse of the New York Stock Exchange.

Great Purges The imprisonment and execution of millions of Soviet citizens by Stalin between 1934 and 1939.

Great Reform Bill (1832) A limited reform of the British House of Commons and an expansion of the electorate to include a wider variety of the propertied classes. It laid the groundwork for further orderly reforms within the British constitutional system.

Great Schism The appearance of two and at times three rival popes between 1378 and 1415.

Green Movement A political environmentalist movement that began in West Germany in the 1970s and spread to a number of other Western nations.

grossdeutsch (gross-DOYCH) Meaning "great German." The argument that the German-speaking portions of the Habsburg Empire should be included in a united Germany.

guild An association of merchants or craftsmen that offered protection to its members and set rules for their work and products.

hacienda (ha-SEE-hen-da) A large landed estate in Spanish America.

Hegira (HEJ-ear-a) The flight of Muhammad and his followers from Mecca to Medina in 622 C.E. It marks the beginning of the Islamic calendar.

heliocentric (HE-li-o-cen-trick) **theory** The theory, now universally accepted, that the Earth and the other planets revolve around the Sun. First proposed by Aristarchos of Samos (310–230 B.C.E.). Its opposite, the geocentric theory, which was dominant until the sixteenth century C.E., held that the Sun and the planets revolved around the Earth.

helots (HELL-ots) Hereditary Spartan serfs.

heretic (HAIR-i-tick) A person whose beliefs were contrary to those of the Catholic Church.

Hieroglyphics (HI-er-o-gli-phicks) The complicated writing script of ancient Egypt. It combined picture writing with pictographs and sound signs. Hieroglyph means "sacred carvings" in Greek.

Holocaust The Nazi extermination of millions of European Jews between 1940 and 1945. Also called the "final solution to the Jewish problem."

Holy Roman Empire The revival of the old Roman Empire, based mainly in Germany and northern Italy, that endured from 870 to 1806.

Home Rule The advocacy of a large measure of administrative autonomy for Ireland within the British Empire between the 1880s and 1914.

Homo sapiens (HO-mo say-pee-ans) The scientific name for human beings, from the Latin words meaning "Wise man." Homo sapiens emerged some 200,000 years ago.

honestiores (HON-est-ee-or-ez) The Roman term formalized from the beginning of the third century C.E. to denote the privileged classes: senators, equestrians, the municipal aristocracy, and soldiers.

hoplite phalanx (FAY-lanks) The basic unit of Greek warfare in which infantrymen fought in close order, shield to shield, usually eight ranks deep. The phalanx perfectly suited the farmer-soldier-citizen who was the backbone of the polis.

hubris (WHO-bris) Arrogance brought on by excessive wealth or good fortune. The Greeks believed that it led to moral blindness and divine vengeance.

Huguenots (HYOU-gu-nots) French Calvinists.

humanism The study of the Latin and Greek classics and of the Church Fathers both for their own sake and to promote a rebirth of ancient norms and values.

humanitas (HEW-man-i-tas) The Roman name for a liberal arts education.

humiliores (HEW-mi-lee-orez) The Roman term formalized at the beginning of the third century C.E. for the lower classes.

Hussites (HUS-Its) Followers of John Huss (d. 1415) who questioned Catholic teachings about the Eucharist.

iconoclasm (i-KON-o-kla-zoom) A heresy in Eastern Christianity that sought to ban the veneration of sacred images, or icons.

id, ego, superego The three entities in Sigmund Freud's model of the internal organization of the human mind. The id consists of the amoral, irrational instincts for self-gratification. The superego embodies the external morality imposed on the personality by society. The ego mediates between the two and allows the personality to cope with the internal and external demands of its existence.

Iliad (ILL-ee-ad) **and the Odyssey** (O-dis-see), **The** Epic poems by Homer about the "Dark Age" heroes of Greece who fought at Troy. The poems were written down in the eighth century B.C.E. after centuries of being sung by bards.

imperator (IM-per-a-tor) Under the Roman Republic it was the title given to a victorious general. Under Augustus and his successors it became the title of the ruler of Rome meaning "Emperor."

imperialism The extension of a nation's authority over other nations or areas through conquest or political or economic hegemony.

imperium (IM-pear-ee-um) In ancient Rome the right to issue commands and to enforce them by fines, arrests, and even corporal and capital punishment.

indulgences Remission of the temporal penalty of punishment in purgatory that remained after sins had been forgiven.

Industrial Revolution Mechanization of the European economy that began in Britain in the second half of the eighteenth century.

insulae (IN-sul-lay) Meaning "islands." The multistoried apartment buildings of Rome in which most of the inhabitants of the city lived.

intendents (in-TEN-duhnts) Royal officials under the French monarchy who supervised the provincial governments in the name of the king.

Intolerable Acts Measures passed by the British Parliament in 1774 to punish the colony of Massachusetts and strengthen Britain's authority in the colonies. The laws provoked colonial opposition, which led immediately to the American Revolution.

Investiture Struggle The medieval conflict between the Church and lay rulers over who would control bishops and abbots, symbolized by the ceremony of "investing" them with the symbols of their authority.

Ionia (I-o-knee-a) The part of western Asia Minor heavily colonized by the Greeks.

Islam (IZ-lahm) Meaning "submission." The religion founded by the prophet Muhammad.

Italia Irredenta (ee-TAHL-ee-a ir-REH-dent-a)   Meaning "unredeemed Italy." Italian-speaking areas that had been left under Austrian rule at the time of the unification of Italy.

Jacobins (JACK-uh-bins)   The radical republican party during the French Revolution that displaced the Girondins.

jacquerie (jah-KREE)   Revolt of the French peasantry.

Jansenism   A seventeenth-century movement within the Catholic Church that taught that human beings were so corrupted by original sin that they could do nothing good nor secure their own salvation without divine grace. (It was opposed to the Jesuits).

Judah (JEW-da)   The southern Israelite kingdom established after the death of Solomon in the tenth century B.C.E.

Julian Calendar   The reform of the calendar by Julius Caesar in 46 B.C.E. It remained in use throughout Europe until the sixteenth century and in Russia until the Russian Revolution in 1917.

July Monarchy   The French regime set up after the overthrow of the Bourbons in July 1830.

junkers (YOONG-kerz)   The noble landlords of Prussia.

jus gentium (YUZ GEN-tee-um)   Meaning "law of peoples." The body of Roman law that dealt with foreigners.

jus naturale (YUZ NAH-tu-rah-lay)   Meaning "natural law." The Stoic concept of a world ruled by divine reason.

Ka'ba (KAH-bah)   A black meteorite in the city of Mecca that became Islam's holiest shrine.

Keynesian Economics   The theory of John Maynard Keynes (CANES) (1883–1946) that governments could spend their economies out of a depression by running deficits to encourage employment and stimulate the production and consumption of goods.

kleindeutsch (kline-DOYCH)   Meaning "small German." The argument that the German-speaking portions of the Habsburg Empire should be excluded from a united Germany.

Kristallnacht   (KRIS-tahl-NAHKT) Meaning "crystal night" because of the broken glass that littered German streets after the looting and destruction of Jewish homes, businesses, and synagogues across Germany on the orders of the Nazi Party in November, 1938.

kulaks (koo-LAKS)   Prosperous Russian peasant farmers.

Kulturkampf (cool-TOOR-cahmff)   Meaning the "battle for culture." The conflict between the Roman Catholic Church and the government of the German Empire in the 1870s.

laissez-faire (lay-ZAY-faire)   French phrase meaning "allow to do." In economics the doctrine of minimal government interference in the working of the economy.

latifundia (LAT-ee-fun-dee-a)   Large plantations for growing cash crops owned by wealthy Romans.

Latium (LAT-ee-um)   The region of Italy in which Rome is located. Its inhabitants were called Latins.

League of Nations   The association of sovereign states set up after World War I to pursue common policies and avert international aggression.

Lebensraum (LAY-benz-rauhm)   Meaning "living space." The Nazi plan to colonize and exploit the Slavic areas of Eastern Europe for the benefit of Germany.

levée en masse (le-VAY en MASS)   The French Revolutionary conscription (1792) of all males into the army and the harnessing of the economy for war production.

liberal arts   The medieval university program that consisted of the trivium (TRI-vee-um): grammar, rhetoric, and logic, and the quadrivium (qua-DRI-vee-um): arithmetic, geometry, astronomy, and music.

liberalism   In the nineteenth century, support for representative government dominated by the propertied classes and minimal government interference in the economy.

Logos (LOW-goz)   Divine reason, or fire, which according to the Stoics was the guiding principle in nature. Every human had a spark of this divinity, which returned to the eternal divine spirit after death.

Lollards (LALL-erds)   Followers of John Wycliffe (d. 1384) who questioned the supremacy and privileges of the Pope and the Church hierarchy.

Lower Egypt   The Nile delta.

Luftwaffe (LUFT-vaff-uh)   The German airforce in World War II.

Magna Carta (MAG-nuh CAR-tuh)   The "Great Charter" limiting royal power that the English nobility forced King John to sign in 1215.

Magna Graecia (MAG-nah GRAY-see-a)   Meaning "Great Greece" in Latin, it was the name given by the Romans to southern Italy and Sicily because there were so many Greek colonies in the region.

Magyars (MAH-jars)   The majority ethnic group in Hungary.

Mandates   The assigning of the former German colonies and Turkish territories in the Middle East to Britain, France, Japan, Belgium, Australia, and South Africa as de facto colonies under the vague supervision of the League of Nations with the hope that the territories would someday advance to independence.

mannerism   A style of art in the mid-to late-sixteenth century that permitted the artist to express his or her own "manner" or feelings in contrast to the symmetry and simplicity of the art of the High Renaissance.

manor   Village farms owned by a lord.

Marshall Plan   The U.S. program named after Secretary of State George C. Marshall of providing economic aid to Europe after World War II.

Marxism The theory of Karl Marx (1818–1883) and Friedrich Engels (FREE-drick Eng-ulz) (1820–1895) that history is the result of class conflict, which will end in the inevitable triumph of the industrial proletariat over the bourgeoisie and the abolition of private property and social class.

Mein Kampf (MINE KAHMFF) Meaning "my struggle." Hitler's statement of his political program published in 1924.

Mensheviks Meaning the "minority." Term Lenin applied to the majority moderate faction of the Russian Social Democratic Party opposed to him and the Bolsheviks.

mercantilism Term used to describe close government control of the economy that sought to maximize exports and accumulate as much precious metals as possible to enable the state to defend its economic and political interests.

Mesopotamia (MEZ-o-po-tay-me-a) Modern Iraq. The land between the Tigris and Euphrates Rivers where the first civilization appeared around 3000 B.C.E.

Messiah (MESS-eye-a) The redeemer whose coming Jews believed would establish the kingdom of God on earth. Christians considered Jesus to be the Messiah (Christ means Messiah in Greek).

Methodism An English religious movement begun by John Wesley (1703–1791) that stressed inward, heartfelt religion and the possibility of attaining Christian perfection in this life.

millets Administrative units of the Ottoman Empire that were not geographic but consisted of ethnic or religious minorities to whom particular laws and regulations applied.

Minoans (MIN-o-ans) The Bronze Age civilization that arose in Crete in the third and second millenia B.C.E.

missi dominici (MISS-ee dough-MIN-ee-chee) Meaning "the envoys of the ruler." Royal overseers of the king's law in the Carolingian Empire.

mobilization The placing of a country's military forces on a war footing.

modernism The movement in the arts and literature in the late nineteenth and early twentieth centuries to create new aesthetic forms and to elevate the aesthetic experience of a work of art above the attempt to portray reality as accurately as possible.

moldboard plow A heavy plow introduced in the Middle Ages that cut deep into the soil.

monophysitism (ma-NO-fiz-it-ism) A Christian heresy that taught that Jesus had only one nature.

monotheism The worship of one, universal God.

Mycenaean (MY-cen-a-an) The Bronze Age civilization of mainland Greece that was centered at Mycenae.

"mystery" religions The cults of Isis, Mithra, and Osiris, which promised salvation to those initiated into the secret or "mystery" of their rites. These cults competed with Christianity in the Roman Empire.

nationalism The belief that one is part of a nation, defined as a community with its own language, traditions, customs, and history that distinguish it from other nations and make it the primary focus of a person's loyalty and sense of identity.

natural selection The theory originating with Darwin that organisms evolve through a struggle for existence in which those that have a marginal advantage live long enough to propagate their kind.

naturalism The attempt to portray nature and human life without sentimentality.

Nazis The German Nationalist Socialist Party.

Neolithic (NEE-o-lith-ick) **Revolution, The** The shift beginning 10,000 years ago from hunter-gatherer societies to settled communities of farmers and artisans. Also called the Age of Agriculture, it witnessed the invention of farming, the domestication of plants and animals, and the development of technologies such as pottery and weaving. The earliest Neolithic societies appeared in the Near East about 8,000 B.C.E. "Neolithic" comes from the Greek words for "new stone."

Neoplatonism (KNEE-o-play-ton-ism) A religious philosophy that tried to combine mysticism with classical and rationalist speculation. Its chief formulator was Plotinus (205–270 C.E.).

New Economic Policy (NEP) A limited revival of capitalism, especially in light industry and agriculture, introduced by Lenin in 1921 to repair the damage inflicted on the Russian economy by the Civil War and War Communism.

New Imperialism The extension in the late nineteenth and early twentieth centuries of Western political and economic dominance to Asia, the Middle East, and Africa.

nomes regions or provinces of ancient Egypt governed by officials called nomarchs.

oikos (OI-cos) The Greek household, always headed by a male.

Old Believers Those members of the Russian Orthodox Church who refused to accept the reforms of the seventeenth century regarding Church texts and ritual.

Old Regime Term applied to the pattern of social, political, and economic relationships and institutions that existed in Europe before the French Revolution.

optimates (OP-tee-ma-tes) Meaning "the best men." Roman politicians who supported the traditional role of the Senate.

orthodox Meaning "holding the right opinions." Applied to the doctrines of the Catholic Church.

Ottoman Empire The imperial Turkish state centered in Constantinople that ruled large parts of the Balkans, North Africa, and the Middle East until 1918.

Paleolithic (PAY-lee-o-lith-ick) **Age, The** The earliest period when stone tools were used, from about 1,000,000 to 10,000 B.C.E. From the Greek meaning "old stone."

Panhellenic (PAN-hell-en-ick) ("all-Greek") The sense of cultural identity that all Greeks felt in common with each other.

Panslavism The movement to create a nation or federation that would embrace all the Slavic peoples of eastern Europe.

papal infallibility The doctrine that the Pope is infallible when pronouncing officially in his capacity as head of the Church on matters of faith and morals, enumerated by the First Vatican Council in 1870.

Papal States Territory in central Italy ruled by the Pope until 1870.

parlements (par-luh-MAHNS) French regional courts dominated by hereditary nobility. The most important was the Parlement of Paris, which claimed the right to register royal decrees before they could become law.

patricians (PA-tri-she-ans) The hereditary upper class of early Republican Rome.

Peloponnesian (PELL-o-po-knees-ee-an) **Wars** The protracted struggle between Athens and Sparta to dominate Greece between 465 and Athens final defeat in 404 B.C.E.

Peloponnesus (PELL-o-po-knee-sus) The southern peninsula of Greece where Sparta was located.

peninsulares (pen-in-SUE-la-rez) Persons born in Spain who settled in the Spanish colonies.

Perestroika (pare-ess-TROY-ka) Meaning "restructuring." The attempt in the 1980s to reform the Soviet government and economy.

petit bourgeoisie (peh-TEE BOOSH-schwa-zee) The lower middle class.

Pharisees (FAIR-i-sees) The group that was most strict in its adherence to Jewish law.

pharoah (FAY-row) The god-kings of ancient Egypt. The term originally meant "great house" or palace.

philosophes (fee-lou-SOPHS) The eighteenth-century writers and critics who forged the new attitudes favorable to change. They sought to apply reason and common sense to the institutions and societies of their day.

Phoenicians (FA-nee-shi-ans) The ancient inhabitants of modern Lebanon. A trading people, they established colonies throughout the Mediterranean.

physiocrats Eighteenth-century French thinkers who attacked the mercantilist regulation of the economy, advocated a limited economic role for government, and believed that all economic production depended on sound agriculture.

Plantation Economy, The The economic system stretching between Chesapeake Bay and Brazil that produced crops, especially sugar, cotton, and tobacco, using slave labor on large estates.

plebeians (PLEB-bee-ans) The hereditary lower class of early Republican Rome.

plenitude of power The teaching that the Popes have power over all other bishops of the Church.

pogroms (PO-grohms) Organized riots against Jews in the Russian Empire.

polis (PO-lis) (plural, poleis) The basic Greek political unit. Usually, but incompletely, translated as "city state," the Greeks thought of the polis as a community of citizens theoretically descended from a common ancestor.

polygyny (po-LIJ-eh-nee) The practice of having two or more wives or concubines at the same time.

polytheism (PAH-lee-thee-ism) The worship of many gods

pontifex maximus (PON-ti-feks MAK-suh-muss) Meaning "supreme priest." The chief priest of ancient Rome. The title was later assumed by the Popes.

Popular Front A government of all left-wing parties that took power in France in 1936 to enact social and economic reforms.

populares (PO-pew-lar-es) Roman politicians who sought to pursue a political career based on the support of the people rather than just the aristocracy.

Positivism The philosophy of Auguste Comte that science is the final, or positive, stage of human intellectual development because it involves exact descriptions of phenomena, without recourse to unobservable operative principles, such as gods or spirits.

Pragmatic Sanction The legal basis negotiated by the Emperor Charles VI (r. 1711–1740) for the Habsburg succession through his daughter Maria Theresa (r. 1740–1780).

predestination The doctrine that God had foreordained all souls to salvation (the "elect") or damnation. It was especially associated with Calvinism.

Presbyterians Scottish Calvinists and English Protestants who advocated a national church composed of semi-autonomous congregations governed by "presbyteries."

presbyter (PRESS-bi-ter) Meaning "elder." A person who directed the affairs of early Christian congregations.

proconsulship (PRO-con-sul-ship) In Republican Rome the extension of a consul's imperium beyond the end of his term of office to allow him to continue to command an army in the field.

Protestant Ethic The theory propounded by Max Weber in 1904 that the religious confidence and self-disciplined activism that were supposedly associated with Protestantism produced an ethic that stimulated the spirit of emergent capitalism.

Ptolemaic (tow-LEM-a-ick) **System** The pre-Copernican explanation of the universe, with the Earth at the center of the universe, originated in the ancient world.

Punic (PEW-nick) **Wars**   Three wars between Rome and Carthage for dominance of the western Mediterranean that were fought from 264 B.C.E. to 146 B.C.E.

Puritans   English Protestants who sought to "purify" the Church of England of any vestiges of Catholicism.

Qur'an (kuh-RAN)   Meaning "a reciting." The Islamic bible, which Muslims believe God revealed to the prophet Muhammad.

racism   The pseudo-scientific theory that biological features of race determine human character and worth.

raison d'etat (RAY-suhn day-TAH)   Meaning "reason of state." Concept that the interests of the state justify a course of action.

realism   The style of art and literature that seeks to depict the physical world and human life with scientific objectivity and detached observation.

Reformation   The sixteenth-century religious movement that sought to reform the Roman Catholic Church and led to the establishment of Protestantism.

regular clergy   Monks and nuns who belong to religious orders.

Reichstag (RIKES-stahg)   The German parliament, which existed in various forms, until 1945.

Reign of Terror   The period between the summer of 1793 and the end of July 1794 when the French Revolutionary state used extensive executions and violence to defend the Revolution and suppress its alleged internal enemies.

relativity   The scientific theory associated with Einstein that time and space exist not separately but as a combined continuum whose measurement depends as much on the observer as on the entities that are being measured.

Renaissance   The revival of ancient learning and the supplanting of traditional religious beliefs by new secular and scientific values that began in Italy in the fourteenth and fifteenth centuries.

reparations   The requirement incorporated into the Versailles Treaty that Germany should pay for the cost of World War I.

revisionism   The advocacy among nineteenth-century German socialists of achieving a humane socialist society through the evolution of democratic institutions, not revolution.

robot (ROW-boht)   The amount of labor landowners demanded from peasants in the Habsburg Monarchy before 1848.

Romanitas (row-MAN-ee-tas)   Meaning "Roman-ness." The spread of the Roman way of life and the sense of identifying with Rome across the Roman Empire.

Romanticism   A reaction in early nineteenth century literature, philosophy, and religion against what many considered the excessive rationality and scientific narrowness of the Enlightenment.

SA   The Nazi parliamentary forces, or storm troopers.

sans-culottes (SAHN coo-LOTS)   Meaning "without kneebreeches." The lower-middle classes and artisans of Paris during the French Revolution.

Schlieffen (SHLEE-fun) **Plan**   Germany's plan for achieving a quick victory in the West at the outbreak of World War I by invading France through Belgium and Luxembourg.

scholasticism   The method of study based on logic and dialectic that dominated the medieval schools. It assumed that truth already existed; students had only to organize, elucidate, and defend knowledge learned from authoritative texts, especially those of Aristotle and the Church Fathers.

scientific induction   Scientific method in which generalizations are derived from data gained from empirical observations.

Scientific Revolution   The sweeping change in the scientific view of the universe that occurred in the sixteenth and seventeenth centuries. The new scientific concepts and the method of their construction became the standard for assessing the validity of knowledge in the West.

scutage   Monetary payments by a vassal to a lord in place of the required military service.

Second Industrial Revolution   The emergence of new industries and the spread of industrialization from Britain to other countries, especially Germany and the United States, in the second half of the nineteenth century.

secular clergy   Parish clergy who did not belong to a religious order.

seigneur (sane-YOUR)   A noble French landlord.

Sejm (SHEM)   The legislative assembly of the Polish nobility.

serfs   Peasants tied to the land they tilled.

Shi-a (SHE-ah)   The minority of Muslims who trace their beliefs from the caliph Ali who was assassinated in 661 C.E.

Sinn Fein (SHIN FAHN)   Meaning "ourselves alone." An Irish political movement founded in 1905 that advocated complete political separation from Britain.

Social Darwinism   The application of Darwin's concept of "the survival of the fittest" to explain evolution in nature to human social relationships.

Sophists (SO-fists)   Professional teachers who emerged in Greece in the mid-fifth century B.C.E. who were paid to teach techniques of rhetoric, dialectic, and argumentation.

soviets   Workers and soldiers councils formed in Russia during the Revolution.

spinning jenny   A machine invented in England by James Hargreaves around 1765 to mass-produce thread.

SS   The chief security units of the Nazi state.

Stoics (STOW-icks)   A philosophical school founded by Zeno of Citium (335–263 B.C.E.) that taught that humans could only be happy with natural law. Human misery was caused by passion, which was a disease of the soul. The wise sought apatheia, freedom from passion.

studia humanitatis (STEW-dee-a hew-MAHN-ee tah-tis)   During the Renaissance a liberal arts program of study that embraced grammar, rhetoric, poetry, history, philosophy, and politics.

Sturm und Drang (SHTURM und DRAHNG)   Meaning "storm and stress." A movement in German romantic literature and philosophy that emphasized feeling and emotion.

suffragettes   British women who lobbied and agitated for the right to vote in the early 20th century.

summa (SUE-ma)   An authoritative summary in the Middle Ages of all that was allegedly known about a subject.

Sunna (SOON-ah)   Meaning "tradition." The dominant Islamic group.

symposium (SIM-po-see-um)   The carefully organized drinking party that was the center of Greek aristocratic social life. It featured games, songs, poetry, and even philosophical disputation.

syncretism (SIN-cret-ism)   The intermingling of different religions to form an amalgam that contained elements from each.

syndicalism   French labor movement that sought to improve workers' conditions through direct action, especially general strikes.

Table of Ranks   An official hierarchy established by Peter the Great in Imperial Russia that equated a person's social position and privileges with his rank in the state bureaucracy or army.

tabula rasa (tah-BOO-lah RAH-sah)   Meaning a "blank page." The philosophical belief associated with John Locke that human beings enter the world with totally unformed characters that are completely shaped by experience.

taille (TIE)   The direct tax on the French peasantry.

"Ten lost tribes"   The Israelites who were scattered and lost to history when the northern kingdom of Israel fell to the Assyrians in 722 B.C.E.

tertiaries (TER-she-air-ees)   Laypeople affiliated with the monastic life who took vows of poverty, chastity, and obedience but remained in the world.

tetrarchy (TET-rar-key)   Diocletian's (r. 306–337 C.E.) system for ruling the Roman Empire by four men with power divided territorially.

Thermidorean Reaction   The reaction against the radicalism of the French Revolution that began in July 1794. Associated with the end of terror and establishment of the Directory.

thesis, antithesis, and synthesis   G.W.F. Hegel's (HAY-gle) (1770–1831) concept of how ideas develop. The thesis is a dominant set of ideas. It is challenged by a set of conflicting ideas, the antithesis. From the clash of these ideas, a new pattern of thought, the synthesis, emerges and eventually becomes the new thesis.

Third Estate   The branch of the French Estates General representing all of the kingdom outside the nobility and the clergy.

Third Reich (RIKE)   Hitler's regime in Germany, which lasted from 1933 to 1945.

Thirty-Nine Articles (1563)   The official statement of the beliefs of the Church of England. They established a moderate form of Protestantism.

three-field system   A medieval innovation that increased the amount of land under cultivation by leaving only one-third fallow in a given year.

transportation   The British policy from the late eighteenth to the mid-nineteenth centuries of shipping persons convicted of the most serious offenses to Australia as an alternative to capital punishment.

transubstantiation   The doctrine that the entire substances of the bread and wine are changed in the Eucharist into the body and blood of Christ.

tribunes (TRIB-unes)   Roman officials who had to be plebeians and were elected by the plebeian assembly to protect plebeians from the arbitrary power of the magistrates.

ulema (oo-LEE-mah)   Meaning "persons with correct knowledge." The Islamic scholarly elite who served a social function similar to the Christian clergy.

Upper Egypt   The part of Egypt that runs from the delta to the Sudanese border.

utilitarianism   The theory associated with Jeremy Bentham (1748–1832) that the principle of utility, defined as the greatest good for the greatest number of people, should be applied to government, the economy, and the judicial system.

utopian socialism   Early nineteenth century theories that sought to replace the existing capitalist structure and values with visionary solutions or ideal communities.

vassal   A person granted an estate or cash payments in return for accepting the obligation to render services to a lord.

vernacular   The everyday language spoken by the people as opposed to Latin.

vingtieme (VEN-tee-em)   Meaning "one twentieth." A tax on income in France before the Revolution.

Vulgate   The Latin translation of the Bible by Jerome (348–420 C.E.) that became the standard bible used by the Catholic Church.

Waldensians (wahl-DEN-see-ens)   Medieval heretics who advocated Biblical simplicity in reaction to the worldliness of the Church.

War Communism   The economic policy adopted by the Bolsheviks during the Russian Civil War to seize the banks, heavy industry, railroads, and grain.

War Guilt Clause   Clause 231 of the Versailles Treaty, which assigned responsibility for World War I solely to Germany.

water frame   A water-powered device invented by Richard Arkwright to produce a more durable cotton fabric. It led to the shift in the production of cotton textiles from households to factories.

Weimar (Why-mar) **Republic**   The German democratic regime that existed between the end of World War I and Hitler's coming to power in 1933.

White Russians   Those Russians who opposed the Bolsheviks (the "Reds") in the Russian Civil War of 1918–1921.

zemstvos (ZEMPST-vohs)   Local governments set up in the Russian Empire in 1864.

Zionism   The movement to create a Jewish state in Palestine (the Biblical Zion).

Zollverein (TZOL-fuh-rine)   A free trade union established among the major German states in 1834.

Index

A

Aachen, 214, 216
Abelard, Peter, 276, 277
Abortion
  Cathars and, 239
  fascist Italy, 1035
  19th century, 824–825
  Roman Empire, 160, 162
  Soviet Union, 1033
  20th century, 1052
Abu Bakr, 207
Academy of Experiments, 464
Academy of Plato, 93, 102–103
Achaemenid dynasty, 63
Achilles, 42, 43
Acrocorinth, 46
Acropolis, 46, 76, 86, 88, *88*
Action Française, 970
Actium, battle of, 143
Acton, Lord, 802
Acts of Supremacy (1534, 1559), 341, 370, 404
Acts of Uniformity (1549, 1552, 1559), 372, 404
Adages (Erasmus), 340
Addison, Joseph, 595, 598
*Address to the Christian Nobility of the German
      Nation* (Luther), 356, 360
Adrian IV, pope, 250
Adrianople, battle of, 176, 196
Adrianople, treaty of (1829), 719
Ad Sacram Sedem, 438
Advancement of Learning, The (Bacon), 455
Aegean area, map of in the Bronze Age, *41*
Aegospotami, battle of, 82
Aeneid (Vergil), 152
Aeschylus, 78, 86
Afghanistan, Soviet invasion of, 1095
Africa
  decolonization, 1048, 1085–1089, *1088*
  early explorations of, 341–343
  imperialism and, 891–893, 895
  slavery in, 560, 741
Africa (Petrarch), 323
Africanus, Scipio, 123, 323
Agamemnon, 42, 43
Agamemnon (Aeschylus), 78
Agesilaus, 83–84
Agincourt, battle of (1415), 295–296
Agon, 43
Agora, 46, 56, *88*, 103
Agricola, Rudolf, 340
Agriculture
  in the Americas, 347–348, 583–585
  Athenian, 54
  Black Death and, 302–303
  Carolingian manor, 217–220, *219*
  collectivization, 984–986, 1038–1039
  18th century, 517–519, 528–531, *530*

enclosures replace open fields, 529–530
  Greek, 54, 58, 59
  Hellenistic, 102
  Middle Ages, 265, 266, 298
  Neolithic Age, 8
  in the 1920s, 967–968
  Roman Republic, 128, 130–132
Agrippa, 141, 143
Agrippina, 162
Aix-la-Chapelle, treaty of (1668), 440
Akhenaten, 24
Akkadians/Akkade, 11, 12, 13
Alais, peace of (1629), 431
Alaric, 197
Alba, duke of, 401, 405
Albanians, 1038
  collapse of Yugoslavia and civil war, 1106,
      1108–1109
Albert, Jeanne d', 391
Alberti, Leon Battista, 326
Albigensians (Cathars), 238–239, 382
Albrecht of Mainz, 358
Albret, Charlotte d', 333
Alcabala, 336
Alcaeus, *60*, 62
Alcibiades, 82
Alcmaeonids, 56
Alcuin of York, 217
Alemanni, 171–172, 175
Alençon, duke of, 403
Alexander I, king of Yugoslavia, 953
Alexander I, tsar of Russia, 674, 685, 717, *717*,
      724, 725
Alexander II, pope, 232
Alexander II, tsar of Russia, 803–805, 807
Alexander III, pope, 243, 250
Alexander III, tsar of Russia, 842, 844
Alexander V, pope, 312
Alexander VI, pope, 332, 333
Alexander the Great (Alexander III), 94, 99–100, *99*,
      101, 188, 930
  campaigns (map) of, *101*
  successors to, 100, 102
Alexandria, 104
Alexandria Eschate, 100
Alexis I, king of Russia, 503, 508, 509
Alexius I Comnenus, 205, 235
Alfred the Great, 241
Algarotti, Francesco, 467
Algeria, French in, 891
Ali, caliph, 206
Alimenta, 158
Almagest (Ptolemy), 451
Alvarado, Pedro de, *344*
Amboise, conspiracy of, 391
Ambrose, bishop of Milan, 179
Americanization of Europe, 1057–1058
American Revolution, 572

C

O